LAW IN JAPAN

LAW IN JAPAN

The Legal Order in a Changing Society

EDITED BY ARTHUR TAYLOR von MEHREN

HARVARD UNIVERSITY PRESS
CAMBRIDGE, MASSACHUSETTS · 1963

Distributed in Great Britain by Oxford University Press, London

Printed in the United States of America
Library of Congress Catalog Card Number: 62–19226

FOREWORD

The essays contained in this volume were prepared for a conference on Japanese law held at the Harvard Law School on September 5–9, 1961. The conference, sponsored by the law schools of Stanford, Michigan, and Harvard universities, was conceived of as an opportunity to consolidate, and reflect upon, knowledge gained through the Japanese American Program for Cooperation in Legal Studies and other cooperative activities involving Japanese and American legal scholars The work of the program, in which the law schools of Stanford, Michigan, and Harvard participated with six Japanese law faculties and the Legal Training and Research Institute, is discussed by David F. Cavers in his introductory essay, "The Japanese American Program for Cooperation in Legal Studies." A few remarks about the conference and the essays prepared for it are appropriate here.

Twelve Japanese legal scholars — professors, judges, and procurators* — came from Japan to attend the conference. Each of them prepared a paper, as did five other legal scholars who did not attend: Judge Abe, Professors Takayanagi, Watanabe, and Kato, and Mr. Uematsu. Three other Japanese legal scholars, who were in Cambridge to begin graduate work at the Harvard Law School, also attended conference sessions: Mr. Nagashima, a practicing lawyer, and Assistant Professors Kaneko and Yoshimura. On the Western side, three American lawyers practicing in Japan, Messrs. Blakemore and Blakeney and the former executive secretary of the program, Mr. Rabinowitz, participated in the conference, as did some thirty scholars from such fields as law, economics, history, anthropology, political science, and philosophy.

The conference proceedings, which were held in sessions spread over five days, are summarized in three essays, each of which relates to one of the parts into which this volume is divided. The commentaries on the proceedings are synthetic in the sense that, though they reflect and are based on the conference discussions, they rearrange the actual discussions and go, at

* The procuracy is the prosecuting arm of the legal profession. Corresponding less to an elected district attorney than to a United States attorney, a procurator is an appointed official of the central government.

various points, somewhat beyond them. Certain comments made at the conference of a rather specific nature, particularly relevant to the discussion of a given essay, are incorporated in that essay in the form of asterisked footnotes.

This volume is divided into three parts: The Legal System and the Law's Processes; The Individual, the State, and the Law; The Law and the Economy. Neither the individual essays nor the three parts are intended to be self-sufficient and themes recur throughout. The arrangement of the essays emphasizes the interconnections with a view to assisting the reader who is approaching Japanese law for the first time.

A word is also in order on the writing of the conference essays. A general plan was developed for the conference and this book; it sought both to explore significant aspects of the contemporary Japanese legal order and to draw on the particular interests of the ten Japanese legal scholars, who had studied, most of them in the period 1954–1956, in the United States under the auspices of the Japanese American Program for Cooperation in Legal Studies: Procurator Haruo Abe,* Professor Kiminobu Hashimoto, Judge Takaaki Hattori, Professor Ryuichi Hirano, Professor Kichiemon Ishikawa, Professor Masami Ito, Professor Shinichiro Michida, Procurator Atsushi Nagashima,† Judge Kohji Tanabe, and Professor Makoto Yazawa. To complete the desired coverage, six other Japanese legal scholars were invited to contribute essays to the conference and to this volume: Judge Hakaru Abe, Professor Yoshio Kanazawa, Professor Ichiro Kato,‡ Professor Takeyoshi Kawashima, Dr. Kenzo Takayanagi, and Mr. Morio Uematsu. Each Japanese author, with the exception of Professor Kawashima, had associated with him an American editorial collaborator. All the editorial collaborators are men who have been particularly interested in Japanese law.

The conference and the publication of this volume were made possible by the generosity of the Ford Foundation, which also had supported the Program in Legal Studies. All those connected with the conference and the book are deeply indebted to the Foundation for its help and continued interest. We hope that the publication of this volume, which makes the conference papers and discussions widely available, will not only contribute to knowledge about Japanese law and society but also advance our thinking with respect to general problems of continuing cultural exchange with Japan and other countries of the Far East.

There remains only the pleasant duty of expressing appreciation to the many persons who worked with me in preparing for the conference and producing this volume. Professor David F. Cavers of the Harvard Law

* In Procurator Abe's case, the period of study in the United States was 1953 to 1955, the 1954–55 academic year being under the auspices of the program.

† Procurator Nagashima studied in the United States in 1956–1958.

‡ Professor Kato's paper was not ready in time for consideration at the conference.

School, who guided the Japanese American Program for Cooperation in Legal Studies, has given guidance and advice at every turn. His counsel and support have been truly invaluable. Professor B. J. George, Jr., of the Michigan Law School contributed much to the planning for the conference and undertook exceptionally heavy duties as a collaborator. Mr. Richard W. Rabinowitz, who served the Japanese American Program for Cooperation in Legal Studies as its Executive Secretary, was in Japan for most of the preconference period. His assistance on the scene in Japan was essential to the conference and the book. Mr. John A. King, Secretary, International Legal Studies, Harvard Law School, discharged with exceptional capacity the many administrative functions that the conference necessitated. In this work, he was supported by the Special Program Division of the Institute of International Education (Mr. Hans Indorf, Director), which administered the Ford Foundation grants for both the conference and the program.

Messrs. Stephen J. Friedman and John C. McCarroll of the Class of 1962 at Harvard Law School served as conference secretaries, performing their duties admirably. Miss Nancy E. Eastham, also of the Class of 1962 at Harvard Law School, and Mr. McCarroll worked with me in the final editing of the conference papers. They discharged their task with great skill and imagination.

Rex Lee Coleman, Research Associate in Law, International Program in Taxation, Harvard Law School, assumed responsibility for the Japanese citations in all the essays. Drawing on his remarkable knowledge of Japanese law, acquired while in Japan on a program fellowship, he contributed greatly to the endeavor to achieve accuracy and consistency in rendering Japanese terms and institutions into English.

Finally, I should like to express appreciation to Mrs. Richard A. Wiley and Miss Marcia Kelly for their excellent secretarial work on materials of unusual difficulty.

Arthur T. von Mehren

Cambridge, Mass.
December 1962

TABLE OF CONTENTS

EDITORIAL COLLABORATORS

Thomas L. Blakemore	—— Kenzo Takayanagi
Ben Bruce Blakeney	—— Ichiro Kato
Robert Braucher	—— Shinichiro Michida
Alexander Calhoun	—— Yoshio Kanazawa
David F. Cavers	—— Hakaru Abe
Rex Coleman	—— Morio Uematsu
Lawrence Ebb	—— Yoshio Kanazawa
Walter Gellhorn	—— Kichiemon Ishikawa
B. J. George, Jr.	—— Haruo Abe
	Ryuichi Hirano
	Atsushi Nagashima
John B. Hurlbut	—— Kohji Tanabe
Richard W. Jennings	—— Makoto Yazawa
Douglas B. Maggs	—— Kiminobu Hashimoto
Nathaniel L. Nathanson	—— Masami Ito
Richard W. Rabinowitz	—— Takaaki Hattori
Max Rheinstein	—— Yozo Watanabe
Timothy S. Williams	—— Hakaru Abe

PARTICIPANTS IN THE CONFERENCE

Abe, Haruo. Procurator, Instructing Officer, Ministry of Justice Comprehensive Research Institute, Ministry of Justice, Tokyo

Beardsley, Richard K. Professor, Department of Anthropology, University of Michigan

Bellah, Robert N. Associate Professor of Sociology and Regional Studies, Lecturer on World Religions, Harvard University

Blakemore, Thomas L. Practicing attorney, Tokyo

Blakeney, Ben Bruce. Practicing attorney, Tokyo

Braucher, Robert. Professor of Law, Harvard University

Broadbridge, Seymour. School of Oriental and African Studies, University of London

Calhoun, Alexander. Practicing attorney, Graham, James and Rolph, San Francisco and Tokyo

Cavers, David F. Professor of Law, Harvard University

Coleman, Rex. Research Associate in Law, Harvard University

Craig, Albert M. Assistant Professor of History, Harvard University

Ebb, Lawrence. Professor of Law, Stanford University

Gellhorn, Walter. Professor of Law, Columbia University

George, B. J., Jr. Professor of Law, University of Michigan

Hall, John. Professor of History, Yale University

Hashimoto, Kiminobu. Professor of Constitutional Law, Chuo University

Hattori, Takaaki. Judge, Tokyo District Court

Hirano, Ryuichi. Professor of Criminal Law, Tokyo University

Ishikawa, Kichiemon. Professor of Labor Law, Tokyo University

Jennings, Richard W. Professor of Law, University of California at Berkeley

Kanazawa, Yoshio. Professor of Economic Law, Hokkaido University

Kawashima, Takeyoshi. Professor of Civil Law, Tokyo University

King, John. Secretary, International Legal Studies, Harvard University

Lockwood, William. Professor of Public and International Affairs, Princeton University

Maggs, Douglas B. Professor of Law, Duke University

Michida, Shinichiro. Professor of Anglo-American Law, Kyoto University

von Mehren, Arthur T. Professor of Law, Harvard University

Morley, James W. Associate Professor, Department of Political Science, Columbia University

Nagashima, Yasuharu. Practicing attorney, Shozawa and Nagashima, Tokyo

Nathanson, Nathaniel L. Professor of Law, Northwestern University

Oppler, Alfred. Retired. Formerly Chief, Legislation and Justice Division, Legal Section, SCAP

Pelzel, John C. Professor of Anthropology and Director, Visiting Scholars Program, Harvard-Yenching Institute, Harvard University

Rabinowitz, Richard W. Executive Secretary, Japanese American Program for Cooperation in Legal Studies, and practicing attorney, Nattier, Anderson, Mori and Rabinowitz, Tokyo

Schwartz, Benjamin I. Professor of History and Government, Harvard University

Smith, Allan F. Dean and Professor of Law, University of Michigan

Steiner, Kurt. Professor, Department of Political Science, Stanford University

Tanabe, Kohji. Judge, Instructing Officer, Legal Research and Training Institute, Supreme Court of Japan

Williams, Timothy S. Practicing attorney, Nattier and Anderson, New York

Wyzanski, Charles. Judge, Federal District Court for Massachusetts

Yazawa, Makoto. Professor of Commercial Law, Tokyo University

Other persons attended one or more conference sessions of particular interest to them. These included: Hiroshi Kaneko, Assistant Professor of Administrative Law, Tokyo University, and Tokushige Yoshimura, Assistant Professor of Civil Procedure, Kyushu University; Robert M. Benjamin of the New York Bar; Livingston Hall, Louis Loss, Frank Sander, and Detlev Vagts, all Professors of Law, Harvard University; Norval Morris, Visiting Professor of Law, Harvard University, 1961–62; Martha T. Henderson, Executive Secretary of the Japan Society of Boston; and George Beckman and John Howard of the Ford Foundation.

THE JAPANESE AMERICAN PROGRAM FOR COOPERATION IN LEGAL STUDIES

David F. Cavers

THE conference on Japanese law of which this volume is the product was the culminating event in the Japanese American Program for Cooperation in Legal Studies, a program that had been initiated seven years before. Many of the conferees had been active participants in the program, and, without the long history of the friendly and scholarly relationships which the program had created, it would have been difficult to achieve either the frank and easy interchange which marked the proceedings of the conference or the editorial collaboration which contributed importantly to the conference papers. Accordingly, it seems appropriate, by way of introduction to this volume, to describe the genesis and nature of the Cooperative Program.

The program, moreover, has been an experiment in cultural exchange which has yielded a number of gratifying results. Although the program was in some respects the product of unique circumstances, the experience gained in its course may have value in guiding future interchange between the legal scholars of the two countries. I shall therefore note some of the problems encountered in the operation of the program and attempt to identify some of its achievements.

The Genesis and Development of the Program

In the winter of 1950–51, the Harvard Law School was asked to be host for three-day periods to two of the many groups of Japanese leaders who at that time were being brought on visits to the United States by the Department of State. The first of these groups to arrive in Cambridge was composed of six judges headed by Chief Justice Kotaro Tanaka of the Supreme Court of Japan.[1] About two months later came the second group which was

Note. Mr. Cavers is Fessenden Professor of Law, Harvard University. B.S., 1923, University of Pennsylvania; LL.B., 1926, Harvard University; D.Jur.Sc. (hon.) 1957, Suffolk University.

[1] The judicial group was comprised of the following: Chief Justice Kotaro Tanaka, Justice Shigeto Hozumi, and Justice Tsuyoshio Mano, of the Supreme Court of Japan; Judge Shuichi Ishizaka, Chief Judge, Sendai High Court; Judge Masaru Higuchi, Tokyo High Court and Chief, Foreign Liaison Section, General Secretariat of the Supreme Court of Japan; Judge Seiichi Kishi, Tokyo High Court and Chief, Criminal Affairs Bureau, General Secretariat of the Supreme Court of Japan. The group was accompanied by Dr. Alfred Oppler, Chief of the Legislation and Justice Division, SCAP, and James Perkins Parker, Escort Consultant.

comprised of six professors from the law faculties of Chuo, Keio, Kyoto, Tohoku, and Tokyo universities.[2] For both of these groups, we arranged programs of meetings with members of the Harvard law faculty to discuss subjects of interest to our visitors.

Whatever benefits our Japanese guests may have derived from these meetings, the exchange was most revelatory to the Harvard participants. We became fully aware for the first time how extensive had been the changes that, under the stimulus or direction of the occupation, had been wrought in Japanese law and how perplexing were the resulting problems to the Japanese judges and scholars who were now being called on to employ and to teach legal doctrines derived from a legal system with which few of them had had any prior acquaintance. Moreover, the problems they faced were immediate and serious; the normal, gradual processes of academic interchange seemed obviously inadequate to overcome them. A cooperative program designed to promote understanding on the part of jurists and scholars in both systems suggested itself. Accordingly, before the professorial group left Cambridge, we inquired whether they would be interested in having us explore the possibility of creating such a program under university auspices. The response was an encouraging affirmative.

As Chairman of Harvard's Committee on International Legal Studies, and subsequently as Associate Dean, I undertook to examine the possibility of developing a program which might advance the building of bridges of mutual understanding and communication between the legal scholars of the two countries. In this work I was aided by William S. Barnes, now Assistant Dean and Director of the World Tax Series, who was then surveying areas for research in foreign law. Our investigation led in 1952 to preliminary proposals to the Institute of International Education and to the Ford Foundation; in the following year, these had advanced to the point where a trip to Japan to consider plans with Japanese legal scholars, judges, and lawyers seemed essential. Accordingly, I obtained a grant from the institute to permit me to go to Japan for this purpose.

I spent five weeks in Japan in the summer of 1953 during which I discussed the organization of a cooperative program with members of the law faculties of the six universities later participating in the program, with the president of the Legal Training and Research Institute, and with a number of leading judges, government officials, and lawyers, including several

[2] The professorial group was comprised of the following: Shigemitsu Dando, Professor of Criminal Law, Tokyo University; Kinsho Katayama, Dean of the Department of Law and Professor of Civil Law and Philosophy of Law, Tohoku University; Shiro Kiyomiya, Professor of Constitutional Law, Tohoku University; Ryuichi Koike, Dean of the Department of Law and Professor of Civil Law and Economics, Keio University; Sanji Suyenobu, Professor of Anglo-American Law, Tokyo University. The group was accompanied by Dr. Kurt Steiner, as SCAP representative.

American lawyers practicing in Tokyo. I was most cordially received everywhere, but I should never have been able to achieve the degree of communication established if I had not had the constant assistance of Richard W. Rabinowitz. He not only aided me in arranging meetings and by interpreting but also was invaluable in explaining the significance of many matters that I would not otherwise have been able to appreciate. Later in this paper I shall report something of the background of this remarkable young lawyer-sociologist who came to play an important role in the program.

I first presented my ideas concerning a scheme of cooperation to Sanji Suyenobu, Professor of Anglo-American Law at Tokyo University, and, in the light of our discussion, formulated a tentative plan which I later submitted to the several law faculties. It was well received, and, upon my return, it was possible to use it with few modifications in developing the American end of the plan, which looked to enlisting the participation of two other American law schools. For these participants, the plan contemplated first-rate law schools situated in different parts of the country in universities that had active programs of Japanese studies. Happily, we were able to induce two law schools which clearly met these criteria, those of the University of Michigan and of Stanford University, to join in the enterprise.

Though we had reason to hope that the program would be aided by Fulbright awards by the United States Educational Commission in Japan, a substantial additional sum was required, and application was made to the Ford Foundation. Because of the large amount of administrative work entailed in a program involving extensive educational exchange, we sought the good offices of the Institute of International Education and proposed that the grant be made to it, to be administered under the guidance of a committee representing the three American law schools. Our application was favorably considered, and a grant was made to the institute in May 1954.

I have already noted the concern from which the idea of a cooperative program grew: our belated realization of the predicament which the bold experiment of the United States in transplanting American laws and legal institutions into the Japanese system had created for the legal profession and the legal scholars of Japan. American law faculties had not been participants in that experiment, nor were they, of course, committed to strive for its success. However, the risk that such an experiment would fail because the transplanted laws had not been properly understood and hence could not be properly employed and evaluated was one to which American law schools, as institutions responsible for the exposition and transmission of the American legal tradition, could not remain insensitive. As I noted in reporting to the institute and the Ford Foundation: "The American laws are not entitled to preservation in the Japanese system simply because of their source or the good intentions with which they were put forward. However, they should be weighed by people who understand them and who can evaluate their usefulness in Japanese society in light of the functions they have played in the United States. This calls for a task of cooperative character in which both Japanese and Americans should participate."

These considerations gave some direction to the development of the program plan: our primary concern was with those areas of law in which the experiment of transplantation had been carried furthest. Both practical and theoretical considerations strongly reinforced this emphasis. For the Japanese, it was in these areas that their "need to know" was greatest and in which they had most to learn from American law schools. For the Americans, these areas offered an absorbing subject for study: the reception of segments of American law into a fully developed but alien legal system operating in a society that differs from the American in many respects.

Needless to say, the emphasis to which these considerations led did not operate to exclude concern with the two systems as wholes. On the contrary, the basic problem of understanding was to understand not simply the provisions of the laws that had been transplanted but how those laws had functioned within the total system from which they had been taken. For American scholars there has been the further problem of achieving an understanding of the total system into which the American laws were introduced, a continuing problem which the conference and this volume should do much to help us meet.

The sense of institutional responsibility for furthering an understanding of the Japanese laws of American origin influenced planning in another respect. How could our limited resources be put to most effective use? This question led to a search for ways in which those resources could be multiplied, and this in turn suggested the desirability of seeking to establish bases for continuing collaboration in a group of law schools in each country rather than simply to subsidize the studies of individual scholars. The decision to pursue this objective led, of course, to the restriction of the program to a relatively small number of universities; a larger number would have spread our resources too thin to achieve the relationships we wished to create. Well-qualified law schools in both countries had to be left out. However, we were reconciled to this necessity by the consideration that we were planning for the needs of a temporary, critical situation, that over a longer range of time there would be no need to channel arrangements in this fashion. Moreover, we were sure that, if our program prospered, its benefits would be shared by other schools and scholars in both countries.

Concern with the immediate problem confronting the Japanese legal profession and law faculties influenced planning in still another way. We were not content to proceed simply on the basis of an exchange of students, even of advanced students. Instead, the plan called for the principal exchange to be at the faculty level. Moreover, when we in the United States came to realize how the task of education for the legal profession was shared in Japan by the judiciary through the Legal Training and Research Institute, we recognized the importance of including the institute along with university law faculties as a participant in the program, a step which we believe did much to enhance the program's usefulness.

THE STRUCTURE OF THE PROGRAM

The plan that was adopted was structurally complex. The program was divided into three subprograms. The first subprogram called for a group of eight Japanese law teachers of junior rank (including judges scheduled to teach at the Legal Training and Research Institute) to come to the United States for a period of two years. The first year they were to spend together as a group at the Harvard Law School; in the second year, they were to be divided between the law schools of Michigan and Stanford. This group upon their return to Japan would constitute a nucleus of teachers familiar with American law and methods of legal education who could cooperate with the Americans coming to Japan on the second and third subprograms.

The second subprogram called for at least one member of the faculty of each of the three cooperating American law schools to go to one of the cooperating Japanese law schools for up to one year, there to engage in teaching and research in which members of the faculties of other cooperating Japanese law schools might also join.

The third subprogram was divided into two parts, each of which contemplated the sending of law-school graduates from one country to spend three years of study in the other country. Eight Japanese were to be sent to the United States, one from each of the cooperating law schools, one from the judiciary, and one from the procuracy. Three American law graduates were to go to Japan, one from each of the cooperating law schools.

The period of three years was regarded as the minimum necessary to enable an advanced student to obtain a real understanding of the law, the language, and the society of the country to which he went. In the case of the American student, it was recognized that he would have to devote much of his time to language study. However, the Japanese legal system confronted him with a less formidable body of learning to master than the American federal-state conglomerate did his Japanese counterpart.

For general policy guidance and for the selection of participants in the three subprograms, two committees were created, each of which was comprised of a representative of each cooperating school,[3] and, in the case of the Japanese committee, the faculty group was supplemented by certain distin-

[3] The American committee was composed of Dean E. Blythe Stason of Michigan (until his retirement in 1961 when Dean Allan F. Smith succeeded him), Dean Carl B. Spaeth of Stanford, and myself.

guished members of the legal profession.[4] To assist the Japanese committee in evaluating the capability of candidates for study in the United States, it created an American advisory committee, including American lawyers practicing in Tokyo.[5] Professor Sanji Suyenobu of Tokyo University served as chairman of the Japanese committee, and I served as chairman of the American committee.[6]

As noted above, financial affairs, travel arrangements, and the like were administered by the Institute of International Education, which sought the guidance of the American committee on questions of policy.

For coordination of the program's activities and to aid both the Japanese going to the United States and the Americans coming to Japan, need was felt for a full-time representative of the program in Tokyo. The person who seemed best qualified to fill this role was Richard Rabinowitz. He was persuaded to accept an appointment as program secretary, with the understanding that he and his wife would accompany the group in the first subprogram to Harvard and, after a year there with them, would return to Tokyo. As my description of the program's activities should make plain, he played a key role in their execution.[7]

[4] The nonfaculty members of the Japanese committee, who were asked to serve by Chief Justice Tanaka, were: Dr. Joji Matsumoto (a lawyer who had been eminent as a professor, business executive, and statesman), Dr. Kenzo Takayanagi (Professor Emeritus of Anglo-American Law at Tokyo University and President of Seikei University) and Dr. Shigehara Matsumoto (a lawyer who had recently become head of the International House in Tokyo). Upon Joji Matsumoto's death, Chief Justice Tanaka enlisted Somei Ugawa, President of Meiji University and President of the International Bar Association of Japan.

The law-faculty representatives were Professor K. Katayama, Chuo University; Dean R. Koike, Keio University; Dean T. Saito, Kyoto University; Dean S. Kiyomiya, Tohoku University; Dean T. Otaka and Professor S. Suyenobu, Tokyo University, and Professor (later President) S. Ohama, Waseda University. Professor Suyenobu was elected chairman.

[5] The American committee, organized in 1954, was composed of James B. Anderson, Ben Bruce Blakeney, and Thomas L. Blakemore of the Tokyo bar, and Dr. W. K. Bunce of the U.S. Educational Commission in Japan (which administered the Fulbright program). In 1955, Alexander Calhoun served in place of Anderson and Jules Bassin, Legal Adviser to the U.S. Embassy, in place of Bunce.

[6] Professor Suyenobu, having become Professor Emeritus at Tokyo University, joined the law faculty of Rikkyo (St. Paul's) University in 1960 but, to the pleasure of those associated with the program, agreed to continue to serve as chairman of the committee.

[7] Richard W. Rabinowitz, a native of New Haven, Connecticut, is a graduate of Yale College and School of Law, receiving an A.B. degree in 1945, an LL.B. degree in 1950, and an M.A. degree in 1951. During World War II, he was assigned to an Army unit which received intensive training in the Japanese language although he did not serve in Japan. During summer vacations while in law school, he joined a group of sociologists who were making a study of the legal profession in a Connecticut city for the American Bar Survey. This work aroused his interest in the sociology of the legal profession, and he conceived the idea of combining his interests in law, sociology, and Japan in a study of the Japanese legal profession. For this purpose, he secured a grant from the Social Science Research Council which enabled him to pursue sociological studies at Harvard. He then obtained a grant from the Ford Foundation which took him and his wife to Japan where he had been less than a year when I interrupted his field study by enlisting his help. Ultimately he completed his dissertation and received a Ph.D. in social science from Harvard University in 1956. A portion of this study was published as *The Historical Development of the Japanese Bar,* 70 HARV. L. REV. 61

The time span conceived for the program was five or six years. However, it proved advantageous to defer the second subprogram until the first had been completed and that fact, plus our inability to schedule the sending of American law teachers to Japan in successive years, made it desirable to extend the program until 1961. This entailed some additional expenditures,[8] and the program might have been financially embarrassed but for the liberality of the Ford Foundation in making a supplementary grant to the institute. Even so, the program would have had to have been curtailed but for the generous support it received from the United States Educational Commission in Japan. Fulbright awards were made to all but one of the Americans going to Japan on the second and third subprograms, and Fulbright travel grants were received by all the eligible Japanese going to the United States on the first and third subprograms.

So much for the structure of the program. In succeeding sections, I shall report with greater particularity on the activities in each subprogram.

The First Subprogram

For the first subprogram, it was understood that an effort would be made to enlist scholars of great promise, preferably assistant professors in their early thirties, who would probably achieve professorial rank soon after their return. In the selection of candidates for this subprogram, it was understood that choice among the university candidates was to be based on the individual applicant's merit and that places would not be apportioned among the cooperating schools. Since the period available for study here was to be limited to two years, considerable emphasis had to be placed on linguistic ability.

The sifting process (which included written, oral, and physical examinations) was conducted by the Japanese committee with the aid of the American advisory committee. It resulted in the choice of six assistant professors, four of whom were from Tokyo University. The six and their fields of principal interest were: Kiminobu Hashimoto, Chuo University (constitutional and administrative law); Ryuichi Hirano, Tokyo University (criminal law and procedure); Kichiemon Ishikawa, Tokyo University (labor law); Masami Ito, Tokyo University (constitutional law); Shinichiro Michida, Kyoto University (constitutional and criminal law); Makoto Yazawa, Tokyo University (commercial law).

From the judiciary two judges were selected by the Judicial Council (composed of justices of the Supreme Court): Takaaki Hattori, who had

(1956). An important adjunct to Rabinowitz' work for the program was the contribution of his wife, Janice, a charming and talented young lady, who, in addition to her busy role as hostess to participants in the program and the program's many visitors, gave instruction in English and in American folkways to wives of the Japanese scholars going to the United States.

[8] A mutually agreeable economy was achieved by an arrangement at the time of the extension which permitted Rabinowitz to devote half his time to law practice in Tokyo.

been a judge in the Tokyo District Court but at the time was serving as head of the First Section of the Civil Affairs Bureau in the Supreme Court General Secretariat, and Kohji Tanabe, who had just been transferred from the Labor Division of the Tokyo District Court to the District Court at Nagoya. Judge Hattori's chief interest related to problems of judicial administration, an area to which the changing role of the judiciary under postwar laws had given great importance. Judge Tanabe was chiefly concerned with the fact-finding process in adjudication and the changes worked in it by the postwar shift from the inquisitorial to the adversary system.

The group did not include any representative of the procuracy, a fact that was noted with regret by the Procurator-General, Tosuke Sato, in a letter to the author. A solution was found through a happy coincidence. A deputy procurator from Hokkaido, Haruo Abe, had come to the Harvard Law School on his own initiative the year before and, having done excellent work, was spending a second year at Harvard, pursuing criminological studies under Sheldon Glueck while carrying a heavy load of outside work. Abe was invited to join the program and a grant made to relieve his financial burden.

Course programs were worked out at Harvard for the eight newcomers to reflect their respective interests, and they were soon subjected to all the stresses and confusion that the case system of legal education imposes on graduate students from other countries, especially those to whom English is not a familiar tongue. However, in the gradual process of mastering this system, they were aided by the guidance of Richard Rabinowitz. Moreover, in many ways, he and his wife, Janice, were able to acquaint the group with American life outside the law school. Illuminating trips and meetings were arranged; informal supper parties with members of the faculty held at the Rabinowitz apartment gave to the group a richer range of contacts than would ordinarily have been possible at a large law school.

As the year drew to an end, plans for the second year of study had to be made. Four of the group, Hashimoto, Michida, Yazawa, and Hattori, elected to go to Michigan; Hirano, Ito, and Tanabe, to Stanford; Ishikawa had found the offerings of the Economics Department and the Graduate School of Business Administration at Harvard of such interest in his study of labor relations that he arranged to spend his second year in Cambridge. Abe, having already completed his second year in the United States, returned to Japan.

In the course of the first year, a decision was reached to enable the wives and children of the group to join their husbands for their second year in the United States. This decision was reached by the American committee with some misgivings — and not only for budgetary reasons. It was feared that the presence of the wives might divert the group from useful informal associations with their fellow students. However, the experiment proved highly successful; the presence of wives and children opened up various points of contact with Americans that would have remained closed to monastic scholars.

The shift from Cambridge to Ann Arbor or Stanford enabled each member of the group making the change not only to encounter a different faculty and university community but also a different section of the United States. To the opportunties afforded by this change in locale must be added those created by the summer traveling in which the group engaged, frequently by car. It was evident that, when the time to return to Japan came, the members of the group took back with them not only a considerable insight into the processes of American law and legal education but also some appreciation of the social context in which those processes operate.

The Second Subprogram

The problem presented by the second subprogram was quite distinct from that posed by the first. The basic difference was that there were no teachers in the three cooperating law schools (if, indeed, in all the law schools of America) who had a command of the Japanese language at all comparable to the knowledge of English possessed by the Japanese teachers who came to the United States in the first subprogram. It was not possible, therefore, to send American law teachers to Japan to study law there in any systematic way. The principal contribution the American law teacher could make in going to Japan would be to present American law and legal experience to Japanese scholars in such a way as to invite comparisons between American and Japanese problems and their legal solutions. Even though neither party to the exchange could penetrate very deeply into the legal system of the other, the successful use of the processes of comparison could enlarge each participant's understanding of his own system's problems. Moreover, even though the American scholar's exposure to Japanese law and legal education would necessarily be restricted, the direct association in a common enterprise with Japanese law teachers and students and with the Japanese legal profession would equip him to communicate more effectively with Japanese scholars and students in the future, especially with those coming to the United States for advanced study.

The most satisfactory medium for teaching for the American law teacher was thought to be a seminar for Japanese law teachers, to which members of the bench and bar could also be admitted. Lectures to students might be welcomed, but it was doubtful how much lasting gain could be expected to result from them. The seminar, however, gave promise of providing an effective two-way interchange, interpretation by seminar members being relied on to surmount language barriers.

The first tests of the seminar technique came in 1956–57 when Professor Arthur T. von Mehren of Harvard and Assistant Professor B. J. George, Jr., of Michigan went to Tokyo University and Kyoto University respectively. Professor von Mehren, whose field is comparative law and who had worked extensively in European legal systems, offered two seminars, one in the judicial process and the other in the reaction of legal systems to social and economic change. Professor George offered a graduate seminar in certain aspects of the American law of criminal procedure and evidence at Kyoto University, and then offered instruction in the same fields to procurators and practitioners in Kyoto.

Both scholars arrived in Japan sufficiently in advance to enable them to join in planning the seminars with the Japanese scholars who were to share in their direction of the seminars — in both instances, participants in the first subprogram. In Tokyo, moreover, Richard Rabinowitz took an active part in the planning process. Von Mehren's first seminar on the judicial process was given under the auspices of the Legal Training and Research Institute. Judge Tanabe shared in its direction, and a number of judges were among the participants. In the second seminar, the sponsorship was that of the Department of Law of Tokyo University. The subject was divided into three areas: industrial accidents, commercial transactions, and labor relations; and the seminar members, chiefly from the faculties of the cooperating schools, were divided into separate groups, coming together for the closing sessions. Professors Ito, Ishikawa, and Yazawa took an active role in the direction of these groups. The emphasis was on Japanese law, with American and European comparisons being introduced by von Mehren as occasion warranted.

The graduate instruction undertaken by Professor George in Kyoto involved a rather systematic study of the Code of Criminal Procedure and the Criminal Procedure Regulations, in which he worked with Professor Michida's aid. In George's work with the procurators and practitioners, comparisons between Japanese and American law inspired extensive questioning. The areas of law to which the two courses were directed were of great practical importance in the Japanese legal system which was then seeking to assimilate the major changes worked in the trial of criminal cases by the postwar legislation.

Disappointments in working out arrangements for sending an American law teacher to Japan in 1957–58 led to a year's hiatus in the second subprogram. In 1958–59, however, Professor Robert Braucher of the Harvard Law School went over for the second half of the year at the invitation of Chuo University. Because of the shorter time at Braucher's disposal, it was important to have preparatory work initiated before he went to Japan. Arrangements were worked out through Rabinowitz for employing the services of Professor Michida of Kyoto who, in addition to being a scholar in the field of criminal law (in which he had aided Professor George), is also expert in commercial law. In the semester before Braucher's arrival, agenda for the seminar were formulated, and he designated certain portions of *Commercial Transactions,* the course books of which he is coeditor,[9] to be used in connection with it. These portions were then translated into Japanese by Michida, comprising a work of about four hundred mimeographed pages, which is now being expanded into a three-volume work for use in Japanese law schools.[10] In addition, Rabinowitz, working with two groups of ten scholars each, devoted weekly sessions to preparatory studies for nearly three months. The resulting faculty seminar (which was attended by faculty members from the four cooperating schools in Tokyo and by selected judges, lawyers, and businessmen) proved highly successful. Subsequently, using the same materials, Braucher conducted student seminars at Tokyo and Chuo universities and a faculty seminar at Keio.

The value of having American legal materials in translation for the use of the seminar members was demonstrated so clearly in Braucher's experience that, the year following, it was decided to follow this precedent for the fourth American law teacher to go to Japan on the second subprogram, Professor John B. Hurlbut of Stanford. In preparation for his seminar, Rabinowitz and Professor Hirano of Tokyo University joined with other university people and representatives of the Legal Training and Research Institute and of the Ministry of Justice (including Atsushi Nagashima, a procurator who had spent two years at Stanford in the third subprogram) in developing agenda and translating Hurlbut's American materials for a seminar to be held at Tokyo University. This seminar undertook to consider problems posed by the privilege against self-incrimination and by hearsay evidence. The seminar was attended by faculty members of the cooperating schools and certain trial judges, procurators, and lawyers. All these branches of the profession were present — though in much larger numbers — in a seminar conducted later in the spring by Hurlbut at the Legal Institute. This brought together some of the outstanding members of the Tokyo bench, bar, and procuracy to discuss problems of criminal procedure and evidence, a combination of the branches of the legal profession much less usual in Japan than in the United States. Both seminars were judged highly successful.

[9] BRAUCHER & SUTHERLAND, COMMERCIAL TRANSACTIONS — CASES AND PROBLEMS (2d ed., 1958); BRAUCHER & SUTHERLAND, COMMERCIAL TRANSACTIONS — TEXT, FORMS, STATUTES (2d ed., 1958).

[10] BRAUCHER & MICHIDA, AMERIKA SHŌ-TORIHIKI HŌ TO NIHON MINSHŌ HŌ (American Law on Commercial Transactions and the Japanese Civil and Commercial Codes), published by the Tokyo University Press. Volume I appeared in 1960 and volume II in 1961. The work is designed for a comparative course in Anglo-American law in this field. It represents a sharp departure from the conventional subject matter of courses in Anglo-American law. In the preface (an English version of which appears on pp. xv–xxi), Michida explains that the materials, first tested in Braucher's seminars at Chuo and Tokyo universities, were given a third test in a symposium on the law of security interests held the following summer by the Japan Private Law Association in which assistance was furnished by professors of Osaka Municipal and Kobe universities, the Tokyo Chamber of Commerce and Industry, and the Ministry of Finance.

In addition to these two seminars, Hurlbut also gave a course for candidates for the first degree in law at Keio University. For this course, Assistant Professor Ryo Taira, who had spent three years in the United States on the third subprogram, had prepared a casebook of Japanese and translated American materials. Professor Hurlbut felt that the students came gradually to enjoy the process of being questioned closely in the manner of an American law class.

Though the most substantial contributions made by the American visitors in the second subprogram were channeled through the seminars and courses I have described, all of them engaged in a considerable amount of lecturing. As recipients of Fulbright awards, they were, of course, expected to visit other parts of the country and to give lectures at universities other than the ones which had sponsored their invitations. Not infrequently these engagements brought them before much larger numbers of lawyers and law students than did the seminars. Moreover, the opportunity to visit other law departments and other parts of the country mitigated in some degree the concentration of attention on the cooperating schools in the Tokyo area.

Experience in the conduct of the second subprogram reinforced the reason for confining the program to a relatively small number of law departments and for not extending it geographically farther from Tokyo than Kyoto in the south and Tohoku at Sendai in the north. Indeed, even with these limitations, it did not prove feasible to assure all the cooperating schools an equal opportunity for participation in the activities of the visiting American teachers. There were simply not enough to go around, and regrettably none was able to offer a seminar at Tohoku.

Although the American law teachers in the second subprogram were kept busy in discharging their responsibilities, they all found the experience a stimulating and enjoyable one. Because they were disqualified by linguistic limitations from pursuing Japanese studies, there had been no reason for them to spend an initial period of study in Japan alone, and provision had therefore been made for them to be accompanied by their wives and children. As in the case of the Japanese scholars, the presence of the families added significantly to the value of the exchange by bringing the American visitors into contact with phases of Japanese life that would scarcely have been observed by professors traveling alone.

The Third Subprogram

The goal of the third subprogram was to assure the existence in each country of a nucleus of legal scholars with a good understanding of the legal system and society of the other country and possessing a sufficient command of its language to permit effective work with its legal materials. Hopefully, a number of the participants would be appointed to the law faculties of their own universities and so would provide a continuing link between those faculties and the cooperating schools in the other country.

The Japanese scholars. The plan contemplated that eight Japanese scholars would be selected from the cooperating institutions, preferably one from each university, one from the judiciary, and one from the procuracy. Moreover, though it was not contemplated that all would go to the United States in the same year, the candidates were all selected at the same time by the Japanese committee, with assistance from the American advisory committee. The result was to give to the candidates whose departure was deferred a chance better to prepare themselves. Allowances were provided to permit them to obtain special instruction in English, and Richard Rabinowitz conducted an informal seminar on American law.

The question arose whether each scholar should spend one year at each of the three cooperating American law schools. This seemed unwise since, with each move, substantial time would be lost in fitting into the new environment and instructional program. Instead, the plan was adopted of having each scholar spend two years at one law school and his third year at another. An effort was made to distribute the participants among the three American law schools so that each school would have about the same degree of association with the group. In some instances, it was possible to assign a scholar to a given school because its course offerings appeared best suited to his individual interest. As in the case of the Japanese in the first subprogram, opportunities were opened up, by means of summer travel and summer-school courses, for the participants to see other universities and other parts of the country.

The first Japanese scholars to come to the United States on the third subprogram were two graduates of the law departments of Keio University in Tokyo and Tohoku University in Sendai. Ryo Taira of Keio was preparing for teaching in the field of Anglo-American law. He spent two years at Michigan, and his final year at Stanford. Yoshito Obuki of Tohoku was interested chiefly in constitutional law. He spent two years at Harvard and his third year at Michigan. Coming to the United States at the same time was an experienced procurator, Atsushi Nagashima. He spent both years of his two-year stay at Stanford, taking advantage in his second year of the opportunity afforded for observation of the California courts.[11]

In 1957–58, three more scholars arrived: Yoshiya Kawamata of Kyoto University; Kensuke Kobori of Chuo University; and Yoichi Nagahama of Waseda University. Kawamata's chief field of interest was admiralty law. After two years at Harvard, where he obtained an LL.M. degree, he completed his work at Michigan. Kobori, a specialist in Anglo-American law,

[11] Nagashima was considerably older than the other Japanese coming in the third subprogram, and for this reason it seemed appropriate to limit his stay to two years.

devoted two years to study at Stanford and the third year at Michigan. Nagahama, whose field was commercial law, spent two years at Michigan and his third year at Stanford.

In 1958–59, the final two visitors on the third subprogram arrived. One of these was Assistant Professor Hideo Tanaka of Tokyo University, whose field was Anglo-American law. He spent his first year at Stanford and the second at Harvard.[12] The other was Judge Yasuo Tokikuni, who was interested in judicial administration. He spent two years at Harvard, obtaining an LL.M. degree, and his third year at Michigan.

On the basis of our experience with the first subprogram, arrangements were made for the married scholars to be joined by their wives and children after the first year in the United States.

The American scholars. The task of enlisting American law-school graduates of high caliber for three years of study in Japan was recognized as a difficulty from the beginning. The principal barriers were two: the problem of language and career uncertainties. The American committee had to explain to applicants that, within the three-year period in Japan, a substantial amount of exceedingly exacting study would have to be devoted to achieving a working knowledge of the Japanese language and that law study would have to be subordinated to this. The committee also had to confess that it could offer no assurances that attractive career opportunities would be opened up by achieving a knowledge of Japanese law and language. Japan does not allow more American lawyers to be added to those already admitted to practice there, of whom about fifteen are still active. The development of comparative studies is still in such a rudimentary stage in American law schools that mastery of another legal system does not open many academic doors. About all that applicants could be told was that, by engaging in this study, they would have acquired a knowledge and skill possessed by few other American lawyers and that this might some day enable them to engage in work which they would find more satisfying than more familiar forms of law practice.

Despite the deterrent effect of these considerations, the committee was successful in enlisting three capable law graduates, one from each of the cooperating schools. In two cases personal considerations reinforced their professional interests: their wives were natives of Japan. In the third case, interest in Japan and Japanese culture had been stimulated by time spent there during military service in the Korean War. Moreover, unlike most of the Japanese scholars, the successful American candidates did not apply primarily with a view to academic careers.

The first applicant to qualify was a graduate of the Stanford University School of Law, Rex Coleman. Coleman stood high in his class and was one

[12] Because he had had a year at Harvard a few years before, Tanaka's fellowship provided for only two years' study in the third subprogram.

of the editors of the *Stanford Law Review*. Arrangements were made to enable him to devote a graduate year exclusively to Japanese study, with much individually directed work, before going to Japan in the summer of 1956. Thanks to that intensive training, Coleman was able to begin law study upon his enrolment in Tokyo University. In his first semester, he took only the course in civil law, the beginning course for Japanese law students. By the end of the semester, he found that his comprehension of the lectures was nearly complete and so, in the next and succeeding semesters, he took a full program of law courses, supplementing this with attendance at courses in the Legal Training and Research Institute. By the end of his three years in Japan, Coleman had completed much more course and seminar work than was required for the degree of master of jurisprudence. The completion of the dissertation required for the degree was facilitated by an arrangement worked out with the International Program in Taxation at the Harvard Law School. He joined in a study of the Japanese tax system that was being undertaken by legal specialists in the Ministry of Finance for inclusion in Harvard's World Tax Series. Coleman, who obtained his M.Jur. from Tokyo University in 1960, is now continuing the tax study at Harvard.

The next applicant to be appointed was an honor graduate of the Harvard Law School, Timothy S. Williams, who went to Japan on a Fulbright fellowship in September 1957. His first year was spent in Tokyo where he pursued the study of Japanese at the Tokyo School for the Japanese Language (commonly known as the Naganuma School), supplemented by specialized tutoring directed to building up a legal vocabulary. He was convinced that a relatively short period of this instruction was worth more than his prior language study in American universities, which, because it had to be subordinated to his law studies, lacked the intensive character of his work in Japan. In retrospect, he regretted the time devoted to language work in America which he felt might better have been spent in more general, cultural studies.

In the fall of 1958, Williams and his wife and infant daughter moved to Kyoto where he began attending a course in civil law, aided by some tutoring from a brilliant senior. Williams continued his studies at Kyoto until the beginning of 1960 when he and his family returned to Tokyo. By 1960, he had made great progress in both language and legal studies, and arrangements were made to permit him to extend his stay in Japan so that he could engage in research in Japanese law and have some law-office experience. In the course of this extension, he was able to translate a considerable body of commercial-law material for a seminar to be given in Tokyo by Professor Richard W. Jennings of the University of California Law School in Berkeley. Another indication of Williams' progress before he returned to the United States in the summer of 1961 was his translation of the paper in this volume on "Education of the Legal Profession in Japan" by Hakaru Abe.

The third American law graduate to go to Japan on the third subprogram was Carl J. Bradshaw, a 1957 honor graduate of the University of Minnesota Law School where he had been a research assistant to Kenneth C. Davis, the author of the leading American treatise on administrative law. With a view to going to Japan for the program, Bradshaw enrolled as a graduate student at the University of Michigan Law School where he obtained the LL.M. degree in June 1958, having specialized in the legal problems of international trade and finance. In September of that year, Bradshaw, who had received a Fulbright fellowship, went with his wife and child to Tokyo. There he too entered the Naganuma School and in less than one year obtained certificates for two years of work, an experience that led him independently to the same conclusion reached by Williams concerning the limited value of attempting to combine Japanese language study with law study in the United States. In the summer of 1959, he entered the Department of Law of Keio University and became a candidate for a master's degree. He was successful in completing the required course work in the summer of 1961, but, in order to obtain some practical office experience in working with Japanese law while completing his dissertation, his period of study was extended to the end of that year. He is, in early 1962, in Tokyo, serving in an apprentice capacity in an American law firm there, and expects in time to return to its office in the United States.

The Conference

As the completion of the Cooperative Program approached, the question arose of whether its gains might not be consolidated by enabling the Japanese scholars who had been here on the first subprogram to come back to the United States for a few months of research in their respective fields. We noted that, if these refresher visits could be scheduled for the summer and fall of 1961, a period of about five years would have elapsed from the end of the first subprogram, a span long enough in duration to provide perspective for the visitors' new observations of the institutions and processes of American law.

When Arthur von Mehren discussed this idea with officials of the Ford Foundation, he coupled it with the suggestion that the occasion of these visits might be used for the holding of a conference that would bring together American and Japanese legal scholars who had been cooperating in legal studies under both the program and other auspices. Moreover, it seemed to him an apt occasion to bring their reflections on developments in contemporary Japanese law to the attention of students of Japanese society from other disciplines and in turn to obtain the benefit of their views.

Both the plan for refresher visits and the plan for the conference were warmly received by John B. Howard, John Scott Everton, and other Ford Foundation officials; an additional grant was made in 1960, and again the good offices of the International Institute were secured for its administration. Although conflicting responsibilities prevented some of the participants in the first subprogram from taking advantage of the full five months of study here that we were prepared to provide, all nine of them were able to come back for at least a month and most of them for several months. Indeed, one scholar, Shinichiro Michida, has worked out arrangements that will permit him to spend about two years in this country, chiefly to enlarge his knowledge of commercial credit and financing devices, a field which had been opened up for him by his active role in Professor Braucher's seminars.

The conference, held early in September 1961, exceeded the hopes of its sponsors. However, in a volume containing both the essays that were presented to the conference and also von Mehren's distillation of its proceedings, there is no need for me to acclaim its merits.

THE EFFECTS OF THE PROGRAM

To identify and appraise the effects of any significant enterprise in the field of education is difficult. If the effects have been important, then their consequences will inevitably manifest themselves over a long span of years. However, during those years, many other forces and factors will have been at work, so that it will become increasingly difficult to disentangle the effects of the educational undertaking under study from the effects of those other influences.

Despite these difficulties, all of which are peculiarly pertinent to any attempt to estimate the effects of the Cooperative Program, I shall hazard some impressions concerning the program's effects that I have derived from discussions and correspondence with participants and with others who, like myself, have had observers' roles.[13] Needless to say, although I have been only an observer of the actual educational processes which I had a hand in administering, I have not been a disinterested observer. Whether consciousness of my bias has led me to lean forward or backward in my estimates is a matter on which I am incompetent to testify.

It is, of course, possible to measure educational achievements, like many other human accomplishments, by reducing them to products that can be counted. The program had an output susceptible of being measured in numerical terms, say, in units of "scholar-years." Using such a yardstick, it could claim to have produced thirty-nine Japanese scholar-years in the United States and eighteen American scholar-years in Japan. Moreover, it would be possible to trace each scholar's career since the completion of his work for

[13] A description and not unsympathetic appraisal of the program appears in BRONFENBRENNER, ACADEMIC ENCOUNTER: THE AMERICAN UNIVERSITY IN JAPAN AND KOREA 96–106 (1961). This work, which surveys seventeen American university programs in Japan and Korea, is based chiefly on interviews from June to December 1958. Much of the evidence on which I have based my own more optimistic evaluation relates to developments after the end of Bronfenbrenner's period of observation.

the program in order to list the posts to which he had been appointed in academic life or within his country's legal system or as an expert in this or that phase of law. If such a measure were used, the program's Japanese participants could point to their records with great satisfaction, especially those who came here on the first subprogram. They have moved up the academic ladder, their views have been sought on public issues, and they have served on various governmental bodies. The younger men who came to the United States on the third subprogram have scarcely had time in which to demonstrate in Japan their capacity for achievement, but of late they have begun to find opportunities to use their new learning in university teaching or in official roles. Of the American participants in the third subprogram, two are already engaging in law-office work involving Japanese problems, and, as was noted above, the third is pursuing research in the Japanese tax system at Harvard.

A number of the Japanese participants have been prolific writers, and, in one instance, a volume by a participant has been singled out for an unusual distinction: in 1959, *Freedom of Speech and Press* by Masami Ito of Tokyo University, a member of the first subprogram, was granted the Japan Academy Award, the first book on a legal subject to receive this highly prized accolade in more than twenty years.[14] However, I have made no effort to compile a bibliography of the publications of the participants in the various subprograms. It would be a long one and it will grow, but I believe more significant measures of achievement must be sought for the program, even though they will not be susceptible of objective measurement.

In describing the genesis of the program, I laid some stress on the sense of responsibility which was felt here to enable Japanese jurists and legal scholars to attain a greater understanding of the elements of American law that had been introduced into the Japanese legal system. Has this objective been materially advanced?

I shall not attempt to answer the question simply in terms of the enhanced understanding of particular individuals; instead, in this and the next few subsections of my essay, I shall point to several developments to which I believe the program has contributed and which should continue to work in Japan toward a more widespread and a more sophisticated knowledge of American law. I hope it is not too great an overstatement that, to quote a letter to me from one observer, "Today one cannot be a 'serious' scholar of law in Japan without dealing with the American law of one's field."

To the extent that this is true, I am sure the development is due in no

[14] ITO, GENRON, SHUPPAN NO JIYŪ, published by Iwanami Shoten. Of this work, Ito wrote in a letter to me, "As you may imagine, it is the consequence of my study under our program. In this book I analyzed the American case law to find the standards determining constitutionality of laws limiting free speech and discussed as to whether these standards would be applicable under the Japanese constitution."

small measure to the achievements of the outstanding scholars of the first subprogram who, in their teaching and writing since their return, have been able to demonstrate both the relevance and the accessibility of American law to the Japanese scholar. This has removed American law from the status of a specialty to be entrusted exclusively to the specialists in Anglo-American law. Once American law is studied not for itself but as an aid to the solution of Japanese legal problems, the necessity of penetrating below the level of textual similarities and dissimilarities to the functional parallels and divergences of the respective laws becomes evident. And, of course, recognition of the substantive relevance of American law for scholarship in many fields of Japanese law multiplies the number of Japanese scholars who will find its study rewarding, if not imperative.

An unexpected consequence of the exposure of Japanese legal educators to the American system of legal education has been the stimulation of a lively interest in its objectives and methods, both of which differ sharply from those traditional to the Japanese law departments. It seems likely to me that the program served to enhance this interest to a significantly greater degree than might have been anticipated from study in this country by an equal number of individual Japanese law teachers. The program constantly fostered group interchange directed to educational problems, whether in the studies pursued by the groups in the first subprogram or in the planning and conduct of seminars with American law teachers in the second subprogram.

No one, of course, would expect that out of a growing Japanese interest in American legal education would come a drastic remodeling of Japanese legal education. However, American ideas may be found in the yeast that appears to be fermenting in the Japanese's thinking about their own legal-educational system. The greater concern of the American law teacher with concrete fact, with the social and economic impact of the laws he is examining and with their relation to the lawyer's role in the legal system, may begin to manifest itself in Japanese law teaching even though no important changes are made in institutional structures or programs.

If trends of this sort become discernible, they should serve in the course of time to make communication easier and more rewarding between the law teachers of the two countries. This naturally would minister to greater understanding of both legal systems.

One of the most striking aspects of the Japanese legal system to the American observer ten years ago was the extent to which the Japanese legal scholars in the universities were isolated from the other branches of the profession: the bench, the procuracy, and the bar. This isolation, of course, was not complete and various postwar measures were already working to reduce it. Nonetheless the contrast was a sharp one. Moreover, it seemed especially unfortunate that this isolation should exist when, after a period of rapid legal change, all branches of the profession were confronted by the necessity of coping with the same new developments in the law from the standpoint of their several responsibilities.

These considerations underlay our suggestion that the program plan of cooperation should extend to the Legal Training and Research Institute, which seemed to be a medium peculiarly well devised for establishing contact with the nonacademic branches of the Japanese legal profession. Influencing this view may have been the fact that in many ways the institute comes closer to the American image of a law school than do the university law departments. In any event, though the idea of including the institute in the program met with ready acquiescence on the part of the university faculties, we have sometimes wondered whether it would have occurred to the latter to propose the institute's inclusion.

The place of the Legal Institute in the program and the return of Judges Hattori and Tanabe to institute posts following the first subprogram resulted in the institute's playing an active role in the organization and conduct of a number of the seminars which I described above in reporting on the second subprogram. The institute's participation meant not merely the contribution of its aid in planning the seminars but also the presence in the seminars themselves of judges, procurators, and lawyers, sitting side by side with university professors and taking an active part in the discussion.

Such a relationship among able men breeds mutual respect and also a greater awareness of what each group has to offer the others. This should create over time a greater concern with concreteness and practicality in Japanese legal scholarship while enhancing the intellectual stature of the bar and the attractiveness of that branch of the profession.

It would be unrealistic to assert that the program's part was a major one among the many influences that are changing relationships among the various branches of the Japanese legal profession — trends on which the essays in this volume throw much light — but I believe one may fairly claim that the program has had more than a makeweight role.

Few prospects could have been more baffling than those confronting the American law teachers who were asked to go to Japan in the second subprogram. Their problem was not simply one of language — for many years scholars in the social sciences and humanities had coped with that problem in, for example, the Tokyo-Stanford summer seminars. The American scholar was expected to direct advanced discussions of legal problems with Japanese scholars trained in a legal system with which he was unfamiliar. He had to base this discussion on his own legal system with which most of them were unfamiliar. This was no easy task.

The ground-breaking work which led to a solution to this problem began with the von Mehren seminars in Tokyo in 1956–57.[15] They demonstrated the importance of careful collaborative planning by scholars who were not themselves subject to the limitations affecting most of the participants. That such scholars were available was due to the first subprogram; moreover, they were strongly reinforced by the participation of Richard Rabinowitz who, more than most, was knowledgeable in both legal systems.

The opportunity to develop the seminar technique was not confined to the visits of the American law teachers on the second subprogram, since other able law teachers were visiting Japan under other auspices — among them Nathaniel Nathanson, Albert Ehrenzweig, Walter Gellhorn, Douglas Maggs, Max Rheinstein, and more recently Richard Jennings and Addison Mueller. However, I think it fair to claim that the program provided much of the motivation and the resources needed for the development of the method. The readers of this essay who will recall my report of the preparatory work that was devoted to assuring effective two-way communication and the identification of significant problems for treatment that lay behind the highly successful Braucher seminars will recognize that this sort of thing does not come about spontaneously.[16]

The reader may, however, ask whether all that work on the part of so many people is justified if it leads only to twenty or thirty hours of seminar sessions. The answer might well be negative, if there were no other fruits. But, apart from the educative value of the preparatory work to those participating in it, a seminar, if it has succeeded, will touch off chain reactions of research and publication. I understand that the Braucher seminars have energized the study of the new techniques for sales financing which the coming of a modern credit economy to Japan is introducing. This study is breaking down conceptual barriers between civil law and commercial law, between academic law and business practice. A substantial professional literature is coming into being, and an important contribution to it are the Braucher materials which Michida has translated.[17] Needless to say, this will have its repercussions in due course on university instruction.

A similar phenomenon appears to have followed the seminars which John

[15] George's seminars in Kyoto were conducted at the same time and along generally similar lines, although they were somewhat more specialized as to both participants and content. Being held in Kyoto, they could not contribute as much to the development of a technique for later use by the Tokyo universities and the Legal Institute.

[16] Excellent preparatory work by a group in the Ministry of Justice enabled Professor Sheldon Glueck and Dr. Eleanor Glueck of the Harvard Law School to conduct an intensive two-week seminar in 1960 in their techniques for the prediction of delinquency. Materials were translated from the Gluecks' writings, supplemented by reports of Japanese studies using the Gluecks' techniques. Procurator Haruo Abe, a member of the first subprogram, who has been active in criminological studies in Japan, was the interpreter for the seminar, and Professor Ryuichi Hirano of Tokyo University, also a member of the first subprogram, was a participant.

[17] See note 10 above.

Hurlbut gave. This time the stimulus came chiefly in the field of evidence law. I should be surprised if carefully prepared seminars for Professors Jennings and Mueller did not have the same effect. With thoughtfully planned agenda, properly translated materials (including Japanese materials translated into English for the visiting teacher), and effective interpretation at the seminar sessions, the barriers of language and differences in legal systems can be broken down, leaving lawyers confronting the universal challenge to their craft — good, tough problems.

As this report has doubtless made plain, the chief thrust of the program was directed toward Japan, a not unnatural development since it was Japan's predicament that had suggested the creation of the program. However, it was hoped that the benefits would be shared by American legal scholarship. I believe that this has occurred, but the effects are limited and difficult to trace. The most immediate beneficiaries were the four scholars who went to Japan in the second subprogram, but the existence of the program, the relationships growing out of it, and the practical experience the program's seminars provided, all served to encourage other American law teachers to accept invitations to teach in Japan under other auspices. Hence, I believe that the program has had some multiplier effect even among American law teachers.

Those who have gone to Japan — and they include some of our most distinguished teachers — all appear to have found the experience intellectually stimulating. However, for the most part, they have not been scholars emphasizing comparative studies in either their teaching or their own research. The Japanese experience is thus likely to influence their thinking in ways that the observer cannot readily identify. However, a striking exception to this generalization is provided by Professor B. J. George, Jr., of Michigan, who since his year at Kyoto has been pursuing the study of Japanese language and law and devoting summers to work in Japan. He will undoubtedly come to be a liaison through which Japanese legal thought can reach American scholars in the fields of criminal law and procedure and of evidence.

Connections made through the program have brought a number of members of the faculties of cooperating American schools into sympathetic contact with Japanese law teachers and advanced students. Through this we have achieved a greater understanding of their problems and a greater ability to guide them here, though their path is still difficult. Moreover, I am sure that the increased interest displayed in the program schools has been parallelled elsewhere, a circumstance that bodes well for continuing interchange despite the program's termination.

THE FUTURE: A NEW PROGRAM?

From time to time, I have been asked whether I thought the Cooperative Program should be renewed. My answer to this question has always been negative, if, as was generally assumed, the plan to be renewed was the plan that had been in operation since 1954. That plan was designed to meet a situation that no longer exists; it seems clear to me that any future instrumentalities for cooperation should not be confined to a small group of institutions in Japan and the United States. Moreover, it may well be that, without more formal planning, enough channels of cooperation will develop to assure the continuation of fruitful intellectual interchange between the legal scholars of the two countries.

Some channels for such cooperation are already coming into existence. I shall note only three. At the University of Michigan School of Law, a program of Japanese studies is being established with a portion of a $3 million grant made by the Ford Foundation to the university, chiefly for non-Western international studies.[18] This program will enjoy the benefit of Professor George's growing command of Japanese law and language. At the University of Washington School of Law, the library of which has possessed since World War II an unusually fine collection on Japanese law, a program on "Law in Asian Countries" is being established under the direction of Professor Dan F. Henderson which will devote special attention to Japan.[19]

At the Harvard Law School, a fellowship program has been developed with the Legal Training and Research Institute under which the institute nominates each year certain of its recent graduates (who may be judges, procurators, or practicing attorneys). The nominee to whom a fellowship is awarded has about a year and a half in which to improve his command of English before coming to the United States. This makes it possible to place less emphasis on present linguistic ability in selecting fellows. The law school has been gratified by the operation of this selection process, which has brought some very capable Japanese fellows to Harvard, ordinarily for one, but occasionally for two, years of study.[20]

Fulbright awards are still available for American law professors to teach and study in Japan, and Professor Addison Mueller of the School of Law of the University of California at Los Angeles is in Japan on a Fulbright grant. If, in his case and in the case of his successors, preparations can be made for seminars of the sort in which the teachers going to Japan in the second subprogram took part, then this effective instrumentality for com-

[18] See Univ. of Mich. Law Quadrangle Notes, Feb. 1962, p. 3: "'The Law of Japan' — Activities being planned include course offerings for American students, comparative research in modern Japanese law, and translation of basic Japanese legal materials."

[19] The program of teaching and research will direct its work initially to Japanese problems. Professor Henderson, a graduate of the Harvard Law School who has practiced in Tokyo and San Francisco, has a Ph.D. degree in political science from the University of California. He expects soon to publish his dissertation on Japanese civil litigation with emphasis on conciliation procedures.

[20] The Harvard-Yenching Institute's visiting-scholars program, which brings to Harvard a dozen or so professors from East Asia each year for one or two years of study, has included some Japanese law professors and so provides still another channel.

munication can continue to function unimpaired. One wonders, however, whether, without a person in the role filled so effectively by Richard Rabinowitz, it may not be difficult to organize the preparatory work that proved so valuable in the conduct of the seminars.

Conceivably, within a looser framework than the program afforded, provision could be made for a legal scholar, American or Japanese, to have a role analogous to Rabinowitz' role. One might imagine the creation in both countries of a Japanese-American Society for Cooperation in Legal Studies, the members of which would be individuals, not institutions. Perhaps such a society could obtain, either directly or through some sponsoring institution, a grant sufficiently large to enable it to appoint a program secretary to serve on, say, a half-time basis. He would have to be familiar with legal education in both countries and be capable of organizing the preparatory work involved in setting up seminars in which visiting American law teachers on Fulbright or other awards would take part. The program secretary could also be a liaison between the executive committees of the society in the two countries and could assist Japanese fellowship recipients to prepare for their work in the United States.

Obviously it is easier to envisage such a development than to bring it to pass; in particular, it would be hard to find a person embodying the organizational, legal, and linguistic talents required of the program secretary. However, the goal of cooperation remains an important one, and, if less organized modes of pursuing it should prove disappointing, I hope the legal scholars in both countries will seek to devise an effective substitute, drawing, as conditions may warrant, on the experience we have gained in the seven years of the Cooperative Program.

I

THE LEGAL SYSTEM AND THE LAW'S PROCESSES

The first of the five essays in Part One, "A Century of Innovation: The Development of Japanese Law, 1868–1961," by Kenzo Takayanagi, centers on constitutional, criminal, and civil law. Sketching the legal, institutional, and human aspects of Japan's massive reception, at least on the level of formal rules and principles, of Western law, Takayanagi concludes with some reflections on the future of Japanese law. Is the process of reception now largely over? In what spirit should Japanese jurists carry their work forward?

In contrast to Takayanagi's detailed account of Japan's formal reception of Western law, Takeyoshi Kawashima's discussion of "Dispute Resolution in Contemporary Japan" deals with the extent to which traditional Japanese society accorded the law a role equivalent to what it has come to have in the West. Did the thinking patterns and general structure of traditional Japanese society provide fertile soil in which Western law could take root and become a vital force in the daily life of the community? How has Western law interacted with Japanese society as that society itself evolves in every area of life in response to pressures exerted by today's increasingly complex world community?

Kohji Tanabe's essay, "The Processes of Litigation: An Experiment with the Adversary System," focuses upon one aspect of the problems discussed by Takayanagi and Kawashima — the institutions and procedures of civil litigation. These fall into the general pattern that emerges from Takayanagi's presentation: heavy reliance before World War II on Continental European, especially German, models which were substantially modified by American influence after 1945. Tanabe also describes the emergence of Japanese solutions from the interaction among conscious borrowings from two quite different Western traditions and Japanese society.

Takaaki Hattori's treatment of "The Legal Profession in Japan: Its Historical Development and Present Situation" complements Tanabe's discussion of civil procedure and raises sharply some problems flowing from the introduction into traditional Japanese society of Western law and legal institutions. Particularly, is a developed and active legal profession a premise of Western law? In this connection, the statistics on the size of the bar stimulate reflection even when placed in perspective by considering the number of legal tasks performed by persons who have a university legal education but are not lawyers in the full or technical sense. Also, has the bar developed less easily and steadily in Japan than have the two other branches of the legal profession — the bench and the prosecuting arm, the procuracy?

The relative strength of bar and bench has, of course, considerable significance for the competing basic philosophies of civil procedure discussed by Tanabe.

The final essay in Part One, Hakaru Abe's "Education of the Legal Profession in Japan," describes the general structure of Japanese legal education, both university and postuniversity, with particular emphasis on the critical role of a unique Japanese institution of relatively recent origin: the Legal Training and Research Institute. Discussing present institutional limitations, the essay also pursues the problem, raised by Hattori, of the appropriate size of the Japanese bar.

A CENTURY OF INNOVATION: THE DEVELOPMENT OF JAPANESE LAW, 1868–1961

Kenzo Takayanagi

ASSISTED BY THOMAS L. BLAKEMORE

THE Charter Oath of Five Articles proclaimed on April 6, 1868, by Emperor Meiji, setting forth fundamental policies for transforming feudal Japan into a modern state, was certainly a document of constitutional importance. It inspired such major reforms as the abolition of fiefs and their conversion into provinces, the adoption of compulsory military service, the establishment of a central taxation system, the abolition of the feudal privileges of the warrior class, and various other piecemeal reforms in the legislative, administrative, and judicial spheres.

The Constitution

The idea of formulating a written constitution incorporating Western principles of government was conceived in the early years of the Meiji regime. It took, however, some twenty years before the Constitution of the Empire of Great Japan was promulgated in 1889. It supplied for half a century the basic principles of Japan's government. During the two decades preceding its enactment, Western political ideas and institutions had been studied with all the ardor of youth by Japanese intellectual leaders in and out of office, and demands for the establishment of a parliament became more and more vigorous. A great number of proposed constitutions were

Note. Mr. Takayanagi is Professor of Law Emeritus of Tokyo University and Chairman of the Constitution Investigation Commission. B.Jur., Tokyo Imperial University, 1912. In 1915–1920 studied law in the United States, England, France, Italy, Switzerland, and Germany. Appointed Member of the House of Peers, 1946; President of Seikei University 1949–1957. Member of the Japan Academy, the Council on the Legal System, the International Academy of Comparative Law, Foreign Honorary Member of the American Academy of Arts and Sciences, Judge of the Permanent Court of Arbitration and a Member of the Asian-African Committee of the Legal Consultative Committee. Author of GENDAI HŌRITSU SHISŌ NO KENKYŪ (Studies in Modern Legal Thought) (1927); HŌRITSU TETSUGAKU GENRI (Principles of Legal Philosophy) (1935); writings in the fields of Anglo-American law and legal philosophy.

Mr. Blakemore is a practicing attorney in Tokyo. B.A., 1936, LL.B., 1938, University of Oklahoma.

Footnotes have been prepared by Rex Coleman and inserted by the editor; they are not the responsibility of the author.

drafted both by the government and by private persons and groups. The outcome of all this was the making of the Constitution of 1889, which is now called the "Old Constitution" or the "Meiji Constitution," as distinguished from the new Constitution of 1946, which is sometimes called the "Showa Constitution." The complicated political history leading up to the former's enactment is now well known to Western scholars through the writings of George Sansom and other able students of Japan's political history.[1]

The Meiji Constitution of 1889

The Meiji Constitution was drawn up with the utmost secrecy and promulgated as a gift of the Emperor to his subjects. Sovereignty resides in the Tennō, the hereditary monarch, not in the people. The Constitution takes scrupulous care to guarantee executive supremacy, which had been the policy of the Meiji government since the Restoration, by recognizing broad imperial prerogatives. This will strike the present generation of Western observers as highly antidemocratic, and political realists are apt to see in the document a selfish attempt to perpetuate, behind a Western constitutional facade, the political power of the oligarchs. The Constitution is certainly conservative; but, compared with the Japanese political regime prior to the Restoration, it was definitely a step forward in the direction of democratizing Japan. It provided for a Diet, including a Lower House, composed of elected representatives. It provided for the usual bill of rights, though "under reservation of the law." It provided for an independent judiciary, though its province was strictly limited, in conformity with the French and Continental traditions, to the trial of civil and criminal cases, and administrative matters were outside its jurisdiction. If it was not the rule of law in the English sense of the term, at least justice according to law was guaranteed.

It is now the Japanese fashion of the day to criticize severely this constitutional document as compared with the more democratic Constitution of 1946. In view of the practical problems that the statesmen of the Meiji era (1867–1912) had to tackle, it is at least debatable whether Japan was not wise in taking a conservative course rather than the progressive or radical line advocated by many Japanese politicians of the time. There were two major tasks to be performed. The first was to create a sovereign state out of the chaos of a feudal state, a task similar to that faced by sixteenth-century European statesmen who had to create a strong centralized government to combat feudal anarchy. The Meiji statesmen had also to take account of the modern democratic developments that had occurred in Europe after the

[1] SANSOM, THE WESTERN WORLD AND JAPAN 310–77 (1951); BECKMANN, THE MAKING OF THE MEIJI CONSTITUTION (1957).

French Revolution — if for no other reason than to ensure the abolition of consular jurisdiction. The two exigencies were, in a sense, antagonistic to each other, and the statesmen of that day chose the more conservative line.

The views of prominent European and American scholars of the time respecting the Meiji Constitution are interesting. After promulgation of the Constitution, Kentaro Kaneko, a graduate of the Harvard Law School who had assisted Prince Ito in the drafting, was sent abroad with the English translation of Ito's Commentaries on the Constitution to obtain the criticisms of eminent political scientists and constitutional lawyers. In England, Kaneko met and heard the views of Herbert Spencer, James Bryce, Henry Sedgwick, William Anson, and Albert Dicey. In Germany, Rudolf von Gneist, who had lectured to Prince Ito, was too ill to give his opinion, but Kaneko met with Rudolf von Ihering. In Austria, Lorenz von Stein, to whose lectures Ito had listened with much admiration, was visited. Kaneko also journeyed to France and there talked to Le Bon, professor of constitutional law at the University of Paris. In the United States, comments were furnished by Professor James Bradley Thayer of the Harvard Law School and Oliver Wendell Holmes, Jr., then Chief Justice of the Supreme Judicial Court of Massachusetts.[2]

Spencer approved both the respect shown by the draftsmen of the Constitution for Japanese historical traditions and their conservative course, which avoided a progressive policy that would be incompatible with the stage of social development in Japan. He observed that European constitutions were all historical products and that it would be a mistake to expect the same results in Japan by translating and enforcing one of these constitutions. He also sounded the warning that, although wisdom and assiduous endeavors of a select few could make a constitution, its enforcement affected the people in general. Consequently, it was several times more difficult to operate a constitution well than to draft a satisfactory document. Specifically citing the case of Irish members of the House of Commons, Spencer opined that participation in public affairs must be conditional on the payment of taxes, for otherwise the discussions of the Diet could degenerate into the mere expression of impractical and irresponsible views.

Bryce favored the conservative policy of concentrating political power in the hands of the Emperor and of separating the executive from the legislature. He felt that changes implicit in the adoption of English cabinet government would be too abrupt for a nation long used to despotic rule. He and Professor Sedgwick took up specifically a number of articles and drew attention to troubles, from the standpoint of the ideal and custom of the English constitution, which might arise under those articles. Sedgwick, then

[2] KANEKO, KEMPŌ SEITEI TO ŌBEIJIN NO HYŌRON (Establishment of the Constitution and Critical Comments Thereon by Europeans and Americans) 197–391 (1937).

over seventy, had been preparing his *Elements of Politics* and was eager to scrutinize the Japanese Constitution in connection with his forthcoming work.

Dicey approved the decision of the drafters to take the German and not the English constitution as their model for the relation between the executive and the legislature. He also advised the adoption of a limited franchise. In addition, he expressed his well-known prejudice against *droit administratif,* saying that the Constitution wrongly adopted the Continental system of administrative courts and that all legal matters should be left to ordinary courts.

Anson expressed his view of a written constitution as nothing more than "a textbook of strategy," whose practical application was to be likened to actual warfare that did not necessarily follow the prescriptions laid down in the textbook. He stressed the importance of political facts rather than of constitutional theories. In his opinion, once a parliamentary system was established, no government could be conducted without the support of political parties, so that, even under the Constitution, Japan might develop a party government. Anson also warned the Japanese government against the danger of relying too much on the Upper House as the bulwark of the government and of minimizing or antagonizing the Lower House.

Ihering said that he was a student of the Roman law, not a constitutional expert; however, his clear logic and his lucid eloquence, as well as his erudition in constitutional lore, seem to have impressed Kaneko deeply. He not only explained in detail the practical working of the Prussian constitution of 1850, but also cited a number of political events in other European countries to support his points. He stressed that, though the Lower House naturally tends to be radical, the government must, lest the state of affairs in Japan lapse into chaos, stick to a conservative policy. Approving the composition of the Upper House, as provided in the House of Peers Order, Ihering recommended that a system of "imperial nominees" be utilized. They should be chosen by the government, to check, as the parliamentary atmosphere suggested, either the ultraconservatism of the nobility or the radicalism of the elected representatives. He also explained Bismark's way of "managing" the Lower House without any resort to dubious methods.

Holmes approved the conservative spirit in which the Constitution was drafted. In introducing constitutional government into Japan, the Constitution should be so drafted as to confine popular participation within narrow limits, with the view, however, of gradually extending this participation. Holmes said that there was no universal principle as to how much popular participation ought to be granted, this being a matter depending on the history of each nation. Although the establishment of constitutional government in Japan was, Holmes believed, a wise step, the Emperor should bear in mind that he himself could not change it at will. Moreover, the Constitution was an ax which would cut the country into several compartments, dividing the people into political parties. Finally, Holmes stressed that the success or failure of the Constitution depended on the political education of the Japanese nation and on the political genius of the Japanese leaders.

Thayer believed that the Constitution could be a success only if Diet members maintained a conservative spirit and refrained from expressing radical opinions. He reminded Kaneko that, immediately after the enactment of the constitution of the United States, Washington became president and his official family consisted of such outstanding men as Jefferson, Adams, and Hamilton — all of whom had served with distinction the cause of American independence — together with other first-rate statesmen; these men followed the policy of gradual progress. In the same way, the first cabinet under the new Japanese Constitution should consist of outstanding statesmen who had rendered meritorious services in the Meiji Restoration and who had enjoyed high prestige in the eye of the entire nation. Kaneko was not a stranger to Thayer and Holmes. Thayer had taught Kaneko constitutional law at Harvard. He was fond of proudly telling American visitors to Japan that Justice Holmes had been his private tutor during his student days in Cambridge.

Thus, all these prominent men of the Western world approved the conservative policy adopted by the Meiji statesmen in drafting the Constitution. English constitutional lawyers did not recommend their own cabinet government. Perhaps they approved the more conservative approach embodied in the Constitution because their historical knowledge indicated that the development of constitutional government was most successful in England and other countries in which the powers of the parliament had originally been limited and only gradually extended. They probably felt that thrusting wide responsibility on parliamentarians before they learned the technique of popular government would be inimical to the sound development of constitutional government. Indeed, the institution of popular government might itself be discredited. The holders of these views were not reactionaries in politics but wise men who never lost historical perspective.

Some of the fundamental institutional arrangements established by the Constitution were soon tested in operation. Perhaps the first to be decisively tried was the independence of the judiciary. Before the Meiji Constitution, the Japanese judiciary had not enjoyed independence; and, just about one year after the Constitution came into effect, the newly guaranteed right was given an acid test.

On May 11, 1891, a policeman made an attempt in Otsu on the life of the Russian crown prince who was then traveling in Japan. The news threw the whole nation as well as the government into consternation, and there was fear of "grave consequences." Since the Penal Code then in force did not specifically regulate offenses against members of a foreign royal household, no penalty heavier than imprisonment for life — the maximum punishment for an ordinary attempt at murder — was available under the code. The government wanted to have the death penalty meted out to the prisoner by an analogous application of provisions concerning offenses against the Japanese imperial household. Great political pressure was brought to bear on Iken Kojima, President of the Great Court of Judicature (the prewar supreme court), as well as on the judges of that Court who went to Otsu to conduct the trial. Rejecting the arguments of the Procurator-General, the Court imposed a sentence of penal servitude for life, not the death penalty. Thus the judges dramatically guarded their independence, rejecting all governmental pressure. Kojima did not preside at the trial. Some historians censured him for having himself infringed judicial independence, considering his urging of the trial judges to reject political pressure an interference with the judicial process. However, Kojima is today looked up to by the Japanese people in general as the embodiment of the spirit of judicial independence.

In a sense, the Otsu affair and its legacy contradict the basic thesis advanced by the Western scholars interviewed by Kaneko; the inclusion in the Constitution of an institution quite foreign to the Japanese scene provided the foundation on which a tradition of judicial independence very quickly emerged. The Otsu judgment remains the most valuable tradition of the Japanese judiciary. Whatever their shortcomings, Japanese judges since then have scrupulously guarded their independence, and the nation has reposed implicit confidence in their integrity and their freedom from corruption, although of course not everyone always likes their decisions.

In another area — the relation between the executive and the legislature — the several predictions of Anson did indeed come true.. The relation between the two branches of government did not develop along the lines, strictly conceived, laid down in the Constitution. Once Western institutions and thinking had acquired a basis within the formal structure of Japanese society, they were able to develop in ways quite incompatible with traditional Japanese thinking and feeling. Unfortunately, however, what had given promise of being a healthy development was cut short in the 1930s.

The draftsmen of the Meiji Constitution envisaged a strong bureaucracy, consisting of civil and military branches, with social prestige and honors emanating from the semidivine emperor. The Diet was not to be allowed any direct control, and even in matters of legislation and finance its authority was to be limited by imperial retention of comprehensive prerogative powers. The conception was a minimum recognition of Western institutions and practices of government while retaining, as far as possible, traditional Japanese institutions and practices.

Yatsuka Hozumi, who occupied the chair of constitutional law at Tokyo Imperial University, interpreted the Constitution in conformity with the intent of its authors, and his interpretation was regarded for some time as authoritative. He made the distinction between *kokutai* (form of state),[3] which is unchangeable, and *seitai* (form of government), which is subject to change. The sovereignty of the Tennō constituted the *kokutai* of the Japanese state that could not be changed. But this theory was challenged by his junior colleague Tatsukichi Minobe, who rejected this metaphysical distinction and adopted the theory, then prevailing among German publicists, that sovereignty resided in the state, of which the Tennō was but an organ, though undoubtedly the highest organ. Although the controversy was an academic and theoretical one concerning the position of the Emperor in the Japanese constitutional system, it concealed a political controversy between proponents of executive supremacy and of legislative supremacy. Hozumi's mantle fell on Shinkichi Uesugi, his successor at the university. Uesugi came to represent the conservative and Minobe the progressive wing of Japanese constitutional theory. If Uesugi could be characterized as a strict constructionist, true to the legislative intent, Minobe was a liberal constructionist, his interpretation being more in conformity with the emerging trend toward parliamentary government. Minobe occupied the chair of constitutional law at the university much longer than his younger rival, and his theory became more influential in the 1920s. However, when political reaction set in with the military ascendency in the 1930s, his "organ theory" was severely attacked as heretical by, among others, ultranationalistic politicians in the Diet.

The statesmen who drafted the Constitution felt, with George Washington and eighteenth-century European statesmen, that political parties were immoral. A similar motive to that which gave rise to political parties in eighteenth-century England — the desire for patronage — stimulated the organization of parties and the mobilization of parliamentary powers. The government endeavored to suppress the opposition by force, but in vain. After the First World War, indications were strong that Japan would evolve a party cabinet of the British type. "Transcendental cabinets," which included men of divergent political beliefs, were discredited in the public mind. By "protection of the constitution" (*goken*) was meant in fact a movement to establish cabinet government. In 1925, the popular basis of Japanese parliamentarism was widened by the adoption of universal suffrage. When the London Naval Treaty was being ratified in 1930, the liberal Prime Minister, Hamaguchi (nicknamed "the Lion"), forced the conservative Privy Council to yield to his iron will. There were even some signs that civilian supremacy might be realized in due course. This, however, proved to be the wishful thinking of Japanese liberals, for a reign of what an English journalist called "government by assassination" ensued.

[3] At times, *kokutai* has been translated somewhat inaccurately as "national polity." See, e.g., BUTOW, JAPAN'S DECISION TO SURRENDER 16 (1954).

At first, the interest in parliamentary affairs was mostly limited to fief leaders, just as in eighteenth-century England active interest in parliamentary government was confined almost entirely to the gentry. The major political parties in Japan, the Seiyūkai and the Minseitō, were, like the Tories and the Whigs in eighteenth-century England, simply factions within the ruling aristocracy. After the First World War, when Japanese capitalism made huge strides, the industrialists headed by the zaibatsu interests, like the Mitsui and the Mitsubishi, entered the political arena using the political parties to promote their own interests. A little later, a political consciousness began to emerge among urban working men and the first proletarian parties were organized. The process of the widening of the popular basis of parliamentarism seen in nineteenth-century England was being repeated in Japan.

This normal development in Japan was checked in the 1930s by the capture of political power by army extremists and by the renewal of bureaucratic absolutism. Following the Great Depression, executive supremacy seemed to be a world-wide trend. Its development in Japan, however, assumed peculiar traits that are little known in advanced Western countries: the use of assassination to express dissatisfaction with the policy of the government or the political opinions of leading statesmen and a gradual erosion of military discipline, which took the form of *gekokujō* (overpowering of seniors by juniors). Indeed, the period between 1934 and 1941, characterized by murderous conspiracy at home and unchecked aggression abroad, was most unpalatable to those Japanese liberals who looked forward to the gradual and peaceful development of constitutional democracy. This period has fairly been styled that of the "Dark Valley" (*kurai tanima*).

The political situation in Japan during World War II followed the course which was taken everywhere else: national unity for success in war. Although the Meiji Constitution was in force until May 3, 1947, when the new Constitution took effect, the political parties had been dissolved, and the Diet in its sittings did nothing but rubber-stamp government-sponsored measures, though it sometimes showed independent judgment in refusing to pass a bill in its original form. A tolerable number of parliamentarians refused to belong to totalitarian parties. Only the judiciary continued to maintain its independence. In that respect the government of Japan was perhaps not as thoroughly totalitarian as that of Nazi Germany.

The text of the Constitution was never amended during the half century of its existence. Japanese political life did not proceed in conformity with the "textbook of strategy" as penned by the Meiji statesmen. The prophesy of William Anson in 1889 proved true.

The New Constitution of 1946

The Constitution of 1946 was drafted during the Allied occupation, with a view to the democratization of Japan. Apart from article 9—renunciation of war — which has a curious history of its own, it is not so radical a document as is often supposed. Like the Meiji Constitution, it is a brief document. Its outward form is similar to that of the old Constitution, but its contents are certainly more democratic. Closely examined, it is a standard constitution befitting a twentieth-century liberal, democratic state. In the first place, the emperorship was retained but only as "the symbol of the State and of the unity of the people."[4] The retention of emperorship was motivated by a due respect for historical continuity. The French Revolution abolished kingship, and this step may logically be more in conformity with the Rousseauist doctrine of "popular sovereignty" (which also is the theory of the new Japanese Constitution), but the British have retained the kingship until the present. If we look back to the constitutional history of the two nations in the nineteenth and twentieth centuries, we cannot say that constitutional development along democratic lines was more successfully effected in France than in Great Britain. Many of the democratic constitutions which in Europe abolished kingship only resulted in political confusion and the emergence of dictatorships.

Under the old Constitution, however, the legitimate source of the Emperor's authority was the mythological and semireligious theory that he was the descendant of the Sun Goddess. Under the new Constitution, his position rests on the secular and political doctrine of popular will. The theory changed, but the institution itself remains. At the end of the Middle Ages, European kings lost much of their actual power, though theoretically they were recognized as the overlords of the feudal system. Similarly, in feudal Japan, the Emperor was theoretically regarded as the head of the nation, but his political power was even weaker and more nominal than that of European kings. He was no more than the symbolic head of the Japanese state. The Meiji statesmen utilized the traditional system to cement the nation and clothed the Tennō with semidivine qualities, just as the sixteenth- and seventeenth-century European statesmen utilized the king as the vicar of God to consolidate national governments.

Even after the Meiji Restoration, the symbolic value of the Emperor was more important for the unity of the whole nation than were his sovereign political powers, which actually rested in the hands of his advisers, constitutional or nonconstitutional. His prerogatives, guaranteed by the Constitution, were really prerogatives of the executive. Viewed in this light, the provisions on the Tennō in the new Constitution are not so revolutionary as it may appear to ardent supporters of the kokutai theory.

In the second place, the executive supremacy contemplated by the old Constitution was replaced in the new by legislative supremacy. This step was not by any means a radical innovation. It was a development which had been taking place in the period of what is popularly called Taisho Democracy

[4] CONST. art. 1.

(1920–1930). The Potsdam proclamation says: "The Japanese Government shall remove all obstacles to the revival and strengthening of democratic tendencies among the Japanese people." The word "revival" was, we are told, inserted at the suggestion of the British government. The historically minded British were probably thinking of the course of constitutional development that Japanese politics had been taking in the 1920s.

In the third place, the constitutional position of the judiciary was considerably elevated, and rule *by* law (*hōchishugi*) under the old Constitution was replaced by rule *of* law (*hō no shihai*). The latter idea seems to be more usually expressed in the United States by such expressions as "government under law," "supremacy of law," or "due process of law." The rule of law provided by the new Constitution is of the type judicially developed in the United States. The classic rights, with some additions, are enumerated by the Constitution and are to be guaranteed by the judiciary. As befits the constitution of a twentieth-century industrial state, the Constitution of 1946 imposes on the state not only the negative duty to refrain from violating human rights and fundamental liberties but also the positive duty to promote the economic and social welfare of its citizens to enable them to enjoy those rights substantively as well as formally.

The idea of the rule of law—tracing back to Bracton's dictum, "the King rules under God and the law," and reminding one of Lord Coke's memorable Sunday morning conference with King James I on November 10, 1612—crossed the Atlantic and crystallized in the institution of judicial review, with which the name of John Marshall is inseparably associated. Albert Venn Dicey expounded the doctrine of the rule of law in his *Law of the Constitution* as a counterweight to the doctrine of parliamentary sovereignty in Great Britain. Dicey's formulation smacks a bit too much of Victorian England and may require a new formulation to fit twentieth-century economic and social conditions. The spirit of the idea, however, endures.

The rule of law is not now an idea solely confined to countries of the common-law tradition; it seems gradually to be becoming international. The Universal Declaration of Human Rights of 1948 declares: "It is essential, if man is not to be compelled to have recourse, as a last resort, to rebellion against tyranny and oppression, that human rights should be protected by the rule of law." The European Convention for the Protection of Human Rights and Fundamental Freedoms of 1950 also contains a phrase about the governments of "European countries which are likeminded and have a common heritage of political traditions, ideals, freedom, and the rule of law."

It seems clear that human rights and fundamental liberties can prosper only under the rule of law and that constitutional democracy cannot successfully function unless the entire nation, the governed as well as the government, has a strong feeling for the law. Although not much commented on by Japanese professors of public law bred in the Continental legal tradition, this transition from rule by law to the rule of law (American in its institutional aspect) is a marked advance in Japan's constitutional history. The success or failure of parliamentary democracy in Japan is still in the lap of the gods, but success depends, in large measure, on the degree to which the spirit of the rule of law becomes the flesh and blood of the nation. Perhaps it might also be said that in this area lies one of the greatest contributions that the common law can make to the legal tradition of Japan, which had been so largely oriented to Continental European law, over which the old Byzantine maxim *Quod principi placuit legis habet vigorem* still casts its shadow.

Criminal Codes

The Old Penal Code

The Penal Code of 1880[5] was based on a draft made by Boissonade. Before coming to Japan in 1873, Émile Gustave Boissonade de Fontarabie had assisted Ortolan in teaching criminal law at the University of Paris. Both men belonged to the neoclassical school. This school followed, in the main, the classical retaliatory doctrine of De Maître and Kant, incorporating, however, the social-defense idea of Beccaria and Bentham. Boissonade himself expressly stated that his *Projet révisé de code pénal pour l'empire du Japon* (1886) was not based solely on the doctrine of absolute justice or solely on the utilitarian doctrine, but on the idea that an act which was both a *mal moral* and a *mal social* was to be made a punishable crime. He aimed at a combination of two basic ideas, "justice" and "utilité." The most "revolutionary" provisions of the code, as far as Japan was concerned, were the following two articles:

Article 2. Nulle action ou omission ne peut être punie, si ce n'est en vertu d'une disposition expresse de la loi.

Article 3. La loi pénale n'a pas d'effet rétroactif sur les infractions commises avant sa promulgation. Toutefois, les dispositions plus douces d'une loi nouvelle sont immédiatement applicables.

These two articles embody the well-known principle of *nullum crimen, nulla poena sine lege* and the principle of banning punishment by an *ex post facto* law. Although expressed in Latin, these are by no means time-honored principles in Continental Europe, and, as far as the judicial process is concerned, they are not honored without exception in contemporary England. They were products of the French Revolution, and nineteenth-century Continental Europe regarded them as fundamental to a civilized concept of justice. These principles were "revolutionary" in Japan because no such

[5] Great Council of State Decree No. 36 of 1880.

general principles were known in the administration of criminal justice in feudal Japan. The Tokugawa statesmen, under the influence of the Confucian conception of government, believed that their primary duty was to teach the governed how to behave according to morality as defined in the feudal period and that the administration of criminal justice was something secondary. Thus orders such as the famous Code of a Hundred Articles (*O-Sadamegaki Hyakkajō*) of 1742[6] took the form of instructions to officials. The texts of the orders were not published. Of course, the people were not kept entirely in the dark regarding punishable conduct, but it was considered a wise policy to keep the correspondence between offenses and penalties an official secret. The new code definitely abandoned this policy.

The code was also revolutionary in establishing the principle of equality before law. The feudal criminal law was an elaborate system. What conduct constituted a crime and what penalties were to be meted out varied according to the social class to which the accused belonged and also according to his family standing and other social relations. The new code swept away all these feudal complexities.

The code established, as its third great innovation, the individualistic principle that guilt was personal. Collective criminal responsibility and guilt by association, which had characterized feudal justice, were abolished. It may be noted that to contemporary Japanese jurists *actus non facit reum, nisi mens sit rea* is not, as in some Western countries, a mere maxim to which lip service is paid. These jurists use a subjective rather than an objective test regarding *mens rea*. Presumptions as to knowledge or belief are unknown to Japanese criminal jurisprudence. Incidentally, a heavy burden of proof is thus put on the public procurator, which accounts, in some measure, for the procurator's tendency to employ inquisitorial methods in the examination of suspects. Punishment for negligent crimes is still today exceptional and cannot be imposed in the absence of an express statutory provision. Although *mens rea* is based on intent, negligence which presupposes lack of intent is treated as similar to *mens rea,* the subjective test also being adopted in determining whether the accused was negligent. Most Japanese lawyers consequently find it difficult to swallow the Anglo-Saxon doctrine of conspiracy, which reminds them of feudal justice. As is well known, rapid industrialization and the related influx of the rural population into large cities in Western countries is giving rise to "public-welfare offenses," punishable without any reference to *mens rea*. However, the influence of the doctrine that guilt is personal, introduced by the Penal Code of 1880, is still so strong that Japanese lawyers experience difficulty in adapting themselves to the era of "eclipse of *mens rea*," to the growing tendency to import strict or absolute liability into the field of criminal justice.

[6] For an English translation, see Hall, *Japanese Feudal Laws III: The Tokugawa Legislation IV,* in 41 TRANSACTIONS OF THE ASIATIC SOCIETY OF JAPAN pt. 5, at 683 (1913).

Finally, it is interesting to note that the code introduced the category of offenses against the imperial household. When, in 1869, a new criminal code was being drafted, the draftsmen provided for the offense of high treason. Upon reading this draft provision, Taneomi Soyejima expressed his indignation and immediately ordered its deletion, saying that such an inauspicious event would never occur in this country. Soyejima's thinking may remind the reader of the ancient Greeks, who refrained from providing for parricide, and of the ancient Persians, who adopted the fiction that any person who committed parricide was born on the wrong side of the blanket. When Japanese legislators found that Boissonade's draft contained the same inauspicious provision, they again vigorously insisted that it be struck out. However, the learned professor finally convinced the legislators that the provision should be retained. Articles 73 to 76 of the Penal Code of 1907[7] also regulated offenses against the imperial household. These provisions were stricken out in 1946, this time on the ground that they were incompatible with the principle of equality before law declared by the new Constitution. The present Penal Code, moreover, also deprives foreign monarchs, presidents, and their envoys of similar privileges.

The Penal Code of 1907

The Penal Code of 1880, which certainly was epoch-making legislation, had been in operation for some twenty-five years when it was radically revised by the 1907 code. Boissonade's project was not a mere translation of the French Penal Code of 1810. He took newer laws into account, introduced novel institutions such as parole, and also incorporated his own personal views on various points. The 1880 code was, however, guided by the old theory that punishment must exactly fit the offense. It adopted the French classification of offenses into "crime," "délit," and "contravention" and provided for each offense and its corresponding penalty in such a way as to leave as small a margin of judicial discretion as possible.

During the operation of the Penal Code of 1880 for over a quarter of a century, the influence of German legal science became more and more marked, even though the code itself was modeled on French law. Students of criminal law who went abroad spent most of their time in Germany. Franz von Liszt's seminar was a source of inspiration to many young Japanese scholars. The battles of various schools of thought, such as that between Birkmeyer and Liszt, were repeated in Japan. Not that French and Italian authors were entirely neglected; but the more systematic method of exposition and the philosophical way in which fundamental problems of punishment were discussed, characteristic of German legal science, deeply influenced Japanese students of criminal law. Out of such academic *Sturm*

[7] Law No. 45 of 1907.

und Drang was born the 1907 code. In it, the subjective theory of punishment advocated by the newer school emerged victorious.

Compared with the former code's 430 articles, the new code was a shorter document consisting of only 264 articles. It abolished the old threefold classification (*crime, délit, contravention*) of criminal offenses. A wider margin was afforded judicial discretion in meting out punishment. Parole had already been recognized in the old code. The new code provided also for the suspension of the execution of sentence, though not yet for the indeterminate sentence.

The absence of a *nullum crimen* provision was conspicuous in the new code. Some Japanese jurists had considered the principle a nineteenth-century doctrine, inadequate for the twentieth-century administration of criminal justice—though they did not go so far as to condemn it as a "bourgeois relic," as Soviet jurists did in the 1920s. The general interpretation of the omission, however, was that an express formulation of the principle was unnecessary because article 23 of the Meiji Constitution provided that "no Japanese subject shall be arrested, detained, tried, or punished, unless according to law." The doctrinal disputes between the old and the new schools thus continued to exist even after the coming into force of the new code, and their differences were reflected in the construction of specific provisions of the new code. The new school of jurists contributed greatly to the progress of criminology in Japan, but the practice of Japanese courts has still not been swayed by the new doctrines. Courts have been inclined, on the whole, to abide by the conservative doctrine, even though the code of 1907 embodied the new school's victory.

After World War I, an attempt was made, as in Germany and Switzerland, to effect a code revision, and a committee was set up for that purpose. But the attempt bore no fruit, nor have a few amendments after World War II affected in any fundamental way the character of the Penal Code of 1907. The deletion of the chapter on crimes against the imperial household has already been mentioned. The provisions respecting the offense of adultery were also amended in view of the constitutional requirements of sexual equality. Under the code of 1907, the wife and her paramour were punishable at the husband's request, while the husband who had intercourse with another woman was not punishable. The alternative for the legislators under the new Constitution of 1946 was either to make husband and wife both punishable or to abolish the offense of adultery altogether. After long debates in the Diet, the latter alternative was chosen. Adultery, however, is now a ground for divorce for both the husband and the wife.

The Code of Criminal Instruction of 1880

The methods of criminal justice employed during the Tokugawa regime were radically changed by the enactment of the Code of Criminal Instruction of 1880,[8] which came into operation simultaneously with the Penal Code on January 1, 1882. The code adopted the French semiinquisitorial method which colored the Japanese administration of penal justice until the end of World War II.

If the administration of criminal justice in Western countries had not evolved so rapidly after the French Revolution, the method of administering criminal justice in feudal Japan might not have been so radically altered. The inquisitorial method, which had come into use in Europe under ecclesiastical influence, became more and more general in the period of absolute monarchy, during which the rights of the state were paramount. The inquisitorial system provided in the famous ordinance of Louis XIV, who identified himself with the state, is no less hideous to the modern mind than the similar method employed during the Tokugawa regime. The Code d'Instruction Criminelle of 1808 was influenced by the spirit of the revolution, and open trials and oral pleading were adopted. However, the essence of the traditional inquisitorial method was retained, and a marked contrast still seems to exist between the Anglo-Saxon accusatory method and the French inquisitorial method. It is well known that Englishmen have, from time to time, adversely criticized French criminal trials, especially during such *causes célèbres* as the Dreyfus case. Not a few learned essays have appeared in English and American legal journals, contrasting the French with the Anglo-American criminal procedure. It is also interesting that, in connection with the abolition of extraterritoriality in Japan. Harry Parkes, the British Minister to Japan, was not enthusiastic over the prospect of subjecting the English-speaking foreigners in Japan, who formed the great majority of the foreign colony, to laws which were mainly French and German in origin. He held that the English legal system should alone have been considered in preparing the new codes. Parkes's attitude was, perhaps, partially motivated by the traditional English prejudice against French criminal trials. In the 1920s, the present writer often heard his American friends criticize Japanese administration of criminal justice. As a matter of fact, this criticism was generally directed against the French procedural institutions adopted by Japan in 1882.

Meiji statesmen early saw the necessity of reforming criminal law and procedure along Western lines. As early as 1869, Rinsho Mitsukuri translated the French Penal Code by order of the government. Piecemeal reforms were achieved: the opening of the courts to representatives of the press (1872),[9] separation of the courts from the procurator's office (1872),[10] prohibition of

[8] Great Council of State Decree No. 37 of 1880.

[9] Based on a statement made to the Great Council of State by the Ministry of Justice in May 1872, representatives of the press were permitted in that year to enter the Ministry of Justice Court and the Tokyo Court. This statement may be found in MEIJI BUNKA SHI: HŌSEI HEN (A History of Meiji Culture: The Legal System) 227 (Ishii ed., 1954).

[10] Justice Staff Regulations and Operating Rules, Great Council of State Notice of August 3, 1872.

the use of torture in civil cases (1872),[11] abolition of class distinctions at court trials (1872),[12] banning of vendettas (1873),[13] restrictions on the use of physical torture (1874),[14] organization of the judicial system along French lines (1875),[15] recognition of appeal (*kōso*) and revision (*jōkoku*) appellate procedure (1875),[16] introduction of the French system of *avocats* (1872) — who were, however, not allowed to appear in criminal cases until 1882[17] — and of *juges d'instruction* (1876),[18] abolition of confession by the accused as a requisite for imposing punishment (1876),[19] the adoption of bail (1877),[20] and total banning of physical torture (1879).[21] All these reforms were largely inspired by French models.

The Penal Code of 1880 and the Code of Criminal Instruction of 1880 were the first "modern" Japanese codes. It is true that in the early years of the Meiji regime, two criminal codes, the Outline of the New Criminal Law (*Shinritsu Kōryō;* 1870)[22] and the Amended Criminal Regulations (*Kaitei Ritsurei;* 1873),[23] had been enacted and were in force until 1881. They considerably humanized the old penalties, but they were largely based on criminal law of Chinese origin and cannot be styled "modern."

The Code of Criminal Instruction provided for the organization and jurisdiction of the criminal courts, as well as for criminal procedure proper. In dealing with the public trial the code adopted the procedure of the modern French type. Indeed, for the first time in Japan an advocate was permitted to appear to defend the accused. The advocate was theoretically on a par with the public procurator under this new procedure, but the latter kept his official dignity by sitting together with the judges on a raised

[11] Ministry of Justice Notice No. 6 of 1872.

[12] Ministry of Justice Notice No. 25 of 1872.

[13] Great Council of State Decrees Nos. 37 and 39 of 1873. However, a subsequent enactment permitted a child or grandchild to kill the murderer of his parents or grandparents on the spot (Great Council of State Decree No. 122 of 1873). This provision was finally repealed by the Penal Code of 1880.

[14] Ministry of Justice Notice No. 19 of 1874.

[15] Rules for the Organization of the Great Court of Judicature and Various Other Courts, Great Council of State Decree No. 91 of 1875.

[16] Appeal and Revision Procedure, Great Council of State Decree No. 93 of 1875.

[17] Justice Staff Regulations and Operating Rules, Great Council of State Notice of Aug. 3, 1872. The Code of Criminal Instruction (1880) authorized for the first time the appearance of the *avocat* in criminal cases.

[18] Provisional Regulations for the Official Duties of Judges of Instruction, Ministry of Justice Notice No. 47 of 1876.

[19] Great Council of State Decree No. 86 of 1876; Ministry of Justice Notice No. 64 of 1876.

[20] Bail Ordinance, Great Council of State Decree No. 17 of 1877.

[21] Great Council of State Decree No. 42 of 1879.

[22] This statute was first given internal distribution within the government to the competent authorities in the manner of the codes and rules that followed the Taika Reform of a thousand years before and of Tokugawa legislation. However, in 1871 private bookstores were authorized to publish and sell copies. It may be found reprinted in [MEIJI 3 NEN] HŌREI ZENSHO ([1870] Complete Laws and Orders) 572.

[23] Promulgated by Great Council of State Decree No. 206 of 1873.

platform as the French tradition of treating judges and public procurators as part of the magistrature was also introduced. (Only after World War II were procurators to sit at the same level as advocates.) The judge had to be very active at trials, behaving more like a confessor than an umpire. The advocate was allowed to crossexamine an adverse witness but only through the judge. Most important of all, the code contained elaborate provisions relative to "preliminary investigation," which reminds one of the old inquisitorial methods. At this preliminary examination counsel was not allowed to assist the suspect; Boissonade, when drafting his project, was naturally unaware of the French law of 1897, which allowed the attendance of counsel at this stage. There were some Japanese critics of the system of preliminary investigation, but most Japanese jurists supported it as a more logical and scientific method for getting at the truth. It is quite natural that, after elaborate investigations by *juges d'instruction,* the accused was presumed in the public mind to be guilty, even if in the eye of the law he is presumed innocent until he is finally found guilty by the court. When an official, for instance, was committed to trial after preliminary investigation, it was customary for him to tender his resignation without waiting for the final judgment. Under this system, therefore, the function of the judge at the trial was to review the findings of the preliminary judge rather than to try the case *de novo.* The importance of this preliminary hearing continued for half a century until its abolition after World War II. However, the code contained many salutary provisions designed to guarantee a fair trial, such as the provision that supporting reasons must be given for all judgments, which provided a check on judicial arbitrariness.

Another point may be noted in connection with this code. The original Boissonade project contained provisions concerning the jury. He explained that it was important to adopt the jury system, in order to put the Japanese legal system on a par with that of other civilized nations. The code would eventually be applied to foreign residents in Japan, and it was desirable to have the jury system inasmuch as they would look upon it as a symbol of impartial justice. There were some Japanese legislators who supported him, but the relevant provisions were finally struck out, chiefly on the ground that it was premature for Japan to adopt the jury system. Boissonade was not satisfied with this decision, and, at the time of the making of the Meiji Constitution, he again advised the government to adopt the jury. Prince Ito, however, refused to accept his proposal.

The Code of Criminal Procedure of 1922

In 1890, after the promulgation of the Meiji Constitution providing for the separation of powers, a separate law relative to the constitution of the judiciary was enacted.[24] Also the renamed Code of Criminal Procedure[25] replaced, with minor changes, the old Code of Criminal Instruction. However, a more fundamental revision of criminal procedure was felt necessary. The reform committee set up for the purpose relied heavily on the German Code of Criminal Procedure of 1877 and on the 1908 and 1920 draft codes. Its work was completed in 1922, although a partial revision had been effected in 1899.[26] The Code of Criminal Procedure of 1922,[27] which came into effect on January 1, 1923, evinces the German influence in ample measure, especially as regards the arrangement of the Code, but the original French influence was not eliminated. The new code also reflected the liberalizing spirit of the 1920s by paying more attention to rights of the accused.

The spirit of the times was further reflected in the enactment of the Jury Law in 1923,[28] which came into force on October 1, 1928. This law, providing for lay participation in criminal justice, took as a model the English jury system rather than the German assessor system. Like the English petit jury, the jury consisted of twelve persons, but the unanimity principle was rejected in favor of the majority principle. The jury had no power to say "guilty" or "not guilty," since this was barred by provisions of the Meiji Constitution guaranteeing the right of Japanese subjects to obtain justice from qualified professional judges. The function of the jury was confined to decisions on questions of fact put by the court. The verdict of a jury, moreover, was not finally binding on the court, which could change the panel as many times as it deemed proper, although the court could not render a judgment contrary to the verdict. If the court accepted the verdict of the jury, its judgment became final and conclusive and no appeal was to be allowed. The jury system did not prosper, although it was at first welcomed as the palladium of liberty. Particularly because of the expense involved and the absence of appeal, waiver of jury trial was the normal procedure. Jury trial was not congenial to the Japanese legal profession, trained in the inquisitorial system, and no serious endeavors were undertaken to make this modified Anglo-Saxon system a success in Japan. The Jury Law was suspended on April 1, 1943,[29] and it has not yet been revived.

The American contribution to the world's legal science — the "juvenile court," established in Chicago at the close of the nineteenth century — was transplanted to Japan by the enactment of the Juvenile Law of 1922.[30] The juvenile court was administered by the Ministry of Justice for over two decades. After World War II, a new Juvenile Law replaced the prewar

[24] Court Organization Law, Law No. 6 of 1890.
[25] Law No. 96 of 1890.
[26] Law No. 73 of 1899.
[27] Law No. 75 of 1922.
[28] Law No. 50 of 1923.
[29] Law Concerning the Suspension of the Jury Law, Law No. 88 of 1943.
[30] Law No. 42 of 1922. These "courts" were known as "Juvenile Determination Boards."

statute,[31] and since 1949 the juvenile court has become part and parcel of Japan's judicial system.[32] Unlike the jury system, this American innovation in criminal justice took firm root in Japan, as it has in many other lands.

The Code of Criminal Procedure of 1948

The new Constitution of 1946 contains no less than nine articles directly affecting criminal procedure. A new Code of Criminal Procedure of July 10, 1948,[33] was accordingly prepared and, supplemented by the Supreme Court Regulation of December 1, 1948,[34] came into operation on January 1, 1949.

The postwar influence of Anglo-American law is most marked in the field of criminal procedure. Rights of suspected and accused persons from arrest to judgment are scrupulously protected, and the old preliminary investigation is now gone. The accusatory procedure replaced the former semi-inquisitorial procedure at trials, though not to such an extent as to sweep away completely the old tradition. Many of the Anglo-American rules of evidence have been incorporated. The art of crossexamination has become the stock in trade of the public procurator as well as the defense counsel. This is not, however, the place to elaborate on those reforms and their practical operation.

The Civil Codes

The late Dean John H. Wigmore of Northwestern University Law School used to tell me that he had been interested in having decisions (in civil cases) of the Tokugawa supreme court[35] translated into English to enable Western scholars to judge for themselves as to whether or not the following conclusions were correct. In the first place, he said, these judgments clearly showed that private law in Japan had been developing in the form of an independent, judicially created system, a phenomenon which clearly distinguished the Japanese from the Chinese legal system. Secondly, among the world's sixteen legal systems, ancient and modern, which he had surveyed, only in the English and the Japanese did official judges decide cases according to judicial precedent. Thirdly, the intellectual level of the Tokugawa judges was on a par with that of English judges of the same period.[36]

During the Tokugawa period there had been judicial law as well as standardized forms of actions through which the government usually

[31] Law No. 168 of 1948.

[32] As a result of the enforcement of the new Juvenile Law on Jan. 1, 1949. The juvenile-court function is now performed by a division of the Family Court.

[33] Law No. 131 of 1948.

[34] Criminal Procedure Regulations, Supreme Court Regulation No. 32 of 1948.

[35] This body was known as the *Hyōjōsho* (Court of Assize).

[36] See Wigmore, Panorama of the World's Legal Systems 481–89, 503–20 (library ed., 1936).

afforded remedies to parties whose legitimate interests were injured. However, a legal science, analogous to the European legal science with which Meiji scholars were confronted, had not emerged.

The pivotal point in the nineteenth-century European legal science of private law was the concept of a "right" — *subjektives Recht, droit subjectif.* This concept was a modern juristic generalization based on schemes of action recognized in both civil and common law — a concept hidden in the interstices of procedure. It may also be noted that in Continental Europe the word *jus* was not used in the distinct sense of a "right" until the end of the sixteenth century. Thus, a science of law with a right as its pivotal point is quite modern. Theoretically, civil justice during the Tokugawa period was administered as a matter of grace, not of right. Practically, however, certain categories of interests were regularly protected by legal process. A jurist might, therefore, have worked out a scheme of rights based on the categories of remedies which had regularly been recognized. But, in contrast to Europe, no such juristic attempts had been made. Japanese legal historians now point out that there was a concept and a term corresponding to a right. At the end of the Heian period (810–1185 A.D.) the word *shiki,* which originally meant "office" and connoted a duty, came to mean a "right in land." This usage, however, became obsolete in the Tokugawa period, except in the term *kabu shiki,* which meant "rights of a licensed trader." In such circumstances, it was quite natural that Meiji students of Western jurisprudence had to coin a new term, *ken ri* (power plus interest) in order to express the concept of a right.

A common-law lawyer who, like Wigmore, had studied the judicial law of feudal Japan might suggest the possibility of drafting a modern civil code out of the old materials of the indigenous law. The Meiji reformers never thought of such a possibility and would have been unequal to such a task even if they had. Moreover, the unification of law and the abolition of extraterritoriality were political exigencies of the first order and allowed of no delay. The reformers, therefore, thought of a quicker way, the importation of a finished legal product — the French Civil Code. Shimpei Eto is said to have ordered Rinsho Mitsukuri to translate the French Civil Code with all possible speed, "never minding mistakes," with a view to promulgating it by replacing the word "French" with the word "Japanese." This was in a way a brilliant idea, but the matter was not so simple. It took some twenty years of arduous endeavors before the so-called Old Civil Code was promulgated in 1890,[37] but it never came into operation. It took eight years more before the present Civil Code came into effect in 1898.[38] This was the

[37] By Laws Nos. 28 and 98 of 1890.

[38] Books I (General Provisions), II (Rights in Things), and III (Obligations) were enacted by Law No. 89 of 1896 and Books IV (Relatives) and V (Inheritance) by Law No. 9 of 1898. The entire code entered into force on July 16, 1898, pursuant to Imperial Order No. 123 of 1898.

new starting point for the further development of private law in Japan.

During the Tokugawa regime some topics, such as the pledge of immovables, were covered by legislation, but, on the whole, private law was determined by custom, either in the shape of judicial decisions or of popular traditions. This state of things continued to exist in the early years of the Meiji era. It is against this background that a decree was issued by the Great Council of State in 1875 providing for the principles and rules of administration of justice. The decree is well known among Japanese lawyers as the Dajōkan (Great Council of State) Decree No. 103 of the Eighth Year of Meiji. Article 3 specifically enumerates the sources of law in civil cases: "In civil trials, those matters for which there is no written law are governed by custom, and those matters for which there is no custom shall be adjudicated by inference from reason (*jōri*)." It is clear from the text of the decree as a whole that French influence strongly affected its draftsman. It also seems clear that article 3 represented a theory of legal sources implicitly accepted during the Tokugawa period.

After the Meiji Restoration, many piecemeal legislative measures showing a marked influence of Western law were taken by the government in the field of private law to meet immediate demands. This piecemeal legislation was "written law" and was the first source of law to be applied. As for "custom," doubt was entertained at first as to whether this meant popular or official custom. It came finally to be taken as including both. There was also some doubt whether "unreasonable" custom was binding.

Courts also encountered difficulties in determining whether to rely on the second or third source of law. The "inference from reason" seems, at first sight, to have been influenced by natural-law thinking of European origin. Yet Japanese legal historians point out the native origin of the idea. They say that the word *jōri* envisaged by this article is synonymous with *dōri,* which served as a supplementary source in the administration of the old codes and rules (*Ritsuryō Kyakushiki*). The word often appears in the laws and judicial decisions of feudal Japan. In reference to the word *dōri,* they sometimes cite a letter addressed by Yasutoki Hojo to the Inspector at Rokuhara (Rokuhara Tandai), written in 1232 at the time of distributing the *Go Seibai Shikimoku* (Formularly for the Shogun's Decision of Suits) for official use. Yasutoki wrote that:

> the document, which set forth "various matters upon which the courts would give their judgments" . . . was not a code of law but merely a list. When it was drafted its authors had wished to give it an imposing title; but this was thought excessive and it was described only as a Formulary (*shikimoku*). People might criticize it, asking upon what ideas it was based; but it had no special basis except in so far as it was compiled in accordance with reason (dōri) . . . although the national law is embodied in the ancient codes and rules . . . not one man in a thousand knows about these. To punish persons for offences under

laws which they do not know gives rise to great hardship, and therefore "we have written this Formulary in such a way that even the most illiterate fellows can understand its meaning. The old laws are like complicated Chinese characters; the new laws are like the simple syllabary [*kana*]." [39]

In Yasutoki's letter, *dōri* was thus not envisaged as a supplementary source of positive law but as the basic principle of legal reform, simplifying the old law. And it may also be pointed out that the word *dōri* was not an expression connoting theological or philosophical doctrines of natural law as in the West. Rather, it meant the common sense of the plain man. By using this word, Yasutoki emphasized not justice according to law but justice according to the simple moral principles prevailing in his time. Even an illiterate man could understand them: the man was to be loyal to his master, the child was to observe filial piety, the wife was to obey her husband, and all in their hearts were to spurn the crooked path and follow the straight.[40]

Meiji lawyers were probably unaware of the complicated history of natural law in Europe, of the position of natural law in the theological system of Thomas Aquinas or in the Age of Reason. They probably understood the "reason" in the decree as the old Japanese lawyers understood *dōri*. Nevertheless, they endeavored to administer justice according to law by importing Western rules and principles for situations in which there were none at home — a course precisely opposite to Tokiyori's idea despite the similarity in terminology.

Still it is clear that *jōri* fulfilled the function of introducing Western law, which was at the time conceived of as the embodiment of civilized justice. It was mainly through this channel, before the enactment of the Civil Code of 1898, that the positive laws of Western countries, especially of France, made their way into Japanese judicial law. Nobushige Hozumi, who lived in this period, writes:

This law flung wide open the door for the ingress of foreign law, and marks an epoch in Japanese legal history. Now, by this time, translations of the French Codes and other law books had appeared, and there were some judges on the Bench, though comparatively few at that time, who had studied English or French law. The rapidly changing circumstances of Japanese society brought many cases before the court, for which there were no express rules, written or customary, and the judges naturally sought to find out "the principles of reason and justice" [this is Hozumi's translation of *jōri*] in Western jurisprudence. The older members of the Bench, who had not been systematically taught in Western jurisprudence, consulted the translations of the French and other European Codes and text books, while the younger judges who had received systematic

[39] 1 SANSOM, A HISTORY OF JAPAN 397 (1958).

[40] Quoted from an earlier letter to the Rokuhara Tandai (then Shigetoki Hojo) translated in *ibid.*, 398.

legal education in the Universities, either at home or abroad, and whose number increased from year to year, consulted Western codes, statute books, law reports, and juridical treatises, and freely applied the principles of Occidental jurisprudence, which in their opinion, were conformable to reason and justice. Blackstone, Kent, Pollock, Anson, Langdel[l], Windscheid, Dernburg, Mourlon, Baudry-Lacantinerie and other text books and the numerous commentaries on European Codes, statute books and law reports were looked upon as repositories of the "principles of reason and justice" and supplied necessary data for their judgments. In this manner, Occidental jurisprudence entered our country, not only indirectly through the *University* and other law colleges, but also directly through the *Bench* and the *Bar* [emphasis in the original].[41]

The Civil Code of 1890

The Old Civil Code of 1890, which never came into effect, was in its arrangement based on the French code. Books II (Property in General), III (Acquisition of Property), IV (Security of Obligations), and V (Evidence) had been drafted by Boissonade. Their contents were mostly French law. Books I (Persons) and III (Inheritance) had been drafted by Japanese jurists. But the French legal influence was marked even in the part dealing with family and inheritance, although the original draft was radically revised prior to promulgation to preserve the old House system. Books II, IV, and V were promulgated on April 27, 1890; Books I and III on October 7, 1890. The entire code was to take effect on January 1, 1893. This was the first modern Japanese code in the field of private law. Since the code affected the social and economic life of the nation in all its aspects, it became a topic of earnest consideration among educated classes. There was heated discussion, especially among lawyers and politicians, as to its merits and demerits. The controversy developed into a dispute between the English and the French schools and finally into a political struggle between conservatives and progressives. The immediate result of this struggle was an eight-year postponement in the enforcement of a civil code.

A few paragraphs are in order to explain the condition of legal education at this period in Japan, since this proved to be an important factor in the factional clash that occurred in connection with acceptance of the Civil Code.

From early Meiji times there had been a law school attached to the Ministry of Justice in which French law was taught. Two or three private law schools also taught French law. Boissonade, who came to Japan in November 1873 and began to teach French law in 1874, was an outstanding figure. He was interested in natural law and lectured on that subject as well as on more technical subjects. In his days the *école d'exégese* was

[41] Hozumi, The New Japanese Civil Code 38–40 (1912). In connection with *jōri*, see Sugiyama, *La loi du juin 1875 sur l'administration de la justice et les sources du droit privé*, 2 Recueil d'Études sur les sources du droit en l'honneur de François Gény 446 (no date).

still dominant in France in the field of private law; the "revival of natural law" in France, which took place at the close of the century, was not yet underway. Boissonade may have read Ahrens' *Cours de droit naturel,* which was first published in 1837 and ran through many editions; and, as is shown by his *Le nouveau code civil italien comparé au code Napoléon,* published in 1868, he had some interest in *législation comparée* before he came to Japan. However, his other works from this period indicate that his main interest lay in the historical aspects of various private-law institutions. Judging from his previous publications, one would suppose that he was a positivist interested in history. It seems that he first began to lecture on natural law in Japan. Was this motivated by his desire to expound his own Weltanschauung in the form of a lecture? Or did it arise from his newly assigned task of drafting modern codes for Japan and making her accept them as an embodiment of natural law? He considered that the system of positive law was, and ought to be, a reflection of natural law, which is in turn a universal idea of mankind and can be discovered by human reason. If there is any discrepancy between positive law and natural law, the positive law was no law but a corruption of law. Boissonade's theory, like Ahrens', is close to that expounded by the seventeenth- and eighteenth-century natural-law jurists. They, unlike the glossators and commentators, considered Roman law binding not because it was based on imperial authority but because it was an embodiment of universal human reason. As is well known, this idea of natural law inspired codification movements in Europe. Although such a theory perhaps served no practical purpose in France after the comprehensive Napoleonic codes had been completed, it could be eminently useful for the Japanese who had the task of codification before them. The natural law expounded by Boissonade seems to have appealed to the Japanese audience because it was very similar to the familiar concept of the Confucian "Way of Heaven." Many Japanese jurists who attended Boissonade's lectures naturally came to believe that the French code was not merely a French national product but an embodiment of natural law — a model of civilized law.

English law had been taught at the Tokyo Kaisei School, which subsequently became Tokyo Imperial University,[42] since the year 1874 by American, English, and Japanese teachers, and it was taught in several other law schools. The methods of legal science in England in those days were analytical-historical, and the school of natural law was looked down upon as outmoded. Henry T. Terry, an American lawyer who for a long time to come was to be familiar around the university as an eminent authority on Anglo-American law, also frowned on natural law. In *First*

[42] From 1877 until 1886 it was called Tokyo University, for a short time thereafter the Imperial University, and still later Tokyo Imperial University. After World War II the title Tokyo University was revived.

Principles of Law, published in 1878, his anti-natural-law sentiment is strongly expressed:

The law of nature or natural law is a species of *pseudo* law which has occupied a great deal of the attention of writers on jurisprudence in the nations of continental Europe, and has been the source of no little confusion and obscurity in the law, and wild and foolish theorizing, and unfortunately of equally wild acting, in the politics of those countries. It is the very tap-root of communism. Fortunately it never took any strong hold of English and American legal thought, though it crops up in the "glittering generalities" of the opening of the Declaration of Independence of the United States and it is the favorite appeal of demagogues of every time.[43]

This book reached fifteen editions and was widely used as a textbook in Japan. His later works, *Leading Principles of Anglo-American Law* (1884) and *The Common Law* (second revised edition, 1898), and his lectures at the university on torts and equity evince, according to Albert Koeourek, an originality and analytic acuteness superior to that of John Austin. It was quite natural that, when the Hohfeldian system and the restatement movement brought about a revival of analytical jurisprudence in the United States, his arrangement of the law and his original analysis of rights drew the attention of American jurists. Terry was adept in analytical jurisprudence and, like Bentham and Austin, favored codification.

Another prominent American jurist who taught Anglo-American law in Japan was John H. Wigmore. He, like Terry, did not uphold natural law. His lectures at Keio Gijuku, his monumental *Treatise on the Law of Evidence,* and his concise summary in *Cases on Torts* attest to his amazing analytic power. Unlike Terry, however, he was also interested in the dynamic aspect of law. His *Panorama of the World's Legal Systems,* the *Evolution of Law* series edited by him, and his highly original planetary theory of legal evolution may be regarded as the later developments of his interest in Tokugawa judicial decisions from the standpoint of comparative legal history. Wigmore was historical and analytical. He followed Henry Maine as well as John Austin.

Japanese jurists of the English school in this period studied not so much the reported cases as they did Bentham, Austin, and Maine and text writers such as Pollock, Holland, Anson, and Terry. They were interested in abstract positive rules and principles as expounded by those text writers. Unlike Savigny and his school, they were not opposed to codification, and, unlike the Germanist branch of the German historical school, they were not upholders of the indigenous law. They were no more "nationalistic" than the jurists of the French school and, like the latter, held Western individualistic jurisprudence in high esteem.

[43] TERRY, THE FIRST PRINCIPLES OF LAW §149, p. 134 (1878).

The objection of the English school of jurists to the immediate enforcement of the Civil Code was scientific rather than political. The code was based exclusively on French Law. The English school did not consider French law the only civilized system of law and believed the English and German systems must also be taken into account. It may be noted in this connection that in 1887, three years before the promulgation of the Old Civil Code, a change had been made in the curriculum of the law department of Tokyo Imperial University. The law school of the Ministry of Justice was transferred to the university in 1885, and the German-law section was newly established in 1887. It may also be noted that German legal science was then acquiring an increased prestige in Japan as well as in other countries.

At first, the case for postponement of the enforcement of the Civil Code beyond 1893 was presented in a scientific spirit. When, however, the question of postponement or immediate enforcement developed into a fight between the two schools, the arguments for opposing immediate enforcement tended to run wild. It was an age of reaction against overrapid westernization, and scholars sometimes appealed to patriotic sentiment. It is also true that some facets of the controversy took on aspects of the controversy between Thibaut and Savigny and of a struggle between the school of natural law and the historical school. However, it was not essentially a conflict of two philosophies, but a conflict of views based on expediency. Nobushige Hozumi, who was himself an English barrister of the Middle Temple and who had also studied at Berlin, was one of the leading champions of the postponement party. Masaaki Tomii, who was a *docteur en droit* of the University of Lyon and an eminent jurist of the French school, also belonged to the postponement group. Kenjiro Ume, who had studied law both at Lyon and Berlin, was a leading champion of the immediate-enforcement party. It is also interesting to note in this connection that in 1892 John Wigmore wrote an article, "New Codes and Old Customs," in the *Japan Mail,* which gave aid and comfort to the enforcement group.

The New Civil Code of 1898

The postponement party won out. A bill to postpone the enforcement of the code was brought before the Lower House. After several heated debates, the bill passed both Houses, and the operation of the code was postponed until December 31, 1896. A new drafting committee of three, consisting of Hozumi, Ume, and Tomii, followed the policy first advocated by the English school and consulted many codes and drafts then available. The net result of their labors was that the arrangement of the new code became entirely German, adopting the Pandekten system rather than the institutional French system. Although its contents are of a composite nature, showing here and there the influence of French and English law as well as the native law, the influence of the first (1887) and second (1896) drafts of the German Civil Code is clearly dominant. The new Civil Code of Japan came into operation on July 16, 1898. Although English, German, and French law continued to be taught at the Imperial University by foreign and Japanese professors, the predominance of German legal science continued down to the end of World War II. Subsequent legislation in other fields of law followed German models. Students of law went mostly to German universities, as German textbooks, commentaries, and court decisions could most conveniently be utilized for the interpretation and application of the codes and statutes in force in Japan.

After the coming into force of the Civil Code of 1898, many special laws were enacted to supplement or modify the provisions concerning real rights and obligations. A committee was set up in 1919 to revise the parts relating to the family and inheritance law, so as to bring them into accord with the "old *boni mores* of our country" (*jumpū bizoku*).[44] Despite the high-sounding proclamation smacking of political reaction, many of the thirty-four proposals for revision in the family law adopted by the committee in 1925, and the seventeen proposals for revising the inheritance law, adopted by it, in 1927, were in various aspects progressive in character. They served, therefore, as valuable material when the Civil Code was revised to bring it into accord with the spirit of the new Constitution.

The Old and New Commercial Codes

As in the case of the Civil Code, there also were an Old Commercial Code and a New Commercial Code. The Old Code was based on a draft written by Hermann Roesler, a German adviser to the government and professor at the Imperial University. Roesler's draft was eclectic and not exclusively French, since German and English law were also taken into account. The Old Commercial Code was promulgated on April 27, 1890,[45] but shared the fate of the Old Civil Code in the heat of the postponement controversy. However, unlike the Old Civil Code, which never came into force but only served as convenient material for the court in exercising "reason," some sections of the Old Commercial Code, especially those parts relating to companies, came into operation on July 1, 1893,[46] and remained in force until the coming into effect of the New Commercial Code. Book III of the Old Commercial Code, which provided for bankruptcy of companies, also came into effect on July 1, 1893, and was in force until replaced by the Bankruptcy Law of 1922.[47] These temporary measures were necessitated by a business panic. The New Commercial Code, drafted by a committee con-

[44] Literally, "gentle ways and beautiful customs."
[45] By Law No. 32 of 1890.
[46] Pursuant to Law No. 9 of 1893.
[47] Law No. 71 of 1922.

sisting of Ume, Okano, and Tabe, was promulgated on March 9, 1899,[48] and took effect on June 16 of the same year.[49]

The Commercial Code of 1899 consisted of five books: General Provisions, Companies, Commercial Acts, Bills, and Maritime Commerce. Book IV, dealing with bills of exchange, promissory notes, and checks, was stricken from the code simultaneously with the enactment of two statutes, one on bills of exchange and promissory notes (1932)[50] and the other on checks (1933).[51] These enactments followed the ratifications of two international treaties entered into at Geneva providing for uniform laws on those topics.

In view of the marked development of industry and commerce after World War I, the Commercial Code, especially Book II, was radically amended,[52] and the amended code came into force on January 1, 1940.[53] A separate statute providing for limited liability companies (*yūgen kaisha*)[54] came into force on the same date,[55] thus amplifying the forms available for business enterprise. The law on companies was again radically revised during the Allied military occupation as one phase of the democratization of Japan, and in this process American corporation law was taken as a model.

Code of Civil Procedure and the Labor Laws

The Code of Civil Procedure was promulgated on April 21, 1890,[56] and came into force on January 1, 1891. The code was almost a literal translation of the German *Zivilprozessordnung;* the translation of *Rechtshängigkeit*—"pending in court"—as *"kenri-kōsoku"*—"fettered right" (in context a meaningless phrase which revealed that the translator thought that *Recht* in the German term "Rechtshängigkeit" had its ordinary sense of "right" rather than the unusual sense of "court")—was a famous laughingstock among old lawyers, though it has now been deleted.

Important amendments to the Code of Civil Procedure were made on April 24, 1926.[57] Unlike the case of the Code of Criminal Procedure, the new Constitution did not necessitate revision of the Code of Civil Procedure. However, a few amendments[58] were made modifying the mode of trial in the court of first instance, and here the Anglo-American influence is conspicuous.

After World War I, Japan's capitalistic economy made marked progress,

[48] By Law No. 48 of 1899.
[49] Pursuant to Imperial Order No. 133 of 1899.
[50] Bills Law, Law No. 20 of 1932.
[51] Checks Law, Law No. 57 of 1933.
[52] By Law No. 72 of 1938.
[53] Pursuant to Imperial Order No. 510 of 1939.
[54] Limited Liability Company Law, Law No. 74 of 1938.
[55] Pursuant to Imperial Order No. 510 of 1939.
[56] By Law No. 29 of 1890.
[57] By Law No. 61 of 1926.
[58] By Law No. 149 of 1948.

and the interest of jurists was drawn to the law in relation to labor. Anton Menger's *Das bürgerliche Recht und die besitzlosen Klassen* (1903) was translated into Japanese by Tadahiko Mibuchi, then a young judge who after World War II became the first Chief Justice of the Supreme Court organized under the new Constitution. Karl Renner's more radical *Soziale Funktion der Rechtsinstitute besonders des Eigentums,* which appeared in 1904 in volume one of *Marx Studien* and was published in a revised edition in 1929 with the title *Die Rechtsinstitute des Privatrechts und die soziale Funktion,* was also studied with much sympathy by students of civil law. After Izutaro Suehiro returned from Europe, he sensed the coming importance of labor law in Japan, began his informal annual lectures on that subject, and published a number of articles in the field. He may indeed be regarded as the father of Japanese labor law. The Factory Law promulgated in 1911,[59] which came into effect in 1916, was the first Japanese labor legislation. A series of social and labor legislation ensued — the Leased Land Law (1921),[60] the Leased House Law (1921),[61] the Leased Land and Leased House Mediation Law (1922),[62] and the Tenant Farming Mediation Law (1924).[63] The period of controlled economy under a series of laws enacted under the National General Mobilization Law of April 1938[64] can be passed over as an outcome of an extraordinary situation. During the military occupation, a trinity of labor laws — the Labor Relations Adjustment Law,[65] the Labor Union Law,[66] and the Labor Standards Law[67] — enacted at the suggestion of American lawyers, brought Japanese labor legislation on a par with American labor law after the New Deal. Lawyers connected with the American occupation were influential in the drafting of labor legislation, as well as in the radical revision of the companies law mentioned above, and in the preparation of the antimonopoly law.[68]

Anglo-American Legal Institutions

The Trust Law[69] and the Trust Business Law of 1922,[70] as well as the Mortgage Debenture Trust Law of 1905,[71] were influenced by Anglo-American trust law. Torajiro Ikeda, who later became president of the

[59] By Law No. 46 of 1911.
[60] Law No. 49 of 1921.
[61] Law No. 50 of 1921.
[62] Law No. 41 of 1922.
[63] Law No. 18 of 1924.
[64] Law No. 55 of 1938.
[65] Law No. 25 of 1946.
[66] Law No. 174 of 1949.
[67] Law No. 49 of 1947.
[68] Law Concerning the Prohibition of Private Monopoly and the Maintenance of Fair Trade, Law No. 54 of 1947.
[69] Law No. 62 of 1922.
[70] Law No. 65 of 1922.
[71] Law No. 52 of 1905.

Great Court of Judicature and who had studied equity under Terry, was chiefly responsible for the drafting of these three laws. The flexible Anglo-American law was not, however, congenial to the rigidly theoretical mind of Japanese civilians and did not make much headway. Reginald Smith's *Justice and the Poor* (1915) made a considerable impression on Japanese lawyers. Many legal-aid societies cropped up. The Tokyo Attorneys' Association set up a section on legal aid and, besides giving consultations, brought suits on behalf of poor clients. This legal-aid work progressed rapidly after World War II, though, compared with the progress made in Great Britain in the 1940s, it still leaves a great deal to be desired, especially in the field of civil litigation. Other Anglo-American institutions influential in this period — the criminal jury and the juvenile court (now part of the Family Court) — have already been mentioned.

JURISPRUDENCE

Japanese Legal Science

The main interest of academic jurists in Japan who participated in codification work lay naturally in *législation comparée* and legislative policies. When they began to lecture on the Civil Code, they used to compare the law adopted by the code with the French, German, and sometimes English law on each topic. The next generation of teachers of private law directed their main endeavors to a systematic and theoretical exposition of the current civil and commercial law, and in this process the influence of German legal scholars was profound; interest in French and Anglo-American law gradually waned. On the whole, their method may be characterized as code positivism, reminding one of the glossators whose efforts were directed to the understanding of the corpus juris in itself, rather than of the commentators whose interest lay in practical applications of the corpus juris to disputes arising out of the social life of the time.

After World War I, the German exegetical method lost its exclusive dominance in Japanese legal science. Let me indicate several signs of this new trend.

A private group was organized in the law department of Tokyo Imperial University for a critical study of the decisions in civil matters of the Great Court of Judicature. This group was headed by two professors of civil law, Shigeto Hozumi and Izutaro Suehiro. Hozumi's father, Nobushige, was the prominent representative of the English school mentioned above. Shigeto Hozumi had been studying under Joseph Kohler at Berlin to prepare himself for a new course on jurisprudence which he was to give when he returned home. Just before World War I broke out in Europe, he reached London and studied the English reports at the Middle Temple library, where his father had read law some thirty years before. There he wrote his monograph,

Sensō to Keiyaku (War and Contracts), in which his study of English cases is amply incorporated. Suehiro stayed a short time in the United States in 1918 and was deeply impressed by the case method in action in the course of attending Dean Hall's lectures on torts at the University of Chicago. I often heard him depreciate his own laborious work on *Obligations: Special Part,* written in the usual German way then prevalent and published before he went abroad. The case-study group was organized after these two professors returned home. Later the work of this group stimulated the formation of similar groups in other fields such as criminal law and public law. This change of emphasis may be compared to a shift from the glossators to postglossators in the study of the corpus juris. The published commentaries on Great Court of Judicature decisions, which they produced, may be compared to the notes published by Sirey and Dalloz in France.

While I was in the United States in 1915, I read Eugen Ehrlich's *Grundlegung der Soziologie des Rechts,* published in 1913, and "Professor Ehrlich's Czernowitz Seminar of Living Law" by Wm. Herbert Page, published in 1914 in *Proceedings of the Fourteenth Annual Meeting of the Association of American Law Schools.* After the end of the War, Ehrlich was an émigré at Berne, Switzerland, where I became friendly with him. Before leaving Berne I asked him to write an article for a Japanese legal periodical with which I was connected. He contributed two articles, one on "Gesetz und lebendes Recht," [72] the other on "Die Soziologie des Rechts." [73] The latter article, which was probably the last essay written by the eminent scholar, appeared in English in the *Harvard Law Review,* in Italian in the *Rivista internationale di filosofia del diritto,* and in Japanese in the *Hōgaku Kyōkai Zasshi* (the latter journal contains the German original as well as the Japanese translation). Ehrlich's articles drew the attention of Japanese jurists to this new field of legal science. They inspired later studies of "living law" in the fields of family law, land law, and mercantile law. Especially after World War II, sociology of law became very fashionable among academic jurists in Japan.

Under the influence of Raymond Saleille's theory of *interprétation évolutif* and Gény's theory of *libre recherche scientifique* in France, on one hand, and of the *Freirechtsbewegung* under Kantorowitz, Ehrlich, and Fuchs in Germany, on the other, Eiichi Makino, an eminent professor of criminal law expounded, in innumerable articles, his "theory of free law" (*jiyū hōron*). Like his French and German predecessors, Makino's theory amounted in practice to the advocacy of equitable interpretation of the codes. Beginning in 1915, the Great Court of Judicature handed down decisions that clearly

[72] Ehrlich, *Gesetz und lebendes Recht,* 38 Hōgaku Kyōkai Zasshi (The Journal of the Jurisprudence Association) 1509 (Japanese), app. at 1 (German) (1920).

[73] Ehrlich, *Die Soziologie des Rechts,* 40 Hōgaku Kyōkai Zasshi 12 (Japanese), no. 1 app. at 1 (German) (1922); 36 Harv. L. Rev. 130 (1922).

indicate an equitable rather than a strict, logical interpretation of the Civil Code.

In this period an interest in Western juristic thought was shown by a group of Japanese jurists. Stammler, Kohler, and Radbruch of Germany; Kelsen, Kaufmann, and A. Merkl of Austria; Del Vecchio and Alessandro Levi of Italy; Hauriou, Gény, and Duguit of France; Vinogradoff, E. Barker, and Laski of the United Kingdom; and Pound, Frank, and Llewellyn of the United States each found a sympathetic or critical exponent. There stood many mansions in the Japanese juristic field — Neo-Kantianism, Neo-Hegelianism, Kelsenianism, Phenomenology, Pragmatism, Neo-Scholasticism — each developing its own ideas. There were, however, few severe *Schulenstreiten,* excepting the Marxists, who severely attacked those jurists, domestic or foreign, holding other views. The net result of this interest in Western juristic thought seems to have been to justify, to use Vinogradoff's formulation, the gradual transition from the individualistic jurisprudence of the Civil Code to the coming socialistic jurisprudence.

Japanese Legal History

John Wigmore used to recall that, when he first came to Japan, most of the Japanese jurists were solely interested in Western law, and the very few experts on Japanese legal history followed an outmoded method. Dozaburo Miyazaki, who studied in Germany in the late 1880s, was influenced by Jacob Grimm; his researches along the lines of comparative philology are remarkable. They were, however, confined to the ancient law of Japan. Study of the history of Japanese private law really began in the 1920s with the resort to modern techniques by Kaoru Nakada and his successor Ryosuke Ishii of Tokyo Imperial University, and by Shuko Miura and Kenji Maki of Kyoto Imperial University.[74] The entire course of Japanese legal history has become tolerably clear through the cumulative efforts of these men and their students, though a school of indigenous law, comparable to the Germanists in nineteenth-century Germany has not emerged.

These varied movements have enriched the writings of legal scholars. The tendency has grown to interpret the Civil Code equitably, according to changing mores, though the impact of German exegetical method is still very clearly seen in the scholars' modes of exposition.[75]

CONCLUSION

The history of Japanese law since the Restoration of 1868 is almost synonymous with an account of the reception of occidental law and legal

[74] Ishii is in 1962 professor at Tokyo University and Maki at Kyoto.

[75] ISHII, NIHON HŌSEI SHI (A History of the Japanese System of Law) (1954). This work is a convenient guide to literature on various topics in Japanese legal history.

science.[76] The fact that Japan became a country of civil law may have been largely due to the historical accident that the common law had no code. As Wigmore opines, had Sheldon Amos' civil code for England become a reality, Japan might have had a common-law-inspired civil code, and the subsequent course of her legal development might have been entirely different. The dominance of Continental, especially German, legal science for over half a century made the common-law world a dark continent for ordinary Japanese lawyers. Then, again by a historical accident — the war and the Allied occupation — Japanese jurists were confronted by a large-scale introduction of rules and principles of common-law origin. They had not been trained in the common law and were naturally not aware either of its historical background or of its techniques of interpretation. It is quite natural that those rules and principles were interpreted by Japanese jurists according to the civilian methods in which they were experts. If one compares commentaries on the Philippine constitution with those on the new Japanese constitution, he will be surprised at the striking difference in the mode of exposition and interpretation, even in cases in which the constitutional text is exactly the same. The former works reveal the mind of common-law lawyers, the latter that of jurists trained in the civil law. Thus Japanese jurists' interpretation of principles of common-law origin has sometimes been justly accused of resembling the interpretation of an English text through canons of German grammar, and, in some cases, serious misinterpretations have resulted. This, however, is inevitable in a transitional period, a period now coming to an end. More and more Japanese lawyers are going to the United States to study law. But what can Japanese civilians now profitably learn from the common law?

Perhaps the first benefit might come from improved techniques of interpretation. The Civil Code of Quebec is said to have borrowed from common law as well as from French law. We are also told by Walton that in interpreting that code the tendency is to follow the French authorities in the case of rules of French origin and the English authorities for principles borrowed from the common law. In the same way, those Japanese jurists whose task it is to interpret constitutional law, company law, labor law, the law of criminal procedure, and other laws of American origin might greatly benefit in their work by studying American law and practice in their respective fields. In view of the fact that Japanese international commerce is mainly with the United States and other countries of the common law, Japanese legislators might in the future find it more convenient to affiliate Japanese commercial law with the common law, just as the Civil Code of Quebec adopted common-law rules in that field because Quebec's commerce

[76] A very detailed and useful account in English of the reception of Western law in Japan in the latter part of the nineteenth century and the first decade of the twentieth is found in Japanese Legislation in the Meiji Era (Ishii ed., 1958).

was exclusively with England, the United States, and Canadian provinces.

Other benefits of common-law studies might be experienced by those lawyers who are now advocating the unification of the bench and bar (*hōsō ichigen*), with a view to improving the administration of justice in Japan. They would find valuable materials in immense abundance in England and the United States. Japanese legal historians have so far endeavored to analyze Japanese legal history through the spectacles of nineteenth-century Continental individualistic jurisprudence, with *Rechtsgeschäft* as the central concept. They have been criticized in some quarters as having distorted the true picture of Japan's legal past. Such historians might rectify the picture in many respects by re-examining the history of Japanese law in comparison with the evolution of modern law from feudal law in England.

Most important of all, Japanese jurists might profitably imbibe the spirit of common law for the improvement of the juridical order of the nation. With the introduction of codified Continental law, Japanese jurists have also inherited the civilians' frame of mind in dealing with the law and its problems — a frame of mind which Lord Macmillan characterized in his *Two Ways of Thinking* as the deductive way of thinking. They now have a tendency to be more interested in legal principles in the abstract than in the close examination of facts and factual nuances in each case. Some jurists have learned much from the lucid and logical Gallic mind. Others have mastered the German art of systematization and philosophical speculation. These qualities are valuable in legal education. Yet, in judicial administration, they can learn a great deal from the surefooted Anglo-Saxon habit of looking at events in concrete terms and of dealing with things legal as they arise instead of anticipating them by abstract formulas.

The introduction of codified Continental law was also accompanied by the authoritarian conception of law as an aggregate of legal rules imposed by sovereign authority rather than as an embodiment of reason and justice. Japanese lawyers and administrators through some seventy years of experience have mastered the art of rule by law. The new Constitution introduced the supremacy of law as one of its basic principles. However, the old authoritarian conception still prevails among the members of the legal profession as well as among the people in general. The spirit of the supremacy of law which views administration as a part of the legal process — a spirit which underlies the thinking of common-law lawyers — is worthy of being absorbed by Japanese lawyers as well as the nation at large. The postwar contact of civil law with common law is deplored in some quarters, but it will not only broaden the vision of Japanese jurists but will afford an occasion for improving Japan's legal order.*

* James W. Morely noted at the conference that, as the transitional phase of modernization comes to an end, the need for massive borrowings in order to utilize law as an instrument of social reform will also end, permitting a development of Japanese law based more largely on indigenous experience.

The divergence of living law from book law is a phenomenon not confined to Japan. It exists not only in codified, civil-law countries such as France and Germany, but also in common-law countries such as the United States. It can be seen not only in private law but in public law as well. Such divergence, however, seems to be more marked in Japan than in Western countries. The reception of Roman law in Germany, for instance, was a gradual process extending over several centuries, and Roman law became part of German customary law. It was, therefore, no contradiction for Savigny, a great Romanist, to have become an upholder of the customary law as reflecting the *Volksgeist* better than the codified law. In the case of Japan, Western law based on assumptions — moral, economic, and cultural — which were widely divergent from the assumptions of the traditional life of the nation was hurriedly transplanted, primarily because of political exigencies. The law in books has been completely westernized, and so has the mode of legal thinking and argument of Japanese lawyers. This undoubtedly has been, and continues to be, an important factor in modernizing the political, economic, and social life of the nation. Such modernization is, however, a gradual process, and it is nonsensical to imagine that the law in books reflects exactly the law in action in Japan.

It has often been pointed out that the elaborate, imported Western apparatus for administering justice and settling disputes has not been utilized in Japan to the same extent as in Western countries. The Japanese people prefer the mediation method to the black-and-white judicial method in the resolution of disputes. Some account for this attitude by the deep influence of the Confucian teaching that "harmony is to be valued," that is to say, by the general feeling that the judicial method is not conducive to abiding harmony between the parties concerned. Others attribute the attitude to the feudal sentiment that it is morally wrong to trouble the mind of the lord about private matters. Still others say it is due to the Japanese national character, that the Japanese people are less assertive of their rights than Anglo-Saxons or Germans, being rather more like the Austrians, to whom Ihering eloquently preached *Kampf ums Recht,* idolizing Shylock, who, it may be noted, is a most abominable figure to Japanese readers of the *Merchant of Venice*. A more prosaic explanation is that the utilization of the judicial apparatus is avoided because it is too expensive and time-consuming — a motive familiar to Western businessmen who prefer commercial arbitration rather than judicial settlement. Each of these explanations may hold an element of truth, but no single explanation can account for the general trend. This trend itself may, however, be a phenomenon in the transitional period. Thus, in the Japanese legal future, *jus* rather than *boni mores* may become the more potent instrument of social control, and the courts may become, as in Western countries, an agency more frequently employed for the resolution of private disputes.

The law laid down in the codes and statutes is Western, but it does not, of course, operate in exactly the same way as in Western countries. The old family system was swept away by the fiat of the new Civil Code; and, while the new rules and principles regarding domestic relations and succession may be in conformity with the sentiments of justice of dwellers in large cities, the situation is otherwise in agricultural areas. There various devices are used to maintain the family-farming system, thus deviating in practice from what the legislators had designed. The new companies law and labor law have American features but these do not work in the same way as in the United States. It is well known that age-old paternalistic ideas color both the conduct of business firms and the practical operation of trade unionism in Japan. It is also well known that the feudal ideas of *oyabun* and *kobun* (paternal leader and subordinates) are still distorting the operation of all political parties and of the Election Law. A discrepancy between the law in books and the law in actual operation is an interesting subject now being discussed by sociological jurists in Japan.

Some forty years ago Ehrlich in his "Statutes and Living Law," a paper specifically addressed to Japanese jurists, warned them against confining their studies exclusively to codes and statutes transplanted from Germany which, though in a way useful, are but statements of abstract principles. He suggested a concrete program for the study of the living private law in Japan. Since then studies along this line, sometimes involving field work, have been made by a few scholars. The majority of academic jurists, however, stick to book law, considering that factual study is outside the province of legal science and within the province of sociology. But sociologists, without adequate training in the law, cannot undertake this work. Although a systematic study of the living law of a nation as a whole transcends the efforts of any individual scholar, however competent, such a study should be done by collaborative efforts and must be continuous, for the living law itself is dynamic and changes constantly. Ehrlich, therefore, suggested that it be undertaken by a state institution, closely affiliated with Japan's Institute of Statistics.[77] Such a systematic study of the law in Japan is, as in other countries, still an ideal, but there is no doubt that its results would enrich and enliven legal education, save judges from *Weltfremdheit,* make administrators less bureaucratic, and render the work of legislators less amateurish, more scientific, and more responsive to social needs.

[77] Ehrlich was apparently referring to the former Cabinet Bureau of Statistics, which should not be confused with the postwar, privately organized Japan Institute of Statistics.

DISPUTE RESOLUTION IN CONTEMPORARY JAPAN

Takeyoshi Kawashima

THERE is probably no society in which litigation is the normal means of resolving disputes. Rarely will both parties press their claims so far as to require resort to a court; instead, one of the disputants will probably offer a satisfactory settlement or propose the use of some extrajudicial, informal procedure. Although direct evidence of this tendency is difficult to obtain, the phenomena described below offer indirect support for the existence of these attitudes among the Japanese people.

FORMAL MEANS OF DISPUTE RESOLUTION: LAWSUITS

During the last years of World War I, when the housing shortage became critical, active speculation in real estate existed and there arose a large number of disputes regarding land and leases, both residential and farm. Because of the patriarchal nature of the traditional lease in Japan, tenants had not previously dared to dispute the terms or meaning of a lease. Thus when tenants began to press these disagreements, the choice of a method for resolution was influenced almost entirely by the advantages and disadvantages of the alternatives. Although the increase of litigation regarding these contracts threatened the government so seriously that the institution of *chōtei* (mediation) was hastily legalized,[1] in the following years the volume of litigation was relatively small when we take into account the seriousness of the housing shortage and the social unrest caused by it. This suggests that only a small portion of the disputes were brought to the courts (see Table 1 at the end of this essay). Furthermore, if we compare the number of mediation cases regarding leases and farm tenancies after mediation was legalized with the lawsuits of the same type, we note that the latter figure is considerably smaller, showing the extent to which mediation was preferred to litigation (Table 1).

Similarly, a comparison of the number of lawsuits and mediation cases

Note. Mr. Kawashima is Professor of Law, Tokyo University. B.Jur., Tokyo Imperial University, 1932; Dr.Jur., Tokyo University, 1959. Visiting Professor at Stanford University, 1958–59. Author of SHOYŪKEN HŌ NO RIRON (Theory of the Law of Ownership) (1949); IDEOLOGY TOSHITE NO KAZOKU SEIDO (The Family System as an Ideology) (1957); writings in the fields of civil law and sociology of law.

[1] By the Leased Land and Leased House Mediation Law, Law No. 41 of 1922.

regarding leases during the years immediately after the Japanese surrender in 1945, when the complete destruction of housing by air raids in most of the cities had produced a serious housing shortage, suggests that litigation was resorted to in only a relatively small number of cases. Mediation was vastly preferred (see Table 2).

It is also indicative in this connection that during the years of economic depression after the panic of 1927—in Japan the depression started two years earlier than in the United States—the statistics do not show any significant increase in the number of lawsuits, although a large number of debtors became insolvent (Table 3). The judicial statistics of the same period of some states in the United States, on the other hand, show a remarkable increase in the number of lawsuits (Table 4). The fairly small number of lawyers in Japan relative to the population and the degree of industrialization suggests that people do not go to court so frequently as in Western countries and that the demand for lawyers' services is not great.[2]

Finally, it is of significance that, according to a survey conducted by this writer, extremely few claims arising from traffic accidents involving railroads and taxis were brought to court, and almost all of the cases were settled by extrajudicial agreements (Table 5). A railroad was involved in a total of 145 traffic accidents which caused physical injury during the period from April 1960 to September 1960; but not a single case was brought to court, and only two cases were handled by attorneys. Of all the accidents of the same company which caused physical injury during the past seven years, only three cases were brought to court, and all three were settled during the course of the litigation. Of the total of 372 accidents which caused physical injury and involved another railroad in 1960, not a single case was brought to court, and only one case was handled by an attorney.

The volume of litigation arising in 1960 from traffic accidents caused by taxis is as follows.[3]

Company	*Personal injury*	*Property damage*	*Total*	*Litigation*
A	221	2,041	2,262	1
B	10	195	205	1
C	4	54	58	0
D	0	appr. 42	appr. 42	0

[2] See Takaaki Hattori, "The Legal Profession in Japan: Its Historical Development and Present State," in this volume.

[3] The following figures from a study by M. A. Franklin, R. G. Chanin, and I. Mark (Columbia University Project for Effective Justice) suggest the significance of these Japanese figures. "Each year in New York City some 193,000 accident victims seek to recover damages for injuries ascribed to someone else's fault. For about 154,000 of these claimants the first step is retaining an attorney, while 39,000 proceed without aid of counsel. Theoretically, a claim is but the first step on the road to the courthouse, but in fact very few of the 193,000 claims ever get that far. Approximately 116,000 are closed without suit, leaving 77,000 that are actually sued. Almost all claimants who have been unable to recover without suit, and who wish to continue, retain an attorney." *Accidents, Money, and the Law: A Study of the Economics of Personal Injury Litigation,* 61 COLUM. L. REV. 1, at 10 (1961).

There are several possible explanations of this relative lack of litigation. On the one hand, litigation takes time (see Table 6) and is expensive, but this seems to be true in almost all countries having modern judicial systems and can hardly account for the specifically strong inclination of the Japanese public to avoid judicial procedures. Or one might point out that monetary compensation awarded by the courts for damage due to personal injury or death in traffic accidents is usually extremely small. In a large number of cases, the damages awarded by the courts for a death caused by a traffic accident were said to be less than 300,000 yen (approximately 833 dollars); thus the Automobile Damage Compensation Security Law[4] when originally enacted provided that the compulsory insurance for a death need cover only 300,000 yen.[5] A more decisive factor is to be found in the social-cultural background of the problem. Traditionally, the Japanese people prefer extra-judicial, informal means of settling a controversy. Litigation presupposes and admits the existence of a dispute and leads to a decision which makes clear who is right or wrong in accordance with standards that are independent of the wills of the disputants. Furthermore, judicial decisions emphasize the conflict between the parties, deprive them of participation in the settlement, and assign a moral fault which can be avoided in a compromise solution.

This attitude is presumably related to the nature of the traditional social groups in Japan, which may be epitomized by two characteristics. First, they are hierarchical in the sense that social status is differentiated in terms of deference and authority. Not only the village community and the family, but even contractual relationships have customarily been hierarchical. From the construction contract arises a relationship in which the contractor defers to the owner as his patron; from the contract of lease a relationship in which the lessee defers to the lessor; from the contract of employment a relationship in which the servant or employee defers to the master or employer; from the contract of apprenticeship a relationship in which the apprentice defers to the master; and from the contract of sale a relationship in which the seller defers to the buyer (the former being expected in each case to yield to the direction or desire of the latter). At the same time, however, the status of the master or employer is patriarchal and not despotic; in other words, he is supposed not only to dominate but also to patronize and therefore partially to consent to the requests of his servant or employee. Consequently, even though their social roles are defined in one way or other, the role definition is precarious and each man's role is contingent on that

[4] Law No. 97 of 1955.

[5] Automobile Damage Compensation Security Law, art. 13; Automobile Damage Compensation Security Law Enforcement Order, Cabinet Order No. 86 of 1955, art. 2. An amendment to the Enforcement Order by Cabinet Order No. 227 of 1960 subsequently increased the amount to 500,000 yen. For a full discussion, see Ichiro Kato, "The Treatment of Motor-Vehicle Accidents: A Study of the Impact of Technological Change on Legal Relations," in this volume.

of the other. Obviously this characteristic is incompatible with judicial decisions based on fixed universalistic standards.[6]

Second, in traditional social groups relationships between people of equal status have also been to a great extent "particularistic" and at the same time "functionally diffuse." For instance, the relationship between members of the same village community who are equal in social status is supposed to be "intimate"; their social roles are defined in general and very flexible terms so that they can be modified whenever circumstances dictate. In direct proportion with the degree to which they are dependent on or intimate with each other, the role definition of each is contingent upon that of the other. Once again, role definition with fixed universalistic standards does not fit such a relationship.[7]

In short, this definition of social roles can be, and commonly is, characterized by the term "harmony." There is a strong expectation that a dispute should not and will not arise; even when one does occur, it is to be solved by mutual understanding. Thus there is no *raison d'être* for the majority rule that is so widespread in other modern societies; instead the principle of rule by consensus prevails.[8]

It is obvious that a judicial decision does not fit and even endangers relationships. When people are socially organized in small groups and when subordination of individual desires in favor of group agreement is idealized, the group's stability and the security of individual members are threatened by attempts to regulate conduct by universalistic standards. The impact is greater when such an effort is reinforced by an organized political power. Furthermore, the litigious process, in which both parties seek to justify their position by objective standards, and the emergence of a judicial decision based thereon tend to convert situational interests into firmly consolidated

[6] The terms "universalistic," "particularistic," and "functionally diffuse" are used here in the sense of the "pattern variables" scheme of PARSONS, THE SOCIAL SYSTEM 62–65 (1951); Parsons & Shils, *Categories of the Orientation and Organization of Action,* in TOWARD A GENERAL THEORY OF ACTION 82–84 (1952).

[7] One of the clues to understanding the social-cultural background of divorce by agreement, which is so characteristic of Japanese culture, is found in this point. Whenever a conflict or a dispute arises between husband and wife, it is most appropriate to attempt to reach agreement through mutual understanding in the context of the complicated and subtle circumstances of the families of both husband and wife, instead of resorting to court for a decision in accordance with universalistic standards.

[8] This principle is still observed today in village communities with regard to a "right of common" in land. To bring about any alteration of rights respecting "common," the mores require unanimous consent of the villagers, and majority rule is not admitted. This traditional principle is recognized as customary law by art. 2 of the Law for the Application of Laws, Law No. 10 of 1898. On this unanimity rule for the "right of common," see Kaoru, *Meiji Shonen no Iriaiken* (The Right of Common in the Early Years of Meiji), in NAKATA, HŌSEI SHI RONSHŪ (Collected Essays on the History of the Legal System) 686–87, 719 (1938). Legal recognition of the unanimity rule makes it extremely difficult for villagers to introduce innovations in the use of common, so that vast areas of common lands are left uncultivated despite a serious shortage of agricultural land.

and independent ones. Because of the resulting disorganization of traditional social groups, resort to litigation has been condemned as morally wrong, subversive, and rebellious.[9]

On the other hand, there were, even in the traditional culture, disputes in which no such social relationship was involved. First, disputes arising outside of harmonious social groups, namely *between* such social groups,[10] have a completely different background. Such disputes arise, so to speak, in a social vacuum. Since amicable behavior from the other party is not to be expected in such a context, both parties to the dispute tend to become emotionally involved to a great extent, and the traditional culture contains no fixed rules of behavior to indicate the acceptable course of action. Yet, even in the absence of a specific tradition of harmony and in spite of strong emotional antagonism, disputes of this type are often settled by reconciliation. If one disputant apologizes, it is postulated by traditional culture that the other party must be lenient enough to forgive him, and, as a matter of fact, emotional involvement is usually quite easily released by the apology of an enemy. Occasionally disputes, usually antagonisms of long standing, are settled because the disadvantage of continuing disagreement outweighs the price of concession. These agreements are usually achieved through the mediation of third parties and are similar in nature to peace treaties. Until and unless such a peaceful settlement is made, sheer antagonism and the rule of power, very often of violence, prevail. Disputes of this kind are also settled when one party can impose a fait accompli by force. In other words, superiority in power establishes a new social order. The only way in which the weaker party can escape from this rule of power is through the lawsuit. For this reason, a large number of suits relating to the "right of common" (*iriaiken*) in land recorded in the law reports of the prewar period were disputes between village communities.[11]

A second class of disputes, those between a usurer and his debtor, lacks from the very beginning a harmonious relationship comparable to that normally found between lessor and lessee or master and servant. Usurers never fail to be armed not only with nonlegal means with which to enforce the factual power situation but also with means founded upon law that enable them to resort to the courts. Since the Meiji era (1867–1912), long before industrialization was under way, official statistics have shown a surprisingly large number of cases involving claims of this sort (see Table 7).

[9] The writer personally knows a farmer in a village near Tokyo whose whole family has been socially ostracized by all the villagers because his deceased father had sued another farmer in a dispute about the boundaries of his farm.

[10] E.g., disputes concerning irrigation rights among various villages, disputes between a village community alleging the existence of customary rights of common or of collective use of land, on the one hand, and an electric-power company denying such rights, on the other.

[11] Hozumi, *Iriaiken ni Kan-suru Sengo Hanrei no Kentō* (An Examination of Postwar Court Decisions Relating to the Right of Common), 31 Hōritsu Jihō (Law Journal) 1546 (1959).

In short, a wide discrepancy has existed between state law and the judicial system, on the one hand, and operative social behavior, on the other. Bearing this in mind, we can understand the popularity and function of mediation procedure as an extrajudicial informal means of dispute resolution in Japan.

This attitude is also reflected in the customary characteristics of contracts. Parties to a contractual agreement are not expected to become involved in any serious differences in the future. Whenever they enter such a relationship, they are supposed to be friendly enough not to consider eventual disputes, much less preparation for a lawsuit. Parties do not, or at least pretend that they do not, care about an instrument or other kinds of written evidence and rather hesitate to ask for any kind of written document, fearing that such a request might impair the amicable inclination of the other party. Even when written documents are drawn up, they do not provide machinery for settling disputes.[12] The contracting parties occasionally insert clauses providing that in case of dispute the parties "may" (instead of "must") negotiate with each other.

Typical examples of the precarious nature of traditional contracts are the following clauses in construction contracts between the government and general contractors before World War II: "If due to act of God [literally "calamity from heaven"] or other appropriate cause it becomes difficult to complete the work within the time in article 2, B [the contractor] may within this time set out a detailed written account of such cause and request an extension from A [the government]. In this case A, if it recognizes the request to be proper, *may* approve it and exempt the damages for delay in article 13." [13] Further, if the government has canceled the contract, "it *may* pay the contractor damages in an amount which the government *considers* adequate." [14] After World War II, these clauses making the legal duties and rights of the contractor dependent on the will of the government were changed into more "democratic" ones (as they are actually called) by which the legal duties and rights of the parties are subject to *ad hoc* agreements between them:

(1) A [the person placing the order], in case it is necessary to do so, may alter the content of the work, or either suspend or discontinue the work. In this case, if it is necessary to alter the fees for the independent work or the time of completion, A and B [the contractor] are to *confer* and settle these matters in writing.

(2) In the case of the prior paragraph, if B has sustained damage, A shall

[12] Von Mehren, *Some Reflections on Japanese Law,* 71 HARV. L. REV. 1486, 1494 (1958), points out "there are still very large areas of Japanese life in which it is difficult to predict whether a dispute will be settled by reference to legal standards (applied either in court or in an out-of-court settlement) or in terms of quite different conceptions. It is often impossible to know in advance whether a party will seek to enforce his legal rights."

[13] Naimu-shō Keiyaku-sho (Ministry of Home Affairs Contract Form), art. 11 in KAWASHIMA & WATANABE, DOKEN UKEOI KEIYAKU RON (A Treatise on Civil Engineering Construction Contracts) 185 (1950). Emphasis added.

[14] *Ibid.*, art. 21. Emphasis added.

compensate him for this damage. The amount of compensation is to be determined by *conferral* between A and B.[15]

(1) If due to act of God or other force majeure damage has arisen concerning the portion of the work already finished or construction materials taken into the work site, the inspection of which has been completed, B, upon the occurrence of this fact, shall, without delay, notify A of the present situation.

(2) In regard to that damage of the prior paragraph which can be recognized as grave, if it can be perceived that B has exercised the care of a good manager, A is to bear the amount of damage. In this case, if casualty insurance or some other form of coverage is present, such amounts are to be deducted from the amount of the damage.

(3) The amount of the damage of the prior paragraph is to be determined by *conferral* between A and B.[16]

These clauses do not assure a solution and lawyers may ask with good reason what would result if the disputing parties could not reach an agreement after negotiation. In practice some agreement is normally reached, though occasionally it is not. The contractual relationship in Japan is by nature quite precarious and cannot be sustained by legal sanctions. If the disputants seek to continue their relationship, some agreement is worked out, even if this means, in rare cases, that one party accepts the status quo imposed by the other. This rarely happens, however, because business and social custom forbids one to terminate a harmonious social tie by selfishly insisting on one's own interests. Usually it is clear that the unilaterally imposed solution is totally inadmissible when no agreement can be reached, and the wronged party is then supported by the moral opinion of the community, leaving the contract breaker in an untenable position. Thus what seems at first glance to be an absurd and serious deficiency in the contractual concept is in actuality only a reflection of the normal way of conducting business transactions.[17] A similar reliance on custom may be seen in the American practice of buying and selling corporate stock through verbal orders.

This emphasis on compromise has produced its own abuses. A special profession, the *jidan-ya* or makers of compromises, has arisen, particularly in the large cities. Hired by people having difficulty collecting debts, these bill collectors compel payment by intimidation, frequently by violence. This is of course a criminal offense,[18] and prosecution of the jidan-ya is reported

[15] Kensetsu Kōji Hyōjun Ukeoi Keiyaku Yakkan (Standard Stipulated Terms for Contracts for Work in Construction Projects), Feb. 21, 1950, Ruling of the Third Meeting of the Central Construction Industry Council, as amended through the Oct. 3, 1956, Ruling of the Twenty-First Meeting, Second Session of the Central Construction Industry Council, art. 16. Emphasis added.

[16] *Ibid.*, art. 22. Emphasis added. Also see Kawashima & Watanabe, note 13, at 57–70, 140–43.

[17] It seems that here we have another clue to an understanding of the social-cultural background of divorce by agreement.

[18] Penal Code arts. 249–50.

from time to time in the newspapers.[19] But their occupation is apparently flourishing. Furthermore, public opinion seems to be favorable or at least neutral concerning this practice; even intimidated debtors thus compelled to pay seem to acquiesce easily and do not indicate strong opposition. This attitude is doubtlessly due to some extent to the delay and expense of litigation, but at the same time the traditional frame of mind regarding extrajudicial means of dispute resolution undoubtedly has had some influence on public opinion toward the jidan-ya. The common use of the term *jidan-ya* seems to suggest that extrajudicial coercion and compromise are not distinctly differentiated in the minds of people.

Finally, the specific social attitudes toward disputes are reflected in the judicial process. Japanese not only hesitate to resort to a lawsuit but are also quite ready to settle an action already instituted through conciliatory processes during the course of litigation. With this inclination in the background, judges also are likely to hesitate, or at least not seek, to expedite judicial decision, preferring instead to reconcile the litigant parties — as is revealed in Table 8 which shows the number of lawsuits actually settled by reconcilement. Complaint about delay in reaching judicial decisions is almost universal, particularly in recent years, and the reasons for the delay are diverse. But one reason may be this judicial hesitancy to attribute clear-cut victory and defeat to the respective parties.[20] It is, though, interesting to note that the percentage of judicial decisions has tended to rise since 1952, while the percentage of judicial proceedings terminated by compromise and successful mediation has tended to fall. It would be incautious to conclude hastily that these figures indicate a popular shift from the traditional attitude to a more individualistic one, but the beginning of such a tendency may be suggested.

Furthermore, it seems that judges are rather commonly inclined to attach importance to the status quo or to a fait accompli. The legal adage, *pereat mundus, fiat justitia,* is apparently alien to the Japanese public as a whole and to Japanese lawyers in particular. Once a certain situation is set, especially when it has been in existence for some time, people are inclined

[19] See, e.g., Asahi Shimbun, Jan. 12, 1962, p. 11, col. 1 (southern Tokyo morning ed.): this item does not appear in the bound ASAHI SHIMBUN SHUKUSATSU HAN for Jan. 1962. Moreover, note the remarks in Nakagawa, *Jidan-ya no Mondai* (The Jidan-ya Problem), HŌGAKU SEMINAR (Legal Seminar) no. 75, at 1 (1962).

[20] In this connection another aspect of this judicial attitude should be pointed out: because of the inclination to avoid attributing to one party clear-cut victory or defeat, judges are apt to attribute some fault to both parties. For instance, in case of a suit for damages based on tort, in which a truck driver, ignoring the right of way of another car, crossed a street and collided with the latter, the court declared that the victim was also negligent in not slowing down his speed, and reduced the amount of damages for personal injury and property damage to 30,000 yen (approximately 83 dollars). Yamaki v. Yūgen Kaisha Kubota Shōji (Kubota Commercial Limited Liability Co.), Tokyo District Court, March 24, 1959, 10 KAKYŪ SAIBANSHO MINJI SAIBAN REISHŪ (A Collection of Civil Cases in the Inferior Courts) 545.

to accept it even if it is not legally permissible. The courts reflect this attitude of the people and then attempt to rationalize the result. Such a tendency also seems to be related to the traditional popular conception of social relationships, which sees them not as something controlled by objective fixed standards but as something precarious depending on and changing with actual situations. An extreme example is the *Kochi Railway* case decided by the Great Court of Judicature on October 26, 1938. In 1929, the Kochi Railway began to lay track across land owned by the plaintiff. The plaintiff obtained a provisional disposition order[21] prohibiting the Kochi Railway from continuing construction, but the order was later withdrawn and the plaintiff was held to be entitled to sue the railroad at any time to compel removal of the railroad facilities from the land if the defendant's construction proved to be a trespass. The plaintiff filed a subsequent suit against the defendant with the District Court which rejected his claim on the ground that the railway served the welfare of the public in that specific locality and, if the railroad facilities in question should be removed, the public would suffer tremendous inconvenience. In such circumstances, the claim of the plaintiff was thought to be an "abuse of property rights." The supreme court sustained the decision of the inferior court.[22]

It is also widely known that the courts are reluctant to admit the existence of unfair labor practices; they prefer to accept the fait accompli and try to reconcile the litigants through extrajudicial negotiations.[23]

Considering these facts, parties in dispute usually find that resort to a lawsuit is less profitable than resort to other means of settlement. A lawsuit takes more time and more expense,* terminates the harmonious relationship between the parties, and gives the plaintiff just as little as, or quite often less than, what he would obtain through extrajudicial means. Who would resort to a lawsuit in view of these disadvantages except pugnacious, litigious fellows?

Jerome Frank has noted that an overwhelmingly large number of lawsuits in the United States are not appealed to a higher court and that nearly 95 percent of the cases come to an end in the trial court.[24] Such finality is in

[21] A remedy similar to the Anglo-American temporary injunction; *einstweilige Verfügung* in German.

[22] Arimitsu v. Kōchi Tetsudō Kabushiki Kaisha (Kochi Railway Co.), Great Court of Judicature, IV Civil Department, Oct. 26, 1938, 17 DAI SHIN IN MINJI HANREI SHŪ (A Collection of Civil Great Court of Judicature Cases) [hereafter cited as DAI-HAN MINSHŪ] 2057, 18 HANREI MINJI HŌ (Civil Case Law) 475 (note Kaino).

[23] See Kichiemon Ishikawa, "The Regulation of the Employer-Employee Relationship: Japanese Labor-Relations Law," in this volume.

* As Thomas Blakemore observed at the conference, in addition to lawyer's expenses, court costs, particularly filing fees which are graduated by the size of recovery claimed, are high. These are recoverable by the winning party, but the necessity of hazarding new capital on the chance of winning the suit is a serious deterrent. The deterrent factor varies directly with the degree of uncertainty as to liability and the amount of probable damage.

[24] FRANK, COURTS ON TRIAL 33 (1950).

striking contrast to the comparatively large number of cases appealed to a higher court in Japan (see Table 9). Presumably this reflects the reluctance of litigants to accept a court decision rendered and imposed upon them without being convinced of the righteousness of its content; in the traditional ways of settling a dispute the solution was, in principle, reached through agreement by both parties. The notion that a justice measured by universal standards can exist independent of the wills of the disputants is apparently alien to the traditional habit of the Japanese people. Consequently, distrust of judges and a lack of respect for the authority of judicial decisions is widespread throughout the nation.

INFORMAL MEANS OF DISPUTE RESOLUTION: RECONCILEMENT AND CONCILIATION

The prevailing forms of settling disputes in Japan are the extrajudicial means of reconcilement and conciliation. By *reconcilement* is meant the process by which parties in the dispute confer with each other and reach a point at which they can come to terms and restore or create harmonious relationships. As stated above, social groups or contractual relationships of the traditional nature presuppose situational changes depending on their members' needs and demands and on the existing power balance; the process of conferring with each other permits this adjustment. Particularly in a patriarchal relationship the superior (*oyabun*) who has the status of a patriarch is expected to exercise his power for the best interests of his inferior (*kobun*), and consequently his decision is, in principle, more or less accepted as the basis for reconcilement even though the decision might in reality be imposed on the inferior. Reconcilement is the basic form of dispute resolution in the traditional culture of Japan. *Conciliation,* a modified form of reconcilement, is reconcilement through a third person.

In the legal systems of Western countries as well as of Japan, dispute resolution through a third person as intermediary includes two categories: mediation and arbitration. In mediation a third party offers his good offices to help the others reach an agreement; the mediator offers suggestions which have no binding force. In contrast, a third party acting as arbitrator renders a decision on the merits of the dispute. In the traditional culture of Japan, however, mediation and arbitration have not been differentiated; in principle, the third person who intervenes to settle a dispute, the go-between, is supposed to be a man of higher status than the disputants. When such a person suggests conditions for reconcilement, his prestige and authority ordinarily are sufficient to persuade the two parties to accept the settlement. Consequently, in the case of mediation also, the conditions for reconcilement which he suggests are in a sense imposed, and the difference between mediation and arbitration is nothing but a question of the degree of the go-between's power. Generally speaking, the higher the prestige and the authority of the go-between, the stronger is the actual influence on the parties in dispute, and in the same proportion conciliation takes on the coloration of arbitration or of mediation. The settlement of a dispute aims to maintain, restore, or create a harmonious "particularistic" relationship, and for that purpose not only mediation but also arbitration must avoid the principles implicit in a judicial settlement: the go-between should not make any clear-cut decision on who is right or wrong or inquire into the existence and scope of the rights of the parties. Consequently the principle of *kenka ryō-seibai* (both disputants are to be punished) is applied in both mediation and arbitration.

If a dispute is very likely to arise and the parties thereto are more or less equal in their status (in other words, the power balance is not sufficient to settle an eventual dispute), they normally agree in advance on a third person as mediator or arbitrator. For example, when marriage takes place, it is a common custom in Japan to have a go-between (sometimes each of the marrying families appoints its respective go-between) witness the marriage and play the role of mediator or arbitrator if serious troubles arise later. Or, when a man is employed (not only as a domestic servant or apprentice of a carpenter, painter, or merchant, but also as a clerk in such business enterprises as steel mills, chemical plants, and banks), it is still common practice for the employer to demand from the employee an instrument of surety signed by a *mimoto hikiukenin* or *mimoto hoshōnin* (literally translated, a person who ensures the antecedents of the employee). Originally this man had to undertake the role of mediator or arbitrator in case of sickness, breach of trust of the employee, or other eventual troubles; in recent years he simply undertakes the obligation as a surety.[25] The reason that a very small portion of disputes are brought to court is to be found,

[25] Though the liability of a *mimoto hikiukenin* was limitless in the traditional contract, in practice it was normal that if the employer sustained damage caused by the employee the scope of liability was defined through an *ad hoc* agreement between the employer and the *mimoto hikiukenin*. Therefore, if the employer sued the *mimoto hikiukenin* in court on grounds of the limitless liability expressed in the language of the contract, it meant that the employer went far beyond the contemplation of the parties to the contract at the time, and consequently, a court would feel the need of making adjustments. The court attempted to mitigate the liability of the *mimoto hikiukenin* under various circumstances — Tanaka v. Kabushiki Kaisha Ōzaki Kyōritsu Ginkō (Ozaki Joint Bank Co.), Great Court of Judicature, I Civil Department, July 4, 1927, 6 DAI-HAN MINSHŪ 436, 7 HANREI MINJI HŌ 328 (note Egawa); Kurihara v. Dai Ichi Kasai Kaijō Hoken Kabushiki Kaisha (First Fire and Marine Insurance Co.), Great Court of Judicature, III Civil Department, May 24, 1933, 12 DAI-HAN MINSHŪ 1923, 13 HANREI MINJI HŌ 346 (note Kaino) — and based on these court practices a law was enacted in 1933 which aimed at mitigating the liability of *mimoto hikiukenin* (Personal Surety Law, Law No. 42 of 1933). Particularly interesting in this connection is the provision of art. 5 which reads as follows: "In determining the liability of a *mimoto hoshōnin* [i.e., a *mimoto hikiukenin*] and the monetary amount thereof, the court shall take into consideration whether there was negligence in the supervision of the employee by the employer, the facts attendant upon the giving of the surety, the degree of care exercised in giving the surety, changes in the duties or status of the employee, and any other circumstances."

as stated above, in the fact that most of the disputes are settled through these informal means.

Kankai

Very soon after the Meiji Restoration, the government was forced to make concessions to this centuries-old practice[26] and accordingly legalized conciliation; in 1876 the government initiated *kankai* (literally, invitation to reconcilement) as a legal court procedure and provided for its preferred usage prior to a regular judicial proceeding.[27] In 1883 the Ministry of Justice issued a directive that kankai should be a compulsory procedure prior to regular judicial process in all except commercial cases.[28]

Kankai — the Japanese word gives the impression that it is a recommendation favoring reconcilement — was actually the imposition of a settlement under authority of the court with the litigants often being in no position to refuse the proposal. A scene of a famous Kabuki drama, *Suitengū Megumi no Fukagawa* (first performance in 1885), by Mokuami presents a very realistic description of the image of kankai then held by the people.[29] The usurer Kimbei comes, accompanied by Yasuzo, a pettifogger, to the home of his debtor Kobei, an indigent former samurai. In front of the debtor's home Yasuzo says to his client: "If the debtor is not likely to pay the debt, let's intimidate him by saying that we will resort to kankai in case he does not deliver a pledge." They enter the house and demand that Kobei deliver them pledges as a substitute for the payment of his debt: "If you are delayed in delivering them, I will bring the case to kankai, have them arrest you and let you enjoy a cool breeze."

Table 10 shows how frequently kankai was resorted to and what an important function it had. Probably this was due to the fact that, in the social chaos of the early Meiji era, the traditional extrajudicial means such as reconcilement and conciliation were insufficient for settling disputes. In 1890 the institution of kankai was abolished by the Code of Civil Procedure. This was but one of the codes promulgated during the 1890s as preparatory measures to bring to an end the privileges of extraterritoriality for alien residents in Japan; and it was with this aim in mind that the government strove to follow the pattern of Western nations in its recognition of judicial institutions. The reactions to the reform can be inferred from the comments on it given thirty years later by members of the House of Representatives when the reinstitution of mediation was under debate.

[26] See Henderson, *Some Aspects of Tokugawa Law,* 27 WASH. L. REV. 85, 98–100 (1952) — a discussion of the pre-Meiji practice.

[27] Ministry of Justice Pronouncement A (*Kō*) No. 17 of 1876.

[28] Ministry of Justice Directive of Oct. 23, 1883 in response to an inquiry from Ibaragi Prefecture.

[29] Mokuami Kawatake is known as a dramatist whose plays give a very realistic description of the Japanese society of his time (the late Tokugawa and early Meiji periods).

> Shotoku Taishi, who drafted the "Constitution of Japan," wrote in article 17 that harmony is to be honored. Japan, unlike other countries where rights and duties prevail, must strive to solve interpersonal cases by harmony and compromise. Since Japan does not settle everything by law as in the West but rather must determine matters, for the most part, in accordance with morality and human sentiment (*ninjō*), the doctrine of mediation is a doctrine indigenous to Japan . . . The great three hundred year peace of the Tokugawa was preserved because disputes between citizens were resolved harmoniously through their own autonomous administration, avoiding, so far as possible, resort to court procedure . . . However, later the justice bureaucrats, assuming upon the appearance of the Code of Civil Procedure that the bureaucracy should attempt to settle all problems in dispute, extremely perverted the thought of the people.[30]

Even after 1945, a leading lawyer, Yoshikata Mizoguchi, now Chief Judge of the Tokyo Family Court, declared in the preface to *Chōtei Tokuhon,* (Mediation Reader; published by the Japanese Federation of Mediation Associations in 1954): "Needless to say, the basic idea of chōtei [mediation] is harmony and since, as Crown Prince Shotoku revealed to us in article 1 of his Constitution of Seventeen Articles enacted 1,350 years ago which stated that 'harmony is to be honored,' respect for harmony is a national trait, the development of the chōtei institution in our country seems natural." We can imagine, then, the popular reaction which followed the abolition of kankai.

Chōtei

During World War I the industrialization and urbanization of Japan developed rapidly and upset the traditional social structure. In such a time of social unrest, the trust in those traditionally in positions of authority, such as employers or landlords, was weakened; and those who had been in an inferior position began to assert their legal rights. The traditional authority and prestige of superiors was no longer effective to prevent, much less to solve, disputes with inferiors. Lawsuits by landlords or lessors against their tenants or lessees, which had been quite rare in the past, were becoming frequent, thus sharpening the antagonism between parties who were supposed to be friendly toward each other. What the government attempted, facing this dissolution of the social structure upon which the political regime had been based since the Meiji Restoration, is interesting from our point of view. Instead of coordinating the conflicting vested interests by legislation,[31] the government reinstituted chōtei, with which the disputes them-

[30] Dai 51 Kai Teikoku Gikai Shūgi In Iinkai Sokkiroku (Stenographic Record of House of Representatives' Committees in the 51st Session of the Imperial Diet), category 5, no. 18, 3rd session, at 2 (1926).

[31] The only exceptions were the Leased Land Law, Law No. 49 of 1921, translated into English in 2 EHS Law Bulletin Series FR 1 (Nakane ed. and trans., 1959); and the Leased House Law, Law No. 50 of 1921, translated into English in 2 EHS Law Bulletin Series FS 1 (Nakane ed. and trans., 1959). These statutes were probably necessitated by the

selves were to be "washed away" (*mizu ni nagasu*) by reconcilement; the emerging individualistic interests of lessees, tenants, and employees were to be kept from being converted into firmly established vested interests independent of the will of their superiors.

A member of the House of Representatives urged, when the Leased Land and Leased House Mediation Law was under debate: "By endeavoring to be sympathetic and by expressing harmony, we amicably reap rights which are not actually rights in themselves."[32] Another member argued:

> Handling this matter as merely a determination of the problem of the rights of a lessee of land or a tenant of a house so that the owner may assert his own rights even to the point of rapacity, in a period such as that of today when a shift in society in the harmony of supply and demand brings only shortages, with anyone being able to assert his own rights exclusively, makes it quite difficult, in the final analysis, to obtain true stability of rights. Therefore, the establishment of the Mediation Law is not so that someone by sticking to the law can determine the relationship of rights among the parties. That is, the relationship between a tenant and a house owner, a land lessee and a landowner differs from that between complete strangers. Therein is the personal expression of sympathy; therein is morality. And in the sense that it attempts to base settlement on these things exists the *raison d'être* of mediation.[33]

The institution of chōtei was to replace the informal mediators of the past who had been mostly men of "face"—for instance, village elders and sometimes even policemen—by mediation committees (consisting of laymen and a judge) and to have parties reach agreement under the psychological pressure derived from the "halo" of a state court. This attempt was quite successful. A large number of disputes arising out of leases were brought to chōtei procedure and not to regular judicial proceedings (see Tables I and II).[34]

---

fact that the traditional contractual relationships between lessors and lessees had been already dissolved, and even in smaller cities it was rather common to resort to a lawsuit to solve disputes arising from these relationships. Table II indicates that in the courts of small local cities the number of lawsuits exceeds the number of mediation cases.

[32] DAI 45 KAI TEIKOKU GIKAI SHŪGI IN IINKAI SOKKIROKU (Stenographic Record of House of Representatives' Committees in the 45th Session of the Imperial Diet), category 5, no. 5, 2nd session, at 4 (1922).

[33] *Ibid.*, 3rd session, at 1 (1922).

[34] In this connection the surveys made by Professor Yoshio Sasaki in Shimane Prefecture are extremely interesting. To his question, "Is it essential in civil mediation to consider whether the contentions of the parties are legally correct or not?" only 28 percent of people listed on the panel of mediation-committee members answered, "It is always essential." To his question asking them "which qualifications they thought most important for a mediation-committee member," only one respondent rated "correct knowledge of the law" as the first qualification, whereas the largest number (approximately 30 percent) of respondents rated it as the last. See Sasaki, *Chihō ni okeru Minji Chōtei* (Civil Mediation in Rural Areas), 32 HŌRITSU JIHŌ 1051, 1054 (1960); Sasaki, *Minji Chōtei ni okeru Hōteki Handan to Jian no Kaimei* (Legal Reasoning and Clarification of the Case in Civil Mediation), 7 MINJI SOSHŌ HŌ ZASSHI (Journal of Civil Procedure Law) 154–57 (1961).

The number of mediation cases concerning land and house leases, farm tenancies, pecuniary debts, and domestic relations increased surprisingly after the institution of mediation,[35] but, remarkably enough, the number of regular judicial cases underwent no significant decrease. In other words, a large number of disputes which had been solved outside of the court or left unsolved were now brought to chōtei, which meant that (1) chōtei was much preferred to regular judicial proceedings, (2) traditional informal means of dispute resolution already had lost their function in this sector of personal relations, and (3) society needed control by a governmental agency of some kind during a period of social disorganization.

The tendency to settle disputes by compromise is also illustrated by the number of suits withdrawn or formally compromised and the number of mediation cases withdrawn (see Table 12). Such a termination takes place when the need for a judicial decision or chōtei disappears; in most such instances, this occurs because the parties have settled the dispute themselves. As the table indicates, the court takes an active role in encouraging settlement at stages short of a final decision. In Summary Courts the number of cases settled by judicial compromise entered in the official record is approximately equal to the number settled without the formal aid of the court and withdrawn. In District Courts, the ratio is lower, but the number of judicial compromises is only a little less than half that of the cases settled privately. Practicing attorneys report that, in a large number of cases, the judge urges the parties to compromise at least once during the course of the trial. Both the tendency of parties to settle and the court's practice of encouraging compromise reflect the general attitude of the people.

In addition to chōtei, there is a long tradition of police intervention in disputes between citizens. Officers act as mediators on the basis of their authority,[36] particularly when another man with sufficient prestige and authority is not available. Chōtei, as legalized by the series of mediation statutes, may in a sense be a modified, perhaps rationalized, form of the type of mediation performed by police officers. But even after chōtei was legalized, mediation by the police did not lessen. With their authority and psychological dominance, particularly under the authoritarian regime of the old Constitution, police mediators were by and large effective and efficient. The total number of cases brought to police officers for mediation is presumed to be still very great, though the exact figures are kept secret. Table 13 shows the considerable quantity of cases brought to the Tokyo police for consultation and the large percentage of them solved through this informal procedure. A certain portion of the cases in which solutions were not reported presum-

[35] That is under the following statutes: Leased Land and Leased House Mediation Law, Law No. 41 of 1922; Tenant Farming Mediation Law, Law No. 18 of 1924; Monetary Obligation Temporary Mediation Law, Law No. 26 of 1932; Personal Affairs Mediation Law, Law No. 11 of 1939.

[36] Hironaka, Hō to Saiban (Law and Trial) 108 (1961).

ably were resolved by party agreement based on the recommendations made. If these are taken into account, the number of cases solved by the police is indeed quite sizable. In my own investigations, I have found that a rather large number of cases in the Family Courts were first brought to police officers for mediation and came to court only after mediation proved futile. Presumably the same may be true for chōtei cases in other courts.

Arbitration

It is characteristic of Japanese culture that arbitration has been a kind of reconcilement. For this very reason, arbitration in the sense of contemporary Western law is alien to Japan. Despite the fact that the Code of Civil Procedure contains provisions for an arbitration procedure, it is seldom used. Clauses specifying that a dispute arising out of a contract shall be settled through arbitration are normally not employed except in agreements with foreign business firms.

The Construction Industry Law[37] provides both arbitration and mediation procedures for disputes arising out of construction contracts, in order to promote the legal disposition of these disputes instead of leaving their resolution to traditional extrajudicial reconcilement. Nevertheless, very few cases of arbitration have been initiated since these provisions came into effect, only two applications for arbitration having been filed with the Ministry of Construction during the period between October 1956 and April 1961, as compared with fourteen applications for mediation. Although the Ministry of Construction is encouraging the use of an arbitration clause in construction contracts (the standard contract stipulations drafted and recommended by the ministry contain a clause of this type), few contracts have made use of it. Contractors and owners have told me that they feel insecure under the provision, since arbitrators might render unfair decisions. Presumably the underlying basis for this feeling of insecurity is not that arbitrators are in fact unfair, but rather that they might make decisions in accordance with universalistic standards; the contractors and owners prefer to settle disputes in accordance with the prevalent psychological climate and the subtle power balance existing between the two parties.

Statistics of labor disputes present an even more interesting picture. Compared to the mediation cases, the number of arbitration cases is surprisingly low (Table 14). Furthermore, it is worthy of note that, out of five arbitration cases filed with the Central Labor Relations Commission, three were withdrawn because the disputes had been settled outside of the administrative proceeding. This again shows that even in the process of arbitration parties are ready, and prefer, to enter into informal reconcilement.

At the same time, however, collective-bargaining agreements, in contrast to construction contracts, apparently tend to familiarize the disputants with

[37] Law No. 100 of 1949, arts. 25-15 to 25-20.

arbitration as a means of dispute resolution. According to an investigation by the Ministry of Labor in 1958, 57 labor agreements from a sample of 532 contained arbitration clauses.[38] In 1961 the Central Labor Relations Commission conducted an investigation of collective labor agreements, and its interim report shows that, from a sample of 280 collective agreements, approximately 20 percent contained arbitration clauses.[39] The sampling methods employed in these surveys were not identical, but indications are that the number of collective agreements containing arbitration clauses nearly doubled over the three years. This figure is indeed impressive, especially in comparison with the extremely few construction contracts or contracts of sale between Japanese citizens containing arbitration clauses (though no supporting statistical figures are currently available). This striking difference is probably due to the fact that the relationship between employer and employee is, unlike most other contractual relationships, more individualistic, each party insisting upon his own interests.

These figures should be compared with those of the international commercial arbitrations administered by the Japan Commercial Arbitration Association. In 1960 there were filed with the association 78 cases of mediation and 93 cases of arbitration. The ratio of arbitration cases to mediation cases is thus 1.19; the ratio of arbitration cases in the Ministry of Construction for the three and a half years between October 1956 and April 1960 is only 0.09, and that in the Central Labor Relations Commission for the entire period from 1946 to 1960 only 0.0027.

Recent Changes

I have tried to show the main features of various forms of dispute resolution, with particular emphasis on their specifically Japanese aspects. However, there are indications of gradual change. Some of these have been touched on above. Since the Meiji Restoration, Japan has been in the process of rapid transition from a premodern, collectivistic, and nonindustrial society. The traditional forms of dispute resolution were appropriate to the old society, whereas judicial decision and arbitration as contemplated in the provisions of the Code of Civil Procedure are alien to it.[40] But all modern societies, including Japanese society, are characterized by citizens with equal status and, consequently, by a kind of check and balance of individual power. It is against this background that traditional relationships serving to make a proposed settlement acceptable have been disrupted and that the need for decisions in accordance with universalistic standards has arisen.

Furthermore, there is another aspect specific to the modern industrialized

[38] Rōdō-shō (Ministry of Labor), Rōdō Kyōyaku Jijō (Actual State of Collective Labor Agreements) (Rōdō Kyōyaku Shiryō (Collective Labor Agreement Materials) No. 51, 1958).

[39] Chūō Rōdō Iinkai (Central Labor Relations Commission), Rōdō Kyōyaku Chōsa (An Investigation of Collective Labor Agreements) 95 (1962).

[40] E.g., Code of Civil Procedure arts. 786–805.

society: the economic value of calculability (*Berechenbarkeit,* as Max Weber calls it) or foreseeability of rights and duties, without which the rational operation of capital enterprise would be seriously endangered.[41] As industrialization proceeds, the need for perfection of the judicial system and of legal precepts becomes both more extensive and more intensive; and the traditional informal means of dispute resolution are found to be disruptive to capital enterprises. In the latter years of World War I, the outward signs of this change were the increase in collective transactions, the growing number of lawsuits involving immovable property, and the development of a new form of labor relations. Though further changes were not apparent under the strong control of the totalitarian regime during the thirties and forties, the large-scale industrialization necessitated by the war in China and later with the Allied powers undoubtedly accelerated the transition. During the whole period of the war, Japanese family life was gradually disorganized, accompanied by dissolution of the social controls exercised by the family. The result was a large number of serious conflicts within families and kinship groups which the traditional means of social control (patriarchal power and the family council) could no longer effectively resolve. The traditional family system being the very basis of the official ideology (*shūshin*) and the power structure of the state, the government adopted chōtei to settle disputes arising from the disorganization of the family. Rather than adjustment through a system of legal rights, disputes were to be "washed away" in order that the family might be strengthened and preserved.

With the collapse of government through the Emperor, the authority of the traditional social institutions as a vehicle of social control was lost or at least greatly weakened. Although various "superiors" still survive to some degree, they are no longer so influential as to be able to solve all controversies arising out of their relationships with their "inferiors." The most conspicuous of these changes is in the area of family disputes. Today neither the authority of the head of the family, the family council, nor the marriage go-between is capable of settling all family disputes. The large number of such disputes brought to the Family Courts in the postwar era suggests this fact.

In 1950 the Ministry of Labor made a very interesting nationwide survey of social attitudes.[42] Among questions on family solidarity, parental authority, selection of a marriage partner, primogeniture, equality of the sexes, and the like, there was this one: "If you checked the weight of rationed sugar [in

[41] A prerequisite for such operations is "full calculability in the functioning of the administrative system and the legal order and dependable *strictly formal* guarantees of all agreements by the political authority (*formal rationale Verwaltung und formal rationales Recht*)." 3 WEBER, GRUNDRISS DER SOZIALÖKONOMIK (III. *Abteilung Wirtschaft und Gesellschaft*) 94 (3rd ed., 1947).

[42] FUJIN SHŌNEN KYOKU (Women and Juvenile Bureau), RŌDŌ-SHŌ (Ministry of Labor), HŌKENSEI NI TSUITE NO CHŌSA (A Survey Regarding Feudal Characteristics) 22 (Fujin Kankei Shiryō Series (Materials Relating to Women Series) No. 7, 1951).

those days sugar was tightly rationed] and found a shortage, would you notify the merchant or not?" This question was designed allegedly to determine the extent to which people would uphold their rights. From a sample of 2808 (randomly selected), 90 percent of the men and 82 percent of the women replied "I would notify him," 9 percent of the men and 16 percent of the women replied "I would not," and 1 percent of the men and 2 percent of the women replied "I don't know." Perhaps this particular question was not entirely appropriate to probe the attitude sought because a deficit in the weight of rationed sugar was of vital importance to everyone in those days of food shortages; thus, while important, one should not overgeneralize from this response. In 1952, the National Public Opinion Institute conducted a nationwide survey, a part of which bears upon our problem.[43] The institute investigated the reaction to the following question: "There is a saying, 'yield to a superior force' [*nagai mono ni wa makarerō:* literally, allow oneself to be enveloped by a long object]. Have you ever heard of this?" Those who replied affirmatively were then asked: "Do you think that the attitude expressed in that saying should be approved and that nothing else can be done?" Purportedly these questions were designed to measure the extent to which people yield to authority or power. Out of 3000 random samples, 51 percent of the men and 30 percent of the women replied that such an attitude should not be approved. Of course, this question simply pertained to the attitude toward authority and did not cover the exact problem under consideration, but it indirectly reveals the attitude of people toward informal means of dispute resolution in which the authority of the go-between plays a significant role.

Probably of greater significance is a change which seems to be taking place in chōtei cases, particularly in the Family Courts of large cities such as Tokyo or Osaka; it is not at all rare for parties to be aware of their legal rights and to insist upon them so strongly that reconcilement becomes at times quite difficult. Parties to chōtei cases have frequently complained that lay mediators did not pay sufficient attention to their rights under the law. From time to time various political leaders complain of the people's awareness of their rights and of the decay of harmony-minded traditions. Whatever their feelings about this may be, the legal institution of chōtei no longer functions to maintain the precarious nature of the interests involved in the traditional social and contractual relationships. The transition is irretrievably in process, and the outcome is clear.

[43] Kokuritsu Seron Chōsajo (National Public Opinion Research Institute), Shakai Kyōiku ni Tsuite no Yoron Chōsa (A Public Opinion Survey Regarding Social Education) (1953).

TABLE 1. Number of Land and House Lease Cases and Farm Tenancy Cases

	I. Land and House										
Prefecture	1916	1917	1918	1919	1920	1921	1922	1923	1924	1925	1926
Tokyo											
DC[a] Land Lease	225	172	145	123	129	118	155	141	243	478	577
House Lease	73	73	137	147	261	382	505	394	390	409	263
LC[b] Land Lease	179	255	212	43	41	58	83	57	196	277	427
House Lease	1,405	1,328	1,603	1,680	1,579	2,145	2,313	2,176	1,937	2,108	2,639
Mediation[c]	—	—	—	—	—	—	97	5,239	8,605	4,608	4,923
Population	2,890,400	2,918,000	3,340,100	3,457,600	3,699,428	3,813,600	3,934,200	4,050,600	3,986,700	4,485,556	4,648,500
Yokohama											
DC Land Lease	8	16	13	70	16	24	9	0	39	42	52
House Lease	6	6	7	16	28	25	34	2	10	11	13
LC Land Lease	52	30	31	13	13	13	38	2	89	93	124
House Lease	293	306	279	392	296	380	466	29	163	271	381
Mediation[c]	—	—	—	—	—	—	11	24	508	682	702
Population	1,178,200	1,189,400	1,246,700	1,268,100	1,323,390	1,342,100	1,361,100	1,379,000	1,307,600	1,416,792	1,436,200
Osaka											
DC Land Lease	64	54	38	45	51	67	73	102	137	143	163
House Lease	36	26	41	88	169	148	128	114	134	132	179
LC Land Lease	72	55	65	58	47	43	48	98	75	113	186
House Lease	694	804	1,126	1,306	1,292	1,201	1,497	1,798	2,064	2,222	3,128
Mediation[c]	—	—	—	—	—	—	83	583	595	892	1,381
Population	2,324,700	2,376,600	2,560,600	2,645,500	2,587,847	2,685,400	2,788,500	2,889,700	2,996,500	3,059,502	3,157,600
Tochigi[d]											
DC Land Lease	0	0	18	1	4	4	9	6	9	8	9
House Lease	1	1	0	0	3	6	8	9	59	4	4
LC Land Lease	29	29	30	17	24	29	17	29	23	21	17
House Lease	88	69	77	44	62	84	70	75	86	133	68
Population	1,039,600	1,054,700	1,054,800	1,067,100	1,046,479	1,060,800	1,075,300	1,089,500	1,109,200	1,090,428	1,099,600
Aomori[d]											
DC Land Lease	0	0	3	7	5	4	3	5	15	14	10
House Lease	0	0	3	2	6	4	1	4	13	7	5
LC Land Lease	26	14	28	36	26	22	26	27	19	24	22
House Lease	45	45	41	38	31	21	34	32	33	54	32
Population	777,900	788,400	786,400	794,400	756,454	764,800	773,200	781,600	791,000	812,977	824,700

TABLE 1 (continued)

Prefecture	1916	1917	1918	1919	1920	1921	1922	1923	1924	1925	1926
					II. Tenant Farming						
Hyogo											
DC	25	29	12	29	28	28	44	51	49	56	71
LC	80	29	41	20	36	9	12	39	26	20	27
Mediation[e]	—	—	—	—	—	—	—	—	2	35	55
Gifu											
DC	0	1	1	3	11	10	18	21	20	15	31
LC	53	40	105	65	90	34	28	66	44	14	70
Mediation[e]	—	—	—	—	—	—	—	—	0	2	30
Aichi											
DC	6	12	21	21	21	23	35	44	69	75	61
LC	32	97	85	102	111	72	56	61	60	43	81
Mediation[e]	—	—	—	—	—	—	—	—	0	28	21
Aomori											
DC	0	1	3	9	6	5	3	3	17	11	12
LC	22	22	41	53	23	26	22	24	12	18	35
Mediation[e]	—	—	—	—	—	—	—	—	0	0	0
Shimane											
DC	0	0	0	0	0	1	1	0	1	5	1
LC	16	22	17	18	23	11	5	6	13	24	50
Mediation[e]	—	—	—	—	—	—	—	—	0	13	49

[a] District Court.
[b] Local Court.
[c] The mediation system began in 1922.
[d] The Leased Land and Leased House Mediation Law was not in effect in Tochigi and Aomori Prefectures during these years.
[e] The mediation system began in 1924.

Source: NIHON TEIKOKU SHIHŌ-SHŌ (Japanese Imperial Ministry of Justice), DAI 42–52 MINJI TŌKEI NEMPŌ (42nd–52nd Annual Reports of Civil Statistics) (1916–1926).

TABLE 2. Number of Postwar Judicial and Mediation Cases Involving Leased Land and Leased Houses

	Judicial cases		Mediation cases	
Year	District Courts	Summary Courts	District Courts	Summary Courts
1950	7,816	1,151	360	23,945
1951	7,433	3,854	591	29,658
1952	8,695	2,979	1,206	23,909
1953	10,449	2,228	1,473	24,411
1954	9,156	4,244	1,474	23,008
1955	8,377	5,891	1,926	25,700
1956	8,955	6,155	1,947	24,811
1957	7,902	7,316	1,888	23,633
1958	7,976	7,635	1,771	23,600
1959	7,313	7,821	1,639	19,597

Source: SAIKŌ SAIBANSHO JIMU-SŌKYOKU (General Secretariat of the Supreme Court), SHŌWA 25–34 NEN SHIHŌ TŌKEI NEMPŌ (1950–1959 Annual Reports of Judicial Statistics), 1 MINJI HEN (Civil Affairs Book).

Table 3. Number of Civil Cases Filed in Japanese Courts

Year	District Courts	Local Courts
1925	51,178	237,731
1926	42,941	260,974
1927	43,306	276,286
1928	43,944	272,631
1929	42,409	268,831
1930	39,756	285,380
1931	38,107	301,774
1932	37,047	333,782
1933	34,027	261,445
1934	32,312	231,705

Source: NIHON TEIKOKU SHIHŌ-SHŌ (Japanese Imperial Ministry of Justice), DAI 51–60 MINJI TŌKEI NEMPŌ (51st–60th Annual Reports of Civil Statistics).

TABLE 4. Number of Civil Cases Filed in Superior Courts in Connecticut

Year	Cases
1927–28	7,822
1928–29	8,387
1929–30	9,523
1930–31	9,535
1931–32	10,503
1932–33	10,396
1933–34	10,711
1934–35	11,194
1935–36	9,824
1936–37	9,461
1937–38	8,967
1938–39	8,158

Source: FIFTEENTH REPORT OF THE JUDICIAL COUNCIL OF CONNECTICUT 16 (1956).

TABLE 5. Extent of Litigation for Traffic Accidents Involving the Japanese National Railways

Litigation and accidents	1953	1954	1955	1956	1957	1958	1959	1960
Number of lawsuits	20	20	22	20	19	18	24	15
Number of victims of physical injury including death	4,645	5,158	5,169	5,451	5,818	6,044	6,317	—

Source: Based upon unpublished materials furnished by the Legal Affairs Section, Japanese National Railways.

TABLE 6. Amount of Time Required for Judicial Decisions

Period required for judicial decisions in the District Courts in 1916 and 1920

	Under 10 days	Under 1 mo.	Under 2 mos.	Under 3 mos.	Under 6 mos.	Under 1 yr.	Under 2 yrs.	Over 2 yrs.	Total
1916	106	1,231	2,047	1,283	1,725	1,142	494	161	8,189
1920	143	1,868	3,646	2,360	2,982	2,023	986	255	14,263

Period required for judicial decisions in 1958 and 1959

	Under 15 days	Under 1 mo.	Under 2 mos.	Under 3 mos.	Under 6 mos.	Under 1 yr.	Under 2 yrs.	Under 3 yrs.	Under 5 yrs.	Over 5 yrs.	Total
					Summary Courts						
1958	576	4,389	11,205	5,791	5,530	2,928	1,526	429	213	17	32,604
1959	434	4,369	10,830	5,668	5,227	2,931	1,853	530	291	30	32,163
					District Courts						
1958	29	582	4,455	3,512	5,136	4,395	4,171	878	1,362	405	25,925
1959	28	499	4,620	3,593	5,091	4,380	4,643	2,094	1,566	545	27,059
					High Courts						
1958	8	21	47	140	458	952	1,091	367	220	56	3,360
1959	14	19	82	167	572	991	1,242	524	247	57	3,915

Supreme Court

	Under 3 mos.	Under 6 mos.	Under 1 yr.	Under 2 yrs.	Under 3 yrs.	Under 4 yrs.	Under 5 yrs.	Under 6 yrs.	Under 7 yrs.	Under 10 yrs.	Total
1958	14	77	96	430	130	22	7	3	3	1	793
1959	4	21	99	289	159	59	—	4	2	5	642

Source: NIHON TEIKOKU SHIHŌ-SHŌ (Japanese Imperial Ministry of Justice), DAI 42, 46 MINJI TŌKEI NEMPŌ (42nd, 46th Annual Reports of Civil Statistics) (1916, 1920); SAIKŌ SAIBANSHO JIMU-SŌKYOKU (General Secretariat of the Supreme Court), SHŌWA 33–34 NEN SHIHŌ TŌKEI NEMPŌ (1958–1959 Annual Reports of Judicial Statistics), 1 MINJI HEN (Civil Affairs Book).

TABLE 7. Lawsuits Concerning Loans of Money and Grain in First-Instance Courts

Year	Hypothecs and pledges of land	Hypothecs and pledges of buildings	Loans of money (Interest-bearing)	Loans of money (Interest discounted)[a]
1878	2,174	233	100,499	9,859
1888	21	1	6,059	481
1905	72	1	4,140	435
1925	43	18	6,843	556
1930	45	13	4,944	—

TABLE 7 (continued)

Year	Loans of grain (Interest-bearing)	Loans of grain (Interest discounted)[a]	Pledges of movable property (Interest-bearing)	Hypothecs of movable property (Interest-bearing)
1878	1,906	1,216	12	254
1888	27	30	0	17
1905	32	20	6	0
1925	23	6	6	0
1930	0	2	11	0

Year	Hypothecs of movable property (Interest discounted)[a]	Total of lawsuits mentioned above (A)	Total of all lawsuits (B)	A/B × 100
1878	1,301	117,523	145,611	80.71
1888	111	8,112	12,098	67.05
1905	50	8,762	22,363	39.18
1925	—	7,567	53,812	14.06
1930	—	5,086	31,082	16.36

[a] These categories are obscure even to scholars of Japanese legal history, but it is presumed that they pertain to loans made with interest discounted in advance.

Source: NIHON TEIKOKU SHIHŌ-SHŌ (Japanese Imperial Ministry of Justice), DAI 4, 14, 38, 51 MINJI TŌKEI NEMPŌ (4th, 14th, 38th, 51st Annual Reports of Civil Statistics) (1878, 1888, 1905, 1925).

TABLE 8. Number of Prewar Lawsuits and Judicial Compromises

Dispute settlement	1920	1925	1930	1935
District Court				
Lawsuits	32,360	53,812	66,411	50,178
Judicial compromise	1,691	3,805	4,522	3,344
Withdrawal of suit	9,293	13,324	14,741	10,322
Total	10,984	17,129	19,263	13,666
Local Court				
Lawsuits	134,391	226,677	692,496	521,258
Judicial compromise	13,324	29,076	45,799	38,956
Withdrawal of suit	34,094	52,002	78,375	61,245
Total	47,418	81,078	124,174	100,201

Source: NIHON TEIKOKU SHIHŌ-SHŌ (Japanese Imperial Ministry of Justice), DAI 46, 51, 56, 61 MINJI TŌKEI NEMPŌ (46th, 51st, 56th, 61st Annual Reports of Civil Statistics) (1920, 1925, 1930, 1935).

TABLE 9. Percentage of Appeals

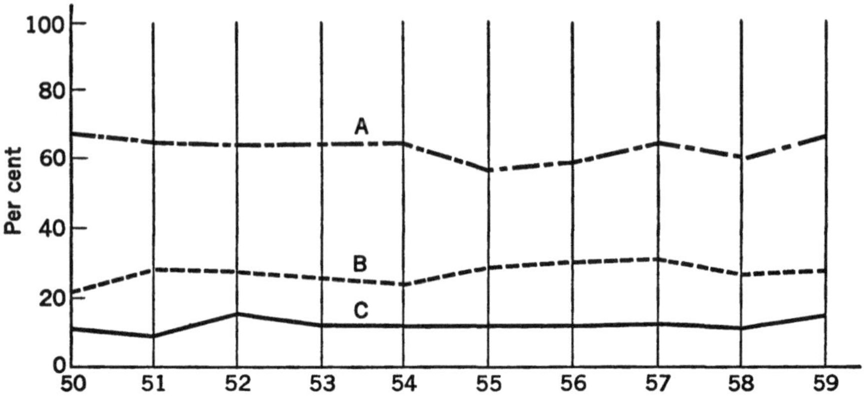

A shows the percentage of appeals of administrative cases in District Courts to High Courts; B the same for ordinary civil cases in District Courts to High Courts; and C the same for all the civil cases in Summary Courts to District Courts.

Source: SAIKŌ SAIBANSHO JIMU-SŌKYOKU (General Secretariat of the Supreme Court), SHŌWA 34 NEN SHIHŌ TŌKEI NEMPŌ (1959 Annual Report of Judicial Statistics), I MINJI HEN (Civil Affairs Book), chart 2.

TABLE 10. Number of Kankai and Lawsuits

Year	Kankai filed	Lawsuits filed
1879	651,604	135,009
1880	675,218	131,813
1881	732,217	130,426
1882	908,932	181,639
1883	1,094,216	238,071
1884	760,106[a]	138,250
1885	592,311	51,873
1886	509,915	49,920
1887	388,215	51,008
1888	327,600	50,707

[a] The reason for this abrupt decrease is not clear.

Source: SHIHŌ-SHŌ (Ministry of Justice), DAI 5–14 MINJI TŌKEI NEMPŌ (5th–14th Annual Reports of Civil Statistics) (1879–1888).

TABLE 11. Lawsuits and Mediation Cases Involving House and Land Leases

Year	Tokyo	Yoko-hama	Yoko-suka	Kyoto	Osaka	Sakai	Kishi-wada
1925							
Mediation	5,050	707	12	251	930	34	9
Lawsuits (DC)[a]	939	55	—	32	273	—	—
Lawsuits (LC)[b]	2,445	309	38	520	2,178	90	29
1930							
Mediation	9,290	1,444	16	2,375	5,487	59	24
Lawsuits (DC)	816	165	—	37	490	—	—
Lawsuits (LC)	3,782	852	118	901	7,163	235	78

Year	Kobe	Itami	Akashi	Himeji	Toyo-oka	Nagoya	Ichino-miya	Okazaki
1925								
Mediation	99	2	5	10	2	226	1	1
Lawsuits (DC)	97	—	—	11	2	124	—	17
Lawsuits (LC)	1,418	72	11	65	8	523	23	19
1930								
Mediation	756	44	11	16	2	1,265	7	23
Lawsuits (DC)	72	—	—	13	1	103	—	10
Lawsuits (LC)	3,200	240	66	127	23	1,799	58	37

[a] District Courts.
[b] Local Courts.
Source: NIHON TEIKOKU SHIHŌ-SHŌ (Japanese Imperial Ministry of Justice), DAI 51 MINJI TŌKEI NEMPŌ (51st Annual Report of Civil Statistics) 338–39, 34–61, 166–237 (1925); NIHON TEIKOKU SHIHŌ-SHŌ, DAI 56 MINJI TŌKEI NEMPŌ (56th Annual Report of Civil Statistics) 38–63, 306–77, 530–31 (1930).

TABLE 12. Postwar Court Mediation and Litigation

I. Mediation cases			
	District Courts		
Year	Filed (A)	Withdrawn (B)	(B/A) 100 (percent)
1952	6,369	483	7.58
1953	8,173	769	9.41
1954	9,629	964	10.01
1955	9,199	1,003	10.90
1956	9,653	1,083	11.22
1957	9,190	999	10.87
1958	9,297	988	10.63
1959	8,644	898	10.39
	Summary Courts		
Year	Filed (A)	Withdrawn (B)	(B/A) 100 (percent)
1950	49,209	11,647	23.67
1951	35,501	12,575	35.42
1952	54,160	11,291	20.85
1953	57,414	11,074	19.29
1954	65,650	12,133	18.48
1955	69,587	13,160	18.91
1956	66,928	12,562	18.77
1957	64,613	11,575	17.91
1958	67,062	11,923	17.78
1959	62,095	11,267	18.14
	Family Courts		
Year	Filed (A)	Withdrawn (B)	(B/A) 100 (percent)
1950	41,412	13,346	32.23
1951	37,920	12,655	33.37
1952	38,187	12,071	31.61
1953	38,351	12,403	32.34
1954	40,023	12,703	31.74
1955	43,109	14,181	32.90
1956	42,711	14,115	33.05
1957	43,358	14,064	32.44
1958	45,906	14,906	32.47

TABLE 12 (continued)

II. Litigation

District Courts

Year	Filed (A)	Withdrawn (B)	Judicial compromise (C)	[(B + C)/A] 100 (percent)
1952	59,815	18,721	10,806	49.36
1953	72,555	22,804	12,368	48.47
1954	74,442	25,563	12,798	51.53
1955	60,360	22,364	10,428	54.33
1956	61,778	24,091	10,661	56.25
1957	63,145	23,375	10,382	53.46
1958	67,232	24,561	11,249	53.26
1959	65,648	24,153	11,474	54.27

Summary Courts

Year	Filed (A)	Withdrawn (B)	Judicial compromise (C)	[(B + C)/A] 100 (percent)
1952	26,493	8,264	8,223	62.23
1953	27,164	8,905	8,374	63.61
1954	58,041	12,848	14,216	50.08
1955	82,675	22,197	23,575	55.36
1956	83,351	25,464	24,206	59.61
1957	87,239	26,207	23,903	57.44
1958	94,633	27,597	26,364	57.02
1959	90,718	28,287	25,765	59.58

Source: Mediation and litigation in the District and Summary Courts: SAIKŌ SAIBANSHO JIMU-SŌKYOKU (General Secretariat of the Supreme Court), SHŌWA 25–34 NEN SHIHŌ TŌKEI NEMPŌ (1950–1959 Annual Reports of Judicial Statistics), 1 MINJI HEN (Civil Affairs Book): 1950, at 114–15; 1951, at 141, 143; 1952, at 63–65, 136–37, 173, 175, 200–01; 1953, at 63, 65, 144–45, 181, 183, 212–13; 1954, at 84, 87, 198–99, 247, 249, 288–89; 1955, at 89, 91, 208–09, 259, 261, 300–01; 1956, at 115, 117, 232–33, 283, 285, 325, 328; 1957, at 141, 143, 310, 315, 363, 365, 408, 411; 1958, at 135, 137, 320, 323, 375, 377, 425, 427; 1959, at 135, 137, 322, 325, 381, 383, 433. Mediation cases in the Family Courts: SAIKŌ SAIBANSHO JIMU-SŌKYOKU, SHŌWA 34 NEN SHIHŌ TŌKEI NEMPŌ (1959 Annual Report of Judicial Statistics), 3 KAJI HEN (Family Affairs Book) 21–25, 34.

TABLE 13. Disposition of Family-Affairs Cases Through Consultation with the Tokyo Police

	Number handled		Satisfactorily solved (%)		Recommendations (%)		Consultation terminated (%)		Transferred to other agencies (%)		Consultation continued (%)	
	1952	1953	1952	1953	1952	1953	1952	1953	1952	1953	1952	1953
I. Family-affairs consultation, 1952 and 1953												
Marriage and adoption	231	182	35.3	19.2	59.7	68.7	4.3	12.1	—	—	0.4	—
Divorce and termination of adoptive relationships	2,274	1,825	30.3	27.9	56.0	60.3	12.1	10.1	0.9	0.7	0.8	0.9
De facto (*naien*) marriages	745	677	36.2	33.8	47.8	51.7	14.6	12.3	0.5	1.2	0.8	1.0
Inheritance	202	204	14.4	10.3	81.7	86.3	3.5	3.4	0.5	0.7	—	—
Support and illegitimacy matters	367	305	40.3	32.1	50.1	59.7	7.6	7.2	1.6	0.7	0.3	0.3
Family registration matters	197	135	24.4	17.0	72.6	77.8	2.5	4.4	0.5	0.7	—	—
Welfare matters	745	515	26.0	28.2	67.5	66.4	3.4	3.1	2.6	1.9	0.5	0.4
Employment matters	228	123	17.1	29.3	79.8	64.2	2.6	2.4	—	4.1	0.4	—
Miscellaneous	3,629	3,075	34.8	33.1	56.1	57.0	7.1	8.0	1.5	1.4	0.5	0.5
Total	8,618	7,041	32.0	30.1	57.8	59.8	8.4	8.4	1.2	1.2	0.6	0.6
Consultation for Prevention of Criminal Actions, 1952 and 1953												
Eviction from buildings	3,903	3,462	33.7	30.6	53.3	57.0	11.6	10.6	0.4	0.3	0.9	1.4
House lease	2,848	2,623	32.6	33.2	56.7	56.1	9.2	9.4	0.8	0.4	0.6	1.0
Land matters	1,837	1,852	27.9	25.3	59.4	62.3	10.6	10.9	0.7	0.3	1.3	1.2
Monetary loans	3,144	2,852	43.7	40.8	37.2	41.2	13.9	14.0	2.4	1.5	2.9	2.6
Matters relating to valuable (negotiable) securities	327	488	41.6	37.7	35.8	36.5	13.5	23.4	3.1	1.0	6.1	1.4
Nonpayment of wages	848	662	49.1	50.6	38.3	34.1	10.4	10.1	1.4	3.5	0.8	1.7
Borrowed goods	468	448	55.3	55.1	27.6	31.0	13.9	11.4	2.4	1.8	0.9	0.7
Nonperformance of contract	3,071	3,487	46.6	43.8	33.1	36.9	14.9	14.5	1.7	1.5	3.7	3.3
Miscellaneous	3,629	2,075	34.8	33.1	56.1	57.0	7.1	8.0	1.5	1.4	0.5	0.5
Total	8,618	7,041	32.0	30.1	57.8	59.8	81.4	8.4	1.2	1.2	0.6	0.6

TABLE 13 (continued)

II. Family-affairs consultation, 1958 and 1959

	Number handled		Satisfactorily solved (%)		Recommendations (%)		Consultation terminated (%)		Transferred to other agencies (%)		Consultation continued (%)	
	1958	1959	1958	1959	1958	1959	1958	1959	1958	1959	1958	1959
Marriage and adoption	152	166	24.3	24.7	64.5	67.5	10.5	5.4	0.7	2.4	—	—
Divorce and termination of adoptive relationships	1,667	1,598	22.6	21.1	69.3	72.0	6.4	5.1	1.4	1.2	0.2	0.7
De facto (*naien*) marriages	907	1,012	34.2	36.4	52.9	52.0	10.4	9.0	2.0	2.4	0.6	0.3
Inheritance	269	286	3.3	8.7	92.6	88.5	2.2	2.8	1.9	—	—	—
Support and illegitimacy matters	205	180	24.4	20.6	67.8	70.6	4.4	5.0	2.9	3.9	0.5	—
Personal problems	2,724	2,900	38.4	38.4	48.7	50.4	6.6	6.7	5.8	4.2	0.4	0.3
Welfare matters	553	405	32.4	38.3	47.2	45.9	7.1	2.5	13.4	13.1	—	0.2
Employment matters	166	134	45.2	45.5	47.0	48.5	3.6	1.5	4.2	4.5	—	—
Miscellaneous	2,400	2,495	34.9	40.9	54.0	51.3	7.6	4.7	3.3	3.0	0.2	0.1
Total	9,043	9,176	32.3	34.3	56.2	56.3	7.1	5.7	4.1	3.4	0.3	0.3
Consultation for Prevention of Criminal Actions, 1958 and 1959												
Eviction from buildings	2,601	2,399	32.8	31.8	55.8	59.2	10.0	7.6	0.8	0.5	0.7	0.8
House lease	2,633	2,584	32.9	30.6	56.2	59.3	9.2	8.0	1.5	1.5	0.3	0.6
Land matters	2,010	2,177	22.9	22.6	65.4	67.3	9.5	8.3	1.1	1.2	1.0	0.7
Monetary loans	2,897	2,757	40.4	38.0	43.7	47.7	11.6	9.8	2.8	2.7	1.5	1.8
Matters relating to valuable (negotiable) securities	572	514	33.0	31.5	41.6	46.5	18.5	15.6	5.1	4.7	1.7	1.8
Nonpayment of wages	890	920	51.6	51.1	32.7	32.2	10.3	11.2	4.6	4.7	0.8	0.9
Borrowed goods	356	361	52.8	54.4	31.5	30.5	10.7	10.2	4.8	4.4	0.3	0.5
Nonperformance of contract	3,495	3,290	45.7	43.5	34.7	35.5	14.4	14.7	3.8	3.8	1.4	2.4
Miscellaneous	6,375	6,830	41.6	39.2	45.8	43.6	9.2	8.4	2.8	3.2	0.6	0.7
Total	21,829	21,885	38.6	36.8	47.1	49.8	10.8	9.7	2.6	2.6	0.9	1.1

Source: HIRONAKA, note 36 in text, at 108–09, 118–19.

TABLE 14. Arbitration and Mediation Cases

Year	Arbitration			Mediation
	C[a]	L[b]	Total	
1946	0	0	0	176
1947	0	2	2	823
1948	0	6	6	1,405
1949	0	4	4	1,296
1950	0	0	0	1,114
1951	0	2	2	1,033
1952	0	1	1	1,051
1953	1	2	3	1,068
1954	1	1	2	1,021
1955	1	1	2	1,123
1956	1	2	3	1,027
1957	0	2	2	1,339
1958	1	3	4	1,174
1959	0	3	3	1,297
1960	0	7	7	1,194
Total	5	36	41	16,141

[a] Central Labor Relations Commission.
[b] Local Labor Relations Commission.
Source: Based upon unpublished materials furnished by the Ministry of Labor.

THE PROCESSES OF LITIGATION: AN EXPERIMENT WITH THE ADVERSARY SYSTEM

Kohji Tanabe

ASSISTED BY JOHN B. HURLBUT

EARLY Japanese civil procedure was strongly influenced by the German system. The first modern Code of Civil Procedure, adopted in 1890, was drafted under the guidance of a German lawyer[1] and in the main was modeled after the German Imperial Code of Civil Procedure of 1877.[2] Al-

Note. Mr. Tanabe is a Judge of the Mito District Court. B.Jur., Tokyo Imperial University, 1944; Dr.Jur., Tokyo University, 1962. Participant, Japanese American Program for Cooperation in Legal Studies at Harvard University, 1954–1955, and at Stanford University, 1955–1956. Assigned to Legal Training and Research Institute, 1956–1962. Author of BEIKOKU MINJI SOSHŌ NO KEIZAI-TEKI HAIKEI (Economic Background of American Civil Procedure) (1957); writings in the fields of civil procedure and labor law.

Mr. Hurlbut is Jackson Eli Reynolds Professor of Law, Stanford University. A.B., 1928, M.A. 1929, University of California at Los Angeles; LL.B., 1934, Stanford University.

[1] In the Meiji era before 1890, Japanese procedure was regulated by a combination of the customary laws developed under the Tokugawa regime and some regulations enacted by the Meiji government (such as rules of pleading, judicial settlement, and appeal) which modified the Tokugawa customary laws along somewhat modernized lines and provided some uniform rules to govern practice. These procedural laws were generally of a strongly inquisitorial nature and applied by judges who were at the same time the administrative officers of the central and local governments.

After 1880, the government made several attempts to draft a code of civil procedure mostly on the model of the French Code of Civil Procedure of 1806, but these attempts never reached the stage of actual legislation. Representative of these attempts are the 1880 draft by the Senate (*Genrōin*) and the incomplete draft by the French scholar Boissonade, a legal adviser to the government. The government finally decided to pattern the code on the German Code of Civil Procedure which was at the time the most recent and most modern one in Europe. Techow, a provincial councilor of Prussia, was invited to serve as an adviser to the government. In collaboration with Japanese officials, he completed his draft in 1886; the draft was adopted by the legislature with some minor modifications, mostly of phrasing. For the detailed legislative history, see JAPANESE LEGISLATION IN THE MEIJI ERA 295–320, 490–511 (Ishii ed., 1958); Kaneko, *Minji Soshō Hō no Seitei* (Enactment of the Code of Civil Procedure), in 2 KANEKO, MINJI HŌ KENKYŪ (A Study of Civil Law) 1 (1942).

[2] In the course of drafting, however, the Japanese background was taken into consideration to some extent. A government report entitled NIHON GENKŌ SOSHŌ TETSUZUKI (The Present Practice of Litigious Procedure in Japan) (Ministry of Justice ed., c. 1882) gave Techow some understanding of the traditional Japanese litigation process. For example, the German system of compulsory representation by counsel was not taken over mainly because of the limited size and function of the Japanese bar at the time. Techow adopted some provisions from European sources other than the German. The French practice of the informal examination of an

though in 1926 an extensive and significant revision of the code was enacted, the basic characteristics of the Japanese system were left unchanged.[3]

THE PREWAR PROCEDURAL SYSTEM AND ITS ADMINISTRATION

The prewar system maximized the responsibility of the trial judge and minimized that of the litigant and his lawyer in the trial of an action. In sharp contrast to Anglo-American procedure, the trial judge had strong directive powers in the processes of fixing issues and of proof taking, and a trial was conducted in piecemeal fashion with several successive hearings often separated by a substantial time interval.

Under the prewar code, after an action was commenced by filing a complaint, the judge either conducted preparatory procedure (that is, a pretrial conference), usually of several hearings, or one or several preliminary sessions[4] for oral argument. In these, he attempted to fix the issues of fact and law by discussing the pleadings with counsel and by rigorously questioning counsel about his version of the facts and the law. When the judge determined that the case (or a particular issue or group of issues) was ready to proceed to the stage of proof, he required the parties to make formal tenders of evidence, specified on the basis of the various tenders the evidence to be heard, and issued an order of proof taking. In the oral argument which followed, the trial court (a single judge in a Local Court[5] or a bench of three judges in a District Court[6]) subpoenaed some (seldom many, not infrequently no more than one) of the witnesses and

---

unsworn party was utilized. But, the basic structure of the code was clearly German. Cf. ISHII, as in note 1 above, at 493–502; 2 KANEKO, note 1, at 10, 13. See also Kaneko, *Nihon Minji Soshō Hō ni Taisuru Furansu Hō no Eikyō* (The Influence of French Law on Japanese Civil Procedure), in 2 KANEKO, note 1, at 17.

[3] The 1926 revision was designed to reduce delays in litigation which had been the subject of complaint by the profession. Under the influence of the Austrian code of 1899 and the later development of the German code, the revision augmented the court's directive powers and sought to prevent prolonged piecemeal trial by making preparatory procedure (a proceeding similar to the American pretrial conference) a required preliminary in the District Court. As we shall see, a concentrated trial was not achieved in actual practice. As to the legislative intent of the revision, see NAGASHIMA & MORITA, KAISEI MINJI SOSHŌ HŌ KAISHAKU (A Commentary on the Revised Code of Civil Procedure) 6 (1930).

[4] The judgment of the court had to be based exclusively on oral pleadings and argument, and proof taking occurring at full-fledged sessions of the court. See CODE OF CIVIL PROCEDURE, Law No. 29 of 1890, arts. 125, 185, 187. The court could also use the early court sessions for the preliminary functions of fixing issues and submitting tenders of evidence. Preparatory procedure, however, was not a full-fledged session of the court but was essentially preliminary; oral pleadings and tenders of evidence could be made but proof taking was not possible. Preparatory procedure was conducted by a single judge who was a member of the collegiate bench of the District Court or the Court of Appeals (now the High Court). At the Local Court (now the Summary Court) preparatory procedure was not required; the District Court could, at its discretion, dispense with preparatory procedure. CODE OF CIVIL PROCEDURE arts. 249 (amended by Laws No. 149 of 1948 and No. 288 of 1950), 250, 254.

[5] In civil cases the jurisdiction of the prewar Local Court covered claims not exceeding 1,000 yen (about 290 dollars) and some other specified cases such as landlord-tenant cases.

[6] The District Court was the court of first instance with general jurisdiction.

examined them with respect to a designated issue or group of issues. As other issues became sufficiently identified for trial, or as the parties sought to introduce additional proof, the court held additional sessions, at which proof taking continued until the court, feeling that the case was "ripe for judgment"[7] (that the parties had sufficiently exhausted their allegations and supporting evidence) would close the process of oral proceedings and render a judgment in writing.

Throughout these successive sessions, both at the pretrial and the trial stages, the court assumed the leadership and responsibility for both fixing and narrowing the issues and for adjusting the pleadings to conform to the proof. This function of the court to continue to "clarify" the matter in dispute[8] was exercised throughout the entire trial process, the court and the attorneys continuing discussions of pleadings and proof at every session. Pleadings were in a constant state of modification and at each stage reflected the results of preceding stages. Amendments of pleadings were freely made at any stage, at least as long as no unreasonable delay would be caused.[9] Litigation was a continuing process of discussion and cooperation between the court and counsel and of direction by the court, rather than a battle between opposing litigants. Needless to say, such a method could exist only because the Japanese system, like most Continental civil-law systems, had no tradition of jury trial.[10]

The pretrial marshaling of evidence and the subsequent presentation of evidence to the court followed the German pattern. Of course, counsel knew his client's version of the dispute. Other witnesses were supposed to be presented to the court "fresh," under no influence of either party. Coaching of or even unintentional suggestion to witnesses was to be scrupulously avoided. Consequently, pretrial interview by counsel of witnesses was considered unethical. Thus the facts of the case became clear to counsel only in the course of their presentation to the court. Furthermore, all examination of witnesses was conducted by the court. Counsel could ask supplementary questions with the judge's permission or submit them to be asked by the court.[11] The responsibility for exploiting the witness and testing his credibility rested almost entirely upon the trial judge. The court could and actually did, though not frequently, subpoena witnesses and other evidence *ex officio*.[12] These prophylactic methods, which tended to

[7] CODE OF CIVIL PROCEDURE art. 182.

[8] CODE OF CIVIL PROCEDURE art. 127.

[9] Even the alteration of a claim was permitted so long as there was "no alteration in the basis of claim" and no considerable delay would be caused. CODE OF CIVIL PROCEDURE arts. 137, 139, 232.

[10] In Japanese criminal procedure a law which assured the defendant the right to a jury trial was adopted in 1923, but its enforcement has been suspended since 1943. A jury has never been used in civil cases.

[11] CODE OF CIVIL PROCEDURE art. 299 (amended by Law No. 149 of 1948).

[12] *Ex officio* proof taking was permitted when the court was not persuaded in either direction

remove the proof from the contagion of client and counsel, were thought to give greater promise that the truth would be revealed than would an adversary system of proof.

The function of the appellate court, particularly that of a court of second instance, was far different from that of the Anglo-American appellate tribunal. The first appellate court (the Court of Appeals for the District Court and the District Court for the Local Court) could, and not infrequently did, examine witnesses who had already been examined by the lower court and receive new testimonial or documentary evidence. Old ground might be replowed and new ground turned in pursuit of old or new lines of inquiry. The process of trial being in general the same as that of the lower court, the appellate court could rely both upon the recorded evidence of the first-instance trial and upon new evidence produced at its own oral hearings.[13] Considering the fact that about one third of the prewar District Court cases disposed of by a formal judgment were appealed, one could say that a trial in the District Court was a sort of prelude to the trial process which terminated in the Court of Appeals. The second and final appellate court (the Great Court of Judicature), except in a few special situations, could review questions of law only.[14]

It is evident that the prewar procedures minimized the lawyer's responsibility for marshaling and presenting evidence. Pretrial interview of witnesses being forbidden and the American type of discovery devices not being available, there was little for a lawyer to do before trial. Instead of making extensive pretrial preparation for a concentrated trial, exploiting his own case and anticipating his adversary's, counsel could expect to develop his pleadings and proof gradually in the course of the piecemeal trial along the guidelines drawn by the judge's "clarification," by examination of witnesses, and by reaction to substantive law questions which the unfolding case suggested. Also, counsel could depend on the skill of an experienced trial judge in draining a witness dry of his usefulness. Quite naturally this system tended to encourage inertia, inactivity, and a casual attitude on the part of the lawyer and to prolong the trial process. Evidence was often

---

by the evidence presented by the parties and on other occasions when the court considered it necessary. CODE OF CIVIL PROCEDURE art. 261 (repealed by Law No. 149 of 1948).

[13] See CODE OF CIVIL PROCEDURE arts. 369, 377.

[14] CODE OF CIVIL PROCEDURE arts. 394 (amended by Law No. 127 of 1954), 403. Concerning matters which the trial court was required to investigate *ex officio* — as, for instance, the issue of the authority of an attorney to represent a party — the supreme court could take proof. CODE OF CIVIL PROCEDURE art. 405. Also a clearly unreasonable finding of fact (called a "contravention of the legal rules for taking evidence") by the trial court was considered to be subject to review by the supreme court as a "question of law." See, e.g., Judgment of March 10, 1930, Great Court of Judicature, I Civil Department, 19 HŌRITSU HYŌRON ZENSHŪ (A Complete Critique of the Law) [hereafter cited HYŌRON], MINSO (Civil Procedure) pt. at 223. See also 1 KANEKO, JŌKAI MINJI SOSHŌ HŌ (Annotated Code of Civil Procedure) 704 (rev. ed., 1956).

scattered throughout the whole process of the two successive trials, and the length of trial frequently exceeded a year.[15]

One may ask why the Meiji government adopted the Continental procedural pattern. It was no accident. With the dramatic mission of changing a country with a deeply rooted feudalism into a modern industrialized nation, the leaders of the Meiji revolution understandably took the fast and efficient way of more or less completely borrowing the systematized codes and statutes of the Continental countries, particularly Germany, rather than the Anglo-American legal patterns found so largely in an enormous and complicated mass of case law. The Code of Civil Procedure was no exception. The hasty Meiji legislation was primarily intended to persuade the Western nations to consent to the proposed revision of the unequal treaties, especially of the provisions for extraterritoriality.[16] Under these circumstances, substantial attention could hardly be paid to traditional feudal litigation processes. The Code of Civil Procedure was a part of the "government-made modernization" of Japan rather than a product of popular needs or pressure. In this setting, the Meiji bureaucrats were attracted to the German pattern of civil procedure in which a trained trial judge plays the role of a vigorous leader rather than to the Anglo-American pattern in which the judge is an umpire in a contest between two adversaries.

It should also be noted that at the time of the adoption of the code, the Japanese people were not litigious. Under the long tradition of unusually strong governmental control and community pressure, the rights consciousness of the Japanese people was very low. Strong social and psychological pressures discouraged the filing of lawsuits, and manifold out-of-court resolution techniques and mechanisms, such as mediation by relatives, court marshals, or local leaders, were commonly used. The compromise of civil disputes was generally regarded as the most desirable solution. In farming villages and small towns, suit against a neighbor was even a moral wrong. In spite of the rapid industrial development of the country since 1900, the development of the people's rights consciousness has been very slow, and the reluctance to use the courts for the resolution of civil disputes remained unchanged throughout the prewar period.[17]

[15] In 1935, of 27,846 civil cases disposed of by the District Courts, 8 percent took more than two years for disposal, 15 percent more than one year, and 22 percent more than six months. About 31 percent of the cases disposed of by formal judgment were appealed to a Court of Appeals, where about 21 percent took more than two years for disposal, 24 percent more than one year, and 27 percent more than six months. Partly due to the presentation of additional evidence at the second instance, about 17 percent of the appealed judgments were modified or reversed by the Court of Appeals. See 61 DAI NIPPON TEIKOKU SHIHŌ-SHŌ (Great Japan Imperial Ministry of Justice), MINJI TŌKEI NEMPŌ (Annual Report of Civil Statistics) (1935).

[16] See Ishii, note 1, at 581.

[17] In 1935, only about 200,000 suits were filed in the District and Local Courts in a country with a population of 70 million. 61 DAI NIPPON TEIKOKU SHIHŌ-SHŌ, note 15, MINJI TŌKEI

In the setting just described, the prestige of the practicing profession could hardly be high. While since 1890 candidates for a career as judge or procurator received special training from the government and were paid a stipend during this apprenticeship period, apprenticeship was required of future practitioners only after 1933, and this training was rather nominal and without regular stipend. These reasons combined with a traditional respect for government officials to produce a tendency among able, ambitious young law graduates to pursue a judge's or procurator's career rather than to enter private practice. Reflecting the all-embracing theme of administrative control, the legal profession was under the administrative supervision of the Ministry of Justice, whose staff consisted of career judges and procurators. Not only the government but also the ordinary citizen, even the educated citizen, was often inclined to consider a lawyer as a trained troublemaker who charged exorbitant fees. It followed that representation of litigants by lawyers was never required, and trials were frequently conducted without counsel. Indeed there was very little recognition of the legal profession as a highly trained professional group.[18] This relative status of judge and lawyer constitutes part of the background in which the prewar civil procedure was designed to operate.

Another facet of the picture deserves emphasis. Traditionally, Japanese big-business firms, unlike those of America, did not use the services of lawyers. In the main their steady flow of legal problems centering around commercial and real-estate transactions and taxation were handled by employees with some legal training. Generally, these employees were graduates of the undergraduate law department of a university. They had not passed the national legal examination;[19] they were without graduate apprenticeship training; and they were not members of the bar and often were not well equipped to cope with the legal problems put in their hands. The Japanese lawyer was thus without that important source of employment and income which supports the American office lawyer. The main function of the Japanese lawyer was as a litigator, and even this function was not enthusiastically recognized by business. Japanese businessmen usually tried to avoid litigation by resorting to informal mediation, often with the intervention of government officials. Consequently, even during a period of dynamic expansion of Japanese capitalism, nothing akin to the

YŌSHI (Summary of Civil Statistics) pt. at 1–2. It should be remembered that in prewar Japan commercial arbitration had not been developed. See the essay by Takeyoshi Kawashima, "Dispute Resolution in Contemporary Japan," in this volume.

[18] The Ministry of Justice consistently opposed legislation enlarging the area of unauthorized practice of law by unlicensed persons, believing that the semilegal practice by "quasi-lawyers," such as the licensed legal document draftsmen known as legal scriveners (*shihō shoshi*), was a necessary service for the ordinary citizen because he could not pay a lawyer's fee.

[19] In the prewar period the national legal examination for the qualification of judges, procurators, and private practitioners was administered by the government as a part of the annual examination for the qualification of senior government officials.

American development of the law firm and the transition of the lawyer "from advocate to counselor" occurred in the prewar years. A Japanese law office with as many as six or seven lawyers was a rarity, and even such an office was usually only a group of independent lawyers sharing the same facilities and taking advantage of a senior attorney's professional reputation. Typical clients were small merchants, tenants, creditors with small unsecured claims, tort victims, divorce-seeking wives, and the like, clients with small claims and modest means. In 1935 about eighty percent of the civil cases filed in the District and Local Courts involved claims of less than 250 yen (about 73 dollars).[20] A lawyer population of only six thousand was adequate to meet the demands of civil litigation as well as of criminal defense.

In the conditions described above, most Japanese lawyers could not afford to litigate on credit and then later charge the client on a time and labor basis. Many clients, on the other hand, could not afford to pay in advance for the lawyer's services. A unique fee arrangement developed; when a lawyer was first retained, the client paid a "commencing fee," which included the expected court costs (the filing fee, postal expenses for the service of the complaints, and such) and a partial fee for services; the balance of the fee was contingent* on success.[21] The client usually did not have to pay before trial for pretrial preparation. In these circumstances the lawyer could hardly be expected to expend much effort in pretrial preparation, least of all in fact investigation. Thus the gradual revelation of the case during the course of the piecemeal trial by the judge's clarification and examination of witnesses meshed nicely with the needs of the lawyer. He did not need to be energetic and resourceful before trial, or indeed even during trial.

Finally, the relative size of the two branches of the profession should be noted. About sixteen hundred well-trained career judges, many of whom were still young and very active, shared the responsibility of trying civil and criminal cases with about six thousand private lawyers (these figures

[20] In 1935 about 90 percent of the civil cases filed in the District and Local Courts involved claims of less than 1000 yen (about 290 dollars). About 72 percent of the civil cases filed in 1935 were for money claims, mostly in contract. In spite of the rapid development of industry and transportation, tort claims accounted for less than 4 percent of the total. 61 Dai Nippon Teikoku Shihō-shō, note 15, Minji Tōkei Yōshi (Summary of Civil Statistics) pt. at 27, 47.

* The contingent-fee concept was originally developed to encourage the use of lawyers. Kohji Tanabe suggested, during the conference discussions, that the uncertainty over the amount that may ultimately be owed still operates as a substantial deterrent even though the liability is contingent on success.

[21] This contingent fee was sometimes charged piecemeal for the results achieved in each instance. The amount of the contingent fee was usually 10 to 30 percent of the amount recovered (or less if the recovery was very large), but the method of fixing the fee varied depending on each lawyer's policy, his personal relation to the client, and the client's financial capacity. The fee standards adopted by the local attorneys' associations indicate that the "commencing fee plus contingent" system was a common practice among Japanese lawyers.

are for 1935). That there should be one judge for every four lawyers will startle the American lawyer. The figures, of course, reflect the division of labor between judge and lawyer contemplated by the prewar procedural system and suggest that the procedural innovations of the Meiji government were well adapted to the social setting in which they were to operate.

POSTWAR CIVIL-PROCEDURE REFORM

The dramatic change in Japan's political climate at the end of World War II produced many fundamental legal reforms. Recognition of the legal integrity of the citizen in his relationship to the state and drastic limitations on the powers of government, individual freedom coupled with individual responsibility, were the basic themes of the "democratization movement" encouraged by the occupation authorities. This movement inevitably elevated the status of the lawyer and strengthened his position in society. The ideal of a "unified legal profession," with judges recruited from the bar was encouraged by the Court Law of 1947[22] under which one third of the justices of the new Supreme Court (which replaced the old Great Court of Judicature) were drawn from the practicing bar. Although, primarily because of insufficient financial inducement, few lawyers would accept appointment to the lower courts, some high judicial positions such as chief judge of a High Court were held by lawyers, something which would have been quite unusual before the war. Since the establishment in 1947 of the Legal Training and Research Institute under the Supreme Court, all prospective members of the profession (lawyers, judges, procurators) are required to engage in two years of intensive graduate apprenticeship. All legal apprentices, including those planning to practice, are paid the same stipend by the government. The autonomy of the bar is well established. It is no longer under the administrative control of the government, and the various bar organizations now exercise a strong influence on judicial administration, legislation, and the conduct of government.

In this new political climate which so greatly strengthened the individual in his relationship to the state, the attractiveness in the field of civil procedure of the Anglo-American adversary system is understandable. Stripping the judge of power and placing the burden of initiative and responsibility on the litigant and his lawyer was felt to be in keeping with the democratic movement. Although most of the Code of Civil Procedure was left unchanged, two important revisions were made in 1948. First, the article giving the trial court the power to take proof *ex officio* was eliminated. Second, a new provision, article 294, put the burden of examining and cross-examining witnesses on the litigants. Of course, as in Anglo-American practice, the trial judge can supplement the litigant's examination of witnesses by

[22] Law No. 59 of 1947, translated into English in 2 EHS LAW BULLETIN SERIES AA 1 (Nakane ed., 1954).

questions of his own, but primary responsibility for the presentation of proof is now placed squarely on the litigant. These two reforms, fragmentary as they were, had far-reaching implications. The abolition of *ex officio* proof taking was generally accepted by the profession as a declaration of the new adversary principle under which the litigant bore the prime responsibility for disclosing the facts, while the trial judge's role was to evaluate passively the merits of the litigant's presentation. Implicit in the shift of responsibility for the examination of witnesses was the intent to make the lawyer the leading figure in the courtroom and to require of him not only skill in the examination and crossexamination of witnesses but also pretrial preparation, especially fact investigation. This last purpose was made doubly apparent by the postwar effort to abandon the piecemeal trial and to establish the concentrated or continuous trial. The Supreme Court regulation of 1954 concerning the continuous trial (later made a part of the court's Civil Procedure Regulations of 1956) declared it to be the duty of the litigant and his lawyer to make a close pretrial investigation of facts, including interviews with witnesses, and to frame the pleadings and present the proof without being urged by the clarification of the judge.[23] The old prejudice against the pretrial contact with witnesses is now officially abandoned and can no longer be an excuse for poor pretrial preparation. This new rule, in an effort to speed up the trial process, requires the court to urge litigants to exhaust their allegations and tenders of evidence at the pretrial stage and severely to limit postponements and various other delaying devices.[24] Clearly, if this new theme was to be successfully translated into action, the Japanese lawyer would have to accept the burden of resourceful pretrial preparation and trial presentation* — burdens almost beyond the imagination of the lawyer accustomed to prewar practice.[25]

These procedural changes, like most of the legislation during the period, were encouraged and even promoted by occupation personnel. The code revisions were the product of close cooperation between the legal section of the occupation force and the staff of the Japanese Ministry of Justice.[26] The Regulations Concerning Continuous Trial in Civil Procedure were drafted by the staff of the Supreme Court along lines suggested by a SCAP direc-

[23] Regulations Concerning Continuous Trial in Civil Procedure, Supreme Court Regulation No. 27 of 1954, art. 2; Civil Procedure Regulations, Supreme Court Regulation No. 2 of 1956, art. 4.

[24] Civil Procedure Regulations, arts. 17, 20, 26.

* The Japanese bar is apparently still experiencing difficulty in adapting to pretrial practice. Judge Takaaki Hattori, now sitting in one of the pretrial divisions in the Tokyo District Court, commented at the conference that the level of preparation was very low. Makoto Yazawa concurred and remarked that perhaps the bar's failure to develop the issues fully can explain some recent decisions in which the court's opinion completely missed the important point.

[25] Under the new rule, "insufficient preparation" is no longer an adequate ground for the postponement of a fixed hearing date. Civil Procedure Regulations, art. 29.

[26] Known during the latter portion of the occupation period as the Attorney General's Office.

tive of October 18, 1950, about the speeding up of civil and criminal trials.[27] It should be emphasized, however, that leading Japanese jurists and lawyers who had responsible roles in the drafting of the reforms seemed to accept or even to embrace this "democratization" enthusiastically. In explaining the objectives of the reforms, two high officials of the Ministry of Justice who drafted the new provisions of the code stated:

> since civil litigation is essentially a dispute concerning private rights, *as a matter of course, the responsibility and duty to present proof rests with the parties; it is neither the responsibility nor the duty of the court* . . . When the necessary facts to maintain the allegation of a party cannot be proven, the disadvantage should be borne by such party, and it is sufficient grounds for the court to issue him an unfavorable determination. The disadvantage is a consequence invited by the party himself, over and beyond which the court should neither assist a party on one side nor interfere.[28]

Many leading Japanese jurists and lawyers who visited the United States soon after the war or who participated in the war-crime trials, were strongly impressed by the vitality of the American trial, particularly by the vigorous role of the American lawyer.[29] Apparently many career judges, who had often complained about the inertia and poor pretrial preparation of the Japanese lawyer, cherished the hope that the challenging assignment given the attorneys under the new system might educate the lawyer to accept and fulfill his new responsibility and free the judge from his heavy burden of

[27] SCAPIN 2127, Oct. 18, 1950, para. 12, NIHON KANRI HŌREI KENKYŪ (Japan Occupation Law Review) no. 34, Directives Section at 26, 32 (in English and Japanese). See also SAIKŌ SAIBANSHO JIMU-SŌKYOKU (General Secretariat of the Supreme Court), MINJI SOSHŌ SOKUSHIN KANKEI HŌKI NO KAISETSU (A Commentary on the Rules of Law Relating to the Speed Up of Civil Litigation) 16 (1951).

[28] OKUNO & MIYAKE, MINJI SOSHŌ HŌ NO KAISETSU (A Commentary on the Code of Civil Procedure) 5–6 (1948); emphasis added. Also, the commentary on the new code published by the Civil Affairs Bureau of the General Secretariat of the Supreme Court states: "In civil litigation the persons, who best know the procedural materials — especially the evidence — and who are in a position where they are best able to gather it together, are the parties. Since a party brings suit in his own direct personal interest, it is enough to entrust the allegations and their proof to the responsibility and efforts of the parties. Excessive interference by the court dampens the zeal of the parties and instead — it being entirely impossible under the present trial system for the court completely to gather all evidence *ex officio* — produces a result which is accidental in nature. *This is the reason why we thoroughly follow the doctrine of party presentation under the new Constitution, in which the freedom and responsibility of the individual is made a fundamental principle*" (emphasis added). MINJI KYOKU (Civil Affairs Bureau), SAIKŌ SAIBANSHO JIMU-SŌKYOKU (General Secretariat of the Supreme Court), KAISEI MINJI SOSHŌ HŌ SHŌSETSU (A Detailed Commentary on the Revised Code of Civil Procedure) 51 (Minji Saiban Shiryō (Civil Trial Materials) No. 9, 1948).

[29] For examples, see INOMATA & OZAWA, TO-BEI HŌSŌ NO KICHŌ KŌEN (Addresses by the Jurists Who Have Returned to Japan from the U.S.) (Shihō Kenshūjo Tokubetsu Kenkyū Sōsho (Legal Training and Research Institute Special Study Series) No. 5, 1951); SATO, TO-BEI HŌSŌ NO KICHŌ KŌEN (Addresses by the Jurists Who Have Returned to Japan from the U.S.) (Shihō Kenshūjo Tokubetsu Kenkyū Sōsho No. 20, 1951); KOZEKI, TO-BEI HŌSŌ NO KICHŌ KŌEN (Addresses by the Jurists Who Have Returned to Japan from the U.S.) (Shihō Kenshūjo Tokubetsu Kenkyū Sōsho No. 25, 1951).

trial supervision.[30] The bar, although somewhat embarrassed by the lawyer's new and challenging responsibility, seemed satisfied with the lawyer's new status as a leading figure in the courtroom. The profession showed perhaps even less resistance in accepting the principle of the concentrated trial. The concentrated trial was not new to the profession because a movement in that direction had been developing since the 1926 revision of the code.[31] Thus, at least during the occupation period, the general reaction of the profession to the postwar changes, as reflected in professional literature and discussions, was generally favorable.[32]

The innovations described, whether wise or unwise, were probably unavoidable in the political circumstances existing during the occupation. It is now possible to look back with some detachment and wonder whether the changes were not made a bit hastily or at least without sufficient recognition of the social and economic background in which they were to operate and without sufficient recognition of the interreaction of these changes with other parts of the legal system. Of course, ingrained behavior of lawyers and judges cannot be changed overnight; no one expected that. But it does seem that the enthusiastic response of the profession to the changes was somewhat naive and much too optimistic. The dynamic rehabilitation and growth of the Japanese economy in fifteen short years is a dramatic chapter in world history. But the social and economic setting in which the innovations have operated is not much different from that which characterized the prewar years.

As has already been noted, the influence and status of the bar has been on the upswing since the war and the capacity of the young lawyer is higher because of the improved training he receives at the Legal Training and Research Institute. The bar is also now attracting more of the most able institute graduates. The lawyer's self-confidence and his responsibilities are on the increase. The size of the bar, however, is only slightly higher than before the war and has not kept pace with the increase in population. In 1960, Japan had about sixty-three hundred lawyers to serve a population of more than eighty million people. In many prefectures with a population of more than a million, there were less than fifty lawyers.[33]

[30] See MINJI KYOKU, note 28, at 51. This feeling is well illustrated by a phrase within the profession in the early postwar period that "under the prewar system a judge draws a heavy wagon while the parties push from behind, but under the new system a judge rides in a carriage drawn by the parties as horses." See MURAMATSU, MINJI SAIBAN NO SHO-MONDAI (Various Problems in Civil Trials) 3 (2nd ed., 1953).

[31] See note 3 above.

[32] It is true, however, that a few judges rather cautiously expressed doubt about the wisdom of the innovations and the capacity of the lawyer to carry his new responsibilities. See KOZEKI, TO-BEI HŌSŌ NO KICHŌ KŌEN (Addresses by the Jurists Who Have Returned to Japan from the U.S.) 40 (Shihō Kenshūjo Tokubetsu Kenkyū Sōsho No. 25, 1951).

[33] There were 6,319 lawyers in Japan in Jan. 1960, with twenty-three prefectures having less than fifty lawyers each and thirty-seven prefectures having less than 100 lawyers each.

Apart from the Supreme Court, the traditional career-judge system continues pretty much as before.[34] The effort to recruit lower-court judges from the bar has almost entirely failed. By the postwar Court Law, ten years of duty as an assistant judge with limited functions (primarily as an associate judge on a collegiate court) are required for appointment to a full-fledged judgeship.[35] Promotion, however, is usually almost automatic. Indeed, because of the shortage of judges, the period of limited function was reduced to five years by special legislation in 1948.[36] The Japanese judiciary is still the same cohesive group of well-trained career judges, in a seniority and promotion system, with the same zeal for achieving justice and establishing truth.

The organization and economic position of the Japanese lawyer has not changed much since the war. Except for a few fairly well-organized firms of the American type (which have developed in response to the need for specialists in such fields as international transactions, labor, and patent practice), the one-man independent practice is the usual pattern;[37] the unique contingent-fee arrangement continues to be widely employed;[38] and the income of lawyers is still not very high.[39]

[34] The number of judges has increased since the war, but the increase was mainly due to the postwar system of the appointment of Summary Court judges without regular qualifications. Under the postwar system the Summary Court judges can be selected and appointed by the Supreme Court after a special screening procedure. They do not have to pass the national legal examination or take the regular apprentice training at the Legal Training and Research Institute. See Court Law, art. 45(1). The number of judges with regular qualifications was 1,601 in 1941 and about 1,900 in 1960. The number of Summary Court judges without regular qualifications was about 300 in 1960.

[35] Court Law, art. 42.

[36] Law Concerning the Special Case of the Official Authority of Assistant Judges, Law No. 146 of 1948, art. 1, translated into English in OFFICIAL GAZETTE, July 12, 1948, extra ed. at 13.

[37] A recent private survey suggests that 90 percent of the Japanese lawyers are practicing alone without associates. Matsui, Makita & Torita, *Bengoshi no Seikatsu to Ishiki — Jittai Chōsa* (The Life and Attitude of Attorneys — A Survey of Actual Conditions), 32 HŌRITSU JIHŌ (Law Journal) 452, 460 (1960). It should be noted that of the 1,000 lawyers questioned, 296 responded.

[38] This is evident from the several lower-court decisions concerning claims for legal fees which fixed the amount on the already described contingent-fee basis. See Karikome v. Suzuki, Tokyo High Court, November 20, 1956, 7 KAKYŪ SAIBANSHO MINJI SAIBAN REISHŪ (A Collection of Civil Cases in the Inferior Courts) 3304; Rules of Fee, Etc., Standards (Hōshū Tō Kijun Kitei), Japanese Federated Attorneys' Association Rule No. 7 of 1955; Matsui, Makita & Torita, note 37, at 461.

[39] The survey mentioned in note 37 revealed that the average monthly income of lawyers in 1960 was approximately 90,905 yen (about 251 dollars), while that of doctors was 149,567 yen (about 415 dollars). That the prejudice against judicial action as the means of settling private disputes continues is suggested by a recent sociological survey which disclosed that about 78 percent of more than 2,000 persons polled preferred an out-of-court solution, particularly mediation by relatives, over litigation. See Sasaki, *Chihō ni okeru Minji Chōtei* (Civil Mediation in Rural Areas), 32 HŌRITSU JIHŌ 1051, 1053 (1960). The number of the informal "consultations" about civil disputes undertaken by the Tokyo Metropolitan Police Office in 1958 numbered 27,210, more than the number of civil actions filed in the Tokyo District Court that year. See Hironaka, *Shimin no Kenri Kakuho to Minji Saiban* (Guarantying Citizens' Rights and Civil Trial), 32 HŌRITSU JIHŌ 1002, 1004 (1960).

Although the rights consciousness of the people has been developing gradually, the traditional reluctance to file a lawsuit and to resort to a lawyer continues strong, and most litigation is still petty when measured by American standards.[40] Apparently the larger part of industrial, commercial, and personal injury disputes are still resolved by out-of-court devices. The traditional reluctance of the large business enterprise to hire lawyers still seems to prevail except in such fields as international transactions and labor disputes.[41] The expense of litigation, particularly the lawyer's fee, and the congestion of the trial calendar in metropolitan centers discourage the filing of actions. It is startling to find that, in 1959, either both or one of the litigants was not represented by counsel in 63 percent of the District Court actions and 91.4 percent of the Summary Court actions.[42] These facts are a large roadblock in the improvement of the economic position of the Japanese lawyer and hinder his ability to carry his new role in litigation.

How could the new system, particularly in its adversary aspects, work well in this setting? How have the new doctrines been interwoven with the old structure which, for the most part, was left unchanged? Is the postwar experiment on the road to success? To consider these questions it is necessary to return to three subjects: (1) the clarification function of the trial court, (2) the new role of the litigant in marshaling and presenting proof, and (3) the problem of the speedy, concentrated trial.

The Court's Clarification Function

Prewar Doctrine

The clarifying function of the trial court has long been considered a basic principle of German civil procedure. A German scholar called it the

[40] The number of actions filed in 1959 (175,439) was less than the annual average (180,838) for the period 1932–1941. In 1959 the average amount of claim was 713,506 yen (about 1,980 dollars) in District Court actions and 44,727 yen (about 124 dollars) in Summary Court actions. Even in the District Courts, 37.6 percent of the actions involved claims of less than 200,000 yen (about 550 dollars) and 69.3 percent less than 500,000 yen (about 1,380 dollars). In spite of the great increase of traffic accidents (in 1959, 371,763 accidents, with 10,097 killed and 230,504 injured), tort claims filed in the District Courts in 1959 accounted for less than 4,282 actions (less than 7 percent of those filed). Although postwar legislation encouraged suits against the state for the annulment of administrative determinations, only 736 actions of this nature were filed in 1959. Saikō Saibansho Jimu-sōkyoku (General Secretariat of the Supreme Court), Shōwa 34 Nen Shihō Tōkei Nempō (1959 Annual Report of Judicial Statistics) 2, 8, 159, 166, 403 (1960). (The postwar Summary Court has jurisdiction over cases not exceeding 100,000 yen and actually handled 57.7 percent of the civil suits filed in 1959; see Court Law, art. 33.)

[41] The survey cited in note 37 also revealed that the overwhelming majority of clients are medium and small concerns and individual citizens, only about 6 per cent being large businesses (Matsui, Makita & Torita, note 37, at 463). The definition of "large business" given by this survey, however, seems to be vague.

[42] Saikō Saibansho Jimu-sōkyoku, note 40, at 160, 404.

Magna Carta of civil procedure, meaning that this function if properly exercised would protect the interests of a litigant who might otherwise suffer the loss of his case or defense because of poor advocacy by his attorney.[43] German courts consider the exercise of the clarifying function a duty.[44] Article 112, paragraph (2), of the first Japanese code (1890), which pretty much copied the corresponding provision of the German code of 1877, stated:

The presiding judge *shall* by questioning cause the clarification of unclear motions, the supplementation of insufficient proof of alleged facts, and the rendering of other statements necessary to settle relationships in the case [emphasis added].

Emphasizing the word "shall" and influenced by contemporary German theory and practice, the Japanese supreme court — the Great Court of Judicature — shortly after enactment of the code declared that clarification was a "duty" of the trial court.[45]

The 1926 revision of the code substituted for article 112, paragraph (2), of the 1890 code the present article 127, paragraph (1):

The presiding judge, in order to clarify the procedural relationships, *may* question the parties concerning matters of fact and law or urge them to present evidence [emphasis added].

The word "may" suggests that the exercise of the clarifying function was discretionary. However, because the code of 1926, despite the change in phraseology of article 127, gave continued emphasis to the trial court's directive powers,[46] Japanese doctrine continued to hold that the power to clarify was indeed the duty to clarify. This doctrine was reinforced by repeated Great Court of Judicature decisions[47] and by the writings of Japanese scholars who continued under the spell of German and Austrian practice.[48]

The duty doctrine was not mere theory; the Great Court of Judicature

[43] BAUMBACH, ZIVILPROZESSORDNUNG §139, comm. 1A (25th ed. Lauterbach, 1958).

[44] See ZIVILPROZESSORDNUNG §139. For a study in English regarding the German situation on "revision" (review by the highest appellate court), see Kaplan, von Mehren & Schaefer, *Phases of German Civil Procedure,* 71 HARV. L. REV. 1193, at 1229 n.145 (1958).

[45] Sasahara v. Mizusawa, Great Court of Judicature, I Civil Department, March 18, 1899, 5 DAI SHIN IN MINJI HANKETSU ROKU (Record of Great Court of Judicature Civil Judgments) [hereafter cited DAI-HAN MINROKU] no. 3, at 23.

[46] The power to take proof *ex officio* was retained. CODE OF CIVIL PROCEDURE art. 261. The judge's power to lead in the unravelling of the case during the pretrial hearings and arguments was emphasized. See HŌSŌ KAI (Jurists' Association), DAI 51 KAI TEIKOKU GIKAI MINJI SOSHŌ HŌ KAISEI HŌRITSU-AN IINKAI SOKKIROKU (Stenographic Record of the Committee on the Code of Civil Procedure Revision Bill in the 51st Session of the Imperial Diet) 437 (1929); HŌSŌ KAI, MINJI SOSHŌ HŌ KAISEI CHŌSA IINKAI SOKKIROKU (Stenographic Record of the Code of Civil Procedure Revision Commission) 529 (1929). Also see NAGASHIMA & MORITA, note 3, at 7, 14, 18.

[47] See the cases cited in notes 58–60.

[48] See MURAMATSU, MINJI SAIBAN NO KENKYŪ (A Study of the Civil Trial) 25–26 (1955) and scholarly writings cited therein at 28–30.

enforced it vigorously. The failure to clarify properly was regarded as an error of law reviewable by that court and as a reversible error if material to the judgment. It became common practice for appellants to urge as ground for reversal that neither the first- nor second-instance court had fulfilled its duty to clarify; many decisions were reversed on this ground and remanded with directions to clarify in accordance with the instructions of the supreme court. A very considerable body of case law developed around the clarification function.[49] The supervisory control of the trial process which the supreme court exercised by this means was significant and firm. This kind of review of the proceedings of the trial court imposed a very heavy burden on the supreme-court judges.[50] It necessitated a meticulous examination of the entire records in both the first and second instances, including the pleadings, the exhibits, and the protocols of each hearing or session.[51] It should also be added that, though many judgments were reversed because of a failure to clarify properly, the Great Court of Judicature never reversed on the ground that the trial judge pursued his clarification duty too vigorously.

The theme which emerged from the decisions is that the trial judge should "make the party win who should win."[52] The general implications are clear. The litigant unrepresented by counsel was obviously assisted. In litigation in which counsel appeared, attorneys approached the initial hearing with only a fuzzy, ambiguous understanding of the case or defense, the underlying facts, the available evidence, and the relevant substantive law. Counsel tendered a chaotic hodgepodge of evidence, the irrelevant along with the relevant. The trial judge had to lead the litigant or his counsel to an effective presentation of the case, bringing to bear not only a refined knowledge of the substantive law, but also leading and directing the litigant into a resourceful marshaling and presentation of proof. By continually clarifying, leading, and directing during the succession of pretrial and trial sessions, the judge developed the full potential of the case or defense.[53] Other

[49] For an extensive collection and analysis of the prewar Great Court of Judicature and postwar Supreme Court cases regarding clarification, see Muramatsu, *Shakumei-ken* (Power to Clarify), in 1 SŌGŌ HANREI KENKYŪ SŌSHO, MINJI SOSHŌ HŌ (Comprehensive Case Study Series, Civil Procedure Law) 97 (1956).

[50] In 1935, 4,069 appeals or actions for revision were filed in the Great Court of Judicature, with 26 judges assigned to civil cases. See 61 DAI NIPPON TEIKOKU SHIHŌ-SHŌ, note 15, at MINJI TŌKEI YŌSHI (Summary of Civil Statistics) pt. at 1.

[51] On the filing of an appeal or action for revision before the former Great Court of Judicature or the present Supreme Court, the whole record of the trial in the first and second instances is sent to the supreme tribunal by the court clerk without any act of the party. CODE OF CIVIL PROCEDURE arts. 369, 399-2, 409.

[52] MURAMATSU, note 30, at 64.

[53] Some illustrations may assist in visualizing the actual administration of the clarifying function of the court. After checking through a complaint, the trial judge might ask at the first session for oral argument: "Counsel, in your complaint you did not mention this fact which is a part of the operative facts of your claim. Are you going to allege it?"; or "This part of your pleading is too abstract [or unclear or inconsistent with other parts of the complaint]. Will you make it more particular?"; or "I am not certain whether you construct your claim in

facets of Japanese practice must be understood before the reasons for decisions concerning the clarification process[54] are clear. It will be recalled that pleadings remain fluid during the pretrial hearings and even during the trial sessions. However, Japanese practice does give emphasis, indeed a strong emphasis, to pleadings. The trial judge prepares an elaborate judgment which meticulously summarizes the pleadings and the evidence and which expounds the legal theories applicable to his findings or facts.[55] Basic to Japanese law is the theory of "party presentation"; a fact not alleged, however well proven, cannot be the basis of a judgment.[56] Japanese pleadings do not stop with the broad general allegations characteristic of so much of modern American pleading, but contain large amounts of what American lawyers would call evidentiary fact.[57] The trial judge should lead the litigant to make the allegations appropriate to support the proof possibly or potentially available. Many judgments were reversed because the trial judge failed to "clarify" the pleadings so as to accommodate proof which might be available to the litigant at the early stage.[58]

---

contract or quasi-contract. Please make your position clear." Counsel might answer the questions immediately or promise to clarify the points at the next session. Exceptionally, the court would order the party to clarify the point in writing before the session commenced. See CODE OF CIVIL PROCEDURE art. 128. A judge, checking the answer, might put similar questions to the defendant or his counsel: "Do you admit this part of the complaint, or not?"; or "You rather vaguely mentioned in your answer that you were 'forced' to sign the contract. Do you mean to present the defense of duress?"

At the proof stage, the judge would often ask such questions as this: "There seems to be some inconsistency between your pleading and the presented documentary evidence. Are you going to amend your pleading?" Discussing tenders of evidence with the proponent, a judge might ask, "Are you going to present any proof regarding this issue?" or he might even ask, "Are you going to present such and such evidence which is usually presented as proof on this issue?"

In general, however, a judge would not urge the party to present a defense such as performance or setoff unless evidence suggesting the defense had already been presented. Most judges were reluctant to suggest that a party had a defense of prescription or the bar of an exclusionary period. Counsel could hardly refuse to clarify a point when requested to do so by the court. A refusal, unless clearly for proper reasons, would either result in the dismissal of an action or defense or lead to a presumption unfavorable to him. Cf. CODE OF CIVIL PROCEDURE art. 185.

[54] See notes 58–60.

[55] CODE OF CIVIL PROCEDURE art. 191.

[56] See Muramatsu, *Benron Shugi* (Principle of Party Presentation), in 2 MINJI SOSHŌ HŌ GAKKAI (Civil Procedure Law Association), MINJI SOSHŌ HŌ KŌZA (Collected Essays on the Law of Civil Procedure) 513 (1954). The article cites numerous cases illustrating this principle.

[57] For example, in actions by an owner to recover possession of property, the plaintiff is required to allege the route by which ownership was acquired (such as by inheritance or purchase) if title is denied by the defendant. Moreover, detailed statements regarding the facts of the case, including important circumstantial evidentiary facts, are often included in the written pleadings.

[58] See, for example, Judgment of Oct. 5, 1943, Great Court of Judicature, I Civil Department, 13 HŌGAKU (Jurisprudence) 5336: Plaintiff P sued defendant D for money alleged to be due on a promissory note endorsed by D's agent A. As an alternative allegation, P simply stated that A had "apparent agency" to endorse but failed to allege any specific facts from which A's apparent authority would follow. The trial court did not examine the evidence offered to prove the alternative allegation, dismissing for defective pleading. On *revision* the Great Court

Moreover, when the evidence presented suggested the existence of a significant fact, the judge was supposed to lead the litigant to tender additional evidence and, if necessary, to amend the pleadings to accommodate the proof.[59] Of course, the completion of trial might thus be further delayed, but this price was not thought too high. And, in the case of variance between pleading and proof (something very common as the case gradually unfolded with the progress of the piecemeal trial), it was a grave error for the trial judge to fail to suggest additional allegations appropriate to the proof.[60] Further, through clarification at both the pretrial and trial stages, the judge should lead the litigants to withdraw groundless allegations, withhold irrelevant proof, and enter into timesaving stipulations.

The trial of an action in the prewar era was thus a very paternalistic operation. If the duty to clarify was fully performed, the law would prevail despite any inadequacy of counsel's advocacy. The process fitted the needs of the Japanese lawyer who did not have the training, tradition, or opportunity for meticulous pretrial investigation of fact and law. Conversely, the development of those traits characteristic of the American lawyer's pretrial preparation was discouraged. The clarification function also made the trial judge an extremely powerful lawgiver. Indeed, one commentator criticized the Great Court of Judicature decisions on clarification as sometimes instructing the trial judge to lead the litigant to allegations "so ingenious and elaborate that neither counsel nor the trial judge could readily

---

of Judicature reversed the judgment and remanded the case on the ground that the trial court had erred in dismissing the action without clarifying the specific content of the alternative allegation.

[59] See, e.g., Ebado v. Fuji Seimei Hoken Kabushiki Kaisha (Fuji Life Insurance Co.), Great Court of Judicature, I Civil Department, July 16, 1931, 20 HYŌRON, MINSO (Civil Procedure) pt. at 559: In an action to recover under an insurance policy, it was disputed whether the insurer had payed a premium. P, the insured, alleged that he had payed it to A, a canvasing agent of the defendant company. Judgment was entered for the defendant because the authority of A to receive the premium was not shown. On *revision* the Great Court of Judicature reversed the judgment on the ground that the trial court had erred in dismissing the action without clarifying whether P would allege that A had apparent authority.

Also, e.g., Takashima v. Muda, Great Court of Judicature, I Civil Department, Feb. 13, 1939, HŌRITSU SHIMBUN (The Law News) no. 4393, at 7: P, a creditor, sued D to recover a debt. D did not raise the defense of performance. In the course of the trial, however, D presented documentary evidence which might have proved performance. The trial court did not take up the defense at all as it was not alleged by D and judgment was entered for P. On *revision* the Great Court of Judicature reversed because error had been committed in dismissing the action without clarifying whether D would allege the defense of performance.

[60] See, e.g., Tsunoda v. Hattori, Great Court of Judicature, I Civil Department, Feb. 22, 1926, 5 DAI SHIN IN MINJI HANREI SHŪ (A Collection of Civil Great Court of Judicature Cases) 99: P filed an action against D for a judgment declaring P's ownership of a house. As a ground for the action, P alleged that he purchased from A the materials of the house — not the completed house which could be the subject of a real estate transaction — and then built a house with these materials and his own funds. The trial court, finding that the house was already completed and owned by A when the purchase was made by P, dismissed the action. On *revision* the Great Court of Judicature reversed the judgment on the ground that the trial court had erred in dismissing without clarifying P's position regarding the variance between P's allegation and the facts proved.

think of them."[61] Finally, with the threat of reversal by the Great Court always present, trial judges tolerated long delays in the tendering of allegations and proof, thus prolonging the trial process.[62] Justice might prevail but it often took a long time.

Postwar Developments

The postwar "democratization" of civil procedure, as described in the first part of this essay, has significant implications for the trial judge and his clarifying function. The elimination of the power to take proof *ex officio* and the placing of responsibility on the parties for the examination of witnesses, as well as the provision of the Regulations Concerning Continuous Trial in Civil Procedure requiring the litigants' ample preparation "without waiting for clarification by the court," seemed to indicate that the trial judge was no longer expected to exercise his prewar directive powers. But article 127 on the clarifying power remains in the code; and the postwar revisions of the code gave no directions to the trial judge respecting the exercise of this function. Consequently, two basic questions were presented to the profession. In the first place, as a matter of statutory interpretation, is the trial court still obligated to exercise its clarifying power, and is the performance of this duty subject to appellate scrutiny? Second, to what extent, as a matter of good trial administration, should the court exercise the clarifying power?

A series of postwar Supreme Court decisions prior to 1954 gave a fairly clear answer to the first question. The trial judge was no longer under the obligation to clarify, and judgments would not be reversed because of his failure to do so. Some appellants argued that the trial judge did not clarify their general or ambiguous allegations so as to lead them into more specific allegations and the tender of supporting evidence. The Supreme Court answered that the trial judge was not under an obligation to determine this question.[63] In more extreme cases, the appellant might argue that the evidence actually tended to establish a fact important to his case or defense and that the trial judge failed to lead him into an elaboration of the matter by further allegations and proof. But the Supreme Court answered that the trial judge is under no duty to lead a litigant to develop even an

[61] Muramatsu, note 49, at 114.

[62] This practice was one of the main reasons for the failure of the attempt of the 1926 revision to speed up trials.

[63] See, e.g., Hirosumi v. Yoneda, Supreme Court, II Petty Bench, Oct. 19, 1951, 5 SAIKŌ SAIBANSHO MINJI HANREI SHŪ (A Collection of Civil Supreme Court Cases) [hereafter cited SAI-HAN MINSHŪ] 612: In a claim for money alleged to be due on a promissory note, D presented the defense of bad faith of P, a holder. The trial court rendered judgment for P, rejecting the defense on the ground that D neither alleged nor presented any evidence of the specific facts constituting bad faith. On *revision* the Supreme Court sustained the judgment of the trial court, stating that the trial court had no duty to clarify whether the party would present further allegations or proof.

apparent cause of action or defense.[64] Seemingly, the Supreme Court had made a 180-degree shift. Now the trial judge commits no error if he tries the case as the litigants present it. He need no longer feel obligated to develop and exploit the litigant's case or defense "to achieve justice." Interestingly, most of the leading scholars and commentators in the field approved this new approach to the trial of a lawsuit.[65]

Although nothing in the code compelled the Supreme Court to abandon the prewar theory of clarification, several elements produced this drastic change of doctrine. First and foremost, the Supreme Court seemed to share the common enthusiasm of the profession for the postwar reforms tending to democratize procedure. Many of the justices had been active leaders in the postwar reforms and undoubtedly had come to think that the older theory was paternalistic and incompatible with the basic philosophy of the new era. Also, one third of the court had been drawn from the bar, and their views may have reflected the lawyer's emerging consciousness of his responsibility. Furthermore, the new Supreme Court's heavy case load made almost impossible the kind of close examination of trial records which adherence to the older theory would have required. The fifteen justices of the Supreme Court[66] had numerous new and difficult questions to adjudicate, such as the constitutionality of legislation and administrative suits. The number of appeals from the High Courts was slowly but steadily climbing.[67] In these circumstances, policing the requirement of clarification would have been most difficult.[68]

[64] See, e.g., Hokkaidō Denki Kabushiki Kaisha (Hokkaido Electric Co.) v. Okuda, Supreme Court, I Petty Bench, Nov. 27, 1952, 6 SAI-HAN MINSHŪ 1062: In an eviction case D, the purchaser of a building on a separately owned piece of land, exercised his right to sell the building to P, the landowner. By statute, P was obligated to buy the building from D (he refused to lease the land to D). Consequently, D acquired the right to refuse to vacate until P paid for the building. But judgment was entered for P on the ground that D did not clearly present this defense in his answer. On *revision* the Supreme Court sustained the judgment on the ground that the trial court had no duty to clarify whether the defendant would rely on the defense. In this decision the Court bluntly stated that "the trial court had no duty to check with or urge the party to exercise a certain right even when the acquisition of that right by the party seemed to be supported by the evidence."

[65] See, e.g., Isomura, *Shakumei-ken* (The Power to Clarify), in 2 MINJI SOSHŌ HŌ GAKKAI (Civil Procedure Law Association), MINJI SOSHŌ HŌ KŌZA (Collected Essays on the Law of Civil Procedure) 473, 491 (1954).

[66] The number of the postwar Supreme Court justices is fixed at fifteen by law (Court Law, art. 5), while the number of judges in the prewar Great Court of Judicature was forty-six in 1935 (twenty-six in the civil departments and twenty in the criminal departments). Partly because of the new recruitment system, the average age of the justices is higher than in the prewar period.

[67] In 1959, 1,284 cases (41.7 percent of the High Court judgments) were appealed. In addition to this, the postwar Supreme Court reviews numerous criminal cases appealed from the High Courts (in 1959 criminal cases involving 3,208 defendants were appealed).

[68] It should be added that from 1950 to 1954, the Court was free by statute to reject appeals which did not present an "important question of law." The Court frequently declared that the claim that the trial judge insufficiently exercised his clarifying function could not be an "important question of law."

Although the Supreme Court seemed to abandon the clarification requirement, it did not necessarily discourage the trial judge from exercising a clarifying function. That remained discretionary, and the court did not indicate how the discretion should be exercised as a matter of good trial administration. It is difficult to generalize about what actually occurs in the trial courts. One thing is clear: the Supreme Court decisions and the then-supporting dicta of the scholars freed these courts from the fear of reversal and the pressure implicit in the requirement. The postwar image of the passive court might appear particularly attractive to trial judges in the metropolitan areas where case loads were becoming increasingly heavy.[69] Also, younger judges, particularly those educated in the immediate postwar years, tended to embrace the adversary philosophy.[70] On the other hand, older judges dedicated to the philosophy that the judge must lead if the litigant is to receive justice were perhaps rather reluctant to give up that philosophy and the status with which it clothed the court. Though the situation during the first postwar decade was thus ambiguous, in general these years saw a less vigorous and active exercise of the clarifying function.[71]

Beginning in around 1954, a reaction gradually set in. The glamor of some phases of the "democratic movement," sometimes misunderstood or ill understood, began to fade. In particular, the illusion that the adversary philosophy was inevitably tied to the development of democratic institutions was exposed. It has been urged that the Japanese bar, for reasons already discussed earlier in this essay, lacks the capacity to make the adversary concept work. Criticism of "excessive emphasis" on the adversary principle has become more and more outspoken. A leading and influential judge of the Tokyo High Court declared that, whereas the prewar Great Court unduly interfered with the trial court's administration, postwar Supreme Court decisions invite the trial judge to allow justice to the litigant to be fortuitous.[72] He urged that the spirit of "making the party win who should win" continue to mold the conduct of the trial judge. The only plausible justification for the new approach, he said, was that the "education of the lawyer through laissez-faire training" requires that he have the experience of losing his case by poor presentation. However, "Why should the interests of the party-citizens, for whom the suit is usually the only experience of litigation

[69] In 1935, 4,796 suits were filed in the Tokyo District Court; in 1955, the number had increased to over 10,000. Many a judge had 300 or 400 cases on his active calendar. See 61 DAI NIPPON TEIKOKU SHIHŌ-SHŌ, note 15, TŌKEI HYŌ (Statistical Tables) pt. at 48; SAIKŌ SAIBANSHO JIMU-SŌKYOKU, note 40, at 135. Cf. notes 34 and 127.

[70] About 1950, the writer heard a District Court judge say to an appellant who complained of the inadequate advocacy of his lawyer at the first-instance trial: "After all, he is your lawyer whom you chose just as you chose your doctor. One should be responsible for the results obtained by his lawyer as well as those obtained by his doctor." The thought expressed would have been unthinkable in the prewar period.

[71] See Niimura et al., *Minji Saiban no Sho-mondai* (Various Problems in Civil Trial), 13 Hōsō Jihō (Journal of the Jurists' Association) 286, 303–305 (1961).

[72] MURAMATSU, note 30, at 23.

throughout their lives, be sacrificed for the sake of the education of lawyers?"[73] Comments in the same vein by senior judges have become common,[74] and various illustrations of undesirable administration (usually by young judges) have been cited.[75]

Interestingly, the opinion of legal scholars (always of considerable influence in Japan) which had generally supported the postwar Supreme Court decisions, is now showing some change. Japanese universities have returned to the prewar practice of sending faculty members to study in Germany and other European countries. Some who came back from Germany were impressed by postwar German civil procedure, which has not only rejected the adversary principle but has even increased the prewar emphasis on the trial judge's guiding role. Their champion is Akira Mikazuki, a Tokyo University professor, who in a recent book advocated a return to the requirement theory of clarification and vigorously criticized the postwar decline of clarification as "an abnormal, isolated movement contrary to the world trend in civil procedure."[76]

Finally, it has been argued that even the Supreme Court may be gradually shifting its position. In a study published in 1960, two scholars, after an exhaustive analysis of all postwar decisions of the Supreme Court, including those not published in the official reports, concluded that since 1954 the court has reversed a considerable number of trial-court judgments because of failure to clarify.[77] It was pointed out that the court carefully avoided the expression "duty to clarify" and used instead a favorite vague term, "insufficient inquiry."[78] It is still too early to say that the Supreme Court is

[73] Muramatsu, note 56, at 534.

[74] See, e.g., Niimura et al., note 71, at 303, 305, 306.

[75] Some judges automatically adopt all offered witnesses without preliminary clarification concerning the relevance of their testimony. For example, in a divorce case a trial judge found a husband to be impotent solely on the basis of the wife's testimony, without suggesting to the defendant that he offer expert testimony on the issue. In another case a trial judge accepted without clarification an allegation that the party had succeeded to the title to immovable property as the "heir to the property of the House," a kind of succession legally impossible under the postwar Civil Code. See MURAMATSU, note 30, at 18; Muramatsu, *Saiban ni Tsuite no Ichi Kōsatsu* (A Study of Trial), 2 MINJI SOSHŌ HŌ ZASSHI (Journal of Civil Procedure Law) 70, 91 (1955); SAIKŌ SAIBANSHO JIMU-SŌKYOKU (General Secretariat of the Supreme Court), DAI ISSHIN KYŌKA NI KAN-SURU MINJI SAIBANKAN KAIDŌ YŌROKU (Record of the Civil Judge Meeting on Strengthening the First-Instance Trial) 81 (Minji Saiban Shiryō (Civil Trial Materials) No. 33, 1953).

[76] MIKAZUKI, MINJI SOSHŌ HŌ (The Law of Civil Procedure) 164–65 (1959). It should be noted that this view is still a minority position among Japanese legal scholars.

[77] SAITO & YASUI, SENGO NO SHAKUMEI-KEN NI KAN-SURU HANREI (Postwar Cases Concerning the Power to Clarify) (1960).

[78] *Ibid.*, 170. "Insufficient inquiry" means that the trial court failed to inquire sufficiently into the case and hence violated the procedural law. This term had often been used by the prewar Great Court of Judicature in reversing judgments of trial courts for failure to clarify. See Isomura, note 65, at 480. It is reported that in one decision not published in the official reports the First Petty Bench of the postwar Supreme Court dared to say that "the trial court erred in not having clarified the point." Judgment of June 25, 1959, Supreme Court, I Petty Bench; see SAITO & YASUI, note 77, at 180.

returning to the requirement theory. Most of the cases cited by these scholars are cases in which the trial court's factfinding was not supported by sufficient evidence or cases in which the trial court violated the party-presentation principle.[79] Reversal was not for a failure to clarify.[80] A close reading of the opinions in these cases, however, does justify the view that since about 1954 the Supreme Court has tended to scrutinize the conduct of the trial court more closely. These writers made an interesting attempt to relate this tendency to a decrease in the case load of the Supreme Court after 1954.[81] Probably more significant, however, is the fact that since 1950 several new justices with long trial-court experience, especially in the High Courts, have been appointed to the Supreme Court,[82] while many of the justices who were more or less identified with the postwar legislation have retired. It may be that the criticism expressed by High Court judges is now gaining direct expression through their colleagues promoted to the Supreme Court bench.

Much can be said in favor of both views respecting trial-court administration of the discretionary clarifying function. The drastic minimization of clarification advocated soon after the last war seems ultimately incompatible with the present procedural system which still assumes the directive power of the trial judge. It should be noted that in addition to the code provision for clarification, several provisions according the judge various directive powers, such as the selection of evidence (article 259) and the *ex officio* examination of a party witness (article 336),[83] remain unchanged. The judge's function both in narrowing the issues before the proof-taking stage and in drafting elaborate judgments assume his active clarification. Moreover, it would be unrealistic to expect career judges with their energy and long tradition to exhibit complete self-restraint. Finally, Japanese litigants continue to look to the judges as well as their lawyers to ensure a full canvas of the facts and ultimate justice.[84]

[79] That is to say, the Supreme Court reversed the trial court for finding, as the basis of its judgment, facts that were not clearly alleged by the party or were not supported by sufficient evidence.

[80] Theoretically, therefore, the trial court on remand was left free to clarify or simply to reject the claim or defense. Practically, however, the usual course would be the former — to clarify.

[81] SAITO & YASUI, note 77, at 194.

[82] Since 1947, three justices who had been judges on a postwar High Court have been appointed to the Supreme Court.

[83] Although art. 261, which had authorized general *ex officio* proof taking, was deleted, art. 336 giving a trial judge discretionary authority to subpoena a party witness *ex officio* was preserved.

[84] One judge has cited an interesting episode involving a citizen who strongly rejected the idea of looking upon his lawyer as "the only doctor in his case" and asserted that both the judge and the lawyer should be his doctors, collaborating to protect his interest. See Someno et al., *Minji Saiban no Hōkō* (The Direction of Civil Trial), 32 HŌRITSU JIHŌ 1022, 1036 (1960). The same episode was cited by another judge as well representing the general feeling of the

On the other hand, it is neither realistic nor desirable to expect the pendulum to swing back to its prewar position. Although the practicing profession has generally recognized the necessity of clarification, a strong feeling of opposition has developed among the postwar lawyers, particularly among younger lawyers who treasure their new role in litigation, to an overly paternalistic exercise of the clarifying function. They fear that continued employment of the clarifying function will frustrate the postwar hope for the development of skill, initiative, alertness, and resourcefulness by the Japanese lawyer.

It has become clear, therefore, that some position between the two extremes should be found. Statements by several presiding judges of the Tokyo courts[85] indicate that the trial judges are now steadily gravitating to a midway approach. What is meant by "midway" is somewhat abstract and hard to describe, but we may summarize the general direction in which the trial judges are moving. They continue to believe that clarification is an indispensable tool for achieving justice. When litigants have only limited capacity and resources, as in Japan, why should the judge not use his skill and knowledge to assure that the case will develop in a proper and fair way? The identification of clarification with an undemocratic, inquisitorial method is firmly rejected. On the contrary, it is believed that all modern litigation systems make provision for clarification in proper cases. The manner and extent of clarification, however, must not strip the litigant and his lawyer of responsibility for the development of the case or defenses. The main objective of clarification, therefore, should be to enable the judge to obtain a clear grasp of the case and to prevent injustice caused by technical defects in the presentation. Clarification should not be used by the court arbitrarily to control the development of the case. The judge should always adjust a variance or settle an inconsistency in the litigant's presentation; but the litigant's ideas should be utilized. The judge's idea should not be forced on the litigant, as was often the case in the prewar practice. Finally, clarification in nonrepresented cases should be very active.

It is not likely that the requirement theory in its prewar form will be revived. So long as the present heavy case load and the urgent need for faster disposal of appeals continues, and only drastic measures could change the situation, the Supreme Court cannot afford to resume a meticulous examination of trial records. Moreover, since such review would again tempt the trial judge to tolerate delays in presentation, it is inconsistent with the Supreme Court's policy adopted in 1956 of "strengthening the first-instance trial" by improving procedures to encourage a concentrated trial

---

ordinary Japanese citizen. See Ishii, *Minji Hōtei Zakki* (Miscellaneous Notes on Civil Courts), HANREI JIHŌ (The Case Journal) no. 249, at 4 (1961).

[85] See Niimura et al., note 71, at 286, 305; Ishii, note 84, at 2; *ibid.*, no. 250, at 2 (1961); no. 251, at 2 (1961); no. 259, at 2 (1961).

and reduce the appeal rate.[86] Here considerations of efficiency prevail. Some scholars and judges argue that under the present system the Supreme Court should reverse the trial court's judgment only in case of clear, manifest injustice — such as an unfavorable judgment because of a minor variance between pleading and proof.[87]

The same considerations of efficiency argue, in the opinion of many scholars and judges, with even greater cogency against the wisdom of active clarification in the second-instance trial.[88] A drastic reduction of clarification by the second-instance court is unlikely in the immediate future, however, because the shortage of judicial personnel still requires that heavy case assignments be given to relatively inexperienced first-instance judges sitting alone, in whom the elder judges of the High Courts do not have complete confidence.[89] The ultimate solution of this problem may lie in eliminating both the trial function of the second-instance court[90] and the hierarchical career-judge system, but these reforms will take a long time to accomplish.

PRETRIAL PREPARATION AND THE EXAMINATION OF WITNESSES

Prewar Practices

Under the prewar Japanese system, the pretrial investigation and marshaling of evidence which characterize the American lawyer's pretrial efforts were largely relegated to the trial stage and the active control of the court. Indeed, the court initiated its inquiry without the benefit of well-informed counsel. Since pretrial interview of witnesses was forbidden, a lawyer's pretrial investigation was largely confined to interviewing his client (and possibly members of his family and his employees) and examin-

[86] See Dai Isshin Kyōka Hōsaku Jisshi ni Tsuite (Concerning the Enforcement of Measures to Strengthen First-Instance Trials), Supreme Court Circular *Sōsō* (General Secretariat, General Affairs Bureau) No. 216, June 7, 1956. See also SAIKŌ SAIBANSHO JIMU-SŌKYOKU, note 75.

[87] See 1 KANEKO, note 14, at 330.

[88] The second-instance court still engages in extensive proof taking that frequently provides a basis for reversing the judgments of the first instance. In 1958 the average number of witnesses examined by High Courts (in cases disposed of by formal judgments) was 4.3. See SAIKŌ SAIBANSHO JIMU-SŌKYOKU (General Secretariat of the Supreme Court), SHŌWA 33 NEN MINJI JIKEN NO GAIKYŌ (The General Condition of Civil Cases in 1958) 16, 36 (1959).

[89] High Court sessions are conducted by a collegiate bench of three judges, each with more than ten years' experience, while District Court cases are, as a rule, handled by a single judge (Court Law, arts. 18, 26). Because of the special law qualifying an assistant judge with more than five years' experience, many young assistant judges with less than ten years' experience handle cases alone. In 1959, 93.6 percent of the District Court cases were handled by a single judge. See SAIKŌ SAIBANSHO JIMU-SŌKYOKU, note 40, at 140. One or two assistant judges with less than ten years' experience may join in the formation of a three-judge bench in the District Court. The average age of district judges is substantially lower than that of the High Court judges. So long as this situation prevails, it seems unrealistic to expect the second-instance judge to refrain from active clarification.

[90] Of course, such a change would take the Japanese procedural system still further from its Continental European antecedents toward Anglo-American arrangements.

ing the documents and any real evidence under the client's control. Even this limited investigation was apt to be done casually, for the lawyer generally received little compensation from his client at the pretrial stage. Moreover, since in most ordinary transactions lawyers were seldom employed, documentary evidence, which might have aided the lawyer in understanding the case, was usually entirely lacking or very poorly drafted.[91] No system corresponding to the modern American discovery apparatus existed.[92]

Unlike the American practice, the court, rather than counsel, actively controlled the preliminary screening of evidence and planned its order of presentation. Since the court acquired a good knowledge of the case, it often exercised a broad discretion in rejecting offers of cumulative evidence or evidence of little probative value; only rarely did the Great Court of Judicature reverse a trial court's judgment on the ground of improper exclusion of evidence.[93] Conversely, when its clarification of the case indicated, the court would frequently suggest that a party present further evidence.

The court exercised control over the selection of witnesses, often selecting some on the basis of a list of "topics to be examined" submitted by counsel in writing.[94] Some judges, contrary to the official policy of the law, sub-

[91] Even commercial transactions involving substantial sums of money were frequently executed without a written contract. To insist upon a meticulously written contract was often regarded as insulting to the other party.

[92] However, there were some devices with functions similar to American discovery procedures. Even before filing suit, a party could request the court to take as proof, for example, the testimony of a seriously ill witness, which might be unavailable at trial (CODE OF CIVIL PROCEDURE arts. 343–351-2). After filing suit, a party could under certain circumstances secure a court order for the production of documentary evidence in the possession of the opponent or a third party (arts. 312–318). Moreover, upon the request of a party, the court would examine the party himself or take proof on certain matters specified by law when necessary to "clarify the procedural relationship" (art. 127).

All these devices were designed either to enable the litigants to secure certain limited types of evidence or to help the court determine the underlying issues. They were in no sense intended to give the litigant an opportunity to engage in broad exploratory operations in the pretrial marshaling of evidence. Of course, during the early stages of the trial itself, the litigant would be helped in marshaling evidence through both the exchange of documentary evidence and discussions concerning the relevance and authenticity of evidence and the contributions that witnesses would make. But being a part of the trial itself, such discovery, unlike American pretrial discovery, was subject to limitations based upon considerations of relevance and trial expedition. Cf. Kaplan, von Mehren & Schaefer, note 44, at 1246 (1958).

[93] Generally the prewar Great Court required that the trial court admit evidence when it was the "only evidence" offered to prove an issue. Gōshi Kaisha Irobe Ginkō (Partnership in Commendam Irobe Bank Co.) v. Matsushita, Great Court of Judicature, II Civil Department, Nov. 12, 1909, 15 DAI-HAN MINROKU 874. For certain exceptions to this rule, see 1 KANEKO, note 14, at 722.

[94] As a legal matter, the list of "topics to be examined" was supposed to be drafted by the court and presented to the witness before examination in order to refresh his memory (CODE OF CIVIL PROCEDURE art. 276). But in actual practice the court always requested the proponent to draft the list. This practice also gave notice to the opponent of expected lines of examination. Art. 31 of the Civil Procedure Regulations of 1956 made the drafting of "topics" mandatory.

poenaed party witnesses before other witnesses had been heard.[95] The court also called its own expert witnesses.

A policy of insulating witnesses from the litigant's influence pervaded the whole trial process. The practice of bringing one's witness to court was never encouraged. Instead, with minor exceptions, the only legal way of securing a witness' testimony was through a subpoena.[96] The witness' fee — a rather nominal one fixed by law — was paid directly by the court.[97] Compensating a witness in excess of the statutory fee for lost time could even suggest solicitation of perjury. However, the prewar system did not entirely preclude the possibility that the litigant and his counsel might have influenced the witness. The litigant was free to interview the witness, and the practice of serving the witness with the topics to be examined (drafted by the proponent) gave the litigant an opportunity to suggest the tenor of the testimony desired. Also, as the case unfolded in the piecemeal trial, prior proof takings might provide the basis for coaching a witness effectively.[98]

In carrying out its responsibility for the examination of witnesses, a court devoted much time to studying the record and preparing questions. The examination itself could cover any matter deemed relevant to the issues or the credibility of the witness, for a court was not hampered by rules of evidence;[99] nor was objection to the judge's examination permitted.

After the judge completed his examination, the parties could ask supplementary questions or request the court to do so.[100] However, the court's examination was generally so exhaustive that supplementary examination by the parties was infrequent and usually of little importance. Consequently, an attorney had little opportunity to develop skill in examining. His main concern was to sense the judge's thinking from the latter's examination as

[95] Art. 336 of the CODE OF CIVIL PROCEDURE states: "If the court is unable to become convinced through the taking of evidence, it may, on motion or *ex officio,* examine the parties themselves. In this case it may cause the parties to take an oath." The Great Court of Judicature declared that the violation of this provision by the trial court would not constitute grounds for reversal of judgment, and in actual practice the parties who had participated in the disputed transaction were almost always examined.

[96] See CODE OF CIVIL PROCEDURE art. 276.

[97] Civil Procedure Costs Law, Law No. 64 of 1890, arts. 9–13, 17. This inflexible and nominal fee system was one of the reasons for the frequent nonappearance of witnesses.

[98] In cases in which testimony was permitted in the appellate court, the danger of coaching was especially great. For this reason, a prewar trial judge stated that such testimony was not very reliable. See SAIKŌ SAIBANSHO JIMU-SŌKYOKU, note 75, at 173.

[99] In actual practice Japanese judges tried to avoid certain kinds of testimony. For example, hearsay was excluded by instructing a witness to relate only what he had experienced. But a judge could admit even hearsay testimony whenever he deemed it necessary and proper without risk of reversal by the appellate court. Beginning in 1907, the prewar supreme court considered that under the "principle of free evaluation" hearsay was fully admissible. E.g., Murakami v. Yamaguchi, Great Court of Judicature, United Civil Departments, April 29, 1907, 13 DAI-HAN MINROKU 458. As for the postwar position of the hearsay rule, see note 116 below.

[100] CODE OF CIVIL PROCEDURE art. 299 (amended by Law No. 149 of 1948). Prior to the 1926 code revision, a party was not permitted to question witnesses. CODE OF CIVIL PROCEDURE art. 315 (2) (amended by Law No. 61 of 1926).

a guide to the presentation of further evidence.[101] The judge's dominant role in the examination of witnesses perhaps reflected the citizen's deference to government officials and a reluctance to cooperate with private lawyers even in the courtroom.

The experience a presiding judge gained by examining numerous witnesses and developing the facts of various cases helped to create a highly skilled judiciary. Observation of a senior judge's conduct and constant discussions of cases with him played a major role in the judicial training of a young associate judge.

However, the development of a highly skilled judiciary may not have compensated for the risks of improper judicial factfinding inherent in the court's extensive control over both the presentation of evidence and examination of witnesses. Lawyers were likely to be less resourceful in the production of evidence. Moreover, supplementary examination might receive little attention from a judge who was overconfident about the skill of his own inquiry; as an investigator preoccupied by his own line of thought, the judge might unconsciously fail to explore important points or lose objectivity in evaluating testimony. There was also the danger that impeaching questions put by the judge would give the appearance of unfairness or partisanship.

The prewar piecemeal trial was not a matter of design; rather it was an accepted fact. The 1926 code revision attempted to achieve a concentrated trial, but the piecemeal trial survived throughout the whole prewar period, for some good reasons. Most important was the litigant's limited capacity for and restricted role in pretrial preparation. Also, the step-by-step inquiry into fact seemed to the court, as well as to the litigants, to be an easier and more natural process of proof than that permitted by the concentrated trial. The presiding judge could hear proof first that would help him to understand the case and prepare him for later examinations. The gradual process of exploration aided an inexperienced member of the court in understanding the case. Moreover, the piecemeal trial effectively prevented such unfair tactics as surprise and, to a considerable extent, succeeded in eventually exhausting the available evidence. The requirement of an elaborate judgment precluded the court from rendering an on-the-spot judgment and in this way somewhat lessened the attractiveness of the concentrated trial.

The piecemeal trial also encouraged settlement during trial, providing time and opportunity for negotiating a fair and acceptable compromise, and thus fitted well the traditional attitudes favoring amicable settlement.[102]

[101] See Somiya, *Soshō Tetsuzuki Tō Kanken* (Some Personal Observations on Litigation Procedure, Etc.), 11 Jiyū to Seigi (Freedom and Justice) no. 4, at 23 (1960).

[102] It is important to notice that landlord-tenant cases occupied a large part of the prewar calendar — in 1935 about 14 percent of the civil cases filed in the Local Courts. In these cases the relation between the opposing litigants was highly personal and settlement was always considered the best solution. In 1935, of 250,787 pending cases in District and Local

Through frequent personal contacts at successive sessions and a growing understanding of the opponent's case, the emotional tension of litigants was thought to be gradually eased and the desirability of compromise encouraged. The judge was to urge settlement whenever the proof suggested its desirability.[103]

However, delay in reaching judgment was the inevitable price of the piecemeal trial. Since the interval between sessions was sometimes as long as two or three months, an ordinary suit might well take a year or more to complete.[104] Unprepared lawyers, nonappearance of expected witnesses, and frequent shifts of judges resulted in many sessions being wasted or postponed, and shrewd defense attorneys often took advantage of the opportunities for delaying tactics. The piecemeal trial also forced the judge to rely very heavily upon recorded testimony that was usually in summary form. The flavor and the details of testimony and the demeanor of witnesses were all but forgotten by the time the judge made his findings. This situation was greatly aggravated by the frequent shifts or promotions of judges.

The principal reason why the 1926 revision did not eliminate the piecemeal trial was the lack of effective methods of pretrial preparation. Although the revised code required the litigants to exhaust their presentations and to fix issues with finality in preparatory procedure,[105] the policy against the pretrial interview of witnesses by counsel was firmly maintained. Moreover, the court itself was not empowered to conduct proof taking at a pretrial stage. Determination of issues was consequently often difficult until the proof-taking part of the trial stage was well under way. When the courts strictly enforced the rule against further presentation at the trial stage, the parties would present all conceivable allegations and offers of proof at the pretrial stage. This naturally prolonged preparatory procedure, multiplied the issues, and made a concentrated trial still more difficult. Furthermore, the courts of first instance were discouraged in their efforts to achieve a concentrated trial by the practice of the second-instance courts of reopening the case to allow evidence that was earlier excluded in strict enforcement of the rule against additional presentations. Accordingly, the trial judges soon gave up the "stage-preclusion policy" of the code, and the whole scheme of concentrated trial collapsed.[106]

Courts, 113,867 cases were disposed of by either judicial settlement or voluntary dismissal (usually on the basis of an out-of-court settlement).

[103] See CODE OF CIVIL PROCEDURE art. 136.

[104] See note 15.

[105] See CODE OF CIVIL PROCEDURE arts. 249 (amended by Law No. 149 of 1948)–255.

[106] For a more elaborate discussion of the experience with the concentrated trial plan of the 1926 code, see Noma, *Benron no Shūchū* (Concentration of Party Presentation), in 2 MINJI SOSHŌ HŌ GAKKAI (Civil Procedure Law Association), MINJI SOSHŌ HŌ KŌZA (Collected Essays on the Law of Civil Procedure) 393 (1954).

Postwar Developments

Unlike the legislative treatment of clarification, the postwar legislation concerning the role of the litigant in the marshaling and presentation of evidence spoke with vigor and clarity. Article 2 of the 1950 Regulations Concerning Continuous Trial in Civil Procedure (re-enacted, with some changes of wording,[107] as article 4 of the Civil Procedure Regulations, 1956) provided:

The parties shall beforehand investigate in detail the factual relationship in regard to the witnesses and other evidence, and without waiting for clarification by the court, exhaust their allegations and their duty to present evidence.

Article 294 of the Code of Civil Procedure, as revised in 1948, provides:

A witness is examined first by the party who has proposed the examination, and after this examination is concluded, the other party may examine him.

The presiding judge may, after examination by the parties is concluded, examine the witness.

The presiding judge may at any time, when he recognizes that it is necessary, carry on an examination himself or permit examination by the parties.

The profession in general accepted this reform with enthusiasm. But its application was quite another matter.

Many difficulties immediately became apparent. Although pretrial interviews with witnesses were now encouraged, citizens were still very reluctant to cooperate with lawyers. Even "neutral witnesses," averse to becoming involved in litigation, often refused to meet with a lawyer. Because communication and transportation were still poor in 1950, simply locating a witness was often very difficult. Also, most lawyers maintained an individual practice involving a number of small cases for modest fees and could not devote much effort to time-consuming investigation. Only some metropolitan lawyers, representing well-to-do clients or big companies were able to engage in effective pretrial investigation.[108] Since the old piecemeal trial still prevailed, lawyers were always tempted to resume the easy method of relying upon "discovery in trial."

Furthermore, though some judges and scholars advocated a pretrial discovery system,[109] the bar showed little interest, perhaps because its

[107] The phrase of art. 2 of the 1950 Regulation, "without waiting for clarification by the court," was eliminated by the 1956 Regulation.

[108] A lawyer representing a well-organized company is usually assigned some of the company's employees for pretrial investigation. This practice helps a lawyer considerably in his preparation.

[109] See, e.g., Kozeki, *Minji Soshō ni okeru Keizoku Shinri* (The Continuous Trial in Civil Procedure), 4 Hōsō Jihō no. 11, at 29, 44 (1952); Tanaka, *Beikoku Rempō Minji Soshō Hō ni okeru Kaiji no Seido* (The System of Discovery under the U.S. Federal Rules of Civil Procedure), 4 Hōsō Jihō no. 11, at 1, 28 (1952).

members saw in discovery devices a substantial additional cost for which they would find it hard to obtain compensation.[110] The setting in which the reform was to operate, then, remained substantially unchanged. Lacking experience, Japanese lawyers were clumsy amateurs in the examination of witnesses. Their questions were apt to be inept and time-consuming; it was said that examination of a witness by a lawyer took twice as long as examination by a judge.[111] For a while after 1948, many lawyers simply read aloud the written "topics" and asked a witness to answer yes or no.[112] The gross leading question was very common. Crossexamination, though frequently used, was often a mere repetition of the direct examination or was unduly argumentative. For many lawyers, crossexamination was a vehicle for arguing the falsity or error of the testimony rather than a vehicle for eliciting additional testimony and for testing the witness' credibility. Objections to improper or irrelevant questions were rarely made, for not only were lawyers unaccustomed to objecting but each had an interest in being able to pose freely leading and "fishing" questions.[113] Older lawyers frequently felt personally insulted by an opponent's objection. Even after the 1956 changes regulated objections and rulings in detail,[114] these difficulties persisted.

The judiciary also had difficulties with the new procedure. Unlike the prewar practice which had permitted the court to plan the progress of the case, many trial judges tended to admit all tendered evidence and to accept the order of proof suggested by the litigants; little judicial direction was given in the trial. But the role of the court under the new rules was the problem that most concerned the judges. It was clear that in nonrepresented

[110] Also, Japanese society, long under the spell of the Continental legal tradition, is not yet ready to accept the notion that the attorney, who is a private person, can exercise the power of compulsory investigation over citizens in the capacity of an "officer of the court." It is still not uncommon for the police to refuse to show the record of a traffic accident to a lawyer conducting a pretrial investigation in a civil case.

[111] See KISHI & YOKOGAWA, JIJITSU SHINRI (Trial of Fact) 87 (1960); Oga, *Minji Soshō Hō Sokushin no Tame ni* (Toward Speeding Up Civil Procedure), JURIST no. 198, at 14, 18 (1960). One judge reported that the average length of time required for examination of a witness in his department of the Tokyo District Court during a two-month period was about thirty minutes. See Azegami, *Minji Soshō ni okeru Hinōritsu* (Inefficiency in Civil Procedure), 11 HŌSŌ JIHŌ no. 1, at 13; no. 2, at 224 (1959). Other judges have found that examinations take even longer in their courts. An additional reason for slowness is the fact that the people lack training in speaking in public.

[112] See Muramatsu, *Shōko ni okeru Benron Shugi* (The Principle of Party Presentation in Proof), in SŌSHŌ TO SAIBAN (Procedure and Trial), IWAMATSU SABURO SAIBANKAN KANREKI KINEN ROMBUN SHŪ (A Collection of Essays in Commemoration of the 61st Birthday of Justice Saburo Iwamatsu) 255, at 273 (Tarumi & Kaneko ed., 1956).

[113] KISHI & YOKOGAWA, note 111, at 75.

[114] Under arts. 34 and 35 of this Regulation, the court can prohibit questions it deems "improper," for example, as abstract, leading, insulting, repetitious, or as on matters that the witness had not observed himself or that require his opinion. Arts. 33–37 of the Regulation and art. 295 of the Code of Civil Procedure regulate the procedure for making objections and rulings.

cases the court should take over the whole examination. But what should be the scope of the court's supplementary questions when counsel is present? Should the court ever prohibit an improper question when the party failed to object? If so, when and by reference to what standards?

The responses of the trial judges to these problems immediately after 1948 were varied. Though some judges actively put supplementary questions and even took over the entire examination, uncertainty and lack of confidence under the new practice generally led to an attitude of restraint. The most extreme approach was the "policy of entire silence"—that is, no supplementary questions at all. In this, some judges were probably misled by the postwar concept of democratic procedure. Also, some judges may have believed that only through such judicial silence would lawyers be educated in the skills of examination, while others thought that supplementary questions would give the appearance of bias.

Judges tended to be lax in prohibiting improper questions. The lack of training in the new rules of evidence often made judges hesitate when quick rulings were required. Moreover, trained under the Continental system of "free evaluation," the judges were naturally inclined to be rather generous in permitting questions that would be considered improper in the American practice; they satisfied themselves by discounting the evidential value of the answers.[115] Some judges adopted the passive policy of waiting for counsel to object, which seldom actually occurred.[116]

Gradually, however, in the decade following the reform the confusion of the early postwar period resulting from judicial restraint and the insufficient skills of counsel gave way to efforts to adjust the new system to Japanese legal traditions. Indicative of this effort was the judiciary's new awareness that it must participate in examinations. Some judges began openly to criticize the policy of judicial silence. They recalled the wisdom

[115] See SHIHŌ KENSHŪJO (Legal Training and Research Institute), SHŌWA 33 NENDO TŌKYŌ-ŌSAKA CHI-SAI GŌDŌ SAIBAN JITSUMU KENKYŪ KYŌGI-KAI YŌROKU (Record of the 1958 Tokyo-Osaka District Court Joint Conference to Study Trial Practice) 28 (1959).

[116] Since an objection to improper questions is seldom raised, little case law has developed. Indeed, when an objection is raised, judges tend to be satisfied with giving a mild warning to counsel.

In connection with the rules of examination, a brief comment on the hearsay rule under the postwar system may be in order. In a 1957 case the appellant argued that since the rule against hearsay evidence is a corollary of crossexamination, such evidence should not be admitted under the postwar system. But the Supreme Court rejected this argument on the basis of the principle of free evaluation. Okano v. Okubo, Supreme Court, II Petty Bench, Feb. 8, 1957, 11 SAI-HAN MINSHŪ 258, [1957] SAIKŌ SAIBANSHO HANREI KAISETSU, MINJI HEN (Commentary on Supreme Court Cases, Book on Civil Affairs) 37 (note Doi). In a 1952 case, the Court rejected appellant's contention that the testimony of a sick witness, whose crossexamination was discontinued when his condition grew worse, was not admissible. Oda v. Minami, Supreme Court, II Petty Bench, Dec. 5, 1952, 6 SAI-HAN MINSHŪ 1217. The majority was composed of two justices with judicial backgrounds; a justice with previous experience in practice wrote a dissenting opinion, emphasizing the significance of the function of crossexamination.

of article 294, which assumes the participation of the trial judge in examination. "If the judge is a mere bystander," one judge challenged, "how can we keep the trust of our citizens who expect not only a lawyer but a judge to be a doctor for the social diseases of their society." [117] At a judicial conference in 1953, the Chief Justice of the Supreme Court, emphasizing the need for resolute trial supervision by the courts, stated that "the time wasted by inefficient trial conduct was neither the litigant's nor the court's, but the taxpayer's time." [118] It was also pointed out that, since witnesses were still often reluctant to tell a lawyer the truth, the judge's active participation in examination was needed.[119]

Thus, it became clear that what was needed was something similar to the "midway approach" adopted with regard to the clarification problem. A Tokyo judge recently remarked that the court's role in examination should be a "middle position between the English and Continental practice." [120] Of course, to find a solution which would preserve the advantages of both the prewar and postwar systems was not easy. The approach varied, and still does, with each judge. But from his trial observations, discussions at judicial conferences, and published statements of trial judges, this writer senses certain major new trends in trial practice.[121]

First of all, the courts are now more resolute in excluding irrelevant or improper questions. Moreover, judges are beginning to inquire into matters that litigants have failed to explore and to share with the litigants the responsibility for testing the credibility of witnesses. Also, many judges now believe that they should exclude tendered evidence that has not been sufficiently clarified and make suggestions, within the proper scope of clarification, concerning the order of presentation of evidence. Of course, the litigant's scheme of examination and presentation should not be interrupted by thoughtless interference on the court's part. The inquiry of the judge should be along the lines of the party's presentation and not the result of his own investigation.

At present judge and counsel collaborate. The bar appreciates the important role that a skilled judiciary can play in the examination of witnesses. The judiciary apparently has learned the basic truth that even the best efforts of judges are no substitute for the resourcefulness of litigants in probing for the facts. As a Tokyo judge recently stated, "The real basis of civil trial is the sufficient preparation of litigants" and "only through encouraging the active role of litigants in examination can good preparation be

[117] Niimura et al., note 71, at 313, 316.

[118] SAIKŌ SAIBANSHO JIMU-SŌKYOKU, note 75, at 142.

[119] See Niimura et al., note 71, at 286, 316.

[120] See Ishii, note 84, no. 245, at 6 (1961).

[121] As the clearest expression of such a view by several Tokyo trial judges, see Niimura et al., note 71, at 313–16.

expected."[122] Though many judges still complain about the present trial conduct of lawyers, they cherish the hope that the gradual improvement of counsel's skill will eventually succeed in making the new system work. At a recent judicial meeting, several leading Tokyo trial judges agreed that the improvement in the lawyer's examination skill in the past five or six years has been both steady and significant.[123] Japanese lawyers, particularly the younger ones educated after the war, now have a lively interest in trial tactics and treasure the role and status that the new system gives them. The fact that attorneys often vigorously object to judicial interference with their plan of examination demonstrates the bar's increasing confidence.[124] Training in examination skills through instruction at the Legal Training and Research Institute is often cited by judges as a justification for the hope that the Japanese lawyer will be able to fulfill his new role in the trial process.

Though progress toward better pretrial preparation remains rather slow, lawyers have shown an increasing interest in this area. Improvement in the lawyer's skill in examination indicates an improvement in pretrial preparation. Though pretrial investigation is still often inadequate, it is being given increasing attention by the bar. For example, neutral witnesses are now more frequently interviewed. Moreover, with more efficient trial preparation as one objective, city lawyers are beginning to establish law firms. Though achievement still falls far short of that which the new regulations contemplate, the prospect is by no means hopeless, and there is no urge to revert to the prewar practice.[125]

Of course, more effective pretrial preparation may carry certain dangers. As the pretrial interview of witnesses becomes more common, there is greater likelihood of witnesses being coached. However, a majority of the profession feels that the advantages gained from the resourcefulness of counsel under the postwar practice of "free preparation" greatly outbalance the possible harm of coaching through the use of pretrial interviews. Correct judicial finding may have been impeded under the old system by testimony of witnesses who were no longer "fresh." Since preservation of testimony close to the original experience is desirable, efforts should be made to encourage active pretrial inquiry under fair procedures, rather than unrealistically to isolate witnesses.

The early postwar period was marked by delay in adjudicating cases.

[122] *Ibid.*, 313.

[123] *Ibid.*, 318.

[124] See Inoue & Wakabayashi, *Tōjisha kara Mita Saibansho* (A Court as the Parties See It), SHIHŌ KENSHŪJO-HŌ (Journal of the Legal Training and Research Institute) no. 25, at 23, 29 (1960).

[125] Since 1948 only one judge and one lawyer have published proposals to abolish the present system and return to prewar judicial examination. They criticized mainly the inefficiency and unskillfulness of the litigant's examination and the danger of coaching. See Oga, note 111; Somiya, note 101. Relatively little attention has been paid to their views.

The situation was very acute in the District Courts, whose jurisdiction had been considerably enlarged by postwar legislation without increasing the number of judges.[126] Despite the fact that the total number of newly filed cases did not exceed the prewar figures, the average case load for a district judge had more than doubled.[127] The shortage of judges was especially felt in the courts of big cities where expanding populations multiplied disputes over housing matters. By 1950, a city judge often had several hundred pending cases on his calendar, and trials frequently extended over two or more years.[128] Consequently, when speed was essential, as in eviction and labor disputes, provisional orders were often used, and perhaps abused, as a substitute for ordinary procedures.[129] Mediation was another frequent substitute.[130] Besides this shortage of judges, the inefficient piecemeal trial procedure was a major cause of delay. Many trials extended over five or more sessions.[131] And, since hearings were frequently postponed, many sessions were unproductive.[132]

In order to expedite adjudication, a concentrated trial was introduced by article 20 of the 1950 regulation and now constitutes article 27 of the Civil Procedure Regulations:

> Where oral argument in a case in which the fixing of issues and evidence has been completed lasts two days or more, it shall be conducted continuously as far as possible until concluded. If it cannot be conducted continuously, the interval from session to session shall be made as short as possible.

[126] The prewar Local Court's jurisdiction included cases involving not over 1,000 yen (about 293 prewar dollars), while that of the postwar Summary Court was changed to 100,000 yen in inflated currency (about 278 postwar dollars).

[127] While the average yearly number of newly filed cases in the District Courts in 1934–1938 was 34,506, in 1958 the number was 72,890. Consequently, the average yearly case load for each district judge increased from 46.5 cases (1934–1938) to 93.93 cases (1958).

[128] In 1959, the average length of trial in the District Courts was 11.9 months, and in the High Courts about 45 percent of the appealed cases (except administrative actions) took more than a year for their disposal. See SAIKŌ SAIBANSHO JIMU-SŌKYOKU, note 40, at 39, 40, 140.

In 1959, 32.3 percent of the formal judgments rendered by the District Courts were appealed to a High Court, where 23.6 percent of those appealed were reversed or modified. See Saikō Saibansho Jimu-sōkyoku (General Secretariat of the Supreme Court), *Shōwa 34 Nen ni okeru Minji Jiken no Gaikyō* (The General Condition of Civil Cases in 1959), 12 HŌSŌ JIHŌ 1152, 1159, 1160 (1960).

[129] In 1959, 31,594 petitions for a provisional order or attachment were filed in the District Courts, while 66,384 ordinary suits were filed in the same year. SAIKŌ SAIBANSHO JIMU-SŌKYOKU, note 40, at 102.

[130] In 1959, 62,095 petitions for mediation were filed in the Summary Courts, only a third less than the 90,718 ordinary actions (*ibid.*, 348).

[131] The average number of oral sessions in the District Courts in 1953 was 7.3. See Iwaguchi, *Soshō Chien no Bōshi ni Kan-suru Jisshō-teki Kenkyū* (A Positive Study Concerning the Prevention of Procedural Delay), 7 SHIHŌ KENKYŪ HŌKOKUSHO (Justice Research Reports) no. 3, at 3–46 (1954).

[132] In addition to these causes of delay, there were such administrative problems as the inefficient organization of personnel, poor clerical facilities, shortage of clerks and reporters, and frequent transfers of judges. Delay was also caused by the generous opportunities for appeal.

Moreover, the regulation, unlike its 1926 predecessor, strongly encouraged and even obliged the litigant to make extensive pretrial preparation, including interviewing witnesses. The court's function of narrowing the issues at the pretrial stage and its strict control over the trial calendar were also emphasized.[133]

The new regulation was enthusiastically received by the legal profession, which believed that an emphasis upon pretrial preparation followed by a concentrated trial might provide an effective way to expedite proceedings. But many local judges immediately found that the contemporary practice did not provide a sufficient basis for the concentrated trial. For judges of large cities, the overwhelming case load made a sudden shift in trial schedules very difficult or impossible.[134] Except in very simple cases, the city and local courts continued to handle cases involving substantial issues in the traditional piecemeal way. Even a Tokyo judge who was enthusiastic about the concentrated trial admitted that in 1952 only 5 percent of his cases could be so handled.[135] Moreover, the legal profession, picturing the concentrated trial as nothing short of a continuous trial, tended to abandon their efforts in that direction whenever the continuous trial failed. Trial time did not decrease after 1950; instead, it steadily increased.[136]

But the major reason for the failure was the insufficiency of preparation. In litigation for which the parties were inadequately prepared, the strict enforcement of a one-session trial always ran the danger of producing injustice. A High Court judge remarked that District Court judges who were too concerned about a tight trial sometimes gave "surprise judgments," which necessitated reopening the case in the High Court.[137]

Achieving a concentrated trial was also made difficult by the old habit of easygoing trial conduct. In 1951, one fifth of the witnesses expected to be examined in the District Court did not appear.[138] Often their nonappearance was due to the failure of counsel to finish prior to trial all the required procedures for securing the witness' attendance,[139] as well as to the common

[133] The 1950 regulation made preparatory procedure discretionary, but, if no preparatory procedure was held, "preliminary oral sessions" were to be conducted to determine the issues in the case before proof taking.

[134] See Iwaguchi, note 131, at 37; Niimura et al., note 71, at 288.

[135] See Kozeki, note 109, at 29. According to a study made by one judge in 1953 of 99 cases in the Tokyo District Court, nine were tried in concentrated trials. See Iwaguchi, note 131, at 3–33.

[136] The average length of trial of ordinary suits tried by the District Courts in 1953, 1955, and 1957 were, respectively, 7.9, 10.4, and 12.0 months. See SAIKŌ SAIBANSHO JIMU-SŌKYOKU, note 40, at 42.

[137] MURAMATSU, note 48, at 124, 126, 128, 130; Niimura et al., note 71, at 293, 299. It was found that the appeal rate was generally high in cases handled by judges strongly enforcing a concentrated trial (see SAIKŌ SAIBANSHO, note 40, at 33).

[138] See Kozeki, note 109, at 53.

[139] For example, a proponent can be required to pay in advance to the court both the charge for service on the witness and the witness fee. CODE OF CIVIL PROCEDURE art. 106.

reluctance of witnesses to cooperate with judicial procedure.[140] But the court's failure to punish defaulting witnesses was a major weakness.[141]

There were many reasons for the lack of a resolute effort on the part of judges and lawyers vigorously to implement the concentrated-trial program. Insufficient understanding of the adversary philosophy by Japanese judges made it difficult for them to carry their responsibility. Younger judges lacked the prestige and experience necessary for controlling dilatory tactics. The still prevailing inclination toward settlement and the belief that it is best accomplished by a gradual exposure of each side to the other's position unconsciously led judges and lawyers to avoid an overly quick disposal of a case.[142] Unfortunately, the friendly settlement was often the best way to recover a claim, for law enforcement in general declined in the postwar years and execution against an unwilling debtor was often difficult.[143]

During the mid-1950s pessimism was widespread within the profession in the face of what appeared to be insurmountable difficulties in the way of achieving the concentrated trial. But gradually efforts toward the development of a modified concentrated-trial scheme emerged. Through the early experience of failure, the profession learned that under the Japanese system, with its lack of jury trial, strict and resolute trial supervision by the court is indispensable. Moreover, as the phrasing of article 27 itself suggests, the concentrated trial, in the strict technical sense of a continuous trial, is neither necessary nor desirable in complicated cases. Consequently, the judges have recently developed their own modified schemes. Though the emphasis varies with each judge, a general pattern has developed.[144] In order to familiarize themselves with the case before entering upon the examination of witnesses, judges hold an extensive preliminary inquiry which includes the examination of relevant documents. Then follow two or possibly three major proof-

[140] The transportation difficulties, the unfavorable attitude of a witness' employer, and the nominal amount of the witness fee were also reasons for a witness' failure to appear. See Iwaguchi, note 131, at 53.

[141] Attorneys too, being afraid of unfavorable testimony as a result of compelling a witness' appearance, are not inclined to request the court to take strict measures. See Nakamura et al., *Minji Soshō no Arikata ni Tsuite* (Regarding What Civil Litigation Ought to Be), 10 JIYŪ TO SEIGI 3–31 (1959).

[142] In 1959, 54 percent of the cases that the District Courts disposed of ended either in consent decrees or in voluntary dismissal (generally as a result of out-of-court settlement).

[143] MURAMATSU, SAIBANKAN TO HŌ (Judges and the Law) 66 (speech given at the May 1958 meeting of the Japan Philosophy of Law Association). For example, the housing shortage immediately after the war made the enforcement of an eviction very difficult. Consequently, a large number of these cases ended in settlement with the active encouragement of the court. The success of out-of-court settlement in these cases, which composed a large portion of the docket, stimulated settlement in other kinds of cases. The enforcement of monetary judgments also met various difficulties because of frequent fraudulent transfers by debtors, archaic judicial sale procedures, lack of effective supplementary procedures, and insufficient search by the lawyer for defendant's property. See Oga, note 111, at 19, 22.

[144] For the expression of such an approach by several Tokyo trial judges, see Niimura et al., note 71, at 294–98, 300.

taking sessions, in close sequence. The final session is designed to give counsel and the court an opportunity to pick up and tie together all the loose ends. All proof-taking sessions are carefully planned after discussion between the court and counsel, and counsel is instructed to follow the arranged schedule. Of course, in planning the trial schedule, the capacity of the parties, the complexity of the case and the necessity for a speedy adjudication are taken into account. Simple cases can often be disposed of in one session.

As one judge remarked, what has emerged is a planned rather than a concentrated trial.[145] This is probably a realistic and workable compromise. The early session of the trial under the new scheme may be used for the purpose of discovery.[146] Furthermore, the two- or three-step process prevents the danger of unfair surprise or premature disposition and often eliminates unnecessary proof taking.[147] Under this scheme, unproductive sessions can be minimized and the interval between sessions shortened. Many courts have gradually decreased the number of proof-taking sessions.[148] In fact, the average length of District Court trials has decreased a little since 1956.[149] Though the situation is still far from satisfactory, this trial scheme gives promise of improving the administration of justice.[150]

Conclusion

Let us now return to the question posed at the end of the first section. Is the postwar procedural experiment on the road to success? I think an affirmative answer is justified.

True, it is much too soon to measure the future confidently or to prophesy the patterns that will ultimately unfold. The experiment is still in progress. The procedural reforms that have been discussed, like many other postwar reforms, were drastic and also complex because of their interaction with diverse facets of the social and political order. Such changes inevitably produce temporary trauma and confusion as well as the need for new understanding and new patterns of thought and action. Accommodation is bound to be slow, a bit painful, and at times faltering. It is, I think, a tribute

[145] *Ibid.*, 298.

[146] Some judges supporting the planned-trial scheme have already started to use the first proof-taking session for this purpose. See *ibid.*, 293, 296.

[147] For example, by dividing proof taking into two parts — one part for the liability issue and the other for the damage issue — the court spares one session if liability is not established. Cf. Hosie v. Chicago & N.W. Ry., 282 F.2d 639 (7th Cir. 1960), *cert. denied*, 365 U.S. 814 (1961), 74 Harv. L. Rev. 781 (1961).

[148] Cf. Shihō Kenshūjo, note 115, at 29–37.

[149] The average trial length of ordinary actions (except administrative suits) in the District Courts was 12 months in 1957, 11.8 months in 1958, and 11.9 months in 1959. See note 128.

[150] As a result of judicial effort, in 1960 in the Tokyo District Court, a 7 percent rise in the appearance rate of witnesses was achieved over the years 1955–1958. See Niimura et al., note 71, at 290.

to the Japanese judge and lawyer that the accommodation has progressed so far and so well in so short a time. The basic themes of the reforms are, I think, in the Japanese law to stay. We may not yet be out of the woods, but progress in adjusting and adapting the changes to the peculiarities of our society will be steady.

The experiment with the adversary system has already produced noteworthy and socially desirable dividends. For the first time in Japanese history the door was opened to the lawyer to become an active, responsible, vital participant in the trial process. Scholars and lawyers have come to believe that heavy reliance upon the initiative, resourcefulness, and responsibility of the litigant is a guarantee that disputes will be judicially determined with fairness and efficiency. The lawyer, upon whom the litigant's burden rests, has acquired a new status not only in the courtroom but also potentially as a lawyer-citizen in the social order. If he pursues his opportunities, he can be a positive and influential force both in the administration of justice and in the affairs of society generally. It is true that the bar is still not well equipped fully to carry its new responsibilities. But there is no reason to be pessimistic. The significant improvement in the training of lawyers (as well as judges and procurators) during the postwar years will continue at an even faster pace. It is true that the bar's capacity to measure up depends in large measure on improvements in the economic position of the lawyer. But there is reason to think that attitudes about lawyers, the role of lawyers in society, and the litigation process held by Japanese business and by Japanese citizens generally will gradually change so that the lawyer's work will become more diversified, more remunerative, and more in demand.

In the applied administration of the postwar procedural reforms discussed in this essay, the gravitation from an exaggerated and extreme version of the adversary concept to what I have labeled a midway position probably suggests the pattern of the future in the District Courts. It seems clear that, as long as most litigants in the Summary Courts are not represented by counsel, the prewar pattern (quite similar to the procedure in many American small-claims courts) will be retained. The midway position is in a real sense a fusion of the Continental and the Anglo-American philosophies. It utilizes nicely the capacity of the judges without putting an undue strain on the potential capacity of the lawyers. Indeed, it may also approach the pattern of modern American nonjury trial as envisioned by such recent enactments as the Federal Rules of Civil Procedure. It is my hope and belief that the unique Japanese postwar experiment will ultimately contribute a new and workable pattern which will be of benefit to all procedural systems.

THE LEGAL PROFESSION IN JAPAN: ITS HISTORICAL DEVELOPMENT AND PRESENT STATE

Takaaki Hattori

ASSISTED BY RICHARD W. RABINOWITZ

UNTIL the collapse of the national policy of isolation toward the end of the Tokugawa regime, when Western civilization began to be introduced into Japan, no thought had been given in Japanese political philosophy to the separation of judicial institutions from general executive authority. The traditional principle, based upon Chinese thinking, was that governmental authorities should also handle judicial matters; as a logical consequence, judicial officers, as distinguished from administrative officials, did not exist.[1] Additionally, in part because a negative attitude in the society toward civil litigation was coupled with an extremely inquisitorial criminal procedure, the feudal regime did not permit representation, at least

Note. Mr. Hattori is a judge of the Tokyo District Court. B.Jur., Tokyo Imperial University, 1935. Appointed to the bench in 1938; served on the Legal Staff of the Ministry of Justice during 1946 and on the Legal Staff of the General Secretariat of the Supreme Court, 1947–1956; assigned as an Instructing Officer for Civil Trial to the Legal Training and Research Institute, 1956–1959. Participant, Japanese American Program for Cooperation in Legal Studies at Harvard University, 1954–1955, and at University of Michigan and Stanford University, 1955–1956; Research at Harvard, 1961. Served as reporter on various committees, including Council on the Legal System of the Ministry of Justice, the Selection Committee for Summary Court Judges, and the Supreme Court Committee for Civil Procedure Regulations. Author of BEIKOKU NI OKERU PRETRIAL OYOBI KAIJI NO SEIDO (The Systems of Pretrial and Discovery in the United States) (1958); writings in the field of judicial administration.

Mr. Rabinowitz is a practicing attorney in Tokyo. B.A., 1945, LL.B., 1950, M.A., 1951, Yale University; Ph.D., 1956, Harvard University.

[1] It was a principle of traditional Sino-Japanese political thought that the administration of justice could not be separated from general administration and, further, that the former was necessarily contained in the latter. See 2 KOBAYAGAWA, MEIJI HŌSEI SHI RON: KŌHŌ NO BU (A History of the Legal System in the Meiji Era: Part on Public Law) 936–37 (1940). Someno states that under the feudal system judicial power came into existence as *jurisdictio,* a part of the feudal lord's authority to govern within his domain and was broader in scope than judicial power as conceived in modern societies. Someno, *Saiban Seido* (The Judicial System), in 6 NIHON KINDAI HŌ HATTATSU SHI (A History of the Development of Modern Japanese Law) 3 (1959).

on a professional basis, in either civil or criminal proceedings.[2] Thus, a legal profession as such did not exist in premodern Japan.

THE PROFESSION IN THE FORMATIVE ERA

Shortly after it came to power in 1867, the new national government proclaimed its intention of adhering to the principle of the separation of powers.[3] However, the system of government actually established in 1869 followed the Ritsuryō institutions, which had existed in Japan many centuries before and were based upon T'ang Chinese models. These were completely inconsistent with the doctrine of Montesquieu which the government had enunciated only two years earlier. One explanation for this apparently surprising reversal is that power came into the hands of conservative leaders who were influenced by traditional Sino-Japanese political ideals; they also desired a general revival of classical traditions, one element of which was the "return" of administrative power to the imperial throne.[4]

However, shortly after he was appointed Minister of Justice, Shimpei Eto, who had a comparatively good understanding of Western judicial systems as well as an unusual enthusiasm for legal reform, and who probably was

[2] Prior to the Meiji Restoration, so-called *kujishi* performed some of the functions now performed by lawyers. However, the policy of the government was to suppress them on the ground that their actions stimulated undesirable litigation. See Rabinowitz, *The Historical Development of the Japanese Bar,* 70 HARV. L. REV. 61, 62–64 (1956); RABINOWITZ, THE JAPANESE LAWYER 26–31 (unpublished thesis in Harvard Law School Library) (1955). These two works are the most comprehensive and reliable studies available about the historical development and present situation of the Japanese bar. Although they are not referred to specifically hereafter for citation purposes, they have been consulted throughout.

[3] The new government announced its basic policies in the Seitaisho (Statement of the Form of Government) of June 11, 1868. Art. 1 read: "The authority of the Dajōkan (Great Council of State) shall be divided into three powers: legislative, judicial and executive."

It is said that the Seitaisho was strongly influenced by the description of the American system of government set forth in *Rempō Shiryaku* (A Brief Account of the Union), a guidebook republished in 1861 from the portion dealing with the United States in an 1838 book on world geography by an American, Elijah C. Bridgman, translated into Chinese as *Hai-kuo T'u-chih* (An Account of Geography Abroad). It contained a general introduction to the history, culture, and the geography of the United States. See MEIJI BUNKA SHI: HŌSEI HEN (A History of Meiji Culture: The Legal System) 110 (Ishii ed., 1954).

[4] "The leaders of the new Meiji government, whether they were conservative or progressive, all grew up under the influence of traditional political ideas in which there was no separation of judicial functions from administrative power. Therefore, although the doctrine of the separation of powers was formally announced at the beginning of the Meiji era, it was not easy for these leaders to think of judicial power as distinct from executive power. Similarly, executive and legislative power were mixed together in their thought. Rather early, however, the ideas of separating these two powers (executive and legislative) became clearly established in their thought because of the antagonism between those who wanted to convene the legislature and those who controlled the executive. Thus, it can be said that the history of judicial independence in the Meiji era (1867–1911) was a process of judicial power being set free from executive domination." KOBAYAGAWA, as in note 1, at 937. See also NORMAN, JAPAN'S EMERGENCE AS A MODERN STATE (1940); this work is perhaps the best source available in English on the characteristics of the Meiji era.

stimulated to some extent by personal ambition,[5] drafted the Shihō Shokumu Teisei (Justice Staff Regulations and Operating Rules, hereafter called Regulations) along quite liberal lines. These Regulations were promulgated into law in 1872.[6] They constituted the first Japanese judicial code and provided not only for the organization of the courts but also dealt with other matters relating to the administration of justice. Particularly to be noted is the fact that they contained provisions for the establishment of Local Courts as separate and distinct judicial institutions and provided for legal officers, both judges and procurators, whose functions were distinguished from those of general administrative officials. The Regulations also authorized so-called *daigennin* or advocates to represent parties in civil actions, thus casting aside the traditional principle that a litigant could not appear in court through a professional representative.

Although the reforms contemplated by the Regulations represented a drastic ideological departure from the traditional ideas briefly noted above, they did not provide for a complete separation of powers. This is most clearly seen in the fact that the Minister of Justice was the presiding judge of the Ministry of Justice Court, the court prescribed in the Regulations as the highest tribunal in the land. Additionally, the Minister of Justice was given complete authority over the appointment and removal of judges, and judgment could not be rendered in criminal cases involving political crimes such as treason until the Minister's approval had been obtained. Finally, the power to supervise the trial of grave crimes was reserved to the cabinet.[7] In practice the situation was made worse by the fact that the Local Courts, which had been established pursuant to the Regulations, were as a rule presided over by local administrative officials, just as the premodern courts

[5] Those who played leading roles in the Meiji Restoration were principally samurai of two of the major feudal fiefs, Satsuma and Choshu. Men from these two fiefs tended to hold disproportionate authority in the executive branch and in the military arm of the new government, believing as they did that leadership in the executive and the military meant assumption of hegemony over the government as a whole. In contrast, those who came from smaller and less powerful fiefs tended to enter the judiciary or take up other occupations within the administration. This inference finds support in the fact that Eto came from the Saga fief. Furthermore, promising young students of law at that time, such as Isobe and Ume, who also came from small fiefs, left Tokyo University, the principal center for the training of higher-echelon administrative officials, and entered the law school attached to the Ministry of Justice. There is also the case of a young Choshu graduate of the Tokyo University law department who gave up private practice and entered the executive at the strong urging of a leader of his fief. In this sense, movements for the independence and strengthening of judicial power at the beginning of the Meiji era can be considered a reflection of opposition by the small clans to Satsuma and Choshu domination. This subject is one of the most interesting and as yet largely unexplored subjects in Meiji legal history. See Someno, note 1, at 14, 61; HARA, BENGOSHI SEIKATSU NO KAIKO (Memoirs of My Life as a Lawyer) 4 (1935); KAINO, SAIBAN (Trials) 217 (1951); KUMAGAI, NIHON KINDAI HŌ NO SEIRITSU (Establishment of Modern Law in Japan) 147–149 (1955).

[6] By Great Council of State Notice of August 3, 1872. "Shihō Shokumu Teisei" is an abbreviation of "Shihō Shokusei Narabi ni Jimu Shōtei."

[7] JAPANESE LEGISLATION OF THE MEIJI ERA 281 (Ishii ed., 1958). This work contains a very detailed account of the legislative history of the Meiji era.

had been, because of an insufficiency of adequately trained personnel.[8] Additionally, there were no provisions in the Regulations or elsewhere prescribing qualifications for judges and procurators. Thus, even full-time judges were appointed principally from among administrative officials who had not been educated in the law.

As a result of a convention held in Osaka in 1875 to adjust divergent opinions among major political leaders concerning the structure of state power, the decision was made anew to operate in accordance with the principle of separation of powers. This would be done by establishing a supreme court at the apex of the judicial system and by authorizing the creation of the Diet as the national legislature. Accordingly, the Great Court of Judicature was established in 1875 as the highest judicial authority, with a president who performed no other functions; the Minister of Justice thus ceased to act as a judicial officer. At least structurally, the Japanese courts since then have been independent of the Ministry of Justice. It would be unwise, however, to lay too much stress on this particular change. Qualifications had not

[8] It is true, however, that, in anticipation of the need for judges, procurators, and the other officials of the Ministry of Justice, the government in 1871 established an institution called the Meihōryō in that Ministry, and in the next year this institution started to train candidates for such positions. It is reported that twenty students were admitted at the outset. At first they were taught the French language; and, after they had a sufficient grasp of the language, they received legal education from French teachers of law. In 1876, this institution was supplanted by the new, better-equipped Shihō-shō Hō Gakkō (Ministry of Justice Law School), which offered preparatory and regular courses, each of four-year duration, and continued legal training under the tutelage of French professors for candidates for positions as judges, procurators, or officials within the Ministry of Justice. Later, in 1885, the Shihō-shō Hō Gakkō was transferred to the Ministry of Education and amalgamated with the Department of Law of Tokyo University where it became the French Law Section. Without question, these two institutions contributed greatly to the development of law in Japan and provided training centers for legal specialists. A tendency to overemphasize French law in these two institutions was matched by a tendency to stress Anglo-American law in the Tokyo Kaisei School (the predecessor of Tokyo University), another institution which provided legal education in the early Meiji era. No definitive explanation has been given for the divergence between the two educational traditions, but the following facts may in part explain the situation.

(1) The Tokugawa government maintained cordial relations with France and had sent a formal diplomatic delegation to France. Things French, including an outline of the French judicial system written in 1867 by Joun Kurimoto, had been made available to the Japanese public. Consequently, Japanese authorities had knowledge of the French legal system very early and their general inclination toward the French caused them to view it sympathetically.

(2) Eight officials, sent to Europe by the Ministry of Justice to study law, stayed in Paris where they studied French law and upon their return occupied important positions in the Ministry.

(3) By virtue of the generally high repute in which it was held abroad, the Code Napoleon was very highly regarded by Japanese observers.

(4) On the other hand, an American law professor, Guido Verbeck, taught in the Tokyo Kaisei School, and he played the leading role in legal education at that school which had on its staff a number of teachers who had studied law in England. See KOBAYAGAWA, note 1, at 1190–1202; NAKAMURA, KINDAI NIHON NO HŌTEKI KEISEI (Legalization in Modern Japan) 26–33 (1956); OSATAKE, MEIJI KEISATSU SAIBAN SHI (History of the Police and the Judiciary in Meiji) 96–98 (1926); TAKAYANAGI, RECEPTION AND INFLUENCE OF OCCIDENTAL LEGAL IDEAS IN JAPAN 6 (Institute of Pacific Relations ed., 1929).

been prescribed for judges and procurators, and until 1877, when administrative officials were prohibited from concurrently acting as judges, the above-mentioned situation in the Local Courts was not improved. Furthermore, since the Minister of Justice continued to hold the absolute power to appoint and remove judges and procurators, the personnel were not independent.[9]

Conspicuous advances were made in the 1884 Hanji Tōyō Kisoku (Regulations for the Appointment of Judges)[10] and the 1886 Saibansho Kansei (Court Organization Regulations).[11] The former made legal study a prerequisite for judicial appointment by providing that judges should be appointed from among those who had passed a legal examination prescribed by the Regulations; the latter contained a similar provision concerning procurators. However, neither of these affected judges or procurators already appointed. Furthermore, the Saibansho Kansei stated that judges could not be removed against their will, or disciplined in the absence of conviction, either in criminal proceedings or through prescribed judicial disciplinary procedures. This guarantee put an end to interference by the executive in the judicial functions through appointment and dismissal of judges, a practice reported to have occurred on occasion even after the separation of the two functions by the 1875 reform.[12]

Although the institutional structure of the judicial system was worked out through the series of reforms discussed above, the judiciary and the procuracy of the day may well have been staffed by individuals without sufficient capabilities or training; it is understandable then that many trials were improperly conducted and mishandled. Perhaps the major reason is

[9] The concept of the courts adopted initially, in accordance with the determination of the Osaka convention, was that they should be independent with "complete" separation of powers in the American sense mentioned above. The government, which contemplated that the position of president of the prospective supreme court would be comparable in status to that of the Prime Minister, requested some of the foremost political figures in the country to assume the presidency, but none were willing. As a consequence, the original scheme was modified so that the supreme court as actually established was placed under the supervision of the Minister of Justice. See Osatake, note 8, at 130. If the original plan had been carried out in 1875 and a major national figure had assumed the presidency, the subsequent history of the Japanese judiciary might have been markedly different.

[10] Great Council of State Notice No. 101 of 1884.

[11] Imperial Order No. 40 of 1886.

[12] For example, some newspapers attacked the government in 1879, charging that influence was being brought to bear on a judge in a forgery prosecution in Osaka because some prominent officials were involved. The day before the case came to trial, the judge was "promoted" to another government office and the case was heard by another judge who found all defendants not guilty. While the truth of the accusations against the government has never been verified, without question this incident provoked suspicion of governmental interference in the administration of justice. Also, in 1881 the Minister of Home Affairs demanded that the Minister of Justice issue a directive to the court having jurisdiction ordering severe punishment in a case in which a supporter of the People's Rights and Freedom Movement was alleged to have insulted a policeman. See Kobayagawa, note 1, at 944–47; Someno, note 1, at 136.

that the reforms were pushed through too hastily, without adequate modification of the social structure and culture, because of zeal to free the country from extraterritoriality.[13] Tsuyoshi Inoue, an able assistant of Hirobumi Ito (frequently regarded as the greatest statesman in the Meiji era), criticized the judges and procurators in the following manner:

> A glance at the courts . . . of today in our country reveals that decisions are not rendered very quickly. They are unable to maintain fair trials . . . This is probably because the courts are not independent; the judges often do not realize the nature of their position and responsibility, they take into account personal considerations and play politics, they are moved by favoritism and attempt to patch up the mistakes of the police and officials, they do not render judgments in accordance with whether or not a fact exists, and many rely upon the mistaken belief that the way to make one's fame and fortune is to give judgments which will ingratiate oneself with the government . . . procurators, too, do not handle a defendant's case pursuant to their beliefs, but are inclined strongly to pressure judges in compliance with the directions of the police.[14]

Another indication of the low repute in which the judiciary and the procuracy were held, and of the failure fully to appreciate the significance of the legal process, was the proposal seriously made in 1887 to appoint foreign lawyers as judges and procurators in Japanese courts in cases involving foreign nationals. True, the measure was an unambiguous expedient to deal with the problem of extraterritoriality, but it could not have been proposed if Japan's leaders, so sensitive to infringements upon national sovereignty in other spheres, had considered the administration of justice an essential part of that national sovereignty.[15]

[13] The fact that a principal impetus for judicial reform in Meiji Japan was the desire to abolish extraterritoriality has also been pointed out by foreign scholars. See WIGMORE, A PANORAMA OF THE WORLD'S LEGAL SYSTEMS 520–21 (library ed., 1936). Extraterritoriality had been conceded to many countries. See KOBAYAGAWA, note 1, at 1129–31. Proposals made by the Meiji government to get the foreign powers to abandon extraterritoriality were often rejected on the grounds of incompleteness of the legal system, incompetence of the judiciary, or lack of judicial independence. See Kiyoura, *Jōyaku Kaisei Zengo no Shihō* (Justice at the Time of the Revision of the Treaties), 15 HŌSŌ KAI ZASSHI (Jurists' Association Magazine) no. 10, at 21 (1937). For example, an Anglo-German project of June 15, 1886, which was submitted jointly to the Japanese government by the British and German commissioners in the course of negotiation for revisions of the treaties, demanded that the Japanese government agree, as a prerequisite to revision, to a new court organization law and new penal, civil, commercial, and civil procedural codes based upon Western principles, to be enacted and in force within two years after treaty revision. NAKAMURA, note 8, at 64, 65. Extraterritoriality was completely given up by August 1899, after many years of negotiation. A very good English-language study of the extraterritorial problem is JONES, EXTRATERRITORIALITY IN JAPAN, 1885–1899 (1931).

[14] 1 HISHO RUISAN, HŌSEI KANKEI SHIRYŌ (Confidential Miscellanea, Materials Pertaining to Legal Matters) 89–90 (Hirobumi Ito ed., 1934).

[15] In 1887, Kaoru Inoue, then Foreign Minister, formulated a plan to the effect that any case, civil or criminal, in which a party was a foreigner would be tried by a collegiate body, the majority of whose members would be foreign lawyers, while, if the action were criminal, a foreign official would act as the prosecuting attorney. His motive in putting forth this plan

It should be noted also that most leading figures in the judiciary and the procuracy at that time either had taken legal training abroad, usually in France, or had been trained in Japan by foreign lawyers.[16] This fact, coupled with the inadequacy of the statutes, on occasion resulted in judicial determinations strongly influenced by foreign legal concepts that were not in accord with circumstances prevailing in Japan.[17]

The development of the bar in Japan followed a different course. While the government was very active in stimulating the development of soundly trained judges and procurators, it did little to develop the advocates (*daigennin*), who were not authorized to represent litigants until 1872 and then only in civil cases. This passive attitude toward the advocates may have derived in part from the poor reputation of the *kujishi,* the precursor of the modern lawyer, as well as from the general tendency during the long feudal period to esteem official position over private occupations.[18] An additional factor was that advocates were less important to the national policy of breaking down extraterritoriality than were judges and procurators.

About the time of the Meiji Restoration, the Western concept of the lawyer was introduced to Japan by observers who went abroad. In 1872, recognition was given for the first time to the principle of representation in civil litigation through advocates.[19] The Sotō Bunrei (Forms for Pleadings) of 1873, regulations which were the precursor of a modern code of civil procedure, provided for some procedures which envisaged the use of advocates.[20] However, qualifications were not established, and any person, except a minor or one under other disability, could act as advocate. As a result,

---

was to overcome opposition of the foreign powers to abolition of the unequal treaties. However, the Inoue program was crushed by strong opposition from some political leaders and the general public. Boissonade was articulate in his opposition. Except for Toru Hoshi, a prominent lawyer, who was convicted for violation of the Publication Ordinance for distributing publications opposing Inoue's plan, Boissonade's position was not supported, at least as far as published materials indicate, by any element in the profession.

[16] The examination prescribed in the Hanji Tōyō Kisoku of 1884 laid stress on English and French law. Its subjects were as follows: (1) criminal law; (2) criminal procedure; (3) English or French law of property; (4) English or French law of contracts; (5) English or French law of evidence.

[17] "In view of the lack of statutes or regulations governing libel in our country, this Court deems it proper to apply the Western rule relating to libel as the guiding principle in rendering judgment in this case. Libel contains five elements: (1) malice; (2) communication in writing; (3) publication; (4) untruthfulness; and (5) defamatory statement." Matsuo v. Masuda, Yokohama Court of First Instance, Oct. 19, 1887, 1 SAIBAN SUISHI (Essential Trial Reports) 146, 150.

[18] In this connection, it should be recalled again that the Meiji Restoration was not a democratic revolution and that many premodern attitudes carried over. An expression which embodies the attitude of superiority of the official is *kanson mimpi* (respect for officials and disdain for the people).

[19] It appears that the first book which presented the Japanese people with some idea of the role of the Western lawyer was GYŌSŌ TSUIROKU (Memoirs Written at Dawn) (1867), by Joun Kurimoto. See OSATAKE, note 8, at 187–89.

[20] Great Council of State Decree No. 247 of 1873.

advocates had no privileges and were dealt with by the courts in the same manner as the litigants themselves. In principle, they were subject to close supervision by the courts; thus they could be fined if they delayed a court session and reprimanded or suspended if they were disrespectful toward the courts. According to available data, they were viewed with substantially the same lack of esteem as had been shown the kujishi in the feudal period.

The creation of the advocate role without the requirement of professional qualifications resulted in entry into the bar of many individuals who were deficient in knowledge of the law or very unethical in their behavior.[21] In 1876, the Ministry of Justice prescribed the Daigennin Kisoku (Advocate Regulations),[22] which for the first time required applicants to pass an examination and obtain the permission of the Minister of Justice as prerequisites to practice. It is worthy of note that, although this examination was required before one was prescribed for judges and procurators, its objective was not to inquire into the knowledge of the law but to exclude persons on grounds of poor character or general lack of education. The very fact that an examination of this type was given is a reflection of the fact that the quality of the advocates was extremely low and that not much was expected from them.[23] Moreover, the examination system did not contribute substantially to improvement in the quality of advocates because the examinations were administered by regional groups and by local administrative officials who were totally unfamiliar with the lawyer's role.[24] In 1880, the examination system was revised in order to make it uniform throughout the country.[25] At the same time, advocates were required to organize into associations in each judicial district for the avowed purpose of raising

[21] Some of the advocates exacted excessive fees from their clients by purposely stressing the weak points of the cases in order to enhance the significance of their own contributions to a successful outcome. There are also reported examples of advocates filing appeals before the judgment of the first instance had been rendered or after the time for appeal had expired. See NIHON BENGOSHI RENGŌ KAI (Japanese Federated Attorneys' Association), NIHON BENGOSHI ENKAKUSHI (A Historical Account of Japanese Attorneys) 22 (1959); HOSOKAWA, NIHON KINDAI HŌSEI SHI (A History of Japan's Modern Legal System) 103 (1961).

[22] Ministry of Justice Pronouncement A (*Kō*) No. 1 of 1876.

[23] The examination merely tested the applicant's familiarity with the outline of governmental decrees, notices, criminal law, and court procedure and inquired into his conduct and personal history.

[24] In the country as a whole, only 34 men passed the first examination. It is reported that most of these were from the former samurai class and were persons who had been practicing law as advocates since the establishment of the daigennin system. See NIHON BENGOSHI RENGŌ KAI, note 21, at 21.

[25] Ministry of Justice Pronouncement A (*Kō*) No. 1 of 1880. The examination subjects were revised somewhat to test the applicant's legal knowledge in civil law, criminal law, procedure, practice, and regulations relating to the administration of justice. It is important to note that examination was waived for graduates of the law department of Tokyo University by Ministry of Justice Notice No. 7 of 1879. This concession, extended later to law graduates of other imperial universities, and retained until 1923, reflects, in a sense, a low level of understanding of the advocate function. It is also an interesting reflection of the traditional bias in favor of the imperial universities.

professional ethics but also perhaps in order to permit the government to exercise control over their activities. Significantly, these associations were responsible to the chief district procurators; they were not autonomous bodies.

While advocates were allowed to act in civil matters, they had not been authorized to defend in criminal cases. However, after the government in 1875 had designated two officials of the Ministry of Justice as *bengokan* (something similar in nature to public defenders), in a case arising out of the assassination of a high government official, it could not continue indefinitely to refuse to extend the same principle to other cases.[26] Thus, under the new Code of Criminal Instruction of 1880, all accused were given the right of counsel.[27]

Although the status of advocates is generally considered to have remained much inferior to that of judges and procurators, it doubtless improved gradually through the above-mentioned reforms, which at least legitimized the activity and gave advocates some recognized functions to perform in the processes of law.

Among other factors improving the status of the advocate was the resignation from official position and the entry into practice of Toru Hoshi, a young and promising official of the Ministry of Finance, who had studied law in England under official orders. In 1887, Hoshi became Japan's first barrister. He handled litigation both for private parties and for the government. Two young and able lawyers, both educated in the United States, followed Hoshi's example and later became leaders of the advocates' association in Tokyo. In 1879, three graduates of Tokyo University's law department, which was generally regarded as the training ground for higher administrative position, entered the bar. Furthermore, some of the leading advocates displayed remarkable ability as defense counsels in criminal cases which arose out of the so-called People's Rights and Freedom Movement. All these factors led to some improvement in the status of the advocate.[28]

The Profession Under the Constitution of 1889

The positions of judge and procurator, which had been developed through frequent but fragmentary reforms, were recognized in the Imperial Consti-

[26] Osatake, note 8, at 191–97.

[27] The Code of Criminal Instruction, Great Council of State Decree No. 37 of 1880, the first modern procedural law, was drafted by Boissonade on the model of the French Code of Criminal Instruction. It contained a provision that a felony could not be tried without defense counsel — art. 381(1) — and that, if the accused were unable to select his counsel, the judge, *ex officio,* would assign defense counsel from among advocates within the jurisdiction — art. 378(2). However, in 1880, there were only 914 advocates throughout the country, and, accordingly, the new provisions could not be enforced. The government, therefore, suspended their application for an indefinite period.

[28] Nihon Bengoshi Rengō Kai, note 21, at 21, 22, 39–44.

The People's Rights and Freedom Movement principally sought early establishment of a national Diet composed of members elected by popular vote.

tution of 1889[29] and the Court Organization Law of 1890,[30] one of the items of legislation that implemented the Constitution.

Upon the recommendation of Hirobumi Ito, who had studied the operation of the constitutions of Western countries for a considerable period of time and had concluded that it was most desirable for Japan to follow the example of the absolute monarchy in Prussia, the Constitution of 1889 was drafted on the Prussian model. As a result, the government also determined to adopt Prussian principles in drafting the Court Organization Law, casting away the previous French models. Thus, Otto Rudorff, then a lecturer on German law at Tokyo University, was ordered to draft an organization law on the model of the *Gerichtsverfassungsgesetz* of January 27, 1877. This shift to German models, however, did not bring about any significant alteration in either the technical functions of Japanese judges and procurators, which had been set in earlier legislation, or in their social status. Both the German and the French systems were within the Continental system of jurisprudence, and, moreover, Boissonade, the French professor and the draftsman of the earlier laws, collaborated with Rudorff in drafting the new organization law.[31] It might have been quite different if there had been a shift to Anglo-American models.

Under the Constitution of 1889 and the Court Organization Law, a judge was guaranteed tenure, and he was required to have knowledge of law and also to have received professional training. Tenure was ensured by the fact that a judge could not be removed, assigned to other courts, suspended, or penalized by reduction in salary unless: (1) he had been convicted of a criminal offense or punished in proceedings as specified in the Judge Disciplinary Law;[32] (2) he had been adjudged incapable of performing his duties because of mental or physical incompetence by the Ministry of Justice, upon a resolution of the judges of the Great Court of Judicature or of the judges of a Court of Appeals sitting in an administrative capacity.[33] Profes-

[29] The Imperial Constitution came into force on November 5, 1890.

[30] Law No. 6 of 1890.

[31] The Court Organization Law did make a remarkable change in court structure, even though it did not alter the status of officials. The following courts (the names of the French courts on which they were based are given in parentheses) had been established at one time or another prior to the enforcement of the Code of Criminal Instruction, note 27: Courts of the Peace (*tribunal de paix*); Courts of First Instance (*tribunal d'arrondissement*); Courts of Grave Offenses (*cour d'assisses*); Courts of Appeals (*cour d'appel*); the High Court (*haute-cour*); and the Great Court of Judicature (*cour de cassation*). Under the Court Organization Law these were superseded by the following (the names of the German courts on which they were based are given in parentheses): Local Courts (*Amtsgericht*); District Courts (*Landgericht*); Courts of Appeals (*Oberlandesgericht*); and the Great Court of Judicature (*Reichsgericht*). Rudorff's draft of the Court Organization Law with his commentary thereon in German can be found in RUDORFF, COMMENTAR ZUM GERICHTSVERFASSUNGSGESETZE FÜR JAPAN (Shihō Shiryō (Justice Materials) No. 259, 1939).

[32] CONST. of 1889, art. 58(2); Court Organization Law, art. 73 (1890); Judge Disciplinary Law, Law No. 68 of 1890.

[33] Court Organization Law, art. 74 (1890).

sional competence was required in that an individual could not be appointed a judge until he had passed an examination and successfully completed three years of professional training as a probationary legal official in the courts and the procurators' offices.[34] The new system did not provide for judicial autonomy because the power of general administrative supervision over the judiciary remained in the hands of the Minister of Justice, although he had no authority over the judges in the exercise of their judicial functions.[35]

It can be said that the structure of the Japanese judiciary, both in its favorable and unfavorable aspects, was stabilized by the Constitution of 1889 and the Court Organization Law.[36] Since that time, by and large, the judiciary has been composed of individuals who entered judicial service immediately after completing their university education, passing the legal examination and taking apprentice training. Thereafter, in the normal course of events, they served until retirement.[37] Thus, the judicial career, quite distinct from other careers in law, came into existence. Both the tradition of complete independence from political influence, which is generally considered to have been established through the famous Otsu case,[38] and a strong

[34] CONST. of 1889, art. 58; Court Organization Law, arts. 57–58 (1890). Law graduates of imperial universities were by art. 65(2) exempted from the judge and procurator appointment examination. In 1923 this exemption was abolished and pursuant to amendment of the Court Organization Law (by Law No. 39 of 1914) and the Attorneys Law (by Law No. 40 of 1914) the examination became the legal section of the senior examination for public officials by combining it with the attorney's examination. It is conjectured that enforcement of the 1914 amendments was postponed because candidates for the bar opposed taking what was considered to be a more difficult examination and imperial university graduates were reluctant to give up the nonexamination privilege.

The professional training system was markedly different from the German *Referendar* system, although created on that model. As to the German *Referendar*, see HAYNES, THE SELECTION AND TENURE OF JUDGES 171–77 (1944). In 1908, the training term was reduced to one and a half years on the ground that three years were not needed for training judges and procurators. It should be remembered that, while three years of training were required for the *Referendar* in Germany, where his apprentice training included work in law firms and administrative agencies, the apprentice training in Japan was limited to work in the courts and the procurators' offices.

[35] Court Organization Law, arts. 135, 143 (1890).

[36] It is manifest from the following data that the quality of judges had improved considerably by the time of the enforcement of the Court Organization Law of 1890; see Kaneko, *Saibansho Kōsei Hō Jisshi Gojūnen ni Atari Shihō Seido no Shokan o Nobu* (Some Impressions on the System of Justice at the Time of the Semi-Centennial of the Enforcement of the Court Organization Law), 17 HŌSŌ KAI ZASSHI (Jurists' Association Magazine) no. 11, at 45, 56–57 (1939). The total number of judges as of Feb. 4, 1892, was 1,255: those who had doctor of jurisprudence degrees from domestic or foreign universities, 1; those who had bachelor of jurisprudence degrees from domestic or foreign universities, 112; those who had passed the examination for appointment as judges, 537; those who had been promoted from among officials of the Ministry of Justice, 558; those who had been appointed from among administrative officials, 42; those who had been appointed from among advocates, 1; and unknown, 4.

[37] Compulsory retirement by reason of age was established for the first time in Law No. 101 of 1921 for both judges and procurators. The retirement age for the president of the Great Court of Judicature and the Procurator-General was 65. For all others the age was 63.

[38] The so-called Otsu case took place in 1891, soon after the Court Organization Law came

sense of professional integrity are manifestations of a consciousness of identity as members of a distinct professional group.[39] The fact that there is not a single recorded instance of judicial corruption, while many bribery cases were reported in the legislative and executive branches particularly at the beginning of this century, and the fact that the judiciary did not yield completely under militaristic and ultranationalistic pressure, even in the critical years of World War II, are further manifestations of this consciousness.[40] In fact, one Japanese authority has called the Japanese judiciary "the most reliable among the branches of government and administrative organizations." [41]

However, one must not evaluate the prewar judiciary and its position too highly. In the first place, as a result of the retention by the Minister of Justice of the power of general administrative supervision over the judiciary, personnel administration within the judiciary inevitably was influenced by

---

into force. The Crown Prince of Russia, later Czar Nicholas II, while on a trip to Japan was attacked and wounded by a policeman at Otsu, a small city near Kyoto. In view of the delicate nature of Russo-Japanese relations at that time, the Japanese government was of the opinion that an act of this gravity should be dealt with by capital punishment. The Japanese Penal Code contained a specific provision that an attempt upon the life of a member of the Japanese imperial family was punishable by death but that the maximum penalty for any other murder attempt was life imprisonment. The government used pressure on the judges of the Great Court of Judicature, in which the case was pending before a department of five judges, but the conscientious and courageous president, Iken Kojima, rejected this attempt at political intervention by refusing to interfere with the action of the department which imposed a life sentence instead of death. Accordingly, President Kojima is called "the god of the defense of justice." See KOJIMA, ŌTSU JIKEN TENMATSU-ROKU (An Account of the Otsu Case) (1931).

[39] DAVID & DE VRIES, THE FRENCH LEGAL SYSTEM 18 (1958), reports a similar phenomenon in France.

[40] The following unreported cases are examples.

(1) In 1942, Yukio Ozaki, a famous liberal politician, made a speech at a campaign meeting conducted for a friend of his in which he said, in part: "There is a proverb, 'A thrifty grandfather, a spendthrift grandson.' See Germany, which fell at the time of Wilhelm III! See Italy! The third Emperor has had his power usurped by Mussolini. We should protect the constitutional government established by the Emperor Meiji, the first Emperor after the Restoration." The militaristic government, taking his speech as a sarcastic reference to the present Emperor, the grandson of the Emperor Meiji, indicted him on a charge of lese majesty. Of course, the military was concerned not only because of the reference to the Emperor but because of the implicit criticism of government policy. The Great Court of Judicature, however, acquitted him on June 27, 1944.

(2) An ardent Christian by the name of Sensaku Asami was accused of violating the Peace Preservation Law because of alleged criticism of the existing form of state under the Emperor in a statement which he made concerning the second advent of Christ. The Great Court of Judicature found him not guilty in June 1945. See SEKINE & NIIMURA, SAIBAN KONJAKU MONOGATARI (Ancient and Modern Tales of Trial) 38–50 (1956).

It should also be noted that during World War II a President of a Court of Appeals sent a strong protest to Prime Minister Tojo, who had made an address at a meeting of the judiciary reproaching it because of its noncooperative attitude toward the militaristic government. In this address, Tojo threatened that he would take necessary remedial action if the judiciary did not alter its attitude. See SAIBAN HIHAN (Trial Criticism) 9 (1957).

[41] KANEKO, SAIBAN HŌ (Law of the Judiciary) 52–53 (1959).

the government. Particularly noteworthy is the fact that the Minister of Justice, by offering greater opportunity of promotion, could induce promising judges and procurators to enter the Ministry to perform general administrative functions. This practice not only resulted in competent jurists leaving the judiciary but also led people to think of the relationship between the Ministry of Justice and the courts in much the same light as that between a central administrative organ and its regional offices.[42] This tendency reinforced by the traditional concept of the judiciary discussed in the preceding section, led to a general evaluation of the status of the judge as inferior to that of the administrative official assigned to a Ministry's head office (though not to a regional office).[43] This in turn led to the view that the judge did not have to be treated as well as the higher administrative official.[44] The Minister of Justice, who had the power to assign judges to particular courts, also sometimes urged them to accept new assignments for the convenience of the government.[45] Furthermore, the judge's status guarantee within the context of a bureaucratic system was accompanied by an unexpected and undesirable result. Whereas the administrative official enjoyed quick promotion and could look forward to a better-paying position in either a public enterprise or a private corporation after relatively early retirement,[46] the judge who remained in the judiciary could reach the

[42] *Ibid.*

[43] The lower esteem of the judge also derived from the exemption from examination for law graduates of the imperial universities. All candidates for the senior administrative ranks, both imperial-university law graduates and others, took an examination corresponding to the legal examination. In this sense, all senior administrative officials "achieved" their status, whereas many of the judicial officials, not having been so tested, had status more of an "ascribed" nature.

[44] A comparison between annual salaries of judges and administrative officials of the Ministry of Justice in 1938 is as follows (in yen — three and a half yen equal one dollar): the President of the Great Court of Judicature received 6,600, while the Minister of Justice received 6,800 and the Vice Minister received 5,800; the Presiding Judge of a department of the Great Court of Judicature and the President of a Court of Appeals, 5,800–4,650; a Judge of the Great Court, 4,650, the Presiding Judge of a department of a Court of Appeals, 4,650–4,050, and the President of a District Court, 4,050, while the Director of a Ministry bureau received 4,650; a Judge of a Court of Appeals, a Judge of a District Court, and senior officials other than a Ministry bureau director all received 4,050–1,130. Hōsō Kai (Jurists' Association), Shihō-bu Shokuin-roku (Directory of Officials in the Justice Branch) 2–3 (1938).

[45] See Date, *Taikan no Ben* (Remarks upon Resignation), Hanrei Jihō (The Case Journal) no. 263, at 2, 4–5 (1961).

[46] The postwar National Public Servants Law, Law No. 120 of 1947, art. 103 (2), translated into English in Official Gazette, Oct. 21, 1947, no. 468, at 1, was designed to prevent this prewar practice: "An official, for two years subsequent to his departure from office, shall not agree to assume or assume a position in a profit-making enterprise which has a close relationship with a national organ, prescribed by regulation of the National Personnel Authority, in which he held office during the five years prior to his departure from office." It will be observed that this provision proscribes entry into profit-making enterprises only and does not prohibit assumption of positions in the many nonprofit public corporations. Many former officials take high positions in such public corporations.

highest salary grade only by a slow and gradual process over a comparatively long period of time, with relatively late retirement. This factor probably tended, as it still does, to discourage some young and able individuals from entering the judiciary, though it cannot be denied that security of assured lifelong work on the bench was an attraction to others.

Secondly, in considering the prewar judiciary one must recognize that the system of the career judiciary, and particularly the exercise of judicial authority by younger men, sometimes met with popular dissatisfaction because of the purported inexperience and immaturity of judges. This dissatisfaction was probably increased by a tendency to expand the number of so-called *Generalklauseln* (statutory provisions cast in broad and highly generalized terms), which required greater maturity of outlook for interpretation than did statutes cast in fairly specific terms.[47] Needless to say, both the requirement of training for three years (since 1908, only one and a half years) before going on the bench and the requirement of a collegiate court composed of at least three judges — except in minor civil and criminal cases where a single judge could preside — was designed and actually served to some extent to reduce this dissatisfaction. Nevertheless, there were many sharp criticisms concerning the "fossilization" or *Weltfremdheit* of the judiciary.[48]

Turning to the procurators, their most notable characteristic under the Court Organization Law of 1890 was the similarity of their status to that of judges. Of course, the procurator differed from the judge in that, as a matter of law, he was subordinate to his superior in performing his duties. However, there was no clear prescription of law determining whether the Minister of Justice, who was not a procurator, could issue instructions to a

[47] For example, new *Generalklauseln* were provided by the revisions of the Leased Land Law, Law No. 55 of 1941 amending Law No. 49 of 1921, translated into English in 2 EHS Law BULLETIN SERIES FR 1 (Nakane ed. and trans., 1959), and the Leased House Law, Law No. 56 of 1941 amending Law No. 50 of 1921, translated into English in 2 EHS LAW BULLETIN SERIES FS 1 (Nakane ed. and trans., 1959). It should also be noted that since the beginning of this century the plea of "abuse of right" had become increasingly frequent largely under the influence of the provision of the Swiss Civil Code of 1907 prohibiting such abuse.

[48] For example, a national meeting of lawyers passed a resolution on November 11, 1936, to the effect that judges should be appointed only from among those who had practiced law for ten years or more. "The present system of appointing judges from probationary legal officials who have entered the judiciary directly from the universities is unreasonable because it does not supply them sufficient opportunity to acquire training and experience as members of living society. It is defective in that it tends continually to create a number of young and immature judges." See NIHON BENGOSHI RENGŌ KAI, note 21, at 191.

Enkichi Oki, who was the Minister of Justice from 1920 to 1922, created a major controversy when he was reported to have made a statement, which is still well known, that judges were "fossils." See HŌRITSU SHIMBUN (The Law News) no. 1716, at 21 (1920). It is apparent that the Leased Land and Leased House Mediation Law, Law No. 41 of 1922, and the conciliation legislation subsequent thereto were designed, in some senses, to correct the supposed defect resulting from the inexperience of judges by creating a system of mediation committees with experienced laymen among their members.

procurator with respect to the disposition of a particular case.[49] Some people, who attached special importance to the integrity of the procuracy, were of the opinion that such attempted exercise of power was illegal. The Minister never tried to exercise this directive power in the prewar days, so the matter remained largely academic. In this sense, the prewar procuracy enjoyed independence similar to that of the judiciary, at least as far as political or other outside pressure was concerned. This comparatively strong guarantee of independence is one of the most important reasons why the procuracy in prewar Japan had a reputation for impartiality and proved itself highly capable in dealing with numerous scandals in political circles — an ability which won it much support from the general public around 1930.

It should be noted, however, that the strong procuracy later was criticized for *kensatsu fassho* (fascism by the procuracy), though it has never been made clear in any objective study whether *kensatsu fassho* really existed or, if it did, exactly what it was.[50]

With regard to professional independence, procurators were selected in a manner substantially similar to judges. Candidates for the procuracy, after passing the same examination as that given the candidates for the judiciary, were appointed probationary legal officials and received the same training as those going on the bench. Procurators were on the same salary scale as judges and probably enjoyed the same prestige.

Notwithstanding the similarity between these two branches of the profession, movement between them was rare because of specialization in function. It is also worthy of note that procurators enjoyed better opportunities for promotion than judges because, though the procuracy was smaller in size,

[49] See Nagashima, *Saibansho Kōsei Hō* (Court Organization Law), in 12 GENDAI HŌGAKU ZENSHŪ (Complete Collection on Contemporary Jurisprudence) 164–68 (1929); *Hōmu Daijin no Shikiken Hatsudō* (Exercise of the Directive Power of the Minister of Justice), JURIST no. 58, at 1–2 (1954).

[50] It is not clear what the phrase means. The Supreme Public Procurators' Office has stated: "*Kensatsu fassho* seems to be generally used to describe the monopoly of the power to prosecute held by the procurators which made it possible for them to exercise this power for political purposes; for example, if they so desired, they could deal with political evils in such a way that the overthrow of a cabinet might result, or at their discretion they could leave the matter as it was." See Saikō Kensatsu-chō Kōhō Bu (Supreme Public Procurators' Office, Public Information Division), *Shin Kensatsu Seido Jūnen no Kaiko* (Ten Years of the New Procuratorial System in Retrospect), 10 HŌSŌ JIHŌ (Journal of the Jurists' Association) 35, 40 (1958).

Idei, a procurator, states: "It can be said that from the middle of the Taisho era to the end of World War II the procurators inclined to remedy the abuses of the times . . . The general public had been very much concerned with the corruption of the political parties since the middle of the Taisho era. It was quite natural that the procurators inclined to correct the abuses from the standpoint of the maintenance of social justice, this being one of the purposes of the procuracy. It seems to me that the disposition of the numerous scandals from the middle of the Taisho era to the beginning of the Showa era was a reflection of this inclination among procurators . . ." IDEI, KENJI MONOGATARI (A Procurator's Tale) 213 (1948).

the number of higher-paying positions was about the same in both branches.[51] Some people have suggested further that public procurators enjoyed greater possibilities of selection as members of the House of Peers or appointment to the position of Minister of Justice. During this period, leadership in the administration of justice reportedly was in the hands of the procuracy.[52]

Turning now to the bar, the Attorneys Law of 1893[53] brought about great changes in organization. Along with the enforcement of the Court Organization Law and the new codes of civil and criminal procedure,[54] the government prepared and introduced to the first session of the Imperial Diet in 1890 a bill to revise the law regulating the bar. Higher regard for the status of the lawyer in a constitutional polity is seen in the following statement by the government concerning the purpose of the revisions:

> Human rights prescribed by the Constitution cannot be fully protected without the activity of lawyers with knowledge, experience and high ethical standards . . . The administration of justice cannot be achieved without full cooperation of judges and lawyers. The purpose of this bill is to establish strict qualifications for the lawyer, protect his rights, respect his position, and supervise his professional conduct.[55]

Although the bill did not become law because of opposition from the *daigennin kumiai* (the professional organization of advocates), a revised bill, which took some of the arguments of the opposition into consideration, was prepared and became law in 1893.[56]

In view of a higher formal evaluation of the lawyer's role, the Attorneys Law of 1893 created a new title, *bengoshi,* for the lawyer to replace *daigennin,*

[51] In this connection, note the following figures for annual salaries in 1938 (in yen — three and a half yen equal one dollar).

Total	*Number receiving 6,600*	*Number receiving 5,800–4,650*	*Number receiving 4,650–4,050*	*Number receiving less than 4,050*
Judges (1,470)	1	15 (1.02%)	52 (3.53%)	1,402 (95.38%)
Procurators (686)	1	11 (1.60%)	51 (7.42%)	623 (90.8 %)

HŌSŌ KAI, note 44, at 2–3; SHIHŌ-SHŌ (Ministry of Justice), SHIHŌ ENKAKUSHI (History of Justice) 543–44 (1939).

[52] IMAMURA, HŌTEI GOJŪ-NEN (Fifty Years Before the Courts) 117, 118 (1948).

[53] Law No. 7 of 1893.

[54] CODE OF CIVIL PROCEDURE, Law No. 29 of 1890; CODE OF CRIMINAL PROCEDURE, Law No. 96 of 1890.

[55] NIHON BENGOSHI RENGŌ KAI, note 21, at 47.

[56] The principal points raised in opposition to the 1890 bill were as follows: (1) The bill provided for separate enrollment for practice before each court, thus placing a limitation on the sphere of activity of the lawyer; one who was practicing, for example, before the Tokyo District Court would not be permitted to argue in a court sitting outside the Tokyo district, in the Court of Appeals in Tokyo, or in the Great Court of Judicature. (2) A fixed period of practice was required before the practitioner became eligible to practice in the higher courts. (3) A high fee was required for enrollment before each court.

a word which sometimes carried a connotation of the shyster or pettifogger. The law also established a new admission examination.[57] In other words, for the first time a demonstration of formal professional knowledge was a prerequisite for qualification as a lawyer in Japan.[58]

Accompanying the legislative changes was a significant change in recruitment. A number of able graduates of the law departments in the universities began to enter the bar, primarily because of the influence of a few leading professors of Anglo-American law,[59] while the private law schools were gradually strengthened and supplied better-trained recruits.[60] Thus, there was a marked increase in the number of individuals with knowledge and ability at the bar, individuals who played an active role in the handling of significant cases and influenced the development of jurisprudence.[61]

Although the status of the bar undoubtedly improved under the Attorneys Law of 1893, many problems remained. In the first place, although lawyers were required to take an examination, it was still separate and distinct from that for judges and procurators, and the former was generally considered, without real basis, easier to pass. In this sense, speaking very generally, it can be presumed that there existed a substantial difference between the caliber of judges and public procurators, on the one hand, and lawyers, on the

[57] The subjects examined, prescribed in the Attorneys Examination Regulations, Ministry of Justice Order No. 9 of 1893, were: civil law, commercial law, criminal law, civil procedure, and criminal procedure.

[58] It must be remembered, however, that there were several important exceptions to the newly established principle of admission by examination. Provision was made for admission without examination of daigennin, some of whom had been kujishi in the Tokugawa period and had become advocates without examination. This could not but have a deleterious effect on the reputation of the lawyer. The previously mentioned exemption of imperial-university graduates also continued.

[59] A number of law graduates of Tokyo University, which had been established (in practice even if not formally) primarily as a training institute for senior administrative officials, entered the bar in the early Meiji era. Two thirds of the law graduates of Tokyo University in 1882 and two fifths in 1890 became lawyers. This was because three prominent professors — Hatoyama, Hozumi, and Okamura — who had studied law either in England or in the United States, impressed the students with the importance of the lawyer's role. See Hara, note 5, at 3–5. However, the situation altered markedly when German law became predominant in the law department of the Imperial University (Tokyo's title between 1886 and the establishment of Kyoto Imperial University in 1897) around 1895. After that date, practice no longer held any appeal for most graduates and relatively few entered the bar.

[60] Among the institutions established were Wafutsu Hōritsu Gakkō (the Franco-Japanese Law School, now Hosei University) in 1879, Meiji Hōritsu Semmon Gakkō (the Meiji Professional Law School, now Meiji University) in 1881, Tōkyō Semmon Gakkō (the Tokyo Professional School, now Waseda University) in 1882, Igirisu Hōritsu Gakkō (the English Law School, now Chuo University) in 1885. See Azuma, Hōgaku Bu Monogatari (The Story of Law Departments) 51, 59, 84, 98 (1958); Takayanagi, note 8, at 6. While many of the graduates of the law department of Tokyo University went into government service, most graduates of private university departments were obliged to go either into private practice or private business.

[61] Nihon Bengoshi Rengō Kai, note 21, at 76–79; Nippon no Hōgaku (Jurisprudence in Japan) 3–16 (1950).

other.[62] This situation continued until 1923, when the two examinations were combined in the legal section of the senior examination for public officials; from that time on, lawyers have had to meet the same standards as their colleagues in the judiciary and procuracy.[63]

A second important factor to be kept in mind when considering the status of the lawyer is that, while both judges and procurators received training as probationary legal officials, one who passed the examination could practice as a lawyer without any further training. The original bill introduced by the government in 1890 had contained a provision requiring apprentice training for applicants who wished to enter the bar, but it was deleted in the Diet on the grounds that lawyers did not need such training. It is clear from scrutiny of the legislative history of the Attorneys Law that many of the lawyers at that time were advocates with relatively little education and that lawyers in general were not regarded as highly as judges or procurators even by members of the Diet.[64] Apprentice training for private practitioners finally was adopted in the 1933 revision of the Attorneys Law which created a system of probationary attorneys (*bengoshi shiho*).[65]

Finally, under the Attorneys Law of 1893 lawyers were subject to significant control and supervision by the Minister of Justice and his regional subordinates, the chief district procurators. Though discipline of lawyers was to be exercised by a disciplinary court for lawyers established in the Court of Appeals having jurisdiction over the attorneys' association to which the lawyer concerned belonged, the right to initiate disciplinary action was reserved to the procurators. The power to approve bylaws of the attorneys' associations, to order the suspension of proceedings of the associations, and to nullify resolutions passed by them was placed in the hands of the Minister of Justice and the chief district procurators. Even if such supervision was perhaps required because of the public nature of the lawyer's functions, its existence was a further manifestation of a lack of confidence in the ability of the bar to control its own affairs.

The Attorneys Law was thoroughly revised in 1933. As already noted, the

[62] The fact that the examination committee for the attorneys' examination was composed of judges, procurators, and senior officers of the Ministry of Justice, but no lawyers, reflects both the poor reputation of lawyers and the idea of "omnipotence of the officials" (*kanken bannō*) which was widely held at that time.

[63] Before the Second World War, an average of about 100 out of 300 successful candidates in the combined examination were appointed probationary legal officials every year, the balance entering private practice. Nagashima, a senior officer of the Ministry of Justice in charge of examination and selection of probationary officials, stated that only those who passed the examination with high grades could be selected as probationary legal officials. See Nagashima, note 49, at 142.

[64] See Nishimura, *Bengoshi Hō no Kaisei ni Tsuite* (On the Revision of the Attorneys Law), in 15 SHIHŌ KENKYŪ (Justice Research) no. 3 (1932).

[65] Attorneys Law, Law No. 53 of 1933, arts. 2–3. However, the system was not fully developed by the time World War II began. The attorneys' associations had begun to implement the legislation, but that was about all.

examination for lawyers was combined with that for judges and procurators and a training system was established. In addition, women for the first time were admitted to practice. It became increasingly common for attorneys' associations to make recommendations to the government or to the courts with regard to legislation and legal reforms or other matters concerning the administration of justice. Prejudice against lawyers still persisted, however, both in the general public and among government officials.[66]

Apart from major legislation — the Court Organization Law of 1890 and the Attorneys Laws of 1893 and 1933 — numerous revisions affecting the various branches of the profession have been made, but the basic character of the profession was not changed until the enforcement of the new Constitution and the implementing legislation after World War II.[67]

THE PROFESSION AFTER THE SECOND WORLD WAR

The Constitution of Japan, enacted in 1946 on the basis of proposals made by the occupation forces, came into effect on May 3, 1947. As in other areas, it brought radical reforms in the judicial system,[68] and the governing statutes and the functions of all branches of the legal profession have undergone considerable change. In the first place, under the new Constitution the courts are the exclusive adjudicators of all legal disputes, including those between citizens and the state arising out of administrative acts. Under the

[66] An indication of such prejudice is the strongly urged advice given some lawyers by the police or military police during World War II when the government required the people to cooperate fully with national policy: "Take up an honest calling." See NIHON BENGOSHI RENGŌ KAI, note 21, at 258.

[67] Particularly noteworthy was the Jury Law, Law No. 50 of 1923, which took effect on October 1, 1928, and provided for a jury in criminal cases punishable by imprisonment or death. It is said that the jury system in Japan was not an outcome of distrust of the professional judge, but was a product of policy considerations that led the government to desire to provide the people with an opportunity to participate in the administration of justice. However, the jury system was not popular in Japan and its use was suspended in 1943. It is generally asserted that the principal causes of the unpopularity were that the accused could have only one appeal if he had been tried by jury instead of two appeals in the nonjury trial, that the accused trusted professional judges more than the lay jurors, and that judges were not necessarily bound by the verdict of the jury. Whatever the cause of unpopularity, the jury system never significantly affected the character of the Japanese legal profession. For the causes of unpopularity of the jury system, see SAIKŌ SAIBANSHO JIMU-SŌKYOKU (General Secretariat of the Supreme Court), WAGA KUNI NI OKERU SAIBANSHO SEIDO NO ENKAKU (Historical Development of the Court System in Our Country) 32 (1957); Miyazawa & Nakagawa, *Hōritsu Shi* (Legal History), in 5 GENDAI NIPPON BUMMEI SHI (Cultural History of Modern Japan) 212 (1944).

[68] For a summary comparison of the old and new Constitutions, see Quigley, *Japan's Constitutions: 1890 and 1947*, 41 AM. POL. SCI. REV. 865 (1947). For summaries of legal reforms in postwar Japan, see Appleton, *Reforms in Japanese Criminal Procedure Under Allied Occupation*, 24 WASH. L. REV. 401 (1949); Blakemore, *Post-War Developments in Japanese Law*, 1947 WIS. L. REV. 632; Gokijo, *The Judicial System of New Japan*, 308 ANNALS 28 (1956); Oppler, *The Reform of Japan's Legal and Judicial System under Allied Occupation*, 24 WASH. L. REV. 290 (1949); Tanaka, *Democracy and Judicial Administration in Japan*, 2 J. INT'L COMMISSION OF JURISTS no. 2, at 7 (1959).

old Constitution the latter disputes were to a very limited extent subject to the jurisdiction of the Administrative Court, but there were frequently no legal remedies available.[69] In contrast, now it is generally believed that "the idea of legal equality, or of the universal subjection of all classes to one law administered by the ordinary courts, has been pushed to its utmost limit," [70] although no such explicit statement is contained in the new Constitution.[71] The only limitation is that disputes concerning qualification of Diet members are left to that body.[72]

Secondly, while the courts under the old Constitution held that the power of judicial review over legislative acts did not exist, though the Great Court of Judicature could review questions concerning the validity of orders,[73] the new Constitution has expressly granted the courts the power of judicial review of legislative acts.[74]

Thirdly, as a corollary of the above, the new Constitution has guaranteed complete independence and autonomy to the courts. The concept of judicial autonomy can be inferred from the provisions in the new Constitution which prescribe the independence of the judiciary, the procedure for disciplining judges (except impeachment), the method of their appointment, and the rule-making power of the Supreme Court which extends not only to procedure and practice but to matters relating to attorneys, the internal discipline of the courts, and the administration of judicial affairs.[75]

Finally, the new Constitution ascribes great importance to human rights. Of course, the old Constitution, too, guaranteed various rights and freedoms of the citizen, but they were always subject to restriction by legislative act, and legislative acts could not be ignored even if they were contrary to the Constitution's spirit. Under the new Constitution, oppressive legislation can

[69] Because of art. 61 of the Constitution of 1889, the ordinary courts were not given the power to adjudicate disputes between citizens and the state arising out of illegal administrative acts. Some of these acts, however, were made subject to the jurisdiction of the Administrative Court, which was established in 1890 and continued until its abolishment at the time of the enforcement of the 1946 Constitution.

[70] DICEY, THE LAW OF THE CONSTITUTION 193 (9th ed., 1959).

[71] The inference can be made from arts. 14(1), 76(2), and 81 of the Constitution. See Court Law, Law No. 59 of 1947, art. 3(1); translated into English in 2 EHS LAW BULLETIN SERIES AA 1 (Nakane ed., 1954).

[72] CONST. art. 55.

[73] Under the old Court Organization Law, the Great Court of Judicature held that it had power to review the question of the ultra vires of orders. See, for example, Sato v. Japan, Great Court of Judicature, III Criminal Department, March 3, 1937, 16 DAI SHIN IN KEIJI HANREI SHŪ (A Collection of Criminal Great Court of Judicature Cases) 193. However, it was generally felt that laws which had been passed by the Diet and sanctioned by the Emperor could not be reviewed by the courts even if they were in contravention of the written constitution. For example, see Shimada v. Japan, Great Court of Judicature, I Criminal Department, July 11, 1913, 19 DAI SHIN IN KEIJI HANKETSU ROKU (Record of Great Court of Judicature Criminal Judgments) 790. See also HAINES, THE AMERICAN DOCTRINE OF JUDICIAL SUPREMACY 15 (rev. ed., 1959).

[74] CONST. art. 81.

[75] CONST. arts. 76(2), 77–78.

be attacked; any law restricting human rights and freedom is invalid.[76] Thus the legal profession clearly has a larger role in protecting human rights than it had before World War II.

Consequently, both organizational and functional changes have occurred in all three branches of the profession, those respecting the judiciary being most significant. In the first place, the judge has been completely freed from the supervisory power of the Minister of Justice, who had exerted an undesirable influence over the prewar judiciary. Now the judiciary is subject only to the general supervision of the Supreme Court, a group of their own professional seniors.[77] Secondly, there is now provision that judges other than Supreme Court justices must be appointed from lists of individuals nominated by the Court.[78] While it is generally agreed that ordinary judges were not appointed for political reasons even under the old Constitution, it is conceivable that appointments to senior judicial position were sometimes, at least in part, motivated by such considerations. The new provision, coupled with the power of the Supreme Court to assign judges among the courts,[79] undoubtedly does much to assure "the right judge in the right position," to say nothing of reducing the undesirable practice of political appointment. In the third place, administration within each court is now in the hands of a conference of judges of the court concerned;[80] under the old system it was in the hands of the president of the court.[81] This revision has eliminated the possibility that a judge, either consciously or unconsciously, will accommodate himself to the particular judge who is his administrative superior. Finally, consideration has been given to compensation of judges; the general principle is that judges should enjoy a higher pay scale than procurators or other government officials.[82]

[76] Cf. chap. 3, CONST. of 1946 and chap. 2, CONST. of 1889.

[77] CONST. art. 77(1); Court Law, art 80. Art. 78 of the Constitution prescribes procedures for the impeachment of judges, something which had not existed under the old Constitution. Impeachment proceedings are conducted by a Court of Impeachment composed of members of the Diet based upon prosecution conducted by the Judicial Prosecuting Committee, also made up of Diet members. Since the enforcement of the new Constitution, two judges have been dismissed by impeachment on the ground of gross default in discharge of judicial duties. See the Judge Impeachment Law, Law No. 137 of 1947; translated into English in 2 EHS LAW BULLETIN SERIES AO 1 (Nakane ed. and trans., 1958).

[78] CONST. art. 80(1); Court Law, art. 40(1).

[79] Judges other than Supreme Court justices are appointed without designation to the court in which they will serve, the right of assignment to a particular court being reserved to the Supreme Court. Court Law, art. 47. Because the power of assignment was in the Minister of Justice before World War II, the possibility of abuse was greater.

[80] Court Law, arts. 12, 20, 29, 35-5.

[81] Court Organization Law, arts. 11(5), 20(1)–(2), 35(1)–(2), 44(1)–(2), 135 (1890).

[82] Law Concerning Temporary Measures for the Compensation, Etc., of Judges, Etc., Law No. 65 of 1947; translated into English in OFFICIAL GAZETTE, April 17, 1947, no. 312, at 3. This was enacted pursuant to arts. 79(6) and 80(2) of the Constitution. The general principle was: (1) The Chief Justice would be paid as much as the Prime Minister, and the associate justices of the Supreme Court as much as an ordinary cabinet minister; (2) judges of

The key question which had to be dealt with in developing a new system was that of the qualifications required for judicial appointment.[83] As Arthur von Mehren has remarked in connection with German judges, it was thought under the prewar system that the Japanese judge had adequately discharged his duties if he were "merely to apply the legislatively given text or, where the text was obscure, to discover the legislator's intent."[84] Under the new Constitution, however, an obligation is imposed upon all judges to do creative and original work, particularly in passing upon the constitutionality of statutes. In the course of drafting the new Court Law, it had been generally accepted, at least as an ideal, that the new judiciary should not "remain in substance a special branch of the general bureaucracy," and that the former system, under which "recruitment is ordinarily by examination" and the "judicial career is usually begun when relatively young,"[85] should be superseded by a system of appointment to the bench of persons of genuine competence, maturity, and considerable professional experience.[86] However, opinions varied widely on the question of where, as a practical matter, new judges could be secured.[87] Moreover, it was almost impossible to carry out a general revamping of the judicial personnel system within the short period of time before the new Constitution was to become operative. The problem was settled by making a compromise among various methods of judicial selection:

---

the inferior courts would be paid not less than vice ministers; (3) the pay scale of procurators should be slightly less than that of judges.

However, it is doubtful whether the second provision has been complied with during the past ten years, for judges as a group probably are not paid more than administrative officials at the present time. Although this reflects in part the fact that postwar efforts to reduce the power of administrative officials have not been fully successful, it also may be attributed to the system of selecting judges, particularly the assistant-judge system which has contributed to the continuation of the career judiciary. This subject is discussed in the text. For a full account of the compensation problem, see Saikō Saibansho Jimu-sōkyoku (General Secretariat of the Supreme Court), *Saikō Saibansho Jūnen no Kaiko* (Ten Years of the Supreme Court in Retrospect), 9 Hōsō Jihō (Journal of the Jurists' Association) 1161, 1174–86 (1957).

[83] A full and very detailed account of the legislative history of the Court Law of 1947 is given in 1 & 2 NAITO, SHŪSEN-GO NI OKERU SHIHŌ SEIDO KAIKAKU NO KEIKA (The Course of Reform in the System of Justice after the End of the War) (1959). A summarized account is found in SAIKŌ SAIBANSHO JIMU-SŌKYOKU, note 67.

[84] VON MEHREN, THE CIVIL LAW SYSTEM 830 (1957). Also see Judge Kishi's statement in SAIBAN HIHAN, note 40, at 55.

[85] VON MEHREN, note 84, at 841, 842.

[86] 1 NAITO, note 83, at II (12–16); SAIKŌ SAIBANSHO JIMU-SŌKYOKU, note 67, at 45, 46, 47. In the course of the drafting of the new Court Law a legal officer of the occupation forces suggested to the Ministry of Justice that judges should be appointed from among persons who had had at least three years' experience in private practice or law teaching. At a meeting of the Legal System of Justice Council (Shihō Hōsei Shingikai), especially established in the Ministry of Justice to deal with the problem of judicial reform after the war, some of its lawyer members persisted in the proposal to revise the selection system so as to require appointment of judges exclusively from among private practitioners. The proposal was rejected on the ground that it was premature.

[87] 1 NAITO, note 83, at II (12–16).

(1) Individuals may not be appointed full judges, qualified to decide all types of cases independently, unless they have had at least ten years' experience as an assistant judge, procurator, private lawyer, or law professor, after having passed the national legal examination and having completed two years of training at the Legal Training and Research Institute.[88]

(2) Assistant judges, appointed from among those who have completed two years of training at the institute, may exercise certain limited judicial powers.[89]

(3) In the case of the Supreme Court, at least ten justices out of the total of fifteen must have been a judge, procurator, private practitioner, or law professor for at least twenty years, while the remaining five need not be "qualified lawyers" as long as they are learned and have some general knowledge of law. The hope was that introduction of nonspecialists would make it possible for the Supreme Court to render judgments which are not merely logical products reached from a narrow, technical viewpoint but are more in accord with community sentiment.[90]

(4) It is particularly noteworthy that justices of the Supreme Court are subject to review in decennial plebiscites held at the time of national elections, while the judges of inferior courts are appointed for ten-year terms.[91] This is a radical departure from the old system of life tenure.[92] It is said that these

[88] Court Law, art. 42. One exception to the general principle concerns judges of the Summary Court, which was established to handle minor civil and criminal cases on the model of the Anglo-American justice-of-the-peace or small-claims court. In view of the unique character of the Summary Court, persons who are not necessarily qualified professionals can be appointed judges. Court Law, art. 45. See SAIKŌ SAIBANSHO JIMU-SŌKYOKU (General Secretariat of the Supreme Court), SAIBANSHO HŌ CHIKUJŌ KAISETSU (An Article-by-Article Commentary on the Court Law) 123 (1958). Some people are critical of this selection system. Cf. *Report of the Committee on Simplification and Improvement of Appellate Practice of the American Bar Association*, 63 A.B.A. REP. 602–03 (1938).

[89] Court Law, arts. 27, 43. Generally speaking, assistant judges cannot try cases independently, although they can be members of the collegiate body in the District Court. Such a system did not exist in prewar days.

[90] Court Law, art. 41. This principle stands in sharp contrast to the situation in England, where all appellate judges are appointed from among barristers, and that in the United States, where judges of the highest courts are, as a general rule, appointed from among qualified lawyers. See HAYNES, note 34, at 139; JACKSON, THE MACHINERY OF JUSTICE IN ENGLAND 231–32 (3d ed., 1960); VANDERBILT, JUDGES AND JURORS: THEIR FUNCTIONS, QUALIFICATIONS AND SELECTION 27–28 (1956).

[91] CONST. arts. 79(2), 80(1); Court Law, arts. 39(4), 40(3).

[92] It is self-evident that the plebiscite system follows the so-called Missouri Plan. In Japan, there are arguments against it in some quarters. See, e.g., Hiraga, *Nihon-koku Kempō to Shihō* (The Constitution of Japan and Justice), in SOSHŌ TO SAIBAN (Procedure and Trial), IWAMATSU SABURO SAIBANKAN KANREKI KINEN ROMBUN SHŪ (A Collection of Essays in Commemoration of the 61st Birthday of Justice Saburo Iwamatsu) 43–59 (Tarumi & Kaneko ed., 1956), where the following points are made: (1) It is not easy for the general public to make informed judgments on the propriety of judicial behavior because judicial duties require a high degree of technical competence which the general public lacks. (2) The general public rarely has an opportunity to acquire knowledge of the activities of any particular justice. (3) A considerable expenditure of public funds is required to review the work of relatively few justices.

limitations on tenure are needed both to reflect the will of the people in the selection of the judiciary and to make it possible to remove incompetent individuals.[93]

(5) In view of the importance attached to judicial duties under the 1946 Constitution, special consideration has been given to the training of judicial officers. In particular, the Legal Training and Research Institute was established to conduct continuing education for younger assistant judges and to provide well-organized professional training for applicants for judicial positions.[94]

Most judges appointed after the postwar reforms were career judges who had been serving under the 1889 Constitution; vacancies have since been filled with young men who are graduates of the Legal Training and Research Institute. Perhaps the aspect of the appointment system that is currently most controversial is the assistant-judge system which necessarily produces a body of career judges.[95]

Changes in the system as it related to the procuracy are exemplified in rather striking fashion by the following phenomena. The public procurators' office, which formerly was located in the same building as the court in each locality, is now situated in a separate building;[96] and the procurator, who formerly sat on the bench at a level with the judge, now sits on the same level as the defense counsel. Sharing of the court building and joint occupancy of the bench may have been nothing more than conventional usage. However, these changes clearly have symbolic significance, for the procurator enjoyed a position superior to the accused or his counsel in the prewar period, a time when the inquisitorial system of criminal procedure vested the procurator with great power in the investigation of crime and when documents

[93] In all plebiscites held so far, votes for dismissal have never reached ten percent of the total and not one justice has been removed. In December 1957, the term of office of a number of judges who had been appointed under the 1946 Constitution expired. Most of them, however, were reappointed, as can be seen from the following list.

	Number terminated	*Reappointed*	*Not reappointed*
Judges	525	465	60
Assistant judges	4	2	2
Summary Court judges	160	147	13
Total	689	614	75

It is generally believed that most of those who were not reappointed retired of their own volition and very few were discharged because of unfitness. See Saikō Saibansho Jimu-sōkyoku, note 82, 10 Hōsō Jihō 52 (1958). The decennial system probably is largely a psychological inhibitant, though its importance cannot be discounted.

[94] Court Law, art. 14. As to the organization and function of the Legal Training and Research Institute, see Matsuda, *The Japanese Legal Training and Research Institute,* 7 Am. J. Comp. L. 366 (1958); Hakaru Abe, "Education of the Legal Profession," in this volume.

[95] Also see Kohji Tanabe, "The Processes of Litigation," in this volume.

[96] Cf. Court Law, art. 6 and Public Procurators' Office Law, Law No. 61 of 1947, art. 2(3), translated into English in 2 EHS Law Bulletin Series BA 1 (Nakane ed., 1953).

prepared by him were treated as competent evidence.[97] These changes signify the complete separation of procuracy and judiciary and the formal procedural equality of prosecution and accused.[98]

Three other noteworthy changes have been made with respect to the status of procurators and the exercise of their authority. In the first place, a procurators' screening committee, composed of members of the National Diet, judges, public procurators, private practitioners, and others, has been established subject to appointment by the Prime Minister in order to screen all procurators every three years to weed out the incompetent.[99] In the second place, a procurator's decision not to prosecute can be reviewed, upon application of complainants or the injured party, by an inquest of prosecution — a committee composed of ordinary citizens picked by lot.[100] If the committee considers a determination unjustified, it recommends prosecution to the chief district procurator. Although a recommendation is not binding, the system clearly provides a check on the arbitrary exercise of prosecuting authority. Finally, a tendency toward excessive independence of the procuracy has been restricted by a provision in the Public Procurators' Office Law that the procurator shall be subject to the direction of the Minister of Justice, through the Procurator-General, even with regard to the disposition of a case.[101]

[97] See CODE OF CRIMINAL PROCEDURE of 1922, Law No. 75 of 1922, arts. 123–124, 126–129, 170, 180–182, 214, 228. Under the postwar law, documents prepared by the procurator are admissible only under limited circumstances.

[98] For the reforms in criminal procedure brought about by the new CODE OF CRIMINAL PROCEDURE, Law No. 131 of 1947, see Appleton, note 68.

[99] Public Procurators' Office Law, art. 23. Prior to the enactment of this statute, a legal officer of the occupation forces suggested to the Ministry of Justice that procurators should be elected triennially in each prefecture. The officials of the Ministry opposed the suggestion on the grounds that the election system was not suited to Japan and that such a system would have hampered strict enforcement of the economic control laws which were in effect at that time. As a consequence, the election system was not adopted. See Saikō Kensatsu-chō Kōhō Bu, note 50, at 44–46.

[100] Inquest of Prosecution Law, Law No. 147 of 1948, arts. 2, 4, 40; translated into English in OFFICIAL GAZETTE, July 12, 1948, extra ed. at 15. The inquest of prosecution seems to derive from the grand jury system in the United States. For a summary of this system, see Meyers, *Japanese Inquest of Prosecution*, 64 HARV. L. REV. 179, 281–86 (1950). The following list provided the writer by the General Secretariat of the Supreme Court presents data on nationwide activities of these committees during the period 1948–1960.

Decisions reviewed	18,748 (100%)
Decisions found improper	1,723 (9.2%)
Decisions found correct	13,617 (72.6%)
Others (withdrawal, etc.)	3,428 (18.2%)

[101] Public Procurators' Office Law, art. 14. In connection with the exercise of directive power by the Minister of Justice, the following well-known case is instructive. In April 1954, when the Tokyo District Public Procurators' Office was investigating a series of bribery cases involving various shipping companies, the then Procurator-General, Tosuke Sato, requested Minister of Justice Takeshi Inukai to allow him to apply to the court for a warrant to arrest Eisaku Sato, the Secretary-General of the Liberal Party, then the party in power. The Minister issued a directive ordering him to refrain from applying for the warrant. The

While it cannot be denied that these reforms have reduced the possibility of arbitrary exercise of prosecuting power by the procuracy and equalized prosecution and defense in the conduct of the trial, the postwar changes respecting the procuracy were clearly less significant than those affecting the other two branches of the profession. The procurator continues to enjoy a reasonably high prestige, is paid comparatively well, and forms a special category of government officials.[102] At the present time, with the Ministry of Home Affairs no longer in existence, the procuracy seems to be nearly "the only centralized bureaucratic organization in the country vested with strong power," [103] and as such it remains of major significance.

To the third branch of the profession, the private practitioner, the 1946 Constitution brought considerable change. Revision was not as quick as it had been in the case of the laws pertaining to judges and procurators;[104] but, unlike previous legislation relating to the lawyer, which always had been introduced through government bills, the postwar bill was introduced as a private member's bill by a lawyer member of the Diet. It was enacted with the active support of the bar. This law clearly represents "a step forward" for the bar as a whole.[105]

There are three points of particular significance in the postwar development of the bar. The first pertains to the enlargement of the scope of a lawyer's activity through new legislation. Apart from "natural" expansion of activity as a consequence of social and economic development, the lawyer's functions have been increased by the constitutional guarantees of human rights. Particularly to be noted are the guarantee of right to counsel in criminal prosecutions*[106] and recognition of the principle that all legal

---

other political parties attacked the directive of the Minister as an abuse of his directive power and challenged it as prompted by partisan considerations. They presented a nonconfidence motion against the Yoshida cabinet to the Diet. As a consequence, the cabinet resigned the following day. This was the first case of the exercise of directive power and provoked a heated controversy throughout the country. See ITO, KENSATSU-CHŌ HŌ SEIGI (A Commentary on the Public Procurators' Office Law) 52–62 (1955).

[102] For example, some of the positions in the table of organization for procurators are for so-called attested officers (*ninshō-kan*), official positions appointed by the cabinet and attested by the Emperor. For the salary of public procurators, see note 82.

[103] KANEKO, note 41, at 238.

[104] Attorneys Law, Law No. 205 of 1949; translated into English in 2 EHS LAW BULLETIN SERIES CA 1 (Nakane ed., 1954). This law was enacted more than a year after the laws concerning the judiciary and the procuracy. It has been suggested that this can be attributed to the fact that "the practice of law is a private profession. As a group, lawyers were not as strong as the other branches of the legal profession, and they have not yet attained an important position in the capitalistic social structure." See NIHON BENGOSHI RENGŌ KAI, note 21, at 292.

[105] For the legislative history of the Attorneys Law of 1949, see NIHON BENGOSHI RENGŌ KAI, note 21, at 293–305; Fukuhara, *Bengoshi Hō no Naritachi to Shōrai no Kaiseiten* (Formation of the Attorneys Law and Points for Future Revision), 32 HŌRITSU JIHŌ (Law Journal) 500 (1960). For the substance of this law, see Woodruff, *The Japanese Lawyer*, 35 NEB. L. REV. 429 (1956), and Rabinowitz' two works referred to in note 2.

* At the conference, Charles Wyzanski and B. J. George stated that the percentage of unrepresented defendants was not high by United States standards. George also remarked that,

disputes on the civil side should be resolved through judicial proceedings.[107]

Second, the bar finally won its struggle for autonomy. The screening of applicants, the enrollment of lawyers, and, in particular, disciplinary action against members are now entrusted to the organized profession rather than to the Minister of Justice, as they had been in the past.[108] Furthermore, for the first time in Japanese history the bar is organized on a national basis with the establishment of the Japanese Federated Attorneys' Association (Nihon Bengoshi Rengō Kai).[109]

The third, and perhaps most significant, point pertains to the reform of the training system for lawyers. Notwithstanding the adoption of the probationary system before the war, training of probationary attorneys was criticized as imperfect and ineffective.[110] By the new Attorneys Law, the probationary program has been merged with the training program for

---

since an immediate plea of guilty is not permitted in Japan, a larger proportion of cases reach the formal-trial stage than do in the United States; this fact may encourage the use of lawyers. It was also observed that, in view of the active role traditionally assumed by Japanese judges, even the unrepresented defendant enjoys a measure of protection.

[106] CONST. arts. 34, 37(3). The extent of representation by counsel in criminal cases during 1960 is shown in the following tabulation prepared by the General Secretariat of the Supreme Court. An asterisk indicates cases in which defense counsel was provided at the expense of the state.

Court	*Represented by defense counsel*				*Unrepresented by defense counsel*
		Selected by the state			
	Selected by accused	*At request of accused*	*For other reasons*	*Total*	
District	33.5%	32.5%*	7.7%	73.7%	26.3%
Summary	16.2%	41.4%*	10.5%	68.1%	31.9%

Shōwa 35 Nen ni okeru Keiji Jiken no Gaikyō (The General Condition of Criminal Cases in 1960), 13 HŌSŌ JIHŌ 1399, 1428 (1961).

[107] CONST. art. 76(2); Court Law, art. 3. Statistics, prepared by the General Secretariat of the Supreme Court, show the total number of administrative cases handled by the courts under the 1946 Constitution: 1947, 478; 1948, 2504; 1949, 2511; 1950, 1746; 1951, 1218; 1952, 1187; 1953, 935; 1954, 1119; 1955, 979; 1956, 838; 1957, 894; 1958, 919; 1959, 896; 1960, 845. *Shōwa 35 Nendo Gyōsei Jiken no Gaikyō* (The General Condition of Administrative Cases in 1960), 13 HŌSŌ JIHŌ 1601, 1638 (1961).

[108] Attorneys Law, arts. 8–9, 31, 45, 51, 59–60. It should be noted that, prior to the enactment of the revised law, opinions varied as to the legality and the propriety of the autonomy of the bar. Autonomy was thought by some to be inconsistent with the rule-making power of the Supreme Court concerning lawyers, clearly prescribed in art. 77 of the Constitution; and fair disciplinary action could not necessarily be expected from trial by one's peers. The latter point has been met by adding judges and procurators to the professional disciplinary committee, while the former remains unsolved. As a matter of fact, in the postwar period the Supreme Court rarely has exercised its rule-making authority with respect to lawyers. See Fukuhara, note 105, at 73–74.

[109] Attorneys Law, art. 45.

In prewar days there was a national federation composed of regional attorneys' associations; but it was merely a voluntary organization to carry out certain activities in which the various attorneys' associations had a common interest. Attorneys Law of 1933, art. 52. Under the Attorneys Law of 1949, the Japanese Federated Attorneys' Association is a statutory organization entrusted with the powers and duties mentioned in the text.

[110] Several reasons have been given for the failure of the probationary-attorney system in the

judges and procurators. Responsibility for the program as a whole is in the hands of the Supreme Court, which supervises the Legal Training and Research Institute.[111] Thus, for the first time the training of Japanese lawyers is treated as part and parcel of training of the whole profession. A desirable byproduct of the joint training program is that prospective judges and procurators now take the training given to private lawyers, thus broadening their perspective.

It is not yet clear how the postwar reforms have changed the professional and social status of the Japanese lawyer. It is generally believed that the work of the Japanese lawyer is still confined primarily to courtroom activity, or at least to litigation, with relatively little general counseling. While this may be so, a number of lawyers are now participating in central or regional governmental and independent commissions and other bodies.[112] Moreover, the Japanese Federated Attorneys' Association is quite active in the study of problems requiring legal reforms and makes frequent recommendations concerning legislation. It is also active in the operation of the legal-aid societies and in such areas as movements for better facilities for the judiciary and for continuing legal education for lawyers.[113]

SOME BASIC PROBLEMS FACING THE PROFESSION

As observed in the preceding section, in the postwar period the Japanese legal profession has been charged with broader and more significant responsibilities than ever before in its history. Generally speaking, the legal profession has improved remarkably and now contributes much to the administration of justice. The question remains, however, whether the profession even now is discharging fully its more comprehensive responsi-

---

prewar period. Shortly after its adoption, the war broke out, and many able lawyers, who might have served as instructors, were called to service. Secondly, no financial support was given by the state. Thirdly, the training of probationary attorneys was left in the hands of the individual attorneys' association without any general systematic program being set up by the bar as a whole.

[111] Attorneys Law, art. 4; Court Law, art. 14. Particularly noteworthy is the fact that the apprentice under the new system receives a stipend from the national treasury even if he contemplates entering private practice. See Court Law, art. 67(2).

[112] It is reported that, as of July, 1958, in 29 out of 46 local labor commissions, the chairman was a lawyer and that lawyers held a fairly high percentage of seats in the national and local legislatures. See Matsui, Makita & Torita, *Bengoshi no Seikatsu to Ishiki — Jittai Chōsa* (The Life and Attitude of Attorneys — A Survey of Actual Conditions), 32 HŌRITSU JIHŌ 452, 458–59 (1960).

[113] The major activities of the association are: (1) Since 1952, it has been very active in the movement for revision of the structure and function of the Supreme Court. (2) With the cooperation of lawyer members of the National Diet, it has campaigned for increases in the court budget. (3) It established the Legal Aid Society in July 1957. Legal aid in civil matters is principally provided by this society and is supplemented by free legal counseling extended periodically by individual attorneys' associations and by municipalities with the cooperation of individual volunteers. However, legal aid in Japan is not yet highly developed because of a shortage of funds. (4) The association conducted a special 50-hour training course for almost all the lawyers in the country in 1950. It also conducts annual summer seminars for its

bilities as stipulated by the 1946 Constitution and as demanded by a growing society.

The Constitution involves a fundamental commitment to a society organized on the rule of law, and the degree of the community's awareness and acceptance of this commitment is basic to any consideration of the legal profession's role in Japanese society.[114] Also, unless persons of sufficient potential are recruited into (and retained in) the profession, legal problems will not be solved in a manner that will satisfy the community's consciousness of law; under such conditions, this consciousness would soon become a sterile thing. Nor will persons of sufficient abilities, once recruited, be able to solve technical law problems well unless they are aware both of the possibilities and the obligations of their roles, given adequate training to perform them well, and then cooperate with one another in performance. Although consideration of society's reception of the premises underlying the new Constitution is beyond my present purpose, the balance of this essay will consider the caliber of personnel in the legal profession and the extent to which its three branches cooperate in discharging their functions.

It is not suggested that Japanese judges have been or are incompetent; on the contrary, as noted earlier, they have been held in high esteem as men of greater integrity and impartiality than those found elsewhere in the bureaucratic structure. This esteem goes back, however, to a day when judges dealt only with disputes between private citizens and were entrusted with the disposition only of ordinary criminal cases; it does not encompass resolution of disputes between the state and private parties or review of legislative and administrative acts for constitutionality. It cannot yet be said that the judiciary has won popular respect in its exercise of the broader judicial powers now entrusted to it; judges under the new system still remain an unknown quantity. If the judiciary is to retain respect, it must recruit extremely able and experienced men, even more so than in the past.[115]

Related to the problem of judicial recruitment is a demand for the "unification of the legal profession." As generally used, the expression includes selection of the judiciary from the bar.[116] A distinguished former

---

members every year in the major cities. (5) It adopted Canons of Professional Ethics in March 1955. See NIHON BENGOSHI RENGŌ KAI, note 21, at 325–45; Mizuno, *Hōritsu Fujo no Jittai* (The Actual Condition of Legal Aid), 11 JIYŪ TO SEIGI (Freedom and Justice) no. 9, at 18 (1960).

[114] As indicated in the preceding sections, the Japanese legal system adopted after the Meiji Restoration was not a "natural" product necessitated by the development of the society itself, but rather a direct import of foreign systems mainly for the purpose of the abolition of extraterritoriality; furthermore, the postwar revisions were undertaken so hastily and drastically that the society could not easily adjust to the transition.

[115] Under the Court Law of 1947, art. 26, the District Court, the court of general jurisdiction, as a general rule handles cases through a single judge; in prewar days all cases in the District Court were tried by collegiate benches of three judges. This shift to one-man courts presupposes judges of maturity and experience.

[116] The expression "unification of the legal profession" (*hōsō ichigen-ka*) is used in various

law professor criticized this demand as it was used before the war as an attempt by the bar, which had long suffered from discriminatory treatment, to gain social equality.[117] Regardless of criticisms and quite apart from its wisdom, it is significant that the same demand is being expressed today, by the Japanese Federated Attorneys' Association[118] with strong support from the Japanese Law Specialists' Association (Nihon Hōritsuka Kyōkai), an unofficial organization of leading judges, procurators, private lawyers, and law professors for the specific purpose of bringing about closer relations among the various branches of the profession.[119]

Although some knowledgeable men are not completely convinced of the cogency of the prounification position, the general proposition that judges should be appointed from among the experienced members of the legal profession seems clearly valid. But appointments from among private practitioners and procurators have not been frequent, despite its feasibility and the fact that so many people spoke of its desirability, particularly in the early postwar period.[120] The principal reasons why experienced and successful

ways. In the broadest sense, the phrase means that those in the various branches of the profession should maintain an awareness of themselves as colleagues within the same profession and that they should form a body to cooperate and contribute to the maintenance in society of a spirit of respect for law. In a narrower sense, it refers to the unification of apprentice training. And, in the narrowest sense, it is the demand that the judiciary be selected from the bar, or at least from those trained in law, and not recruited directly from among graduates of the Legal Training and Research Institute. These, however, do not exhaust the ways in which the expression has been used. For example, it is sometimes used in connection with a demand that procurators as well as judges be selected from the bar or that the judiciary be recruited only from the procuracy and the bar.

[117] KANEKO, note 41, at 261.

[118] In 1954, the Federated Attorneys' Association announced a program for the unification of the legal profession. A summary of this program is as follows: (1) Judges and procurators should be appointed from among lawyers who had practiced for a considerable period of time. (2) The Legal Training and Research Institute should be under the control of the association. (3) The system of assistant judges should be abolished.

[119] The Japanese Law Specialists' Association was organized on April 15, 1952, to promote the administration of justice, contribute to the progress of jurisprudence, and improve professional standards. As of June 1961, its members included 201 judges, 65 procurators, 557 private practitioners, and 45 professors and others.

On June 9, 1961, the association's Committee for the Unification of the Legal Profession adopted a resolution that judges should be appointed from among experienced private practitioners and the procurators. See Saikō Saibansho Jimu-sōkyoku (General Secretariat of the Supreme Court), SAIBANSHO JIHŌ (The Court Journal) no. 331, at 7, 9 (1961).

[120] According to statistics prepared for the writer by the General Secretariat of the Supreme Court, the total number of judges appointed from among private practitioners during the period 1947–1960 is as follows.

	1947	*'48*	*'49*	*'50*	*'51*	*'52*	*'53*	*'54*	*'55*	*'56*	*'57*	*58*	*'59*	*'60*
Justices of Supreme Court	5	—	—	—	1	1	—	—	—	1	1	—	—	1
Judges	13	43	47	14	14	12	18	8	4	1	9	5	7	7
Assistant judges	5	8	13	6	4	4	4	4	0	3	4	7	5	3
Summary Court judges	59	41	35	23	16	14	4	7	4	6	5	8	10	8
Total	82	92	95	43	35	31	26	19	8	11	19	20	22	19

private practitioners are unwilling to go on the bench are these. (1) They would face a substantial diminution in income.[121] (2) They would be at a severe disadvantage in respect to retirement pensions.[122] (3) Since Japanese lawyers practice independently, they would have to start afresh if and when they withdraw from judicial service because they would not have firms to which they could return.[123] (4) They would find it difficult to deal with a host of unfamiliar tasks presented upon entering a new career at a relatively

---

So few procurators and professors have been appointed judges that the statistics are omitted.

As far as the Supreme Court is concerned, it is an accepted principle, though not a legal requirement, that one third of the justices are to be appointed from among career judges, another one third from among private practitioners, and the balance from among procurators, law professors, or others trained in the law. The former positions of the justices as of December 31, 1960, are as follows: judges of inferior courts, 5; private practitioners, 5; others, 5 (2 law professors, 1 procurator, 1 director of the Cabinet's Legal System Bureau, 1 director of the Diet's Legal System Bureau). See SAIBANSHO JIHŌ no. 224, at 6 (1957); no. 258, at 8 (1958); no. 316, at 16 (1961); no. 320, at 16 (1961); and HŌSŌ KAI (Jurists' Association), SHIHŌ TAIKAN (A General View of Justice) 1–4 (1957). The high social prestige of Supreme Court justices, the particular demand for men of talent as justices of the court of last resort, and other similar factors make the appointment of individuals other than career judges to the Supreme Court easier than to the inferior courts.

[121] There is no authoritative material with regard to the income of private practitioners in Japan. However, according to a survey conducted by HŌRITSU JIHŌ, a private law journal, using the stratified sampling method, the average monthly income of private practitioners in 1959 was 98,939 yen. See Matsui et al., note 112, at 460–61. Compare this with the following figures relating to monthly judicial salaries in the same year (360 yen equal one dollar): Chief Justice of the Supreme Court, 150,000; associate justice of the Supreme Court, 110,000; full judge of inferior courts, 100,000–53,200 (all judges receive certain allowances in addition to the above salaries).

[122] Under the present system, individuals who have served as public officials for twenty years or more are eligible to receive annual pensions. Those who serve for lesser periods receive only a lump-sum retirement allowance. See the National Public Servants Mutual Aid Societies Law, Law No. 128 of 1958, arts. 76, 80; National Public Servants, Etc., Severance Allowance Law, Law No. 182 of 1953, art. 3.

[123] According to the Attorneys' Directory of 1960, published by the Federated Attorneys' Association, the organization of law practice in Tokyo was as follows.

Number of lawyers in same office	*Number of offices*
15	1
13	1
12	2
9	1
8	2
7	3
6	5
5	8
4	2
3	54
2	106

A total of 550 lawyers were thus practicing in some form of association; the total number of practitioners registered in Tokyo in 1960 was 2,882. Many of the law offices with two or more lawyers are not law firms but merely involve office sharing.

advanced age.[124] The result is that the overwhelming majority of vacancies in full judgeships have been filled during the entire postwar period by assistant judges directly from the Legal Training and Research Institute, and the Japanese judiciary remains very much a career judiciary.[125]

A career judiciary clearly has some merit. A career judge has the possibility of greater independence from pressure-group influences, be they from politicians, business groups, labor organizations, or others; and there is more opportunity to train him adequately for trial work.[126] However, a very practical, and perhaps fatal, defect of the system is that it tends to bring down the salary scale of the judiciary to the same level as that of administrative officials in general, and, as a consequence, it is much more difficult to attract successful private practitioners to the bench. This is truly a vicious circle. Indeed, the assistant-judge system, adopted as a compromise or transitional measure to meet the immediate needs of the postwar period by providing a pool of young career judges, has become an obstacle to the further development of judicial recruitment from the profession at large.

Not only does it appear virtually impossible for the judiciary to attract the able and experienced lawyers, but the legal profession as a whole does not necessarily recruit the most promising graduates of the law departments.[127] There are probably numerous reasons for this failure. Some of them, related to the historical background of the Japanese legal profession discussed in the preceeding sections, have been discussed by Rabinowitz.[128]

[124] It is generally considered that the work load of Japanese judges is comparatively high. Some contributing elements are: (1) Prewar procedure was influenced by the inquisitorial principle under which the judge's duties are much heavier than they are in a system in which the principle of party presentation prevails. Although the fundamental procedural philosophy has been changed (at least in a formal sense) since the war, the judge is still expected to carry the principal burden of moving litigation forward. (2) The absence of a jury system requires the judge to be the finder of fact in all cases. (3) A very high percentage of cases in Japanese courts are ones in which the parties are not represented by lawyers. This situation is a striking contrast, for example, to that in England. See JACKSON, note 90, at 234–35.

[125] Initial positions taken by graduates of the Legal Training and Research Institute is shown in Table 1 at the end of this essay. The table was prepared by the General Secretariat of the Supreme Court at the request of this writer (also see note 120 above).

[126] For the need for special training of trial judges, see FRANK, COURTS ON TRIAL 247–53 (1949).

[127] KANEKO, note 41, at 260–61. According to mimeographed material prepared and distributed by the Tokyo University Press, the scholastic records of Tokyo University law graduates classified by their first employment in 1959 were as follows. For those who became government officials, the average number of top grades was 31; for those who became legal apprentices, the number was 25. Conclusions cannot be drawn from such scanty evidence, particularly because traditionally many able law graduates of Tokyo University enter the government or large private enterprises. However, the data do suggest the general situation to some extent.

[128] Rabinowitz, note 2, at 78–81. He pointed out the following factors retarding development of the legal profession in Japan: (1) The Japanese lawyer lacks a tradition and, as a consequence, the role of the lawyer is at best imperfectly understood. (2) There has been great reluctance to establish a sphere of occupational monopoly for the lawyer. (3) Professional organization and responsibility have never been strong. (4) Legal education was not adequate. The higher education that the lawyer has received has not been designed to help him meet the exigencies of practice.

Perhaps more important today is the discouraging effect upon university law graduates of the narrowness of the sole gate to the legal profession, the national legal examination.[129] It is extremely difficult for law graduates to succeed in the examination unless they undertake further extensive studies after they complete their university education. Furthermore, so few applicants pass the examination that many capable individuals, who might otherwise be attracted, seek other careers. Many able graduates of the law departments choose other vocations, such as the civil service or employment in large public and private enterprises, which do not involve comparable delays and hazards. These tendencies are further encouraged by the fact, already discussed, that a successful legal career does not necessarily assure higher prestige or income. A thorough re-examination of the screening system of applicants for the legal profession, and the legal education provided them, is imperative if sound remedial measures are to be taken.

Turning now to the question of roles and functions among various branches of the profession, and to the problem of cooperation among the several branches, not much needs to be said about the judiciary and the procuracy. Both branches have been part of officialdom and, for historical reasons, have closely cooperated with one another; indeed, cooperation has been at times so close as to cause misunderstanding and suspicion on the part of the public.

The more significant aspect of this problem — cooperation between the courts and private practitioners — is not discussed to indict either the courts or the lawyers for past failures, which were probably due to the historical background. In the prewar period, relations between the bench and the procuracy, on the one hand, and the bar, on the other, were not very good.[130]

What cooperation there was in the past was largely of a very passive nature: compliance with requests of the courts or obedience to the orders of judges. Cooperation did not take the form of adequate advance preparation of cases, either on the facts or on the law, or of active assistance to the court in effective disposition of its business. Nor did the courts do much to foster a more cooperative attitude on the part of practitioners. The inadequate advance preparation and the lack of active assistance to the court in effectively disposing of its business were not as severe a problem when litigation was

[129] According to statistics supplied this writer by the Ministry of Justice, the number of applicants and the number of successful candidates in the legal examination in 1958, 1959, and 1960 are as follows.

	1958	*1959*	*1960*
Number of applicants (appr.)	7,000	7,800	8,300
Number of successful candidates (appr.)	346	319	345
Percent successful (appr.)	4.85	4.09	4.16

[130] Matsuda, note 94, at 375; Tanaka, *Hōsō Ichigen-ka no Rinen* (The Idea of Unifying the Legal Profession), in Hō no Shihai to Saiban (The Rule of Law and Trial) 436–37 (1960).

handled under the inquisitorial principle, which laid stress on the judge's directive, clarifying, and expediting functions.[131]

Attitudes and practices developed under the old system have carried over into the new. Even now that active cooperation — in particular, adequate advance preparation of cases — is clearly required by court rules with a view to fairer and speedier disposition of cases,[132] judges frequently complain about noncompliance by the lawyers although, it must be confessed, little is done to improve the situation.[133] It is sometimes said that lawyers are too busy to cooperate fully, but the Japanese bar is still very small.[134] Its smallness is due to a variety of historical, social, and political factors which cannot be explored in full here. For example, there is good reason to believe that even in present-day Japanese society, probably under the influence of traditional ethical and religious precepts, great emphasis is placed upon the solution of disputes through "what has been called 'smoothness in human relations'" rather than strict legal procedure.[135] Second, as pointed out by von Mehren, "Japanese law is not the product of centuries of slow, organic growth," [136] a generalization to which even the postwar legal reform is not an exception. Thus, "the law's role," and, hence, the lawyer's role, "in modern Japanese society is markedly different from its role in Western societies." [137] Third, for a long period of time prior to the Meiji Restoration the criminal trial was extremely inquisitorial in nature. On the other hand, civil dis-

[131] For example, under the Code of Civil Procedure of 1890, the clarification of the matter in dispute became, through numerous Great Court of Judicature decisions, a judicial duty and nonperformance thereof a ground of reversal of the judgment; the trial court was authorized to take proof *ex officio;* witnesses were examined by the judge and not by the parties or their lawyers. It is also important to note that Japanese procedural law contains no provision for pretrial discovery devices. The lack thereof constitutes another inhibitant to advance preparation on the part of those who otherwise might be inclined to so prepare. See Kohji Tanabe, "The Processes of Litigation: An Experiment with the Adversary System," in this volume.

[132] See Civil Procedure Regulations, Supreme Court Regulation No. 2 of 1956, arts. 3–4.

[133] See, for example, MINJI SAIBANKAN KAIDŌ YŌROKU (Record of the Civil Judges Meeting), held December 11, 1950, at 122, 129; February 26, 1953, at 75; March 25, 1954, at 188; March 17, 1955, at 33; March 26, 1957, at 40.

[134] The number of lawyers in Japan is set forth in Tables 2 and 3 at the end of this essay.

[135] Von Mehren, *Some Reflections on Japanese Law,* 71 HARV. L. REV. 1486, 1493 n. 22 (1958). Former Chief Justice Tanaka has stated that the relatively low prestige of law administrators in Japan has some relation to the speculative and aesthetic tendencies of the Japanese people. See TANAKA, SHIHŌKAN RON (A Treatise on the Judicial Officer) 18–19 (Shihō Kenshūjo (Legal Training and Research Institute) ed., 1958). In this regard, the emphasis upon mediation procedures in Japan is especially worthy of note. Consider the following facts in this connection: the total number of original civil actions filed during 1960 was 147,468; the total number of mediation cases filed during 1960 was 64,731. Although it is said that the popularity of mediation is due primarily to the fact that inexpensive and speedy settlement of dispute is possible, it probably also reflects the basic psychological orientation of the Japanese people. See *Shōwa 35 Nendo Minji Jiken no Gaikyō* (The General Condition of 1960 Civil Cases), 13 HŌSŌ JIHŌ 1710, 1744, 1746, 1747 (1961); Kawashima, "Dispute Resolution in Contemporary Japan," in this volume.

[136] Von Mehren, note 135, at 1491.

[137] *Ibid.,* 1493.

putes, particularly disputes with respect to pecuniary matters, either could not be brought to the authorities for solution or, if they could be so presented, settlement by mutual compromise was encouraged.[138] Until some ninety years ago, representation on a professional basis of the parties in both civil disputes and criminal proceedings was strictly prohibited under the feudal government. Claims of right by private citizens were thus extremely limited; traditionally, disputes were resolved without reliance upon legal procedures or the legal profession. Fourth, certain nonlawyer specialists perform functions which otherwise would be discharged by lawyers. The *benrishi* (patent specialist) can act as an attorney or give counsel with regard to patent, utility model, design and trademark questions; the *zeirishi* (tax specialist) can draft tax returns, file applications for review concerning assessments, and counsel on tax questions.[139] The *shihō shoshi* (legal scrivener) is licensed to draft legal documents to be filed with the court, the procurators' office, or the regional offices of the Ministry of Justice.[140] In addition to these specialists, most governmental agencies and large enterprises have their own legal staffs manned by individuals who, though graduates of university law departments, are not qualified to practice. These legal departments handle such matters as the drafting of legislation, contracts, and other legal documents.[141] Fifth, the lawyers themselves often have opposed, or at least have been reluctant to see, an increase in the size of the bar for fear of "excessive" competition.[142] The small size of the profession is due to these factors among others.[143]

[138] 2 MIURA, HŌSEI SHI NO KENKYŪ (Studies in the History of the Japanese Legal System) 463–64 (1944).

[139] Patent Specialist Law, Law No. 100 of 1921, art. 1; Tax Specialist Law, art. 2, Law No. 237 of 1951, translated into English in OFFICIAL GAZETTE, June 15, 1951, no. 1565, at 1. Certified public accountants in Japan, as elsewhere, also handle tax problems that otherwise might be handled by lawyers.

[140] Legal Scrivener Law, Law No. 197 of 1950, art. 1; translated into English in OFFICIAL GAZETTE, May 22, 1950, no. 1242, at 2.

In addition to the *shihō shoshi*, the *gyōsei shoshi* (administrative scrivener) is authorized to draft documents to be submitted to administrative agencies. See Administrative Scrivener Law, Law No. 4 of 1951, art. 11; translated into English in OFFICIAL GAZETTE, Feb. 22, 1951, no. 1471, at 1.

[141] The total number, as of Dec. 31, 1960, of nonlawyer specialists, excluding those performing legal functions in government agencies and private enterprises, according to information made available to the writer, was: patent specialists, 1,086 (figure from Patent Agency, Ministry of International Trade and Industry); tax specialists, 10,617 (figure from National Tax Agency, Ministry of Finance); legal scriveners, appr. 12,000 (figure from Ministry of Justice); administrative scriveners, appr. 6,000 (figure from Ministry of Autonomy); certified public accountants, 1,508 (figure from Ministry of Finance).

[142] See MATSUDA, HŌSŌ KYŌIKU (Professional Legal Education) 31 (1960); 1 NIHON HŌRITSUKA KYŌKAI (Japanese Law Specialists' Association), HŌSŌ ICHIGEN TOKUBETSU IINKAI KIROKU (Record of the Proceedings of the Special Committee on the Unification of the Legal Profession) 65 (1956).

[143] A rough comparison of the number of judges and lawyers in selected countries, based upon statistics provided by the General Secretariat of the Supreme Court, may be found in Table 4 at the end of this essay.

The current shortage of lawyers poses the problem of how to educate the public about the services a lawyer has to offer without creating expectations which the bar cannot meet. Paradoxical as it may sound, the public makes relatively little use of lawyers while lawyers are too busy to give proper attention to many legal matters.* The 1946 Constitution has placed new duties on the bar, and a modern society creates an increasing demand for legal services; yet the bar is presently too small to perform these various functions.[144] In addition, the shortage, perhaps reinforced by the traditionally unfavorable attitudes toward the bar dating from the time of the kujishi, means that the lawyer is only infrequently used in handling daily transactions and the way is thus paved for disputes that could have been avoided if lawyers had been involved in the prospective structuring of the transactions rather than being brought in only at the dispute stage. Court appearances without counsel are also frequent. Evidence suggests that neither party is represented by counsel in nearly one third of all District Court cases.[145] Such conditions not only increase the burden upon the court but also greatly inhibit the efficient administration of justice. Once again a vicious circle develops: inadequate judicial machinery, or the failure adequately to utilize such judicial machinery as does exist, leads the general public to utilize informal and less satisfactory techniques of dispute resolution and increases dissatisfaction with the law and its administrators. Finally,

* At the conference, this point was made in different contexts. Shinichiro Michida remarked that one problem with private practitioners is that they are much too busy and "always out." Yasuharu Nagashima, who is himself a practicing lawyer, stated that lawyers are too busy to meet all the demands of the big companies. Kichiemon Ishikawa reported that trade-union lawyers were too busy to protect adequately the unions or their members.

[144] According to statistics prepared for this writer by the General Secretariat of the Supreme Court, as of June 1961, 32 out of 240 cities or towns where branches of the District Court (the court of general jurisdiction) are located and 202 out of 680 cities and towns where the Summary Courts (the courts having jurisdiction over small claims and minor criminal offenses) are located have no lawyer practicing within their territorial jurisdiction. Particularly critical is the situation of the profession outside the metropolitan centers, since most graduates of the institute prefer to practice in larger cities. The distribution as of June 1961 of younger lawyers who have graduated from the institute, according to statistics which have been prepared by the General Secretariat of the Supreme Court is as follows: Tokyo, 999; Osaka, 245; Nagoya, 62; Yokohama, 46; Fukuoka, 40; two attorneys' associations, 20–39; six attorneys' associations, 10–19; ten attorneys' associations, 5–9; twenty-six attorneys' associations, 1–4.

[145] The percentage of representation in civil cases in 1960 is shown in the following tabulation prepared by the General Secretariat of the Supreme Court.

Court	*Total*	*Represented by lawyer*			*Both parties not represented by lawyer*
		Both parties	*One party*	*Total*	
District	100%	39.6%	33.0%	72.6%	27.4%
Summary	100%	9.3%	20.3%	29.6%	70.4%

Shōwa 35 Nendo Minji Jiken no Gaikyō (The General Condition of 1960 Civil Cases), 13 Hōsō Jihō 1710, 1726, 1734 (1961).

the shortage of lawyers inhibits the development of specialization, which is essential to the competent disposition of the complex domestic and international problems produced by industrialization and the general economic development of modern Japanese society.[146] Although some of the functions which would be performed by lawyers are being discharged by the nonlawyer specialists mentioned above, the latter are not necessarily well trained in law and sometimes they do not discharge their duties adequately.[147]

The shortage of lawyers in Japan is not due to a scarcity of applicants. Japanese universities produce over thirteen thousand law graduates annually — though not all aspire to the legal profession[148] — and over seven thousand people annually take the national legal examination.[149] But very few pass the examination, and many able law graduates are not attracted to the profession. The very restrictive admission policy of the examination is based, at least in part, upon a frequently articulated, though probably quite specious, belief that a less restrictive policy would inevitably lower the quality of the legal profession and that a significant expansion in numbers is neither necessary nor desirable. This second assumption is the key to the seeming paradox: because the current bar fears the competition that would arise from expanded opportunities for admission, many duties that should be performed by lawyers are undertaken, by default, by quasi-lawyers. When these latter groups perform inadequately, public confidence in the entire legal structure is weakened, leading to further search for quick and satisfactory means of achieving the desired end. If the bar, in general, were to recognize the potential self-generating consequences and expand to accept some of these responsibilities, the presumably higher quality of service would further increase public demand. Given the fact that the Legal Training and Research Institute is a state-supported enterprise, however, the ultimate solution depends upon a significant increase in the state's budgetary allowance for the institute. Such support cannot be anticipated without greater general understanding of the importance of the role of the legal profession and until

[146] See note 123. Although modern medicine was introduced to Japan at about the same time as the Western legal system, by world standards the former would today probably be considered to have developed to a much higher level. Doctors number 101,449 as of Dec. 21, 1959, and they are highly specialized in urban areas.

[147] Judge Matsuda, the former President of the Legal Training and Research Institute, has stated that, according to his experience, the members of the legal staffs of government agencies who are law graduates but not lawyers tend to draft legislation containing provisions which, in his opinion, are unreasonable, dubious, or difficult to interpret. See MATSUDA, note 142, at 32. The implication, perhaps well founded, is that qualified lawyers might do better.

[148] The following figures are from MATSUDA, note 142, at 6–7:

	National	*Municipal*	*Private*	*Total*
Universities	2,021	193	10,951	13,165
Graduates	12	2	22	36

[149] See note 129.

the respective roles in legal education of the universities and the institute have been more carefully worked out.[150]

In the last analysis, the fundamental problem facing the legal profession in Japan today is deceptively easy to state. How in a functional sense can Japan's judges, procurators, and lawyers adequately perform those roles which the new Constitution formally assigns to them? It is of the essence that a sufficient number of highly competent individuals be attracted to the profession, for unless they are it is unlikely that the spirit of the 1946 Constitution will be maintained. Nor will the demands of the emergent social and economic orders for rational structuring be met. It is true that some attempts are being made to deal with the problem. For example, the Legal Training and Research Institute implicitly appealed, through publication of a report on the number and distribution of lawyers in Japan, for a larger legal profession. The appeal obtained the support of well-informed individuals and produced a slight increase in the number of legal apprentices.[151] This institute and the Ministry of Justice Integrated Research Institute conduct special training courses for assistant judges and procurators so that they can acquire further technical training and become more thoroughly acquainted with their own society and its place in the contemporary world.[152] Additionally, some of the leading members of the profession are trying to further cooperation among all branches of the profession through such institutions as the Japanese Law Specialists' Association. Contact with the

[150] A leading law professor has stated, in summary: "The university law department, which was reformed after World War II on the model of the American college system and which today requires many courses on general culture, is unable to find enough time for legal education to train the legal profession adequately. On the other hand, the subjects and the requirements of the legal examination are as they were before . . . Thus, it is extremely difficult for university law graduates to pass the examination without doing further and extensive study after graduation from the university. As a consequence, most of the able graduates who cannot afford to spend years for such further study are obliged to choose careers other than law . . . To remove this bottleneck, we should consider the reform of the legal-examination system, strengthening of legal education in the university, particularly the extension of the term of school years in the law faculty . . ." See KANEKO, note 41, at 260, 261. Some people suggest an alternative solution: That the role of the institute be made less central so that other avenues into the profession might be opened.

[151] See SHIHŌ KENSHŪJO (Legal Training and Research Institute), HŌSŌ JINKŌ MONDAI NI KAN-SURU KENKYŪ (A Study Concerning the Problem of the Professional Legal Population) (Shihō Kenshūjo Chōsa Sōsho (Legal Training and Research Institute Research Series) No. 1, 1955). This study, conducted in 1953, showed that even the program for 350 trainees per year will not contribute much toward a substantial increase in the numbers in the legal profession (including the judiciary, the procuracy, and the bar). The following facts from the study project the increase in the total number of judges, procurators, and private practitioners that would result from the 350-trainees program: for 1953, 8,591; 1963, 9,476; 1973, 9,983; 1983, 10,813; 1993, 11,633. After the study, the number of legal apprentices admitted to the institute, which ranged between 220 and 250 annually, was gradually increased; since 1959, about 350 a year have been admitted. For a current commentary on the same problem see Amano, Yoshikawa, Tanabe, Matsuda & Mikazuki, *Hōsō Jinkō* (The Professional Legal Population), JURIST no. 249, at 40 (1962).

[152] See Matsuda, note 94, at 375–76.

legal profession abroad has been established and is being continued, thus serving in some measure to familiarize the profession in Japan with both the potentialities and shortcomings of the profession elsewhere.

Nevertheless, one cannot be very sanguine about prospects for the profession. Traditional attitudes toward law and the role of the legal profession are not easily modified and, until they are, it is quite unlikely that more competent men will choose careers in law. Furthermore, recruitment of the competent in and of itself is no answer; unless more adequate training is given, such recruitment will be largely meaningless. The basic requisite to the proper training of an increasing number of candidates is a willingness, both within the profession and in society generally, to accept fundamental institutional changes in the relation between the lawyer and society. Yet it will be difficult to change the ideas that legal training is something for a small elite and that legal services are used only as a last resort. Also, change will be required in order to bring about a functional integration of the legal profession so that the traditional tendency toward exclusiveness among the branches will be broken down and so that the judiciary will be able to attract personnel primarily from among individuals with experience in law.

There is no doubt that we can anticipate increased understanding by the public of the role of law and of its administrators, an understanding which will grow with the social, political, and economic development of Japan. However, unless remedial measures of the type suggested above are taken, it is unlikely that the spirit of the 1946 Constitution will be maintained and the demands of modern society satisfied.

TABLE 1. Initial Positions Taken by Graduates of the Legal Training and Research Institute

Year	Judges	Procurators	Lawyers	Others
1948	74	38	17	4
1949	62	40	29	0
1950	92	60	85	0
1951	83	69	128	2
1952	55	76	105	2
1953	50	67	96	2
1954	42	46	136	1
1955	64	58	113	1
1956	73	49	89	3
1957	77	45	142	0
1958	65	45	144	2
1959	69	51	157	5
1960	81	44	166	0
1961	84	48	216	1
Total	971	736	1,623	23

Source: unpublished research conducted by the General Secretariat of the Supreme Court.

TABLE 2. Total Numbers in the Legal Profession

Year	Judges[a]	Procurators[a]	Lawyers[a]	Total[a]	Total population[b]
1890[c]	1,531	481	1,345	3,357	39,902,000
1895	1,221	385	1,589	3,195	41,557,000
1900	1,244	473	1,590	3,307	43,847,000
1905	1,179	379	2,008	3,566	46,620,000
1910	1,125	390	2,008	3,523	49,184,000
1915	898	386	2,486	3,770	52,752,000
1920	1,134	570	3,082	4,786	55,752,000
1925	1,116	564	5,673	7,353	59,179,000
1930	1,249	637	6,599	8,485	63,872,000
1935	1,391	648	7,075	9,114	68,662,000
1940	1,541	734	5,334	7,609	71,400,000
1945[d]	1,189	658	—	—	72,200,000
1950	2,261	930	5,883	9,074	83,142,000
1955	2,327	1,000	5,994	9,321	89,837,000
1960	2,387	1,044	6,458	9,889	93,408,000

[a] The number of judges, procurators, and lawyers prior to 1940 is from SHIHŌ-SHŌ (Ministry of Justice), SHIHŌ ENKAKUSHI (History of Justice) 542–46 (1939).

[b] Provided this writer by the Bureau of Statistics, Prime Minister's Office.

[c] Numbers and populations prior to 1940 include those in Okinawa Prefecture and Karafuto (southern Saghalien).

[d] The number of lawyers in 1945 is not available.

TABLE 3. Number of Private Practitioners by District (December 1960)

District	Practitioners	Population	Population per practitioner
Tokyo	2,882	9,675,000	3,400
Kanagawa	156	3,442,000	22,100
Saitama	58	2,430,000	41,900
Chiba	81	3,306,000	28,400
Ibaragi	53	2,046,000	38,600
Tochigi	59	1,513,000	25,700
Gumma	42	1,578,000	37,600
Shizuoka	85	2,756,000	32,400
Yamanashi	36	781,000	21,700
Nagano	57	1,981,000	34,800
Niigata	64	2,442,000	38,200
Osaka	750	5,504,000	7,300
Kyoto	159	1,993,000	12,500
Hyogo	197	3,906,000	14,800
Nara	16	780,000	48,800
Shiga	18	842,000	46,800
Wakayama	38	1,001,000	26,400
Aichi	227	4,206,000	18,500
Mie	39	1,484,000	38,100
Gifu	41	1,638,000	40,000
Fukui	29	752,000	26,000
Ishikawa	42	973,000	23,200
Toyama	26	1,032,000	39,700
Hiroshima	106	2,184,000	20,600
Yamaguchi	60	1,602,000	26,700
Okayama	86	1,670,000	19,400
Tottori	25	599,000	24,000
Shimane	25	888,000	35,600
Fukuoka	187	4,006,000	21,400
Saga	34	942,000	24,800
Nagasaki	51	1,760,000	34,500
Oita	50	1,239,000	24,800
Kumamoto	65	1,856,000	28,600
Kagoshima	47	1,962,000	41,800
Miyazaki	28	1,134,000	40,500
Miyagi	81	1,743,000	21,500
Fukushima	58	2,051,000	35,400
Yamagata	28	1,320,000	47,200
Iwate	24	1,448,000	60,400
Akita	33	1,335,000	40,500
Aomori	29	1,426,000	49,200
Hokkaido	128	5,039,000	39,400
Kagawa	35	918,000	26,300
Tokushima	30	847,000	28,200
Kochi	42	854,000	20,300
Ehime	51	1,500,000	29,400
Total	6,458	93,408,000	Average 14,500

Source: figures for practitioners, Japanese Federated Attorneys' Association; figures for population, 1961 ASAHI NENKAN (1961 Asahi Yearbook) 592.

TABLE 4. Number of Judges and Lawyers in Selected Countries

Country	Total population	Judges	Lawyers	Population per judge	Population per lawyer
Japan[a]	93,160,000	2,387	6,490	39,028	14,354
Great Britain[b]	51,680,000	20,274	24,544	2,549	2,105
United States[c]	182,714,000	48,850	250,710	3,740	728
Canada[d]	18,020,000	1,299	13,192	13,872	1,366
West Germany[e]	54,300,000	15,502	17,190	3,502	3,012
France[f]	44,500,000	2,936	7,713	15,156	5,769
Italy[g]	48,483,000	12,741	30,000	3,805	1,601

[a] The number of judges and lawyers is as of March 1960.

[b] Judges include about 20,000 justices of the peace; lawyers include both barristers and solicitors. Numbers are as of 1959.

[c] The number of judges includes about 45,000 justices of the peace and is as of 1957; the number of lawyers is as of August 1960.

[d] The statistics were provided by the Canadian government through the Canadian Embassy in Tokyo in May, 1961 at the request of the Supreme Court.

[e] Judges include justices of the peace and municipal judges of the land of Baden-Wuertemberg; the number is as of 1958.

[f] Lawyers include avocats and avoués; the number is as of 1958.

[g] Judges include about 8,000 justices of the peace; the number is as of 1957.

Source: unpublished research conducted by the General Secretariat of the Supreme Court.

EDUCATION OF THE LEGAL PROFESSION IN JAPAN

Hakaru Abe

ASSISTED BY DAVID F. CAVERS AND TIMOTHY S. WILLIAMS

THE theme of this paper is legal apprenticeship, that is, the postgraduate legal training given to legal apprentices by the Legal Training and Research Institute, an agency of the Supreme Court of Japan. Because the training given in Japan by the institute to legal apprentices most nearly corresponds to the legal education given by the American law school, which has as its objective the training of the legal profession only, it does not seem unreasonable to emphasize the education given apprentices in explaining the education of the legal profession in Japan. While the present Legal Institute also has the important functions of the advanced education of judges and the supervision of their research, this essay will deal only with its role in training apprentices.[1]

Introduction

Outline of the History of Legal Education in Japan

The distinguishing characteristic of prewar Japanese professional legal education was its dual system of training, that is, the distinction between the education of probationary attorneys and that of probationary legal officials. This was based on the rigid separation between lawyers on the one hand and judges and procurators on the other. Under this system, the modes of

Note. Mr. Abe is a judge serving as President of the Legal Training and Research Institute. B. Jur., Tokyo Imperial University, 1918. Appointed to the bench in 1920. President, Yokohama District Court, 1946–1947. Chief Judge, Fukuoka High Court, 1947–1952, Osaka High Court, 1952–1955, Tokyo High Court, 1955–1958. The author wishes here to express his appreciation to all of those connected with the Legal Institute, in particular to Judge Kohji Tanabe, for advice and cooperation in the preparation of this essay.

Mr. Cavers is Fessenden Professor of Law, Harvard University. Mr. Williams is a practicing attorney, New York City; A.B., 1951, Cornell University; LL.B., 1957, Harvard University.

[1] For a more detailed discussion of the history, organization, and training program of the institute by its former president, see Matsuda, *The Japanese Legal Training and Research Institute*, 7 Am. J. Comp. L. 366 (1958).

appointment and the professional careers of the two groups received entirely separate regulation.

The prewar system had its origins in the period before 1923, when even the qualifications for lawyers were separately established from those for judges and procurators. In 1923 these distinctions were abolished, and all who aspired to become judges, procurators, or lawyers were required to qualify by taking the legal section of the senior examination for public officials. But the system of apprentice training after qualification continued to separate the education of lawyers from that of legal officials. For those wishing to become judges or procurators, the probationary-legal-official system was derived in 1890 from the German *Referendar* system. The Ministry of Justice selected each year from among those who had passed the legal section of the senior examination a certain number of probationary legal officials and, after giving them training for a period of a year and a half, appointed judges and procurators from among them. The probationary legal officials were treated as public officials and received a certain salary from the government. They were assigned to the various District Courts and were given practical training in the civil and criminal departments and in the procurators' offices. The training was centered on the drafting of judgments and indictments under the direction of individual judges and procurators and emphasized an apprenticelike training by personal contact with senior judges and procurators. In 1939 the Legal Research Institute was established under the Ministry of Justice.[2] One of its functions was the guidance of the probationary legal officials, and all of them gathered there for training for about two months prior to their final examination. However, this final instruction had as its principal objective the adjustment of differences in level of training arising from the periods of regional training. It was simply supplementary to the training supervised by the District Courts and the attached procurators' offices.

For lawyers, on the other hand, there was no systematic training even after 1923. Actually, most of them, after qualifying by examination, entered the office of a senior lawyer for an apprenticeship of several years and then established themselves independently. Legally, however, one could, after passing the examination, immediately establish an independent practice, and in fact not a few did so. In 1936 the probationary-attorney system was established to improve the quality of the bar; and it became necessary, in order to become a lawyer, to go through a training period of a year and a half. The training, however, was chiefly conducted by placing the probationary attorneys under the individual guidance of various lawyers, and its content differed considerably according to the guiding lawyer, in some cases leaving the probationer much to his own devices. The probationary attorney was uncompensated or received only a small allowance, and thus his liveli-

[2] By Imperial Order No. 445 of 1939.

hood was not guaranteed. Moreover, no institution was established for centralized training and research, like the Legal Research Institute mentioned above. Under these circumstances it was natural that considerable differences should exist between the training given lawyers and that received by judges and procurators, and one may say generally that the education of the probationary legal officials was fuller and more systematically carried out. Again, almost no opportunity was given to either group to receive training in the other's field.

After the war the role of law was strengthened under the new Constitution, and the status and authority of the courts, with the Supreme Court at their head, were markedly raised. The importance of the social function of the bar also gradually became recognized. Along with these developments, the ideal of "unification of the legal profession," which will be discussed later in some detail, was strongly advocated. Those supporting this principle held that judges, procurators, and lawyers should cooperate as a single body for the improvement of the administration of justice. In the field of legal education, they strongly urged the professional training of the three groups to be conducted under a unified apprenticeship system. In response to these demands, the new Court Law of 1947 abolished the distinction between probationary legal officials and probationary attorneys, established a unified legal apprenticeship for both, and provided for the Legal Training and Research Institute under the Supreme Court as the agency to supervise the entire training process.[3] The institute began its work on May 7, 1947, with the promulgation of the new Constitution. Since the institute was established under the postwar Allied occupation, it had to be approved by the occupation authorities. However, although the basis of the institute may have derived from the systems of various other countries, it did not result from positive suggestions of the occupation authorities. It was entirely the independent, original conception of those of the Japanese legal profession who were chiefly responsible for legislation at that time.[4]

The Present System of Training for the Legal Profession

Under the new system, those who aspire to the legal profession must first pass the national legal examination and complete a two-year process of legal training.[5] The more important part of the legal examination is the second examination which tests the specialized capacity of the candidates. A

[3] Court Law, Law No. 59 of 1947, arts. 14, 55–56; for an English translation, see EHS LAW BULLETIN SERIES AA 1 (Nakane ed., 1954). See also Court Law, arts. 43, 66–68; Public Procurators' Office Law, Law No. 61 of 1947, art. 18, translated into English in 2 EHS LAW BULLETIN SERIES BA 1 (Nakane ed., 1953); Attorneys Law, Law No. 205 of 1949, art. 4, translated into English in 2 EHS LAW BULLETIN SERIES CA 1 (Nakane ed., 1954).

[4] See Matsuda, as in note 1 above, at 368 n. 10.

[5] Court Law, arts. 66–67; Legal Examination Law, Law No. 140 of 1949, translated into English in OFFICIAL GAZETTE, May 31, 1949, extra ed. no. 57, at 33.

candidate can qualify to take the second examination either by completing the general-education curriculum of a university or by demonstrating adequate general cultural knowledge and academic capacity by passing the first examination.[6] In practice most candidates for the second examination are university graduates, particularly from departments of law.[7] Most of these apprentices had received, under the postwar educational system, six years of primary school, three years of middle school — both compulsory — three years of high school, and four years of university education. The latter had in most cases included an initial year and a half to two years of general cultural education and two to two and a half years of specialized instruction, including legal subjects. As will be later explained, the education given by the law department of a Japanese university is not intended only for those students who will enter the legal profession, but is directed broadly to those who will become public officials or company employees and need a general knowledge of law. Centering on the Six Codes — the Constitution, the Civil Code, the Penal Code, the Commercial Code, the Code of Civil Procedure, and the Code of Criminal Procedure — this instruction emphasizes understanding of the fundamental principles of law. Instruction is chiefly by lectures to large classes. As a result, graduates of the law departments generally have little knowledge concerning the practical application of law.

Although most who take the examination have come through the law departments in this way, the high standard required makes qualification extremely difficult. For example, of about 8,000 candidates who took the second examination in 1960, only 345 (about 4 percent) qualified. The examination is graded by scholars and members of the profession appointed by the Ministry of Justice to the Legal Examination Control Committee, and those candidates achieving a prescribed grade are qualified. The examination is essentially a qualification test; but, since of course the grading standards of the committee members are not perfectly consistent, the examinations accepted may vary to some degree according to the strictness and approach of the individual examiner. The examination is divided into written and oral parts. The written part is in general composed of essay-type questions[8] requiring discussion of specified topics, but occasionally questions based on simple hypothetical cases are also given. The subjects examined center on the Six Codes mentioned above.

All those who qualify by passing the examination, with a few exceptions

[6] Legal Examination Law, arts. 2–4.

[7] Of about 8,000 persons who took the second examination in 1960, only 50 had qualified by passing the first examination. Of the 333 apprentices who entered the institute in 1961, 319 were university graduates, and almost all of these had been graduated from departments of law or similar departments of law and political science or law and economics.

[8] By this term is meant a question that requires a brief discussion, in the manner of an article in a legal periodical, directed to a specified topic, such as: "Discuss the relation between the right to work and the union-shop agreement."

for such causes as physical defects, are accepted as legal apprentices and train for two years under the supervision of the Legal Training and Research Institute. The number of apprentices entering the institute each year ranged between about 200 and 250 until about 1956 but, after 1957, gradually increased. In 1959 the number was about 350; in 1961, 333 apprentices entered.[9]

During the first and the last four-month periods of training all apprentices attend the institute for classroom instruction. During the intervening sixteen months they receive apprentice training in actual practice in the civil and criminal departments of the various District Courts, the district procurators' offices, and perfectural attorneys' associations. Each apprentice spends four months with each of the four types of institution responsible for training. Under the General Plan for the Guidance of Legal Apprentices[10] established by the institute in 1954, the first four-month period of training at the institute has an introductory function; the apprentices are given a general basic understanding of the legal practice of the judiciary, the procuracy, and the bar. The last four months are employed to round off the training, and the content of the instruction is at a higher level than that of the first period. For the two periods of instruction at the institute, the apprentices are divided into classes of about fifty, and five instructing officers including persons from the judiciary, the procuracy, and the bar are assigned to each class. The basic courses are conducted as joint research of a very practical nature and center on cases, using such techniques as drafting of documents used in litigation and problem discussions. To these are added the introductory lectures of the first period, lectures on special legislation and supplementary sciences, seminars on special subjects, and finally a general cultural program.

The content of these courses will be discussed more fully below, but drafting is the most important one, occupying most of the apprentices' time and demanding their greatest effort. As a rule, each instructor handles subjects in his own field, but, where the topic embraces all aspects of the legal profession, instruction is also given jointly by all instructors assigned to the class. The time devoted to subjects taught by the various instructors individually is divided in a ratio of three:two:two:two among civil-court work, criminal-court work, prosecution, and advocacy.[11]

The sixteen months of field training involves chiefly apprentice study

[9] For the figures before 1957, see Matsuda, note 1, at 369 n. 13.

[10] Nikki-hatsu (Legal Training and Research Institute Daybook Entry) No. 320 of 1954 (circular issued by the president of the institute).

[11] The regular program in 1960 had a total of approximately 340 units (a unit ranges from 2 to 2.5 hours, but in seminars and lectures on general cultural topics is, as a rule, 1.5 hours). Of the 340 units, about 120 were devoted to the drafting and criticism of judgments, pleadings, and indictments. Problem discussions occupied about 23 units, lectures on law and related sciences about 130 units, seminars about 46 units, and the general cultural program about 21 units.

under the guidance of individual judges, procurators, and lawyers who are handling actual cases. For example, while training at a court, the apprentice would be assigned to a judge to observe the proceedings in cases which that judge was hearing, read the records, and draft judgments for criticism by the judge. This involves observing all the work of his senior and, so far as possible, performing the same work himself. In addition, lectures on practice are also given during this period. This field training, conducted in accordance with instructions prepared by the institute, is entrusted to the various District Courts, procurators' offices, and attorneys' associations, under the supervision of the heads of these agencies. To coordinate this training the institute holds several conferences each year of the responsible persons from the various districts.

When the apprentice has completed the training outlined above and passed the final examination, he is qualified to become an assistant judge, a deputy procurator, or a lawyer. This examination is divided into written and oral parts, the former consisting of drafting and analysis of problems based on a record and the latter of practical questions based on specific cases and other questions on matters of general culture. Until 1952 there were some persons who did not qualify in this final examination, but, thanks to the selection of the legal apprentices through the rigorous national legal examination, no one has failed the final examination during the past eight years.

The apprentices who pass the final examination may decide, in the light of their observations of each field during the previous two years, to become judges, procurators, or lawyers. However, because the number who may become assistant judges or procurators is fixed, a few are unable to enter the fields of their choice. Of the 349 graduates (including eleven women) in 1961, 84 became judges, 48 procurators, and 214 lawyers. One of the remaining three continued his career as a scholar in his specialty. At present (May 1961), there are 9,803 persons in the Japanese legal profession (1,992 full judges and assistant judges, 1,143 procurators, and 6,668 lawyers).[12] Among these are 3,242 graduates of the institute, including 930 judges, 711 procurators, 1,546 lawyers, and 55 others.[13] Institute graduates total more than 30 percent of the entire legal profession. Finally, it should be noted that the institute since its founding has been the sole source of supply for the Japanese legal profession.

Although legal apprentices are not public officials, they receive from the government salary approximately equivalent to that received by newly appointed public officials who are university graduates, as well as health

[12] These figures do not include the number of the Summary Court judges who have not taken the regular apprentice training and were appointed through a special screening procedure.

[13] Some of these 55 others entered government departments or businesses. Some of them are pursuing academic careers as law teachers.

insurance and certain other privileges of public officials. They also assume such obligations as the preservation of secrets.[14]

The Legal Training and Research Institute is an agency of the Supreme Court. The president and the instructing officers are appointed by the Court. The present president is from the judiciary, and the thirty-five instructors other than the president include seven judges from both the civil and criminal benches, seven procurators, seven lawyers who have handled criminal cases, and seven who are experienced in civil matters. The procurators and lawyers are appointed on the recommendation of the Ministry of Justice and the Japanese Federated Attorneys' Association, respectively. It is thought that instructors should have had ten years' experience in the profession, and the experience of many extends to from twenty to thirty years. The president of the institute has ultimate authority in the management of its affairs, but all important matters relating to education are decided in consultation with a committee composed of all the instructors. Legally the president is responsible to the Chief Justice of the Supreme Court, but as a practical matter all educational plans are determined by the institute itself.[15]

The foregoing is only a brief description of the education given legal apprentices by the present Legal Training and Research Institute. It should be evident, however, that the postwar system does not represent merely an increase in the length of training over the prewar system. The content of the instruction and its organization have been greatly improved, and in particular the training given lawyers has been strikingly reformed. Many persons have recognized that the postwar system — based on equality of the judiciary, the procuracy, and the bar — has advanced understanding and cooperation among the three branches of the profession and that the general level of legal practice is rising through improvement in the caliber of the younger members of the profession. Nevertheless, Japanese professional legal education actually faces now a number of fundamental problems and will face more difficult questions in answering the demands of a new period.

Legal Professional Education under the Postwar Education System

Education in the University Law Departments and the National Legal Examination

As explained above, the law departments of the Japanese universities are unlike the American law schools in that they do not have as their principal objective the training of persons who will enter the legal profession. The

[14] Regulations Concerning Legal Apprentices, Supreme Court Regulation No. 15 of 1948, arts. 2–3, translated into English in Official Gazette, August 18, 1948, no. 715, at 2.

[15] Court Law, arts. 55–56; Legal Training and Research Institute Rules, Supreme Court Rule No. 8 of 1947, art. 4.

departments of law, even though called by that name, ordinarily give instruction in political science, administration, and economics, as well as law; and most graduates of the law departments have expected from the beginning of their studies to enter government or to find employment with private companies. In 1959, 36 universities in Japan gave instruction in law; their law or similar departments in that year graduated 13,165 students. In the same year about 8,000 persons took the national legal examination, and 319 qualified. In 1961 only eight universities sent more than ten legal apprentices to the institute.[16] Thus, most of the universities in Japan which offer instruction in the law send none or at most a few of their students into the professional legal world, and, even in those universities that have a fair number of graduates who become legal apprentices, these represent only a small portion of all their graduates. As a result, legal education in the universities resembles that of American undergraduate political-science departments rather than American law schools and must be limited to the fundamentals necessary for students considering positions in government or industry.

The universities, using chiefly the lecture method, explain the principal academic views relating to the legislative bases, the interpretation, and the structure of the fundamental codes and the Constitution. From this instruction the student can acquire a general knowledge of the content and interpretation of these codes and become familiar with the method of interpretation of legal rules and the processes of legal reasoning. However, because of the insufficient length of university education, because of the low proportion of professors to students, and because of the necessary assumption that most students will not become professionals, detailed examination and study based on analysis of the facts of individual decisions and specific cases are generally not attempted. There is rather a tendency to emphasize the systematic development of theory from a certain academic viewpoint, particularly that of the professor lecturing. It is also unusual to discuss in much detail the social background of changes in decisional and statutory law.

[16] The numbers of the graduates of various universities who entered the Legal Institute in 1961 are:

Chuo University (private)	106
Tokyo University (national)	41
Kyoto University (national)	32
Waseda University (private)	19
Meiji University (private)	18
Kyushu University (national)	17
Tohoku University (national)	12
Nippon University (private)	11
All other schools (less than 10 each)	77
Total	333

For a complete list of the applicants from various universities, and of those who passed the required examination, 1949–1961, see Fujishima, *Shihō Shiken no Genkyō* (The Present State of the Legal Examination), JURIST no. 249, at 28, 32–33 (1962).

However, since the war, under the influence of Anglo-American law, there has been a tendency among the university scholars also to emphasize the explanation of cases and to conduct case-method study and criticism of decisions in seminars or other small classes. However, since there is limited capacity to handle such seminars, not all students can participate in them, and resort to the lecture system, with a content as described above, apparently continues to be the prevailing tendency. As a matter of fact, one cannot say that such a legal education is entirely inadequate for the majority of students, who will not enter the formal legal profession but will, in government and in companies, acquire skill in general legal matters not involving litigation, such as the drafting of contracts and the handling of business relating to taxes and stock transactions. The fundamental legal knowledge necessary for such quasi-lawyers is taught very efficiently in a short time along with courses in administration, government, economics, and other fields. Since case law is not yet well established in such fields as commercial acts, taxes, and company law, matters of practice are frequently carried out by such graduates in accordance with the particular academic views learned at the universities. For these students who will not spend their lives working within the profession, a more complete grasp of law may not be necessary. To American lawyers it is a surprising fact that procedure is frequently an elective course and that many students who have not studied procedure are graduated from the law departments.

It is thus clear that in Japan graduation from the law department of a university does not at all imply legal knowledge at a professional level or a capacity for legal thinking of a professional character. Furthermore, the postwar reform of the educational system has lowered the level of scholarly attainment. Before the war, the university law faculty gave a legal education of three years' duration to students who had completed a preparatory general education consisting of six years of primary, five years of middle, and three years of high-school training. Under the new postwar system, however, the university must include in a four-year course both general and specialized education, including law. The distribution of this four-year period between general and specialized training varies somewhat from university to university, but, because of the shortened period of education prior to entrance into the universities, the preparation of the entering students is less adequate than before the war, and the universities must devote some time to the teaching of language and other general subjects. As a result, the time which the law departments can allocate to specialized legal study is in practice normally about two and a half years. When one considers that, in addition to this reduction in the period of training, the content of law has become more complex and varied since the war, the level of legal knowledge transmitted to the students is almost certainly lower than in the prewar period.

It is difficult to avoid concluding that there is a gap between the standard of legal knowledge which should naturally be demanded of the professional apprentices and the level of legal knowledge imparted by the universities. However, since one must qualify in the national legal examination to become a legal apprentice, it may be that this gap is in fact narrowed to some degree by the special study of law undertaken by students in preparing for the examination. This, however, is accompanied by some undesirable consequences. Since the examination covers the major codes, the candidate must begin rather early to emphasize the courses relating to them if he wishes to qualify before leaving the university. Many begin such study even before attending the relevant lectures. Because this is a heavy burden on the student, there is a tendency to concentrate on courses preparatory to the examination at the sacrifice of courses in social sciences and the liberal arts. However, since the examination is difficult, requiring about the same high level of knowledge of law as before the war, most students are unable to qualify before graduation from their universities and a rather large number of *rōnin* (masterless scholars)[17] study for the legal examination. The average age of the 333 persons who became legal apprentices in 1961 was 27.1 years (if one progresses normally in his education, he might graduate from a university at 22),* and among them only 65 (18.8 percent of the total) had qualified while university students.[18] Not a few of these "masterless scholars" take the examination a third and a fourth time,[19] and many study for it while working as clerks in law offices or as secretaries to the courts.†

It is certainly true that this laborious preparation for the national legal examination enlarges to some degree the student's knowledge of law, but one may doubt whether it actually assists the development of either a good legal sense or a capacity for legal thinking. The questions in the examination are of the type found in the examinations of the various courses of the university law departments, and, since they are chiefly essay questions,[20] the

[17] This is a play on the term used for masterless samurai in the feudal period, who were known as *rōnin*.

* David Cavers pointed out during the conference discussions that the five-year gap between the average age of graduation from the universities and the average age of entering students in the institute represents a loss to society of legal resources.

[18] It should also be noted, however, that a considerable number of apprentices are persons who, after having some years' experience in government or business, have decided to join the legal profession — sometimes even after retirement from their governmental or business careers. In 1961, 62 among 333 entering students were over 30 years old (15 over 35, 4 over 40). On the other hand, the median age of those entering the institute in the same year was also 27.

[19] Applicants may take the examination as many times as they wish; there is no legal limit.

† The loss of time and the general pressure on the educational system resulting from the lack of a limitation on the number of times the examination may be taken led Cavers to suggest that important economies could be effected by not allowing applicants to take the examination more than three times.

[20] See note 8. Since 1956, multiple-choice questions concerning basic legal concepts or

candidates tend to prepare by memorizing academic interpretations and theory to be able to get down a good outline in a short time. Accordingly, one must question to what extent the depth of the candidate's knowledge of law and his capacity for legal thinking are developed by this sort of preparation, particularly if it is repeated for several years. Furthermore, the fundamental function of university education is distorted by this sort of study for the examination: students are deprived of a grounding in general culture and in other social sciences.

Of course it must be recognized that the existence of the national legal examination maintains the capacity of the legal apprentices at a rather high level. Recently, particularly since a number of practitioners have been named as examiners and the proportion of simple hypothetical case problems requiring a legal solution has increased, the kind of preparation required is tending to develop that ability in legal analysis which is not always sufficiently nourished in the universities. It is also true that, because of the examination, a good many young men with a capacity for serious and diligent study and who are able to undergo this long trial are entering the legal profession. Nevertheless, since the sort of study they pursue is not conducted in a planned manner under good teachers and, moreover, is often repeated with the same content each year for several years, it clearly constitutes irrational and inefficient work.

In view of these circumstances, and particularly in order to draw a larger number of talented persons into the legal profession, the Legal Examination Law was amended in 1958 with the objective, among others, of making it possible for students to qualify for the examination while still in the universities.[21] The amendment became effective on January 1, 1961. It eliminates from the subjects formerly required either civil or criminal procedure, as the candidate may elect, and permits the candidate to elect any one of several specified nonlegal subjects, such as political science or economics. Such changes effect an important reformation of the examination method. Yet the modifications have been criticized as failing to reach the heart of the problem since there is no change in the basic method of study. Moreover, they present one important difficulty in that legal apprentices can now enter the institute without having been examined in civil procedure or, alternatively, in criminal procedure. Given the importance of procedure to the professional in law, it cannot be denied that in one sense the gap between university and professional training has been widened. It is expected, as a consequence, that the institute will be compelled to give much more systematic instruction in procedural law.

---

institutions have been included, and only the answers to essay questions of those who pass the multiple-choice section are graded.

[21] By Law No. 180 of 1958. The amendment was also aimed at improving the general cultural knowledge of the applicants.

Instruction in the Legal Training and Research Institute

As explained above, the gap between the attainments required of a professional man of law and the legal education furnished by the universities is rather wide, and, in the end, the burden of filling this gap falls on the education presently given by the Legal Training and Research Institute. Thus the institute must now, whether it cares to or not, go beyond strictly technical education in procedural practice and pursue positively, to some degree, the kind of legal training which is basically the function of the university, such as the training of the analytical "legal mind" through case study. As a result, the nature of the instruction of the present institute is coming to be qualitatively different from that of the prewar training given probationary legal officials and probationary attorneys.

First, in the initial part of the first four-month period at the institute, instructors from various fields present rather detailed analyses, from the viewpoints of judge, procurator, and lawyer, both of the actual functioning of civil and criminal procedure and of the process by which procedural law and substantive law are applied. For this purpose, not only actual records of cases but also very practical texts prepared by the institute are used as teaching materials, and the legal apprentices are given audio-visual instruction through films of trials and through mock proceedings. Starting with this active instruction, the apprentices learn how the body of law which was spread before them as students in its theoretical aspect only is realized in actual proceedings.[22]

After this orientation period, the most important work assigned the apprentices is the drafting of judgments, complaints, indictments, and answers. This is felt to be the most effective method of instruction for the development of the analytical mind which the university has not sufficiently trained. The apprentice must review all the pleadings and evidence in actual cases[23] which the instructors have selected from all parts of the country and prepare appropriate judgments, complaints, and other procedural documents. Hence they are given a burden which is in some ways even heavier than that of the American law student working under the case method. They must note carefully the details of pleadings and proof scattered through the unorganized record, investigate painstakingly the decisions and the academic authorities, and, mobilizing both their legal knowledge and their imagination, conceive a suitable result. Moreover, since they must make determinations of fact as well as investigations of the legal problems presented, they must at times give attention even to commercial custom or to the supplemen-

[22] In 1960, 23 units (more than 50 hours) were devoted to this instruction during the first period.

[23] The printed records of the actual cases are given to students. These contain written pleadings, summaries of oral pleadings, testimony (sometimes a verbatim record, sometimes a summary), documentary evidence, and other procedural documents.

tary sciences. Again, because their drafts are reviewed in detail and corrected by the specialist instructors and returned with criticisms, the apprentices must take up their pens with care. They often have cause to reflect on the crudity of their own inferences. The apprentices are ordinarily released from formal instruction for a half day or a day when assigned a drafting problem and are encouraged to consult with one another. Such discussion shapes the legal mind and develops skill in the techniques of argument, as well as affording the apprentices the stimulation of contact with their most able fellows. In the second period of study at the institute frequent drills are given which require study of records and preparation of drafts in limited time in the classroom. The instructors, too, particularly since their number has been increased to seven in each field, face their classes after careful discussion and specialized consideration of the records. Since these officers have had rather extensive professional experience and have become skilled in conducting discussion in the course of a year at the institute, the discussion with the apprentices in the classroom is brisk and thorough. Most of the apprentices are experiencing this sort of thorough case-method training for the first time; but they acquire in a short time, quite effectively, the capacity for legal thinking and the habit of careful attention and learn methods of persuasion and techniques of expression.

Another aspect of the instruction, not seen in the prewar probationer's training, is reflected in the preparation, especially in recent years, of a succession of systematic texts and reference materials by the instructors of the institute for use as teaching materials. The titles include *Explanation of First-Instance Civil Procedure,*[24] *Guide to Drafting Civil Judgments,*[25] *Outline of First-Instance Criminal Trial Procedure,*[26] *Outline Lectures in Prosecution,*[27] and *The Psychology of Testimony.*[28] Such materials, besides assisting the apprentices in obtaining a theoretical grasp of practice, have made it possible to reduce the time formerly devoted to instruction in the detailed technical points of drafting. These texts and reference materials are distinguished from most books on law by their extremely practical content.

In addition to these materials, lectures on such subjects as government, economics, history, or literature and seminars on foreign law (foreign cases and documents, especially constitutional decisions) are included in the curriculum. These are needed because the apprentices, under the pressure of preparation for the national legal examination, may reach the institute with insufficient grounding in general subjects and in such fields as foreign

[24] SHIHŌ KENSHŪJO (Legal Training and Research Institute), MINJI DAI ISSHIN SOSHŌ TETSUZUKI KAISETSU (rev. ed. 1959).

[25] SHIHŌ KENSHŪJO, MINJI HANKETSU KIAN NO TEBIKI (1958).

[26] SHIHŌ KENSHŪJO, DAI ISSHIN KŌHAN TETSUZUKI NO GAIYŌ (1958).

[27] SHIHŌ KENSHŪJO, KENSATSU KŌGI-AN (1957).

[28] SHIHŌ KENSHŪJO, KYŌJUTSU SHINRI (Shihō Kenshūjo Jijitsu Nintei Kyōzai Series (Legal Training and Research Institute Factfinding Instructional Materials Series) No. 1, 1959).

language and foreign law. Lectures by specialists and scholars on areas of law not sufficiently covered in the university curriculum are also given, emphasizing particularly matters covered by special legislation.

The educational program described above, integrated with the sixteen-month period of field training in handling actual cases, has been very effective in increasing the ability of the apprentices to think in legal terms and in developing their knowledge of law. Actually it is not too much to say that the intensive training, which seeks to prepare the apprentices adequately in a two-year period to stand independently as members of the legal profession, roughly closes the gap between the education of the universities and the requirements of the profession.

It is true, of course, that the assumption by the institute, which started as basically a center for practical apprenticeship, of such important educational functions has resulted in difficulties. Since few of the instructors are professional educators, there are insufficiencies in such matters as the organization of the curriculum, the method of conducting discussion, and the selection of materials. There may also be a good deal of unnecessary duplication of material taught by the universities. Moreover, since the instructors generally have not engaged in research on a specialized subject in the manner of university professors and since their time is limited, the content of the instruction they offer is not always sufficiently broad and well prepared. To make up these deficiencies, much time is devoted to conferences in preparation for evaluating drafts and for editing materials and to appropriately specialized work by the instructors concerning each topic. Also, since the initiation in 1953 of a system under which assistant judges and lawyers are attached to the institute, the work of young members of the profession (at present, eight persons) assigned to the institute to prepare basic instructional materials and to do long-term research has effectively supplemented the teaching and research of the instructors. From time to time, the institute has also invited specialists in education to give their opinions concerning its instruction and has conducted meetings with professors from the law faculties to exchange views on the content of the education offered by their respective institutions.

Despite these efforts, conditions of instruction at the institute are insufficient in many respects; in particular the assurance of facilities and time for research by the instructors is a pressing problem. It would also be desirable to provide for systematic participation by scholars in the work of the institute, to publish more detailed educational materials, and to provide more books, materials, classrooms, and study areas for the apprentices. Finally, continued attention must be given a fundamental problem: the extent to which an institution like the Legal Institute should share the burden of the training which should be central to legal education, namely, the development of the capacity to employ legal processes of thought. This problem can be truly solved only if it is earnestly considered in the broad perspective of the relationship between the institute's training and the education conducted by the law departments of the universities.

The Relation of Education to the Ideal of Unification

I shall not discuss in depth here the postwar ideal of the unification of the legal profession since that subject has been considered in detail in the essay by Takaaki Hattori. It will be sufficient to mention here only the relation of the apprentice system in the postwar Legal Institute to unification and the influence that the institute has had on this ideal.

The Influence of the Legal Training and Research Institute

The specific content of the idea of unification of the legal profession, much emphasized by members of the profession in Japan since the war, is not entirely clear, and its advocates do not always use the concept with the same meaning. However, it is clear that, as first expressed, it was based on the Anglo-American system for the selection of judges, a system under which nearly all judges are chosen from persons with considerable practical experience as lawyers. Before the war the bench, the bar, and the procuracy were separated in Japan. There was little intercourse among them and even a certain sense of antagonism between the judiciary-procuracy group and the lawyer group. Accordingly, "unification of the legal profession" in its original form meant integration of this sharply divided legal profession into a single group, raising the status and authority of the courts by appointing senior members of the group to the bench and thereby establishing the prestige of the courts as required by the Constitution.

However, for various reasons — the principal one being economic — this ideal of choosing judges from the bar has been realized only to a limited extent: one third of the justices of the Supreme Court are selected from the bar, and a few lawyers have become chief judges of the District Courts and High Courts. However, almost all the present lower-court judges have followed the career path from legal apprentice to assistant judge to judge, and most of the procurators are career men. There are few interchanges of personnel among the three branches of the profession, as, for example, when retired or resigned judges or procurators take up the practice of law. It may be that the new Court Law, although much influenced by the ideal of unification of the profession, retains the assistant-judge system as a compromise resulting from recognition of the difficulty of realizing the pure form of the concept.[29]

[29] Under the present law, judges of the lower courts may be appointed from among persons with more than ten years' experience as assistant judges, procurators, or lawyers (professors of law are also eligible). Court Law, art. 42. In practice almost all judges at present have been either assistant judges or judges under the prewar system. In addition a large number of assistant judges with more than five years' experience have been given, pursuant to the special legislation of 1948, authority nearly equal to that of full judges.

Accordingly, a modified and more realistic form of unification is now advanced. While it is recognized that the three branches of the profession will each be composed of career specialists, it is urged that fair and efficient operation of the judicial system can be effected by cooperation among the three branches based on development of a sense of unity as members of the same profession, on mutual understanding, and on elimination of the prewar antagonisms. "Unification of the legal profession" in this sense is reflected in the organization of the Supreme Court, which includes equal numbers of former lawyers and career judges as well as men of academic and general experience.

Since the Legal Training and Research Institute trains all branches of the legal profession, it might have become a link in a program to establish a wholly unified profession (in the sense first described above) by taking as the focus of its training the parties to litigation as is done in the American law school. Apparently some people were thinking in this direction. Because training is functional, however, the institute's program continues to encourage specialization; but since all receive identical training prior to the selection of a specialty, the institute seems well suited to the realization of the second, modified form of unification based on promoting cooperation and mutual understanding among the profession's three branches. Its contributions have in fact been of this nature. The legal apprentices are, until they have made their choice of work at the end of their training, simply young professional comrades, sharing during their two years of stiff training the common life of the classrooms and dormitories. The understanding and friendship resulting from this experience lasts after the apprentices have entered their chosen fields and produces a strong feeling of the unity of the profession. This is evidenced by the fact that many judges, procurators, and lawyers who have studied together at the institute hold meetings in the various districts to renew friendships and exchange thoughts and experiences concerning their work. This sense of association is not limited to graduates of the same classes at the institute but extends to all those who have been apprentices under the postwar system. In 1951 a general alumni organization known as the Association of Former Classes (Zenkikai), composed of the entire body of graduates, was formed. The association as a whole has not yet become very active, but the fact that its membership already numbers nearly one third of the entire legal profession indicates that it may be a most influential body. On occasion, officers of local attorneys' associations have been elected on recommendation by the lawyer members of the local Association of Former Classes. These relationships would have been unimaginable before the war, and the institute's part in ending the prewar antagonism between those "in office" and those "outside" and in advancing the unity of the three branches of the profession is immeasurably important. In the future, when the legal profession must face as one body important reforms in the judicial system, the structure of the Association of Former Classes and the postwar sense of professional unity will be of great importance.

Second, the institute's training advances functional understanding among the three branches in many ways. The institute gives the same instruction in judgment, prosecution, and advocacy to all apprentices, regardless of the fields they hope to enter in the future. The apprentices thus gain a broader perspective and experience which will be of much value to them, whichever branch of the profession they enter. At the same time they are given an adequate basis for understanding the actual work, difficulties, and responsibilities of the other branches of the profession. In particular it is of great significance for the protection of human rights that those who will become judges and procurators should have a chance to know the actual circumstances of lawyers and their clients. It is not too much to say that, in this sense, the original ideal of unification has been at least partially realized.

Third, the system developed through the institute has ended the unequal educational treatment of the prewar probationary legal officials and probationary attorneys. By thus equalizing the skills of the three branches, it has succeeded in providing a basis for cooperation and mutual understanding among equals. Before the war, the status of the official was high, and, since many persons wished to enter the government service, the Ministry of Justice was able to select the probationary legal officials from among those who qualified with high scores in the legal section of the senior examination for public officials. Hence the legal officials were generally thought to be superior to the lawyers, at least in knowledge of law, and, in those days of "respect for officials and disdain for the people" [30] and general lack of understanding of the lawyer's work, the judge and the procurator tended to feel a certain superiority over the lawyer. This the lawyer repaid with an antipathy toward these officials.

However, since under the postwar system those who are to become judges and procurators and those who are to become lawyers receive identical treatment both economically and in the content of their training, the prewar inequality has entirely disappeared. Moreover, as the function of the lawyer as a defender of human rights has come to be understood and as the high esteem for officialdom has declined, many ambitious and enterprising young men of talent have been drawn into practice. They present an interesting contrast to the many more sober and scholarly young men who have preferred to become judges. Almost all the judges are agreed that, in richness of legal knowledge and in active conduct of litigation, the young lawyers who have been graduated from the institute outdo the prewar members of the profession. Thus, as the ability of the lawyers rapidly improves, the young

[30] *Kanson mimpi.*

lawyers come to have the confidence of full equality with the judges and procurators. Taken as a whole, the lawyers do not now fall below the judges and procurators in quality and capacity.

Needless to say, this improvement in the status and capabilities of the lawyers has been of great service to furthering cooperation among the three branches. Furthermore, this development is laying a foundation which may make possible the unification of the profession in more basic terms, that is, through the appointment of lawyers as judges. In the past, the special qualities of judicial work, in particular the importance of the elaborate technique of drafting judgments, have been emphasized as an objection to appointing judges from the bar. However, since the postwar lawyers have as apprentices also been trained in judicial techniques and since the level of their knowledge of law is high, this obstacle is no longer of much importance. Nor should it be forgotten that, as the skill of those representing the parties to litigation develops, there is a corresponding growth of an adversary system of litigation, and the ground is prepared for a trial system in which the judge acts as a senior umpire. In any event, it may be expected that, as the number of good lawyers increases, the lawyers will not be satisfied with the present three branch system and may seek appointment as judges. It seems fair to say that the improvement in the skill and confidence of the bar, together with the mutual understanding and sense of unity of the institute's graduates, is preparing the way, however slowly, for a true unification of the profession.

Finally, I should like to add that the new training system is doing much to promote a sense of affinity among members of the prewar generation of the three branches by bringing them together as instructors at the institute or in field training — an unexpected byproduct of the postwar system. Institute instructors enjoy particularly close cooperation, and the number of leading judges, procurators, and lawyers who have served as instructors has now reached about 145. These men form an influential group within the profession. Already two lawyers who had served as instructors have been named to the Supreme Court. Mutual understanding and familiarity among instructors from different fields has been particularly advanced by cooperative teaching in such recently inaugurated institute programs as the seminar in examination of witnesses, mock trials, and the summer joint-training project.[31]

Some Problems and Plans

I think it clear from the above that the institute is playing an important role in the realization of the ideal of unification of the legal profession. It should not be assumed, however, that no problems have arisen. First,

[31] It may incidentally be noted that three graduates of the institute have already themselves been appointed instructors.

some apprentices who have determined in advance which branch of the profession they wish to enter tend to become negligent in their studies relating to the other branches. This is seen particularly among those who intend to become lawyers. Aspirants to the judiciary and the procuracy take the examination which concludes the training rather seriously, but those wishing to become lawyers are not so earnest. Particularly since in recent years almost no one has failed this examination, many tend to become less diligent in courses concerning the judiciary and procuracy and in those which are not of immediate use upon entering practice. The institute continually warns the apprentices against falling into this error of shortsightedness, but it is hard to correct the tendency entirely.

Again, it is said that the instruction in the practice of the lawyer is the least adequate part of the institute's training. While the judicial and procuracy instructors devote full time to the institute, the lawyer instructors are all on a part-time basis, and, as a rule, their busy schedules permit them to devote only one day a week to their teaching duties. Although a large number of excellent and experienced lawyers have served as instructors, it is hard to avoid the conclusion that, in matters such as preparing lectures and materials and in cooperative work with other instructors, they do not measure up to the other instructors. Also some local attorneys' associations find it hard to conduct organized field training equal to that of the courts and procurators' offices. Although the ratio of instructors at the institute is two judges to one procurator to two lawyers, the ratio of instruction time assigned to each field in both periods of training at the institute is five for court's work (three civil and two criminal) to two for prosecution and two for advocacy (one civil and one criminal). One reason for this is the limited time the lawyer instructors have available. Another reason for such a distribution of field-training time may lie in the limited capacity of the attorneys' associations to arrange systematic instruction for the apprentices.

This is disturbing, whether considered from the viewpoint of unification of the profession or in light of the fact that more than one half of the apprentices become lawyers. Of course, training in court work and prosecution is of great help to those who are to become lawyers, but nevertheless, in view of the ideal of unification, education relating to the attorney's work should be fundamental to professional legal education and should certainly not be inferior to that in other fields. Moreover, except for short-term projects in which relatively few persons take part, there are almost no refresher programs for the education of lawyers like the research programs established for judges and procurators already embarked on their careers.[32] The initial education a lawyer receives at the institute is therefore of great importance for the preservation of the level of skill of the bar. Some urge even today

[32] As to the program of training and research for judges under the institute, see Matsuda, note 1, at 376.

that, for unification of the profession, the institute should center its training on advocacy, leaving instruction in the special techniques of the judge's work and of prosecution to later in-service training. It has been suggested that, as things now stand, the influence of the judicial and procuracy instructors will naturally become strong in the administration and general instruction of the institute. For example, attorney instructors have pointed out that in the field of civil litigation the apprentices are easily influenced by the manner of viewing cases of the instructors from the judiciary. The latter draw the apprentices' attention to concise drafting of documents for litigation and to elaborate theoretical analysis but tend to neglect the careful pleading of circumstantial facts and the tactics of litigation essential to the lawyer.

Of course, it would be most desirable for the ultimate solution of these problems to provide full-time instructors in advocacy but it appears hard, in the present conditions of law practice, to realize this solution immediately. Accordingly, efforts are being made to correct the situation within the limits of existing conditions. For example, all important educational policies are determined by instructors' meetings attended by the attorney instructors; and the recently established institutions committee, now studying basic changes in the apprentice system, includes representatives of the attorney instructors and is attempting to reflect their views. Also the attorney instructors are continuing earnest work on the preparation of materials to improve instruction in advocacy. Recently a guide to the drafting of documents for litigation with respect to civil pleading has been published. In fact, the time devoted by the attorney instructors to the editing of materials, the holding of prelecture conferences, and consultation on educational plans has increased somewhat. Since 1959 a system under which capable young lawyers are attached to the institute has been in effect, and at present two are assisting the attorney instructors in the editing of materials and in other ways. Again, while the plan noted above for joint instruction by instructors from all three fields contemplates training through the cooperation of specialists from each area, its main objective is drill in the activities of the litigant parties to proceedings. Thus it may also be considered an effective measure to improve the present instruction in advocacy.

Finally, it must be recorded that, despite the institute's efforts to further unification of the legal profession, actual realization remains rather difficult. Frequent appointment of judges from the profession at large must await growth in the size of its membership and the development of organized law practice. Obstacles exist even to achieving cooperation among the three branches. On the one hand, a sense of unity among the young members of the profession is being nurtured by the institute. On the other hand, the strength of long tradition and the influence of life as members of a single branch undeniably tend to erect barriers to mutual understanding even among graduates of the institute as they adopt the attitudes of their respective branches of the profession. It is, in the end, a mistake to assume that the problem of unification of the profession can be solved by the efforts of the institute alone. Ultimate solution depends on the will and efforts of the entire profession to achieve a better system of justice. The institute can do no more than offer encouragement and prepare the ground for such efforts to find a fundamental solution.

The Bearing of Postwar Changes on Legal Professional Education

Changes in the Status and Responsibility of the Legal Profession

Since the prewar Japanese legal profession was considered a body of legal technicians employed primarily in litigating criminal and civil actions, it could scarcely be expected to occupy a leading directive role in society. However, since the realization of the rule of law has become a fundamental objective of democratization in postwar Japanese society, the legal profession has come to the fore as an extremely important group. For example, lawyers' groups are frequently asked for their views concerning important social problems, and lawyers are from time to time appointed to high positions in government agencies and administrative commissions. The high position of the Supreme Court in the functioning of the system of law has been firmly established, and the people are gradually beginning to realize that the courts are the ultimate protectors of human rights, with powerful authority derived from the Constitution to overturn acts of the legislative and executive branches of the government.

These great changes, which have occurred since the war and have elevated the political and social functions of the legal profession, demand skill and training superior to that considered adequate before the war. The members of the legal profession are no longer simply procedural technicians. They must now have both a strong consciousness of human rights and the determination to protect them. They must be men of independent character. It is of particular importance that judges and procurators think of themselves truly as citizens, putting aside bureaucratic conceptions. Lawyers must assume important responsibilities for the proper functioning of the legal system and the judicial process and for the maintenance of order under law. Accordingly, not narrow legal professionalism but leadership — statesmanship — with a broad social perspective is demanded of the legal profession. Naturally this must be grounded in knowledge not only of law but of such fields as politics, economics, labor, and administration.

Naturally, too, an education for the legal profession that is broad enough to meet these needs must basically be a function of the educational process prior to entrance into the Legal Institute. It can be readily and successfully provided only by the universities with their specialists in every field and their experts in education, within their tradition of academic freedom and independence. Again, it is not enough to rely solely on education; the problem cannot be truly solved unless measures are devised at the same time to draw into the profession large numbers of particularly talented persons. Although the objectives — realization of the rule of law and preservation of order under law — may be intimately related to practical aspects of law, their attainment ultimately must have its roots in the basic attitudes of the members of the profession. This essential foundation must be provided by the universities and the schools which precede them in the educational process. The Legal Institute exists to give instruction in practice and technique to students who have finished a general education in jurisprudence. But it has only eight months during which the students are gathered within its walls for direct instruction. The instructors, furthermore, are nearly all professionals and not specialists in scholarship or education. Since the institute is essentially an agency of the government, supported by the national budget and directed principally by men who are public officials, it would be mistaken to expect from it broad education of the sort discussed above.

Nevertheless, the institute at present must assume responsibility for a certain amount of broad education appropriate to the new image of the profession. First, as previously indicated, many apprentices show a rather marked deficiency in general cultural fields other than law as a result of such factors as the reduction in the length of the period of university training and the difficulties of qualification through the national legal examination. Second, legal instruction in the universities is limited in time and confined to relatively abstract legal theory. Therefore, it cannot be expected to deal adequately and specifically with such problems as the concrete realization, through judicial proceedings and the work of the profession, of such ideals as protection of human rights, the rule of law, or the role that law should play in the new society. Third, the professors of the universities usually have had no practical experience with the law, and the main thrust of their instruction is directed to the training of quasi-lawyers who will not enter the legal profession. It is hard, therefore, for the law departments to give to those who wish to enter the profession adequate guidance concerning their new role in society.* The institute must accordingly assume the function of closing this educational gap, and many persons expect it to do so.

In response to this demand, the institute now includes within its limited curriculum measures directed to broader educational needs. Both periods of instruction at the institute include lectures by noted specialists, particularly by men from fields other than law and by men of affairs, concerning such

* Richard Rabinowitz suggested at the conference that the large number of law-department students not ultimately entering the institute indicates the need for a rethinking of the value of law as an ingredient in liberal education on the undergraduate level.

themes as the rule of law and the constitutional rights of the people. A certain amount of time is also devoted to lectures by first-rate specialists in fields such as economics, sociology, history, natural science, and belles-lettres.[33] Great care is taken in selecting instructors for these courses to find men of balanced convictions based on adequate study. The lecturers include not only scholars but also experts with abundant experience in practical affairs, journalists, and others. In 1960 a series of lectures was offered entitled "The Courts and the Public," which included lectures by many persons from nonlaw fields. Generally speaking, the institute, taken as an agency of the government, has secured adequate freedom in its educational policies; there has been no interference from any agency with the right of the president of the institute to determine who shall give the lectures described above.

I should like to add that, as already discussed, the unification at the institute of the three branches of the profession also assists in many ways the formation of the new image of the profession. Through receiving instruction as lawyers from senior members of the bar and having the opportunity to associate closely with those of their colleagues who will become lawyers, future judges and procurators in Japan are now able to acquire a consciousness of human rights like that of the general public outside the bureaucracy. Again, since the ages of the present apprentices vary from twenty-two to sixty, with an average age of twenty-seven, they bring to their studies a wide range of experience. The future judges and procurators thus share the life of the classroom and dormitory with many kinds of men, engaging in frank and close discussion with them. Conversely, through their frequent attendance at the courts and procurators' offices and close contact with judges and procurators, the future lawyers can develop attitudes of full responsibility to the society as a whole rather than purely negative, critical philosophies. It is not too much to say that for these reasons the members of the profession who have been trained since the war have been given the opportunity to surpass the prewar generation in breadth of perspective and sense of responsibility.

Next I must mention the emphasis given in the institute's program to education in legal ethics which is designed to develop the character of the members of the profession by encouraging a strong sense of professional responsibility. Because of the postwar growth of the interest of society in the life of the profession, criticism by older lawyers of the professional attitudes of their juniors, and the defiant attitude taken by some lawyers to the judges of some of the criminal courts, the need for instruction in legal ethics has been pressed upon the institute from all quarters. The lawyer instructors have been devoting a limited amount of time in both periods of instruction (a total of four hours in the first period of 1960) to lectures on

[33] In 1960, about 21 units (about 40 hours) of a total of 340 units, were devoted to these subjects in the two periods of instruction.

general professional ethics. The lectures have included such matters as the mental preparation of the attorney and his attitudes toward the courts, his clients, and the general public. To prevent these lectures from becoming nothing more than tiresome moral preachment, the instructors employ various devices, relating to the apprentices episodes from their own long experience or discussing the attitudes which the lawyer should take with respect to specific cases. They might question the apprentices, for example, on the way in which a lawyer should deal with a defendant who confesses his guilt to the lawyer. They might ask the apprentices to criticize a recently submitted petition for appeal in which the lawyer stated that "the judgment of the lower court is correct — the defendant's criminal action cannot be socially sanctioned." In the 1958–59 second period of instruction, seminars in professional ethics were conducted three or four times. In addition, lectures of this sort are frequently given during the periods of field training by the local attorneys' associations. Again, instructors from each of the three branches of the profession, using specific examples of courtroom technique, discuss in seminars the technique of examining witnesses and, in their comments on the mock trials, the manners of the judge, procurator, and lawyer in court and the way in which all should cooperate to preserve order in the courts. Such instructional materials in professional ethics as Hanai's *The Lawyer's Duty of Good Faith*[34] and Drinker's *Professional Ethics* (in translation)[35] are distributed to the apprentices and employed in their training. Of course, close observation of the speech and actions of superior senior members of the profession in the courts, procurators' offices, and attorneys' associations is the most effective sort of training for development of high personal qualities.

The foregoing describes the institute's earnest efforts to meet the demands of a new age. However, there is obviously a limit imposed by its structure and capacity on what the institute can do in this direction. It should be understood that the ultimate solution of these problems must await such basic resolutions as the reform of university education, the strengthening of professional bodies, and the understanding of the rule of law by society at large.

Expansion of the Area of Legal Affairs Managed by the Profession

The legal affairs handled by the profession before the war centered chiefly on litigation and like measures in the process of dispute resolution. So-called preventive-law functions, such as the offering of general legal advice and opinions outside the courts, the drafting of contracts, and the conduct of

[34] Hanai, *Bengonin no Shinjitsu Gimu*, in CHŪŌ DAIGAKU GOJŪ SHŪNEN KINEN ROMBUN SHŪ, HŌRITSU NO BU (A Collection of Essays in Commemoration of the Fiftieth Anniversary of Chuo University, Part on Law) 415 (1935).

[35] Translated as DRINKER, HŌSŌ RINRI (Muto trans., 1958).

commercial negotiations, were generally undertaken not by members of the profession but by the quasi-lawyers who entered companies and the government ministries on graduation from the university law departments. This tendency has not been markedly altered since the war. It should be noted, however, that it has gradually become common for lawyers to draft contracts and take part in the negotiation of international transactions with foreign companies. Again, as the risk that litigation will develop from labor disputes has increased, both companies and unions have tended to seek early legal advice. In such fields the demand for lawyers to perform preventive and advisory functions is gradually increasing. Generally, society has been rather slow in this respect, but realization of the need for legal advice is growing little by little. Recognition of the need to seek the advice of specialized lawyers in such fields as tax, patent, and private international law in particular will increase in the future. I believe that at present the portion of the Japanese lawyer's work which is devoted to advising outside the courts is larger than it is generally thought to be.

However, if the tendency toward increasing use of the lawyer's counseling role continues, both the universities and the institute will have to give instruction not only in the process of litigation but also in the rendering of legal advice and opinions in broad areas of law to enable the profession to cope with these new functions. Actually, not only do the universities almost entirely omit instruction in these areas, but the institute is also extremely weak in the same fields, though it has ultimately the responsibility for practical training. I think this results from the following factors.

In the first place, since instruction in the work of judges and procurators, who devote themselves almost entirely to judicial proceedings, occupies an important part of the institute's training, the importance of instruction in the preventive functions described above is easily overlooked. Particularly since training in criminal matters forms a rather large part of the program (more than half of the entire curriculum), it is hard to give great weight to instruction in the business of advising, which involves chiefly private law problems.

Second, while instruction in preventive functions requires a great deal of research and preparation, the time of the attorney instructors who properly should do most of the teaching in this field is rather limited.

Third, the lawyers trained before the war are not always familiar with the techniques of rendering legal advice. It becomes particularly hard to find lecturers who have both sufficient knowledge and adequate experience in giving advice on areas of law involving special legislation. Moreover, the scholars who deal with these fields in the universities are not always particularly well informed concerning matters of practice. Hence the institute has difficulty even in locating a sufficient number of lecturers in specialized areas to conduct instruction in the offering of legal advice.

Fourth, the capacity of the institute's curriculum has already reached its limit with instruction relating to judicial proceedings alone. In view of its nature and time limitations, it cannot offer training in the broad areas of law important to the advisory functions of the lawyer.

Of course, despite the above difficulties, the attorney instructors sometimes devote a part of their schedule for the first and second periods of instruction to the drafting of contracts and opinions. The attorneys' associations also, in their field-training program, attempt to afford some opportunity for practical training or observation of such matters as management of the legal affairs of companies or the giving of advice concerning the law. The attorneys' associations in the large cities have arranged during the periods of field training specialized lectures on such nonlitigious matters as preparation of opinions, patent procedures, and tax practice. Again, in response to the growing demands of practice with international aspects, an international legal-practice seminar — still at an elementary level — was initiated by the institute in 1958. These measures, however, are insufficient, and, if instruction in these fields is considered hereafter to be necessary, either the universities must establish appropriate chairs or the kind and the length of study at the institute must be fundamentally altered.

The Growing Importance of Judicial Administration and Procedure

Legal education in the Japanese universities, both before and after the war, has placed extreme emphasis on the theoretical interpretation of law. It has given little attention to such problems as the acceleration of proceedings, determination of facts, techniques of trial, and the administration of the judicial system. In the prewar training of the probationary legal officials and probationary attorneys, such matters as the drafting of documents for litigation were systematically taught to some degree. However, such problems of judicial administration as those noted above were left, as matters of discretion, to observation by the probationers during the period of training or to later accumulation of experience and insight as practitioners; they were almost never studied or taught in terms of systematic analysis.

However, with the rapid advance of the natural sciences and sociology, statistics, and psychology since the war, the need for the introduction of science into the traditional judicial process or for the rationalization of judicial procedures by positive methods has gradually come to be recognized. These forces made themselves felt rather quickly in the legal profession, and the postwar establishment of the Family Courts, the provision for probation officers, social workers, and medical-affairs offices, the positive studies of juvenile delinquency by the predecessors of what is now the Ministry of Justice Integrated Research Institute, and the collection of detailed statistics on the legal system were all attempts to realize the ideal of the introduction of science into judicial proceedings.

In the traditional fields of civil and criminal judgments, also stimulated by these trends, the need for more systematic study of judicial administration gradually came to be stressed by members of the profession. Added to this was the increased interest of the public in judicial proceedings. Criminal proceedings such as the *Matsukawa*[36] and *Yakai*[37] cases, which centered on disputes concerning the determination of facts, drew strong public attention. The risk of erroneous judgment was sharply described and led many to believe in the necessity of scientific study of the factfinding process. Again, "efficiency" of business became a catchword and, with the rationalization of all affairs and the markedly increased tempo of social life which accompanied the remarkable postwar development of the Japanese economy, strong criticism was raised against the inefficiency of the traditional judicial system. In particular, the inordinate delay in civil proceedings in the large cities was criticized by the public, which is gradually becoming conscious of its rights. Movements arose within the profession calling for study of the causes of delay in litigation and for appropriate measures for its reduction. Certain measures are already under consideration.

One extremely important point concerns the dramatic shift, supplementary to the postwar reform of the general legal system, from the Continental to the Anglo-American systems of civil and criminal procedure with the adversary and concentrated-trial procedures. Because of this the legal profession has faced many doubts and difficulties in dealing with judicial administration. Extensive study of trial supervision by the judge and of the courtroom techniques of the parties (matters which formerly had been beyond the sphere of academic interest and had been left to the "discretion" of individual judges and attorneys) was felt to be indispensable in order to digest rapidly the alien system and adjust to the new circumstances. For example, to effectuate the concentrated trial, a carefully prepared plan of trial based on cooperation between the judge and the parties and on the analysis of their experiences was necessary. It was of course essential to the success of the adversary system that lawyers and procurators study the technique of procedure, particularly the examination of witnesses. In addition, in cases involving such matters as labor disputes and public security, which have

[36] Japan v. Suzuki, Fukushima District Court, Jan. 12, 1951, 13 SAIKŌ SAIBANSHO KEIJI HANREI SHŪ (A Collection of Criminal Supreme Court Cases) [hereafter cited SAI-HAN KEISHŪ] 1749, *reversed on appeal* Sendai High Court, Feb. 23, 1954, 13 SAI-HAN KEISHŪ 2111, *reversed on revision and remanded* Supreme Court, Grand Bench, Aug. 10, 1959, 13 SAI-HAN KEISHŪ 1419, *modified on rehearing* Sendai High Court, Aug. 8, 1961, JURIST no. 239, at 97 (1961).

[37] Japan v. Ato, Yamaguchi District Court, Iwakuni Branch, June 2, 1952, HANREI JIHŌ (The Case Journal) no. 127, at 53, *affirmed on appeal* Hiroshima High Court, Sept. 18, 1953, HANREI JIHŌ no. 127, at 56, *reversed on revision and remanded* Supreme Court, III Petty Bench, Oct. 15, 1957, 11 SAI-HAN KEISHŪ 2731, *modified on rehearing* Hiroshima High Court, Sept. 23, 1959, HANREI JIHŌ no. 201, at 11, *reversed on revision and remanded* Supreme Court, I Petty Bench, May 19, 1962, 16 SAI-HAN KEISHŪ 609.

rapidly increased in number since the war, the litigants have on occasion disrupted the order of the courts and refused to follow the instructions of the judges. Study of the control of proceedings in such cases is therefore also an important problem. Systematic training and knowledge in judicial administration is essential in order to realize the new image of the profession.

The Legal Institute as an agency for the training of the profession consequently must adopt instruction in judicial administration if it is to be responsive to these postwar requirements. It has in fact exerted considerable effort in this area, and it might be said that this has recently been the main emphasis of its instruction. First, in the drafting study, which is a most important part of the curriculum, emphasis was formerly placed on problems of the interpretation of law, the legal bases of procedure, and the expressions and terms used in drafting, but recently, especially in areas such as criminal-judgment drafting, a great part of the time has come to be devoted to lectures and discussion concerning the determination of fact. These attempt detailed study of the inferences to be drawn from all the circumstantial evidence and, drawing on the results of related sciences such as psychology, the analysis of testimony and other evidence. Various materials have been prepared for use in such instruction. For example, a casebook, *The Psychology of Testimony*,[38] which includes recent judicial decisions, reports by practitioners, and excerpts from works of judges, procurators, and psychologists, has been published by the institute and is distributed to the apprentices for reference use.

Active criticism of the direction of proceedings by judges and of the methods of argument and presentation of evidence by lawyers, as these appear in records of proceedings, is carried on. In the courses involving study in drafting criminal judgments, consideration of the sentencing problem in specific cases forms an important part of the instruction. This instruction in sentencing is made necessary by the broad discretion in setting punishment given to the judge by the Japanese Penal Code. In order to provide an objective basis for the determination of sentences, the institute has published an extensive study, national in scope, of the sentencing practices of the courts in recent murder and similar cases, arranged and classified according to the particular circumstances of each case.[39] The text mentioned earlier, *Explanation of First-Instance Civil Procedure*,[40] contains many descriptions of, and comments on, the role of the judge in directing proceedings. The instructors in classes on drafting technique and problem discussion frequently com-

[38] See note 28.

[39] SHIHŌ KENSHŪJO, SATSUJIN NO TSUMI NI KAN-SURU RYŌKEI SHIRYŌ (Materials on Assessing the Penalty in Regard to the Crime of Homicide) (Shihō Kenshūjo Chōsa Sōsho (Legal Training and Research Institute Research Series) No. 5, 1959); SHIHŌ KENSHŪJO, SHŌGAI CHISHI NO TSUMI NI KAN-SURU RYŌKEI SHIRYŌ (Materials on Assessing the Penalty in Regard to the Crime of Inflicting Fatal Bodily Injury) (Shihō Kenshūjo Chōsa Sōsho No. 6, 1959).

[40] See note 24.

ment on the appropriateness of the actions of judges in directing proceedings with reference to such matters as orders for clarification and selection of evidence.

In the area of trial technique for litigants, the text *Outline Lectures in Prosecution,*[41] edited by the procurator instructors, offers many similar explanations. Materials relating to the techniques of civil pleading, prepared by the attorney instructors, have just been published. Perhaps the most remarkable effort in this area is the series of instructional programs, initiated in 1958, centering on demonstrations of trial activity. Since the first period of instruction in 1959, a mock civil trial has been presented to each group of new apprentices by some of the most recent graduate judges and lawyers. This is intended to represent a typical civil proceeding employing the concentrated trial and lasts for a full day. A movie of a model criminal trial prepared by a group of prominent Tokyo practitioners is also shown to the apprentices. In the second period, seminars in the technique of examination of witnesses in civil proceedings and in mock criminal proceedings, in both of which the apprentices themselves are called upon to perform, are allotted considerable time.[42] Almost all the apprentices participate in these seminars, and, in addition to taking parts in the proceedings themselves, are frequently required to draft conclusions based on their observation of the cases. These seminars employ the special resources of the institute, using materials prepared after the instructors have made a selection of the most appropriate cases from the courts of the entire country. A second particularly useful quality of these seminars is the thorough criticism of the apprentices' performances by instructors from the judiciary, the procuracy, and the bar and occasionally by judges assigned to Tokyo who participate specially. These criticisms, based on long experience in various branches of the profession, are perhaps a once-in-a-lifetime opportunity for most of the apprentices. A third factor of importance in these seminars lies in the fact that, since the apprentices have by then completed sixteen months of field training, it is possible to give guidance in direction of proceedings and trial techniques at a rather high level.

The object of these seminars is not, like the American model trial, purely instructional, seeking merely to show the students the actual conduct of a legal proceeding. Legal reform is also served. The purpose is to offer practice which will reform and explore, by cooperative effort and mutual criticism and with a scientific attitude, the activities of the trial, which tend to be left to the experience of the individual members of the profession, and to offer stimulation for further study by the apprentices. The seminars should also

[41] See note 27.

[42] The sessions are conducted on a class basis and often occupy a whole afternoon. Students are required to make extensive preparation for the sessions. In 1960, the civil seminars were conducted four times and the criminal twice.

direct the apprentices, who, perhaps because of the instruction in drafting which relies on the records of proceedings, tend to fall into the habits of the prewar documentary examination, to the postwar objective of "judgment based on seeing and hearing." These differences in objective are perhaps possible because the Japanese legal apprentice has, unlike the American law student, experienced a valuable period of field training and is thus already familiar with actual trials.

In other fields, although the time allotted may be insufficient, instruction in related sciences such as legal medicine, the psychology of the witness, psychiatry, and accounting is offered by visiting lecturers of the first rank. Lectures are also given on interviewing technique and written expression. Moreover, in the second period of instruction elective seminars are offered, under the guidance of specialists, in such subjects as polygraph testing, criminology (including the psychology of confession), and criminal-law policy. In 1958 a seminar dealing with the acceleration of civil proceedings was offered by Tokyo District Court judges and first-line lawyers. The institute's strong point, the fact that it is the sole agency in the country devoted to professional training in law, is apparent throughout this program in that it has not been at all difficult to obtain the cooperation of first-rate specialists from both the academic world and the world of practical affairs.

It would perhaps be desirable to include within the institute's educational program instruction in the system of judicial appointment, the structure of the courts, the administration of professional bodies, and even broader aspects of judicial administration, but at present these points are touched upon only in a few lectures by senior members of the profession. However, a study prepared in 1955 by the institute is noteworthy in this connection. This inquiry, *A Study Concerning the Problem of the Professional Legal Population,*[43] publishes the results of a detailed statistical investigation of the legal profession and points out the insufficiency of its numbers.

As will be appreciated from the foregoing pages, the Legal Training and Research Institute has, for the past seven or eight years, expended great efforts to produce a new legal profession with a grounding in and concern for judicial administration. Of course, it is rather hard to compress instruction on such broad lines into the already crowded eight-month schedule, and there is a risk that in the end the effects may be only superficial. However, the apprentices have as a rule completed the training of the university law departments and, moreover, they observe the practice of the profession for a period of sixteen months during their apprenticeship. Thus, even if the seminars and lectures described above do no more than stimulate a proper interest and indicate apt methods for further study, their educational effects can be very great, having a continued impact on the apprentices after they

[43] SHIHŌ KENSHŪJO, HŌSŌ JINKŌ MONDAI NI KAN-SURU KENKYŪ (Shihō Kenshūjo Chōsa Sōsho No. 1, 1955).

have left the institute and entered the profession. In fact, this instruction has already stimulated strong interest in further study of judicial administration among young members of the profession, as may be well illustrated by the translations of works of Jerome Frank, *Not Guilty*[44] and *Courts on Trial*,[45] recently completed by two young graduates of the institute. It nevertheless remains true that the institute cannot, within its present curriculum, attempt a broader and more thorough treatment of judicial administration; this problem, as well, can be solved only by altering the institute's basic structure and term of instruction.

Legal Professional Education in the Future

As may be seen from the preceding sections of this essay, the postwar world of the legal profession has made great demands on the Legal Training and Research Institute, and the institute has endeavored to meet these demands. There are, nevertheless, not a few insufficiencies in the present pattern of instruction at the institute, and there are many fundamental problems which require attention. Since these problems have been discussed at appropriate points earlier, I shall not consider them again here, but I do wish to point out two or three basic issues which the institute must inevitably face and to indicate various proposals that have been offered for their solution.

It may perhaps be said that the character of a nation's legal profession is determined by the social function it is expected to perform in the present and in the future. If it is true, then, as suggested above, that the social role of the legal profession in Japan has been expanding both qualitatively and quantitatively since the war, problems concerning the size and composition of the profession inevitably arise. For example, the number of complex judicial proceedings has increased with the proliferation of conflicts over rights which has accompanied the rapid postwar changes in social life. Delay in proceedings in the large cities has become most serious; it is now urged from all quarters that the number of judges be increased. If this is correct and the number of judges must be increased, it would seem that, in view of the present adversary form of proceedings, the number of lawyers must also be increased and that in effect it may be necessary to increase the size of the entire profession. Again, if lawyers are in the future more frequently called upon to perform advisory functions, and if, as Jiro Matsuda, a former president of the institute, has suggested, it would be desirable for future graduates of the institute to take employment with companies and the government ministries in their professional capacities as is done in the United States and Germany, it follows inevitably that the profession must be much larger than it is now. It is also strongly urged that it is utterly impossible for sixty-seven hundred lawyers in a nation with a population of

[44] Translated as Frank, Muzai (Kojima trans., 1959).

[45] Translated as Frank, Sabakareru Saibansho (Koga trans., 1961).

ninety million — a ratio much lower than that of other advanced nations — to protect adequately the rights of the public throughout the country or to realize effectively the rule of law.

Of course, there has yet been no scientific study to determine just how great the latent demand for the legal services of lawyers is in Japanese society and, consequently, to determine the size of the legal profession which may be required; there are those who do not approve increasing the size of the profession at the risk of lowering its quality. However, the 1955 study of the professional legal population conducted by the institute indicates clearly that at least three hundred and fifty apprentices must be admitted annually simply to maintain the present ratio between the size of the profession and that of the general population.[46] When one considers the demands being made upon the profession from all sides, the growing rights consciousness of the public and the increasing complexity of social life and of the laws, one must conclude that a certain increase in the numbers of the profession cannot be avoided. It must be anticipated that the training required will at the least strain the capacity of the present staff and facilities of the institute, and it may be that difficulty would be encountered in providing reasonable stipends for all apprentices from the national budget. Moreover, even if these difficulties could be overcome, a fundamental problem would remain. Is the institute, an agency of the government, the proper place in which to concentrate the education of the large numbers of lawyers who are to bear important responsibilities for protecting the rights of the public and to assume positions as leaders of the society? In short, is it the most appropriate center for the education of a legal profession — and especially a body of lawyers — composed of independent individuals?

As I have indicated, it is now generally argued that, as a result of the postwar reduction in the years of attendance at the universities and the increase in the number of courses dealing with such areas as special legislation, the time allotted to university training in law is insufficient. The institute as well suffers from restrictions on time and the increasing burdens imposed on its instructors. The problem of the overcrowded curriculum, common to the universities and the institute, most certainly results from the strong pressures placed on these institutions to perfect the education given a legal profession that is subjected to the increasing demands of this new age. Although the problem might be solved by increasing the length of the combined university-institute program, proposals to follow this policy will encounter strong opposition, based on the fear that the entry of talented men into the profession would be impeded by the increased financial burden on the students and the reduced attractiveness of a career demanding longer training.

If for the present the combined period of instruction — now about four

[46] SHIHŌ KENSHŪJO, note 43, at 187.

and one-half years[47] — is not to be altered, the question remains as to the manner in which this period is to be divided between the universities and the institute. Furthermore, in connection with the problem of increasing the period of study in the law departments, questions arise whether a special, concentrated legal education for those who wish to enter the profession can be offered or whether the present instruction directed to a broader group of students including the quasi-lawyers should be continued. Indeed, the problem of reconstructing legal education in the broadest meaning of the term, in such a way that it will be brought into better balance with the size and composition of the profession, is the most important issue now confronting those engaged in Japanese legal education.

The determination of the agencies which are to be responsible for legal education is naturally related to the above problems concerning the distribution of the task. A great many views have been put forward on this point. Some lawyers, taking as their premise the ideal of unification of the profession in the strict sense, argue that the institute should be directed by the Federated Attorneys' Association.[48] Others, including Chief Judge Matsuda, who base their view on the modified and perhaps at present more realistic view of unification as the cooperation and reconciliation of the three branches of the profession, respond that, if a bar-association-like body including judges, procurators, and lawyers should be formed, then it should be entrusted with operation of the institute.[49] Both of these views assume that, as at present, practitioners should be responsible for professional legal education. Some scholars, on the other hand, suggest that the university law-department curriculum be lengthened by one year and that the period of instruction at the institute be reduced by a year and devoted to training of a purely practical and technical nature.[50] This seems in effect to be an argument that some portion of the present instruction in law should be shifted to the universities, which are considered specialists in legal education. However, there are also eminent scholars who feel that the university law departments should continue to give a basic legal education to both those who will enter the profession and those who will not, but that the structure and facilities of the institute should be perfected — and if possible the period of instruction lengthened as well

[47] That is, in a department of law and the institute following a year and a half of general university education.

[48] In 1954 the Japanese Federated Attorneys' Association adopted a resolution in which it proposed to change the Legal Training and Research Institute into a training institution for lawyers under the federation. See MATSUDA, Hōsō Kyōiku (Professional Legal Education) 11 (1960).

[49] On June 9, 1961, the Japanese Law Specialists' Association (Nihon Hōritsuka Kyōkai), a privately organized body for the unification of the legal profession consisting of leading judges, procurators, lawyers, and legal scholars, adopted such a resolution and proposed as a future plan to operate the Legal Institute under the auspices of the Federated Attorneys' Association.

[50] See the remarks of Sakae Wagatsuma, Jiro Tanaka, Teruhisa Ishii, and Hajime Kaneko in *Kore kara no Hōritsugaku* (Legal Studies from Here On Out), JURIST no. 217, at 141, 154–158 (1961).

— to provide a more concentrated specialized legal training at the post-graduate level.[51]

Adoption of any of these proposals would profoundly affect the Japanese legal profession, and probably no one can predict with confidence the course which will be followed. However, I think that a majority feel that for the present, because of the lack of practical professional experience in the universities, many difficulties would be encountered in assigning the training of professionals to them and that, since there is now no strong body of the bar-association type and since the attorneys' associations lack the structural and financial resources necessary to enable them to undertake the training of the profession, the present division of the educational function between the universities and the institute should be continued.[52] This is perhaps correct insofar as it is based on present circumstances. In looking to the future, however, I think we should bear two considerations in mind. First, it is most desirable that high-level professional training be undertaken by specialists in education in pluralistic institutions with developed traditions of freedom and individuality. Second, if the size of the profession is increased to any substantial degree, only a larger number of specialized educational institutions will be able to handle adequately the training which will be required.

Finally, if for the present the form of legal education is not to be altered, it is of the utmost importance that the educational program of the institute be further improved. This, in brief, means that the institute must advance its instruction from the hands of amateur educators — legal professionals temporarily directed to teaching — to the hands of true professional educators. Various measures must be pressed to this end: the instructors should be assured of time and facilities for research and given a grounding in the field of education; perhaps more advice can be obtained from educational specialists for the development of a method and system of rational education suited to the youth of the new generation. Those responsible for legal education in the universities may be consulted concerning the division of instruction between the universities and the institute, and the instructional materials can be further developed. Probably the relationship between the first and second periods of instruction at the institute and the field training should be re-examined. To study these problems and the broader basic problems of professional legal education and to consider important reforms, an institutions committee was established within the institute in November 1960. Since its formation, it has been engaged in collecting the views of persons representative of professional and academic circles.

Thus the Legal Institute, despite its many deficiencies, will presumably

[51] See the statement of Sakae Wagatsuma, professor emeritus of Tokyo University, in NIHON KŌHŌ GAKKAI–NIHON SHIHŌ GAKKAI (Japanese Public Law Association–Japanese Private Law Association), HŌGAKU KYŌIKU (Legal Education) 129–131 (1959).

[52] See MATSUDA, note 48, at 11, 12 n.7.

continue its earnest endeavor to meet the demands of postwar Japanese society. It may be said, perhaps, that an educational institution can preserve its life and vitality only if it correctly perceives the needs of the times and responds to them sensitively and with composure. To be sure, the institute has substantially improved the content of its instruction since the war, but this improvement has depended greatly on the basic assumption of the present system — that is, on the assumption that human and material resources are to be freely concentrated in the training of only somewhat more than three hundred apprentices. When this premise is changed, then the institute must respond with resolution and with new conceptions. Perhaps it may be said that the Japanese legal profession has a bright future to the extent that the institute responds perceptively and judiciously to the broadening of the rule of law in this new age and to the increasing social demands on the profession.

COMMENTARY: PART I

Arthur Taylor von Mehren

SINCE the conference discussions were primarily directed to Japanese institutions and experience and no comprehensive criticism of Western law was undertaken, criticism of Japanese law and legal institutions does not imply a judgment on comparative merit. Indeed, legal systems can hardly be evaluated on a universalistic scale; the relevant inquiry is whether a particular practice or institution is well suited to its own social setting. To do more is to evaluate social structures and ways of life — matters on which it is difficult, if not impossible, to pass beyond personal intuition to objective knowledge based on considered premises.

Discussions, both Japanese and Western, tend to proceed in terms of dichotomies: the Anglo-American and Continental European legal systems, modern and premodern Japan, and Japanese and non-Japanese elements. For example, Kenzo Takayanagi considers in detail the impact, through borrowing and conscious adaptation, on the Japanese legal structure of Continental European and, later, Anglo-American law. Such contrasts are useful in exposition and often suggestive. But, unless used with caution and a full awareness that they were not formulated with special reference to the development of contemporary Japanese law, these dichotomies may obscure a much more complex reality — a law that is a unique and specifically Japanese product arising from all the circumstances of Japanese life.

In the same vein, the discussions emphasized at several points that the tides running in the modern world do not pose the law's problems in terms of borrowing but, rather, in terms of adapting the institutions and processes of Japanese society, firmly caught up in the contemporary world, to the various societal changes occurring.[1] This task often requires state action, typically legislation, and a spirit of flexibility and pragmatism. Individuals are needed who, unwedded to the stereotypes employed to bring order into

Note. Mr. von Mehren is Professor of Law, Harvard University. B.S., 1942, LL.B., 1945, Ph.D., 1946, Harvard University.

At various places throughout this commentary, the conference participant who suggested or particularly emphasized a point is named.

[1] Professor Cavers.

past history, are sensitive to problems and solutions that do not fit comfortably within the older patterns.

The experience of other societies in handling similar problems can be of great benefit to processes of adaptation and development. Particularly in taxation[2] and certain branches of commercial law, where solutions are needed for problems common to all modern societies, specific techniques and institutions can be adopted.[3] But where a particular legal rule or institution is inextricably connected with a society's legal order and background, the process of adaptation is much more complex and subtle and the results necessarily less predictably beneficial.

One should also remember that Japan's experience differs radically from that of Western legal orders, which have grown more slowly and organically, developing rules and institutions in response to felt needs and experiences. True, Roman law was "received" in Continental Europe, but this reception involved a body of rules and principles that was, in many areas of life, ancestral to the receiving societies. Moreover, Roman law was thoroughly reworked and integrated over time into each receiving society's total legal order; materials derived from Roman and other sources could be slowly assimilated in an epoch when the pace and depth of change were most moderate by contemporary standards. In Japan, as Takayanagi makes clear, a massive, eclectic borrowing of foreign law took place, in part for purposes of reform, in part for reasons of survival and national independence; and there has been relatively little time in which to achieve mutual accommodation. Moreover, Japan has used law far more consciously and pervasively than the West as an instrument for general social change (as distinguished from specific amelioration). The era of massive borrowing to advance rapid and broad social change may now be over.[4] As the process of accommodation and interpenetration between the law and the society continues,[5] more specifically Japanese experience will be accumulated, out of which new rules and institutions can be forged without the need to draw so extensively on the experience and institutions of other systems.[6]

[2] Mr. Coleman commented that, in the tax field, great emphasis has been placed on the experience of other legal systems. By and large, tax rules and practice are not closely meshed with the general legal system. Japanese tax officials not only find suggestive experience in other systems; they also utilize rules and practices of foreign systems to suggest changes they would like to introduce on other grounds. Professor Yazawa remarked generally that, judging by his work on a law-revision commission, the emphasis in Japan is on practical problems encountered in drafting laws rather than on theoretical disputes over competing legal systems.

[3] Judge Tanabe.

[4] Professor Morley.

[5] In this connection, consider Judge Tanabe's remark that in some fields — for example, criminal law — the courts have a far greater body of experience than in others — for example, tort law. In the former areas, the process of accommodation and interpenetration has been carried forward by judicial decision at the level of formal law; in the latter areas, adjustments have been largely extralegal.

[6] Professor Hall pointed out that the degree to which law in Japan develops along

A comparison of Takayanagi's essay, which describes the official legal structure as borrowed from Western sources, with Takeyoshi Kawashima's description of the unofficial view of the legal system illustrates the extent of the adjustment yet to be made. Japan has long emphasized law's prescriptive function as distinguished from its function in the resolving of concrete problems. James Morley asserted at the conference that the codes are today among the chief expressions of the society's values and as such, carry considerable moral force.[7] Kawashima pointed out that Japan has a long tradition of seeing in the body of law a statement of morals; the government always used the codes as a basis of moral education — *shūshin* — and law is still so regarded today by the people. Thus members of the legal profession generally, and particularly professors and judges, are considered teachers of morals.[8]

Kawashima's essay poses problems which constantly recurred in the conference discussions, particularly his proposition that in traditional Japanese society (and, to a lesser extent, today) relatively little reliance is placed on the formal legal order as an agency for adjusting disputes and channeling human energy and capacity. The structure of traditional Japanese society was such that most disputes were seen as arising within a group relationship. Reinforced by the Confucian ethic's insistence on harmony in human relations,[9] the prevalent values sanctioned the maintenance of the group — in particular the family, which in a sense provided the basic pattern for the entire social structure — rather than the delineation or vindication of individual rights. In such a setting, the obligations attached to social status and the pressures exerted by the group — taking, in extreme situations, the form of ostracism — performed the task of maintaining and restoring the society's equilibrium, a task the West has, in recent centuries, substantially assigned to a body of law operating on individualistic principles.

In the absence of any mechanism or principles of institutional adjustment, disputes between, rather than within, groups were resolved either through sheer power or through mediation. Consequently, traditional Japan never evolved techniques of dispute resolution appropriate for controversies arising in an individualistic setting. On the other hand, Western law has given most of its attention to precisely this range of problems, developing relatively generalized norms and principles administered by impartial, official agencies of society. Thus traditional Japan, in the last decades of the nineteenth century, began to import Western law, with its individualistic premises and its generalized and abstract principles, into a society whose approach to dispute resolution had the following characteristics: (1) its principal tech-

---

specifically Japanese lines is likely to vary directly with the degree to which the area of life in question involves specifically Japanese practices and attitudes.

[7] Judge Tanabe agreed.

[8] Professor Morley and Judge Tanabe.

[9] Professor Schwartz.

nique was mediation or adjustment, not litigation; (2) each situation was resolved in terms of its highly specific and often exceedingly complex social setting, instead of by the application of generalized principles; (3) the dangerous rule of raw power and violence could prevail whenever the social fabric proved inadequate to resolve a dispute or whenever a dispute's setting transcended a single group.

Accepting this picture of traditional Japan, the conference centered on the evolution under way since the Meiji era. Discussion proceeded on essentially two levels: a dispassionate, sociological analysis assessing the effect of social change on dispute resolutions; and value judgments about the extent to which the individual should be the basic unit of society, the importance of regulating the rights and duties of individuals in terms of relatively generalized principles, and the role of litigation in vindicating the rights and duties so regulated.

There was general agreement that, as Japan's traditional social relations dissolve or alter, especially in response to urbanization and industrialization, the traditional forms of dispute resolution become increasingly less apt and effective. In some areas of life, indeed, reliance on traditional mechanisms may today be a mere reflex, a moribund social form lacking the vitality that attaches to functional appropriateness. Often, however, no feasible alternatives have yet emerged. In particular, judicial resolution on universalistic principles is neither generally nor fully accepted, and the transitional phase may well emphasize the underlying power situation — expressed in social or economic terms[10] — more than would either the traditional society or Western law.

These general propositions can perhaps be illustrated by the process of settlement common in Japan in cases of personal-injury claims arising from automobile accidents, an area in which, in view of the number of accidents, remarkably few cases are litigated.[11] In response to a question,[12] Kawashima outlined the procedure utilized for most taxi accidents causing personal injury. A representative of the taxi company visits the victim (or his family) and apologizes. Some compensation will ordinarily be paid, but the amount is typically less than the hospitalization costs and loss of income during the period of incapacitation. The respective legal rights of the parties, as they could be vindicated through litigation, play little if any role in the settlement. The basic explanation is perhaps that the taxi company, ordinarily the economic and social "superior," can take advantage of anachronistic attitudes. The injured party does not want his associates to think him queer and troublesome.[13]

[10] Professor Nathanson reported that a Japanese lawyer had told him that informal arbitration or mediation was a bad system because the decisions usually favored those higher on the social scale.

[11] See the statistics given by Kawashima in his essay, pp. 42 and 63.

[12] By Professor Gellhorn.

[13] Procurator Abe.

Traditionally the apology served as an expiation for the injury and allowed reintegration of the wrongdoer into the social group of which both he and the victim were members; but since it is unlikely that the taxi victim and the taxi company (or driver) belong to the same group, such reintegration no longer has such significance. Of course, the vindication of the injured party's rights under the written law is of less functional significance in Japan than it is in Western societies, particularly the United States. The persistence of traditional values means that no psychic cost attaches to the failure to vindicate; indeed, vindication would presumably entail such costs. To the extent that cohesive family unity still provides a substitute for compensation or social security, the injured party is effectively cared for. Furthermore, Western tort law's function of compensating the victim for his out-of-pocket expenses is performed, for medical expenses, by legislation establishing a comprehensive insurance scheme.

The most basic force operating to change this situation is the emergence of new attitudes; changing social forms increasingly devitalize the traditional attitudes toward dispute resolution. These new attitudes will probably emphasize the consciousness of rights and a reliance on general rules administered by official judicial agencies as functionally appropriate for a society that is increasingly tending toward the atomistic individualism characteristic of the contemporary West. Particularistic forces are also at work. The increasing use of the automobile itself, because of its destructive attributes, tends to foster a climate of attitudes and experience conducive to the pursuit and payment of claims. And the related and probably inevitable growth of insurance (indeed, Japan has recently adopted a system of compulsory liability insurance), with its business need for calculability based on general experience, provides an institution admirably designed to nourish the sense of individual rights. Within limits, both the ethical and the economic dynamics of the insurance relationship require claims and their payment — otherwise the insurance enterprise performs no function and fails to demonstrate its importance to society. Other elements which will affect the evolution toward rights consciousness and universalistic principles include the size of the bar, its general attitude toward the lawyer's role, and the availability of a relatively inexpensive and effective system of civil procedure. We shall return to these later.

A more emotionally charged counterpoint arises to this sociological discussion. To what extent should the individual form the basic unit of society; how humanly and socially valuable is a consciousness of rights; and what are the connections, if any, between political democracy and a sense of rights?

It was recognized at the conference that the courts must decide cases in terms of the formal law. Accordingly, Japanese judges are committed to individualism as a basic value. Kohji Tanabe emphasized that compromises, to the extent that they occurred under court control, were formulated by reference to the legally relevant standards and considerations. At the close of the final session of the conference, he eloquently stated his view that economic and social justice, as well as political democracy, derive support from rights consciousness and the availability of tribunals in which the individual's rights can be vindicated in terms of objective and impartial justice.

In general, the Japanese participants seemed to see in law a major instrument for moving their society still closer to the industrialized democracies of the West. Sounding a note of partial dissent, Haruo Abe suggested that new techniques of mediation, based on casework methods, might be developed to the nation's advantage. This course might develop a system of preventive casework designed to keep civil disputes from emerging.

The opinions of the American participants on these issues were more varied and less assured. Some thought that greater consciousness of rights was essential to social justice and political democracy in Japan.[14] Others sought to define more precisely the relationship between rights consciousness and political democracy.[15] Still others questioned the implicit acceptance by many conference participants, both Japanese and non-Japanese, of the proposition that, given contemporary Japanese conditions and economic aspirations, a high degree of individualism was desirable.[16] It was urged that greater attention should be given to whether traditional Japanese values might not be more compatible with several of the principal goals of contemporary Japanese society.[17]

Although all the essays are relevant, through specific examples or experience, to these general themes, the remaining three essays in the first group deal with the processes and personnel of the legal system.

Kohji Tanabe's essay, "The Processes of Litigation: An Experiment with the Adversary System," deals with the institutions and procedures for handling civil litigation. Japan's procedural system initially drew heavily on Continental European, especially German, models. After the Second World War, there was conscious, and often more or less imposed, borrowing from the American system, in particular the adversary form of litigation. More recently, attention has been given to adapting these procedural imports to function more effectively in their Japanese setting.

Tanabe pointed out that the elements of the American adversary system

[14] Professors Nathanson and Gellhorn were particularly outspoken on this question.

[15] Professor Schwartz pointed out that some nondemocratic societies have a relatively high level of individual rights consciousness. He suggested that dispute resolution through the techniques of Western law was relevant for democracy only in areas in which the parties did not enjoy a rough equality in wealth and power. Judge Wyzanski remarked, though in a context not directly relevant to this point, that Americans are, and throughout their development have been, "an incredibly lawyer-minded people." In other societies some of the American lawyer's tasks might be performed better by nonlawyers.

[16] Mr. Rabinowitz emphasized this issue.

[17] In this connection, Professor Pelzel's remark that social solidarity is becoming increasingly important in the United States is interesting.

introduced in Japan did not function very well for several reasons. The practicing lawyers, once the pretrial preliminaries had been completed, were not prepared to assume the burden of preparing to present the case to the court consecutively and uninterrupted by adjournments. Moreover, in a system without a jury, concentration of the trial into a single episode is not institutionally required but depends on strict judicial control. In Tanabe's view, the courts are slowly realizing that, at least in the Japanese context, the adversary system cannot mean an inactive court.

In order to achieve greater concentration in litigation, the Tokyo District Court has established two pretrial divisions which will formulate the issues in the cases and ensure proper pretrial preparation, thereby freeing the judge's attention for the problems of the trial.[18] The new divisions are frankly experimental. They will process a certain proportion of the total case load so that a judgment can be made as to the effectiveness of the new arrangements. Takaaki Hattori stated that many lawyers said they opposed the innovation because they believe it prolongs the procedure; but, in his judgment, lawyer opposition really springs from a reluctance to give the time necessary for pretrial preparation.

Two general problems were raised about the procedural system described by Tanabe. Do the post-1945 innovations encourage the use of legal machinery in dispute resolution? To what extent do the innovations find a secure basis in the organization, economic situation, and general outlook of the Japanese bar?

It was noted that the American and English systems tend, even after appropriate adjustments are made for different living standards, to be relatively more expensive for individual litigants than are the Continental European systems from which Japan originally borrowed in the procedural field. Of course, the differences in the expense of litigating relate in substantial measure to the higher compensation received by Anglo-American lawyers. The Anglo-American system may, however, be intrinsically more time-consuming, though there was no clear agreement on this point[19]; in any event, since it is more demanding on the lawyer (the judge bears a far greater burden in European systems), it would seem to follow that greater skill would be required on the lawyer's part; and, as a corollary, larger

[18] Thanks to the attendance at the conference of Judge Hattori, who will preside over one division, the conference was given a preview of this recent innovation.

[19] Some participants argued that the total lawyer's time expended in each system would be roughly equivalent, so that the two systems would be equally costly. Others suggested that the degree of preparation is necessarily greater in the American system; since a mistake or omission can be fatal, every avenue, no matter how unpromising, had to be explored fully. Moreover, few cases are settled before full preparation has taken place. In the Japanese context, on the other hand, settlement in court is less dependent on a full knowledge of the facts on each side. Indeed, for the Japanese, the episodic nature of the trial is more conducive to compromise than is a concentrated proceeding because the basis for settlement tends to be the relations established between the parties rather than the precise factual situation.

compensation would be demanded. Certainly, Anglo-American systems are far less conducive than the European systems to a litigant's conducting his own case.

The use of legal machinery in Japan is further inhibited by relatively high court costs (a feature of Continental European rather than of Anglo-American procedure). These are graduated according to the size of the recovery claimed and are ultimately paid by the losing party. (Lawyers' fees, on the other hand, are not so recoverable.) The relatively large initial outlay and the risk of nonrecovery probably deter recourse to the courts.

The second general problem suggested above carries the discussion to Takaaki Hattori's essay, "The Legal Profession in Japan: Its Historical Development and Present State." One specific difficulty connected with the organization of legal practice deserves mention before we turn to a general discussion of the essay. Although there are some law firms of the American type, the typical Japanese lawyer was pictured to the conference participants[20] as an extremely busy man, usually practicing alone and handling a very general practice. Because he does not have a collaborator and cannot specialize, a lawyer may not have the specialized skill and the time requisite for adequate pretrial preparation in cases of reasonable complexity. Indeed, it is hard to see how the individual practitioner, handling many matters, can be adequately prepared for a concentrated trial on the American model, a task which even the experienced American trial lawyer finds difficult when practicing alone.

Several participants[21] in discussing Hattori's essay emphasized that the small bar was supplemented by a much larger group of persons performing legal functions. Thus, many persons with university legal training — very few of whom, however, have been eligible to study at the Legal Training and Research Institute and achieve admission to the legal profession — are employed in the bureaucracy, for example, in the National Tax Agency. Corporate legal departments — which, it should be borne in mind, are conceived of as specialized clerical departments rather than as professional legal staffs — are staffed with individuals having a university legal education.[22] Tax specialists and patent specialists perform particular functions, involving a good deal of legal work. Numerous legal scriveners and administrative scriveners furnish various kinds of legal services, except those requiring actual courtroom appearances.

Even with the work of these groups, however, the number of persons in Japan doing legal work remains small by Western standards. Particularly in rural areas, legal advice is a scarce commodity. In general, the size of the

[20] Especially by Mr. Nagashima and Professor Yazawa.

[21] Especially Messrs. Coleman and Blakemore and Professor Yazawa.

[22] Mr. Blakeney noted that, in his experience, corporations sought relatively little legal advice. He sensed a change in the direction of more advice in the areas of commercial law, international transactions, and, to a degree, tax matters.

Japanese bar — in 1960, there were 6,458 practicing lawyers in the entire country — and related nonprofessional groups reflects the restricted role of law in dispute resolution and may, as well, provide new grounds for the maintenance of traditional attitudes; overly busy lawyers may not attract a timid or hesitant client. Also according to Hattori's statistics, the great majority of the persons admitted to the bar in recent years practice in either the Tokyo or Osaka areas. Thus, attorneys' associations in other areas are not only small but are composed of older, less energetic men who share more of the prewar Japanese attitudes toward the role of law in society.

The size of the bar has many implications which were brought out at the conference. Traditionally the lawyer in American society has been trained to adopt a broader view of legal problems than has the nonlawyer in contact with the law. It was suggested that the reliance of the government and corporations in Japan on nonlawyers means that the answers are drawn from a narrow and specialized background, with little chance for perspective on the particular problem. Moreover, does not membership in a profession help to impart to the lawyer a conception of his role and function significantly different from that held by the nonprofessional? [23] At the same time, it was suggested that the Legal Training and Research Institute does not do as much as it should to help the graduate toward a deeper understanding of law and of the law's potential contribution to the rational ordering of human affairs; but this question is best considered along with Abe's essay on legal education.

Another consequence of the relatively small size of the Japanese bar is that very few lawyers are available to handle certain significant tasks, in particular litigation, exclusively reserved to lawyers.[24] The scarcity of lawyers may, for example, significantly impede the more active protection of human rights. The size and character of the Japanese bar are not such as to encourage lawyers to conceive of their profession in activist terms or to do very much to promote the consciousness of rights in their society.

Agreement seemed general that Japanese society was evolving in directions that would require a greater use of professional lawyers. In this connection, David Cavers pointed to the growing incidence of industrial and traffic accidents, to the increasing depersonalization of the employment relation, and to the developing awareness on the part of the business community that nonprofessional legal advice is likely to be less informed and perceptive than

[23] Judge Tanabe remarked that the corporate quasi-lawyers are involved in organizations for their own distinct purposes; using their knowledge and skill largely to further their own interests within the organization, they lose contact with the societal aspects of law. Similarly, career government men are so immersed in their careers and the exercise of state power that they lose touch with the people and the evenhanded administration of the laws.

[24] Mr. Nagashima remarked that "the lawyers are too busy even to meet the demands of the big companies." Professor Ishikawa stated that "even trade-union lawyers are too busy to protect the unions or their members adequately, and some unions, therefore, refrain from using counsel and thus lose their remedies."

that of members of the bar. The question central to Abe's essay on legal education remains. Does the Japanese system of legal education and admission to the bar adequately meet the demands that are now or will be placed on the legal profession? Also, do the nonprofessionals who furnish many legal services receive a satisfactory preparation in their university legal education?

In the discussion, university legal education was criticized from the point of view of both the future professional and the future quasi-lawyer. This education follows European patterns and is subject to the same criticisms. The instruction does not provide a satisfactory vehicle for either general or professional education; rather, it tends to fall between the two. Instruction is largely expository; the student seeks to commit material to memory, not to evaluate or criticize.[25] Legal education is essentially static, concerned with a description of existing rules and institutions rather than with imparting an understanding of the processes of development or the direction of change. This deficiency will be increasingly felt as law becomes more significant in Japanese life. Moreover, to the extent that those performing legal tasks lack the vision of law as a way both of ordering human relations to avoid or minimize conflict and of coordinating human effort in harmonious and mutually advantageous patterns, society and the economy lose the benefit of much creative thinking.

The deficiencies in university legal education are the product of a whole complex of forces. They are partly due to traditional Japanese attitudes toward the role of law in society; furthermore, the tone of Japanese legal education is rooted in the psychological situation of scholars who must study and expound a body of formal rules neither indigenous to their own society nor congenial to its practices and attitudes. Confined initially by budgetary considerations, university legal education must mold itself into general educational patterns which may be inappropriate to its particular requirements. In the context of existing educational arrangements in Japan, legal education perhaps cannot be more professional in its emphasis; it probably must continue to deal with relatively large classes in which only a small minority will be motivated by a professional interest in law.

The question remained of the Legal Training and Research Institute's role in professional legal education.[26] Accepting the premise that the legal profession (bench, bar, and procuracy) could not be adequately nourished by the institute's yearly output of less than three hundred and fifty graduates,

[25] Procurator Abe particularly emphasized the degree to which Japanese legal education was memory-oriented.

[26] In principle, all prospective members of the Japanese legal profession (bench, bar, and procuracy) must graduate from the Legal Institute. It provides eight months of classroom instruction and supervises sixteen months of apprentice training in actual practice under the various District Court civil and criminal departments, the district procurators' offices, and prefectural attorneys' associations.

the conference explored various remedies. Considerable support emerged for a substantial expansion of the Legal Institute or the creation of other institutes. It was felt by many that, if the need were perceived, the required additional financial resources could be obtained.

Ryuichi Hirano, in a drastic proposal, would maintain the institute but end its monopoly of the training of lawyers. He suggested a national legal examination to qualify all applicants; the institute would continue to train future judges and procurators, and some future lawyers as well, but other law schools would train the large majority of lawyers. This professional education might be supplemented by some kind of apprentice system followed by a final examination. Judge Hattori objected because the proposal would destroy the sense of professional unity which now results from the common institute training received by all future members of the bench, bar, and procuracy.

Thomas Blakemore presented an alternative plan, which he developed in some detail. He would amend the Attorneys Law to create a new category of lawyer, similar to the English solicitor, who would not be qualified for general courtroom practice (though he might well be allowed to appear at simpler legal proceedings such as Summary Court and mediation proceedings). These lawyers would be admitted by way of a national examination given under the supervision of either the Supreme Court or the Federated Attorneys' Association. In principle, no specific educational preparation would be required for admission to the examination. In practice, the candidates would presumably be drawn primarily from among university law graduates who had received additional professional training at a special graduate school or course established at designated universities. In addition, after passing the qualifying examination, successful candidates might be given a brief course of formal training which would, in a small way, resemble the broader course of instruction provided by the institute. These lawyers, after a period of actual practice, could become full-fledged members of the bar by taking still another examination.

In addition to creating a new source of competent legal advisers to meet Japan's urgent and increasing needs, this plan would, in Blakemore's opinion, gradually bring under the profession's control many current abuses resulting from the giving of legal advice by inadequately trained men. The cost of this plan would be relatively modest. Such a proposal would be more acceptable to the Japanese bar than one calling for an immediate and large increase in the number of full-fledged lawyers. Businesses might be encouraged to hire individuals from this new group to perform legal services, thus improving the quality of corporate legal advice. The work and role of the Legal Training and Research Institute could continue unchanged. Finally, by offering less arduous and less restrictive avenues of admittance, new groups, particularly ones of varied specialized backgrounds (for example, tax specialists and maritime experts), would be attracted into the enlarged legal profession.

The Hirano and the Blakemore proposals both stimulated considerable interest. Clearly, they involve important questions about the whole character of the Japanese legal profession. For example, would such an enlargement change the attitude of the bar toward the lawyer's role, perhaps stimulating a more aggressive search on the part of some members for ways in which legal services might be of value to individuals and to business enterprises? Moreover, would the relaxing of admission to the profession result in attracting different, and more varied, personality types into the legal profession? In particular, does recruitment into the profession through the very rigorous entrance examination to the Legal Training and Research Institute perhaps give the Japanese legal profession a caste of mind too exclusively intellectual and reflective at the expense of more activist attitudes? [27]

[27] For a recent discussion of these same two proposals in Japan, see Amano, Yoshikawa, Tanabe, Matsuda & Mikazuki, *Hōsō Jinkō* (The Professional Legal Population), JURIST no. 249, at 40, 53–63 (1962), and *Poor Lawyer Ka No Lawyer Ka* (Poor Lawyer or No Lawyer?), JURIST no. 250, at 39 (1962).

II

THE INDIVIDUAL, THE STATE, AND THE LAW

Part Two, The Individual, the State, and the Law, comprises seven essays which collectively consider the legal ordering of the most significant relationships between the individual and his society.

The first pattern of relationships discussed is that of the individual to the government in its general aspects. Masami Ito's essay, "The Rule of Law: Constitutional Development," and Kiminobu Hashimoto's essay, "The Rule of Law: Some Aspects of Judicial Review of Administrative Action," both examine the extent to which Japanese society relies on law, especially the judicial process, to ensure that certain minimum standards of fair conduct are observed by government in its legislative, executive, and administrative dealings with the governed. The rule-of-law concept insists on formal legality, a correspondence between the formal source and the specific exercise of governmental power, and implies social acceptance and institutionalization of values that accord a certain primacy, up to the point at which the state's survival is at stake, to the individual when his interests and claims conflict with those of the society. These essays on the constitutional and administrative aspects of the rule of law thus again raise the problem, as Hashimoto expresses it, of "the right balance between private rights and the necessities of government."

"The Accused and Society: Some Aspects of Japanese Criminal Law" by Ryuichi Hirano, "The Accused and Society: The Administration of Criminal Justice in Japan" by Atsushi Nagashima, and "The Accused and Society: Therapeutic and Preventive Aspects of Criminal Justice in Japan" by Haruo Abe, all consider the relationship between the individual and society in the fairly specific context of the criminal law. Western law has had in criminal law its most varied and most intense experience with the right balance between private rights and the necessities of government. Treating Japanese criminal law and Japanese attitudes toward sentencing and rehabilitation in a detailed and comprehensive fashion, these three essays shed light on specific problems and give insight into the law as an instrument of social control in Japanese society.

"The Family and the Law: The Individualistic Premise and Modern Japanese Family Law" by Yozo Watanabe, considers the contemporary legal status and regulation of the key institution of society in traditional Japan — the family. The essay is also relevant to other topics, such as dispute resolution or labor and business law; it is included in this section of the volume because the discussion of the shift away from the family toward the individual as the basic unit of society is critical to the change now occurring in Japanese thinking and sociological patterns.

The first five essays in Part Two discuss legal rules and institutions that, by and large, premise an individualistic society. Watanabe discusses the measures taken to foster individualism through a substantial weakening of the family. This weakening produces problems in its turn, particularly in fields such as criminal law, and the essay thus illuminates, from various perspectives, the general subject under consideration.

The final essay included in Part Two, "The Treatment of Motor-Vehicle Accidents: The Impact of Technological Change on Legal Relations" by Ichiro Kato, deals with a problem of legal ordering that is increasingly perplexing for modern societies. Japan's solutions include interesting innovations and may represent an area of law in which Japanese experience can furnish suggestive guidance for many Western countries facing the legal and social problems created by mechanized transportation.

THE RULE OF LAW: CONSTITUTIONAL DEVELOPMENT

Masami Ito

ASSISTED BY NATHANIEL L. NATHANSON

ACCORDING TO Albert Venn Dicey's famous definition, the rule of law "has three meanings, or may be regarded from three different points of view": controls are exercised through regular law instead of arbitrary power; the law of the land is administered by the ordinary law courts equally for all people; constitutional law is not the source but the consequence of the rights of individuals, as defined and enforced by the courts.[1] This threefold definition reflects the constitutional ideas and the individualistic thought peculiar to nineteenth-century England and has inevitably been criticized from the perspective of the circumstances and ideas of the present century.[2] But these attacks have been directed toward specific aspects of Dicey's definition, such as his denial of administrative law and administrative tribunals,[3] and, on the whole, the concept of rule of law survives in English constitutional law as a rejection of control by arbitrary power. Even if the concept is only a politically oriented one, lacking the definite content which might be expected of a legal concept,[4] it does not lose its real value in establishing that

Note. Mr. Ito is Professor of Law, Tokyo University. B.Jur., Tokyo Imperial University, 1943; Dr.Jur., 1960; participant, Japanese American Program for Cooperation in Legal Studies at Harvard University, 1954–1955, and at Stanford University, 1955–1956. Award of the Japan Academy, 1960. Secretary-General, Japanese National Committee of International Association of Legal Science, 1956– ; member of Tokyo Metropolitan Labor Relations Commission, 1962– . Author of GENRON SHUPPAN NO JIYŪ (Freedom of Speech and Press) (1959); HŌ NO SHIHAI (The Rule of Law) (1954); IGIRISU KŌHŌ NO GENRI (Principles of English Public Law) (1954); writings in the fields of constitutional and comparative law.

Mr. Nathanson is Professor of Law, Northwestern University. B.A., 1929, LL.B., 1932, Yale University; S.J.D., 1933, Harvard University.

[1] DICEY, LAW OF THE CONSTITUTION 202 (10th ed., 1959).

[2] The most severe criticism was made in JENNINGS, THE LAW AND THE CONSTITUTION 305–17 (5th ed., 1959). Even the Committee on Ministers' Powers, *Report,* CMD. No. 4060 (1932), in general favorable to Dicey's theory, proposed several revisions in his analysis.

[3] In this respect, Dicey himself partially acknowledged his misunderstanding, in *The Development of Administrative Law in England,* 31 L.Q. REV. 148 (1915). This article contained what have been called "handsomer concessions" by Frankfurter, *The Task of Administrative Law,* 75 U. PA. L. REV. 614–15 (1927).

[4] JENNINGS, as in note 2 above, at 311, suggests that Dicey's theory is a rule of policy for Whigs.

notion of "government under law" which Western democracy seeks to realize.[5]

Recently, rule of law has been much discussed from the point of view of comparative law, where it is understood as requiring the exercise of governmental power to be controlled by legal rules.[6] Without this principle, a free society cannot exist. Thus, in spite of differences of tradition and social background, the nations which seek to be truly democratic have to include, expressly or implicitly, the concept of rule of law in their constitutions.

The Meiji Constitution of 1889 may be considered a modern constitution because it met at least the minimum requirements of constitutionalism — separation of powers and guarantees of individual rights. However, it is doubtful whether anything approximating a true rule of law existed under the old Constitution. What separation of powers was provided was camouflaged in a sense; for, although the legislative, executive, and judicial powers were assigned to the Diet, the Cabinet, and the courts, respectively, the Emperor (Tennō) stood above all three. Thus all governmental powers were concentrated in the hands of one person. The rights of the people were guaranteed by constitutional provisions; but there was protection only against executive invasion because a law enacted by the Diet could abridge any freedom or right. Moreover, as the prewar history of Japan showed, the government often ignored the constitutional limitations, and no means of checking such exercises of power existed. Generally speaking, the Meiji Constitution did not place the government under the law, and, therefore, the principle of rule of law in its first and most traditional meaning — that no arbitrary exercise of governmental power shall be permitted — was neglected. But the idea of *Rechtstaat,* that any governmental power ought to be derived from the positive law, could be found.[7]

The present Constitution has deprived the Emperor of sovereign power and established the sovereignty of the people. But, as Roscoe Pound has said, the superiority of law over power — an idea which has been maintained by the common-law courts — should be insisted upon even against the majority will of the people.[8] In England, with its mature democratic forms, the doctrine of rule of law may be protected by the electorate itself. Ivor

[5] See generally GOVERNMENT UNDER LAW (Sutherland ed., 1956); *Post-war Thinking about the Rule of Law,* 59 MICH. L. REV. 485–613 (1961) (symposium).

[6] The International Association of Legal Science dealt with the rule of law in Western and Eastern countries at its Chicago conference (Sept. 8–19, 1957) and the principle of legality which seems to be similar to the rule of law in socialist countries at the Warsaw conference (Sept. 10–16, 1958). The International Commission of Jurists "is dedicated to the support and advancement . . . of the Rule of Law." STATUTE OF THE INTERNATIONAL COMMISSION OF JURISTS (1955); see Marsh, *The Rule of Law as a Super-National Concept,* in OXFORD ESSAYS IN JURISPRUDENCE 223 (Guest ed., 1961); Bishop, *The International Rule of Law,* 59 MICH. L. REV. 553 (1961).

[7] For a discussion of the Meiji Constitution, see Kenzo Takayanagi, "A Century of Innovation: The Development of Japanese Law, 1868–1961," in this volume.

[8] POUND, THE SPIRIT OF THE COMMON LAW 63–64 (1921).

Jennings says that "so long as there are free elections, it is always possible to compel the Government to exercise its powers not too partially, for there is an Opposition to draw attention to abuses and to persuade the electorate that because of those abuses, if not for other reasons, the Government should be turned out . . . The fundamental liberty is that of free elections, and the others, including some at least of their limitations, follow from it."[9] Where the voters' consciousness of political responsibility is not so high, however, as in Japan, the sovereignty of the people tends to introduce arbitrary control by the majority, with the result that the rights of the minority groups are easily abrogated. Accordingly, the new Japanese Constitution quite properly includes rule of law as a constitutional precept.[10]

The makers of the Constitution, though they do not mention the doctrine in express words, intended the relation between government and law to be based and built upon the rule of law. In this sense it can be said that the Japanese Constitution purports to realize the rule of law through legal means, whereas the modern English constitution secures the supremacy of law through political measures.[11] The Japanese Constitution legalizes the doctrine in two ways. In the first place, fundamental human rights receive strong guarantees against arbitrary exercise of any governmental power. Under the present Constitution, even a law enacted by the Diet, which under article 41 of the Constitution is the highest organ of state power, shall not have legal force when it invades the constitutional area of individual freedoms and rights.

In the second place, judicial review of legislation is recognized. Modeled after American constitutional practice, article 81 vests the courts, especially

[9] JENNINGS, note 2, at 279.

[10] While not expressly attacking the rule of law as such, representative of a somewhat divergent view also current in Japan are the remarks made by Hisatada Hirose, a member of the Constitution Investigation Commission and former Diet member, before the seventy-fifth plenary meeting of the commission on the afternoon of March 20, 1962, in opposition to a statement by Chairman Kenzo Takayanagi that "a constitution exists not against the public but against those who govern through the exercise of political power, and therefore there is a threat that clearly indicating public duties attached over a broad area will tend to weaken the rule of law." Hirose said: "The present Constitution strikes out boldly for the guarantee of the people's rights, but only lightly presents the people's duties upon which these rights are premised. Therefore, provisions on the people's duties which harmonize with the provisions guaranteeing the people's rights should be clearly indicated . . . Under the existing democratic Constitution, those who govern and the public are essentially one and the same. There are bounds even to the people's rights; rights without duties attached are in and of themselves dangerous." Asahi Shimbun, March 21, 1962, p. 2, col. 8 (morning ed.).

[11] In England, too, at the period when the modern constitution was in the making, some lawyers tried to establish the rule of law through legal processes. Their leading representative is Sir Edward Coke, as seen from his famous dicta in Dr. Bonham's Case, 8 Co. 114a, 2 Brownl. 225, 77 Eng. Rep. 646, 652 (C.P. 1610). But as the result of the revolutions of the seventeenth century, which introduced the principle of sovereignty of Parliament, the English moved from a legalistic to a political approach in securing the rule of law. Coke's thinking, however, is said to have been transplanted to the United States. Plucknett, *Bonham's Case and Judicial Review*, 40 HARV. L. REV. 30, 61–68 (1926).

the Supreme Court, with the power to determine the constitutionality of any law, order, regulation, or official act. The power of judicial review seems to be the most universally typical institution embodying rule of law. "It was Coke's version of the supremacy of the common law principles as exemplification of rules of reason and of justice that served as a convenient precedent when American justices were confronted with the demand that limits must be placed on legislative powers in order to safeguard individual rights and privileges." [12]

It would have been appropriate for an essay dealing with the rule of law in the Japanese Constitution to discuss both of these topics, but in view of space limitations the following pages are confined to a study of the fundamental human rights guaranteed by the Constitution.[13]

STRUCTURE OF GUARANTEES OF FUNDAMENTAL RIGHTS IN THE JAPANESE CONSTITUTION

The Japanese Constitution contains substantial guarantees, both quantitatively and qualitatively, of various freedoms and rights. Chapter III, Rights and Duties of the People, contains some thirty articles. Only four of these, all without legal effect in a strict sense, are duties of the people;[14] the remainder are, as article 11 states, "eternal and inviolate rights." The protection of fundamental rights is clearly one of the basic principles of the Constitution. In order to explain fully the legal nature of fundamental rights, each freedom or right would have to be analyzed; but, since such a detailed inquiry is not feasible here, I shall first discuss general rules applicable to all these rights and then analyze in detail a specific right, freedom of expression.

The Constitution occasionally includes rules which may be called political directives. They cannot be applied to determine a concrete case judicially, and, since they are not legal norms, they are only constitutional "usages." If such constitutional provisions are violated, any resulting controversy would be settled through political rather than legal processes.[15] Other constitutional provisions can be looked upon as rules addressed to the judiciary in view of

[12] HAINES, THE AMERICAN DOCTRINE OF JUDICIAL SUPREMACY 36 (2nd ed., 1932).

[13] The problem of judicial review with respect to administrative action is dealt with in detail in Kiminobu Hashimoto, "The Rule of Law: Some Aspects of Judicial Review of Administrative Action," in this volume.

[14] The duties of the people provided in the Constitution are (1) the general duties to maintain the constitutional freedoms and rights by constant endeavor, to refrain from abuse of them, and to utilize them for the public welfare (art. 12); (2) the obligation to see to it that all boys and girls under their protection receive ordinary education (art. 26); (3) the obligation to work (art. 27); and (4) the liability to taxation (art. 30). These duties are either purely moral obligations or the other side of rights guaranteed by the same articles.

[15] For example, art. 53 provides that when a quarter or more of the total members of either house so demand, the Cabinet must convoke an extraordinary session of the Diet. But in the past such demands of the minority party having more than a quarter of the total membership were often ignored. Though the Cabinet might be criticized for acting unconstitutionally, the controversy could be settled only through political processes.

the power of judicial review. The most important examples are the guarantees of fundamental rights.[16] In interpreting chapter III, we must not forget that these provisions are real legal norms.

A general analysis of the legal norms relating to fundamental rights contained in chapter III must consider two problems. Does a presumption of constitutionality exist? What standard is the court to apply in determining the constitutionality of legislation that limits a fundamental right? I propose to classify the various types of rights into four groups and to discuss the characteristics of each group with regard to these two problems. The classification is my own and does not derive from decisions of the Japanese Supreme Court.

The Fundamental Right of Existence

Article 25, a typical example of a "fundamental right of existence," provides that "all people shall have the right to maintain the minimum standards of wholesome and cultured living." Such constitutional provisions are hortatory provisions, and they are new, assume the welfare state, and are suited to twentieth-century constitutions. They have little legal meaning, however. They do not vest in each individual person a concrete right which can be enforced through judicial processes. Such concrete rights can come into being only through implementing legislation. The state is under a political, or rather moral, obligation to enact laws to ensure, so far as possible, that the people enjoy a decent standard of living. But the people cannot force legislation by seeking judicial review.

To take one example, in order to meet food shortages immediately after the end of the last war, the Japanese government adopted a severe food-control policy. A man who was indicted for breach of the Food Control Law[17] argued that it was contrary to the provisions of article 25 that the prohibition of purchase and transportation of staple foods made it impossible for him to supplement his deficient ration, and that he was thus denied the fundamental right of existence ("right to live"). The Supreme Court upheld the conviction:

> the provision in article 25, paragraph 2, of the Constitution that "in all spheres of life, the State shall use its endeavors for the promotion and extension of social welfare and security, and of public health" declares that it is one of the tasks of the state to endeavor to expand and reinforce social institutions, which are positivistic government, in accordance with the aforesaid changes in social life. Then paragraph 1 of the same article declares that it is the responsibility of the state to conduct an administration which is able to maintain the minimum standards of wholesome and cultured living for all people. For the most part, this is

[16] In the United States, the most important problems relating to the federal constitution are the relation between federal and state governments (questions of federalism) and the relation between government and individuals (questions concerning the Bill of Rights). Since Japan has a unitary system of government, no federal questions arise and problems concerning fundamental human rights present the leading constitutional issues.

[17] Law No. 40 of 1942.

to be done through the enactment and enforcement of social legislation, but it is assumed too that the maintenance and extension of the related standard of living is also one of the tasks of the state. Thus, while the state bears a general responsibility to the populace of the nation at large, which is a task in national administration, it has no specific and actual duty to individual members of the public. In other words, individual members of the public directly possess no specific and actual rights against the state under these provisions. Only pursuant to social legislation and the creation and expansion of social institutions are the specific and actual livelihood rights of individual members of the public established and perfected for the first time.[18]

This interpretation is correct.[19] Indeed, although the Indian constitution contains a very similar provision, it is found not in the part labeled "Fundamental Rights" but in that called "Directive Principles of State Policy." Any law relating to the right of existence must be presumed to be constitutional. The presumption can only be overcome by showing that the state is actively interfering with private life and clearly invading the right to live — such legislation would be unthinkable under the present political structure.[20] Because the actual content of this right is formulated only through legislative action, an improper or insufficient formulation can be corrected only by appeal to the legislature. In other words, the presumption of constitutionality cannot be overturned by counterevidence in such a case. It follows that the second problem — the standard for determining the validity of a law which limits the right of existence — is not reached. Generally speaking, therefore, the guarantee of the right to live is almost meaningless when we consider constitutional law as rules for judicial determination.

Fundamental Economic Rights

Fundamental rights and freedoms securing the basis of economic life of individuals are important in modern constitutions. The fundamental right

[18] Nakano v. Japan, Supreme Court, Grand Bench, Sept. 29, 1948, 2 SAIKŌ SAIBANSHO KEIJI HANREI SHŪ (A Collection of Civil Supreme Court Cases) [hereafter cited SAI-HAN KEISHŪ] 1235, at 1237–38.

[19] The Supreme Court has always so interpreted art. 25. But a few scholars find a more positive meaning in the guarantee of the right of existence. The *Asahi* case (see note 20) reflects this kind of thinking.

[20] Asahi v. Kōsei Daijin (Minister of Welfare), Tokyo District Court, Oct. 19, 1960, 11 GYŌSEI JIKEN SAIBAN REISHŪ (A Collection of Judicial Precedents Concerning Administrative Cases) 2921, is interesting with regard to art. 25. Asahi, a patient in a hospital, received 600 yen a month as living and medical allowance from the state, but after his brother started to send him 1500 yen a month voluntarily, the head of the social-welfare office decided to end the monthly allowance, leaving Asahi 600 yen for daily necessaries and collecting the remaining 900 yen for hospital expenses. Asahi contended that, since he could not afford the minimum standards of wholesome and decent living at only 600 yen (less than 2 dollars) a month, the ruling of the chief of the Tsuyama City Social Welfare Office was invalid. The Tokyo District Court decided in favor of the plaintiff, holding that the maximum amount of 600 yen for daily necessaries was undoubtedly insufficient to maintain the minimum standard of decent living and so did not satisfy the requirement of art. 8 of the Livelihood Protection Law, Law No. 144 of 1950. The court also suggested that the chief's ruling was contrary to the spirit of art. 25 of the Constitution.

of existence just discussed relates to an aspect of economic life, but it differs from fundamental economic rights in that the latter are to be free from governmental interference and constitute the foundation of the capitalistic system. These rights have long been recognized (for example, John Locke emphasized the importance of the guarantee of property).

The "right to own or to hold property" and to "just compensation" guaranteed by article 29 for private property taken for public use are typical of these fundamental economic rights. These provisions are by no means "hortatory": they establish concrete and legal rights. Therefore, any law abridging these legal rights—such as the right to own private property—involves a constitutional question as a matter of course and can be held unconstitutional and invalid by the judiciary. When the law restricting the transportation of staple foods was attacked as invading the right of existence, the court could avoid review because the issue was only one of policy; but if it is contended that the same law conflicts with guarantees of fundamental economic rights, the courts have to inquire into its substantive content and decide the constitutional question. The Supreme Court, after so inquiring, held that the law was constitutional because it was for the benefit of the public welfare, namely, securing food for the people in general.[21]

A law relating to fundamental economic rights is presumed to be constitutional. Today, property rights are not considered the most valuable natural rights; thus regulation of the economic life of the people depends upon governmental policy. A specific policy formulated by the duly elected representatives in the National Diet is quite properly assumed to be proper, suitable, and constitutional. Accordingly, anyone contending that a law is in contravention of the guarantees of economic rights must prove his case without the benefit of a presumption. For example, when the compensation for property taken for public use is attacked as unjust under article 29, paragraph 3, the party challenging the law must bear the burden of proving that the compensation is unreasonable. The very words of article 29, paragraph 2, "property rights shall be defined by law, in conformity with the public welfare," give a formal basis for a presumption of validity with regard to these economic regulations. These provisions recognize that the basic property right shall, even though article 29, paragraph 1, makes the right to own and hold property inviolable, be regulated by legislation guided by the public welfare.

The approach of the Japanese Constitution to the right of property, which may have been prompted by the reflection that the United States Supreme Court had declared a number of New Deal laws unconstitutional, allows the state to place some restrictions on property rights in order to promote the interest of society as a whole. A law enacted by the majority of a representative legislature ordinarily intends to secure the interest of society and con-

[21] Kim v. Japan, Supreme Court, Grand Bench, Nov. 22, 1950, 4 SAI-HAN KEISHŪ 2389.

forms to the public good. We can conclude, then, that any law regulating fundamental economic rights will be held valid unless proved to be completely arbitrary and contrary to reason. It is very often difficult to determine whether specific legislation is reasonable, and a court must reach its decision by comparing the conflicting societal interests. Since the present Constitution accepts the system of private property as one of the basic conditions of society, the provisions of article 29, paragraph 1, are not the exception, but the rule. Any law ignoring this rule — for example, a law depriving a person of the right to enjoy his property substantially, even though not formally, without paying compensation — would be invalid as a denial of rights.[22]

However, such an unconstitutional law will be rare. On the one hand, it is not difficult to find a reasonable foundation for almost all economic legislation; on the other hand, it is not easy to prove that a law is arbitrary. Accordingly, only in exceptional cases will a limitation imposed upon these fundamental economic rights be held invalid. This view corresponds with the current social acceptance of broad governmental intervention in a wide sphere of individual economic activities. In the United States, since 1937 when the precedents unfavorable to economic legislation were overruled, the "reasonableness" standard has been applied in favor of regulatory powers. I have been unable to find a single case in the United States Supreme Court since that date in which a federal law was held invalid because of an invasion of fundamental economic rights guaranteed by the due-process clause. Robert Stern has written, "only restrictions which were in fact arbitrary, or not reasonably related to a proper legislative purpose . . . would be held unconstitutional in the future . . . Since it is difficult to conceive of any statute for which some rational basis may not be found, this test means that the due process barrier to substantive legislation as to economic matters has been in effect removed — although it still stands in theory against completely arbitrary legislative action."[23] Such views are also appropriate for interpreting the Japanese Constitution.

[22] Cf. Portsmouth Harbor Land & Hotel Co. v. United States, 260 U.S. 327 (1922).

[23] Stern, *The Problems of Yesteryear — Commerce and Due Process*, 4 VAND. L. REV. 446, 449 (1951). The Prostitution Prevention Law, enacted in 1956 as Law No. 118 of that year, prohibited the carrying on of prostitution as a business. This law destroyed a vested right without compensation, but such regulation or forfeiture may be justified by the government's police power. Moreover, it is noteworthy that art. 31 of the Indian Constitution, originally similar to art. 29 of the Japanese Constitution, has undergone considerable change through amendment. See SHUKLA, COMMENTARIES ON THE CONSTITUTION OF INDIA 101–18 (3rd ed., 1960). In the first place, when a law provides for the acquisition of a person's property for a public purpose, he cannot challenge the validity of that law in a court on the ground that the legislature has not provided for payment of just compensation. Secondly, the obligation of the state to pay compensation arises only in one case, namely, where the property is transferred directly from the private owner to the state or a state agency. When property is regulated or even destroyed by the police action of the state, no obligation to pay compensation will arise. These provisions of the Indian Constitution may anticipate the future of guarantees of property rights.

The Freedom to Express Oneself

One of the fundamental principles of modern constitutions is to protect the intellectual activities of human beings against governmental interference. This kind of freedom has often been discussed en bloc, but it seems proper to distinguish between external and internal freedom. Of course, intellectual life is primarily internal by nature and as such is not suitable for legal regulation; however, insofar as intellectual activity involves external results it can raise legal, and not merely moral, questions. By the guarantee of external intellectual freedom, I mean constitutional protection of the external expression of intellectual activities, apart from internal movement of mind. The freedoms of speech, press, assembly, and association guaranteed by the provisions of article 21, paragraph 1, are typical of these rights.

No presumption of constitutionality should exist as regards a law abridging rights of this kind. Constitutionality presupposes the principle of representative democracy that the law is the expression of the will of the majority and should therefore be considered to be reasonable. Why then should this rule be excluded in the case of limiting the freedom of expression? This has been much discussed in the United States as a problem of the so-called double standard.[24] In Japan there are two reasons, one formal and one substantial, for constitutional interpretation that distinguishes between economic rights and intellectual freedoms. Formally, the constitutional provisions relating to fundamental economic rights anticipate explicitly their restriction for the benefit of the public welfare while the provisions relating to intellectual freedoms do not; at least in words, the Constitution apparently intends to give absolute protection to them.

The substantial reasons are similar to those submitted for the preferred position of first-amendment freedoms in American constitutional law.[25] Most modern constitutions — including the Japanese — adopt a system of representative democracy, based upon the principle of self-government by the people, and freedom to express oneself, especially freedom of speech and press, are indispensable to such a system. Democracy requires that all sorts of political opinions be freely communicated to the public and that the public should then choose freely. Furthermore, laws abridging freedom of expression restrict the possibilities for those aggrieved to obtain relief through appeal to the political process. Thus freedom of expression connects closely with the principle of sovereignty of the people — a principle of the first importance in the Japanese Constitution. Fundamental economic rights, on the other hand, do not have this immediate relation to political democracy.[26]

[24] See, e.g., McKay, *The Preference for Freedom*, 34 N.Y.U.L. REV. 1182 (1959).

[25] Cf. Freund, *Competing Freedoms in American Constitutional Law*, in CONFERENCE ON FREEDOM AND THE LAW 26, 27–36 (Conference Series No. 13, 1953).

[26] Especially, MEIKLEJOHN, POLITICAL FREEDOM, THE CONSTITUTIONAL POWER OF THE PEOPLE (1960), has emphasized the close connection between the freedom to express political ideas and the principle of self-governance.

If this view is correct, a law limiting an individual's freedom to express himself should not be presumed constitutional; the party asserting that such a law is invalid presents, so far as he proves this freedom to be restricted, an issue sufficient to impose upon the court the duty of determining the constitutional question involved. Though not accepted as orthodox theory in the United States, the opinion of Justice Murphy is suggestive in interpreting the Japanese Constitution. He said that the freedoms of speech and press "are to be presumed to be invulnerable and any attempt to sweep away those freedoms is prima facie invalid. It follows that any restriction or prohibition must be justified by those who deny that the freedoms have been unlawfully invaded."[27]

In this case, what is the standard for adjudicating whether the law limiting an individual's freedom to express himself is valid? One answer is that the standard of "reasonableness" can also be applied in this case: the validity of law is sufficiently upheld if it is shown that the restriction imposed by such law is reasonable. But this standard does not seem to be proper under Japanese constitutional law. Because of the higher value placed on intellectual freedoms, stricter requirements should be satisfied before accepting the constitutionality of a law abridging them. The difficult problem of what tests or requirements are acceptable is considered in the next section.

The Right of Intellectual Freedom

The freedom to express oneself relates to the constitutional guarantee of the external expression of intellectual activities. We now turn to the problem of safeguarding the interior activities of the human mind. Article 19—"freedom of thought and conscience shall not be violated"—is an example of this kind of freedom. In its broadest aspects, this freedom is nothing but the essential right of man to think and constitutes the basis of all freedoms to express oneself. However, the specific application of article 19 is to cases in which a person is subject to legal sanctions because of his internal thought, apart from any external action, or is required to affirm a position contrary to his principles.

Freedom of thought and conscience means freedom for intellectual activities that express the personality of the human being. These activities have two aspects—rational and logical, on the one hand, and subjective and ethical, on the other. Freedom of thought safeguards the former, freedom of conscience the latter, and together they secure the unhampered development of human personality. It follows that article 19 does not protect intellectual activities, such as cultivation of personality, which do not belong to the fundamentals of spiritual life.

Two cases decided by the Supreme Court support this view. The first

[27] Prince v. Massachusetts, 321 U.S. 158, 173 (1944) (dissenting opinion).

case relates to the so-called Missouri plan for appointment of judges.[28] The Japanese Constitution provides that the appointment of justices of the Supreme Court shall be reviewed by the people every ten years and that, when a majority of the voters favor the dismissal of a justice, he will be dismissed. The details of the review are regulated in a statute entitled Supreme Court Justice Popular Review Law;[29] every voter who takes part in the general election of members of the House of Representatives is given a ballot on which the names of the justices to be reviewed are listed, and the voter must mark an *x* opposite the names of justices whom he wants dismissed. The plaintiff in one case, a voter, argued that this law was in conflict with the guarantee of freedom of thought and conscience in that it deprived him of freedom of thought without justifiable grounds because, even if he did not feel able to decide whether a particular judge should be dismissed, he had to vote yes or no and so could not express his true position ("I don't know"). Consequently, a legal effect different from what he really intended might attach to his vote. The Supreme Court refused revision, saying that a contention that the way of voting provided by the law might not be the most desirable method does not establish an invasion of freedom of thought and conscience. The Court's opinion also pointed out that, since the voter could decline to cast any ballot with respect to judges, no question of compulsory voting was presented.

The second and more interesting case is concerned with the remedy of compulsory apology for defamation.[30] The Civil Code provides in article 723 that "a court, pursuant to the claim of the injured party, may, in place of damages or together with damages, order a person who has injured the reputation of another to carry out measures appropriate to restore his reputation." The courts have long considered compulsory apology to be an appropriate measure. The trial court, though it denied the claim of the plaintiff to have the apology broadcast over the radio, ordered the defendant to publish the apology in specified newspapers. The defendant, after the High Court sustained the decision of the trial court, sought revision by the Supreme Court, saying that "the appellant, even now, possesses a firm conviction that the content of his address was true and that the appellant's speech was made for the benefit of the people's happiness; so to require such an appellant to publish in a newspaper under the appellant's name a statement contrary to the intention of the appellant infringes upon the appellant's freedom of conscience . . . Compelling the people, by a judicial judgment,

[28] Sasaki v. Yamashita, Supreme Court, Grand Bench, Feb. 20, 1952, 6 SAIKŌ SAIBANSHO MINJI HANREI SHŪ (A Collection of Civil Supreme Court Cases) [hereafter cited SAI-HAN MINSHŪ] 122, 72 HŌGAKU KYŌKAI ZASSHI (Journal of the Jurisprudence Association) 310 (note Ito).

[29] Law No. 136 of 1947.

[30] Okuri v. Kageyama, Supreme Court, Grand Bench, July 4, 1956, 10 SAI-HAN MINSHŪ 785, 74 HŌGAKU KYŌKAI ZASSHI 539 (note Ito).

to correct what they feel in good conscience to be a just belief directly contravenes the purport of article 19 of the Constitution."[31]

The majority opinion of the Supreme Court rejected the argument, holding that if the court order imposed upon the appellant a servile submission, or required him to go contrary to his own conscience or principles, his freedom of conscience might have been infringed; but a confession of the truth and expression of regret does not infringe the freedom and may be compulsorily enforced against the defendant's will as an appropriate measure to restore the plaintiff's reputation.[32] This holding determined only that the apology in this specific case was not prohibited by the Constitution; it did not make clear either what might constitute a breach of freedom of conscience or the content of this freedom.

In a concurring opinion, Justice Kuriyama said that freedom of conscience in the Japanese Constitution means only the freedom to select a religious belief. He cited several foreign constitutions, including the constitutions of California, India, and Burma, in which the freedom of conscience is interpreted to mean the freedom to select one's religion.[33] Considering article 19 historically, this view may be correct, but it seems too narrow. Chief Justice Tanaka wrote another concurring opinion, saying that "conscience" in article 19 does not include moral compunction or the feeling of honesty which should be the basis of apology and that the provisions of article 19 require the state to be indifferent to religious belief and other such intellectual activities.[34] According to this view, the compulsory apology as a special judicial remedy for defamation has nothing to do with the freedom of conscience guaranteed by the Constitution. This opinion approximates my own view. It should be noted, however, that Justices Fujita and Tarumi dissented. Fujita said that "the state, by such action as ordering this appellant to manifest publicly an ethical determination that his act was wrong and again by ordering him to manifest publicly a moralistic intention to 'apologize' or 'beg forgiveness,' through operation of the power of a judicial judgment, encroaches upon the so-called 'freedom of conscience' of article 19 of the Constitution."[35]

During the period of occupation after the last war, two cases were litigated concerning freedom of thought and conscience. One, in which Minister of Agriculture and Forestry Rikizo Hirano contested the validity of a determination by the Purge Board that he should be purged, related to an order of the Supreme Commander for the Allied Powers removing all militarists, extreme nationalists, and supporters of aggression from public

[31] *Ibid.*, at 808.
[32] *Ibid.*, at 786–88.
[33] *Ibid.*, at 791–94.
[34] *Ibid.*, at 788–91.
[35] *Ibid.*, at 799.

office.[36] This order clearly imposed a disadvantage on some persons because of their purely personal beliefs.[37] Probably these very general measures would be held unconstitutional if their validity were decided on the merits. Indeed, the Tokyo District Court set aside the law as unconstitutional. However, the Supreme Court never reached the merits; the Chief Justice issued a declaration that the question was beyond the jurisdiction of the Japanese judiciary.[38]

The other case involved the so-called Red purge.[39] General MacArthur wrote a letter to the Prime Minister of Japan, advising that all Communists and pro-Communists had to be dismissed from important industries and certain other positions. The plaintiff, who lost his job at the Kyodo Press as a result of this letter, insisted that such a dismissal was invalid as an invasion of freedom of thought. The Supreme Court held that the Allied commander had absolute power in governing Japan and that, therefore, Japanese law, including constitutional law, lost its effect to the extent that it was contrary to his order. But for MacArthur's letter, the dismissal of plaintiff would, it is universally believed, have been unconstitutional, since it deprived a person of his job because of his ideas. These two decisions both reflect the special circumstances of the occupation period. With the exception of such special cases, freedom of thought and conscience is considered an absolute right, any invasion of which is unconstitutional. Therefore, no further refinement of the standard or test for adjudicating the validity of a law limiting these individual freedoms is required.

I have considered the four types of fundamental rights guaranteed by the Japanese Constitution. However, this fourfold classification omits several rights. In the first place, personal freedoms, which are mainly guarantees of procedural justice in criminal cases, require mention.[40] The Japanese

[36] Hirano v. Naikaku Sōri Daijin Katayama (Cabinet Prime Minister Katayama), Tokyo District Court, Feb. 2, 1947, SAIBANSHO JIHŌ (The Court Journal) no. 5, at 1. Some scholars take the view that, because the idea of ultranationalism — which was the cause of the war and so came to be the object of purge — is absolutely in conflict with the principle of democracy in the new Constitution, the guarantee of freedom of thought does not cover such an idea.

[37] Memorandum concerning Removal and Exclusion of Undesirable Personnel from Public Office, Jan. 4, 1946, SCAPIN 550, NIHON KANRI HŌREI KENKYŪ (Japan Occupation Law Review) no. 7, Directives and Memorandum pt. at 17.

[38] Circular from the Secretary-General of the Supreme Court to the Chief Judges of the District Courts, *Saikō Saibansho Gyōsei Kō* (Supreme Court, Administrative Bureau A) No. 4, Feb. 6, 1948. The circular cited a letter from General Whitney, head of the Government Section of SCAP, to the Chief Justice in which Whitney confirmed that the Japanese courts had no jurisdiction over purge cases.

[39] Zen-Nippon Shimbun Rōdō Kumiai Kyōdō Shibu (All-Japan Newspaper Labor Union, Kyodo Local) v. Kyōdō Tsūshin Sha (Kyodo Press), Supreme Court, Grand Bench, April 4, 1951, 6 SAI-HAN MINSHŪ 387.

[40] OPS. LEG. & OP. ASS'T ATT. GEN. 536 states that the personal freedoms are the most valuable among the fundamental rights guaranteed by the Constitution. See McNabb v. United States, 318 U.S. 332, 347 (1943) (Frankfurter, J.): "the history of liberty has largely been the history of observance of procedural safeguards."

constitutional provisions, almost identical with the corresponding provisions of the American Bill of Rights,[41] are, as compared with other rights, very detailed and concrete; problems of interpretation are settled through analysis of the provisions of each article. These rights, if they are to be included in our fourfold classification, would fall under a freedom to express oneself, because, like these freedoms, they are indispensable conditions for true democracy. Secondly, the right to equality guaranteed by article 14 must be noted. This right does not relate to the substance of the object to be safeguarded. It is concerned with the form of legal regulation, for it prohibits discriminatory treatment in all aspects of life, political, economic, or social. Accordingly, the requirement of equality before the law is connected with all four categories of rights in our classification. Thirdly, what scholars call the fundamental remedies for securing fundamental rights — for example, the right in article 17 to claim damages from the state for torts committed by public officials — do not fit into our classification because they are supplementary and secondary rights.

Other rights can be assigned to one of the four categories, the specific category being determined by a judgment that the right in question is most analogous to the typical rights or freedoms of that category. Once the category is determined, the standard for adjudicating the validity of a law limiting the right is also established.

Let us consider some examples. The article 26 right to receive an education belongs, in view of the language of the provision as well as the nature of the right, to the fundamental right of existence. Freedom to choose an occupation in article 22, paragraph 1, is a fundamental economic right because it provides the basis for individual economic security; freedom to choose and change one's residence, mentioned in the same article, is both an economic right and a personal right closely related to freedom of association. Significantly, the provisions relating to this freedom are accompanied by the express words of restriction: "to the extent that it does not interfere with the public welfare." This public-welfare limitation has formed the basis for Supreme Court decisions upholding laws limiting free trade in narcotics or stimulants,[42] or requiring one to obtain a license before carrying on businesses such as pawnbroking, secondhand dealing, or operating

[41] The jury system is the exception. See Kohji Tanabe, "The Process of Litigation: An Experiment with the Adversary System," in this volume. Japan adopted the petty jury in criminal cases before the war, but now the Jury Law is suspended. Art. 3(3) of the Court Law, Law No. 59 of 1947, translated into English in 2 EHS LAW BULLETIN SERIES AA 1, provides that "the provisions of this Law do not prevent the establishment elsewhere by law of a jury system for criminal cases."

[42] Pak v. Japan, Supreme Court, Grand Bench, Dec. 26, 1956, 10 SAI-HAN KEISHŪ 1746; Nagata v. Japan, Supreme Court, Grand Bench, Sept. 11, 1956, 10 SAI-HAN KEISHŪ 1341; Tsukuba v. Japan, Supreme Court, Grand Bench, July 13, 1956, 10 SAI-HAN KEISHŪ 830.

public baths.[43] According to my interpretation, freedom of religion in article 20 means freedom of religious activities, the freedom to choose one's own religious belief being guaranteed by the freedom of conscience as an individual right. From this point of view, freedom of religion under article 20 corresponds to the freedom of speech and press and is a freedom to express oneself. Academic freedom, protected in article 23, is also such a freedom and means freedom of the outward activities of learning—for example, freedom for the professor to lecture and for the scholar to publish the results of his research.

The classification of rights of workers raises the most controversial issues. Some scholars insist that these rights are absolute because, in the present economic situation, the rights of workers are the most valuable means for realizing the happiness of the people and they should, therefore, be superior to other rights. But a fundamental right not subject to any limitation must be one that is indispensable to the very existence of a person as a human being. The rights of workers are not indispensable in this degree. They are important and many recent constitutions safeguard them in express words; but, at least under the current constitutional system, these rights do not occupy the same position as freedom of thought and conscience. Since these rights are subject to some legal limitations, how should they be classified? This question cannot be answered by the explicit words of the Constitution; we must inquire into the content of the rights.

The rights of workers have been developed through a process of modifying the principles of modern law according to "socialistic" ideas (in the sense of an emphasis on social welfare). To classify these rights as a whole ignores the different substantive nature of each. The right to work mentioned in article 27, paragraph 1, because it lacks the concreteness necessary for guarantee through the judicial process, is a fundamental right of existence. Article 27, paragraph 2, provides that standards for wages, hours, rest, and other working conditions shall be fixed by law. These provisions, which are probably included because of the American experience in having labor legislation held unconstitutional, indicate that the determination of labor standards depends upon the legislative policy of the state and that, even when specific legislation is deemed unsatisfactory by the workers, amendment must be sought through the legislative process; an individual worker has no basis for contesting the validity of such a law in court. The rights to organize and to bargain and act collectively, provided in article 28, are, together with property rights, means for obtaining economic security. The Constitution presupposes that the economic life of the person is sustained by labor as

[43] Shimizu v. Japan, Supreme Court, Grand Bench, Jan. 26, 1955, 9 SAI-HAN KEISHŪ 89 (public bath); Manabe v. Japan, Supreme Court, Grand Bench, March 18, 1953, 7 SAI-HAN KEISHŪ 577 (secondhand dealer).

well as by property. Accordingly, the right of workers to bargain collectively has a constitutional position similar to that given to private-property rights; it should be classified in the group of fundamental economic rights.[44] Therefore, although reasonable restrictions are permitted, arbitrary interferences ought to be held invalid. The employees of the Japanese National Railways are forbidden by law to strike. These laws were challenged as unconstitutional abridgements of the rights guaranteed by article 28. The Supreme Court sustained the legislation, holding that these rights are subject to limitations imposed for the benefit of public welfare and that, since a public corporation such as the Japanese National Railways is closely connected with the national economy and public welfare, the limitations imposed by these laws must be adjudged reasonable.[45]

Lastly, it cannot be overlooked that among these rights of workers are found rights whose nature is closer to intellectual freedom and to freedom to express oneself than to economic rights. For example, the right of workers to organize is, in some instances, closely akin to the right of association guaranteed in article 21; a law limiting the very right to organize would, therefore, be handled in the same way as a restriction on freedom to express oneself. Peaceful picketing also has the function of informing the public of the real situation of a strike and of enlisting general sympathy for the activities of the workers: it is an act which expresses a specific idea. It follows that such picketing should be safeguarded in fundamentally the same manner as freedom of speech.[46]

This kind of analysis of the rights of workers develops proper theoretical standards for determining the validity of laws which affect them.

FREEDOM TO EXPRESS ONESELF: ANALYSIS OF THE DECISIONS OF JAPANESE COURTS

This section considers the problem of the tests or standards that should determine the validity of a law limiting the freedom of expression guaranteed by the Japanese Constitution. Compared to the wealth of cases decided by the courts of the United States, Japanese courts have handled relatively little litigation in this area; it is too early, therefore, to come to definite

[44] See Takeuchi v. Japan, Supreme Court, Grand Bench, July 22, 1955, 9 SAI-HAN KEISHŪ 1189.

[45] Noguchi v. Nihon Kokuyū Tetsudō (Japanese National Railways), Supreme Court, Grand Bench, Sept. 15, 1954, 8 SAI-HAN MINSHŪ 1606; Hasegawa v. Japan, Supreme Court, Grand Bench, April 8, 1953, 7 SAI-HAN KEISHŪ 775.

[46] Cf. Thornhill v. Alabama, 310 U.S. 88 (1940). Subsequent decisions, however, have placed limitations on the sweeping principles of the *Thornhill* case. See, e.g., International Teamsters Union v. Vogt, Inc., 354 U.S. 284 (1957); International Bhd. of Teamsters v. Hanke, 339 U.S. 470 (1950); Giboney v. Empire Storage & Ice Co., 336 U.S. 490 (1949). For a more extensive discussion of the Japanese treatment of the problem, see Kichiemon Ishikawa, "The Regulation of the Employer-Employee Relationship: Japanese Labor-Relations Law," in this volume.

conclusions. But I shall pursue my analysis with as much attention as possible to the case law, taking scholarly discussion into account as well.

The Public-Welfare Test

The fundamental test applied by the Supreme Court is that any restriction is valid unless it exceeds the limit of reasonableness or the necessities of public welfare. The Supreme Court has consistently held that restrictions may be imposed to protect the public welfare. Article 12 provides that "the people . . . shall always be responsible for utilizing [freedoms and rights] . . . for the public welfare," and article 13 states that "their right to life, liberty, and the pursuit of happiness shall, to the extent that it does not interfere with the public welfare, be the supreme consideration in legislation and in other governmental affairs." The Supreme Court finds in this language a sufficient basis for the interpretation that even freedom to express oneself can be limited upon a reasonable basis to the extent justified. For example, the decision holding valid the Tokyo Metropolitan Ordinance regulating parades and demonstrations in the streets or in other public places[47] — this case will be considered in detail later — includes the following:

> The freedoms of assembly and association as well as speech, press, and all other forms of expression provided for in article 21 of the Constitution belong to the eternal and inviolate rights, namely fundamental human rights, and it need not be reiterated that their complete guarantee is a fundamental principle of democratic government and that here in particular is the most important characteristic which distinguishes democracy from totalitarianism. Moreover, in that the people shall refrain from any abuse of these freedoms and shall always be responsible for utilizing them for the public welfare, they do not differ from other forms of fundamental human rights [see Const., art. 12]. Therefore, under the Constitution of Japan it is the task of the courts in individual concrete cases to protect freedom of expression while at the same time preventing its abuse, to harmonize it with the public welfare, and to delineate the proper boundary between freedom and the public welfare.[48]

These words, considered abstractly, are not objectionable. However, in the Supreme Court's practice, the public-welfare test has come to be a justification for supporting the constitutionality of any law limiting freedom to express oneself. This way of thinking deprives the constitutional guarantee of free speech of its substantial significance, for whenever a law is enacted some kind of danger to the public welfare can be easily found as a legal regulation would rarely, if ever, be imposed in case no danger exists. Therefore, under the public-welfare test, only extremely arbitrary restrictions upon

[47] Ordinance Concerning Assembly, Parades en Masse, and Mass Demonstrations, Tokyo Metropolitan Ordinance No. 44 of 1950.

[48] Japan v. Ito, Supreme Court, Grand Bench, July 20, 1960, 14 SAI-HAN KEISHŪ 1243, 1247.

this freedom are invalid. This attitude loses sight not only of the distinction between intellectual freedom and its external expression, on the one hand, and economic freedom, on the other, but also between the new Constitution, which guarantees the freedom of expression in absolute words, and the old Constitution which had protected it only to the extent permitted by law.

This way of thinking may recall the "clear and present danger" test of American constitutional law.[49] In a society in which the traditional idea of free speech has been firmly established, even a standard favorable to legal restriction on freedom, such as a public-welfare test, can be administered reasonably and without fear of abuse. However, in Japan, where the higher value of free speech has not been recognized, legal restrictions upon this freedom may, as the sad history of the prewar period illustrates,[50] be too easily accepted by the people. One well-known writer compared freedom of speech to "a reed asway in the wind."[51] Hence the stricter standard may be required in Japan.

Even though the Court seems to adopt the unqualified reasoning that the public welfare justifies legal restriction upon freedom to express oneself, it in fact pays attention to the substance of such restrictions and compares the value of free expression with the social value sought to be protected by the legislation. For example, a trial court penalized, under the law dealing with contempt of court,[52] a photographer who took a picture of the accused in the courtroom in spite of the judge's prohibition.[53] The photographer contended that this action of the trial court was illegal as an unconstitutional restriction of freedom of news reporting. The Sapporo High Court sustained the judgment of the trial court, saying that "the so-called freedom to report is none other than one form of the freedom of expression provided for in article 21 of the Constitution, but while the taking of the photograph in this case should be called an act of gathering materials, it is a preparatory act for the purpose of reporting, not the act of reporting itself."[54] The Supreme Court affirmed, saying:

[49] Schenck v. United States, 249 U.S. 47 (1919); cf. Dennis v. United States, 341 U.S. 494 (1951).

[50] The most striking example was the Peace Preservation Law, enacted originally as Law No. 46 of 1925 and not repealed until after the war. Designed to prevent activities seeking to change the form of government or to destroy the private-property system, the offenses punishable under this law were vaguely defined and the procedures were arbitrary; the development of freedom of expression and association was inhibited, particularly during the war period, when every kind of thought unfavorable to the government could be suppressed. Subject to this statute, the notorious Special High Police (Tokubetsu Kōtō Keisatsu) exercised arbitrary power.

[51] From the title of the book KAZE NI SOYOGU ASHI (A Reed Asway in the Wind) by Tatsuzo Ishikawa, which described oppression of free speech prior to and during the war.

[52] Law Concerning the Maintenance of Order in Court, Etc., Law No. 286 of 1952.

[53] *Ex parte* Chida, Kushiro District Court, Dec. 10, 1953, 7 KŌTŌ SAIBANSHO KEIJI HANREI SHŪ (A Collection of Criminal High Court Cases) [hereafter cited KŌ-HAN KEISHŪ] 81.

[54] *Ex parte* Chida, Sapporo High Court, Feb. 15, 1954, 7 KŌ-HAN KEISHŪ 77, 80.

On the whole, it goes without saying that the reporting of truth by a newspaper belongs to the freedom of expression recognized in article 21 of the Constitution and that activities gathering materials for this purpose must be authorized. However, although it is a freedom guaranteed to the people by the Constitution, since the people shall not abuse it and shall always be responsible for utilizing it for the public welfare [Const., art. 12], this freedom cannot be called unrestricted. Thus, because the purpose of the provisions in the Constitution that in a trial party confrontation and judgment are to take place in open court is none other than to guarantee that the proceeding will, in general, be open and that the trial will be performed fairly, even if it is admitted that the circumstance of a public courtroom is in itself an action for gathering materials in order that they may be reported at large, where such action is of a sort that it disturbs judicial order in the public courtroom and infringes the proper interests of the defendant and other parties involved in litigation, it, of course, cannot be permitted. Therefore, there being a danger that taking photographs in a public courtroom will, depending upon the particular time and place, produce the aforesaid undesirable results, article 215 of the Criminal Procedure Regulations has entrusted approval of the taking of photographs to the discretion of the court and made clear that acts of this sort may not be performed as long as they are not in accordance with such approval; these provisions do not violate the Constitution.[55]

The Supreme Court thus followed its usual way of reasoning, recognizing the superiority of public welfare to freedom, but it went on to analyze the concept of public welfare and concluded that the social interest involved in maintaining a fair trial was included in the public welfare.

The Criminal-Offense Test

Let us consider cases in which the expression of intellectual activity constitutes *mala in se*—for example, intimidation, defamation, and obscenity. The view that freedom of expression should be absolute would probably recognize that an act constituting any of these crimes can be punished without invading constitutional safeguards. The Supreme Court of the United States, through Justice Murphy, said that "there are certain well-defined and narrowly limited classes of speech, the prevention and punishment of which have never been thought to raise any Constitutional problem. These include the lewd and obscene, the profane, the libelous, and the insulting or 'fighting' words."[56] Although some scholars in Japan consider that expression has nothing to do with constitutional freedoms in such cases, the Supreme Court has taken the view that these expressions can raise constitutional questions, though the Court has always upheld the conviction on the ground that, since the criminal act affects the public welfare, its punishment is constitu-

[55] *Ex parte* Chida, Supreme Court, Grand Bench, Feb. 17, 1958, 12 SAI-HAN KEISHŪ 253, 255–56.

[56] Chaplinsky v. New Hampshire, 315 U.S. 568, 571–72 (1941).

tional. For example, the Court, rejecting the appellant's assertion that his acts of intimidation could not be constitutionally punished because they did not constitute a clear and present danger either to the body or mind of others, said:

However, although intimidation is a notification (expression) to another by written document, word of mouth, or gesture, it is a notification which includes the threat of injury to another's life, person, liberty, reputation, or property and therefore a crime under article 222 of the Penal Code. The deed of "a number of persons who jointly . . . [commit] the crime of article 222 of the Penal Code," being essentially the same, is an aggravated offense punishable under article 1 of the Law Concerning the Punishment of Acts of Violence, Etc.,[57] and since it is, in actuality, . . . an antisocial immoral act injurious to the public welfare, omitted from the boundaries of freedom of speech and expression guaranteed by the Constitution, needless to say, a judgment punishing it as a crime under article 1 of the same law does not violate article 21 of the Constitution.[58]

In another case relating to defamation, the Court rendered the very short opinion that

article 21 of the Constitution does not unrestrictedly guarantee freedom of speech. Therefore, as decided in the first-instance judgment affirmed by the judgment below, defaming another by publishing a news item in a newspaper and distributing it is an abuse of freedom of speech, which we cannot recognize as being within the scope of freedom of speech guaranteed by the Constitution.[59]

However, I prefer the reasoning of Justice Murphy, that "it has been well observed that such utterances are no essential part of any exposition of ideas, and are of such slight social value as a step to truth that any benefit that may be derived from them is clearly outweighed by the social interest in order and morality,"[60] to the attitude of the Supreme Court of Japan that the public welfare overrides freedom to express oneself. The former line of reasoning recognizes that the criminal sanction would conflict with constitutional guarantees of free speech if it restricted expressions which, as a step to truth, are of greater social value than is the social interest in order and morality. We are required to compare the value contained in the expression and that protected by the criminal sanction (for example, the reputation of another person). We may be led into error if we follow the simpler approach that any act can be treated as a crime if it contravenes the public welfare. The Penal Code provides in article 230-2 that:

[57] Law No. 60 of 1926.

[58] Watanabe v. Japan, Supreme Court, III Petty Bench, April 22, 1958, 12 SAI-HAN KEISHŪ 1118, 1123.

[59] Kono v. Japan, Supreme Court, I Petty Bench, April 10, 1958, 12 SAI-HAN KEISHŪ 830, 831; see also Okuri v. Kageyama, note 30, at 786.

[60] Chaplinsky v. New Hampshire, note 56, at 572; see CHAFEE, FREE SPEECH IN THE UNITED STATES 150 (1948).

When it is recognized that the act . . . [which defames another person by publicly alleging facts] pertains to facts involving the concern of the public and that it was committed for a purpose solely in the public interest, if in determining the truth or falsity of the facts they are proven true, it is not to be punished.

In regard to the application of the provisions of the prior paragraph, facts relating to the criminal act of a person against whom a public action has not yet been instituted are deemed facts involving the concern of the public.

When the act of paragraph (1) of the prior article pertains to facts relating to a public servant or a candidate for public office through public election, if in determining the truth or falsity of the facts they are proven true, it is not to be punished.

These provisions presuppose that even expressions defaming another person may contain social values superior to the protection of individual reputations.[61]

The most interesting case bearing on this problem is the *Lady Chatterley's Lover* case. The translator and the publisher of the Japanese translation of *Lady Chatterley's Lover* were prosecuted for obscenity. The Tokyo District Court held that, though a literary work having artistic value ordinarily does not belong to the class of obscene writing proscribed by article 175 of the Penal Code, various parts of the book are very close to what is clearly obscene writing. The court held that the book, which had been sold on a large scale and with sensational advertisements, stimulated the sexual desires of readers and destroyed or weakened the control of reason over sexual impulses; it concluded that such publication amounted to obscene writing as punished by article 175. The Court imposed a fine of 250,000 yen on the publisher, but found the translator not guilty because he expected the book to be bought only by persons who would read it as literature and so did not participate in the publisher's criminal act.[62]

The Tokyo High Court, to which both the publisher and the prosecution

[61] Formerly the defamation of the Tennō or a member of the imperial family was severely punished. At the time of the food shortage after the war, in the case of a "give us more rice" demonstration near the imperial palace, a participant lifted up a placard which stated, "His Majesty eats his fill. You, dear subjects, starve to death!" He was prosecuted for lese majesty. But General MacArthur ordered the Japanese government to repeal the provisions relating to lese majesty as contrary to democratic principles and the accused was acquitted. Today, an expression defaming the Tennō or a member of the imperial family is punished as ordinary defamation upon complaint made by the Prime Minister. See PENAL CODE art. 232. Fukasawa, the novelist, published in 1960 *Fūryū Yume Monogatari* (The Tale of an Elegant Dream) in which he described the heads of the Tennō and his family being cut off and rolled in the street. The Prime Minister decided not to seek public action for prosecution, probably because such fiction was not considered to constitute defamation. I think this decision of the Prime Minister was correct, for the novel, though a bit imprudent, does not lower the reputation of the Tennō. Moreover, it has some value as an expression of a specific view on the Tennō system. But the rightists were most indignant, a boy belonging to one extreme faction murdering the maid of the publisher and wounding his wife in February of 1961. This tragic incident shows the immaturity in acceptance of the idea of free speech in Japan.

[62] Japan v. Koyama, Tokyo District Court, Jan. 18, 1952, 5 KŌ-HAN KEISHŪ 2524.

appealed, sustained the conviction of the publisher and, reversing the acquittal of the translator, imposed upon him a fine of 100,000 yen, reasoning as follows. First, in cases in which the translator performed the task of translation at the request of the publisher and the latter printed the manuscript without alteration, the translator is considered to be a coprincipal. Secondly, the trial court was mistaken in its view that this book became obscene writing by virtue of the methods of sale and advertisement; the translation itself constitutes the offense of obscenity prohibited by the Penal Code.[63]

The Supreme Court sustained this decision of the High Court. The essential parts of its rather long opinion follow:

> In short, according to the cases, to constitute an obscene writing it is required that it offend the sense of shame, give rise to the stimulation and excitation of sexual desire, and violate the notions of virtuous sexual morality . . .
>
> . . . although what we refer to is the stimulation and excitation given to the general reader by the work and the degree that this reader entertains a feeling of shame, these matters must be determined by the court. The court's standard for making this determination is the good judgment employed by society at large, i.e., the "common sense of society" . . .
>
> Yet the common sense of a society regarding sex in general is not the same from time to time and place to place, and even within the same society it is subject to various vicissitudes. It is not unusual in modern society, for example, to exhibit pictures and sculpture, whose display was not formerly permissible, or to print publicly novels whose publication was not formerly acceptable . . . However, despite the fact that such changes are now either present or occurring in society's common sense concerning sex, undeniably certain recognized and generally maintained norms exist in all societies as to the bounds beyond which one may not go. This is the principle of privacy in sexual conduct referred to above. To this extent we cannot find any marked change in the common sense of society to the effect that what was formerly regarded as obscene has become today regarded generally as no longer obscene . . .
>
> . . . on examining the translation in this case, it is not true that we cannot discover an artistic quality different from pornographic literature [literally, "spring books"] in the depiction of the twelve sexual scenes pointed out therein by the public procurator, but even so these are quite bold, detailed, and realistic. They contravene the principle of privacy in sexual conduct and offend the feeling of shame to the extent that one would hesitate to read them aloud in not only the family circle but at a public gathering as well . . . Therefore, the determination by the judgment below that the translation in this case in and of itself is an obscene writing within article 175 of the Penal Code is proper, and the gist of the grounds for revision attacking it, that the court disregarded the common sense of society and rendered its judgment in accord with the dogmatism of the judges, fails to satisfy us . . .
>
> . . . The artistic character of this book must be recognized not only in regard to the work as a whole but also for the twelve parts portraying sex indicated by

[63] Koyama v. Japan, Tokyo High Court, Dec. 10, 1952, 5 KŌ-HAN KEISHŪ 2429.

the procurator. But artistry and obscenity are concepts belonging to separate and different dimensions that are not incompatible . . . A high level of artistry does not necessarily purge obscenity from a work . . .

The presence of obscenity must be determined purely objectively, namely from the literary work itself, and is not influenced by the subjective intention of the author . . . The honesty of a work does not always purge its obscenity . . .

. . . However, irrespective of whether or not the possibility of restraint is clearly indicated in each respective provision relating to the various fundamental human rights guaranteed by the Constitution, their abuse is prohibited under the provisions of articles 12 and 13 of the Constitution, and this court has often ruled that standing subject to the limits of the public welfare they are not absolutely unrestricted[64] . . . since there is no room to doubt that preservation of sexual order and maintenance of a minimum level of sexual morality are encompassed within the public welfare, the judgment rendered below finding the translation in this case to be an obscene writing, the publication of which is contrary to the public welfare, is proper . . .[65]

Hence, both the publisher and the translator should be held criminally liable for the offense of obscenity, and the provisions of the Penal Code punishing it are not invalid even if to some extent they happen to restrict artistic expression.

I agree with the Court's ruling that the provisions relating to punishment of obscene writing are constitutional; but, when the writing in question contains some social value, this value must be analyzed in the application of these provisions. Freedom to express oneself is diminished to the extent that careful comparison of the societal interests in conflict is omitted on the basis of the simplistic logic that legal and artistic values are, in their nature, so different as to be incommensurate. Historically, the suppression of free speech often has been started under the pretense of prohibition of obscene writing. The following minimal considerations must be taken into account in the application of the provisions relating to obscenity. In the first place, the court must judge a literary work as a whole, as the recent English

[64] At this point the Supreme Court cited the following precedents: Ishii v. Japan, Supreme Court, Grand Bench, Aug. 6, 1952, 6 SAI-HAN KEISHŪ 974; Endo v. Japan, Supreme Court, Grand Bench, Jan. 9, 1952, 6 SAI-HAN KEISHŪ 4; Sakabara v. Tōkyō Kyūkō Dentetsu Kabushiki Kaisha (Tokyo Express Electric Railway Company), Supreme Court, Grand Bench, April 4, 1951, 5 SAI-HAN MINSHŪ 214; Kim v. Japan, Supreme Court, Grand Bench, Oct. 11, 1950, 4 SAI-HAN KEISHŪ 2029; Itamoto v. Japan, Supreme Court, Grand Bench, Sept. 27, 1950, 4 SAI-HAN KEISHŪ 1799; Takahashi v. Japan, Supreme Court, Grand Bench, May 18, 1949, 3 SAI-HAN KEISHŪ 839; Araki v. Japan, Supreme Court, Grand Bench, Dec. 27, 1948, 2 SAI-HAN KEISHŪ 1951; Murakami v. Japan, Supreme Court, Grand Bench, March 12, 1948, 2 SAI-HAN KEISHŪ 191.

[65] Koyama v. Japan, Supreme Court, Grand Bench, March 13, 1957, 11 SAI-HAN KEISHŪ 997, translated into English in JUDGMENT UPON CASE OF TRANSLATION AND PUBLICATION OF LADY CHATTERLEY'S LOVER AND ARTICLE 175 OF THE PENAL CODE (Series of Prominent Judgments of the Supreme Court upon Questions of Constitutionality No. 2; General Secretariat of the Supreme Court trans., 1958).

statute provides.[66] The prosecutor insisted that twelve scenes in *Lady Chatterley's Lover* were obscene; these parts should have been considered not severally but in relation to the entire work. Secondly, the judges who are supposed to represent the "common sense of society"—the standard that determines obscenity—must avoid the attitude of censors. For me, the most unsatisfactory part of the *Lady Chatterley* opinion is the dictum to the effect that, if the sensibility of society to obscenity is paralyzed, the judges must "assume a critical attitude against the sickness and degeneration and play a clinical role."[67] This kind of thinking may lead to a judicial censorship that is hostile to freedom of expression. The translation of the works of de Sade have been prosecuted as obscene. This case is now pending in the Tokyo District Court, and the authority of the *Lady Chatterley* decision will probably be re-examined.[68]

The Clear-and-Present-Danger Test

In the cases discussed above, the specific exercises of freedom to be controlled constitute, in a sense, *mala in se* so that their social value, if any, is slight. Accordingly, these restrictions do not generally raise serious constitutional problems; in other words, the social interest in protecting order or morality is, as a rule, taken to be greater than the value of the specific exercise of the freedom. The incitement of undesirable acts presents a more difficult question. In the first place, since the very idea of incitement is vague and the commission of the act incited is not necessary for conviction of the inciter, the broad scope of punishable incitement may offer a greater threat to freedom of expression. Secondly, the act to be incited is often *mala prohibita*—not morally blameworthy but made punishable for the sake of a specific policy of government. Thirdly, in many cases the inciting speech is connected with the expression of some political idea;[69] historically, criticisms of governments in power have been suppressed under the pretense of

[66] Obscene Publications Act, 1959, 7 & 8 Eliz. 2, c. 66 §1. See, generally, Clark, *Obscenity, the Law and Lady Chatterley,* 1961 CRIM. L. REV. 156, 224; also, Grove Press, Inc. v. Christenberry, 276 F.2d 433 (2d Cir. 1960).

[67] Koyama v. Japan, note 65, at 1007.

[68] Yukio Mishima, the well-known novelist, wrote UTAGE NO ATO (After the Banquet), a thinly veiled account of Hachiro Arita, the Socialist candidate for governor of Tokyo in the 1960 election, and his former wife. This work was highly praised in literary circles, but Arita brought an action for violation of his right of privacy. The right of privacy has been unknown in Japanese tort law up to now, although some scholars have argued that it ought to be recognized. This case, now pending in the Tokyo District Court, may present an interesting issue requiring a choice between the freedom of literary expression and the right to be left alone. For the plaintiff's complaint, see 33 HŌRITSU JIHŌ (Law Journal) 574 (1961). The same issue contains a number of articles on the right of privacy. A summary of the respective positions of the parties also appears in Asahi Shimbun, Jan. 12, 1962, p. 10, col. 1 (morning ed.). An English translation of this book, bearing the same title, was published in the United States by Alfred A. Knopf in early 1963.

[69] Justice Holmes said that "every idea is an incitement." Gitlow v. New York, 268 U.S. 652, 673 (1925) (dissenting opinion).

punishing incitement. The social value that may be contained in expressions inciting some kind of illegal act must, therefore, be carefully assessed. The clear-and-present-danger test seems to be the most valuable standard for harmonizing the value of the expression and the danger of the act the expression seeks to incite.

At the time of a serious shortage of food immediately after the last war, the accused attended a meeting in Bippu Village, Kamikawa Township, Hokkaido, at which about three hundred farmers were assembled. He told them, regarding the delivery quota of the rice they produced, that "it is selfish of the government one-sidedly to determine the price for rice that we as farmers raised and harvested ourselves and compel us to hand it over. The submissive attitude taken by us up to now is no good! Since the farmer has been cheated up to now, there is no damn need to deliver the rice." [70] He was prosecuted in the Asahikawa Local Court under the Food Emergency Measures Order[71] because these words constituted the offense of inciting nondelivery of staple foods to the government; he was sentenced to six months' imprisonment. After the Asahikawa District Court dismissed his appeal [72] and the Sapporo High Court his request for revision,[73] he again sought revision in the Supreme Court, insisting that his speech was a protest against the maladministration of the present government and that, if the order were construed to prohibit such speech, it would be unconstitutional as an abridgment of freedom of speech. The Supreme Court rejected the argument:

> criticism of government policies and attack upon its maladministration by the people, so long as the method is not a breach of the public peace, belongs under freedom of speech and all other forms of expression. However, concerning the sale of staple foodstuffs to the government pursuant to the Order based on the provisions of the Food Control Law prescribed in order to prepare for the carrying out of the anticipated purpose of the same law, which was enacted by the state under today's food shortage conditions to assure staple foods for the public as a whole, action instigating one not to do so fails to stop at merely criticizing the policies of the government and attacking its maladministration, but, as herein related, goes on to urge the nonperformance of an important legal duty borne as a member of the nation and to violate the public welfare. Thus, since deeds of this sort depart from the bounds of freedom of speech guaranteed in the new Constitution and ought to be condemned morally in our social life, a rule of law punishing them as a crime does not contravene the terms of article 21 of the new Constitution.[74]

These reasons are not convincing. The Court used its familiar but vague notion of "public welfare" as a panacea for curing the alleged unconstitu-

[70] Takahashi v. Japan, Asahikawa District Court, n.d., 3 SAI-HAN KEISHŪ 843.
[71] Food Emergency Measures Order, Emergency Imperial Order No. 86 of 1946.
[72] Takahashi v. Japan, Asahikawa District Court, note 70, at 843.
[73] Takahashi v. Japan, Sapporo High Court, July 20, 1948, 1 KŌ-HAN KEISHŪ 189.
[74] Takahashi v. Japan, Supreme Court, note 64, at 840–41.

tionality of the law. This decision, rendered in 1949 only two years after the new Constitution came into force, played a pioneer role in the course which the Supreme Court has developed toward laws restricting freedom of expression.

The Court should have analyzed the clear and actual danger of the speech, which was made in the presence of a large number of farmers who owed a duty to deliver rice to the government at a time of almost inconceivable food shortage. The defendant contended that his speech did not constitute the crime of incitement. Nevertheless, the Court, presupposing that his act was punishable, discussed the legal question whether the Food Emergency Measures Order was valid and upheld its validity under the public-welfare test.

The Supreme Court followed the same line of reasoning in the second case relating to incitement. The Local Public Servants Law[75] prohibited anyone from inciting local public officials to sabotage. The defendant distributed a pamphlet to local police officers encouraging them to resist the orders of foreign imperialists and of a traitorous government and to join in the battle for national independence. The Supreme Court upheld the conviction of the defendant;[76] the expression in question was contrary to the public welfare and beyond the scope of the freedom guaranteed by the Constitution, as shown by the case involving the Food Emergency Measures Order. Significantly, however, the court suggested that incitement, insofar as it did not involve a danger of arousing sabotage, was not a crime. This proposition seems clear, and I would agree that, even though some degree of danger exists, the freedom should be protected unless the danger carries some overriding actual evil. However, the Court advanced one step further in dealing with the free-speech problem because it recognized the probability of social value being included even in the inciting expression and thought that the existence of danger had to be taken into consideration. Justice Kuriyama's concurring opinion is of special interest. He proposed that the degree to which the expression would arouse substantial evil to society should determine whether such an expression is an abuse of freedom.[77] Of course, his test is much less strict than the clear-and-present-danger test; however, since it requires the prosecution to show objective circumstances indicating some degree of danger, it considers that freedom of expression may be violated by punishment for incitement and thus proposes a standard stricter than the public-welfare test.

Nondelivery of staple foods at a time of serious food shortage and inciting public officials to sabotage — the results sought by incitement in these cases — are of fairly definite content; provisions punishing incitement of such

[75] Law No. 261 of 1950.

[76] Takahashi v. Japan, Supreme Court, II Petty Bench, Aug. 29, 1952, 6 SAI-HAN KEISHŪ 1053, 1054–56.

[77] *Ibid.*, at 1056.

undesirable results may thus be less dangerous to free speech. In other words, in these situations, we can rather easily compare the value of the speech and the value of the social interest to be protected against the abuse of free speech. The problem becomes much more difficult and delicate in cases in which the result sought by incitement is indefinite.

A typical example of this kind of problem is brought out by the Subversive Activities Prevention Law, enacted in 1952.[78] This law follows the Smith Act of the United States.[79] Article 38 provides punishment for incitement to insurrection, for inducement of foreign aggression, or assistance to the enemy for the purpose of causing another person to perform any of these crimes, and also for incitement to such acts as riot, arson, homicide, or robbery in order to cause another person to perform any of these crimes for political purposes. Since the act which is the object of incitement constitutes a criminal offense, such incitement can cause a danger to society, but at the same time incitement through speech or publication has a close connection with expression of political ideas. Therefore, the legal control imposed by this law should be placed in a strict framework lest the law violate the freedom to express political opinions. Unlike the case of an instigator, the inciter may be punished even if the person incited does not commit the act. Moreover, in this law the object of incitement is rather indefinite. For these reasons, some scholars consider the law unconstitutional. Whether it is or not, a loose standard such as the public-welfare test should not be used in applying its provisions to concrete cases. It is significant that all the decisions of the lower courts, though none of them held the law invalid, acquitted those who were prosecuted under it through the application of the clear-and-present-danger test.

The Kyoto District Court, after considering the development of the clear-and-present-danger rule in the United States and suggesting that the view of Chief Justice Vinson in the *Dennis* case[80] — which altered the test substantially — should not be adopted, went on to say:

> In article 2 of the Subversive Activities Prevention Law, since this Law has an extremely important relationship with the fundamental human rights of the people, it is only natural that it is expressly provided that it is to be applied only to the minimum extent necessary to assure the public safety and that it shall not be expanded. These words indicate no less than that this Law should be applied in accordance with the so-called clear and present danger rule of Justices Holmes and Brandeis.[81]

In another case, the Kushiro District Court said:

[78] Law No. 240 of 1952.
[79] 18 U.S.C. §2395 (1958).
[80] Dennis v. United States, note 49, at 502–11.
[81] Japan v. Sugahara, Kyoto District Court, Dec. 27, 1956, HANREI JIHŌ (The Case Journal) no. 112, at 1, 31.

Freedom of speech is the essential prerequisite for eliminating all rule by force and despotism and for fostering the development of sound democracy. Therefore, even admitting that freedom of speech may at times be overdone, we have to exercise caution in restricting it through penal sanctions. We must conclude that in imposing restrictions this freedom should be limited if a clear and present danger to society's public safety and welfare arises, but where we can do no more than logically affirm the possibility that sometime in the future society's public safety and welfare will be impaired, it cannot be restricted.[82]

And the Tsu District Court wrote in another decision:

The "clear and present danger principle," brilliantly enunciated by Justice Holmes as the standard for restricting speech, coincides with "the minimum extent necessary to assure the public safety" in article 2 of the Subversive Activities Prevention Law and should be adopted and applied as is, we believe, to "the purpose of causing the execution of the crime of insurrection" in article 38, item (ii), of the Law. In other words, where there is no clear and present danger that the relevant evils will be brought about, restricting freedom of speech merely on idle speculation that a threat exists that such evils will arise in the future contravenes the fundamental principles of democracy.[83]

Although the Supreme Court has not yet disclosed its view with respect to this problem, I think the clear-and-present-danger test adopted by the lower courts suggests a correct way of harmonizing the value of free speech with the value of the security of society.

The Prior-Restraint Test

Article 21, paragraph 2, of the Constitution provides that "no censorship shall be maintained." Although the second half of this paragraph is concerned with the secrecy of means of communication, it must be interpreted to mean that censorship is prohibited as regards all kinds of speech and publication. Censorship is no doubt the classical and most severe form of restriction upon free speech and is typical of prior restraint. If paragraph 2 can be construed liberally, the new Constitution may be taken to prohibit all prior restraint upon the exercise of intellectual freedom.[84] The old Constitution had permitted various types of prior restraint on the expression of ideas. For example, though censorship of the publication of books and newspapers was not formally permitted, it occurred because the Publication Law[85] and the Newspaper Law[86] permitted the Minister of Home Affairs to prohibit the sale or the distribution of books or newspapers and to seize

[82] Japan v. Shimamura, Kushiro District Court, Sept. 15, 1954, HANREI JIHŌ no. 36, at 3, 5.

[83] Japan v. Arai, Tsu District Court, Feb. 28, 1955, HANREI JIHŌ no. 48, at 3, 15.

[84] The traditional attitude of the common law was that freedom of speech meant no previous restraint. See 4 BLACKSTONE, COMMENTARIES *151–52. For a history of the freedom of press in England, see Holdsworth, *Press Control and Copyright in the 16th and 17th Centuries*, 29 YALE L. J. 841 (1920).

[85] Law No. 15 of 1893.

[86] Law No. 41 of 1909.

them if he found that they disturbed security and order or injured morality; moreover, his determination was final.[87] It is natural that these powers were abolished under the new Constitution.

Nevertheless, certain kinds of censorship do exist. Article 21 of the Customs Tariff Law[88] vests in the superintendent of the customhouse the power to prohibit the importation of books and pictures injurious to public security or morality. This law, enacted under the old Constitution, is still enforced under the new Constitution. The customhouse inspects imported motion-picture films and sometimes orders the cutting of portions; if the importer does not obey such an order, the importation is not permitted. Almost all constitutional-law scholars take the view that this inspection of films by the customhouse is the same as censorship and regard the provisions of article 21 of the Customs Tariff Law as unconstitutional.[89] But, probably because the importers fear taking a strong attitude, no customhouse order has been questioned in the courts. Hence we cannot know how the court would decide the issue.[90]

In the *Niigata Ordinance* case,[91] the Supreme Court admitted, to some extent, the validity of the doctrine of prior restraint under the new Constitution. The ordinance requires prior permission from the City Public Safety Commission for parades and demonstrations in the streets.[92] The commission

[87] The Recourse Law, Law No. 105 of 1890, and the Administrative Trial Law, Law No. 48 of 1890, enumerated the forms of administrative action (disposition) which could be contested. They did not cover a determination by the Minister of Home Affairs, which accordingly was final.

[88] Law No. 54 of 1910.

[89] MIYAZAWA, KEMPŌ II (Constitutional Law II) 359 (Hōritsu-gaku Zenshū (Complete Collection on the Law) ed. 1960); UKAI, KEMPŌ (Constitutional Law) 103 n. 12 (1956); Ito, *Zeikan Kenetsu to Kempō Nijūichi Jō* (Customhouse Censorship and Article 21 of the Constitution), JURIST no. 223, at 6 (1961).

[90] Several reasons have been given supporting the validity of inspection of imported films by the customhouse. For example, it is argued that the freedom of expression is qualified by censorship only to the extent necessary to protect the public welfare. But this argument ignores the significance of the constitutional prohibition of censorship. A view which seems more worthy of consideration is that films, being a kind of commercial good, are not protected by art. 21. Purely commercial expression may have nothing to do with increasing knowledge, and it is not given a preferred position in the constitutional law. See Valentine v. Chrestensen, 316 U.S. 52 (1942); Resnick, *Freedom of Speech and Commercial Solicitation*, 30 CALIF. L. REV. 655 (1942). The Japanese Supreme Court recently held a law prohibiting the advertisement of the business of masseurs, acupuncturists, and moxicauterists valid on the ground of public welfare, in particular, as protecting the public from exaggerated propaganda. Judge Tarumi's concurring opinion advanced an interesting argument. He said that such advertisements were purely commercial expressions, whose constitutional position was the same as that of economic rights, and that therefore the Court should presume that the law was a reasonable regulation. Ono v. Japan, Supreme Court, Grand Bench, Feb. 15, 1961, 15 SAI-HAN KEISHŪ 347, 350. I agree with this opinion. Such commercial criteria, however, can be applied only to purely commercial expression, and films are not *necessarily* wholly commercial. For example, the newsreel is similar to the photographs of a newspaper.

[91] Yamaoka v. Japan, Supreme Court, Grand Bench, Nov. 24, 1954, 8 SAI-HAN KEISHŪ 1866.

[92] Ordinance Concerning Parades and Mass Demonstrations, Niigata Prefectural Ordinance No. 4 of 1949, art. 1.

is to give permission if there is no ground for apprehension that the parade or demonstration will injure public safety.[93] The defendant was prosecuted for violating the ordinance. The Supreme Court upheld the validity of the ordinance and, in so doing, developed general principles for determining the constitutionality of regulations of freedom of assembly or other forms of mass expression.

Since parades or mass demonstrations (hereinafter referred to as "such activity"), insofar as they do not rely upon an improper purpose or method, concern essentially a freedom of the people, aside from where just a system of notification is fixed by Ordinance regarding such activity, it is proper to construe that prescribing a general approval system and making this a prior restraint is an impermissible violation of the purport of the Constitution. However, although such activity is involved, we cannot conclude where, in order to maintain public order or to prevent a marked invasion of the public welfare, one must complete in advance the receipt of approval or the making of a notification under reasonable and well-defined standards in regard to the specific place or method, that the establishment of rules in an Ordinance to the effect that in such cases the activity may be prohibited directly constitutes an improper restriction of a freedom of the people guaranteed by the Constitution. In the final analysis, the provisions of the Ordinance concerned do not in any way generally restrict such activity, but instead merely, from the previously indicated viewpoint, go no further than to recognize restrictions as to specific places and methods.[94]

This holding is the first to propose a rather definite standard for determining the constitutionality of laws limiting fundamental freedoms. A general prior restraint would be unconstitutional; but a limited prior restraint administered under reasonable and well-defined standards with regard to place or method of mass activities is not necessarily invalid.

The Supreme Court concluded that the Niigata ordinance was not a general approval system, but rather a regulation, under reasonable and well-defined standards, of the specific place or method of the parade or demonstration. The Court would have preferred the abstract standard—"apprehension of injury to public safety," which could give wide discretionary power to the Public Safety Commission—to have been supplemented by a clearer and more concrete standard. Judge Fujita's argument in dissent seems much more persuasive than that of the Court.[95] He would

[93] *Ibid.*, art. 4.

[94] Yamaoka v. Japan, note 91, at 1872. Immediately after the quoted sentence, the Court said: "Again, when a fact can be foreseen regarding such action which will amount to a clear and present danger to the public safety, it must be construed that the establishment of provisions to the effect that it will not be approved or that it may be prohibited does not directly constitute an improper restriction of a freedom of the people guaranteed by the Constitution" (at 1872–73). This sentence could have proved significant had the Supreme Court showed a favorable attitude toward the clear-and-present-danger test. But the Supreme Court has not further developed this line of thought.

[95] *Ibid.*, at 1876. Nathanson, *Constitutional Adjudication in Japan*, 7 AM. J. COMP. L. 195, 208, said the dissenting opinion of Judge Fujita was "a breath of fresh air."

hold the ordinance unconstitutional because it imposes a general regulation covering almost all kinds of parades and demonstrations. In all events, the line of reasoning adopted in *Niigata Ordinance* won the support of many scholars who expected the Supreme Court to give up the simple public-welfare test and to develop the subsequent case law along the lines suggested by the decision.

However, about six years later, the Supreme Court, in the *Tokyo Ordinance* case,[96] reverted to its traditional attitude. It reversed the decision of the lower court, the Tokyo District Court, which held the Tokyo ordinance invalid under the general principles enumerated in *Niigata Ordinance.* The Tokyo ordinance controlling parades and demonstrations prohibits any assembly or parade in a street or other public place and any demonstration in any place unless advance permission has been obtained from the Public Safety Commission. Excursions, games of students, festivals, and other customary events are exempted.[97] The Commission is to grant the application unless it considers that such mass activities would immediately endanger the maintenance of public security.[98] The Tokyo District Court considered that the ordinance imposed a general prior restraint upon freedom of expression.[99] But the Supreme Court, in disregard of *Niigata Ordinance* and with two justices dissenting, supported the validity of the ordinance under the public-welfare test. The Court explained:

In short, mass activity — particularly mass demonstrations — subject to this Ordinance is that which disturbs serenity and involves physical force having the danger of developing into violence, omitted from the scope of the use of pure freedom of expression which must have regard for order under general tranquillity; consequently, some degree of legal control concerning it cannot be called unnecessary. *A fortiori* the state and society must pay maximum respect to freedom of expression, but we must recognize that obtaining foreknowledge prior to an event of activity likely to break down peace and order through mass action on the pretext of freedom of expression, or activity tinged with such a tendency, and devising appropriate measures to prepare against unforeseen contingencies is after all inescapable. Of course, it cannot be said that even this Ordinance contains absolutely no danger at all of violating through its operation the guarantee of freedom of expression assured by article 21 of the Constitution. Naturally, the utmost care must be taken to see that the Public Safety Commission in carrying out the operation of the Ordinance does not abuse its authority and proceed to suppress peaceful and orderly mass activity on the pretext that it is maintaining the public peace. However, it is improper to assume that just because the possibility of a threat of abuse exists, the Ordinance in question is unconstitutional.[100]

[96] Japan v. Ito, note 48, at 1250–51.
[97] Ordinance Concerning Assembly, Parades en Masse, and Mass Demonstrations, art. 1.
[98] *Ibid.*, art. 3.
[99] Japan v. Ito, Tokyo District Court, Aug. 8, 1959, 14 SAI-HAN KEISHŪ 1282, 1290.
[100] Japan v. Ito, note 48, at 1250–51.

I cannot agree with this reasoning. In the first place, the logic is too simple: because parades and demonstrations tend to affect the public safety and so cannot be left to take their own course without limitation, this ordinance must be considered indispensable and valid. The real issue is not a choice between the denial and the support of legal control on mass activities — almost all views admit that some legal regulation may be imposed upon these activities[101] — but whether a severe prior restraint such as that imposed by the Tokyo ordinance is permissible under the Constitution. The reasoning through which this real issue is supplanted by the question of whether any legal control is admissible represents a kind of word magic.

Furthermore, it is true the Supreme Court recognized, at least in the words of its decision, that only the minimum extent of regulation would be permitted; but its brief explanation does not persuade us that the Court attaches real importance to this qualification. For example, according to the Court, since the permission is denied only in an exceptional instance, the ordinance can be considered a notification system rather than a license (approval) system;[102] but this easy rationalization loses sight of the essential difference between the two systems.[103] The wide discretionary power of the commission is thought of as indispensable in regulating mass activities; yet the protection of freedom of expression requires that, so far as possible, the exercise of discretionary power be restrained by clear and definite standards. Justice Tarumi in his dissent mentions various examples of standards available for preventing the arbitrary exercise of such power.[104] Moreover, even

[101] Even previous restraint may be imposed on this type of expression, though such regulation seems exceptional and must be pursuant to an equally definite standard. Cf. Poulos v. New Hampshire, 345 U.S. 395 (1953); Cox v. New Hampshire, 312 U.S. 569 (1941).

[102] "The Public Safety Commission must approve the carrying out of mass activity other than 'where it can be clearly recognized that [this] . . . will amount to a direct danger from the standpoint of maintaining the public peace' (art. 1). In other words, approval is imposed as a duty and cases of nonapproval are strictly limited. Therefore, while this Ordinance on the face of the wording of its provisions adopts an approval system, this approval system, in substance, does not differ from a notification system. It does not matter whether the condition for mass activity is approval or notification provided the essential point that it does not become an improper restriction of freedom of expression exists." Japan v. Ito, note 48, at 1249.

[103] The notification system is a kind of subsequent punishment because any person can enjoy the freedom of expressing his ideas simply upon notice to a public official, and, if exercise of the freedom causes a breach of law, he is punished according to law. Of course, even such a regulation might raise a constitutional question. Cf. Thomas v. Collins, 323 U.S. 516 (1945). But the issue raised by it is, generally speaking, not as serious as pure prior restraint. Cf. Emerson, *The Doctrine of Previous Restraint,* 20 LAW & CONTEMP. PROB. 648 (1955).

[104] Judge Tarumi mentioned examples of English, French, and West German regulations having reasonable and definite standards. He also indicated what he considered constitutional methods of regulating mass activities: for example, prohibition of mass activities between twelve o'clock midnight to four A.M.; prohibition of parades of more than *x* meters in width in streets less than *x* meters wide; prohibition of "scrimmage" or snake-dancing parades lasting more than forty minutes and occupying the entire street. Japan v. Ito, note 48, at 1272–73. Whether or not his proposals are practical, his effort deserves commendation.

the majority opinion admits that legal remedies against denial of permission by the commission are unsatisfactory. Of course, insufficiency of legal remedies does not always lead to the invalidity of legislation; but it seems that the Court should have explained in more detail why the ordinance was, in spite of this deficiency, valid. Considering these points, it is difficult to conclude that the regulation provided by the Tokyo ordinance does not go beyond what is necessary to maintain public peace.

Although, as the majority opinion points out, mass activities in public places are distinguishable from speech and publication because such activities are accompanied by physical force which may turn into violence,[105] the Supreme Court overemphasized the unsound side of mass activities and did not fully understand that parades and demonstrations are the sole form of expressing political ideas open to the common people who ordinarily do not have access to the media of speech and press. Through this form of expression the potential political ideas of the people may be communicated. Moreover, the ordinance intends to control only parades and demonstrations having something to do with political ideas, for ordinary processions which might equally disturb traffic on the streets are exempted. Is it too much to say that the Supreme Court was showing its hostility to those forms of expression which involve mass activities? As the dissenting opinion of Justice Fujita said, "We must not lose sight of the essence of freedoms guaranteed by the Constitution as a result of being dazzled by the necessity for control."[106]

Then, of course, it is not suitable for the Court to disregard its own precedent in so cavalier a manner. The fact that more than half of the fifteen justices were appointed after the *Niigata Ordinance* case probably weakened its binding force. Moreover, generally speaking, the binding force of constitutional cases may be less strict than those of ordinary cases, as a number of the American scholars assert.[107] But sufficient reasons should be shown before a precedent is disregarded. If, as in this decision, a precedent is wholly ignored—*Niigata Ordinance* was not even cited—and is substantially overruled, the constitutional case law cannot perform its function of stabilizing the interpretation of the Constitution.

Finally, the reasoning of the *Tokyo Ordinance* case is that the necessity

[105] Another difference between mass activities and ordinary speech and publication is that the former are much more likely to injure the rights of others. A parade in the streets might obstruct the right of way enjoyed by the public. But this reason cannot explain why festival parades and student excursions are exempted. The effect of these exemptions is to render the ordinance applicable only to mass activities relating to expression of some creed or opinion. This consideration seems to explain why the Supreme Court did not mention the obstruction of another person's legitimate rights as a reason for supporting the ordinance.

[106] Japan v. Ito, note 48, at 1256.

[107] VON MOSCHZISHER, STARE DECISIS, RES JUDICATA AND OTHER SELECTED ESSAYS 16–17 (1929); 3 WARREN, THE SUPREME COURT IN UNITED STATES HISTORY 470–71 (1923); Douglas, *Stare Decisis,* 49 COLUM. L. REV. 735 (1949). See also the dissenting opinions of Justices Brandeis and Stone in Burnet v. Coronada Oil & Gas Co., 285 U.S. 393, 401, 405 (1932).

of maintaining peace and order is superior to the freedom to express oneself and that, in spite of the unconstitutionality of separate parts of the law, if the law as a whole is thought reasonable it should be held valid. This kind of reasoning gives all legislation a strong presumption of constitutionality;* at least under normal circumstances, we cannot imagine the legislature being so arbitrary as to produce a law unreasonable enough to overcome this presumption. Accordingly, as long as the Supreme Court thinks in this way, it cannot be expected to hold a law in this area unconstitutional.[108] At this point it would seem that there are many difficulties to overcome before the power of judicial review, transplanted by the new Constitution, can grow up on the soil of Japan.

* Kohji Tanabe at the conference explained sociologically the reluctance of the Japanese appellate courts to strike down legislation. The relatively low prestige of the bench and the public antipathy toward the bureaucrat mean that, as an institution, the Supreme Court must tread lightly in overthrowing the popular mandate.

[108] Since art. 81 of the new Constitution recognized the power of judicial review, the Supreme Court has only twice held a law unconstitutional: Nomura v. Yamaki, Supreme Court, Grand Bench, July 6, 1960, 14 SAI-HAN MINSHŪ 1657 (compulsory arbitration case); Sakagami v. Japan, Supreme Court, Grand Bench, July 22, 1953, 7 SAI-HAN KEISHŪ 1562 (1953) (Cabinet Order No. 325 of 1950 case). The laws held invalid in both cases had already lost their legal force at the time of decision. Of course, the number of decisions holding laws unconstitutional does not always indicate the efficacy of judicial review. Excessive use of judicial review might threaten the progress of democracy in Japan. In this sense, I cannot support the very high value that some attach to judicial review as a technique of constitutional government. As stated in my introduction, in a great many situations the political process, not the judicial process, should be relied upon to realize the rule of law. It is for this reason that, in spite of the critical attitude of many scholars, I supported the decision of the Supreme Court in the *Sunakawa* case — Japan v. Sakata, Supreme Court, Grand Bench, Dec. 16, 1959, 13 SAI-HAN KEISHŪ 3225, translated into English in 4 JAPANESE ANN. INTL. L. 103 (1960) — which, reversing the decision of the Tokyo District Court, held that the Security Treaty Between Japan and the United States — Sept. 8, 1951, [1952] 3 U.S.T. & O.I.A. 3329, T.I.A.S. 2491, 136 U.N.T.S. 211 (April 28, 1952) — permitting the stationing of American armed forces in Japan, was not in conflict with art. 9 which renounces war. A highly political issue, such as what approach should be adopted for defending the nation, must be determined politically. I agree with Nathanson's remark: "I am inclined to view with considerable more sympathy than these Japanese critics the timidity or caution of the Japanese Court in meeting constitutional questions" (note 95, at 216). But this generous view of the Court cannot be applied to the *Tokyo Ordinance* case. With regard to *Niigata Ordinance,* which is more favorable to freedom of expression, Nathanson said, "the policy of postponing or avoiding constitutional questions can be indulged too far, and I would agree that in some instances the Japanese Court seems to have erred in that direction" (*ibid.*). After the decision of *Tokyo Ordinance,* the Chief Justice told news reporters that, even if there were no decisions holding laws to be unconstitutional, the very existence of the power of judicial review would have a psychological effect in persuading the legislature to respect the Constitution. This kind of thinking may well paralyze judicial review.

THE RULE OF LAW: SOME ASPECTS OF JUDICIAL REVIEW OF ADMINISTRATIVE ACTION

Kiminobu Hashimoto

ASSISTED BY DOUGLAS B. MAGGS

THE Meiji Constitution of 1889 was modeled on the Prussian constitution and represented a compromise between absolute monarchy and modern democracy. The Constitution granted certain rights to the people, but these rights were each subject to restraints enacted by law and were thus only nominally guaranteed. The principle of separation of powers was purportedly adopted, but in reality the idea of checks and balances was rejected. History shows that the traditional subordination of the individual to the Emperor or to those ruling in his name led the people to submit to domination by a strong government. Because of the highly nationalistic and scarcely democratic tendencies and of the combination of archaic and modern features in the political structure, the rule of law in its true meaning did not exist.

Introduction

Commentators inclined to the view that the Meiji Constitution adopted to some extent the Continental notion of the *Rechtsstaatsprinzip* (to be distinguished from the Anglo-American concept of the rule of law). Strictly speaking, however, the Meiji Constitution did not establish a *Rechtsstaat* in its full meaning. Let us examine the main defects of the pre-1945 legal structure, especially those fundamentally affecting administrative law.

Note. Mr. Hashimoto is Professor of Law, Chuo University. B.Jur., Chuo University, 1942; Dr.Jur., 1960. Participant, Japanese Delegation to the United States on University Education in Public Administration, 1951; participant, Japanese American Program for Cooperation in Legal Studies at Harvard University, 1954–1955, and at University of Michigan, 1955–1956; guest auditor at Heidelberg University and Munich University, 1956–1957. German Ambassador Prize, 1942. Director of Japan Public Law Association; Specialist of Special Commission on Administrative Organization and Management. Author of Beikoku Gyōsei Hō Kenkyū, Gyōsei Kōi ni Tai-suru Shihō Shinsa (A Study of U.S. Administrative Law, Judicial Review of Administrative Action) (1958); Kempō Genron (Principles of Constitutional Law) (1959); cotranslator, with Inomata, Ukai, and Wada, of Gellhorn, Individual Freedom and Governmental Restraints (1960); writings in the field of constitutional and administrative law.

Mr. Maggs, until his death in September 1962, was Professor of Law, Duke University. A.B., 1922, J.D., 1924, University of California; S.J.D., 1926, Harvard University.

The formal or structural component of the *Rechtsstaatsprinzip* requires that administrative power be exercised in accordance with laws enacted by the legislature. This principle of legality (*Prinzip der gesetzmässiger Verwaltung* or *Prinzip der Gesetzmässigkeit der Verwaltung*) is deemed essential to modern government. However, the principle was narrowly limited under the Meiji Constitution. In the first place, the executive retained broad independent power to make substantive laws. Subordination of administration to laws enacted by the legislature could not, therefore, be achieved. In the second place, delegation of broad legislative power to the executive was accepted and so widely practiced that the principle of legality could not serve to check administrative power. Even the theoretical limitations of delegated legislative power were quite often disregarded by the administrative authorities.

Furthermore, the remedies against illegal administrative action were extremely limited in prewar Japan. A basic principle of the Anglo-American idea of the rule of law is that one whose legal rights have been invaded by administrative action may challenge its legality in a court of justice. Although there is still considerable controversy about the extent and scope of judicial review, nobody can deny its important role in America. But the Meiji Constitution established instead an Administrative Court with a narrowly restricted jurisdiction to review the legality of administrative action.[1] In this way, the Constitution sought to secure the independence of the executive from the judiciary; expert administrative judges reviewed a limited segment of administrative activity. Administrative law in prewar Japan was thus based on the existence of a special law for cases involving the administration and of a special court to decide them.

However, the prewar system had defects that prevented it from achieving the principle of legality of administration and the protection of the rights of the people. First, the jurisdiction of the Administrative Court was quite narrowly restricted. A man adversely affected by illegal administrative action could bring an action before the Administrative Court only when a statute permitted him to do so. The legality of administrative action in many fields was thus not subject to challenge in the Administrative Court. Second, because only one administrative court was set up, this institution could not exercise effective control by reviewing a substantial number of cases. Third, influenced by a strong bureaucratic tradition, the administrative judges were favorably disposed toward the executive and not inclined to protect the rights of the people. Fourth, there were few procedural safeguards in the proceedings of the Administrative Court.

[1] Art. 61 of the Meiji Constitution provided: "Litigation alleging an infringement of rights through an illegal disposition by the administrative authorities, which shall come under the judgment of an administrative court separately prescribed by Law, does not come within the purview of the courts of justice." See HIROBUMI ITO, COMMENTARIES ON THE CONSTITUTION OF THE EMPIRE OF JAPAN 108–12 (Miyoji Ito trans., 3rd ed., 1931).

In short, the subordination of administration to the law was not sufficiently guaranteed under such an imperfect system of review. The inevitable result was a dangerous tendency toward arbitrary exercise of administrative power. Legality of administration was, in practical effect, a mere maxim of political morality. Needless to say, the rule of law could not exist under such a system.

The Constitution of 1946 abolished the Administrative Court and introduced the Anglo-American system of judicial review. Paragraphs 1 and 2 of article 76 provide:

> The whole judicial power is vested in a Supreme Court and in such inferior courts as are established by law.
>
> No extraordinary tribunal shall be established, nor shall any organ or agency of the Executive be given final judicial power.

Although a few scholars insist that the new Constitution does not prohibit the establishment of a system of administrative courts alongside the judicial courts, their attempts to construe the Constitution in this traditional way have not been found persuasive. Japanese jurists generally agree that the Constitution has introduced the idea of the rule of law, which is understood by them to have two features: the principle of legality (that is, that governmental action is invalid unless based on law); and the principle that the ordinary law courts must be available to persons who wish to challenge the validity of an administrative act.[2]

Dissatisfied with mere assertion of the *Rechtsstaatsprinzip* in its formal or structural sense, Japanese scholars and jurists have accepted this notion of the rule of law and sought to establish effective control of administrative action by the judicial courts. Article 3 of the Court Law[3] provides: "The courts, except where it is especially so provided in the Constitution of Japan, are to adjudicate all legal disputes and possess such other authority as is particularly provided by Law."

The system of judicial review of administrative action has wrought an epochmaking reformation of Japan's administrative law. Since the establishment of the new system, a large number of actions seeking review have been brought in the courts.[4] As a result, judge-made law has been steadily

[2] This view of the rule of law accords with that of some American writers. See, e.g., SCHWARTZ, FRENCH ADMINISTRATIVE LAW AND THE COMMON-LAW WORLD 111–12 (1954).

[3] Law No. 59 of 1947, translated into English in 2 EHS LAW BULLETIN SERIES AA 1 (Nakane ed., 1954).

[4] The statistics, reported in SAIKŌ SAIBANSHO JIMU-SŌKYOKU (General Secretariat of the Supreme Court), GYŌSEI JIKEN SOSHŌ JŪNEN SHI (A History of a Decade of Litigation in Administrative Cases) 1–39 (1961), are as follows. The administrative cases in all courts from May 3, 1947, to Dec. 31, 1957, totaled 17,916. The number of administrative cases brought in courts of first instance in each year was as follows: 478 in 1947; 2,504 in 1948; 2,511 in 1949; 1,746 in 1950; 1,218 in 1951; 1,187 in 1952; 935 in 1953; 1,119 in 1954; 978 in 1955; 838 in 1956; 894 in 1957. This report classifies these 14,408 cases as follows: 7,925 agricultural land cases (55.0%); 2,243 tax cases (15.6%); 704 election cases (4.9%); 686

increasing in the field of administrative law.[5] The judicial courts play a role much more important than that played in the past by the Administrative Court.

All courts are faced with many difficult questions in discharging their responsibility for protecting the rights of the people from illegal administrative action and guaranteeing the principle of legality of administration. It should be borne in mind that Japanese experience in this field has been very short as compared to that of the American courts and that many important questions still remain untouched or unsettled.

An abstract conception of the rule of law cannot serve as a useful guide to the solution of questions in this area. We should not equate the rule of law with the maximum degree of judicial review. Needless to say, the judiciary cannot, does not, and should not attempt either to dominate or supervise the executive. We must, therefore, admit the existence of some nonreviewable administrative action and the need for an allocation of functions between judicial courts and administrative agencies. Attempts to draw a clear-cut line between these functions on the basis of theoretical analyses of the nature of judicial power have not been successful. In this essay, I have taken into account practical considerations which affect judicial decisions, and I have attempted to arrive at a theoretical formulation by this pragmatic approach.

The judicial decisions analyzed here reveal, I submit, that judges in reviewing administrative action have realized that, on the one hand, protection must be given to persons whose rights are adversely affected by administrative action and that, on the other hand, the performance by government of its necessary functions must not be unduly hampered. The legislature in its statutes and the judges in their opinions are attempting, not always with success, to devise an allocation of functions between courts and administrative

---

local government cases (4.8%); 412 industrial property cases (2.8%); and 2,438 other cases (16.9%). [Editor's note: It was pointed out at the conference that the agricultural land cases are a postwar phenomenon growing out of the occupation land reform which compelled the large landowners to sell to the government, which in turn resold land to create a small-farmer class. The universal reaction of the landowners was to seek relief in the courts. Also, some comparative tax statistics are revealing. Rex Coleman pointed out at the conference that in Japan (figures for 1961) the number of cases entering the nonnegotiating administrative stage (the conference groups) exceeds, adjusted for population, the comparable level in American tax administration — that is, adjustments referred to informal conference with the group chief of the examining officer in the first adjustment stage (figures for 1952). But, when the action reaches the judicial stage, there is a sharp reversal, with about 1,800 suits filed annually in the Court of Claims and the federal District Courts, while only about 400 were filed in Japan. The American judicial figures would probably even be higher if it were not for the Tax Court which has about 6,000 petitions annually. Japan has no comparable administrative tribunal. It should be recognized, however, that in addition to the two administrative appeals available in Japan, the nonlawyer tax specialist is not permitted to appear in court and the use of *bengoshi* considerably increases the expense of litigation.]

[5] Despite this, the great bulk of administrative law is still, and will continue to be, created by the legislature and by administrative interpretation. The legislature will continue to play a significant role in reforming administrative law.

agencies which will not only ensure judicial protection of rights against executive infringements but will also ensure governmental power to enforce the rights conferred by the Constitution and the laws. Such an allocation of functions is essential to the rule of law, as I conceive it.[6]

The problems discussed here raise additional questions. Is judicial review of administrative action now too greatly restricted in Japan by the courts' use of the concept of administrative discretion? Should judicial review of administrative action be restricted more than it is now by wider substitution of the substantial-evidence rule for the currently normal trial *de novo* of administratively determined questions of fact? *

An abstract theoretical or conceptual approach to these subjects would lead us to overly simple and unrealistic conclusions. The judicial review which the rule of law calls for differs as the governmental functions involved differ and as the rights affected differ. Hence, I shall analyze several cases involving some typical administrative functions in order to determine (1) what administrative choices or judgments in the application of statutes should be exempt from judicial review, and (2) to what extent judicial review of administrative findings of fact should be restricted to the question of whether there is substantial supporting evidence in the administrative record.

Unreviewable Administrative Judgment in the Exercise of Statutory Authority

The usual statement of the basic principle of review runs somewhat as follows. As far as action is by law committed to the agency's discretion, administrative action is final and non-reviewable unless discretion was exceeded. In other words, the agency can determine conclusively, within the area committed to its discretion, what action should or should not be taken; the courts can determine solely whether the challenged administrative action is illegal, not whether it is appropriate. An administrative agency derives authority from a statute. The courts, in judicial review of administrative action, enforce limitations which the statute, interpreted in the light of the Constitution, expressly or by implication, imposes on that authority. Within these limitations, the statutes provide for "discretion" — unreviewable administrative choice or judgment in the selection of the appropriate action. "Exceeding the scope of discretion" is the courts' label for a violation of the limits that are least explicit in the statute, limitations which are really read

[6] Davis discusses the variousness and vagueness of the meanings of the term rule of law and warns us against using it loosely in 1 Davis, Administrative Law §1.08 (1958). Surely, it is either useless or harmful to use the concept as a tool for solving questions of judicial review, without first defining it in terms of its purpose.

* Judge Kohji Tanabe indicated at the conference that the Japanese version of trial *de novo* is that described by the German word *Berufung*, a potentially full redoing of the case, including rehearing former witnesses and hearing new ones.

by the courts into the statute in order to achieve what they believe to be the objective of the rule of law—the right balance between private rights and the necessities of government. The courts give different weights, in this balancing process, to different governmental interests and to different private rights.

Nearly all the law concerning administrative discretion is judge-made. Hence, instead of making a futile attempt to draw a clear-cut line between administrative discretion and arbitrary action, I shall discuss court decisions involving different administrative functions, for the courts themselves must draw the line in different places.[7]

Discipline Cases

An outstanding example of a disciplinary action is *Fukuda v. Kyōto Furitsu Ika Daigaku-chō* (President of Kyoto Prefectural Medical University).[8] The plaintiffs, students, were expelled from the university because they had interfered with a faculty meeting of the Women's Professional Department attached to the school. They brought an action in the Kyoto District Court, asking that the disciplinary action be set aside (1) because the plaintiffs were not given an opportunity to be heard before the action was taken and therefore the disciplinary proceeding was unlawful, and (2) because the defendant had no discretionary power to discipline students. The defendant answered that the disciplinary proceeding was lawful and that disciplinary action was committed to his discretion.[9] The District Court held that in a disciplinary proceeding the faculty can decide the method

[7] We should bear in mind that the legislature does not have unlimited power to commit administrative action to agency discretion. Certainly there are, with respect to some constitutional rights at least, minimum requirements of judicial review.

[8] Kyoto District Court, July 19, 1950, 1 GYŌSEI JIKEN SAIBAN REISHŪ (A Collection of Judicial Precedents Concerning Administrative Cases) [hereafter cited GYŌSAI REISHŪ] 764.

[9] Art. 11 of the School Education Law, Law No. 26 of 1947, provides: "Principals and teachers, when they recognize that it is necessary from the standpoint of education, may discipline their students, pupils, and children as prescribed by the supervising government office. Provided, however, that they may not impose corporal punishment."

School Education Law Enforcement Regulations, Ministry of Education Order No. 11 of 1947, art. 13(3) provides that dismissal may be carried out under any one of the following items:

"(i) Persons, recognizable as being of bad character and conduct, for whom there is no prospect of improvement.
(ii) Persons, recognizable as being of inferior scholastic ability, for whom there is no prospect of successful completion.
(iii) Persons habitually absent without a suitable reason.
(iv) Persons who have disturbed the order of the school or otherwise violated their position as a student or pupil."

Art. 34 of the Kyoto Prefectural Medical University College Regulations provides: "The President, upon a resolution adopted at a faculty meeting, is to discipline a person whose act is recognized as contrary to his position as a student. Discipline takes three forms: admonition, suspension, and expulsion."

No statute makes any provision for the method to be adopted by a faculty investigation.

or manner of investigating the facts and that an opportunity to be heard is not required in this proceeding; but the court further held that defendant erroneously had exercised a discretionary power of discipline:

Of course, if there is an act by a student contrary to his position as such, there is nothing to prevent the construction that whether or not this is to be subjected to discipline — i.e., whether or not the disciplinary power will be invoked — is entrusted to their [the school authorities'] free discretion,[10] but in any invocation of disciplinary power it is not enough merely to decide objectively whether the said act is contrary to the position of a student; if it is contrary, the specific circumstances determining which, among these three forms imposed as a discipline, is most appropriate in accordance with the common sense of society, viewed from the educational standpoint, must be weighed precisely and then disposition befitting the said act imposed . . . Therefore, within these fixed limits the president possesses discretionary power and herein only the questions of wrongfulness and impropriety arise, but when he goes beyond the specified limits and selects a heavy class of discipline that is undeserved, we must state that this is illegal discipline, not stopping at the question of wrongfulness and impropriety, which constitutes a mistaken exercise of discretionary power. The disposition of expulsion is subject to legal discretion[11] and if in the selection of expulsion a mistake is made regarding this, its illegality . . . is clear . . .

Hence, since the defendant's disposition of expulsion against the six plaintiffs is illegal, we must uphold the claim of the plaintiffs in this case seeking its annulment.[12]

The Osaka High Court reversed the judgment, saying:

We must state both that where there has been an act by a student meriting discipline, whether or not disciplinary power ought to be invoked should be decided by educators from the educational viewpoint pursuant to their own free discretion, and that where they invoke this discretionary power, whether the act of the student deserves punishment or, again, which among the prescribed disciplinary dispositions ought to be employed are naturally matters that may be determined by the person with disciplinary power in accord with his own free discretion based on the educational viewpoint . . .

However, despite our reference to the free discretion of the person with disciplinary power, this does not mean that the matter is left entirely to his peculiar whims for there are certain built-in limitations and a disposition which has exceeded these limitations becomes illegal . . .

Thus, since we cannot construe that the disposition imposed by the appellant expelling the above five respondents pursuant to article 34 of the College Regula-

[10] In Japan, as in Germany, "absolute" as opposed to "legal discretion" is technically referred to as "free discretion" (*freies Ermessen*). Concerning the distinctions involved see 1 TANAKA, GYŌSEI HŌ (Administrative Law) 154–56 (Yuhikaku Zenshū (Yuhikaku's Complete Collection) ed., 1956); 4 DAVIS, ADMINISTRATIVE LAW §§28.02, 28.16 (1958); DAVIS, ADMINISTRATIVE LAW 847 n. 195 (1951).

[11] See note 10 above.

[12] 1 GYŌSAI REISHŪ at 787–92.

tions for the aforesaid acts . . . in recognition of its necessity from the educational viewpoint, is markedly improper viewed from the common sense of society, we cannot conclude that the disposition expelling the above five respondents is illegal.[13]

This judgment was affirmed by the Supreme Court:

Disciplinary disposition against university students is none other than a self-regulating device recognized in order to maintain internal order within the university as an educational establishment and to achieve educational purposes. In determining whether an act deserves to be disciplined or which disposition ought to be selected from among disciplinary dispositions upon the invocation of discipline against a student's act by a university president with the power to discipline, besides the gravity of the said act it is necessary to take into account various factors such as the character and past conduct of the principal party, the influence of the act on other students, and the impact of the disciplinary disposition on this person and other students as a deterrent, and it is clear that if the determination of these points is not entrusted to the discretion of one, well-versed in conditions within the university and at the immediate center of education, an appropriate result cannot be anticipated. Therefore, it is proper to construe that the determination of whether discipline will be invoked against a student's act or which disposition will be selected from among the disciplinary dispositions — except where it can be recognized that this decision is not in any way founded upon a basis in fact or that it is conspicuously lacking in propriety as conceived by society and exceeds the scope of the discretionary power entrusted to the person with authority to discipline — is left to the discretion of him who has this power. The conclusion reached by the court below that the disposition expelling the appellants is an act within the scope of the discretionary power of the president, the one with the power to discipline, is correct and the argument presented does not merit adoption.[14]

In this case, it is apparent that the courts successively involved considered and weighed the students' interest in retaining their status as such and the university's interest in its educational function. The three courts agreed that a university president has discretionary power to a certain extent. One obvious reason why the courts admitted administrative discretion is that an educator is better qualified than a court to make a choice among several kinds of discipline. Considering the university's educational function, the courts recognized the need for effective and flexible disciplinary action. The courts did not disregard the students' interests, however, in judging whether the university president exceeded his discretion; they sought the right balance between the students' interests and the university's educational function.

[13] Kyōto Furitsu Ika Daigaku-chō v. Fukuda, Osaka High Court, April 30, 1953, 4 GYŌSAI REISHŪ 986, 1005–08.

[14] Fukuda v. Kyōto Furitsu Ika Daigaku Gakuchō, Supreme Court, III Petty Bench, July 30, 1954, 8 SAIKŌ SAIBANSHO MINJI HANREI SHŪ (A Collection of Civil Supreme Court Cases) [hereafter cited as SAI-HAN MINSHŪ] 1501, 1502–03.

It is submitted that the Kyoto District Court attached too much importance to the students' interests in the balancing process. The conclusions of the Osaka High Court and of the Supreme Court seem more reasonable from the viewpoint of common sense.

We should note how the courts used the concept "exceeding the scope of discretion." Although the courts theoretically cannot review administrative action[15] which is committed by law to the discretion of an agency or officer, in practice they do just this. A court usually conducts a trial *de novo* to determine whether the administrative action was excessive from the viewpoint of common sense; if so, the action is held to have surpassed the permissible bounds of discretion. When the court holds that the scope of discretion was exceeded, the administrative action must be set aside; when the court finds the exercise of discretion not excessive, the administrative choice in the employment of lawful authority is upheld.

In another leading case, the Osaka City Police Department Police Personnel Hearing Commission found that Nakatsugawa, a policeman, continued a friendly relationship with the wife of one Hirase despite Hirase's demand that Nakatsugawa give up the friendship; further, knowing that Hirase was a gambler and a swindler, Nakatsugawa lent him money and borrowed clothes from him. Nakatsugawa was dismissed for misconduct[16] and sought judicial relief. The Osaka District Court conducted a trial *de novo* and held that the dismissal exceeded the scope of discretion:

Generally speaking, in dealing with a disciplinary incident, one should begin by making a proper determination objectively as to whether an incident does exist and then based on this determination select a disposition from among the

[15] Technically referred to as "administrative disposition." In Japan "administrative disposition" is used in a sense similar to "agency action" in the United States. See Recourse Law, Law No. 105 of 1890, art. 2; Law for the Special Situation of Litigation in Administrative Cases, Law No. 81 of 1948, art. 1; Administrative Exceptions Review Law, Law No. 160 of 1962, art. 2(1); Administrative Case Litigation Law, Law No. 139 of 1962, art. 3(2); Administrative Procedure Act, §2(g), 60 Stat. 238 (1946), 5 U.S.C. §1002(g) (1952).

[16] Local Public Servants Law, Law No. 261 of 1950, art. 29 provides:

"(1) In a case where an employee comes under any one of the following items, as disciplinary disposition therefor, the disposition of admonition, reduction in pay, suspension, or dismissal may be taken:

(i) Where he has violated this Law or a Law that has prescribed the special cases provided for in article 57, or based thereon an Ordinance, Regulation of a local public body, or Rule prescribed by an organ of a local public body.

(ii) Where he has violated the duties officially required of him or neglected his official duties.

(iii) Where there has been misconduct on his part unworthy of the entire servant body.

(2) The procedure and effect of disciplining an employee shall be prescribed by Ordinance other than where they are specially prescribed by Law." (An English translation of this statute may be found in the OFFICIAL GAZETTE, Dec. 13, 1950, no. 1415, at 1.)

Art. 136 of the Osaka City Police Department Basic Rules provides that the Hearing Commission must endeavor so far as possible during its inquiry to conduct a close and fair investigation.

prescribed disciplinary dispositions appropriate thereto, and if there is a conspicuous lack of propriety in determining the existence of an incident or error in selecting the disposition which results in too heavy a burden, the disposition must be designated illegal. Appropriateness in selecting a disposition should be decided in accordance with the common sense of society after examining such matters as the nature of the incident, its significance, the nature of the duties of the person subject to the disposition, the importance of his status based thereon, his professional history, his performance record, and the extent of his repentance.[17]

Then the court analyzed the facts and concluded:

Regarding incident (1) . . . we are able to recognize respectively that the association of the plaintiff with Matsuko Hirase began in the autumn of 1947 when the plaintiff became acquainted with the husband and wife Masao and Matsuko Hirase, who are not parties to this suit, through Yoshiyatsu Todaka, who is also not party to the suit, that because the plaintiff and the nonlitigant Matsuko Hirase both came from Kagoshima Prefecture they became good friends and moreover this same nonlitigant expressed sympathy for the plaintiff over the circumstance that he was separated from his wife with five children to care for all alone by himself, that over a period the plaintiff visited the nonlitigant Hirases and, during Masao's absence, the nonlitigant Matsuko Hirase a number of times, eating or remaining overnight together with them or her upon occasion, that from these facts the nonlitigant Masao Hirase came to harbor suspicions that an improper sexual relationship existed between the plaintiff and Matsuko and in April 1950 proposed that they sever their association with the plaintiff, and that subsequently, sometime after July 24th of the same year, the plaintiff and the nonlitigant Matsuko Hirase happened to meet by chance at a restaurant in Shin Sekai and dine together, but as luck would have it the nonlitigant Masao Hirase, who had followed Matsuko because of his aforesaid doubts concerning her, spotted them at this place thus deepening his suspicions all the more; and there is no other evidence affecting these findings. Assuming such to be the case, can we say that merely because the nonlitigant Masao Hirase came to distrust his wife's conduct due to the above sort of association, misconduct unbecoming to a police official is present on the part of the plaintiff? Of course, it possibly can be said that in terms of the highest moral standards it is unwise to eat and drink in broad daylight with another man's wife on one's day off. But, is it not true that if we look at this matter as an average man would (even one designated as a "police official" is an average man), we would not be too highly critical? When all is said and done, disciplinary incident (1) in this case was a product of the nonlitigant Masao Hirase's jealousy and the conclusion of the Hearing Commission adopting it as a grounds for discipline in this case, where we are unable to recognize that it was deliberately provoked by the plaintiff, is irrefutably illegal. Regarding incident (2), upon considering . . . the testimony . . . we are able to recognize that in the summer of 1949 the plaintiff lent 6,000 yen to the nonlitigant Matsuko Hirase and borrowed a bathing suit from this same nonlitigant,

[17] Nakatsugawa v. Ōsaka-shi Keishi-chō Keishi Sōkan (Superintendent-General of Police of the Osaka City Police Department), Osaka District Court, May 9, 1952, 3 GYŌSAI REISHŪ 840, 848.

and that similarly, at the end of the same year, he borrowed girl's New Year's clothing from her, but there is not sufficient evidence to recognize that the nonlitigant Masao Hirase is a habitual gambler and swindler . . . because regarding incident (2) as well we cannot conclude that the plaintiff forgot his high-minded position as a police official and that there was an act on his part unbecoming to a police official, we must decree that the ruling by the Hearing Commission in this case, arising from a different view, is illegal.[18]

The Osaka High Court affirmed the judgment.[19] But, in *Ōsaka-fu Keisatsu Hombu-chō* (Chief of the Osaka Prefectural Police Headquarters) *v. Nakatsugawa,*[20] the Supreme Court reversed the judgment:

On the whole, disciplinary disposition against a public servant in an administrative agency is a function of the administrative supervisory power — based on a so-called "special power relationship" [*besonderes Gewaltverhältnis* in German] — for the purpose of preserving order in regard to the services performed by the officials attached, enforcing official discipline, and causing the public servants to perfect the execution of their duties. It is imposed on violations of this person's official duties or other misconduct unbecoming to a public servant, and it is proper to construe that determination as to whether the person with power to discipline should invoke disciplinary disposition or as to which disposition he should select from among the disciplinary dispositions — except where it can be recognized that this disposition is not in any way founded upon a basis in fact or that it is conspicuously lacking in propriety as conceived by society and exceeds the scope of the discretionary power entrusted to the person with authority to discipline — is left to the discretion of the one who has this power.[21]

Then the Court concluded:

Thus, the administrative disposition in this case was performed . . . based on the recommendation of an inquiry commission . . . and since it cannot be called an illegal disposition in excess of the scope of the discretionary power of the person with authority to discipline, the first-instance judgment annulling it as illegal and the judgment in the court below affirming the first-instance decision must be described as clearly contrary to the laws and orders affecting these judgments and neither can escape being quashed; since, as stated above, under the facts established by the judgment below the respondent's claim is without reason, we hereby quash that claim . . .[22]

This case shows that the courts sought, in the same way as in the students' discipline case, the right balance between the private and public interests involved — here, between the policeman's interests and the necessities of

[18] *Ibid.*, at 848–50.

[19] Ōsaka-shi Keisatsu Hombu-chō (Chief of the Osaka City Police Headquarters) v. Nakatsugawa, Osaka High Court, Sept. 2, 1954, 5 Gyōsai Reishū 2169.

[20] Supreme Court, II Petty Bench, May 10, 1957, 11 Sai-han Minshū 699.

[21] *Ibid.*, at 701. At this point the Supreme Court cited Fukuda v. Kyōto Furitsu Ika Daigaku Gakuchō, as in note 13 above, at 1502.

[22] 11 Sai-han Minshū at 701–02.

order in the public service and of enforcement of official discipline. After careful consideration of these interests, the lower courts substituted their own judgment for the administrator's. But the Supreme Court, taking a much more reserved position, refrained from interfering with the executive. In other words, the Supreme Court gave more weight to the governmental interests than to the private interests in this case. The basic idea of the Supreme Court's decision is that, in exercising supervisory power, an administrator may and should consider these interests in determining whether and how to discipline his subordinates, and that a court is no better equipped and qualified to determine the matter than is the administrator. Although the Supreme Court thus substantially restricts judicial review, it does not exempt administrative discretion from all review; administrative discretion can be overturned, but only when the court finds action in excess of discretion.[23] The reasonableness of the decision of the Supreme Court seems problematical, in light of the facts established in the trial *de novo*.

Passport Cases

Article 22 of the Constitution provides:

> Every person shall have freedom to choose and change his residence and to choose his occupation to the extent that it does not interfere with the public welfare.
>
> Freedom of all persons to move to a foreign country and to divest themselves of their nationality shall be inviolate.

Freedom to travel abroad is thus guaranteed as a constitutional right. This freedom, however, has been subjected to some statutory restrictions. Article 13(1) of the Passport Law[24] states:

> The Minister of Foreign Affairs or a consul may refuse to issue a general passport or add further destinations in a case where the person seeking to obtain the issuance of the general passport or the addition of the further destinations comes under any one of the following items . . . (v) Other than those dealt with in each of the prior items, persons for whom there is sufficient suitable reason for the Minister of Foreign Affairs to recognize that there is a danger that they will perform acts which would injure markedly and directly the interests or public safety of Japan.

On the basis of this provision, the Foreign Minister has often refused to issue passports to persons who planned to travel to Communist countries. In several cases dealing with the denial of passports, courts have been faced with questions of constitutional right and of administrative discretion.

[23] The reader will note the similarity of the "in excess of discretion" principle to the American "abuse of discretion" doctrine. On the latter, see 4 DAVIS, ADMINISTRATIVE LAW §28.16 (1958).

[24] Law No. 267 of 1951.

Jiichiro Matsumoto, a former Vice President of the House of Councillors, applied in 1952 for a passport to Communist China. He had received an invitation to the Asian Pacific Area Peace Conference, scheduled to be held in Peking. The Foreign Minister refused to issue a passport on the ground that the applicant's travel to Communist China would "injure markedly and directly the interests of Japan." In an action against the Foreign Minister, Matsumoto contended that his travel would further the interests of Japan.

In *Matsumoto v. Gaimu Daijin* (Minister of Foreign Affairs),[25] the Tokyo District Court held that the issuance and denial of passports are matters within the area of diplomatic policy and that the Foreign Minister's judgment about the effect on "the interests of Japan" is not subject to judicial review:

Japan, in September 1951, concluded a peace treaty with the majority of the former Allied powers, i.e., the United States, the United Kingdom, and the other so-called democratic states, and what is more concluded a Security Treaty with the United States, but no peace treaty has been established between Japan, the Soviet Union, and the minority of other so-called Communist nations nor has intercourse been opened, as will be commented on later, with the government of Communist China. Thus, promotion of friendly relations with the U.S., U.K., and other democratic nations and reliance for the most part on American military power for the country's safety have been set as the supreme aims of the Japanese nation. These are the aims of the present government headed by Premier Yoshida and are based upon facts approved by the National Diet, the highest organ of state power . . .

. . . As far as the courts are concerned, they must respect the aforesaid supreme aims of the Japanese nation, established pursuant to the approval of the Diet, as settled, and then, with this as a premise, consider whether "the interests of Japan" are or are not injured . . .

. . . However, whether or not a passport ought to be issued to the plaintiff is in itself alone a matter not unrelated either to the foreign policy of the state — where these measures will have some impact — or to the country's future course and embraces problems supervised by those responsible for governing the nation. But, the courts do not hold a position of responsibility regarding the administration of the state, particularly foreign policy. It must be recognized that in the taking of evidence by the courts materials for determining various conditions relating to national administration and foreign diplomacy are insufficient at times. Therefore, where a court hands down a judgment on these matters, it must be extremely cautious about overturning a decision rendered by the Minister of Foreign Affairs. Such a decision must be assumed justifiable as long as the determination generally satisfies people, there is no error in the facts upon which it is premised, and the process by which a conclusion is reached from these facts seems a logical one.[26]

[25] Tokyo District Court, Sept. 27, 1952, 3 Gyōsai Reishū 1863.
[26] *Ibid.*, at 1876, 1881.

In another leading case, *Hoashi v. Japan*,[27] Kei Hoashi, former member of the House of Councillors, received an invitation to the International Economic Conference held in Moscow in 1952. He applied for a passport to the Soviet Union, but his application was denied on the ground relied on in the *Matsumoto* case. Hoashi than applied to a court for provisional disposition[28] and, when it was denied, he brought an action for damages. The Tokyo District Court dismissed the action.[29] The Tokyo High Court reached the same conclusion:

As alleged by the appellant, freedom to travel abroad is one of the fundamental human rights guaranteed by article 22 of the Constitution. But this same article also expressly declares that this guarantee hinges on the requirement that it does not interfere with the public welfare. Therefore, since it is clear that the performance of acts which would injure markedly and directly the interests or public safety of Japan after one has travelled abroad is an interference with the public welfare, the provisions of article 13, paragraph (1), item (v), of the Passport Law, which, in order to restrict the travel of those persons for whom there is sufficient suitable reason to recognize that there is a danger that they will perform such acts, have provided that issuance of a general passport or addition of further destinations may be refused, do not strike us as unconstitutional legislation . . . thus, we should not forthwith treat the disposition of the Minister of Foreign Affairs refusing to issue a passport in this case as illegal, and, excepting the situation where the Foreign Minister's refusal to issue a passport is arbitrary, so long as there is neither serious error in his understanding of the facts upon which his decision is premised nor marked irrationality in the reasoning processes by which he reached his conclusion, we as a court must respect his decision where it is based on his own judgment and convictions. Here must be drawn the boundary line for what can be determined in court. The courts must not, for reasons of propriety or impropriety, unnecessarily interfere with the Foreign Minister's exercise of authority within his sphere of responsibility.[30]

The Supreme Court affirmed the decision:

Under the factual relationships recognized in the decision below — particularly the international situation with which our nation was confronted under occupation rule — it was determined that there was a danger that participation in the Moscow International Conference would injure markedly and directly the interests or public safety of Japan; here too, in this Court as well, we are able to agree with the judgment handed down in the decision below to the effect that the Foreign Minister's disposition refusing to issue a passport could not be called illegal.[31]

[27] Supreme Court, Grand Bench, Sept. 10, 1958, 12 SAI-HAN MINSHŪ 1969.

[28] Hoashi v. Gaimu Daijin (Minister of Foreign Affairs), Tokyo District Court, March 24, 1952, 3 GYŌSAI REISHŪ 415, *protest rejected sub nom.* Hoashi v. Japan, Tokyo High Court, March 27, 1952, 3 GYŌSAI REISHŪ 418.

[29] Hoashi v. Japan, Tokyo District Court, n.d., 12 SAI-HAN MINSHŪ 1983.

[30] Hoashi v. Japan, Tokyo High Court, Sept. 15, 1954, 12 SAI-HAN MINSHŪ 1995–96.

[31] 12 SAI-HAN MINSHŪ at 1971–72.

Although freedom to move to a foreign country is guaranteed by the Constitution, this freedom is subject to the restrictions imposed by the Passport Law, and in practice the Foreign Minister exercises his authority to issue or deny passports so as to control travel abroad. As a matter of fact, a passport is not merely a travel document which establishes the identity and the nationality of the traveler, but also a document which represents governmental permission for departure from and re-entry into Japan. Despite this, the courts have hesitated to interfere and have tended to accept the Foreign Minister's exercise of power almost as uncontrollable. But, it is submitted, the case law should be reconsidered, lest freedom of movement be destroyed by recognition of the Foreign Minister's unbridled discretion.

In dealing with this question, the Tokyo District Court took a more positive attitude in 1960. In 1956, Kenji Miyamoto, Communist leader and novelist, and three other writers received invitations from the Chinese People's Foreign Cultural Association and the Chinese Writers' Association to visit Communist China. The Foreign Minister issued passports to two of the writers but denied Miyamoto's and one other's application, relying on the *Matsumoto* and *Hoashi* cases. In *Miyamoto v. Gaimu Daijin* (Minister of Foreign Affairs),[32] the Tokyo District Court set aside the decision of the Foreign Minister:

Freedom to travel abroad involves a fundamental human right of the people guaranteed in the Constitution. Since the provisions of article 13, paragraph (1), item (v), of the Passport Law should be interpreted as an exception restricting freedom of travel and prescribing that issuance of a passport can be refused only in the instance where, from the standpoint of maintaining the public welfare in terms of the nature of the trip, there is a danger that due to the travel of the passport applicant the interests or public safety of our country will be markedly and directly injured, an interpretation that a trip directly infringes our national interests in the aforesaid provisions merely because the destination is a country which has not yet re-established diplomatic relations with our country must be described, considered from the process of the enactment of the above provisions and their operation, as a far too broad construction, resulting in actually denying the people's freedom of travel, which we feel cannot be permitted. Therefore, in construing these rules we must interpret them as requiring an adequate concrete examination and review of what sort of influence the international and domestic situation in which our country is currently placed and the said applicant's trip have on our national interests . . .

Pursuant to the above recognized facts, unavoidably we come to the conclusion that the defendant in refusing the plaintiff's and Nakano's passport applications attached significance to the point that these persons, unlike the others, Honda and Usui, who applied at the same time for the same purpose, are both members of the Communist Party of Japan, and, as recognized above, the defendant's

[32] Tokyo District Court, April 28, 1960, 11 GYŌSAI REISHŪ 1217.

indication that he intends to authorize concurrently the issuance of passports to Honda and Usui shows that he himself does not believe that a trip to China in general would markedly and directly injure our national interests . . .

. . . As explained above, the defendant's disposition refusing to issue a passport here must be characterized, in this case where the presence of a suitable reason cannot otherwise be found, as an illegal disposition improperly usurping one's freedom to travel abroad: an action which cannot escape being overruled.[33]

The basic proposition of the *Miyamoto* case is that freedom of movement is one of the fundamental liberties of the people, of which an applicant for a passport cannot be deprived solely because of his beliefs, associations, or the ideology to which he adheres. It is arguable that this position is more consonant with the principles of the Constitution and the literal meaning of the provisions of the Passport Law than is the position taken in the *Matsumoto* and *Hoashi* cases. But the *Miyamoto* case is not the leading case. Presumably the Supreme Court will continue to adhere to the view it adopted in the *Hoashi* case, that the Foreign Minister has a much broader discretion.

If international tension should become more acute, it seems likely that the Foreign Minister would stretch to its fullest extent the authority to deny passports as a means to prevent people from traveling to certain countries and to prevent leftists from traveling abroad; and the courts probably would not check the minister's actions. If international tension lessens, restrictions on freedom of movement are likely to be relaxed, and there may be no more court decisions involving them.

It is submitted, however, that the Foreign Minister's discretion to issue or deny passports should not be completely unchecked. The discretionary theory of passport authority adopted in the *Matsumoto* and *Hoashi* cases gives more weight to the executive's interests and the Foreign Minister's expertness than the preservation of effective government requires, and it gives too little weight to the interests of individuals in freedom of movement. The courts should have greater regard for constitutional liberty and should infer from it greater limitations upon the statutory grant of power to the Foreign Minister.[34]

In Japan, as compared with the United States, there is far less interest in procedural safeguards. This is true not only of the courts but also of the legislature, of administrators, and even of lawyers. The Passport Law provides merely that, when a passport is denied, the applicant must be notified and that he may then appeal to the Foreign Minister. These safeguards are quite nominal, and serious defects are left uncured. The Passport Law fails to assure an applicant a hearing of any kind. The administrative reasons

[33] *Ibid.*, at 1235–38.

[34] Cf. the attitude of the United States Supreme Court in a similar situation but without the explicit constitutional provisions, in Kent v. Dulles, 357 U.S. 116 (1958).

for denial of a passport are not stated with any specificity. There is no provision for separation of functions in the Foreign Ministry. It is curious that the lack of a fair procedure has never been challenged in any case and never criticized by any scholar. In light of this serious deficiency in procedural safeguards, judicial decisions that the Foreign Minister has almost unbridled discretion could give a fatal blow to freedom of movement.

Cases Involving Special Permission to Stay in Japan

Any alien who has entered Japan illegally may be deported in accordance with the procedure prescribed in the Emigration and Immigration Control Order.[35] Unlike the Passport Law, this order prescribes a rather fair procedure. An alien who has been notified of an unfavorable decision, which is made, after a hearing, by a special hearing officer, may file an objection with the Minister of Justice.[36] Article 50, paragraph (1), of the Emigration and Immigration Control Order provides:

> The Minister of Justice, even where he recognizes that the motion of objection to the determination of paragraph (3) of the prior article is without reason, may, if the said suspect comes under any one of the following items, specially approve this person's stay . . . (iii) When the Minister of Justice otherwise recognizes circumstances for which his stay ought to be specially approved.

This provision has been construed by courts to give discretionary power to the Minister of Justice. In several cases a question arose as to the extent of his discretion.

Ko Lin-mai v. Tōkyō Nyūkoku Kanri Kyoku Shunin Shinsakan (Chief Inspector of the Tokyo Immigration Control Bureau) is an interesting case.[37] The plaintiffs, natives of Taiwan, entered Japan in 1952 and thereafter lived with their son and brother, permanent residents of Japan. In 1954 defendant issued an order for their deportation after the relief they had sought by filing a motion of objection with the Minister of Justice had been denied. They brought an action in the Tokyo District Court for annulment of the deportation order, relying upon evidence they had given that deportation would jeopardize their lives. The court held that the deportation order had been issued illegally and set it aside:

> Thus, when we consider the provisions of article 50 of the Control Order and article 35 of the Order's Enforcement Regulations together, the Minister of

[35] Cabinet Order No. 319 of 1951.

[36] When an immigration guard officer detains a suspect after investigation, an immigration inspector is to review the matter promptly. If the immigration inspector finds that the suspect entered Japan in violation of the Order, he must immediately give the suspect notice in writing of his findings, a statement of the grounds therefor, and notice of the right to a hearing. An oral hearing before a special hearing officer is guaranteed to every suspect. If the special officer finds that there is no mistake in the finding, the suspect may file an objection with the Minister of Justice. *Ibid.*, at arts. 47(2)–(3), 48–49.

[37] Tokyo District Court, April 25, 1957, 8 Gyōsai Reishū 754.

Justice, upon issuing a determination on a motion of objection, possesses discretionary authority to decide whether or not a special approval of stay should be granted. Accordingly, the above determination must be rendered not only in regard to the propriety of the special hearing officer's decision alone, but also after deliberating the point whether a special stay should be approved. Since it is proper to construe that this discretionary authority was bestowed upon the Minister of Justice from the viewpoint of its appropriateness to such purposes as administrative convenience and the fair control of emigration and immigration provided for in article 1 of the Control Order, aliens entering or leaving Japan have a corresponding legal interest, and where the Minister of Justice departs from the scope of his authority and renders a determination that is conspicuously unfair and lacking in propriety, we must conclude that his disposition issuing a written deportation order based thereon is illegal and that its annulment may be sought . . .

. . . Nevertheless, the declaration in the second paragraph of the preamble to our Constitution that all people have the right to live in peace, free from fear and want, must be regarded applicable per se to aliens visiting our country. Therefore, where it is clear that by deporting persons who at present continue to live peaceably in Japan the lives of such persons would be immediately placed in jeopardy, it is proper to assume that even though such persons' presence is illegal, because they have ceased to possess immigration status, deportation in response thereto cannot be permitted.

Consequently, in this case where the aforesaid findings exist regarding the plaintiffs, it must be recognized that the determination on the plaintiffs' motion of objection, confirming the propriety of the deportation and stating that their motion of objection is without reason, is a measure which is conspicuously unfair and lacking in propriety.[38]

The basic rationale of the Tokyo District Court in this decision is this: article 50 does not confer absolute discretion upon the Minister of Justice; the courts must determine the extent of the discretion conferred upon him by interpreting article 50 in the light of its objective; the courts should decide, by relating this objective to the special circumstances of each case, whether he has exceeded his discretion; and when administrative action not essential to the attainment of its proper objective infringes seriously on a fundamental right, the administrative action is unlawful and should be set aside. The court wisely avoided the concept of grace (privilege) that too often leads courts to uphold the administrative action as a matter of course, without making any attempt to achieve the right balance between private interests and governmental interests.[39]

The Tokyo High Court, however, reversed on the grounds, first, that the Minister of Justice has discretionary power and, second, that a foreigner has no right to stay in Japan:

[38] *Ibid.*, at 762–66.

[39] Cf. Jay v. Boyd, 351 U.S. 345, 354 (1956), construing a similar statute to be a matter of grace and within the absolute discretion of the sovereign.

when we consider that it is accepted customary international law that so long as a special treaty does not exist approval of the entry of aliens into a country and their stay therein is entrusted to the free discretion of the state concerned (see Supreme Court [A] No. 3594 of 1954, decided June 19, 1957[40]), it is proper to construe that the special approval of stay, premised on the suspect's meeting certain specified conditions, is left to the discretion of the Minister of Justice as freely exercised by him . . . Of course, there are certain built-in limitations in free discretion and, needless to say, the unbridled exercise of free discretion through arbitrary decisions cannot be permitted, but when the Minister of Justice has seen fit, within his sphere of responsibility, to rule that one's stay cannot be specially approved, that ruling should be respected. Particularly, when we take into account that those suspects specified in article 50 of the Order are persons already ordered to be deported who have no other course open to them and that the special approval of their stay is, so to speak, a matter of grace, not right, vain discussion as to the merits of the Minister of Justice's discretionary judgment on this point constitutes an unwarranted interference with executive power that ought not to be performed by the courts.[41]

The Tokyo High Court seems to have reached its decision by characterizing the special permission sought as "a matter of grace"; the court in effect adopted the privilege doctrine of American law without regard to its limitations. According to this holding, the Minister of Justice has absolute discretion. It is submitted that if the court had subjected the privilege doctrine to a critical analysis, it would have concluded that its application is often unsound[42] and would have affirmed the decision of the Tokyo District Court, approving its approach and the balance it struck between the private and public interests involved in the case.

Liu Sun-chin v. Ōsaka Nyūkoku Kanri Jimusho Shunin Shinsakan (Chief Inspector of the Osaka Immigration Control Office)[43] is another interesting

[40] The case referred to is Lin Jung-kai v. Japan, Supreme Court, Grand Bench, June 19, 1957, 11 SAIKŌ SAIBANSHO KEIJI HANREI SHŪ (A Collection of Criminal Supreme Court Cases) [hereafter cited SAI-HAN KEISHŪ] 1663. Appellant, a native of China, entered Japan illegally in 1951 and was indicted for violation of the Alien Registration Order, Imperial Order No. 207 of 1947, art. 3 (translated into English in OFFICIAL GAZETTE, May 2, 1947, extra ed. at 2), which forbade an alien to enter Japan without permission from SCAP. Appellant was found guilty as charged and was sentenced to imprisonment for six months. The judgment was affirmed by the Tokyo High Court. Seeking revision in the Supreme Court, appellant contended that the order was invalid under art. 22 of the Constitution. The Supreme Court held: "it must be said that article 22 of the Constitution makes no provision concerning the entry of aliens into Japan, and the matter can be interpreted to be the same as the notion under customary international law that approval of the entry of aliens into a country may be determined in accordance with the free discretion of the nation concerned and that no state, as long as a special treaty does not exist, bears a duty to approve alien entry. Therefore, we have to state that the purport of the argument alleging the unconstitutionality of the provisions of the aforesaid Alien Registration Order is without reason." 11 SAI-HAN KEISHŪ at 1664–65.

[41] Tōkyō Nyūkoku Kanri Jimusho Shunin Shinsakan (Chief Inspector of the Tokyo Immigration Control Office) v. Ko Lin-mai, Tokyo High Court, Oct. 31, 1957, 8 GYŌSAI REISHŪ 1903, 1907.

[42] See 1 DAVIS, ADMINISTRATIVE LAW §§7.11–7.19 (1958).

[43] Osaka District Court, Oct. 16, 1957, 8 GYŌSAI REISHŪ 1900.

case. Since 1953, Liu had lived in Japan with governmental permission to reside there for a temporary period; he had married a Japanese woman and had had two children. In 1957, his deportation was ordered because his application for renewal had been denied. Because one of Liu's children suffered from polio and was under medical treatment, permission was given to Liu's wife to stay in Japan until 1959. Liu sought suspension of enforcement of the order for his deportation, alleging that, if the order were enforced, he would be placed in jeopardy of his life directly after his deportation; that his sick child, two years old, would not be able to get medical treatment; and that his wife and children would be in distress for lack of support. The Osaka District Court coldly denied the interim relief sought, on the grounds that no foreigner has a right to get permission to stay in Japan and that the power to grant such permission is committed to agency discretion.[44]

Clearly this court fell into the simple conceptualism of the privilege doctrine, disregarding human rights by refusing to read into article 50 of the Order limitations on the extent of the discretionary power it confers upon the Minister of Justice. On appeal from the decision, the Osaka High Court reversed and ordered suspension of enforcement of the deportation order:

> even if the above discretionary authority of the Minister of Justice is construed to be a disposition under free discretion, naturally this free discretion is subject to the rational restrictions of the administrative purpose involved, and when an exercise of discretionary judgment disregards the purpose for which the discretionary disposition was recognized and is conspicuously lacking in fairness, it is, of course, not only a wrongful act, but one subject to suit for annulment as an illegal act.[45]

In this case the court thus developed the theory of judicial review along the line taken by the Tokyo District Court in the *Ko Lin-mai* case.

These deportation cases show that the Tokyo and Osaka High Courts differ about the extent of the discretion vested in the Minister of Justice by article 50 of the Emigration and Immigration Control Order, a question that is still unsettled. The courts agreed that the minister has discretion to give or deny special approval of stay; their opinions differed on the question whether the minister's discretion is unbridled or not. The approach taken by the Tokyo District Court in the first case and by the Osaka High Court in the second is a valuable contribution to the development of the theory of judicial review in this field; it is to be hoped that the Supreme Court will follow suit.

[44] *Ibid.*, at 1902.

[45] Liu Sun-chin v. Ōsaka Nyūkoku Kanri Jimusho Shunin Shinsakan (Chief Inspector of the Osaka Immigration Control Office), Osaka High Court, Dec. 12, 1957, 8 GYŌSAI REISHŪ 2281, 2283.

Cases Involving Denial of a Permit to Demonstrate

Article 21 of the Constitution provides: "Freedom of assembly and association as well as speech, press and all other forms of expression are guaranteed." Several interesting cases deal with the denial of an application for a permit to hold a meeting in a public park.

Anyone who desires to hold an assembly or a demonstration at any "national public park" is required, under article 4 of the National Public Park Control Regulations,[46] to get a permit from the Minister of Welfare. The Japanese General Council of Labor Unions (Sōhyō) applied to the minister for permission to hold an assembly at the Imperial Palace Plaza, such a park, on May Day, 1952. The Minister of Welfare refused the permission, and the General Council of Labor Unions sought judicial relief. The minister contended that his refusal was unreviewable because he had discretionary power to give or deny permission and also that the park would be considerably damaged by the hours-long demonstration of a tremendous crowd of people (estimated at half a million). In *Nihon Rōdō Kumiai Sō-hyōgikai* (Japanese General Council of Labor Unions) *v. Kōsei Daijin* (Minister of Welfare),[47] the Tokyo District Court held that the minister's denial of permission was unlawful and set it aside:

The disposition of approval or disapproval by the Minister of Welfare under article 4 of the National Public Park Control Regulations purports to be no more, as related above, than an imposition of controls on the use of national public parks for the purpose of the Minister of Welfare preventing, from the standpoint of national public parks, the creation of impediments to their preservation and supervision. The provisions of article 4 of these Regulations cannot escape being unconstitutional and void if we assume that they grant authority in excess of this to the Minister of Welfare. Therefore, the Minister of Welfare is not to consider maintenance of public safety and other such purposes of state, but instead only may examine whether use ought to be permitted wholly in the light of the essential purpose of national public park facilities, or whether it ought not to be permitted because there is a danger of impairing the function of national public parks.[48]

The Court concluded:

As touched upon above, utilization of the Imperial Palace Plaza for assembly and parade en masse does not conflict with the Plaza's intrinsic character of being "devoted to public use," and must be permitted so long as it does not impair the function of the park . . . Thus considered, the disposition of disapproval in this case, as made clear in our explanation up to this point, erred in the application of the National Public Park Control Regulations and is, in turn,

[46] Ministry of Welfare Order No. 19 of 1949, translated into English in OFFICIAL GAZETTE, May 31, 1949, no. 948, at 7.

[47] Tokyo District Court, April 28, 1952, 3 GYŌSAI REISHŪ 634.

[48] *Ibid.*, at 639.

quite illegal, for it violates the provisions of article 21 of the Constitution which guarantee freedom of assembly, etc.[49]

The Tokyo High Court reversed the decision on the ground that the Japanese General Council of Labor Unions no longer had a legal interest in the case because May Day of 1952 had already come and gone.[50] The Supreme Court affirmed the decision and, in obiter dicta, remarked:

Again, the power to administer national property adheres in the head of each ministry and agency . . . and the manner and the extent to which property employed in the public welfare is to be utilized for the people comprises this power, but of course approval of this utilization, so long as the utilization complies with the property's purpose devoted to public use, is not such that it falls within the mere free discretion of the administrator; the administrator should, in accord with the nature of the said property and taking into account its scale and equipment, exercise his power to administer property in such a way as to adequately accomplish its mission as property employed in the public welfare, and we must conclude that if he errs in this exercise, he cannot escape illegality, for he has interfered with the people's utilization . . . the Minister of Welfare, standing in the position of one who is attempting to accomplish the public park's mission as such, made his disapproval disposition after adequately considering the sundry points to be taken into account in applying article 4 of the National Public Park Control Regulations and by no means depended upon mere free discretion; nor are we able to perceive that he erred in the proper application of his power to administer.[51]

When constitutional rights such as freedom of assembly are involved, the case law shows that the courts are reluctant to concede the existence of unreviewable administrative discretion. Their reason obviously is that they believe the placing of restrictions on the exercise of fundamental human rights should be committed to administrative discretion only in very exceptional cases; hence, they interpret the statutes involved in the light of the relevant constitutional provision and find implied limits on the authority conferred that closely confine administrative choice or judgment.[52]

Conclusions About the Cases

These cases concerning administrative discretion show that the courts enforce limitations that they believe the statute expressly or implicitly imposes on the administrative authority. Within these limitations, the courts concede

[49] *Ibid.*, at 648.

[50] Kōsei Daijin (Minister of Welfare) v. Nihon Rōdō Kumiai Sō-hyōgikai (Japanese General Council of Labor Unions), Tokyo High Court, Nov. 15, 1952, 3 GYŌSAI REISHŪ 2366.

[51] Nihon Rōdō Kumiai Sō-hyōgikai (Japanese General Council of Labor Unions) v. Kōsei Daijin (Minister of Welfare), Supreme Court, Grand Bench, Dec. 23, 1953, 4 GYŌSAI REISHŪ 3288, at 3292–94.

[52] However, because of the present unavoidable delays in litigation, in practice judicial relief is almost never available for one who is denied a permit to hold a demonstration in a public park; judicial review is denied on the ground that the passing of the date sought for the assembly has made the action moot. Until a more expeditious procedure is devised, the theoretical right to judicial review will be of little avail.

the existence of unreviewable choice or judgment in the application of statutes. The proposition can be expressed in a formula: administrative discretion can be overturned only when the court finds administrative action in excess of, and therefore in abuse of, the discretion contemplated by the statutes. This theory may, in the abstract, well be beyond challenge, but we should bear in mind that its thoughtless application can deprive individuals of judicial remedies. The courts should not rely on this theory to facilitate refusal of judicial review; they should critically examine the statutory language and meaning and seek the right balance between private rights and the necessities of government.

It should be borne in mind that in Japan courts usually have no concern for the procedural basis of the challenged administrative action, except when statutes provide explicitly for fair procedure. It is submitted that, even though statutes authorize administrative functions without expressly requiring procedural safeguards for the individuals affected, administrative discretion ought to be exercised only after fair procedure, as far as that is possible.

Judicial Review of Administrative Findings of Fact

Although Japan has adopted the principle of review of administrative action by the judicial courts from America, the Japanese law governing the scope of review of administrative findings of fact is extremely different from American law. In the United States, as Davis has written, "The debate of the 1930's over scope of review was largely between those who wanted broad review or even de novo review and those who wanted narrow review or even no review; the extremists, however, moved from both ends toward the middle,"[53] and now "nearly all judicial review of evidence in the federal courts and most of it in the state courts is governed by the substantial-evidence rule."[54] In Japan, however, judicial review generally proceeds by trial *de novo,* and this is true even when the administrative findings of fact were made by experts and were based on evidence adduced at a hearing and set forth in a record available to the reviewing court.

A few statutes do provide for the substantial-evidence rule. At first, Japanese lawyers had very little idea what kind of review these statutes called for. The courts, however, tried to avail themselves of American experience and gradually developed case law. Judicial interpretation of these few statutory provisions, though still somewhat confused and uncertain, has brought into being a method of judicial review that approximates the usual American method. But, unless a statute expressly enacts the substantial-evidence rule, the courts conduct trials *de novo* and do not restrict the scope of review.

Needless to say, trial *de novo* is the only kind of judicial review feasible if an administrative finding of fact was not made on the basis of evidence

[53] 4 Davis, Administrative Law §29.01 at 116 (1958).
[54] *Ibid.,* §29.11 at 186.

adduced at a hearing and set forth in a record available to the reviewing court. In this section, therefore, I shall discuss only judicial review of administrative findings of fact which were thus made after a trial-like hearing.

The limitation imposed on judicial review in the few statutes that provide for the substantial-evidence rule has been attacked as an unconstitutional restriction on judicial power. According to traditional theory of the judicial power, courts must find the facts as well as apply the law to the facts. Therefore, a statutory provision that, for instance, "facts found by the Fair Trade Commission are binding upon the court when there exists substantial evidence proving them,"[55] is regarded by some scholars as an invalid restriction. The prevailing view is to the contrary, however, most scholars being inclined to follow American case law.

Views in the two countries diverge greatly as to the area to which the substantial-evidence rule ought to apply. When highly technical matters are involved, the courts are not as well qualified to determine disputed questions of fact as are expert administrative agencies, and it may be wise to delegate to the latter the initial determination of such questions, with only limited judicial review. The courts, however, are certainly qualified to determine questions of fact not involving these specialized matters. The legislature's adoption in statutes of the substantial-evidence rule, and judicial acceptance thereof, are mainly based on this recognition of "the comparative qualification of the agency and of the court to decide the particular issue."[56] Another justification for the adoption of the substantial-evidence rule is that it conserves time and money from the point of view of both courts and litigants.

In determining what kind of administrative procedure and what kind of judicial review should be adopted, the legislature should seek the right balance between governmental interests and private interests. Theoretically, the courts may and should consider these matters independently of legislative determinations. The case law shows, however, that Japanese courts adopt the substantial-evidence rule only when directed to do so by an explicit statutory provision.

Interpretation of Statutory Provisions Adopting the Substantial-Evidence Rule

Article 80 of the Law Concerning the Prohibition of Private Monopoly and the Maintenance of Fair Trade (hereafter called the Antimonopoly Law) provides:

[55] Art. 80(1) of the Law Concerning the Prohibition of Private Monopoly and the Maintenance of Fair Trade, Law No. 54 of 1947. An English translation may be found in 2 EHS LAW BULLETIN SERIES KA 1 (Nakane ed. and trans., 1960).

[56] Davis' expression, "the comparative qualifications of courts and of agencies," is surely a useful guide in this matter. 4 DAVIS, ADMINISTRATIVE LAW §30.08 at 240; see also §30.14 at 269 (1958).

In regard to a suit provided for in article 77, paragraph (1), facts found by the Fair Trade Commission are binding upon the court when there exists substantial evidence proving them.

The existence or not of the substantial evidence provided for in the prior paragraph is to be determined by the court.[57]

The procedure to be followed by the Fair Trade Commission is fully prescribed in the Antimonopoly Law and in the Regulations Concerning Inquiry and Hearing by the Fair Trade Commission;[58] the provisions dealing with investigations and subsequent proceedings are set forth in the margin,[59]

[57] For similar provisions, see art. 99 of the Radio Law, Law No. 131 of 1950, and art. 52 of the Law to Establish the Land Adjustment Commission, Law No. 292 of 1950.

[58] Fair Trade Commission Regulation No. 5 of 1953.

[59] The citations "art. 46," "art. 47," etc., in this note refer to provisions of the Antimonopoly Law. Art. 46 (Compulsory Disposition for the Purpose of Investigation) provides:

"(1) The Fair Trade Commission, in order to conduct a necessary investigation regarding a case, may carry out a disposition dealt with in any one of the following items:

(i) Ordering the appearance of parties concerned with the case or participants therein, questioning them, and collecting opinions or reports from these persons.
(ii) Ordering the appearance of experts and causing them to give their expert opinion.
(iii) Ordering the custodian of accounting books, documents or other physical things to produce the said thing and retaining physical things so produced.
(iv) Conducting an on the spot inspection of the place of operations or other necessary places of the parties concerned with the case, and examining the condition of their activities and property, accounting books and documents, and other physical things.

(2) The Fair Trade Commission, when it recognizes that it is proper to do so may, as prescribed by Order, designate a staff member of the Fair Trade Commission as investigating officer and cause him to carry out the dispositions of the prior paragraph.
(3) In a case where a staff member is required to conduct an on the spot inspection or an examination pursuant to the provisions of the prior paragraph, he shall carry with him an identification card."

Art. 47 (Preparation of a Protocol) provides: "The Fair Trade Commission, when it has conducted a necessary investigation regarding a case, shall enter the gist thereof in a protocol and, when, in particular, there has been a disposition provided for in the prior article, clearly put down the results thereof."

Art. 50 (Matters to Be Entered in a Written Ruling Instituting Adjudication) provides in part: "(2) Adjudication procedure is instituted upon service of a transcript of the written ruling instituting adjudication on the person who committed the said act of infraction (hereafter referred to as the "respondent") as provided for in article 48, paragraph (1)."

Art. 51 (Submission of a Written Answer) provides: "The respondent, when he receives service of the written ruling instituting adjudication, shall, without delay, submit to the Fair Trade Commission a written answer in response thereto."

Art. 52 (The Respondent's Right to Present a Defense and His Representative) provides in part: "(1) The respondent or his representative may at the hearing express reasons why measures ordered regarding the said case by the Fair Trade Commission pursuant to the provisions of article 7, 8-2, 17-2 or 20 are improper and submit materials proving this; request the Fair Trade Commission to question essential participants, to order experts to give their expert opinion, to order the custodian of accounting books, documents, or other physical things to produce the said thing, or to conduct an on the spot investigation of a necessary place and examine the condition of activities and property, accounting books and documents, and other physical things; or question participants or experts ordered by the Fair Trade Commission to appear."

as are the articles of the Antimonopoly Law that provide for the transmission to the reviewing court of the administrative record and for remands to the commission for the reception of new evidence.[60] The Radio Law and the Law to Establish the Land Adjustment Commission prescribe much simpler but substantially similar procedures to implement their adoption of the substantial-evidence rule.

The first case involving interpretation of this statutory provision was *Nihon Shuppan Kyōkai* (Japan Publishing Association) *v. Kōsei Torihiki Iinkai* (Fair Trade Commission).[61] Article 5(1) of the Businessmen Organization Law[62] provided in part:

Art. 53 (Open Hearings and the Stenographic Record Thereof):

"(1) The hearings shall be public. Provided, however, that if it is recognized that it is necessary in order to protect the business secrets of the businessman or if it is recognized that it is necessary in the public interest, they need not be public.
(2) A stenographer shall be present during the hearings and record the testimony." [Art. 60 of the Regulations Concerning Inquiry and Hearing by the Fair Trade Commission provides as follows: "(1) The Commission or trial examiner, when it or he perceives the necessity, may take evidence other than at a hearing session. In this case the investigating officer and the respondent shall be accorded an opportunity to be present. (2) The Commission or trial examiner, when it or he has carried out the taking of evidence in the prior paragraph, shall prepare a protocol. In the protocol shall be entered the results of the taking of evidence and other necessary matters, the staff member conducting hearing affairs shall add his signature and seal, and the Chairman of the Commission or the trial examiner shall affix his seal of approval. (3) The protocol of the prior paragraph shall be exhibited at a hearing session."]

Art. 57 (Form of the Written Decision):

"(1) The decision shall be rendered in writing, the facts found and the Laws and Orders applied in regard thereto by the Fair Trade Commission shall be indicated in the written decision, and the Chairman of the Commission and Commissioners present in the collegiate body shall affix their signatures and seals.
(2) A minority opinion may be appended to the written decision."

[60] Art. 78 (Transmission of the Case Records) provides: "When an action is brought, the court shall, without delay, request the Fair Trade Commission to transmit the records of the said case (including the protocol of the interrogation of the parties concerned with the case, participants or experts, the stenographic record, and all other items that might constitute evidence on trial in court)."

Art. 81 (Offers of New Evidence and Remand) provides:

"(1) A party may, only in cases coming under any one of the following items, offer to the court new evidence which is related to the said case:

(i) Where, without suitable reason, the Fair Trade Commission did not accept the said evidence.
(ii) Where the said evidence could not be submitted at the hearing of the Fair Trade Commission and moreover there was no negligence in this non-submission.

(2) In a case dealt with in any item of the prior paragraph, the party shall make clear the cause thereof.
(3) The court, when it perceives the necessity of examining new evidence pursuant to the provisions of paragraph (1), shall remand the said case to the Fair Trade Commission and order it to take appropriate measures after examining the said evidence."

[61] Tokyo High Court, Aug. 29, 1953, 4 GYŌSAI REISHŪ 1898.

[62] Law No. 191 of 1948, translated into English in OFFICIAL GAZETTE, July 29, 1948, no. 698, at 5. "Businessmen organization" is the Japanese term for trade association.

A businessmen organization shall not perform an act coming under any one of the following items:

> (i) Controlling or attempting to control production or distribution through the allocation of raw materials or orders or any other means, and preparing for the government or submitting to it a plan or program concerning the allocation of raw materials, merchandise, or facilities.[63]

The commission found that the Japan Publishing Association had made plans, for the government, for the allocation of paper and submitted them to the government:

> The facts in the aforementioned 1. are undisputed and recognized by the respondent; the facts of 2. are clear in the light of the results of this Commission's investigation and the respective testimony of the participants Ichiro Haneba, Isamu Kobayashi, Taro Mimasaka, Hideo Shinoda, Tsunetaro Kinoshita, and Sotaro Tsuchiya. Again, the facts of 3. can be recognized from the results of this Commission's investigation and the respective testimony of the participants Tsunetaro Kinoshita, Sotaro Tsuchiya, Tadashi Takayama, Ayao Amamiya, Hideo Shinoda, Hidekazu Kuzuhara, and Shigenori Yoshihara, and the facts of 4. too can be recognized from the results of this Commission's investigation and the respective testimony of the participants Sotaro Tsuchiya and Tadashi Takayama.[64]

The association was ordered to cease and desist from controlling paper allocation by any method.

A suit challenging the order was instituted in the Tokyo High Court; the association contended that the commission's decision was not supported by "substantial evidence." The association argued, among other things, (1) that the substantial-evidence rule requires that the record must contain some reliable evidence supporting the commission's finding of facts, that the record must not contain any credible contradictory evidence, and that the record must show that the plaintiff was afforded an opportunity to present such contradictory evidence in the proceeding before the commission; and (2) that these three requirements of the substantial-evidence rule had not been satisfied.[65]

The Tokyo High Court dismissed the action:

[63] This provision was later altered extensively by Law No. 291 of 1952. In turn the entire Businessmen Organization Law was repealed by Law No. 259 of 1953.

[64] Nihon Shuppan Kyōkai (Japan Publishing Association), Fair Trade Commission, May 9, 1950, 1949 (Han) No. 5, 4 GYŌSAI REISHŪ 1932, 1936. Note that this vague statement did not make clear upon what evidence obtained in its investigation the commission had relied. Later the commission changed its practice. At present, the commission specifies in its decisions all the items of evidence on which it relies in support of its findings.

[65] The association did not present this argument very clearly. It made no assertion that the commission had denied it an opportunity to present evidence. The whole argument may sound strange to American lawyers. But the substantial-evidence rule was unknown in prewar Japan; it was introduced in the occupation era entirely on the initiative of SCAP. Inevitably, Japanese lawyers had little idea what the substantial-evidence rule meant.

Upon reflection it is hardly necessary to mention that it is essential that substantial evidence exist in regard to the facts found by the decision, but there is no reason always to limit such evidence only to that which can be found in the records after the institution of the said case's adjudication procedure; it also includes that prior to instituting administrative adjudication and it is sufficient if it exists within all the records concerning the said case, that is anywhere within those referred to in article 78 of the Anti-Private Monopoly Law which are to be transmitted by the defendant as "records of the said case." Substantial evidence means proof that can form a rational basis for the facts found by the decision. In other words, if it is such that a reasonable man thinking rationally would arrive at this finding of fact based on this proof, the proof must be denominated as substantial evidence. Naturally, the problems of whether certain evidence cannot possibly be believed in terms of human experience and whether the choice to accept or reject proof made by the defendant — mutually inconsistent evidence being present within the records of the said case — does not contravene human experience must both be reviewed by a court . . . the choice to accept or reject proof is to be made by the defendant, who possesses authority respecting the finding of fact, and if the defendant's judgment on the evidence does not contravene human experience and is reasonable, it even binds the courts, but when this is not the case, the courts may on these grounds annul the defendant's decision as illegal . . . Of course, the defendant, in regard to its choice to accept or reject evidence in adjudication procedure, must accord the plaintiff an opportunity to submit what evidence he desires, but in the records of this case there is no indication that the defendant suppressed the submission of evidence by the plaintiff.[66]

The court achieved considerable success in its effort to make clear the basic notion that an administrative finding of fact is not to be judicially disturbed if the record contains rationally credible evidence which, after a rational weighing of it against any contradictory evidence, tends to support the finding. But the court's interpretation of the statute's words, "records of the said case," to include those of evidence "prior to instituting administrative adjudication" is highly questionable. As I have already pointed out, the commission said in its decision that it had based its findings of fact on the "Commission's investigation" as well as on the testimony of specified witnesses. Nothing in the report of the case indicates that the association had an opportunity to know of the evidence (if there was any) adverse to it in the record of the earlier investigation and to rebut it. A party whose rights are at stake in a proceeding before either a court or an administrative agency surely should have such an opportunity.[67] By not saying a word about whether the association was afforded this right by the commission, the court seemingly sanctioned a practice which denies fundamental fairness to

[66] 4 GYŌSAI REISHŪ at 1931–32.

[67] Cf. Mazza v. Cavicchia, 15 N.J. 499, 105 A.2d 545 (1954), holding, after extensive examination of the problem, that a party had a right to know the material in a preliminary investigation. For a discussion of the case, see JAFFE & NATHANSON, ADMINSTRATIVE LAW 658–63 (2nd ed., 1961).

parties against whom the commission institutes proceedings. Perhaps the court failed to consider this matter thoroughly because it was eager to frame a definition of the substantial-evidence rule after it had examined some American decisions.

The second fundamental decision was *Nihon Sekiyu Kabushiki Kaisha* (Japan Oil Co.) *v. Kōsei Torihiki Iinkai* (Fair Trade Commission).[68] Japan Oil and other oil companies were ordered by the Fair Trade Commission to cease and desist from creating unfair restraints on competition by price-fixing agreements. The Tokyo High Court dismissed an appeal from the order:

> the allegations of the plaintiffs concerning this point constitute an attack upon the defendant's judgment as to the credibility of the evidence or its choice to accept or reject proof made by the defendant. The meaning of article 80 of the Law Concerning the Prohibition of Private Monopoly and the Maintenance of Fair Trade (hereafter referred to as the "Anti-Private Monopoly Law") is that a court's scope of review concerning a finding of fact by the Fair Trade Commission is restricted to whether or not substantial evidence exists proving this fact, and the judgment of the Fair Trade Commission as to the credibility of the evidence is binding upon the court unless it can be determined that it is irrational to believe it for the reason that the evidence cited by the Fair Trade Commission is, in and of itself, contrary to actual human experience or its credibility is precluded on comparison with the contrary evidence cited by the plaintiffs.[69]

In this case, the court was more successful than it had been in the first case in making clear the meaning of the substantial-evidence rule.

De Novo *Review of Administrative Findings of Fact*

The question now to be discussed is whether, in the absence of a statutory prescription of the substantial-evidence rule, a reviewing court should always deem itself required to hold a trial *de novo*. In cases where a trial-like hearing was not held by the administrative agency, trial *de novo* is the only kind of judicial review that is feasible. This much is beyond dispute. But with respect to cases in which there is a record embodying the evidence on which the administrative agency based its findings of fact, and the affected person was given an opportunity to go before the agency, have it consider evidence favoring him, and rebut adverse evidence, it is arguable that a reviewing court should adopt the substantial-evidence rule.

Japanese case law shows, however, that the courts deem themselves bound, even in part, by the agency's findings only when there is a statutory prescription of the substantial-evidence rule. When there is none, a trial *de novo* is conducted and the evidence in the administrative record is considered by the court only if introduced again in the court proceeding. Even though the case involves a highly technical matter, with which the administrative agency

[68] Tokyo High Court, Nov. 9, 1956, 7 Gyōsai Reishū 2849.
[69] *Ibid.*, at 2862.

is especially competent to deal, the court seems to feel obliged both to proceed wholly on the evidence produced in court by both parties and to make its own independent judgments about the credibility, the probative value, and the weight of the evidence.

In *Osawa v. Tokkyo-chō Chōkan* (Director-General of the Patent Agency),[70] plaintiff appealed from a decision of a trial examiner of the Patent Agency, which had dismissed plaintiff's application for a patent. There had been a trial-like administrative hearing.[71] The disputed issue was the patentability of plaintiff's invention, and the questions of fact seemingly involved a highly technical matter within the administrative experts' special competence. The Tokyo High Court, nevertheless, conducted a trial *de novo,* and received and relied upon new evidence introduced by the defendant Patent Agency.[72] The court dismissed the action after making its own findings. The appellant appealed to the Supreme Court, which rejected the appeal:

> It is argued that in a suit seeking to annul a decision of a patent protest adjudication the allegation and proof of new facts not submitted at the administrative protest adjudication hearing should not be permitted, but since the original instance in court is the trial of fact instance, it is not illegal to allege newly facts not alleged at the administrative adjudication — facts not made a basis for its decision by the administrative tribunal — and it is in no way illegal for a court to adopt such facts as the basis for its judgment.[73]

Thus, the Supreme Court made clear its view that the parties, in the trial of a court action for revocation of a decision of patent trial examiners, may submit new allegations of fact and new evidence, which had not been submitted to the agency and on which its decision was not based. The Tokyo High Court followed this precedent in a trademark case, *Hatogaya Shōyu Gōshi Kaisha* (Hatogaya Soy Sauce Partnership in Commendam Co.) *v. Tokkyo-chō Chōkan* (Director-General of the Patent Agency).[74]

[70] Tokyo High Court, July 31, 1951, 2 GYŌSAI REISHŪ 1290.

[71] The Patent Law of 1921, Law No. 96 of 1921, which was superseded by the current Patent Law, Law No. 121 of 1959, provided for a hearing and gave the private party opportunity to introduce evidence (ch. V). The law also provided that, in case of a lawsuit, the whole record should be transmitted from the Patent Agency to the court (art. 128-4).

[72] 2 GYŌSAI REISHŪ at 1292–94.

[73] Osawa v. Tokkyo-chō Chōkan (Director-General of the Patent Agency), Supreme Court, II Petty Bench, Oct. 16, 1953, 4 GYŌSAI REISHŪ 2424, 2425.

[74] Tokyo High Court, Nov. 5, 1953, 4 GYŌSAI REISHŪ 2702. But the same court has since taken a different view in Kureha Bōseki Kabushiki Kaisha (Kureha Spinning Co.) v. Tokkyo-chō Chōkan (Director-General of the Patent Agency), Tokyo High Court, Aug. 9, 1955, 6 GYŌSAI REISHŪ 2007. The Patent Agency dismissed plaintiff's application for a patent on a kind of vacuum cleaner, on the ground that this apparatus was already in public use. Plaintiff appealed from the decision, and defendant submitted a new allegation of fact. The court held that the parties "may not lawfully allege in the principal action to try and adjudge whether the above administrative decision was illegal or not" new facts on which the administrative decision was not based (*ibid.,* at 2021). See also Nishioka v. Tokkyo-chō Chōkan (Director-General of the Patent Agency), Tokyo High Court, Feb. 27, 1958, 9 GYŌSAI REISHŪ 266.

In reviewing decisions of the High Marine Disaster Determination Agency, the Tokyo High Court, which alone has jurisdiction, always conducts a trial *de novo,* although the applicable statute provides in detail for a hearing.[75] *Terui v. Kōtō Kainan Shimpan-chō* (High Marine Disaster Determination Agency)[76] is an example. The plaintiffs' licenses as seamen were suspended by a decision of the marine agency. The question in the case was whether fault on the plaintiffs' part had caused the collision of two ships. On appeal, the Tokyo High Court conducted a trial *de novo,* although highly technical matters were involved, and the agency's findings of fact were based on evidence produced at a trial-like hearing. The court dismissed the action after making its own findings, and the Supreme Court affirmed the decision.[77]

In cases involving review of decisions of a labor relations commission, made under a statute which provides in detail for a trial-like hearing,[78] the court follows the same principle. In *Ogawa v. Chūō Rōdō Iinkai* (Central Labor Relations Commission),[79] the Tokyo District Court held:

> We should examine the extent to which the court is able to review the Labor Commission's findings of facts. The following argument can be made: "Decisions of the Labor Commission are apparently different from the administrative actions of the ordinary executive organs . . . In judicial review of orders of the Labor Commission, the court should examine solely whether the Commission's findings are supported by substantial evidence, and the court should not examine the evidence and determine the fairness of the Commission's findings . . ." But it must be noted that the Labor Union Law has no provisions such as articles 80 to 82 of the Anti-Private Monopoly Law; that the qualifications required of a member of a Labor Commission are not set strictly as compared with those required of a member of the Fair Trade Commission; that for restricting the scope of judicial review, statutory provision is needed, such as article 78 of the Anti-Private Monopoly Law, which provides for transmission of the record from the administrative commission, but that there is no such provision here. We conclude, therefore, that under the Labor Law the court should examine the evidence, find the facts, and determine whether the Commission's decision is lawful or not.[80]

[75] The Marine Disaster Determination Law, Law No. 135 of 1947, art. 40-3. Art. 40-3 states specifically: "Findings of fact shall be in accordance with evidence investigated at hearing sessions."

[76] Tokyo High Court, Feb. 17, 1950, 5 SAI-HAN MINSHŪ 408.

[77] Terui v. Kōtō Kainan Shimpan-chō (High Marine Disaster Determination Agency), Supreme Court, III Petty Bench, July 3, 1951, 5 SAI-HAN MINSHŪ 399. Another example is Kawaguchi v. Kōtō Kainan Shimpan-chō Chōkan (Director-General of the High Marine Disaster Determination Agency), Tokyo High Court, June 12, 1957, 8 GYŌSAI REISHŪ 1136.

[78] Central Labor Relations Commission Regulations, Central Labor Relations Commission Regulation No. 1 of 1949, translated into English in OFFICIAL GAZETTE, Aug. 4, 1949, no. 1004, at 17.

[79] July 29, 1952, 3 RŌDŌ KANKEI MINJI SAIBAN REISHŪ (A Collection of Civil Cases Concerning Labor) 253.

[80] *Ibid.,* at 269–70.

Japanese and American Judicial Review of Administrative Findings of Fact

The main difference between American and Japanese judicial review of administrative findings of fact is that in Japan trial *de novo* is far more frequently used than it is in America, while review in accordance with the substantial-evidence rule is far less frequent. These are, in my opinion, the principal reasons for this difference.

(1) In Japan judicial power traditionally means the power of a court to determine not only questions of law but also questions of fact. In other words, the court (which always sits without a jury) must find the facts and apply the law to them. It is widely accepted that the power to find facts cannot be taken away from the courts. If a statute undertakes to deprive the courts of this power, it will be challenged as unconstitutional. The Antimonopoly Law, trying to avert such a challenge, states in the second paragraph of article 80 (the first paragraph of which prescribes the substantial-evidence rule) that "the existence of the substantial evidence provided for in the prior paragraph is to be determined by the court." One supporter of this law explains that the substantial-evidence rule it prescribes does not wholly deprive the court of the power to find the facts, but merely lessens the court's responsibility for ascertaining them.

In American law, not only the distinctions drawn between questions of fact and questions of law but also the substantial-evidence rule derive from the jury system. The division of functions between judge and jury is that the jury decides questions of fact and the judge decides questions of law; the judge may set aside a jury verdict (except one for the accused in a criminal case) if he believes it contrary to the weight of the evidence, and he is obligated to set it aside if he believes that no jury could reasonably infer from the evidence the findings of fact implied by the verdict.

(2) Another fundamental difference between American and Japanese courts may be found in their attitudes toward the law-creating function. In American legal thinking, it is well understood that the courts create law. Even when a statutory provision is applicable, it is recognized that its interpretation is more than a merely deductive process. The proportion of statutory to common law has greatly increased and continues to increase; nevertheless, judge-made law continues to dominate nearly all branches of administrative law. In traditional Japanese legal thinking, on the contrary, the legislature creates the law by enacting statutes, and the courts merely interpret and apply the law to the facts. Of course, under cover of this convention, the courts necessarily do more than interpret statutes by a deductive process; they also exercise the power of making law in concrete cases. But the fiction that judges merely apply the law affects not merely the judges' opinions; it also affects their decisions. When we compare Japanese and American decisions in a particular branch of the law, we notice that a remarkable dis-

similarity has resulted from this difference in judicial attitudes. In general, Japanese courts are inclined to feel themselves closely bound by statutory provisions in the field of administrative law. American courts feel freer to make law that is not deducible from the applicable statutes. For example, in areas in which there are no statutory provisions establishing the substantial-evidence rule, or conferring a right to be heard, Japanese courts do not attempt to create law about these matters. Hence, there is but little judge-made law concerning the substantial-evidence rule or administrative procedure.

(3) Most Japanese judges still hesitate to place their trust in administrative officials. Even when factual questions relate to highly technical matters which may more appropriately be dealt with by specialized administrative experts, judges seem to be reluctant to rely much upon administrative competence.

(4) This attitude of the courts may be a reflection of the people's general lack of trust in administrative agencies. Japan suffered from the excesses of bureaucratic government for many years; it still fears strong administrative authority and, hence, looks with disfavor on restricting the scope of judicial review. The degree of popular confidence or lack of confidence in administrative agencies may well be one of the most vital factors affecting the scope of judicial review in Japan.

(5) Finally, statutory and case law concerning administrative procedure is still immature. Moreover, the Japanese cannot afford enough well-qualified trial examiners. The time is perhaps not ripe for broader adoption of the substantial-evidence rule.

Conclusion

Since the new Constitution was established in 1946, Japanese law has developed in the direction of American law. Thus, judicial review of administrative action is and will remain a central legal institution in Japan. Although the historical, political, economic, and social backgrounds of Japan and America differ greatly, this new system is proving its fitness. Case law in this area has been developing rapidly.

The basic idea of judicial review of administrative action is that the principle of legality of administration must be guaranteed by the courts. In other words, every person whose rights are adversely affected by administrative action should have a judicial remedy to challenge the legality of that action. The term "the rule of law" is not, in itself, a useful guide toward the solution of the many problems that exist in this area. We must consider what the rule of law means in the light of the objectives we seek to serve by its adoption.

As governmental responsibilities have multiplied, complicated case law concerning judicial review of administrative action has arisen. The courts seek by judicial review to afford adequate protection to private interests without unduly hampering the government in the discharge of its functions. The fundamental character of rights guaranteed by the Constitution must be respected, but the necessities of government, without which rights would be unenforceable, cannot be ignored. In the determination of the proper roles of administrative agencies and courts, their respective qualifications must be considered. The right balance between private and public interests does not always require the maximum of judicial review.

The conventional analysis of the case law concerning unreviewable administrative discretion is that, as far as action is by law committed to agency discretion, the administrative action is final and only reviewable if it is in excess of discretion. The courts can determine only whether the challenged administrative action is illegal or not; they cannot determine whether the administrative action is inappropriate. In this essay, another analysis of the cases has been advanced. The courts enforce limitations which they believe that the statute, interpreted according to the Constitution, expressly or implicitly imposes on that authority. Exceeding discretion is the courts' label for a violation of the limitations read into the statute by the courts in order to achieve what they believe to be the objective of the rule of law — the proper balance between private rights and the necessities of government. The courts give different weights, in this balancing process, to different governmental interests and to different private rights. It is difficult to draw a clear-cut line of demarcation between reviewable and discretionary actions, and the courts are likely to uphold administrative action as discretionary when the subject matter is so highly political or technical that administrators seem to be better qualified to deal with it. But when fundamental human rights are involved, the courts are likely, through interpretation of the Constitution and the statutes, to limit administrative discretion.

Japanese case law concerning judicial review of administrative findings of fact may be summarized more succinctly: when a statute prescribes the substantial-evidence rule, the reviewing court limits itself to determining whether the administrative finding of fact was reasonably derived from the evidence in the administrative record. If the substantial-evidence rule is not prescribed by statute, the reviewing court assumes full responsibility for finding facts, conducting a trial *de novo*.

By way of reforms, I would suggest that it would be wise for Japan to avail itself of American experience. In order to protect human rights from the unlawful exercise of state power, despite the continuing growth of administrative functions, the courts and the administrative agencies should cooperate, each carrying out its own proper task. Provision should be made for fair administrative procedure to safeguard the rights and liberties of the people. There are, of course, some procedural provisions in individual statutes, but two committees have been formed to draft a general law for administrative procedure: the Recourse System Investigation Commission, which recommended more judicialized procedures, and the Council on the Legal System of the Ministry of Justice, which proposed an administrative litigation law eliminating the doctrine of exhaustion of remedies.[81] Also, measures should be taken to staff the agencies with a sufficient number of competent administrators, well educated and trained before appointment.* This must all take place step by step. After these conditions have been satisfied, the courts may be able to move from *de novo* review of administrative action to judicial review that is restricted by the substantial-evidence rule.

[81] These proposals were enacted into law on May 16, 1962 as the Administrative Case Litigation Law, Law No. 139 of 1962, and on Sept. 15, 1962 as the Administrative Exceptions Review Law, Law No. 160 of 1962.

* At the conference Rex Coleman offered a somewhat different view. He believed that Japanese public service suffered not from a lack of well-trained officials but rather from too many. As a generalization, he felt that Japanese governmental officials are more able than American officials at comparable levels. Traditionally, the top graduates of the leading law departments have entered the executive branch of the government rather than becoming lawyers or judges. Such persons tend to look down upon the members of the judiciary as men of lesser ability and therefore feel that they are better qualified to interpret the law. Moreover, in many instances the officials construing a statute or order are also those who actually drafted it and thus consider themselves best able to understand its meaning. The result is that administrative action in Japan often ignores judicial precedent. Although the courts may overrule the decision of the administrator, this possibility does not constitute much of a constraint since the slowness of litigation deters appeals and normally an unfavorable precedent can be soon removed by a recommendation to the Diet to enact new legislation. The courts, in turn, are particularly unhappy about the tendency of administrators to disregard the courts' power of review and accordingly retaliate by being unwilling to abdicate any of their authority. The extreme self-confidence of government officials and its, at times, unpleasant outward manifestation are, of course, by no means confined to Japan, but they may appear in a different segment of the society. In the United States, for example, the same characteristics are occasionally visible among judges and senior members of the older well-established law firms.

THE ACCUSED AND SOCIETY: SOME ASPECTS OF JAPANESE CRIMINAL LAW

Ryuichi Hirano

ASSISTED BY B. J. GEORGE, JR.

IT IS not a simple matter to set forth in short compass the essential characteristics of a country's penal law. An attempt to express the special characteristics of Japanese criminal law, however, might focus on one question. Is it true that Japanese criminal law is subjective?

This question is an important one today particularly in the context of criminal procedure. When Japan entered the Meiji era (1867–1912), criminal law and procedure, like other areas of the law, were initially under French legal influence. Thereafter Japanese law was generally influenced by German law; both the currently effective Penal Code of 1907[1] and the Code of Criminal Procedure in effect from 1923 to 1948[2] were based on the corresponding German codes. Consequently, the law of criminal procedure embodied what German scholars called "a semiaccusatorial principle."[3] After the Second World War, the Penal Code was left intact, but under the influence of the occupation authorities the American adversary system formed the basis of the present Code of Criminal Procedure of 1948.[4]

Under the Continental semiaccusatorial system, at successive stages of the inquiry an investigating official and a judge interrogate the suspect or defendant, and each has a considerable opportunity to obtain a statement from him in the form of a confession or otherwise. In this way, there is

Note. Mr. Hirano is Professor of Law, Tokyo University. B.Jur., Tokyo Imperial University, 1942; Dr.Jur., Tokyo University, 1962. Participant, Japanese American Program for Cooperation in Legal Studies at Harvard University, 1954–1955, and at Stanford University, 1955–1956. Research at Free University of Berlin, 1962. Member of the Council of Direction of the International Society of Criminology. Author of KEIJI SOSHŌ HŌ (Law of Criminal Procedure) (Hōritsu-gaku Zenshū (Complete Collection on the Law) ed., 1958); writings in the fields of criminal law and criminology.

Mr. George is Professor of Law, University of Michigan. B.A., 1949, J.D., 1951, University of Michigan.

[1] Law No. 45 of 1907.

[2] Law No. 75 of 1922 [hereafter cited CODE OF CRIMINAL PROCEDURE OF 1922].

[3] See GNEIST, VIER FRAGEN ZUR DEUTSCHEN STRAFPROCESSORDNUNG 5 (1874).

[4] Law No. 131 of 1948.

provided a direct method of determining those subjective and psychological elements of a crime that often can be definitively proven only by the defendant's statement of them. Thus, despite the fact that German substantive criminal statutes contain a great many subjective elements, cases can be and are successfully prosecuted. On the other hand, it is extremely difficult to establish the subjective elements of a crime under the adversary system of criminal procedure, in which an opportunity is only rarely given either to the judge or to the investigating official to interrogate the defendant or suspect. Consequently, in American criminal law substantive criminal proscriptions embody objective elements which are relatively easy to prove, as well as presumptions adverse to the defendant by which the required subjective elements may be established. Because of this discrepancy between the requirements of the substantive law and the allowances of the procedure, it is asserted either that the Penal Code must be revised completely along the lines of American criminal law or that the Code of Criminal Procedure must be amended to correspond to German law or the prewar Japanese code.

However, the form of a criminal law should probably not be looked at solely in relation to the regulation of criminal procedure. Whether a criminal law can be classified as objective or subjective depends to some extent on the theory of punishment which its drafters had in mind. The approach that the sole purpose of punishment is deterrence stands in opposition to that approach which stresses as one leading purpose of punishment the rehabilitation of the offender. This antithesis is ordinarily referred to as the division between the classical and the modernist schools of thought on theories of punishment. In Japan, however, this antithesis is often expressed in terms of a conflict between the "objective principle" and the "subjective principle," since the modernist group in Japan stresses the subjective elements of the act as material constituents of the crime. The modernist school in Europe and in the United States does not necessarily do so, however. Thus the question of whether Japanese criminal law is subjective involves an inquiry into the influence of the modernist idea of punishment on Japan's substantive criminal law.

The problem can also be considered from an even broader perspective—the sociolegal aspects of criminal law, or the function of the criminal law as a medium of social control. Along with other norms such as religious beliefs, morals, and convention, criminal law controls certain kinds of antisocial behavior; the role played by criminal law varies according to the culture of each country. An acquaintance with these interrelationships is thus necessary to an understanding of Japanese criminal law.

With these perspectives in mind, we may now more closely consider the question of the subjectivity of Japanese criminal law. It seems likely that no single conclusion is possible, for it must depend upon the particular aspect of the criminal act that one has in view. The following three propositions show the basic subjective-objective dichotomy present in the Japanese law.

(1) In the sense that punishment is rarely inflicted unless serious harm has actually been caused to society, Japanese criminal law tends to be objective.

(2) Since even actual harm is not punished unless an element of intent is present, Japanese criminal law is also subjective.

(3) Japanese criminal law is also subjective in that, if a criminal offense involves concert among several individuals, the person who committed the objectively harmful act may be considered morally less blameworthy, and hence be less severely punished, than those who psychologically or morally encouraged him.

INJURY TO SOCIETY

By special statutory provisions, Japanese law punishes attempts only in connection with particular crimes. In many other countries, all attempts are punished except those pertaining to certain minor offenses; in France and Germany, for example, all attempts to commit major crimes are punishable, while attempted minor crimes are punished only under special provisions.

Once they are determined to be criminal, attempts under Japanese law generally receive the same punishment as the completed offense; punishment may, not must, be reduced.[5] There is a certain inconsistency between the idea that criminality of attempts is exceptional and the approach that, as a general principle, the criminal attempt is punished in the same way as the completed crime. The explanation seems mainly historical. French penal law recognized no distinction between attempt and the completed crime; when French law was taken over in the Japanese Penal Code of 1880,[6] the only substantial modification was to authorize mitigation of the penalty. Probably this change was made by legislators who found it difficult in terms of Japanese attitudes to accept the general proposition that attempts and crimes should be treated alike. Most judges today still seem to feel that the attempt ought to be punished less severely than the completed crime.[7]

The Japanese codified definition of attempt, patterned after the French, differentiates preparation from attempt according to whether there is "commencement of execution" (*commencement d'exécution*). A number of scholars, particularly those who advocate the so-called subjective principle, maintain that attempt ought to be recognized at an early stage, that the

[5] "The punishment of a person who commences in the execution of a crime but does not complete it may be reduced. Provided, however, if he has desisted from it in accordance with his own will, his punishment is to be reduced or remitted." PENAL CODE art. 43.

[6] Great Council of State Decree No. 36 of 1880.

[7] The table at the end of this essay of the number of individuals sentenced for four types of crime in 1959 illustrates the judicial attitude.

commission of the crime should begin when there is "activity manifesting an actual criminal intent."[8] According to judicial precedent, however, attempt comes into being rather late. For example, when a man merely enters a room in an effort to steal something, an attempt has not yet been made.[9] Attempts have been found when the would-be thief forced his way into a silkworm nursery looking around with a flashlight for food[10] and when an offender approached a bureau to ransack it for valuables.[11] The criterion in these cases is popularly known as the "search test." The mailing of a poisonous substance with the intent of committing homicide does not constitute an attempt; an attempt occurs only when the addressee receives the substance and he and his family are thereby placed in a situation in which they are able, and likely, to consume it as food.[12] Even some of the advocates of the objective theory question this decision, on the ground that, at a certain stage of activity turned toward achieving a proscribed harm, it ought to be considered an attempt.[13] But the cases hold that there is an attempt only when there is imminent danger that the desired results will be achieved.

European courts have recognized attempt at a much earlier stage. In Germany, a man who tried to kill a watchdog, with the purpose of committing theft, was convicted of an attempted theft.[14] Scholars consider that the mailing of a threatening letter would amount to the commencement of a criminal act.[15] In Austria, it was held to be attempted theft to send a

[8] See, e.g., 1 MAKINO, NIHON KEIHŌ (Japanese Criminal Law) 254 (major rev. ed., 1937); MIYAMOTO, KEIHO TAIKŌ (General Features of Criminal Law) 179 (1935); KIMURA, KEIHŌ SŌRON (Criminal Law — General Part) 344 (1959).

[9] Japan v. Umemura, Great Court of Judicature, IV Criminal Department, Oct. 19, 1934, 13 DAI SHIN IN KEIJI HANREI SHŪ (A Collection of Criminal Great Court of Judicature Cases) [hereafter cited DAI-HAN KEISHŪ] 1473. The Great Court of Judicature — the Dai Shin In — was the highest court in the prewar judicial system. Its jurisdiction resembled very closely that of the French Cour de Cassation, on which it was in fact patterned. The present Supreme Court — Saikō Saibansho — was established with a revised appellate jurisdiction as part of the postwar judicial system. In addition see Kawai v. Japan, Tokyo High Court, Dec. 10, 1949, 2 KŌTŌ SAIBANSHO KEIJI HANREI SHŪ (A Collection of Criminal High Court Cases) [hereafter cited KŌ-HAN KEISHŪ] 292.

[10] Japan v. Umemura, as in note 9 above.

[11] Endo v. Japan, Supreme Court, I Petty Bench, April 17, 1948, 2 SAIKŌ SAIBANSHO KEIJI HANREI SHŪ (A Collection of Criminal Supreme Court Cases) [hereafter cited SAI-HAN KEISHŪ] 399, 402.

[12] Japan v. Fujimoto, Great Court of Judicature, III Criminal Department, Nov. 16, 1918, 24 DAI SHIN IN KEIJI HANKETSU ROKU (Record of Great Court of Judicature Criminal Judgments) [hereafter cited DAI-HAN KEIROKU] 1352. Also to the same effect see Japan v. Kagauri, Great Court of Judicature, II Criminal Department, Aug. 28, 1916, 22 DAI-HAN KEIROKU 1332.

[13] See, e.g., 1 ONO, KEIHŌ KŌGI (Lectures on Criminal Law) 106 (new rev. ed., 1950); DANDO, KEIHŌ KŌYŌ (Elements of Criminal Law) 265 (1957).

[14] Judgment of April 1, 1919, Reichsgericht, II Strafsenat, 53 Entscheidungen des Reichsgerichts in Strafsachen [hereafter cited R.G.S.] 217 (Ger.); see also SCHÖNKE-SCHRÖDER, STRAFGESETZBUCH: KOMMENTAR 208–13 (10th ed., 1961).

[15] See SCHÖNKE-SCHRÖDER, note 14, at 210.

telegram luring away the proposed victim;[16] in Switzerland, to set out in the direction of the predetermined spot;[17] and in France, to lie in wait for a person carrying cash receipts near the doorway of a building from which he was to emerge.[18]

The recent legislative thinking of some European countries has tended either to recognize attempt as coming into being prior to the commencement of the "execution" or to adopt a subjective concept of when the "execution" commences.[19] But the Japanese Draft Penal Code of 1961, with its use of the terminology "commenced in the execution" as the essential requirement for attempt, shows no broadening of the judicially determined concept of attempt.[20]

In the area of impossibility, the use of punishment is also rather restricted. The decisions say that there shall be no punishment in cases in which accomplishment of the intended result is "absolutely impossible." [21] The expression of the differing results in these cases in terms of absolute impossibility and relative impossibility has been criticized;[22] but the problem here is not to

[16] Judgment No. 2969, Kassationshof, June 20, 1904, 6 Entscheidungen des k.k. Obersten Gerichts — als Kassationshofes (new series) 219 (Austria); see also 1 RITTLER, LEHRBUCH DES ÖSTERREICHISCHEN STRAFRECHTS 262 (2d ed., 1954).

[17] Regierungsrat Aargau v. Regierungsrat Glarus, Bundesgerichtshof, April 1, 1908, 34(I.) Entscheidungen des Schweizerischen Bundesgerichtes 288, 292 (Switz.); see also Germann, *Die Rechtsprechung über den Versuch nach schweizerischem Strafgesetzbuch,* 60 SCHWEIZERISCHE ZEITSCHRIFT FÜR STRAFRECHT 1, 14 (1946).

[18] Prévost et Coulond, Cour de Cassation, Ch. crim., Jan. 3, 1913, [1913] Sirey Recueil Général I. 281 (Fr.); see also DONNEDIEU DE VABRES, TRAITÉ DE DROIT CRIMINEL ET DE LEGISLATION PÉNALE COMPARÉE 134 (3d ed., 1947).

[19] See, e.g., PROJET DE LOI PORTANT REFONTE DU CODE PÉNAL (Draft Code), No. 4287, art. 106 (Chambre des Députés, 1938): "Toute tentative de crime qui aura été manifestée par un commencement d'exécution, ou par des actes tendant directement à le commettre, . . . est considérée comme le crime même . . ." (Every attempt to commit a crime which has been manifested by a commencement of the execution, or by acts tending directly to its commission, . . . is considered as the crime itself).

ENTWURF EINES STRAFGESETZBUCHES E1960 (Draft Code) §26 (1960) [hereafter cited German Draft Penal Code of 1960]: "(1) Eine Straftat versucht, wer den Vorsatz, die Tat zu vollenden, durch eine Handlung betätigt, die den Anfang der Ausführung bildet oder nach seiner Vorstellung von den Tatumständen bilden würde, aber nicht zur Vollendung führt" (A person attempts a crime who demonstrates the intention to complete the crime by engaging in an action which constitutes a commencement of execution or which, under his conception of the circumstances, would constitute such a commencement, but which does not lead to full execution).

"(2) Der Anfang der Ausführung bildet eine Handlung, durch die der Täter mit der Verwirklichung des Tatbestandes beginnt oder unmittelbar dazu ansetzt" (An action constitutes a commencement of execution when through such action the actor either begins to fulfill the constituent elements [of the crime involved] or directly sets out to do so).

[20] KAISEI KEIHŌ JUMBI SŌAN (Preliminary Draft of the Revised Penal Code) art. 22(1) (1961) [hereafter cited Japanese Draft Penal Code of 1961], to be found in 34 HŌRITSU JIHŌ (Law Journal) no. 2, supp. at 7: "A person, who has commenced in the execution of a crime but has not completed it, has perpetrated a criminal attempt."

[21] Fujino v. Japan, Supreme Court, I Petty Bench, Aug. 31, 1950, 4 SAI-HAN KEISHŪ 1593, 1594.

[22] See, e.g., KIMURA, KEIHŌ SŌRON (Criminal Law — General Part) 352–53 (1959).

determine the propriety of using the term "absolute impossibility," but rather to determine what kinds of cases in practice fall outside the area of punishability. There has been only one case in which a judgment of not guilty was rendered on the grounds of impossibility by either the prewar Great Court of Judicature or its successor, the Supreme Court.[23] In that case the criminal tried to kill his victim by having him drink sulphur; the criminal obviously thought that sulphur was a deadly poison. The comments on this case, even by advocates of the so-called objective theory, express the view that this conduct ought to have been punished as an attempt.[24] On the basis of this one case, at least, the Japanese courts appear to have adopted an extreme objective standard — that criminality first occurs only when the danger becomes quite real. The absence of cases decided on the grounds of impossibility does not mean that punishment has been freely assessed in other cases in which this defense has been raised. In marginal cases of impossibility, the procurator tends not to institute public prosecution, probably because he does not feel very strongly the necessity of imposing punishment.

In the area of *Mangel am Tatbestand* (absence of a constituent element [of the crime involved]), the decisions hold that it is attempted theft to put one's hand into an empty pocket,[25] but a court would probably acquit in a case involving an attempted abortion on a nonpregnant woman.[26] In contrast, French and German courts have punished as attempted abortion both an effort to produce an abortion by administering *eau de cologne* and an effort involving a woman who was not pregnant.[27] The German courts have also held that the buying of goods which the accused incorrectly believes have been stolen constitutes an attempt to receive stolen property.[28]

Recent foreign legislation, such as the Swiss Penal Code[29] and the German

[23] Kanazawa v. Japan, Great Court of Judicature, II Criminal Department, Sept. 10, 1917, 23 DAI-HAN KEIROKU 999, 1003. Some scholars also cite the Judgment of June 20, 1927, Great Court of Judicature, V Criminal Department, 6 DAI-HAN KEISHŪ 216, 221, as a second case in which impossibility blocked guilt. Uematsu, *Funōhan* (Impossibility), in 3 SŌGŌ HANREI KENKYŪ SŌSHO — KEIHŌ (Comprehensive Case Study Series — Criminal Law) 121, at 155.

[24] See, e.g., 1 ONO, note 13 above at 192.

[25] E.g., Japan v. Hanagasaki, Great Court of Judicature, III Criminal Department, July 24, 1914, 20 DAI-HAN KEIROKU 1546, 1547.

[26] In the Judgment of June 1, 1927, Great Court of Judicature, I Criminal Department, 6 DAI-HAN KEISHŪ 208, at 215, the Court in obiter dicta declared that if the embryo had already been dead, the act would not have constituted a punishable attempt at abortion.

[27] E.g., Époux Fleury v. Ministère public, Cour de Cassation, Ch. crim., Nov. 9, 1928, [1929] Dalloz Jurisprudence I. 97 (Fr.); Judgment of Feb. 27, 1888, Reichsgericht, I Strafsenat, 17 R.G.S. 158, 159; Judgment of May 24, 1880, Reichsgericht, Vereinigte Strafsenate, 1 R.G.S. 439.

[28] E.g., Judgment of March 25, 1930, Reichsgericht, IV Strafsenat, 64 R.G.S. 130.

[29] See, e.g., SCHWEIZERISCHES STRAFGESETZBUCH art. 23 (1958): "Ist das Mittel, womit jemand ein Verbrechen oder ein Vergehen auszuführen versucht, oder der Gegenstand, woran er es auszuführen versucht, derart, dass die Tat mit einem solchen Mittel oder an einem solchen

Draft Penal Code of 1960,[30] shows a strong tendency toward subjectivity. The Japanese Draft Penal Code of 1961, however, with its provision that "if an act was such that by its nature it was generally impossible for it to produce an effect, it is not to be punished as a criminal attempt,"[31] would exempt cases which are definitely criminal under the above-mentioned European codes.

The Japanese code provides that "a person who has instigated and caused another to execute a crime" becomes punishable.[32] When the person who is instigated does not commit the crime, the instigator is not punished; in such a case the instigation is considered neither an attempt nor a preparatory act. In Europe, however, such conduct is very often criminal. For example, the Swiss Penal Code[33] and the German Penal Code[34] punish attempts to induce major crimes. In Japan, the statement of general principles of the Penal Code revision of 1926 stated that the new code should include a provision making attempted inducement independently criminal; but the 1940 and 1961 drafts did not consider worthy of punishment most attempts to induce criminal acts and went no further than to punish attempted inducement to insurrection and homicide.

In England and the United States one very subjective crime exists — conspiracy. The Japanese Penal Code follows the European countries,[35] however, and provides only for conspiracy to commit insurrection, foreign aggression, or private war.[36]

The problem thus far has been to determine at what point an act becomes so imminently dangerous to certain legally protected interests that it warrants punishment. The question of what kinds of interests should be protected by criminal sanctions is a different problem, although the two are interrelated since they both bear on the fundamental question of how far the bounds of control can properly be extended through the criminal law. It is not practical to make an extended list of all punishable acts and then to compare them in detail. But even a cursory glance reveals that a large number of acts, particularly those involving sexual crimes and crimes

---

Gegenstande überhaupt nicht ausgeführt werden könnte, so kann der Richter die Strafe nach freiem Ermessen mildern (art. 66)" (If the means, with which a person attempts to commit a crime or a misdemeanor, or the object on which he attempts to carry it out, is such that the act with such a means or on such an object could not be carried out, the judge can, in his discretion, reduce the punishment). "Handelt der Täter aus Unverstand, so kann der Richter von einer Bestrafung Umgang nehmen" (If the actor acts out of a lack of understanding, the judge need not impose any punishment).

30 See German Draft Penal Code of 1960, §§26, 27(3).

31 Japanese Draft Penal Code of 1961, art. 23.

32 PENAL CODE art. 61(1).

33 SCHWEIZERISCHES STRAFGESETZBUCH art. 24(2) (1958).

34 STRAFGESETZBUCH [hereafter cited StGB] § 49(a) (32nd ed. C. H. Beck, 1961).

35 The German Penal Code does, however, punish conspiracies to commit felonies. ST GB § 49(a).

36 PENAL CODE arts. 78, 88, 93.

against the family, fall outside the bounds of criminality in Japan although they are rather widely punished in Europe and the United States.

Homosexuality, incest, and sodomy are not punishable; the crime of adultery was abolished after the war. Bigamy is punishable but, since many socially acceptable "marriages" are not legal marriages because the marriage is not recorded in the family register,[37] the constituent elements of the crime of bigamy are often lacking. Indeed, punishment for bigamy has been imposed in only four cases in the postwar period. Abortion in general is punishable under the Penal Code, but the Eugenic Protection Law[38] promulgated after the war legalized abortion within broad limits. In particular, this law provides that an abortion can be performed whenever, in the judgment of a single authorized physician, "it is feared that continued pregnancy or childbirth will for physical or economic reasons markedly injure the health of the mother's body."[39] Under this provision there were 1,120,000 legally authorized abortions performed in 1957,[40] while in the same year only five cases were punished under the abortion statute.[41] Maintenance of houses of prostitution was prohibited in 1957,[42] but the act of prostitution itself is not treated as a crime.[43] The Supreme Court of Japan held that *Lady Chatterley's Lover* was an obscene publication,[44] but obscene literature is not strictly controlled in Japan.[45]

[37] See Yozo Watanabe, "The Family and the Law: The Individualistic Premise and Modern Japanese Family Law," in this volume.

[38] Law No. 156 of 1948.

[39] Eugenic Protection Law, art. 14(1) (iv). It was recently reported in the Diet that foreign women posing as tourists are coming to Japan to get abortions because the Japanese techniques are superior and the cost is low. See Asahi Shimbun, March 22, 1962, p. 1, col. 7 (evening ed.); Asahi Evening News, March 22, 1962, p. 1, col. 1. However, upon later inquiry by the press, the Diet member making this assertion could not substantiate it. Asahi Evening News, March 23, 1962, p. 1, col. 2.

[40] DAIJIN KAMBŌ (Office of the Minister), KŌSEI-SHŌ (Ministry of Welfare), KŌSEI HAKUSHO SHŌWA 33 NENDO BAN (1958 Welfare White Paper) 173 (1958).

[41] SAIKŌ SAIBANSHO JIMU-SŌKYOKU (General Secretariat of the Supreme Court), SHŌWA 32 NEN SHIHŌ TŌKEI NEMPŌ (1957 Annual Report of Judicial Statistics), 2 KEIJI HEN (Criminal Affairs Book) pt. 1, at 49 (1958).

[42] Prostitution Prevention Law, Law No. 118 of 1956, arts. 11–12; translated into English in BAISHUN TAISAKU NO GENKYŌ (The Present Condition of Anti-Prostitution Measures) 518 (Baishun Taisaku Shingikai (Anti-Prostitution Policy Council) ed., 1959).

[43] While the statute states that "no person shall engage in prostitution nor become the other party thereto," no criminal sanctions are imposed for violation of this rule. See Prostitution Prevention Law, art. 3.

[44] Koyama v. Japan, Supreme Court, Grand Bench, March 13, 1957, 11 SAI-HAN KEISHŪ 997.

[45] One possible answer to this seeming inconsistency may be the following:

"B. But why are the pulp magazines free from restraint while an action is brought against *Chatterley*?

"D. They're not completely free from restraint; actions are brought against some . . .

"D. It seems to me that the *Chatterley* action also has the following meaning. With a pulp magazine or a Japanese author who writes something of this sort, I believe that since they are evaluated by society in general as trash and in no way first class works, even if they seem to have literary value, they are not openly read and parents can prevent children reading them, but because Lawrence is a leading foreign author, supported by our tendency to make

Punishment for violations of the duty of financial support is also quite restricted. In many countries, one charged with a duty under the Civil Code to provide maintenance can be punished if he does not fulfill that duty. But the Penal Code of Japan makes criminal a failure to support only in a case in which the life of an infant, sick person, or elderly person is endangered.[46] Failure to fulfill the duty to support one's wife is not punishable.

The above discussion has dealt with the scope of criminal law as contained in statutory definitions of criminal activities. The scope of criminal law as actually applied is even more limited. Prosecuting officials have broad discretion as to whether to institute prosecution.[47] Among the criminal cases handled in 1957 by procurators only 46.1 percent resulted in prosecutions; in 1958, the figure did not exceed 50.2 percent. These figures do, however, show a marked increase in comparison with the 25 percent rate encountered around 1953.[48] Even in cases of homicides, prosecution is not always instituted. Of course there are also a great many cases in which no complaints are made. As a result, in 1959 only 11 persons were punished for abandonment; 18,690 for assault; and 3,860 for gambling. In 1956, there were 10 cases of abandonment; 14,435 of assault; and 5,000 of gambling.[49] The Minor Offenses Law[50] enumerates 34 separate offenses, but punishment was actually imposed in only 209 cases in 1959.[51]

CRIMINAL INTENT

Even in cases in which important legal interests are impaired, in the Japanese view criminality does not immediately attach. In order to impose punishment, a certain state of mind — the intent to infringe upon a particular legal interest — is also required. In the United States criminal intent or negligence is not required in so-called public-welfare offenses. Such absolute liability is not recognized in Japan. At a minimum, negligence is necessary, and in most cases criminal intent is required.*

a fetish out of foreign literature, we socially lack the strength to hold at an appropriate line and must employ instead, unavoidably, the power of the public procurator." Hirano, *Chiyatarei Saiban Hihyō* (A Critique of the Chatterley Trial), JURIST no. 4, at 12, 17 (1952).

[46] PENAL CODE arts. 217–19.

[47] CODE OF CRIMINAL PROCEDURE art. 248: "When pursuant to the offender's character, age and surroundings, the gravity and circumstances of his crime, and his conduct after the crime it is felt unnecessary to prosecute, a public action need not be instituted."

[48] HŌMU SŌGŌ KENKYŪJO (Ministry of Justice Integrated Research Institute), HŌMU-SHŌ (Ministry of Justice), HANZAI HAKUSHO — SHŌWA 35 NENBAN (1960 White Paper on Crime) 148 (1960).

[49] SAIKŌ SAIBANSHO JIMU-SŌKYOKU (General Secretariat of the Supreme Court), SHŌWA 34 NEN SHIHŌ TŌKEI NEMPŌ (1959 Annual Report of Judicial Statistics), 2 KEIJI HEN (Criminal Affairs Book) pt. 1, at 129–30, 352 (1960).

[50] Law No. 39 of 1948.

[51] SAIKŌ SAIBANSHO JIMU-SŌKYOKU, note 49, at 308.

* At the conference Robert Braucher stated that this absence of absolute responsibility was an achievement of Japanese law which should be applauded. He commented later that a law

The basic principle of the Penal Code is that "unintentional acts are not to be punished." This principle does not apply, however, if there are special provisions to the contrary in the Penal Code or in other statutes.[52] Thus the question arises whether the term "special provisions" requires specific terms or whether they can be implied. The Supreme Court has not yet been confronted by a case requiring a definite answer to this question, but lower courts following the precedents of the Great Court of Judicature have nearly always limited the exceptions to specific terms.[53]

During the period after the Second World War, when there was a shortage of alcoholic beverages in Japan, intoxicants containing methyl alcohol or methanol appeared in the cities, causing death or blindness in a great many cases. The occupation authorities then promulgated an order punishing those who violated its provisions stating that "foods and beverages containing methanol or lead tetraethyl may not be sold, assigned, manufactured, or kept in one's possession."[54] The authorities probably intended that the order should impose strict liability, but the Japanese judges and procurators all interpreted the language as making punishable only those who sold, assigned, manufactured, or kept in their possession something that they *knew* contained methanol.[55] Consequently, the order was immediately revised to make it clear that it covered both intentional and negligent performance of the prohibited activities.[56]

The former law on road traffic imposed punishment only on knowing violators of its provisions. Problems have arisen under its statutory rule authorizing a fine against the operator of a motor vehicle who fails to have his driver's license in his possession while operating his vehicle.[57] The Tokyo High Court held that a negligent failure to have a driver's license in one's possession was punishable.[58] This was an exceptional case, however, and many commentators argued that even in this situation punishment should

---

which holds a man guilty for acts he could neither control nor prevent debases the moral force of law generally in the eyes of most people.

[52] PENAL CODE art. 38(1). One may contrast this with the Danish Criminal Code, which states: "As regards other offences [other than those dealt with in the Criminal Code], the appropriate penal sanction shall apply, even where the offence has been committed through negligence, unless otherwise provided." DANISH CRIMINAL CODE art. 19 (Giersing trans., 1958).

[53] Tomizaki v. Japan, Great Court of Judicature, I Criminal Department, May 17, 1918, 24 DAI-HAN KEIROKU 593, 594.

[54] Poisonous Foods and Beverages Control Order, Imperial Order No. 52 of 1946, art. 1(i). Art. 4(1) provided that "a person who has violated the provisions of article 1 is to be punished by imprisonment at forced labor for between three years or more and fifteen years or less or by a fine of between two thousand yen or more and ten thousand yen or less."

[55] See, e.g., Sagawa v. Japan, Supreme Court, II Petty Bench, March 20, 1948, 2 SAI-HAN KEISHŪ 256, 258.

[56] Imperial Order No. 325 of 1946 added the following sentence to art. 4(1): "It is the same for a person who has violated the provisions of the same article through negligence."

[57] Road Traffic Control Law, Law No. 130 of 1947, arts. 9(3), 29(i).

[58] Japan v. Hagiwara, Tokyo High Court, June 16, 1959, 12 KŌ-HAN KEISHŪ 635, 639.

be inflicted only for intentional violation of the statute. The problem was settled by a new statute in 1960 which authorized the imposition of a light fine of 10,000 yen (28 dollars) on the basis of negligence in this and a number of other cases.[59]

Absolute liability also appears in Anglo-American law in the form of vicarious responsibility. In Japanese law as well criminal liability is sometimes imposed on an employer for the acts of his employees, but this liability is limited to those cases in which there are special provisions to this effect. Some of these special provisions allow exoneration of the employer by proof that he exercised due care in the selection and supervision of his employees. In cases in which such special exoneration is not provided, the courts first held the employer's liability to be an absolute one.[60] Recently, however, the Supreme Court has held that even in such cases the statute should be interpreted to permit exoneration by proof that the employer was free from negligence in selecting and supervising his employees.[61] Absolute liability has thus been extinguished.

The felony-murder rule is another form of absolute liability found in American law. This rule is often ridiculed by Continental and Japanese lawyers. But in Japan, if a person dies as the result of a train wreck, rape, or robbery, the death penalty or life imprisonment is imposed on the one who committed the original criminal act. A killing in connection with arson is not specifically punished, but arson itself carries the death penalty. The term "murder" is not used in these cases, but in fact the same results are reached as under the felony-murder rule. However, most scholars argue that even in these cases negligence turned toward the graver harm on the part of the actor should be required.[62] The 1961 Draft Penal Code adopts this view.[63]

Anglo-American law thus recognizes objective liability even for such serious offenses as homicide. In other manifestations of absolute liability a certain state of mind must be found in order to establish the offense; the criterion is not whether the defendant in the case actually was aware of the material facts but whether a reasonable man would have been so aware. Anglo-American law applies, for example, the label of murder not only to

[59] Road Traffic Law, Law No. 105 of 1960, arts. 95(1), 121(1) (x).

[60] See, e.g., Fujimoto v. Japan, Great Court of Judicature, III Criminal Department, Sept. 16, 1942, 21 DAI-HAN KEISHŪ 417; Tatsuke v. Japan, Great Court of Judicature, II Criminal Department, Dec. 18, 1941, 20 DAI-HAN KEISHŪ 709; Ueno v. Japan, Great Court of Judicature, III Criminal Department, March 4, 1938, HŌRITSU SHIMBUN (The Law News) no. 4248, at 13; Judgment of Feb. 27, 1923, Great Court of Judicature, I Criminal Department, 2 DAI-HAN KEISHŪ 134.

[61] Kambayashi v. Japan, Supreme Court, Grand Bench, Nov. 27, 1957, 11 SAI-HAN KEISHŪ 3113, 3116 (violation of the criminal provisions of the Admission Tax Law).

[62] See, e.g., 1 ONO, note 13 above at 178; DANDO, note 13, at 248.

[63] Japanese Draft Penal Code of 1961, art. 21.

cases involving a specific intent to kill but also to cases in which the intent is to inflict "grave bodily injury." This doctrine has not been excluded even under the 1957 English Homicide Act.[64]

In some jurisdictions in the United States murder is found not only when there is an actual intent to harm but also when the act is "wanton" and evinces a depraved mind. Opinion as to what "wanton" means is not uniform, but the prevailing view seems to be that it is enough if the defendant knew facts which would cause a reasonable man to judge that there was a substantial danger of death.[65] Ordinarily when there is an awareness of the facts, one can foresee what results are likely to arise. Especially in the case of drunkenness or mental abnormality, there is apt to be a discrepancy between the power to recognize facts and the power to foresee. Fatigue or inattention may also result in the loss of foresight. The objective theory would probably say that cases in the former group should lead to heavy punishment because of their particular dangerousness, while the defense of the lack of requisite state of mind should be rejected in the latter group of cases because such a defense might be too easily raised in every prosecution.

In Japan it is criminal homicide only when the possibility that death may result is actually realized by the actor. According to the prevailing theory, criminal intent has two elements: one cognitive, the other volitional. The first means that the accused is not criminally responsible for a homicide unless he knew that death was a possible consequence of his act; the second signifies that he must willingly accept this possibility. Both of these elements can be established by proof that the actor at the time believed that death was an inevitable consequence of his act. If this state of mind cannot be established, however, each element must be proved separately. If it is proven that the actor, although he knew death was a possible consequence of his act, trusted to luck and truly believed that death would not in fact occur, the volitional element is lacking; but that element is established by a showing that the accused accepted the risk of death and chose to act in spite of it. This is the theory of *dolus eventualis.*

The crime of receiving stolen property furnishes another example of the two different approaches to "intent." In order to commit that crime in Japan, the defendant must realize and admit that the goods might well be stolen property. In the United States this subjective element is not an element of the crime in some instances. If there is good reason to believe that the goods are stolen, the defendant may be punished even though he did not in fact realize that the property might have been stolen. In states where the "good reason" test is not applied, knowledge is often presumed if certain facts are

[64] Homicide Act, 1957, 5 & 6 ELIZ. II, c. 11.

[65] MORELAND, THE LAW OF HOMICIDE 36 (1952).

shown.[66] Also under the German Penal Code, which usually rejects presumptions, the crime of receiving stolen property occurs "in cases in which the defendant ought to have known from the circumstances that the goods were stolen." [67]

There are many other presumptive provisions in England and the United States, but the Japanese penal statutes contain almost no provisions creating presumptions respecting the subjective elements of crimes. The only exception[68] is an old 1884 decree which penalizes traffic in explosives and imposes a light punishment upon a defendant found in possession of explosives who does not prove that he did not have an intent to kill or injure by their use.[69] Consequently, Japanese procurators envy the many presumptive provisions of Anglo-American law, especially in cases of receiving stolen property and of governmental corruption.[70]

The fact that under Japanese law acts are not criminal unless there is a subjective element present logically implies that punishment cannot be imposed unless it is possible to impute moral blame to the actor. Although

[66] See, e.g., MODEL PENAL CODE §206.8 (Tent. Draft No. 4, 1955):

"(1) *In General.* A person who receives stolen movable property otherwise than for the purpose of restoring it to the owner commits theft if he knows that it is stolen property or, in the case of a dealer, if he believes that it is probably stolen property . . .

"(3) *Dealer Defined.* Dealer means:

"(a) a person found in possession or control of movable property stolen on separate occasions from more than two persons;

"(b) a person who has received stolen movable property in two other transactions within the year preceding the receiving with which he is charged;

"(c) a person who is in the business of selling or using property of the sort received.

"(4) *Presumption of Knowledge or Belief.* The requisite knowledge or belief shall be presumed when:

"(a) the actor is a dealer within paragraphs (a) or (b) of the preceding subsection;

"(b) the actor is a dealer within paragraph (c) of the preceding subsection, acquires the property from one under the age of 16 or for substantially less than reasonable value, and fails to notify either the police or any person whose identity and probable interest in the property appear on or from the nature of the property;

"(c) the actor had been convicted of theft, by receiving or otherwise, or attempted theft, within three years preceding the receiving with which he is charged."

[67] STGB §259.

[68] Art. 207 of the Penal Code may be another exception: "In a situation where through the use of violence by two or more persons they injure another, if it is impossible to know the gravity of the injury or if it is impossible to know which person caused the injury, they are to be dealt with as in the case of accomplices even though they are not joint actors."

[69] Explosives Control Penal Rules, Great Council of State Decree No. 23 of 1884.

[70] The English Prevention of Corruption Act, 1916, 6 & 7 GEO. V, c. 64, §2, states: "Where . . . it is proved that any money . . . has been . . . given to or received by a person in the employment of His Majesty . . . by or from a person . . . holding or seeking to obtain a contract from His Majesty . . . the money . . . shall be deemed to have been paid or given and received corruptly . . . unless the contrary is proved." Whether this substantive-law emphasis on subjective elements justifies the semiaccusatorial or inquisitorial system of criminal procedure is another problem. (See Kohji Tanabe, "The Processes of Litigation: An Experiment with the Adversary System," in this volume.) In my view, the significance of this aspect of the substantive law for procedural arrangements is very small and has been rather overemphasized by procurators.

moral blame cannot be imputed to a defendant unless he was able to choose between legal and illegal courses of activity, the Japanese Penal Code has no provisions exempting compelled acts from criminal responsibility. When the defendant had no real chance to choose between legal and illegal activity, however, the Japanese law seems to take the position that punishment should not be imposed. This is the principle of *Zumutbarkeit* (imputability). The Supreme Court has not yet faced the problem, but the lower courts have utilized this principle and have handed down rulings of not guilty.[71]

Since in Japanese law there is an emphasis on moral blameworthiness, it would be expected that the courts would require as an element of crime that the accused must have had knowledge of the illegality of his act; but the courts have stopped short of this and have taken the view that *ignorantia juris non excusat.*[72]

Absolving a defendant of criminal liability for an act which would otherwise be criminal because he had no choice as to his conduct may seem somewhat extreme. In all cases, however, the degree of moral blameworthiness is an important consideration in the assessment of punishment. The Japanese Penal Code fixes punishment within rather broad limits, providing, for example, that homicide may be punished by death, life imprisonment, or imprisonment for a fixed term in excess of three years.[73] The punishment actually imposed is intended to correspond to the degree of the actor's responsibility.[74] But in some of the United States, where murder is classified as either first or second degree, first-degree murderers

[71] E.g., Hayashi v. Japan, Tokyo High Court, Oct. 29, 1953, 6 KŌ-HAN KEISHŪ 1536–40; Hirose v. Japan, Tokyo High Court, Oct. 28, 1950, KŌTŌ SAIBANSHO KEIJI HANKETSU TOKUHŌ (High Court Criminal Decisions Special Reporter) no. 13, at 20, 21; Kabushiki Kaisha Obayashi-gumi v. Japan, Tokyo High Court, Oct. 16, 1948, 1 KŌ-HAN KEISHŪ supp. at 18, 19.

[72] E.g., Komatsu v. Japan, Supreme Court, III Petty Bench, Nov. 28, 1950, 4 SAI-HAN KEISHŪ 2463, 2465; Yoshida v. Japan, Supreme Court, Grand Bench, July 14, 1948, 2 SAI-HAN KEISHŪ 889, 891; Shiozaki v. Japan, Great Court of Judicature, III Criminal Department, Sept. 13, 1933, 12 DAI-HAN KEISHŪ 1619, 1634; Judgment of Aug. 5, 1924, Great Court of Judicature, I Criminal Department, 3 DAI-HAN KEISHŪ 611, 616. However, in a handful of cases the Great Court of Judicature adopted the view that the accused should not be punished if he had reasonable grounds to believe that his act was lawful. E.g., Oshima v. Japan, Great Court of Judicature, III Criminal Department, Feb. 10, 1934, 13 DAI-HAN KEISHŪ 76, 80; Matsumoto v. Japan, Great Court of Judicature, I Criminal Department, Aug. 4, 1932, 11 DAI-HAN KEISHŪ 1153, 1157. The Japanese Draft Penal Code of 1961, art. 20(2), provides for the incorporation of such a rule into substantive law. Moreover, it also should be noted that from time to time both the Great Court and the Supreme Court have made a distinction between mistakes of law and of fact as well as mistakes of penal law and of nonpenal law, acquitting an accused by declaring his error to be in the area of fact or nonpenal law. E.g., Judgment of June 9, 1925, Great Court of Judicature, I Criminal Department, 4 DAI-HAN KEISHŪ 378; Judgment of April 25, 1924, Great Court of Judicature, VI Criminal Department, 3 DAI-HAN KEISHŪ 363.

[73] PENAL CODE art. 199.

[74] Leniency in punishing offenses against life and limb, compared with those against property, may also be explained by the fact that the courts take the blameworthiness of the actor's motive fully into consideration. Offenses against life and limb are often a result of twisted human relations in the community and the victim is also partially responsible.

receive the mandatory death penalty. The English Homicide Act of 1957 enumerates several types of murderers on whom the mandatory death penalty is imposed.[75] These acts were selected with a view to deterring professional criminals. But consider, for example, a case of homicide committed by shooting: since there are various motives and causes for such an act, the 1957 Homicide Act unjustly imposes the death penalty across the board. Efforts are made to achieve just results in such cases in England and the United States by the use of pardons after the courts have entered a final death sentence. The law is supposed to contemplate the reasonable, average man and weigh the acts according to objective standards; the special circumstances surrounding an individual offender apparently enter only into the consideration of pardon. The *Mignonette* case, involving the hapless English cabin boy,[76] has been used to show the difference between Anglo-American criminal law and that of Germany on the issue of whether the courts or some other agency make the conclusive determination concerning responsibility.[77] The case would serve as well to illustrate the differences in this area between Japanese and American criminal law.

THE PROBLEM OF ACCOMPLICES

The Japanese Penal Code divides accomplices into coprincipals, instigators, and accessories; it provides that "two or more persons who have jointly executed a crime are all principals," that a "person who has instigated and caused another to execute a crime" is an instigator, and that a "person who has assisted a principal is an accessory." [78] An instigator is punished within the same statutory limits as provided for a principal, but an accessory always benefits from a statutory reduction of punishment. It thus appears that the drafters of the code thought that criminals ought to be classified according to the objective factors of acting, encouraging, and aiding, and that the gravity of punishment should be weighted according to the classification. This system follows the lines of the French and German codes.

The Japanese cases have gone beyond the limits set by the Penal Code, however, and have developed the concept of a "conspiratorial coprincipal." [79] Once a conspiracy to commit a crime has been entered into, those who actually carried out the acts constituting the crime as well as those who did not are treated as principals. The Great Court of Judicature first developed this theory in a case in which A suggested and planned the crime of intimidation but got B to agree to go to the victim's house. The Court held

[75] Homicide Act, 1957, 5 & 6 ELIZ. II, c. 11, §§5–6.

[76] The Queen v. Dudley & Stephens, 14 Q.B.D. 273 (1884).

[77] See RADBRUCH, DER GEIST DES ENGLISCHEN RECHTS 74–81 (2d ed., 1947). We should note, though, that English law takes into account the reluctance of a single judge to impose capital punishment as a sentence.

[78] PENAL CODE arts. 60–62.

[79] *Kyōbō kyōdō seihan.*

that it was proper to impose heavy punishment as a principal on one who took charge of the "commission of an intellectual crime" of this kind and who contributed such great "psychological impetus" to its commission.[80]

Since the code says that an instigator can be punished within the same statutory limits as the principal, in strict theory A, treated as an instigator, could have been punished just as B was or even more severely. However, the Court apparently felt that such treatment would be hard to justify in practice unless A's blameworthiness were emphasized by a label such as "principal offender."

As Justice Jackson said about conspiracy,[81] once a principle is recognized the tendency is to carry it to its logical extreme. Thus in a 1936 decision of its united criminal departments the Great Court of Judicature determined that even in crimes of violence such as robbery conspirators could be held as principals.[82] The extension of the original doctrine was due in part to considerations of convenience of proof, in that it did away with the necessity of proving the acts done by each individual. Accordingly, today it is standard to institute prosecution in a form such as: "Defendants A and B conspired to kill X and killed X at a certain time and place." Under this charge it is unnecessary to prove whether A or B struck the blow. Thus the subjective element of conspiracy has come to have great importance.

The conspiratorial-coprincipal theory has much in common with the Anglo-American law of conspiracy.[83] In the first place, it is not necessary under the American law to determine whether all the conspirators knew who the others were. Japanese courts have taken the same view and have admitted the possibility of there being a "conspiratorial coprincipal through an intermediate link."[84] Secondly, a tacit agreement is sufficient to constitute conspiracy.[85] This tendency is perhaps stronger in Japan than in the United States. The concept of the conspiratorial coprincipal has been developed through cases interpreting the provisions covering coprincipals.

[80] Judgment of April 18, 1922, Great Court of Judicature, I Criminal Department, 1 DAI-HAN KEISHŪ 233, 235.

[81] Krulewitch v. United States, 336 U.S. 440, 445 (1949) (concurring opinion).

[82] Kuki v. Japan, Great Court of Judicature, United Criminal Departments, May 28, 1936, 15 DAI-HAN KEISHŪ 715, 734. Carrying this tendency even further, courts have treated as accomplices those who have actually carried out the crime. In a case involving a violation of a provision in the Food Control Law that rice shall not be transported without permission, the Supreme Court held that the person who did the planning and ordered the rice to be transported was the principal, and the person who carried the rice was only an accomplice. Aoyagi v. Japan, Supreme Court, I Petty Bench, July 6, 1950, 4 SAI-HAN KEISHŪ 1178, 1180.

[83] On the American law of conspiracy, see *Developments in the Law — Criminal Conspiracy*, 72 HARV. L. REV. 920 (1959). The Anglo-American law of conspiracy has been described as reflecting in its development the contemporary tendency of "infusing morals into the law." Sayre, *Criminal Conspiracy*, 35 HARV. L. REV. 393, 400 (1922).

[84] Suemura v. Japan, Great Court of Judicature, II Criminal Department, June 18, 1936, 15 DAI-HAN KEISHŪ 805, 812.

[85] See Sumiyoshi v. Japan, Supreme Court, III Petty Bench, June 27, 1950, 4 SAI-HAN KEISHŪ 1096.

In cases involving coprincipals, cooperative action provides sufficient basis for inferring an intent to participate, as a sort of tacit agreement.[86] This inference has been extended to cover cases in which conspirators are treated as coprincipals.[87] As a result, the tendency in lower courts has been to punish as conspiratorial coprincipals even those who merely had the facts constituting the conspiracy confided to them.[88]

It is still undecided whether a conspiracy is an act or a state of mind. According to Judge Kusano, who wrote the 1936 decision referred to above, a conspiracy is a state of mind;[89] consensus should exist when the criminal act was perpetrated, but it does not matter when and where the consensus was formed. Later cases of the Great Court of Judicature and the Supreme Court seem to have taken a different view, however. The Great Court of Judicature held that the place at which the conspiring itself occurred, even though the contemplated act was perpetrated elsewhere, was the place where the crime was committed, so that the court of that district has jurisdiction over the crime.[90] A recent decision of the Supreme Court seems to have ruled that it is necessary not only to prove the existence of a state of mental agreement but also to produce enough evidence to show the act of forming the conspiracy, including the time and place of formation.[91] There is, however, a fundamental difference between the Japanese approach and the Anglo-American law of conspiracy. The conspiratorial-coprincipal theory requires that the criminal activity progress beyond the simple overt act to a stage where actual harm is done to society before criminal liability attaches.

THE RELATION BETWEEN RESTRAINT AND SUBJECTIVITY

In comparison with Western systems, then, Japanese criminal law is characterized both by restraint in the sense of a consciousness of practical limitations on the law's effectiveness and by subjectivity in the form of a pronounced emphasis upon the defendant's moral blameworthiness.

The restraint found in Japanese criminal law undoubtedly stems from the

[86] E.g., Shinkai v. Japan, Supreme Court, III Petty Bench, Dec. 14, 1948, 2 SAI-HAN KEISHŪ 1751, 1753.

[87] E.g., Sano v. Japan, Supreme Court, II Petty Bench, Feb. 8, 1949, 3 SAI-HAN KEISHŪ 113, 114.

[88] But see Japan v. Ando, Tokyo District Court, Dec. 25, 1958, HANREI JIHŌ (The Case Journal) no. 177, at 5, 8, where Judge Akio Date attempted to restrict the conspiratorial-coprincipal doctrine. This case is regarded as an exception to the general line of precedent.

[89] See Kusano, *Keihō Kaisei Sōan to Kyōhan no Jūzokusei* (The Draft Revising the Penal Code and the Accessory Nature of Accomplices), 50 HŌGAKU KYŌKAI ZASSHI (Journal of the Jurisprudence Association) 959, 978 (1932).

[90] Toyoda v. Japan, Great Court of Judicature, V Criminal Department, Dec. 9, 1936, 15 DAI-HAN KEISHŪ 1593.

[91] Yajima v. Japan, Supreme Court, Grand Bench, May 28, 1958, 12 SAI-HAN KEISHŪ 1718, 1723; Suzuki v. Japan (The Matsukawa Case), Supreme Court. Grand Bench, Aug. 10, 1959, 13 SAI-HAN KEISHŪ 1419, 1441.

underlying character of traditional Japanese culture. In Europe, criminal law originally developed to satisfy the desire for retribution. But in tracing the history of criminal law in Japan prior to the importation of Western institutions, one does not encounter retributive law, probably because the highly developed and nonretributive penal law of T'ang China was taken over at a very early period in Japanese legal development. A brief examination of Japanese myths in comparison with those of ancient Germany illustrates the differences between Japanese and Western culture. This original difference became even greater as the Western European tradition was influenced by the strict individualistic morality of Christianity while Japanese culture derived its inspiration from permissive Buddhism and practical Confucianism. The fact that from 818 to 1156 the death penalty was officially prohibited in Japan is a symbolic manifestation of this difference. Also, sexual taboos were weak in traditional Japan in comparison with Europe.

Nor was it necessary for traditional Japan to depend on criminal law to the same extent as the Western societies did, since control and discipline through the family and local community were — and are — very strong.* Prior to the Meiji Restoration the villages were separate governmental units, each holding its own independent right to impose punishment for offenses. Banishment was the strongest form of coercion, but when certain impediments arose against the use of banishment, social ostracism — a concerted breaking off of social and commercial relationships as the result of the decision of a village meeting — was quite widely employed as a coercive measure. After the Restoration, social ostracism was legally abolished, and punishment for intimidation could be imposed for social ostracism not based on reasonable grounds. Nevertheless, the custom is still not extinct today; there were 139 cases in 1951 and 135 cases in 1952 in which villagers who had been ostracized sought relief from Human Rights Protection Commissioners.[92]

Even before the Meiji era, the head of a family held no legally recognized right to inflict punishment. In practice, he was accorded the power to shut a criminal or a mentally abnormal individual in a locked room without being punished for false imprisonment. Today this power to control members of the family has become very weak in metropolitan areas, but it probably is still invoked to some extent in rural districts, especially in

* In fact, as Albert Craig suggested during the conference, it is not the awareness of punishment which serves to deter a Japanese so much as the awareness of the impact which the fact of his involvement in criminal proceedings would have on himself and, more important, on his family.

[92] See Maeda, *Murahachibu no Sho-keitai* (Various Forms of Murahachibu), 5 KINKI DAIGAKU HŌGAKU (Kinki University Jurisprudence) 30, 44 (1957); Iwasaki, *Murahachibu ni Tsuite* (Concerning Murahachibu), 6 KEIHŌ ZASSHI (Journal of Criminal Law) 162, 193 (1956)

cases of mentally abnormal persons.[93] Japan has not yet adopted the system widely recognized in other countries under which persons found not guilty by reason of criminal insanity are committed to institutions. Japanese practices in this area are behind the times, which may be a partial result of the survival of the practice of keeping the mentally ill person within the family.

The state law is a standard imposed from without which stands at times in opposition to criteria of local morality. Japanese laws were copied from French or German codes in order to achieve quickly the respectability expected of a modern nation as regards legal rules and practices. If these codes had been strictly enforced in their original form, the extent to which they ran counter to popular standards would have been exposed at once. It is true that criminal codes contain a great many provisions reasoned from basic human nature, and there are no major differences among nationalities in truly basic traits; but it is impossible to avoid a number of subtle differences. Moreover, because the judges, procurators, and police charged with enforcing the law were newly created officials, their intervention, even though for the purpose of enforcing traditional and popularly accepted standards, was considered meddling from outside.

If such extreme limitations characterize the social function of Japanese criminal law, how then do we explain its strong emphasis on moral blameworthiness?

The Meiji government, though it took the form of a modern state, was patriarchal in its essence. The government was expected to dictate the society's moral standards, which, incongruously enough, were based on Western individualism, and to foster the economic activities of individuals — an ideology which Japanese political scientists call "national liberalism." Under such a system, law is not clearly distinguished from morality and the courts tend to judge the inner moral culpability of the accused. This tendency is usually held somewhat in check, however, by the characteristic restraint of Japanese criminal law.

The development of the interrelation between the two characteristics has been particularly interesting in the area of cases involving direct injury to the government. At first, especially in cases of crimes against the Emperor, criminal law entered an extremely subjective domain. Under the now repealed article 73 of the Penal Code, "a person who inflicts or attempts to inflict injury on the Emperor . . . is to suffer the death penalty." The term "attempt" extended to all acts expressing an intent to inflict injury. By virtue of this provision, twenty-four anarchists were sentenced to death in 1910

[93] This may be inferred from the fact that there were 450,000 mentally ill persons in Japan in 1957, but only 2.5 percent of that number were committed to mental institutions. DAIJIN KAMBŌ, note 40 above at 292.

for plotting the death of the Emperor.[94] Also, under former article 76 of the Penal Code, persons who committed acts showing disrespect toward the imperial family were punished. Under this statute, punishment was inflicted even against a defendant who merely wrote comments critical of the imperial family in a private diary.[95]

The Peace Preservation Law[96] was a suppressive measure against Communists. Either the death penalty or some lesser penalty was to be imposed on those who "organized a society for the purpose of revolutionizing the form of state or of repudiating the institution of privately owned property," those who formed a group or organized a society for the purpose of preparing for the organization of such a society or of supporting such a society, those who joined such a society, and those who performed acts to facilitate the accomplishment of its objectives. These provisions had a decidedly negative effect in that freedom of speech in political matters was seriously oppressed.

However, after World War II, the crimes of high treason and disrespect were abolished, and acts against the heads of government are punishable today only as battery or defamation, as they would be if directed against any ordinary citizen. The Subversive Activities Prevention Law,[97] a descendant of the Peace Preservation Law, in addition to punishing solicitation for revolutionary societies and inducement of acts against the government, imposes punishment on persons who, with the object of bringing about acts of insurrection, "print, distribute, or publicly post documents or posters asserting the propriety or necessity of such acts."[98] Up to now there have been four prosecutions instituted for violations of this statute, all against Communists, but each resulted in a judgment of acquittal because the courts found no "clear and present danger."[99] Thus, even in the area involving injury to the government the objective principle of restraint is now emerging.

The interrelationship between objective restraint and the emphasis on subjective moral blameworthiness has been important also in the context of punishment. Around the end of the last century, the so-called modernist

[94] Japan v. Kotoku, Great Court of Judicature, Special Criminal Department, Jan. 18, 1911 (not officially reported). See SHIODA & WATANABE, TAIGYAKU JIKEN (The Treason Case) (1961).

[95] Hashiura v. Japan, Great Court of Judicature, I Criminal Department, March 3, 1911, 17 DAI-HAN KEIROKU 258, 263.

[96] Laws No. 46 of 1925 and No. 54 of 1941. The death penalty was introduced through amendment of the 1925 statute by Imperial Order No. 129 of 1928. The new 1941 law abolished it.

[97] Law No. 240 of 1952.

[98] *Ibid.*, art. 38(2)(ii).

[99] Japan v. Kim, Gifu District Court, January 27, 1959, HANREI JIHŌ (The Case Journal) no. 183, at 5, 33; Japan v. Shimamura, Kushiro District Court, Sept. 15, 1954, HANREI JIHŌ no. 36, at 3, 9; Japan v. Sugahara, Kyoto District Court, Dec. 27, 1956, HANREI JIHŌ no. 112, at 1, 32; Japan v. Arai, Tsu District Court, Feb. 28, 1955, HANREI JIHŌ no. 48, at 3, 15.

school arose in Europe. On the one hand, this school stressed the desirability of making punishment more humanitarian and scientific, while, on the other, it expressed a strong concern for the protection of society and tended occasionally to ignore the civil rights of criminals. The subjective nature of European criminal law is an expression of this concern to protect society. But if we emphasize, as did the great criminologist Franz von Liszt, that the criminal law is the Magna Carta of criminals, then the criminal law should probably be made as objective as possible. This position does not necessarily rule out the idea of the modernist school, which is that it is the actor who should be punished, not the act. It would be rather superficial to consider that the subjective elements of a criminal act in themselves always reveal the actor's personal characteristics; the personality of a criminal can be made clear only after a full investigation. The definition of crime which first gives rise to the opportunity for diagnosis and treatment can be an objective one and yet still give effect to the idea of rehabilitating the offender.

In Europe the modernist school appeared after the criterion that the individual is the fundamental value in society had been fully accepted. But this was not the case in Japan, where patriarchal concepts survive to this day. It should be noted that the patriarchal idea of punishment and that of the modernist school take the same form in some respects. It may be for this reason that the modernist school in Japan rather naively denies the principle of *nulla poena sine lege,* interprets the provisions in the Penal Code subjectively, and maintains that attempts at instigation should be punishable *de lege lata.* In this they are even more thoroughgoing than European scholars of the same school. As a result of the tendency in Japanese society not to rely so much on law for the protection of society, however, the concepts of the modernist school did not exert so great an influence on the law as they would have in a society which depended more on law for its protection.

The modernist school in Japan has had a major influence on those trends of a humanitarian and punishment-reducing nature, such as suspension of prosecution, suspension of the execution of judgment, and parole. These reforms were comparatively easy to achieve in Japan where the sense of retributive justice has not been nearly so strong as it is in Europe. Suspension of prosecution was permitted in all criminal cases under the 1922 Code of Criminal Procedure.[100] Suspension of the execution of judgment has been recognized since 1906 in the case of all crimes punished by confinement of less than two years,[101] and it was expanded by the 1947 amendments[102] to cover crimes punishable by incarceration of less than three years. Within these limits, suspension of execution is possible for almost all crimes. In 1959,

[100] CODE OF CRIMINAL PROCEDURE OF 1922, arts. 279, 292.
[101] PENAL CODE art. 25, amended by Law No. 124 of 1947.
[102] Law No. 124 of 1947.

43,498 of the 90,830 persons convicted of crimes punishable by imprisonment, or about 48 percent, received suspension of the execution of punishment.[103] Looking at homicide cases alone, 405 out of 1,483 convicted defendants received suspension of the execution of the judgment against them.[104]

Parole is allowed under the Penal Code whenever one third of the term of imprisonment has been served.[105] The leniency of this is striking when compared with European countries such as Switzerland where two thirds of the sentence must have been served. In 1959, 14,949 served their full sentences, while 31,180 were paroled, although 21,365 of that number served four fifths or more of their maximum terms.[106]

Even today, however, there are no provisions in Japan authorizing indeterminate sentences or preventive detention against repeated offenders, nor are there special measures for the treatment of mentally abnormal criminals.

The striking aspects of present-day Japanese criminal law have been described above, and some overgeneralization is unavoidable in such a short statement. Prediction for the future is more uncertain than is diagnosis. Whether it is an improvement or not, Japan is rapidly becoming urbanized and industrialized, and this development will probably not be halted. As a result, the role of criminal law as an instrument of social control will become more pervasive, since nonlegal forms of control such as the family and community will surely become less and less powerful. At the same time, criminal law will become more functional and less moralistic, and increasing emphasis will be placed on techniques of treatment as distinguished from punishment. Because of the complex nature of Japanese society, however, uncritical acceptance of the so-called scientific method in penology will be dangerous for Japan.

[103] Saikō Saibansho Jimu-sōkyoku, note 49, pt. 2, at 202, 262.

[104] *Ibid.*, at 254.

[105] Penal Code art. 28.

[106] 61 Hōmu-shō (Ministry of Justice), Gyōkei Tōkei Nempō Shōwa 34 Nen (Annual Report of Penal Administration Statistics — 1959) 8, 280 (1960).

Number of Individuals Sentenced for Four Types of Crime, 1959

Sentence	Homicide		Attempted homicide		Theft		Attempted theft	
Death	0.58%	5	0.00%	0	0.00%	0	0.00%	0
Life imprisonment	2.09	18	0.00	0	0.00	0	0.00	0
20 years or less	0.00	0	0.00	0	0.00	0	0.00	0
15 years or less	8.48	73	0.32	2	0.00	0	0.00	0
10 years or less	21.37	184	1.13	7	0.01	4	0.00	0
7 years or less	21.14	182	3.37	21	0.05	21	0.00	0
5 years or less	17.65	152	16.38	103	0.82	363	0.00	0
3 years	20.44	176	40.99	255	1.81	785	0.52	4
2 years or more	6.04	52	31.03	193	8.31	3,664	4.00	31
1 year or more	0.81	7	6.43	40	57.24	24,532	49.93	387
6 months or more	1.39	12	0.16	1	30.69	13,153	43.49	337
Under 6 months	0.00	0	0.00	0	0.79	339	2.06	16
Total	100.00%	861	100.00%	622	100.00%	42,861	100.00%	775

Source: SAIKŌ SAIBANSHO JIMU-SŌKYOKU (General Secretariat of the Supreme Court), SHŌWA 34 NEN SHIHŌ TŌKEI NEMPŌ (1959 Annual Report of Judicial Statistics), 2 KEIJI HEN (Criminal Affairs Book) pt. 2, at 70 (1961).

THE ACCUSED AND SOCIETY: THE ADMINISTRATION OF CRIMINAL JUSTICE IN JAPAN

Atsushi Nagashima

ASSISTED BY B. J. GEORGE, JR.

THE purpose of this essay is to discuss the major difficulties encountered in the administration of criminal justice in Japan by judges, procurators, and practicing lawyers under the present Code of Criminal Procedure and the Criminal Procedure Regulations. Investigation of four areas may serve to highlight these difficulties: the discretionary power of the public procurator, the changing role of defense counsel, the status of the defendant before the trial court, and the conduct of trial by judges.

It must be kept in mind throughout that Japanese criminal procedure was patterned after Continental law for about seventy years prior to 1949. In 1880, the Code of Criminal Instruction[1] was promulgated, having as a model the French Code d'Instruction Criminelle. In 1890 the Code of Criminal Procedure[2] was enacted, under both French and German influence. After 1895 there was strong pressure for a new code, which led to the enactment in 1922 of the second Code of Criminal Procedure,[3] which had a German foundation. Finally, in 1949 the present Code of Criminal Procedure[4] became effective; this was greatly influenced by Anglo-American criminal procedure. Because of the strength of the tradition of Continental law, however, some fields of procedure were not much altered under this new code, such as the functions of the public procurator and the status of the defendant. The Anglo-American influence was felt in the enlargement of the scope of defense counsel's functions and in the introduction of the ad-

Note. Mr. Nagashima is Counselor, Criminal Affairs Bureau, Ministry of Justice. B.Jur., Kyoto University, 1941. Participant, Japanese American Program for Cooperation in Legal Studies at Stanford University, 1956–1958. Alternate participant in the United Nations Seminar on Human Rights held in Tokyo, 1960, and in Wellington, New Zealand, 1961. Participant in the United Nations Consultative Group on the Prevention of Crime and Treatment of Offenders in Geneva, 1961. Author of KEIJI SOSHŌ HŌ (The Law of Criminal Procedure) (1956); writings in the fields of criminal law and the law of criminal procedure.

[1] Great Council of State Decree No. 37 of 1880.

[2] Law No. 96 of 1890.

[3] Law No. 75 of 1922.

[4] Law No. 131 of 1948.

versary form of trial, including the use of rules of evidence such as the hearsay rule. Use of the jury system has been suspended for the past twenty years, however,[5] and trial judges consequently have suffered under the heavy burden of four duties: keeping order in the court and presiding over the trial; determining the facts in the case as trier of fact; determining and applying the appropriate standards in deciding guilt and innocence; and setting the penalty where necessary. The main difficulties in the administration of criminal justice in Japan seem to derive from the conflicting origins and fundamental principles contained in the present hybrid code. In the thirteen years of experience under the new code, however, one can see certain trends toward new administrative and legislative policies in the law of criminal procedure which may solve some of these difficulties.

THE DISCRETIONARY POWER OF THE PUBLIC PROCURATOR

One of the unique characteristics of Japanese procedure is the very wide discretionary power granted to public procurators. A decision not to prosecute may be based not only on the ground of insufficient evidence to support conviction, but also on the ground of the undesirability or inappropriateness of prosecution. In a word, the procurator may decline prosecution whenever he deems it proper to do so.[6]

The post of public procurator was first created in 1872. In 1880, the function of the procurator was described as follows: "The procurator has the power to request the investigation of a crime, but he does not have the power to make an investigation himself."[7] During the period 1897 to 1916, the practice was gradually established for the procurator himself to make a thorough investigation. The reason for the change was not that the procurator wanted to strengthen his own powers, but that the people in general wanted him to investigate crimes so that he would not institute proceedings with insufficient evidence to support conviction of the defendants; the percentage of acquittals entered by the courts was amounting to nearly 30 per-

[5] See Haruo Abe, "The Accused and Society: Therapeutic and Preventive Aspects of Criminal Justice in Japan," in this volume.

[6] CODE OF CRIMINAL PROCEDURE art. 248: "When pursuant to the offender's character, age, and surroundings, the gravity and circumstances of his crime, and his conduct after the crime it is felt unnecessary to prosecute, a public action need not be instituted." This code can be found in English translation in MINISTRY OF JUSTICE, THE CONSTITUTION AND CRIMINAL STATUTES OF JAPAN 86 (1960) [hereafter cited CRIMINAL STATUTES]. This publication contains English translations of the Constitution, Penal Code, and other codes relating to the administration of criminal justice.

[7] KIYOURA, ZUICHŌ ZUIHITSU (Things Heard and Jotted Down at Random) (1880), quoted in Idei, *Kensatsu no Jissen-teki Settoku Kinō* (The Practical Persuasive Function of Prosecution), JURIST no. 223, at 10–11 (1961). The author, Kiyoura, was a famous politician. He became Vice Minister of Justice in 1892 and was Minister of Justice for most of the period from 1896 to 1903. In 1924 he became Prime Minister.

cent of the total cases.[8] The effort was successful, for in 1916 the rate of acquittals was only 7 percent by examining magistrates[9] and 2.5 percent in the trial courts.[10] This practice has continued to the present, and procurators do not institute proceedings unless they themselves have a firm belief in the guilt of the defendant. This strict attitude has been strongly supported by the public. Since it is not unusual for a procurator who fails to obtain a conviction to be blamed for inefficient investigation, no case is now brought unless the procurator has made a full investigation of facts surrounding the crime prior to the filing of the information. Thus it is not surprising that convictions are entered in 99 percent of the cases which procurators have presented for trial in recent years.[11]

Another, more important, aspect of the discretionary powers of the procurator is his role in rehabilitation. Before the second Code of Criminal Procedure, there was no provision giving procurators a discretionary power of nonprosecution. Nevertheless, it gradually became general usage for the procurator to decline prosecution of less serious crimes. Because the investigation and disposition of the matter were carried out by the procurator in closed chambers, the identity of the offender against whom prosecution was declined was rarely disclosed to the public; consequently the offender could continue in the community as a good citizen rather than with the stigma of a criminal. This system contributed so much to the rehabilitation and re-entry of the offender into society that it was explicitly approved and extended in the second code. Even an offender who had committed a rather serious crime might be relieved from prosecution if he was a first offender, if the injuries caused by the offense were compensated for, and if there was reasonable ground to believe that he would not commit another offense.[12] In large cities, procurators' offices set up so-called offenders' rehabilitation

[8] Shihō-shō (Ministry of Justice), Dai 23 Keiji Tōkei Nempō — Meiji 30 Nen (23rd Annual Report of Criminal Statistics — 1897) 403 (1899); Shihō-shō, Dai 24 Keiji Tōkei Nempō — Meiji 31 Nen (24th Annual Report of Criminal Statistics — 1898) 408 (1900); Shihō-shō, Dai 25 Keiji Tōkei Nempō — Meiji 32 Nen (25th Annual Report of Criminal Statistics — 1899) 411 (1901); Shihō-shō, Dai 26 Tōkei Nempō — Meiji 33 Nen (26th Annual Report of Criminal Statistics — 1900) 413 (1902).

[9] Under the first Code of Criminal Procedure, Japan had a system of examining magistrates, or *juges d'instruction,* who held a preliminary examination of serious or complicated cases referred to them by public procurators. They decided whether a *prima facie* case for the prosecution had been made out and then entered rulings either to refer the case to the trial courts or to discharge the accused.

[10] Shihō-shō (Ministry of Justice), Dai 42 Keiji Tōkei Nempō — Taishō 5 Nen (42nd Annual Report of Criminal Statistics — 1916) 34, 66–67 (1918).

[11] Saikō Saibansho Jimu-sōkyoku (General Secretariat of the Supreme Court), Shōwa 35 Nen Shihō Tōkei Nempō (1960 Annual Report of Judicial Statistics), 2 Keiji Hen (Criminal Affairs Book) pt. 1, at 50 (1961).

[12] The relevant provision of the second Code of Criminal Procedure of 1922 (art. 279) was almost identical to article 248 of the present code cited in note 6 above. The only change was the addition of "gravity" to the "circumstances of his crime."

sections through which volunteer probation officers and other volunteer social workers assisted discharged offenders by providing lodging and board, procuring employment, and so on. Although the offenders' rehabilitation sections have been replaced by probation offices, the assistance program still continues with great success. In 1958, prosecution was declined in 49.8 percent of the total cases disposed of during the year. Of these, 11.2 percent were based on the insufficiency of the evidence, while 38.6 percent were attributable to the exercise of the discretionary power of procurators based on criminological considerations.[13]

Not unrelated to discretionary prosecution is the traditional closing statement of the procurator at the trial. Article 293(1) of the Code of Criminal Procedure provides merely that "after the examination of evidence has been completed, the public procurator shall state his opinion in regard to the facts and the application of the law," but it has been a longstanding practice in Japan, as well as in some European countries, for the procurator at that time to express his opinion as to the appropriate penalty or other safety measures to be imposed upon the defendant. Usually procurators request the court to decree a specific penalty, such as two years' imprisonment or a 10,000 yen fine. The procurator has wide discretionary power in selecting from among a variety of sanctions: various terms of imprisonment, fines in varying amounts, suspension of the execution of sentence, probationary supervision, and protective measures.[14] Nevertheless, the recommendations tend to be uniform and in accord with popular feeling because of the subordination of the procurators to the general direction of the Procurator-General, who is mindful of public opinion and issues directives from time to time.[15] The court gives serious consideration to the recommended penalty—in part because the procurator can appeal the sentence if he feels that it is inadequate.[16]

Although the functions of the public procurator in the administration of

[13] HŌMU-SHŌ (Ministry of Justice), DAI 84 KENSATSU TŌKEI NEMPŌ — SHŌWA 33 NEN (84th Annual Report of Prosecution Statistics — 1958) 105 (1959).

[14] For example, protective measures for adult offenders are provided for in article 17 of the Prostitution Prevention Law, Law No. 118 of 1956, translated into English in BAISHUN TAISAKU NO GENKYŌ (The Present Condition of Anti-Prostitution Measures) 518 (Baishun Taisaku Shingikai (Anti-Prostitution Policy Council) ed., 1959):

"(1) When against a woman of 20 years of age or more who has committed the crime in article 5, execution of imprisonment at forced labor or confinement, pertaining to the crime of the same article or another crime, is suspended, this person may be placed under guidance disposition.

"(2) A person placed under guidance disposition is to be committed to a Women's Guidance Home and given the guidance necessary for her rehabilitation."

[15] These directives are usually issued orally at the national conference of public procurators which is held at least once every two months. The Minister of Justice also expresses his opinion on these occasions concerning principles of administration of criminal justice.

[16] Appeal to a High Court may be taken from a judgment of the trial court by either the accused or the public procurator. It is constitutional — that is, not in violation of article 39 of the Constitution forbidding double jeopardy — to give to the procurator the right to appeal even against a judgment of acquittal. Ishizaki v. Japan, Supreme Court, Grand Bench, Sept.

criminal justice in Japan are very broad, his power has not attracted much attention or criticism from practicing lawyers and scholars until very recent years. The reason may lie in the fact that Japanese procurators have occupied a status equivalent to that of judges, in which their independence and impartiality have been protected by law. The procurator in Japan has been thought to be the impartial representative of the public interest, like his French counterpart, the *procureur de la république*.[17]

27, 1950, 4 SAIKŌ SAIBANSHO KEIJI HANREI SHŪ (A Collection of Criminal Supreme Court Cases) [hereafter cited SAI-HAN KEISHŪ] 1805. If the defendant is the only party to appeal, the appellate court cannot pronounce a sentence heavier than the original one. CODE OF CRIMINAL PROCEDURE arts. 402, 414.

If an appeal is taken solely by the prosecution and is found groundless, the state indemnifies the accused for the expenses he has incurred. CODE OF CRIMINAL PROCEDURE art. 368. In 1958, the ratio of appeals for improper imposition of penalty to the total appeals was 63.5 percent for public procurators and 73.5 percent for defendants. In the same year, the rate of quashing original judgments when the public procurators appealed was 69.1 percent; in view of the fact that the total rate of quashing appeals during the same year was 26.3 percent, it seems that appeals made by public procurators receive a higher rate of support by appellate courts than those of defendants. HŌMU SŌGŌ KENKYŪJO (Ministry of Justice Integrated Research Institute), HŌMU-SHŌ (Ministry of Justice), HANZAI HAKUSHO — SHŌWA 35 NENBAN (1960 White Paper on Crime) 161, 163 (1960).

[17] Public Procurators' Office Law, Law No. 61 of 1947, art. 4, translated into English in CRIMINAL STATUTES 403. "Public procurators, in regard to criminal affairs, prosecute public actions, claim the proper application of law in court, and supervise the execution of judgments; in regard to other matters subject to the authority of a court, when they perceive the necessity from the standpoint of their official duties, they seek the advice of, or express their opinion to, the court; or as representatives of the public interest, they conduct affairs placed under their authority by other Laws and Orders." Two systems which have bearing upon the discretionary powers of the procurator have been introduced under the present code. One is the system of the inquest of prosecution which might be said to be a halfway step toward the grand-jury system. Inquest of Prosecution Law, Law No. 147 of 1948; see also "Commentary: Part II," in this volume. Under this system, if the injured party is not satisfied with the decision of the procurator not to prosecute the offender, he can petition to the inquest of prosecution, which consists of eleven laymen selected by lot and whose term of office is for six months. On receipt of the complaint, the inquest of prosecution will examine the documentary evidence presented by the procurator and summon the witnesses. After hearing the case, the inquest can recommend that prosecution be instituted. Eight votes are required for such a recommendation. Upon receipt of such recommendation, the procurator must re-examine the case and, if he deems it proper, he then institutes prosecution. Between 1949 and 1958, approximately 14,000 applications were received by inquests of prosecution, of which about 1,500 cases were referred to the procurators advising the institution of prosecution. Of these, about 260 resulted in prosecution and, in the ensuing trials, 180 defendants were found guilty and 36 not guilty. Hōmu-shō (Ministry of Justice), *Shōwa 32 Nendo Kaiko to Tembō* (1957 in Retrospect and Future Prospects), KENSATSU GEPPŌ (The Monthly Prosecution Report) no. 106, at 1, 12 (1958); Hōmu-shō, *Shōwa 34 Nendo Kaiko to Tembō* (1959 in Retrospect and Future Prospects), KENSATSU GEPPŌ no. 128, at 1, 21 (1960).

This rate of acquittal was much higher than in ordinary cases.

The other system is the so-called quasi-prosecution procedure, under which the injured party may apply to the court to try the case when he is dissatisfied with the determination of nonprosecution by the public procurator. If the collegiate court which hears the application finds it to be well grounded, the court must commit the case to a competent District Court for trial (CODE OF CRIMINAL PROCEDURE arts. 262–69). During the period 1949 to 1958, there were 624 such applications. Of these, 5 cases were committed to District Courts for trial; in 2 cases the defendants were sentenced to imprisonment, and in 1 case a pronouncement of acquittal was made. HŌMU SŌGŌ KENKYŪJO, note 16, at 149.

In recent years, however, there have been several proposals designed to restrict the powerful functions of the procuracy.* The first is that the procurator should refrain from investigative work, leaving that to the police, and should concentrate upon conducting the trial as an attorney for the government. Many police officials and judges, as well as some scholars, seem to support this suggestion.[18] The basis for their view is threefold. In the first place, police officials point to article 189(2) of the Code of Criminal Procedure, which provides: "Judicial police officials, when they feel that a crime exists, are to search for and investigate offenders and evidence."† On the other hand, article 191(1) provides: "A public procurator, when he perceives the necessity, may search for and investigate crime on his own initiative." Thus, it is contended, the first and primary responsibility for criminal investigation lies with the police; the procurator's function in this respect is merely supplementary and one for which he is not properly trained. In contrast with the old procedure by which the procurator presented to the court, prior to the opening of the trial, all the documents and other evidence which he had gathered, the procurator must now examine and crossexamine witnesses in open court. In addition, the new code introduces many complicated rules of evidence covering confessions, hearsay, and so on. Because of such changes, the time which the procurator must consume in preparation for trial as well as in court has become greatly increased. Finally, the adversary system of the new code requires that the procurator be the attorney for the government; thus he cannot be an impartial party to the trial. Instead he must concentrate on obtaining a conviction and a heavy penalty against the defendant. Whether desirable or not, the procurator must become the attorney for the prosecution and nothing else.

The second proposal is that the discretionary power of the procurator to institute proceedings should be restricted. The proponents of this view[19]

* At the conference, Ryuichi Hirano stated his feeling that the wide and largely unreviewed discretion accorded the procuracy leaves open many possibilities of abuse. For example, suspects are now placed on an unofficial form of probation in some cases as a prerequisite to the procurator's declining to prosecute. Even though the accused consents, such a practice poses a threat to the civil liberties of the defendant.

[18] See, for example, Nakabu, *Kensatsukan to Shihō Keisatsu Shokuin to no Kankei ni Tsuite* (On the Relationship Between Public Procurators and Judicial Police Officials), in KAISEI KEIJI SOSHŌ HŌ (Revised Code of Criminal Procedure) 246, 248 (Nihon Keihō Gakkai (Japan Criminal Law Association) ed., 1953) (scholar); Kiriyama, *Keisatsukan no Sōsa to Kensatsukan no Sōsa* (Investigation by Police Officers and Investigation by Public Procurators), 21 KEISATSU KENKYŪ (Police Research) no. 1, at 45, 50–51 (1950) (police official); Yokokawa, *Sōsa to Shin Keiso* (Investigation and the New Criminal Procedure), 21 HŌRITSU JIHŌ (Law Journal) no. 10, at 3, 5 (1949) (judge).

† Although the present code requires the police to investigate all suspected crimes, Atsushi Nagashima reported to the conference that they do exercise discretion and do not investigate all who are suspected of minor offenses.

[19] Hirano, *Shikkō Yūyo to Senkoku Yūyo — Jumbi Sōan to Keiji Seisaku-jō no Sho-Mondai* (Suspended Execution and Suspended Sentence — The Preliminary Draft and Various Policy Problems), 32 KEISATSU KENYŪ no. 2, at 25, 26 (1961).

advocate a reconsideration of the strict attitude of procurators in evaluating evidence and in declining prosecution when they fear an acquittal by the court. It is thought to be contrary to the public interest that a conviction might have been entered against some of the offenders who escaped prosecution because of the personal and perhaps groundless belief of the procurator as to the insufficiency of the evidence.

The opponents of these proposals[20] insist first that, in the actual situation in Japan, it is impossible to institute prosecution with reliance solely on the evidence collected by the police, since in a number of cases deficiencies in police investigation have necessitated a supplementary investigation by the procurator. Moreover, there may be cases in which the police cannot make a sufficient investigation because of their lack of legal knowledge or because of powerful political or community influences. In the latter case, no one except a public procurator who is protected in his independence by law can possibly make a thorough investigation. Under the new code, there is no question but that the procurator must devote a great portion of his time to preparation for trial and to trial work itself; but this does not negate the necessity of his investigative function. Further, the adversary system does not necessarily produce a partial procurator. The procurator as an impartial representative of the public interest and justice sometimes withdraws prosecution or expresses an opinion in his closing statement that the defendant should be acquitted because of his clear innocence or because of the insufficiency of the evidence. Moreover, in Japanese practice, the procurator participates in the sentencing process, by introducing all relevant evidence known to him even though some of it may favor the defendant, and in his closing statement the procurator comments on this evidence impartially. The standards used by the procuracy in evaluating evidence and in instituting prosecution have been supported for a long time by the Japanese people. Furthermore, criminological considerations involved in the exercise of his discretionary power of nonprosecution have contributed greatly to the rehabilitation of the offender and his reentry into society; and there is no reason whatsoever to leave criminological considerations solely to the courts.

In spite of this controversy, there has been an increasing tendency in the public procurators' offices to put more and more stress on criminological considerations in handling cases, especially in cases involving adolescents, prostitutes, or drug addicts.[21] Some offices have set up special protective offices for adolescents or prostitutes; probation officers, voluntary social caseworkers, procurators, and women police officers work in these offices

[20] Idei, note 7, at 13.

[21] Directives issued by the Minister of Justice and the Director of the Ministry's Criminal Affairs Bureau at the national conferences of public procurators held in Tokyo June 24, 1960, May 29, 1961, and May 28, 1962. Also see Nagashima, KEIHŌ ZASSHI (Journal of Criminal Law) no. 12, at 136 (1962).

and assist offenders who are not prosecuted. Personnel of the public procurators' offices and often the caseworkers assigned to these offices cooperate with the procurator in investigating the environmental circumstances of the suspect. Psychiatrists and psychologists are consulted more frequently than ever before by the procurators in examining the mental and psychological condition of suspects. Thus an increasing amount of thorough, impartial, and scientific information is collected, which not only makes the exercise of discretion by the procurator more rational and criminologically sound, but which also helps the court in passing sentence. It is not easy to forecast the method that will be followed by procurators in the future. But one thing seems clear: the traditions of the procuracy in Japan are firmly rooted, and the public reliance on the discretionary powers of procurators will not soon change.

THE CHANGING ROLE OF DEFENSE COUNSEL

The history of criminal procedure may be called the history of the enlarging functions of the defense attorney. This is particularly true in Japan, where the new code greatly enlarged the scope of the defense counsel's functions. In the first place, under the new code, any person who is under investigation may select defense counsel whether he has been arrested or not.[22] Secondly, the new code gives defense counsel the right of confidential communications with his client, whether defendant or suspect, while under arrest or detention.[23] Thirdly, the new code enlarged the scope of the right to have counsel provided by the state.[24] Of the 149,639 defendants tried before the courts in 1958, 105,476 or 64.5 percent had the assistance of counsel. Defendants for whom attorneys were appointed at government expense numbered 70,190 or 40.9 percent of the total. Counsel for the other 23.6 percent were selected by defendants at their own expense.[25]

Under the old code, the defense attorney had no powers during the process of investigation. After the filing of the case before the court or examining judge, he could read and copy the documents presented to the court by the procurator and he could interview the defendant with a guard present. In such circumstances, the functions of the defense attorney were very restricted. As a matter of practice, his preparation for trial was concentrated on the examination of the documents prepared in the course of

[22] CODE OF CRIMINAL PROCEDURE art. 30; see HIRANO, KEIJI SOSHŌ HŌ (Law of Criminal Procedure) 73–82 (Hōritsu-gaku Zenshū (Complete Collection on the Law) ed., 1958).

[23] CODE OF CRIMINAL PROCEDURE art. 39 (1948). Also see CODE OF CRIMINAL PROCEDURE OF 1922, arts. 43, 334–35.

[24] CODE OF CRIMINAL PROCEDURE arts. 36–38.

[25] CIVIL LIBERTIES BUREAU, MINISTRY OF JUSTICE, SYSTEM OF CIVIL LIBERTIES COMMISSIONERS AND LEGAL AID IN JAPAN 13–14 (1960) (throughout this volume the agency referred to here as the Civil Liberties Bureau is translated as the "Bureau for the Protection of Human Rights" and Civil Liberties Commissioners as "Human Rights Protection Commissioners").

investigation to discover discrepancies. It was quite unusual for defense counsel himself to investigate the case beyond questioning the defendant about the facts charged, or interviewing relatives and acquaintances of the defendant to collect information which might be submitted at the trial to obtain a more lenient sentence or suspension of the execution of sentence. It was believed to be contrary to professional ethics to interview prospective witnesses for the prosecution.[26]

The situation has changed completely under the new code.* Now the defense attorney selected by the suspect has a very important function in protecting his client. He must not obstruct the investigation, but he may protest against improper investigative procedures. He should collect and present to the investigating officers or to the procurator any evidence that is favorable to the suspect. Thus the defense counsel must have free access to his client and must be able to interview him without any guard present. Private conference is vitally important at the early stages of the investigation, especially when the suspect wants his attorney's advice as to whether he should make a factual statement or remain silent. The role of the defense counsel under these circumstances is delicate and requires finesse; he may tell the suspect about his constitutional right against self-incrimination, but he should not suggest or establish any false story. In fact, in a number of cases the suspect has become silent after an interview with his counsel, with the result that the investigating officer has encountered difficulties. For this reason, investigating officers and procurators do not like the fact that defense counsel may interview the suspect, especially in the early stages of the investigation when its success or failure depends greatly upon the voluntary cooperation of the suspect and other witnesses. A serious controversy thus exists between procurator and defense counsel, which might be said to be between the public interest, represented by the procurator, in prompt discovery of the crime and the criminal, and the interest of the suspect in protecting himself against prosecution and conviction. Article 39(3) of the Code of Criminal Procedure draws the line between the conflicting interests:

A public procurator, a procuratorial administrative officer, or a judicial police official (this refers to members of the judicial police and judicial constables, . . .), when it is necessary for purposes of search and investigation, may in regard to the interview or delivery and receipt of [documents in] paragraph (1), as long as it is prior to the institution of the public action, designate the date,

[26] TANAKA, SHŌKŌ HŌ (The Law of Evidence) 289 (1953); Shimomitsu, *Hōtei ni okeru "Uso"* ("Lies" in Court), 33 HŌRITSU JIHŌ 1318, 1319–21 (1961); Honda, *Keiji Soshō Hō ni okeru Riron to Jissai* (Theory and Actuality in the Law of Criminal Procedure), 9 HŌRITSU NO HIROBA (The Legal Plaza) no. 9, at 22, 25 (1956).

* Alfred Oppler suggested, however, that even today defense counsels adopt a similar approach of advising a plea of guilty with mitigating circumstances, and that this course is followed because of a fear that a plea of not guilty would unsettle the attorney's relations with the judge or procurator.

place, and time. Provided, however, this designation shall not be an improper restraint on the right of the suspect to prepare his defense.

It is natural that a controversy exists as to the interpretation of this article.[27] The investigating authorities construe the provision to mean that the designation of the date and place may be made not only when a public procurator or police official is actually questioning the suspect, but also when these officials deem the restrictions necessary to the investigation. On the other hand, private attorneys insist that the provision may be applied only when a public procurator or police official is actually questioning the suspect; otherwise it is an intolerable interference with the activities of defense counsel and hence with the right to counsel of the suspect. In practice, this power of designation is exercised mostly with regard to those suspects against whom a court order has been obtained forbidding them from interviewing persons other than their defense counsel on the ground that escape might be attempted or evidence destroyed.[28] The Sapporo High Court supported the view taken by the investigating authorities, holding that the clause "when it is necessary for purposes of search and investigation" includes the necessity to make inquiries of the suspect.[29] But in a case in which the suspect was in the custody of the police under a warrant of detention, and his interview with his defense counsel was limited to two or three minutes, the Supreme Court reacted as follows: "even assuming that there was a reason for imposing time restrictions, we can conclude generally that this designation was an improper measure, the time being far too short for the suspect to prepare his defense—an accepted right."[30] The Japanese Federated Attorneys Association has commented on the problem from time to time and has requested the Minister of Justice to change the Criminal Procedure Regula-

[27] Kanai & Kishimoto, *Sekken Mondai ni Kan-suru Kensatsukan-soku to no Iken Kōkan Kai* (A Meeting to Exchange Opinions With the Procuracy Concerning the Interview Problem), 4 JIYŪ TO SEIGI (Freedom and Justice) no. 12, at 31, 33, 35, 37 (1953); Ono & Otsu, *Hikokunin, Higisha to Bengonin no Sekken no Futō na Seigen ni Tsuite* (On Improper Restraints on Counsel's Interview of Defendants and Suspects), JURIST no. 51, at 14 (1954).

[28] CODE OF CRIMINAL PROCEDURE art. 81: "A court, when sufficient suitable reason exists to suspect that there will be an escape or that evidence of a crime will be destroyed or concealed, may, on the claim of the public procurator or ex officio, prohibit the interview of the defendant being detained by a person other than those provided for in article 39, paragraph (1) [i.e. his attorney or a person who may become such], examine the documents or other things to be delivered and received therewith, prohibit their delivery and receipt, or attach them. Provided, however, the receipt and delivery of food may not be prohibited or attached."

[29] Baba v. Japan, Sapporo High Court, Dec. 15, 1950, KŌTŌ SAIBANSHO KEIJI HANKETSU TOKUHŌ (High Court Criminal Decisions Special Reporter) no. 15, at 188. The court held that the designation of the times for interviews made by the procurator in this case, three times during a ten-day detention, was proper: the first, twenty minutes on the third day of detention; the second, thirty minutes on the eighth day of detention; the third, thirty minutes on the ninth day of detention.

[30] Hongo v. Japan, Supreme Court, II Petty Bench, July 10, 1953, 7 SAI-HAN KEISHŪ 1474, 1477.

tions implementing article 39 of the code to provide that the date and time of interview shall be designated so as to allow counsel to interview the suspect at the latest on the day following the day on which the request for interview is made, and that the time of the interview shall not be shorter than thirty minutes.[31]

Another important problem is the right of defense counsel to force disclosure of evidence held by the procurator. Under the old procedure, as mentioned above, the documentary and real evidence prepared or seized during investigation was presented to the court together with the information containing the facts charged, and the defense counsel thereafter had free access to these items of evidence before the trial began. The procurator was supposed to present to the court all the evidence which he had, whether unfavorable or favorable to the defendant. Thus disclosure before trial was complete. The situation was changed completely by the new code, under which prosecution ("public action") is begun by filing an information with the court. In order to avoid prejudicing the court, the presentation of documents and other evidence is prohibited until the appropriate point in the trial is reached. In furtherance of the new adversary system, the new code provides the means by which both parties can obtain the information necessary for the preparation of the trial. Article 299 of the code provides that the public procurator and the accused or the defense counsel must each give the opposing party, in advance, the names and addresses of the prospective witnesses if requested. If documentary or real evidence is to be produced before the trial court, the other party must be afforded an opportunity to inspect it in advance. The Criminal Procedure Regulations state in article 178-3 that generally such disclosure shall be made at least five days (three days in Summary Courts) before the first day of the public trial, provided that the period may be ignored if no objection is raised by the adverse party. These provisions are not intended to force the procurator to disclose all the evidence in his hands, but to give each party free access to the evidence on which the other intends to rely in making out his case before the trial court. Thus the disclosure under the code does not reach to the name and residence of witnesses or to documentary or real evidence when these are to be used in rebuttal or only by consent of the adverse party.

[31] The president of the Japanese Federated Attorneys Association, in a letter dated December 24, 1959, requested the Minister of Justice to cooperate with his proposal to change the Criminal Procedure Regulations by adding an article as follows: "Article 30-2. When an attorney asks a public procurator for an interview with the suspect, the procurator must designate a date and place so that the attorney may interview the suspect not later than the following day. The length of the interview must be not less than thirty minutes on each occasion." ZENKOKU KŌHAN-KAKARI KENJI KAIDŌ HAIFU SHIRYŌ OYOBI ZENKOKU KENSATSU CHŌKAN KAIDŌ HAIFU SHIRYŌ (Materials Distributed at the National Meeting of Procurators in Charge of Public Trials and Materials Distributed at the National Meeting of Chief Public Procurators) 35 (Keiso Kankei Shiryō (Materials Relating to Criminal Procedure) no. 7, 1961).

It should be noted that since the new code introduced the hearsay rule,[32] most of the written statements gathered by the procurator cannot be used as evidence in the trial court unless the adverse party consents. Such documents will not be reached by disclosure proceedings.

These changes in the use of evidence have caused much difficulty for the defense counsel in preparing his case. In the first place, for a long time he was accustomed to prepare by reading and examining the documentary or real evidence presented to the court prior to the trial. Secondly, private attorneys in Japan, even in the major cities, are rarely organized into large law firms and thus do not have sufficient staffs to investigate a case and to interview prospective witnesses for the opposing party. Thirdly, the investigation, search, and seizure by police and procurator are so thorough and efficient that there is rarely much evidence left to be collected by defense counsel. In such circumstances, it is natural that a general practice has been established by which the public procurator discloses all the evidence he has to the defense attorney prior to the first session of public trial. This attitude on the part of the procurator has been welcomed not only by private attorneys but also by trial judges; it has helped to expedite trial since the issues in controversy can be clarified beforehand, so that the parties to the trial can concentrate their efforts on those problems alone. Furthermore, the court can reduce the number of witnesses to be summoned, using in their stead written statements submitted by the parties under stipulation or consent.

There have been many cases, however, in which the procurator strictly invoked the provisions of the code and refused to disclose evidence to the defense beyond the limits stipulated by law: (1) when evidence might be lost, for example, by threats to the prospective witnesses inducing them to perjure themselves or not to testify at all; (2) when the trial is of such a kind, mostly those involving or arising out of labor disputes or subversive activities, that defense counsel cannot be expected to cooperate with the procurator and, occasionally, not even with the judges; and (3) where the complexity of the case and the evidence requires the procurator to use special tactics in introducing and rebutting evidence in order to persuade the trial court. This attitude on the part of procurators has caused severe criticism from among practicing lawyers and scholars. In 1953, the Japan-

[32] The hearsay rule and its exceptions are spelled out in CODE OF CRIMINAL PROCEDURE arts. 320–28.

It is generally believed that art. 37(2) of the Constitution, which grants the accused a full opportunity to examine all witnesses, requires the hearsay rule to be introduced in criminal-trial proceedings. The exceptions to the rule are much broader than those under Anglo-American law, however. This may be explained by the fact that Japanese public trial is conducted before judges and not before lay jurors. Jurors may be influenced by unreliable hearsay evidence when judges may not be, because the latter are much more experienced in distinguishing facts. Therefore, exceptions to the hearsay rule may be permitted much more widely under a system of trial by judges.

ese Federated Attorneys Association asked the Supreme Court and the Minister of Justice to take necessary steps to enact a law or promulgate an order which would permit defense counsel the right of free access to all the documents and real evidence in the hands of the procurator.[33] The Osaka District Court in a pretrial order in 1959 directed the procurator to disclose all the evidence in his possession to defense counsel.[34] The procurator filed in the Supreme Court a "special protest" against this ruling,[35] insisting that the District Court had exceeded its judicial power in making such an order. The Supreme Court nullified the order of the inferior court,[36] declaring *inter alia* that article 299 of the code and article 178-3 of the regulations are concerned only with whatever evidence the party definitely intends to introduce in the trial court and do not impose upon a party any obligation to disclose all the evidence in his hands; nor do they give the trial court the power to order such disclosure. This decision of the Supreme Court quieted somewhat the controversy between procurators and defense counsel; but the pressure for new legislation to give defense counsel free access to all the evidence in the hands of procurators has been increasing among private attorneys, scholars, and judges. The most vigorous opponent of such new legislation is, of course, the procurator, who argues three points.[37] First, the new code introduced the adversary trial proceeding and thus made a fundamental change in the process of factfinding. Under the old code the trial judge himself had enough time to read and examine the documentary and real evidence presented by the procurator prior to the first day of public trial; in effect the *prima facie* case for the prosecution was presented before the trial began. The trial proceedings themselves were then really a process of reconfirming the probative value of the evidence presented beforehand. The trial judge himself examined the defendant at length in court and often summoned witnesses on his own initiative. In such circumstances it was feasible for the judge to discover the truth even from

[33] See 4 JIYŪ TO SEIGI no. 3, at 62 (1953) and HANREI JIHŌ (The Case Journal) no. 202, at 22 (1959). The president of the Federated Attorneys Association, also in his letter of December 24, 1959 (see note 31), requested the Minister of Justice to introduce the following article as an amendment to the Code of Criminal Procedure: "Article 40-2. Subsequent to the institution of the public action, the defense attorney may, in the public procurators' office, inspect or copy documents or other articles of evidence which are possessed by or are in the custody of the public procurators. Provided, however, that he must obtain the permission of the procurators in order to copy any article of evidence."

[34] Japan v. Doishita, Osaka District Court, Oct. 3, 1959, HANREI JIHŌ no. 202, at 22–23.

[35] Pursuant to CODE OF CRIMINAL PROCEDURE art. 433. The "special protest" is akin to the German *Beschwerde,* described in Kaplan, von Mehren & Schaeffer, *Phases of German Civil Procedure II,* 71 HARV. L. REV. 1443, 1444–47 (1958).

[36] Takehara v. Doishita, Supreme Court, III Petty Bench, Dec. 26, 1959, 13 SAI-HAN KEISHŪ 3372.

[37] Honda, *Shōko Shorui no Etsuran Tōsha* (Inspection and Copying of Evidenciary Documents), 12 HŌRITSU NO HIROBA no. 11, at 4 (1959); Ishikawa, *Shōko Shiryō no Teishutsu o Kensatsukan ni Kyōsei Dekiru Ka* (Can the Public Procurators Be Compelled to Produce Evidenciary Materials?), 10 HŌRITSU NO HIROBA no. 5, at 14 (1957).

conflicting evidence. But the situation has changed completely under the new code; now the judge is supposed to be the last man to learn the truth of the case. The rule which requires the judge to be free from any bias or prejudice forbids him to have access to any evidence until it is introduced properly in the course of the trial. He must listen to the oral testimony of the witnesses and the reading of written documents as they are presented, and gradually reach his own conclusions. The procurator and defense counsel stand before the trial judge, neither having any priority over the other, yet the procurator has the ultimate burden of proving the deeds allegedly committed by the defendant. Although the criminal trial is not a game or combat before the trial judge, tactics play an important role in determining the verdict. These tactics involve, among other things, techniques of introducing evidence. If evidence is not hidden from the eyes of the other party, therefore, such tactics cannot be effectively employed. Secondly, the proponents of the new legislation insist that real equality before the trial court cannot be obtained unless all the evidence in the hands of the prosecution is disclosed to the defense counsel, since the procurator has powerful official machinery available to help him collect evidence in support of his case. This contention is not true, however, because the procurator has a heavy burden of proving the facts charged while defense counsel need not prove the innocence of the defendant but need only raise some doubt about the truth of some of the allegations. Moreover, if disclosure is required only of the procurator and the defense counsel is free of any such obligation, it strengthens the actual inequality between the procurator and defense counsel and puts the former at an often insurmountable disadvantage. Lastly, if the procurator is required to disclose all the evidence in his hands, information might be discovered which will disclose techniques or sources of investigation or reveal other investigative activities being undertaken at present or to be undertaken in the future. There is no doubt that such discovery could hamper very seriously the functions of investigation and prosecution. Despite this opposition, the question of pretrial disclosures will be one of the main subjects to be considered by the National Diet in the near future.

THE POSITION OF THE DEFENDANT BEFORE THE TRIAL COURT

The defendant has two positions before the trial court under the new code as well as under the old. One is his status as a party to the trial; the other is his status as the object of questioning by the public procurator, defense counsel, and trial judge. Under the old code, the defendant was more the object of an inquisitorial proceeding than a party to the trial. Now, however, the defendant has the full powers of a party. Even if defense counsel is assigned to him, the defendant himself may crossexamine witnesses or may request the judge to summon witnesses.[38] Sometimes this

[38] CODE OF CRIMINAL PROCEDURE arts. 298, 304.

system hampers the prompt completion of trial, especially when the defendant crossexamines in anger and at length the adverse witnesses, who often are the police officers or procurators who have interrogated him in the course of investigation or prosecution; usually he does this to establish the involuntary nature of his own confession. Some persons contend that the right of the defendant to crossexamine witnesses should be restricted to cases in which he is not represented by counsel.[39]

The new code has wrought fundamental changes in the second position of the defendant. Under the old codes, the trial judge questioned the defendant at length at the beginning of the trial about the facts charged, in an inquisitorial manner. Under the new Constitution and code, the defendant has a right against self-incrimination throughout the proceedings from the beginning of the criminal investigation to the end of the trial.[40] The investigating officers, procurators, and trial judges must inform the defendant of this right prior to inquiry or trial.[41]

The questioning of the defendant during trial is of two kinds. The first is the questioning by the judge at the opening stage of trial. As provided in article 291(2) of the code, the defendant is afforded the opportunity to make brief preliminary statements about the facts charged against him.[42] The inquiry by the trial judge on this occasion is designed not to extract a confession from the defendant but to clarify the excuse or defense being made; this is similar to the arraignment proceeding in the United States, in which the judge tries to ascertain whether a plea of guilty by the defendant is reliable and voluntarily made. The questioning at this point is usually very short and is supposed to be as noninquisitorial as possible. The second kind of questioning is that during the course of trial by the trial judge, defense counsel, and procurator. Although article 311 of the code does not limit the stage at which this inquiry may be made,[43] the practice has been established that it usually comes after the other evidence has been

[39] Idei, *Shōnin no Hogo* (Protection of Witnesses), JURIST no. 31, at 2–3 (1953).

[40] CONSTITUTION art. 38; CODE OF CRIMINAL PROCEDURE arts. 146, 311; see DANDO, SHIN KEIJI SOSHŌ HŌ KŌYŌ (Essentials of the New Law of Criminal Procedure) 84, 239 (4th rev. ed., 1951); HIRANO, note 22, at 196–200.

[41] Criminal Procedure Regulations, Supreme Court Regulation No. 32 of 1948, art. 121.

[42] CODE OF CRIMINAL PROCEDURE art. 291(2): "The presiding judge, after he has notified the defendant following the completion of the reading of the information aloud that he may be silent at all times or refuse to make a statement in response to individual questions and of other matters prescribed by the regulations of the court necessary for the protection of the defendant's rights, shall accord the defendant and his attorney an opportunity to make a statement concerning the defendant's case."

[43] CODE OF CRIMINAL PROCEDURE art. 311:

"(1) The defendant may be silent at all times or may refuse to testify in response to individual questions.

"(2) Where the defendant testifies voluntarily, the presiding judge may at any time seek the defendant's testimony in regard to essential matters.

"(3) An associate judge, the public procurator, the attorney, a codefendant, or his attorney may, upon notifying the presiding judge, seek the testimony in the prior paragraph."

received, except that defense counsel may question the defendant earlier with reference to the testimony of the other witnesses. Also, the procurator may crossexamine the defendant at any time with reference to his answers to questions posed by the judge and defense counsel or his statements made in crossexamining other witnesses.

It must be clearly understood that the defendant cannot be a formal witness in his case and that he has the right to be silent at all times and to refuse to answer any question, whether the answer might incriminate him or not. In addition, article 197(1) of the regulations provides *inter alia* that the defendant may at any time make a statement which may be used as evidence for or against him. Thus the defendant has an absolutely free hand in answering questions or in making statements. Even if he makes a false statement, he cannot be prosecuted or punished as a perjurer because he does not make his answer or statement as a witness under oath; yet his answer or statement may be used as evidence for him just as the testimony of a witness under oath. Moreover, the defendant must be afforded the opportunity to speak last at the trial.[44]

The defendant is thus completely protected during the course of trial. In fact, many defendants abuse these rights. In such circumstances, it is natural that there are those who contend that the defendant should not be allowed to make any statement during the course of the factfinding process unless he voluntarily takes the witness stand under oath and undergoes proper crossexamination by the procurator. The very favorable status now enjoyed by the defendant would have been eminently fair in trial proceedings under the old code, in which the trial judges displayed an inquisitorial attitude, but, under the accusatorial and adversary procedure introduced by the present code, it is illogical that the defendant may lie with impunity and is exempt from crossexamination by the procurator, even though his statements or answers to questions may be used as evidence on his behalf. In addition, prolonged statements by defendants — sometimes including political speeches — have contributed to the increased length of criminal trials in Japan, as shown in Table 1 at the end of this essay.

THE CONDUCT OF TRIAL BY JUDGES

Jury trial was introduced in Japan for the first time by the Jury Law of 1923.[45] For five or six years several cases were tried before juries, but thereafter jury trial was rare; it was suspended altogether in 1943.[46] The system of that time was modeled after the Continental trial jury. The

[44] Criminal Procedure Regulations, art, 211: "The defendant or his attorney shall be accorded an opportunity to make a statement at the very end."

[45] Law No. 50 of 1923.

[46] Law Concerning the Suspension of the Jury Law, Law No. 88 of 1943.

presiding judge had the opportunity to read and inspect all evidence presented by the procurator prior to and at the trial. The judge himself questioned the defendant in detail concerning the facts charged. In his instructions to the jury, the judge commented not only on the law to be applied to the case, but also on the details of the evidence. The verdict of the jury was not a general verdict of guilty or not guilty, but a special verdict containing answers to questions posed by the judge. This verdict did not bind the judge, who had the power to order retrial of the case. The parties to a jury trial could not appeal to a Court of Appeals and could appeal only to the Great Court of Judicature on the ground of erroneous application or interpretation of law. There were several reasons why the jury system was not popular in Japan. In the first place, people had then been accustomed for a long time to trial by judges, in whom they had great confidence. Conversely, the people, including defendants and defense counsel, were uneasy about the verdict of laymen, who usually did not have as much training and experience in factfinding as did the judges. This uneasiness was increased because of the limitation on the right of appeal in jury-trial cases. The added expense of jury trial and the inconvenience to the jurors, who were obliged to stay throughout the period of the trial in an annex to the courthouse, were not insignificant factors. Finally, there is reason to believe that trial by jury did not suit the inquisitorial proceedings of that time; the judges overwhelmed the jurors to a very great degree.[47] Under the new code, however, the adversary proceeding has been embedded in Japanese criminal procedure. It is natural, therefore, that there has been an increasing demand for the jury system in recent years.[48]

More than 90 percent of the cases processed by formal public trial are conducted by a single judge.[49] The collegiate court, which consists of three

[47] Art. 95 of the Jury Law provided that "the court, when it perceives that the verdict of the jury is improper, may by a ruling, no matter which stage in litigation has been reached, once more subject the case to the deliberations of another jury." Trial judges thus had a free hand in accepting or rejecting the jury's findings. During the period 1928 to 1942, 378 defendants were found guilty in jury proceedings and 81 not guilty. In 17 cases of the 378 and 6 of the 81, the final determinations required more than two presentations of the matter to a jury. SHIHŌ-SHŌ (Ministry of Justice), DAI 58 KEIJI TŌKEI NEMPŌ — SHŌWA 7 NEN (58th Annual Report of Criminal Statistics — 1932) 31 (1934); SHIHŌ-SHŌ, DAI 63 KEIJI TŌKEI NEMPŌ — SHŌWA 12 NEN (63rd Annual Report of Criminal Statistics — 1937) 33 (1939); SHIHŌ-SHŌ, DAI 68 KEIJI TŌKEI NEMPŌ — SHŌWA 17 NEN (68th Annual Report of Criminal Statistics — 1942) 32 (1944).

[48] Yokokawa, *Keiji Saiban to Baishinsei no Zehi* (Pros and Cons of the Jury System and Criminal Trial), 9 JIYŪ TO SEIGI no. 6, at 2 (1958).

[49] SAIKŌ SAIBANSHO JIMU-SŌKYOKU (General Secretariat of the Supreme Court), SHŌWA 32 NEN SHIHŌ TŌKEI NEMPŌ (1957 Annual Report of Judicial Statistics), 2 KEIJI HEN (Criminal Affairs Book) pt. 1, at 68 (1958); SAIKŌ SAIBANSHO JIMU-SŌKYOKU, SHŌWA 33 NEN SHIHŌ TŌKEI NEMPŌ (1958 Annual Report of Judicial Statistics), 2 KEIJI HEN (Criminal Affairs Book) pt. 1, at 152 (1960); SAIKŌ SAIBANSHO JIMU-SŌKYOKU, SHŌWA 34 NEN SHIHŌ TŌKEI NEMPŌ (1959 Annual Report of Judicial Statistics), 2 KEIJI HEN (Criminal Affairs Book) pt. 1, at 152 (1961).

judges, tries very serious cases such as murder, rape, and arson, as well as any other case which the court deems it proper to try. It is generally believed that a collegiate court is more reliable than a single-judge court, partly because the presiding judge of a collegiate court is usually more experienced than a single judge and partly because discussions and votes among the three judges may neutralize peculiarities or personality traits of the individual judges in factfinding and sentencing. The congestion of the docket, however, especially in the large cities, obliges trial courts to dispose of more and more cases through a single judge, as shown by Table 2 at the end of this essay.

The functions of the judge may be divided into three phases. The first is maintaining order in the courtroom and presiding over the trial proceedings. The second is rendering a judgment embodying facts found in the case. The third is pronouncing a specific penalty or other measure against the defendant who has been found guilty.

The judge is responsible for seeing that there is a speedy and fair trial; for this purpose, he must maintain order and preside over the trial proceedings skillfully, efficiently, and in a spirit of fairness. In recent years, there have been a number of cases in which defense counsel did not obey the orders of the trial judge. Some of them were punished by the judges for contempt of court. Since contempt penalties had never been applied to defense attorneys, the firm attitude displayed by judges caused some controversy among practicing lawyers; but the support of a majority of lawyers led to a declaration by the Federated Attorneys Association urging its members to observe professional ethics and to cooperate with the trial judge.[50]

[50] The general meeting of attorneys held on May 27, 1961, by the Japanese Federated Attorneys Associations adopted the following resolution: "Judges, procurators, and private attorneys must join together in maintaining order through law. It is most regrettable that trial proceedings have sometimes been hampered. We must adhere to the Canons of Legal Ethics and prevent similar cases from occurring in the future." 12 JIYŪ TO SEIGI no. 6, at 53 (1961).

Under the Law Concerning the Maintenance of Order in Court, Etc., Law No. 286 of 1952, a judge has the power to inflict nonpenal sanctions similar to those exercised by Anglo-American judges in proceedings for civil contempt of court. For there to be contempt of court, a person must, in the presence of a judge or in a nearby place within the perception of a judge, disobey a judicial order aimed at maintaining order in the judicial proceedings, or interfere with the exercise of the functions of a court by means of contemptuous utterances, violent acts, or noisy or otherwise improper behavior; or otherwise impair the dignity of trial. The nonpenal sanctions are confinement not exceeding twenty days or a fine not exceeding 30,000 yen, or both (art. 2(1)). In recent trials, one private attorney was sentenced to twenty days' confinement and another to a 30,000 yen fine by judges of the Tokyo District Court because of their contemptuous utterances in the presence of the judges, who were stating in open court their reasons for detention of the suspects before trial. See HANREI JIHŌ no. 235, at 4–10.

The problem of how far criticism of the factfinding of a trial judge is permissible has been a subject of great controversy in recent years. Note, for example, former Chief Justice Kotaro Tanaka's admonitory address at the May 1960 National Meeting of Chief Judges of High and District Courts, SAIBANSHO JIHŌ (The Court Journal) no. 306, at 1 (1960). It is generally agreed that there is no reason that the judicial system and its general administration should

The judge, or three judges in a collegiate court,[51] is the trier of fact. He has the responsibility of determining what part of contradictory evidence is true, and he cannot convict a defendant unless he concludes that the facts are proved beyond a reasonable doubt. It is generally thought in Japan that the trial judge is not only an impartial umpire of the trial but also a personification of justice, in that he is able to discern the true from the false so as to convict the real offender and discharge the innocent. Thus judges have been especially eager to determine the truth. This attitude may explain some characteristics of the judge's activities in the trial. In the first place, he is very eager to hear, read, and examine all evidence relevant to the case. To that end he often sustains the admissibility of evidence which might be excluded under a strict application of exclusionary rules.[52] Sec-

---

not be open to criticism. Also, it is desirable for the development of legal thought that the decisions of the courts should be commented on and criticized from a legal viewpoint. The situation was thought to be quite different, however, when Hiroshi Masaki, a private attorney, while his client's case was pending before the Supreme Court, published in 1955 a book entitled *Saibankan* (A Judge), in which he criticized the judgment of the lower court that his client had committed murder. Many lawyers held the view that a judge should not be influenced by any opinion or organized movement outside the courtroom and were strongly opposed to publications of that kind. Chief Justice Tanaka expressed the opinion before a national conference of judges that he greatly regretted such a publication, which tended to decrease the faith of the people in the judiciary by criticizing in detail a pending case and by casting aspersions on the competence and knowledge of the trial judge. See SAIBANSHO JIHŌ no. 184, at 1 (1955).

[51] For a discussion of the distinction between single judge and collegiate courts, and the workings of the latter, see Kohji Tanabe, "The Process of Litigation: An Experiment with the Adversary System," in this volume.

[52] Some examples may be cited from the judgments of the Supreme Court. Concerning the rule requiring corroboration of a confession, the Court held that the corroborative evidence need not be sufficient, independent of the confession, to establish the whole of the corpus delicti, but only enough to support the truth of the confession. Okubo v. Japan, Supreme Court, II Petty Bench, Oct. 30, 1948, 2 SAI-HAN KEISHŪ 1427. Several years ago there was a case in which the issue was whether the confession of a suspect made before a public procurator was admissible. In that case the suspect was in the custody of the police under a warrant of detention, and his interview with his defense attorney allegedly had been limited to two or three minutes and had been attended by a police officer, in violation of the right of confidential communication between the suspect and his attorney. The Court held that even if that were the case, the mere fact that illegal measures were taken against the suspect did not necessarily lead to the conclusion that the confession was made involuntarily. Hongo v. Japan, note 30. Similarly, in cases in which confessions were obtained from suspects under illegal arrest or without notification of the privilege against self-incrimination, the Court held that such facts did not necessarily make the confession involuntary. Tsukahara v. Japan, Supreme Court, III Petty Bench, Nov. 25, 1952, 6 SAI-HAN KEISHŪ 1245; Pak v. Japan, Supreme Court, III Petty Bench, Nov. 21, 1950, 4 SAI-HAN KEISHŪ 2359. As for admissibility of illegally obtained evidence, the Court held that real evidence may be admissible even though it has been obtained through illegal search and seizure, because the substance of the real evidence will not be modified thereby. Judgment of Dec. 13, 1949, Supreme Court, III Petty Bench, Dec. 13, 1948, *Re* (Criminal Revision Case) No. 2366 of 1949. Very recently, in a narcotics case, six justices of the Supreme Court expressed doubt about the above decision and took the position that illegally obtained real evidence is not admissible if fundamental human rights have been seriously infringed. Japan v. Arima, Supreme Court, Grand Bench, June 7, 1961, 15 SAI-HAN

ondly, he is a very active participant in the trial. It is not unusual that the judge himself puts questions to the witnesses and the defendant. He may urge the parties to the trial to produce further evidence as well as summoning witnesses at his own discretion; indeed, not infrequently the High Courts have quashed decisions of trial courts on the ground that the trial judges tried the cases insufficiently, in that they failed to make the parties obtain additional evidence or to summon easily available and indispensable witnesses.[53] Thirdly, a trial judge may permit or order a procurator to add, withdraw, or change counts in the information if he deems it proper, provided that the new count retains the fundamental identity of the old one.[54] The court may thus convict a defendant on a count other than that originally charged by the prosecutor.

In light of these judicial activities, some scholars maintain that the fundamental character of Japanese criminal procedure even under the new code may be deemed inquisitorial, in the sense that it is fundamentally different from the Anglo-American accusatorial procedure.[55] This contention is supported by the practice of trial judges of setting the dates for public trial not continuously but with intervals of two weeks to six months or more between hearings in a single case.[56] Thus the judge's view of the facts is influenced not so much by the oral testimony of the witnesses at the trial

---

KEISHŪ 915, 927 (supplementary opinion of Tarumi, J.), 930 (opinion of Yokota, C. J.), 933 (opinion of Fujita and Okuno, JJ.), 935 (minority opinion of Kotani and Kawamura, JJ.).

The attitude of the courts in interpreting the exceptions to the hearsay rule has been very liberal. Thus a written statement made before a public procurator by a person other than the accused may be used as substantive evidence where the testimony of the witness before the trial court is different from his previous statements, provided the court finds that the previous statements are more credible than the testimony given before the trial court. Shiraishi v. Japan, Supreme Court, III Petty Bench, Jan. 11, 1955, 9 SAI-HAN KEISHŪ 14. See CODE OF CRIMINAL PROCEDURE art. 321(2).

[53] Japan v. Hanawa, Tokyo High Court, July 1, 1952, 5 KŌTŌ SAIBANSHO KEIJI HANREI SHŪ (A Collection of Criminal High Court Cases) [hereafter cited KŌ-HAN KEISHŪ] 1111; Japan v. Takahashi, Tokyo High Court, June 7, 1951, 4 KŌ-HAN KEISHŪ 641.

[54] CODE OF CRIMINAL PROCEDURE art. 256:

"(1) Institution of a public action shall be performed by filing an information.

"(2) The following matters shall be entered in the information: (i) The name of the defendant and other matters sufficient for identifying the defendant. (ii) Facts of the public action. (iii) Name of the crime.

"(3) The facts of the public action shall be entered, the cause of action being clearly indicated. Clear indication of the cause of action shall be performed by specifying, as far as possible, through the means of the date, place, and method, the facts constituting the crime."

CODE OF CRIMINAL PROCEDURE art. 312:

"(1) A court, when there is a claim by the public procurator, shall, to the extent that it does not impair the factual unity of the public action, permit the addition, withdrawal or alteration of the causes of action or penal provisions entered in the information.

"(2) A court, when it recognizes that it is proper in view of the course of the trial, may order that a cause of action or penal provision should be added or altered."

[55] ONO, HANZAI KŌSEI YŌKEN (The Constituent Elements of Crime) 167 (1953).

[56] On the discontinuous nature of Japanese proceedings, see the essay by Kohji Tanabe in this volume.

as by the transcript of the proceedings, which he reads carefully between hearings. This system does not differ very much from the factfinding process under the old code, in which the judge reached his conclusions mainly on the basis of the defendant's confession and written statements of the witnesses. Indeed, the judge's conclusions under the present procedure may be based even less on in-court evidence than under the old code: formerly the judge could direct his attention at the trial toward examining the probative value of the evidence he had seen before the trial; but now the judge has no prior knowledge about the case, so that when he admits evidence at the trial he cannot evaluate its probative value at the time. Thus his determination of its value must be based on his reading and examination of the evidence admitted and the transcript during the interval between court sessions. This tends to make the trial somewhat more complicated and the judge more confused.

There has been an increasing tendency in recent years to have trials conducted continuously and to have more stress put upon the oral testimony of the witnesses in court instead of relying on their written statements. Several judges, mostly in the Tokyo District Court, have experimented along these lines with quite promising results.[57] Their success, however, has been due to a great extent to the cooperation of the parties to the trial, who have had to prepare their cases very carefully before trial, attend pretrial conferences with the judge in especially complicated cases, stipulate before trial the admissibility of written statements, and have their witnesses present in court. Nevertheless, the success of the experiment appealed to trial judges, practicing lawyers, and most procurators, with the result that very recently the Criminal Procedure Regulations were amended in regard to public actions instituted after January 1, 1962 (January 1, 1963 for the Summary Courts).[58] There are six main points in the new regulation. (1) Each party has a duty at his earliest convenience to disclose for the use of the opposing party the documentary and real evidence which he is planning to produce at the trial.[59] (2) Each party has a duty to examine the evidence thus disclosed by the opposing party and to indicate whether he is going to stipulate the admissibility of the documentary evidence at the trial.[60] (3) Both parties must make a reasonable effort to have their witnesses present at the trial.[61] (4) The procurator must return the articles seized in the course of investigation to the owner, custodian, or other possessor, permanently or temporarily, in order that the defense may use them for preparing for trial, provided that the articles seized are not necessary for the prosecution.[62] (5) Both parties

[57] For example, Judges Seiichi Kishi, Toshio Yokokawa, and Masaru Higuchi.

[58] By Supreme Court Regulation No. 6 of 1961.

[59] Criminal Procedure Regulations art. 178-6(1)(i), (2)(iii).

[60] *Ibid.* art. 178-6(1)(ii), (2)(ii).

[61] *Ibid.* art. 178-8.

[62] *Ibid.* art. 178-11.

must contact each other for the purpose of clarifying the issues in the case and must report to the trial court the time which should be allocated to the trial.[63] (6) When it deems it proper, the trial court may request both parties to be present at a pretrial conference and may confer with them about such trial matters as the designation of trial dates, allocations of time to the procurator and defense counsel, the order in which evidence will be produced by the parties, and so on. The conference may not touch on any matter which might prejudice the court, however.[64]

These provisions have as their main objective continuous and speedy trials. Some judges anticipate that, if the amended regulations are followed, nearly 80 percent of all cases will each require only a single day of trial, and yet each trial itself will be more complete in substance than before.[65] Thus the proponents of the new regulation call it the "regulation for condensed trials" rather than "for continuous and speedy trials." [66] It is clear that the new rule marks an epoch in its introduction of real adversary forms of procedure to Japan after thirteen years of practice under the new code. There will be many obstacles in the path of the new regulation, however. In the first place, the inadequate number of procurators and defense attorneys, especially in the small cities and towns, makes it difficult as a practical matter for the trial judge to require the parties to prepare the case fully ahead of trial so that he can set consecutive dates for the hearings. Secondly, there is the fundamental problem whether this adversary system of procedure requires a jury to try the facts. Logically speaking, the answer is no. Yet in fact the trial judge who has two functions to perform, one of supervising the trial process and the other of factfinding, sometimes experiences difficulties. If he puts too much emphasis on a fair and speedy trial, he may lose sight of the facts of the case. Moreover, if there is a sharp dispute as to the admissibility of evidence, for example, and the judge rules on the matter favorably to one of the parties, then the judicial fact determination may be claimed to be partial. Furthermore, if he is too eager to find the real facts in the case, he may easily tend to become an inquisitorial trier of fact and thus lose his impartial attitude. To keep the proper balance between these two functions is not easy, and it is inescapable that individual judges will differ to some degree in the attitudes which they bring to individual cases. To lessen these difficulties of the trial judge and to further the adversary system of trial, it might be best to take from the judge the major responsibility for factfinding and to leave that function primarily to a jury. Nevertheless, it is not likely that the jury system will be reinstituted in Japan in the near future, not because people feel that trial

[63] *Ibid.* art. 178-6(3).
[64] *Ibid.* art. 178-10.
[65] Symposium, *Keiji Saiban no Sho-Mondai* (Various Problems in Criminal Trial), 13 Hōsō Jihō (Journal of the Jurists' Association) no. 5, at 43 (1961).
[66] *Ibid.*, at 35.

by judges is more proper in its nature than trial by jury, but rather because they feel uneasy about trial by jury in that jurors selected by lot from among the laymen of Japan might be more easily influenced by emotional factors than by the evidence produced at the trial. In a word, they believe that factfinding by judges is more reliable than that by jurors. Thus trial judges will probably remain the trier of fact for some time to come.

Two problems must be mentioned with regard to the third role of the trial judge, that of deciding the penalty to be imposed upon guilty persons.[67] The trial procedure has no separation of factfinding and sentencing, and the system of presentence investigation has not yet been introduced (except for juvenile offenders before the Family Courts).[68] These two problems should have been solved by the new code, since they present a major deficiency in the administration of criminal justice. Under the adversary system of trial, whether by jury or not, some rules of evidence, such as the hearsay rule, must be followed in order to protect the fundamental rights of the defendant and to maintain a proper balance between the parties. Thus some evidence which is clearly relevant to the case must be excluded for the purposes of factfinding. This same evidence need not necessarily be excluded during the sentencing process, however. On the contrary, it is claimed by some that the presentence investigation report of a probation officer may be used for sentencing, even though it may contain information which falls within the scope of the hearsay or some other exclusionary rule.[69] The combination of these two processes, therefore, makes the application of the rules of evidence quite complex. Trial judges have shown two different attitudes. Some emphasize the adversary character of the procedure and readily exclude evidence by virtue of the hearsay rule and the like, even though the evidence is introduced solely for the purposes of sentencing.[70] The information to be considered for sentencing thus becomes quite inadequate. Other judges admit any information without applying the rules of evidence insofar as it is produced in connection with sentencing.[71] This liberal attitude has the serious defect that there is no safeguard except the

[67] See generally, Haruo Abe, "The Accused and Society: Therapeutic and Preventive Aspects of Criminal Justice in Japan," in this volume.

[68] There are special probation officers (known as "Family Court investigation officers") in each Family Court. See Court Law, Law No. 59 of 1947, art. 61-2. In making their investigation before sentencing, they are required to make efficient use of medical, psychological, educational, sociological, and other technical knowledge, especially the results of physical and mental examinations conducted in the Juvenile Classification Center, in regard to the conduct, career, temperament, and environment of the juvenile, his guardians, or other persons concerned. Juvenile Law, Law No. 168 of 1948, art. 9.

[69] Eriguchi, *Keiji Saiban ni okeru Hanketsu Zen–Chōsa ni Tsuite* (On Prejudgment Investigation in Criminal Trial), Hō no Shihai (The Rule of Law) no. 1, at 87, 93-94 (1959).

[70] See 1 Kishi, Keiji Soshō Hō Yōgi (The Essentials of Criminal Procedure Law) 160–61 (1961).

[71] 1 Aoyagi, Keiji Soshō Hō Tsūron (A General Treatise on the Law of Criminal Procedure) 254 (completely rev. ed. 1954).

self-restraint of the judge himself against his using the hearsay evidence in making the fact determination in the case.

There is a more basic objection to the combining of the factfinding and sentencing processes. Sentencing should be governed not by the tactical maneuvering found in the adversary system, but by scientifically sound techniques for the rehabilitation of the defendant. In actual practice, however, the procurator presents material such as any record of former convictions or affiliation with delinquent gangs which tends to support his opinion concerning the penalty to be imposed, while the defense counsel does his best to collect and introduce whatever materials might lead to a more lenient penalty. Thus judges, even those who are very diligent in attempting to ascertain the true facts and manifest an inquisitorial attitude during the process of factfinding, have tended to refrain from collecting on their own initiative evidence pertaining to the sentencing process. Perversely enough, the sentencing process thereby tends to be carried on in a more adversarial form than the factfinding process is.

In light of these considerations, it is not surprising that the system of presentence investigation has not yet been introduced. The situation has been changing gradually, however, and the proponents of such a system have been increasing among judges, procurators, lawyers, and scholars.[72] Nevertheless, the strong influence of the opposition, especially among private attorneys, should not be underestimated.[73] This opposition may be explained by the fact that defense counsel are often concerned mainly with obtaining a lenient sentence for the client rather than getting him acquitted;[74] introduction of a presentence-investigation system would tend to restrict the activities of defense attorneys. Another influential stand in opposition has been taken by many procurators.[75] This opposition is not against the introduction of presentence investigation itself, but rather against the proposed organization of the investigation officers. The General Secretariat of the Supreme Court proposes that the officers should be attached to the trial courts,[76] while the procurators insist that they should be under an independent committee, or some organization other than the trial courts,[77] because the procurator should utilize the reports of these officers

[72] See Eriguchi, *Hanketsu Zen–Chōsa Seido ni Tsuite* (On the Prejudgment Investigation System), 10 JIYŪ TO SEIGI no. 12, at 2 (1959); Abe, *Hanketsu Zen–Chōsa wa Dō Arubeki Ka* (What Sort of Prejudgment Investigation Should There Be?), 72 KIKAN KEISEI (Quarterly Journal of Criminal Law and Criminology) no. 3, at 12 (1961).

[73] Suzuki, *Hanketsu Zen–Chōsa Seido ni Tsuite* (On the Prejudgment Investigation System), 10 JIYŪ TO SEIGI no. 12, at 12 (1959).

[74] See the essay by Haruo Abe in this volume.

[75] Izumi, *Baishun Bōshi Hō Kaisei ni Shitagau Hanketsu Zen–Chōsa Seido Setchi Mondai* (The Problem of Establishing a Prejudgment Investigation System Pursuant to Amendment of the Prostitution Prevention Law), JURIST no. 152, at 57 (1958).

[76] Eriguchi, note 69, at 94.

[77] Abe, note 72, at 17.

in exercising his discretionary powers of nonprosecution and in expressing his opinion at the trial about the penalty to be imposed. This dispute derives from a fundamental difference of opinion over the relative functions of judges and procurators in enforcing the criminal policy of the nation.

It is submitted that the first step to be taken to solve these problems is to revise the present code so as to divide the process of factfinding from that of sentencing and to make clear the extent to which the rules of evidence are to be applied at each stage. A second step might be to set up whatever system of presentence investigation is most suitable to the fundamental character of criminal procedure and to the proper functions of judges, procurators, and defense counsel.

Conclusion

The first point to be mentioned in conclusion is the fact that the administration of criminal justice in Japan has been changing clearly and steadily from an inquisitorial to an accusatorial process. Perhaps this trend will be strengthened in the future by the increasing support given it by judges, procurators, private attorneys, and scholars. Public procurators and defense counsel will be increasingly careful in their preparation for trial. A court consisting of a single judge will be replaced gradually by a collegiate court. Judges will become more strict in keeping order in the court and will take steps toward becoming impartial umpires of the trial rather than inquisitorial exposers of the truth. Thus the road will be opened, eventually, to the introduction of the jury trial. Finally, more and more stress will be placed on criminological considerations throughout the administration of criminal justice.[78] Thus the discretionary power of the procurator to decline prosecution will be exercised more scientifically through the aid of social caseworkers, psychiatrists, and probation officers, who will investigate the environmental and personal characteristics of individual delinquents and help in the rehabilitation of suspects discharged from prosecution. The use of the presentence investigation will be introduced in the process of sentencing, which will be separate from the factfinding process. The second point to be mentioned here is that the status of the defendant in the process of factfinding will perhaps be modified so that he is qualified to be a voluntary witness in his own case but will thereby be subjected to crossexamination by the procurator.

Changes such as these should go far toward the creation and preservation of a fair, scientifically sound system of criminal procedure in Japan.

[78] See also the essay by Haruo Abe in this volume.

TABLE 1. Increased Length of Criminal Trials

I. Duration of trials under the old code

Year	Duration from the filing of information to the disposition: Within 15 days	Within 1 month	Within 2 months	Within 3 months	Within 6 months	Over 6 months
1927	51.8%	27.3%	14.5%	3.4%	2.0%	0.9%
1932	52.0	26.0	15.0	3.6	2.4	1.0
1936	54.9	26.1	12.4	2.8	3.0	0.9

II. Duration of trials in District Courts under the new code

Year	Total number of dis-positions	Duration from the filing of information to the disposition: Within 1 month	Within 2 months	Within 3 months	Within 6 months	Within 1 year	Within 2 years	Over 2 years
1954	60,352	16.6%	30.0%	15.9%	17.2%	9.6%	7.1%	3.6%
1955	64,943	16.0	28.9	16.9	20.0	9.3	4.3	4.7
1956	56,597	14.8	27.3	16.1	18.7	10.8	7.0	5.3
1957	51,508	13.6	27.8	18.0	21.5	8.9	5.6	4.7
1958	52,854	12.8	29.1	19.0	21.5	9.3	4.0	3.9

III. Duration of trials in collegiate courts in 1958

Total number of dis-positions	Duration from the filing of information to the disposition: Within 1 month	Within 2 months	Within 3 months	Within 6 months	Within 1 year	Within 2 years	Within 3 years	Over 3 years
8,432	1.4%	12.5%	18.8%	31.7%	17.8%	7.6%	3.2%	6.5%

Source: Part I: SHIHŌ-SHŌ (Ministry of Justice), DAI 53 KEIJI TŌKEI NEMPŌ – SHŌWA 2 NEN (53rd Annual Report of Criminal Statistics — 1927) 234 (1927); SHIHŌ-SHŌ, DAI 58 KEIJI TŌKEI NEMPŌ — SHŌWA 7 NEN (58th Annual Report of Criminal Statistics — 1932) 276 (1934); SHIHŌ-SHŌ, DAI 62 KEIJI TŌKEI NEMPŌ — SHŌWA 11 NEN (62nd Annual Report of Criminal Statistics — 1936) 308 (1938).

Part II: SAIKŌ SAIBANSHO JIMU-SŌKYOKU (General Secretariat of the Supreme Court), SHŌWA 29 NEN SHIHŌ TŌKEI NEMPŌ (1954 Annual Report of Judicial Statistics), 2 KEIJI HEN (Criminal Affairs Book) pt. 1, at 110–11; SAIKŌ SAIBANSHO JIMU-SŌKYOKU, SHŌWA 30 NEN SHIHŌ TŌKEI NEMPŌ (1955 Annual Report of Judicial Statistics) 2 KEIJI HEN (Criminal Affairs Book) pt. 1, at 142–43; SAIKŌ SAIBANSHO JIMU-SŌKYOKU, SHŌWA 31 NEN SHIHŌ TŌKEI NEMPŌ (1956 Annual Report of Judicial Statistics), 2 KEIJI HEN (Criminal Affairs Book) pt. 1, at 142–43; SAIKŌ SAIBANSHO JIMU-SŌKYOKU, SHŌWA 32 NEN SHIHŌ TŌKEI NEMPŌ (1957 Annual Report of Judicial Statistics), 2 KEIJI HEN (Criminal Affairs Book) pt. 1, at 122–23; SAIKŌ SAIBANSHO JIMU-SŌKYOKU, SHŌWA 33 NEN SHIHŌ TŌKEI NEMPŌ (1958 Annual Report of Judicial Statistics), 2 KEIJI HEN (Criminal Affairs Book) pt. 1, at 152–53.

Part III: SAIKŌ SAIBANSHO JIMU-SŌKYOKU (General Secretariat of the Supreme Court), SHŌWA 33 NEN SHIHŌ TŌKEI NEMPŌ (1958 Annual Report of Judicial Statistics), 2 KEIJI HEN (Criminal Affairs Book) pt. 1, at 152.

TABLE 2. Number of Cases Disposed of by Collegiate Courts in Comparison with Dispositions by Single-Judge Courts

Year	Total number	By collegiate courts	By single-judge courts
1957	51,508	8,185 (16%)	43,323 (84%)
1958	52,854	8,432 (16%)	44,422 (84%)
1959	55,655	8,967 (16%)	46,688 (84%)

Source: SAIKŌ SAIBANSHO JIMU-SŌKYOKU (General Secretariat of the Supreme Court), SHŌWA 32 NEN SHIHŌ TŌKEI NEMPŌ (1957 Annual Report of Judicial Statistics), 2 KEIJI HEN (Criminal Affairs Book) pt. 1, at 68; SAIKŌ SAIBANSHO JIMU-SŌKYOKU, SHŌWA 33 NEN SHIHŌ TŌKEI NEMPŌ (1958 Annual Report of Judicial Statistics), 2 KEIJI HEN (Criminal Affairs Book) pt. 1, at 152; SAIKŌ SAIBANSHO JIMU-SŌKYOKU, SHŌWA 34 NEN SHIHŌ TŌKEI NEMPŌ (1959 Annual Report of Judicial Statistics), 2 KEIJI HEN (Criminal Affairs Book) pt. 1, at 152.

THE ACCUSED AND SOCIETY: THERAPEUTIC AND PREVENTIVE ASPECTS OF CRIMINAL JUSTICE IN JAPAN

Haruo Abe

ASSISTED BY B. J. GEORGE, JR.

THE PROBLEM of crime and delinquency is as old as human history. A Japanese myth starts with the story of the Sun Goddess' younger brother who, for his persistent misbehavior, was finally expelled to the earthly world by a unanimous verdict of the celestial assembly.[1] Continuous efforts have been made to cope with crime and delinquency. Unfortunately, however, they have been as fruitless as an attempt to sweep back the rising ocean tide with a wornout broom.

The administration of criminal justice, even under modern practices, has

Note. Mr. Abe is Public Procurator and Instructor on Law and Criminology, the United Nations Asia and Far East Institute for the Prevention of Crime and Treatment of Offenders, Tokyo. B.Jur., Tokyo Imperial University, 1943; B.Jur., Tokyo University, 1949; LL.M., Harvard University, 1955; Fulbright grantee at Harvard, 1953–1954. Appointed to the procuracy in 1951. Participant, Japanese American Program for Cooperation in Legal Studies at Harvard, 1954–1955; visiting lecturer at Michigan Law School, comparative criminal-procedure seminar, 1962. Japanese delegate to the United Nations Seminar on Human Rights, Ceylon, 1959 and to the Criminal Law Administration Seminar, Northwestern University, Chicago, 1960. Coauthor with Higuchi of GLUECK HANZAI YOSOKU-HŌ NYŪMON (An Introduction to the Glueck Crime Prediction Method) (1959); author of KEIJI SOSHŌ HŌ NI OKERU KINKŌ TO CHŌWA (Balance and Harmony in the Law of Criminal Procedure) (1962); writings in the fields of criminal procedure and criminology.

[1] This is the well-known legend of the *Kamu-yarai* (divine banishment) of Prince Susa-no-o. The eight hundred myriad deities decided to impose on him an immense fine of "a thousand tables." After submitting the expiatory gifts required for purification, he is exiled from the realm of the heavens, with his beard shaven off and nails pulled out. CHAMBERLAIN, TRANSLATION OF "KO-JI-KI" OR "RECORDS OF ANCIENT MATTERS" 71 (2nd ed. ann. by Aston, 1953); NIHONGI 48 (Aston trans., 1956). This ostracism in the ancient history of Japan should not be understood solely in the light of retributive or expiatory punishment as used in a less primitive society. It may be explained as a ritual process of exorcism (*harae*). Crime was abhorred because it might pollute the whole community, which in turn might possibly incur divine wrath. Ritual processes, such as bathing and sacrificial offerings, were frequently used. Sometimes a criminal had to be exiled in order to purify the pollution. Counterparts of such tribal ostracism are also found among American Indians. See, e.g., LLEWELLYN & HOEBEL, THE CHEYENNE WAY (1941).

not been equipped with a criminology and penology which are sufficient to solve the riddle of the etiology of crime and the pathology of aberrant human behavior. In such circumstances, the emotional reactions to rising crime rates have often driven unenlightened rulers and administrators toward simple reliance upon deterrent and retributive punishment.

In the Middle Ages in Japan, feudal regimes apparently recognized various kinds of barbarous punishment, including crucifying, burning, and boiling. Execution of the death penalty was often designed to inflict the maximum pain on the offender. For example, an outraged feudal lord,[2] who narrowly escaped an attempted assassination, ordered his assailant to be sawed to death. The unfortunate would-be assassin was buried in the middle of a highway with his head above ground. A big bamboo saw was placed beside him so that passersby could take turns at sawing his neck. It is said that it took seven days and seven nights for the man to be put out of his misery.

Cruel punishment, however, soon proved to be useless. It was not a deterrent. Revenge led to further revenge; hatred multiplied hatred. The vicious cycle of retaliatory actions served only to dull the sense of humanity.[3] Over two hundred years ago a Japanese Kabuki playwright mocked the folly of shocking punishment through the lips of a robber-hero[4] who, while being boiled to death with his little son in his arms, uttered the following words: "Though you may be able to exhaust the sands of the stony river shore, the seed of the thieves of this world is inexhaustible."[5]

There is no doubt that the classical penal system based on a metaphysical criminology is almost bankrupt and that something new is urgently needed. The futility of traditional criminal justice has been particularly felt in recent times, when the incidence of juvenile delinquency has reached an unprecedented high. The rate of juvenile crime since World War II has been about three times that of the prewar level.[6] The incidence of rape, assault,

[2] Oda Nobunaga (1534–1582).

[3] It should not be concluded that the prevalence of uncivilized administration of criminal justice is a characteristic peculiar to Oriental criminal law. Even in the Western world, where the soil of rationalism is generally more fertile than in the East, the administration of criminal justice has been and still is characterized by the relative dominance of a metaphysical type of penology. One of the characteristics of this type of penal philosophy is a blind belief in freedom of the will. It starts from the postulate that a human being equipped with a free will can choose between right and wrong by weighing in advance the pleasures and pains which will follow his chosen behavior.

[4] The play was *Ishikawa Goemon*, about the notorious bandit of this name, who is believed to have lived from 1558 to 1594.

[5] These words may be found in a version of the play edited by Jidayu Matsumoto in 8 TOKUGAWA BUNGEI RUISHŪ (A Compilation of Tokugawa Literature), JŌRURI pt. at 146, 163 (1914). They contain a play on words. Since the Ishikawa family name meant "stony river," "sands of the stony river" implied the execution of the criminal's children and relatives. It should be noted here that by virtue of the system of *enza* (criminal responsibility by relationship) innocent family members and relatives were often punished in Japan prior to the Meiji era.

[6] See p. 352 below.

and robbery committed by juveniles has been some eighteen, thirteen, and five times, respectively, that of the prewar levels.[7] Such phenomena may be attributed to the large-scale social disorganization which characterized Japan immediately after the war. They eloquently prove the fact, however, that rampancy of crime and delinquency is almost beyond the control of outmoded systems of criminal law. Theoretically, retribution is no longer the dominant objective of criminal law; reformation and rehabilitation have become important goals of modern criminal jurisprudence. But, in practice, the oldfashioned theory of crime and punishment which is retribution-oriented appears still to be prevalent in the administration of justice.

What is slowing the wheels of progress? Both the immaturity of the science of criminology and the lack of enlightenment on the part of the general public are retarding factors. But a more serious hindrance appears to be the legal profession itself; legal and judicial conservatism has been greatly responsible for the retardation of penal reform. The Japanese legal profession, with its chronically inflexible thinking, has been prone to lag behind other professions in a world which is advancing into the nuclear age. To illustrate, when a Japanese politician who had had a long career as a railroad engineer was appointed Vice Minister of Justice, he could hardly stomach the legal dogmatism which was dominant among lawyers and which was hampering his attempts at innovation. He finally uttered these words, using a metaphor from his past career: "Why, the legal profession is coasting on inertia!"

The following pages describe how the "locomotive of justice" has slowly puffed its way through the decades, although some streamlining of the administration of criminal justice has been accomplished. What exists, however, always has some reason behind it, whether justifiable or not. The cause of this slow process of judicial innovation appears to consist, at least partially, of sociocultural factors which are inherent in Japanese society. These require careful analysis from beyond a mere legal viewpoint.

CHARACTERISTICS OF THE SENTENCING PROCESS IN JAPAN

Legal and Human Elements

In Japanese criminal procedure, the process of sentencing is not clearly separated from that of factfinding. This derives from the fact that the Japanese trial court is not equipped with a jury.[8] A trial court, consisting of

[7] See p. 352 below.

[8] Japan has had a jury law since 1923. Jury Law, Law No. 50 of 1923 (fully enforced on Oct. 1, 1928). It was suspended in 1943 for certain practical reasons, however. See MINISTRY OF JUSTICE, CRIMINAL JUSTICE IN JAPAN 13 (1960).

either one or three judges according to the gravity of the offense,[9] hears evidence which throws light not only on the commission or noncommission of the crime but also on the circumstances which reveal the culpability of the act of the accused and his personality and background. When both parties have completed the presentation of evidence and the proceeding is ripe for judgment and possible sentencing, the court concludes the hearing and fixes the date when judgment and any sentence shall be pronounced. The court is the trier of fact as well as the body responsible for the application of law and the assessment of sentence. Thus rendering judgment of conviction or acquittal and setting the punishment are both included in the functions of the court.

Combining two such heterogeneous processes causes considerable inconvenience.[10] On the one hand, the process of judicial evaluation of the evidence purporting to establish guilt may be contaminated by the information about the character of the offender, even though in practice the court receives such information after it has heard all the evidence. On the other hand, the linking of the two processes causes some difficulties for the public procurator who wishes to inform the court of unfavorable aspects of the personality or background of an offender. In theory, the procurator may feel free to introduce such information, insofar as it pertains to the sentencing process; but, in fact, he must be somewhat hesitant to do so since every shred of information which purports to cast light on the personal background of the accused may have an effect on the factfinding process.[11]

[9] For a full description of Japanese courts and their organization, see *ibid.;* Court Law, Law No. 59 of 1947, arts. 1–38, translated into English in MINISTRY OF JUSTICE, THE CONSTITUTION OF JAPAN AND CRIMINAL STATUTES [hereafter cited as CRIMINAL STATUTES] 371 (1960); SUPREME COURT OF JAPAN, OUTLINE OF CRIMINAL JUSTICE IN JAPAN 3–6 (1959).

[10] See Atsushi Nagashima, "The Accused and Society: The Administration of Criminal Justice in Japan," in this volume.

[11] The procurator's hesitancy comes partially from an awareness of the fact that any written or oral testimony given by an expert or layman on the personality and background of the accused contains a great many hearsay elements. Theoretically, hearsay-evidence rules do not strictly apply to evidence providing information for sentencing. This exception has been implied from a decision of the Supreme Court in a prosecution for violation of the Food Control Law, Law No. 40 of 1942, under the Code of Criminal Procedure of 1922, Law No. 75 of 1922. In that case the Court decided that documentary evidence informally received was properly considered in determining the propriety of suspension of sentence. Sato v. Japan, Supreme Court, II Petty Bench, Feb. 22, 1949, 3 SAIKŌ SAIBANSHO KEIJI HANREI SHŪ (A Collection of Criminal Supreme Court Cases) [hereafter cited SAI-HAN KEISHŪ] 221. This doctrine was reiterated and given further emphasis by the Supreme Court in a case under the present Code of Criminal Procedure. Japan v. Matsuoka, Supreme Court, II Petty Bench, April 25, 1956, *A* (Criminal Revision Case) No. 1672 of 1955. Practical public procurators, however, are usually reluctant to prove sentencing data by means of statements containing hearsay evidence. The adoption of a system of presentence investigation seems to be hampered for the same reason. It has been suggested that one way to avoid this difficulty is to adopt a system of intermediate judgment under which the court may declare the result of the factfinding process in the form of a judgment of guilty or not guilty before it commences the sentencing process.

Some thirty years ago two American scholars of criminal law cited a provision of the criminal law of Massachusetts as a typical example of the absurdity of the system which still survived in the twentieth century.[12] It provided that:

Whoever steals . . . the money or personal chattel of another . . . shall, if the value of the property stolen exceeds one hundred dollars, be punished by imprisonment in the state prison for not more than five years or by a fine of not more than six hundred dollars and imprisonment in jail for not more than two years; or, if the value of the property stolen does not exceed one hundred dollars, shall be punished by imprisonment in jail for not more than one year or by a fine of not more than three hundred dollars; or, if the property was stolen from the conveyance of a common carrier or of a person carrying on an express business, shall be punished for the first offense by imprisonment for not less than six months nor more than two and one half years, or by a fine of not less than fifty nor more than six hundred dollars, or both, and for a subsequent offense by imprisonment for not less than eighteen months nor more than two and one half years, or by a fine of not less than one hundred and fifty dollars nor more than six hundred dollars, or both.[13]

Such a provision, which is designed to keep the amount of punishment mathematically commensurate with the value of the property stolen, is a remnant of the eighteenth-century Beccarian philosophy which tried to restrict the arbitrariness of feudal magistrates. Although such inflexibility in sentencing standards was originally an implementation of the principle of legality, *nulla poena sine lege,* and therefore played an important role in the development of modern criminal law, it has in subsequent generations proved to be a stumbling block in the path of the movement toward individualization of punishment. It is unfortunate that in modern society there still survive outmoded statutory provisions under which the nature or size of a sentence to be imposed is made to hinge upon such haphazard factors as the value of the property that happened to be stolen and the person or place from which it was taken, rather than upon the makeup or environment of the offender or other circumstantial factors which reflect the real seriousness of the offense committed or the true danger of the person who committed it.

In the latter part of the nineteenth century, the administration of criminal justice in Japan was fettered by sentencing standards which were even less flexible than those quoted above. One of the provisions of the Outline of the New Criminal Law (*Shinritsu Kōryō*) of 1870, for example, set out a

[12] Glueck & Glueck, *Predictability in the Administration of Criminal Justice,* 42 HARV. L. REV. 297, 327–28 (1929).

[13] MASS. GEN. LAWS ch. 266, §30 (1921). This provision has not been substantially modified to date.

meticulously detailed sentencing scheme.[14] In 1882 the oldfashioned criminal law, designed to fetter the discretion of judges, was superseded by the Penal Code of 1880.[15] The latter still retained the basic concept of standardized punishment, but it allowed the sentencing judge to exercise some discretion. For example, with regard to simple theft it provided that "a person who steals property owned by another person commits the crime of larceny and is to be punished by heavy confinement for two months or more or four years or less,"[16] and this was followed by several standard-setting provisions dealing with certain types of aggravated or repeated theft punishable by heavier penalties.[17] The Penal Code of 1907 went a step forward in relaxing its sentencing standards to give the judge even more discretionary power.[18]

This last Penal Code of Japan, effective at present, emphasizes the discretionary power of the judge in order to provide a more satisfactory individualized justice. As a matter of both law and theory, therefore, the judge seems to have absolute authority to fix sentence within the broad framework stipulated by statute.

In a homicide case, for example, the Penal Code provides that "a person who has killed a human being is to be punished by the death penalty or imprisonment at forced labor for an indefinite term or three years or more."[19] Moreover, when there are certain extenuating circumstances, the court may even suspend the execution of the sentence and put the offender under probationary supervision.[20]

As a matter of practice, however, the judge is not the sole actor in the sentencing drama. The dynamic process of sentencing comprises three human beings — the procurator, the defense counsel, and the judge. The

[14] Enforced in 1870 but never promulgated. However, a copy may be found in [Meiji 3 Nen] Hōrei Zensho ([1870] Complete Laws and Orders) 572. A translation in English under the title "New Code" will be found in Longford, A Summary of the Japanese Penal Codes (5 Transactions of the Asiatic Society of Japan pt. 2, 1877). This provision set out the sentencing standards for ordinary theft substantially as follows: Whoever steals the property of another shall, if the value of the property is under one ryō, be punished by 60 lashes; if it exceeds one ryō, 70 lashes; if 10 ryō, 80 lashes; if 20 ryō, 90 lashes; if 30 ryō, 100 lashes; if 40 ryō, penal servitude for 1 year; if 50 ryō, penal servitude for 1.5 years; if 60 ryō, penal servitude for 2 years; if 70 ryō, penal servitude for 2.5 years; if 80 ryō, penal servitude for 3 years; if 90 ryō, first-degree "transportation" (banishment to a remote island, occasionally accompanied by forced labor); if 110 ryō, third-degree transportation; if 250 ryō, death by hanging. The value of the ryō is equivalent to 2.69 United States dollars today. The value measured by its purchasing power, however, equals 10 United States dollars or more.

[15] Penal Code of 1880, Great Council of State Decree No. 36 of 1880.

[16] *Ibid.*, at art. 366.

[17] *Ibid.*, at arts. 367–83.

[18] See, e.g., Penal Code, Law No. 45 of 1907, art. 235: "A person who steals the property of another commits the crime of larceny and is to be punished by imprisonment at forced labor for 10 years or less."

[19] Penal Code art. 199. "Indefinite term" (*muki*) is the Japanese terminology for life imprisonment and is to be distinguished from an indeterminate sentence (*futeiki*).

[20] Penal Code arts. 25–25-2, 27; see also p. 357.

process may be characterized as one of bargaining. The procurator usually proposes a high "price" for an offense, as if he were a seller. The defense attorney, as the buyer, usually tries to "discount" it. Finally, the judge, as a mediator, fixes the "price" somewhere in the middle.

The law provides only that, in his closing argument, the procurator must state his opinion about the facts which should be found and the law which ought to be applied. As a matter of practice, however, he usually suggests the sentence he thinks the court should fix. The procurator's recommendation of an appropriate sentence has been conventionally called *kyūkei* or "request for punishment"; it often constitutes one of the highlights of a trial. The procurator, who regards himself as a protector of society and a representative of the public interest, is apt to request a rather stiff sentence, particularly if he is one of the "oldtimers." The closing argument of the defense is generally aimed mainly at the reduction of the sentence suggested by the procurator.*

From experience, defense counsel well knows that it is strategically more effective to appeal to the emotions rather than to the reasoning processes of the judge. Of course, if guilt is seriously in doubt, defense counsel will try to persuade the judge to render a favorable judgment, or at least a moderate sentence, by attacking logically and factually the weak points of the prosecution's case. In most cases, however, it is wiser for the defense to admit the guilt of the accused and to place the accused on the mercy of the court. The defense counsel often resorts to the favorite technique of presenting a witness who appeals to the softheartedness of the judge; it is particularly important to show the judge that the defendant is remorseful and is making efforts to rehabilitate himself.[21] Thus an able and eloquent defense counsel sometimes succeeds in obtaining a very lenient sentence for a man whose personality and background, if examined scientifically, would prove in fact too questionable to warrant early release from prison.

The position of the judge is somewhat delicate. Since as an umpire of the trial he is supposed to protect society and represent the public ideal of justice, he should be neither too sympathetic toward the defense nor too cooperative with the prosecution; but most judges, sensitive about judicial independence and superiority, are eager to demonstrate their judicial broadmindedness by reducing the sentence suggested by the prosecution. Thus it has become almost a fixed practice for the judge to "discount" the sentence

* At the conference, Kichiemon Ishikawa suggested that the procurators are quite lenient in making the decision to prosecute; similarly, Nagashima points out that procurators tend to prosecute only when they are quite sure of a conviction. In fact, the conviction rate is 99.6 percent. Thus, one reason defense attorneys concentrate on mitigating circumstances would seem to be that only ironclad cases are ever brought to trial.

[21] A Japanese must appear apologetic and willing to reform, even if feignedly, in order to be reaccepted into society. The same is true if the procurator is to exercise his discretion to drop the case under the CODE OF CRIMINAL PROCEDURE, Law No. 131 of 1948, art. 248. An English translation of the code can be found in CRIMINAL STATUTES 86.

suggested by the prosecution even in cases in which such a course of action is not absolutely required by justice.

Judicial Leniency

Since an ingenious pilot study reported in 1939,[22] more than a dozen scholars and lawyers have attempted scientific approaches to sentencing problems. Although their findings have been varied, they have generally concurred in the belief that Japanese judges are too lenient. This corroborates the feeling generally held by the Japanese public and practical-minded lawyers that judicial leniency, especially as it is coupled with generous parole eligibility,[23] frustrates the deterrent and segregative effect of punishment in Japan.[24]

[22] FUWA, KEI NO RYŌTEI NI KAN-SURU JISSHŌ-TEKI KENKYŪ (A Positivistic Study Concerning Penalty Assessment) (1939).

[23] A prisoner becomes eligible to be considered for parole when he has served one third of a fixed sentence of imprisonment or 10 years of a life sentence ("indefinite term"). See PENAL CODE arts. 28, 30. In 1959, 67.6 percent of the prisoners discharged were parolees. It is also reported that in 1959 about 48 percent of parolees whose original sentences were imprisonment over three years were paroled before they had served 80 percent of their time. See HŌMU SŌGŌ KENKYŪJO (Ministry of Justice Integrated Research Institute), HŌMU-SHŌ (Ministry of Justice), HANZAI HAKUSHO—SHŌWA 36 NENBAN (1961 White Paper on Crime) [hereafter cited 1961 WHITE PAPER ON CRIME] 168, 171 (1961).

[24] The following cases were decided by the Tokyo District Court during 1960 and 1961:

The defendant, D, a 40-year-old man, was prosecuted for homicide. He was a construction worker and an army veteran without a family. During the afternoon preceding the tragedy, he had some time off and had a drink with his fellow workers, including V, the victim, and M, with whom D had had some difficulties the day before. At that time D shared a room with V and M. In the course of the drinking party, V, who was drunk, implied that he intended to fight D, using M as an accomplice, and displayed a hostile attitude toward D. D became indignant and went out to buy a butcher knife. About midnight he returned home with the knife and a bottle of sake and went to bed, concealing the knife under the covers. About 12:10, V returned home, very drunk. He burst into the room, crying aloud, "Hey, hit the deck!" and, according to D, kicked D in the stomach. D lost his temper, reached for the concealed knife, and started fighting with V. In the course of the fighting, D stabbed V in the side and struck him over the head with the knife, causing instantaneous death. D had three prior convictions. In two of them, he had unintentionally killed someone in a fight and had been sentenced to imprisonment, once for two years and once for six years. In the present case the finding was not murder, but infliction of bodily injury resulting in death. D was sentenced to imprisonment for 10 years. Japan v. Iriguchi, Tokyo District Court, Jan. 31, 1961 (unreported case).

D, a 28-year-old man, was prosecuted for "robbery resulting in bodily injury," the penalty for which is imprisonment for life, or seven years or more, unless mitigating circumstances exist. He had embezzled 60,000 yen from his employer and departed for Tokyo to escape a criminal investigation. After a period of idling about, he became destitute and decided to commit robbery. He broke into a dormitory room where a 69-year-old woman lived as a housekeeper and robbed her of 300 yen, striking her on the back of the head with a heavy metal bar and injuring her seriously. D had had no previous trouble except the unprosecuted embezzlement case mentioned above. He was sentenced to imprisonment for 5 years. Japan v. Oka, Tokyo District Court, April 28, 1960 (unreported case).

D, a 35-year-old owner of a small factory, was prosecuted for negligently hitting persons while driving a car at night in a state of intoxication. D, heavily intoxicated, was driving a car greatly in excess of the legal speed limit when he approached a spot in the middle of the highway where another accident had already occurred. He did not notice a policeman

One characteristic of judicial leniency in Japan is that it has increased over the years. A long-range statistical survey of cases of homicide from 1909 through 1940 reveals that the tendency towards leniency steadily became more pronounced.[25] For the decade from 1909, the average ratio of homicide cases in which the death penalty was imposed was approximately 3.4 percent of all homicide cases; whereas, for the decade ending in 1940, the incidence of capital sentences decreased to about 0.7 percent.[26] This tendency has also been noticeable in recent years. During the decade from 1949 through 1958, the death penalty was imposed in 0.66 percent of all cases in which defendants were found guilty of homicide.[27] Furthermore, from 1952 through 1958, imprisonment for a fixed term of more than ten years and less than fifteen years was imposed in 4.9 percent of all homicide cases resulting in convic-

---

waving a torch as a warning. About ten yards behind the policeman the scene of the accident had been closed off by a reflective barrier serving as a warning. Several people were working behind the barrier, including Police Inspector A, who was investigating the accident; B, the driver involved in the previous accident; and C, a medical intern who was voluntarily helping officers in investigating the scene. D, observing neither the barrier nor the people working, drove directly into the middle of the group. The policeman with the torch narrowly escaped, but A, B, and C, having no time to jump aside, were knocked down by the wild vehicle. B was killed instantly and A and C were seriously injured. D had four previous convictions, including two traffic offenses, one of which involved speeding. D was sentenced to confinement for 8 months. Japan v. Kim, Tokyo District Court, Oct. 21, 1960 (unreported case).

If these cases had been tried in the United States, it seems likely that the defendants would have incurred far heavier penalties than they actually received. The author has not yet systematically tested the psychological reactions which ordinary Japanese citizens may have to the sentences in these cases; but generalizing from the reactions of certain people to whom these cases have been outlined, it seems that laymen would feel that the defendants should have been punished at least twice (ten times, in the third case) as severely as they actually were.

For expressions of the view that the Japanese judiciary is extremely lenient see FUWA, note 22, at 59, 72, 85, 87–88, 115, 131; Uematsu, *Eijisatsu ni Kan-suru Hanzaigaku-teki Kenkyū* (A Criminological Study Concerning Infanticide), in 2 KEIJI HŌ NO RIRON TO GENJITSU (The Theory and Reality of Criminal Law), ONO HAKASE KANREKI KINEN ROMBUN SHŪ (A Collection of Essays in Commemoration of the 61st Birthday of Dr. Ono) 351, 354, 365, 400 (1951); SOGABE, RYŌKEI NO KENKYŪ (A Study of Penalty Assessment) 92–93 (Hōmu Kenkyū Hōkokusho (Ministry of Justice Research Reports) Ser. 46, No. 1, 1958).

[25] SAIKŌ SAIBANSHO JIMU-SŌKYOKU (General Secretariat of the Supreme Court), RYŌKEI NO HENSEN NI TSUITE (On Transitional Changes in Penalty Assessment) 43 (Keiji Saiban Shiryō (Criminal Trial Materials) No. 65, 1952). Infanticide cases are not included except for the year 1924.

[26] Similarly, in the same period from 1909 through 1940, the number of homicide cases in which there was a sentence of imprisonment for a fixed term of 10 years or more but less than 15 years was reduced by more than one half (from 17.6 percent to 6.85 percent). The relative decrease in heavier sentences was, of course, balanced by a relative increase in lighter sentences. Thus, for the decade starting with 1909, the average percentage of homicide cases in which sentences for imprisonment for less than 3 years were imposed was 16.9 percent of all homicide cases, whereas the ratio for the decade ending with 1940 was 37.6 percent; in the three decades the incidence of lighter sentences doubled. See *ibid.*

[27] SAIKŌ SAIBANSHO JIMU-SŌKYOKU (General Secretariat of the Supreme Court), SHŌWA 34 NEN SHIHŌ TŌKEI NEMPŌ (1959 Annual Report of Judicial Statistics), 2 KEIJI HEN (Criminal Affairs Book) pt. 1, at 46 (1961). Infanticide cases are excluded for the purposes of the present analysis.

tion;[28] and from 1949 through 1959, imprisonment for less than three years was imposed in 23.2 percent of such cases.[29]

Secondly, judicial leniency in Japan is characterized by a tendency toward a high frequency of sentences imposed at the minimum prescribed by statute. Apparently sentencing judges have paid little attention to the penal framework, particularly the maximum thereof, set by the legislature. For example, for ordinary theft the Penal Code prescribes imprisonment at forced labor for not more than ten years and not less than one month.[30] One might presume that the majority of sentences for theft would be fixed somewhere around two or three years, but in fact this is not so. During the six-year period from 1950 through 1955, approximately 324,000 sentences were pronounced by District Courts in theft cases. It is surprising to observe that about 87 percent of the total were sentences of imprisonment at forced labor for not more than one year. The tendency of sentences to cluster near the bottom of the sentencing scale provided by statute is particularly conspicuous in bodily-injury cases, for which the law prescribes either imprisonment at forced labor for not more than ten years and not less than one month, or a fine.[31] About 80 percent of all such cases prosecuted from 1947 through 1955 led to sentences of imprisonment at forced labor, but 69.4 percent of the terms of imprisonment were less than one year, and 23.16 percent were only six months.

When the legislature has stipulated a minimum penalty, the judge is not supposed to go below in fixing sentence, unless certain particularly extenuating circumstances exist.[32] The rising tide of judicial leniency, however,

[28] Thus the rate of more severe sentences for homicide became only about two thirds of the rate for 1940. See note 26 above.

For the basic figures used in this analysis, see SAIKŌ SAIBANSHO JIMU-SŌKYOKU (General Secretariat of the Supreme Court), SHŌWA 24–26 NEN KEIJI SAIBAN TŌKEI NEMPŌ (1949–1951 Annual Reports of Criminal Trial Statistics); SAIKŌ SAIBANSHO JIMU-SŌKYOKU, SHŌWA 27–32 NEN SHIHŌ TŌKEI NEMPŌ (1952–1957 Annual Reports of Judicial Statistics), 2 KEIJI HEN (Criminal Affairs Book) pt. 2; SAIKŌ SAIBANSHO JIMU-SŌKYOKU, SHŌWA 33–34 NEN SHIHŌ TŌKEI NEMPŌ (1958–1959 Annual Reports of Judicial Statistics), 2 KEIJI HEN (Criminal Affairs Book) pt. 1. Infanticide cases are excluded. The same sources are used for the analysis in later paragraphs unless otherwise noted.

[29] Thus the rate of lighter sentences for homicide (23.2 percent) increased by one half over the rate for 1909 to 1918 (16.9 percent). See note 26.

[30] PENAL CODE arts. 12, 235. The statistics on sentencing which follow are from SOGABE, note 24, at 118.

[31] PENAL CODE arts. 12, 204.

[32] Under the Penal Code of Japan there are two types of authorization for lowering the minimum level of penalty prescribed by statute. One is a statutory reduction of penalty, which the court may or ought to make only in cases where the law specifically so provides. Art. 43 of the Penal Code, for example, provides that the court may make such a reduction in the case of an attempted crime. Another possibility is discretionary reduction, which the court may make whenever it believes that there is some mitigating circumstance. PENAL CODE arts. 66–67. When reduction is made, whether statutory or discretionary, the prescribed framework of punishment is modified in the following manner: the death penalty is changed to imprisonment at forced labor for life or 10 years or more; life imprisonment is lowered by reducing the minimum penalty by one half (arts. 68, 71). Thus imprisonment for 7 years or more

very easily evades the barriers set by statute. For example, the Penal Code prescribes the minimum penalty for the crime of robbery resulting in bodily injury as imprisonment for seven years. Yet in 1958, of 870 defendants who were found guilty of this crime, 783, or 90 percent, were sentenced to imprisonment for seven years or less; and 61.7 percent were sentenced to imprisonment for five years or less.

A similar phenomenon is found with regard to the crime of parricide, for which the Penal Code prescribes life imprisonment or death. In 1950 to 1955, only 14 percent and 2 percent of persons found guilty of this crime were actually sentenced to life imprisonment and death, respectively.[33]

Judicial leniency in Japan is also characterized by generosity in placing the convict on probation.[34] In the postwar period from 1953 through 1958, of about 587,000 people sentenced to imprisonment, approximately 275,000, or 46.8 percent, were placed on probation; in the prewar period from 1927 through 1932, of about 198,000 people sentenced to the same category of penalty, about 33,000, or only 16.67 percent, were put on probation.[35] The probation ratio is remarkably high in cases involving certain offenses,[36] even some serious ones. For example, from 1953 through 1958, 31 percent of all persons convicted of homicide and 47 percent of all extortionists were placed on probation.[37]

---

may be reduced to imprisonment for 3.5 years. If both reductions are made, imprisonment for 7 years or more may be reduced to as low as imprisonment for not less than 1 year and 9 months.

[33] The relevant Penal Code provision is art. 200. The absolute figures were 32 persons sentenced to life imprisonment and 5 to death out of 233 convicted. SAIKŌ SAIBANSHO JIMU-SŌKYOKU (General Secretariat of the Supreme Court), SHŌWA 30 NEN SHIHŌ TŌKEI NEMPŌ (1955 Annual Report of Judicial Statistics), 2 KEIJI HEN (Criminal Affairs Book), pt. 1, at 44–45.

[34] See PENAL CODE arts. 25–27. On this point it must be noted that under Japanese law the mode of placing the convict on probation is not necessarily the same as in the United States. If the judge finds the accused guilty, he must pronounce an appropriate sentence. If the judge sees fit, however, he may, under certain limitations, suspend the execution of the sentence for a certain period. He may then place the probationer under the supervision of a probation officer, but this is not a mandatory step except in certain cases prescribed by law. The term "probation" is used here in its broader sense.

[35] HŌMU SŌGŌ KENKYŪJO (Ministry of Justice Integrated Research Institute), HŌMU-SHŌ (Ministry of Justice), HANZAI HAKUSHO—SHŌWA 35 NENBAN (1960 White Paper on Crime) [hereafter cited 1960 WHITE PAPER ON CRIME] 173–74 (1960).These figures exclude life-imprisonment cases.

[36] E.g., drafting false private documents by a doctor, 100 percent; abuse of authority by a public officer, 100 percent; defamation, 100 percent; violence and mistreatment by a special public official, 90 percent. These figures are averages for 1949 through 1955.

[37] The probation rate in homicide cases is based upon the SAIKŌ SAIBANSHO JIMU-SŌKYOKU (General Secretariat of the Supreme Court), SHIHŌ TŌKEI NEMPŌ (Annual Report of Judicial Statistics), 2 KEIJI HEN (Criminal Affairs Book) for the following years at the page given: 1953, at 166; 1954, at 166; 1955, at 182; 1956, at 196; 1957, at 120; 1958, at 70.

The rate for extortion cases is from the same source for the following years and pages: 1953, at 164; 1954, at 164; 1955, at 180; 1956, at 196; 1957, at 120; 1958, at 70.

Reference to the probation rates in the United States and West Germany will give some basis for comparison. It is reported that in the year ending June 30, 1955, the probation rate

Such growing leniency as reflected in the high probation rate may mean either that Japanese judges are paying increasing attention to scientific considerations in sentencing or else, more likely, simply that judicial indulgence has been growing, irrespective of any scientific foundation. The latter interpretation is at least partially supported by the fact that the rate of unsuccessful probation, as reflected in the ratio of revoked probation, seems to have been increasing.[38]

Finally it seems that more leniency is observed in cases of offenses against personal safety or dignity than of offenses against property rights. For example, median terms of imprisonment imposed in theft and bodily injury cases during the year 1958 were 13.8 months and 6.7 months, respectively, although both types of crime are punishable by the same term of imprisonment.[39]

Some may favor the theory that judicial leniency in Japan reflects a general leniency in the Japanese mentality. Such a generalization, however, does not represent the true picture. It is indeed true that the Japanese people, being kind and merciful in general, do not like to impose punishment of a vindictive or retaliatory nature, and they are usually ready to forgive.[40] Numerous historical facts, of course, contradict such a simplified generalization.

Nevertheless, some aspects of judicial leniency may be explained in terms of sociopsychological elements which are peculiar to Japanese society in general. For example, the fact that heavier penalties have been imposed for offenses against property rights than for offenses against personal safety or dignity, even in cases in which the legislature provided for similar degrees of punishment in both types of offense, may be largely attributed to a pattern of thinking which has been long cultivated by the difficult socioeconomic situation faced by the Japanese people.

---

for the entire federal jurisdiction in the United States was 34.5 percent, the district rates ranging from 5.5 percent in Arizona to 84.2 percent in New Hampshire. U.S. BUREAU OF PRISONS, DEPT. OF JUSTICE, FEDERAL PRISONS: 1955, at 92 (1956). It is also reported that in 1957 the rate of suspended sentence for adults in Germany was about 17 percent. In Germany, as in Japan, the mode of placing the convict on probation in a regular court is the suspension of the execution of sentence. In 1957 in West Germany, 54,382 defendants, including 49,288 adults and 5,094 quasi-adults, were convicted in regular courts, and execution of sentence was suspended for 9,401 convicts, or 17.29 percent, including 8,360 adults and 1,041 quasi-adults. BUNDESMINISTERIUM DER JUSTIZ, BEWÄHRUNGSHILFESTATISTIK 15 (Bonn 1957).

[38] In one prewar period (1927–1932), the rate of revoked probation was about 7.5 percent, whereas in one postwar period (1953–1958) the rate was about 16.8 percent. See 1960 WHITE PAPER ON CRIME 175.

[39] SAIKŌ SAIBANSHO JIMU-SŌKYOKU (General Secretariat of the Supreme Court), SHŌWA 33 NEN SHIHŌ TŌKEI NEMPŌ (1958 Annual Report of Judicial Statistics), 2 KEIJI HEN (Criminal Affairs Book) pt. 1, at 254, 258 (1960). Both are punishable by a maximum of 10 years of imprisonment and a minimum of 1 month of imprisonment. PENAL CODE arts. 12, 204, 235.

[40] They are particularly ready to forgive those who admit their guilt, apologize, and work hard to rehabilitate themselves. Cf. note 21.

It was not until the 1880s that the people of Japan had their first contact with the Western philosophy of individualism. For centuries before that time, they had been accustomed to the view that the rights of subjects are of far less importance than the dignity or interests of the rulers. The eighty-year period of modernization has not been enough to eliminate the remnants of their premodern mode of thought. Moreover, for many centuries the Japanese have suffered from difficult conditions arising from the narrowness of the land, the lack of natural resources, and frequent natural calamities such as typhoons, floods, earthquakes, and tidal waves. From these continual disasters and the ensuing marginal living standards, the common people were quick to learn the lesson that a grain of rice is sometimes more valuable than human dignity. Certain ruthless militarists took advantage of such an attitude of resignation on the part of the people; the value of a soldier's life was once figured to be one and a half sen,[41] that is, the cost of postage for a military order to call a person into service.

Thus it is not unfair to conclude that the weaker judicial reaction to offenses against human dignity than to offenses against property rights is derived from sociopsychological elements which have been deeply rooted in the minds of the people. Beyond this point, however, it would be inaccurate to explain the fact of judicial leniency in terms of the Japanese mentality. This characteristic should rather be attributed to a peculiarity of the Japanese judiciary. The prevailing impression of the Anglo-American legal system is that juries generally show a more sympathetic attitude than judges, particularly in cases that have special appeal to the emotions. In Japan the situation appears to be the opposite. In most criminal cases Japanese judges, or sometimes even public procurators, react more moderately than ordinary citizens. This is one of the reasons why the Jury Law was suspended after fifteen years of operation.[42] It was reported that 98 percent of the accused waived trial by jury;[43] at least one of the motives for such waiver was the general assumption by the accused that the jury, which participated in both the factfinding and sentencing process, would be harsher than the judge.

The leniency of Japanese jurists as compared with lay citizens was confirmed by an ingenious study carried out by Tadashi Uematsu, a jurist and psychologist, about twenty years ago.[44] The purpose of his study was to find out the possible relation between the gravity of sentences imposed and the

[41] One hundred sen equal one yen.

[42] See note 8.

[43] Okahara, *Baishin Hō Teishi ni Kan-suru Hōritsu ni Tsuite* (On the Law Concerning the Suspension of the Jury Law), 21 HŌSŌ KAI ZASSHI (Jurists' Association Magazine) no. 4, at 10, 17–18 (1943).

[44] UEMATSU, *Kei no Ryōtei ni Kan-suru Jisshō-teki Kenkyū* (A Positivistic Study Concerning Penalty Assessment), in SAIBAN SHINRIGAKU NO SHOSŌ (Various Aspects of Trial Psychology) 99 (newly rev. ed., 1958).

backgrounds and attitudes of those imposing sentence. He showed eight different infanticide cases, in the form of eight brief statements of charges, to a sample group of people comprising twenty-five trial judges, seven public procurators, thirteen primary-school teachers, and ten university students. From the findings of the study, the following five points merit particular attention. First, the judges were found to be the most moderate in their reactions to the cases and the students the least; the order of degrees of leniency, from highest to lowest, was judges, public procurators, teachers, and students. Second, the sentences proposed by the legally trained group (judges and public procurators) were markedly milder than those advocated by the lay group (teachers and students). Third, there was a great similarity between the sentences proposed by the judges and those assessed by the public procurators, not only in leniency but also in the way in which circumstantial factors were considered. Fourth, disparity in actual sentences was far less in the legally trained group than in the lay group. Fifth, the rate of granting probation was far greater in the legally trained group than in the lay group: procurators, 62.5 percent; judges, 61.1 percent; teachers, 24.0 percent; and students, 22.5 percent.[45]

Limited space does not permit a detailed discussion of Uematsu's study. To give at least a partial picture of it, however, one of his correlation tables is reproduced as Table 1 at the end of this essay. Although the size of the sample used is too small to permit one to draw any scientific conclusions from it, the pilot study is at least somewhat corroborative of the common feeling that judicial leniency in Japan derives from certain personality attributes cultivated in the social milieu of the Japanese legal profession.

Although it is still too early to make any conclusive statements concerning the possible psychological grounds on which judicial leniency has been developed,[46] I would suggest five tentative possibilities. First, professional training enables judges and public procurators to have a sharper insight into the real causation of crime and delinquency. These men well know that crimes are not exclusively attributable to the immorality of the offenders, but rather result from certain hereditary or environmental factors which are not easily controlled by the unfortunate offenders themselves. Thus attitudes within the legal profession tend to be more sympathetic toward offenders than are those of laymen.

Second, professional calmness and objectivity prevent judges and procurators from being emotionally shocked by cruelty in the commission of offenses. At the sight of the bloody corpse of the victim, lay people are easily excited and are prone to cry out, "Hang the criminal!" But it is much more difficult

[45] This point was not clearly mentioned by Uematsu but can be inferred from his data.

[46] Judicial leniency is, of course, paralleled by the leniency of the public toward a repentant criminal who has apologized and shown a sincere intention to rehabilitate himself through hard work.

to deprive professional people of their objectivity in reaching a judgment.

Third, professional lawyers, particularly judges, know that punishment has very limited educative power. They are often skeptical or pessimistic about the effects of long-term imprisonment, and they expect more from extramural treatment, such as probation and parole, than from incarceration. This attitude naturally makes them reluctant to impose a heavy penalty.

Fourth, an awareness of human rights — a humanitarian impulse — is much stronger in the legal profession than in the public at large. The lawyer has been specially trained in humane ways of handling offenders. Some modern judges believe that the most important role of the judiciary lies in the protection of offenders from severe and unreasonable punishment.*

Fifth, whether consciously or unconsciously, judges sometimes want to demonstrate their judicial broadmindedness by lenient sentencing. This sense of "judicial patronage" has at least contributed to the gradual lowering of the sentencing norm in Japan.

These five elements may be thought to be indicative of progress in judicial attitudes. It may be thought that there is no reason why judicial leniency should be indicted; leniency is better than harshness and may even be a sign of the first step toward enlightenment. But it must be borne in mind that judicial leniency without a scientific basis cannot solve the fundamental problems of crime. Such an attitude based on a pretentious humanitarianism actually amounts to an evasion and abdication of the judicial function. The judicial cruelty in the feudal age and the judicial leniency in modern times are nothing but the two opposite extremes of the same pendulum of judicial sentimentalism. True justice will be served not by stereotyped leniency but by truly individualized treatment. The accused should receive whatever penalty or treatment his particular situation merits. Unscientific leniency, though laudable from a short-run humanitarian standpoint, contributes very little toward reduction of the crime rate.

Disparity in Sentencing and Efforts toward Standardization

Some years ago a Harvard professor of law reminded federal judges of an old complaint about the haphazard nature of sentencing, by telling the story of a village magistrate who used to fine the accused in the amount of whatever price he happened upon in a mail-order catalogue.[47] When an unlucky out-of-state victim was brought in for violating the traffic law, the

* Kohji Tanabe commented at the conference on the judicial attitude prevalent at a time before World War II, when the judiciary had a far greater responsibility, under the inquisitorial procedure, for developing the evidence. Then the trial was a moral experience, perhaps somewhat analogous to confession in the Roman Catholic Church, with the judge and the accused as the principal participants. The judge took personal responsibility for the success of the sentence, frequently visiting the criminal in jail to encourage repentence.

[47] Glueck, *The Sentencing Problem,* 20 Fed. Prob., Dec. 1956, p. 15.

learned jurist opened up his mail-order catalogue, cleared his throat, and pronounced a sentence of $14.98. When the defendant protested that he had never before paid more than $10.00 for speeding, the arresting officer whispered in his ear, "Ye'd better shet up. Y're dern lucky Hizzoner put his finger on 'pants' instead of 'pi-anos.'" A solemn reality implied in this seeming nonsense is often proved by facts. In the United States much has been written about the problem of disparity in sentencing,[48] a disparity which in some cases is almost incredible.[49] Although it is generally agreed that this is also the case in Japan, the situation there is not so extreme because of the characteristic judicial leniency. For example, it has been reported that almost 90 percent of all arson cases incur imprisonment for five years or less.[50] Uematsu reported that 77 percent of 52 infanticide cases involving unmarried mothers resulted in exactly the same sentence, imprisonment for two years suspended for three years.[51] The prevailing stereotyped leniency tends to make rigorous judges conspicuous. At the general meeting of the Japan Criminal Law Association in May 1961 in Tokyo, a practicing lawyer discussed the current inconsistent sentencing behavior of Tokyo judges and pointed out that some trial divisions presided over by rigorous judges are feared by defense lawyers as *Jigoku-dani* (Valleys of Hell).

Although no systematic surveys have been made of individual differences in sentencing behavior, an informative study has been made of area deviations in sentencing in theft cases.[52] The conclusions pointed out *inter alia*

[48] For major contributions in the period 1958–1960, see, e.g., Bennett, *The Sentence—Its Relation to Crime and Rehabilitation,* 1960 U. ILL. L. REV. 500; Devitt, *Improvements in Federal Sentencing Procedures,* 35 N.D.L. REV. 185 (1959); George, *Comparative Sentencing Techniques,* 23 Fed. Prob., March 1959, p. 27. See also STAFF OF HOUSE COMM. ON THE JUDICIARY, 85TH CONG., 2D SESS., FEDERAL SENTENCING PROCEDURES (Comm. Print, 1958); S. REP. No. 1478, 85th Cong., 2d Sess. 23 (1958).

[49] For example, J. V. Bennett, Director of the Federal Bureau of Prisons, recently reported that early in 1960, a 32-year-old Army veteran had been sentenced to 15 years in the penitentiary for forging a $58.40 check, whereas at about the same time a 36-year-old Navy veteran had been sentenced to 30 days of imprisonment for forging a $35.20 check. Records disclosed that the histories and offenses of these two men were practically identical. It was also shown that the former acted under more extenuating circumstances, that is, his wife had just suffered a miscarriage and they needed money for food and rent. Moreover, the latter had a more unfavorable record, that is, two small previous convictions, whereas the former had previously had only one court martial for misconduct. Yet the former received a sentence which was 180 times more severe. Bennett believes the difference existed "simply because they appeared before two different judges." Bennett, *Sentences Are Inconsistent; Forgery Conviction Means From 30 Days to 15 Years, Depending on Your Judge,* Pacific Stars and Stripes, May 9, 1961, p. 15, col. 1. For a more systematic description of sentencing disparity in the United States, see Bennett, note 48.

[50] FUWA, note 22, at 107. Art. 108 of the Penal Code provides with regard to arson that a person who sets fire to and burns a building inhabited by someone shall be punished with "death or imprisonment at forced labor for an indefinite term or five years or more."

[51] Uematsu, note 24, at 183, 211.

[52] Takahashi, *Settōzai ni Tai-suru Ryōkei no Chiikisa ni Tsuite* (On Regional Differences in Penalty Assessment for Theft), 3 KEIHŌ ZASSHI (Journal of Criminal Law) 364, 387 (1953).

that in 1949 rates for suspension of execution of sentence ranged from a high of 52.7 percent in the Maebashi District to a low of 28.3 percent in the Otsu District,[53] and that rates for sentences of imprisonment for three years or over ranged from a high of 15.6 percent in the Tottori District to a low of 0.5 percent in the Asahigawa District. Since there are no circumstances supporting an assumption that theft cases in Otsu and Tottori are of an especially grave nature, the cause of such disparity must be found in the differences in the behavior of different judges.

There are three possible approaches to achieving uniformity in sentencing: organizational, legislative, and statistical.

The first method is to organize the judiciary into a unitary sentencing body, which is then more apt to adopt standardized practices. Japan approaches this organization more closely than does the United States. This fact may explain in part why there is less disparity in sentencing in Japan.

One standardizing factor is that Japan has a unitary court system, with only one territorial jurisdiction and without the dualism of federal and state jurisdictions. Thus the same Penal Code and the same Code of Criminal Procedure are applied in all the courts throughout the country. Furthermore, the Japanese judiciary consists of a centralized body of well-trained and officially appointed judges and assistant judges. Although their status is protected by the Constitution, as a matter of personnel administration they are transferred at certain intervals from one place to another, that is, from rural courts to urban courts, from lower courts to higher courts, and vice versa, so that there is a constant circulation of judges. No doubt this system, which fosters constant homogenization of individual experiences, contributes a great deal toward the formation of standardized sentencing practices.

Like the United States with its federal court system, Japan has a pyramid-shaped judicial hierarchy consisting of three levels of courts.[54] Unlike most courts of appeals in the United States,[55] however, Japanese appellate courts generally have the power to reverse unreasonable sentences imposed by

[53] Compare this with the situation in the United States federal jurisdiction. U.S. Bureau of Prison reports show a wide range in the probation rate. See note 37 reporting the rate for 1955. In 1958 the probation rate varied from 68.5 percent in Eastern Pennsylvania to 11.8 percent in the First Division of Alaska. Rates within a single circuit, the Eighth, varied from 68 percent in South Dakota to 12 percent in Southern Iowa. U.S. BUREAU OF PRISONS, DEPT. OF JUSTICE, FEDERAL PRISONS: 1958, at 114 (1959).

[54] The three-level structure of the Japanese court system consists of a Supreme Court, eight High Courts, and numerous courts of first instance (49 District Courts and 570 Summary Courts). See Court Law, arts. 1–38; Abe, *Criminal Justice in Japan: Its Historical Background and Modern Problems,* 47 A.B.A.J. 555 (1961).

[55] Note B. J. George's contention on this point: "we are the only country in the free world where a single judge may, without being subjected to any review of his determination on the merits, decide absolutely the minimum period of time during which a convicted offender must remain in prison." George, note 48, at 27. See also Bennett, note 48, at 505, citing Address by U.S. Assistant Attorney General Doub, American Bar Association Annual Meeting, Miami Beach, Florida, Aug. 1959.

lower courts;[56] even the Supreme Court has discretionary power to review the propriety of sentencing by lower courts.[57] In 1958, whereas 7,828 appeals were made to High Courts on the ground of inappropriate sentencing, 1,961 were reversed on that ground.[58] About 70 percent of all appeals taken to High Courts in Japan are based on the ground of allegedly inappropriate sentence, and about 70 percent of all reversals of inferior-court judgments are based at least in part on inappropriate sentencing.[59] Thus appeal in Japan is widely used as a method of achieving uniformity in sentencing.

The second main device for achieving uniformity in sentencing is detailed legislative prescription of criteria to be applied by the judge in assessing the length and nature of the sentence. As mentioned above, this method is outmoded when the details relate to the amount stolen and similar criteria.[60] The more modern approach, however, is to establish flexible criteria, relating to more general aspects of the offense, containing somewhat more elastic standards for sentencing. An illustration of such a legislative attempt may be found in the Italian Penal Code Project of the late Enrico Ferri.[61] The Italian project proposed the adoption of an elaborate schedule of "conditions of greater danger" and "conditions of lesser danger," to be prescribed by the code in advance and to be applied by the judge as a basis for computation of individual penal treatment.[62] Although theoretically the Ferri system appears precise and efficient, it is too mechanical to attain a realistic individ-

[56] See CODE OF CRIMINAL PROCEDURE arts. 381, 386, 393, 397, 402.

[57] *Ibid.*, art. 411. In 1958, however, despite 1,346 appeals made to the Supreme Court on the ground of allegedly inappropriate sentencing, only 19 were reversed for that reason. SAIKŌ SAIBANSHO JIMU-SŌKYOKU (General Secretariat of the Supreme Court), SHŌWA 33 NEN SHIHŌ TŌKEI NEMPŌ (1958 Annual Report of Judicial Statistics), 2 KEIJI HEN (Criminal Affairs Book) pt. 2, at 232, 264.

[58] *Ibid.*

[59] *Ibid.*

[60] The primitive form of such legislative efforts to set up criteria for sentencing was found in the old Beccarian attempt to fetter the judge with an inelastic control apparatus. In such a stage of development, the criteria were designed to make detailed degrees of punishment mechanically correspond to detailed degrees of apparent gravity of the criminal act. People soon realized, however, that such an approach did not actually help to achieve true uniformity in sentencing and permitted but a poor counterfeit of scientific individualization, although it is useful for confining judicial arbitrariness within prescribed limits. See pp. 328–329 and note 14.

[61] 1 FERRI, RELAZIONE SUL PROGRETTO PRELIMINARE DI CODICE PENALE ITALIANO (1921). See also Glueck, *Principles of a Rational Penal Code*, 41 HARV. L. REV. 453 (1928), in CRIME AND CORRECTION 72 (1952).

[62] The Italian project of Ferri listed seventeen "circumstances which indicate a greater danger from the offender," and eight "circumstances which show less danger" as criteria to be applied in assessing individual sentences. His code further provided numerous directives regarding the method of applying these criteria to individual cases. These explained how to assess a sentence between the maximum and the minimum penalty set forth for the offense committed by the accused, depending on the presence of one or more circumstances of greater or lesser danger. The Italian project in addition provided an elaborate system of punishments which were to be taken into consideration by judges in connection with the conditions of greater and lesser danger, thus further complicating the process of individualization. See Glueck, note 61, at 471–75, in CRIME AND CORRECTION at 90–94.

ualized treatment. Moreover, since the Italian project does not suggest any relationships among the many different conditions of danger, the judge may still have to resort to his own "hunch" when he has more than two conditions before him.

A less mechanical system is attempted in the sentencing provisions of the Model Penal Code which is being drafted by the American Law Institute.[63] It tries to provide more flexible criteria for sentencing, leaving greater latitude for criminological considerations by the judge. It is likely that judges customarily take into account such criteria as are included in the draft code; but a legislative enumeration of some essential criteria for sentencing is useful to remind judges to consider systematically the various matters deemed relevant by the legislature. Such a listing of pertinent considerations will in the long run bring about greater uniformity in sentencing and treatment. Judicial discretion still remains, however, and a judge must depend upon his own individual experience or hunch in the crucial process of weighing and integrating various factors.

As stated above, the present Penal Code of Japan, enacted in 1907, decisively abandoned the attempt to maintain in the sentencing system a mechanical correlation between detailed degrees of penalty and detailed degrees of apparent gravity of criminal acts. Under the new legislation, sentencing judges began to enjoy almost unhampered freedom in assessing punishment. Depending solely upon his own limited experience, however, each judge now had to grapple with a new and more difficult problem, that of achieving uniformity in sentencing while attaining true individualization of treatment. Under the present code, conscientious judges must sometimes feel as if they were floating on an ocean without a compass. A few attempts to rescue them have been made by draftsmen of proposed penal codes. In 1940, for example, a governmental commission published the text of a Provisional Draft of the Revised Penal Code,[64] which enu-

[63] E.g., MODEL PENAL CODE § 7.01 (Tent. Draft No. 4, 1955): "(1) The Court may deal with a person who has been convicted of a crime without imposing sentence of imprisonment if, having regard to the nature and circumstances of the crime and to the history and character of the defendant, it deems that his imprisonment is unnecessary for protection of the public, on one or more of the following grounds." The draft then enumerates eight types of extenuating conditions, such as lack of a previous criminal record, want of serious harm, unlikelihood of a recurrence of the circumstances prompting the criminal act, strong provocation, the victim's consent, the defendant's advanced age or poor physical condition, and good character indicating a high probability of no recidivism.

The draft then provides other criteria to be taken into account in the imposition of fine or imprisonment. For example, the criteria for imposing a sentence of an "extended term of imprisonment" include such items as (1) "a persistent offender," (2) "a professional criminal," and (3) "a dangerous, mentally abnormal person." MODEL PENAL CODE § 7.03. See also MODEL PENAL CODE §§ 7.02, 7.04.

[64] KAISEI KEIHŌ KARI-AN, Keihō Narabi Kangoku Hō Kaisei Chōsa Iinkai Sōkai Ketsugi oyobi Ryūho Jōkō, Shōwa 15 Nen Happyō (Resolution and Reservation of a Plenary Session of the Penal Code and Prison Law Revision Investigation Commission, Published 1940) [hereafter cited Japanese Draft Penal Code of 1940], reprinted in ROPPŌ ZENSHO SHŌWA 35 NENBAN (Complete Six Codes 1960 Edition) 1260 (Wagatsuma & Miyazawa ed., 1960).

merated several aggravating and extenuating circumstances to be taken into account in assessing sentences. It also provided in article 57 a set of general criteria for fixing sentence.[65] The proposed draft was not approved by practitioners, however. They thought that these criteria were simply those which they had taken into account as a matter of routine for many years. What they needed was not a table of factors to be considered in assessing penalties, but rather rules or formulas which would determine the interrelationship among such differing considerations. Consequently, the Penal Code Revision Preparation Commission submitted a Preliminary Draft of the Revised Penal Code (1961),[66] which contained an article providing general standards for sentencing.[67] There has been much discussion about the usefulness of such general standards, and most lawyers are apparently skeptical about the practical value of such abstract criteria.[68]

The search for some new device to help judges behave more scientifically in the process of individualization of punishment leads to the third and

[65] Japanese Draft Penal Code of 1940, art. 57:

"In applying punishment consideration shall be given to the offender's character, age, and surroundings, the circumstances of his crime, and his conduct after the crime, and in particular the following items shall be taken into account:

(i) The career, habits, and heredity of the offender.
(ii) The strength of his criminal determination.
(iii) Whether the motivation for his crime is blameworthy or pardonable from the standpoint of loyalty, filial piety, or other moral precepts, or the public interest.
(iv) Whether his crime is founded upon fear, surprise, excitement, panic, provocation, intimidation, group suggestion, or some other similar cause.
(v) Whether he committed the crime or caused the crime to be committed through abuse or disdain for kinship, guardianship, the master-pupil relationship, employment, or some other similar relationship.
(vi) Whether the method of his crime is cruel and cunning.
(vii) The quantity of planning for his crime and the gravity of the danger or actual harm produced as a result of the crime.
(viii) Whether after committing the crime he was penitent and endeavored to indemnify the damage or otherwise lighten the actual harm."

[66] Kaisei Keihō Jumbi Sōan, reprinted in 34 Hōritsu Jihō (Law Journal) no. 2, supp. at 1 [hereafter cited Japanese Draft Penal Code of 1961].

[67] Japanese Draft Penal Code of 1961, art. 47:

"(1) Punishment shall be assessed commensurate with the culpability of the offender.

"(2) In applying punishment, the age, character, career, and environment of the offender, the motive, method, effect, and social impact of the crime, and the attitude of the offender subsequent to the crime shall be considered, and the purpose shall be to suppress the crime and reform and rehabilitate the offender.

"(3) The type and amount of punishment shall not exceed the degree necessary to maintain legal order. Application of the death penalty shall be performed with particularly great care."

[68] This problem was listed as one of the major issues on the agenda of the general meeting of the Japan Criminal Law Association held in May 1961 in Tokyo. In a plenary session of this meeting, Professor Hideo Ichikawa of Chuo University, one of the reporters, doubted the substantial usefulness of such abstract standards, although he recognized some value in this legislative attempt to emphasize, though secondarily, educative aspects of penal treatment. He thought that this sort of provision could not help much unless "logical interrelationships" among the prescribed conditions were expressly stated. His position appeared to have wide support. Pessimism seemed to be the dominant feeling of the conference.

last suggested resort, an attempt to construct statistical correlation tables. Such a device certainly may be useful in accelerating the slow movement from hunch to science. But the paths of science are always beset by many theoretical and practical difficulties.

One of the greatest barriers to a scientific approach to reasonable sentencing standards is the long-standing conflict between retributive and educative theories of penal law. Under the retributive philosophy of punishment, it is important to keep the degree of punishment mathematically commensurate with the gravity of the criminal act, which reflects the moral culpability of the actor. Following the educative philosophy of punishment, however, it is more important to choose the treatment which is best fitted to the rehabilitation of the offender to sound citizenship. This conflict may perhaps be resolved by an eclectic approach which gives considerable priority to the educative view of punishment.[69]

In assessing sentence the judge should first consider what type of penal treatment is most effective in promoting the rehabilitation of the offender. The choice may be between fine and imprisonment, or it may be between probation and incarceration; as a matter of practice, the judge is most frequently confronted with the latter choice. Insofar as priority is given to the educative theory of punishment, the criteria for the choice must be the relative probabilities of successful rehabilitation. If, for example, the judge thinks that a higher probability of success in rehabilitation of a particular offender is to be expected under extramural treatment, he has good reason to place that defendant on probation. The problem then arises as to how to estimate or predict the probability of successful rehabilitation.

A promising way to solve this problem has been suggested by Sheldon Glueck of the Harvard Law School:

> The question presented is whether there is available, for the purposes of scientific differentiation of treatment, an instrument that can aid the judge in determining which factors have been shown, by systematic analysis of past experience, to be *truly relevant to the expectable behavior of various offenders, and how much weight to give such factors in the particular case before the judge for sentence.*[70]

He then proposed a method of controlling sentencing by means of a recidivism-prediction table. His proposal for promoting individualization of treatment has been gradually accepted by practitioners and researchers in Japan. Most specialists have begun to realize the importance of follow-up investigation as the first step toward construction of correlation tables which show the relationship between success or failure of rehabilitation and the

[69] Although priority should be given to the educative view of punishment, it is wrong to disregard totally the retributive or deterrent view of punishment. In order to control certain aspects of human behavior, deterrence sometimes proves useful.

[70] Glueck, note 47, at 21.

characteristics and environmental background of persons subjected to various kinds of treatment, including different types and lengths of sentence and subsequent treatment.[71] Certain pilot studies in this direction have already been carried out by a few researchers.[72]

Still, the retributive view of punishment, with its emphasis on a correlation between penalty and culpability, has predominant currency in theory and practice in the administration of criminal justice in Japan,[73] although Eiichi Makino[74] and his followers have fought against this situation for many years. It would seem that one should be able to place considerable emphasis on the retributive aspect of punishment if it becomes clear that little reformative effect can be expected from extramural treatment. The problem then becomes to find some device for determining the penalty that reasonably corresponds to the gravity of the antisocial behavior of the defendant. It seems likely that systematic analysis of sentences actually pronounced and the data used in fixing them will enable construction of a table which shows the correlation between the sentences and "circumstantial indices" which reflect the moral culpability of individual defendants. In order to make such a table significant, a preliminary study must be made to determine which circumstantial factors have actually been considered in judicial assessment of penalty.

Recently I carried out a pilot investigation directed toward the construction of such a correlation table, which shows sentencing tendencies in the past and, therefore, can be used as a sentencing standard in the future. This preliminary inquiry was limited to bodily-injury cases, excluding those resulting in death. The 190 bodily-injury cases disposed of by the Tokyo District Court from May to December 1961 were checked; and pertinent data was obtained on 155 cases. With this data an inquiry was

[71] For the remarkable work accomplished by the Gluecks, see, e.g., GLUECK & GLUECK, PREDICTING DELINQUENCY AND CRIME (1959). This book includes all their tables — youth and adult, male and female — covering all types of treatment: probation with and without suspended sentence of imprisonment, industrial schools, men's and women's reformatories, prisons, jails, houses of correction, and parole — everything except the results of the imposition of simple fines.

[72] See Takeuchi, Juvenile Delinquency in Japan — Characteristics and Preventive Programs 10–15 and nn. 25–39 (London, 1960) (mimeograph of a speech prepared for the Second United Nations Congress on Prevention of Crime and the Treatment of Offenders). For a comprehensive list of publications concerning prediction studies in Japan, see Kenkyū Bu (Research Divisions), Hōmu Sōgō Kenkyūjo (Ministry of Justice Integrated Research Institute), Hōmu-shō (Ministry of Justice), Bibliography of the Publications in Japan Concerning the Theories of the Gluecks and Related Studies (1960) (mimeographed).

[73] This position, resting on a culpability principle, has been clearly incorporated in art. 47 (1) of the Japanese Draft Penal Code of 1961. Art. 47 places primary emphasis on the correspondence of punishment to the degree of culpability, and only secondary attention is paid to the educative value of punishment. See note 67.

[74] Eiichi Makino has been in effect editor-in-chief of *Kikan Keisei* (Quarterly Journal of Criminal Law and Criminology) since 1952. His educative view of punishment has been clearly reflected in this publication. Each number of the journal contains an English summary of a leading article written from a philosophical viewpoint congenial to Makino's approach.

made as to the relation between the sentences actually imposed and the incidence of circumstantial factors that seemed to be relevant to sentencing.[75] By the use of statistical techniques, the following factors were found to be significantly enough associated with the gravity of sentences to pass mathematical tests: (1) remedial period; (2) motivation given by victim; (3) reconciliation and restitution; (4) gang association; and (5) previous criminal record.[76] Each factor was then divided into three subcategories and a "significance score" (0, 1, or 2) was given to each subcategory so that each of the five significant factors had a score scale.[77]

The total significance score of each individual case was then computed by adding up scores calculated for each case on the basis of the five score scales. The total scores thus obtained were "circumstantial indices" which "significantly" represented different degrees of moral culpability of the offenders involved. Theoretically, these circumstantial indices could have ranged from 0 through 10, but their actual distribution was 0 through 8. The final step was to construct a correlation graph showing the relation between gravity of sentences imposed and the circumstantial indices (see Table 2). Degrees of circumstantial indices were scaled on the horizontal axis and degrees of gravity of sentences on the vertical axis; individual cases were assigned to appropriate spots (the two arrowed dots appear to be deviations). Following a similar procedure, Table 3 was constructed to show the correlation between the gravity of sentences proposed by the public procurator and the gravity of culpability as expressed in circumstantial indices.

[75] These factors were: ethnic origin, sex, age, type of injury, remedial period, physical defect remaining, method, number of offenses, number of accomplices, leadership in offense, state of mind, motivation, scheme of offense, drunkenness, motivation given by victim, age and sex of victim, reconciliation and restitution, occupation, gang association, previous criminal record of the same nature, previous criminal record of a different nature.

[76] The tabulation below, for example, shows the statistical relation found between "previous criminal record" and the gravity of sentences imposed in 155 bodily-injury cases decided by the Tokyo District Court from May through December 1960.

	Sentence suspended		*Sentence not suspended*		
Criminal record	*Imprisonment for less than 8 months or fine*	*Imprisonment for 8 months or over*	*Imprisonment for less than 8 months or fine*	*Imprisonment for 8 months or over*	*Total*
None	26	19	4	4	53
Of different nature	9	9	12	11	41
Of the same nature	7	14	19	21	61
Total	42	42	35	36	155

[77] (1) *Remedial period:* within two weeks, 0; within one month, 1; over one month, 2. (2) *Motivation given by victim:* recognizable or slightly recognizable, 0; no information, 1; none, 2. (3) *Reconciliation and restitution:* made, 0; no information, 1; not made, 2. (4) *Gang association:* none, 0; no information, 1; some, 2. (5) *Previous criminal record:* none, 0; of different nature, 1; of the same nature, 2.

These tables are primarily experience tables which tell something about the sentencing tendency in the past.[78] But if one accepts the postulate that the past is repeated in the future, these diagrams may also be used as prediction tables or as sets of sentencing standards on which judges and public procurators can generally rely. The curves in Tables 2 and 3 show the tendencies of past sentences imposed by judges and requested by procurators; an assessment of sentences along these lines may prevent unreasonable deviation. If some judges or procurators are unwilling to follow blindly such standards, they may easily consider as modifying elements particular factors which are not represented in the tables, or modify the basic score scales by weighing particular factors. By reading their concepts of policy into the tables, they will be able to individualize sentence, yielding neither to arbitrariness nor to formalism.

This initial effort toward standardization of sentencing through correlation tables based on the pretrial performance of the particular offender is, of course, far from perfect. It may be full of defects and errors, theoretical and factual. But this statistical method of measuring the gravity of sentence by a scale of circumstantial indices suggests the possibility of creating a scientific device which aids, but does not direct, judges in the process of individualization of punishment. It is submitted that sentencing judges in the future could be furnished with two sets of predictive charts as explained above,[79] together with a presentence-investigation report containing sufficient data for an efficient application of such charts. By this method judges may be able to replace their traditional method of assessing sentence on the basis of personal hunch by a scientific system.

Presentence Investigation

Even a precisely organized sentencing mechanism cannot function well if it lacks a presentence-investigation system which furnishes the sentencing body with a detailed picture of the personality and background of the convicted man. The present universal trend toward the adoption of presentence investigation is understandable not only from the narrow, technical viewpoint but also in the broad context of the general process of judicial modernization.

[78] For example, Table 2 indicates that, if the index exceeds 5, suspended imprisonment becomes exceptional. It shows also that the ceiling for sentences in bodily-injury cases is about 1 year and 6 months, despite the fact that the law allows latitude from fine up to imprisonment for 10 years.

[79] One would be retribution-oriented and the other rehabilitation-oriented (that is, based upon the concept of recidivism-expectancy). Recently Professor Glueck wrote me as follows: "It occurs to me that with further development and refinement, it might ultimately be possible to subject each serious case to two sentence-assessing tests: (1) an appraisal in terms of data deemed relevant by the legislature from the point of view of culpability or blameworthiness (*i.e.*, an essentially retributive-oriented screening), followed by (2) an assessment in terms of the relationship of background factors to recidivism-expectancy. A good presentence investigation report should contain both types of data, with printed definitions, at the bottom of the 'face-sheet,' of each item included." Letter from Sheldon Glueck, Oct. 3, 1961.

We are now in a transitional stage in judicial development from an old system of punitive tribunals to a new system of therapeutic, or treatment, tribunals. It is clearly unsatisfactory to vest in the judge, as a nonexpert in the behavioral sciences, the exclusive power to determine the nature of the treatment that the offender will receive. But it is also clear that the science of criminal behavior is not mature enough at this point to enable reliance solely upon the administrative decision of a correctional board. It is possible that eventually a purely administrative therapeutic board will be able to take over the sentencing functions now exercised by judicial tribunals.[80] Meanwhile, however, judicial tribunals must suffice, assisted by teams of experts, including psychiatrists, psychologists, sociologists, and social caseworkers. This seems to be the philosophy underlying presentence-investigation systems.

Japan already has a well-organized system for presentence investigation in juvenile-court proceedings, which is administered by caseworkers attached to the court and clinicians working with the Juvenile Classification Centers.[81] With regard to adult proceedings, however, a presentence system has not yet been created.

The demand for such a system in Japan has been growing, however, stimulated by the general trend in the administration of criminal justice and particularly encouraged by the development of the probation system in the United States. The necessity for such a system was especially felt when the possibility of enacting provisions for an adult-probation system was seriously discussed in 1951.[82] Most specialists thought that adult probation without presentence investigation would be somewhat like a boat without a rudder.[83] Debate on the necessity of presentence investigation was revived when the

[80] An interim stage toward this ideal situation is the use of the indeterminate sentence administered by a parole board. The prevailing use of the indeterminate sentence in the United States, particularly under recent federal legislation, suggests that the stated possibility is not a mere dream. See 18 U.S.C. §4208(a) (1958); Devitt, note 48; Tappan, *Sentencing Under the Model Penal Code,* 23 LAW & CONTEMP. PROB. 528, 532 (1958).

[81] See also Atsushi Nagashima, "The Accused and Society: The Administration of Criminal Justice in Japan," in this volume.

[82] Thus in May 1951, the Council on the Legal System (an advisory commission on legislation), in winding up its deliberations on an adult-probation system, passed a resolution asking its subcommittee on criminal procedure to consider the enactment of a law to provide a presentence-investigation system administered by caseworkers attached to the courts. See HŌMU DAIJIN KAMBŌ (Office of the Minister of Justice), HANKETSU ZEN-CHŌSA SEIDO KANKEI SHIRYŌ, SONO 2 (Materials Relating to the Prejudgment Investigation System, 2) 15 (23 Shihō Seido Chōsa Shiryō (Materials for Investigation of the System of Justice), 1960). The subcommittee was reluctant to consider such an enactment, however, because it might require a fundamental change in the traditional structure of criminal procedure. In 1953, the present adult-probation system was enacted into law, but it included no provisions relating to presentence investigation. PENAL CODE arts. 25(2), 26–26-3, added by Law No. 195 of 1953.

[83] See, for example, Symposium, *Hanketsu Zen-Chōsa o Megutte* (Around About Prejudgment Investigation), in HŌMU DAIJIN KAMBŌ (Office of the Minister of Justice), HANKETSU ZEN-CHŌSA SEIDO KANKEI SHIRYŌ (Materials Relating to the Prejudgment Investigation System) 73 (20 Shihō Seido Chōsa Shiryō (Materials for Investigation of the System of Justice), 1959).

creation of Women's Guidance Homes was considered by a committee of the National Diet.[84] In 1958 the law creating the homes was enacted,[85] but again the adoption of a presentence system was postponed.

The General Secretariat of the Supreme Court, which is especially concerned about the absence of a system of presentence investigation, organized a special committee to deal with this problem. In 1959 the committee recommended the adoption of such a system, under which presentence investigators should be attached to a court and to no other agency. However, other groups in the legal profession did not agree with the proposal.

The Japanese Federated Attorneys Association, a coordinating body of practicing lawyers throughout the country, was particularly antagonistic to the proposal. A special committee of the Association concluded that the Supreme Court proposal was dangerous because a system of presentence investigation carried out by caseworkers attached to a court by implication suggests the beginning of a return to the old inquisitorial judicial system.[86]

The Ministry of Justice was at first not very enthusiastic about the creation of a presentence system, but soon changed its attitude. In 1959 Yoshitsugu Baba, Administrative Vice Minister of Justice, created a committee to inquire into the possibility of legislating such a system. After nearly two years of intensive study, the committee concluded its activities by recommending its own presentence-investigation system.[87] For several reasons the Ministry

[84] Judge Sugao Eriguchi of the General Secretariat of the Supreme Court proposed an amendment to the government bill to enable judges to use a presentence investigator attached to the court. See Naito, *Keiji Jiken ni okeru Hanketsu Zen-Chōsa ni Tsuite* (On Prejudgment Investigation in Criminal Cases), in Hōmu Daijin Kambō, note 83, at 47. Although this proposal was rejected, the Committee on Justice of the House of Representatives passed a resolution on March 3, 1958 emphasizing the necessity of presentence investigation. Hōmu Daijin Kambō, note 82, at 19.

[85] The Women's Guidance Home Law, Law No. 17 of 1958, translated into English in Criminal Statutes, supp. at 15. These homes are correctional institutions for former prostitutes.

[86] *Hanketsu Zen-Chōsa Seido ni Kan-suru Nichibenren Iinkai no Ikensho* (A Statement of J.F.A.A. Committee Concerning the Prejudgment Investigation System), in Hōmu Daijin Kambō, note 82, at 21. Also see 10 Jiyū to Seigi (Freedom and Justice) no. 12, at 25 (1959). This view is, of course, an exaggeration of the fear that the adoption of a system of presentence investigation carried out by the court officers might impair the spirit of the adversary system. It is thought that the judge is likely to depend more on data collected by his own assistant investigators than on information presented by the adversary parties. The true reason for the opposition on the part of the bar, however, seems to be more subtle and deepseated. First, they are afraid that an allegedly scientific investigation carried out by the court-supervised caseworker would hamper defense counsel's professional activities of gathering data favorable to the defendant, thus eventually impairing income sources of private lawyers. Second, they fear that the court might be unreasonably influenced by the "pseudo-scientific" report prepared by its own presentence investigator. This misgiving derives largely from lawyers' skepticism concerning modern behavioral sciences.

[87] In reporting to the Vice Minister, the committee pointed out the universal trend toward presentence-investigation systems and emphasized their importance for criminal justice. The basic proposal of the committee is to create five-member committees under the Ministry of Justice, each consisting of a judge, a public procurator, a practicing attorney, and two experts in social science. Such a committee would carry out a presentence investigation through a

of Justice experts seem reluctant to accept the organizational proposal made by the Supreme Court committee.[88]

In theory, there is a general consensus on the desirability of a presentence-investigation system. But, in practice, legislative agencies are not very enthusiastic about its enactment. There are probably two major reasons for this inconsistency. One is insufficient knowledge. Most lawyers think that traditional procedures for collecting and producing circumstantial evidence can supply relevant data quite as adequately as presentence investigations can.[89] Moreover, most practitioners fear that a thorough presentence investigation and report necessitate systematic postponement of sentence.[90] These views, however, are erroneous.

The second factor hampering the adoption of a presentence-investigation

team of caseworkers attached to the committee or through specialized agencies. The investigation could be begun upon the request not only of the court but also of prosecuting attorneys or defense lawyers. Hōmu-shō (Ministry of Justice), Hanketsu Zen-Chōsa Seido no Kenkyū no Kekka ni Tsuite (On the Results of the Study of the Prejudgment Investigation System) (mimeographed report submitted Oct. 15, 1960 by Juhei Takeuchi, Director of the Criminal Affairs Bureau).

[88] First, they think that a presentence investigation carried out by court officers alone is inconsistent with the fundamental philosophy of the adversary system. This is particularly the case with regard to Japanese criminal procedure in which the sentencing process is not clearly separated from the factfinding process. Second, they think that presentence investigations carried out by court officers constitute a judicial encroachment into a field properly belonging to the executive branch of the government. In this connection it must be noted that in Japan matters concerning probationary supervision of adult probationers come under the jurisdiction of an administrative agency, the Ministry of Justice. Some maintain that since probation officers belonging to the Ministry of Justice are in charge of probationary supervision over adult probationers, the presentence investigation of adult persons should also be handled by the same probation officers or their colleagues.

They also point out that the public procurator who has discretionary power to discharge an offender because of criminological considerations, the probation officer who is responsible for the supervision of a probationer, the correctional officer who is responsible for the reformation of a prisoner, and the defense attorney who is very much concerned with the sentence imposed on his client should have equal opportunity to request the committee to carry out an investigation. In view of the fact that the supply of experts who are able to carry out a presentence investigation is quite limited in Japan, it seems to be not only unfair but also uneconomical to allow the judiciary to monopolize the presentence-investigative facilities. See Izumi, *Baishun Bōshi Hō Kaisei ni Shitagau Hanketsu Zen-Chōsa Seido Setchi Mondai* (The Problem of Establishing a Prejudgment Investigation System Pursuant to the Amendment of the Prostitution Prevention Law), JURIST no. 152, at 57, 60–61 (1958); Abe, *Hanketsu Zen-Chōsa o Meguru Sho-Mondai* (Various Problems Surrounding Prejudgment Investigation), 30 HŌRITSU JIHŌ 1288, 1293 (1956).

[89] True individualization of treatment is not attainable through the use of superficial information about the defendant's moral attitude as shown by ordinary circumstantial evidence collected by a person who is not a specialist in human behavior. The scientific determination of the type of treatment that will be best suited to the defendant requires a detailed expert report covering the makeup and background of the defendant. The sentencing judge may obtain miscellaneous data concerning the defendant through the trial process. But this information is meaningless unless he learns, through an expert report, which elements are not relevant in the particular case before him.

[90] Such a postponement may be beneficial, however, particularly in cases involving especially repulsive crimes, because the emotional state that they arouse interferes with the calm and reflective evaluation of the facts.

system is the bureaucratic egotism of interested agencies, which want to set up an investigation facility which is only for their own use. Such an overzealous bureaucratic attitude must be strongly condemned.[91]

UNWORKABILITY OF THE TRADITIONAL MACHINERY OF CRIMINAL JUSTICE

Recidivism and Juvenile Delinquency in Postwar Japan

A long-range statistical survey reveals that there has been a remarkable increase in the crime rate in postwar Japan.[92] The total number of adult offenders investigated by the police in 1941, when Japan entered World War II, was 281,618.[93] It went up to 543,602 in 1951, when Japan was still in a state of postwar confusion. This means that the number of adult offenders increased by 93 percent in ten years. In 1958 the crime rate appeared to be subsiding, but the number of adult offenders was still very high (420,000). A closer analysis, however, may reveal that the increase itself is not a serious problem. If the steady increase in general population is taken into account, the increase in adult crime rates does not appear substantial.[94]

The real problem in adult criminality in Japan is the sharp increase in recidivism.[95] During the period from 1952 through 1955 about 57 percent of all newly received prisoners have been in prison before, whereas from 1947 to 1952 about 35 percent of offenders admitted to prisons were recidivists. Moreover, it is reported that in recent years about 13 percent of all repeaters have four or more prior convictions.[96] A statistical study made on a follow-up basis reveals further that about 40 percent of all discharged prisoners returned to prison within two years, while about 47 percent returned within five years.[97]

[91] What is important to them seems to be not the facilitation of scientific administration of criminal justice, but rather their own bureaucratic concern with efficiency, superiority, and prestige. Thus draftsmen of the system of presentence investigation are burdened with the task of drafting a bill which satisfies all agencies concerned—an impossible job. I submit that a neutral presentence investigation committee, consisting of a judge, a public procurator, a practicing attorney, and a few specialists in behavioral sciences, which conducts an investigation through attached teams of caseworkers, should be created as a public facility.

[92] The basic data was taken from the 1960 WHITE PAPER ON CRIME. For other sources, see note 28. These materials supply the data for the statistical analysis in the following paragraphs unless otherwise stated.

[93] The term "adult offenders" here means persons of twenty years of age or older who have committed offenses covered by the Penal Code and who have been formally investigated by the police.

[94] The rate of adult offenders per 1,000 population was 7.4 in 1941, 9.8 in 1951, and 7.8 in 1958. If the index for the basic year 1941 is fixed as 100, the indices for 1951 and 1958 are 132 and 105, respectively. 1960 WHITE PAPER ON CRIME 29, 417.

[95] Under the Japanese Penal Code a recidivist or "repeating offender" ordinarily means a person who is convicted within five years of the day on which his former sentence of imprisonment terminated. See PENAL CODE art. 56.

[96] 1960 WHITE PAPER ON CRIME 45; HŌMU-SHŌ (Ministry of Justice), DAI 57 GYŌKEI TŌKEI NEMPŌ — SHŌWA 30 NEN (57th Annual Report of Penal Administration Statistics — 1955) 8 (1956).

[97] 1960 WHITE PAPER ON CRIME 250.

A recent study of the recidivism rate of discharged prisoners shows that of 504 discharged first offenders, about 32 percent relapsed within a given period.[98] All these facts support the presumption that no less than 50 percent of all discharged offenders will eventually resume their antisocial careers.

The rate of juvenile delinquency markedly increased after World War II. In 1941 the number of juvenile offenders[99] was 42,601. The number went up to 133,656 in 1951 and 124,379 in 1958. This means that the number of juvenile crimes in the postwar period has been about three times that of the prewar level. The factor of increase in the juvenile population as a whole does not change the picture very much. The rate of juvenile offenders per 1,000 population was 4.7 in 1941, whereas it was 12.8 in 1951 and 11.1 in 1958. If the index for the basic year 1941 is fixed at 100, the indices for 1951 and 1958 are 272 and 236, respectively. This means that in seventeen years the juvenile crime rate rose to about two and a half times that of the prewar level.[100]

The real problem with juvenile delinquency, however, is represented not so much by its quantitative as by its qualitative aspects. Juvenile offenders constituted 22.8 percent of all offenders in Japan in 1958.[101] With regard to some types of serious offenses, however, the rate of juvenile offenders to total offenders is well over 22.8 percent. For example, of 8,569 rapists, 4,605, or 54 percent, were juveniles. Of 1,962 persons committing indecent assault, 797, or 41 percent, were juveniles. Of robbers and thieves, 38 percent and 32 percent, respectively, were juveniles.[102] Moreover, while the number of crimes committed by juvenile delinquents increased about three times between 1941 and 1958, the rates of increase were not uniform for all kinds of offenses. For certain types of serious offenses, the rates were particularly high; for example, in 1958 the incidence of rape, assault, robbery, indecent assault, and murder committed by juveniles were, respectively, 18, 13, 5.4, 4.4, and 3.4 times those of the levels in 1941.

Postwar juvenile delinquency has been characterized also by its sharp increase among young teenagers in urban areas. For example, in the five-year period from 1954 to 1958, the incidence of the crime of extortion committed by members of the fourteen- and fifteen-year-old age groups increased 6.3 times. Also, the postwar crime waves involve juveniles not only from families of low economic status but also from middle- and upper-class families.

[98] 1960 WHITE PAPER ON CRIME 251. The study involved 504 prisoners selected at random discharged throughout Japan between 1947 and 1949. Relapse was determined as of January 1, 1951.

[99] The term "juvenile offenders" here means persons under twenty years of age who have committed crimes covered by the Penal Code and who have been formally investigated by the police.

[100] 1960 WHITE PAPER ON CRIME 417.

[101] 1960 WHITE PAPER ON CRIME 289, 417.

[102] 1960 WHITE PAPER ON CRIME 292–93.

In attempting to find out the causes of juvenile delinquency, scholars and specialists have approached the problem from various angles.[103] But thus far no fully adequate suggestions have been made concerning the causes of crimes or possible methods of repressing juvenile delinquency.

Confronted with data indicating the growing menace of recidivism and juvenile delinquency, people have become aware that the traditional machinery of criminal justice is insufficient. The urgent call for a re-examination of the crime-prevention system has been augmented by sensational journalism, which has exaggerated the violent aspects of juvenile crimes. As a result, the process of revolutionary change in the outmoded mechanism of criminal justice has begun in the area of juvenile delinquency. The Juvenile Law,[104] the basic philosophy of which is education rather than punishment, tries to solve the problem of delinquency through a juvenile-court system.[105] One difficulty with this solution, however, is that the system is not yet set up to use scientific methods which facilitate diagnosis and treatment of juvenile delinquency. In the incipient stages of the juvenile-court movement, idealistic humanitarianism rather than scientific realism was emphasized.[106]

Problems Resulting from Postwar Innovations in the Treatment of Offenders

Since 1945, Japan has been struggling toward the ideal of a modern democratic state. The trends toward new systems in the fields of crime prevention and the treatment of offenders are a part of this struggle. These movements have frequently been confronted by unexpected difficulties,

[103] See Keiji Kyoku (Criminal Affairs Bureau), Hōmu-shō (Ministry of Justice), Shōnen Hō Kaisei ni Kan-suru Mondai-ten to Iken no Yōshi (The Essentials of the Issues and Opinions Concerning Revision of the Juvenile Law) 2–7 (Shōnen Hō Kankei Shiryō (Materials Relating to the Juvenile Law) No. 14, 1959).

The following may be suggested as probable social causes of the sharp increase in juvenile delinquency in postwar Japan: (1) Breakdown of the traditional family system and the consequent weakening of family control over children; (2) collapse of the traditional value system based upon a hierarchical social structure with the Emperor at the apex, and the consequent ethical vacuum and moral confusion (a gap in thought and attitude between older and younger generations); (3) unhealthy materialism resulting from rapid westernization after the war; (4) unfettered liberalism and immature democracy (freedom without responsibility); (5) economic instability as an aftermath of the war; (6) moral deterioration of adults (children as a mirror of parents); and (7) untamed energy of youth in leisure time plus immoral influences of mass communication.

[104] Juvenile Law, Law No. 168 of 1948, translated into English in Criminal Statutes 323.

[105] The Family Court performs the functions of a juvenile court. *Ibid.*, art. 3.

[106] The Juvenile Law was sometimes called the "Law of Love" by a group of people who held to a spiritual approach. But people soon realized that love, even religious love, is not a cureall for a chronic state of delinquency. A few years ago a woman member of the Diet believed lack of motherly love to be the real cause of juvenile delinquency. Motivated by pure idealism, she donated so-called motherhood bells to reform schools throughout Japan. The beautiful sound of the bells chiming morning and evening was supposed to remind inmates of their mothers and to encourage them toward living honest lives. But the real, deepseated psychological difficulties of these inmates were hardly eliminated by chiming bells. There has been no sign of a declining rate of juvenile recidivism since the day the bells started chiming.

which apparently have derived from one major source — a discrepancy between idealism in ends and the practical difficulties of achieving those ends. The inability to resolve such a conflict often comes from an inadequate perception of the actual situation. This is true of the present juvenile-court system in Japan.

When American military occupation advisers sought to democratize Japan, they were doubtless motivated by idealism and good will. But the best intentions unaccompanied by knowledge and wisdom are sometimes dangerous. The American advisers thought that any system based on a centralized administration was tainted with military totalitarianism and was therefore a potential menace to human freedom. Thus they regarded the traditional structure of treatment of juvenile delinquency in Japan as undesirable because of its centralized administrative character.

The Juvenile Law of 1922,[107] which basically followed the Scandinavian system, provided for Juvenile Determination Boards (*Shōnen Shimpan-jo*) as quasi-judicial authorities for determining treatment and protection of juvenile delinquents.[108] Since most "juvenile determination officers" had backgrounds as experienced jurists, there was no apprehension of possible infringement of human rights. The Juvenile Boards functioned very satisfactorily and contributed much to the rehabilitation of juvenile offenders. But occupation advisers, eager to reform the traditional regime on an American model, strongly urged that the old system be replaced by a juvenile court.

This abrupt change in the juvenile system, carried out more or less in disregard of Japanese tradition, has given rise to three major problems. First, the system of a competent authority which used to have a unitary jurisdiction over juvenile delinquents has been split into two systems.[109] Second,

[107] Law No. 42 of 1922.

[108] *Ibid.*, arts. 15–25. Each board was made up of a certain number of "juvenile determination officers," who were usually appointed from among experienced judges, juvenile probation officers, and court clerks. Each determination officer was responsible not only for disposing of cases in the best interests of the children, but also for checking on their conduct afterwards. A variety of nonpunitive dispositions, including placement on juvenile probation, was available. The juvenile determination officer at his discretion could change or modify a previous disposition in light of the subsequent conduct of the child. In reaching their decisions, juvenile determination officers were sometimes assisted by clinicians affiliated with the board.

[109] One is the juvenile-protection system under the present Juvenile Law; the other is the juvenile-welfare system under the Child Welfare Law, Law No. 164 of 1947. The former is centered around the Family Courts, whereas the latter is administered by Child Consultation Centers and related agencies which are operated under prefectural governors and supervised by the Ministry of Welfare. As a rule, the Family Court has jurisdiction over offenders of fourteen years or over, whereas the Child Consultation Center has jurisdiction over those under fourteen years of age. This dual system often results in overlapping and conflict, however, and makes the process of juvenile protection complicated. For the organization and functions of the Family Court (strictly speaking, the juvenile division), see GENERAL SECRETARIAT OF THE SUPREME COURT, GUIDE TO THE FAMILY COURT OF JAPAN (1957); MINISTRY OF JUSTICE, JUVENILE DELINQUENCY AS SEEN IN THE FAMILY COURT (1957); MINISTRY OF JUSTICE, JUVENILE DELINQUENCY IN JAPAN (1957).

the halfway "judicialization" of the control mechanism has impaired the unity of the probation system.[110] Third, with the creation of the new court system, integrity and elasticity of treatment have been lost.[111]

The new Juvenile Law brought about some change in emphasis in treatment. Under the new system, the principles of protection and education are particularly stressed, and punitive measures are only rarely taken, even against offenders who have committed the more serious crimes.[112]

The new system strengthened the practice of protectionism by investing the juvenile court exclusively with the power of screening juveniles for punitive treatment. Of the total number of cases handled by juvenile courts today, only about 4 percent are sent back to public procurators for ordinary criminal prosecution.[113] The sharp increase in the rate of juvenile delinquents prosecuted in ordinary criminal courts is a good indication that the new system is operated primarily on the progressive principle of educative treatment. But there is a question as to whether the attitude of juvenile-court judges is supported by truly scientific thinking or merely motivated by sentimental humanitarianism. An analysis of recent statistics indicates that there has been a considerable tendency toward the latter.[114]

[110] The new Juvenile Law created a juvenile-court system assisted by court probation officers. These court probation officers, however, are "social investigators" who are responsible only for presentence investigation and have nothing to do with probationary supervision. The function of probationary supervision is carried out solely by official probation officers and voluntary probation officers who work under the Ministry of Justice. Moreover, the function of investigating the mental condition or personality of juvenile offenders is exercised by Juvenile Classification Centers, which are also under the jurisdiction of the Ministry of Justice. Thus the system of juvenile probation which used to function smoothly under the Juvenile Determination Boards has been split into two separate systems—judicial and administrative.

[111] Whereas under the old system a type of treatment determined by the determination officer might be modified according to the results of the treatment, a judicial disposition of a case made under the new system is not subject to any administrative (or even judicial) alteration. An effort to escape from these confines has created a rather abnormal practice, according to which the juvenile court withholds or postpones formal decision and orders the social investigator to exercise an "experimental supervision" over the juvenile delinquent. This new practice has been criticized on the ground that it not only constitutes a judicial infringement of administrative functions but also makes the legal status of these delinquents uncertain.

[112] Under the old Juvenile Law considerable emphasis was placed upon education rather than punishment. But under the old system the public procurator had the discretionary power to make the preliminary selection of those juveniles who deserved punitive treatment. Thus, in the prewar period, of the total number of juvenile offenders referred by the police to public procurators, about 20 percent were prosecuted in the ordinary adult criminal courts and 80 percent were sent to Juvenile Determination Boards for protective treatment.

[113] 1960 WHITE PAPER ON CRIME 339–40. Traffic violation cases are excluded from this tally. If included, the figure would be about 6 percent.

[114] Today, over 50 percent of the juveniles coming before the Family Court are dismissed or discharged without being subjected to any reasonable educative measures. For example, in 1958 of 157,265 juveniles dealt with by a Family Court (excluding traffic cases), 33.6 percent (52,804) were dismissed and 23.7 percent (37,300) discharged. In the case of traffic offenses the juvenile dismissal rate reached as high as 71 percent (285,307 out of 363,561). 1960 WHITE PAPER ON CRIME 339. Moreover, statistics reveal that the rate of recidivism is far from low among juveniles discharged or dismissed. In 1959, 35.8 percent (61,286) of 171,728

Generally speaking, nonpunitive treatment is better than punitive. Extramural treatment may by and large be most suitable for the rehabilitation of juvenile offenders. Dismissal and discharge have the advantage of not stigmatizing the young offender. But nonpunitive treatment cannot be effective unless it is supported by careful prognosis.

Practical-minded people in Japan today are disturbed both by the organization of the treatment system and contemporary juvenile-court practices, characterized as they are by excessive idealism and overprotectionism. Although an idealistic attitude is perhaps necessary to some degree in the administration of criminal justice, sentimental idealism is intolerable when it overwhelms reality. Criticism of the unbalanced philosophy of the juvenile-court system became stronger after the revision of the Juvenile Law in 1951,[115] which raised the upper age limit of offenders to be handled by the juvenile court from eighteen to twenty years.[116] This extension of the age jurisdiction follows a universal tendency to push upward the age limit of offenders entitled to treatment as juvenile delinquents. Nevertheless, some lawyers in Japan seriously doubt the value of nonpunitive treatment of older teenagers unaccompanied by well-organized casework service. Thus there have been some voices raised recommending the modification of the present system along the lines of the German youth-court system which appears to be based upon a moderate, elastic, and realistic philosophy of treatment.[117]

---

juvenile offenders (excluding traffic cases) were recidivists, and 35.2 percent (21,554) and 23.2 percent (14,259) of these persons were dismissed or discharged respectively. 1961 WHITE PAPER ON CRIME 34. These figures raise considerable doubt as to the care with which the juvenile courts examine the cases before them and the educative value of dismissal and discharge.

[115] By Law No. 72 of 1951.

[116] Progressive criminologists even suggest that the age limit be raised to twenty-three or twenty-five so that juvenile-court jurisdiction covers young adults. As a matter of theory, I agree with this proposal.

[117] See Jugendgerichtsgesetz (Juvenile Court Law), August 4, 1953, [1953] 1 BUNDESGESETZBLATT 751 (Ger. Fed. Rep.). Under this law, a juvenile (*Jugendlicher*) is a person who, at the time of committing an offense, is fourteen but not eighteen years of age (§1). "Youth Courts" (*Jugendgerichte*) mean (1) a career judge as youth judge (*Amtsrichter als Jugendrichter*); (2) a lay-judge court (*Schöffengericht,* or *Jugendschöffengericht*), consisting of one youth judge and two youth lay judges (*Jugendschöffen*); and (3) a criminal chamber (*Strafkammer,* or *Jugendkammer*), a criminal division of the *Landgericht,* consisting of three judges and two youth lay judges. Of the two lay judges, one should always be a woman (§33). Juvenile offenders are prosecuted in one of the three youth courts according to the nature of the offense and the offender. Juvenile criminal law, as distinguished from ordinary criminal law, is applied to juvenile cases. The youth courts can apply the following measures: (1) educative measures, (2) disciplinary measures, and (3) juvenile punishment, including a type of indeterminate sentence. The youth court has jurisdiction also over "quasi-adults" (*Heranwachsende*), who are persons of eighteen but not yet twenty-one years of age at the time of committing an offense (§1). In the youth courts, ordinarily adult criminal law is applied to quasi-adult cases, with certain limitations as to kind and length of punishment. But juvenile criminal law is applied to such cases if it seems appropriate because of the personality of the offender or the nature of the offense (§105). Thus the German youth courts may apply either punitive or educative measures to quasi-adult offenders. In 1957, German youth courts applied juvenile criminal law to 33.5 percent of all quasi-adult cases. See STATISTISCHES BUNDESAMT, ABGEURTEILTE (1957).

The disturbing effect of excessive idealism is also felt in postwar innovations in the probation and parole systems in Japan. Three major changes may be mentioned. First, the Bureau of Protection — the agency charged with supervising rehabilitation which used to be a small section in the Bureau of Correction — became a full bureau of the Ministry of Justice. This new bureau was given extensive authority over the administration of probation and parole. In view of the growing significance of probation and after-care, this is an important reform; but, as an expanded administrative agency without a solid budgetary and personnel base, the bureau has been confronted with many unexpected and difficult problems.

Second, the occupation authorities ordered the dissolution of the juvenile protection organizations and other similar post-treatment agencies for juvenile offenders which had been run on a nongovernmental basis. Consequently, all the private reform institutions for juveniles were reorganized into government training schools. This reform was aimed at standardizing and strengthening reformation and rehabilitation services for juveniles and at eliminating the possible exploitation of juvenile labor by corrupt private organizations; but, as a result of this radical step, most of these useful social resources disappeared altogether.

Third, an adult-probation system was adopted in the amendment of the Penal Code in 1953. The newly enacted article 25-2 of the code[118] authorized placing an adult convict under the supervision of a probation officer. Before this innovation, the execution of a sentence pronounced by a regular court might be suspended for a certain period and the offender put on "probation," for the purpose of providing the convict with the chance to rehabilitate himself, but there was no probationary supervision. The adoption of adult probation was enthusiastically welcomed by progressive lawyers. But here again some difficult practical problems have arisen.[119]

Insofar as technical aspects are concerned, the correctional system in Japan, having already reached the level of Western systems, did not experience any substantial innovations after the war; even before the war the correctional system in Japan nearly reached the level required by the standard minimum rules subsequently adopted by the United Nations. It is true that in the years since the war the physical facilities for treatment have been markedly modernized, the attitudes of prison administrators have become less authoritarian, and methods of classification of inmates have been improved. The process of democratization of correctional services was par-

[118] By Law No. 195 of 1953.

[119] There have been two major related problems hampering the smooth development of the adult-probation system. One is the insufficient number of trained probation officers. Today, about 85,283 adults on probation are handled by 510 probation officers throughout the country (these figures are as of the end of 1958). Thus, the caseload per officer is about 167 probations. In this connection, it must be noted that the probation service is assisted by about 50,000 voluntary probation officers (posts for 52,500 exist but not all are filled). The latter, however, are far from being trained caseworkers. Another difficulty is the scantiness of educational facilities to train social caseworkers. See 1960 White Paper on Crime 264–65.

ticularly advanced by the American advisers who during the occupation period tried to reduce the authoritarian aspects of the Japanese administration. These changes, however, are nothing but a continuation of the development carried on for several decades under the leadership of Japanese penal reformers.

The modern appearance of the correctional administration has little value unless the recidivism rate of former prisoners proves low;[120] the criterion of a good correctional service is not an apparent efficiency of the prison administration but a high rate of successful rehabilitation of discharged offenders. If such a criterion is applied, it is clear that the penal system in Japan leaves a great many things yet to be accomplished. The most serious problems confronting progressive correctional administrators in contemporary Japan are the following: how to develop new techniques of treatment, such as individual counseling and group psychotherapy, under a less authoritarian system; how to attain a minimum security system in compliance with the universal trend toward open institutions; and how to make prison officers into correctional caseworkers, well versed in modern scientific techniques.

CONCLUSION

In concluding a speech delivered before the second United Nations Congress on the Prevention of Crime and the Treatment of Offenders,[121] Juhei Takeuchi,[122] a delegate from Japan, made the following statement:

> In the first part of our century, most progressive criminologists were guided by the concept that as soon as the state receives a criminal in its peno-correctional institution its obligation to rehabilitate him as a good citizen begins. Today, I believe, the leading philosophy is that every government of the world should make constant efforts not to let young people pass through the gate of the peno-correctional institution. For the implementation of this ideal, however, all nations of the world must develop intensive and realistic works and studies in the field of prevention of crime and treatment of offenders.[123]

[120] The recidivism rate of former prisoners is fairly high in Japan (see pp. 351–53). A recent follow-up study conducted by the Ministry of Justice Integrated Research Institute revealed that, of 7,142 juveniles released in 1957 from Juvenile Homes throughout Japan, 79.7 percent (5,688) were arrested for a new offense within three years and that during this same period 54 percent (3,862) were not only arrested but also recommitted to Juvenile Homes. The fact of arrest was ascertained from fingerprint cards on file with the Police Agency. Actually, the total number of juveniles released from Juvenile Homes in 1957 was 7,855, but for various technical reasons 712 cases had to be eliminated from consideration. YOSHIZAWA, TSUCHIMOCHI & SATO, ZENKOKU SHŌNEN IN SHUTSUINSHA NO NARIYUKI CHŌSA HŌKOKU, DAI IPPŌ (An Investigative Report of the Path Taken by Persons Released From Juvenile Homes Throughout the Entire Country, First Report) 5–12 (Hōmu Sōgō Kenkyūjo Kenkyū Bu Shiryō (Ministry of Justice Integrated Research Institute Research Divisions' Materials) No. 7, 1962).

[121] Held in August 1960 in London.

[122] Director of the Criminal Affairs Bureau of the Ministry of Justice.

[123] See Takeuchi, note 72.

As Takeuchi suggests, the prophylactic approach to the problem of delinquency and the development of research following that approach are two foundation stones on which the new crime-prevention program is being established. In furtherance of this new program, the Ministry of Justice has devoted a great deal of time and energy to the establishment of an administrative headquarters and of research centers directed toward the better administration of preventive criminal justice.[124]

In order to make the preventive approach effective, the method of "character prophylaxis" must be used. Such treatment will be most effective if it is applied to a person still in early childhood and therefore easier to reform. Character prophylaxis is not an easy task, however, and should be founded on organized experience derived from careful follow-up studies rather than on unproven and oversimplified theories of crime and delinquency.

As the concept of character prophylaxis grows more important, the role of lawyers in the crime-prevention program must change. Lawyers will need more and more cooperation from scientists in related fields — psychiatrists, psychologists, sociologists, and social caseworkers. Legal studies in the field of administration of criminal justice will be more frequently reinforced by interdisciplinary research involving several branches of science. Thus it seems likely that, by the early part of the next century, the functions of lawyers in crime-prevention programs may be largely replaced by interdisciplinary activities carried out by various scientific experts. To survive this development, criminal law must emerge as a coordinator among sciences rather than as a final determinant of logical analyses of concepts of crime. If such a situation develops, one of the most important functions of criminal law and criminal lawyers will be that of mediating between scientific techniques and human dignity. This, I believe, will truly fulfill the coming purpose and function of law and the lawyer.

[124] In 1960 the Youth and Juvenile Section of the Criminal Affairs Bureau was created in the Ministry of Justice to serve as an administrative headquarters and information center for the delinquency-prevention program. Ministry of Justice Organization Order, Cabinet Order No. 384 of 1952, art. 16. In 1959, the First and Second Research Divisions, concerned with criminological research, were established as an integral part of the Ministry of Justice Integrated Research Institute. Ministry of Justice Integrated Research Institute Rules of Organization, Ministry of Justice Order No. 2 of 1952, art. 3(2)–(3). In 1961 the Asia and Far East Institute for the Prevention of Crime and Treatment of Offenders was established in Tokyo by the Japanese government jointly with the secretariat of the United Nations for research and training in the field of prevention of crime and treatment of offenders. Agreement Between the United Nations and Japan for the Establishment of the Asia and Far East Institute for the Prevention of Crime and the Treatment of Offenders, March 15, 1961, Treaty No. 4 of 1961, U.N.T.S. No. 5706.

TABLE 1. Distribution of Sentences for an Infanticide Case Involving the Accused M, Hypothetically Pronounced by Different Groups of Sentencing Parties

	Sentencing party			
Penalty	Judges	Public procurators	Primary-school teachers	Students
Death			1	1
Life imprisonment			2	2
Imprisonment for				
15 years			1	1
13 years			1	
11 years				1
10 years			3	1
9 years				1
8 years			1	
7 years			2	
6 years				1
5 years	1		1	1
4 years	2		1	1
3 years	3	1		
2 years	7	2		
1.5 years	5			
2 years, susp. for 5 years	3	3		
2 years, susp. for 4 years	2			
2 years, susp. for 3 years	3	1		
2 years, susp. for 2 years	1	1		
	—	—	—	—
Total	27	8	13[1]	10
Representative penalty	1.5 or 2 years (5)	2 years (5)	10 years	10 years

Source and note. UEMATSU, note 44, at 113. This table was constructed from the various responses made to the following hypothetical charge of infanticide: "In the summer of 1930, the accused, M, a 30-year-old village woman, had carnal knowledge with U, her brother, at his urging, and continued this illicit and immoral relation with him from that time on. In the spring of 1933 she developed another illicit relationship with one K of the same village, in order to conceal the relationship with her brother. She continued to have illicit relations with the two men until she became pregnant by U. She suffered day and night for fear of her pregnancy's becoming known, because she knew of a current rumor in the community about the carnal relations between her brother and her. When the time of childbirth drew near, she rented a room and cohabited with K as *de facto* husband and wife in order to camouflage temporarily the fact of pregnancy from the eyes of the public. She gave birth on the evening of July 2, 1933, and immediately thereafter she pressed heavily on the neck and chest of the baby until it died."

(Note to Table 1 continued)

It was explained to the test group that possible sentences were death, life imprisonment, imprisonment from 1.5 to 15 years, or imprisonment from 1.5 to 2 years, with the execution of sentence suspended for 1 to 5 years. The charge was shown to the subjects of this experiment as a hypothetical case, but it was adopted from a real case decided by the Keijo (now Seoul) District Court. The penalty actually imposed by the court was imprisonment at forced labor for 2 years. It should be noted that, at the time this experiment was carried out, Japan was involved in warfare in China and that the government's policy favored an increase in the national population. Judgment of Oct. 16, 1934, Keijo District Court (unreported case), noted in FUWA, note 22, at 24.

As a representative value of penalty for each group of sentences, Uematsu employed a median value. The figure in parentheses indicates the number of years during which the execution of the sentence is to be suspended. It is interesting to note that the median value of the hypothetical sentences of the legally trained group are very close to the sentence — two years — actually handed down in the case on which the hypothetical case was based.

TABLE 2. Correlation Table of Sentences and Circumstantial Indices
Graph showing the correlation between the gravity of sentences imposed and the gravity of circumstantial indices, constructed on the data from 155 bodily-injury cases tried by formal proceeding in the Tokyo District Court from May through December 1960.

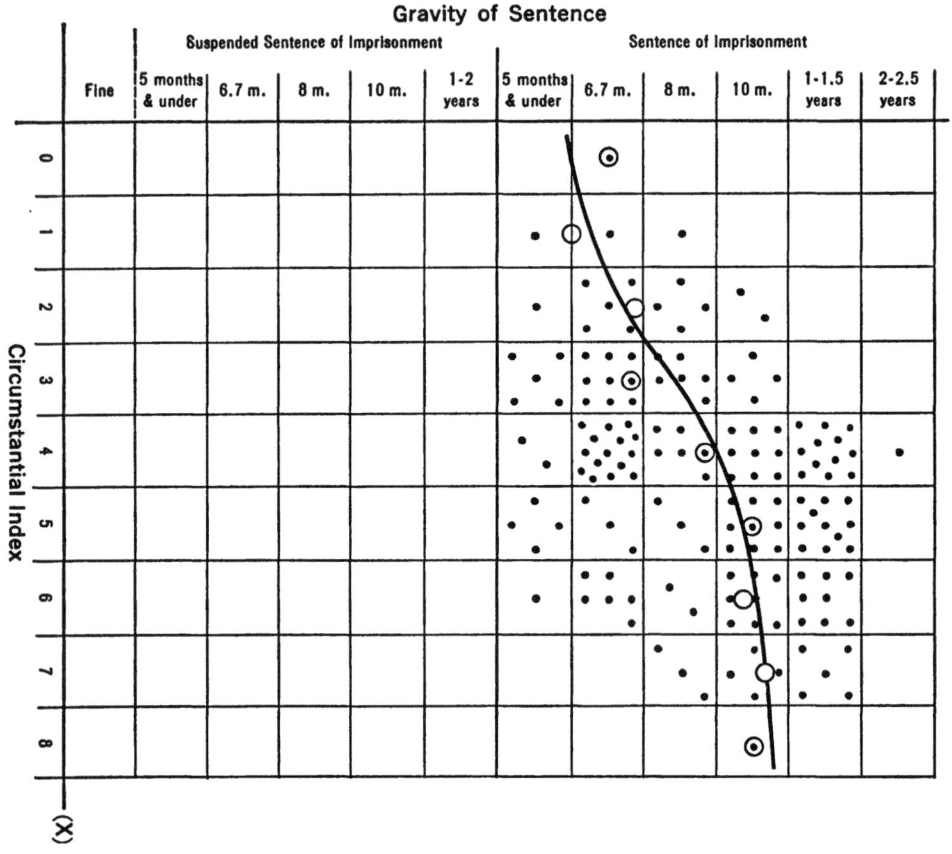

Source and note. This table is based on a study conducted by the author. See p. 345–47 above and Abe Yamamoto, *Sōkanhyō no Ōyō ni yoru Kei no Ryōei no Kagaku-teki Kenkyū* (A Scientific Study of the Assessment of Penalty by the Application of Correlation Tables), JURIST no. 248, at 36 (1962). The black dots represent individual cases and the circles the median. When the median falls at the same point as a single case, the black dot appears within the circle.

TABLE 3. Correlation Table of Sentences Requested and Circumstantial Indices
Graph showing the correlation between the gravity of sentences requested by the prosecution and the gravity of circumstantial indices, constructed on the data from 155 bodily-injury cases tried by formal proceeding in the Tokyo District Court from May through December 1960.

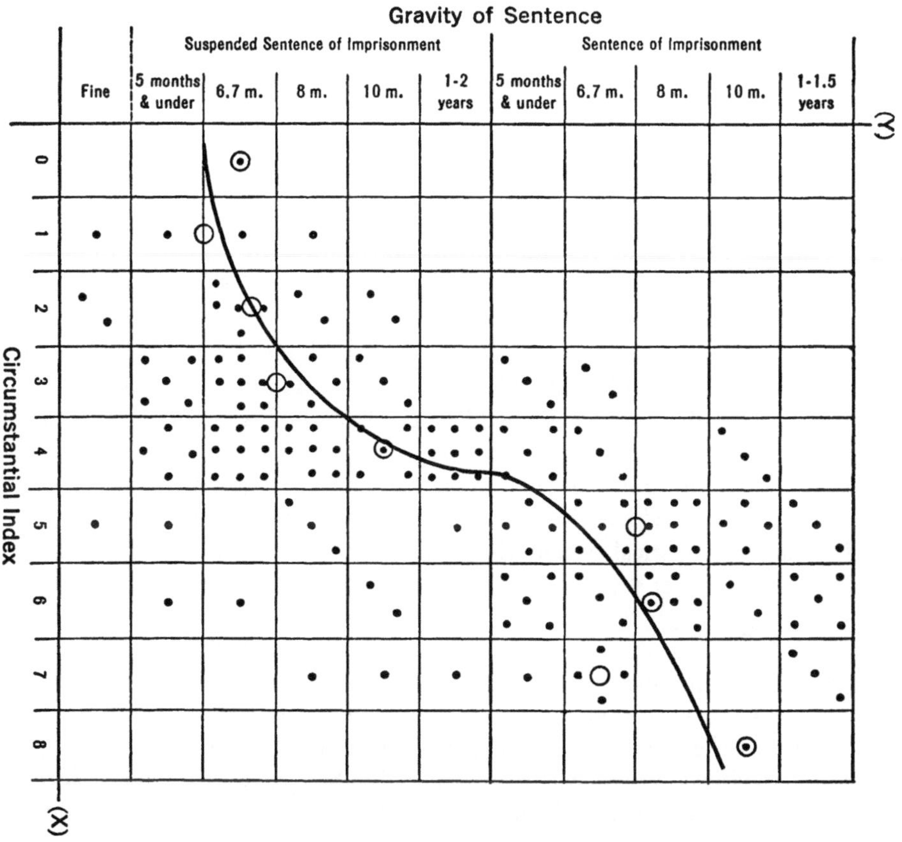

Source and note. *Ibid.*

THE FAMILY AND THE LAW: THE INDIVIDUALISTIC PREMISE AND MODERN JAPANESE FAMILY LAW

Yozo Watanabe

ASSISTED BY MAX RHEINSTEIN

BEFORE World War II, the primary unit of Japanese society was the family rather than the individual, and within the family group the relationship of one member to another was one of inequality. The relationship between parent and child, husband and wife, or eldest brother and younger siblings was that of superior and subordinate. Each family was in turn subject to the head of the "large family," or House. The patriarchical order of the family system extended beyond domestic life: political organization was also based upon a familial type of rule and subordination. The parent-child relationship was the symbol for all aspects of society. Because of the reinforcement which the hierarchical family system afforded the similarly structured political system, the government attempted to strengthen the existing social order by giving the family system both moral and legal support.

The Imperial Speech on Education of October 30, 1890, established a scheme of "moral education" according to the spirit and tenets of the family system, and the family system itself was formally incorporated as a legal institution in the Civil Code of 1898.[1] This unique feature of the Japanese legal and political system was fundamentally changed by the legal reforms enacted shortly after World War II. But only after studying the inequalities

Note. Mr. Watanabe is Assistant Professor of Law, Social Science Institute of Tokyo University. B.Jur., Tokyo University, 1947, Dr.Jur., 1962. Director of the Japanese Association of Legal Sociology, 1952. Author of Nōgyō Suiri-ken no Kenkyū (A Study of Agricultural Water Rights) (1954); Hō Shakaigaku to Hō Kaishakugaku (Sociology of Law and Philosophy of Law) (1959); coauthor with Ushiomi et al., Nihon no Nōson (Japanese Farm Villages) (1957); writings in the fields of civil law and the sociology of law.

Mr. Rheinstein is Max Pam Professor of Comparative Law, University of Chicago. Dr. Utr. Iur., 1924, University of Munich; Juris Doktor (hon.), 1957, University of Stockholm; Dr. iur. (hon.), 1960, University of Basel.

[1] Books IV (Relatives) and V (Inheritance) of the Civil Code were enacted by Law No. 9 of 1898 [hereafter cited Meiji Civil Code]. An English translation of the imperial speech may be found in Sansom, The Western World and Japan 464 (1951).

under the prewar law will the reader be able to appreciate the full significance of these reforms.[2]

Family Law Before the War

Marriage and Divorce

Traditionally, marriage was a transaction between two families rather than the creation of a union based on mutual love between two individuals. Marriage involved the intrusion of a stranger — the new wife — into the husband's House. Since each House had its own peculiar customs, the choice of a wife affected a far larger group of people than simply the marriage partners themselves. Consequently, free choice was largely eliminated. A new marriage frequently was considered tentative during a trial period to see whether the wife would really fit in with the family, in particular, with the family head and his wife. Under the Meiji Civil Code[3] as well as under the modern code,[4] a marriage is legally concluded when a formal "report" is made to the proper governmental authorities. In the popular view, however, a marriage is concluded by the performance of the customary ceremony. If the report is postponed for some time after the ceremony, the interval can be used as a trial period; and if the new wife should not fit in with her husband's family, she can be expelled from it unilaterally and without the possibility of judicial recourse. Although the trial marriage still exists, its use has decreased with the legal and social breakup of the family system.

Under the prewar system, there were other reasons for entering an informal, or *naien,* marriage. Because of the importance of a marriage to the family, severe restrictions, both legal and informal, were placed on an individual's freedom to contract a marriage. Neither a man under thirty years of age nor a woman under twenty-five could validly conclude a legal marriage without parental consent,[5] and no member of a House could marry at all without the consent of the head of the House except upon pain of possible expulsion from the House and the attendant serious pecuniary

[2] A very thorough account of Japanese marital law in English, including a number of quotes from scholars concerning concepts touched upon in this essay, will be found in Coleman, *Japanese Family Law,* 9 Stan. L. Rev. 132 (1956).

[3] Meiji Civil Code art. 775.

[4] Law No. 222 of 1947, art. 739 [hereafter cited New Civil Code]. This law completely revised the prior Meiji statute. In form, though, it merely constituted an amendment of Law No. 9 of 1898 which remains the official citation for the books of Relatives and Inheritance and not an entirely new re-enactment. Technically, then, 1947 did not give rise to a new Civil Code, the current code still being that of 1898. However, in accord with the usage of scholars and the supplementary provisions to the 1947 law (Law No. 222 of 1947, supp. prov. art. 3), I have designated the law prior to 1947 as the Meiji Civil Code and that afterwards as the New Civil Code.

[5] Meiji Civil Code art. 772.

and moral disadvantages.[6] Informal marriages represented a way to circumvent these limitations.[7] Ordinarily these marriages would be legalized as soon as permission could be obtained. Unlike the common-law marriage in the United States, however, a naien marriage received no official recognition at any time,[8] and the wife was not protected to the same extent as a legal spouse was.[9]

The husband's dominant position was reflected in the perquisites of marriage. A man, although not acquiring title to his wife's property upon marriage, acquired the right to the possession and management of the property and to the enjoyment of rents and profits in a fashion similar to the common-law estate *iure uxoris*.[10] He, of course, bore all expenses of the family.[11] In many cases a married woman could not enter a legal transaction without the prior consent of the husband.[12] The criminal law showed a similar disparity of treatment. While adultery committed by or with a married woman could be punished criminally,[13] extramarital intercourse by a married man with an unmarried woman was no crime because it would not affect the purity of the family lineage. Not only did a wife adopt her

[6] MEIJI CIVIL CODE art. 750.

[7] *Naien* is a concept developed by the Japanese courts in order to give some protection to the parties to the *de facto* marriage which results when a wedding ceremony is performed but no official report is made. It was first recognized in Taninaka v. Nozawa, Great Court of Judicature, United Civil Departments, Jan. 26, 1915, 21 DAI SHIN IN MINJI HANKETSU ROKU (Record of Great Court of Judicature Civil Judgments) [hereafter cited DAI-HAN MINROKU] 49. On naien generally, see Coleman, as in note 2 above, at 138–42.

[8] That is, the naien relationship has never been dealt with expressly in the Civil Code, nor is it regarded as a fully valid lawful marriage. NEW CIVIL CODE art. 742(ii). However, a number of special statutes provide for the naien spouse: Workmen's Accident Compensation Insurance Law, Law No. 50 of 1947, art. 15(1), translated into English in MINISTRY OF LABOR, JAPAN LABOR LEGISLATION [hereafter cited LABOR LEGISLATION] 365 (1959); Workmen's Accident Compensation Insurance Law Enforcement Regulations, Ministry of Labor Order No. 22 of 1955, art. 16(1), translated into English in LABOR LEGISLATION 381; Labor Standards Law, Law No. 49 of 1947, art. 79, translated into English in LABOR LEGISLATION 199; Labor Standards Law Enforcement Regulations, Ministry of Welfare Order No. 23 of 1947, art. 42, translated into English in LABOR LEGISLATION 233; Welfare Annuity Insurance Law, Law No. 115 of 1954, art. 63(1)(ii); National Annuity Law, Law No. 141 of 1959, art. 5(3); Day Laborer's Health Insurance Law, Law No. 207 of 1953, art. 3(2)(i); Ship's Crew Insurance Law, Law No. 73 of 1939, art. 50-4(ii), translated into English in MINISTRY OF WELFARE, THE SEAMEN'S INSURANCE LAW 1 (1954); Health Insurance Law, Law No. 70 of 1922, arts. 49, 56. But see Inheritance Tax Law Basic Circular, National Tax Agency Circular, *Chokushi* (Direct Tax Division — Assets Tax Section) 10, Jan. 28, 1959, art. 123.

[9] However, if one naien spouse deserts the other, for example, to enter into a legal marriage, damages may be recovered in an action identical to a breach of promise suit. Naien spouses can establish a "privilege" against each other for necessaries, and they have a duty of mutual support. Moreover, the relationship may be dissolved by a judicial proceeding known as naien divorce, with the plaintiff recovering damages for injury to his or her estate due to the failure of the defendant to enter into a legal marriage. Coleman, note 2, at 140–42.

[10] MEIJI CIVIL CODE arts. 801–06.

[11] MEIJI CIVIL CODE art. 798.

[12] MEIJI CIVIL CODE arts. 14–18.

[13] See PENAL CODE, Law No. 45 of 1907, art. 183, repealed by Law No. 124 of 1947.

husband's name upon becoming one of his family,[14] but the husband alone chose their place of residence.[15] The only exception to this pattern was in the case in which the groom was a *mukoyōshi* and the bride herself the head of a family; then the husband entered her family and assumed her name.[16] In the premodern period, divorce was an exclusively male privilege,[17] which a husband could exercise simply by handing his wife a letter, traditionally of three and a half short lines, announcing the divorce — a *mikudari-han*.[18] This unilateral divorce was abolished during the Meiji era.[19] Unless the wife consented, a husband could obtain a divorce only for adultery or other serious marital misconduct.[20] For the first time, the wife was permitted to divorce her husband; this could be done for cruel treatment, desertion, or other serious misconduct on the husband's part — not for infidelity.[21] Although an improvement, the new system did not go far enough and was easily abused by husbands or heads of the husbands' House. Divorce by agreement did not — nor does it under the present law — require any judicial cooperation or control.[22] The system seems to correspond well with modern ideas of individual liberty. It is easy, however, to exert pressure to induce a wife to permit her seal to be added to the simple instrument which is all that must be sent to the authorities to perfect the divorce.[23] Effective controls still do not exist even as to the genuineness of the wife's purported signature. In marked contrast to the Christian idea of marriage, the Japanese idea of marriage and divorce is neatly expressed by the proverb: "Those who have put themselves together separate themselves."

[14] MEIJI CIVIL CODE arts. 746, 788(1).

[15] MEIJI CIVIL CODE art. 789(1).

[16] See MEIJI CIVIL CODE arts. 746, 788(2).

[17] It has been pointed out that, although such divorces are described "as a 'system of exclusively privileged divorce,' this did not mean that the one-sided will of the husband was invoked entirely independently; rather there was a union of the husband's intent to divorce and the wife's willingness to be divorced which took the form of an agreement." Takayanagi, *Meiji Izen no Rikon Hō* (Divorce Law Prior to Meiji), in 3 KAZOKU MONDAI TO KAZOKU HŌ (Family Problems and Family Law) 110, 118–19 (Nakagawa, Aoyama, Tamaki, Fukushima, Kaneko, Kawashima eds., 1958).

[18] There were, of course, some minor exceptions to this general principle. Thus, a wife might obtain a divorce after taking sanctuary in the temple nunneries at the Tokeiji in Kamakura or the Mantokuji in Nitta, Kozuke Province (now in Gumma Prefecture). See Ishii, *Engiridera* ("Divorce Temples") (pts. 1–3), 76 HŌGAKU KYŌKAI ZASSHI (Journal of the Jurisprudence Association) 401, 77 HŌGAKU KYŌKAI ZASSHI 127, 412; ISHII, *Engiridera no Koto* (On the "Divorce Temples"), in EDO JIDAI MAMPITSU (Random Notes on the Edo Period) 152 (1959).

[19] By Great Council of State Notice No. 209 of 1875.

[20] MEIJI CIVIL CODE art. 813(i)–(ii),(iv)–(ix).

[21] MEIJI CIVIL CODE art. 813(i),(iii)–(x).

[22] The importance of this divorce form is shown by the fact that even today agreement divorces comprise more than 90 percent of all divorces occurring in Japan.

[23] NEW CIVIL CODE arts. 764, 739; Family Registration Law, Law No. 224 of 1947, art. 76; Family Registration Law Enforcement Regulations, Ministry of Justice Order No. 94 of 1947, arts. 57(1), 59, app. form no. 13.

The value to women of the judicial divorce thus introduced was greatly diminished by the failure to accord the divorced wife custody of the children or an adequate financial settlement. Even when the father was at fault, he retained custody of the children.[24] Although the wife could take with her any property which had belonged to her before the marriage, if she could prove title,[25] the concept of permanent alimony or even a separation settlement was unknown under the Meiji code. In rare cases of outrageous conduct, a husband was compelled to pay damages if he had caused the wife any pain and suffering.[26] In addition to these legal disadvantages, a woman would be deterred from taking the initiative toward a divorce by the strong moral disapproval that she was likely to incur, for to bear everything and to obey her husband in all respects was regarded under the family system as the supreme virtue of a wife.

Parent and Child

Under the Confucian ideology of filial piety (*kō* in Japanese, *hsiao* in Chinese), a child is to obey his parents unconditionally, to gladden them in all ways, and to serve them in every respect. But there were no corresponding parental duties in traditional ideology. A child was subject to a far-reaching parental power even beyond the age of majority if the child continued to depend upon his parents for support. This power lent itself to abuse and was even apt to engender a popular belief that in a certain sense a child was property. He could even be "sold" by his parents and at least in fact, although not in law, bound for life to such a profession as that of prostitute or acrobat. Perhaps the sense of possession constitutes one psychological basis of those cases occurring even today in which a parent determined to commit suicide also kills his children.

Filial piety found a most striking expression in the selection of a spouse. *Kō* went beyond the legal requirement of parental consent to the marriage of a man under thirty or a woman under twenty-five and required as a moral duty that a child submit to his parents' wishes without reference to his own. Although filial piety was owed by the child to both parents, the exercise belonged in law as well as in fact to the father alone; only under exceptional circumstances, when the father was dead or otherwise incapacitated, did the mother exercise such power.[27]

Under the family system, adoption was a necessary and widely used means

[24] Provided that there was no agreement to the contrary or that a court did not so order for the benefit of the child. MEIJI CIVIL CODE arts. 812(1), 819.

[25] MEIJI CIVIL CODE art. 807(1).

[26] Hagiwara v. Sho, Great Court of Judicature, I Civil Department, March 26, 1908, 14 DAI-HAN MINROKU 340. But a wife who failed to make a claim for damages at the time she entered into divorce by agreement might be regarded as having abandoned any right to present such a claim later. Watanabe v. Muto, Great Court of Judicature, V Civil Department, Feb. 16, 1940, HŌRITSU SHIMBUN (The Law News) [hereafter cited SHIMBUN] no. 4536, at 10.

[27] MEIJI CIVIL CODE art. 877.

to provide for the perpetuation of a family line in cases of failure of male issue or even in cases in which none of the natural issue was regarded as worthy to assume the family headship. But adoption, too, was susceptible of abuse. Adoption was simply a private transaction like divorce by agreement, often between the two family heads concerned, conceivably without regard to the wishes of the adoptee. There was no judicial control whatever, and adoption could thus be used to cover the sale of a human being for purposes of gain and exploitation.

In the criminal law one again finds that the interest of a parent is given special protection. Article 200 of the Penal Code prescribes a more severe punishment when one has slain an ascendant than for other kinds of killings.

Under the family system, the *Ie* or House meant a supragenerational group which continued from forefathers to descendants.* It also meant that the position of the head of the House as ruler was passed from parent to child and from generation to generation. Thus the heir presumptive as head of the family was allowed a privileged status and was called the "heir of the House." In principle, the eldest son was to become the heir and received better care than the other brothers and sisters. On becoming the head of a family, he succeeded to the property of the House, which had been owned under the name of his father. The younger sons and the daughters had no rights to inherit the House property whatsoever. These inequalities of rights were also accompanied by inequalities of duties: the eldest son bore the heavy responsibility to support his parents, as well as his younger brothers and sisters. Ordinarily each member of the family had little individual property and lived on the House property. Thus the eldest son, on becoming the new owner, was expected to direct and manage the efforts and work of the others so that the House property would support all.

Preservation of the Family System and Prewar Changes

Why did twentieth-century Japan maintain the nondemocratic family system based on the inequality principle? Why did the state show such a strong interest in its preservation? In explanation Japanese scholars have pointed out the following main points. The political system established after the Meiji Restoration was not democratic but authoritarian and demanded that the people be uncritically obedient and docile. Consequently, the government spared no effort to develop such traits through moral education, religious inculcation, and legal sanctions. The discipline a man undergoes within his family from infancy on forms his character and his morals, and the government largely relied upon family discipline to bring up citizens who would submit to governmental authority. It is not surprising that a

* Takeyoshi Kawashima pointed out at the conference that authority was truly concentrated in the head of the family only in the families of the samurai; in middle- and lower-class families the power tended to be diffused among the elders of the group.

man or a woman is, without misgiving, blindly obedient to authoritarian government once he has been taught to obey the orders of the House head and his parents unconditionally and made firmly to believe that unquestioning obedience is the supreme virtue.*

Governmental policy could not have maintained the family system, however, had it not been the basis of certain traditions of Japanese society. Post-Meiji Japanese society had not fully accepted the idea that the individual citizen's worth is to be determined by his own efforts. Important determinants of status were taken over into the post-Meiji order, such as the hierarchy and stratifications of birth and of various types of associations. Especially in rural districts the village community called *mura* survived and firmly controlled the lives of farmers. Men were not allowed to live as independent individuals but were expected to act always as members of the mura. At times the influence of the mura went so far as to control a man's vote in elections and thus penetrated into a sphere in which, if anywhere, the individual's free decision ought to prevail. The mura was organized around its Houses, and the order of the mura was thus closely connected with the family. The effect of such associations extended beyond the rural districts to various spheres of city life. A company was likely to be considered a sort of family, with its director as a parent and its employees as so many sons. A school, too, was a family, with the teacher as the parent and the pupils as the children. Ultimately the whole state became a family, with the Emperor as the parent and the subjects as his children. According to such a social structure, it was only natural that the individual's interest was neglected in favor of the community's.

Finally, the mura performed certain economic functions in society. Japanese capitalist economy of post-Meiji times developed without the liquidation of the feudal ownership of land in agriculture or the pattern of small-scale management. Each family was a production unit, and management was completely in the hands of the family heads. Other members were but to toil as ordered by the family heads, and without any pay other than maintenance. Industrial pay tended to be meager and insufficient to permit adequate savings for periods of unemployment, sickness, or other emergency. Moreover, the Japanese social-insurance system was poor. The workers, mainly migrant and from rural areas, had nowhere to go but to their families when they fell ill, became unemployed, or reached old age. Thus the city workers were interested in maintaining the stability of their "families" in the countryside.

Although political, economic, and social conditions in prewar Japan com-

* Takeyoshi Kawashima commented during the conference discussions that, because Japanese family life has a corporate nature in which the interest of the group is paramount, the individual Japanese, more than individuals in other societies, fears separation from the group with which he identifies. Therefore, the totalitarian regime required the active support of only relatively few persons; the remainder of each group followed from fear of ostracism.

bined to preserve the family system, the fifty years of the Meiji Civil Code were years of social change and development. Especially after the First World War, Japanese society saw the rise of a popular movement demanding democracy, which caused a certain weakening of the authoritarian regime and undermined the power of the various feudal groups and communities. Democracy's incompatibility with the family system came to be recognized by an ever increasing number of people and the demand for reform grew steadily. But this provoked fears of a total collapse of the social structure based upon the family system and resulted in reactionary efforts to strengthen the system. In 1919 the government appointed a council to consider the revision of the Civil Code and to prepare an appropriate draft.[28] The council was deeply split. One group, regarding the family system as essential for Japan, wished to strengthen that system by eliminating from the code those modest concessions to individualism which it contained; the other group, regarding the family system as obsolete, wished to break it down by radical changes in the law. The latter group was in the majority, but its recommendations were not adopted by the government.

While the effort to modernize the text of the law failed, however, the actual content of the law underwent changes through judicial interpretation. The courts, after all, could not help being influenced by the changes in the climate of public opinion. Although the Great Court of Judicature in the Meiji era held that the wife of a naien marriage was not entitled to any damages when the relationship was unilaterally terminated by the husband after many years of life together,[29] this attitude changed after World War I. In its decision of January 26, 1915, the Court held that the breach of a promise of formal marriage constituted, in some circumstances, a default of obligation. This rule was applied to the wife of an informal marriage.[30] Later the naien wife was included in the group of persons who have a "privilege" against each other for necessaries as provided in article 310 of the Civil Code,[31] and she was permitted to recover damages from the person responsible for the wrongful death of her husband.[32]

In another line of decisions, the Great Court of Judicature tried to mitigate the inequality of husband and wife with respect to marital fidelity. A husband's adultery, if committed under particularly aggravating circum-

[28] The Temporary Council on the Legal System (Rinji Hōsei Shingikai) established pursuant to Imperial Order No. 332 of 1919.

[29] Hiramatsu v. Ide, Great Court of Judicature, I Civil Department, March 25, 1911, 17 DAI-HAN MINROKU 169.

[30] Taninaka v. Nozawa, Great Court of Judicature, United Civil Departments, Jan. 26, 1915, 21 DAI-HAN MINROKU 49.

[31] Nippon Bōeki Shintaku Kabushiki Kaisha (Japan Trading Trust Co.) v. Fujio, Great Court of Judicature, III Civil Department, June 3, 1922, 1 DAI SHIN IN MINJI HANREI SHŪ (A Collection of Civil Great Court of Judicature Cases) [hereafter cited DAI-HAN MINSHŪ] 280.

[32] Ishino v. Hanshin Denki Tetsudō Kabushiki Kaisha (Hanshin Electric Railway Co.), Great Court of Judicature, I Civil Department, Oct. 6, 1932, 11 DAI-HAN MINSHŪ 2023.

stances, was held a sufficiently grave insult to the wife to entitle her to a judicial divorce,[33] and in another case it was considered a tort entitling the wife to damages.[34]

A third example of judicial reform limited parental power by expanding the doctrine of abuse of right. The exercise of an adoptive father's right to take the child away from his former wife of a naien marriage was held by the Great Court to constitute an abuse of right when done for no acceptable reason.[35] By an extensive interpretation of article 888 of the Meiji Civil Code (now article 826), which provides that a parent whose interest is adverse to his child's interest cannot act as the representative of the child, the Court sought to protect the child's property interest. In 1914, the Court held that the holder of parental power could not act as the legal representative in hypothecating immovable property of the child to secure a debt of his own.[36] The Court held invalid the parent's act making the child a codebtor in a credit transaction undertaken exclusively in the parent's interest.[37] Especially noteworthy is the decision of the Nagasaki Court of Appeals in which parental power was declared to be forfeited by a parent who had tried to "sell" his daughter into prostitution.[38]

Although the reaction of the political leaders of the time even went so far as a proposal in 1940 to limit the franchise to heads of Houses, the actual revision of the Meiji code made in 1941 in fact reduced the hold of the family system.[39] The war economy had induced large numbers of rural youths to flock to the cities to work in the war plants, and it was necessary to abolish the power of rural family heads to recall these war workers to the farms. Consequently, the right of House heads to determine the abode of all the members of the family was considerably reduced in scope. Thus the war, brought about by the political leaders themselves, resulted in a considerable weakening of that system which they wished to fortify.

FAMILY LAW AFTER THE WAR

Enactment of a New Law

Japan's defeat in the Second World War destroyed the bases of the old political system, clearing the ground for far-reaching reforms. The new

[33] Iida v. Iida, Great Court of Judicature, II Civil Department, March 1, 1929, SHIMBUN no. 2976, at 14.

[34] Judgment of July 20, 1926, Great Court of Judicature, I Criminal Department, 5 DAI SHIN IN KEIJI HANREI SHŪ (A Collection of Criminal Great Court of Judicature Cases) 318, 6 HANREI MINJI HŌ (Civil Case Law) 332 (note Hozumi).

[35] Morishita v. Morinaga, Great Court of Judicature, II Civil Department, Nov. 29, 1923, 2 DAI-HAN MINSHŪ 642, 3 HANREI MINJI HŌ 479 (note Hozumi).

[36] Kishigawa v. Yamada, Great Court of Judicature, II Civil Department, Sept. 28, 1914, 20 DAI-HAN MINROKU 690.

[37] Judgment of Oct. 24, 1933, Great Court of Judicature, V Civil Department, HŌRITSU SHIMPŌ (The New Law Report) no. 344, at 9.

[38] Yoshida v. Hamashima, Nagasaki Court of Appeals, Feb. 6, 1922, SHIMBUN no. 1954, at 9.

[39] By Law No. 21 of 1941.

Constitution, drafted in conformity with the Potsdam Declaration, aimed at the democratic reconstruction of Japan; article 24 established the equal rights of husband and wife, equality of the sexes, and the inviolability of the individual. Article 14 pronounced equality for all persons before the law. Thus the legal foundations of the family system, based on the inequality principle, were abolished. Further, the spirit of the new Constitution would not allow the continuance of such institutions as the House, rights of House heads, or inheritance of the headship of a House. A new family law was enacted into the Civil Code in 1947 and took effect on January 1, 1948.[40] The attitude within conservative circles toward the new law, as toward all postwar democratic reform, was anything but positive. But since the democratic reforms were supported by the Allied forces occupying Japan, their opposition was of no avail.

At first, even the government had no clear policy as to the implications of the constitutional changes for the family system. At the Ninetieth Session of the Imperial Diet, which adopted the new Constitution, Prime Minister Yoshida declared in the House of Representatives: "[The new Constitution] does not negate such things as the rights of the head of a House, the family, or inheritance . . . Japan's inheritance of the House headship, etc., is one of the 'good ways and beautiful customs' peculiar to Japan. There is no particular provision on this point [in the Constitution.]"[41] When the Prime Minister himself saw no contradiction between the family system and the spirit of the new Constitution, it was indeed unlikely that conservative politicians would understand the necessity of changing the system. But the family system was widely regarded by scholars as a hindrance to social progress and as already in a state of collapse. Hence these men eagerly supported a revision of the Civil Code which would undermine the family system, leading to its eventual dissolution. Heated arguments ensued, and the result was a compromise. As a legal institution the family system was to be abolished; its tenets were no longer to be enforceable by the law. But "the beautiful system" would continue as a custom upheld by moral suasion. Many critics of firm democratic conviction opposed this compromise, demanding not only that the family system be abolished as a legal institution but also that steps be taken actually to eliminate it from social life. The strength of the opposition made such an aim impossible of achievement, however, and the concessions obtained were welcomed by all concerned, including the more radical reformers.

The Equality Principle in the New Family Law

Marriage is now recognized as a union of two individuals based exclusively on their free agreement rather than the creation of a tie between

[40] Law No. 222 of 1947, supp. prov. art. 1.

[41] Dai 90 Teikoku Gikai Shūgi In Honkaigi Sokkiroku (Stenographic Record of the Plenary Meetings of the 90th Session of the Imperial Diet) 81 (June 27, 1946).

two families. Those provisions of the old law which required the consent of parents and House heads for the marriage of persons of full age[42] have, of course, disappeared, and with them the conditions which formerly induced many people to enter into a naien marriage.

The new law also provides for the complete separation of the wife's property from that of the husband.[43] The wife has not only title but also the power to manage and receive the profits from her assets; transfers no longer require the consent of the husband. Consequently, all the former limitations on the legal capacity of a married woman are gone. But the wife now has to contribute to the expenses of married life[44] and together with the husband is jointly and severally liable for debts incurred with respect to daily household matters.[45]

Under the new law, the wife has been elevated to the status of a full and equal partner in marriage. A husband's adultery now constitutes a ground for judicial divorce, and the inequality of the criminal law, under which adultery of a married woman constituted a crime while adultery committed by the husband went unpunished, was eliminated by abolishing punishment for adultery altogether.[46] While formerly the wife had to assume her husband's family name, article 750 of the new code provides that the couple may select either the husband's or the wife's family name. Similarly, the marital residence is chosen by mutual consultation.[47]

The Meiji institution of divorce by agreement conforms well to equality between husband and wife and was continued under the new law. However, reforms needed to increase the practical feasibility of divorce for the wife were introduced. The first step was to permit the wife to receive custody of the children. The parties may agree upon custody; or, failing agreement, the Family Court will award custody to one, depending on the merits of the individual case.[48] If the wife receives custody, the husband is required to contribute to their support. A mother need no longer consider the loss of her children as the price of divorce. Secondly, article 768 of the new code introduces a property settlement—*zaisan bunyo,* which may be translated as a "division and distribution of property." Ordinarily the parties themselves determine which, if either of them, should receive this settlement and in what amount. Most commonly the husband, who would usually control the bulk of the property, makes the payment to the wife. If they cannot reach an agreement, an award, generally modest, is made by the Family

[42] MEIJI CIVIL CODE arts. 750, 772.
[43] NEW CIVIL CODE art. 762.
[44] NEW CIVIL CODE art. 760.
[45] NEW CIVIL CODE art. 761.
[46] By Law No. 124 of 1947, repealing PENAL CODE art. 183.
[47] Cf. MEIJI CIVIL CODE arts. 788–89, and NEW CIVIL CODE art. 752. Also see Coleman, note 2, at 148 n. 123.
[48] NEW CIVIL CODE art. 766.

Court. Zaisan bunyo is far from being an equivalent of alimony, for the idea that a divorce should not entail lasting obligations of one spouse toward the other still dominates Japanese law. But the right to a kind of severance settlement eases the difficulties of postdivorce adjustment and thus facilitates a wife's decision to seek a divorce.

Another important improvement in the position of married women has occurred in the wife's status in intestate succession. Under the Meiji Civil Code, title to the property of the House belonged to the House head and passed to his heir, usually the eldest son. A wife could succeed to the headship of the House only under exceptional circumstances; and if, as was frequently the case, all her husband's property was House property, she had no rights of succession.[49] Even for individual property, succession rights of a wife were regarded under the family system as unnecessary because it was expected that the widow would be taken care of in the House by the successor to the headship; consequently, the wife could succeed only if the decedent was not survived by any descendants. Since the abolition of the House, all property owned by individuals is now individual property; upon the death of the owner, the surviving spouse is entitled to an intestate share, even if the decedent is survived by descendants. Under article 900 of the new Civil Code the surviving spouse's intestate share is determined as follows: (1) if there are descendants of the decedent, one third; (2) if there are no descendants of the decedent but ascendants, one half; (3) if neither descendants nor ascendants of the decedent survive but there are brothers or sisters or descendants of brothers and sisters, two thirds; (4) in all other cases, the entire estate.

Parental power, once almost exclusively the father's, is now exercised jointly with the mother over children who have not yet completed the twentieth year of age. As soon as the child reaches majority, he is the equal of his parents before the law.[50] The basic nature of parental power, once a form of dominion belonging to the parents for their own interest, has been transformed into a kind of trust to be used and exercised by the parents in the best interest of the child. Parental power may be forfeited for selfish abuse.[51] A parent or guardian can no longer receive a minor's wage for him, and special provisions of the Labor Standards Law of 1947 were enacted to prevent exploitation of a minor's earning power by parents. A parent cannot conclude a labor contract for a minor,[52] and the minor can now receive wages without parental consent.[53]

Finally, the institution of adoption, once a device to secure the continuation

[49] See MEIJI CIVIL CODE arts. 969–85.

[50] See NEW CIVIL CODE art. 818.

[51] NEW CIVIL CODE art. 834. This provision is substantially unchanged from MEIJI CIVIL CODE art. 896.

[52] Labor Standards Law, art. 58.

[53] Labor Standards Law, art. 59.

of a House, is now an instrument of child welfare. The adoption of a child below the age of majority can no longer be made by simple agreement of the natural and the adoptive parents, but requires the approval of the Family Court, which must determine whether the adoption will promote the best interests of the child.[54]

Although inequalities in the field of private family law have been eradicated, some have survived in the criminal law. Article 200 of the Penal Code, which provides for especially severe punishment in the case of the homicide of an ascendant as distinguished from any other person, continues, but this provision has been severely criticized as incompatible with the principle of equality as pronounced in article 14 of the Constitution. The Supreme Court upheld the constitutionality of the provision by a five-to-four vote in its much discussed decision of October 11, 1950.[55]

The reforms also abolished the various rules which guaranteed the eldest son a predominant position as an heir to the House. Most important, the system of household inheritance, the very center of the inheritance system under the old law, was changed to ensure for the first time that all children are now successors in the same order[56] and of equal shares[57] to the property left by a deceased parent.* But the principle of equal succession of all children is modified by two important exceptions. One is for the custom of ancestor worship, or *sosen saishi*. The ownership of the genealogical table, the utensils for the ancestor-worship ceremonies, and the family tombs still descends to the heir of the House.[58] This provision is under severe criticism because it is thought to recognize the family system as custom and preserve the idea of the heir. Another exception is that, although a recognized illegitimate child has the right to inherit, its share amounts to only one half that of a legitimate child.[59] The problem of how to deal with the illegitimate child is common to many countries, and in Japan opinions were divided as to what was proper treatment. Some thought that legitimate and illegitimate children should be treated alike. The unequal treatment is not, it should be noted, due to the family system.

With equality of rights all children now bear equal filial duties. Under the old law the heir to the House alone had to bear the duty to support the

[54] NEW CIVIL CODE art. 798.

[55] Actually the decision was in regard to death resulting from bodily injury under PENAL CODE art. 205(2), which provides in the case of ascendants a heavier penalty similar to art. 200. Japan v. Yamato, Supreme Court, Grand Bench, October 11, 1950, 4 SAIKŌ SAIBANSHO KEIJI HANREI SHŪ (A Collection of Criminal Supreme Court Cases) 2037; commented on in Steiner, *A Japanese Cause Célèbre: The Fukuoka Parricide Case*, 5 AM. J. COMP. L. 106 (1956).

[56] NEW CIVIL CODE art. 887(ii).

[57] NEW CIVIL CODE art. 900(iv).

* Thomas Blakemore noted at the conference that some precedent for the rule of equal division may be found in the principle contained in the Meiji code that personal as contrasted with House property passes to all the children in equal shares.

[58] See NEW CIVIL CODE art. 897.

[59] NEW CIVIL CODE art. 900(iv).

parents, but now all children have an equal support obligation. When there are several children, the distribution of the burden of the support to be provided the parents must be decided among them. When no agreement is reached, an allocation is made by the Family Court.[60]

The Impact of Postwar Social Changes on Family Order

As far as the law is concerned, the family system of Japan has been abolished. But to what extent does the state of the law correspond to the realities of social life? Generally speaking, the entire social order in Japan has undergone far-reaching transformations in the immediate postwar period. Because the family system was an intimate part of the political, social, and ideological life of prewar Japan, the changes have necessarily had effects even more significant than those wrought by the diminished legal recognition.

The most significant fact in the political sphere is the removal of the authoritarian form of government exercised in the name of the Emperor. Those political groups which believed that they had to rely on the family system as the major guarantee of their power were swept away by the force of events, and for the first time in history the Japanese people were free to criticize the government openly. Not needing or expecting blind, unquestioning obedience, the government no longer needs to maintain the family system as the cradle of a docile populace. The new political atmosphere has engendered new ideas about the ends of education; the aim is now the development of free, self-reliant citizens. This democratic system of education is gradually expelling those ideals which lay at the bottom of the family system. The old predilection for collective association, which has been so characteristic of Japan, is dissolving. The effects of the changing attitudes and those of the legal reforms cannot be clearly distinguished; the two interact and reinforce each other. The land reform, for example, dealt a mortal blow to those large, high-caste landowners, who traditionally exercised the dominant influence in the mura. In the face of the loss of legal backing and the changing attitudes toward collectivism, the mura has lost its integrating force in the countryside, thus contributing in turn to the rise of individualism.

In new Japan, wealth is gradually supplanting the traditional foci of social values: lineage, status, and parent-child ties. The growing importance of property has been strikingly illustrated by the recent marriage of the Crown Prince. The imperial family of the Tennō, the oldest House in Japan, the very paragon of the family system, has dared to break with tradition and to accept as a daughter-in-law the child of an industrialist, whose family is distinguished by wealth rather than by traditional status. The emergence of materialistic values has resulted, in part, from changes in the Japanese

[60] See New Civil Code art. 878.

economy. The land reform, which doomed the system of feudal land ownership, also radically altered Japan's rural economic pattern. Before the land reform, more than one half of the peasants were tenant-farmers bound to deliver about one half of their crops — principally rice — to their landlords.[61] The part retained was used primarily for subsistence; little was offered for sale in the open market. Now very few farmers rent; rents must be paid in cash; and any crops not needed by the farmers themselves can be marketed. Having been exposed to a market economy, farmers are beginning to be guided by the profit motive, and this has changed their entire outlook, especially their attitude toward the land. No longer is the family homestead primarily viewed as the site of a long ancestral tradition; it is a means of production, a tool to make money. The agricultural worker now claims the wages he believes he is worth, and there is no longer a place for unpaid family labor under patriarchal authority. The impact of the land reform has been reinforced by introduction and propagation of machinery in farming, and the younger generation has been active in using it. Those parents who could not understand the efficiency of the machine and its use lost their influence in the management of mechanized farms. The young men grew in self-confidence and began to feel that they could express their opinions on an equal footing with their parents. Mechanization has thus had a dual impact. The success of new equipment has contributed to development of wealth as a criterion of social status, thereby weakening the old system of values. In addition, the failure of the older generation to adapt to the innovations has provided children with an element of superiority in a relationship which postulates the inferiority of children; this reversal of position has seriously diminished parental prestige and consequently weakened the family system.

Developments in Japan since 1945 show clearly that the ideals of the new civil law have become part of the reality of social life and that the equality principle has gradually influenced family relationships. But at the same time one must not overlook the continued vitality of political forces that work to preserve the family system. Because Japan was still under Allied occupation at the time of the enactment of the new Civil Code, these groups did not openly oppose the legislative abolition of the family system. But when Japan regained independence, they missed no opportunity to express their desire to revive the system. The Outline Draft of Revision of the Constitution of Japan, by the Liberal Party — the conservatives — published on November 5, 1954, was typical of these efforts.[62] The draft did not, of course, insist

[61] See OUCHI, NIHON SHIHON-SHUGI NO NŌGYŌ MONDAI (Agricultural Problems in Japanese Capitalism) 17 (1948).

[62] JIYŪTŌ KEMPŌ CHŌSA KAI (Liberal Party Constitution Investigation Committee), NIHON-KOKU KEMPŌ KAISEI YŌKŌ-AN (An Outline Draft of Revision of the Constitution of Japan) (1954) [hereafter cited LIBERAL PARTY DRAFT CONSTITUTION] reprinted in *Kempō Kaisei* (Constitutional Revision), HŌRITSU JIHŌ (Law Journal), Bessatsu (Separate Issue), June 25,

upon the full revival of the family system; in particular, no attempt was made to restore the authoritarian powers of House heads. But the two principal features of the draft were thoroughly reactionary. It provided for the restoration of the duty of filial piety of children toward parents and attempted to re-establish the institution of family ownership of farm land.[63]

The Liberal Party's actions engendered violent opposition, centering in the women's organizations. The opposition considered the enactment of the provision requiring filial piety as an initial step in an attempt to revive the "feudalistic" ideology of *kō,* which had been one of the principal tenets of the family system; it was thought that such a retrogression would return women and children to an inferior status. Similarly it was feared that the institution of family property would result in a revival of the old system of family inheritance which gave a pre-eminent position to the oldest male descendant. Ever since the violent opposition to the plan to revise the Constitution, neither the Liberal Party nor its successor, the Liberal-Democratic Party, has dared to advocate openly the revival of the family system.

Yet the idea of the family system is by no means dead. The institutional reform was achieved when the democratic consciousness was not yet sufficiently mature. The country was stunned by its defeat and occupied by the victors. The thoughts and ideas of the nation lagged behind the official reforms. Although all aspects of Japanese democratization have been similarly affected, this lag has been of special significance in connection with the problem of the family system, which had taken such deep root in the life of the nation. Large parts of the nation were not prepared to accept the change and have not attempted to understand its implications.

One of the most important factors operating to preserve the family system has been the continuance of the small-enterprise system in farming. Land reform affected the title to land but not the form of agricultural enterprise;

1956, p. 200. Representative of the views of the committee of the Liberal Party which prepared the draft are the following remarks of its chairman Nobusuke Kishi, who subsequently became Prime Minister: "Since the concept of the *Ie* is completely nonexistent in the present Civil Code, the *Ie* — the 'family' [at this point Kishi used English] — itself is being lost; the ideas of commemorating one's ancestors, of respecting one's lineage, and of passing this on to one's children and grandchildren are all gone forever. Seated for the wedding ceremony we call out 'Drink up for the two Houses of such-and-such and so-and-so,' but from the viewpoint of the Civil Code the two Houses of such-and-such and so-and-so today no longer exist. Just because we say that marriage is a union between a man and a woman, is such an individualistically centered approach really proper? We say that children have no responsibility to care for their parents and thus we find that all the old folks have gone off to homes for the aged. Is this the course that ought to be followed to meet national conditions in Japan? I believe that the existence of the *Ie,* which so well befits Japan's traditions, its customs, and its national conditions, is essential. It is based on the spirit of the *Ie* that the state is constituted, while at the same time it forms the foundation for the state's advance internationally." *Kempō Kaisei ni yoru Kazoku Seido no Fukkatsu o Fusegō* (Let's Prevent the Revival of the Family System by Constitutional Revision), FUJIN KŌRON (The Woman's View), June 1954, p. 95.

[63] LIBERAL PARTY DRAFT CONSTITUTION, Kokumin no Kenri oyobi Gimu (Rights and Duties of the People) no. 4.

large-scale modernization of management and market-determined payment of labor has taken firm hold only in orchard farming and stock breeding. In the main sphere of Japanese agriculture, rice farming, the small-scale family enterprise still predominates, thereby limiting the use of agricultural machinery (which requires fairly large-scale utilization to be economical). The pervasive "parent-child" relations have continued to exist, especially between an employer or supervisor and his subordinates. This attitude has been steadily diminishing in force, but it still exercises influence upon Japanese life. Similarly, while the rural mura has been considerably weakened, it has by no means disappeared; and in the cities and in business, numerous enterprises based upon family ties and the idea of "one enterprise, one family" still exist. Even in larger industry, the tradition of cheap labor has not disappeared, and wages are still determined in some instances by the worker's social status rather than by the free interplay of market forces. The workers have been suffering not only from poor wages but also from housing shortages, inadequacies in the social-security system, and instability of the labor market, conditions which still cause workers to rely upon the ties with their rural families. Finally numerous "cliques" based upon family ties still exercise considerable influence and power in all spheres of social activity, including finance, politics, education, artistic circles, and the bureaucracy.

POPULAR ACCEPTANCE OF THE PRINCIPLE OF EQUALITY

In postwar Japan, the action and counteraction of the process of dissolving the conventional family system and the forces at work to reverse the process are responsible for the present chaotic confusion of the family order. In few countries, if any, is public opinion so widely divided on this fundamental issue as in Japan.[64] In addition, the data are not sufficient to permit accurate analysis of the impact of the reforms. In the pages to follow, we must, therefore, be content with taking up some problems on the basis of hypotheses drawn from the limited stock of available research data.

Generally speaking, the family system tends to find more supporters among the aged than among the young, among men than among women, among farmers and shopkeepers than among employees and workers, among those economically badly off than among the well-to-do. The intermingling of these factors determines an individual's attitude toward the family system. For instance, a well-educated married couple with a good income and liberal political views are almost completely free from the influence of the family system. On the other hand, an old farmer, with limited educational background and sympathy for the conservative party, is almost completely imbued with the old ideal. Between these extremes there is a spectrum of conscious-

[64] An extremely interesting and careful account of the ideological approach toward the family system in Japan will be found in KAWASHIMA, IDEOLOGY TOSHITE NO KAZOKU SEIDO (The Family System as an Ideology) (1957).

ness depending on varying combinations of the determining factors. Of these factors, age and education have been most important in the postwar spread of democratic ideas that tend to militate against the old system. Women are direct beneficiaries of its abolition and, not surprisingly, are staunch supporters of reform. In the last analysis, then, the question is how to account for the large percentage of supporters of the family system among farmers, shopkeepers, and the economically weak. Before attempting to answer this question, we shall examine the extent of popular acceptance of the Civil Code principle of equality among family members.

Equality between Husband and Wife

Takashi Koyama conducted an investigation into the period of time prior to registration after an informal marriage in a mountain village and in an urban apartment-house area.

Table 1, at the end of this essay, shows that only about 12 percent in the village and about 37 percent in the apartment-house area registered the marriage within ten days of the wedding ceremony. The rural districts are particularly marked by belated marriage registration, as the table indicates, a phenomenon traceable to the survival of trial marriage in mountain and farm villages. These statistics should be considered together with a study made by Professor Takanashi of Nippon University in which he investigated 705 cases of unregistered *de facto* marriages to find the reason for the failure to register (see Table 2).

The data which were obtained in the period 1947–51 soon after the introduction of the new law and are now somewhat obsolete* must be used for want of more recent ones. The reasons for nonregistration listed indicate that the notions prevalent under the family system still have a substantial impact on the decision to register. It need hardly be pointed out that reasons such as "to wait until the wife becomes pregnant," "to see how the wife gets along with the husband's parents," "to wait till the wife's nature is better known," have in view the interests of the husband. This means that the husband, and the husband alone, has retained power in a substantial number of cases to determine whether to register the marriage.

Although far more of those people willing to express an opinion are now

* Rex Coleman pointed out at the conference that these figures were compiled only a short while after the new reforms went into effect and are not very helpful in understanding the feeling in Japan today, almost a decade later. Based on his own limited experience in the country areas of Fukushima and Miyagi prefectures and Hokkaido in 1959 and 1960, he found general approval of the postwar changes, combined with a strong dislike of the family system, widespread among both rural and urban segments of the populace up to about age forty; persons above this age level commonly expressed nostalgia for the former institutions. More up-to-date statistics on naien as well as many other matters relating to marriage, divorce, zaisan bunyo, parent-and-child, adoption, and support, given in almost eighty English and Japanese bilingual graphs, charts, and statistical tables, may be found in KATO, ZUSETSU KAZOKU HŌ (Graphic Family Law) (1963).

in favor of equality of the sexes as a principle than against it (see Table 3), definite supporters of the equality principle in rural districts are still short of 50 percent, the negative and "don't knows" together amounting to as much as 56 percent — a fact which suggests that the equality principle has not yet been generally recognized in those areas. Even in *danchi,* as apartment-house areas are commonly called in Japan, where the most liberal viewpoint would be expected, about 25 percent are opposed to equality of the sexes. These officially expressed opinions may not, however, be an accurate gauge of the extent to which equality of the sexes is realized in actual married life; in fact, it may be assumed that the percentage of those who actually practice it is lower than that of those who purport to accept it as a principle. But there are no data to substantiate the assumption. As to the management of property, the wife is generally entrusted with the management of daily household matters, but the determination of legal acts of importance and assignment of proprietary benefits accruing therefrom are more frequently in the hands of the husband alone. This aspect of inequality, however, may be attributable more to the conditions of modern family life than to the influence of the family system.

One reform accepted, at least by the women, is the increased possibility for a woman to obtain a divorce. According to a survey conducted by the Women and Juvenile Bureau of the Ministry of Labor in 1958 with regard to 1,940 women who obtained agreement divorces, there are a greater number of cases of divorce initiated by wives than by husbands. Among the wives divorced by agreement, 60 percent personally signed and sealed the registrations, but more than 70 percent had sought advice from their relatives and friends before filing. Some 60 percent of them were without any arrangement about the terms and conditions of divorce; about 25 percent had such agreements in writing; and only 60 percent of those who had agreements had them actually performed. In an opinion poll on divorce by agreement, 36 percent approved, while 40 percent disapproved.[65]

The potentialities of zaisan bunyo as a means of supporting a divorcée either permanently or until she is self-supporting do not seem to have been realized. As Table 4 shows, zaisan bunyo does not exceed such small amounts as 100,000 yen, 50,000 yen, or even 30,000 yen. Unfortunately, the courts have not articulated the basis on which an award of zaisan bunyo is made. Because they ordinarily award less than 200,000 yen even when the marriage has lasted twenty years, zaisan bunyo is apparently not being used to divide property which the wife could be considered to have helped to accumulate by keeping the house while the husband worked. Furthermore, there is no indication that the courts have made awards to compensate the petitioning

[65] FUJIN SHŌNEN KYOKU (Women and Juvenile Bureau), RŌDŌ-SHŌ (Ministry of Labor), RIKON NI KAN-SURU ISHIKI CHŌSA KEKKA GAIYŌ (An Outline of the Results of the Survey of Feeling Regarding Divorce) (1961).

party for injuries, mental or physical, endured during the marriage. Because a wife is likely to be unprepared to support herself immediately after divorce, since any skills she has have been unused for so long and since she may not be aware of the opportunities available to her, zaisan bunyo might well be considered a means of providing for her support. Estimated in terms of the cost of living in Japan in 1961, any amount less than 100,000 yen is nothing but a token payment, and divorced wives, it seems, would need the minimum amount of 1,000,000 yen if zaisan bunyo is really meant to support them for the rest of their lives.[66] Generally, however, they receive as little as one fifth or even one tenth of that amount. The lesser amounts could be justified if zaisan bunyo was supposed to provide support only for the period until the wife should become self-supporting. The courts, however, have not indicated that this is the basis of awards and have not attempted to ascertain the amount needed for such a period. These small amounts of zaisan bunyo are indicative of the still low social status of Japanese wives as well as of the low economic standard of Japan in general. In one case a *de facto* wife demanded a million yen at the dissolution of her unregistered marriage but was awarded only 15,000 yen by the decision of a District Court, whose decision, however, was reversed and remanded by a High Court for defective reasoning.[67]

Equality between Parent and Child

Eiichi Isomura of Tokyo Metropolitan University conducted research on opinions concerning parent-child relations among students of high schools and girls' junior colleges in Tokyo, sending the same questionnaire to their parents (see Tables 5, 6, and 7). According to his results, it seems to be a very widely held opinion that, when parents and children disagree, the parents should not arbitrarily force their will on the children as to either marriage or occupation. The answers, "Decision should be reached through mutual consultation" and "The child should take initiative in the decision," predominated. It cannot be overlooked, however, that among the parents there are about 20 percent who still adhere to the family-system principle that parents should take initiative in choosing the spouses of their children.* The stronger influence of the family system in agricultural villages can be seen by comparing the answers from the Tokyo region to the questions about the course to be taken when parent and child disagree about choosing a

[66] At the official rate of exchange, 360 yen equal one dollar; however, in terms of Japanese living standards, the purchasing power of the yen is much greater than the exchange rate would indicate.

[67] Hayashi v. Kawamata, Tokyo High Court, Jan. 24, 1958, 11 Kōtō Saibansho Minji Hanrei Shū (A Collection of Civil High Court Cases) 329.

* At the conference, Richard Beardsley suggested that the difference in opinion between old and young may result not only from the greater "modernity" of the latter but also from the natural difference in outlook and interests which comes with age.

spouse with those given in farm villages around Okayama City and Akita City (Tables 8 and 9).[68] Taken together the responses to both questions indicate that about one half of the respondents in the rural districts of Okayama and Akita denied the child a voice in the selection of his mate and required that he obey his parents without question. Unfortunately, there are no statistics indicating the degree of correlation between parents denying the child a voice in the selection of his spouse and those requiring unquestioning obedience. That both ideas are survivors of the family system suggests that the correlation would be high. More recent investigations by Professor Koyama indicate that the degree of acceptance of the reforms continues to be much lower in agricultural areas than in urban communities (see Table 10). The table indicates clearly the marked differences between agricultural or forest villages and nonagricultural groups, particularly urban communities. In the agricultural families the eldest son is treated by the parents in a considerably different manner from his brothers and sisters. Parental intervention in marriage of the eldest son is still active, and about 2 percent of those who answered adhered to the traditional idea that parents can arbitrarily select the spouse for their eldest son or daughter. Even those who advocate "consultation between parents and children" seem to desire, although in a more moderate form, to reserve some room for intervention in their children's marriages. Thus those parents who want to retain a say in the eldest son's marriage actually comprise about 60 percent of the total. The degree of parental participation in the spouse selection of younger sons and daughters is somewhat lower: about 50 percent for daughters and about 40 percent for younger sons.

On the other hand, there is scarcely any distinction between the treatment of the eldest son and that of younger sons and daughters in nonagricultural families even if the family lives in a farm village; the extreme view of absolute parental discretion in spouse selection is held by less than 10 percent. The same figure for urban apartment dwellers falls to about 5 percent. Also, in the latter group, the idea of allowing children substantial free choice in selection of spouses is supported by 60 to 70 percent of the respondents, showing the fairly wide acceptance of the ideal of the new family type.

Equality among Siblings

An examination of opinions about the abolition of the House head and the accompanying inheritance of House property further illustrates the dichotomies between the agricultural and nonagricultural groups and between generations. Among those presently occupying the status of House head, one half are against the abolition of either the position of head of the

[68] More recent material that is also illustrative of the difference in attitudes about these matters in urban and rural communities is found in Table 10.

House or the system of inheritance to the House, and only 10 to 15 percent actively support the abolition. On the other hand, less than 10 percent of the young men are against the abolition of head of the House, and more than half of them actively support such changes. Only one third of the young men, however, actively support abolition of inheritance (see Diagrams 1 and 2). The same division can be seen in the results of the similar urban poll conducted by Isomura (see Table 11). Even though few openly support the primogeniture system of inheritance to the House, many parents are still inclined to give some preference to the eldest son, and those who support equal division in inheritance barely exceed 50 percent. Over 70 to 80 percent of the children, however, are in favor of equal division. It seems that the younger generation in cities accepts the idea of equal inheritance as something perfectly natural.

In contrast, the ratio of supporters of equal division among agricultural householders in the Okayama and Akita districts is found to be markedly lower, reaching a low of 14 percent in Akita (Table 12). Similarly, Koyama's findings (Table 13) indicate that in agricultural families about 70 to 80 percent believe that the eldest son should receive a larger share of the property than the other children; further, about one half of this group — especially in the case of the agricultural families in agricultural villages — actively assert that the law should be revised. On the other hand, among the urban apartment dwellers nearly 40 percent say that there is no need to give the eldest son a larger share. If those of the opinion that "as a principle, equal division is desirable, but it may have to be modified according to the circumstance" are added, the supporters of equal division amount to about one half. In contrast, revision of the civil law is supported by only 14 percent.

The strong antipathy harbored by the agricultural and mountain villagers for equal division in inheritance has its roots in the fear that equal inheritance would divide the land into plots too small to be farmed. Equal inheritance, of course, means equal shares in value and does not require an actual division of the land. In normal cases, these parents give the land to the eldest son, while providing other children with schooling expenses, bridal trousseaus, or the funds to set up a branch family, thus letting each child enjoy a considerable share in the parental property. Although the eldest son is not the sole recipient of parental largesse, nevertheless it is usual that the land and other properties necessary for cultivation will constitute the main part of the whole estate. When they are taken over by the eldest son alone, his share naturally becomes considerably larger than those of the other children. If the eldest son, who has monopolized the agricultural land, tries to compensate the others in money, equal division will be effected. An increased cash payment, however, makes the management of the farm more difficult. Thus the problem is one of making equal division in inheritance compatible with the maintenance of farm management. This dilemma, a recurrent political issue during the seventeen years of postwar Japan, has not yet been satisfactorily resolved.

In fact, in a predominantly large number of agricultural families, the eldest son alone succeeds to the property, and the other children waive their rights of inheritance. In such a case the actual situation has not changed much since the Meiji Civil Code. Nevertheless, shrinkage in the size of the landed property among the lower stratum of the agricultural population has tended to produce a "landless proletariat"—a group of agricultural laborers without land of their own. Although this phenomenon is primarily the result of other economic conditions, the influence of equal inheritance undoubtedly has had some impact. Without lands to divide, this group has little interest in supporting primogeniture. The upper stratum of agricultural families, generally in possession of cash, bonds, forests, and other properties besides agricultural land, can divide these among the younger sons and daughters and still retain the agricultural land as a unit. For this reason, these families are beginning to accept the principle of equal division in inheritance. On the other hand, the middle stratum of owner-cultivators constitutes the bulk of Japanese agricultural families, and these families usually have little more than their agricultural assets to be divided among the children. Their cash income from wages is very small and their degree of dependence on the land high. In such a situation, it is not possible to divide the agricultural land itself. Both in reality and in general attitude, it is among this category of the agricultural population that the system of primogeniture is most vigorously supported and tenaciously retained. The conservative party's recurrent attempts to restore a system of patrimony have been made in response to the demands of this attitude.

The desire of the parents to give a larger share to the eldest son seems to be closely related to their expectation that the eldest son will support them in old age. Diagram 3 shows that the principle that every child is responsible for supporting his or her parents, as laid down by the new law, is accepted by a slight majority and that one third of the total population holds the view that the eldest son should take sole responsibility for the support of the parents. Isomura's research (Table 14) indicates that about 40 percent of the parents think that the eldest son should support the parents, while only 17 percent of the sons agree. About 40 percent to 50 percent of the parents consider that all children are responsible for the maintenance of the parents or that only those who can afford the expense should maintain them, in harmony with the new Civil Code, while 60 to 70 percent of the children accept this principle.

Table 15, representing agricultural opinion, roughly agrees with the findings concerning primogeniture. Of the agricultural householders in rural and mountain villages, about 70 to 80 percent advocated sole responsibility for the eldest son, and those who think that all children should bear equal responsibility were less than 10 percent. Among the urban dwellers, at least a majority felt that all children should bear equal responsibility for support, and only 20 percent thought that the eldest son alone should be responsible. This contrast may be due to the fact that in agricultural villages maintenance involves living with the parents, while in cities this is not necessarily the case. However, in Japan, where welfare facilities for old people are still deficient and there is an acute and general housing shortage, even in cities most of the aged parents may have to live with the adult (usually married) children and be taken care of by them. Research conducted in 1954 revealed that, on the average for the whole country, 80 percent of the old people live with their children.[69] In Osaka City, 92 percent of the old people having a child or children live with them.[70] Among those living with their children, roughly 60 percent live with the eldest son, roughly 10 percent with one of the younger sons, and roughly 20 percent with daughters. In view of the previous status of daughters, the latter fact may reflect the influence of the new law. On the whole, however, the traditional pattern of the eldest son living in his parents' house and supporting them still predominates.

Conclusion

From what has been said in the preceding pages, the reader will have realized the diversity of the contemporary attitudes among the Japanese toward the question of equality among family members. The greatest postwar change is in the relation between parents and children, except with respect to the duty of support. The patriarchal authority formerly enjoyed by the parents was derived mainly from political, social, and ideological conditions. Therefore, with the change of these conditions, parental authority lost its supports. On the other hand, the children reared under the postwar educational system differ fundamentally from their parents in manners of thinking. These two factors have brought about a drastic change since 1945.* In rural villages, where modernization of farm management and mechanization were accompanied by confirmation of the son's leadership in running the farm, the position of children has markedly improved. Of course, generally speaking, remnants of the ideology of the family system still linger in the

[69] Kokuritsu Seron Chōsajo (National Public Opinion Research Institute), Rōgō no Seikatsu ni Tsuite no Seron Chōsa (A Public Opinion Survey of Life in Old Age) (1954).

[70] Shakai Fukushi Kenkyūshitsu (Social Welfare Laboratory), Ōsaka Shiritsu Daigaku (Osaka Municipal University), Ōsaka-shi Rōjin Seikatsu Jittai Chōsa (A Field Survey of the Life of the Elderly in Osaka City) (1954).

* Haruo Abe stated at the conference that the juvenile-delinquency rate in Japan has tripled since the end of the last war. He viewed this rise not as a sign of the disintegration of moral fabric, but as an expression of the new freedom the children are now enjoying. A return to the old system would be inimical to democratic values, and the present problem is one of filling the vacuum left by the disappearance of the virtues of filial piety.

minds of parents. With the further progress in modernization of agriculture, however, parental authority will be steadily and further undermined.

The degree of change in husband-wife relations is next to that in the parent-child relation in importance. Not only has the wife's status been raised to one of equality, but the position of women in general has been elevated through the granting of suffrage and a general improvement in working conditions. In spite of this progress, equality of men and women cannot yet be achieved because many women do not have equivalent training or economic opportunity.* Now the focus of the problem is gradually shifting away from the institutional discrimination of the family system to inequality caused by economic factors.

The smallest postwar change is in the privileged position of the eldest son centering around his right of inheritance and the obligation to support the parents. In actual practice, the eldest son continues to succeed to the principal items of property, a result approved by the majority of the population. Is the survival of the family-system ideology particularly tenacious in regard to inheritance and support of parents? The answer should probably be in the negative. These two aspects of the family life are most closely related to economic problems; without solving these, it is impossible to solve the connected problems in family relations. In Japan, a paucity of progressive agricultural policies forces cultivators to cling to their land, making them supporters of primogeniture succession. And the failures to provide adequate housing or old-age insurance force the eldest sons of the lower-income groups, whose members are in pressing need of such assistance, to live with and support their parents; substantial support consequently remains for the traditional way of supporting parents. The future course of the systems of inheritance and support of parents depends largely on the development by the government of remedial agricultural and social policies.

* At the conference, Rex Coleman questioned whether there was any country in the world in which women in general have training and economic opportunity equal to that of men. Even in the United States, which is often described in the Japanese popular press as a woman-dominated "ladies-first" country, this is certainly not the case. In this respect Japan may not in fact be too different from the nations of the West. Coleman did not believe that the percent of women college and high-school graduates is considerably less among the younger members of the population than in the United States, while Japan may to some extent lead Western Europe in this area. Economically all professions are today open to women, and, although the female "tycoon" has not yet appeared, women form a respectable portion of the doctors, lawyers, and elected government officials.

TABLE 1. Length of Time before Registration of Informal Marriage

Period	Otamba (Mountain-village area)	Toyama (Urban apartment-house area)
Within 10 days	12.9%	37.2%
Within 3 months	33.3	26.4
Within 6 months	16.7	11.7
Within a year	8.1	7.8
Within two years	3.3	1.7
More than two years	1.4	6.1
Forgotten	19.5	6.9
Not yet	0.5	0
Others	4.3	2.2
	100.0%	100.0%

Source: KOYAMA, GENDAI KAZOKU NO KENKYŪ (A Study of the Modern Family) 113 (1960). The research was conducted during 1955–56. Toyama is in Shinjuku Ward and Otamba in Okutama Town, Nishi Tama Township, both located within the Metropolis of Tokyo.

TABLE 2. Selected Results of an Inquiry about Why Naien Marriages Had Not Been Registered

Reasons	Number of cases
Because both husband and wife are heirs to their respective households	169
Because both husband and wife are heads of their respective households	85
Registration is not necessary	60
To wait until the wife becomes pregnant	49
Because everything is left to parents	46
To see how the wife gets along with the husband's parents (or, less frequently, how the husband married into the wife's family gets along with her parents)	33
Because of nationality	27
Because of custom	21
Cannot register because a former marriage is still officially recorded	19
Didn't know about registration	19
To wait until the wife's nature is better known (or, less frequently, until the nature of the husband married into the wife's family is better known)	18
To see how the wife gets along with the husband and his former wife's children	18
Total	564

Source: TAKANASHI, NIHON KONIN HŌRON (A Legal Treatise on Japanese Marriage) 127 (1957).

TABLE 3. Attitudes toward Equality of the Sexes in Marriage

Attitude	Otamba (Mountain-village area)	Toyama (Urban apartment-house area)
Positive	40.5%	59.8%
Negative	25.7	20.4
Don't know	30.0	13.4
No answer	3.8	0.4
	100.0%	100.0%

Source: see Table 1, at 148.

TABLE 4. Zaisan Bunyo: Amount Demanded and Awarded of Distributed Property (yen)

Amount demanded	Total number of cases	0	Up to 10,000	Up to 30,000	Up to 50,000	Up to 100,000	Up to 200,000	Up to 300,000	Up to 500,000	Up to 1,000,000	Over 1,000,000	Others	Unde-cided
Tota cases	13,733	2,201	259	695	644	801	476	251	155	69	29	205	7,928
0	5,800	1,440	55	92	95	101	53	31	19	5	2	46	3,861
Up to 10,000	47	4	14	2	—	1	—	—	—	—	—	1	25
Up to 30,000	150	13	17	59	2	1	—	—	—	—	—	3	55
Up to 50,000	377	52	34	78	62	6	2	1	—	1	—	2	139
Up to 100,000	1,042	119	35	137	137	142	9	2	1	1	1	12	446
Up to 200,000	1,049	93	27	104	104	143	96	3	—	—	—	6	473
Up to 300,000	956	80	16	61	92	132	67	63	1	—	—	7	437
Up to 500,000	1,076	79	7	53	66	102	113	64	52	2	—	7	531
Up to 1,000,000	565	34	5	19	23	55	49	27	32	31	—	2	288
More than 1,000,000	254	12	—	2	5	6	13	13	8	13	13	3	166
Others	1,041	117	21	38	33	43	31	14	14	5	6	97	622
Unknown	1,376	158	28	50	45	69	43	33	28	11	7	19	885

Source: statistical data of the Family Courts for 1956.

TABLE 5. Survey Opinions on the Proper Extent of Filial Obedience

Family member responding	Should obey as much as possible	Child's will should also be respected	Need not be obeyed blindly	Should talk over the differences	No answer
Parent					
Father	17.0%	44.5%	—	31.5%	7.0%
Mother	11.9	16.7	2.4	64.0	5.0
Child					
High school	7.0	24.0	—	69.0	—
Junior college (girls)	4.6	17.2	1.7	76.5	—

Source: KAZOKU NO FŌUY (Support of a Family) 43 (Isomura, Kawashima & Koyama ed., 1956).

TABLE 6. Survey Opinions on Parental Importance in the Selection of a Spouse

Family member responding	Parent should decide	Parental initiative	Consul-tation	Child's initiative	Child should decide	Don't know	No answer
Parent							
Father	—	18.5%	46.3%	29.7%	1.9%	1.8%	1.8%
Mother	4.8	16.7	35.7	38.0	2.4	2.4	—
Child							
High school	—	—	41.4	37.8	10.4	7.0	3.4
Junior college	0.9	12.1	31.8	50.8	3.5	0.9	—

Source: see Table 5, at 43.

TABLE 7. Survey Opinions on Parental Importance in the Selection of a Child's Occupation

Family member responding	Obey parent's opinion if possible	Parental initiative	Consultation	Child's initiative	Child's decision	No answer
Parent						
Father	—	—	35.3%	57.4%	1.8%	5.5%
Mother	—	2.4	42.7	50.0	2.5	2.4
Child						
High school	—	—	65.5	31.1	3.4	—
Junior college	—	1.7	48.2	49.2	0.9	—

Source: see Table 5, at 44.

TABLE 8. Survey Opinions on Parent-Child Disagreements, by Geographical Region

District	Should obey parent	Child's opinion should also be respected	Need not blindly obey parent's opinion	Don't know
Tokyo	11.9%	31.2%	49.7%	7.3%
Okayama	46.8	26.3	22.2	4.4
Akita	51.2	32.1	13.8	2.7

Source: see Table 5, at 51. The research in Akita and Okayama was conducted in 1953; in Tokyo in 1954.

TABLE 9. Survey Opinions on Parental Importance in the Selection of a Spouse, by Geographical Region

District	Parent's opinion	Consultation	Child's opinion	Don't know
Tokyo	15.9%	42.5%	36.5%	5.5%
Okayama	48.7	38.4	11.3	1.4
Akita	47.9	36.7	13.6	1.6

Source: see Table 5, at 51.

TABLE 10. Survey Opinions on Parental Importance in the Selection of a Spouse

Question / Respondent	Otamba (Mountain-village area)			Komae (Agricultural families in farm areas)			Komae (Nonagricultural families in farm areas)			Toyama (Urban apartment-house area)		
	Spouse for: E.s.	Y.s.	D.	Spouse for: E.s.	Y.s.	D.	Spouse for: E.s.	Y.s.	D.	Spouse for: E.s.	Y.s.	D.
Parents, parental initiative												
Father	22.1%	10.7%	20.4%	21.2%	10.9%	15.9%	7.9%	7.9%	12.7%	4.5%	3.9%	5.3%
Mother	21.5	10.3	20.0	21.5	9.2	10.9	9.1	9.1	10.9	6.4	3.9	7.1
Consultation between parent and child												
Father	39.4	31.1	33.0	33.3	31.3	36.5	38.1	30.2	33.3	30.8	26.8	29.3
Mother	34.6	29.9	33.3	52.3	41.5	54.7	45.5	36.4	38.2	34.0	30.3	33.3
Total												
Father	61.5	41.7	53.4	54.5	42.2	52.4	46.0	38.1	46.0	35.3	30.7	34.6
Mother	56.1	40.2	53.3	73.9	50.8	65.6	54.6	45.5	49.1	40.4	34.2	40.4
Child's initiative												
Father	26.9	36.9	32.0	36.4	45.3	38.1	31.8	34.9	27.0	49.6	51.2	51.1
Mother	29.0	35.5	28.6	13.8	32.3	18.8	32.7	34.5	34.5	46.8	50.0	46.8
Child's decision												
Father	11.6	21.3	14.6	9.1	12.5	9.5	22.2	27.0	27.0	15.1	18.1	14.3
Mother	14.9	24.3	18.1	12.3	16.9	15.6	12.7	20.0	16.4	12.8	15.8	12.8
Total												
Father	38.5	58.2	46.6	45.5	57.8	42.6	54.0	61.9	54.0	64.7	69.3	65.4
Mother	43.9	59.8	46.7	26.1	49.2	34.4	45.4	54.5	50.9	59.6	65.8	56.6

Source: see Table 1, at 106. Komae is a town in Kita Tama Township, Metropolis of Tokyo, located between Chofu City and Setagaya Ward. E.s. is eldest son; Y.s. is younger son; D. is daughter.

TABLE 11. Survey Opinions on Appropriate Testamentary Division of Property, by Age (inquiry within a city)

Family member responding	Eldest son only	Equal division among sons	A larger share for the eldest son	Equal division among children	Donation to welfare works	Don't know	No answer
Parent							
Father	1.85%	—	37.0%	53.7%	1.85%	1.9%	3.7%
Mother	—	—	38.5	47.5	—	7.15	7.15
Child							
High school	—	—	7.0	86.2	3.4	3.4	—
Junior college	0.9	—	28.4	69.8	0.9	—	—

Source: see Table 5, at 39.

TABLE 12. Survey Opinions on Appropriate Testamentary Division of Property, by Geographical Region

District	Mainly to the eldest son	Equal division among children	Don't know
Tokyo	35.1%	55.1%	9.8%
Okayama	58.5	38.7	2.5
Akita	80.8	14.0	4.9

Source: see Table 5, at 51.

TABLE 13. Survey Opinions on Appropriate Testamentary Division of Property, by Geographical Region

Opinion	Otamba (Mountain-village area)	Komae (Agricultural families in farm areas)	Komae (Non-agricultural families in farm areas)	Toyama (Urban apartment-house area)
Larger share for the eldest son				
Law should be revised	33.7%	48.4%	15.8%	14.0%
No need of law revision	23.3	25.7	25.0	20.1
Don't know about law	16.6	9.9	8.3	5.8
No need to give a larger share to the eldest son	16.1	11.4	37.6	40.1
A larger share for the eldest son if required by circumstances	2.2	3.8	6.7	3.7
Equal share according to circumstances	0	0	0.8	1.7
Other ways of division according to circumstances	2.7	0.8	5.0	10.9
No answer	5.4	0	0.8	3.7
	100.0%	100.0%	100.0%	100.0%

Source: see Table 1, at 79.

TABLE 14. Survey Opinions on Who Should Support Dependent Parents, by Age

Family member responding	Eldest son	Mainly eldest son, with other children helping	Who-ever can afford	All the children	Old people's home	Don't know	No answer
Parent							
Father	1.8%	40.7%	22.3%	24.1%	3.7%	1.9%	5.5%
Mother	—	42.7	19.2	33.3	2.4	—	2.4
Child							
High school	—	17.3	27.6	48.3	3.4	3.4	—
Junior college	1.7	31.0	25.8	38.8	1.7	0.8	—

Source: see Table 5, at 39.

TABLE 15. Survey Opinions on Who Should Support Dependent Parents, by Geographical Region

Opinion	Otamba (Mountain-village area)	Komae (Agricultural families in farm areas)	Komae (Non-agricultural families in farm areas)	Toyama (Urban apartment-house area)
Eldest son	81.6%	74.2%	36.7%	20.4%
Eldest son and independent sons	4.0	6.1	5.8	8.5
All children	8.1	12.9	35.0	52.7
Others	4.5	5.3	21.7	16.0
No answer	1.8	1.5	0.8	2.4
	100.0%	100.0%	100.0%	100.0%

Source: see Table 1, at 79.

DIAGRAM 1. Pros and Cons on the Law Revision Abolishing the System of the House

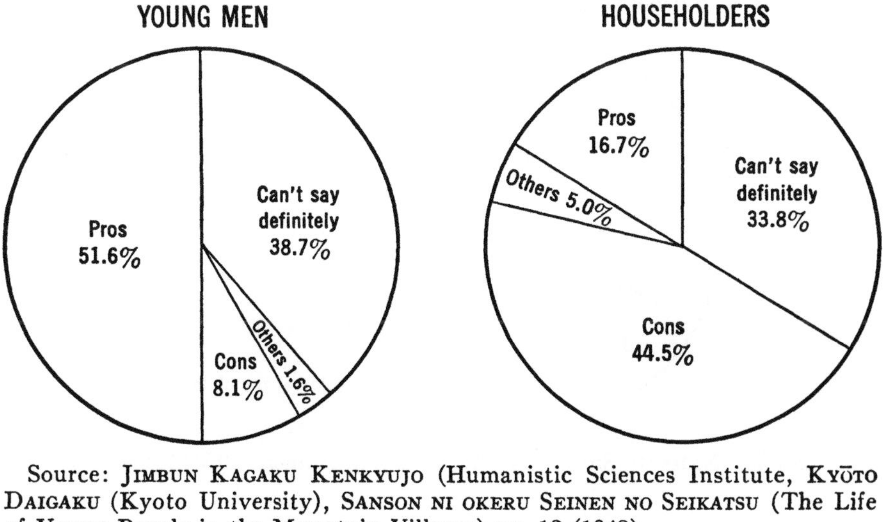

Source: JIMBUN KAGAKU KENKYUJO (Humanistic Sciences Institute, KYŌTO DAIGAKU (Kyoto University), SANSON NI OKERU SEINEN NO SEIKATSU (The Life of Young People in the Mountain Villages) no. 12 (1948).

DIAGRAM 2. Pros and Cons on the Law Revision Abolishing the System of Inheritance of House Property

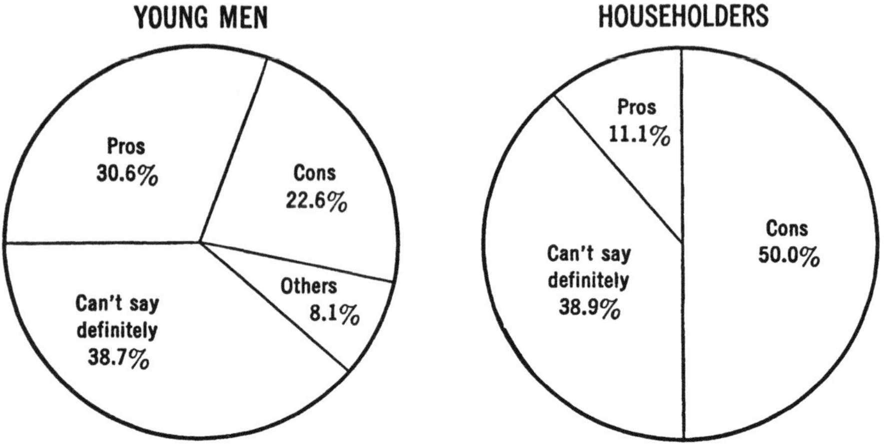

Source: see Diagram 1.

DIAGRAM 3. Survey Opinions on Who Should Support Dependent Parents

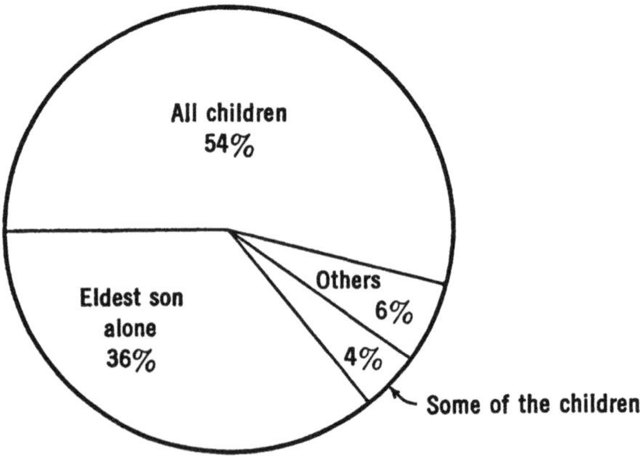

Source: JIJI NENKAN, SHŌWA 28 NEN (The Jiji Annual, 1953) 289 (1953).

THE TREATMENT OF MOTOR-VEHICLE ACCIDENTS: THE IMPACT OF TECHNOLOGICAL CHANGE ON LEGAL RELATIONS

Ichiro Kato

ASSISTED BY BEN BRUCE BLAKENEY

THE THEME of this essay is the evolution of the law of motor-vehicle-accident liability in the course of the modernization and "motorization" of Japan. In developing the theme, it will be necessary to touch on several aspects of Japanese tort law in general, as well as the specific acts rather recently passed.

Background: Laws and Motor Vehicles in Japan

Until 1955, when the Automobile Damage Compensation Security Law was enacted,[1] liability for motor-vehicle accidents was regulated solely by articles 709 through 724 of the Civil Code relating to "unlawful acts," or torts. The keystone of tort liability in the code is fault; the Automobile Damage Law prescribes a special liability which approaches liability without fault. It also establishes compulsory motor-vehicle liability insurance. But since the law prescribes only the basic conditions for liability and leaves all other problems to resolution in accordance with the Civil Code, it is necessary to understand the outlines of civil responsibility under that code.

Other laws are also relevant. The Road Traffic Law[2] prescribes, enforceable by penal sanctions, many rules for driving: the requirement of a driver's license, the rule of keeping to the left side of the road, speed limits, and

Note. Mr. Kato is Professor of Law, Tokyo University. B.Jur., Tokyo Imperial University, 1943; Dr.Jur., Tokyo University, 1961. Secretary of the Civil Law Subcommittee of the Council on the Legal System; member of the Subcommittee on Transactions of the Ministry of International Trade and Industry Industrial Rationalization Council; member of the Ministry of Welfare Medical Care Investigation Commission. Author of Fuhō Kōi (Torts) (1957); Fuhō Kōi Hō no Kenkyū (Studies in the Law of Torts) (1961): writings in the fields of civil law, especially the law of torts, family law, inheritance law, and agricultural land law.

Mr. Blakeney, until his death in early 1963, was a practicing attorney in Tokyo and Lecturer in American Law at Tokyo and Chuo Universities. A.B., 1929, University of Oklahoma; LL.B., 1932, Harvard University; Dr.Jur. (hon.), 1962, Chuo University.

[1] Law No. 97 of 1955 [hereafter cited as the Automobile Damage Law].

[2] Law No. 105 of 1960.

like matters. Theoretically, a driver who violates one of these rules is not deemed *ipso facto* negligent so as to establish his liability under the Civil Code; but as a matter of practice courts usually do presume negligence. The Penal Code provides penalties for accidental infliction of injury and homicide.[3] Generally speaking, in case of injury or death resulting from a motor-vehicle accident, if the putative wrongdoer settles amicably with his victim, either the police do not send the report to the procurators' office or the procurators do not prosecute unless there has been reckless driving. Thus the Penal Code provisions serve indirectly to ensure compensation for injury.

The Japanese people tend to avoid litigation and to settle claims out of court.[4] This is also true of injury and property-damage claims arising from motor-vehicle accidents, although these are somewhat more often litigated than other claims. The Japanese are reluctant to go to court for several reasons. In the first place, controversies have traditionally been settled amicably within restricted communities through mediation by village elders, neighborhood leaders, and policemen; something of this spirit of settlement remains. Secondly, the Japanese prefer a solution by compromise and do not fully accept the "all or nothing" result of litigation. A famous and still current Japanese proverb declares that in a quarrel both parties are to blame; this suggests that a consciousness of the concept of individual rights is not yet fully developed in Japan and reveals a psychology peculiar to the Japanese people. Finally, the ordinary man hesitates to resort to the courts because litigation is expensive and time-consuming. Even in the few suits which are brought, the proceedings are very different from those in the typical American personal-injury litigation, since there is no jury and the judge tends to play a more significant role than the attorneys.[5] In the ensuing discussion, only relatively few references to judicial proceedings are possible; thus much greater reliance must be placed on theoretical discussions than is usual in American legal scholarship.

The enactment in 1955 of the Automobile Damage Compensation Security Law was a natural result of the motorization of Japan. In the period 1950–1961, the number of motor vehicles in Japan increased more than ten times, as shown in Table 1 at the end of this essay. From Table 2 we see that only a little over ten percent of the total number of motor vehicles are ordinary four-wheeled passenger cars; in 1961 there was still only one ordinary passenger car per 157 people. But there are also many small motor vehicles with two or three wheels, as well as about two million motorbikes and many more regular bicycles. This great variety makes the regulation of

[3] Law No. 45 of 1907, arts. 209–11.

[4] See generally Takeyoshi Kawashima, "Dispute Resolution in Contemporary Japan," in this volume.

[5] See Kohji Tanabe, "The Process of Litigation: An Experiment with the Adversary System," in this volume.

road traffic very difficult and thus is one cause of the large number of accidents in Japan.

In the period from 1948 to 1959, motor-vehicle accidents increased by more than 1,000 percent, as seen in Table 3. This remarkable increase is due mainly to the expansion of the number of motor vehicles. The increase in trucks, motorcycles, and motor scooters is especially significant, since their drivers tend to be both somewhat unskilled and rather oblivious to danger. In addition, Japanese roads are not suited to handle the increase in traffic. City streets and trunk roads are paved, but these comprise only 15 percent of all roads. The driver is often handicapped by an uneven and narrow road; the pedestrian frequently has no sidewalk.

Most fatal motor-vehicle accidents in Japan occur between motor vehicles and pedestrians or bicycles; the rate of fatalities resulting from collisions between motor vehicles remains rather low, as shown in Table 4. The rate of fatal accidents involving old people and children is comparatively high. Since these victims have little or no income, their families cannot claim large damages; their low recoveries reduce the average amount of damages recovered for personal injuries in accidents.

Liability Under the Civil Code

Conditions of Civil Liability

The basic provision of the Civil Code regulating liability is article 709, which provides: "A person who, wilfully or negligently, has injured the right of another is bound to compensate him for the damage which has arisen therefrom."

Intent or negligence on the part of the defendant is thus basic to liability (the *Verschuldungsprinzip* of German law); and the burden of proof of fault lies with the plaintiff. Typically, automobile accidents do involve fault. In most cases the plaintiff can prove the defendant's fault; and even when it cannot be fully proven the judge may be able to presume it. In a few cases, however, the plaintiff cannot establish fault and thus loses. The fault requirement is probably even more significant in cases settled out of court, since it gives the defendant a legal argument to use in negotiation. Stricter principles of liability for motor-vehicle accidents were thus urged and were adopted in the Automobile Damage Compensation Security Law.

Article 722(2) of the Civil Code, dealing with the plaintiff's negligence, provides: "If there has been fault on the part of the injured party, the court may take it into account in determining the amount of compensation for damages." This is the civil-law rule of comparative negligence; fault on the part of the injured party does not necessarily extinguish the wrongdoer's liability, but only reduces the damages he must pay. Thus if a pedestrian or a cyclist who was injured by an automobile was himself at fault, the damages are reduced according to the degree of fault of the parties and at the discretion of the court. When two automobiles collide, reciprocal liabilities generally arise. The court then reduces the amount of the damages owed to each party under the principle of comparative negligence, and the difference is paid by the party owing the larger amount. These computations are often difficult to make and may in some cases hinder or prevent settlement out of court.

When a driver is employed by a taxi company, a trucking company, or an individual, the employer is ordinarily liable for injury caused by the employee, assuming that the latter would be held liable under article 709. Article 715(1) of the Civil Code prescribes the employer's liability:

A person who employs another for the purpose of any undertaking is bound to compensate for damage which his employee has inflicted on a third party in the execution of this undertaking. Provided, however, that this does not apply if the employer has exercised adequate care in the selection of the employee and the superintendence of the undertaking, or if the damage would have arisen even though adequate care had been exercised.

Literally, this provision exempts an employer from liability if he can prove that his selection and supervision of the driver were faultless; but the courts have long refused to allow such proof. The employer who has paid such compensation may demand reimbursement from the employee, however, under article 715(3), although often he does not do so.

When an employed driver drives an automobile for his private use, it is unclear whether he acts "in the execution of this undertaking." The courts have tended to hold the employer vicariously liable when the driving falls within a sphere which, objectively viewed, would seem to be under his own control. For example, the Supreme Court held the state liable for injuries inflicted by a driver engaged by the Ministry of International Trade and Industry, although he was driving on the private business of a secretary at the time; the Court reasoned that objectively the driving was within the scope of the employee's work, although subjectively it was done for the nonbusiness purposes of the secretary.[6]

Another kind of connected situation is that in which someone is injured by a person who is practicing driving preparatory to securing a license. The Great Court of Judicature at first held that the employer was not liable because he had not ordered the driving.[7] In a later case, the Court imposed liability on the ground that the driving was objectively within the scope of

[6] Hoya v. Japan, Supreme Court, I Petty Bench, Dec. 22, 1955, 9 SAIKŌ SAIBANSHO MINJI HANREI SHŪ (A Collection of Civil Supreme Court Cases) [hereafter cited as SAI-HAN MINSHŪ] 2047.

[7] Katsube v. Maruhachi Jidōsha Kabushiki Kaisha (Maruhachi Automobile Co.), Great Court of Judicature, I Criminal Department, Jan. 21, 1919, 25 DAI SHIN IN KEIJI HANKETSU ROKU (Record of Great Court of Judicature Criminal Judgments) 42.

the driver's employment, even though the driver had in fact disobeyed the instructions of his employer.[8] Thus liability can apparently be based on the objective manifestations of the employee's acts — a theory which benefits the injured person.[9]

Assessment of Damages

The injuries caused by motor-vehicle accidents fall into three categories: property damage, physical injury to the person, and injury in the form of mental pain and suffering.

When property has been damaged or destroyed in a motor-vehicle accident, its owner can claim compensation for the damage done. The measure of damage is ordinarily the cost of repairs; if the property cannot be repaired or has been destroyed, however, its value as of the time of damage or destruction can be recovered.

In case of bodily injury, medical expenses may be recovered; further, if the accident was fatal, the family of the deceased is entitled to reimbursement for funeral expenses. These damages are analogous to those allowed for harm to ordinary property.

In addition, when the injured person will be unable to work in the future because of his injury or when his earning capacity is reduced, he may claim damages for loss of earnings. If the victim has died, to determine the amount to be paid his survivors his average living expenses are deducted from his monthly gross earnings to determine his net earnings; if the victim is still alive, the measure of damages depends on his gross earnings as reduced by what he can now expect to earn. The lost monthly earnings thus ascertained represent his monthly damages. If the victim is dead, payment in monthly installments is, of course, impossible; even if he is alive, damages are ordinarily paid in Japan in a lump sum. Thus the victim's life expectancy must be determined so that his total lost earnings may be obtained. This amount is then converted into a lump sum to be given to the plaintiff by subtracting the interest component according to Hoffman's method.[10]

[8] Yanagi v. Egami Jidōsha Gōshi Kaisha (Egami Automobile Partnership in Commendam Co.), Great Court of Judicature, IV Civil Department, Feb. 12, 1938, 17 DAI SHIN IN MINJI HANREI SHŪ (A Collection of Civil Great Court of Judicature Cases) [hereafter cited DAI-HAN MINSHŪ] 203, 18 HANREI MINJI HŌ (Civil Case Law) 52 (note Katsumoto); Kenjo v. Arama, Great Court of Judicature, I Civil Department, Sept. 12, 1932, 11 DAI-HAN MINSHŪ 1765, 12 HANREI MINJI HŌ 476 (note Suehiro).

[9] See KATO, FUHŌ KŌI (Torts) 182 (22 Hōritsu-gaku Zenshū (Complete Collection on the Law), 1957).

[10] Under this method, if we represent the net lost earnings of the injured person, calculated for his normal life, by A, his life expectancy at his age by N years, and the interest rate per annum by R (5 percent in Japan), we obtain the present lump sum X by the following formula: $X = A/(1 + NR)$. Matsumoto v. Kōbe-shi (Kobe City), Great Court of Judicature, II Civil Department, Jan. 26, 1926, 5 DAI-HAN MINSHŪ 71, 6 HANREI MINJI HŌ 55 (note Hirano). All courts formerly used this formula, even though it reduces substantially the interest element in the final award. Recently, in order to remove this inequity, a number of courts have turned to a new formula, in which the net monthly earnings of the victim are represented

In practice, the amount of damages awarded for loss of earnings is usually very small. Indeed, the limit on insurance payments under the Automobile Damage Law was originally fixed at 300,000 yen (now 500,000 yen[11]), since the damages awarded in death cases had generally been under that figure or even less than 200,000 yen. These low recoveries are largely owing to the relatively low level of individual income in Japan and to the fact that the persons injured are mainly pedestrians consisting of old people, children, or people in low-income groups. In some cases the very modest recoveries result from an unfavorable method of assessing damages; for example, the estimate is often low when there is difficulty in proving the total income, or excessive reductions are made for living expenses if the victim has died. But many jurists, as well as the general public, have strongly criticized this low evaluation of the price of life, and assessing practices are beginning to be more reasonable. Moreover, individual incomes have been generally increasing and, because of the growing number of collisions between motor vehicles, persons of substantial income are more frequently injured in automobile accidents. Recently a court assessed the loss of earnings of a thirty-three-year-old man who was killed in an automobile collision at about 6 million yen; the decedent, a photographer, had a working-life expectancy of thirty-two years and a monthly income of 35,000 yen, about the average middle-class income in Japan.[12] This decision may well presage a future liberal trend in the assessment of damages.

The claim for loss of earnings is a right accruing to the victim of the accident. Thus in a case of serious injury, the right to damages first accrues to the injured person and then passes to his heirs upon his death.[13] If death is instantaneous, however, since the right of the deceased theoretically ripens only upon death he does not die with a right to damages, and there is nothing to pass to his heirs; they would receive damages only for loss of support

---

by a: $a/[1 + 1(R/12)] + a/[1 + 2(R/12)] + \ldots + a/[1 + n(R/12)]$. It is very troublesome to calculate separately each term in this series, however, and the courts in practice resort to a table of index numbers for months — for example, 97.14515218 for 120 months. Thus, when the life expectancy of the injured person is 10 years, we can obtain the present lump-sum damages by multiplying the monthly earnings by this index number. See, e.g., Nakayama v. Yamaichi Suisan Kabushiki Kaisha (Yamaichi Marine Products Co.), Kofu District Court, April 24, 1959, 10 KAKYŪ SAIBANSHO MINJI SAIBAN REISHŪ (A Collection of Civil Cases in the Inferior Courts) [hereafter cited KAKYŪ MINSHŪ] 820; Iwai v. Japan, Sapporo District Court, Nov. 14, 1960, 11 KAKYŪ MINSHŪ 2449.

[11] Automobile Damage Compensation Security Law Enforcement Order, Cabinet Order No. 286 of 1955, art. 2, as amended by Cabinet Order No. 227 of 1960.

[12] Nakayama v. Yamaichi Suisan Kabushiki Kaisha, as in note 10 above. Also see note 32 below.

[13] Ito v. Hanshin Denki Tetsudō Kabushiki Kaisha (Hanshin Electric Railway Co.), Great Court of Judicature, IV Civil Department, Aug. 1, 1928, 7 DAI-HAN MINSHŪ 648, 8 HANREI MINJI HŌ 316 (note Egawa); Okutani v. Nomura, Osaka High Court, Jan. 20, 1960, 13 KŌTŌ SAIBANSHO MINJI HANREI SHŪ (A Collection of Civil High Court Cases) 10.

in their own right.[14] The courts have avoided the practical anomaly of this situation, however, and have affirmed the right of successors to recover the decedent's lost earnings in all cases.[15] Recovery for loss of support by the deceased is always open to the successors; thus the decedent's family usually has a choice between the two remedies. In most instances it is more advantageous to claim damages as heirs of the rights of the deceased, since loss of earnings is more easily established than is loss of support; moreover, the amount of support is usually less than the amount of earnings. Consequently, heirs almost always claim damages as successors to the decedent's rights.

The injured party may also claim solatium for his mental suffering. Article 710 of the Civil Code provides that a person who is bound to compensate damage "is required to make such compensation even for damage which is other than pecuniary, irrespective of whether it was a case of injury to the body, liberty, or honor of another, or a case of injury to his property rights." But where property rights are invaded, the injured party must generally be satisfied with damages for the loss of property, except in rare cases such as that of intentional damage to property having sentimental value. In practice, therefore, solatium is paid only in case of bodily injury or death.

The standards for setting the amount of solatium are not exact; the amount has been fixed according to the usual practices and principles of equity. The function of solatium is theoretically to satisfy the injured party, although in practice its main object is to supplement the inadequate damages awarded for loss of earnings and property. The solatia today are too small and too regularized to fulfill these functions, however. Usually the amount awarded is not over 100,000 yen in case of bodily injury, and from 100,000 to 200,000 yen in case of death.

If the victim dies, his parents, spouse, and children may claim solatium in their own right under article 711 of the Civil Code. It is disputed, how-

[14] One case denied the succession to the right to damages for loss of earnings of the deceased while suggesting that an independent right might accrue to the successors, but the case has not been influential. Murata v. Japan, Great Court of Judicature, III Civil Department, March 10, 1928, 7 Dai-han Minshū 152, 8 Hanrei Minji Hō 65 (note Suginohara).

[15] E.g., Endō v. Gōshi Kaisha Homma-gumi (Homma Group Partnership in Commendam Co.), Great Court of Judicature, IV Civil Department, Dec. 27, 1941, 20 Dai-han Minshū 1479, 21 Hanrei Minji Hō 412 (note Kaino); Terauchi v. Tōriku Jidōsha Unyu Kabushiki Kaisha (Toriku Motor Transport Co.), Great Court of Judicature, II Civil Department, May 8, 1936, Hōritsu Shimbun (The Law News) [hereafter cited Shimbun] no. 3987, at 17; Sato v. Meiki Tetsudō Kabushiki Kaisha (Meiki Railway Co.), Great Court of Judicature, V Civil Department, March 25, 1932, 21 Hōritsu Hyōron Zenshū (A Complete Critique of the Law), Mimpō (Civil Law) pt. at 251; Iwasaki v. Japan, Great Court of Judicature, II Civil Department, Feb. 16, 1926, 5 Dai-han Minshū 150, 6 Hanrei Minji Hō 102 (note Hirano); Yoshinaga v. Tsunoda, Great Court of Judicature, I Civil Department, April 20, 1920, 26 Dai Shin In Minji Hanketsu Roku (Record of Great Court of Judicature Civil Judgments) [hereafter cited Dai-han Minroku] 553.

ever, whether these near relatives may succeed to the decedent's right to solatium. The courts have said that, if before his death the deceased declares his intention to claim solatium from the wrongdoer, his right thereto becomes complete and passes upon his death to his heirs.[16] The declaration of intention may be found under questionable circumstances; for example, one court decided that the decedent had declared his intention to claim solatium by crying "zannen, zannen!" ("it's awful, awful!") on his deathbed.[17] Many jurists criticize this decision as based on a fiction; they insist that the right to solatium accrues at once to the injured person without any declaration on his part and that it should always pass to his heirs. On the other hand, a minority view asserts that the right to solatium is entirely personal and thus should never pass to a man's heirs.[18]

Practically speaking, however, it ordinarily makes little difference whether the relatives of the deceased can claim solatium only in their own right, under article 711, or succeed as well to the deceased's claim. Since these rights are largely congruent, under the majority view the heirs ordinarily have an option between the two forms of relief, with about equal damages under both. But in some situations the overlapping is not complete; for example, if the deceased had children, his parents cannot claim solatium as his heirs,[19] but only in their own right under article 711. Furthermore, when the successors are not the near relatives prescribed in article 711 — for example, if they are grandchildren or siblings — they can recover solatium only as heirs.

THE AUTOMOBILE DAMAGE COMPENSATION SECURITY LAW

The Damage Law can be best discussed broken down into three topics: liability, compulsory liability insurance, and governmental compensation of injured persons not otherwise compensated through insurance.

Liability

Article 3 of the law provides as follows:

A person who, for his own benefit, places an automobile in operational use, if he has injured the life or body of another, is bound to compensate him for the

[16] There are many precedents; e.g., Murata v. Japan, note 14; Honda v. Kabutomori, Great Court of Judicature, II Civil Department, June 5, 1919, 25 DAI-HAN MINROKU 962; Kozawa v. Keihin Denki Tetsudō Kabushiki Kaisha (Keihin Electric Railway Co.), Great Court of Judicature, II Civil Department, Oct. 3, 1910, 16 DAI-HAN MINROKU 621.

[17] The famous *Zannen* ("It's awful") case is Imai v. Yamato Unyu Kabushiki Kaisha (Yamato Transfer Co.), Great Court of Judicature, I Civil Department, May 30, 1927, SHIMBUN no. 2702, at 5.

[18] Representative of the general view is WAGATSUMA, JIMU KANRI, FUTŌ RITOKU, FUHŌ KŌI (Management of Affairs, Unjust Enrichment, Tort) 213 (1940), while KATO, note 9, at 259–62, takes the minority view.

[19] Arts. 887, 889–90 and 900 of the Civil Code prescribe inheritance in the following order: (1) lineal descendants (taking two thirds altogether) and spouse (one third); (2) lineal ascendants (one half) and spouse (one half); (3) brothers and sisters or their lineal descendants (one third) and spouse (two thirds).

damage which has arisen therefrom. Provided, however, that this does not apply if he can prove that he and the driver did not neglect care in the operation of the automobile, that there was willfulness or negligence on the part of the injured party or a third party other than the driver, and that there was no structural defect nor functional disorder in the automobile.

Article 3 thus shifts the burden of proof of fault from the injured party to the defendant. Since proof of the several defenses is difficult if not impossible, the law has created a liability which is closely akin to liability without fault.

Some concepts in article 3 are used in a special sense. The term "automobile," as defined in article 2(2) of the Road Transport Vehicle Law,[20] includes almost every kind of motor vehicle except motor-bikes, that is, passenger cars, trucks, buses, motorcycles, and motor scooters.

The "owner of an automobile or a person otherwise having the right to use an automobile, who, for his own benefit, places an automobile in operational use" is defined as a "holder" of a motor vehicle.[21] This term does not include an unauthorized operator, such as a thief. However, the broader language of article 3 is less restrictive and embraces the unauthorized operator as well. But a mere "driver" engaged by an owner, since he is not operating the vehicle "for his own benefit," is not liable under article 3 but only under the Civil Code.[22]

"Operation" is defined in article 2(2) of the Damage Law as the ordinary use of a motor vehicle without regard to whether it is used in the transportation of persons or goods. This definition is applied somewhat arbitrarily, however. If an unoccupied motor vehicle starts moving because it was improperly parked, or if a pedestrian is injured when a door of a parked vehicle is opened, any injury inflicted results from the "operation" of the vehicle. But when one driver, working on his vehicle at a service station, ignited a fire by dropping a spark that fell on a gasoline can, the injured service-station attendant was held to have no rights under the law because the accident did not result from the operation of a motor vehicle.[23]

Article 3 covers injuries to taxi passengers, for there are no specified injured persons who can claim recovery. As is pointed out below, however, it is disputed whether article 3 applies to injuries suffered by passengers who are either guests or members of the holder's family.

Coverage under article 3 is limited to the damages arising from death or personal injury; accordingly, the provisions of the Civil Code govern claims

[20] See note to Table 1.

[21] Automobile Damage Law, art. 2(3).

[22] For similar terminology see the German Motor Vehicle Law (Gesetz über den Verkehr mit Kraftfahzeugen), Law of May 3, 1909, art. 7, commented on in VON MEHREN, THE CIVIL LAW SYSTEM 436 (1957). Also see JIDŌSHA SONGAI BAISHŌ KENKYŪ KAI (Automobile Damage Study Group), JIDŌSHA SONGAI BAISHŌ HŌ NO KAISETSU (A Commentary on the Automobile Damage Compensation Security Law) 41 (1955).

[23] Arai v. Kyōei Kasai Hoken Sōgo Kaisha (Kyoei Mutual Fire Insurance Co.), Kobe District Court, April 18, 1959, 10 KAKYŪ MINSHŪ 781.

for property damage.[24] The exclusion of property-damage coverage in the law is due to the heavy economic burden on holders of motor vehicles that would result from nearly strict liability and compulsory insurance for property damage.

The holder bears the liability under article 3. Thus, if an employer is the holder, he must prove not only the absence of fault in his employee, but also other matters such as the fault of the injured person. The liability of the driver to his employer remains under article 715(3) of the Civil Code, if the employer can prove the fault of the employee. This right of indemnification, however, comes into existence only when the total damage exceeds the amount covered by the compulsory insurance, because the insurance covers both the holder and the driver.[25] Other matters not specifically mentioned in article 3, such as the measure of damages and comparative negligence, are still governed by the provisions of the Civil Code.

Compulsory Liability Insurance

No one is to operate a motor vehicle unless it is covered by insurance as required by article 5 of the law. When a contract of liability insurance has been concluded, the insurance company issues a certificate to the insured; the document must be kept in the vehicle during operation and must be presented to the proper administrative officers upon request and when any interest in the vehicle is to be transferred.[26] An insurance company may not refuse to write a contract of liability insurance.[27] In order to make these provisions effective, violation of any of them is punishable by fine or imprisonment;[28] for example, operating an uninsured vehicle may be punished by a fine of not more than 30,000 yen or imprisonment for not more than three months.[29]

The law does not provide who shall procure the policy of liability insurance; in practice, the holder generally takes it out.

Under the liability-insurance system, the insurer must indemnify the holder for any liability he has under article 3, up to certain limits.[30] The amount of insurance payments are prescribed by article 2 of the Enforce-

[24] Art. 4 of the Automobile Damage Law provides as follows: "The liability to compensate for damage of a person who, for his own benefit, places an automobile in operational use, besides being governed by the provisions of the prior article, is governed by the provisions of the Civil Code." Thus, while the Automobile Damage Law, being a special statute, supersedes the Civil Code, pursuant to art. 4, when an express provision is lacking in the former law, the Civil Code applies.

[25] See Automobile Damage Law, art. 11.

[26] Automobile Damage Law, arts. 7–9, 85.

[27] Automobile Damage Law, art. 24.

[28] Automobile Damage Law, arts. 87–91.

[29] Automobile Damage Law, art. 87.

[30] Automobile Damage Law, art. 11.

ment Order, implementing article 13 of the law, as follows: for death, 500,000 yen; for serious injury, 100,000 yen; for slight injury, 30,000 yen. These are the maximum benefits payable under compulsory insurance; when actual damages are less than those amounts, payments equal to the actual damages are to be made.[31]

We hardly need observe that these benefits are too low. Originally, indeed, the amount payable for death was only 300,000 yen, an amount which reflected the generally low level of damages in Japan and which was felt sufficient to cover damages in normal cases. But this valuation of life was often criticized, and in numerous cases damages were awarded that exceeded the insurance coverage. As a result, the coverage was raised in September 1960, but only to 500,000 yen.[32]

The premium for liability insurance must be approved by the Minister of Finance with the concurrence of the Minister of Transportation.[33] The Minister of Finance is not to give his approval unless the proposed rates are sufficient to ensure an efficient business operation without providing a profit.[34]

In the course of drafting the law, some legislators favored placing liability insurance under governmental management; but the insurance companies resisted that idea, and the responsibility for the insurance was ultimately entrusted to them. Although the operation is profitless and under government supervision, the insurance companies wanted it both because they wished to keep the government out of the insurance business and because they thought the sale of additional coverage on which they would earn a profit would be stimulated.

Premiums for compulsory insurance are based on a classification of motor vehicles, the figures being set in accordance with the approximate amount of loss caused by each category of vehicle. In the period 1955–1960, premiums have twice been raised.[35] For example, the annual premium for a taxi in Tokyo has risen from 7,880 to 19,960 yen; for a truck of normal size, from

[31] Automobile Damage Law, art. 15.

[32] By Cabinet Order No. 227 of 1960. Examples of damage awards made prior to 1960 exceeding the insurance coverage may be found in the following cases: Nakayama v. Yamaichi Suisan Kabushiki Kaisha (Yamaichi Marine Products Co.), note 10 above (an award of 4,100,468 yen); Uematsu v. Kusui, Takamatsu District Court, Nov. 5, 1958, 9 KAKYŪ MINSHŪ 2182 (an award of 430,000 yen); and Hiruma v. Japan, Tokyo District Court, Oct. 22, 1957, 2 FUHŌ KŌI NI KAN-SURU KAKYŪ SAIBANSHO MINJI SAIBAN REISHŪ (A Collection of Civil Cases in the Inferior Courts Concerning Torts) 247 (an award of 657,866 yen).

[33] Automobile Damage Law, arts. 25, 28.

[34] Automobile Damage Law, art. 25.

[35] According to statistics kept in the Automobile Bureau of the Ministry of Transportation, the total deficit incurred by the liability-insurance fund in 1955–1960 was about 4,294,000,000 yen. The largest deficit in this period, 1,778,000,000 yen, was incurred in 1959. Despite the opposition of the Ministry of Transportation, which was under pressure from taxi and truck operators, this deficit compelled the government to raise the premium rates.

5,030 to 8,900 yen; and for a private passenger car, from 2,410 to 2,780 yen.[36] The rate of rise, which has been resisted particularly by the taxi and trucking interests, reflects the relative increase in accidents and in resulting injuries, particularly the constantly increasing number of accidents caused by taxis, as well as by ordinary trucks, dump-trucks loaded with gravel, and concrete-mixer trucks, and the increase in 1960 of the minimum death payment from 300,000 to 500,000 yen.

Claims by an injured person are usually settled with the injurer, as mentioned above. Then the insured, the holder or the driver of an automobile, may demand payment from the insurance company to the extent that he has actually paid damages to the injured man.[37] An injured man, however, may claim compensation up to the amount of the insurance coverage from the insurance company directly; this right is provided in article 16(1), one of the excellent provisions of the law. When an insurance company has paid compensation to the injured person, it is deemed to have indemnified the insured under the policy.[38]

The insurance company ordinarily has no duty to indemnify under a contract of liability insurance if the damage was caused maliciously by the insured.[39] This is a solution resulting from the general principles of insurance law. So that the victim in such cases will not lose his rights to redress, however, article 16(4) provides that he can demand compensation directly from the insurance company. In such a case, the company can demand indemnification from the government, which is in turn subrogated to the right of the injured person to recover damages from the malicious tortfeasor.[40]

Before trial or final settlement, under article 17(1) an injured person may demand provisional payment of compensation from the insurance company; such anticipatory payments on direct demand give the victim temporary relief. The amounts of provisional payment are: for death, 120,000 yen; for serious injury, 20,000 or 10,000 yen, according to the degree of injury; for slight injury, 2,000 yen. Since these amounts correspond to the normal minimum damages recovered in litigation, the insurer generally need not fear an overpayment. If the amount of provisional payment should exceed the amount of compensation given by a court under article 16(1), the insurance company may demand repayment of the excess from the injured person.[41] But if the court found that the holder was not liable in

[36] See Automobile Damage Compensation Liability Insurance Rate Validation, Ministry of Finance Notification No. 466 of 1955, as amended by Ministry of Finance Notifications No. 22 of 1958, No. 140 of 1959, and No. 181 of 1959.

[37] Automobile Damage Law, art. 15.

[38] Automobile Damage Law, art. 16(3).

[39] Automobile Damage Law, art. 14.

[40] Automobile Damage Law, arts. 72(2), 76(2).

[41] Automobile Damage Law, art. 17(3).

damages, the insurance company need not attempt to recover from the injured person but may demand indemnification for the provisional payment from the government, which must in turn seek repayment from the injured person.[42]

The provisions on compulsory insurance do not apply to motor vehicles operated by the state, public corporations, prefectural governments, and the five major Japanese cities.[43] These holders presumably have the means to pay damages and are willing to do so. For holders of large fleets of vehicles, the law provides a system of self-insurance instead of liability insurance. Such possessors must obtain the approval of the Minister of Transportation; the standards for the grant of approval are ownership of more than two hundred vehicles (a bus being treated as two vehicles), the ability to pay damages, and the absence of danger of frequent accidents.[44] Regulations provide that the self-insurer must maintain a reserve fund and must manage the assets thereof in order to meet whatever motor-vehicle liability it might incur.[45]

Government Compensation

In the usual case the injured person has no difficulty in obtaining compensation for his injuries to the extent of the coverage of the liability insurance, but in some exceptional cases there is no such coverage. In these, the government pays compensation to the injured person, just as insurance companies often make direct payment to injured persons. Then the government is subrogated to the injured person's rights and may seek reimbursement from the injurer, who remains primarily liable. Thus an injured man always has the benefit of some kind of liability insurance. Governments do not ordinarily pay compensation for injuries incurred through an accident between private persons—in Japan, the only other example is the case of damage from atomic energy[46] — and this exceptional and progressive provi-

[42] Automobile Damage Law, arts. 17(4), 72(2), 76(3).

[43] Automobile Damage Law, art. 10. The cities are Osaka, Nagoya, Kyoto, Yokohama, and Kobe. Local Autonomy Law, Law No. 67 of 1947, art. 252-19(1); Cabinet Order Concerning the Designation of the Designated Cities of Article 252-19, Paragraph (1) of the Local Autonomy Law, Cabinet Order No. 254 of 1956. Tokyo comes under the head of "prefectural governments."

[44] Automobile Damage Law, arts. 55–56.

[45] Automobile Damage Law, art. 58; Automobile Damage Compensation Security Law Enforcement Regulations, Ministry of Transportation Order No. 66 of 1955, art. 20.

[46] Damage resulting from the employment of atomic energy is dealt with by two laws, both enacted in 1961: the Law Concerning Compensation of Atomic Energy Damage, Law No. 147 of 1961, and the Law Concerning Atomic Energy Damage Compensation Indemnification Contracts, Law No. 148 of 1961. The former establishes strict liability of the entrepreneur for injury arising from the employment of atomic energy. The entrepreneur is required to take out insurance against liability in the amount of 5,000,000,000 yen; in the event of injury not covered by the liability insurance — for example, damage resulting from earthquake, volcanic eruption, or normal operation, or when a claim is made after the ten year contractual restraint on the right to payment of insurance has run — the state will indemnify him

sion shows that the relief of persons injured in motor-vehicle accidents is considered a problem of vital importance.

The government compensates injured persons for loss of life or personal injuries resulting from the operation of a motor vehicle in two types of cases.[47] The first is that in which the injured person cannot demand damages under article 3 because the holder of the vehicle is unknown, that is, the case of the hit-and-run driver. Even if the driver or the holder of the automobile was covered by liability insurance, the injured person cannot take the benefit of the insurance. The second case is that in which the required coverage has not been taken out, either because the holder has not obtained liability insurance, whether forgetfully, neglectfully, or intentionally, or because the accident was caused by a thief or other unauthorized driver whom the compulsory insurance does not cover.

It is not unusual for the holder to fail to procure liability insurance. In 1959 only 78 percent of all motor vehicles were covered, and only 63 percent of the total number of motorcycles and scooters were insured.[48] The percentage of coverage has been gradually falling, owing in large measure to inadequate supervision. Perhaps better results would be obtained if the police were to take over this responsibility from the Ministry of Transportation.

Many accidents have thus been caused by uninsured vehicles. But in such cases, the possessor, fearful of the penalties for lack of liability insurance, often pays damages voluntarily. Therefore, as Table 5 at the end of the essay shows, the government has had to pay compensation in only a relatively small number of cases other than those involving a hit-and-run.

In a given case, the amount of governmental compensation is the same as the amount of liability-insurance benefits, and it has the same limits. When the government has paid, it is subrogated to the rights of the person compensated.[49] Obviously the government may demand reimbursement from a hit-and-run driver only when he has been identified; in fact, however, the percentage of arrests has proved quite high (60 to 67 percent).[50]

The funds for government compensation are provided through liability assessments paid by insurance companies and self-insurers to the govern-

---

for damages he pays. The state may enter into a contract with the entrepreneur for such indemnification; the state also renders to him assistance so that he can pay claims over 5,000,000,000 yen. These provisions are all aimed at the protection of the entrepreneur as well as of persons injured.

[47] Automobile Damage Law, art. 72(1).

[48] JIDŌSHA KYOKU (Automobile Bureau), UNYU-SHŌ (Ministry of Transportation), JIDŌSHA SONGAI BAISHŌ NEMPŌ, SHŌWA 36 NEN (Automobile Damage Compensation Annual Report, 1961) 2.

[49] Automobile Damage Law, art. 76.

[50] KEISATSU-CHŌ (Police Agency), SHŌWA 35 NEN KŌTSŪ JIKO TŌKEI (1960 Traffic Accident Statistics) 59. The percentage of arrests has been rising and in 1960 reached 67 percent for fatal accidents and 65 percent for accidents causing personal injuries.

ment, along with assessments paid by motor-vehicle holders who are excepted from liability insurance, such as public corporations and prefectural governments.[51] The state also keeps up a special fund equivalent in amount to assessments on its vehicles.[52] The amount of the yearly assessments paid on each vehicle is set by cabinet order.[53] The theory of the fund thus accumulated is that all motor-vehicle users should help injured persons who would otherwise probably not receive compensation. As it is, the state appropriates a considerable sum each year to cover part of the administrative expenses incurred by these compensation operations.[54]

When compensation has been paid because of an accident caused by an uninsured injurer, the government may levy a "negligence fine" against the persons liable.[55]

Some Problems of Motor-Vehicle Liability

Compulsory Liability Insurance in Practice

More than six years have passed since the adoption of the Automobile Damage Compensation Security Law. The law has been administered for the most part by insurance companies, which have established joint offices for assessment and handling of common problems. In addition to the ordinary compulsory liability insurance, the companies manage the compensation by the government. Thus they have become directly concerned with questions of civil liability under article 3. Something can be learned, therefore, about the way in which motor-vehicle accidents are handled under the law by examining the practices of the insurance companies.[56]

Since the adoption of the law, disputes over whether civil liability exists have decreased, both because it is very difficult to disprove all liability under article 3 and because any liability is covered by insurance in the normal case. But some legal problems relating to civil liability remain.

Many problems arise in connection with the assessment of damages, whether in a court action or in a settlement with the company. Some of these are practical; for example, steady losses from their compulsory-insurance operations, because of the increase in the number of accidents

[51] Automobile Damage Law, art. 78.

[52] Automobile Damage Law, art. 82(1).

[53] Cabinet Order Fixing the Amount of Automobile Damage Compensation Security Business Assessment, Etc., Cabinet Order No. 316 of 1955.

[54] Automobile Damage Law, art. 82(2).

[55] Automobile Damage Law, art. 79. This "negligence fine" is in the nature of an administrative penalty, differing from the Scandinavian concept. See Ehrenzweig, "Full Aid" Insurance for the Traffic Victim 30 & n.172 (1954).

[56] The following description of insurance-company practices is based on information furnished by the Joint Headquarters for Automobile Damage Compensation Liability Insurance. An account of some of these measures may be also found in Kimura, *Jidōsha Jiko to Songai Baishō* (Automobile Accidents and Damage Compensation), Jurist no. 172, at 44 (1959).

and the lag in raising premiums, have put great pressure on the companies to reduce insurance payments, with a resulting tendency for them to seek low settlements and verdicts. Other problems respecting the assessment of damages are theoretical; these are discussed below.

As can be seen in Table 6, which gives statistics of payment of insurance benefits, there has been a radical increase in motor-vehicle injuries, with a gradual rise in insurance payments. The latter results mainly from rises in prices and in earnings, but public opinion has played some role. The sudden rise in payments for death in 1961 resulted from the September 1960 increase in coverage to 500,000 yen; it will probably be yet higher in 1962, since the increased coverage applied only to contracts concluded thereafter, and the period of liability insurance is usually one year.

Insurance is normally paid to the injurer after he has paid damages; direct payment to the injured person is rare, both because the system is not widely known and because insurance companies prefer not to deal with the matter directly and often advise claimants who do come to them to talk with the injurer. When an insurance company does pay directly, it often demands that the injured person sign a document agreeing that he will not claim further damages or releasing the right to make such a claim. Such a document may bar further recoveries even if the injuries prove worse than was thought, or if the victim proves to be permanently injured. In my opinion, although the courts have not yet so held, the effect of such a document is doubtful in a case in which the victim was compelled by economic necessity to execute it and when the conditions have substantially changed.

Guest Passengers and Family Members

When an injured passenger is a guest or a member of the family of the injurer, it is disputed whether liability exists. Because there are no well-settled precedents or ruling theory, one can describe only the practice of the insurers in settling claims. That practice is to deny that a spouse — including a *de facto* spouse[57] — and the lineal relatives — the parents, children, grandparents, or grandchildren — have any right to recovery from the injurer. Siblings and more distant relatives are recognized as having a right. Guests have been dealt with on a case-to-case basis. Generally speaking, if a group of friends which is driving a rented car incurs an accident, they are regarded as common holders and as having no right to damages *inter se;* the same result is reached when a holder of a car drives with a friend in pursuance of a common plan, as, for example, to a mutually agreed destination and with expenses shared. But if someone is casually riding in a friend's automobile, he may claim damages from the holder.

[57] For a discussion of unregistered *de facto* marriages — so-called *naien* marriages — see Yozo Watanabe, "The Family and the Law: The Individualistic Premise and Modern Japanese Family Law," in this volume.

These results have considerable practical justification, but their theoretical basis is not clear. It would be quite logical to have a rule that a nonpaying passenger should not recover damages, in which case all the persons above would be excluded; such a rule, however, has not been developed so far in Japanese tort law. The principle might also be that a possessor of an automobile should be liable under any circumstances so long as he had injured another person; this approach would harmonize well with the provisions of the Civil Code respecting torts, which do not differentiate the rights of guests and family members. The middle position taken by the insurance companies is thus perhaps the most difficult one to justify doctrinally, although it may ultimately be accepted by the courts.

Assessment of Damages

The practice of insurers in assessing damages likewise has relatively little basis in established doctrine. Precedents are available, but it is usually very difficult to arrive at uniform principles for assessing damages from these cases. Insurance practice thus involves new standards that are not firmly based on decided cases.

In determining monthly earnings in cases of total disability, insurance practice takes the mean of the earnings of the preceding three months and adds to it one twelfth of any special earnings, such as bonuses, in the preceding year. The expected future earning period is fixed at the period remaining before age sixty if the injured person is under fifty, or, if he is over fifty, one half of his remaining life expectancy. The gross-earning loss is then figured by multiplying these two factors. The main objection to this technique, as some jurists point out, is that retirement or "severance pay" and expected future increases in monthly earnings are not taken into account in computing the gross loss of earnings.[58]

This figure must be reduced by any living expenses of an individual, separated from the family or household expenses. Insurance practice today allots expenses to each family member according to an index of consumption as follows: for the injured person, 1.0; for his spouse, 0.9; for a child under five, 0.3; for a child over five but under eleven, 0.4; and so on. In the case of a single man, 80 percent of his earnings is regarded as the amount of his living expenses. The index appears to be based on statistics of cost of living. The practice, because it is based on fixed figures, has the virtue of avoiding excessive reduction of gross earnings for living expenses, something that often happened in the past.

The gross figure must also be reduced for interim interest. Insurance practice uses Hoffman's method, deducting interest during the whole period

[58] KATO, note 9, at 227; KATO, FUHŌ KŌI HŌ NO KENKYŪ (Studies in the Law of Torts) 159 (1961); Sato, *Songai Baishō-gaku no Santei ni Tsuite* (On Assessing the Amount of Compensation for Damages), 75 KAIKEI (Accounting) 658, 665–70 (1956) (Sato is an accountant).

from the sum of earnings. This approach should be abandoned in favor of the approach now adopted by some courts of calculating the interest yearly, or, better yet, monthly, so as not to reduce the gross figure excessively.

If the injured person had no earnings — for example, if he was unemployed, a housewife, an old person, a student, or a child — it is not possible to calculate earnings according to the above principles. The expected earnings, or the average earnings for the victim's age, may be estimated on the assumption that he would have worked; in the case of a housewife, a value may be assigned to her services in the household. But these calculations are difficult and have not been generally adopted by the courts. Insurance practice takes certain fixed amounts to be the loss of earnings: for the housewife and the college student, 200,000 yen; for the high-school student, 150,000 yen; for the schoolboy, the rentier, or the unemployed person, 100,000 yen; and for the small child under school age (six years), 50,000 yen. These amounts seem unduly low. Although it is very difficult to find any standards, the amount of damages to be paid by the government in case of injuries caused by American military forces, for example, is two or three times as large, being at least 300,000 yen (except 250,000 yen for a small child).[59]

In insurance practice, there is a fixed amount for solatium according to the category into which the injured or killed person falls. The amounts paid are unfortunately not made public, but are certainly quite low. In any event, a fixed amount cannot be adequate; these damages should be fixed according to ages, the circumstances of the injury, and, if feasible, the status of the deceased person.

Table 7 shows total damages, including loss of earnings, solatium, and medical expenses. These figures were compiled from the statistics of the amount of insurance payments to various age groups during a two-year period. With respect to insurance payments for death, it should be noted that the current limit of 500,000 yen, and even the former limit of 300,000 yen, are higher than the average amount of recovery per person.

CONCLUSION

The great increase in recent years in motor-vehicle accidents can be attributed only in part to the rapid growth of the Japanese economy; a failure to change — particularly the lack of a modern street and highway system — has also contributed to the increase. Thus, even if higher damages had been provided, the deterrent effect of the Automobile Damage Security Compensation Law could not have brought about a startling decrease in

[59] Nihonkoku to Amerika Gasshūkoku to no aida no Anzen Hoshō Jōyaku ni Motozuki Chūryū-suru Amerika Gasshūkoku Guntai ni yori Songai o Uketa Mono ni Tai-suru Hoshō-kin narabi ni Mimai-kin no Shikyū ni Kan-suru Ken (Matter Concerning the Provision of Indemnification and Condolence Money to Persons Who Have Been Subjected to Damage by American Military Forces Present under the Security Treaty Between Japan and the United States of America), Cabinet Decisions of May 16, 1952 and Oct. 2, 1956.

the number of accidents, although the enactment of the law may have helped to reduce the totals. With all its shortcomings, however, the law has assisted persons suffering injuries. Prior to its enactment, the victim often received minimal damages or dropped his claim; now an injured person can always obtain compensation up to the amount of liability insurance and he can more easily recover additional damages.

Although the law's system of compensation, based on compulsory liability insurance and government compensation, is one of the most advanced in the world today, it still has several shortcomings. The amount of the insurance is inadequate, particularly in case of death. Even at the time the law was drafted some jurists argued that the coverage should be greater, but the point of view of the business world prevailed. Those who favored higher limits were content to establish the principle of compulsory insurance, with the expectation that the limits would gradually be raised. Regrettably, only one increase has been made. Of late, press campaigns have aroused public concern for the problem of motor-vehicle accidents; pressure is building up for an increase in coverage. In my view, the limit for a death payment should be set at not less than a million yen, preferably two million or more.

Another defect in the law is that it does not cover property damage. This exclusion stems from the insistence of the business world that premiums be as low as possible. But it is not logical that an injurer remains subject to normal liability under the Civil Code for damage to property while he is subjected in the same accident to the stricter liability for injury to the person under the Damage Law.

In time, this law will have a liberalizing effect on Japanese legal thinking in various areas, including the assessment of damages. Japanese doctrine and jurisprudence tend to be concerned with theoretical problems; practical details are too often ignored, such as the precise criteria under which damages are to be set or the principles regulating liability to nonpaying passengers and family members. The law inevitably and increasingly directs attention to such practical matters and should stimulate Japanese courts and scholars to give greater thought to the more concrete issues that arise in daily life.

TABLE 1. Number of Motor Vehicles in Japan

Year	Number of motor vehicles	Index
1950	413,732	100
1951	531,570	129
1952	759,757	184
1953	1,094,784	265
1954	1,338,195	323
1955	1,501,740	363
1956	1,775,120	429
1957	2,069,143	500
1958	2,404,118	581
1959	2,898,479	701
1960	3,573,168	864
1961	4,440,100	1,073

Note. "Motor vehicle" here is equivalent to the statutory concept of "automobile" — the term used in the Automobile Damage Law (see art. 2(1)) — defined in article 2(2) of the Road Transport Vehicle Law, Law No. 185 of 1951, as "a contrivance manufactured for the purpose of movement on land by means of a motor, which does not use a track or a trolley wire, or a contrivance manufactured for the purpose of movement on land by being drawn thereby, other than . . . motorbikes . . ." This definition includes almost every kind of automotive vehicle — the passenger car, the truck with three, four, or more wheels, the bus, the motorcycle, and the motor scooter.

Source. 1950–60: CHŌSA KYOKU (Investigation Bureau), KEIZAI KIKAKU-CHŌ (Economic Planning Agency), KEIZAI YŌRAN 1962 (1962 Economic Survey) 140 (1961). 1961: Unpublished statistics supplied by the Ministry of Transportation.

TABLE 2. Types of Motor Vehicles in Japan

Type	1950	1961
Total	413,732 (100%)	4,440,100 (100%)
Trucks, total	278,800 (67)	1,543,961 (35)
Ordinary trucks	120,385 (29)	271,575 (6)
Small trucks (with 4 or 3 wheels)	155,624 (38)	1,265,542 (29)
Trailers	2,791 (1)	6,844 (0)
Autobuses	19,812 (5)	65,418 (2)
Passenger cars, total	100,977 (24)	2,742,558 (62)
Automobiles with 4 wheels	44,428 (11)	602,344 (14)
Small automobiles (with 3 or 2 wheels)	11,351 (3)	45,903 (10)
Motor scooters or miniature automobiles	44,798 (11)	2,094,311 (42)
Automobiles for special uses	14,043 (3)	88,163 (2)

Source. 1950: CHŌSA KYOKU (Investigation Bureau), KEIZAI KIKAKU-CHŌ (Economic Planning Agency), KEIZAI YŌRAN 1962 (1962 Economic Survey) 140 (1961). 1961: Unpublished statistics supplied by the Ministry of Transportation.

TABLE 3. Results of Motor-Vehicle Accidents

	Accidents		Individuals killed		Individuals injured	
Year	Number	Index	Number	Index	Number	Index
1948	16,506	100	2,342	100	13,465	100
1949	20,089	122	2,214	95	16,139	120
1950	28,347	172	2,779	119	21,827	162
1951	36,623	222	3,157	135	27,556	205
1952	53,642	325	3,437	147	29,304	218
1953	74,095	449	3,761	161	54,426	404
1954	86,534	524	5,187	221	66,154	491
1955	85,237	516	4,623	197	67,351	500
1956	110,486	669	5,486	234	90,220	670
1957	130,448	790	6,209	265	108,028	802
1958	148,345	899	6,735	288	124,410	924
1959	173,888	1,053	8,218	351	146,841	1,091
1960	400,527	2,427	9,689	414	236,303	1,755
1961	435,689	2,640	10,146	433	246,268	1,829

Note. Accidents not involving motor vehicles are those between streetcars, trolley buses, motorbikes, bicycles, and pedestrians. The figures after 1960 include minor accidents involving motor vehicles and the dramatic increase of that year over 1959 is due in part to this inclusion.

Source. 1948–60: KEISATSU-CHO (Police Agency), SHŌWA 35 NEN KŌTSU JIKO TŌKEI (1960 Traffic Accident Statistics) 11. 1961: Unpublished statistics supplied by the Police Agency.

TABLE 4. Individuals Killed, by Type of Motor-Vehicle Accident

Type	1950	1960
Total	3,046 (100%)	13,293 (100%)
Collision with another motor vehicle	32 (1)	678 (5)
Collision with pedestrian	1,857 (61)	5,441 (41)
Collision with bicycle	216 (7)	1,706 (13)
Collision with train	150 (5)	663 (5)
Other collisions	53 (2)	161 (1)
Running off the road	150 (5)	620 (5)
Overturning on the road	95 (3)	168 (1)
Motorbike accidents	80 (3)	3,478 (26)
Other accidents	413 (14)	378 (3)

Source. 1950: Kōsei Tōkei Kyōkai (Welfare Statistics Association), *Kokumin Eisei no Dōkō — Shōwa 36 Nen* (Trends in National Health — 1961), 8 KŌSEI NO SHIHYŌ (Welfare Indices) no. at 10, 34. 1960: Unpublished statistics supplied by the Ministry of Transportation.

TABLE 5. Number of Demands for Government Compensation (February 1956 to March 1961)

Type of injury	Hit-and-run driver	Uninsured (A)[a]	Uninsured (B)[b]	Total	Compensation[c]
For death	831	377	32	1,240	7
For serious injury	2,639	460	35	3,134	13
For slight injury	2,005	95	12	2,112	1
Total	5,475	932	79	6,486	21

[a] Injuries caused by automobiles not covered by liability insurance.
[b] Injuries caused by unlicensed drivers who are not insured.
[c] Compensation to insurance companies under Automobile Damage Law, art. 72(2).
Source. JIDŌSHA KYOKU (Automobile Bureau), UNYU-SHŌ (Ministry of Transportation), JIDŌSHA SONGAI BAISHŌ NEMPŌ, SHŌWA 36 NEN (Automobile Damage Compensation Annual Report, 1961) 91.

TABLE 6. Payments of Liability Insurance

	For death			For serious injury			For slight injury		
Year[a]	Number of persons	Amount of benefits	Per person	Number of persons	Amount of benefits	Per person	Number of persons	Amount of benefits	Per person
1955[b]	3,502	830,930,380	237,273	19,021	1,088,825,910	57,243	20,619	200,224,058	9,711
1956	4,961	1,225,511,215	247,030	26,905	1,596,522,807	59,339	26,186	284,778,562	10,875
1957	5,735	1,419,406,569	247,499	33,152	1,974,359,091	59,555	30,776	333,252,801	10,828
1960[c]	8,269	2,147,181,680	259,666	46,797	2,833,498,947	60,549	38,474	432,674,090	11,246
1961 (to June)	769	234,517,059	304,964	4,360	271,758,501	62,330	3,211	36,935,027	11,503

[a] This is the Japanese fiscal year, from April 1 through March 31.
[b] Figures for 1955 through 1957 cover only payments (made in the period ending in March 1960) under contracts of liability insurance concluded in those years.
[c] Figures for 1960 and 1961 (to June) cover all insurance payments actually made in those periods, regardless of when the contracts were concluded.
Source. 1955–57: JIDŌSHA KYOKU (Automobile Bureau), UNYU-SHŌ (Ministry of Transportation), JIDŌSHA SONGAI BAISHŌ NEMPŌ, SHŌWA 36 NEN (Automobile Damage Compensation Annual Report, 1961) 84–86. 1960–61: JIDŌSHA SONGAI BAISHO SEKININ HOKEN KYŌDŌ HOMBU (Joint Headquarters for Automobile Damage Compensation Liability Insurance), ZENKOKU KYŌDŌ SATEI JIMUSHO TSUKIBETSU SATEI KETTEI-GAKU ICHIRAN HYŌ (The National Joint Assessment Office Monthly Tables of Assessed Amounts).

TABLE 7. Amount of Insurance Payment by Age Groups

		For death		For serious injury		For slight injury	
Age	Sex	Number of persons	Payments per person	Number of persons	Payments per person	Number of persons	Payments per person
Under 6	Male	519	152,244	1,223	43,784	1,278	7,601
	Female	348	147,764	695	44,815	712	6,698
	Total	867	150,446	1,918	44.158	1,990	7,278
6–16	Male	483	194,948	2,644	48,213	2,462	7,924
	Female	205	193,615	1,166	48,438	1,240	7,484
	Total	688	194,551	3,810	48,404	3,702	7,777
16–21	Male	348	266,715	2,757	55,837	2,573	9,149
	Female	95	258,417	848	55,610	1,042	9,149
	Total	443	264,936	3,605	55,784	3,615	9,549
21–31	Male	809	287,798	5,328	62,206	5,538	11,097
	Female	114	272,239	1,404	57,538	1,681	10,120
	Total	923	285,876	6,732	61,233	7,219	10,869
31–41	Male	516	294,520	3,075	64,297	3,114	12,982
	Female	91	287,129	924	59,298	1,121	11,250
	Total	607	293,431	3,999	63,142	4,235	12,523
41–51	Male	531	293,311	2,793	67,596	2,548	13,434
	Female	143	286,953	927	62,895	935	11,305
	Total	674	291,959	3,720	66,424	3,483	12,862
51–61	Male	575	290,306	2,547	66,259	2,169	13,968
	Female	158	277,382	961	60,673	773	11,515
	Total	733	287,520	3,463	64,782	2,942	13,324
61–71	Male	480	278,499	1,665	65,346	1,309	13,466
	Female	150	237,526	737	60,355	479	10,788
	Total	630	268,744	2,402	63,814	1,788	12,748
Over 71	Male	266	238,985	571	62,063	424	11,866
	Female	166	202,882	483	60,070	240	10,240
	Total	432	225,112	1,054	61,150	664	11,279
Total	Male	4,527	258,585	22,603	60,430	21,415	11,306
	Female	1,470	222,444	8,100	56,568	8,223	9,766
	Total	5,997	249,743	30,703	59,411	29,638	10,918

Note. This table shows payments from April 1958 to March 1960 to persons insured under contracts concluded in the fiscal year 1958.

Source. JIDŌSHA KYOKU (Automobile Bureau), UNYU-SHŌ (Ministry of Transportation), JIDŌSHA SONGAI BAISHŌ NEMPŌ, SHŌWA 36 NEN (Automobile Damage Compensation Annual Report, 1961) 69.

COMMENTARY: PART II

Arthur Taylor von Mehren

COMMENTING on the pessimism shown in Masami Ito's paper about the future of judicial review in Japan, Douglas Maggs remarked that the Supreme Court of the United States, after *Marbury v. Madison*,[1] did not hold another congressional act unconstitutional until the *Dred Scott* case some fifty years later.[2] Ito replied that he was not concerned that only two statutes had been held unconstitutional. The results would be acceptable if the court's reasoning indicated sufficient concern for individual safeguards, particularly in the field of human rights, the subject of his paper, but the public-welfare test applied to this class of cases emphasizes the interests of the state and always seems to require a holding of constitutionality. The comments of others[3] revealed similar concern that the Supreme Court would interpret the concept of the nonjusticiable "political question" too broadly, to the detriment of fundamental human rights.

On the other hand, in criminal due-process cases the Supreme Court has gone rather far in protecting defendants.[4] For example, a person cannot be convicted on the basis of his confession alone, and confessions made after long detention (apparently a fairly typical practice of Japanese law-enforcement authorities) are set aside. This area does not involve the constitutionality of legislation and thus the public-welfare doctrine; instead, the concept of what is due process expresses the society's recognition of man, even the criminal, as a sentient being.[5]

The conference recognized that judicial review cannot be discussed abstractly, torn out of the social context within which it operates. In some respects judicial review of legislation in America has developed to a degree not paralleled anywhere else, even in other parts of the Western world, and thus does not provide an appropriate standard against which to compare other systems. The American institution depends in large measure upon

Note. At various places, the conference participant who suggested or particularly emphasized a point is named. The essay by Ichiro Kato, "The Treatment of Motor-Vehicle Accidents: The Impact of Technological Change on Legal Relations," was not available at the conference and is, therefore, not discussed in this commentary.

[1] 1 Cranch (5 U.S.) 137 (1803).

[2] Dred Scott v. Sandford, 19 How. (60 U.S.) 393 (1857).

[3] Especially Professor Hashimoto.

[4] As pointed out by Mr. Oppler and Mr. Coleman.

[5] See Tanabe, "The Process of Litigation: An Experiment with the Adversary System," in this volume.

the society's tendency to frame political and economic questions in terms of legality, upon the American habit of entrusting perplexing questions of policy and values to the legal profession for articulation and resolution, and upon the prestige of law and of the legal profession. Reinforcing these habits is the American's tendency to be litigious when he feels his rights have been ignored or infringed.[6] These characteristics are rooted in the particular political and social history of the United States, and none of these elements is present in the social setting within which the Japanese Supreme Court approaches judicial review. Furthermore, the willingness to entrust important decisions to the judiciary may depend on the widely shared, although unexpressed, belief that the judiciary will act in accordance with the accepted purposes and principles of the society. The judiciary, an unrepresentative group in the sense that it is not responsible to the people through a genuine election — the essentially symbolic control exercised over Supreme Court judges by the constitutionally provided popular review can hardly substitute for an election — is not well adapted to selecting fundamental principles. It is not clear whether even today Japan's democratic institutions represent a consensus on these fundamental principles.[7]

In this context the achievements of the Japanese Supreme Court are quite remarkable.

The relatively short experience with judicial review is reflected in the attitudes of all parts of the legal profession toward constitutional problems. In contrast to the American experience in which civil rights were evolved in a series of pragmatic compromises between the requirements of the state and the needs of the individual, in Japan such rights, now constitutionally guaranteed, were "suddenly handed down from above to the people." [8] It is not surprising, then, that Japanese judges, like Japanese society as a whole, tend to view these rights, expressed as they are in unqualified language, rather abstractly and absolutely.[9]

[6] Mr. Oppler made the related statement that before human rights can be protected through judicial processes, the Japanese must be persuaded to litigate these matters.

[7] Professors Schwartz and Craig emphasized this point. Craig remarked that at times the degree of ideological polarization in Japan seems so great as to lead to pessimism respecting the future of democratic institutions.

[8] Procurator Abe.

[9] Procurator Abe advanced, as examples of such an abstract and absolutist approach, the District Court decisions in the *Sunakawa* and *Tomabechi* cases. Japan v. Sakata, Tokyo District Court, March 30, 1959, 1 KAKYŪ SAIBANSHO KEIJI SAIBAN REISHŪ (A Collection of Criminal Cases in the Inferior Courts) 776 (holding that the stationing of United States forces in Japan under the security treaty between the two nations is unconstitutional under art. 9 of the Japanese Constitution) — for an English translation of the decision, see 4 JAPANESE ANN. INT'L. L. 97 (1960); Tomabechi v. Japan, Tokyo District Court, Oct. 19, 1953, 4 GYŌSEI JIKEN SAIBAN REISHŪ (A Collection of Judicial Precedents Concerning Administrative Cases) 2540, *reversed on revision*, Supreme Court, Grand Bench, June 8, 1960, 14 SAIKŌ SAIBANSHO MINJI HANREI SHŪ (A Collection of Civil Supreme Court Cases) 1206 (holding the dissolution of the Diet ineffective because one member of the cabinet had given only oral consent to, and had not signed, the instrument of dissolution).

As with any institution, the work of the Supreme Court of Japan is affected by its structure and membership.[10] The Court is composed of fifteen justices, of whom five are, as the tradition has developed, to be career judges and five lawyers. Both the conception of the law held by this group and its conditioning experiences lead the lawyers and career judges to be hesitant to declare legislation unconstitutional or to interfere with governmental process on constitutional grounds.[11] The suggestion that the Japanese bar does not prepare the complex issues of constitutional litigation in such a manner as to facilitate wise resolution by the courts[12] may also reflect inexperience with this type of case. Generalization is of course difficult, and a high level of appellate presentation is shown in some cases. But in many cases, and especially in the field of criminal procedure, the briefs and arguments are deficient.[13] Furthermore, academic discussion does not seem to perform the role of contributing to a mature understanding of the issues. The assistance given the Supreme Court in the *Sunakawa* case[14] by the scholarly comments contrasts with the usual discussion, which tends to be dogmatic, abstract, and ideologically oriented.[15]

The work of the Japanese courts described in Ito's essay, and in Kiminobu Hashimoto's discussion of judicial review of administrative action as well, was also considered to be of potentially great significance for the development of a consciousness of rights and for a more thoroughgoing legalization of dispute resolution. The mere fact that public discussion and controversy can center on legal questions is significant.[16] Takeyoshi Kawashima noted the relatively large amount of litigation involving these public-law problems as compared with the paucity of litigation in private areas. The explanation of this phenomenon is in part political—the opposition political parties have encouraged and supported litigation with a view not only to fostering broader acceptance of their thinking and principles but also to harassing the

[10] This was emphasized by Judge Tanabe.

[11] See Judge Tanabe's remarks quoted on p. 238 above.

[12] Mr. Rabinowitz.

[13] Professor Hashimoto.

[14] Japan v. Sakata, Supreme Court, Grand Bench, Dec. 16, 1959, 13 SAIKŌ SAIBANSHO KEIJI HANREI SHŪ (A Collection of Criminal Supreme Court Cases) 3225—for an English version of the decision, see 4 JAPANESE ANN. INT'L L. 103 (1960) and GENERAL SECRETARIAT, SUPREME COURT OF JAPAN, JUDGMENT UPON THE CASE OF THE SO-CALLED "SUNAKAWA CASE" (1960). The decision is discussed in Oppler, *The Sunakawa Case: Its Legal and Political Implications*, 76 POL. SCI. Q. 241 (1961); Yokota, *Renunciation of War in the New Japanese Constitution—As Interpreted by the Supreme Court in the Sunakawa Judgment*, 4 JAPANESE ANN. INT'L L. 16 (1960).

[15] Mr. Coleman. Particular reference was made to Professor Ito's article prior to judgment on the problem of the case. See Ito, *Jōyaku no Iken Shinsa* (Reviewing the Unconstitutionality of Treaties), 31 HŌRITSU JIHŌ (Law Journal) no. 5, at 120, 124–25 (1959).

[16] Professor Craig. Mr. Oppler observed that a case like the *Sunakawa* decision, which involved the whole future of the government and of the Liberal-Democratic Party, must have made an impression on many ordinary citizens.

government.[17] But the explanation for the relatively greater amount of litigation in the public-law domain may lie deeper and relate to the general problem of rights consciousness in Japan. Perhaps the public-law field is a particularly apt arena for the emergence of rights consciousness in a society such as Japan. As indicated in the discussion of Kawashima's essay,[18] the traditional Japanese approach to dispute resolution assumes controversies arising within a group. However, the emergence of the modern state, with its political assumptions and its governmental apparatus, has produced a public law that considers the individual and the state as its basic units. If any group, in the traditional sense, exists today in the public-law area, the group is coextensive with the society (or, if the particular problem is not approached on the national level, with the social group that corresponds to the relevant governmental subdivision). Consequently, public-law disputes can only rarely be said to arise within a group that is capable, sociologically speaking, of effecting reconciliation in the traditional sense. Moreover, a solution in terms of power hardly recommends itself; the state's position vis à vis the individual is always overwhelmingly superior. The situation is one that requires new techniques and machinery through which dispute resolution can be effected; the law and the courts offer just such an alternative. The attitudes thus fostered by public-law controversies can, in time, hardly fail to influence the individual's thinking about dispute resolution in the private-law area.[19]

The conference discussion next focused more intensively on Kiminobu Hashimoto's essay, "The Rule of Law: Some Aspects of Judicial Review of Administrative Action." Judicial review of administrative action, though less dramatic than review of the constitutionality of legislation, is probably far more significant in protecting the rights of citizens.

Because the government is constantly affecting an individual through a myriad of relations, the rights he is supposed to enjoy and the procedure of vindicating these rights in a court or before some impartial body have enormous immediate, practical significance. It is not only actual litigation which protects the otherwise largely defenseless citizen against positive administrative abuse; the mere possibility of litigation disciplines and curbs the conduct of administrative bodies.

Though much of the post-1945 discussion of Japanese administration has been in American terms, it should be remembered that the tasks of the Japanese administration are, in many respects, significantly different from those of the federal agencies in Washington around whose work so much

[17] Professor Maggs remarked that dissident or minority groups, such as the Jehovah's Witnesses and the National Association for the Advancement of Colored People, have contributed largely to the development of American constitutional law.

[18] "Dispute Resolution in Contemporary Japan."

[19] Mr. Steiner emphasized this last point.

of American administrative law has evolved. In the United States, federal agencies are entrusted with regulatory powers over large sectors of the economy. In Japan significantly less governmental regulation of this kind occurs. The Japanese economy is highly regulated, but regulation tends to take unofficial and informal forms. Consequently, Japanese administrative law is developing in a setting very different from that of the federal administrative law in the United States.

The discussion of the three criminal-law papers began with consideration of the degree to which Japanese society uses criminal law as a means of social control. In traditional Japan,[20] criminal laws were considered the impositions of a remote, political authority rather than as acts of agents of the people, and local communities held values and standards that diverged from those of the criminal law and had recourse to nonlegal sanctions — ostracism, rumor, and boss-authority. These attitudes and practices still persist to some extent. For example, Kawashima described a famous case of ostracism in modern times. The daughter of a local policeman reported an election scandal, involving major political leaders in the village, to the public procurators' office. Following the arrest of these leaders, the policeman's family was ostracized. At first the procurators' office praised the girl's courage; but gradually, as public criticism was increasingly felt, not only the police but also the Bureau for the Protection of Human Rights withdrew their support of the girl. Finally, the girl's teacher became involved, because she should have taught the girl better manners, and was forced to resign.

Japanese opinion at the conference was unanimous in holding that these extralegal standards and practices should be supplanted by the criminal law. Some Western scholars were less certain that this course was necessarily desirable. Norval Morris asserted that, in many respects, unofficial community control is more satisfactory than social control through the criminal law. If this is so, the decline in control resulting from the dismantling of these unofficial controls may be potentially more dangerous than the present aspects which are disapproved.

In discussing more particular characteristics of Japanese criminal law, it was remarked[21] that the Japanese law, as compared with criminal law in the United States, recognized relatively few social-welfare crimes; that is to say, situations in which responsibility attaches to an objective state of fact without regard to the defendant's state of mind. The Japanese approach doubtless relates in part to an element in traditional thinking — the very high degree of recognition of other persons as sentient human beings. This is an element often overlooked in emphasizing another strand of traditional thinking —

[20] As Professor Kawashima pointed out.
[21] By Professor Braucher.

the imposition of collective responsibility.[22] John Pelzel offered the tentative hypothesis that the emphasis on subjective elements in Japanese criminal law reflects both a belief that each individual's consciousness is of primary importance in maintaining the social order and the absence of any conception of right or wrong in an absolute sense. Kohji Tanabe commented that the emphasis on the subjective elements of guilt also relates in part to the manner in which trials were conducted in prewar Japan. A trial was a very "moral" experience, in which the judge attempted to lead the accused to a state of repentance and frequently visited him in prison after conviction.

Another aspect of Japanese criminal law and its administration that aroused considerable interest was the role of the procuracy — in particular, the procurator's very wide discretion with respect to the initiation of prosecution.[23] Atsushi Nagashima stated that no indictment was brought in 60 percent of the cases brought to the public procurators' office; on the other hand, conviction was obtained in 99.6 percent of the cases prosecuted. Perhaps because of the traditionally lenient attitude of Japanese society toward offenders and the availability of nonlegal modes of deterrence and rehabilitation — in particular the family and, more generally, a close-knit, stable, and very homogeneous community — this wide discretion seems to have met with rather general approval. First offenders are especially likely to be released without indictment. The feeling is that prosecution brands a person as a criminal and should not occur unless the suspect deserves such a reputation. Moreover, once a person is so branded, his rehabilitation becomes much more problematic and difficult.

Interestingly enough, the exercise of discretion by the procuracy developed rather gradually and without any specific statutory basis. There was no clear legal basis for the exercise of such discretion until 1924. The so-called Inquest of Prosecution was introduced after World War II to act as a check on the exercise of this discretion.[24] This "embryonic grand jury" has an advisory power to recommend indictments. Its report is sent to the procurator's superior and made public. Nagashima stated that, between 1949 and 1958, 14,000 applications were made for review by the Inquest of Prosecution, and 1,500 complaints of nonprosecution were returned. Of these, 260 were ultimately prosecuted and 180 found guilty.[25] In evaluating the high degree of discretion exercised by the procuracy, it is of great significance that the

[22] Professor Pelzel.

[23] It should be noted that, by law, the police have no discretion but must investigate all suspected crimes and report the results to the public procurator. In fact, as is inevitable and doubtless desirable, the police exercise a considerable discretion in investigating and reporting.

[24] Described by Mr. Oppler.

[25] The practice, as reported by Procurator Nagashima, is for the chief procurator, after receiving such a recommendation, to assign the case to another procurator for further investigation and re-evaluation. The rate of conviction obtained when such cases are prosecuted is 83.3 percent, strikingly lower than the 99.6 percent conviction rate ordinarily achieved.

procurators are career professionals who receive the same basic training as judges and enjoy a high degree of independence. The procuracy, headed by the Procurator-General, is technically under the Minister of Justice; however, he does not exercise any direct control over an individual case. Each procurator enjoys full independence with respect to prosecution. Haruo Abe stated that, in his experience, no superior had ever sought to influence the handling of a case.

Allan Smith contrasted, in terms very favorable to the Japanese procedure, the career procuracy with the district-attorney system of the United States. The Japanese system almost eliminates the risk, inherent in American arrangements, of the prosecutor's discretion being exercised to further political ends. The disposition of cases without attaching the formal stigma of guilt — which, modern penology teaches us, inhibits rehabilitation — is facilitated. Finally, official recognition of the discretionary element, which a procurator must always exercise in some degree, raises the prestige and importance of the office and provides a basis for accumulating experience and insight that can be transmitted in the form of a tradition. The esprit thus fostered may well attract better men to the profession.

Others were more reserved in their evaluation. Ryuichi Hirano, basing his position upon the principle of the rule of law, asked whether the judicial process should not play a larger role in the handling of suspects. The enormous powers exercised by the procuracy can be abused. Indeed, certain current practices pose, in Hirano's opinion, a threat to civil liberties. The procuracy often offers to release a suspect without prosecution if he will accept a kind of voluntary probation.[26] Despite attempts by the Ministry of Justice to formalize the procedure, it is still totally unregulated. Thus a person may be placed in a status normally thought to be that of a lawbreaker on grounds totally inadequate to obtain a conviction. Because of the procuracy's tendency to emphasize deterrence while the courts are more interested in rehabilitation, the practice, Hirano suggests, does not operate harmoniously with the formally accepted penology. It was also suggested that the practical consequence of the procurator's high degree of discretion, coupled with a conviction rate of close to 100 percent, might be a tendency for the procurator to confuse his role with that of the judge. To the extent that the procurator considers prosecution equivalent to conviction, he may find it hard to exercise his broad discretion wisely.

Alfred Oppler agreed, suggesting that, in his judgment, Abe and Nagashima somewhat idealized the procurator's role. In prewar Japan, the procuracy dominated the enforcement process because the judiciary did not exercise a fully independent judgment. The creation after World War II of a completely independent judicial branch was partly motivated by the

[26] Procurator Nagashima confirmed this practice, at least in Kanagawa prefecture, which includes the city of Yokohama.

procuracy's previous dominance. Even so, in Oppler's opinion, the old habit of following the procurator's recommendation still retains some strength. The very high rate of convictions obtained by the procuracy is also due, in part, to the view of many defense attorneys (a view connected with the traditional Japanese attitude toward law) that their clients should plead guilty with mitigating circumstances to avoid upsetting the judges and procurators and to emphasize their repentance and desire to be reintegrated into the group.

Even if criminal law is considered from the broader angle of its general impact on society, it was suggested that criminal law in action has to be defined more in terms of the operations of the procuracy than the judicial administration of the Penal Code. Moreover, it appears that the procuracy's decisions with respect to prosecution are based on many considerations other than the applicability to the particular situation of the substantive criminal law, which means that criminal law in practice may be quite different from the code.

The institutional framework of Japanese criminal justice, with its corps of highly trained professionals in the procuracy, seems much better adapted than the American system, which lacks such a group, to the introduction of those facets of contemporary criminological thinking that emphasize treatment. A shift to a highly individualized approach to crime, emphasizing predictions with respect to the defendant's chances of rehabilitation and relying on "treatment" rather than punishment, can pose serious threats to individual liberty and raises problems, still largely unexplored, for the rule of law. To the extent that Japan moves along this road, it may find in the procuracy an institution capable of providing a much needed "judicial" element in a very new pattern of relations between the individual and the state.

An understanding of the family and of the patterns of family activity gives insight into many aspects of the society and of the lives of its members. Yozo Watanabe's essay on "The Family and the Law: The Individualistic Premise and Modern Japanese Family Law" thus casts light on many aspects of Japanese life and of the influence of legal rules and institutions on that life.

Before World War II, Japanese family law emphasized the hierarchical nature of the family.[27] Today, family law focuses more on the individual, with consequent subordination of the interests of the family as a collectivity.[28] Just as before World War II, the present legal patterns do not fully correspond with the reality. Traditionally, the family was less hierarchical than is usually assumed; a far more significant characteristic was the emphasis on

[27] Professor Beardsley.

[28] Professor Kawashima. He also remarked that, though the prewar family law related to the samurai family, many other kinds of families were to be found in Japan. In the nonsamurai families, the hierarchical element was less strong, with power being diffused rather widely among the elders. But the emphasis on the collectivity remained great.

the group's interest to the derogation of individual needs or desires.[29] Today, the hierarchical element in the Japanese family has been still further weakened by social change, economic developments, and provisions of newly enacted laws. The collectivist tendency — the emphasis on the group's good — still remains strong, however.[30]

Basically, postwar Japanese family law destroys much of the legal structure that supported the hierarchical and collectivist conception of the family.[31] As Watanabe's essay points out, contemporary Japanese family law no longer legally subordinates the individual's interest to that of the family group. These legal changes do not, sociologically speaking, make certain the decline of the family group. In large measure, they do no more than remove possible legal impediments to a growing emphasis on individualism flowing from westernization, urbanization, and industrialization.

These social changes do mean that much of the functional basis for the hierarchical and collectivist family has disintegrated. As the economy and the culture become more diverse, increasing opportunities for individual financial independence will encourage individualism at the expense of the family.[32] These changes have reached even into the countryside, though the rural areas are still significantly less individualistic than the cities.[33] Thus, while in the old days the eldest son had to stay on the farm, greater flexibility exists today; he can go to college and take up a professional career while the second son takes the farm.[34]

Takeyoshi Kawashima described a study undertaken in 1951–53 by the Japanese Federated Attorneys' Association. In postwar family law, equal division of the parent's property among the children is the rule.[35] The purpose of the study was to determine the effect of the new rule on the inheritance of land. Division of the farm property on the parent's death was not uncommon in some parts of rural Japan even before World War II in districts in which the farmer had an opportunity to earn a supplementary income from office or factory work. If this arrangement was possible, the

[29] Professor Pelzel. Professor Kawashima agreed, asserting that the principle of corporate solidarity was definitely more important than the hierarchical element.

[30] Professor Kawashima.

[31] Professor Cavers.

[32] Professor John Hall.

[33] Professor Beardsley. The explanation, aside from a slower rate of cultural change generally in rural areas, is perhaps largely found in the economic necessity of preserving the existing small units. Division means fragmentation of land holdings and economic units too small to be viable. Mr. Steiner remarked that, in spite of the equal-division rule, excessive division of farm property has been almost entirely avoided by the practice of filing waivers. In urban areas, family property is more readily divisible and equal division is more usual.

[34] Mr. Steiner.

[35] Mr. Oppler remarked that the occupation had left this decision to the Japanese. In his opinion, the abolition of the traditional system, in which the collective house property passed from eldest son to eldest son, was mainly due to militant feminists, particularly the women members of the legislative committees preparing Diet legislation.

eldest son often preferred to divide up the farm because part-time farm work plus factory or office employment would yield a larger total income than he could derive from full-time work on the farm. This tendency toward part-time farming increased during the last war because of the shortage of animals and of manpower. During the period of the 1951–53 study, such economic considerations were responsible for all except one of the land divisions considered. In only one case, did a family member insist on his legal right to equal division. The study suggests that, at least in this area, the formal legal rule is of relatively little observable significance in shaping the conduct of family members. Of course, as social attitudes conducive to a hierarchical and collectivist view of the family increasingly break down, the existence of a legal right to equal division may well take on added significance, perhaps accelerating the change in Japanese attitudes respecting the proper relations between the individual and the family group.

Discussion of the collectivistic element in traditional and, though to increasingly lesser extent, modern Japanese family life, led to a consideration of the decision-making process in Japan. John Pelzel, speaking generally, commented that group decisions in Japan tend to be reached not by majority vote but by consensus or unanimity. He suggested that the extent to which majority rule was used in Japan might serve as a useful index of social change. In his view, families and small businesses almost always reach decisions through discussion — with the "boss" then announcing the conclusion — or through consensus without dissent being expressed. Makoto Yazawa stated that in corporate-shareholder meetings in Japan there is generally no formal, final vote — even though the minutes typically reflect such a vote — decisions being reached through a kind of consensus. Moving from private groups to the public arena, Kawashima remarked that a member of a council of a small village once told him that, by long tradition, the council never took a formal vote. Recently, however, the council had been forced to reach decisions by majority rule because of the recalcitrance of a Communist member. The nonvoting tradition is thus also strong in the public sector. Kohji Tanabe noted that, in his experience, Japanese judges rely on voting and the majority principle. Richard Jennings speculated that the continual claim by the minority Japanese political parties of tyranny of the majority might derive from this tradition of consensus.

To assist in putting some of these observations in perspective, Charles Wyzanski drew the conference's attention to some attributes of decision making in the United States. The appropriate processes are intimately related to the size of the group. Justice Cardozo once remarked that the seven-man Court of Appeals of New York State could discuss while the nine-man Supreme Court of the United States could only vote. President Lowell of Harvard had also been convinced that more than seven individuals could not effectively deliberate on difficult intellectual problems. In Wyzanski's experience, the governing bodies of corporations tend to reach decision by consensus. Dissent is usually recorded only if there is some reason to fear investigation by an outside body. Wyzanski also emphasized that the picture of the judicial decisional process as one of majority rule revealed by the opinions of the Supreme Court of the United States is most misleading. In the highest state courts, published dissents are infrequent. Richard Beardsley, returning to the family, added that families in all societies operate as informal consensus groups.

However, behind these general uniformities in the decision-making process lies a significant difference between Japan and the United States: in Japan, unanimity has a value in itself.[36] It is now perhaps eroding, but it remains significant.[37] This value operates in the family situation to mute the voices of family members, thus giving added weight to the views expressed by those whose formal position entitles them to exert leadership.[38]

The Japanese family is changing, and will continue to change, not only because the economic and social realities and the human attitudes upon which its traditional forms were based are disappearing, but also because of a growing individualism and consciousness of rights, particularly on the part of the younger generation, the women especially.[39] In postwar Japan, many important reforms have come about through the activities of women's clubs. Young educated women are very conscious of their rights under the family law. For example, they are fully aware of the woman's rights in the event of divorce.

As women and children develop increasing contacts outside the family circle, the strength of the family's authority is weakened, particularly that of parents over children. It is perhaps to be expected that any such relaxation of familial authority in favor of more individualistic patterns would produce an increase in juvenile delinquency, and Haruo Abe remarked in this context that the current rate of juvenile delinquency is three times the prewar rate.[40] Recognizing clearly that the family is the most important source of a child's moral education, Japanese thinking is increasingly concerned with the growing incidence of juvenile delinquency and the problem of bolstering or replacing the declining influence of the family.[41]

William Lockwood reflected on the possible significance of these developments for the general Japanese political scene. Much of the postwar ferment with respect to Japanese family law has derived from a desire to foster

[36] Mr. Steiner.

[37] Mr. Steiner noted that in 1956 the Liberal-Democrats, the guardians of Japanese tradition, had a real fight over the election of their president.

[38] Professor Kawashima.

[39] Mr. Coleman.

[40] Professor Beardsley noted that the Japanese rate is today only 3 to 4 percent, though it is growing, as compared with the American rate of 10 to 12 percent (percentage of adults in the total population who had some brush with the law as juveniles).

[41] Professor Kawashima.

individualism. This desire is based in good measure on the historic association in the West between the spread of individualism and the rise of democracy. In Lockwood's view, Japan has achieved equalization (in class and business relations, for example) more rapidly than it has individualism. He raised the question of whether such a climate is favorable to the development of political democracy. Or does governmental stability depend upon a broad base of small corporate groups which are, in themselves, quite stable? In the German experience, part of the instability of the Weimar Republic derived from the difficulty of imposing the forms of political democracy on structures (particularly, the family and business) that were quite authoritarian in nature. A stable society requires a basic consistency among the community's various authority structures.

III

THE LAW AND THE ECONOMY

Part Three, The Law and the Economy, has a somewhat more limited and intensive focus than Parts One and Two. The five essays in this section consider the relation between the law and legal institutions on the one hand and the Japanese economy on the other. Although the subject matter of three of the essays takes us rather deeply into technical legal issues, the treatments of labor law and the regulation of monopolies discuss fundamental social and economic issues for which legal technicalities are not so important.

Kichiemon Ishikawa's essay, "The Regulation of the Employer-Employee Relationship: Japanese Labor-Relations Law," considers the conduct of Japanese labor relations under the postwar legislation drawn from American experience. Not surprisingly, his study reveals that the institutional patterns developed for American society require some adjustments when applied to employer-employee relations in Japan. The goals and values of Japanese labor-union leadership are, for example, far more ideological and political than those traditionally pursued by American unions, and this difference changes profoundly the character of Japanese labor relations. The particular experience in labor relations is also illustrative of the problems likely to be encountered in any attempt to channel Japanese social or economic life by legal prescription and of the difficulties and possible dangers inherent in large-scale borrowing of legal rules and institutions — the leitmotiv of several of the conference papers.

Japan also drew widely from American experience after World War II in the regulation of monopolies, and Yoshio Kanazawa's treatment of "The Regulation of Corporate Enterprise: The Law of Unfair Competition and the Control of Monopoly Power" continues, in this new context, many of Ishikawa's themes. The borrowed legal patterns of antitrust law were also superimposed on a society whose traditions and current economic patterns are vastly different from those that produced the adopted legal machinery. In particular, economic life and organization did not develop in an ideological and institutional environment favoring individual enterprise and strong competition. Although monopoly regulation is far less an ideological battleground than Japanese labor relations, the results and reactions in the two fields to the imported law are quite comparable.

The rather more technical legal focus of the remaining three essays — Shinichiro Michida, "The Legal Structure for Economic Enterprise: Some Aspects of Japanese Commercial Law," Makoto Yazawa, "The Legal Structure for Corporate Enterprise: Shareholder-Management Relations Under Japanese Law," and Morio Uematsu, "Computation of Income in Japanese

Income Taxation: A Study in the Adjustment of Theory to Reality"—provide an opportunity to observe rather closely the workings of Japanese law in areas which seem, if Western experience is a reliable guide, to lend themselves to the development of a highly developed and well-coordinated body of rules and principles. That these areas are susceptible to the creation of a "lawyer's law" does not, as a little reflection will make clear, detract from the importance and interest of the problems discussed, for this characteristic affects only the type of solution available. Moreover, the fascinating question of the significance of the law on the books for the actual conduct of affairs remains; as has been noted before, the question is of heightened importance in Japan where the law on the books frequently represents an alien tradition.

THE REGULATION OF THE EMPLOYER-EMPLOYEE RELATIONSHIP: JAPANESE LABOR-RELATIONS LAW

Kichiemon Ishikawa

ASSISTED BY WALTER GELLHORN

MOUNTAIN ranges are the products of convulsive pressures associated with the earth's cooling or with the release of explosive forces beneath its crust. The jagged bits and pieces become softened in time by erosion and abrasion; trees and plants take root; water courses make pathways; the mountains become familiar and habitable. But new mountains have still a harshness, a sharpness, a somewhat chaotic massiveness less often associated with the more ancient ranges. Japanese labor-relations law may fairly be said to resemble somewhat a recently created volcanic mountain.[1]

That this should be so is not surprising. Until 1946 Japanese labor law did

Note. Mr. Ishikawa is Professor of Law, Tokyo University and a Public Commissioner of the Public Corporation, Etc., Labor Relations Commission. B.Jur., Tokyo Imperial University, 1943. Participant, Japanese American Program for Cooperation in Legal Studies at Harvard University, 1954–1956. Public Commissioner, Tokyo Metropolis Local Labor Relations Commission, 1953, 1957–1962. Author of writings in the field of labor law.

Mr. Gellhorn is Betts Professor of Law, Columbia University. A.B. 1927, Amherst College; LL.B. 1931, Columbia University; L.H.D. 1952, Amherst College.

[1] I confine myself to the labor-relations law of present-day Japan. In this category are art. 28 of the Constitution, the Labor Union Law, Law No. 174 of 1949, the Labor Relations Adjustment Law, Law No. 25 of 1946, the Public Corporation, Etc., Labor Relations Law, Law No. 257 of 1948, the Local Public Enterprise Labor Relations Law, Law No. 289 of 1952, the Law Concerning the Regulation of the Method of Acts of Dispute in the Electricity Business and the Coal Mining Industry, Law No. 171 of 1953, and several articles in the National Public Servants Law, Law No. 120 of 1947, and the Local Public Servants Law, Law No. 261 of 1950, which prohibit certain kinds of labor activity (so-called acts of dispute) by public servants, national or local. Important articles of some of these laws are set out in Appendix A at the end of this essay.

The other category of labor law, which includes all legislation having no direct relation to the labor unions as such — legislation concerning maximum hours, minimum wages, safety, pensions, unemployment, vocational training, and so on — is not discussed. In these areas, there is little difference between Japan and the United States in the approach or way of thinking, although the degree of protection afforded differs considerably in the various fields. In sum, the standards of these protective statutes may be said to approximate those embodied in the Versailles Treaty of 1919 as the then-acceptable minimums. Japan is a member of the International Labour Organization, but has not yet ratified all the conventions promulgated by that body. The titles of several protective acts are set out in Appendix B at the end of this essay.

not exist at all in any meaningful sense. In the early 1930s as many as four-hundred thousand Japanese workers had some sort of union affiliation, and a few unions were actually engaged in collective bargaining despite governmental and managerial hostility.[2] But by the time Japan entered the war in 1941, unions had virtually disappeared. Military and other reactionary pressures had been brought to bear on leaders and members alike to discourage voluntary associations of workers. When the war had run its tragic course, not a single union and not a single union member existed in all Japan, as far as is known. Then, in a burst that may well be likened to an eruption, labor-relations law emerged as a major component of Japan's social and economic structure. Within twenty months of the beginning of Japan's occupation, more than five million men and women had been enrolled as members in seventeen thousand unions whose formation had been encouraged, and whose protection had been assured, by the occupying forces.[3]

Elsewhere in the world, modern labor law may be justly regarded as a consequence rather than as the generator of organized labor activity. In the United States, for example, the ancient concepts of trespass and conspiracy, which had at first given an air of lawlessness to concerted efforts by workers to improve their lot, were reshaped by statutes such as the Norris-LaGuardia Act of 1932,[4] limiting the issuance of injunctions in labor controversies, and the National Labor Relations Act of 1935,[5] compelling employers to recognize their employees' right to organize and to bargain collectively through chosen representatives. The new laws facilitated union growth, but they built upon a wealth of experience growing out of relationships between employee organizations and management. The very fact of their enactment testifies to the political strength of the unions. Leadership existed, both nationally and locally; new units could be placed in an already solid structure; a common vocabulary was in wide use, so that the terminology of labor relations was understandable to all those concerned.

In Japan, all was different. Neither management nor labor — nor, for that matter, government — could draw on past experience to deal with the new issues. When the Supreme Commander for the Allied Powers (SCAP) induced the adoption of laws to nurture the unionization of Japan's work-

[2] It is true that before the war there had been laws relating to the labor movement, but they were intended to suppress it — as in article 17 of the Peace Police Law, Law No. 36 of 1900, the Administrative Execution Law, Law No. 84 of 1900, and the Peace Preservation Law, Law No. 46 of 1925 — or, realizing that total suppression was impossible, to bring labor disputes affecting the public welfare to solutions as soon as possible — as in the Labor Disputes Mediation Law, Law No. 57 of 1926. Up to the outbreak of the Manchurian Incident in 1931, however, the attitude in the Imperial Diet was gradually shifting in favor of a sounder conception of labor-management relations.

[3] Careful accounts of the prewar and postwar labor movements will be found in LEVINE, INDUSTRIAL RELATIONS IN POSTWAR JAPAN (1958) and SUEHIRO, NIHON RŌDŌ KUMIAI UNDŌ SHI (History of the Japanese Labor Union Movement) (1950).

[4] 47 Stat. 90 (1932), 29 U.S.C. §101 (1956).

[5] 49 Stat. 449 (1935), 29 U.S.C. §151 (1956).

ers, an entirely new set of social organisms came into being at a stroke. Literally in a matter of moments the labor relations law began to function, without the softening effects of tradition, without sophisticated understanding on the part of those responsible for its application, and, indeed, without an initial comprehension of the very words in which the new laws were couched. The significance of the developments in the period 1946–1961 cannot be grasped unless one keeps firmly in mind the volcanic recency of this branch of Japanese law.

Characteristics of the Labor Movement

Establishment of Unions

To an extent believed to be unparalleled in Western industrial nations, Japanese labor unions are based upon individual establishments rather than upon larger craft and industrial groupings. The shipping industry provides the only example of industrial unionism.[6] There, all ranks from the common seaman to the first mate — and the captain as well if he so chooses — are members of a single union. Elsewhere the core of Japanese union organization is quite literally its members' place of employment. Typically, the appropriate "bargaining unit" [7] is establishment-wide. Much less frequently it is company-wide, embracing a number of separate plants of a single manufacturer. It is not industry-wide; nor is it determined by the occupational identification of workers, such as electricians, machinists, or teamsters. Moreover, not only the members of the union but its officers as well are drawn from the place of immediate employment. This intensive localization brings about a certain lack of sophistication concerning labor goals and methods, since the officers' range of past experience is necessarily somewhat narrow. Also unions often fail to achieve the compensating virtue of a close-knit relationship between the unions' leadership and their members. In many instances the local union officials are young men who are heavy readers, somewhat doctrinaire in outlook, and convinced that they constitute an elite group whose duty it is to guide the less socially conscious

[6] Levine says: "The structural feature most characteristic of Japanese trade unionism has been its 'enterprise' basis of organization. Probably more than 85 per cent of all basic union units, embracing almost 80 per cent of total union membership, are organized along enterprise lines; that is, their members are confined to a single shop, establishment, or enterprise. The remainder are divided about equally between industrial unions and craft organizations in which the local units are not based simply on enterprise membership" Levine, note 3, at 90. This calculation reflects the vagueness of the structure of Japanese unions once the confines of the individual establishment are exceeded. Moreover, even those unions which are said to have a craft or industry basis depend far more than their American counterparts on their connection with particular establishments. It may be a slight exaggeration to characterize the seamen's union as the only industrial union. The teachers' union is perhaps another example, but it is *sui generis,* having almost no resemblance to craft, industry, or even establishment unions.

[7] Japanese labor law does not recognize the notion of "bargaining unit." At this point I use the term for convenience, without assigning any legal meaning.

members. Members are not encouraged to share in shaping union policies; as a result, they remain indifferent to union problems until acute crises arise.

The establishment — factory, shop, store, office — as the basis of organization is historically explicable. While, as already noted, Japan had not a single union at the war's close, it had imported from its German ally the institution of the labor front, a device for rallying the workers of each employment unit to outdo themselves in productivity. The labor fronts met to discuss operational difficulties, to receive announcements of plans and goals, and to stimulate patriotic fervor by mutual exhortation as well as by discouraging grumbling about current conditions. When unionization was decreed, the simplest way in which to link millions of workers into labor organizations was to transform the labor fronts into unions. This was done so rigorously and with so little genuine understanding of what was involved that, for a very short period of time, many owners or chief executives of places of employment dutifully became presidents of labor unions instead of chairmen of labor fronts, which they had been before.

Because the establishment union is the norm, some seven and a half million workers now form over forty thousand separate and distinct unions in Japan.[8] These are not company unions in the sense that they are management-created or management-dominated, though undoubtedly some are responsive to managerial advice. They are not administrative subunits of larger organizations as are the locals of nationwide unions in the United States. Each one has its own conception of what its function should be, its own officers, and its own duty to represent the employees who comprise its membership. Moreover, since a union's members are determined by place of employment rather than by type of work performed, unions typically embrace white-collar workers as well as production workers.[9]

Union Federations

So localized a type of organization cries out for means of amalgamation, so that bargaining power may be increased, information may be exchanged, and policies may be coordinated. Three types of union confederation may be noted. First are confederations of unions representing employees of a single employer, though in a number of separate locations; thus, for example, six unions whose members are employed by the Mitsui Kōsan Kabushiki Kaisha

[8] In the United States, over 52,000 labor organizations come under the jurisdiction of the Labor Management Reporting and Disclosure Act, 73 Stat. 519 (1959), 29 U.S.C. §401 (1962). Most of these organizations are "locals," but unlike the Japanese unions they are mainly segments of a larger organization (that is, a national or international union). For the number of Japanese unions and union members, see Table 1 at the end of this essay.

[9] According to one careful estimate, 60 percent of the unions have both blue-collar and white-collar members; 15 percent are composed entirely of production workers; 25 percent consist entirely of clerical and other office employees. These exceptional groupings reflect the composition of the work force in the establishment, rather than through some exclusionary policy or a principle similar to craft unionism. See LEVINE, note 3 above, at 91.

(Mitsui Coal Mining Company) in six of that company's mines have formed a working alliance so that in appropriate circumstances they may act together. Second, unions within a single industry have sometimes banded together to form a single organization, such as the Nihon Tankō Rōdō Kumiai (Japan Coal Mining Labor Union) or the Zenkoku Seni Sangyō Rōdō Kumiai Dōmei (National Confederation of Textile Industrial Labor Unions). These confederations somewhat resemble American industrial unions such as the United Mine Workers or the Textile Workers of America, but they differ in tightness of organization, power of central officers, and authority to require local-union adherence to nationally determined policies. Finally, Japanese unions have from prewar days banded together in national federations designed to mobilize the political power of union members.

The history of these national federations comprises in a sense one of the most important aspects of the history of postwar politics in Japan. During the early days of the occupation, two nationwide groups, Sambetsu[10] (All-Japan Congress of Industrial Labor Unions) and Sōdōmei[11] (Japanese General Confederation of Labor Unions), struggled for leadership of the working class. Persons who were Communists or who were thought to be particularly friendly to Communism acquired positions of great importance in Sambetsu, though that organization was never professedly Communist. With the help of SCAP, the assertedly Communist elements were purged from the labor movement, beginning in 1950; with their disappearance, Sambetsu virtually collapsed. Sōdōmei, which was led chiefly by moderates who had been unionists many years before in the prewar period, did not thrive, perhaps because its leaders were too conservative, too unaggressive, and too Western in outlook.

To provide a center for the entire labor movement, a new federation, Sōhyō[12] (Japanese General Council of Labor Unions), was created in 1950 with strong support from SCAP. Sōhyō, contrary to SCAP's expectation, proved to be under left-wing, though non-Communist, leadership. Sōhyō remains the most important voice of Japanese labor, for it speaks for local unions with a total membership of 3.7 million. It is no longer the spokesman for all, however. In 1953 several unions seceded from it, dissatisfied with Sōhyō's radicalism. They created yet another confederation, Zenrō[13] (All-Japan Labor Union Congress), in order to pursue a more cautious course. Zenrō now claims an affiliated membership of 900,000 workers. A third national federation, Shin Sambetsu (New All-Japan Congress of Industrial Labor Unions) links together unions with a total membership of 45,000 workers. The remaining 3 million unionists are unaffiliated.

[10] An abbreviation of "Zen-Nippon Sangyō-betsu Rōdō Kumiai Kaigi."
[11] An abbreviation of "Nihon Rōdō Kumiai Sōdōmei."
[12] An abbreviation of "Nihon Rōdō Kumiai Sō-hyōgikai."
[13] An abbreviation of "Zen-Nippon Rōdō Kumiai Kaigi."

None of the three existing national federations has individual members. They are associations of autonomous unions, each of which may have members of widely varying political orientation. Sōhyō and Zenrō attempt to function as grand strategists in the "labor struggle." They identify goals to be sought and then, as tacticians, suggest the means by which those goals may be attained. Sōhyō has been the more determinedly political. While not structurally connected with the Socialist Party (the principal opposition party in Japan at present), it is that party's main source of financial support and carries great weight in its councils. Moreover, Sōhyō's concepts of labor-management relations have so far been heavily influenced by Marxist analysis of the class struggle. Partly as a consequence, it seems at times to be more interested in sweeping issues of governmental policy than in immediate gains through collective bargaining. By contrast, Zenrō, which is to the Democratic Socialist Party what Sōhyō is to the Socialist Party, functions more on the economic than on the political plane, dealing with current needs and with gains that can be won immediately.[14]

THE LEGALITY OF UNION ACTIVITIES

Much of Japanese labor-relations law today turns on the question of legality of "acts of labor dispute," a term without exact counterpart in American law.[15] Acts which in other circumstances would be deemed illegal, under criminal law or civil law or both, have been viewed as permissible within the context of labor-management strife. This unusual evaluation of conduct derives from legal language that was inspired, if not actually composed, by Americans whose thinking, unlike that of the persons to whom the texts were addressed, had been shaped by long exposure to industrial-relations problems. The words as they were written were probably not intended to have the meanings their readers gave them, but, for good or ill, the terminology has shaped a new conception of the limits of allowable conduct by organized labor.

[14] The main issue when Zenrō was formed was the alleged overemphasis on politics by Sōhyō's leaders. At the same time, Zenrō itself was concerned with political issues; it simply had a different opinion concerning them. For example, Zenrō supported early signing of a peace treaty, which Sōhyō opposed. Zenrō, like Sōhyō, opposed the security treaty with the United States. In general, Zenrō's leaders may be characterized as somewhat conservative trade unionists. When Sōhyō was created, it was markedly anti-Communist in tone. It then planned to become affiliated with the International Confederation of Free Trade Unions. As time has passed, however, Sōhyō has lost interest in becoming linked with the Western world and has concentrated upon Japanese politics while increasingly espousing positions taken by neutralist countries or, though with somewhat less frequency, by the USSR in world affairs. But I believe that Sōhyō will become more aware of its responsibility and that a change, whether professed or not, will occur in its policies and outlooks.

[15] This term is reminiscent of the "concerted activities" protected by section 7 of the National Labor Relations Act. But there is a great distinction between concerted activities in the United States and acts of dispute in Japan.

Constitutional Provisions

The fundamental text is article 28 of the Japanese Constitution, adopted on November 3, 1946, and effective six months later: "The right of workers to organize and to bargain and act collectively is guaranteed." The words, it will be observed, are unqualified. To Americans, who long ago learned that absolute language rarely means what it seems to say, this wording would have caused little difficulty. "Congress shall make no law respecting an establishment of religion, or prohibiting the free exercise thereof; or abridging the freedom of speech, or of the press; or the right of the people peaceably to assemble, and to petition the Government for a redress of grievances." This is as unqualified as is possible, but the courts have managed to read into these words of the first amendment to the United States Constitution the implied thought that Congress may make no law that is *unreasonable.*[16] Section 10(f) of the National Labor Relations Act of 1935 said broadly that the findings of fact made by the National Labor Relations Board should not be disturbed "if supported by evidence"; the United States Supreme Court read "evidence" as meaning "substantial evidence" and then went further: "Substantial evidence is more than a mere scintilla. It means such relevant evidence as a reasonable mind might accept as adequate to support a conclusion."[17] The Sherman Antitrust Act of 1890, section 1, says that "every . . . combination in restraint of trade," without exception, shall be a criminal offense and shall subject participants to severe civil liabilities; the courts quickly revised the statutory language by reading into it the "rule of reason," so that Congress was held to have meant to outlaw only those combinations found to be unreasonable in their restraining effects.[18] Article I, section 17, of the Constitution of the State of New York, in words that are perhaps the origin of article 28 of Japan's Constitution, declares that "employees shall have the right to organize and to bargain collectively through representatives of their own choosing,"[19] but these sweeping terms have not been regarded as immunizing the labor movement against the nondiscriminatory application of legal restraints.

In Japan, by contrast, judges and scholars have tended to give absolute words an absolute interpretation. In part, their doing so may be attributable to mere misunderstanding of the Western concept that had been thrust into Japanese law. Foreign military authorities, whose pronouncements were not likely to be closely questioned, told the Japanese that labor had "rights" that must be recognized and honored. Few Japanese scholars and even

[16] See Schenck v. United States, 249 U.S. 47 (1919).

[17] Consolidated Edison Co. v. NLRB, 305 U.S. 197, 229 (1938).

[18] See Standard Oil Co. v. United States, 221 U.S. 1 (1911).

[19] For other examples of constitutional provisions closely akin to Japan's, see N.J. Const. art. 1, §19; Mo. Const. art. 1, §29.

fewer Japanese judges had any knowledge of Western labor relations, nor were they able at once to obtain documentary materials that would have enhanced their understanding. Moreover, the condition of wage earners was little short of desperate in the early occupation period owing to currency inflation and supply shortages; sympathy with the workers' severe hardships led many legally trained persons to seize eagerly upon theories seemingly advantageous to the underprivileged without giving them as much critical scrutiny as they might have otherwise.

In any event, whatever may be the full explanation, the postwar Constitution was widely accepted as not merely legalizing the previously forbidden labor unions, but as conferring upon them a collective privilege to act in ways for which individuals would be liable or punished.*

Statutory Provisions

The constitutional provision discussed above was soon supplemented by statutes. Chief among them, for purposes of the present discussion, was the Labor Union Law of June 1, 1949,[20] which has not been changed in the portions relevant here, despite numerous subsequent amendments.

Article 1(1) of the Labor Union Law declares its purposes to include the following:

> to elevate the status of workers through promoting equal standing for workers in their negotiations with their employer;
>
> to protect the election by workers of their own representatives for the purpose of negotiating the conditions of their work and the self-organization of and association in labor unions in order to carry out other collective action; and
>
> to encourage the practice and procedure of collective bargaining in order to conclude collective labor agreements governing relations between employers and workers.

To assure that unionization would emerge from the shadow of prewar illegality, article 1(2) declares that "appropriate collective bargaining and other acts of a labor union, performed in order to attain the purposes enumerated in the prior paragraph," should be deemed covered by article 35 of the Penal Code.[21] That article provides, in part, that no person shall be penalized for acts done "in accordance with . . . an appropriate business function." The Labor Union Law adds in article 1(2), however, that "in no case shall the use of violence be construed an appropriate act of a labor

* During the conference discussions, the prevailing literal attitude toward the constitutional provision was further illustrated by Kiminobu Hashimoto's reference to the university teachers' union — the Zenkoku Daigaku Kyōju Rengō (National Union of University Professors). Professors are considered "workers," although the faculty governs the university.

[20] An English translation of this statute will be found in MINISTRY OF LABOR, JAPAN LABOR LEGISLATION [hereafter cited LABOR LEGISLATION] 83 (1959).

[21] Law No. 45 of 1907.

union." Article 7(i) forbids discriminating against or discharging an employee for organizing or joining a union or for his having "performed an appropriate act of a labor union." Article 8 says that an employer cannot recover against a union or its members in a civil action for "damages incurred due to a strike or other acts of dispute which are appropriate."

Thus the law protects a union against criminal and civil liability for acts that are "appropriate," while its adherents may not be disciplined for having engaged in "an appropriate act of a labor union." The practical application of the somewhat amorphous word "appropriate" is discussed in the pages that follow.[22]

Acts of Dispute by Workers

As in Western countries, the strike is the chief weapon of Japanese workers. Considerable inventive skill has been used to refine that weapon and to adapt it to Japan's special conditions, however. Three of those special conditions must be noted especially, for they have a great effect on the interests of Japanese unions and the behavior of their members. First, the notion of "exclusive bargaining representative" has gained no recognition at all; interunion strife can be continuous because each union is free to bargain for whatever members it may have within the establishment. Second, Japanese labor agreements, in general, deal only with major matters such as wage rates and working hours. Detailed thought is not devoted to issues that may arise during the life of the contract; thus no effort is made to prevent later friction by spelling out completely the parties' respective rights. Third, unions and employers have not yet come to use arbitration as a means of adjusting grievances. Contractual gaps, coupled with the absence of machinery for the voluntary determination of contractual obligations, encourage continuous combat in place of the attention to "legal rights" that now characterizes American labor relations. Further comment upon these matters appears below, but they should be borne in mind throughout the following discussion.

A central ingredient of any strike is, of course, the withholding, or, in the Japanese term, the "nontender," of labor. The mere fact that workers combine together to give their "nontender" cogency does not render a strike illegal if the work stoppage is for a legal purpose and is not accompanied by conduct that, in the absence of a labor dispute, would be deemed lawless. Such is the meaning, in Western law, of guaranteeing the right to strike. The "guarantee" is merely that civil and criminal liability shall not attach to acts done in unison when those same acts would be permissible if done by a worker as an individual. The Japanese identification of appropriate acts rests on somewhat broader conceptions.

[22] The Japanese term here translated by the English word "appropriate" is *seitō na*.

Seisan Kanri

Seisan kanri has no English synonym.[23] Basically it means the seizure of a place of business by those who work there, the expulsion of the management, and the continuing conduct of the business by its captors. In the years immediately following the war, this type of concerted activity occurred with considerable frequency. A steel mill, for example, was operated by striking employees for over a month; orders were taken, existing orders were completed, and the strikers paid themselves their wages out of the employer's funds.[24]

A printing plant, in which seisan kanri had occurred, continued in business. When the usurpers were no longer able to meet the payroll, its occupiers began to sell bits of surplus equipment in order to eke out their wages.[25]

To argue that seisan kanri is an appropriate act because it is merely an aspect of a labor dispute, or because done by a union as a collective action in order to give workers "equal standing . . . in their negotiations with their employer," may at first seem to be simply a play on words. The Supreme Court of Japan rejected the argument as early as 1950[26] in the steel-mill case mentioned above, which involved several union officials who were accused of misappropriating the employer's funds during the seisan kanri. The Court's reasoning, which is discussed more fully below, was that seisan kanri would undermine the private-property system on which the present legal order rests, as stated in article 29 of the Constitution. Despite this assertion of the Supreme Court, however, a number of lower courts and perhaps a majority of scholars in the labor-law field persistently contend otherwise.

Those who approve of seisan kanri purport to find justification in the Labor Relations Adjustment Law of September 27, 1946.[27] That statute has as its purpose the prevention or settlement of labor disputes in order to maintain industrial peace and further economic development. To that end it defines the powers and duties of the labor-relations commissions, indicates certain circumstances in which prior notice must be given of intent to perform an act of dispute, and provides "emergency adjustment" procedures when the Prime Minister deems a dispute to be dangerous to the nation's well-being. Article 7 defines "acts of dispute" as meaning "strikes, slow-

[23] Literally these words mean "production control."

[24] Odaka v. Japan, Supreme Court, Grand Bench, Nov. 15, 1950, 4 SAIKŌ SAIBANSHO KEIJI HANREI SHŪ (A Collection of Criminal Supreme Court Cases) [hereafter cited SAI-HAN KEISHŪ] 2257. It should again be noted that most unions include office staffs as well as production workers and that many managerial employees below the top-management level also are unionists. Hence continuity of operations is more feasible than it would be if no union member understood the paperwork phase of modern industry.

[25] Kitao v. Japan, Supreme Court, II Petty Bench, Feb. 22, 1952, 6 SAI-HAN KEISHŪ 288.

[26] Odaka v. Japan, note 24 above.

[27] An English translation will be found in LABOR LEGISLATION 107.

downs, lockouts, or other acts or counteracts, performed by the parties to labor relations for the purpose of realizing their claims, which hamper the normal operation of a business." Seisan kanri undoubtedly falls within this definition, but whether its being an act of dispute within the jurisdiction of the commissions legitimatizes it for all purposes is quite another question.

Discussion of that question in Japan is somewhat beclouded by the intrusion of philosophical issues, which, though of great intrinsic importance, are irrelevant to analysis of statutory and constitutional verbiage. Marxism is an active element in current scholarly debates[28] and, even when not openly proclaimed, it colors many legal commentaries.* Strikes and other labor controversies are skirmishes connected with the grand battle for ultimate mastery. Victories in these skirmishes are important not as ends in themselves but as steps toward a larger triumph. What conduces to victory is desirable. In the present context, Marxist scholars—and some others as well—assert that the obvious purposes of Japanese statutes are to nurture the organization and to raise the living standards of workers. According to this theory, what is necessary to achieve these purposes is beyond legal challenge, for it would be anomalous to state a desirable social goal and at the same time render civilly or criminally actionable the steps that might achieve it.

This equating of necessity with legality seems to overlook two perplexing problems. The first is simply deciding what is necessary. No Japanese judge or scholar has yet argued, for example, that a killing in the course of a labor dispute is to be excused because it was deemed necessary to the achievement of the union's ends. At some point mere necessity does not suffice. The proponents of the theory outlined above have not stated the determinants of justifiable necessity as contrasted with unlawful means of attaining victory.[29] The second problem arises from the fact that social goals are plural and often conflicting. As already noted, Japan's Constitution provides in article 28 that collective bargaining and other joint action are guaranteed; thus it states as a fundamental proposition that labor should be free to organize in

[28] Marxism sees labor law merely as an instrumentality in the basic class struggle. Workers are to be prepared for revolution rather than for amelioration of conditions within the framework of capitalist institutions.

* Richard Jennings and the author pointed out at the conference that Marxian thinking is not limited to Marxists. Most economists in Japan, whatever their political inclinations, are trained in Marxian economics.

[29] Reference may here be made again to article 1(2) of the Labor Union Law, which, while declaring appropriate acts of trade unions to be beyond the reach of penal statutes, adds that "in no case shall the use of violence be construed an appropriate act of a labor union." This proviso is steadfastly ignored by those who defend the legality of seisan kanri and other uses of force in labor disputes. The defenders of seisan kanri criticize article 1(2) on two grounds: its application would tend to narrow the sphere of appropriateness; it is a national shame to have such a clause because it gives foreigners the false impression that the Japanese unions frequently resort to violence. It would be preferable if the impression were in fact false as asserted.

order to advance workingmen's interests. The very next article of the same Constitution provides, however, that "the right to own or to hold property is inviolable." The reasoning that has led some scholars to justify seisan kanri — which, in essence, is that the end justifies the means — might be used with equal force to support severe repressive measures, on the ground that they were necessary to effectuate the promised inviolability of property.

In general, the Supreme Court has adopted the view that labor law intermeshes with other branches of law. Thus, in the steel-mill case referred to above, the court said:

The Constitution at the same time that it guarantees workers the right to organize and to bargain and act collectively also guarantees all of the people such fundamental human rights as equality, liberty, and property; it neither recognizes the complete exclusion of these various fundamental human rights before the unrestrained exercise of the worker's right to dispute nor, vice versa, the absolute priority of the latter over the former. Rather, it seeks harmony between these various general fundamental human rights and the rights of labor, and the appropriate limits of the right to dispute are at a place where this harmony is not disturbed. The point at which harmony is to be found must be determined by considering the spirit of the legal system as a whole. Naturally those rights referred to as the employers' rights of liberty and property are not absolutely unlimited, for they are to some extent subject to restrictions for the benefit of workers' rights such as the right to act collectively, but we conclude that it is not permissible to suppress the free will of employers and to interfere with their control over their property to the extent decreed by the trial court . . .

The private-property system forms the mainstay of our country's present legal order, profit and loss from a business being attributed to the capitalist. Therefore, the management of an enterprise and orders directing the course of production come under the authority of the capitalist or his representatives in charge of management. Even assuming, as asserted, that workers are responsible for an enterprise along with the entrepreneur, it does not follow as a matter of course that workers have the right to use and receive the profits of the enterprise or that they possess authority in the power of management. Thus, workers may not be allowed methods of dispute which undermine the very mainstay of private property in the entrepreneur.[30]

Wave Strike, Time Strike, and Designation Strike

Among contemporary industrial inventions are means of disrupting work schedules without engaging in a full-fledged strike. Prominent examples in Japan are the wave strike (or, as it is sometimes called, the piston strike), the time strike, and the designation strike.

A wave strike involves repetitive work stoppages at intervals planned in advance. For example, the operations of a chemical manufacturing plant can be rendered difficult and in some instances virtually impossible by a twenty-

[30] Odaka v. Japan, note 24, at 2260–61.

four-hour strike which is renewed after the passage of three days. Meanwhile, the workers report for duty and demand (and receive) full wages despite the disturbing effect of work stoppages upon continuous production processes.

A time strike is a shorter variant of the wave strike. By previous design, those who engage in a time strike cease productive activity for an agreed period, such as two hours. They then resume work until the next day, when, at the same hour, a time strike again occurs. In these instances the strikers remain at their work places.

A designation strike (the term is mine and has no precise American counterpart) involves a work stoppage by one employee or a group of employees in accord with union instructions or, to put it differently, a stoppage by designated workers. For example, a truck driver was instructed to "go on strike" by abandoning his truck, heavily laden with the products of the company, just as he was leaving the plant to deliver them to a customer. This caused great trouble for the company, which thereafter discharged several officers of the union. In reply to the union's complaint that this was an "improper labor act" (unfair labor practice), the company asserted that resort to a designation strike was not an appropriate act of a labor union. Although it deplored the union's tactics, the Central Labor Relations Commission ordered the company to reinstate the discharged officers, holding that, upon consideration of the whole situation, the discharge had been motivated by a desire to undermine the union.[31] The commission carefully refrained from deciding the legality or appropriateness of the designation strike as such. It should be noted that, if it had so wished, the commission in this instance could have condemned the designation strike while reinstating the officers on the ground that in fact their discharge was not referable to this particular union activity. In two other cases, bill collectors were ordered by their union to commence a strike at the moment their rounds had been completed but before their cash collections had been delivered to the employer; the union further directed the designated strikers to deposit the employers' money in the union president's bank account "for safe keeping." In one case the union did not return the money to the employer promptly after the dispute was over; in the other, the union returned the money to the employer at once when the controversy was settled. When the union officers who had received the employers' funds were subsequently prosecuted for embezzlement, the Supreme Court of Japan held in the first case that the union's conduct was not an appropriate act of a labor union and remanded the matter to the lower court for further investigation of the facts;[32] in the

[31] Nihon Kayaku Kabushiki Kaisha (Japan Chemical Co.) v. Nihon Kayaku Rōdō Kumiai (Japan Chemical Labor Union), Central Labor Relations Commission, July 18, 1959, RŌDŌ IINKAI SOKUHŌ (Labor Relations Commissions Rapid Reporter) no. 467, at 236.

[32] Yamamoto v. Japan, Supreme Court, II Petty Bench, Sept. 19, 1958, 12 SAI-HAN KEISHŪ 3127.

second case, the Court expressed no opinion concerning the union's conduct but held that it did not amount to an embezzlement.[33] It is not clear how the Supreme Court would have decided the second case if the employer had discharged the designated strikers or the president of the union.

Factory Occupation

Factory occupation is, in American parlance, a sit-down or stay-in strike. Unlike seisan kanri, factory occupation connotes no usurpation of managerial functions by the unionists in order to continue operations. It does, however, connote the physical expulsion of top management and the continuing occupation of business premises by those who normally work there. In no instance has this seizure of the work place been clearly upheld as legal; on the other hand, a number of courts have struggled to find means of avoiding holding it to be illegal.

Factory occupation has been commonplace in small- or medium-sized enterprises but not in the larger industrial plants. In smaller establishments the organization of a union is often accomplished in absolute secrecy. When the union group feels sufficiently confident of its cohesiveness, it suddenly informs the employer of its existence and demands almost immediate collective bargaining about issues it has formulated. Typically if the new union's wishes are not at once fulfilled, a strike is declared and, in many instances, made effective by factory occupation. The process is exceedingly abrupt, with little genuine negotiation before the strike occurs.[34]

Factory occupation, although in form aimed at the employer, is in fact also a means of preventing work by nonsympathizers; by seizing the work place the strikers force nonstrikers as well as the employer to take heed of the union's wishes. In this sense it is closely linked with picketing, to which we now turn.

Picketing

Picketing in Japan is not a means of communication intended to give information and to appeal for support. It is rather a means for enforcing

[33] Japan v. Kamada, Supreme Court, II Petty Bench, Sept. 19, 1958, 12 SAI-HAN KEISHŪ 3047.

[34] It should be noted here that there is yet another type of strike in which negotiation occurs after rather than before the work stoppage. Major unions or a federation of unions (such as those related to steel production or private railways) agree in advance that they will synchronize their demands upon their respective employers. A list of various demands is then drawn up. Each union presents the demands to its employer, scarcely expecting that they will be wholly acceptable. Usually each union then goes on strike on the predetermined date. Piston strikes or time strikes are often called in such cases. This tactic is called a "scheduled strike," a term which is now a Japanese expression. Recently the labor movement itself has become somewhat skeptical about the utility of scheduled struggles that ignore entirely the possibility of peaceable negotiations; but such strikes continue to be an accepted labor tactic, especially among some of the larger unions affiliated with Sōhyō.

the will of those who have commenced a strike.[35] It is the building of a human wall to prevent access to the work place; it is the application of raw power. The line is effective not because sympathizers will refuse to cross it, but because nonsympathizers will fear to do so;[36] the pickets' purpose is to repel opponents rather than to gain adherents. Thus factory occupation can be likened to picketing; there, in a sense, the mass picketers have simply stationed themselves inside instead of outside the gates.

Picketing accompanied by implied or actual threats of violence is regarded by the majority of Japanese scholars and a few judges as being beyond the reach of the law. The typical method of picketing in Japan is for the picketers to form a line by tightly linking arms in order not to allow "a single ant to enter." High company officials are usually allowed to pass through the line, but it requires great courage for customers or nonmember workers to break the pickets. It is utterly impossible for those workers who have seceded from the union during the strike or who have become highly critical of the incumbents' policies to defy the pickets without facing a physical fight. The law does declare that "in no case shall the use of violence be construed an appropriate act of a labor union." [37] But some apologists for Japanese-style picketing engage in verbal subtleties to distinguish between picketing that is "violent" and picketing that simply involves "might," thus a distinction might be drawn between a picket's shooting a nonstriker, which would no doubt be regarded as an act of violence by even the most tolerant, and a picket's brandishing a loaded gun before a nonstriker and threatening to shoot him if he gives the picket trouble. Although the illustration is extreme, it exposes the inadequacy of the theory that might is permissible though violence is not. Nevertheless, the might theory continues to prevail among those who, as in the case of

[35] A typical definition of the aims of picketing in Japanese labor disputes is: (1) to watch the conduct of union members, high officials of the employer, and nonmember workers; (2) to persuade those workers who have seceded or who are going to secede from the union to come back or remain; (3) to prevent the employer from using means to break up the union; (4) to prevent nonmember workers or "scabs" from entering into or working in the establishments; (5) to prevent the employer from delivering raw materials or finished or semifinished products into or from the premises; and (6) to discourage the employer from using strikebreakers. CHŪKAI RŌDŌ KUMIAI HŌ (A Commentary on the Labor Union Law) 83 (Azuma ed., 1959).

[36] Japanese labor still rarely concerns itself with seeking to arouse sympathy for its demands. Consumers and the public at large are not looked upon as potential allies whose economic power could be used to strengthen the labor movement. On the contrary, the prevailing attitude is one of "we stand alone against all the world," which is perhaps understandable if each strike is perceived as an episode in the class struggle rather than as an effort by employees to win a favorable contract. Because strikers make little appeal to others for support, but rather defy them to interfere, the boycott is unknown. Nor, so far, has any Japanese union or confederation of unions ever engaged a public-relations consultant who might advise them concerning means of educating the public about issues labor deems vital.

[37] Labor Union Law, art. 1(2).

seisan kanri, maintain that an act of labor dispute is "appropriate" if it is necessary. Moreover, the view has often been expressed that if the Labor Union Law were to be interpreted as forbidding effective picketing—taken by hypothesis to mean mass picketing that can override opposition, that is, the kind of picketing described above—the statute would be invalid because it would conflict with article 28 of the Constitution, guaranteeing "the right of workers to organize . . . and act collectively."

The Supreme Court seems unimpressed by the might theory, however. All the cases concerning picketing which have come up to the Supreme Court have been criminal proceedings, chiefly involving union officials accused of interference with the employer's or other workers' business. The Court's judgments have reflected two approaches. The first one is that neither "acts which by violence or intimidation seek to obstruct action by employers who attempt to continue to carry on their business" nor "acts which suppress the free will of employers or interfere with their control over their property" are permissible.[38] This seems to be the same view that prevails in the United States, but it is modified by a second theory: "in a case where during the prosecution of a strike by a union, which is utilizing its right to carry on a dispute, a portion of its union members withdraw from the strike and participate in production, it goes without saying that the union (consequently, the union officials and union members who comply with their will) may by peaceful means of persuasion request, orally or in writing, that these persons starting work cease to do so, but causing such persons to suspend starting work by means of violence, intimidation, or force must be construed as illegal generally. Naturally, though, whether an act bringing about a suspension of starting work is to be recognized as illegal or not must be carefully determined by particularly taking into account the various circumstances at the time the appropriate strike or other acts of dispute are being carried on."[39] This "various circumstances" theory is hard to apply. In practice the Supreme Court seems inclined to adopt as lawful any means that fall within the "peaceful means of persuasion" category.*

The might theory, which is thought to be highly prolabor, does not prove to be so in actual practice. A long-continued strike engenders strong emotion among its supporters and deepening dissatisfactions among those who become disillusioned with the union's leadership. Those who are dissatisfied are likely to split off from the union to form a new group. If might is

[38] Tokiyasu v. Japan, Supreme Court, Grand Bench, May 28, 1958, 12 SAI-HAN KEISHŪ 1694, 1696–97.

[39] Japan v. Hirata, Supreme Court, III Petty Bench, Dec. 11, 1956, 10 SAI-HAN KEISHŪ 1605, 1608–09.

* Conference discussion pointed out that the courts have been very hesitant formally to disapprove mass picketing. Instead, the cases, particularly reinstatement cases, are decided without reference to the propriety of mass picketing; usually the employee is simply ordered reinstated. Consequently many workers believe that mass picketing is fully legal.

permissible, pitched battles between "loyal" unionists and defectors become inevitable, with victory going to whichever side may be the more effectively violent. The intralabor warfare thus encouraged is socially undesirable, as are other breaches of the peace. It is doubly unfortunate from the standpoint of organized labor because the wounds inflicted by workers arrayed against fellow workers are slow to heal. Thus, although the allowance of might may appear to be advantageous to unions in the short run, over time it might well jeopardize labor unity.

Acts of Dispute by Employers

Although the statutes referred to in the preceding pages provide a basis for the unions' claim to legal powers and immunities, no similar laws can be seized upon as justification for employers' actions during a labor dispute.[40] That does not mean, of course, that Japanese employers remain wholly inert when confronted by labor strife. Some of them, like some of their counterparts in the United States, seek openly or subtly to undermine their employees' union solidarity despite laws that forbid employer intrusion into union affairs; in so doing they may commit improper labor acts, which are discussed below. Often even without employer connivance the workers are so disunited that an employer may be able to continue his plant's operations by utilizing the services of nonunionists or seceding union members; but never in recent times has a Japanese employer sought to discharge all striking employees and replace them with newly hired personnel. Professional strikebreakers and amateur "scabs" are as yet unknown in Japan.

The employer's chief weapon of economic pressure or counterpressure is the lockout, a term to which certain special meanings have attached. In Great Britain and Germany, for example, a lockout is essentially a "strike" by management against labor. Lockouts are condoned and condemned in basically the same circumstances as are normal strikes.[41] They may violate existing contracts, in which case they may give rise to damage claims. Subject to such limitations, an employer may in theory use a lockout as an

[40] Art. 7 of the Labor Relations Adjustment Law includes lockout among the labor disputes which a competent labor commission should adjust. The statute gives no intimation whatsoever that a lockout is proper or legal, however; article 7 merely recognizes that if a lockout occurs, then, *de facto*, a labor dispute exists.

The Public Corporation, Etc., Labor Relations Law, art. 17, translated into English in Labor Legislation 125, and the Local Public Enterprise Labor Relations Law, art. 11, translated into English in Labor Legislation 147, also mention lockouts. These statutes declare that lockouts shall not occur in publicly owned enterprises. They say nothing directly about the legality of lockouts in private enterprises, though perhaps the conclusion may be drawn that their explicit illegalization in one area connotes their legality elsewhere.

[41] In Great Britain, there seems to be no feeling that strike and lockout must, for legal purposes, be treated differently. Thus, the Trade Disputes and Trade Unions Act of 1927, 17 & 18 Geo. 5, c. 22, repealed in 1946, prohibited both political lockouts and political strikes.

In Germany, under the federal constitution, freedom to lock out exists to the same extent as freedom to strike. See 2 Hueck & Nipperdey, Lehrbuch des Arbeitsrechts 30 (1957).

economic weapon and shut down operations, close the doors of the work place, and decline to pay wages until a new agreement has been reached concerning the terms and conditions of employment.

Until 1935 the situation in the United States was the same as the present European position. Since the enactment of the Wagner Act, however, employers cannot lock out their employees as freely as the unions can strike; an employer who does try a lockout ordinarily runs the risk of committing an unfair labor practice, although there have been substantial changes in the attitudes of the National Labor Relations Board and the courts.[42]

Also in Japan employers are not so free to "strike" as are their employees. Curiously, however, no case has decided that a lockout is an improper labor act. Great differences exist between the American and the Japanese positions, though, concerning the legal requisites and effects of a lockout. Moreover, while in the United States a lockout has no special position as a matter of civil or criminal law, under Japanese law it gives rise to many difficult and peculiar problems in the fields of civil and criminal law.

Effecting a Lockout

Effecting a lockout in the United States may not be easy as a matter of practical labor relations, but it is simple as a matter of law. The employer simply notifies the employees that work is suspended and that they are forbidden to enter the premises until further notice. Those who ignore this prohibition may be ejected as trespassers, for a worker has no right of entry except as it may have been secured by contract or other consent. Dispute about the propriety of a lockout is thus transferred to a court or to arbitration.

Such is not the case in Japan. The lockout has become a test of physical strength rather than an expression of the employer's will. It is not enough for the employer to declare a suspension of work; he must take "effective measures" to prevent entry to his property and to forestall the employees' performing their usual services. This means, in essence, that to achieve the desired lockout the employer must close all gates, post guards, erect barricades if necessary, and otherwise be prepared to prevent the employees from entering his premises. This view of the lockout seems to be traceable to a scholarly comment on the Labor Union Law.[43] The thrust of the comment was that it was contrary to the dictates of common sense to convict for illegal entry those workers who had gone to their customary work stations despite a notice that operations had been suspended. Because the explanation of the comment was unclear, however, some lower courts adopted the

[42] See NLRB v. Truck Drivers Union, 353 U.S. 87 (1957); Buffalo Linen Supply Co., 109 N.L.R.B. 447 (1954). For detailed analysis, see Metzler, *Single-Employer and Multi-Employer Lockouts Under the Taft-Hartley Act*, 24 U. CHI. L. REV. 70 (1956).

[43] TŌKYŌ DAIGAKU RŌDŌ HŌ KENKYŪ KAI (Tokyo University Labor Law Research Society), CHŪKAI RŌDŌ KUMIAI HŌ (A Commentary on the Labor Union Law) 32 (1949). As one of the coauthors of the book, I must confess regret over the result.

view that the charge of illegal entry was inappropriate not only in criminal cases but also in civil cases in which employers sought provisional orders ousting the employees. Scholars quickly seized upon this view as a basis for their argument that a lockout could never be a matter of employer intent, but must always be a matter of employer achievement; if the employer could not himself prevent the workers from coming to work, he had not succeeded in locking them out, regardless of how clear his desire or how explicit his orders might be, since the law would not aid him in removing the offending employees from the premises. In some factories, either because of their physical location or because of the manner of their operations (for example, three-shift operation), "effective measures" are a virtual impossibility; in such situations, the lockout is deemed to be altogether barred.

The effective-measures theory is a plain invitation to violence.[44] In one case, for example, a mining corporation decided to lock out its employees.[45] Mindful of the prevailing theory, the management placed essential miners' equipment such as caplights in a storeroom and stationed guards at its doors. Clashes quickly developed between the guards and union members who attempted to break into the storeroom. After considerable damage to persons and property, the workers failed to break the locks; thus the employer's measures proved to be effective measures for preventing the resumption of work.

Fortunately, criticism of the effective-measures theory has persisted precisely because of the likelihood that it would generate disorderly battles.[46] In March 1961, the Tokyo District Court held clearly that a lockout did not require the employer's mobilizing of a plant constabulary.[47] Thus it is

[44] Cf. Arita v. Dai Nippon Kōgyō Kabushiki Kaisha Hatsumori Kōgyō-jo Rōdō Kumiai (Great Japan Mining Company Hatsumori Mine Labor Union), Akita District Court, Sept. 29, 1960, 11 RŌDŌ KANKEI MINJI SAIBAN REISHŪ (A Collection of Civil Cases Concerning Labor) [hereafter cited RŌ-MINSHŪ] 1081, 1101, JURIST no. 219, at 70 (note Ishikawa): "That is since forcing work [work against the will of the employer] is an effective action employed by the union as a countermeasure to check the enforcement of a lockout before the event, a directive [by the union] to force work in itself certainly cannot be called illegal." Rarely has a member of the judiciary issued a clearer invitation to use force.

[45] *Ibid.*

[46] CHŪKAI RŌDŌ KUMIAI HŌ, note 35, at 245.

[47] Kabushiki Kaisha Meguro Seisakujo (Meguro Manufacturing Co.) v. Sōhyō Zenkoku Kinzoku Rōdō Kumiai Tōkyō Chihō Hombu Meguro Seisakujo Honsha Shibu (Sōhyō National Metalworkers Labor Union, Tokyo Local Headquarters, Local for the Main Meguro Manufacturing Co.), Tokyo District Court, March 28, 1961, 12 RŌ-MINSHŪ 161. The case involved the Meguro Manufacturing Company, a manufacturer of automotive parts. A lengthy strike led to a splitting of the union. About half of the work force desired to resume work, but the others, under union leadership, occupied the factory and continued the strike. Meguro then notified the union that it intended to close the plant for an indefinite period and that the union's members should vacate the premises. When they refused, the employer sought a District Court order to compel the occupants to leave. An order to do so was issued by the court, but the strikers ignored it. The court marshal, who went to the factory to secure compliance, was refused admittance. The police then arrested the strike leaders for disobedience of the court's order.

Cf., however, my discussion of factory occupation as an act of labor dispute on p. 452.

possible that the judicial tide is turning. Lockouts may be undesirable—like strikes, they are often unnecessary interferences with normal productivity—but their legality should not be made to turn upon the relative muscularity of the opposing parties.

The Employer's Liability during a Lockout

Although in general the employer's duty to pay wages ceases when work has been discontinued pursuant to his command, liability for wages may exist in some circumstances.

Article 536(2) of the Civil Code says: "If performance [of a contract] becomes impossible in consequence of a cause for which the creditor is responsible, the debtor does not lose his right to receive counterperformance. Provided, however, that if he has obtained a benefit due to being relieved of his obligation, he is required to restore it to the creditor." As applied to an individual labor contract, this would seem to mean that a worker who stands ready to perform an agreed-upon service could not be deprived of his wages if the employer prevented the rendition of the service for which wages were to be paid. As this has been interpreted, however, the issue to be considered in connection with an employer's liability during a lockout is whether the employer's act in forcing suspension of work was justifiable in labor-dispute terms. The answer to that question seems clear if the purpose was illegal—for example, to damage a union and thus to discourage membership, which the employer is prohibited from doing by article 7 of the Labor Union Law—or violated an existing collective labor agreement. In the latter event a lockout seems no more an "appropriate act of dispute" than a strike would be in the same circumstances. Whether liability to pay wages exists in other circumstances remains unsettled; there is no decision of the Supreme Court on this point. In the lower courts three trends may be discerned. For several years after the war, some courts denied demands for wages on the ground that "it is a matter of course from both the principle of trustworthiness [*Treu und Glauben*] in bilateral contracts and the principle of equality in labor disputes that during a period of lockout employers have no duty to pay wages."[48] Strictly speaking, this view regards lockout as not falling within the purview of article 536(2) of the Civil Code and resembles the prevailing thinking in the European countries in equating lockout and strike. The other two views regard lockout in the light of article 536(2) but differ in the next step. One leniently acknowledges the nonliability of the employer;[49] the other holds that lockout exempts the

[48] Ōzuru Kōgyō-jo Rōdō Kumiai (Ozuru Mine Labor Union) v. Kishima Tankō Rōdō Kumiai (Kishima Coal Mining Labor Union), Saga District Court, May 30, 1950, 1 RŌ-MINSHŪ 341, 348.

[49] Dōwa Kōgyō Rōdō Kumiai Rengō Kai (Federation of Dowa Mining Labor Unions) v. Dōwa Kōgyō Kabushiki Kaisha (Dowa Mining Co.), Tokyo District Court, Aug. 7, 1951, 2 RŌ-MINSHŪ 258.

employers from paying wages only when it is done in a defensive way, that is, "in the case of an unavoidable lockout imminently necessary to defend the enterprise from a marked injury arising or likely to arise owing to acts of dispute where the labor organization to which the employees belong resorts to acts of dispute which will markedly injure the employer or it is clear that it will resort to such acts of dispute." [50] In other words, a lockout may be instituted with impunity if its purpose is to forestall a threatened factory occupation, seisan kanri, or the like, by a union, but not if its purpose is to achieve an affirmative desire of the employer, such as a lowering of wage rates. The majority of scholars seems to have adopted the last view.[51]

The Rights of the Locked-Out Workers

It is generally understood that the contract between the employer and his employee is not terminated by lockout or strike. According to some scholars, a worker need not leave his work place. Unless he himself has by misconduct or omission forfeited his right to remain there, he is deemed to have a right of possession or something akin to it and cannot be proceeded against for trespass, even if he ignores the employer's lockout by entering into or remaining on the employer's premises. This approach seems perhaps somewhat metaphysical, but it has a number of adherents, though it has not yet gained the support of judicial decisions. It is understandable in the domain of criminal law because, under the maxim of ***nulla poena sine lege,*** article 130 of the Penal Code can be construed not to cover such cases, stress being laid on the existence of "reason." [52] The Tokyo District Court has held that

> the issue before us is whether, in a case where during a dispute an employer—based on his right to control a building—demands that his employees leave and the union members—directly bearing the duty to depart—contravene this duty, they thereby give rise to the crime of nondeparture. As far as this court is concerned, on this point, it does not feel that these facts alone create the crime. This is because, since the union members need to carry on collective bargaining, etc., during this dispute, we believe that it would be unduly harsh to say that the mere fact that the members remained in the building in and of itself immediately gives rise to the crime of nondeparture. But, if the circumstances should be such that—in a case where there has been a demand for departure based on the right to control a building—the union members, on their part, plan to go beyond appropriate acts of dispute in order to interfere with the employer's execution of his business functions and moreover such acts have emerged, we must construe that the constituent elements of criminal nondeparture have been met: namely, failure to leave without reason.[53]

[50] Kamezaki v. Japan, Tokyo District Court, Jan. 14, 1957, 8 Rō-MINSHŪ 109, 127.

[51] See, e.g., MIYAJIMA, LOCKOUT RON (A Treatise on Lockout) 416 (1960).

[52] "A person who, without reason, intrudes upon a human habitation or upon the guarded residence of a person, a structure or a vessel, or who will not leave such place upon demand is to be punished." PENAL CODE art. 130.

[53] Judgment of Aug. 29, 1958, Tokyo District Court, HANREI JIHŌ (The Case Journal) no. 168, at 28.

Nevertheless, the approach seems unsupportable once it goes further and asserts that workers have rights akin to possession and that, therefore, the court cannot order the workers to leave the employer's premises.

Some scholars argue that, once a strike or lockout has begun, an employer may not properly resume operations at a later time with newly hired personnel, for, as mentioned above, the employer-employee relationship is not severed by a strike or a lockout. The presumed continuity of relationship merges imperceptibly into a supposed contractual obligation to go on treating an individual as an employee in all spheres, including the continuance of wages.[54]

INTRAUNION AND INTERUNION CONFLICTS

Divisions and dissensions within the labor-union movement are in no sense peculiar to Japan. The United States has experienced major ruptures, such as the breaking off of the Congress of Industrial Organizations from the American Federation of Labor in 1937, as well as schisms within individual unions.[55] Many of the presently dominant British trade unions are the products of "breakaway." [56] But the splitting of unions may have become quantitatively more significant in Japan than elsewhere. Quite apart from the large divisions to which reference has been made in an earlier context,[57] almost every prominent labor dispute causes the fragmentation of some existing union and the growth of new organizations. Japanese law is absolutely silent about the consequences of a union split, despite the frequency with which members secede from one group in order to form another which then lays claim to its predecessor's assets or prerogatives.

On the other hand, Japan is more fortunate than the United States in that so far it has not had any jurisdictional disputes among the unions, and it is unlikely that the country will suffer from this kind of problem in the near future.[58] The nature of the Japanese unions, particularly the pre-

[54] The gaps in this theorizing will be clear to anyone schooled in Western conceptions of contract. At the May 1961 meeting of the Japan Labor Law Association, however, the position was strongly asserted and widely endorsed that employers must continue to pay some allowance even to employees who are actively on strike. The employees' contract of labor, it was maintained, does not abate by reason of their going on strike, a constitutionally protected activity for which they may not lawfully be subjected to penalty; if the unfounded principle of "no work, no pay" were to prevail, there would be little value in the constitutional guarantee of the right to strike. See *Nihon Rōdō Hō Gakkai Dai 22 Kai Taikai Kiji* (Proceedings of the 22nd Convention of the Japan Labor Law Association), RŌDŌ HŌ (Labor Law) no. 18, at 108, 119.

[55] See 24 NLRB ANN. REP. 27 (1959).

[56] See Bell, *Trade Unions,* in THE SYSTEM OF INDUSTRIAL RELATIONS IN GREAT BRITAIN 174 (Flanders & Clegg ed., 1954).

[57] See the previous discussion of the major labor federations, Sōhyō and Zenrō, on p. 443.

[58] In the United States, § 8(b)(4)(D) of the National Labor Relations Act is intended to reduce jurisdictional disputes. As a matter of fact, however, there are still many such disputes, explicit or implicit.

dominance of the establishment-wide union, accounts for this phenomenon.

Disintegration of a union is usually an incident of a long-continued and frustrating strike. Members who have grown skeptical of their leaders' judgment or motives proceed secretly to organize a rival union. Then, when they think the moment propitious, they reveal the existence of the new union, denounce the leaders of the old, and — often only after a violent physical struggle with pickets who have remained loyal to the old union — return to work on terms agreeable to them or, quite often, even before such terms have been agreed upon.[59] Once this has been done, the new union usually succeeds in procuring the membership of a majority of the workers; the old union is absorbed and becomes an embittered minority faction, sometimes reduced to only two or three diehards but occasionally still including close to half of the employees.

Japanese workers are not unique in their dissatisfaction with long strikes. Back-to-work movements are actual or possible threats to union solidarity in most prolonged labor disputes in the United States and elsewhere. Strike leaders must devote much care to "educating" both the workers themselves and their families as well, in order to maintain morale and to encourage unity during the hardships and uncertainties of a lengthy work stoppage. What is perhaps peculiar to Japan is the failure of its labor movement to create intraunion mechanisms that make possible the airing of the members' doubts and disagreements, and the failure to create an atmosphere in which the union members would think of utilizing such mechanisms when they do exist. Typically Japanese unions do not function as member-controlled bodies. The members usually meet yearly to elect officers and to reformulate general policies. The leaders direct the members from this point on; they do not receive and execute the members' instructions. Moreover, the leaders command rather than advise. Choices are not debated and put to a vote; they are made by the elected leaders and announced to the followers.

In these circumstances, disagreement necessarily expresses itself by rebellion and leads to disruption of the organization, rather than merely causing the adoption of new policies or the supplanting of officers who have

[59] Some scholars maintain that no union member is free to withdraw during a strike. To abandon the union at such a time, they say, is an act of treachery to the proletariat of which the worker is a part. They contend that art. 28 of the Constitution guarantees the right of workers to organize and, at the same time, the right of the resulting organizations to function in their organizers' behalf. If the right of the individual workers comes into conflict with the right of the union, the latter must prevail. As a consequence, the union must be deemed free to take harshly repressive — that is to say, necessarily violent — action against traitors who have sought to retire from the union and who wish to terminate the strike. The theory just described has not yet received judicial endorsement, but it is strongly urged by many scholars. See, e.g., NUMATA, DANKETSU-KEN YŌGO RON (A Treatise on Defense of the Right to Organize) 227 (1952); Minemura, *Danketsu-ken* (Right to Organize), in DANKETSU TO KYŌYAKU NO HŌRI (Legal Principles of Organization and Collective Agreement) 13 (1954).

lost their popular support. The absence of genuine democracy in Japanese labor unions explains their fragility. They shatter into pieces because they lack the elasticity to respond to internal pressures.

The question then arises as to why the union does not protect itself, as in the United States, by insisting upon a "union security" provision in its contract with the employer. The question may be answered in terms of the union situation.

Closed-shop agreements are virtually impossible in Japan since an employer cannot promise to recruit new employees only from among a union's members; the members of an establishment union are by definition only those persons who have already been employed.

However, no similar impediment stands in the way of a union-shop contract, which would make it the duty of the employer to dismiss employees who have failed to join or to remain members in good standing of the union with which the contract has been made. This agreement is thus very popular in Japan; it is said that over 80 percent of the collective labor agreements have a union-shop clause. But here again a peculiar situation exists. Almost all the union-shop agreements are "soft" ones, meaning that the employer is relieved from the duty of discharging employees who have quit the union or have been ousted from it if he deems their services necessary for his business. The unions' readiness to concede this very large escape hatch indicates that they do not greatly prize the contractual security. Apparently, though the mere existence of union-shop provisions may have some effect upon uninformed workers, such provisions are rarely enforced. The unions have demanded rarely that employers dismiss workers who have seceded whether in connection with a major split or the defection of only a few members.

The legality of union-security provisions seems to be reasonably clear, however. The Labor Union Law provides in article 7(i) that, whereas no worker may be discriminated against by reason of his union affiliation or, by implication, his lack of union affiliation,

> in a case where a labor union represents a majority of the workers employed at a factory or place of business, this [prohibition] does not preclude [an employer] concluding a collective labor agreement which imposes as a condition of employment that these workers be members of this labor union.

A few commentators have expressed doubt that this statutory approval of union-shop contracts is consonant with the constitutional guarantee of the workers' freedom to organize as they may wish, but most observers have no doubt that the statutory and constitutional provisions are harmonious.[60]

[60] The Tokyo District Court recently expressed the view that a union which had lost its majority following could not seek enforcement of a union-shop provision by demanding the ouster of workers who had resigned from the union. The court reasoned that the basis on which the legality of the union shop stood had been lost. Kabushiki Kaisha Meguro Seisakujo

The possibility remains, therefore, that Japanese unions may in the future seek more energetically than they have in the past to claim the protection which the law puts within their reach.

Disposition of a union's property after it has split is a highly contentious matter. The problem has given rise to heated litigation in the United States without a clear resolution of the issues.[61] It is not surprising, therefore, that in Japan—where the problem has more recently emerged and where clarifying litigation is less frequent—considerable confusion remains concerning conflicting claims to a disrupted union's funds.

The only expression of the Japanese Supreme Court in this field has evoked much derision and scant approval. Five hundred of the six hundred members of a union representing workers in a plant seceded from the union and established a rival organization. The newcomer demanded that the old union turn over to it five sixths of the union's assets. When the demand was rejected, an ordinary civil action was brought to recover property which allegedly was being wrongfully withheld from its rightful owner. After much deliberation, the Supreme Court finally rejected the newcomer's claim on the ground that, "since the property of an association without capacity of rights is in actuality subject to the so-called 'collective ownership' [*Gesamteigentum*] of all the members composing the association, it is proper to conclude that so long as a decision to dissolve the collective ownership or dispose of this property is not made with the common consent of all the members, neither the present nor the original members automatically possess a co-ownership interest right or a right to claim partition regarding this property." [62] The term "collective ownership," so obligingly and appropriately adopted by the Court from a German model, means essentially that property held in common by a group may be transferred only by the unanimous agreement of its owners. The proposition developed out of the customary law of tribes that once roamed the woods of old Germania. Its applicability to the affairs of a many-membered association of workers in modern industrial society seems highly doubtful.[63]

Some lower courts, approaching the problem more realistically, have tried to divide the assets in accordance with the number of members in the

(Meguro Manufacturing Co.) v. Sōhyō Zenkoku Kinzoku Rōdō Kumiai Tōkyō Chihō Hombu Meguro Seisakujo Honsha Shibu (Sōhyō National Metalworkers Labor Union, Tokyo Local Headquarters, Local for the Main Meguro Manufacturing Co.), note 47 above. Were this view to prevail, 7(i) would lose much of its significance. The union's majority status and, consequently, its eligibility to make a union-shop contract must be determined as of the time when the contract was made, not as of the time when it is applied. Otherwise the entire purpose of the union-security provision would be defeated.

[61] See Greenberg, *Disposition of Union Assets upon Disaffiliation*, 33 TEMP. L.Q. 152 (1959).

[62] Tanaka v. Shinagawa Shiro Renga Kabushiki Kaisha Okayama Kōjō Rōdō Kumiai (Shinagawa White Brick Company Okayama Factory Labor Union), Supreme Court, I Petty Bench, Nov. 14, 1957, 11 SAI-HAN MINSHŪ 1943, 1944.

[63] The decision is criticized in CHŪKAI RŌDŌ KUMIAI HŌ, note 35, at 303–07.

respective unions. Difficult problems still remain, however. For example, in order that the courts not interfere with an intraunion battle by prematurely dividing the organization's assets, they must determine under what circumstances a union split may be considered sufficient to justify such a division. Courts also face a problem in ascertaining the exact number of members in each union, since often a single worker is counted by both unions.

IMPROPER LABOR ACTS

The concept of unfair labor practice originated in American law and was exported to Japan during the occupation. It experienced a number of sea changes while in transit, however, so that the Japanese development, known as "improper labor acts," has only a slight resemblance to the original American model.

The legal framework can be quickly stated. The Labor Union Law in article 7 forbids as improper certain acts of employers. Japanese law thus, unlike American, does not recognize the possibility of an unfair labor practice by a union. The most frequently heard accusation is of discrimination against unionists. Employer domination, interference in the affairs of a union, and refusal to bargain collectively are other causes of complaint.[64] Articles 19 through 26 create various labor-relations commissions and describe their composition and function. Article 27 provides that the appropriate commission shall act upon complaints alleging a violation of article 7, making such investigations and holding such hearings as may be needed to determine whether an employer has engaged in antiunion activities as charged. Article 28 sets forth penalties for disregard of a labor commission's final order that has been affirmed upon judicial review; and article 32 imposes similar penalties for violation of a court order directing compliance with a commission order.

Concurrent Jurisdiction

A striking aspect of Japanese law is that, unlike its American counterpart, it gives to courts as well as to labor-relations commissions full jurisdiction to deal with an alleged improper labor act, at least with respect to discrimination cases.[65]

A worker who asserts that he has been dismissed from his job because of union activity may file a petition with the appropriate labor commission. This is not merely a charge, to be investigated by the commission as a preliminary to its filing a complaint against the employer if the charge appears to have substance. A petitioner can initiate proceedings before the labor

[64] See Table 4 at the end of this essay.

[65] With respect to other types of improper labor acts, such as interference or refusal to bargain, some scholars hold that the courts cannot decide cases because the problems are not susceptible of judicial handling. This view has been expressed to the author by Professors Teruhisa Ishii of Tokyo University and Mitsutoshi Azuma of Hitotsubashi University.

commission just as he can initiate a lawsuit in a civil court; the commission does not have control over its intake of cases as does the United States National Labor Relations Board.

If the worker prefers, he may file an action in one of the forty-nine District Courts, which are courts of general jurisdiction. The relief usually sought in such a lawsuit is an order of "provisional disposition," requiring the employer to revoke the alleged act of discrimination. If the act was a discharge, the order would require the employer to rescind the discharge and treat the worker as an employee. Provisional disposition may be likened to a temporary restraining order; it reflects no judgment on the merits, but is an exercise of discretionary power to prevent undue hardship until the merits can be determined. Its ready availability in matters of this type tends to make the courts a favored forum for the consideration of allegedly wrongful acts of employers.[66]

Although recourse to the courts is usual, some cases of this type still appear before labor commissions and, in a few instances, before a court and a commission simultaneously. Occasionally the separate tribunals have reached contrary conclusions. Thus, one labor-relations commission held that an employer had not improperly discharged a worker who began a hunger strike at the factory entrance because, in the commission's opinion, the hunger strike was not an "appropriate act of a labor union";[67] but in the very same case a District Court decreed that the worker's discharge violated items (i) and (iii) of article 7 of the Labor Union Law and was "contrary to public order in labor relations."[68] In the known instances of inconsistent decisions, the parties have reached compromises, thus preventing further exploration of this juridical anomaly. The embarrassments that may flow from jurisdictional nonexclusivity have not yet aroused the concern of the courts or the Diet. Conflicting decisions are blandly excused on the ground that courts and commissions have different functions; a court considers a discharged worker's complaint as a civil case whereas a labor commission regards it as an administrative case; thus the two tribunals utilize different

[66] The courts' jurisdiction to deal with such cases is not spelled out explicitly anywhere. The generally prevailing theories in support of jurisdiction are, first, that a discharge because of union affiliation is contrary to the spirit of art. 28 of the Constitution and therefore violates art. 90 of the Civil Code, a catchall provision that declares that "a juristic act which has as its object a matter contrary to public order or good morals is void"; and, second, that such a discharge is nothing more than an abuse of right and thus falls within the interdiction of article 1(3) of the Civil Code ("Abuse of rights is not permitted"). On one theory or another, the courts do assume jurisdiction and no serious objection to their doing so has been voiced. In no instance, as far as I know, has a court dismissed a suit on the ground that recourse to a labor commission was meant to be an exclusive remedy for a discriminatory discharge.

[67] Honda Giken Saitama Rōdō Kumiai (Honda Giken Saitama Labor Union) v. Honda Giken Kōgyō Kabushiki Kaisha (Honda Giken Industrial Co.), Saitama Local Labor Relations Commission, Oct. 9, 1958, Rōdō Iinkai Sokuhō no. 438, at 6.

[68] Chijiiwa v. Honda Giken Kōgyō Kabushiki Kaisha (Honda Giken Industrial Co.), Tokyo District Court, Nov. 24, 1958, 9 Rō-minshū 1013.

decisional criteria. Whether this verbalistic mumbo jumbo will prove permanently satisfying to scholars, let alone to the much more critical body of laymen who may be affected by such proceedings, is highly doubtful.

Appellate Proceedings

Appeal from an adverse judicial decision may be taken to a higher court, as provided in the Code of Civil Procedure. The steps are simple and are well understood by lawyers.

Appeal from an unfavorable labor relations commission's decision is far more complex. The Labor Union Law contemplates a local commission in each one of Japan's forty-six prefectures and a Central Labor Relations Commission.[69] A petitioner begins his action before the local commission having jurisdiction over the place in which the alleged improper labor act has occurred or where the employer's place of business is located.[70] The unsuccessful party can then appeal to the Central Labor Relations Commission. The loser before the central commission can seek judicial review by the Tokyo District Court, then if still interested, by the Tokyo High Court, and ultimately by the Supreme Court, which also sits in Tokyo. Under article 27(6), when the employer does not petition the central commission for review, he may also institute suit in accordance with the procedural rules set down in the Administrative Case Litigation Law. This means that the employer can seek judicial review in the proper District Court sitting in the prefecture without first obtaining administrative review of the order by the local commission. For the employees, however, there is no such provision; a person who has sought an administrative remedy must exhaust every procedure open to him. Accordingly a worker must be prepared to file a petition and attend a hearing at the prefectural seat, and then to make possibly repeated trips to Tokyo for further administrative- or judicial-review proceedings that may last as long as five years. A process more calculated to thwart the worker's attempts to assert his rights is hard to imagine. Those who contemplate pursuing Justice through all the labyrinthine paths along

[69] Labor Union Law, art. 19(2). That same statute creates the Mariners' Central Labor Relations Commission and twelve Mariners' Local Labor Relations Commissions. *Ibid.* The Public Corporation, Etc., Labor Relations Law, art. 19 creates the Public Corporation, Etc., Labor Relations Commission. I omit these specialized bodies from the present discussion for the sake of simplification. The description of procedures and problems of the central and local commissions is largely applicable to the special commissions as well.

[70] In some instances, therefore, the employee can choose the particular local commission which he thinks is most favorable to him or to labor at large, or most competent to handle improper-labor-act cases. "The Central Labor Relations Commission takes precedence in assuming jurisdiction in regard to the conciliation, mediation, arbitration and disposition of cases involving two or more metropolises, circuits, urban prefectures or prefectures or pertaining to a problem important nationally." Labor Union Law, art. 25(1) (second sentence).

which it totters are generally believed to be millionaires' sons or psychopathic personalities with a passion for litigation.

Organization and Methods of Commissions

Despite the forbidding procedures just described, labor relations commissions do perform some functions.

Each commission is tripartite. The central commission and the local commissions in Hokkaido Circuit, Tokyo Metropolis, Osaka Urban Prefecture, and Fukuoka Prefecture consist of seven public commissioners, seven employer commissioners, and seven labor commissioners; the other local commissions have five members from each group. The term of office is one year, but reappointments are frequent. Appointments of employer and labor commissioners are made on the basis of recommendations by employers and labor organizations; and the public commissioners must be appointed with the consent of the employer and labor members.[71]

The commissions have two duties. One is to adjudicate complaints of improper labor acts, which includes deciding whether a union is eligible to participate in the formal procedures provided in the Labor Union Law and be accorded the remedies provided therein.[72] The public commissioners alone engage in these tasks.[73] The other is to adjust labor disputes by conciliation, mediation, or, if both parties agree to it, arbitration.

Each commission has the assistance of clerks, but there are no field investigators or hearing officers. In the larger commissions, the chairman assigns each case to an individual public commissioner, who then conducts whatever inquiries or hearings may be suitable. The Tokyo Metropolis Local Labor Relations Commission disposes of about eighty cases annually, divided among its seven public commissioners. Some local commissions in smaller prefectures have only one or two proceedings each year, and sometimes none at all. When a case does arise, all five public commissioners are likely to sit *en banc* to hear it, a practice some cynics believe functionally justified only by the fact that it produces prestige for the sitters. The annual number of all petitions is around 400,[74] a strikingly low figure when

[71] Labor Union Law, art. 19(7).

[72] Labor Union Law, art. 5(1): "Unless a labor union submits evidence to a labor relations commission and proves that it is complying with the provisions of article 2 and paragraph (2), it is not eligible to participate in the procedures provided for in this Law nor may it be accorded the remedies provided for in this Law. Provided, however, that this is not to be construed as denying any individual worker the protection under the provisions of article 7, item (i)."

[73] Labor Union Law, art. 24: "Only the public commissioners of a labor relations commission participate in a disposition concerning cases pursuant to the provisions of articles 5, 7, 11 and 27, and article 42 of the Labor Relations Adjustment Law. Provided, however, that this does not preclude the employer and labor commissioners participating in hearings held in advance of a ruling."

[74] See Table 2 at the end of this essay.

compared with the United States, in which there were 7,723 charges against employers in 1960.[75]

The number of hearings varies from case to case but generally there are at least five, each lasting from two to as many as eight hours. In article 27(1), the statute prescribes that during the hearing the "employer and petitioner shall be accorded adequate opportunity to submit evidence and crossexamine witnesses." Those who conduct hearings tend to allow the proceedings to move at the pace the parties set. In one recent case to determine whether a single employee had been unfairly dismissed, thirteen hearings were spread over a period of two years. In another instance, the hearings had not been concluded after twenty-one sessions.

Ordinarily about six months elapse between the filing of a petition and a local commission's rendering of its order. The commission may grant the relief sought, reject the complaint on the merits after hearing, or dismiss the complaint either because of procedural defects or because it shows on its face that no improper labor act has occurred.[76]

Orders, like those of the National Labor Relations Board in the United States, are designed to fit the needs of the particular case. For example, they may compel reinstatement of a worker with back pay, direct an employer to engage in collective bargaining, or command him to refrain from interfering with or dominating union affairs. Several important differences exist between these orders and those of the NLRB, however. First, the Japanese order is much shorter.[77] Second, many Japanese orders merely require the employers to post notices.[78] Third, in Japan reinstatements without full back pay are very infrequent, having occurred only twice. Japanese administrative practice thus disregards an employee's earnings from other sources during the period in which he was not working for the employer who wrongfully discharged him. Recently, however, the Tokyo High Court launched the novel theory that article 536(2) of the Civil Code[79] applies to such cases and, therefore, that the employee's earnings during the period of discharge had to be deducted from the back pay awarded him by the commission's order.[80] Whether this approach will be generally accepted remains to be seen.

[75] See 25 NLRB ANN. REP. 12 (1961).

[76] Cf. Table 2 and Table 3 at the end of this essay.

[77] A typical order is as follows: "The company must withdraw the discharge of the petitioner, dated April 1, 1961, and reinstate him in his former job. The company also must pay the petitioner a sum equivalent to the wages he would have earned but for the discharge." It should be noted that in Japan, unlike the United States, no difficulties have been encountered in determining what amount of back pay is due.

[78] In the United States a requirement to post a notice is always part of an order; consequently, the NLRB never issues an order which merely requires the employer or labor organization to post a notice.

[79] CIVIL CODE art. 536(2). See p. 458.

[80] Kamezaki v. Japan, Tokyo High Court, Jan. 30, 1961, 12 RŌ-MINSHŪ 37 (this case involved a lockout at the U.S. Army Kokura General Supply Depot in northern Kyushu).

Substantive Issues

Japan has many problems in the area of improper labor acts that are not yet solved; only a few of these can be mentioned here. For example, one current question involves the "intent" of the employer. This matter has long been an important issue in the United States as well, but the law there is now fairly clear. An unfair labor practice exists without regard to the employer's intent under section 8(a)(1) of the National Labor Relations Act, which prohibits employer interference with the rights of employees guaranteed in section 7, such as the right to bargain collectively through representatives of their own choosing; on the other hand, the employer's state of mind is relevant to the determination of an unfair labor practice under section 8(a)(3), which prohibits discrimination by employers.[81] In 1949 the Supreme Court of Japan, with respect to article 7(iii) of the Labor Union Law, expressed the view that an employer who had in fact exercised domination over a union was guilty of an improper labor act even though he did not intend to crush the union.[82] This decision has attained little popularity, however, even among the lower courts; there has been no decision citing it. The Supreme Court has not yet given its view with respect to article 7(i). The general opinion seems to be that in every instance the employer's intent is an indispensable ingredient of an improper labor act.[83] A few scholars criticize this conclusion by pointing out that it is too much influenced by the theory of intent in criminal law; they assert that the employer's intent should not be regarded as an essential component of an improper labor act since issuing orders in such cases is not intended to penalize employers but to bring about better relations between management and labor.[84] This view, however, is still that of the minority.

In 1958 the Tokyo District Court rendered a decision which has led to much discussion and criticism among scholars and practitioners.[85] A creditor company demanded of a debtor company that the latter discharge an employee who, in his capacity as union president, had joined in an effort to

[81] Such an intention will be presumed where the discrimination inherently has the effect of an unfair labor practice, as where it is based on union membership or lack thereof. Where discrimination does not inherently encourage or discourage union membership, however, the employer's unlawful motivation must be shown by independent evidence. See Radio Officers' Union v. NLRB, 347 U.S. 17 (1954); 25 NLRB ANN. REP. 65 (1961).

[82] Yamaoka Nainenki Kabushiki Kaisha (Yamaoka Internal Combustion Engine Co.) v. Shiga Ken Chihō Rōdō Iinkai (Shiga Prefecture Local Labor Relations Commission), Supreme Court, II Petty Bench, May 28, 1954, 8 SAIKŌ SAIBANSHO MINJI HANREI SHŪ (A Collection of Criminal Supreme Court Cases) 990.

[83] Minakawa v. Mitsui Seimei Hoken Sōgo Kaisha (Mitsui Mutual Life Insurance Co.), Tokyo District Court, Nov. 28, 1957, 8 RŌ-MINSHŪ 1003.

[84] See, e.g., Ishikawa, *Danketsu-ken to Futō Rōdō Kōi* (The Right to Organize and Improper Labor Acts), HŌGAKU SEMINAR (Legal Seminar), no. 40, at 44, 46 (1959).

[85] Fujita v. Yamae Mokuzai Kabushiki Kaisha (Yamae Lumber Co.), Tokyo District Court, Dec. 24, 1958, 9 RŌ-MINSHŪ 984.

organize the workers of yet a third company in which the creditor was interested. The debtor, under great pressure, finally did dismiss the employee, acknowledging that it did so only because his activities in the labor movement had earned the creditor's enmity. The court refused to issue an order of provisional disposition commanding the discharged employee's reinstatement, saying that the employer had not acted in order to penalize a unionist but simply to preserve its credit standing. The case should not have been regarded as raising any question of intent, but rather as whether an innocent employee should be without redress because coercion by a third party had robbed the employer of free will. The very fact that this case is thought by many scholars[86] to be one relating to employer's intent, even though the court carefully refrained from using the term, reflects the present majority feeling that active intent is an essential ingredient of an improper labor act just as intent is an element of most crimes.

Another current issue is involved with the dissolution of a number of smaller enterprises in order to avoid dealing with a union, when these have soon thereafter reappeared under an altered name with a full roster of nonunion supporters drawn from the employment lists of the predecessor firms. In Japan, as in the United States, an effort is made to determine the real substance of the transaction, with the result that successors and assignees have been held liable for improper acts against a predecessor corporation's employees.[87] Sometimes a complete dissolution actually occurs; a businessman simply decides that he will shut his doors forever rather than deal with a union. Some courts have held, with the approval of many scholars,[88] that the dissolution is null and void in such circumstances because the employer's purpose was to discourage the workers' organization and collective bargaining.[89] A few scholars maintain, with the support so far of only one lower court decision,[90] that a line must be drawn between a business enterprise that engages in trickery to avoid fulfilling its legal obligations to employees and a business enterprise that is terminated in good faith in order to avoid unwelcome obligations.[91]

As in the United States, an employer's freedom of expression in connection with improper labor acts has been a controversial issue. There is no statutory

[86] See, e.g., KIKAN RŌDŌ HŌ (Quarterly Labor Law) no. 31, at 150, 156 (note Momii).

[87] Fukuoka Kokusai Kankō Hotel (Fukuoka International Tourist Hotel) v. Yonekura, Fukuoka District Court, May 2, 1952, 3 RŌ-MINSHŪ 125.

[88] For example, KIKAN RŌDŌ HŌ no. 23, at 91 (note Yokoi).

[89] E.g., Shinohara v. Kabushiki Kaisha Ōta Tekkōjō (Ota Ironworks Co.), Osaka District Court, Dec. 1, 1956, 7 RŌ-MINSHŪ 986.

[90] Denki Rōren Hōjō Chiku Gōdō Rōdō Kumiai (All-Japan Federation of Electrical Equipment Labor Unions, Hojo District United Labor Union) v. Kabushiki Kaisha Obata Tekkōjō (Obata Ironworks Co.), Kobe District Court, Yashiro Branch, July 12, 1960, 11 RŌ-MINSHŪ 763.

[91] See, e.g., Ishikawa, *Kaisha no Kaisan Ketsugi ga Futō Rōdō Kōi Toshite Mukō to Naru Ka* (Is a Resolution to Dissolve a Company Void as an Improper Labor Act?), JURIST no. 126, at 42 (1957).

provision similar to section 8(c) of the United States National Labor Relations Act.[92] The Osaka High Court held in one case that the freedom of expression guaranteed in article 21 of the Constitution is limited, in some cases and to some extent, by the rights of workers guaranteed by article 28.[93] The judgment was affirmed by the Supreme Court.[94] The Tokyo District Court has held that "generally, in labor disputes, mutual persuasion and attack upon the assertions of the other as improper through speech comes within the area of freedom of speech permitted both workers and employers." [95] There is a slight difference between these two decisions: the former view, which now represents the prevailing opinion in Japan, imposes a somewhat greater limitation upon the employer's freedom of expression. Indeed, although the courts and the labor commissions have never gone this far, Japanese employers fear that any expression of their views during a labor dispute may constitute an improper labor act. The results of this attitude have been unfortunate. A union may freely say whatever it thinks helpful to its cause during a labor dispute; inevitably much of what it says is exaggerated, tendentious, or false. The employer, feeling unable to respond by speech or writing, may ultimately be driven by desperation and frustration to respond by violence. An explicit recognition of the employer's freedom to speak would thus be a wholesome development.

A final current issue to be considered is the problem of the absence of any provision for determining either what constitutes an appropriate bargaining unit or which union is the representative of a majority of the workers and thus entitled to speak for them all. This situation exposes an employer to almost continuous negotiations. At the time of fixing the year-end bonus, for example, an employer may have to deal simultaneously or consecutively with three or four unions. A union that admittedly represents only two employees is entitled as a matter of law to the same attention as that given to a more truly representative group, although of course such a small union is rarely in a position to exert heavy economic pressure. Several years ago, the government sought to introduce the "appropriate bargaining unit" system, but the attempt was unsuccessful since both labor and management were opposed to it. Moreover, the system was generally thought to be unconstitutional because it would deprive the workers of their free choice of unions.

[92] Section 8(c) of the American statute says: "The expressing of any views, argument, or opinion, or the dissemination thereof, whether in written, printed, graphic, or visual form, shall not constitute or be evidence of an unfair labor practice under any of the provisions of this Act, if such expression contains no threat of reprisal or force or promise of benefit."

[93] Yamaoka, Nainenki Kabushiki Kaisha (Yamaoka Internal Combustion Engine Co.) v. Shiga Ken Chihō Rōdō Iinkai (Shiga Prefecture Local Labor Relations Commission), Osaka High Court, Aug. 22, 1952, 3 Rō-MINSHŪ 304.

[94] Yamaoka Nainenki Kabushiki Kaisha v. Shiga Ken Chihō Rōdō Iinkai, note 82.

[95] Takano v. Chūō Rōdō Iinkai (Central Labor Relations Commission), Tokyo District Court, July 3, 1953, 4 Rō-MINSHŪ 281.

CONCLUSION

The Japanese labor movement was born in a time of national dislocation when the economy was staggering if not prostrate, when the previously acknowledged patterns of authority had been torn asunder, and when force and violence had become the norm rather than the aberration of organized society. From its infancy in the troubled times of the early postwar years, it has grown into adolescence—a period of awkwardness, emotional instability, somewhat uncontrolled strength, impatience, and limited experience.

Labor law, which has developed during the same span of years, shares many of the characteristics of the movement whose emergence in the postwar era brought this branch of law into being. It, too, is gawky, insecure, and at times mistaken because uninformed. Such law as exists is administered in part by judges who have had little opportunity to gain understanding of the difficult problems with which they now must deal.

Moreover, academic consideration of both the labor movement and labor law has been much influenced by persons whose enthusiasm for certain socioeconomic goals has consciously or unconsciously colored their writings. The validity of those goals is not the topic now under discussion; nor is any opinion expressed concerning their ultimate desirability. Nonetheless, the point must be made that open or covert political ax grinding is not the best means of developing labor law for practical use in present-day Japan. Much of what purports to be professional analysis has, unfortunately, been a calculated or careless obfuscation, intended to give aid to a protagonist rather than to advance genuine understanding.

All of this has contributed to a poor start for Japanese labor law. Debates about what the law should be are insufficiently differentiated from debates about what the law is.* What is thought to give some immediate advantage in a dispute of the moment too often has excluded consideration of the parties' own long-range interests, let alone the nation's interest in maintaining public order, remedying injustices, and nourishing economic advancement.†

The outlook for the future is not dark, however; adolescents do ultimately mature. The labor movement, labor law, labor lawyers, and judges seem constantly to be learning by experience. Unions are themselves showing

* Considerable conference discussion was directed to the problem of scholarly objectivity. There was general agreement that, although everyone quite properly and necessarily has a value commitment which affects his writings, a scholar dealing with legal institutions has an obligation to state such commitments if they are fundamentally different from those underlying the legal institutions being discussed.

† Alfred Oppler noted that in Japan there is no fundamental general agreement on philosophical bases of society or government such as is found in the United States.

signs of impatience with some of their more dogmatic sympathizers.[96] In increasing numbers, labor leaders apparently realize that essential weaknesses must be faced rather than simply glossed over with the aid of strained legal reasoning. The years ahead will no doubt be full of turmoil as Japan's growing economy and tempestuous politics reflect themselves in relations between unions and employers. If, however, both sides become persuaded that they must indeed live together for a long time to come, the chances are good that they will seek to develop a more elaborate system of legal relationships than has emerged during the past two decades. For their own benefit, management and labor alike may well conclude that closer attention to procedures will be more productive than continuation of the present incessant and often chaotic struggle.

[96] Recently, Kaoru Ota, president of Sōhyō, wrote an article in which he bitterly criticized the metaphysical revolutionalism of many scholars. He said: "Generally speaking, there is a peculiar tendency in the Japanese labor movement toward a wild youthfulness which propels itself forward by means of its own agitation. This trend seems to be strengthened by the fact that scholars often intrude into and make pronouncements upon problems of organization which are outside their sphere of professional competence. Since scholars have very little experience in mass movements and think only in the abstract, they can make up quickly within their minds all sorts of plans for revolution or what have you. They possess the impatience to which the intelligentsia is peculiarly prone, and, mistaking the radical conduct of workers — which has burst forth from their dissatisfaction with their low wages and occupational standing — as the height of political consciousness, they attempt to apply their plans. Since the present leadership does not comply with their demands, they loudly proclaim that this leadership is untrustworthy. Such persons assert that the existing leadership has no ability whatsoever and that the only hope is the explosive conduct of the masses and the catastrophe which it will produce and that reliance can be placed nowhere else but on the passionate leadership which will emerge after the prior leadership has been thrown off during this chaos. It goes without saying that this view smacks of the theory of armed uprising." Ota, *Sōhyō no Shin Rosen Sengen* (Declaration of a New Course for Sōhyō), 76 Chūō Kōron (Central Review) no. 6, at 112, 115 (1961).

TABLE 1. Number of Unions and Members

Year	Number of unions	Number of members
1946	17,000[a]	5,000,000[a]
1947	23,323	5,692,179
1948	33,926	6,677,427
1949	34,688	6,655,483
1950	29,144	5,773,908
1951	27,644	5,686,774
1952	27,851	5,719,560
1953	30,129	5,842,678
1954	31,456	5,986,168
1955	32,012	6,166,348
1956	34,073	6,350,357
1957	36,084	6,606,275
1958	37,827	6,881,581
1959	39,303	7,077,510
1960	41,561	7,516,316
1961	45,096	8,154,176

[a] Approximate figure.

Source: RŌDŌ-SHŌ (Ministry of Labor), RŌDŌ HAKUSHO–SHŌWA 36 NENBAN (1961 White Paper on Labor) 288 (1962).

TABLE 2. Number of Petitions

Year	Number of complaints	Number of petitions by unions
1949 (June–Dec.)	320	103 (32%)
1950	526	193 (37%)
1951	287	147 (51%)
1952	320	169 (53%)
1953	394	241 (61%)
1954	445	312 (70%)
1955	397	282 (71%)
1956	367	282 (77%)
1957	429	344 (80%)
1958	443	351 (79%)
1959	374	302 (81%)
1960	392	339 (86%)

Source: Figures based on statistics given in CHŪŌ RŌDŌ IINKAI (Central Labor Relations Commission), DAI 15 KAI RŌDŌ IINKAI NEMPŌ (15th Annual Report of the Central Labor Relations Commission) 163 (1961).

TABLE 3. Disposition of Improper Labor Acts Litigation by Labor-Relations Commissions

Year	Number of cases disposed of by ruling	Number of cases compromised or withdrawn
1949 (June–Dec.)	68	42
1950	132	100
1951	166	95
1952	141	58
1953	133	56
1954	185	85
1955	236	86
1956	197	78
1957	250	69
1958	189	71
1959	209	82
1960	217	106

Source: *Ibid.*, at 40.

TABLE 4. Grounds of Petition under Labor Union Law

Year	Art. 7(i) Discrimination because of union activity	Art. 7(ii) Refusal to bargain	Art. 7(iii) Interference or domination	Art. 7(iv) Discrimination because of testimony, etc.
1949 (June–Dec.)	275	42	55	0
1950	453	74	110	0
1951	268	33	104	0
1952	272	35	126	1
1953	305	51	177	4
1954	355	67	215	4
1955	307	77	154	4
1956	288	91	172	6
1957	301	96	228	5
1958	329	100	239	7
1959	283	84	194	10
1960	256	130	203	4

Source: *Ibid.*, at 163.

Appendix A. Important Labor Provisions

CONSTITUTION OF JAPAN (1946)

Article 28. The right of workers to organize and to bargain and act collectively is guaranteed.

Article 29. The right to own or to hold property is inviolable.

Property rights shall be defined by law, in conformity with the public welfare. Private property may be taken for public use upon just compensation therefor.

LABOR UNION LAW, LAW NO. 174 OF 1949

Article 1 (*Purpose*).

(1) The purpose of this law is to elevate the status of workers through promoting equal standing for workers in their negotiations with their employer; to protect the election by workers of their own representatives for the purpose of negotiating the conditions of their work and the self-organization of and association in labor unions in order to carry out other collective action; and to encourage the practice and procedure of collective bargaining in order to conclude collective labor agreements governing relations between employers and workers.

(2) The provisions of article 35 of the Penal Code are applicable to the appropriate collective-bargaining and other acts of a labor union, performed in order to attain the purposes enumerated in the prior paragraph. Provided, however, that in no case shall the use of violence be construed an appropriate act of a labor union. [Article 35: "Acts done in accordance with Laws and Orders or an appropriate business function are not punishable."]

Article 7 (*Improper Labor Acts*).

An employer shall not perform the acts dealt with in each of the following items:

(i) To discharge or otherwise treat a worker unfavorably because the worker is a member of a labor union, has attempted to join or form a labor union, or has performed an appropriate act of a labor union; or to impose as a condition of employment that he not join a labor union or withdraw from a labor union. Provided, however, that in a case where a labor union represents a majority of the workers employed at a factory or place of business, this does not preclude concluding a collective labor agreement which imposes as a condition of employment that these workers be members of this labor union.

(ii) To refuse to bargain collectively with the representatives of the workers employed by the employer without an appropriate reason.

(iii) To dominate or interfere with the formation or administration of a labor union by his workers or contribute financial support relating to the payment of expenses necessary for the administration of the labor union. Provided, however, that this does not preclude an employer permitting workers to confer or negotiate with him during working hours without loss of time or pay, and the employer's contributions to welfare funds or benefit or other funds actually used for payments to prevent or relieve economic distress or misfortune and his furnishing of minimum office space are excepted.

(iv) To discharge or otherwise treat a worker unfavorably for the reason that the worker petitioned a labor-relations commission alleging that his employer had violated the provisions of this article, that he petitioned the Central Labor Relations Commission to review an order pursuant to the provisions of article 27, paragraph (4), or that the worker submitted evidence or proffered testimony in a case where a labor-relations commission was conducting an investigation or a hearing pertaining to these petitions or a labor dispute was being adjusted pursuant to the provisions of the Labor Relations Adjustment Law.

Article 8 (*Compensation for Damage*).

An employer may not claim compensation from a labor union or its members because of damages incurred due to a strike or other acts of dispute which are appropriate.

Article 27 (*Orders, Etc., of a Labor-Relations Commission*).

(1) A labor-relations commission, when it has received a petition alleging that an employer has violated the provisions of article 7, shall without delay conduct an investigation and, when it has perceived the necessity, conduct a hearing as to whether or not the said petition is reasonable. The procedure of this investigation and hearing shall be in accordance with the regulations of procedure prescribed by the Central Labor Relations Commission pursuant to the provisions of the prior article and in the hearing proceeding the said employer and petitioner shall be accorded adequate opportunity to submit evidence and crossexamine witnesses.

(2) A labor-relations commission, when the petition of the prior paragraph pertains to a case for which one year has elapsed since the date of the act (with consecutive acts, the day they ended), may not accept it.

(3) A labor-relations commission, where it is conducting the hearing in paragraph (1), may, on motion of the parties or ex officio, require the appearance of witnesses and question them.

(4) A labor-relations commission, when it completes the hearing procedure in paragraph (1), shall make findings of fact and based on these findings issue an order either granting in whole or in part the relief pertaining to the petitioner's claim or rejecting his petition. These findings of fact and the order shall be in writing and copies thereof delivered to the employer and the petitioner. This order becomes effective from the date of delivery. The procedure under the provisions of this paragraph is to be in accordance with the regulations of procedure prescribed by the Central Labor Relations Commission pursuant to the provisions of the prior article.

(5) The employer, when he has received the delivery of an order of a local labor-relations commission may within fifteen days (when there is an unavoidable reason such as a natural calamity or other event why a petition for review was not made within this period, within a period of one week calculated from the day

following the day this reason came to an end) petition the Central Labor Relations Commission for review. Provided, however, that this petition does not stay the effectiveness of the said order and this order will cease to be effective only when the Central Labor Relations Commission annuls or modifies it as a consequence of review pursuant to the provisions of article 25.

(6) When the employer does not petition the Central Labor Relations Commission for review regarding the order of the local labor-relations commission or when the Central Labor Relations Commission has issued an order, the employer may within thirty days from the date of delivery of the said order institute suit for the annulment of the said order. This period is an unalterable period.

(7) When the employer has petitioned the Central Labor Relations Commission for review pursuant to the provisions of paragraph (5), he may institute a suit for annulment only against the order of the Central Labor Relations Commission responding to this petition. The provisions of article 12, paragraph (3), of the Administrative Case Litigation Law do not apply in regard to this suit.

(8) In a case where an employer has instituted suit in a court pursuant to the provisions of paragraph (6), the court accepting the action may by a ruling, on petition of the said labor-relations commission, order that the employer comply in whole or in part with the order of the labor-relations commission pending the judgment of the court becoming final and conclusive, or, on motion of the parties or ex officio, rescind or modify such ruling.

(9) When an employer does not institute suit regarding the order of a labor-relations commission within the period in paragraph (6), the order of the labor-relations commission is final and conclusive. If the employer does not comply with the order of the labor-relations commission in this case, the labor-relations commission shall so notify the District Court at the location of the domicile of the employer. This notification may also be made by a worker.

(10) When pursuant to a final and conclusive judgment based on a suit in paragraph (6) the order of a local labor-relations commission is sustained in whole or in part, the Central Labor Relations Commission may not review the order of the local labor-relations commission.

(11) The provisions of paragraph (5), in regard to a petition for review made by a labor union or worker to the Central Labor Relations Commission, and the provisions of paragraph (7), in regard to a suit for annulment instituted by a labor union or worker as prescribed in the Administrative Case Litigation Law, respectively, shall be applied correspondingly.

(12) The provisions of paragraphs (1), (3), and (4) shall be applied correspondingly to the review procedure of the Central Labor Relations Commission.

LABOR RELATIONS ADJUSTMENT LAW, LAW NO. 25 OF 1946

Article 7 (*Acts of Dispute*).

In this Law "acts of dispute" refer to strikes, slowdowns, lockouts, or other acts or counteracts, performed by the parties to labor relations for the purpose of realizing their claims, which hamper the normal operation of a business.

Appendix B. Protective Labor Legislation

1. Article 27 of the Constitution:
   "All people shall have the right and the obligation to work."
   "Standards for wages, hours, rest and other working conditions shall be fixed by law."
   "Children shall not be exploited."
2. Labor Standards Law, Law No. 49 of 1947.
3. Workmen's Accident Compensation Insurance Law, Law No. 50 of 1947.
4. Minimum Wage Law, Law No. 137 of 1959.*
5. Health Insurance Law, Law No. 70 of 1922.
6. Welfare Annuity Insurance Law, Law No. 115 of 1954.
7. Unemployment Insurance Law, Law No. 146 of 1947.
8. Occupation Stabilization Law, Law No. 141 of 1947.
9. Vocational Training Law, Law No. 133 of 1958.
10. Emergency Unemployment Countermeasures Law, Law No. 89 of 1949.
11. Medium and Small Enterprise Severance Pay Mutual Aid Law, Law No. 160 of 1959.

* It was observed at the conference that the Minimum Wage Law is not very effective because small industry cannot afford the wage levels of the larger enterprises, particularly in the export field. The law is almost voluntary, permitting an industry to establish a minimum wage if its members so desire.

THE REGULATION OF CORPORATE ENTERPRISE: THE LAW OF UNFAIR COMPETITION AND THE CONTROL OF MONOPOLY POWER

Yoshio Kanazawa

ASSISTED BY LAWRENCE F. EBB AND ALEXANDER D. CALHOUN, JR.

IN this essay I shall first outline the political and economic setting in which modern Japanese industry was created as government enterprise and discuss the cartelization of that industry following its transfer to private ownership. Then I shall consider in greater detail the 1947 Law Concerning the Prohibition of Private Monopoly and the Maintenance of Fair Trade[1] — the Antimonopoly Law — as interpreted by the Fair Trade Commission and the courts and as amended, both directly and by exemptive legislation. Finally, an explanation will be offered for the unsatisfactory state into which the field of law covered by this statute has fallen.

From its very inception, modern Japanese industry has been regarded as an instrument of national policy. The manufacture of iron and armaments and shipbuilding were begun before the end of the Tokugawa era for defensive purposes. Private interests were not in a position to carry these developments forward because of the absence of a capitalistic class with experience in industrial undertakings. Officials of the Saga, Tosa, Satsuma, and other *han* (fiefs), as well as of the Tokugawa Shogunate itself, undertook to develop the desired industries with the assistance of foreign engineers and technicians.

Following the overthrow of the Tokugawa Shogunate in 1868, the Meiji government continued and greatly intensified the previous efforts at industrialization, primarily to enhance its military power. For example, a pro-

Note. Mr. Kanazawa is Professor of Law, Hokkaido University. B.Jur., Tokyo Imperial University, 1938; Dr.Jur., Tokyo University, 1961. Author of Bōeki Kankei Hō (Law Relating to Trade) (1956), Suihō (Water Law) (1960), and Keizai Hō (Economics Law) (1961).

Mr. Ebb is Professor of Law, Stanford University. A.B., 1939 A.M., 1940, LL.B., 1946, Harvard University. Mr. Calhoun is a practicing attorney in San Francisco. A.B., 1949, Harvard University; LL.B., 1952, George Washington University.

[1] Law No. 54 of 1947 [hereafter cited Antimonopoly Law].

posed railroad from Tokyo to northern Honshu was justified because it "will make it profitable to reclaim waste and uncultivated tracts of moors and plains, and still more important advantage will be that, in cases of sudden emergency, it will be possible to dispatch troops quickly to put down disturbances." [2]

Moreover, Japan's trade balance became extremely unfavorable after the tariff convention of 1866, which lowered duties to approximately 5 percent ad valorem.[3] The resulting loss of gold and foreign exchange led to the issuance of paper currency not backed by specie and was soon followed by inflation and depreciation of the currency. Both the government itself and the samurai class suffered from the decline in the value of paper money. Much of the government's income was derived from a fixed land tax payable in paper currency, and the samurai received an important portion of their income from government bonds bearing fixed interest, also payable in paper money. Furthermore, the competition of foreign imports threatened Japan's important handicraft industry with ruin. Since the nation's tariffs were under international control and could not be raised, the only hope of balancing the international payments seemed to be to drive foreign manufactured goods out of the domestic market by producing competitive locally manufactured goods and to build up export industries.[4]

Because of the necessity of focusing economic development on those areas of immediate national concern and because there was no alternative leadership available, the state provided most of the initial impetus for industrial growth. The Meiji government was active in the establishment of the early telegraph and railroad systems and also played a dominant part in mining, in shipbuilding, and in the manufacture of machinery and building materials such as glass and cement. To assist in the modernization of the important silk-reeling and cotton-spinning export industries, the government brought in technicians from France and established modern silk-reeling and cotton-spinning mills.[5] On November 5, 1880, however, a fundamental change of

[2] *Memorandum on the Advantages To Be Gained from the Construction of Railways*, in CORRESPONDENCE RESPECTING AFFAIRS IN JAPAN: 1868–70, at 97 (70 British Parl. Papers, Japan No. 3, 1870), as quoted in SMITH, POLITICAL CHANGE AND INDUSTRIAL DEVELOPMENT IN JAPAN: GOVERNMENT ENTERPRISE, 1868–1880 42 (1955).

[3] *Ibid.*, at 24–31.

[4] In 1875 Finance Minister Masayoshi Matsukata, in words which have a contemporary ring, stated: "If henceforth we strongly endeavor to expand the production of goods and work to reduce the purchase of foreign products we must expect that after a decade we will inevitably obtain good industrial growth in commodities and attain, by ourselves, the establishment of the basis for a sound economy. If we do not do this and continue unceasingly to buy foreign products with specie, and, while the government and people together rush forward in superficial progress . . . we continue to be swayed by and propagate the evils of easy living, the importation of western goods will rapidly increase day by day until finally we will not even know where to begin to bring it to an end." 1 MEIJI ZENKI ZAISEI KEIZAI SHIRYŌ SHŪSEI (A Compilation of Public Finance and Economic Historical Materials From The Early Meiji Era) 284 (Ōkura-shō (Ministry of Finance) ed. 1931).

[5] See 3 *ibid.*, at 383–84.

policy occurred; the Dajōkan[6] ordered the various departments of the government to sell the enterprises under their jurisdiction to private interests. Within a few years, most of the government enterprises, with the exception of the railroads, telegraph companies, and arsenals, had been turned over to private interests which expanded upon this industrial base until they became the zaibatsu of later days. This transfer signaled the end of the era in which the Meiji government participated directly in industrial development as entrepreneur and manager.

ZAIBATSU CARTELIZATION AND GOVERNMENT REGULATION

This essay cannot treat in detail the expansion of the purchasers of the industrial enterprises established by the Meiji government into the dozen or so zaibatsu combines which dominated finance, trading, and large-scale industry in Japan after 1920.[7] But it is worth noting that each combine tended to operate in a number of markets, in some of which it was strong, in others weak.[8] In these circumstances, competition in one market might easily lead to retaliation in another and thus ultimately to unrestrained economic warfare. This situation placed a premium upon the achievement of stability through cartel understandings and organizations. Moreover, in this period as in postwar Japan, a substantial segment of economic activity—approximately one quarter of total factory output—was that of small, keenly competitive home industries, too small to offer competition where the combines sought to restrict production. The first notable Japanese laws in modern times regulating corporate enterprise—the Export Society Law[9] and the Important Export Commodities Industrial Society Law[10]—were enacted in 1925 to reverse a decline in exports by assisting exporters. The first law authorized the establishment of cartels of traders; the second permitted cartels of producers. These cartels could fix prices, establish quotas, curtail production, and allocate markets.[11] Furthermore, the minister having jurisdiction over the particular trade in question was authorized to order firms not party to the cartel agreement or association to observe the terms of the agreement.[12] These laws are considered the first in modern times to provide for compulsory adherence to cartels.[13] In them the Japanese government moved affirmatively to support and strengthen the cartels which had

[6] The Great Council of State of the early Meiji government.
[7] For such an explanation see DEPARTMENT OF STATE, REPORT OF THE MISSION ON JAPANESE COMBINES (Far Eastern Series 14) (1946).
[8] See BISSON, ZAIBATSU DISSOLUTION IN JAPAN 11–17 (1954).
[9] Law No. 27 of 1925.
[10] Law No. 28 of 1925.
[11] Arts. 1 and 3 of both laws. Cf. the McGuire Act authorizing resale price maintenance in the United States. Ch. 745, 66 Stat. 631 (1952), 15 U.S.C. §45(a) (1958).
[12] Export Society Law, art. 9; and Important Export Commodities Industrial Society Law, art. 8.
[13] EGGMAN, DER STAAT UND DIE KARTALLE 32 (1945).

independently arisen throughout Japanese economic society without formal governmental sanction.

By 1937, when the Export Society Law was replaced by the Trade Society Law,[14] which permitted the formation of import as well as export societies,[15] more than eighty export societies had been established.[16] Similarly, numerous manufacturers' organizations had also been organized under the Important Export Commodities Industrial Society Law, the title of which was changed to the Industrial Society Law in 1931.[17] The success of cartels under the early laws led the government to extend the policy of statutory governmental support of cartels to almost all major industries in the economic depression of the 1930s. The newly named Industrial Society Law broadened the scope of the Important Export Commodities Industrial Society Law to include the production of important industrial goods, whether for the domestic or export markets.[18] In 1932 the Mercantile Society Law authorized cartels among wholesalers and retailers.[19] The most extensive of these laws, however, was the Law Concerning the Control of Important Industries of 1931,[20] which authorized support of cartel agreements (called "control agreements") among producers generally.[21] It was in practice primarily applicable to large-scale producers and provided for the filing with the ministry having jurisdiction over the industry involved of cartel agreements restricting production, fixing prices, or allocating markets. The minister then had authority to require both the modification of the agreement and its observance by firms that were not members of the cartel.[22] While in effect, this law applied to cartels in twenty-six industries, including coal mining, cement, and various light industries such as textiles.

A number of similar laws were enacted concerning particular industries: for example, the Petroleum Industry Law of 1934,[23] and the Machine Tool Manufacturing Business[24] and Aircraft Manufacturing Business Laws of 1938.[25]

During World War II, the government forced mergers in a number of

[14] Law No. 74 of 1937.

[15] *Ibid.*, art. 1.

[16] 2 SHŌKŌ GYŌSEI SHI (History of Administration in Commerce and Industry) 435 (Shōkō Gyōsei Shi Kankō Kai (History of Administration in Commerce and Industry Publishing Society) ed. 1955).

[17] Law No. 62 of 1931.

[18] Industrial Society Law, art. 1, as amended by Law No. 62 of 1931.

[19] Law No. 25 of 1932, arts. 1, 3.

[20] Law No. 40 of 1931.

[21] Law Concerning the Control of Important Industries, art. 3. For the industries covered see 2 SHŌKŌ GYŌSEI SHI, note 16, at 411.

[22] *Ibid.*, art. 2. Such orders were issued by the Minister of Commerce and Industry to the cement industry in the years 1934 through 1936. 3 SHŌKŌ GYŌSEI SHI, note 16, at 172.

[23] Law No. 26 of 1934.

[24] Law No. 40 of 1938.

[25] Law No. 41 of 1938.

industries to increase efficiency by coordinating production and eliminating competition. Authority to do this was given in the National General Mobilization Law of 1938.[26] The same law provided for government enforcement of cartel agreements among both members and nonmembers of the cartel[27] and the establishment of industry-wide associations, in which membership was compulsory, controlling activities in almost every field of commerce and industry.[28] The Commerce and Industry Society Law,[29] enacted in 1943, provided for the establishment of smaller cartels controlling a particular subdivision of industry. These wartime "control" associations[30] were patterned after similar organizations, the *Wirtschaftsgruppen,* found in Nazi Germany. Their distinguishing features were compulsory establishment, enforced membership, and the development and regulation of association policy by a single director appointed by the government (*Führerprinzip*), instead of by the decision of a majority of the members of the association. This of course contrasts sharply with regulation by government agencies operating under statutory standards.

THE ANTIMONOPOLY LAW OF 1947

Following the end of World War II and the occupation of Japan, one of the first concerns of the Supreme Commander for the Allied Powers was the deconcentration of the centralized economic structure which had resulted from prewar policies and conditions. Several broad and far-reaching steps were taken to reorganize the pattern of the Japanese economy. The zaibatsu holding companies were liquidated by the Holding Company Liquidation Commission.[31] Interlocking relationships among the various zaibatsu enterprises through personnel, share ownership, loans, and other contractual ties were forbidden by the Imperial Order Concerning the Restriction, Etc., of Securities Holdings by Companies of 1946.[32] A number of major industrial

[26] Law No. 55 of 1938, art. 16.

[27] National General Mobilization Law, art. 17.

[28] National General Mobilization Law, art. 18.

[29] Law No. 53 of 1943.

[30] Important Industry Organizations Order, Imperial Order No. 831 of 1941, arts. 4–50; Commerce and Industry Society Law, arts. 7–51; called in Japanese *tōsei-kai* and *tōsei kumiai.*

[31] Memorandum Concerning Dissolution of Holding Companies, Nov. 6, 1945, SCAPIN 244, NIHON KANRI HŌREI KENKYŪ (Japan Occupation Law Review) no. 5, Directives and Memorandums pt. at 9; Memorandum Concerning Amendment of AG 004 (6 Nov. 45) ESS/ADM, Nov. 8, 1945, SCAPIN 250, NIHON KANRI HŌREI KENKYŪ no. 5, Directives and Memorandums pt. at 13; Holding Company Liquidation Commission Order, Imperial Order No. 233 of 1946, translated into English in OFFICIAL GAZETTE, April 20, 1946, no. 14, at 1; Holding Company Liquidation Commission Order Enforcement Regulations, Cabinet, Ministry of Finance and Ministry of Justice Order No. 1 of 1946, translated into English in OFFICIAL GAZETTE, Aug. 8, 1946, no. 107, at 1; Law Concerning Adjustment, Etc., of the Disposition of Valuable Securities, Law No. 8 of 1947, translated into English in OFFICIAL GAZETTE, Jan. 18, 1947, no. 239, at 2.

[32] Imperial Order No. 567 of 1946.

enterprises, including some resulting from wartime mergers, were broken up under the Elimination of Excessive Concentration of Economic Power Law.[33] Personnel closely associated with the zaibatsu were forbidden to hold any positions with zaibatsu companies under the Law for Elimination of Zaibatsu Family Control.[34] Finally, most of the wartime compulsory control associations were dissolved pursuant to the Closed Institutions Order of 1947.[35]

Having thus established, or so they thought, the conditions for industrial competition, the occupation authorities sought to prevent any reversion to the prewar oligopolistic structure of Japanese industry in which cartels regulated almost every major field of activity. To this end, the Japanese government was induced to enact the Law Concerning the Prohibition of Private Monopoly and the Maintenance of Fair Trade in 1947 and the Businessmen Organization Law in 1948.[36]

The Antimonopoly Law originally included provisions based on those of the Sherman Act, the Clayton Act, and the Federal Trade Commission Act[37] and on the judicial interpretation of these acts.[38] Detailed rules were also set forth governing mergers, interlocking directorates, and intercorporate shareholdings. Article 3 prohibited private monopolies and improper restraints of trade generally. Furthermore, under Article 4[39] the following concerted practices were specifically defined to be improper restraints and illegal per se unless their effects upon competition within a particular field of trade were negligible: fixing, maintaining, or increasing prices; restricting the volume of production or sales; restricting technology or products or allocating markets or customers; restricting the construction or expansion of facilities or the use of new technology or methods of production. Article 8[40] authorized administrative orders designed to eliminate substantial disparities in bargaining power that were not the result of willful monopolization. All private international agreements containing any restriction on freedom of trade proscribed by article 4 were prohibited, and all international agreements had to be filed within thirty days after coming into effect.[41] The

[33] Law No. 207 of 1947.

[34] Law No. 2 of 1948.

[35] Imperial Order No. 74 of 1947. For a detailed study see BISSON, as in note 8 above, at 191–96.

[36] Law No. 191 of 1948.

[37] Ch. 647, 26 Stat. 209 (1890), as amended, 15 U.S.C. §§1–7 (1958); ch. 323, 38 Stat. 730 (1914), as amended, 15 U.S.C. §§12–27 (1958); ch. 311, 38 Stat. 717 (1919), as amended, 15 U.S.C. §§41–51 (1958).

[38] See, generally, HANDLER, CASES ON TRADE REGULATION 84–185 (3rd ed., 1960).

[39] Repealed by Law No. 259 of 1953.

[40] Completely revised by Law No. 259 of 1953.

[41] Antimonopoly Law, art. 6. The requirement that international agreements be filed with the FTC was not applied in the case of agreements covering a single transaction or of those merely conferring a power of agency. Art. 6(3), as amended by Law No. 214 of 1949 and Law No. 259 of 1953.

Antimonopoly Law also prohibited unfair methods of competition such as boycotts, price discrimination, dumping, and exclusive dealing or tying contracts.[42] The Fair Trade Commission could also, after considering the views of the public and of those in a particular line of business, designate certain other competitive methods as being unfair.[43] Article 9 forbade holding companies. Detailed and stringent restrictions were placed on intercompany loans and shareholding,[44] on interlocking directorates, and even on a person's serving as an officer of more than one company.[45] Mergers and acquisitions between competitors were forbidden by article 15.

To administer these provisions of the Antimonopoly Law, the Fair Trade Commission was created.[46] This is a novel administrative and quasi-judicial body which is independent of all ministries and administratively responsible directly to the Prime Minister.[47] Its members are named by him, originally with the consent of the lower house and later that of both houses of the Diet.[48] The FTC has primary jurisdiction to administer the Antimonopoly Law and related laws. It receives complaints and investigates violations of the law. If satisfied that there is a violation, the FTC can enter a consent decree at any time before the conclusion of a hearing,[49] or if, after a full hearing, it finds a violation, it can issue a cease-and-desist order,[50] enforceable by criminal proceedings which may be commenced by the FTC's filing a complaint with the Procurator-General.[51] Decisions of the FTC are appealable to the Tokyo High Court.[52] The commission's findings of fact are binding

[42] Antimonopoly Law, arts. 2(6)(i)–(vi), prior to complete revision by Law No. 259 of 1953 (now art. 2(7)(i)–(vi)), 19. Law No. 259 of 1953 replaced the words "unfair methods of competition" (*fukōsei na kyōsō hōhō*) with the term "unfair trade practices" (*fukōsei na torihiki hōhō*).

[43] Antimonopoly Law, arts. 2(6)(vii), repealed by Law No. 259 of 1953, 71–72.

[44] Antimonopoly Law, arts. 10, 11, 12, repealed by Law No. 214 of 1949.

[45] Antimonopoly Law, art. 13.

[46] Antimonopoly Law, arts. 27–76.

[47] Antimonopoly Law, arts. 27(2), 28.

[48] Antimonopoly Law, art. 29, amended by Law No. 91 of 1947 and Law No. 257 of 1952.

[49] Antimonopoly Law, arts. 48, 53-3. Consent decrees constitute by far the most numerous of the decisions issued by the Fair Trade Commission, particularly in the early years of its existence when it was actively pursuing the enforcement of the Antimonopoly Law. It is noteworthy that art. 53-3 places upon the respondent the responsibility for putting forward a concrete plan to remedy his admitted violation of the law, which plan may be accepted or rejected by the commission.

[50] Antimonopoly Law, art. 54.

[51] Antimonopoly Law, art. 96. However, because the concepts of the Antimonopoly Law are novel to Japan and there is no general feeling that violation of its strictures is morally wrong, cases of such criminal prosecution are extremely rare; I am aware of only three: Japan v. Nōrin Renraku Kyōgikai (Agriculture and Forestry Liaison Conference), Tokyo High Court, April 27, 1951 (unreported case); Japan v. Ōkawa Gōmei Kaisha (Okawa Partnership in Commendam Co.), Tokyo High Court, May 12, 1952 (unreported case) (dismissed under the amnesty proclaimed with the Peace Treaty); Japan v. Yamaichi Shōken Kabushiki Kaisha (Yamaichi Securities Co.), Tokyo High Court, Dec. 28, 1951 (unreported case) (prosecution withdrawn).

[52] Antimonopoly Law, art. 85.

upon the court if they are supported by substantial evidence,[53] but it can grant compensatory damages to private parties[54] and assess criminal penalties for violations first considered by the FTC.[55]

The Businessmen Organization Law of 1948, which became part of the Antimonopoly Law when the latter was amended in 1953,[56] required all businessmen organizations (trade associations) to file copies of their articles of association, any changes in organization or dissolution, and other information with the FTC;[57] and it generally restricted the scope of operations permitted to such associations.

No sooner had the Antimonopoly Law been enacted than agitation began for its amendment. The principal criticisms were directed at the categorical prohibition of cartels for the restriction of production, fixing of prices, and allocation of markets and customers and at what were characterized as overly stringent restrictions on mergers, stockholdings, and holding of multiple directorships and officerships. It was said that the Antimonopoly Law was more severe than the American antitrust legislation from which it was derived; it was inappropriate, the argument went, to Japanese economic circumstances, which required strong combinations of local producers and exporters in order to compete more effectively with foreign producers on the international scene. On the other hand, no public opposition was voiced to the proscription of the holding-company system by which the zaibatsu controlled their financial, commercial, and industrial empires.[58] Ultimately, some changes were necessary to induce foreign investors to invest in Japanese companies and to enable the government to dispose of the large amount of stock it had acquired upon the dissolution of the zaibatsu concerns. The general effect of the first major revision of the Antimonopoly Law in 1949[59] was conditionally to permit intercorporate

[53] Antimonopoly Law, art. 80.

[54] Antimonopoly Law, arts. 25, 26, 84, 85(ii). I know of only one example of the payment of compensation for damages arising from violations of the Antimonopoly Law: Kabushiki Kaisha Kosaka Yakkyoku (Kosaka Medicine Co.) v. Taishō Seiyaku Kabushiki Kaisha (Taisho Pharmaceutical Co.), Tokyo High Court, Feb. 19, 1958, 9 KŌSEI TORIHIKI IINKAI SHINKETSU SHŪ (A Collection of Fair Trade Commission Decrees) [hereafter cited SHINKETSU SHŪ] 162 (compromise settlement reached out of court).

[55] Antimonopoly Law, arts. 85(iii), 89–91.

[56] By Law No. 259 of 1953.

[57] Businessmen Organization Law, art. 3 (now Antimonopoly Law, art. 8(2)–(4)), and Regulation Concerning Notification Pursuant to the Provisions of the Law Concerning the Prohibition of Private Monopoly and the Maintenance of Fair Trade, Fair Trade Commission Regulation No. 2 of 1953. These requirements are patterned on the recommendations of the Temporary National Economic Committee. TNEC, FINAL REPORT AND RECOMMENDATIONS 38 (1941).

[58] See Ashino, *Experimenting With Anti-trust Law in Japan,* 3 JAPANESE ANNUAL OF INT'L L. 31, 35–39 (1959).

[59] By Law No. 214 of 1949. Japanese technically categorize this change as the "second revision," Law No. 91 of 1947, enacted three months after the initial statute, being referred to as the "first." In addition, minor amendments were incorporated in the following legislation: Law No. 195 of 1947, Laws No. 207 and 268 of 1948, and Laws No. 103 and 134 of 1949.

shareholding and multiple directorships if the positions were not obtained by unfair trade practices and did not tend substantially to lessen competition between the companies concerned or in any particular field of trade.[60] Mergers and acquisitions were permitted providing that they were not brought about by means of unfair practices and did not result in a monopolistic situation with disparity in bargaining power or in the lessening of competition in any field of trade;[61] since a report was required to be filed thirty days in advance of a merger, the FTC had this period within which to oppose the consolidation.[62]

Although these amendments were substantial, they did not affect the prohibition of cartels.[63] Pressure for further amendment of the Antimonopoly Law continued. In 1951, in anticipation of the peace treaty, an inquiry commission was appointed to review the laws enacted during the occupation; the first subject it took up was the Antimonopoly Law. Following the issuance of the report of the commission,[64] the law was further amended in 1953.[65] The provision for the elimination of substantial disparities in bargaining power by administrative action was dropped, as was the provision making certain practices illegal per se; only international agreements containing improper restraints of trade or unfair trade practices were forbidden.[66] Moreover, two important exceptions were made to the general prohibition of cartels.[67] The Fair Trade Commission was authorized, after consultation with the pertinent minister, to approve ("validate") in advance the establishment of a cartel when the price of a commodity fell below its average production cost, thus posing the danger that a substantial number of its producers may go out of business. Such so-called antidepression cartels may restrict production and sale of the commodity and, if that is not sufficient,

[60] Antimonopoly Law, arts. 10, 14. "Unfair methods of competition," rather than "unfair trade practices," was used prior to 1953. See note 42 above.

[61] Antimonopoly Law, arts. 10, 15.

[62] Antimonopoly Law, art. 15(2)–(4).

[63] Exceptions to this prohibition were originally limited by art. 24 to cooperatives established pursuant to the various cooperative society laws and by art. 22 to certain industries in the nature of public utilities.

[64] This commission was called the Cabinet Orders Inquiry Commission, but it reexamined all legislation and not just cabinet orders. A summary of its report presented to the Prime Minister on June 29, 1951, known as *Keizai Hōrei no Kaihi ni Kan-suru Iken* (Opinion Concerning Revision and Abolition of Economic Laws and Orders), is given in IZUMOI, SHIN DOKUSEN KINSHI HŌ NO KAISETSU (An Explanation of the New Antimonopoly Law) 39–41 (1953).

[65] By Law No. 259 of 1953. This is called the "fourth revision"; Law No. 257 of 1952 was the "third." Other minor intervening changes were Laws No. 192 and 211 of 1951, Cabinet Order No. 261 of 1951, and Law No. 268 of 1952. For a comparative table of the 1949 and 1953 amendments, see Fair Trade Institute, FAIR TRADE no. 3, at 8–31 (1958).

[66] Antimonopoly Law, art. 6(1).

[67] These were patterned after similar provisions in the then-pending draft of the Law Against Restriction of Competition (Gesetz gegen Wettbewerbsbeschränkungen), [1957] I BUNDESGESETZBLATT 1081, adopted by West Germany in 1957. Arts. 5 and 8 of that law provide for rationalization and depression cartels, respectively.

fix the price at which it is sold by members of the cartel. However, such action must not exceed what is necessary to overcome the threatened depression, must not harm unduly the interests of the consumer or of related trades, must not be unjustly discriminatory, and must be voluntary.[68] Because of the difficulty of meeting these conditions, only a few small anti-depression cartels have been approved, such as those restricting the sales of hemp yarn and of chloride vinyl and the allocation of raw materials among yeast producers.[69] As of 1962, no effective antidepression cartel existed.

The Fair Trade Commission was also authorized, after consultation with the pertinent minister, to validate cartels for the rationalization of an industry by the improvement of technology, the sharing of transportation or storage facilities, or the utilization or purchase of byproducts, waste, or scrap.[70] However, the proposed action must not harm unduly the interests of the proponent's customers, of the consumer, or of related trades; must not be unjustly discriminatory; must be voluntary; and, in the event production is allocated among the members of the cartel, must not unduly concentrate the production of any particular product in any one member firm.[71] Rationalization cartels have been formed to purchase scrap iron and copper, to limit production of certain textile products, to allocate production of bearings, and most recently to rationalize production of dyestuffs. At the present time, there are five rationalization cartels approved and in effect.[72]

In addition, the 1953 amendments authorized resale-price-maintenance agreements for copyrighted articles such as books and phonograph records and a narrow range of other commodities — to be designated by the Fair Trade Commission — which must be in daily use by the general consumer, easily identifiable (as, for example, by their trademark), and in free and open competition with other similar commodities.[73] Since 1953, the FTC

[68] Antimonopoly Law, art. 24-3.

[69] Details concerning the antidepression cartels will be found in the Kōsei Torihiki Iinkai (Fair Trade Commission), Nenji Hōkoku (Annual Report) for the following years at the pages given: 1955, at 44; 1956, at 60; 1958, at 23–24, 26; 1959, at 21–22, 24; 1960, at 18.

[70] Antimonopoly Law, art. 24-4 (1)–(2).

[71] Antimonopoly Law, art. 24-4(3).

[72] Information on these cartels will be found in the Kōsei Torihiki Iinkai (Fair Trade Commission), Nenji Hōkoku (Annual Report) for the following years at the pages given: 1954, at 44; 1955, at 45–46; 1956, at 60; 1960, at 21–22. The cartel on dyestuffs was approved by the FTC on August 1, 1961, but has not yet been recorded in an Annual Report.

[73] Art. 24-2 provides in part:

"(1) The provisions of this Law do not apply to legitimate acts of an entrepreneur who produces or sells merchandise, designated by the Fair Trade Commission and easily identifiable as being identical in nature, which fix with the opposite entrepreneur in the sale of the said merchandise the resale price of this merchandise (this refers to the price at which the opposite entrepreneur or an entrepreneur, who purchases and sells the said merchandise sold by this opposite entrepreneur, sells this merchandise; hereinafter the same) and are done in order to maintain that price. Provided, however, that this does not apply where the said act improperly injures the interests of the general consumer and where by the acts done by has authorized resale-price-maintenance agreements covering cosmetics, hair tint, tooth paste, household soap, liquor, caramel candy, medicines, cameras, and shirts.[74] Finally, the 1953 amendments also further relaxed the restrictions on intercorporate shareholdings, interlocking directorates, and multiple officerships. The provisions of the Businessmen Organization Law, incorporated into the Antimonopoly Law, were also made milder.[75]

These 1953 changes were the last major amendments to the Antimonopoly Law,[76] although in 1958 further amendments were proposed which would have greatly eased the requirements to be met before a cartel could be established.[77] Those proposals were opposed by the Socialist Party and representatives of consumers, farmers, small businessmen, and labor. Nevertheless, it is probable that they would have been adopted had not the major political issue of the Police Duties Execution Bill intervened and disrupted temporarily all legislative activity, leading the government to abandon for the time being its efforts to amend the Antimonopoly Law.

THE ADMINISTRATION OF THE ANTIMONOPOLY LAW

Shortly after the enactment of the Antimonopoly Law, the Fair Trade Commission, consisting of seven commissioners assisted by a secretariat of three hundred, was established. The commissioners have since been reduced to five and the staff to approximately two hundred and fifty.[78] The term of

---

the entrepreneur selling the merchandise the will of the entrepreneur manufacturing the merchandise is contravened.

"(2) The Fair Trade Commission shall not make a designation pursuant to the provisions of the prior paragraph unless it is a case coming under any of the following items:

(i) That the said merchandise is a thing in daily use by the general consumer.

(ii) That free competition is being carried on in regard to the said merchandise."

It is interesting to compare these provisions with the language of the Miller-Tydings Amendment, ch. 690, 50 Stat. 693 (1937), 15 U.S.C. §1 (1958), from which they are apparently derived. The United States Supreme Court held that the Miller-Tydings Amendment did not legalize the application of resale-price-maintenance contracts to nonsigners, Schwegman Bros. v. Calvert Distillers Corp., 341 U.S. 384 (1951); and some Japanese scholars reject the argument that the "nonsigner" clause is validated by the definition of the resale price as "the price at which the opposite entrepreneur or an entrepreneur, who purchases and sells the said merchandise sold by this opposite entrepreneur, sells this merchandise." See. e.g., IMAMURA, DOKUSEN KINSHI HŌ (Antimonopoly Law) 170 (52 Hōritsu-gaku Zenshū (Complete Collection on the Law) ed. 1961).

[74] Designation of Merchandise Provided for in Article 24-2, Paragraph (1) of the Law Concerning the Prohibition of Private Monopoly and the Maintenance of Fair Trade, Fair Trade Commission Notification No. 18 of 1953.

[75] For the present text of the law in English together with a discussion of its adoption and amendment, see Restrictive Trade Practices Specialists Study Team, Japan Productivity Center, Control of Restrictive Trade Practices in Japan (mimeograph, 1958).

[76] Minor changes were brought about by Law No. 127 of 1954, Laws No. 120 and 134 of 1956, Laws No. 142 and 187 of 1957, Law No. 129 of 1959, and Law No. 111 of 1961.

[77] Ashino, note 58, at 46–47.

[78] Of the several administrative commissions established during the occupation on the American model (such as the Holding Company Liquidation Commission, the Fair Trade Commission, the Securities Exchange Commission, the Foreign Investment Commission, the

office of a commissioner is five years. Recently, commissioners who had previously served in regular government departments, such as the Ministry of International Trade and Industry, have tended to have a relatively negative attitude toward the underlying philosophy of the Antimonopoly Law. Reports of the commission's activities indicate a sharp decline in total activity and a shift in emphasis in what activity remains from the enforcement of the Antimonopoly Law's prohibition of restraints on competition to enforcement of the provisions in that law proscribing certain unfair trade practices.* The extent of this shift can be seen from the following statistics comparing the number of consent and ordinary decrees.[79]

	Monopolization or illegal restrictive practices		*Unfair competitive practices*	
Year	*Ordinary decrees*	*Consent decrees*	*Ordinary decrees*	*Consent decrees*
1947	0	5	0	0
1948	0	2	0	0
1949	1	8	0	1
1950	3	32	2	3
1951	6	9	0	0
1952	3	5	1	1
1953	1	8	1	2
1954	1	0	2	2
1955	2	4	2	2
1956	1	3	0	2
1957	0	2	0	5
1958	0	2	0	1
1959	0	1	0	1
1960	0	1	0	0

"Monopolization or illegal restrictive practices" includes cases of vertical restrictions such as resale-price-maintenance agreements, even though Japa-

---

Public Utilities Commission), the FTC is the only one left in the economic field. Administrative control has been restored to its traditional place in the ministries and agencies under the Cabinet, while the public interest is now represented by some fifty-five consultative councils attached to the particular governmental agencies concerned. For a list of these councils, see KANAZAWA, KEIZAI HŌ (Economics Law) 65 (52 Hōritsu-gaku Zenshū (Complete Collection on the Law) ed. 1961).

* Although the FTC has ceased active enforcement of the antimonopoly laws, it publishes an annual report indicating the extent to which competition is restricted in certain industries. Makoto Yazawa remarked at the conference that, by simply keeping people informed, the FTC might be preparing for future reforms.

[79] "Consent decree" here includes both "recommendation decrees" pursuant to Antimonopoly Law, art. 48, and "consent decrees" issued under art. 53-3. "Ordinary decrees" refer to cease and desist orders issued pursuant to art. 54.

nese legal doctrine holds that such agreements ordinarily constitute an "unfair trade practice," since they unjustly restrict the business activities of the dealers;[80] the term "improper restraint of trade" is generally used only for horizontal restraints between producers or dealers.[81] However, in *Hokkaidō Butter Kabushiki Kaisha,*[82] the FTC ruled that a resale-price-maintenance agreement concluded between the Hokkaido Butter Company and its eight principal wholesalers was an improper restraint since the arrangement involved horizontal restrictions among the wholesalers as well as vertical restrictions between the producers, Hokkaido, and Hokkaido's wholesalers. In sharp contrast, the Tokyo High Court, in *Kabushiki Kaisha Asahi Shimbun Sha* (Asahi Newspaper Co.) *v. Kōsei Torihiki Iinkai* (Fair Trade Commission),[83] which involved an agreement among newspaper publishers allocating their dealers' territories, reversed the FTC, holding that the agreement among the publishers did not restrict "their" business activities as forbidden by article 2(6), since only the activities of the dealers were restricted, and that the vertical allocation of territories by the publishers to the dealers also did not violate the article since the arrangement only forbade horizontal agreements among entrepreneurs. As construed by the Tokyo High Court, the prohibition against restraints of trade in the Antimonopoly Law is substantially narrower than the similar prohibition (section 1) of the Sherman Act.[84]

[80] Art. 2(7) of the Antimonopoly Law provides:

"In this Law an unfair trade practice refers to an act which comes under any one of the following items and is designated by the Fair Trade Commission from among those acts feared to hinder fair competition:

(i) To discriminate improperly in the treatment of other entrepreneurs.

(ii) To carry on transactions at an improper price.

(iii) To induce or coerce improperly the customers of a competitor to deal with oneself.

(iv) To carry on transactions with conditions which improperly bind the business activities of the opposite party.

(v) To carry on transactions with an opposite party by improperly utilizing one's bargaining position.

(vi) To impede improperly a transaction between another entrepreneur, who is in a competitive relationship within the country with oneself or a company in which one is a shareholder or officer, and the opposite party to the transaction, or in a case where the said entrepreneur is a company, to induce, instigate or coerce improperly the company's shareholders or officers to do an act disadvantageous to the company."

[81] Art. 2(6) of the Antimonopoly Law provides: "In this Law an improper restraint of trade refers to a substantial restraint of competition in a particular field of trade, contrary to the public interest, due to an entrepreneur, whether by contract, agreement or under some other name, in conjunction with other entrepreneurs, mutually binding or executing his business activities in such a way as to fix, maintain or raise prices, or to restrain quantity, technology, products, equipment or the opposite parties to transactions."

[82] Fair Trade Commission, Sept. 18, 1950, 2 SHINKETSU SHŪ 103 (consent decree).

[83] Tokyo High Court, March 9, 1953, 4 GYŌSEI JIKEN SAIBAN REISHŪ (A Collection of Judicial Precedents Concerning Administrative Cases) [hereafter cited GYŌSAI REISHŪ] 609, *annulling* Kabushiki Kaisha Asahi Shimbun Sha, Fair Trade Commission, April 7, 1951, 3 SHINKETSU SHŪ 4.

[84] Ch. 647, 26 Stat. 209 (1890), as amended, 15 U.S.C. §1 (1958).

In the late 1940s and early 1950s — the years just after the law was passed — the FTC considered a number of problems and issued opinions which indicate the scope which might have been afforded the commission had not amendments and a change in public sentiment restricted its operations. One of the most noteworthy decisions concerns the definition of unfair trade practice found in article 2(7). In *Kabushiki Kaisha Yomiuri Shimbun Sha* (Yomiuri Newspaper Co.),[85] the FTC held that the use of a lottery to sell newspaper subscriptions tended "to induce or coerce improperly the customers of a competitor to deal with" the newspaper conducting the lottery. Following this decision, the FTC conducted hearings and designated, pursuant to article 71, specific unfair trade practices applicable to the newspaper industry.[86] Similar designations of specific unfair practices have been made for other industries, such as textbooks,[87] miso,[88] soy sauce,[89] marine transport,[90] and, most recently, canned meat.[91] This last involved the sale of canned whale meat with a label showing a herd of cattle and the words "beef style." The FTC on February 1, 1961, issued a notification designating this type of deception a specific unfair trade practice in a particular field of trade (the canned-meat industry), on the ground that it unduly induced the customers of a competitor to deal with the firm engaging in these practices. In the absence of any showing that such practices actually do have such a result, it is doubtful whether the Antimonopoly Law is properly used for the sole purpose of protecting the consumer.[92] Deceptive acts should be regulated under an amended Food Sanitation Law[93] — the law's scope is now limited to cases affecting public health — or the addition of a clause to the Antimonopoly Law patterned on section 5 of the American Federal Trade Commission Act.[94] Since the FTC is the administrative agency charged with responsibility for protecting the general interests of the consumer, this addi-

[85] Fair Trade Commission, Dec. 8, 1955, 7 SHINKETSU SHŪ 96 (consent decree), *following an emergency suspension ruling,* Kōsei Torihiki Iinkai (Fair Trade Commission) v. Kabushiki Kaisha Yomiuri Shimbun Sha (Yomiuri Newspaper Co.), Tokyo High Court, Nov. 5, 1955, 6 GYŌSAI REISHŪ supp. at 3.

[86] Specific Unfair Trade Practices in the Newspaper Industry, Fair Trade Commission Notification No. 3 of 1955.

[87] Specific Unfair Trade Practices in the Textbook Business, Fair Trade Commission Notification No. 5 of 1956.

[88] Specific Unfair Trade Practices in the Miso Industry, Fair Trade Commission Notification No. 13 of 1953. Miso is a fermented soy bean paste used as a base for a kind of Japanese soup.

[89] Specific Unfair Trade Practices in the Soy Sauce Industry, Fair Trade Commission Notification No. 12 of 1953.

[90] Specific Unfair Trade Practices in the Marine Transport Industry, Fair Trade Commission Notification No. 17 of 1959.

[91] Specific Unfair Trade Practices in the Animal and Whale Meat, Etc., Canning Industry, Fair Trade Commission Notification No. 1 of 1961.

[92] See IMAMURA, note 73, at 110 n.1.

[93] Law No. 233 of 1947.

[94] Ch. 311, 38 Stat. 719 (1914), as amended, 15 U.S.C. §45 (1958).

tional responsibility could appropriately be given to it, at least to the extent that no other ministry is already so charged.

A number of cases have considered whether an exclusive distributorship, or exclusive dealing contract, constitutes an unfair trade practice in that it "improperly binds the business activities" of the distributor. The first case, *Marukin Shōyu Kabushiki Kaisha* (Marukin Soy Sauce Co.),[95] involved the appointment of an exclusive dealer in Hawaii with, apparently, some provision for territorial restrictions as well. The appointment was disallowed. The next case, *Nippon Kōgaku Kōgyō Kabushiki Kaisha* (Japan Optical Industrial Co.),[96] upheld the appointment of an exclusive distributor in the United States because in the particular circumstances of the case there was no substantial restraint on competition. However, this decision was followed by three cases in which exclusive dealing contracts were held to constitute substantial restraints on trade and to violate article 2(7)(iv) of the Antimonopoly Law: *Chūkyō Lion Hamegaki Seizō Kabushiki Kaisha* (Chukyo Lion Toothpaste Manufacturing Co.),[97] *Taishō Seiyaku Kabushiki Kaisha* (Taisho Pharmaceutical Co.),[98] and *Kabushiki Kaisha Hokkaidō Shimbun Sha* (Hokkaido Newspaper Co.).[99]

A number of cases involve price-fixing agreements among competitors.[100] One of the most interesting and earliest is *Kabushiki Kaisha Teikoku Ginkō* (Imperial Bank Co.),[101] in which the defendant banks were found guilty of having fixed maximum rates of interest on loans and deposits in violation of articles 3 and 4. Following this decision, the long-established practice of self-regulation by the banks was replaced by direct governmental regulation; the Extraordinary Interest Adjustment Law authorized the Minister of Finance

[95] Fair Trade Commission, March 20, 1949, 1 SHINKETSU SHŪ 129 (consent decree).

[96] Fair Trade Commission, Sept. 3, 1955, 4 SHINKETSU SHŪ 30 (ordinary decree).

[97] Fair Trade Commission, March 7, 1953, 4 SHINKETSU SHŪ 106 (consent decree).

[98] Fair Trade Commission, Dec. 10, 1955, 7 SHINKETSU SHŪ 99 (recommendation decree).

[99] Fair Trade Commission, May 18, 1953, 5 SHINKETSU SHŪ 5, *affirmed* Kabushiki Kaisha Hokkaidō Shimbun Sha v. Kōsei Torihiki Iinkai (Fair Trade Commission), Supreme Court, I Petty Bench, Jan. 26, 1961, 15 SAIKŌ SAIBANSHO MINJI HANREI SHŪ (A Collection of Civil Supreme Court Cases) [hereafter cited SAI-HAN MINSHŪ] 116. Cf. United States v. White Motor Co., 194 F. Supp. 562 (N.D. Ohio 1961); Note, *Restricted Channels of Distribution under the Sherman Act*, 75 HARV. L. REV. 795 (1962).

[100] E.g., Yuasa Mokuzai Kabushiki Kaisha (Yuasa Lumber Co.), Fair Trade Commission, Aug. 30, 1949, 1 SHINKETSU SHŪ 62 (fixing of prices on plywood sold to the Japan Procurement Agency for use by the occupation forces); Tamura Koma Kabushiki Kaisha (Tamura Koma Co.), Fair Trade Commission, May 12, 1950, 2 SHINKETSU SHŪ 34, translated into English in Restrictive Trade Practices Specialists Study Team, note 75, at 145 (fixing of prices for the purchase of silk by textile wholesalers from the Textile Export Trade Public Corporation; consent decree); Nihon Sekiyu Kabushiki Kaisha (Japan Petroleum Co.), Fair Trade Commission, Dec. 1, 1955, 7 SHINKETSU SHŪ 70, development of the case summarized in English in Restrictive Trade Practices Specialists Study Team, note 75, at 176 (fixing of prices of petroleum products; the Standard Vacuum Oil Company was the only defendant which was discharged by the FTC).

[101] Fair Trade Commission, Dec. 22, 1947, 1 SHINKETSU SHŪ 1 (consent decree).

to have the Policy Committee of the Bank of Japan establish maximum interest rates.[102]

The film industry has also occasioned some interesting decisions. In *Shōchiku Kabushiki Kaisha* (Shochiku Co.),[103] an agreement among the leading distributors to include in their film-rental contracts clauses forbidding double features of dramatic films was struck down as a violation of article 3 of the Antimonopoly Law. A second *Shōchiku Kabushiki Kaisha* case[104] disapproved certain kinds of block booking and other practices. In *Tōhō Kabushiki Kaisha* (Toho Co.),[105] the FTC and the courts considered and ruled upon issues as to the relevant market, both in geographical terms and with relation to the particular commodity involved, within which to measure a "substantial restraint of competition." The courts disapproved a long-term rental of the Subaru and Orion theaters by Toho because they would give Toho 57.9 percent of the seating capacity in the relevant geographical market of the Yuraku-cho, Marunouchi, and Ginza entertainment districts of Tokyo and, further, because Toho would acquire an even greater degree of control with respect to the seating capacity in theaters showing the kind of high-quality imported and roadshow films in which these two theaters specialized.

Noda Shōyu Kabushiki Kaisha (Noda Soy Sauce Co.)[106] is a remarkable case. The FTC found that, because of its dominant position in the market and as a price leader, Noda controlled through its resale-price-maintenance program the price at which the products of its competitors were sold in the Tokyo market, thus achieving private monopolization and restraining trade improperly in violation of articles 3 and 2(5) of the Antimonopoly Law.

A recent case considered the right of indemnification afforded, under articles 25 and 26 of the Antimonopoly Law, to one who has been injured by an "entrepreneur who has effected private monopolization or improper restraint of trade or who has employed unfair trade practices." The FTC refused to investigate charges of violations of the Antimonopoly Law made by a consumers' organization, stating that, while a group of newspaper publishers may have effected in the past a cartel to increase the price of their newspapers, the cartel was no longer in existence at the time the charges were brought; consequently, the consumers' group was precluded from

[102] Law No. 181 of 1947, art. 2.

[103] Fair Trade Commission, May 12, 1948, 1 SHINKETSU SHŪ 18 (consent decree), translated into English in Restrictive Trade Practices Specialists Study Team, note 75, at 131.

[104] Fair Trade Commission, Feb. 27, 1950, 1 SHINKETSU SHŪ 114 (consent decree).

[105] Fair Trade Commission, Sept. 29, 1950, 2 SHINKETSU SHŪ 150, *affirmed on different grounds* Tōhō Kabushiki Kaisha v. Kōsei Torihiki Iinkai (Fair Trade Commission), Tokyo High Court, Sept. 19, 1951, 2 GYŌSAI REISHŪ 1562, *affirmed* Supreme Court, III Petty Bench, July 20, 1954, 8 SAI-HAN MINSHŪ 950.

[106] Fair Trade Commission, Dec. 27, 1955, 7 SHINKETSU SHŪ 108, translated into English in FAIR TRADE no. 4, at 18 (1958), *affirmed* Noda Shōyu Kabushiki Kaisha v. Kōsei Torihiki Iinkai (Fair Trade Commission), Tokyo High Court, Dec. 25, 1957, 8 GYŌSAI REISHŪ 2300.

claiming indemnification under the Antimonopoly Law because the decision required by article 26 was wanting. The consumers thereupon filed suit in the Tokyo High Court asking that the FTC be compelled to investigate the charges and make a finding as to past violations. The court refused the requested relief, holding that the FTC decision was within its discretionary power.[107] The same consumers' organization is now suing the newspaper publishers for damages under article 709 of the Japanese Civil Code, the general provision on tort liability.

THE STEADY INCREASE OF "EXEMPTED ACTIVITIES"

The many statutes exempting various industries and activities from the Antimonopoly Law are of more practical importance than are the amendments of that law.[108] Consumers' and farmers' cooperatives and public utilities are exempted by the terms of the Antimonopoly Law itself.[109] The first of a mushrooming collection of independent exemptive laws was passed almost immediately following the enactment of the Antimonopoly Law. The first exemption was designed to permit the establishment and operation of a joint-rate-making association by nonlife-insurance companies.[110] Shortly thereafter a law patterned after the American Shipping Act of 1916[111] was adopted to exempt conference activities of shipping companies from the Antimonopoly Law.[112] This law was further amended in 1959 to permit certain practices still forbidden by the American law. Shipping conferences are allowed to exclude applicants for admission if the trade is already adequately served, and in some circumstances a conditional deferred-rebate system may be used to meet the competition of outsiders.[113] Finally, aviation companies were subjected to regulation by the Ministry of Transportation and exempted from the Antimonopoly Law.[114]

These exempted industries are, for various reasons inherent in their nature and structure, exempted in every country to a greater or less degree from legislation designed to promote free competition. As early as the spring of 1952, however, industries with a less clear case for special treatment began to receive exemptions. The cotton and synthetic-textile industries, at the

[107] Zenkoku Shōhisha Dantai Rengō Kai (National Federation of Consumers' Organizations) v. Kōsei Torihiki Iinkai (Fair Trade Commission), Tokyo High Court, April 26, 1961, 12 GYŌSAI REISHŪ 933.

[108] English translations of many of the exemptive provisions are to be found in Restrictive Trade Practices Specialists Study Team, note 75, at 63–111.

[109] Arts. 21 and 24.

[110] Law Concerning the Organization for Computation of Casualty Insurance Premium Rates, Law No. 193 of 1948; this organization is exempt under the Law Concerning Exclusion from Application, Etc., of the Law Concerning the Prohibition of Private Monopoly and the Maintenance of Fair Trade, Law No. 138 of 1947, art. 2(ii)(h).

[111] Ch. 451, 39 Stat. 728, as amended, 45 U.S.C. §§801–42 (1958).

[112] Marine Transportation Law, Law No. 187 of 1949, art. 28.

[113] *Ibid.*, art. 30(iv), (vi).

[114] Aviation Law, Law No. 231 of 1952, art. 111.

urging of officials of the Ministry of International Trade and Industry (MITI), took measures to restrict their operations, with a resultant reduction of production, in order to meet an overproduction crisis resulting from the conclusion of the Korean War. In August 1952, the Medium and Small Enterprise Stabilization Law[115] was enacted to legalize this action. Furthermore, at the same time, the Export-Import Transactions Law[116] was adopted for the asserted purpose of enabling exporters to stabilize the prices and volume of exports and forestall complaints of dumping activities, the complaints coming mainly from the United States.[117] The fact that the United States itself permitted the establishment of export associations[118] as an exception to its antitrust laws was used in support of the adoption of this statute.

The Export-Import Transactions Law states that its purpose is "to prevent unfair export transactions, establish order among export and import transactions and thereby provide for the sound development of foreign trade."[119] The law authorizes exporters and importers in certain circumstances to agree upon prices, quantity restrictions, and similar matters relating to exports and imports.[120] Originally, MITI had to approve agreements with the concurrence of the FTC before they became effective, but at present export agreements become effective ten days after they are filed with MITI.[121] Similar agreements may be concluded relating to domestic trade in goods of a kind being exported[122] and among producers of or dealers in goods for export,[123] if the validation of MITI is first obtained. Societies may also be formed to establish prices, quantity restrictions, and similar regulations for exports and imports.[124] In certain circumstances MITI may by order prescribe the terms of such agreements or societies and may make those terms effective for all exporters and importers.[125] Ironically, the establishment of these export associations has been encouraged to a very considerable extent by the American government, which has sought to meet the opposition of domestic American industry to Japanese imports by obtaining "voluntary quotas" that restrict the volume and maintain the price of Japanese exports to the United States.[126]

[115] Law No. 294 of 1952, art. 32, repealed by Law No. 185 of 1957.

[116] Law No. 299 of 1952; originally entitled Export Transactions Law, it was given its present title by Law No. 188 of 1953.

[117] *Ibid.*, art. 33 excludes the application of the Antimonopoly Law.

[118] See Webb-Pomerene Export Trading Act, ch. 50, 40 Stat. 516 (1918), 15 U.S.C. §§61–65 (1958).

[119] Export-Import Transactions Law, art. 1.

[120] *Ibid.*, arts. 5, 7-2.

[121] *Ibid.*, art. 5(1).

[122] *Ibid.*, art. 5-2.

[123] *Ibid.*, art. 5-3.

[124] *Ibid.*, arts. 11, 19-4.

[125] *Ibid.*, arts. 28–31.

[126] Particularly so since the legality of such arrangements may be questionable under the following American statutes: Sherman Antitrust Act §1, ch. 647, 26 Stat. 209, as amended,

In 1957, the Medium and Small Enterprise Stabilization Law was replaced by the Law Concerning the Organization of Medium and Small Enterprise Organizations,[127] which broadened the coverage of the earlier law to include dealers and service enterprises as well as producers. Pursuant to its provisions, large enterprises are permitted to combine with small and medium enterprises to restrict production, fix prices, and allocate markets. By June, 1961, 634 commerce and industry societies existed. Furthermore, MITI can order both members and nonmembers of the society to observe restrictions on competition imposed by MITI to accomplish the purposes of the society[128] and order medium and small enterprises which are nonmembers of the society to enter it.[129] The parallel with the prewar statutory-supported cartels is obvious: once again the government is lending a hand to support and direct privately regulated competition,* particularly in the export industries.[130]

---

15 U.S.C. § 1 (1958); Wilson Tariff Act §73, ch. 349, 28 Stat. 570 (1894), as amended, 15 U.S.C. §8 (1958); see 31 OPS. ATT'Y GEN. 545, 553–57 (1910); cf. United States v. R. P. Oldham Co., 152 F. Supp. 818 (N.D. Calif. 1957); United States v. Watchmakers of Switzerland Information Center, 133 F. Supp. 40, 46–48 (S.D.N.Y. 1955).

[127] Law No. 185 of 1957.

[128] Medium and Small Enterprise Stabilization Law, art. 29(1)–(2) (these provisions remain in effect pursuant to Law No. 185 of 1957, supp. prov. art. 9); Law Concerning the Organization of Medium and Small Enterprise Organizations, arts. 56, 57. Similar provisions include Export-Import Transactions Law, arts. 28–31; Law Concerning the Promotion of the Export Marine Products Industry, Law No. 154 of 1954, art. 26 (order of the Minister of Agriculture and Forestry); Law Concerning Normalization of the Operation of Enterprises Related to Environment Sanitation, Law No. 164 of 1957, art. 57 (order of the Minister of Welfare).

[129] Law Concerning the Organization of Medium and Small Enterprise Organizations, art. 55; this provision greatly enhances the cartel's power to police the restrictions ordered by MITI, or adopted on the cartel's own initiative. However, no instance of the issuance of such an order has been reported.

* Because the Ministry of International Trade and Industry has the power to exempt groups from the antimonopoly laws, its suggestions respecting the formation of cartels have great force. In fact, Alexander Calhoun pointed out at the conference, private industry and MITI tend to work together in encouraging cartels. MITI formulates broad policies while individuals suggest and seek approval for particular acts.

[130] Compare the support given by the Swiss Government to the watchmaking industry as described by Jolidon, Cartels and Restrictions on Freedom of Commerce in Swiss Law (unpublished paper submitted to the 1958 Cologne Conference of the International Bar Association): "This industry, almost entirely oriented towards exports, is extremely vulnerable, while at the same time having a substantial importance for the Swiss economy generally. Hit by serious crises between 1920–1930, crises due essentially to 'chablonnage' (that is, the exportation of watch movements and of certain spare parts) and due to price cutting, the watch industry undertook to organize itself. Great associations of manufacturers of spare parts and of finished products were created and bound themselves together by special conventions for which a single collective convention was subsequently substituted. The 'cartel reciprocity,' which prohibits members of the associations from buying or selling watch movements or spare parts of a watch from houses that are not members of the convention, and the establishment among these associations of price schedules and obligatory terms of payments for the members, have comprised from the outset and still are, along with the prohibition of the principle of 'chablonnage,' the three pillars of the cartel thus established. But this system turned out to be imperfect because of the dissidence that existed. The public authorities then intervened to facilitate the periodic renewal of the collective convention, and, more directly, by financing in part in 1931 the establishment of a powerful company which bought up and wholly absorbed some watch factories and certain factories producing spare parts. However, that did not suffice to effectuate the desired purifica-

This legislation does not go to the extremes of compulsory establishment and the *Führerprinzip* (abolition of majority rule) embodied in Japanese wartime legislation for associations in the fields of economic activities. But the "organizations" for which the Law Concerning the Organization of Medium and Small Enterprise Organizations provides are not entirely free from the danger of totalitarian tendencies, although they purport to be autonomous and democratic.

Article 55 of this law provides for compulsory cartel membership for the first time since World War II; it must, therefore, be examined in the light of article 21 of the Japanese Constitution which guarantees freedom of association. Since freedom of association may be restricted for reasons of public welfare, article 21 does not necessarily render article 55 unconstitutional; a finding of "a marked impediment to the sound development of the national economy" is required before the clause permitting compulsory membership can be invoked. The absence of detailed statutory standards will make it extremely difficult, however, to decide a concrete case involving compulsory membership. The national legislature, with the constitutional problem in view, inserted a rather clumsy "attestation" clause[131] which provides that those who do not want to join a cartel may remain outside, even if an administrative order for compulsory membership is in force, by seeking "attestation" from the competent administrative authorities. But attested outsiders are subject to the restrictions that are established for the commerce and industry society. If they violate these measures, they are liable to monetary penalties imposed by the society. Such penalties seem improper because the monetary penalty is imposed directly by the society, a private body. Moreover, members have no freedom of secession[132] so long as the administrative order for compulsory membership remains in force. Therefore, the attestation clause does not change the character of the law in regard to the freedom of association.

Over and beyond the question of the validity of the Law Concerning the Organization of Medium and Small Enterprise Organizations under the freedom-of-association provision of the Japanese Constitution, there may be

tion of the industry because of the dissidence that persisted and new dissidence that arose; these dissenters were not bound by the undertakings that the 'conventional' organizations had undertaken. Accordingly, the Federal Council [the Swiss federal executive of seven men, each one in charge of a government Department] issued in 1934 a decree requiring a license for the opening of a new enterprise in the watch industry, or for increase in the number of workers, or for expansion and transformation of existing enterprises, as well as for the export of 'chablons,' watch movements, and watchmaking supplies. However, the dissidents, ignoring the price schedules adopted by the member organizations in the convention, continued the practice of price cutting. This led the Federal Council in 1936 to adopt a new decree supplementing the previous one and making obligatory, even for the dissidents, after approval by the relevant Department, the minimum price schedules established by the cartel or organizations adhering to the convention."

[131] Law Concerning the Organization of Medium and Small Enterprise Organizations, art. 55(4).

[132] *Ibid.*, art. 63.

a further question as to the sufficiency of the statutory standards laid down by the Japanese legislature. Is the establishment of such standards an unconstitutional delegation of legislative power? The same basic constitutional considerations led the United States Supreme Court, in *A.L.A. Schechter Poultry Corp. v. United States,*[133] to hold that the determination of what constitutes "fair competition" may not be left with the industry affected, subject to approval by the President, since such an arrangement constitutes an excessive delegation of legislative power in the absence of sufficiently detailed and intelligible statutory standards. The codes promulgated under the American legislation would have had the standing of statutes, as the cartel agreements appear to have under the Japanese law. In holding the code-making authority to be an unconstitutional delegation of legislative power, the Supreme Court reasoned that "Congress cannot delegate legislative power to the President to exercise an unfettered discretion to make whatever laws he thinks may be needed or advisable for the rehabilitation and expansion of trade or industry."[134] Although the decision in *Schechter Poultry* has not been mentioned frequently by the Supreme Court of the United States, there seems little doubt as to the continued vitality of the Court's holding with respect to the impropriety of the delegation of legislative power in the absence of adequate statutory standards.[135] Since article 41 of the Japanese Constitution confers the sole lawmaking authority upon the National Diet—just as article I, section 1, of the Constitution of the United States vests the legislative power in Congress—the reasoning of the American Supreme Court in *Schechter Poultry* may well be applicable to any consideration by Japanese courts of the validity of the delegation of compulsory cartelization powers under the Law Concerning the Organization of Medium and Small Enterprise Organizations.

Other laws have specifically exempted concerted activity among packers in the export of canned goods[136] and among producers of ammonium-sulphate fertilizer.[137] Still other laws provide for the reorganization and consolidation of particular industries in the form of cartels formed pursuant to the directions of the responsible government ministry.[138] Even more

[133] 295 U.S. 495, 529–42 (1935).

[134] *Ibid.*, at 537–38.

[135] See, e.g., 1 DAVIS, ADMINISTRATIVE LAW §§2.07–.08 (1958); GELLHORN & BYSE, ADMINISTRATIVE LAW 98–102, 114–20 (4th ed. 1960). See also Lathrop v. Donohue, 367 U.S. 820, 854–55 (1961) (Harlan, J., concurring); *ibid.*, at 878 n.1 (Douglas, J., dissenting); United States v. Sharpnack, 355 U.S. 286, 298–99 (1958) (Douglas, J., dissenting).

[136] Law Concerning the Promotion of the Export Marine Products Industry, art. 27.

[137] Ammonium Sulphate Industry Rationalization and Ammonium Sulphate Export Adjustment Extraordinary Measures Law, Law No. 173 of 1954, art. 14.

[138] Coal Mining Industry Rationalization Extraordinary Measures Law, Law No. 156 of 1955, arts. 25, 62, 63, 67; Fiber Industry Equipment Extraordinary Measures Law, Law No. 130 of 1956, arts. 24, 28, 30; Machinery Industry Promotion Extraordinary Measures Law, Law No. 154 of 1956, arts. 6, 10; Electronic Industry Promotion Extraordinary Measures Law, Law No. 171 of 1957, arts. 7–11.

recently, the merger of wholesalers with the approval of the Minister of Agriculture and Forestry has been permitted,[139] and associations of public bathhouses, theaters, restaurants, hotels, beauty parlors, and similar enterprises can fix prices, hours, and other business conditions for the ostensible purpose of raising sanitation standards.[140]

Before going on to a more detailed explanation of the system of voluntary export quotas, I should mention another device which has been widely employed to effect cartelization in the purely domestic market. This is the "recommended restriction of production" whereby an official of one of the ministries, usually MITI,* recommends to each of the firms in an industry that it observe certain restrictions on its production or pricing practices. The official has no authority in law to enforce his recommendations, and the effectiveness of his suggestions probably depends on two factors. In the first place, the proposals may be followed because of the time and expense necessary to resist whatever official pressure might be brought and because, other things being equal, a producer may feel that his long-run interests are served by cooperating with the government agency that regulates him. More important, however, may be the underlying desire of the industry group in question to reach some form of agreement. If such is the case, the governmental suggestion offers a convenient focus for compromise of the individual claims of each producer.[141] Furthermore, an industry which suffers from overproduction or excessive competition and desires to create a cartel may find it difficult to obtain the cooperation of a sufficient proportion of producers; in these circumstances the industry may turn to the ministry concerned for assistance in the form of a "recommendation." Such a recommendation is particularly effective when the ministry is in a position to exercise a persuasive influence through its control over the import of necessary raw materials. It is estimated that following the 1957 recession such recommended restrictions on production were applied in over twenty domestic industries, including those producing such basic commodities as steel products, oil, coal, textiles, and pulp and paper, as well as in the marine-transportation field.[142]

139 Central Wholesale Market Law, Law No. 32 of 1923, art. 15-2.

140 Law Concerning Normalization of the Operation of Enterprises Related to Environment Sanitation, arts. 8, 16.

* Both William Lockwood and Alexander Calhoun commented at the conference on the MITI preference for operating through informal pressures. Calhoun went on to suggest that a simple suggestion is frequently sufficient to bring compliance by the industry involved.

141 This latter view appears to be that held by a former member of the FTC, Ashino, note 58, at 44–45. However, certain laws do provide for an exemption from the Antimonopoly Law in the case of concerted action taken pursuant to the recommendation of the responsible ministry. E.g., Law Concerning the Preservation of Liquor Tax and Liquor Industry Societies, Etc., Law No. 7 of 1953, art. 93.

142 This is based on information furnished me directly by MITI. Also see Kanazawa, *Dokkin Hō to Gyōsei-chō no Kankoku* (The Antimonopoly Law and the Recommendations by Administrative Agencies), Kōsei Torihiki (Fair Trade) no. 136 (1962).

EXPORT QUOTAS AND THE LAW

Voluntary export-quota systems have been established to restrict the export of such commodities as textiles, stainless-steel flatware, and plywood to American markets. Their purpose is to forestall the erection of mandatory barriers to such imports by the United States government at the behest of domestic producers of these commodities.[143] While the United States government has participated in discussions of, and has strongly supported, these various voluntary export quotas, only the quota for the cotton-textile industry has been formalized by the exchange of diplomatic notes. Quotas and standards of price and quality can be established by exporters on their own initiative under articles 5[144] and 11[145] of the Export-Import Transactions

---

Among the matters currently being investigated *In the Matter of the Grand Jury Investigation of the Shipping Industry,* Misc. No. 5–60, United States District Court for the District of Columbia, is the possibility that certain shipping companies including Japanese, may have "secretly and concertedly fixed rates on many of the so-called open rate items" which they carried from Japan to the United States and may have established quotas on the tonnage of such items lifted on each sailing. Previously, the Japanese Ministry of Transportation, responding to an inquiry on the same question, took the position that such sailing quotas and uniformity of rates may have existed but that those were put into effect independently by each of the Japanese shipping companies involved in response to "recommended restrictions" put forward by that ministry.

[143] This move is urged in spite of the probable violation of American antitrust laws. See note 126 above.

[144] Art. 5 provides:

"(1) An exporter, upon reporting it to the Minister of International Trade and Industry up to ten days prior to the date of its conclusion, may conclude an agreement regarding price, quantity, quality, design, or other matters in an export transaction involving specific kinds of goods being exported to a specific destination.

"(2) The Minister of International Trade and Industry, if he ascertains, in a case where he has had a report pursuant to the provisions of the prior paragraph, that the agreement pertaining to the report fails to comply with any of the following items, shall, prior to the conclusion of the agreement, order the exporter to alter the agreement or prohibit its conclusion:

(i) That there is no fear that it violates a treaty or other arrangement concluded with a foreign government or international agency.

(ii) That there is no fear that it will injure the interests of the importer or related businessmen at the destination and that it will markedly injure the international credit of exporters in this country.

(iii) That besides the prior two items, there is no fear that it will cause hindrance to the sound development of export trade.

(iv) That its content is not improperly discriminatory.

(v) That participation in the agreement or withdrawal from the agreement is not improperly restrained.

(vi) That there is no fear that the interests of either related persons engaged in agriculture, forestry, and fishing, related medium and small entrepreneurs and other related businessmen, or the general consumer will be improperly injured."

[145] Art. 11 provides in part:

"(1) An export society may carry on the following enumerated business activities. Provided, however, an export society, other than an export society in which an investment is made by the members (hereafter referred to as an "investment export society"), may not carry on the business activities in item (iii).

Law; or by MITI under article 28 of the same law if, as often happens, the exporters are unable to reach an agreement on these points. In either case, MITI can assist in the implementation of the established quotas through its licensing of exports pursuant to the Foreign Exchange and Foreign Trade Control Law.[146]

The cotton-textile industry is illustrative of the export-quota system. Speaking of the quotas placed on cotton exports to the United States beginning on January 1, 1956, Kojiro Abe, Chairman of the All-Japan Cotton Spinners' Association [Society], told the Boggs subcommittee of the House Committee on Ways and Means, at a meeting with Japanese business leaders held by the subcommittee in Tokyo:

> It may be appropriate to point out at the outset that, as with the total balance of trade between our two countries, Japan purchases far more raw cotton from the United States than Japan exports to the United States in the form of textile products . . .
>
> While it is true that our total of all cotton products to the United States — fabrics, garments, and even including such minor specialty items as gloves and brassieres — have increased to 270 million square yards, it is also true that the United States produced some 10 billion square yards of cotton fabrics, not including most of the specialty articles that are included in Japan's total. Thus, it is difficult for us to conceive that our niggardly export volume could cause serious injury to the American industry which outproduced and outsold Japanese imports by such an impressive margin that there was no comparison. It might be more realistic if the United States industry looked to other than Japanese imports as the cause of their current problems . . .
>
> In passing, it should be repeated that judged against the facts at least as we see them, we cannot understand the clamor and the condemnation of Japanese textile imports on the part of our counterpart industry in the United States.
>
> Nevertheless, when the Japanese Government advised us that these outcries, however unfounded, were endangering cordial relations between our two countries, the Japanese textile industry imposed voluntary quotas or export adjustment measures in order that international friendship and comity might be preserved between the United States and Japan.
>
> The Japanese textile industry felt that the maintenance of international

---

(i) Prevent unfair export transactions by the members belonging to the export society (this refers to persons directly or indirectly composing the export society; hereafter the same).

(ii) Establish facilities for the purpose of furthering the common interest of the members belonging to the export society.

(iii) Loan funds to society members (including the discount of notes) and borrow them for the benefit of society members.

"(2) An export society, upon reporting to the Minister of International Trade and Industry up to ten days prior to the date of its establishment, may, as prescribed in its articles of association, fix matters, other than those prescribed in the prior paragraph, to be observed by its members regarding price, quantity, quality, design, or other matters in an export transaction of specific kinds of goods being exported to a specific destination."

[146] Law No. 228 of 1949.

good will transcended the aspirations of any single industry or combination of industries.

When the exportation of certain articles that are in demand overseas is restricted by self-imposed quotas in a nation that believes in free enterprise, we submit that these represent real sacrifice and hardship to our industry. This is particularly true with such items as velveteens, blouses, and ginghams, for they are manufactured by the smaller companies whose very existence is threatened by the reduction in orders from abroad.

These voluntary measures of self-restraint represent a terrible threat to our own industry in another way; if we imposed them voluntarily to maintain cordial relations with the United States, then other nations may also expect us to impose similar restrictions on our exports to them; the precedent established may well serve to reduce our free-world markets. And yet this was the price that we were willing to pay for Japanese-American friendship.[147]

Nevertheless, the domestic American industry maintained its opposition to Japanese cotton-textile imports. The industry demanded that mandatory import quotas be instituted and filed numerous petitions with the United States Tariff Commission under section 7 of the Trade Agreements Extension Act of 1955, requesting escape-clause relief for the domestic gingham, blouse, pillowcase, and velveteen industries; recommendations to the President by the Secretary of Agriculture, under section 22 of the Agricultural Adjustment Act of 1935, for the imposition of quotas on cotton-textile imports were demanded, and boycotts and discriminatory legislation in a number of states were supported. Because of these pressures, discussions were held between the Japanese and American governments and a decision was reached that these voluntary quotas should be extended.

As previously pointed out, it is possible that in certain circumstances a voluntary system of export quotas to the United States would violate that country's antitrust laws.[148] In the case of the Japanese cotton-textile industry, certainly the involvement of both governments in negotiating and fixing the overall quotas makes it most unlikely, as a practical matter, that any such question will ever be raised. Nevertheless, it appears that the allocation of the quotas is effected by the export societies concerned, pursuant to articles 5 and 11 of the Export-Import Transactions Law rather than by MITI under article 28 of the same law. It is possible that this allocation itself may be shown to exercise a restraint on competition. In other industries, the overall quota for exports to the United States, as well as its allocation, is decided by the export society (with the concurrence of MITI). In such cases and in the absence of previous discussions with the Department of State, it could well be that a thoroughly well-intentioned attempt to stabilize

[147] *Hearings on the Administration and Operation of Customs and Tariff Laws and the Trade Agreements Program Before the Subcommittee on Customs, Tariffs and Reciprocal Trade Agreements of the House Committee on Ways and Means*, 84th Cong., 2d Sess., pt. 4, at 2080–82 (1956).

[148] Note 126 above.

the marketing of certain goods in the United States would run afoul of that country's antitrust laws.

Conclusion

Although it is obvious that the trend has been strongly toward the creation of exceptions to the Antimonopoly Law, particularly in the export industries, it would be a mistake to conclude that the Antimonopoly Law has not had and does not still have a considerable influence in Japan. Its enforcement is anemic today, but the text of the statute and the decisions implementing it in the past remain and could be resuscitated easily by an administration sympathetic to their principles. There is, of course, no immediate prospect of this happening. At the very least, however, the law has served as a restraining influence on the seemingly natural inclination of Japanese big business to form cartels.

A more difficult question is whether such legislation serves a useful function in the social and economic environment of Japan.* The export industries have the strongest claim to a broad exemption from the antimonopoly requirements. Collaboration is required in order to meet massive foreign competition in such fields as heavy machinery and to accomplish the orderly penetration of foreign markets without provoking retaliatory opposition. Furthermore, many of these industries are comprised of many relatively small, and therefore fiercely competitive, producers which occupy a much more important position in the Japanese economy than they would in the economy of the United States.[149] Thus it appears that these producers must also have some exemption from the Antimonopoly Law.

In 1962 the Japanese government is still obliged to put into effect various measures to reduce the consumption of goods and services by the domestic market in order to redress the country's balance of payments. In such circumstances, antitrust legislation may be an anomaly since one of its principal purposes is supposed to be to keep prices lower and thereby increase the

* General discussion at the conference brought out several aspects of this conflict between policies favoring competition and those favoring cartel rationalization. Charles Wyzanski drew a comparison with American industries associated with the public interest, such as railroads, which are subject to regulation which both restricts competition and requires it to a certain extent. William Lockwood commented that Japan's high growth rate in recent years indicated that, while cartels may be on the increase, there must be extreme competition in the areas not subject to them. There was disagreement about the effects of the present exchange restrictions and import quotas. Alexander Calhoun thought their importance overstated since they do not control distribution of the supplies once they have entered the country. Makoto Yazawa and Yoshio Kanazawa thought these restrictions very important; in fact, there is serious concern, Yazawa said, about how to fill the gap in control that will probably result if Japan complies with the recommendation that the International Monetary Fund is expected to make, namely, to abolish exchange restrictions (this recommendation was made in early 1963).

[149] In 1958, manufacturers with less than 300 employees accounted for 52.7 percent of total Japanese production. Chūshō Kigyō-chō (Medium and Small Enterprise Agency), Chūshō Kigyō Tōkei Yōran (A Survey of Medium and Small Enterprise Statistics) 58–59 (1961).

consumption of goods and services. But the consumption of the Japanese domestic market has expanded tremendously since the adoption of the Antimonopoly Law, and the vigorous opposition in 1958 to its amendment by consumer groups undoubtedly reflected their belief that it serves to keep prices lower than they would otherwise be and that this is desirable insofar as they are concerned.[150]

Because of this sentiment, it appears unlikely that any substantial amendment will be made to the Antimonopoly Law itself. However, a failure to amend will not prevent the continued expansion of exempted activities pursuant both to particular legislation and to such schemes as the "recommended restrictions" put forth by various industries. Nor should the sentiment prevent certain further amendments that are necessary to adjust the Antimonopoly Law to its Japanese environment. Unfortunately, there is no immediate prospect that the FTC will be able to revitalize itself and assume a positive role in the administration of the law. It is to be hoped that, with the continued expansion of domestic consumption, such revitalization will be possible and appropriate amendments will by then have been made better to fit the Antimonopoly Law to its social environment. In particular, the Antimonopoly Law itself should permit restrictive practices when they demonstrably benefit the Japanese economy or society as a whole, as in the case of the export industries and of industries composed of many relatively small producers.

[150] Some Japanese economists believe that the Antimonopoly Law has contributed to the country's phenomenal economic growth since the end of World War II.

THE LEGAL STRUCTURE FOR ECONOMIC ENTERPRISE: SOME ASPECTS OF JAPANESE COMMERCIAL LAW

Shinichiro Michida

ASSISTED BY ROBERT BRAUCHER

DURING the past century, Japanese law and society have been undergoing revolutionary change and development. From our position in the midst of this continuing process, we are unable to estimate accurately the rate of change. Instead we must view the process in order to pick out those features or elements that are most likely to have contemporary and future significance. Perhaps the main feature of the social development has been the decentralization of power, leading toward a more "pluralistic" society. The legal development has followed a parallel course; it seems likely that its direction will continue to be toward the production of a body of law which is flexible enough to meet the demands of a pluralistic society.

The pluralism of modern Japanese society had its tentative beginnings before the Meiji Restoration of 1868; but the Western influence in the latter decades of the nineteenth century both produced the social patterns and provided the legal and institutional framework on which a new society was established and on which the industrial development of contemporary Japan depends. A merchant class had arisen over a period of centuries, but the development of a legal structure for economic enterprise began only in the Meiji era. During that period business stock companies were formed for the first time in Japan;[1] banks began to discount bills of exchange and

Note. Mr. Michida is Professor of Law, Kyoto University. B.Jur., Kyoto University, 1949; Dr.Jur., 1962. Participant, Japanese American Program for Cooperation in Legal Studies at Harvard University, 1954–1955, and at University of Michigan, 1955–1956; research at Harvard, Michigan, and other American law schools, 1961–1963. Coauthor of BRAUCHER & MICHIDA, AMERIKA SHŌ-TORIHIKI HŌ TO NIHON MINSHŌ HŌ (American Law on Commercial Transactions and the Japanese Civil and Commercial Codes) (1961); author of writings in the fields of commercial and criminal law.

Mr. Braucher is Professor of Law, Harvard University. A.B., 1936, Haverford College; LL.B., 1939, Harvard University.

[1] See KANNO, NIHON KAISHA KIGYŌ HASSEI SHI NO KENKYŪ (A Study of the History of the Emergence of Japanese Company Enterprise) 110–51 (1931).

promissory notes before maturity to provide credit for merchant holders.[2] Bills of exchange had been in use long before Meiji. Indeed, during the Tokugawa period expansion of credit had often been effected through their use, so that 60,000 or 70,000 ryō in paper could be issued with a capital of only 10,000 ryō.[3] According to one writer, "in the 15th and 16th centuries Japan was a great maritime nation with trade centers all along the Eastern seaboard of Asia, and with colonies of settlers as distant as Java and Siam."[4] One is often reminded by writings in English on Japanese history that the city merchants in Tokugawa Japan accumulated fortunes and attained financial power, establishing themselves mostly before the Genroku era (1688–1703). These facts raise a question as to why a legal structure for corporate enterprise did not develop before the Meiji era.[5]

ELEMENTS OF THE LEGAL STRUCTURE

The Tokugawa Repression

The answer to this question may properly be regarded as a task for the economic historian rather than for the lawyer, but the answer is of key importance in understanding the Japanese legal structure. Medieval commercial capital did not generally go into the organization and means of production. Loans were made primarily to finance future commercial activity or as advances against future nonindustrial production. Small merchants were willing to borrow at usurious rates to carry on business, although there were a number of laws governing usury. The typical pattern of borrowing money was for the borrower-merchant to use land or warehouse receipts for rice as security; then the merchant was able to use the borrowed funds to buy goods, which were in turn used as security to borrow money to buy more goods, and so on. Moreover, economic conditions also forced the feudal overlords to borrow large sums from the lending merchants in order to survive. Thus capital was being used for primarily nonindustrial purposes. Indeed, only in the last years of the Tokugawa period

[2] The first clearing house in Japan, the Osaka Clearing House, was established in 1879, and the Tokyo Clearing House was established in 1887. In Tokyo in 1887, the Yasuda Bank listed the discounting of bills and notes as one of its services. YASUDA GINKŌ (Yasuda Bank), YASUDA GINKŌ ROKUJŪ NEN SHI (A Sixty-Year History of the Yasuda Bank) 83 (1940).

[3] See SHELDON, THE RISE OF THE MERCHANT CLASS IN TOKUGAWA JAPAN 78–79 n.52 (1958).

[4] NORMAN, JAPAN'S EMERGENCE AS A MODERN STATE 19 n.18 (1940).

[5] See SHELDON, as in note 3 above, at 64. See also HONJO, THE SOCIAL AND ECONOMIC HISTORY OF JAPAN (1935); 1–3 TAKEKOSHI, THE ECONOMIC ASPECTS OF THE HISTORY OF THE CIVILIZATION OF JAPAN (1930); TAKIZAWA, THE PENETRATION OF MONEY ECONOMY IN JAPAN (1927). Of course, in medieval Japan various professional guilds known as *Za* had existed, one of which composed of silver merchants has left its name in the Ginza area of Tokyo, while joint ventures similar to the medieval Italian *commenda* can be found in Tokugawa Japan. On the *Za,* see 2 SANSOM, A HISTORY OF JAPAN 192–94 (1961), while KANNO, note 1, at 22–32, gives examples of joint ventures.

was there a shift from a system of "cottage industry" to a system of manufacture in small factories.

The most important single obstacle to the development of industrial capital was the fact that the domestic economy lacked the stimulation that foreign markets, especially new colonial markets, normally provide. Such markets were closed to Japan after 1638 because of the isolationist policy of the Tokugawa government. Thus commercial capital had to batten exclusively upon internal trade, which, at least, was as highly organized as feudal restrictions permitted. As a result, Japan's emergence as a modern state was postponed: "the Tokugawa ban on foreign trade, together with the pettifogging restrictions devised by feudal prejudice, served to retard the development of the Japanese merchant class, especially in its accumulation of capital, wherein it lagged far behind the great trading companies of 17th and 18th century Britain and Holland."[6]

This forcible stunting of the growth of a capitalist class deprived the merchant and banker class of its progressive spirit, and it tended to preserve family enterprise intact and essentially unchanged. It also brought with it continued intervention from the government. These effects can still be seen in the law, particularly in certain technical rules of the law of negotiable paper and security interests, and may help to explain the fact that the attitude of Japanese bankers toward legal protection in such transactions resembles the attitude of English or Continental bankers more than that of American bankers. Perhaps less direct but more important is the effect of the stunting on the whole legal climate of modern Japan, which fostered the borrowing from Continental legal systems of a general legal structure. The new banking laws adopted in Meiji Japan were borrowed entirely from the American national banking law, and the need for a stock company law was advocated with great urgency by people who had visited the United States.[7] But in the process of building a modern system for Japan, Continental patterns of legal thought were adopted with enthusiasm.

The Role of "Special" Statutes

When the Meiji Restoration undertook to develop a new capitalistic society in Japan, the necessary legal structure began with special statutes designed to meet particular problems. The first great task was the development of the market and the centralization of capital. This meant the abolition of tariff barriers and tolls among the fiefs, the establishment of freedom of trade and occupation, the unification of the monetary and banking system, and the encouragement of the formation of business stock companies. The slogan of the period, both inside and outside of the government, was *Shoku-san kō-gyō!* which means literally, "Plant and raise industries!"

[6] NORMAN, note 4, at 19.

[7] See KANNO, note 1, at 35–48, 290–93.

In the first two decades a number of steps were taken. In 1869, the second year of the Meiji era, for the purpose of facilitating exchange and credit as well as centralizing the available capital, the government encouraged and assisted the formation of trading and exchange companies in several cities.[8] In 1871, the government published two books on the mechanism of the stock company and the advantages of enterprise in corporate form;[9] one of them was based primarily on information about American corporations.[10] In 1872, the National Bank Ordinance was enacted,[11] in 1874, the Stock Exchange Ordinance[12] with rice commodity exchange companies directed to follow its provisions,[13] and in 1882, the Bills of Exchange and Promissory Notes Ordinance.[14] For the purpose of facilitating transactions in immovable property, a Recording Law was enacted in 1886.[15]

The substance of such special statutes, which are still being enacted today, is complex, constituting a delicate and dynamic reflection of national policy. The Foreign Exchange and Foreign Trade Control Law, enacted in 1949,[16] and the Law Concerning Foreign Investment of 1950[17] are good modern examples. In Japan, as elsewhere in the world today, enterprise in company form is seriously concerned with agreements relating to technical assistance and foreign investment; such transactions are entirely governed by special statutes. In practice they present very difficult legal problems; skill and judgment in dealing with these and similar problems are of primary importance to economic enterprise.

However, the importance of the vast body of such statutes and regulations is often underestimated and sometimes ignored. The acts have not greatly affected general legal thought or teaching curricula, but have remained the specialty of government and company experts and a few specialized lawyers and scholars. The unrealistic attitude of the academic community may be explained by two factors: first, the traditional isolation of that community; and second, the traditional emphasis on "general laws" as opposed to "special laws."

The Commercial Code[18] is a special law as compared with the Civil

[8] Trading companies (*tsūshō kaisha*) and exchange companies (*kawase kaisha*) were formed in Tokyo, Osaka, and several other cities in 1869.

[9] FUKUCHI, KAISHA-BEN (Companies) (Ōkura-shō (Ministry of Finance) ed., 1871), reprinted in 5 NIHON KINYŪ SHI SHIRYŌ MEIJI-TAISHŌ HEN (Japanese Monetary Historical Materials: Meiji-Taisho Compilation) 1 (Nihon Ginkō Chōsa Kyoku (Bank of Japan Research Bureau) ed., 1956); SHIBUSAWA, RIKKAI RYAKUSOKU (Principles of Forming a Company) (Ōkura-shō ed., 1871), reprinted in 5 NIHON KINYŪ SHI SHIRYŌ MEIJI-TAISHŌ HEN 23.

[10] That is the RIKKAI RYAKUSOKU.

[11] Great Council of State Decree No. 349 of 1872.

[12] Great Council of State Decree No. 107 of 1874.

[13] By Great Council of State Decree No. 138 of 1874.

[14] Great Council of State Decree No. 57 of 1882.

[15] Law No. 1 of 1886.

[16] Law No. 228 of 1949.

[17] Law No. 163 of 1950.

[18] Law No. 48 of 1899.

Code,[19] but it is a general law as compared with a statute such as the Foreign Exchange and Foreign Trade Control Law. Early in their course of study, law students are taught that a special law prevails over a general law if the terms of both apply to a specific case. But it is common for professors and lawyers to overemphasize the extent to which the structure is provided by the Civil Code, the Commercial Code, and such basic statutes as the Bills Law[20] or the Immovable Property Recording Law.[21] Such general laws are often treated as if they were the entire law, perhaps partly because of the traditional view that a code is a self-sufficient whole.

A foreigner may ask questions about Japanese law which can be answered solely by reference to special statutes. Certainly an understanding of the Japanese legal structure for economic enterprise requires some knowledge of such statutes. Except for specific questions on international aspects of commercial transactions, however, the questions most often asked relate to the Japanese law on agency, sales, checks, or the validity or priority of a security interest. Such questions require recourse to a code, even though a special statute may also be involved.

The Development of the Codes

In academic legal circles, perhaps more than among practicing lawyers, the codes, particularly the Civil Code and the Commercial Code, are viewed as the basic and fundamental elements of the legal structure. But, when the codes are viewed in the context of the historical emergence of Japan as a modern state at the time of the slogan "Shoku-san kō-gyō," they do not seem so important. To indicate their true position, it is necessary to give some explanation of why Japanese law did become codified.

Had there been a national private law and an independently organized bar with a vested interest in the law,[22] the code-making process in Japan might well have been quite different. It is said that "the French Civil Code of 1804 and the German Civil Code of 1900 are fresh starts for their legal systems."[23] The Commercial and Civil Codes of Japan might also be viewed as a fresh start for the Japanese legal order. A closer look at the legislative process, however, shows that the principal function of the codes was to demonstrate Japan's potentialities as a world power and to provide a basis for the abolition of the unequal treaties signed at the end of the Tokugawa period.[24]

During the first thirty years of the Meiji era, the primary task of for-

[19] Law No. 89 of 1896 and Law No. 9 of 1898.

[20] Law No. 20 of 1932.

[21] Law No. 24 of 1899.

[22] Cf. von Mehren, The Civil Law System 11 n.39 (1957).

[23] *Ibid.*, at 13.

[24] After a thirty-year struggle, in 1899 the national consciousness awakened in the Meiji Restoration was finally crowned with success by the revision of these treaties. On the treaty-revision movement, see Sansom, The Western World and Japan 444 (1951).

eign policy was to prove to the Western powers that Japan was a modern nation ruled by law. At the same time, Japanese capitalism was passing through its formative stage, and the Meiji leaders became conscious of the need for a codified law to govern it. In 1881, the government made a formal commitment to ask a German, Hermann Roesler, to draft a commercial code. Promulgated in 1890, Japan's first Commercial Code followed the Continental pattern and regulated separately various commercial matters; in 1,064 articles it provided for the treatment of bills and notes, sales, commercial contracts, companies, carriers, maritime commerce, bankruptcy, and other subjects. During the same period, a Civil Code was being drafted by a Frenchman, Gustave Émile Boissonade.

The codes were delayed from becoming effective because of attacks upon their contents, made primarily by nationalistic groups objecting to the large-scale borrowing of foreign elements. Despite the controversy, a need was felt for prompt enactment of statutes on companies, bills and notes, and bankruptcy, so that in 1893 the articles on these subjects were made effective as separate statutes.[25] The Civil Code was made effective in 1898;[26] it covered contracts, hypothecs, pledges, privileges (liens), sales, agency, immovable and movable property, relatives, and inheritance. A new Commercial Code, effective in 1899,[27] consisted of five books: General Provisions, Companies, Commercial Acts, Bills, and Maritime Commerce. The book on Bills was repealed in 1934[28] when the laws on bills and checks were enacted pursuant to the Geneva Conventions Providing a Uniform Law on Bills of Exchange and Promissory Notes[29] and a Uniform Law on Cheques.[30]

Thus, the coverage of the codes was the product of borrowings primarily from Continental legal systems and of modernization that was also in Continental terms, as shown in the Geneva laws, this being the result of national eagerness for the status of an independent power. The codes are conventionally viewed as fundamental, but serious dangers are involved in clinging to the statutory text and paying exclusive homage to its foreign sources. What is needed is not adherence to the law of any particular country but breadth of viewpoint and eclecticism in legal thought — at the legislative level, in judicial holdings, and in the classroom.

Foreign Influences in Legal Administration

An eclectic approach to formulating and interpreting a legal structure makes available types of solutions and bodies of experience that have per-

[25] By Law No. 9 of 1893.

[26] By Imperial Order No. 123 of 1898.

[27] By Imperial Order No. 133 of 1899.

[28] By Bills Law, art. 80 and Checks Law, Law No. 57 of 1933, art. 64.

[29] Convention Providing a Uniform Law for Bills of Exchange and Promissory Notes, June 7, 1930, Treaty No. 4 of 1933, 143 L.N.T.S. 257.

[30] Convention Providing a Uniform Law for Cheques, March 19, 1931, Treaty No. 7 of 1933, 143 L.N.T.S. 355.

haps been ignored in the past. The legal structure for economic enterprise, to be serviceable in modern times, must be formed by a rational choice made from among all the possible alternatives. Foreign influences on Japanese law thus far have not been as broad as they might have been, or indeed as they may seem. For example, a single transaction in the ordinary course of the business of a company enterprise, perhaps involving a contract for sale, the sending of a check, and the acceptance of some form of security interest as a basis for an extension of credit, may be seen to be governed by laws from several sources. But these elements have traditionally been treated as involving three distinct legal topics: the law of sales, negotiable paper, and security interest. The foreign influence on each of these has been somewhat one-sided.

With respect to the use of a check, the Geneva Uniform Laws on Bills and Cheques have been accepted in Japan as embodying ideal solutions to problems of negotiable instruments. Comparative studies of the Geneva and the American provisions were published in the *Harvard Law Review* in 1931[31] and in the *Yale Law Journal* in 1938,[32] which can be found in many Japanese libraries. But it was only in 1960, after a lapse of more than twenty years, that such studies were really introduced into the Japanese legal world.[33] Under American law, payment in good faith does not discharge the payer of order paper if an endorsement has been forged. In England, the paying banks were successful in obtaining protection under a provision on discharge by bona fide payment inserted as section 19 of the Stamp Act;[34] collecting banks found protection in the crossed check, provided for in the Bills of Exchange Act.[35] Still broader protection is given by the English Cheques Act of 1957.[36] The Checks Law of Japan introduced the crossed check,[37] but experience has shown that the risk of theft is not small, and the solution of forgery problems involving crossed checks is in fact still complicated and difficult.

Turning to security interests, the German law on chattel security, with no requirement of public notice, was treated in Japanese legal discussion until 1959 as the only possible solution to legal problems respecting security interests in a merchant's stock in trade. The Enterprise Security Law[38] in-

[31] Hudson & Feller, *The International Unification of Laws Concerning Bills of Exchange,* 44 HARV. L. REV. 333 (1931).

[32] Kessler, *Forged Indorsements,* 47 YALE L.J. 863 (1938).

[33] See Michida, *Tegata Kogitte Hō no Kokusai-teki Bunretsu to Riron no Rieki to Daishō* (The International Schism in the Law of Bills and Checks and the Advantages and Cost of the Theories), 66 HŌGAKU RONSŌ (Treatises in Jurisprudence) no. 5, at 1, 7–12, 32–37 (1960), in NICHIBEI SHŌJI HŌ NO JISSAI (Reality in Japanese American Commercial Law) 43, 49–54, 76–81 (Michida ed., 1961).

[34] Stamp Act, 1853, 16 & 17 Vict., c.59, §19.

[35] Bills of Exchange Act, 1882, 45 & 46 Vict., c.61, §§76–82.

[36] Cheques Act, 1957, 5 & 6 Eliz. 2, c.36, §4.

[37] See Checks Law, arts. 37–38.

[38] Law No. 106 of 1958.

troduced into Japanese law in 1958 the English floating charge, but restricted its use to securing bonds issued by stock companies. Before 1959 there was apparently no attention paid to the American law on the continuing general lien or floating lien.[39]

With respect to sales, English law on sale of goods has often been the subject of Japanese legal studies, but the first study of American sale law was in 1960.[40] The sale law traditionally taught in Japan treats liability for latent defects in specific goods as a liability imposed by operation of law rather than by contract. The legal profession has only recently learned of the American theory that warranty liability is contractual.

The Concept of the Merchant in the Commercial Code

It would be quite natural for any foreign-trained lawyer, confronted with a question of Japanese commercial law, to look for an answer in the Commercial Code. The reading of the code has a rather limited utility for such a purpose, however; considerable familiarity with cases, theories expounded in treatises, and practices outside of the code provisions is also required. But a brief discussion of the logic behind the Commercial Code may at least assist in the reading of the code itself.

The Commercial Code of Japan assumes that commercial law should exclude nonmercantile law in accordance with the traditional distinction of the Continental method of legal codification. The European codifications of commercial law centered on the concept of "merchant," which was relatively easily definable by reference to membership in the merchant class, a semi-political category. Largely following this pattern, article 4(1) of the Commercial Code of Japan provides that "in this Code 'merchant' refers to a person who in his own name performs commercial acts as a business." But since commercial activities often involved nonmerchants in old Japan, the scope of the term was made to turn not on membership in a class but on the definitions of a commercial act provided in other articles of the code. For example, articles 501–503 are concerned with a number of acts which are mercantile per se. Thus "merchant" embodies objective criteria as well as the personal criterion.

In 1938, a provision (paragraph (2)) was added to article 4 to the effect that "a person who engages in the sale of goods as a business through a shop

[39] See the report on American security interests, delivered at the symposium on "Assignment as Security" held by the 23rd Convention of the Japan Private Law Association, October 14, 1959, published in part as Michida, *Jōto Tampo — Amerika Hō* (Assignment as Security — American Law), SHIHŌ (Journal of Private Law) no. 21, at 153 (1959); another part of the report is published in 2 BRAUCHER & MICHIDA, AMERIKA SHŌ-TORIHIKI HŌ TO NIHON MINSHŌ HŌ (American Law on Commercial Transactions and the Japanese Civil and Commercial Codes) 456–60, 656–60 (1961).

[40] 1 *ibid.* (1960). Publication of the first volume of this work, which dealt with sales, created demand for Michida to hold a series of sessions on sales contracts with company experts in Tokyo and Osaka.

or other equipment similar thereto, or who carries on a mining business, even if he does not perform commercial acts as a business, is hereby deemed a 'merchant.' It is the same for the companies of article 52, paragraph (2)." This addition was an attempt to broaden the personal criterion and meant clearly that enterprise in company form was to be regulated by commercial law.

The determination whether a party is a "merchant" is important, since the Commercial Code sets up a number of rules different from those of the Civil Code in the same matters; several examples of such differences will be seen with regard to agency and formation of contracts. On the other hand, article 1 of the Commercial Code provides that "regarding commercial matters not provided for in this Code, commercial customary law applies, and when there is no commercial customary law, the Civil Code applies." Furthermore, article 3(1) provides that "in regard to an act which is a commercial act for a party on one side, this Code applies to both sides." It would seem that special rules for merchants might be applicable under article 3 to transactions between a merchant and a casual or inexperienced seller or buyer, and that this would be detrimental to the nonprofessional. But the code also adopts a policy of expressly stating special rules applicable only to transactions "between merchants," as does the Uniform Commercial Code.[41] For example, the code's requirements for prompt correspondence and quick decision, integral to modern mercantile speed and exactitude, are relaxed for nonmerchants by the qualifying words "between merchants" in article 526. A similar qualification appears in articles 524 and 527, among others.

Agent, Broker, and Factor

Agency and the Codes

The development of industry in Meiji Japan naturally resulted in an increasing utilization of agents in carrying on business enterprises. These included not only those agents whose tasks were primarily manual or mechanical, such as workmen engaged in production or other such company employees, but also those, such as insurance or traveling agents, whose tasks involved the creation of new legal relations between the employer and third persons. The Meiji government recognized the necessity of keeping the legal relationships among the principal, the agent, and the third person certain and uniform, regardless of commercial customs. Before Hermann Roesler made a draft of the Commercial Code, the government in 1881 appointed a committee for the investigation of commercial customs in Japan. This committee collected numerous statements on various commercial

[41] See Uniform Commercial Code §§2-104, 2-201(2), 2-207(2), 2-605(1)(b) (1958 official text).

matters from businessmen, trade associations or societies, and county offices all over the nation. The statements about agency showed that the legal consequences of acts done by the three parties involved in agency transactions under various circumstances were not always clearly understood.[42] The Roesler report on the Draft of the Commercial Code stated that this lack of uniformity and clarity was the reason that commercial customs were not incorporated into the code.[43]

The imposition of legal consequences upon actions by the three parties depends largely on the Civil and Commercial Codes; yet these codes have rather few provisions on agency. For example, although a particular statute or another code may include special provisions on insurance agents, there is nothing in the Commercial Code on such agents, either in the chapter on insurance (articles 629–683) or in the chapter on commercial agents (articles 46–51). The latter chapter defines commercial agent and provides for the agent's duty to give notice of his transactions, the agent's duty to avoid competitive occupations, the agent's right to receive notice of claims or performance of his transaction, the termination of the contract of mandate (agency contract), and the agent's right of retention (possessory lien); but it does not include provisions concerning the agent's authority. The business of insurance agents may be widely varied: some may have authority only to solicit applications; others may also have authority to complete, countersign, and issue policies. It is thus very important for a person who is going to negotiate with an insurance agent to know what kind of protection is given to him if the agent exceeds his authority or has no authority at all.

The familiar English terms "apparent authority" and "breach of warranty of authority" are not found in the Japanese statutes, but similar doctrines are expressed in different phraseology in articles 109–112 and 117 of the Civil Code.[44] The transactions with respect to which this code imposes legal consequences are not necessarily "commercial acts." On the other hand, the Commercial Code, in the chapter on general provisions for commercial acts, provides rules for cases of unnamed or undisclosed principals and for cases of death of the principal if the agency dealing relates to a commercial act (articles 504 and 506). The provisions of these codes together, however, even including article 715 of the unlawful acts (tort) chapter of the Civil Code respecting the liability of employers, are still too scanty to resolve the complex question of whether the insurance company should be liable for damage caused to third persons through actions of its agents, who may be executives

[42] NIHON SHŌJI KANREI RUISHŪ (A Compilation of Japanese Commercial Customs) (Shihō-shō (Ministry of Justice) ed., c.1883–84).

[43] *Ibid.*, preface.

[44] The comparable Japanese terms are "apparent agency" (*hyōken dairi*) and "exceeding authority" (*kengen yuetsu*).

and employees of the company directly; persons employed by executives or employees; or persons, including juridical persons (legal entities), to whom the insurance company, its executives, or its employees entrust various activities. Consequently, a separate statute, the Law Concerning the Control of Insurance Solicitation of 1948,[45] was enacted; in article 11 it contains provisions as to the insurance company's liability for damages caused by each of the several categories of persons referred to above.

The absence of the term "warranty" in the phraseology of the code provisions regarding agency, with the resultant necessity of dealing with the problems of authority in other ways, is not a unique situation in Japanese law. Rather it is a common occurrence, reflecting the fact that the warranty doctrine is underdeveloped and that other approaches are used in resolving similar problems throughout the whole structure of current Japanese law.

Brokerage Transactions

Utilization of others in carrying on a business may take the form of broker as well as agent transactions. A broker is defined in article 543 of the Commercial Code, and his rights and duties are provided in articles 544–550. The reading of article 546 by a man familiar with Anglo-American law may raise questions in his mind as to the precise aim of the first paragraph:

> When an act has been effected between the parties, the broker, without delay, is required to prepare documents in which have been entered the full personal or trade name of each party, the date of the act, and the gist thereof, and after signing, deliver them to each party.

It might seem that this could be the Japanese version of the Anglo-American Statute of Frauds. But recently, as indicated by comment 1 to section 2-201 of the Uniform Commercial Code, the tendency with respect to the requirements of content of the writing necessary to satisfy the American Statute of Frauds is that there need be included neither all the material terms of the contract nor an indication of which party is the buyer and which the seller. The writing need afford only a basis for believing that the offered oral evidence rests on a real transaction.

The aim of the requirement of article 546 was tested in 1933 in a case before the Great Court of Judicature. The broker had not made the required writing, and it was argued that the contract was therefore unenforceable. The Court ruled as follows:

> Of course, the statute does not purport to make the order to the broker to perform the prescribed procedure in Commercial Code art. 308 [now art. 546] a requisite for the formation of a contract, but rather seeks to prevent conflicting

[45] Law No. 171 of 1948.

argument in the future in a case where a contract is concluded pursuant to the agreement of the parties. Thus, in the instant case, even if the above prescribed procedure of the Commercial Code is not fulfilled, a concurrence between the parties as to their declarations of intention must result in the establishment of a sale. So long as we are able in fact to find this agreement, allegations such as those of the appellant above, except where by special stipulation the parties make performance of the said procedure a condition for the formation of the contract, are in and of themselves without reason.[46]

Although this requirement of a writing may thus be evidentiary, the code is not much concerned with matters of evidence. Indeed, nowhere in Japanese law is there such a thing as a parol-evidence rule, substantive or evidentiary. Thus an assertion of oral agreement may negate written provisions, depending upon the judge's finding from the evidence in any particular situation. Article 546 itself, despite the Great Court's characterization of it as an evidentiary rule, may be said to be simply a codification of a model business standard for the brokerage business.

Factors and Foreign Trading Companies

Business may also be transacted through a factor, defined by the Commercial Code in article 551. In the United States, the functions of the classical factor have been assumed by the commission merchant and the financier; today a factor is statutorily defined to include anyone who lends money against a pledge of goods, whether or not he is employed to sell them. But under the Japanese statutory definition, " 'factor' refers to a person who in his own name engages as a business in the sale or purchase of goods for the benefit of other persons."

In Japan there are thousands of trading companies engaged in foreign trade, several of them having grown into big businesses. They manage the sales of imported goods, making large advances to domestic principals against inventory and accounts receivable. In importing the goods from foreign sellers, the companies have computed a price-fluctuation reserve under the tax law by treating as sales their transactions with their principals, both domestic manufacturers and distributors. As to imports of raw sugar, however, the National Tax Agency has recently taken the view that a trading company which in its "own name engages as a business in the . . . purchase of goods for the benefit of other persons" in fact concludes a factor contract, as provided in articles 551–558 of the Commercial Code, even though in form there is a contract of sale. In legal effect, therefore, regardless of how the bills of lading are handled, the transaction is effected for the sugar-refinery company, which then may compute the price-fluctuation reserve as of the

[46] Judgment of April 25, 1933, Great Court of Judicature, V Civil Department, 2 HŌGAKU (Jurisprudence) 1486.

time that the trading company obtained the title to the raw sugar from the foreign shipper.[47]

The question of whether a particular transaction of a trading company is a factor transaction, an agent transaction, or a transaction on its own account is often a difficult one. But if what has been regarded as a transaction on its own account is now to be considered as a factor transaction in imports of goods other than raw sugar, the big trading company will be treated to a considerable extent as a commission merchant. The problem is not limited to tax matters, but involves a change in the traditional structure of commerce and industry, in which the trading companies have played a large and an integrating role since early in the Meiji era. Thus this problem, like so many others, poses a narrow legal question in a much broader economic setting.

Sales and Contracts

The Codes

In the Civil Code, contracts are supposed to be covered in one chapter of the book entitled Obligations, while separate chapters are supposed to cover the management of affairs without mandate, unjust enrichment, and unlawful acts (torts). Contracts are divided into thirteen types of enforceable, purely consensual transactions, one of which is sales; these are all regulated in articles 549–696. More general rules applicable to all these types of contracts are set out in a section on general provisions for contracts, consisting of twenty-eight articles (articles 521–548). But provisions concerning contracts, management of affairs without mandate, unjust enrichment, and unlawful acts are also covered in a separate chapter of General Provisions for obligations (articles 399–520). Also, as in the case of agents, the Commercial Code sets up separate rules for "commercial acts"—for example, formation of contracts in articles 507–509 and sales in articles 524–528.

Under American statutes, the concept of "property in the goods" or "title to the goods" is important. Once title or property passes, the seller may recover the sale price; the risk of loss is on the buyer; and the buyer has the remedies of an owner. In Japan, sales of goods are primarily governed by the Civil Code, which provides for the passing of title and risk of loss in articles 534–536. But the provisions as to the seller's remedy for the price and the buyer's remedy as an owner do not center on the explicit words "passing of title." Instead, the code provisions are stated simply in terms of

[47] See Concerning the Treatment of the Price Fluctuation Reserve for Imported Raw Sugar, Etc., National Tax Agency Circular, *Chokuhō* (Direct Tax Division—Juridical Persons' Tax Section) 1-32, Feb. 10, 1958. For further details concerning this reserve for price fluctuations, see the essay by Morio Uematsu, "Computation of Income in Japanese Income Taxation: A Study in the Adjustment of Theory to Reality," pp. 604–06, in this volume.

the legal relations, the "obligations" between the "debtor" and "creditor." For example, article 414(1) provides, "if a debtor does not voluntarily carry out performance of his obligation, the creditor may claim its compulsory performance from a court"; and article 415 provides, "if a debtor does not carry out performance in accordance with the tenor of his obligation, the creditor may claim compensation for his damage." Both articles may apply to give remedies either to the seller or to the buyer.

Identification and Appropriation of Goods

Under American statutes, legal questions on sales often turn on "appropriation" or "identification" of goods, if goods are to be made or selected after the contract is made. Under the Japanese law, such questions are governed by article 401 of the Civil Code,[48] a provision in the chapter on General Provisions for obligations; none of the provisions in the section of the Civil Code on sales or in the chapter of the Commercial Code on sales is applicable. A case involving the sale of liquid tar in a storage tank provides a good example of the practical operation of the Japanese law of sales.

The agreement between the buyer and the seller in that case provided for the sale of 2,000 tons of tar from February 1946 through January 1947 on the buyer's demand for a specified quantity and the seller's notification of the place of delivery. The tar was kept in a storage tank on the premises of the seller's supplier, and the seller placed watchmen there. After some tar had been delivered in August, the buyer refused to receive further deliveries on the ground of the tar's poor quality. Sometime in October the seller withdrew the watchmen; the remaining tar was then disposed of by employees of the seller's supplier. The buyer sued the seller for loss of the tar, claiming a violation of the duty to preserve the goods, imposed by article 400 of the Civil Code. The District Court and the High Court held for the buyer, but the judgment was quashed by the Supreme Court on two grounds. One was that the lower courts did not sufficiently examine the effect of failure of performance of the contract by the buyer, that is, his refusal to take the tar. The other was stated as follows:

> viewed in such terms as the nature and quantity of the subject matter of the sale, in this case, where no special circumstances are perceptible, it is proper to find that the sale performed was that of a nonspecific thing . . . Next, the trial court has held that, in any event, the subject matter in this case was specific, but we are unable to discern from the language of the trial judgment what facts

[48] CIVIL CODE art. 401 provides as follows:

"(1) If, in a case where the subject matter of an obligation is designated only by species, its quality cannot be determined by the nature of the juristic act or by the intention of the parties, the debtor is required to deliver a thing of average kind and quality.

"(2) If in the case of the prior paragraph the debtor has completed the acts necessary for the delivery of a thing or has, obtaining the consent of the creditor, designated a thing to be delivered, henceforth this thing is assumed to be the subject matter of the obligation."

constitute "the debtor [a person who] has completed the acts necessary for the delivery of a thing." As pointed out in argument, it is clear that a mere verbal tender made by the appellant in regard to the undelivered portion of the subject matter in the case did not constitute completion of the acts necessary for the delivery of a thing. Therefore, the point that the subject matter in the instant case, no matter which of the above types of obligation happens to cover it, does not yet deserve to be characterized as specific under the facts in the judgment of the trial court has merit, and we must state, moreover, that the trial court's conclusion that the appellant came to bear the duty of care of a good manager in regard to the subject matter is erroneous.[49]

The decision of the Supreme Court seems right on the first point, but its reasoning on the second point is quite dubious under a view of strict adherence to the letter of the code: "the acts necessary for the delivery of a thing." The case illustrates the difficulty of foreseeing the legal consequences of a transaction under Japanese law.

In analyzing the uncertainty of legal consequences, several points may be worth mentioning by way of comparison with the American law. In the first place, there is no provision in the Japanese statutes like section 51 of the Uniform Sales Act on the buyer's liability for failing to accept delivery; instead, that subject is assumed to be governed by the terms of the obligation and the language of article 413 of the Civil Code. Secondly, the provision on appropriation, article 401, provides, "if, in a case where the subject matter of an obligation is designated only by species . . . the debtor has completed the acts necessary for the delivery of a thing or has, obtaining the consent of the creditor, designated a thing to be delivered, henceforth this thing is assumed to be the subject matter of the obligation." It does not further state that such consent may be implied as well as expressed; nor does it state that "unless a different intention appears," the article provides the rule for ascertaining the intention of the parties as to appropriation and identification, as does the Uniform Sales Act in section 19. Thirdly, there is a provision which provides, "if the creditor has refused its acceptance in advance or if an act of the creditor is required in regard to the performance of the obligation, it shall be sufficient to notify him that the preparations for fulfillment have been made and admonish[50] its acceptance." This provision, article 493, should be considered in the interpretation of "the acts necessary for the delivery of a thing" of article 401 or in the interpretation of article 413, because article 493 provides a test for tender of fulfillment (performance) or "delivery." But article 493 was not considered in the tar-sale case,

[49] Tsuneno v. Iwate Ken Gyogyō Kyōdō Kumiai Rengō Kai (Iwate Prefecture Federation of Fishing Cooperative Societies), Supreme Court, III Petty Bench, Oct. 18, 1955, 9 SAIKŌ SAIBANSHO MINJI HANREI SHŪ (A Collection of Civil Supreme Court Cases) [hereafter cited SAI-HAN MINSHŪ] 1642, 1644.

[50] The Japanese term *saikoku*, herein translated as "admonish" or "admonishment," corresponds to the German concept of *Mahnung*.

perhaps because it occurs in the part of the Civil Code dealing with the extinction rather than the subject or effect of an obligation. Finally, the absence of a definition of the acts necessary to make the goods ready for delivery should be noted, whereas section 76(4) of the Uniform Sales Act provides that "deliverable state" means "such a state that the buyer would, under the contract, be bound to take delivery of them."

Although even in America it is said that the meaning of the word "appropriation" is puzzling and that the courts and text writers have not made it clear,[51] the difficulties of foreseeing legal consequences and the uncertainties of sales transactions under the Japanese law seem primarily to be a result of the method of codification.

Warranties

Although in Japan product-liability cases for personal injuries are very rare,* commercial claims between merchants for breach of warranty are many. As was pointed out above in the discussion of agency, however, there is no term in the Japanese statutes that may be translated literally as "warranty." The absence of the word in the statutes reflects the fact both that the doctrine of warranty is underdeveloped and that a different approach is preferred. This is not to say that there is no such word in the Japanese language. Indeed, the contract forms in use by the various companies for sales of durable consumer goods like television sets or refrigerators contain warranty clauses and disclaimer clauses;† they use the Japanese term *hoshō,* which means warranty or guarantee.

In contrast, the American Uniform Sales Act, as early as 1906, recognized the need to analyze product liability in terms of warranty, taking into account the patterns of behavior of buyers and sellers and providing expressly for the legal consequences of such usual behavior. Even more remarkable to a Japanese observer is the case-law growth in America along the lines that warranties need not be confined either to sales contracts or to the immediate parties to such a contract.

The Japanese analogs to the American provisions on warranties in the statutes are two: article 415 of the Civil Code, in General Provisions for obligations, and article 570 of the Civil Code, a provision on sales. According to the case law the former is applicable to cases of the buyer's nonacceptance

[51] BRAUCHER & SUTHERLAND, COMMERCIAL TRANSACTIONS—TEXT, FORMS AND STATUTES 24 (2nd ed., 1958).

* Robert Braucher commented at the conference that the litigation in Japan in recent years of even a few claims for personal injury based on breach of warranty represents an increase; previously such litigation was nonexistent.

† Makoto Yazawa commented at the conference that contractual warranties existed not because of the code provisions but as byproducts of competition between manufacturers.

of goods and the latter to his acceptance of goods having a latent defect.[52]

Primary Remedies in Sales

Section 2-712 of the American Uniform Commercial Code, emphasizing the commercial feasibility of replacement of undelivered goods, introduced a new concept of the buyer's right to "cover." The Japanese codes have not adopted any such concept in those terms, but in practice when a seller breaks a contract it is normal for the buyer to procure substitute goods and to claim as damages the difference between the cost of cover and the contract price, together with any incidental or consequential damages. Therefore, though the codes do not explicitly recognize the buyer's procurement of substitute goods, the matter is dealt with entirely as a problem of the scope of damages as defined in article 416 of the Civil Code.[53]

Under the Uniform Commercial Code, the seller's equivalent of the buyer's right to cover is the right to resell. Under Japanese law, the seller's right to resell is provided by the Commercial Code in article 524, but it is not dealt with by any of the provisions of the Civil Code on sales or obligations. The Japanese right of resale is very much restricted in its operation in comparison with the seller's right under section 60 of the Uniform Sales Act or section 2-706 of the Uniform Commercial Code. Article 524 of the Japanese Commercial Code permits resale only if: (1) the transaction is between merchants; (2) an admonishment is given to the buyer, except where the goods are perishable; and (3) the sale is at public auction. Under the American Uniform Commercial Code, on the other hand, the seller's right of resale is strengthened by section 2-704, which permits the seller to identify goods for resale. Moreover, the resale may be at private sale if it is commercially reasonable. It is apparent that the Japanese right of resale is unreasonably restricted. Indeed, more than twenty-five years ago the Council on the Legal System put forth the suggestion in its Principles for Commercial Code Revision that the seller's right should be extended to transactions in which either party is a merchant and that resale should be allowed at private sale under certain conditions.[54]

[52] See, e.g., Akazaka v. Shindō Seizō Kabushiki Kaisha (Shindo Manufacturing Co.), Great Court of Judicature, II Civil Department, March 13, 1925, 4 DAI SHIN IN MINJI HANREI SHŪ (A Collection of Civil Great Court of Judicature Cases) [hereafter cited DAI-HAN MINSHŪ] 217, 5 HANREI MINJI HŌ (Civil Case Law) 156 (note Funabashi); Tōyō Kanzume Kabushiki Kaisha (Oriental Canning Co.) v. Oishi, Great Court of Judicature, II Civil Department, April 15, 1927, 6 DAI-HAN MINSHŪ 249, 7 HANREI MINJI HŌ 210 (note Komachiya). Also see 1 BRAUCHER & MICHIDA, note 39, at 72–73.

[53] See Suwa v. Aoki, Tokyo District Court, Feb. 14, 1916, HŌRITSU SHIMBUN (The Law News) [hereafter cited SHIMBUN] no. 1103, at 24.

[54] Hōsei Shingi Kai (Council on the Legal System), Shōhō Kaisei Yōkō (Principles for Commercial Code Revision) art. 209 (1935), reprinted in KYŪ-HŌREI SHŪ (Collection of Former Laws and Orders) 353 Yuhikaku Roppō Zensho Henshūiin (Editors of the Yuhikaku Complete Six Codes) ed., 1957).

SECURITY INTERESTS AND CREDIT

Security Devices in the Codes

The legal machinery demanded for Meiji Japan had to provide devices for security suitable for the financing of the merchants' stock in trade and for the development of productive capital. But the legal system for merchant credit that is now the heart of modern business is ignored in the Commercial Code; and only certain aspects of the system are covered by the Civil Code. The latter provides for a hypothec on immovables (real-estate mortgage) (articles 369–398, chapter X of Book II, Rights in Things); the pledge of movables, immovables, and property rights (articles 342–368, chapter IX); privileges (nonpossessory liens) (articles 303–341, chapter VIII); the right of retention (possessory liens) (articles 295–302, chapter VII); assignment of claims, commercial papers, accounts receivable, and the like (articles 466–473, section IV, chapter I, of Book III, Obligations); and sureties (articles 446–465, also chapter I). Among these devices, the hypothec on immovables, the pledge of property rights (in particular, on investment securities), the assignment of claims, and suretyship have been in use for secured credit for merchants as well as consumers. In the scheme of the Civil Code, however, there is no pledge of a movable (chattel pledge) unless the creditor takes and holds possession, and the hypothec is not available for movables. Thus, if the debtor desires to hold possession and to use consumer goods, equipment, or inventory, there is no way for him to get credit by using the goods as security. One of the reasons, perhaps the determinative one, for the limited recognition of security devices in the Meiji codification is the fact that the leading businesses at that time were obtaining a great deal of credit from the government in subsidies and other forms. Hence, they did not depend heavily upon credit from nongovernmental sources and were not sharply conscious of the need for comprehensive codification of security interests.

It was felt among certain groups of people, fairly soon after the enactment of the codes, that the provision for only a limited number of types of security devices was an obstacle to further development of Japanese industry. A search was thus begun for security devices that would make possible sufficient credit for the rapidly advancing business of the period.

Blanket Hypothecs and Enterprise Security

The practical necessity of financing the development of Japanese industry in the early twentieth century drove the government to the enactment of a series of special statutes on various kinds of blanket hypothecs ("estate" or "foundation hypothecs").[55] The closest analogy to these hypothecs among

[55] *Zaidan teitō.*

the traditional security devices in the United States is the mortgage covering both real estate and forms of personal property. In 1905, the first of these statutes — the Factory Hypothec Law,[56] the Railroad Hypothec Law,[57] and the Mining Hypothec Law[58] — were enacted and are still in force.

Under article 370 of the Civil Code, a hypothec attaches either to land or to a building; it cannot attach to both, nor can it attach to business equipment together with land or a building. From the standpoint of business, however, the placing of a number of separate hypothecs on the immovable property or other assets of a going concern is undesirable for at least two reasons: first, the recording is troublesome; second, the possible piecemeal seizure of assets threatens a breakdown of the going-concern value.

Under the Factory Hypothec Law, an owner of a factory or factories can establish a foundation (*zaidan*),[59] composed of all or any part of the land; structures; machinery, implements, electric poles and lines, sundry conduit pipes, tramways, and other accessories; superficies; leases; industrial property (patents, etc.); dam-use rights; and registered automobiles belonging to the company, by recording the foundation at the proper government office.[60] The foundation so established, even though its components may be located all over Japan, can be the subject of a single factory hypothec. This was a remarkable innovation in legal technique. The recording office for a factory hypothec covering a single factory is the Legal Affairs Bureau or Local Legal Affairs Bureau of the Ministry of Justice or the branch bureau or suboffice that has administrative jurisdiction over the situs of the factory.[61] The recording office for a hypothec covering rights and property at several factories located in different prefectures is one of the relevant Legal Affairs Bureaus, designated by the Minister of Justice.[62] All the property covered by a recorded factory hypothec is deemed a single parcel of immovable property, as the law expressly provides.[63]

Article 2 of the Factory Hypothec Law made another extension in the law of security interests; if, instead of creating a factory hypothec under the statute, an owner simply places a hypothec on land on which a factory is located or on a building that belongs to the company, the hypothec covers the "machinery, implements, and other things put to use in the factory installed on the land," or machinery, implements, and other things in the building. This is so even for after-acquired property, although the language of article 2 does not explicitly so provide. The leading case dealing with this

[56] Law No. 54 of 1905.

[57] Law No. 53 of 1905.

[58] Law No 55 of 1905.

[59] In Continental European law, a "foundation" is a conglomeration of property set aside for a fixed purpose.

[60] Factory Hypothec Law, arts. 8, 9, 11, 13-2.

[61] Factory Hypothec Law, art. 17(1).

[62] Factory Hypothec Law, art. 17(2); Immovable Property Recording Law, art. 8(2).

[63] Factory Hypothec Law, art. 14(1).

problem is a 1920 Great Court of Judicature decision in which a hypothec on a factory was held to cover a boiler acquired after the attachment of the hypothec.[64]

The Railroad Hypothec Law also provides for the creation of a recorded blanket hypothec but differs from the Factory Hypothec Law both as to the property covered and the recording office. Under the Railroad Hypothec Law, a local railroad may include in the hypothecated foundation its tracks, warehouses, factories, electric-power control towers, offices, communication facilities, business equipment, immovable property rights used for business purposes (as defined in article 3), and after-acquired property (article 11), but not its intangible industrial property. The recording office is always the Ministry of Transportation in Tokyo. The differences under this law derive from the nature of the railroad company as a public utility.

Because of its effectiveness and usefulness, the technique of establishing an enlarged foundation for security purposes has been extended to other lines of business and industry. The Canal Law in 1913,[65] the Fishing Industry Foundation Hypothec Law in 1925,[66] the Automotive Traffic Business Activities Law in 1931,[67] the Harbor Transport Business Activities Law in 1951,[68] and the Road Traffic Business Activities Hypothec Law in 1952[69] each provided for such hypothecs. The Automotive Traffic Business Activities Law was supplanted in 1951 by the Automobile Hypothec Law.[70]

Hypothecs under these special statutes have been used a great deal for long-term credit, but the reported cases on them are few since the agreements have been formed between fairly big companies and banks, trust banks, or other financial institutions, with the result that the agreements are well drafted and the obligations performed. In the financing of small or medium businesses, the hypothec provided by article 2 of the Factory Hypothec Law may well have greater significance.

The blanket security has also had significance in company financing through the issuance of bonds. The Commercial Code provides for company bonds in the chapter on stock companies (articles 296–341-5), but the provisions relate to unsecured bonds and not to mortgage debentures; unsecured bonds were of little use for financing expanding industry. As a result, in the same year in which the first three blanket-hypothec laws were enacted

[64] Watanabe v. Kitai, Great Court of Judicature, I Civil Department, Dec. 3, 1920, 26 DAI SHIN IN MINJI HANKETSU ROKU (Record of Great Court of Judicature Civil Judgments) [hereafter cited DAI-HAN MINROKU] 1928.

[65] Law No. 16 of 1913, art. 13.

[66] Law No. 9 of 1925.

[67] Law No. 52 of 1931, arts. 38–49.

[68] Law No. 161 of 1951, arts. 23–28.

[69] Law No. 204 of 1952.

[70] Law No. 187 of 1951.

(1905), the Mortgage Debenture Trust Law was enacted,[71] following a study of the English law of trusts. Originally the act adopted the closed-mortgage system. Under this system, if a company wants to issue mortgage debentures at several different times, it must either divide its assets or differentiate first, second, and succeeding mortgages.[72] In the former case, the procedure for division is complex and the going-concern value of the assets is threatened. In the latter, the position of the holders of the succeeding mortgages becomes progressively weaker and the mortgage bonds subsequent to the first issue are not attractive to investors. To remove these weaknesses in the corporate-mortgage system, after study of the open-end mortgage in the United States, the act was amended in 1933[73] to make possible the use of the same collateral as security for several different issues of bonds on an equal footing.

The kinds of collateral for mortgage bonds recognized under the Mortgage Debenture Trust Law were originally limited to seven: pledges of movables, hypothecs on immovables, pledges of obligation paper provided by the Civil Code, the ship hypothec provided by the Commercial Code (now in article 848), and hypothecs under the three 1905 statutes. Since then, the notion and technique of foundation hypothecation has shown its remarkable utility for security purposes, and the types of collateral have been expanded to eighteen (article 4), including blanket hypothecs under the special statutes listed above.

A serious defect in the special statutes providing for blanket hypothecs is the complexity of the description of the collateral that the statutes require for recording. Because of this defect, attempts were made to evolve a system which would provide sufficient notice to the public and yet still be manageable. For example, in 1938, when Nippon Seitetsu Kabushiki Kaisha (Japan Steel Co.), a company formed by statute, was planning to issue bonds for the first time, the participating syndicate of banks demanded that the company record the establishment of a foundation for use as collateral. The company refused to comply with the demand, however, alleging the difficulties of compliance with the statute, and insisted that the bonds be unsecured. To make an adjustment between the two stands, the law providing for the establishment of the steel company was finally amended to provide that the

[71] Law No. 52 of 1905.

[72] Because of the derivation of this system from Anglo-American law, the word "mortgage" is used at this point to translate the Japanese words *butsujō tampo,* which actually are a synonym for the French term *sûretés réeles* and might be more accurately rendered in English as "property security." Butsujō tampo cover all security interests in things such as, for example, pledges and hypothecs. The reader should keep in mind that I do not refer here to a concept which encompasses all the technical attributes of a mortgage in the Anglo-American sense.

[73] By Law No. 44 of 1933.

bondholders and specified lenders were entitled to share in the assets of the company as persons with a privilege (lienholders) subordinate only to the rights of particular privilege holders specified in the Civil Code.[74] This special privilege has been termed both in business circles and in legal discussion a "general mortgage." [75] The general mortgage has been used also in other cases, usually involving the issue of bonds by companies under special governmental protection and supervision and the guarantee of payment of the bonds by the government.[76]

In 1949, the Federation of Economic Organizations made public its *Opinion Calling for the Simplification of the Procedure for Organizing a Foundation,*[77] and in 1950 the federation staff began a study of the general mortgage.[78] In the same year, the Ministry of International Trade and Industry made a proposal with respect to the general mortgage.[79] The Ministry of Justice in 1952, adopting some of the demands of the Economic Federation, took action to amend the Factory Hypothec Law, and a committee was set up to study the floating charge in England, with a view to the enactment of a statute on general mortgage. Various institutions and associations, governmental and nongovernmental, participated in examining and testing several proposals or drafts of a new general-mortgage law; and further studies were made of the English system. In 1958 these efforts culminated in a new law, the Enterprise Security Law.

The law provides for a floating charge adapted from English law. The security interest attaches to the entire assets of a stock company as they vary from time to time (article 1), and the interest is to be recorded in the stock company register covering the situs of the head office of the company (article 4). Insofar as these aspects of the statute are concerned, the law seems to establish a streamlined, modern security device. But it can be

[74] Japan Steel Stock Company Law, Law No. 47 of 1933, art. 5-3, as amended by Law No. 63 of 1941. Similar provisions were also placed in the statute abolishing the Japan Steel Company in regard to the assets of its successor companies: Fuji Iron & Steel and Yawata Iron & Steel. See the Law Repealing the Japan Steel Stock Company Law, Law No. 240 of 1950, supp. prov. arts. 5, 8.

[75] Again, in reference to Anglo-American concepts, but without the full technical connotations of the Anglo-American mortgage. See note 72 above. Japanese statutes employ the words *ippan tampo* or "general security."

[76] See Public Utilities Order, Cabinet Order No. 343 of 1950, art. 52, translated into English in OFFICIAL GAZETTE, Nov. 24, 1950, extra no. 124, at 8, expired Oct. 24, 1952; International Telegraph and Telephone Stock Company Law, Law No. 301 of 1952, art. 7; Electric Resource Development Promotion Law, Law No. 283 of 1952, art. 25.

[77] Keizai Dantai Rengō Kai (Federation of Economic Organizations), *Zaidan Sosei Tetsuzuki no Kanso-ka ni Kan-suru Yōbō Iken* (Opinion Calling for the Simplification of the Procedure for Organizing a Foundation), Keizai Rengō (Bulletin of the Federation of Economic Organizations), Dec. 1949, p. 16.

[78] This study was undertaken by the Keizai Dantai Rengō Kai Tampo Seido Kenkyū Kai (Federation of Economic Organizations Security System Study Group), which reached certain general conclusions but did not publish any definite recommendations based on its research.

[79] This was the Ippan Tampo Hō Yōkō (Main Points of a General Security Law) prepared by the Ministry's Business Enterprise Bureau.

used only to secure company bonds and certain loans involving the Nihon Kaihatsu Ginkō (Japan Development Bank); it cannot be used to secure a company's other indebtedness or the debts of borrowers that are not stock companies.

During the first three years of the law's life, twelve stock companies have used the Enterprise Security Law to provide security for their bonds. Some of these have issued bonds at twenty different times during the three years; others have just recently used the law for only a few issues. All the issues have been successful; but the high degree of success is probably attributable largely to the fact that all of the issuing companies are among the leading business companies in Japan, and most of them are even preparing to register American Depositary Receipts in order to sell their shares on the American stock market.[80]

The reason that the use of enterprise security has been limited to big business is that such security interests have a low priority; thus bankers would be reluctant to accept as collateral a share in the assets of a company which was not among the leading concerns of the country. According to the provisions of the law, the secured interest is subordinate to the privileges (liens) of articles 306 through 341 of the Civil Code and to specific privileges, pledges, and hypothecs on particular collateral taken by creditors other than the holder of the enterprise security interest (article 7). Even if the enterprise-security interest is recorded first, it is subject to other interests affecting the assets of the company which are perfected afterward (article 6).

There is some support for the adoption of a different system of floating charges. In particular, the Tokyo Chamber of Commerce and Industry, after a series of meetings over a period of years before the passing of the law, took the view that the use of enterprise security should not be restricted to the securing of company bonds and that the priority of the secured interest should be strengthened and made equal with specific privileges or hypothecs following only the order of perfection.[81] The present form of the law was favored by the bankers and is the result of their influence; but nonbanking business companies also tend to agree with the Tokyo Chamber of Commerce and Industry. In 1961, for example, bond and hypothec specialists from the twelve companies mentioned above, those

[80] These companies are Fuji Seitetsu Kabushiki Kaisha (Fuji Iron & Steel Co.), Yawata Seitetsu Kabushiki Kaisha (Yawata Iron & Steel Co.), Nihon Kōkan Kabushiki Kaisha (Japan Steel & Tube Co.), Nihon Tsūun Kabushiki Kaisha (Japan Express Co.), Tōkyō Gasu Kabushiki Kaisha (Tokyo Gas Co.), Sumitomo Kinzoku Kōgyō Kabushiki Kaisha (Sumitomo Metal Industry Co.), Kabushiki Kaisha Hitachi Seisakujo (Hitachi Manufacturing Co.), Tōkyō Shibaura Denki Kabushiki Kaisha (Tokyo Shibaura Electric Co.), Tōyō Rayon Kabushiki Kaisha (Oriental Rayon Co.), Shin Mitsubishi Jū-kōgyō Kabushiki Kaisha (New Mitsubishi Heavy Industry Co.), Mitsubishi Denki Kabushiki Kaisha (Mitsubishi Electric Co), Ōsaka Gasu Kabushiki Kaisha (Osaka Gas Co.).

[81] Tōkyō Shōkō Kaigisho (Tokyo Chamber of Commerce and Industry), Kigyō Tampo Hōan ni Kan-suru Yōbō Iken (Views Regarding the Enterprise Security Law Bill), April 9, 1957.

which have used enterprise security as well as the older blanket hypothec, gathered informally for the purpose of preparing a proposal to amend the present law to permit more extensive use of enterprise security. Thus the law in this area may well change in response to the dynamics of banking and business in Japan.

Security Interests in Chattels

The Civil Code covers certain secured transactions, but it provides no device at all for security interests in movables unless the creditor takes and holds possession. But the credit economy of today assumes that the debtor and not the creditor will take possession of goods in the ordinary course of commerce. The company may buy goods for its own use as business equipment or for resale to others; in either case the purchase may be possible only on a credit basis. Unless there is a security device that makes possible the debtor's possession for business purposes, the development of the credit economy is restricted.

In an attempt to meet the need for such a device, a statute was enacted in 1933 providing for hypothecs on agricultural equipment.[82] In 1951, another statute provided for hypothecs on motor vehicles;[83] in 1953, for hypothecs on aircraft;[84] and in 1954, for hypothecs on construction equipment.[85] But these statutes met only a small portion of the practical need for chattel credit.

For years, recourse has been had to a device known as *jōto tampo* (assignment as security), which is based upon assigning the ownership of goods to the creditor. This device has been upheld in decisions of the Great Court of Judicature and the Supreme Court of Japan since about 1906,[86] but a Great Court decision of 1916 stated that it had been in use since about 1885.[87] Jōto-tampo transactions are of various kinds. Some correspond to the American chattel mortgage; some to the American conditional sale; some to the American factor's lien; some to the consignment; some to the assignment of ac-

[82] Agricultural Movables Credit Law, Law No. 30 of 1933, arts. 12–17.

[83] Automobile Hypothec Law, Law No. 187 of 1951.

[84] Aircraft Hypothec Law, Law No. 66 of 1953.

[85] Construction Machinery Hypothec Law, Law No. 97 of 1954.

[86] E.g., Kondo v. Yamada, Great Court of Judicature, II Civil Department, Oct. 7, 1912, 18 DAI-HAN MINROKU 815 (transaction involving business equipment); Nishizawa v. Machida, Great Court of Judicature, July 8, 1912, II Civil Department, 18 DAI-HAN MINROKU 691 (transaction involving land); Shirono v. Higashi, Great Court of Judicature, II Civil Department, Oct. 5, 1906, 12 DAI-HAN MINROKU 1172 (transaction involving 1,000 tons of coal).

[87] Kawano v. Kawano, Great Court of Judicature, III Civil Department, Nov. 8, 1916, 22 DAI-HAN MINROKU 2193, 2204. Similar devices are recognized in a number of Continental countries. Thus, Germany has *Sicherungsübereignung* and *Sicherungskauf,* while in the Netherlands a technique known as "transfer of property as security" is employed. On the latter see Dainow, *Civil Code Revision in the Netherlands: Some New Development in Obligations and Property,* in XXTH CENTURY COMPARATIVE AND CONFLICTS LAW 172, 182–85 (Legal Essays in Honor of Hessel E. Yntema; Nadelmann, von Mehren & Hazard ed. 1961).

counts receivable; some to the pledge; and some exactly to the trust receipt.[88] In these transactions, the goods — inventory, equipment, or consumer goods — are in the possession of the debtor or the buyer, while the title to the goods vests or remains in the creditor or the seller. There is no statute providing for recording or filing of the rights of the creditor or seller in jōto-tampo transactions; consequently, there have been a few cases in which the rights of a competing secured party or the rights of attaching creditors were unreasonably prejudiced by the hidden rights of a jōto-tampo holder.

In one case, two lenders advanced money to one debtor, taking the same movie projectors and equipment as security.[89] The first lender and the debtor entered into a jōto-tampo agreement which left the security in the possession of the debtor; since there was no recording system, no notice of the transaction was given to the public. Then a second lender advanced money to the debtor, taking actual possession of the security. In determining which party had priority, the Supreme Court held that the second lender was subordinate to the first lender, regardless of the actual possession, since article 183 of the Civil Code provides that "when an agent has declared his intention that a thing in his possession shall thereafter be possessed on behalf of his principal, the principal thereby acquires a possessory right." *

This result is contrary to what would be expected in the United States. For example, section 9-205 of the Uniform Commercial Code provides that "this section does not relax the requirements of possession where perfection of a security interest depends upon possession of the collateral by the secured party or by a bailee." And comment 2 to section 9-305 states that "possession may be by the secured party himself or by an agent on his behalf; it is of course clear, however, that the debtor or a person controlled by him cannot qualify as such an agent for the secured party."

The hidden right of the jōto-tampo holder may prevail not only against conflicting security interests but also against the rights of attaching creditors. In a leading Great Court of Judicature case in 1914,[90] unsecured creditors sought to levy execution against a debtor's business equipment; another creditor, who had entered into a jōto-tampo agreement, objected to the execution and because of his ownership of the goods the agreement was upheld. Article 549(1) of the Code of Civil Procedure provides that "when a third person alleges ownership in regard to the subject matter of compulsory execution . . . he shall assert his objection to this compulsory execution by

[88] For a comparison between American security devices and jōto tampo and a description of the various forms of the latter see 2 BRAUCHER & MICHIDA, note 39, at 315–18, 460–83.

[89] Masuko v. Sakazume, Supreme Court, I Petty Bench, June 2, 1955, 9 SAI-HAN MINSHŪ 855.

* At the conference, Takaaki Hattori expressed his disagreement with the decision of the Supreme Court in this case; in his opinion, the bona-fide-purchaser clause of the Civil Code should have protected the second lender.

[90] Hida v. Kume, Great Court of Judicature, II Civil Department, Nov. 2, 1914, 20 DAI-HAN MINROKU 865.

means of an action against his creditor."[91] Under the traditional theory of the jōto tampo as the transfer of the title to the good and not simply the giving of a security interest, the assertion of objection to the execution entirely frustrated the execution proceedings brought by the unsecured creditors.

One lower-court decision in the same kind of case did not follow the traditional title theory as to jōto tampo, however, but adopted a security theory instead.[92] The case was held to be governed by article 565(1) of the Code of Civil Procedure, which provides that "even though a third person may hold security rights in rem in regard to a thing subject to attachment, this may not preclude attachment. However, the right to claim preferential satisfaction out of the proceeds of sale by means of an action in accordance with the provisions of article 549 is not thereby precluded."

There has been intensive debate among scholars over whether the jōto tampo constitutes the transfer of title or property to the creditor or merely gives him a security interest. Specialists in civil law have tended to look at the agreement purely in terms of the contract and its effect between the parties; their writings have not questioned the adequacy of a change in title or property-ownership theory.[93] But specialists in civil procedure have tended to look at the agreement in terms of the consequences of the execution of the contract in relation to other creditors' rights; their writings have cast doubt on the adequacy of the title theory and have favored a security theory.[94]

The National Tax Collection Law of 1959 struck a strong blow for the security theory.[95] Article 24(1) of that act provides that, if a person who is a jōto-tampo debtor fails to pay his taxes, the claim for taxes may be collected out of the collateral transferred to the creditor by the jōto-tampo transaction. This provision assumes that the transaction creates a security interest only, and it subordinates that interest to the government's right of priority in tax collection. But under articles 15 and 24, a jōto-tampo transaction entered into before the due date of the tax payment can be given priority — either by recording under the immovables recording system or by use of the notarial instrument provided by the Public Notary Law,[96] a document with the date stamp of a recording or public notary's office or a document certified by the post office in accordance with article 63 of the Postal Law.[97]

[91] Law No. 29 of 1890.

[92] Ishii v. Kobayashi, Tokyo District Court, Aug. 8, 1936, SHIMBUN no. 4113, at 7.

[93] See, e.g., 2 BRAUCHER & MICHIDA, note 39, at 595–96 n. 3; Mikazuki, *Jōto Tampo to Sozei* Assignment as Security and Taxes), SHIHŌ no. 22, at 4 (1960).

[94] *Ibid.*

[95] Law No. 147 of 1959. Before this law, jōto-tampo transactions were thought to be quite often misused to escape tax liability.

[96] Law No. 53 of 1908.

[97] Law No. 165 of 1947, translated into English in OFFICIAL GAZETTE, Dec. 12, 1947, no. 512, at 7.

Article 24 of the National Tax Collection Law is thus the first statutory bridgehead for the security theory; it takes a successful step toward a security-interest rationale for a device which in origin depended entirely upon title. The American Uniform Commercial Code adopts a scheme of provisions by which the rights and duties of the parties to a security transaction and of third parties are stated without reference to the location of the title to the collateral: under section 9-202, title to collateral becomes immaterial.

The task of the Japanese law with respect to security interests in movables seems to be twofold: first, to provide a comprehensive public-notice system; second, to rationalize the whole scheme of the existing laws on statutory hypothecs and jōto tampo. Thus, it would be helpful to be able to scrutinize the floating lien under a simple workable notice-filing system like that provided by article 9 of the Uniform Commercial Code. This system assumes that the notice indicates merely that the secured filing party may have a security interest in the collateral described and that further inquiry from the parties concerned will be necessary to disclose the total situation. The closest Japanese analog to the American notice-filing system is the recording of enterprise-security interests, which has been used only in recent times and which is quite restricted in scope. All other Japanese movable-security statutes establish complex formal requisites, very much like many of the American chattel-mortgage statutes prior to the Uniform Commercial Code. A legislative movement toward a simplified and tenable notice-filing system for movable security in general will probably encounter resistance, particularly from the bankers, who oppose an extension of the Enterprise Security Law.

Secured Transactions in the Distribution of Consumer Goods

A discussion of the credit system in Japan cannot be confined to an explanation of security devices in terms of the legal structure. Something must also be said about the actual mechanics of financing the distribution of merchandise from producer to consumer. The distribution of durable consumer goods provides a good example.

The manufacturers of electrical appliances have subsidiary companies for the distribution of their products to wholesalers and for installment sales directly to consumers. For example, in one actual instance, a manufacturing company has designated a single subsidiary as the distribution company for its household electrical appliances and a number of others, scattered throughout various parts of the country, as installment-sales companies to finance their purchase. The credit men of the distribution company keep a check on the wholesale distributors by using a variety of standard forms for reporting credit information. Inventory security in the United States commonly takes the form of conditional sale, chattel mortgage, trust receipt, or sometimes consignment. But in Japan distribution of these fairly expensive articles takes the form of a straight sale on credit, accompanied by a clause providing for acceleration and cancellation upon default and for return to the distribution company of title to the inventory in the buyer's possession. Payment of the price of the articles sold and delivered is on a monthly basis, either in cash or by promissory notes with a three-month maturity. The distribution company takes some security, but the transaction is largely on an unsecured basis. The security takes the form of a cash deposit of a certain percentage, varying from one to ten, of the expected sales to the wholesale distributor; alternatively or additionally, the distribution company takes investment securities or hypothecs on immovables. The appraised value of the investment securities amounts to only one half of the total of cash deposits, and the appraised value of the immovable hypothecs comes to only two thirds. The distribution company also advances money to the distributors for other purposes, usually taking immovable hypothecs. The obtaining of credit information and subsequent policing are carefully done, and the records of the particular distribution company studied show that there has been no case of an insolvent wholesale distributor.*

The transactions between the wholesale distributor and the retail dealer follow approximately the same pattern as those between the distribution company and the distributor. In the course of dealer distributions, the consumer sometimes pays cash for the goods. If the consumer wants to pay by installments, however, an agreement is made between the buyer and the installment-sales company; the dealer gets only a commission, and the title to the goods is retained by the installment-sales company for the purpose of securing payment of the obligation. In a separate agreement, independent from that between the installment-sales company and the consumer, the dealer becomes a surety for the performance of the consumer's debt. In consequence, the flourishing installment sales system for consumer goods depends heavily upon credit inquiry and credit information about the consumers.

Credit for Small and Medium Businesses

The role played by small and medium-size business in the Japanese industrial structure is very important.[98] The business-establishment statistics of the Prime Minister's Office for 1960 show that 99.8 percent (3,556,675) of the total number of Japanese establishments classified (3,561,743, not in-

* The experience of this company illustrates a further aspect of credit practice in Japan, as noted at the conference by Shinichiro Michida. Not relying on legal guards, creditors seek to prevent abuses and losses by careful control of the choice of debtors to whom credit is extended.

[98] I wish to acknowledge and express appreciation for the information and materials, used in writing this portion, which were made available to me by the Chūshō Kigyō Kinyū Kōko (Public Medium and Small Enterprise Finance Depository).

cluding agriculture, forestry, or fishery) have fewer than 300 employees,[99] while a report prepared by the same office based on the 1957 statistics reveals that small and medium businesses hire 84.9 percent of all employees (15.1 million) throughout the nation.[100] But the credit capacity of these enterprises is poor in comparison with that of big business. In prewar days, wholesale merchants used to meet the credit needs of small and medium-size manufacturers and traders through loans and long-term credit sales, but since the war the financial power of wholesale merchants has been weakened. Consequently, business has had to rely heavily upon borrowing from financial institutions, most of which are willing to lend to the smaller concerns. Commercial and private banking institutions make nearly 60 percent of the total amount of loans extended to such enterprises. The remainder is furnished by other types of institutions which specialize in financing these businesses only.

A predecessor of the modern institutions specializing in the financing of small and medium businesses is the *mujin,* a method of finance by which members of a group pay shares in regular installments into a pool and the funds thus collected are advanced periodically to a member or members chosen by lot or bidding. The members so financed continue to pay their own installments as before the advance, in the same amount and manner.[101] The system of mujin is said to have been initiated in the Kamakura period (1192–1333), and it flourished during the Tokugawa period (1603–1867) as a system of mutual financial aid. It achieved still more remarkable progress in the Meiji era as mujin companies emerged and developed which were eventually licensed under the Mujin Business Law of 1931.[102] In 1951 the overwhelming majority of monetary mujin companies were reorganized into their present form as mutual savings and loan banks (*sōgo ginkō*—literally "mutual banks") under the Mutual Bank Law,[103] promulgated for the purpose of promoting the sound development of this system.[104] The banks number more than seventy, and the percentage of the

[99] Tōkei Kyoku (Bureau of Statistics), Sōrifu (Prime Minister's Office), Nihon Tōkei Nenkan Shōwa 36 Nen (Japan Statistical Yearbook 1961) 66 (1962). Total establishments, classified and otherwise, amounted to 3,668,659.

[100] 3 Chūshō Kigyō Kenkyū (A Study of Medium and Small Enterprise) 692–95 (Chūshō Kigyō Chōsa Kai (Medium and Small Enterprise Investigation Committee) ed., 1960). The figure given for the total number of employees does not cover company or organization officers, individual proprietors, and family employees. When these persons are also included, the total number of persons employed in 1957, excluding agriculture, forestry, and fisheries, amounted to 20.8 million. *Ibid.*, at 684.

[101] An account in English of the similar Chinese institution may be found in Gamble, *A Chinese Mutual Savings Society,* 4 Far Eastern Q. 41 (1944).

[102] Law No. 42 of 1931.

[103] Law No. 199 of 1951.

[104] Commodity mujin were not covered by the Mutual Bank Law and still continue to function under the Mujin Business Law. Moreover, private mujin organized between friends and not as a commercial undertaking still exist throughout Japan.

number of loans out of the total number granted to small and medium-size business was 18.5 percent at the end of March 1958.

Cooperative financial institutions for loans to small and medium enterprises emerged around 1887, first as nonlegal credit organizations, receiving deposits from and granting loans to their members only. The institutions developed and began to receive deposits from nonmembers. In 1951, the Credit Depository Law[105] was enacted in order to protect depositors and to meet other needs. The credit depositories (*shinyō kinko*) are now more than 540 in number; and at the end of March 1958, they were granting 12 percent of the total amount loaned to small and medium businesses.

Credit societies (*shinyō kumiai*)[106] started to develop around 1890; and the enactment of the Industry Society Law of 1900[107] instituted the system of such institutions, which today number about 450. Under the Medium and Small Enterprise and Others' Cooperative Societies Law[108] and the Law Concerning Financial Business Activities by Cooperative Societies,[109] they are not allowed to deal with nonmembers. Perhaps partly for that reason, their loans are a low percentage of total credit.

Since 1936, there has been a central bank dealing exclusively in the financing of small and medium businesses, the Commerce and Industry Societies Central Depository (Shōkō Kumiai Chūō Kinko). The Commerce and Industry Societies Central Depository Law[110] restricts its business dealings to cooperatives and organizations of similar nature, including their members. The Central Depository operates through more than fifty branches, in all the seats of prefectural government and in some other commercially important cities. Approximately half of its original capital was paid by the government, the remainder by the cooperatives and similar organizations entitled to borrow from it; its funds are raised primarily through the issuance of private bonds.

One of the peculiarities of the financing of small and medium businesses is the difficulty of getting long-term loans like those readily granted by banks to big concerns. In 1953, the Public Medium and Small Enterprise Finance Depository (Chūshō Kigyō Kinyū Kōko) was formed for the purpose of providing the long-term credit which ordinary financial institutions, including mutual banks, find it difficult to supply.[111] Its funds are entirely supplied by the government both by capital grants and loans. The Public Depository has several branches and utilizes about 600 financial

[105] Law No. 238 of 1951.

[106] A body similar in organization to the American credit union.

[107] Law No. 34 of 1900, repealed by Law No. 200 of 1947. Note that "industry societies" (*sangyō kumiai*) should be distinguished from the "industrial societies" (*kōgyō kumiai*) of the Industrial Society Law, Law No. 62 of 1931.

[108] Law No. 181 of 1949.

[109] Law No. 183 of 1949.

[110] Law No. 14 of 1936.

[111] Public Medium and Small Enterprise Finance Depository Law, Law No. 138 of 1953.

institutions as agents, including the Commerce and Industry Societies Central Depository, commercial banks, mutual banks, and credit societies; including these agents, about 5,200 offices were handling its loan business in February 1958.

In 1949, under the People's Finance Public Depository Law,[112] the old Commoner Depository (Shomin Kinko) and the Pension Depository (Onkyū Kinko) were merged into the People's Finance Public Depository (Kokumin Kinyū Kōko). The object of the Public Depository is to serve people who find it difficult to obtain business loans from banks and other financial institutions. Article 18(2) provides that a person is eligible for a loan from the Depository if he has an appropriate scheme for a business to be carried out independently; the funds are not to be used for relief for poverty-stricken people. The funds of the Public Depository come entirely from the government; despite its name, it receives no deposits but exists solely to make loans. Besides making ordinary loans, it extends loans on pension security, generally prohibited by article 11 of the Pension Law;[113] there is a separate statute for pension-security finance by the People's Finance Public Depository.[114]

As briefly summarized above, there have been important changes and remarkable developments during the postwar years in the financing of small and medium businesses, although the financial difficulties of such concerns are not peculiar to that period. The rehabilitation and development of the Japanese economy in the postwar period has been carried out so hastily that even big business has been largely dependent upon borrowed capital; the wholesale merchants, who supplied financing to small and medium businesses in prewar days, are now themselves dependent upon financial institutions. The problems of financing small business are many, difficult, and controversial; further change is to be anticipated.

Commercial Paper and Investment Securities

"Yūka Shōken" and Negotiable Instruments

A commercial transaction often involves the giving of a check or draft, for example, in payment of the purchase price of goods. Instead of goods in the ordinary sense, a transaction may involve stocks or bonds, and some aspects of such a transaction may be different from the sale of ordinary goods. Thus a discussion of commercial law as a whole requires some mention of the laws governing checks, drafts, stocks, and bonds. A commercial transaction may also involve a bill of lading or warehouse receipt or

112 Law No. 49 of 1949.

113 Law No. 48 of 1923.

114 Law Concerning Pension Security Financing Carried On by the People's Finance Public Depository, Law No. 91 of 1954.

both, if the goods are shipped or stored. American lawyers would call bills of lading and warehouse receipts "documents of title" and would distinguish them from checks, drafts, or bonds, which are called "negotiable instruments." Company stock certificates have sometimes been treated as negotiable instruments, but traditionally they have been considered as constituting a separate category.

Japanese scholars deal with a different concept, *yūka shōken,* which would be translated as "valuable securities," originally derived from the German *Wertpapier*. The term is often used in statutes, for example, the Commercial Code, articles 285, 501, 518, 519, 578; the Code of Civil Procedure, articles 430, 559, 581, 594, 664; the Penal Code, articles 162, 163; and the Securities Exchange Law, article 2. Yet there is no statutory definition of the term and there is no single statute dealing with it. Rather it is a term of Japanese jurisprudence in the sense of an integrated scheme of legal thought and interpretation separate from the statutory scheme.

The term is broad in coverage, taking in not only checks, drafts, bonds, and stocks but also bills of lading, warehouse receipts, and immovable hypothecation securities issued by recording officers under the Hypothecation Securities Law;[115] it excludes statements of indebtedness, ordinary receipts, postage stamps, and carriers' and innkeepers' checks for baggage. Probably the interpretation of yūka shōken has been the most controversial single aspect of the jurisprudence of commercial transactions. Just as the legal consequences of sales are stated in terms of the broader general concepts of debtor and creditor instead of the narrower concrete concepts of buyer and seller, so the legal consequences of transactions involving checks or other instruments that are understood to be yūka shōken are generally treated by scholars according to which theory of yūka shōken they find the most satisfactory.

In the United States, there are basically two separate classes of negotiable instruments: (1) commercial paper, consisting of bills, notes, and checks; and (2) investment securities, mainly stocks and bonds. To avoid the obstacles to the full negotiability of corporate securities found in judicial decisions under the Uniform Negotiable Instruments Law, article 8 of the Uniform Commercial Code has provided a new set of criteria for negotiability which are not dependent upon the traditional formal requisites of negotiable instruments. The code speaks of the two categories of negotiable instruments mentioned above, including stock in the class of "investment securities," which in section 8-105 are declared to be negotiable instruments.

In Japan, although the term "commercial paper" (*shōgyō shōken*) is used in article 501 of the Commercial Code, there is no statutory definition of it nor is there a body of rules concerning the concept. The laws on commercial paper in the sense of the Uniform Commercial Code are pro-

[115] Law No. 15 of 1931.

vided in the Bills Law and the Checks Law, both effective in 1934, which adopted the Geneva Uniform Laws. Thus the works mentioned earlier comparing the Geneva laws and the American rules of negotiable instruments[116] are helpful in the study of the Japanese law of negotiable instruments.

Investment Securities and Circulation

The laws on investment securities are provided only to a limited extent by the Commercial Code of Japan. The American code provides in section 8-204 that "unless noted conspicuously on the security a restriction on transfer imposed by the issuer even though otherwise lawful is ineffective except against a person with actual knowledge of it." Contrary to this and section 15 of the American Uniform Stock Transfer Act, the Commercial Code of Japan provides in article 204(1) that "the assignment of a share of stock may not be prohibited or restricted even by a provision in the articles of association." The present policy of the code, disapproving any restriction on the transfer of shares, is a result of its amendment in 1950;[117] a policy demanded by the General Headquarters of SCAP on the theory that it would help to break up the prewar concentration of economic power. Before the 1950 amendment, the article 204(1) had provided that the assignment of shares could be restricted by the provisions of the articles of association.[118]

The amendment has been criticized in its application to the small, family-owned stock company. But restriction of transfer may be legitimate not only because of the size or type of the company but also because of the nature of its business; special statutes have sometimes been enacted in order to give effect to such restrictions. For example, a stock company whose business is to issue a daily newspaper is allowed to restrict the transfer of its shares under a 1951 law,[119] if the restriction is noted on the stock certificates. The Japan Air Lines Company is allowed to restrict transfer under the law establishing that company,[120] while more than half of the stock of the International Telegraph and Telephone Company may not be owned by aliens and foreign juridical persons under its enabling law.[121]

On the other hand, there is no provision in the Commercial Code requiring the free transferability of bonds. Free transferability seems to be assumed,

[116] Hudson & Feller, *The International Unification of Laws Concerning Bills of Exchange*, 44 Harv. L. Rev. 333 (1931); Kessler, *Forged Indorsements*, 47 Yale L.J. 863 (1938).

[117] By Law No. 167 of 1950.

[118] This language had been introduced into art. 204(1) by Law No. 72 of 1938.

[119] Law Concerning Restrictions, Etc., on the Assignment of Shares of Stock and Interests in Stock Companies and Limited Liability Companies Whose Purpose Is to Issue Daily Newspapers, Law No. 212 of 1951, art. 1.

[120] Japan Air Lines Stock Company Law, Law No. 154 of 1953, art. 2(3)–(4).

[121] International Telegraph and Telephone Stock Company Law, art. 4(1).

but since bonds do not entitle the holders to participate in the management of the company, issuers do not try to restrict their transfer.

Article 307 of the Commercial Code provides for the transfer of nominative bonds (registered bonds) that registration of the transfer in the books of the company perfects it as against the issuer or third persons. In actual practice, however, bearer bonds are far more common; there is no provision on the transfer of bearer bonds in the section of the code dealing with bonds (articles 296–341-5). The statutory rule on the transfer of these bonds is found instead in the Civil Code. Article 86(3) provides: "Bearer claims are hereby deemed movable property." Article 178 provides: "An assignment of rights in rem concerning a movable may not consequently be set up against a third party unless the movable is delivered." One interpretation of these provisions is that a transfer of a bearer bond becomes effective between the parties upon agreement, but it cannot be perfected as against a third person until the bond certificate has been delivered. This interpretation was approved by scholars until recent times,[122] when another school of reasoning became popular: that the transfer of a bearer bond, since it is a "valuable security," cannot take place until the delivery of the certificate.[123] The latter view, like the new criteria of the Uniform Commercial Code, rests upon customary commercial dealing in bonds as instruments valuable in themselves.

Free circulation of investment securities does not depend solely upon the principle of nonrestriction of transfer expressed in article 204(1) of the Commercial Code; it also rests heavily upon the special protection, not given to purchasers of ordinary contracts, which is given to the bona fide purchaser of securities. To carry out the principle of free circulation, investment securities have to bear some resemblance to money both in law and in practice. This special protection or concept of negotiability has two aspects, issuer's defenses and adverse claims.

For stock transfer, the Commercial Code provides in article 229 for the rights of the bona fide purchaser, stating that "the provisions of article 21 of the Checks Law shall be applied correspondingly" to the bona fide purchase of stocks. With respect to endorsements, the Commercial Code provides in article 205(2) that "the provisions of articles 12 and 13, article 14, para-

[122] MATSUMOTO, NIHON KAISHA HŌ RON (A Treatise on Japanese Company Law) 362 (1929); IZAWA, CHŪKAI SHIN KAISHA HŌ (The New Company Law Annotated) 547 (1952); K. TANAKA, KAITEI KAISHA HŌ GAIRON (A General Treatise on the Revised Company Law) 464 (1955).

[123] This approach is often taken in a discussion of the pledge of bearer bonds; see, e.g., OSUMI, KAISHA HŌ RON (A Treatise on Company Law) 388 (1940); ISHII, SHASAI HŌ (The Law of Company Bonds) 199 (1950); 2 SANEKATA, KAISHA HŌGAKU (The Legal Study of Companies) 391 (1952); HATTORI, TEISEI KAISHA HŌ TEIYŌ (Essentials of the Revised Company Law) 261 (1955); S. TANAKA, KAISHA HŌ (Company Law) 430 (1955); OMORI, KAITEI KAISHA HŌ KŌGI (Lectures on the Revised Company Law) 245 (1956); MATSUDA, SHIN KAISHA HŌ GAIRON (A General Treatise on the New Company Law) 270 (1957). On the point of transfer generally, see OHOTORI, SHASAI HŌ (Company Bond Law) 163 (1958).

graph (2), and article 16, paragraph (1), of the Bills Law shall be applied correspondingly to the endorsement of stock certificates."

Thus the negotiability of stocks is made to depend upon the two laws cited.

Article 307 is the only specific provision dealing with transfers of registered bonds. Endorsement and the rights of bona fide purchasers are governed by the general provisions of article 519 for yūka shōken: "The provisions of article 12 through article 14, paragraph (2) of the Bills Law and article 5, paragraph (2), article 19, and article 21 of the Checks Law shall be applied correspondingly to valuable securities which have for their object a particular performance[124] in money, other things or valuable securities." Consequently, the negotiability of registered bonds depends upon the laws dealing with bills, notes, and checks.

Negotiability and Forgery

Bills and notes are negotiable, both in the United States and in Japan, only if certain formal requirements are met. Although this is not the place for the study of such requirements, one of the differences between American and Japanese law in this respect may be worth stating because of its practical significance. In the United States, notes are quite often payable in monthly installments, following the pattern of the development of the credit economy through payment on time. But under article 33(2) of the Japanese Bills Law, "bills of exchange . . . payable by installments are null and void," and article 77 makes article 33 applicable to promissory notes. Thus, if it is agreed that payment is to be made in monthly installments, the use of notes means that a separate note which complies with the formal requirements must be made out for each installment.

The negotiability of an instrument under any system of law is vitally affected by the attitude adopted toward forgery. Outside the Anglo-American world, the Geneva rule carries the principle of free circulation to its logical end by protecting the bona fide purchaser of order paper rather than the real owner; if the chain of endorsements on order paper appears to be regular, the purchaser's title is not impaired by the fact that an endorsement has been forged. In the United States, on the other hand, if an endorsement is forged, no right to retain the instrument, to give a discharge for it, or to enforce its payment can be acquired.

Under both systems, there is no doubt that the bona fide purchaser of bearer paper, like the holder of money, takes free of the rights of former owners. But in the United States, the bank which purchases or pays a check payable to order on a forged endorsement may be compelled to make good the loss of the real owner, while under the Geneva rule the bank need not.

The typical Japanese reaction toward the American law on forged endorse-

[124] *Leistung* in German.

ments would be that the Geneva solution, adopted in Japan, in attempting to promote the negotiability of order paper, emphasizes the security of transactions, or "dynamic security," while the American law gives priority to the security of property ownership, or "static security." But the typical American viewpoint would be that, under Japanese law, order paper is very similar in its practical effect to bearer paper; many Americans would refuse to use checks in situations in which there is a risk of loss by theft. It is commonly understood that the greatest difference between the American and the Geneva laws relates to the problem of forgery of endorsement.[125] Although scholars in Japan advocate the Geneva solution for free negotiability, the fact is that the use of order checks amounts to only about 10 percent of the total volume of checks in Japan.* Thus the Geneva solution of the forged-endorsement problem has not in fact accomplished the purpose of promoting the use of order paper through increased negotiability, as far as checks are concerned.[126]

Many social and historical factors underlie adherence to the present Japanese solution; in this connection, the relative lack of a progressive spirit among Japanese bankers when compared with American bankers has particular significance. Banks normally issue check books printed in bearer form; by using this method, a bank can easily avoid almost all of the troubles peculiar to checks in order form, since if a Japanese customer wants to use such a bearer-form check as an order-form check he must strike out the word "bearer." Thus the customer rarely transforms the check into order paper. The framers of the American Negotiable Instruments Law did not follow section 60 of the Bills of Exchange Act of England, which protected the bank paying on a forged endorsement, even though most of the rest of the law followed the English act. Moreover, "there was scarcely any support whatever, even among the banks, for the English rule sanctioning payments of demand instruments made over forged endorsements," according to the results obtained from a questionnaire sent out in 1928 to some two hundred and fifty American banks.[127] In Japan, however, the bankers' desire for ease in check transactions seems to be stronger.

Another reason for the continuation of the present Japanese solution is that a change in the law of forged endorsements would require the accel-

[125] See, e.g., Braucher, *Commercial Law in Japan and America*, 47 A.B.A.J. 150, 153 (1961).

* It was noted at the conference that the fact that the order check is an unsatisfactory instrument of payment has led to the development of alternative means; in some cases the depositor issues directly to his bank a list of "consolidated" or "collected written payment requests" calling for the payment of specific enumerated creditors, the so-called *sōgō furikomi iraisho* or *furikomi ikkatsu iraisho*. Robert Braucher commented, however, that such substitutes are not really satisfactory in an advanced economy. Concerning the operation of *furikomi* see Michida, note 33, at 43, in NICHIBEI SHŌJI HŌ NO JISSAI at 88.

[126] See Michida, note 33, at 14–16, in NICHIBEI SHŌJI HŌ NO JISSAI at 55–57.

[127] Turner, *A Factual Analysis of Certain Proposed Amendments to the Negotiable Instruments Law*, 28 YALE L.J. 1047, 1051 (1929).

erated development of doctrines with respect to warranties on presentment and transfer; there is no provision in the Japanese statutes on negotiable instruments like section 3-417 of the Uniform Commercial Code, codifying such warranties. Also, there has been no development of insurance against forgery in Japan as there has been in America.

Negotiability involves other problems as well as those of forged endorsements. A careful study of the various problems suggests that the principle of free negotiability, which is supposed to have been carried to its logical conclusion in Japan, is not consistently applied throughout the whole structure of the Japanese law of negotiable instruments.

Under the Uniform Commercial Code, a person who makes use of a signature stamp or other automatic signing device, and is negligent in looking after it, is precluded from asserting lack of authority against a holder in due course of an instrument bearing a signature made by such a device. In Japan there was a contrary decision in 1952. A drawer whose signature was forged by the use of a seal which he entrusted to the forger for use in a real-estate transaction was held not liable to a bona fide purchaser of the instrument, even though he was negligent in entrusting the seal.[128] In a 1957 case, on the other hand, a company was held liable when an officer's signature was forged by the chief of the accounting division; the forger's duties included preparation of instruments but not the affixing of a signature or seal.[129] The holding depended upon article 715(1) (main sentence) of the Civil Code: "A person who employs another for the purpose of any undertaking is bound to compensate for damage which his employee has inflicted on a third person in the execution of this undertaking." Consequently, the purchaser was protected, but only on the basis of a provision outside the Bills Law.

Alteration and Certification

Under section 3-407 of the Uniform Commercial Code, fraudulent alteration is a personal defense of the party whose contract is changed by the alteration, and a holder in due course may always enforce the altered instrument according to its original tenor. But where negligence of the obligor has substantially contributed to the alteration, section 3-406 gives the holder the right to enforce the instrument as altered. According to comment 3, "negligence usually has been found where spaces are left in the body of the instrument in which words or figures may be inserted." In such cases the obligor has no defense against a bona fide purchaser.

The Japanese law is similar. In a case decided in 1956, the plaintiff took a cashier's check in good faith, without knowledge that the date had been

[128] Murakami v. Ikeda, Supreme Court, III Petty Bench, Oct. 21, 1952, 6 SAI-HAN MINSHŪ 841.

[129] Mitsukoshi Hōsei Kabushiki Kaisha (Mitsukoshi Sewing Co.) v. Chabatake, Supreme Court, III Petty Bench, July 16, 1957, 11 SAI-HAN MINSHŪ 1254.

altered, and presented it within the proper time from the altered date. It was held that enforcement was barred by the expiration of the time for presentment, computed as running from the original date. The original November date had been inserted by rubber stamp; it had been altered to a December date by the addition of a small dash to the Chinese character. Plaintiff insisted that the bank should have used a different and more complex Chinese character on its rubber stamp, but the court held that the bank had not been negligent and was not precluded from asserting the alteration against the purchaser in good faith.[130]

A personal check rests on the credit of the issuer; a cashier's check issued by a bank is much stronger. A bank can put its credit behind a personal check by certifying it, thus making the check more attractive and more easily circulated. The Geneva law does not provide for certification, but the Japanese Checks Law does, in articles 53–58, make use of a reservation as permitted under the Geneva law. The reason for this reservation was the prevalence of the American practice of check certification in Japan long before the adoption of the Geneva law; the Great Court of Judicature had occasion to render a decision on the liability of a certifying bank as early as 1911.[131] As stated in the beginning of this essay, the new banking law adopted in Meiji Japan was entirely borrowed from the American national bank laws. But the legal consequences of certification differ from those in the United States. Article 56 of the Checks Law provides that "the drawer and other debtors on a check are not discharged from liability through certification of payment." Under section 3-411 of the American Uniform Commercial Code, a certification procured by the drawer leaves him liable; but when a holder procures certification, the drawer and all prior endorsers are discharged.

CONCLUSION

Scholars hold the view that Japan is a country of statutory or codified law, and a logical order deriving from the interrelation of the various codes and statutes provides the basis and determines the scope of the teaching curriculum. From the point of view of the extent and elaboration of the statutory scheme for economic enterprise, however, the picture is askew. Too often the codes do not lead to precise predictability with respect to modern business transactions. Nor does the structure maintained by the present statutes necessarily promote business efficiency. For example, the rule on forged endorsements coupled with conservative banking practices results in the

[130] Motohashi v. Kabushiki Kaisha Nippon Kangyō Ginkō (Japan Hypothec Bank), Tokyo District Court, Dec. 25, 1956, 7 KAKYŪ SAIBANSHO MINJI SAIBAN REISHŪ (A Collection of Civil Cases in the Inferior Courts) 3754.

[131] Chūō Shōgyō Ginkō (Central Commercial Bank) v. Harada, Great Court of Judicature, II Civil Department, March 20, 1911, 17 DAI-HAN MINROKU 139.

effecting of payments by an enterprise's sending agents who deliver bearer-form checks and return with signatures on prepared receipts. Checks payable to order are not often used, since they have both the disadvantages of bearer instruments and disadvantages of their own. The situation somewhat resembles the eighteenth-century English banking practice, before the establishment of clearing houses, of clearing bills and notes by sending messages from bank to bank, although the banking business in Japan today has the benefits of the clearing-house system and business in general takes advantage of the administrative efficiencies made possible by machines. Demands for a more efficient payment device exist, and *furikomi iraisho,* a close analog of the English traders' payment, are often used with regard to instruments other than bills, notes, and checks. Other areas of retarded legal development are insurance against forgery, the doctrine of warranty, and product-liability insurance. Future business experience in Japan may develop the insurance arrangements needed for business activities, just as the demands for an efficient payment device produced the furikomi. In all events, development of a fully articulated legal structure for economic enterprise will require close study of the actual practice and problems of business administration.

Sometimes the results of litigation in Japan have seemed absurd and unreasonable to an observer who is familiar with the American law of commercial transactions, particularly in its most modern version, the Uniform Commercial Code. But if a Japanese lawyer prepares his case in a more eclectic way, taking into account the fact that many traditional legal concepts exist to serve the needs of commerce and can be molded to that end, the Japanese courts will be likely to respond in similar fashion. Nevertheless, a carefully considered and modernized codification of the law applicable to commercial transactions is needed, although there is yet no institutionalized movement for new legislation revising that which now covers the whole area of commercial law.[132]

The production of a body of law which is flexible and adaptable enough to meet the needs of a highly developed industrial society depends basically upon the intellectual quality of the society's legal profession. The profession must avoid a provincial focus on the concerns of only its own country. In this connection, it is regrettable that the history of modern Japanese commercial law over the last hundred years discloses not a single lawyer or scholar with comprehensive knowledge of the American law of commercial transactions, while many lawyers and scholars have been thoroughly familiar with Continental commercial law. This is all the more regrettable in view of the fact that interchange between the United States and Japan on the subject of corporate and banking law had made a good beginning at the

[132] Piecemeal changes, of course, continue to take place as in the instance of the new legislation revising the provisions of the Commercial Code dealing with the keeping of accounting records. Law No. 182 of 1962.

opening of the Meiji era. There is today a resumption of the interchange after the hundred-year lapse, which may be one facet of the current shrinking of the world, accelerated by industrialization and agitated by the contact of nations and cultures. In a changing world, the study of various legal systems is requisite to the successful building of an effective body of law for any one nation.

THE LEGAL STRUCTURE FOR CORPORATE ENTERPRISE: SHAREHOLDER-MANAGEMENT RELATIONS UNDER JAPANESE LAW

Makoto Yazawa

ASSISTED BY RICHARD W. JENNINGS

THE purpose of this essay is to explore some of the major current legal problems in shareholder-management relationships in Japan. These relationships are regulated by various provisions of the Commercial Code[1] and the Securities Exchange Law.[2]

The Commercial Code was transplanted from Germany to Japan in 1899 as a part of the general acceptance of Western law in the Mejii era. This drastic move, which had the effect of replacing almost all elements of Japan's indigenous law merchant with an alien system, was made primarily for the purpose of obtaining for Japan reciprocal treatment from Western powers in trade and commerce. Subsequent amendments to the code in 1911, 1933, and 1938 in the field of company law, necessitated by the rapid development of the Japanese economy, continued to reflect German developments.[3]

Note. Mr. Yazawa is Professor of Law, University of Tokyo. B. Jur., Tokyo Imperial University, 1943; Dr. Jur., Tokyo University, 1962. Participant, Japanese American Program for Cooperation in Legal Studies at Harvard University, 1954–55, and at the University of Michigan, 1955–56. Research at Harvard and Michigan and other American Law Schools, 1961. Member, Subcommittee of Legal Committee on Hire-Charter and Aerial Collision, International Civil Aviation Organization, 1960, 1961. Legal Adviser, Japanese Delegation, Conference on Air Law, Guadalajara, Mexico, 1961. Delegate, International Conference on Restrictive Business Practices, Chicago, 1958, Frankfurt-am-Main, 1961, Washington, D.C., 1962. Coauthor of Blakemore & Yazawa, *Japanese Commercial Code Revisions Concerning Corporations*, 2 AM. J. COMP. L. 12 (1953); writings in the fields of commercial law, air law, and antitrust law. The writer wishes to extend his appreciation to Professor Louis Loss of Harvard Law School, and to Richard W. Rabinowitz for their helpful comments.

Mr. Jennings is Coffroth Professor of Law, University of California at Berkeley. A.B., 1927, Park College; A.M., 1934, University of Pennsylvania; LL.B., 1939, University of California.

[1] Law No. 48 of 1899 [hereafter cited COMMERCIAL CODE].

[2] Law No. 25 of 1948. For an English translation of the text of the law as amended to date, see 6 EHS LAW BULLETIN SERIES MA 1 (Nakane ed. & trans., 1957) [hereafter cited Securities Exchange Law].

[3] See CODE TRANSLATION COMM. OF THE LEAGUE OF NATIONS ASSN. OF JAPAN, *Historical Introduction*, in THE COMMERCIAL CODE OF JAPAN, ix-xliii (1931).

Under the prodding of the American authorities, during the occupation after World War II a number of new limbs of Anglo-American origin were grafted onto what had been a code of exclusively Continental origin.[4] The amendments in 1950, sponsored by the occupation authorities, had the objective of promoting "corporate democracy" through strengthening the position and rights of shareholders. At the same time, Japanese initiative promoted redistribution of corporate powers among the shareholders, the board of directors, and the corporate auditors, as well as provision for a new method of attracting and inducing capital investment. As a result of this amendment, shareholder-management relationships have changed greatly, at least on the statute books.

The Securities Exchange Law was enacted as a condition imposed by the occupation authorities on the reopening of the securities exchanges, which had been closed at the beginning of the occupation.[5] This law, enacted in 1948, is a modified version of the Securities Act of 1933 and the Securities Exchange Act of 1934 of the United States. It contains substantially similar provisions for the disclosure of corporate information through a registration system for the public issue and sale of securities and for the regulation of the securities markets, both on organized exchanges and over the counter, through mandatory registration of dealers, brokers, securities dealers' associations, and securities exchanges. Within the corporate structure, proxy solicitation and insider trading are subject to regulation which follows the pattern found in the Securities Exchange Act of 1934. In Japan as in the United States this system of securities regulation has exerted a considerable influence on shareholder-management relations in publicly held corporations.[6]

More than ten years have elapsed since the adoption of this general corporate and securities legislation. The decade has seen an unprecedented expansion of the Japanese economy, accompanied by a vast increase in the number of corporations and in the number of investors in publicly held corporations. For example, the number of stock companies in 1959 was

[4] For the occupation policies and the 1950 amendments to the Commercial Code, see Blakemore & Yazawa, *Japanese Commercial Code Revisions Concerning Corporations*, 2 AM. J. COMP. L. 12 (1953).

[5] For the occupation policies and content of the Securities Exchange Law, see ADAMS, JAPANESE SECURITIES MARKETS (1953).

[6] Although not strictly correct as a matter of Japanese legal terminology, the term "corporation" is used throughout this essay in the sense in which it is most commonly employed in the United States, that is, as a synonym for the Japanese term "stock company." In Japan, following the legal structure typical in Continental European law, legal entities in the broadest sense are known as "juridical persons" (*hōjin*) and those governed by commercial law as "companies" (*kaisha*). The latter concept includes "partnership under a common name companies" (*gōmei kaisha;* a form of general partnership), "partnership in commendam companies" (*gōshi kaisha;* a form of limited partnership), "stock companies" (*kabushiki kaisha*), and "limited liability companies" (*yūgen kaisha;* a form similar to the British private company and based on the German GmbH).

267,345, five times the number in 1945 and twice that in 1950.[7] The number of stock companies listed on the securities exchanges rose from 677 in 1950 to 789 in 1959.[8] The Securities Exchange Law, to which many unlisted companies are subject, was applicable to some 1,544 corporations as of the end of 1960. This rapid increase in the number of stock companies, especially close corporations,[9] resulted largely from a revision of the tax laws adopted in 1950 following the recommendations of the Shoup Mission of 1949 and 1950.

Prior to Japan's defeat in World War II, shares of large corporations were closely held by a small number of individuals or concerns, usually either the banks of zaibatsu combines or holding companies, while public savings were deposited in the zaibatsu banks or other financial institutions. The elimination of the zaibatsu,[10] and the heavy capital levy in 1947 which forced the sale of assets, spread the ownership of shares more widely. This diffusion of stock ownership has been greatly accelerated during the last ten years as a result of the rapid increase in the market price of shares, which has attracted large numbers of individuals into the securities markets for the first time. Now shares are distributed among ordinary citizens almost as widely in Japan as in the United States.[11] Since this dispersal did not occur by a gradual

[7] The number of stock companies and limited liability companies in Japan has been as follows:

	1935	*1945*	*1950*	*1959*
Stock companies	24,566	47,093	134,064	267,345
Limited liability companies (governed by Law No. 74 of 1938)		19,507	36,133	183,004

[8] When stock exchanges were first established in Japan in 1878, the number of issues traded thereon was 52, made up mainly of government bonds and shares of banks and exchanges. By 1938 the number of issues traded on the exchanges had increased to 200. See also note 11 below.

[9] Called "family companies" (*dōzoku kaisha*) in Japan. On the tax aspects of the increase in companies, see Morio Uematsu, "Computation of Income in Japanese Income Taxation: A Study in the Adjustment of Theory to Reality," in this volume.

[10] See BISSON, ZAIBATSU DISSOLUTION IN JAPAN (1954); U.S. DEPARTMENT OF STATE, REPORT OF THE MISSION ON JAPANESE COMBINES (Far Eastern Series 14, 1946).

[11] Data on the dispersion of stock ownership in the listed companies in Japan shows the following:

	1946	*1950*	*1959*
Number of shareholders			
Number of listed companies	631	677	789
Investment trusts	—	—	1,935
Foreign individuals	—	—	17,705
Individuals	1,673,828	4,190,523	9,706,839
Number of shares held by			
Investment trusts	—	—	1,483,861,865
Foreign individuals	—	—	123,011,402
Individuals	235,427,487	1,382,473,596	11,046,130,111

The number of individual shareholders owning shares in listed corporations in the United States was said to be 12,490,000 in 1959. N.Y. STOCK EXCHANGE, SHARE OWNERSHIP IN AMERICA: 1959, at 5.

evolutionary process as in the United States, the resulting need for investor protection is even greater in Japan. The new Japanese legislation in the corporate field was designed to meet this need.

The basic assumption of the occupation authorities in suggesting this corporate and securities legislation might be said to be the belief that what had worked in the United States would work in Japan and that what was suitable for one would be beneficial for the other. No account was taken of the roots of these American concepts, however, and no question was raised with regard to the congeniality of the soil into which the new legislation was transplanted. It is doubtful, for example, that German law had earlier been accepted and applied in Japan as it was administered in Germany. As one specialist in comparative law has noted:

> It is thus perhaps fair to generalize that, from the point of view of official rules, institutions, and legal education, the Japanese legal system is closer to the civil law than to the common law. In many ways, however, the Japanese legal order is markedly different from the Western legal orders, common and civil law alike.[12]

This general observation seems valid in the corporate-law field. It seems appropriate, therefore, to evaluate the actual efficacy and functioning of these new regulations, as well as to appraise the older legislation which has remained unchanged, as they relate to some of the central problems in the area of shareholder-management relationships.

SHAREHOLDERS' PARTICIPATION IN CORPORATE GOVERNMENT

The crux of the shareholder-management problem is to make more effective the exercise of the stockholders' rights at general meetings, especially the right to "hire and fire" the directorate.

The most important aspect of the shareholders' right to "hire" the directors is regulating the solicitation of proxies by management. The widespread distribution of shares,[13] with the concomitant separation of ownership and control, puts the shareholders' meeting at the mercy of the proxy system. This mechanism invites and fosters a self-perpetuating management. Those engaged in revision of corporation law throughout the Western world, including the British, the French, and the Germans, are at this time seeking methods for effective regulation of the proxy machinery. The Commercial Code permits a shareholder to give a proxy only with respect to a particular shareholders' meeting, thus prohibiting the general proxy.[14] However, the proxy-solicitation process is now more effectively controlled through the extension of the Securities Exchange Law to this field. Pursuant to article

[12] Von Mehren, *Some Reflections on Japanese Law*, 71 HARV. L. REV. 1486, 1491 (1958).

[13] The "big three" among the Japanese corporations — Hitachi, Yawata Steel, and Toshiba — have shareholders numbering respectively 321,006; 267,393; and 251,106. See also note 11 above.

[14] COMMERCIAL CODE art. 239 (3)–(4).

194 of the law, proxy regulations were adopted in 1948,[15] which were an almost literal version of Regulation X-14 issued by the United States Securities and Exchange Commission pursuant to section 14 of the 1934 Securities Exchange Act. As a result of subsequent amendments in Japan in 1949[16] and 1955,[17] however, the differences between the Japanese and American regulations have become greater.

The first point of divergence relates to the contents of the proxy statement which must be given to each solicited person. The Japanese regulations specify items to be disclosed in the proxy statement with respect to each proposal that is a proper subject for shareholder action under the Commercial Code.[18] Regarding the election of directors, the cardinal requirements are concerned with a disclosure of the relationship between the nominees for director and their corporation. There is no specific requirement governing disclosure of management remuneration and transactions of directors with the corporation, except the very vague element of "interest which the nominees for director have or have had with the . . . company."[19] This requirement is actually a dead letter, however: the enforcement agency can give no explanation as to what is required by this provision, and the general practice has been simply to write "no interest." Although financial statements are not required to be included in a proxy statement for the election of directors, under the Commercial Code they must be approved at the annual meeting at which directors are elected,[20] so that indirectly they are required as a part of the proxy statement. False statements in proxy statements are a cause for suspension of the solicitation by the Ministry of Finance, which is now in charge of enforcement.[21] On the other hand, in the United States annual financial reports to shareholders need not be filed with the SEC[22] and do not lead to statutory liabilities for omissions or misstatements.

Secondly, when the proxy regulations were originally adopted, three preliminary copies of the proxy statement and form had to be filed with the Securities Exchange Commission at least ten days before the final material

[15] Regulations Concerning the Solicitation of Proxy of Listed Shares [hereafter cited Proxy Regulations], Securities Exchange Commission Regulation No. 13 of 1948.

[16] Security Exchange Commission Regulations No. 1 and No. 2 of 1949.

[17] Security Exchange Commission Regulation No. 196 of 1955.

[18] Proxy Regulations, art. 2. There is no problem concerning the questions of what is a proper subject for shareholder action — a serious problem in the United States — for in Japan there is only one corporation statute which clearly determines the power of the shareholders' meeting. See COMMERCIAL CODE art. 230-2; see also 2 LOSS, SECURITIES REGULATION [hereafter cited Loss] 901–12 (2d ed., 1961).

[19] Proxy Regulations, art. 2 (iii) (c); cf. SEC Schedule 14A, item 7, 17 C.F.R. 173 (Supp. 1961); 2 Loss 888–89.

[20] COMMERCIAL CODE art. 283.

[21] In Japan the Securities Exchange Law was first administered by the Securities Exchange Commission, an independent agency of the government. In 1952, this agency was abolished and the administration of the law was entrusted to the Ministry of Finance.

[22] SEC Rule 14a–3(c), 17 C.F.R. §240.14a–3(c) (Supp. 1961); see 2 Loss 886–88.

was used. In practice, the commission at the outset seems not to have used the waiting period as a device for enforcing a higher standard of compliance, and there was in fact no case of suspension of the use of the proxy statement as filed. As a result, by the 1949 amendment, the waiting period was made subject to acceleration by the commission for good cause; and by the 1955 amendment, a copy of the material to be sent to the shareholders need be filed with the Ministry of Finance only at the time of use.[23] There is no reported case in which the commission or the ministry has asked the court to enjoin the use of material because of deficiencies; nor is there any case in which a shareholder has brought an action to enjoin or set aside a resolution adopted at a shareholders' meeting where the solicitation was made in violation of the proxy regulations. This lack of court activity would seem to indicate either that the requirements are so lax that no violations occur or that no shareholder or his lawyer has been concerned over a violation. Since, quite unlike the situation in the United States, in Japan a lawyer does not prepare the proxy statement, the profession is not generally familiar with the securities law and regulations.

Thirdly, the regulations require use of the two-way proxy, which permits a shareholder to choose between approval or disapproval of any proposal.[24] Under the American proxy regulations administered by the SEC, shares represented by a proxy must be voted in accordance with the directions given on the proxy.[25] In Japan, however, there are corporations in which the proxy holders selected by management do not vote any proxy in which the shareholder has given a direction to vote against a management proposal, or they simply ignore that direction and vote in favor of the proposal.[26] Some scholars approve this procedure, relying upon certain agency theories.[27] Because of a conflict of views among scholars as to the acceptable practice, the original requirement to vote in accordance with the shareholders' direction as specified in the proxy was deleted by the 1949 amendments. There is still a difference of opinion as to whether the proxy holder should be bound by the shareholders' direction. Certainly where the practice of ignoring the instructions persists, at the least the shareholders are thereby deprived of the benefits of the two-way proxy. Another interesting difference between the two systems is that the two-way-proxy requirement also applies in Japan in the case of corporate elections,[28] although it is not so effective in this case unless shareholders are permitted to propose candidates.

[23] Proxy Regulations, art. 6; cf. SEC Rule 14a–6(a), 17 C.F.R. §240.14a–6(a) (Supp. 1961).

[24] Proxy Regulations, art. 3; cf. SEC Rule 14a–4(b), 17 C.F.R. §240.14a–4(b) (Supp. 1961).

[25] SEC Rule 14a–4(e), 17 C.F.R. §240.14a–4(e) (Supp. 1961).

[26] Among 347 corporations, 100 followed this practice in 1960.

[27] These scholars argue that, if an agent is bound by the direction of his principal, he becomes a mere tool of the principal and therefore cannot be an "agent."

[28] Under the United States proxy rules, the two-way proxy is not applicable to election of directors. SEC Rule 14a–4(b), 17 C.F.R. §240.14a–4(b) (Supp. 1961).

Lastly, a shareholder-proposal rule, which went beyond the American system to include election of directors, was a part of the original regulations,[29] but, since it had never been used, it was deleted by the 1949 amendment. Clearly a resolution proposed by a shareholder has virtually no chance of passing without an independent proxy solicitation. But the right of minority shareholders to compel the convening of a meeting to consider matters specified by them is often used as a substitute for the former shareholder-proposal rule, as is explained below.[30] Moreover, in the absence of public-spirited citizens like Lewis D. Gilbert or Wilma Soss, so-called professional shareholders in Japan have been known to prefer the method of extorting money from management by blackmail tactics in connection with the shareholders' meeting.

It has been said that in a Japanese zaibatsu company a proxy fight was "not simply unusual; it borders on the inconceivable." [31] Recently, however, battles for control have been growing more frequent in Japan.[32] Most such skirmishes are conducted through a quiet purchase of shares; the *Shirokiya* case is about the only one which entailed a proxy campaign as such. Even in cases resembling *Shirokiya,* the struggle will probably not be resolved by a conventional contest for votes. Rather, in order to prevent competition by voting, both sides may scheme to struggle over the chairmanship and disrupt the meeting; or the opening of the meeting may be rendered impossible by one side withdrawing and thus breaking the quorum, or by filling the meeting place with persons other than shareholders, so that the majority voting power held by the other side cannot prevail. Later one side usually brings an action to set aside, on the basis of irregularity, any resolutions actually adopted.[33] In these situations the problem is one not of proxy solicitation but of the conduct of the meeting, so that there is as yet no movement to set up special regulations governing proxy contests like those adopted in the United States in 1956.[34]

Although the proxy regulations have advanced "corporate democracy," Japanese shareholders and the legal profession have not yet fully explored the regulations and the remedies afforded by them. One of the most debated

[29] Proxy Regulations, art. 8(3), repealed by Security Exchange Commission Regulation No. 1 of 1949; cf. SEC Rule 14a–8, 17 C.F.R. §240.14a–8 (Supp. 1961).

[30] See pp. 554–55 below.

[31] U.S. DEPT. OF STATE, note 10, at 22.

[32] E.g., Tokyo Electric Power Company (1952); Shirokiya Department Store (1954); Tokyo Sugar Refinery Co. (1959).

[33] Even in the United States some of these techniques (notably that of breaking the quorum) were used to such an extent in one recent merger — that of Textron, American Woolen, and Robbins Mills — that one writer called it "the most acrimonious and tricky of recent mergers — a sort of running demonstration of business judo." Saunders, *The Stormiest Merger Yet,* Fortune, April 1955, p. 136, at 137.

[34] SEC Rule 14a–11, 17 C.F.R. §240.14a–11 (Supp. 1961); SEC Schedule 14B, 17 C.F.R. 178 (Supp. 1961); see Note, *SEC Regulation of Proxy Contests,* 69 HARV. L. REV. 1462 (1956); 2 LOSS 894–900.

questions concerns the merits of cumulative voting for the election of directors, a right granted to shareholders by the 1950 amendment of the Commercial Code.[35] Unless voting is otherwise restricted by the articles of association,[36] directors must be elected by cumulative voting upon the request of any shareholder. Even if voting is restricted by the articles, this method may be used by any shareholder if a request is made by shareholders representing one fourth of all outstanding shares.[37] No instance has in fact been reported in which cumulative voting has been used, although there have been several cases in which shareholders have made the request. With very few exceptions,[38] an exclusion of cumulative voting is provided in the articles of association of every Japanese corporation. Moreover, proposals to abolish the right of cumulative voting are frequently made by business groups. This climate of opinion in opposition to cumulative voting is fostered by the common practice of having a board of directors wholly or largely composed of individuals who are also full-time executives of the corporation.

Under the Japanese Commercial Code, the right to "fire" the directors is a very important one and is used quite frequently in battles for control. A director may be removed from office at any time by a shareholders' resolution, while in most parts of the United States the stockholders have no power to remove a director, in the absence of misconduct, until the expiration of his term of office. And if the meeting has rejected the removal of a director, shareholders holding more than 3 percent of all the outstanding shares for a period of six months may bring an action to remove the director in case of misconduct.[39] Moreover, any shareholders having the same qualifications may demand that a general meeting be convened, and if the directors fail to take the necessary steps without delay, or to send notice of the meeting dated within six weeks after the demand, such shareholders may convene the meeting with the permission of the court.[40] On the other hand, under some American statutes the shareholders cannot call a special meeting for any purpose unless the bylaws so provide and, even in states which give such right to shareholders, the qualifications are much more severe.[41] A Japanese

[35] Law No. 167 of 1950.

[36] The articles of association are equivalent to the American corporate charter or articles of incorporation.

[37] COMMERCIAL CODE arts. 256-3–256-4. This solution represents a compromise between the occupation authorities, who asked for the adoption of an unconditional mandatory provision, and the Japanese, who opposed making cumulative voting mandatory.

[38] It was reported that, in the case of one joint-venture corporation organized by Japanese and American corporations, a mandatory cumulative-voting clause was included in the articles of association.

[39] COMMERCIAL CODE art. 257.

[40] *Ibid.*, art. 237.

[41] E.g., 10 percent (N.C., Tex.); 20 percent (Cal., D.C., Pa.); 25 percent (Md., Ohio). See BAKER & CARY, CASES ON CORPORATIONS 178 (3d ed., 1959). Before the 1950 amendment, it was 10 percent in Japan, while in California it was 10 percent before the 1933 amendment of the California Corporations Code.

court has gone so far as to grant a temporary injunction[42] to restrain directors from exercising their powers between the date of the shareholders' demand and the actual meeting for the purpose of removal.[43] These procedures for the removal of directors and the calling of general meetings are very familiar to Japanese lawyers and are quite extensively used. They may be regarded as a partial substitute for a shareholder-proposal rule and as a more effective weapon than the newly adopted injunction proceeding by shareholders, which will be discussed later.

Fiduciary Obligations of Directors

Although as a practical matter the removal of the incompetent director will be of more significance than the pursuit of the dishonest one, it is also important that management should not reap a personal profit at the expense of public shareholders. The 1950 amendment included a provision expressly stating the duty of loyalty of directors,[44] but the prevailing view of legal scholars construes this as constituting merely the classical duty of care and diligence of a good manager, applicable generally to fiduciary relationships, and does not regard it as very significant. No case determining the effect of the 1950 amendment has yet been reported.

There have been, however, three sets of regulations, both before and after that amendment, for the purpose of preventing breach of the duty of loyalty. These include the regulation of competition of a director with the corporation, transactions between the director and his corporation, and executive compensation. In the first place, a director who, on his own behalf or on behalf of a third person, intends to effect a transaction that comes within the class of business carried on by the corporation must disclose all the material facts about that transaction at the general meeting and obtain the stockholder's approval.[45] The courts, unlike Anglo-American courts, have not enlarged this principle to prevent directors from taking any personal advantage of a corporate opportunity.

Secondly, when a director seeks to borrow money from his corporation or to effect any transaction with the corporation on his own behalf or that of a third person, he must obtain the approval of the board of directors;[46] any such transaction without the approval of the board has been interpreted by the courts as null and void.[47] Accordingly, this provision is quite often used

[42] More correctly, "provisional disposition," a remedy similar to the Anglo-American temporary injunction. See Code of Civil Procedure, Law No. 29 of 1890, arts. 755–63.

[43] Sumitomo v. Chuma, Chiba District Court, Oct. 12, 1953, 4 Hanrei Times (The Law Times Report) no. 9, at 43; see Commercial Code art. 270.

[44] Commercial Code art. 254-2 (cf. old code, art. 254); Civil Code art. 644.

[45] Commercial Code art. 264.

[46] Commercial Code art. 265.

[47] See, e.g., Kabushiki Kaisha Nihon Kōshō Ginkō (Japan Industrial and Commercial Bank Co.) v. Eguchi, Great Court of Judicature, I Civil Department, June 21, 1904, 10 Dai Shin In Minji Hanketsu Roku (Record of Great Court of Judicature Civil Judgments) 956.

as a defense by the corporation against a contract action brought by the director or the third party. This provision may be avoided, however, by routing the transaction through a subsidiary corporation. Furthermore, there is not adequate regulation of all the common directors' situations. Nonetheless, the Japanese law is stricter than the American in some respects. Contracts even in part authorized on behalf of the corporation by an interested director's vote are void,[48] whereas such contracts are merely voidable under the prevailing American view. Japanese courts also do not permit a director to defend the contract by establishing his good faith and the fairness of the transaction, as do some American courts.

Finally, "the compensation to be received by the directors" must be authorized by a resolution of the general meeting, provided that its "amount is not prescribed in the articles of association." [49] The code is silent on whether the amount of renumeration of each director must be fixed or whether the specification of a total amount is sufficient. Furthermore, the provision does not make clear whether the remuneration to be set by the articles or resolution covers services as a director only or whether it covers services as an executive employee as well.* The opinion of most legal scholars is that only a total amount need be fixed by articles of association or resolution, but there is disagreement as to whether the compensation covers services of directors in all capacities. In one early case a provision in the articles gave the board of directors the authority to determine the remuneration of the president and vice president, who also were directors, without setting a maximum limit. In a shareholder's suit attacking this provision, the prewar Great Court of Judicature sustained its validity and stated that it was not intended to leave the fixing of the top executives' remuneration to the unlimited discretion of the board, but only to permit the board to fix their compensation within a reasonable range.[50] This interpretation might have implied that courts will examine the reasonableness of the amount of compensation to be received by directors. Since then, however, the Japanese courts have held that, if the total amount of remuneration of directors is not fixed in either the articles of association or by resolution, the action of the board is null and

[48] COMMERCIAL CODE art. 260-2.

[49] *Ibid.*, art. 269.

* It was pointed out at the conference that, under the Commercial Code, a direction that the general meeting was to fix compensation for directors was interpreted as applying only to the fairly nominal amounts paid directors for attending meetings and did not refer to compensation for acting as officers. Richard Jennings commented further that companies considered the amount of compensation paid officers such a business secret that they preferred not to reveal it even though they would lose a tax deduction available only if the amount of compensation were disclosed.

[50] Furukawa v. Kabushiki Kaisha Shōkin Ginkō (Specie Bank Co.), Great Court of Judicature, III Civil Department, June 5, 1929, 18 HŌRITSU HYŌRON ZENSHŪ (A Complete Critique of the Law), SHŌHŌ (Commercial Law) pt. at 702.

void. These holdings imply that Japanese courts will not develop a standard of reasonableness like that applied by American courts.[51]

Japanese courts and legal scholars adhere to the theory that directors do not stand in a fiduciary position toward individual shareholders; they have scarcely begun to develop the doctrine now applied by most American courts that "special facts" may impose such a fiduciary obligation. The only exception is the insider-trading rule of the Securities Exchange Law.[52] The underlying theory of this legislation, however, is so foreign to Japanese thinking about the nature of the corporate structure and the relationship between management and shareholders that no shareholder has ever used this remedy. Moreover, the 1953 amendments of the law deleted the provision requiring periodic reporting of insider transactions, purportedly for the very vague reason of "lack of practical effect." This amendment blunted this weapon in the shareholders' arsenal beyond all effectiveness. It is regrettable that the reporting provision was eliminated, since some abuses of insider position have been recently reported in the press.

A special characteristic of Japanese regulation of the fiduciary obligations of directors entails reliance more on such procedural guarantees as approval by shareholders or the board of directors than on the use of judicially applied standards of fairness or reasonableness through the derivative suit. The lack of development of such standards seems related to the system of legal education, the training of judges, and the administration of justice. Career judges have never been engaged as lawyers in a business practice so as to gain a practical knowledge of corporate management, and there is no supporting body of tradition or flexible case law comparable to that in the United States or in England. Moreover, lawyers do not usually give preventive counsel prior to business decisions but confine their activities largely to litigation. The lack of adequate discovery procedures imposes a barrier to obtaining evidence of "fairness or reasonableness" in many of these complicated business situations. In these circumstances, it is unfortunate that the proxy regulations do not clearly require the disclosure of compensation of directors or transactions of directors with the corporation as in the United States, since disclosure, of all procedural techniques, has perhaps the most significant self-enforcing effect.

It is more difficult to evolve a satisfactory procedure for enforcing the director's duties than it is to set up the substantive standard. The 1950 amendments of the Commercial Code introduced new shareholders' remedies—the derivative suit for damages or injunction and the nonderivative

[51] See, e.g., Murayama v. Kyōei Seimoku Kabushiki Kaisha (Coprosperity Fine Lumber Co.), Tokyo District Court, April 28, 1951, 2 Kakyū Saibansho Minji Saiban Reishū (A Collection of Civil Cases in the Inferior Courts) [hereafter cited Kakyū Minshū] 566.

[52] Securities Exchange Law, art. 189.

suit for injunction in the event that shares are issued illegally or on grossly unfair terms. Any six-month shareholder may institute an action to enforce the liability of directors.[53] This system replaced a much less effective one whereby an auditor, upon the demand of minority shareholders whose request had been refused at a shareholders' meeting, could bring such an action against directors. Before the 1950 amendment, it was observed that "stockholder suits to recover damages, to compel payment of dividends, or to remove management in such corporations are scarcely within the scope of Japanese conception." [54] Even since the amendment, derivative actions have been uncommon. In the only reported case, the court confined the suit purely to the enforcement of the liability of directors as prescribed in the Commercial Code;[55] the court refused to compel a director to transfer to the corporation the title of a building registered in his name and purchased on account of the corporation, since the code recognized only actions for damages to enforce directors' liability.[56] Quite recently a shareholder of the Yawata Steel Company brought a derivative action against directors who contributed a considerable amount of corporate funds to both major political parties and to some of their candidates. Because securities are now so widely held and corporate activity is so intense, it seems probable that more derivative actions will be brought in the future, but it is doubtful whether these actions will succeed, primarily because of judicial unwillingness to invade the realm of business judgment and also because of the dearth of lawyers with the special skills and training needed in this area of the law.

The derivative suit for injunction is available to any six-months stockholder when a director engages in an *ultra vires* or illegal act from which a reasonable fear arises that irreparable damage will be done the corporation. The shareholder may demand that the director refrain from such acts and, if necessary, may enforce such a demand through a court proceeding.[57] This new remedy has never been used, since a temporary injunction to prevent the directors from exercising their powers pending election or removal proceedings[58] is far more effective than a proceeding to enjoin specific acts. The 1950 amendment also afforded shareholders an individual, nonderivative suit for injunction in the event of the illegal issuance of shares or of issuance in a grossly unfair manner or at a grossly unfair price.[59] Such actions have been brought quite often.

The paucity of litigation involving derivative actions and derivative in-

[53] COMMERCIAL CODE arts. 267–68-3; cf. old code, art. 268 (before amended by Law No. 167 of 1950).
[54] U.S. DEPT. OF STATE, note 10, at 22.
[55] COMMERCIAL CODE arts. 266, 280-13.
[56] Haung v. Li, Tokyo District Court, Oct. 19, 1956, 7 KAKYŪ MINSHŪ 2931.
[57] COMMERCIAL CODE art. 272.
[58] *Ibid.*, art. 270.
[59] *Ibid.*, art. 280-10.

junctions may be due to lack of experience on the part of trial lawyers. More fundamentally, it is hard to expect small shareholders to bring an action without the opportunity of obtaining direct recovery rather than benefiting only indirectly through a derivative suit. Even in the case of close corporations, where derivative actions produce far more direct benefits, the more practical remedies are the traditional actions to remove directors rather than the newly allowed derivative suits or injunction proceedings.*

Shareholders' Access to Financial Information

A stockholder is at a great disadvantage vis-à-vis management with respect to the corporate information at his disposal. If reasonable access to financial information is not guaranteed by law, he can neither exercise intelligently his right to hire or fire the directorate nor use effectively the derivative action or injunction. Something can be achieved by compelling disclosure to shareholders through annual financial statements. Under the Commercial Code, financial statements prepared by the directors, together with a report thereon by an auditor appointed by the shareholders, must be submitted to the shareholders' meeting for approval. These financial statements and reports are open for inspection by any shareholder or creditor for one week prior to the annual meeting; the approved balance sheet must also be published in a newspaper, although in practice closely held corporations do not usually comply with the publication requirement. After the financial statements have been approved at a shareholders' meeting, the directors are discharged from liability for damages, except those arising from dishonest acts, caused by any omissions or misleading or false information in the financial statements unless action is taken by the corporation within two years.[60]

The first defect in this mechanism of disclosure lies in the position of the auditor. There is no requirement that the auditors be independent; nor need they be professional accountants, as British auditors are, since there exists no disqualification except that they may not be directors or employees of the corporation.[61] Moreover, in practice, the auditorship is either a sinecure or is used as a training ground for young executives.

A second defect is that legal requirements as to the form and content of financial statements are very lax and archaic. They have been limited to

* There was considerable disagreement at the conference about where the responsibility rests for the relatively poor development of the shareholder's legal remedies. Alfred Oppler noted the similarity between Japanese and German legal training in that both are deficient in economic education. In Germany, however, the wide experience of the bar largely corrects this defect. Judges Hattori and Tanabe suggested that although the bench was competent to handle these problems, the bar did not bring them to the courts. Yasuharu Nagashima, a practicing attorney, stated that few shareholders are willing to litigate these questions. Tanabe added that perhaps only a government agency could make the various provisions effective.

[60] *Ibid.*, arts. 281–84.

[61] *Ibid.*, art. 276.

fixing standards of valuation of fixed or deferred assets and to the requirement of legal reserves or surpluses. The intent at the time of the 1938 amendment was to prescribe minimum forms and items for the financial statements; but this objective has not yet been attained by reason of inaction on the part of the Ministry of Justice, which was given implementing authority.[62] At the end of World War II, it was observed that the balance sheets made available to shareholders were "curiosities in obscurity and evasion," the profit and loss statements were as obscure as the balance sheets, and consolidated financial statements were not to be found in Japanese accounting.[63]

The Securities Exchange Law has made a great advance in requiring publicity and in supplying some details at least in the case of publicly held corporations. Issuers who file registration statements must submit annual reports, including financial statements, to the Ministry of Finance; those issuers whose securities are listed on an exchange must also submit their reports to the exchange. These reports must remain open to public inspection either at the office of the Ministry of Finance and the business offices of the issuer or at the exchange.[64] The form and content of financial statements included in these reports, as well as registration statements and prospectuses, are strictly regulated by the regulation issued by the Securities Exchange Commission,[65] which is an adaptation of SEC Regulation S-X in the United States. These financial statements must be certified by independent certified public accountants.[66] The accounting standard required by these regulations is so high that recently the Sony Company succeeded in registering in the United States under the Securities Act of 1933 without much difficulty.* The regulations relating to accounting and auditing are the most successful of the corporate legislation transplanted from the United States in the postwar period. There are, however, two important defects in the Japanese regulations, both of which have been mentioned previously: the absence of requirements of consolidated financial statements and of the disclosure of the interest of management in transactions with the corporation.

Following the lead of the regulation of securities, the Ministry of Justice

[62] Law Enforcing the Commercial Code Amendment Law, Law No. 73 of 1938, art. 49.

[63] U.S. DEPT. OF STATE, note 10, at 26–27.

[64] Securities Exchange Law, arts. 24–25, 118. The government printing office (the Ministry of Finance Printing Bureau) has just begun to print and sell all of these annual reports as a result of requests for copies by members of the public.

[65] Regulations Concerning the Terms, Form, and Method of Preparing Financial Statements, Etc., Securities Exchange Commission Regulation No. 18 of 1950, issued under Securities Exchange Law, art. 193.

[66] Securities Exchange Law, art. 193-2; Ministerial Order Concerning the Certified Audit of Financial Statements, Ministry of Finance Order No. 12 of 1957.

* At the conference Thomas Blakemore dissented. Despite the high standards of the Japanese law, the Sony Company had had difficulty in filing its registration statement because Japanese and American accounting practices are quite different.

recently proposed amendments to the accounting provisions of the Commercial Code. These include the prescription of standards for valuing assets in accordance with sound accounting principles so as to forestall the use of secret reserves, as well as the regulation of the form and content of the financial statements now required to be published under the code. The proposed amendments have the practical effect of extending the same kind of control as is required by regulations concerning the preparation of financial statements to those stock corporations which are not subject to the Securities Exchange Law.[67]

Although this pattern of disclosure may enable a shareholder to exercise his voting right intelligently through the detection of the symptoms of disease in the corporate body, it is not likely to reveal the cause of the disease. It will certainly not give him the evidence necessary for bringing a lawsuit against those whom he suspects to have caused the trouble. He needs some means of finding out whether his suspicions are well founded. Under the 1950 amendment of the Commercial Code, the right to inspect the files and books of a corporation was given to holders of more than 10 percent of all outstanding shares. Under previous law, no shareholder had a right of access to corporate books and records. The new requirement represented a compromise between the occupation authorities, who pressed for giving such right to individual shareholders without limitation, and the Japanese, who refused to accept an unlimited right of inspection because of the possibility of abuse and who urged as an alternative that such shareholders be permitted to apply to the court for the appointment of an inspector of the books and records. Before the amendment, an interesting solution had been to confer power upon the court to appoint an inspector to investigate the affairs and property of a corporation upon application by holders of 10 percent of the shares when there was any reason to suspect misconduct of directors,[68] an approach which is very close to the British system.[69]

There have been very few cases in which shareholders have sought to use this new right to inspect the books and records. Thus the fear of the Japanese legislators appears to have been groundless and the remedy has not proved to be too useful. In the only case reported, the court refused to grant an order placing the corporate records in the custody of a court officer and held that, in order to obtain evidence of misconduct of a director, an application for an inspector to investigate the company's affairs is a more appropriate remedy than the shareholders' right of inspection, which the

[67] These amendments were enacted by Law No. 82 of 1962. See Suzuki, Yazawa, Ueda & Ajimura, *Shōhō no Ichibu Kaisei* (Partial Revision of the Commercial Code), JURIST no. 247, at 10 (1962) (symposium).

[68] COMMERCIAL CODE art. 294.

[69] Companies Act, 1948, 11 & 12 GEO. 6, c. 38, §§164–75. Advantages of this system are discussed in Gower, *Some Contrasts Between British and American Corporation Law*, 69 HARV. L. REV. 1369, 1388–89 (1956).

court regarded as too limited for this purpose.[70] The opinion is revealing with respect to the attitudes and the thinking of the Japanese legal profession in this area.

CORPORATE FINANCE

Management has a wide discretion in determining the method of financing the corporation, including the terms of issuing shares. The task of the legislators in this field will be to preserve the rights of existing shareholders, who might be injured by a dilution of their equity interests caused by the issuance of shares at an inadequate price, while protecting incoming shareholders, who might suffer a loss because of lack of knowledge regarding the shares offered to them. Until the zaibatsu were dissolved, the capital requirements of large corporations were met almost entirely by means of the issuance of shares to carefully selected subscribers, usually either the banks or the holding companies of combines. With dissolution of the holding companies and the separation of investment and commercial banking,[71] this whole structure disappeared. As a result, borrowing from commercial banks was at first the only practical channel open for financing the corporation. But gradually Japanese corporations became aware that substantial new capital could be obtained directly from their own shareholders and the public generally.[72] The government has also been taking measures, including the granting of tax advantages, to stimulate financing by way of equity capital rather than debt.

In the 1950 amendment, the authority to issue shares, which theretofore had been vested in the shareholders, was delegated to the board of directors.[73] This concept of authorized but unissued stock, as well as the concept of stock without par value, was taken over from American corporate practice and law for the purpose of providing flexibility in corporate financing. The same amendment sought to protect existing shareholders by prohibiting the issuance of shares below a fair price unless existing shareholders were given a pre-emptive right.[74] Although there has been an increase in the number and

[70] Sakamaki v. Kabushiki Kaisha Ogikubo Ichiba (Ogikubo Market Co.), Tokyo High Court, May 2, 1960, 11 KAKYŪ MINSHŪ 965.

[71] Securities Exchange Law, art. 65.

[72] Changes in the methods of corporate financing occurred as follows (in percents):

	1934–1936	*1950*	*1955*	*1960*
Government sources	1.2	12.6	13.0	7.5
Banks	17.9	72.7	68.9	71.2
Bonds	0.5	8.5	3.9	5.2
Shares	80.4	6.2	14.2	16.1

For the regulation of foreign investment, see Ishii, *Japan,* in LEGAL ASPECTS OF FOREIGN INVESTMENT 318 (Friedmann & Pugh eds., 1959).

[73] COMMERCIAL CODE art. 280-2.

[74] COMMERCIAL CODE arts. 280-3, 280-10–280-11.

percentage of shares sold to the public other than existing shareholders,[75] it is still the custom for Japanese corporations always to issue shares to existing shareholders at par regardless of the market price. As a consequence, in Japan the pre-emptive right is of utmost importance to shareholders.

The 1950 amendment also introduced a unique and extremely troublesome requirement that in the articles of association a corporation must provide for the existence of, restriction on, or exclusion of pre-emptive rights to authorized but unissued shares. This is the compromise reached between the occupation authorities, who advocated the recognition of a general pre-emptive right, and the Japanese, who were opposed to it. This new provision was put in issue five years later, when the Tokyo District Court held null and void the most common type of clause in articles of association, giving the shareholders a general pre-emptive right but allowing the board of directors to sell a part of a new issue to the public or to give an option to executives or employees of the corporation. The rationale behind the decision was that, because there was no limit on the number of shares which the board of directors at its discretion might exempt from the general pre-emptive right of the shareholders, the clause was too illusory to fulfill the statutory requirement.[76]

The Diet subsequently took quick action to amend the Commercial Code; under the present law the board of directors may determine whether preemptive rights are to be given to existing shareholders unless otherwise provided by the articles of association.[77] If, however, an option is to be given to persons other than the shareholders, the board must obtain the authorization at a shareholders' meeting. This amended provision relating to the option posed a problem quite recently when the Sony Company entered into an underwriting agreement with investment bankers for the issuance of its shares on the American market; the question was whether an underwriting agreement without shareholder authorization entails giving an option to the underwriters and thus violates the new provision relating to options. Although the *Sony* case did not result in a shareholders' suit because the company obtained shareholder approval when the point was raised, such suits have been brought against other corporations.

Because of the wide distribution of shares and the increase in share transfers, the 1950 amendment introduced the institution of the transfer agent in order to facilitate such transfers. The first professional transfer agent in

[75] The ratio of public issues to "rights" issues in terms of the issue price has been as follows: 1955 — 0.07 percent; 1959 — 2.1 percent; 1960 — 2.4 percent; 1961 (up to July) — 4.3 percent. It is usual to combine a public issue with a "rights" issue, in which event the public issue is generally about 10 percent of the entire issue.

[76] Furukawa v. Denki Kagaku Kōgyō Kabushiki Kaisha (Electrochemical Industrial Co.), Tokyo District Court, Feb 28, 1955, 6 KAKYŪ MINSHŪ 361.

[77] COMMERCIAL CODE art. 280-2, as amended by Law No. 28 of 1955.

Japan began operation in 1954, but by 1961 there were eight, handling stock transfers for some 423 corporations. Also, a few years ago the securities exchanges undertook a pilot operation of keeping stock in a central location to solve the difficulties entailed in the delivery of the tremendous numbers of shares traded on the exchange. Although this operation is so far limited to ten issues, the stock exchanges plan to extend it to all listed issues. Thus the transfer of shares will be further facilitated.

Merger is a special method of corporate finance and is extensively used in Japan. The 1950 amendment gave the shareholders the right of appraisal, affording a dissenting shareholder an opportunity to demand payment for his shares in case of a purchase or sale of the assets of a corporation as well as in case of a merger or consolidation.[78] This provision was modeled after the United States appraisal statutes, but the Japanese law has progressed one step beyond its prototypes in that the right of appraisal is also given to the shareholders of the transferee corporation. In practice, however, no instances have been reported in which payment was made to dissenting shareholders of either the transferee or the transferor corporation, although there have been several cases in which a demand was made.

Disclosure of corporate information before subscription is insufficient under the existing corporation law. A prospectus is not required, the only information given being that in the subscription slip which, except in the case of subscriptions by the promoters, must be included in the subscription contract to render the latter valid. This subscription slip, which is to be prepared by the promoters or directors, must disclose the essential facts required by law,* such as the name, object, and location of the business offices of the corporation; information concerning its capital structure; and the conditions of subscription.[79] The same facts are made public through filing with a competent registry administered by the Ministry of Justice.[80] The information disclosed at the time of filing with this office will not protect a subscriber in the case of preincorporation subscription, however, since the registration can take place only after the subscriptions have been received.

If shares are to be issued in exchange for property other than cash, the name of the subscriber, the description and valuation of the property, and

[78] COMMERCIAL CODE arts. 245-2–45-4, 408-3.

* Makoto Yazawa commented at the conference that the information required is not sufficient to provide a basis for intelligent judgment. Moreover, in Europe, where the same kind of regulation exists, any advantage this technique might possibly have over a prospectus is nullified, Louis Loss noted, by the fact that usually a stock purchaser will have his bank sign the subscription slip, so that he never sees it.

[79] COMMERCIAL CODE arts. 175, 280-6; cf. Securities Act of 1933, Schedule A, paras. 1, 3, 8–9, 11, 17 C.F.R. §230.610a (1), (3), (8), (9), (11) (Supp. 1961).

[80] COMMERCIAL CODE arts. 9, 188. Filing takes place at all Legal Affairs Bureau and Local Legal Affairs Bureau offices, established by the Ministry of Justice, which have jurisdiction over the head and branch offices of the corporation. Non-Litigious Cases Procedure Law, Law No. 14 of 1898, art. 139.

the number of shares allotted to him for the property must also be disclosed in the subscription slips to be furnished to other subscribers; these facts are also subject to investigation by an inspector appointed by the court.[81] The transaction may be modified by court order or by a resolution adopted by an organizational meeting of subscribers. The same system of inspection applies to an agreement by which the corporation acquires property during the process of organization, to arrangements conferring special advantages on any promoters, to organizational expenses to be charged to the corporation, and to the compensation of promoters. These regulations are quite strict, but in practice the promoters will usually engineer the transaction so as to avoid inspection.

The Japanese Securities Exchange Law requires more thorough and effective disclosure by requiring a registration statement and prospectus. The registration procedure and the contents of the statement and prospectus are quite similar to those of the United States Securities Act of 1933. Both provide sanctions, civil and criminal, for misstatements or material omissions.

As regards civil remedies, the Japanese securities law differs from the United States law in that it has no provisions concerning liabilities of underwriters or of directors who sign the registration statement; these problems are left to the Commercial Code or to the general tort rules of the Civil Code.[82] Another difference is that the Japanese courts have not yet been called upon to develop the "implied liability" doctrine, which the federal courts have put into the Securities Exchange Act of the United States, to the effect that one who violates a criminal provision designed to protect a particular class of persons (such as investors) is by implication civilly liable to a member of the class damaged by the violation even though the statute is silent as to civil liability.[83] Indeed, not only has no doctrine of implied civil liability emerged, but the Japanese courts have ruled that the issuance of shares before registration with the Ministry of Finance is not void even if the issuance violates the Securities Exchange Law.[84] Litigation in this area has not proved so attractive in the Japanese system as in the American; so far there have been no reported cases concerning civil liabilities or criminal prosecutions arising out of misstatements or omissions.

These *ex post facto* sanctions, however, are far less effective than the initial scrutiny of the prospectus by an administrative agency in order to assure compliance with registration requirements. In Japan this important task has

[81] Commercial Code arts. 173, 181, 280-8.

[82] See Commercial Code art. 266-3; Civil Code art. 709.

[83] See 3 Loss 1759–97.

[84] E.g., Kawase v. Gōdō Shōken Kabushiki Kaisha (United Securities Co.), Tokyo High Court, Sept. 26, 1956, 7 Kakyū Minshū 2625; Irinaka Shōken Kabushiki Kaisha (Irinaka Securities Co.) v. Furusho, Tokyo District Court, Oct. 4, 1954, 5 Kakyū Minshū 1662; Kyōto Dai Ichi Shōken Kabushiki Kaisha (Kyoto First Securities Co.) v. Imamura, Kyoto District Court, Dec. 16, 1952, 3 Kakyū Minshū 1778.

been entrusted to the Ministry of Finance. Although there has been no formal stop-order case reported, the "deficiency letter" practice has been efficiently used to obtain compliance through informal means, as in the United States, and in practically all cases the issuer will accept the changes in the registration statement and prospectus "suggested" by the Ministry of Finance. It is to be noted that, in Japanese practice, lawyers neither prepare the registration statement nor participate in the negotiations with the Ministry of Finance.

CONCLUSION

The rights and remedies of shareholders introduced by the 1950 amendments to the Commercial Code as well as the new regulations under the Securities Exchange Law have not yet been fully explored by Japanese investors. Although fourteen years have elapsed since the enactment of the law and twelve years since the amendment of the code, few cases have been reported and no stop order or injunction has been issued under the authority of the Securities Exchange Law. The fears that the new shareholders' remedies and rights afforded by corporation law might be used as weapons for blackmail have not so far materialized, but some doubts do exist that these new remedies are workable only in the case of close corporations. Even in such corporations, the shareholders will usually resort to the classical remedies of an action to set aside the resolutions adopted at the shareholders' meeting or of seeking a temporary injunction to prohibit the directors from acting as directors. As far as the new securities regulations are concerned, in spite of a paucity of reported civil, criminal, or administrative enforcement proceedings, the disclosure philosophy has proved to be highly effective when compared with the old regulatory philosophy of corporation law. Annual reports of registered or listed corporations have become very much more informative than ever before through the improvement in accounting standards.

The time is ripe for reappraisal and amendment of the legislation relating to the shareholder-management relation, taking into account past experience and the American roots of these concepts. Indeed, such currents of thought and action are now found within the government and among business groups.

COMPUTATION OF INCOME IN JAPANESE INCOME TAXATION: A STUDY IN THE ADJUSTMENT OF THEORY TO REALITY

Morio Uematsu

ASSISTED BY REX COLEMAN

A TAX system, like other human institutions, must make compromises with the needs of realistic and efficient operation. The best of all possible systems on paper can be one of the worst in practice, for the intricacies involved in its application may go beyond the facilities and the ability of those called upon to administer it. Again, despite the undeniable fact that achievement of tax equity is a highly desirable goal, the realistic demands of national economic policy may dictate the adoption of certain measures antithetical to this ideal. The history of Japanese taxation over the past twelve years has been one long record of just such efforts to adjust pristine theory to hard reality.[1]

On invitation of the Supreme Commander for the Allied Powers, in 1949

Note. Mr. Uematsu is Chief of the Direct Tax Division, Tokyo National Tax Bureau, National Tax Agency. B.Jur., Tokyo Imperial University, 1944; Legal System and Opinion Counselor, Legal System and Opinion Bureau, Attorney General's Office, 1949–1951; Assistant Chief, First Tax System Section, Tax Bureau, Ministry of Finance, 1956–1961; Chief, Temporary Office for Tax Law Reform, Tax Bureau, Ministry of Finance, 1961–1962; Official in Charge of the Japanese Delegation to the United States to Negotiate Tax Treaty Revision, 1960, 1961. Principal writer of ZEISEI CHŌSA KAI (Tax System Investigation Commission), TŌMEN JISSHI-SUBEKI ZEISEI KAISEI NI KAN-SURU TŌSHIN (ZEISEI CHŌSA KAI DAI ICHIJI TŌSHIN) OYOBI SONO SHINGI NO NAIYŌ TO KEIKA NO SETSUMEI (Report Concerning Tax System Revision That Should Be Enforced Immediately (First Report of the Tax System Investigation Commission) and an Explanation of the Content and Progress of Deliberations) (1960), author of various writings in the field of tax law, and contributor to the HŌREI YŌGO JITEN (Dictionary of Terms Used in Laws and Orders) (Sato & Hayashi ed. 1959).

Mr. Coleman is Research Associate in Law, Harvard University, and Editor, World Tax Series, International Program in Taxation, Harvard Law School. A.B., 1951, LL.B., 1955, Stanford University; M.Jur., 1960, Tokyo University.

[1] The remarks contained in this essay describe the income tax system as of June 1, 1962.

and 1950 a body of distinguished American tax scholars visited Japan[2] and prepared two reports recommending a sweeping reconstruction of the Japanese tax system along the lines of what was then the best current American theory on tax policy; both reports have since come to bear the name of the leader of the mission, Professor Carl S. Shoup of Columbia University.[3] The Shoup Reports' outstanding service in the modernization of Japan's tax structure and administration deserves only the highest praise, and without question their rich legacy, even today, molds and shapes every aspect of taxation in Japan. Yet, while we must not fail to render them the great honor that is their proper due, it is equally undeniable that at some points they did make proposals divorced from the concrete needs and practices of Japanese society. This struggle between theory and reality, so characteristic of post-occupation Japanese taxation as a whole, is clearly evidenced in the changes that have subsequently taken place in the Shoup approach to the concepts underlying the computation of income for purposes of income taxation.

Nowhere were the reports more thoroughgoing than in their treatment of income and its computation. Here they sought to carry the global tax system, introduced two years earlier by officials of the occupation, to its logical limits. No distinction was to be made between salaried income and other forms (special measures for various categories of income also being eliminated); every capital gain was to be fully taxed with capital losses fully deductible; and all transfers of assets, even gratuitous ones by gift, bequest, or inheritance, were to be taxable as capital gains.[4]

The Shoup proposals, of course, were not made in a vacuum. Japan had

[2] The members of the mission and their professional affiliations at the time of their trip to Japan were as follows: Dean Howard R. Bowen, College of Commerce and Business, University of Illinois (subsequently President of Grinnell); Professor Jerome B. Cohen, Department of Economics, College of the City of New York; Mr. Rolland F. Hatfield, Director of Tax Research, Department of Taxation, St. Paul, Minnesota; Professor Carl S. Shoup, School of Business and Graduate Faculty of Political Science, Columbia University; Professor Stanley S. Surrey, School of Jurisprudence, University of California (subsequently of Harvard Law School and now [1963] Assistant Secretary of the Treasury); Professor William Vickrey, Graduate Faculty of Political Science, Columbia University; Professor William G. Warren, School of Law, Columbia University (subsequently Dean). Only Professors Shoup, Surrey, Vickrey and Warren actually made the 1950 trip.

Although by no means the first such mission of tax experts to another country, this was probably the first to be composed of so many eminent scholars. For a list of tax missions, see U.N. TECHNICAL ASSISTANCE ADMINISTRATION, TAXES AND FISCAL POLICY IN UNDER-DEVELOPED COUNTRIES 111–18 (E/CN.8/67, ST/TAA/M/8) (1954) and U.N. TECHNICAL ASSISTANCE ADMINISTRATION, TAXES AND FISCAL POLICY IN UNDER-DEVELOPED COUNTRIES, SUPPLEMENTARY LIST OF REPORTS OF TECHNICAL ASSISTANCE MISSIONS TO UNDER-DEVELOPED COUNTRIES IN THE FIELD OF PUBLIC FINANCE (ST/TAA/M/8/Add.1) (1961).

[3] SHOUP MISSION TO THE SUPREME COMMANDER FOR THE ALLIED POWERS, REPORT ON JAPANESE TAXATION (Tokyo 1949) [hereafter cited FIRST SHOUP REPORT]; SHOUP MISSION TO THE SUPREME COMMANDER FOR THE ALLIED POWERS, SECOND REPORT ON JAPANESE TAXATION (Tokyo 1950) [hereafter cited SECOND SHOUP REPORT].

[4] Aside from the Shoup Reports themselves, a summary of the Shoup recommendations is given in Sundelson, *Report on Japanese Taxation by the Shoup Mission*, 3 NAT'L TAX J. 104 (1950).

had more than sixty years of experience with the income tax when Shoup and his associates arrived upon the scene. Accordingly, before going into a discussion of the state of income computation in Japan today and the current significance of the Shoup recommendations, it would seem well to insert a few words concerning what had gone before.

History of Income Taxation in Japan

National Income Taxation

The Meiji leaders did not ignore the tax field in their general ardor for borrowing new ideas from the forefront of advanced Western thought. To these men, engaged in the almost insurmountable tasks of "nation building," the income tax seemed a most attractive source of additional revenue.[5] Thus, in 1887[6] Japan became one of the first states in the world to possess a national income tax.[7] The tax enforced was completely global in structure, but the progression in rates went from only 1 to 3 percent, with the result that only meager amounts of revenue were raised.[8] Furthermore, no provision was made for the individual characteristics of the taxpayer or for the presence of dependents.[9]

[5] For a good account of the financial difficulties of the early Meiji government see SMITH, POLITICAL CHANGE AND INDUSTRIAL DEVELOPMENT IN JAPAN: GOVERNMENT ENTERPRISE, 1868–1880, at 72–85 (1955).

[6] Income Tax Law of 1887, Imperial Order No. 5 of 1887.

[7] The only states to introduce an income tax before Japan were Great Britain (1799), Switzerland (1840), Prussia (1851), the United States (1862), Italy (1864), Serbia (1884), and South Australia (1884). This list is based on that given in SHIOMI, JAPAN'S FINANCE AND TAXATION 1940–1956, at 139–41 (1957), but Prussia, which was omitted by Shiomi, has been added.

[8] In 1887 the income tax produced 527,724 yen (406,347 dollars) and in 1888 1,066,894 yen (789,502 dollars) — 0.8 and 1.8 percent of the total tax revenues for these years respectively. By comparison, the revenue from the land tax in the same two years was 42,152,171 yen (32,457,172 dollars) and 34,650,528 yen (25,641,391 dollars). 6 MEIJI TAISHŌ ZAISEI SHI (A History of Meiji-Taisho Public Finance) 530–32 (Ōkura-shō (Ministry of Finance) ed. 1937). The dollar-yen rate of exchange is taken from ANDO, GAIKOKU KAWASE GAIRON (A General Treatise on Foreign Exchange) app. Table 11 (1957).

[9] A complete history of the development of Japan's tax system from the Meiji era on will be found in Japanese in WATANABE, ZEI NO RIRON TO JISSAI (Tax Theory and Actuality), 1 JISSAI HEN (Actuality Part) 173–273 (1956), and of national income taxation since its inception in English in SHIOMI, note 7, at 113–49. An English-language account of the first income tax is also available in Ikeda, *The Establishment of the Income Tax in Japan (A Historical and Sociological Study)*, 12 PUBLIC FINANCE 145 (1957). The entire language of all the Income Tax Laws from Imperial Order No. 5 of 1887 to Law No. 8 of 1926 and the various orders thereunder, as well as relevant commentary, may be found in 6 MEIJI TAISHŌ ZAISEI SHI, note 8, at 977–1221. Similar information is available for the Income Tax Law of 1940, Law No. 24 of 1940, and the Juridical Persons' Tax Law of the same year, Law No. 25 of 1940, in 5 SHŌWA ZAISEI SHI (A History of Showa Public Finance) 491–590, 779–803, 806–13 (Ōkura-shō Shōwa Zaisei Shi Henshū-shitsu (Ministry of Finance History of Showa Public Finance Editorial Office) ed. 1957). Also a summary of all substantive changes in the Income Tax Law and the Juridical Persons' Tax Law, including rates, is given in chart form in 1 SHUZEI KYOKU (Tax Bureau), ŌKURA-SHŌ (Ministry of Finance), NAIKOKU ZEI NO KAZEI HYŌJUN, ZEIRITSU OYOBI NŌKI TŌ NI KAN-SURU ENKAKU TEKIYŌ (A Historical Résumé Concerning the Tax Base, Tax Rate and Time of Payment, Etc., of Domestic Taxes) 1–187 (1954).

An interesting point is that, since a systematic organization of legal entities had not yet been established (the first Commercial Code of 1890 still being in the future), the tax applied only to the income of natural persons. Corporate bodies were not to escape long, though, for the sudden rise in capitalism following the nation's victory in the Sino-Japanese War (1894–1895) generated a new Income Tax Law of 1899 with expanded coverage to include all juridical persons (corporations).[10] However, this statute did seek to avoid "double taxation" of the same increment of income by both the corporate and personal taxes through a provision exempting dividends from taxation.[11] It had another aspect also, which was of no less significance from the standpoint of Japanese tax history than the innovation of the corporate taxpayer; it first introduced "withholding" — a tax on interest from public and private bonds becoming subject to collection at source.[12]

Emerging from the First World War as one of the victors, Japan found itself not only ranked among the "great powers" of the world, but a nation saddled with ever-increasing expenditures to meet new demands, such as the expansion of armaments. In order to provide sufficient revenue to satisfy the state's fiscal needs, in 1920 the income tax was completely revised[13] and the maximum progressive rate raised to a new high of 36 percent.[14] There was also an attempt to make the structure more equitable and responsive to the peculiar situation of each taxpayer by the establishment for the first time of a system of deductions for dependents.[15] The continued rapid development of corporate enterprise was taken into account by repealing the nontaxation of dividends received by individuals and by specifying that henceforth these

[10] Law No. 17 of 1899, arts. 1, 3; translated into English in MOGAMI, *The Income Tax Law*, in THE REVISED TAX LAWS OF JAPAN 1–14 (1913). Regarding the concept of "juridical persons," see the essay by Makoto Yazawa, "The Legal Structure for Corporate Enterprise: Shareholder-Management Relations Under Japanese Law," note 6, in this volume.

[11] Income Tax Law of 1899, arts. 4(2), 5(vii).

[12] *Ibid.*, arts. 3, 4(ii), 42(2).

[13] Income Tax Law of 1920, Law No. 11 of 1920; translated into English in DE BECKER, JAPANESE INCOME TAX LAW (1926), and SEBALD, *The Income Tax Law*, in THE PRINCIPAL TAX LAWS OF JAPAN 1–29 (1938). A commentary in English on the provisions of this statute will be found in DE BECKER, A SURVEY OF SOME JAPANESE TAX LAWS 1–20 (1931).

[14] Income Tax Law of 1920, art. 23(1). The increase to 36 percent was, of course, the culmination of a number of gradual increases over the years. These changes in the maximum rate and the statutes enacting them were as follows (the dollar-yen rate of exchange is from ANDO, note 8, app. Table 11): 3 percent of 30,000 yen (22,314 dollars) income or more (Imperial Order No. 5 of 1887), 5.5 percent of 100,000 yen (49,630 dollars) income or more (Law No. 17 of 1899), 9.35 percent of 100,000 yen (48,940 dollars) income or more (Law No. 3 of 1904), 20.35 percent of 100,000 yen (49,120 dollars) income or more (Law No. 1 of 1905), 22 percent of 100,000 yen (49,380 dollars) income or more (Law No. 13 of 1913), 30 percent of 200,000 yen (103,000 dollars) income or more (Law No. 5 of 1918), and 36 percent of 4,000,000 yen (1,967,600 dollars) income or more (Law No. 11 of 1920). In 1920 the maximum United States federal personal income tax rate was 73 percent of 1,000,000 dollars income or more (Revenue Act of 1918, ch. 18, §§210–11, 40 Stat. 1057), but by 1926 this had been reduced to 25 percent of 100,000 dollars income or more (Revenue Act of 1926, ch. 27, §§210–11, 44 Stat. 9).

[15] Income Tax Law of 1920, art. 16.

sums should be subject to the global levy imposed by the personal income tax at the individual shareholder level — certain special deductions being allowed.[16] Moreover, a second form of tax base was added for entities with the introduction of an "excess income" (excess profits) tax on juridical persons.[17] Income received by the juridical person was carved up into brackets fixed at a percentage of its stated capital, and the excess income tax was then imposed at a progressive rate on income falling within these brackets. This formula remained, in essence, a feature of Japanese corporate income taxation until it was finally abolished pursuant to the Shoup Reports. The 1920 statute confirmed the position of the income tax as a permanent feature of the tax system and made it Japan's largest single revenue-producing tax: receipts collected under the heading "income tax" (including both corporate and personal taxation) accounted for more than 20 percent of the total national tax revenue.[18]

Throughout the following years, the world darkened day by day, with signs of upheaval leading the way to crisis and a breakdown in the "Versailles order." Inside Japan the influence of the militarists grew in strength; in 1931 the pressure of chronic depression brought the "Manchurian incident," and in 1937 the force of circumstances resulted in the outbreak of the "China incident." In this setting, at first several successive tax reductions were enacted as a link in the retrenchment policy of the temporary period of reaction immediately following the First World War, but later the gradual shift of the economy from a semiwar footing to full wartime status, ending at last in the final catastrophe of the Pacific war, brought one tax increase after another.

For two decades the basic format established in 1920 remained substantially unchanged, but in 1940, on the eve of the Pacific conflict, a major tax revision was carried out at both the central and local levels to prepare the nation's finances for war.[19] Together with the subsequent alteration inspired by Shoup, the 1940 changes formed one of the two most far-reaching tax reforms in modern Japanese history. The tax on entities was transformed into a new independent "juridical persons' tax,"[20] while the term "income tax," in a formal legal sense, came to mean only the tax imposed on individuals.[21]

[16] *Ibid.*, art. 14(1) (v).

[17] *Ibid.*, arts. 5, 21(1)A.

[18] 1920 revenue from the income tax was 190,344,151 yen (93,630,288 dollars) and from all national taxes 660,329,546 yen (324,816,104 dollars). 6 MEIJI TAISHŌ ZAISEI SHI, note 8, at 538–40; ANDO, note 8, app. Table 11.

[19] For a more thoroughgoing description of the 1940 changes, see Shiomi, *The Reform of the Tax System*, 15 KYOTO U. ECON. REV. no. 2, at 36–52 (1940).

[20] Juridical Persons' Tax Law of 1940, Law No. 25 of 1940; translated into English in 4 TOKYO GAZETTE 252, 296 (1940–1941).

[21] Income Tax Law of 1940, Law No. 24 of 1940; translated into English in OVERSEAS DEPARTMENT, DOMEI TSUSHIN SHA, *Income Tax Law*, in WARTIME LEGISLATION IN JAPAN 200–63 (1941) and 3 TOKYO GAZETTE 493 (1940), 4 TOKYO GAZETTE 34, 85, 125, 166, 207 (1940).

The outstanding change in the personal income tax was the adoption of a bipolar system, similar to that found in France at the time, which employed schedular taxes and a unitary or global tax simultaneously.[22] Under the schedular income tax concept, different deductions and rates are established for various types of income classified according to their particular nature; on the other hand, a unitary or global tax unites all forms of income into one grand total, so that the taxpayer's ability to pay relative to the amount of his income may be taken into account, and then applies a progressive rate to the portion exceeding a certain specified minimum. From quite an early time, the idea had been vigorously held in Japan that ability to pay differs with the type of income — it is strongest with income from assets (capital), stronger with business income from assets and labor combined, and weakest with earned income — and that in taxing income classified rates should be established to take these distinctions into consideration. Pursuant to this line of thinking, taxes on profits, such as the land tax, house tax, enterprise profits tax, and interest from capital tax, were treated as levies supplementary to the income tax. Actually, though, the principal reason for adopting this form of income tax was to assure revenue elasticity; whenever required, the needs of wartime finance could be met through raising the proportional rates of the schedular taxes.[23] This revision also expanded the withholding system to cover wages in accordance with the large increase that had taken place in the number of wage-earning taxpayers, laying the cornerstone for the highly complex system of today.[24] It is interesting to note that the United States introduced the same form of system in 1943,[25] while Britain set up its P.A.Y.E. contemporaneously with Japan in 1940.[26]

Despite the fact that the course of the war was marked year after year by a steady spiral upward in tax rates, before the cessation of hostilities no alteration was made in the fundamental principles underlying the system itself. The radical change in conditions following hard upon the nation's defeat naturally meant, however, that the tax structure carried forward

[22] *Ibid.*, arts. 10–33. On the former French system, which was substantially revised in 1959, see WORLD TAX SERIES, TAXATION IN FRANCE 5/1.1 (to be published in early 1964). This system is also common among Latin American countries. For example, COMMISSION TO STUDY THE FISCAL SYSTEM OF VENEZUELA, THE FISCAL SYSTEM OF VENEZUELA: A REPORT 87–111 (Shoup ed. 1959).

[23] Income tax, juridical persons' tax and total tax receipts in 1941, rounded to the nearest thousand, were as follows: 1,401,363,000 yen (328,479,000 dollars), 530,782,000 yen (124,-415,000 dollars) and 4,930,526,000 yen (1,155,715,000 dollars). This, however, did not constitute all 1941 national revenue of an income tax nature since several extraordinary and special taxes on various types of profit were also in effect. 5 SHŌWA ZAISEI SHI, note 9, Materials II pt. at 10; ANDO, note 8, app. Table 11.

Also, in 1940 the maximum rate of the global tax reached 65 percent of 800,000 yen (187,520 dollars) income or more. Income Tax Law of 1940, art. 33(1).

[24] Income Tax Law of 1940, art. 72.

[25] INT. REV. CODE OF 1939, §§1621–32, added by ch. 120, §2(a), 57 Stat. 126 (1943).

[26] Finance Act, 1940, 3 & 4 Geo. 5, c.48, §11. Also see WORLD TAX SERIES, TAXATION IN THE UNITED KINGDOM 2/2.5, 8/1.18 (1957).

through wartime was fated for major modification, and such a reform did finally materialize two years after the surrender. This 1947 revision, formulated under the guidance of the occupation forces, had a strong American flavor to it.[27] It abolished the bipolar schedular-unitary tax of 1940 and replaced it with a purely global tax with highly progressive rates.[28] The change was justified on various grounds: successive increases during and after the war had stretched the rates of the schedular taxes—originally thought to be rich in elasticity—to their breaking point, resulting in a loss of the elasticity function; and different taxation of varying categories of income could not escape the criticism of being founded upon strictly arbitrary distinctions. Global taxation was strengthened and expanded structurally by providing for the unified taxation of all income, including capital gains[29] and windfall or casual receipts,[30] while at the same time a technique was adopted to soften the effect of progressive taxation upon irregular income.[31] Moreover, the United States plan of taxing income on a current basis[32] replaced the prior Japanese policy of imposing tax on income of the year before,[33] and the celebrated American "self-assessment" system[34] superseded the traditional method of government assessment and collection.[35] Finally, the introduction of detailed tax tables for withholding at source on wages and the year-end adjustment device[36] built a guaranty into the system that taxes

[27] Income Tax Law, Law No. 27 of 1947, translated into English in OFFICIAL GAZETTE, March 31, 1947, extra no. 2 at 1; Juridical Persons' Tax Law, Law No. 28 of 1947, translated into English in OFFICIAL GAZETTE, March 31, 1947, extra no. 2 at 32. A more detailed account of the 1947 reform, presented from the occupation viewpoint, may be found in Shavell, *Taxation Reform in Occupied Japan*, 1 NAT'L TAX J. 127 (1948).

[28] Income Tax Law, arts. 9–15, prior to amendment by Law No. 142 of 1947.

[29] *Ibid.*, art. 9(1)(vii), prior to amendment by Law No. 142 of 1947.

[30] *Ibid.*, art. 9(1)(viii), as amended by Law No. 142 of 1947, but prior to amendment by Law No. 107 of 1948.

[31] *Ibid.*, art. 9(1)(iii), (v)–(vii), prior to amendment by Law No. 142 of 1947.

[32] *Ibid.*, arts. 30–43, prior to amendment by Law No. 142 of 1947.

[33] Income Tax Law of 1940, arts. 12(1), 30(1).

[34] Income Tax Law, arts. 21–36, prior to amendment by Law No. 142 of 1947; Juridical Persons' Tax Law, arts. 18–25, prior to amendment by Law No. 107 of 1948.

[35] Income Tax Law of 1940, arts. 34–39; Juridical Persons' Tax Law of 1940, arts. 18–19, 22. Strictly speaking, Japan had had some limited experience with self-assessment prior to 1947. In 1945, immediately before the end of the war, because of the shortage of government tax personnel, a form of self-assessment was adopted for certain large companies in order to handle accelerated tax collections.

[36] Income Tax Law, art. 40, prior to amendment by Law No. 142 of 1947. The "year-end adjustment" device is a system whereby an employer is required to make adjustments at the end of each calendar year, based on materials furnished him by his employees, for individual differences between the amount of tax withheld from wages under the detailed tables and the actual tax liability of his employees, thus eliminating the need, so far as possible, for refunds or further assessment. For a short explanation of its operation, see TAX BUREAU, MINISTRY OF FINANCE, AN OUTLINE OF JAPANESE TAX 1962 at 76–80 (1962). West Germany possesses a similar year-end adjustment system, but it was not enforced until 1949. WORLD TAX SERIES, TAXATION IN THE FEDERAL REPUBLIC OF GERMANY 8/1.5a (1963), and 2 BLÜMICH-FALK, EINKOMMENSTEUERGESETZ 1789–92 (8th ed. 1960).

would be computed and paid correctly, thus freeing tax-paying wage earners from the intricacies of self-assessment.

The 1947 changes completely recast the language and organization of the Income Tax Law and Juridical Persons' Tax Law in a new framework. Although these statutes have been amended innumerable times since — so much so that in many areas the original 1947 content can scarcely be discerned — the formal basic make-up determined at that time still governs Japan today. But, even though 1947 clothed the arrangement of tax law in new dress, it neglected to lower taxes. The rapid advance of postwar inflation automatically increased the burden of the income tax, while the juridical persons' tax bore down ever more heavily on corporate income computed in accordance with pre-inflation book values. The whole nation watched and waited for a reduction in taxes and a fundamental reformation of the system itself. In 1949 and 1950, SCAP commissioned Shoup and his associates to propose a remedy for this situation.[37]

Initially, the tax structure was rebuilt from top to bottom in accordance with the Shoup design. However, not long thereafter, the practice of imposing amendment after amendment upon the original legislation began, a trend which has not yet fully run its course even at this late date.[38] "Repeated tax reduction and reconstruction of the Shoup plan" has characterized the route taken by the tax system, but it still remains impossible to discuss the state of taxation in present-day Japan without considering the Shoup proposals. Therefore, an account of the mission's recommendations as they affect computation of income will be deferred until the general discussion of that topic.

[37] Prior to the Shoup amendments, the maximum personal income tax rate was 85 percent on 5,000,000 yen (13,889 dollars) or more. Income Tax Law, art. 13(1), prior to amendment by Law No. 71 of 1950. Commensurate with the enactment of a wealth tax, this was dropped to 55 percent of 500,000 yen (1,389 dollars) or more (by Law No. 71 of 1950), but abolition of that tax meant another raise in the upper brackets. Today (June 1, 1962), it stands at 75 percent of 60,000,000 yen (166,667 dollars) or more. Income Tax Law, art. 13(1).

In 1951, rounded to the nearest million, the income tax generated 225,672,000,000 yen (627,000,000 dollars), the juridical persons' tax 183,881,000,000 yen (511,000,000 dollars), and all national taxes 723,144,000,000 yen (2,009,000,000 dollars). For fiscal year 1962, these same figures are estimated at 497,933,000,000 yen (1,383,000,000 dollars), 699,964,000,000 yen (1,944,000,000 dollars), and 2,232,848,000,000 yen (6,202,000,000 dollars) respectively. SHUZEI KYOKU (Tax Bureau), ŌKURA-SHŌ (Ministry of Finance), ZEISEI SHUYŌ SANKŌ SHIRYŌ SHŪ 1962 (A Collection of Major Tax System Reference Materials 1962) 17–18 (1962). (All dollar amounts are computed at the official rate of 360 yen to the dollar.)

For a more extensive discussion of the current state of tax revenues and burdens in Japan, the reader should refer to UEMATSU, THE INCOME TAX SYSTEM OF JAPAN AND ITS ADMINISTRATION (Coleman ed. & trans., in preparation at the International Program in Taxation, Harvard Law School).

[38] Bronfenbrenner and Kogiku have carefully recorded the subsequent changes made in the Shoup plan through 1956, but their analysis of the underlying causes is open to question on a number of points. Bronfenbrenner and Kogiku, *The Aftermath of the Shoup Tax Reforms* (pts. 1–2), 10 NAT'L TAX J. 236, 345 (1957). A commentary will be found in UEMATSU, note 37.

Local Income Taxation

Income taxation in Japan is not only a national measure but also a local one, for it takes place on the prefectural and municipal level in the form of an "inhabitants' tax" and a "business activity tax." [39] The origin of the former goes back, even prior to the inception of the national income tax, to the creation of the "household rate" as a prefectural impost in 1878.[40] After ten years its benefits were extended to the municipalities, which were authorized to impose a tax supplement on top of the amount levied by the prefectures,[41] and in 1926 it was converted into a purely municipal tax.[42] The household rate was assessed on the head of a house or persons having an independent livelihood apart from the house.[43] At first the assessment was made by the tax officials in accordance with the antiquated technique of merely estimating what they thought proper,[44] but later they took into account the resources of the taxpayer and his family — the computation being based on the amount of the family's income, the floor space of the

[39] A complete compilation of all Japanese local tax statutes, orders, and numerous other related materials between 1868 and 1953 may be found in the seven volumes of JICHICHŌ (Autonomy Agency), CHIHŌ ZEI SEIDO SHIRYŌ (Local Tax System Materials) (1961). Local tax legislation, with extensive commentary and statistics, is also given in 7 MEIJI TAISHŌ ZAISEI SHI, note 8, at 1049–1224 (1878 to 1926) and 14 SHŌWA ZAISEI SHI, note 9 (1926 to 1946). For a careful collection of tax legislation prior to 1868 see SOZEI KYOKU (Tax Bureau), ŌKURA-SHŌ (Ministry of Finance), DAI NIPPON SOZEI SHI (Great Japan Record of Taxes) (1926).

[40] Local Tax Regulations of 1878, Great Council of State Decree No. 19 of 1878, art. 1. The household rate can even be traced back prior to 1878 through the "civil duties" of early Meiji to the town and village "dues" of the Tokugawa period. During Tokugawa, besides the taxation imposed by the Bakufu or the feudal lords within their respective domains, local municipal bodies assessed a variety of "dues" (*nyūhi*) to meet their particular needs. These dues might be determined at a specified rate household by household or according to either the amount of or the recorded yield of land held by a household. After the Restoration, the municipalities continued to meet their revenue requirements in this fashion, while the new prefectures, established in the Bakufu territory in 1868 and in place of the former fiefs in 1871, finding that the "prefectural taxes" allocated to them by the state were insufficient, imitated the municipalities and initiated the imposition of similar levies. About 1872 the municipal dues began to be referred to as "civil duties" (*mimpi*), and in the following year this term was extended to include all prefectural imposts other than national treasury grants and "prefectural taxes." It was employed in contradistinction to "official duties" (*kampi*) or the various legal "taxes" imposed by the state and its subdivisions. Thus, civil duties gathered for strictly local purposes were regarded as funds raised for the private benefit of the people and not the official objectives of the state. The Local Tax Regulations of 1878 expressly replaced the "prefectural taxes" and civil duties with a new system of "local taxes." 7 MEIJI TAISHŌ ZAISEI SHI, note 8, at 1049–55; MEIJI BUNKA SHI: HŌSEI HEN (A History of Meiji Culture: The Legal System) 174–77 (Ishii ed. 1954). Also see note 56 below.

[41] Organization of Cities, Law No. 1 of 1888, arts. 90, 123(vii); Organization of Towns and Villages, Law No. 1 of 1888, arts. 90, 127(vii).

[42] Law Concerning Local Taxes, Law No. 24 of 1926, art. 22.

[43] Local Tax Regulations, Great Council of State Decree No. 16 of 1880, art. 1; Notes on the Local Tax Regulations, Ministry of Home Affairs Communication of May 27, 1880, art. 1; Law Concerning Local Taxes, art. 23.

[44] Notes on the Local Tax Regulations, art. 1.

family's dwelling, and the state of the family's assets.[45] Eventually, those few municipalities in which it was difficult to assess the rate were authorized to replace it with a supplement on the national income tax, provided they obtained the approval of the Ministers of Finance and Home Affairs.[46]

In 1940, one segment of the tax reform enacted in that year called for a municipal inhabitants' tax to take the place of the rate, its scope being expanded to cover, besides the former taxpayers, the business offices of individuals and juridical persons.[47] In the beginning this tax was, for the most part, a broad per-capita levy on all inhabitants, but during the war, in order to increase revenue, more and more it came to take ability to pay into account. Finally in 1946, shortly after the end of the conflict, an identical prefectural tax was instituted.[48]

Shoup recommended that the inhabitants' tax be restricted to the municipalities and that it contain both a per-capita and an income element, the latter constituting a local income tax.[49] These proposals were enacted and the amount imposed was considerably increased in order that the tax might function as the principal source of city, town, and village tax revenue.[50] Liability encompassed "inhabitants" in an extremely broad sense.[51] In the taxation of individuals the municipalities were permitted to select from among several alternative tax bases founded upon either national income or the amount of national income tax. With juridical persons the impost was first set at a fixed per-capita amount,[52] but a year later, in 1951, a rate applied against the amount of juridical persons' tax due was added.[53] Also, in

[45] Law Concerning Local Taxes, arts. 24–27; Matter Concerning Enforcement of the Law Concerning Local Taxes, Imperial Order No. 339 of 1926, arts. 21–24; Enforcement Regulations of the Law Concerning Local Taxes, Ministries of Finance and Home Affairs Order of Nov. 27, 1926, art. 20.

[46] Law Concerning Limitation of Local Taxes, Law No. 37 of 1908, art. 3(3), as amended by Law No. 25 of 1926.

[47] Local Tax Law of 1940, Law No. 60 of 1940, arts. 63(1), 64. Apparently the title originally adopted for this tax, *shi-chō-son minzei* which we have translated in English as "municipal inhabitants' tax," was meant to be a Japanese version of the German term *Bürgersteuer* and possibly might be rendered more exactly as "citizens' tax." The statutes still employ *minzei,* whether for prefectures (*to-dō-fu-ken*) or municipalities (*shi-chō-son*), but general usage has come to refer to the prefectural and municipal taxes together as the "inhabitants' tax" (*jūmin zei*). Since from its inception it has applied to all inhabitants, whether citizens or not, and the Japanese word *min* is somewhat vague in meaning, in an attempt to avoid increasing the reader's confusion I have decided to translate the name of the tax in all its various forms as "inhabitants' tax."

On the 1940 local tax reforms generally, see Shiomi, *The Reform of the Local Tax System* (pts. 1–2), 16 KYOTO U. ECON. REV. no. 3, at 51; no. 4, at 42 (1941).

[48] Local Tax Law of 1940, art. 48-2, as amended by Law No. 16 of 1946.

[49] 2 FIRST SHOUP REPORT 182–87; SECOND SHOUP REPORT 15–16, 88–92.

[50] Local Tax Law, Law No. 226 of 1950, arts. 292–340, prior to amendment by Law No. 95 of 1951; translated into English in OFFICIAL GAZETTE, July 31, 1950, extra no. 94 at 1.

[51] *Ibid.*, art. 294, prior to amendment by Law No. 95 of 1951.

[52] *Ibid.*, art. 311, prior to amendment by Law No. 95 of 1951.

[53] *Ibid.*, art. 313, as amended by Law No. 95 of 1951.

the same year, a form of withholding against individuals was introduced.[54] 1954 brought another major change when, in a reallocation of the sources of tax revenue among local governments, a portion of the municipal tax was cut away to create a new prefectural inhabitants' tax.[55]

Somewhat more restricted in the sort of income taxable, but equally as old as the inhabitants' tax, is the business activity tax, which can also be traced back to 1878 when the prefectures first imposed an "enterprise tax" on various forms of commercial activity—taxpayers including from the very outset both natural and juridical persons.[56] A little later, cities, towns, and villages were authorized to place a tax supplement on top of this prefectural impost.[57] In 1896 the tax was split into a national tax on various major industries (subsequently called the "enterprise profits tax"),[58] subject to a tax supplement levied by the prefectures and municipalities,[59] and a local tax (retaining the old name) for all other forms of industry. The enterprise profits tax was required to use the amount of business profit as its base,[60] but the local enterprise tax could employ either a fixed amount or flat rates founded on certain external standards, such as sales, number of employees, building rent, and capital.[61]

[54] *Ibid.*, art. 321-3, as amended by Law No. 95 of 1951.

[55] *Ibid.*, arts. 23–71-6, as amended by Law No. 95 of 1954.

[56] Local Tax Regulations of 1878, art. 1; Sorts of and Restrictions on the Enterprise Tax and Miscellaneous Taxes Among Local Taxes, Great Council of State Decree No. 39 of 1878, art. 1. Also, as in the case of the household rate (note 40 above), this tax actually antedates its official establishment in 1878. In the Tokugawa period taxes imposed by the Bakufu and daimyō were classed as land taxes, miscellaneous taxes, and labor services. Among the miscellaneous taxes were included innumerable "offerings" (*myōga*) and "donations" (*unjō*) required to be paid by merchants associated in the same sort of business or for various kinds of business operations, supposedly in thanks for the benevolence of their lord in permitting them to carry on nonproductive activities. A list of these taxes which number over a thousand, given province by province, may be found in 2 Dai Nippon Sozei Shi, note 39, at 450–516, while a general account of their nature appears in Honjo, *Views in the Taxation on Commerce in the Closing Days of Tokugawa Age,* 16 Kyoto U. Econ. Rev. no. 3, at 1 (1941). The new Meiji government decreed in its first year, 1868, that other than the land taxes, donations and offerings affecting sake and soy sauce, and national services, all former Bakufu and fief taxes should be levied by the prefectures (and until 1871, fiefs). These taxes, although unaltered in substance after the Tokugawa period, came to be known as "prefectural taxes" (*fu-ken zei*) and were finally repealed by the Local Tax Regulations of 1878. Clearly the enterprise tax enacted by these regulations merely served to continue the old "donations" and "offerings." 7 Meiji Taishō Zaisei Shi, note 9, at 1049–55.

[57] Organization of Cities Law, arts. 90, 123(vii); Organization of Towns and Villages Law, arts. 90, 127(vii).

[58] Enterprise Tax Law of 1896, Law No. 33 of 1896, translated into English in Mogami, note 10, 25–33; Enterprise Profits Tax Law, Law No. 11 of 1926, translated into English in Sebald, The Principal Tax Laws of Japan 56–63 (1938). A commentary on this statute appears in De Becker, A Survey of Some Japanese Tax Laws 24–35 (1931).

[59] Enterprise Tax Law of 1896, art. 36.

[60] Enterprise Profits Tax Law, art. 3. Prior to the enactment of this statute in 1926, the national tax also employed external standards.

[61] Law Concerning Local Taxes, art. 18; Matter Concerning Enforcement of the Law Concerning Local Taxes, art. 14; Enforcement Regulations of the Law Concerning Local Taxes, art. 2.

The two taxes were recombined in 1940 into a single enterprise tax collected by the nation on behalf of local governments (the receipts later being "restored" to local government),[62] and, at the same time, a system of tax supplements, directly imposed by the local government, was instituted.[63] Net profits from business became the tax base and have so remained to the present day.[64] After the war, the tax once again took the form of an independent prefectural impost,[65] and in 1948 its name was changed to the "business activity tax."[66] Today, it covers not only the traditional forms of business enterprise, but also the free professions — medicine, law, and so on.[67] Shoup suggested that it be replaced by a value-added tax,[68] but in the end his proposals failed to bear fruit.[69]

GENERAL ASPECTS OF THE INCOME TAX SYSTEM

The Legal Basis

Nationally the fundamental legislation governing the income tax and the juridical persons' tax is contained in an Income Tax Law and a Juridical Persons' Tax Law imposing the taxes; a National Tax Common Provisions Law[70] specifying certain general rules for all national taxes; a Tax Special Measures Law[71] dealing with short-term policy measures affecting taxation (principally the income and juridical persons' taxes); a National Tax Collection Law[72] fixing collection procedures; and a National Tax Violations Control Law[73] containing the principles applicable to tax crimes. These basic rules, following the pattern of most Japanese statutes, are filled out by supplementary legal provisions prescribed in cabinet orders (established by the Cabinet) and ministerial orders (issued by the Minister of Finance).[74]

[62] Enterprise Tax Law, Law No. 33 of 1940.

[63] Local Tax Law of 1940, arts. 44, 57.

[64] Enterprise Tax Law, arts. 3–4.

[65] By Law No. 29 of 1947.

[66] Local Tax Law of 1948, Law No. 110 of 1948, arts. 46, 63; translated into English in OFFICIAL GAZETTE, July 7, 1948, extra no. 1 at 100.

[67] Local Tax Law, art. 72.

[68] 2 FIRST SHOUP REPORT 197–204; SECOND SHOUP REPORT 17–19.

[69] Local Tax Law, arts. 23–74, originally provided for a value-added tax, but enforcement was postponed. Finally, by Law No. 95 of 1954, these provisions were repealed without ever actually having come into operation. See Bronfenbrenner, *The Japanese Value-Added Sales Tax,* 3 NAT'L TAX J. 298 (1950).

[70] Law No. 66 of 1962.

[71] Law No. 26 of 1957.

[72] Law No. 147 of 1959.

[73] Law No. 67 of 1900.

[74] Cabinet and ministerial orders prescribe in statute-like language the particulars for executing the provisions of a law and certain matters delegated by the law. Although normally a cabinet order is established directly under a law and then a ministerial order under the cabinet order, a ministerial order may also exist immediately under a law. As long as the law fails to specify expressly the manner in which the mandate is conferred, there is no clear line of demarcation between the respective areas of competence for cabinet and ministerial orders, but in most cases ministerial orders deal with procedural details and other items too minor for cabinet orders.

Tax law has undergone a remarkable change in its make-up since the end of World War II. Before the war, laws and orders were written in a peculiar formal style known as "literary language," which was entirely different from the popular spoken tongue, while an attempt was made to formulate laws as concisely as possible. They settled only the broad features of a topic as a whole—provision of concrete rules was delegated first to imperial orders (equivalent to today's cabinet orders) and from them to ministerial orders (however, orders too were subject to the general idea that skill in draftsmanship required conciseness and brevity). During the occupation, the American authorities strongly criticized this sort of "continental" legislation. At every turn they pursued the thesis that an unflagging effort should be made to squeeze shut all openings for a delegation to orders while filling out the statutes in the smallest possible detail. This approach conformed to the spirit of the new Constitution which states that the National Diet is "the sole lawmaking organ of the State."[75] Although at the time Japanese experts in legislation deplored this practice—deeming it destructive of the character of laws and orders as deeply meaningful and extremely discerning instruments carefully prepared by highly qualified legislative technicians—law in Japan was rewritten on a grand scale in accordance with the policy of General Headquarters, SCAP.

Tax law was caught in the very center of the torrent. Together with the other major features of postwar taxation, such as the unprecedented public consciousness regarding tax legislation stirred up by the heavy tax burden, expansion of the democratic movement away from authoritarian administrative practices, and ever more intensive study of the various facets of the system, the incredibly detailed and complex provisions of the written law mark a startling change from conditions before the war.[76] Without doubt

[75] CONST. art. 41.

[76] The following, which is the first of five paragraphs in art. 9-6 of the Juridical Persons' Tax Law, is typical of provisions existing in present day Japanese tax statutes:

"Where a juridical person in any business period has received from a domestic juridical person (excluding associations, etc., without personality; hereinafter the same in this article and article 17, paragraph (3), item (ii)) a dividend, a distribution of surplus, or a distribution of the gains of a securities investment trust (excluding public and company bond investment trusts; hereinafter the same in this paragraph), if, in a return pursuant to the provisions of articles 18 through 21 or article 22-2, or a late return, in which has been entered the matters provided for in these provisions, a declaration is entered (including in the situation where a declaration has not been entered, when it is recognized by the Government that there are special circumstances for not entering the declaration) regarding the amounts received due to the said dividend or distribution of surplus or the amounts, within an amount received due to the distribution of the gains of a securities investment trust, computed in the way prescribed by Order as pertaining to dividends or distributions of surplus that are received from a domestic juridical person (if the stock, investment, or beneficiary securities constituting their principal have been acquired within one month prior to the final day of the basic period for computing the dividend, distribution of surplus, or distribution of the gains of a securities investment trust (excluding those owned until an elapsed date two months from the said final day), the 'amounts received due to the said dividend or distribution of surplus,' other than the case of amounts dealt with in one of the items of paragraph (2), are the portion the Shoup Reports, permeated throughout as they are with American conceptions of an ideal tax system—which is to be expected—served as major stimuli in this direction. For example, income tax law today consists of a Law of 117 articles, a Cabinet Order of 226 articles, and a Ministerial Order of 66 articles plus attached forms. Upon comparison with West Germany, we find that the total number of articles in this law and these orders far exceeds the similar provisions in that country's income tax law.[77] Of course, despite the undenied Americanization of the manner in which legislation is presented, many instances still remain where a tax statute confers a mandate of authority upon an order, numerous provisions dealing with the computation of income for the juridical persons' and income taxes having been placed in cabinet orders and not laws. The traditional Japanese view of written law balks at overloading a statute with a multitude of diverse and extremely technical rules, but to the American lawyer, the product of a different background, this convention of completing legislation through a delegation of certain matters to cabinet orders and a further delegation of details to ministerial orders may well appear both difficult and unduly cumbersome.

While cabinet and ministerial orders either create or particularize items

within these amounts, computed as prescribed by Order, equivalent to the period that the stock, investment, or beneficiary securities constituting the principal have been owned; hereinafter these will be referred to as 'the amounts received due to a dividend, etc.', the said amounts received due to a dividend, etc. (if there is interest on a debt necessary in order to acquire the stock, investment or beneficiary securities constituting their principal, the amount remaining after the amount of interest computed as prescribed by Order has been deducted from the said amounts) are not to be included in proceeds in the computation of the income of article 9, paragraph (1)."

[77] In 1961 the *Einkommensteuergesetz,* in the version of Aug. 15, 1961, [1961] 1 BUNDESGESETZBLATT 1253, had 73 sections and the *Einkommensteuer-Durchführungsverordnung,* in the version of April 7, 1961, [1961] 1 BUNDESGESETZBLATT 382, 94 sections.

A comparison with American statutory law is equally interesting. The Internal Revenue Code of 1954 contains 454 sections dealing with personal and corporate income taxation. The provisions of the Income Tax Law, the Juridical Persons' Tax Law, the Tax Special Measures Law, the National Tax Common Provisions Law, and the Cabinet and Ministerial Orders under these laws on the same subject are contained in 1,104 articles (117 in the Income Tax Law, 74 in the Juridical Persons' Tax Law, 104 in the Tax Special Measures Law, 96 in the National Tax Common Provisions Law, 226 in the Cabinet Order under the Income Tax Law, 168 in the Cabinet Order under the Juridical Persons' Tax Law, 106 in the Cabinet Order under the Tax Special Measures Law, 36 in the Cabinet Order under the National Tax Common Provisions Law, 66 in the Ministerial Order under the Income Tax Law, 61 in the Ministerial Order under the Juridical Persons' Tax Law, 45 in the Ministerial Order under the Tax Special Measures Law, and 5 in the Ministerial Order under the National Tax Common Provisions Law). The Orders involved are as follows: Income Tax Law Enforcement Regulations, Imperial Order No. 110 of 1947; Juridical Persons' Tax Law Enforcement Regulations, Imperial Order No. 111 of 1947; Tax Special Measures Law Enforcement Order, Cabinet Order No. 43 of 1957; National Tax Common Provisions Law Enforcement Order, Cabinet Order No. 135 of 1962; Income Tax Law Enforcement Rules, Ministry of Finance Order No. 29 of 1947; Juridical Persons' Tax Law Enforcement Rules, Ministry of Finance Order No. 30 of 1947; Tax Special Measures Law Enforcement Regulations, Ministry of Finance Order No. 15 of 1957; National Tax Common Provisions Law Enforcement Regulations, Ministry of Finance Order No. 28 of 1962.

prescribed abstractly or not at all by a law, unlike the Internal Revenue Code Regulations in the United States they do not indicate the government's official interpretation. Nevertheless, no matter how detailed one may seek to make their content, it is very nearly impossible to provide an exhaustive explanation in laws and orders themselves. Consequently, some such additional commentary is essential, especially in the case of the intricate and difficult-to-comprehend rules affecting taxation. In Japan this function is performed by circulars issued by the Director-General of the National Tax Agency, Ministry of Finance.[78]

The Director-General uses circulars to furnish subordinate revenue officers with a precise construction of the law based on his official view. Since these circulars indicate the line that all within the National Tax Agency will follow in administering taxation, they set standards universally employed by the tax authorities, but they do not in themselves possess binding force as law. A taxpayer who believes that the content of a particular circular departs from the proper rules of tax law may challenge its application at any time. Actually, though, objections of this sort are rare, and accordingly the circulars function as the basic norm under which tax law operates. In any inquiry into the content of Japanese tax law, an investigation of the National Tax Agency's circulars is indispensable.[79] They cover all areas of taxation, new ones being issued each time the statutes are amended and old ones revised whenever necessary. Their content is, in principle, open to the general public, and important ones are published in the Official Gazette (as are laws and orders).[80] Professional tax services also exist which make

[78] The National Tax Agency is an external organ of the Ministry of Finance in charge of the administration of national taxes, performing a function similar to that of the Internal Revenue Service in the United States. It is headed by a Director-General equivalent to the U.S. Commissioner of Internal Revenue. Inside the main office of the ministry, entirely independent of the agency, is also a Tax Bureau responsible for formulating national tax policy and legislation, as well as dealing with international tax operations.

[79] The detailed nature of these circulars can be shown by a comparison similar to that employed above in regard to written provisions of law. As of February 1961, United States Treasury Regulations, both "final" and "proposed," include approximately 1,348 subsections on personal and corporate income taxation covering about 1,600 pages of text. Japanese circulars on these same two topics, giving a general basic interpretation of law and not merely reporting a ruling on a specific case before the tax authorities, contain some 3,455 separate items in about 1,000 pages of text. The larger number of headings in a shorter space on Japan's part can be explained by the fact that most Japanese items are only one paragraph in length while the American subsections are normally several paragraphs long.

[80] Formerly these circulars were secret and only distributed to tax officials as a kind of "hornbook" to acquaint the skilled revenue officer with the secrets of his trade. During the period when tax officials determined the amount of tax payable, government assessment procedures were not open to the public, but maintenance of secrecy was clearly contrary to the spirit of the new postwar "self-assessment" method. Shoup urged publication of such circulars and his recommendations were promptly put into operation. See 4 First Shoup Report D47–48, D65. Today confidential circulars are still issued occasionally on matters of internal administration and in regard to the disposition of individual cases affecting governmental policy, but these constitute the exception, all general interpretative circulars and most individual rulings being published.

new circulars quickly available to their subscribers.[81] For some statutes, the National Tax Agency has prepared its circulars in the form of an article-by-article commentary,[82] but in the case of those laws, such as the Income Tax Law and the Juridical Persons' Tax Law, whose provisions are subject to repeated amendment and repeal, the Agency has issued separate circulars for each change and compiled them chronologically without adequate systematic organization.

There are, however, innumerable private publications which compile tax laws, orders, and circulars correctly and systematically;[83] but Japan does not yet have anything like the American CCH *Federal Tax Reporter* which collects and keeps up to date not only statutes, regulations, and circulars, but also court opinions and related tax materials.[84]

So far my remarks have been restricted to national taxation. A final word might also be said about the sources of the inhabitants' and business activity taxes. These taxes are imposed pursuant to the inherent powers of local government through ordinances enacted by their legislative bodies for this purpose, but a nationally prescribed Local Tax Law sets certain limits on their authority to tax and fixes a skeletal system within which they must operate. Similar to the pattern found in national taxation, this law is complemented by a cabinet order[85] and a ministerial order,[86] and the Tax Affairs Bureau of the Ministry of Autonomy issues interpretative circulars. Moreover, on the local level, the ordinance actually imposing the taxes is often supplemented by a regulation issued by the governor or mayor of the local governmental entity involved.[87]

[81] For example, the KOKUZEI SOKUHŌ (Rapid National Tax Report) published biweekly by the Ōkura Zaimu Kyōkai, a private association affiliated with the Ministry of Finance. Circulars therein are printed from the same plates originally used to print the circulars for internal use within the National Tax Agency.

[82] For example, Concerning the Establishment of the National Tax Collection Law Basic Circular, National Tax Agency Circular, *Chōchō* (Collection Division — Collection Section) 4–5, Jan. 27, 1960.

[83] One such is ZEI KANKEI HŌREI HANREI TSŪTATSU SHŪ. (A Collection of Laws, Orders, Cases, and Circulars Relating to Tax), published by the Dai Ichi Hōki Publishing Company, which compiles all tax laws, orders, and circulars in a twelve-volume looseleaf set kept up to date through bimonthly supplements. Despite its title, it contains only a scattered sampling of court decisions.

[84] Nevertheless, a looseleaf collection digesting court decisions on taxation does exist: SOZEI HANREI (Tax Cases) (Nakagawa ed.), published by Sankōsha of Kyoto. Besides the regular court reporters, the complete decisions are also available in ZEIMU SOSHŌ SHIRYŌ (Tax Litigation Materials), issued annually by the National Tax Agency.

[85] Local Tax Law Enforcement Order, Cabinet Order No. 245 of 1950.

[86] Local Tax Law Enforcement Regulations, Prime Minister's Office Order No. 23 of 1954. Initially a Prime Minister's Office Order was issued because in 1954 local taxation was under the supervision of an agency of that office: the Autonomy Agency. In 1960 this agency was reconstituted as a ministry and since July 1 of that year the Local Tax Law Enforcement Regulations have been amended by means of its ministerial orders.

[87] See the model ordinances proposed by the Ministry of Autonomy: Prefectural Tax Ordinance (Model Provisions), Autonomy Agency Circular, *Ji-hei Fu-hatsu* No. 30, Aug. 1, 1955; Municipal Tax Ordinance (Model Provisions), Autonomy Agency Circular, *Ji-otsu Shi-hatsu* (Tax Affairs Bureau—Municipal Tax Section) No. 20, May 14, 1954.

Taxpayers

Natural persons constitute the taxpayers of the income tax and juridical persons those of the juridical persons' tax.[88] A distinctive feature of Japanese tax law is the fact that all bodies possessing legal personality under the Commercial Code,[89] the Civil Code,[90] and other laws, regardless of the particular form in which they are constituted, are subject to the juridical persons' tax. Included are not only stock companies but "partnership-under-a-common-name-companies" [91] (which, despite the possession of legal personality, are organized in the same manner as simple partnerships of the Civil Code), various cooperative societies, juridical persons in the public interest established pursuant to the Civil Code,[92] and other types of special juridical persons. However, the profits of a joint venture (that is, a simple partnership) without legal personality[93] carried on by individuals are taxed by the income tax as the personal income of the partners, irrespective of whether the profits are retained in the partnership or distributed. The same treatment is also accorded the members of a "secret partnership." [94]

A problem, however, is presented by those bodies which, in spite of their lack of legal personality, act not as a mere collection of individuals but are subject, instead, to a single will and whose continued existence transcends the individuality of the various component members: namely, the so-called "associations and foundations without personality." Because the Juridical Persons' Tax Law was formerly quite formalistic in the way in which it determined the entities to be taxed, and because the income tax by nature concerned only natural persons, for a long while the taxation of these bodies formed a legal blind spot. To be sure, since organizations of this sort are apt to act through legally fixed representatives, in some cases in actual tax administration the income tax was imposed as if the organization's income belonged to the representative — such income being separated, however, from the representative's own personal income. Gradually, astute tax experts came to recognize that the manner in which these bodies were being treated constituted a very large loophole in the tax structure. Consequently, to remedy the situation, in 1957 legislation was enacted providing that associations or foundations without personality, in which a representative or ad-

[88] Income tax (not juridical persons' tax) is withheld at source on interest for deposits or public and company bonds and on dividends whether the recipient of payment is a natural or juridical person. To this extent, juridical persons also constitute formal taxpayers of the income tax.

[89] COMMERCIAL CODE, Law No. 48 of 1899, arts. 52–500.

[90] CIVIL CODE, Laws No. 89 of 1896 and No. 9 of 1898, arts. 33–84.

[91] *Gōmei kaisha.* These are the same as French *société en nom collectif* and German *offene Handelsgesellschaft.*

[92] CIVIL CODE art. 34.

[93] *Kumiai.* See CIVIL CODE arts. 667–88.

[94] *Tokumei kumiai. Stille Gesellschaft* in Germany and *association commerciale en participation* in France. See COMMERCIAL CODE arts. 535–42.

ministrator has been fixed and which are carrying on a profit-making business activity — among those specifically provided by tax law — that is continuous at an established place of business, are deemed to be juridical persons and that the proceeds of their profit-making business activity shall be taxed by the juridical persons' tax.[95]

In keeping with the general world-wide practice, the state, local governments, and other specified public organizations are not taxed.[96] But, since the Shoup Reports,[97] domestic juridical persons whose purpose is charity, education, learning, religion, or other activities in the public interest are relieved of taxation only in regard to nonprofit-making activities as determined by law.[98] Their profit-making business activities are taxed by the juridical persons' tax at a reduced rate.[99] Equivalent foreign juridical persons may obtain the same treatment through a special designation by the Minister of Finance on grounds of reciprocity.[100]

What has been said so far applies equally well to the taxpayers of the local inhabitants' and business activity taxes. These two taxes also cover both natural and juridical persons,[101] although the latter is limited solely to profits derived from certain enumerated businesses and professions.[102]

Like most nations, Japan divides taxpayers according to their particular status into unlimited and limited categories. Individuals resident for a year or more or domiciled in Japan are unlimited taxpayers and all others limited taxpayers; nationality is immaterial.[103] Tax law calls the former "residents" and the latter "nonresidents." The tax liability of a juridical person is not determined by the location of its "central control and management," as in many European countries,[104] but rather, as in the United States, by its formal place of establishment (incorporation) — that is, juridical persons having a head office or main office within Japan bear unlimited liability as "domestic juridical persons" and those which do not are "foreign juridical persons" with limited liability.[105]

[95] Juridical Persons' Tax Law, art. 1(2), as amended by Law No. 28 of 1957; Income Tax Law, art. 1(7), as amended by Laws No. 27 of 1957 and No. 44 of 1962; Income Tax Law Enforcement Regulations, art. 1-13; National Tax Common Provisions Law, art. 3.

[96] Juridical Persons' Tax Law, art. 4; Juridical Persons' Tax Law Enforcement Regulations, art. 1-9; Income Tax Law, art. 3(1) (i)–(vii).

[97] 1 FIRST SHOUP REPORT 114–18.

[98] Juridical Persons' Tax Law, art. 5; Juridical Persons' Tax Law Enforcement Regulations, art. 1-11; Juridical Persons' Tax Law Enforcement Rules, art. 1-3; Income Tax Law, art. 3(1) (viii)–(xiii).

[99] Juridical Persons' Tax Law, art. 17(1)(i).

[100] Juridical Persons' Tax Law, arts. 4(v), 5(1)(viii); Juridical Persons' Tax Law Enforcement Regulations, arts. 1-10, 1-12; Income Tax Law, art. 3(2); Income Tax Law Enforcement Regulations, art. 1-12.

[101] Local Tax Law, arts. 24, 72, 294.

[102] *Ibid.*, art. 72(1), (5)–(7).

[103] Income Tax Law, art. 1(1)–(2).

[104] See, for example, WORLD TAX SERIES, TAXATION IN THE UNITED KINGDOM 5/2.2 (1957).

[105] Juridical Persons' Tax Law, arts. 1(1), 2(1). Tax law uses the term "main office" (*shutaru jimusho*) together with "head office." At times the former has been mistakenly

Generally speaking, unlimited taxpayers are obliged to pay tax on all income irrespective of its source.[106] But, after 1957, resident individuals who do not intend to remain in Japan permanently (persons who do not continuously possess a residence or domicile within the country for more than five years) have been classified as "nonpermanent residents," and their income from foreign sources not paid within nor remitted to Japan is excluded from income taxation.[107] This change constituted the first new element in Japan's means of allocating tax liability since the 1899 adoption of a year or more of residence or mere domicile as the standard.[108]

Limited taxpayers are only liable for income tax or juridical persons' tax on income derived from assets or a business activity situated in Japan or on other types of income legally prescribed as having its source within Japan.[109] Here the concept of "income having its source within Japan" had been unknown to Japanese tax law prior to 1952, when it was imported in imitation of the United States doctrine.[110] The same concept also appears in the Income Tax Agreement for the Avoidance of Double Taxation concluded between Japan and the United States in 1954.[111]

Computation of Income

Computation of income for purposes of the inhabitants' tax and the business activity tax is based substantially on the income and juridical persons'

---

translated into English as "principal place of business," but actually *shutaru jimusho* has exactly the same meaning as "head office"; it does not mean the principal place where business activities are in fact being conducted. Both terms appear in tax law because the various statutes recognizing the establishment of juridical persons are not uniform in their terminology. Thus, the Civil Code refers to the "main office" while the Commercial Code speaks of the "head office." The head office or the main office is the place formally designated in a juridical person's articles of association and registered as such. Under Japanese law, all juridical persons which have their head or main office in Japan are treated as juridical persons established pursuant to that law.

106 Income Tax Law, art. 2(1); Juridical Persons' Tax Law, art. 2(1).

107 Income Tax Law, art. 2(2), as amended by Law No. 27 of 1957; Income Tax Law Enforcement Regulations, arts. 1-9–1-11.

108 Income Tax Law of 1899, art. 1.

109 Income Tax Law, arts. 1(2)–(3), (6), (8), (10), 2(3); Income Tax Law Enforcement Regulations, arts. 1–1-2, 1-6–1-8; Juridical Persons' Tax Law, arts. 1(3)–(4), (6), 2(1); Juridical Persons' Tax Law Enforcement Regulations, arts. 1–1-4.

110 By Law No. 53 of 1952. Prior to the 1952 amendment, other than income from assets or a business activity within the country, Japan employed the place of payment as the sole test to determine the liability of nonresidents and foreign juridical persons. Thus, only items, such as dividends or interest, paid within Japan were taxed.

111 Convention With Japan for the Avoidance of Double Taxation and the Prevention of Fiscal Evasion With Respect to Taxes on Income, April 16, 1954, art. XIII, Treaty No. 1 of 1955, [1955] 1 U.S.T. & O.I.A. 149, T.I.A.S. No. 3176, 238 U.N.T.S. 39 (effective April 1, 1955).

On the taxation of limited and unlimited taxpayers generally, see Uematsu, Hikyojūsha, Gaikoku Hōjin oyobi Gaikoku Zeikaku Kōjo ni Kan-suru Kaisei Zeihō no Kaisetsu (An Explanation of the Revised Tax Law Concerning Nonresidents, Foreign Juridical Persons and the Foreign Tax Deduction) (Kokuzei-chō (National Tax Agency) ed. 1962).

taxes.[112] Therefore, the subsequent discussion is limited solely to the national taxes. The reader, though, should keep in mind that what is said applies, for the most part, to the local taxes also.

Computation of Income for the Income Tax

The general principles governing computation of the income tax require that all income acquired by an individual be combined, various personal deductions made, and then progressive tax rates applied against the remainder (known as "taxable income"). Here "computation of income" refers to the computation process prior to the personal deduction stage. In terms of American tax law, it is equivalent to the calculations necessary to reach "adjusted gross income."

Normally, computation of income takes place each calendar year. Individual entrepreneurs are not permitted to select special accounting periods for taxation.

The Income Tax Law classifies income into ten categories: (1) interest income, (2) dividend income, (3) income from immovables, (4) business income, (5) remuneration income, (6) severance income, (7) forestry income, (8) assignment income (capital gain), (9) occasional income, and (10) miscellaneous income. This classification is chiefly a matter of convenience to assist in working out the amount of one's income and tax in accordance with the intrinsic character of the income involved. It is not a device, as was the former schedular tax, for the employment of discriminatory rates in the belief that differences in degree of ability to pay depend on the type of income; nor is it the same as the classified listing found in the British and West German income taxes which do not tax income falling outside the area covered by the schedules. Item (10) — miscellaneous income — is a catchall embracing all income not picked up by items (1) through (9),[113] and thus denotes that tax, as in the United States, is imposed on all income from every possible source. However, at no point do the statutes give a definition of the meaning of "income" itself, with the consequence that determination of the bounds of the concept still remains a problem.

Since the content of each income category is fairly well indicated by its title, I shall merely touch on a few points that merit particular attention. "Interest income" does not specify all interest in the economic sense, but only interest which is most readily susceptible to withholding, namely, that produced principally by private saving: interest on bank deposits and public and company bonds.[114] "Dividend income" covers both stock dividends and the gains of securities investment trusts investing chiefly in shares of stock.[115] "Business income" is not restricted to income from commerce and in-

[112] See Local Tax Law, arts. 23, 32, 51, 72, 72-12, 72-14, 72-17, 292, 297, 313.
[113] Income Tax Law, art. 9(1)(x).
[114] *Ibid.*, art. 9(1)(i).
[115] *Ibid.*, art. 9(1)(ii).

dustry; it is a broad concept including also income from agriculture, fishing, and the free professions such as medicine and law.[116] However, income from the assignment of fixed assets employed in a business, not being of a regular recurring nature, is classified as "assignment income" (capital gain) and not "business income."[117] Fundamentally, "remuneration income" is compensation for rendering personal services under a contract of employment, but besides compensation paid during the course of employment it encompasses pensions and annuities paid by one's prior employer following retirement.[118] Moreover, annuities obtained after retirement from certain specified mutual-aid societies organized by wage earners, annuity benefits received pursuant to the social-insurance system, and annuities paid out of a fund similar to the British and American pension funds, established by a firm as prescribed by tax law, are deemed "remuneration income."[119] "Severance income" refers to a single lump-sum payment made under a system prevalent in Japan to a wage earner upon his leaving work or retiring.[120] "Forestry income" is income from the felling or assignment of timber provided that the income recipient has held the timber for at least one year.[121] "Occasional income" consists of casual or windfall gains such as gambling receipts and prize money, but it never includes consideration for services even if only a one-time affair.[122]

From what has been said it is apparent that "income" in the Income Tax Law is an extremely broad concept comprising receipts from every possible source. It is interesting to note that, as far as gifts are concerned, the term is even more inclusive than that employed in the United States, for in Japan a gift is considered income since it increases the economic power of the donee. Of course, because the Inheritance Tax Law provides a separate gift tax on gifts by individuals,[123] such transfers are expressly excluded from taxation under the income tax,[124] but gifts from juridical persons are not so privileged, being considered occasional income.[125] Again, all remuneration paid in kind is income;[126] no special treatment, comparable to that existing in American law, is available.[127] It has been extremely difficult, however,

[116] *Ibid.*, art. 9(1)(iv), Income Tax Law Enforcement Regulations, art. 7-3.

[117] Income Tax Law, art. 9(1)(iv); Income Tax Law Basic Circular, National Tax Agency Circular, *Chokusho* (Direct Tax Division—Income Tax Section) 1–1, Jan. 1, 1951, 135.

[118] Income Tax Law, art. 9(1)(v).

[119] *Ibid.*, arts. 8(8)(ii), (iv), (vi)–(vi-v), (vii-iii)–(vii-iv), (viii), 9(2); Income Tax Law Enforcement Regulations, art. 7-12; Juridical Persons' Tax Law, art. 2(2).

[120] Income Tax Law, art. 9(1)(vi).

[121] *Ibid.*, art. 9(1)(vii).

[122] *Ibid.*, art. 9(1)(ix); Income Tax Law Basic Circular, 142–43, 146–47.

[123] Inheritance Tax Law, Law No. 73 of 1950, art. 1-2.

[124] Income Tax Law, art. 6(xiii).

[125] Income Tax Law Basic Circular, 150.

[126] Income Tax Law Enforcement Regulations, art. 9-2; Income Tax Law Basic Circular 210, 212.

[127] E.g., INT. REV. CODE OF 1954, §§107, 109, 119. Also see WORLD TAX SERIES, TAXATION IN THE UNITED STATES 8/1.3 (1963).

in terms of tax administration, to preserve this framework strictly. Many concessions have in fact been recognized.[128] Reflecting the confused state of the economy after the war, the National Tax Agency in many sectors through its circulars enlarged the area of nontaxation beyond reasonable bounds.[129] On the other hand, Japan, like the United States and unlike Great Britain and West Germany, does not deem the imputed rent of taxpayers owning their own dwellings to be income.

Computation of the amount of income takes place first within each income category. In accordance with the common practice of most tax systems, income is computed in principle by deducting necessary expenses from total receipts. Personal, family, and related expenditures are regarded as disposal of income rather than necessary expenses and, therefore, are not deductible.[130] The business activity tax and the fixed assets tax on property

[128] As in Great Britain, from time to time the Japanese National Tax Agency announces, by means of a circular, extrastatutory concessions which it will make in favor of all taxpayers in applying tax law. The concessions represent deviations from strict statutory requirements for reasons of administrative convenience or to avoid manifest inequity not contemplated by the statute. While there is no legal basis for this practice, it has been followed for a number of years without being attacked in the Diet or in the courts. The measures described in the text and in the following footnote fall within this area. On the comparable British practice, see WORLD TAX SERIES, TAXATION IN THE UNITED KINGDOM 1/3.1b. (1957).

[129] These circulars, besides treating certain payments in kind as nontaxable for the convenience of employers, placed the provision of commutation railroad passes, meals, and low-rent housing, within specified limits, beyond the area subject to tax, and even accorded tax-free status to the payment of small amounts for serving as a day or night watchman in addition to one's regular duties. See, for example, Income Tax Law Basic Circular, 210; Concerning the Operation of the Basic Circular Relating to the Income Tax Law (Collection at Source Portion), National Tax Agency Circular, *Chokusho* (Direct Tax Division—Income Tax Section) 2–62, July 5, 1951, 5; Concerning the Revision of the Treatment of Payment in Kind, Etc., of Commutation Passes, National Tax Agency Circular, *Chokusho* 2–109, Nov. 2, 1961; Concerning the Treatment of the Income Tax on Day and Night Watchmen Fees, National Tax Agency Circular, *Chokusho* 2–12, Feb, 15, 1954; Concerning the Treatment of the Income Tax on Day and Night Watchmen Fees, National Tax Agency Circular, *Chokusho* 2–28, March 12, 1955; Concerning the Treatment of Remuneration Income for an Amount Equivalent to the Rent of Company Houses, Dormitories, Etc., National Tax Agency Circular, *Chokusho* 2–78, Aug. 13, 1951; Concerning the Treatment of Remuneration Income for an Amount Equivalent to the Rent of Company Houses, Dormitories, Etc., National Tax Agency Circular, *Chokusho* 2–109, Oct. 24, 1951; Concerning the Treatment of Remuneration Income for an Amount Equivalent to the Rent of Company Houses, Dormitories, Etc., National Tax Agency Circular, *Chokusho* 2–61, Aug. 11, 1952; Concerning the Evaluation of an Amount Equivalent to the Rent of Company Houses, Dormitories, Etc., National Tax Agency Circular, *Chokusho* 2–94, Nov. 4, 1952.

A discussion of this problem may be found in ZEISEI CHŌSA KAI (Tax System Investigation Commission), TŌMEN JISSHI-SUBEKI ZEISEI KAISEI NI KAN-SURU TŌSHIN (ZEISEI CHŌSA KAI DAI ICHIJI TŌSHIN) OYOBI SONO SHINGI NO NAIYŌ TO KEIKA NO SETSUMEI (Report Concerning Tax System Revision That Should Be Enforced Immediately (First Report of the Tax System Investigation Commission) and an Explanation of the Content and Progress of Deliberations) [hereafter cited FIRST REPORT OF THE TAX SYSTEM INVESTIGATION COMMISSION], TŌSHIN BESSATSU (Separate Volume of the Report) [hereafter cited SEPARATE VOLUME] 77–80, 358–61 (1960).

[130] Income Tax Law, art. 10(2); Income Tax Law Enforcement Regulations, art. 10-25 Income Tax Law Basic Circular, 262–64.

employed in a business are necessary expenses,[131] but not the income and inhabitants' taxes.[132] In general, the accrual basis has been adopted to determine the point at which a taxpayer's receipts and necessary expenses arise.[133] With agricultural income, though, for reasons of administrative convenience income is deemed realized on the harvest of the agricultural product.[134] Consequently, contrary to the American rule, farm products consumed personally by a farmer and his family are not excluded from income subject to tax.

There are numerous exceptions to the above fundamental principle of income computation. Although interest on a debt necessary to obtain the capital invested may be deducted in determining dividend income,[135] interest income is considered by its very nature not to require expenses — the amount of receipts being looked upon as "pure" income.[136] Nor are necessary expenses available for either remuneration or severance income, certain special deductions being recognized instead.[137] In the case of remuneration income, first 10,000 yen (28 dollars) is subtracted from the amount of receipts, then 20 percent from the portion remaining up to and including 400,000 yen (1,111 dollars), and finally 10 percent from the excess up to and including 700,000 yen (1,944 dollars).[138] While in some respects this deduction resembles the blanket deduction for employment income (income from non-independent work) connected expenses in West Germany's Income Tax Law,[139] it operates not merely as a substitute for the deduction of expenses but also in a manner similar to the special deduction for "earned income relief" [140] in Great Britain.[141]

[131] Income Tax Law, art. 10(2); Income Tax Law Basic Circular, 253.

[132] Income Tax Law, art. 10(4).

[133] Income Tax Law, art. 10(1)–(2); Income Tax Law Basic Circular, 194–206, 217.

[134] Income Tax Law Enforcement Regulations, art. 9.

[135] Income Tax Law, art. 9(1)(ii).

[136] *Ibid.*, art. 9(1)(i); Income Tax Law Basic Circular, 67.

[137] The 1962 tax revision introduced special treatment for funds similar to qualified pension trusts in the United States and approved superannuation funds in Great Britain. Payments made out of such a fund, known as a "qualified retirement annuity fund," are taxable as remuneration income, but the contributions of an employee thereto are deductible in computing the employee's remuneration income and it is only after this amount is subtracted that the special deductions recognized in lieu of expenses apply. This deduction is an exception permitted only in regard to this sort of remuneration income. Income Tax Law, art. 9(2); Income Tax Law Enforcement Regulations, art. 7-17.

[138] Income Tax Law, art. 9(1)(v)(a)–(c).

[139] See WORLD TAX SERIES, TAXATION IN THE FEDERAL REPUBLIC OF GERMANY 6/1.6f. (1963).

[140] "Earned income relief" is recognized in British law for all "earned income" — that is, not only remuneration from employment, but also compensation for personal services rendered and income from business. See WORLD TAX SERIES, TAXATION IN THE UNITED KINGDOM 12/1.2j. (1957).

[141] Unlike the situation in the United States, there is a strong tendency in Japan to construe a taxpayer's expenditures for daily travel to and from work (commuting expenses) as necessary expenses, but for wage earners administrative difficulties are avoided by regarding this amount as taken care of by the remuneration income deduction. As the other side of the coin, travel allowances paid to wage earners for a business trip are treated as nontaxable income. Income Tax Law, art. 6(iii).

This "remuneration income deduction" was first introduced by the 1920 revision and thus has a long history among Japanese tax measures.[142] Today it functions as an allowance incorporating the following elements: (1) a blanket deduction to replace necessary expenses incurred while working, (2) an adjustment for the fact that the ability-to-pay-tax of recipients of remuneration income (which is consideration for nonindependent work) is not so strong as that of those who receive asset and business income, (3) a "squeeze" deduction to compensate for the relatively more complete collection of tax from remuneration income made possible by withholding, and (4) a form of interest adjustment because the imposition of withholding creates an earlier payment date for remuneration income taxpayers than others.[143] At the time the deduction was established, withholding against wages had not yet been enacted and so it would seem that the initial intention was probably the grounds given in (2), but after the war, with an increased tax burden and a period of tax administration beset by confusion, we may presume that the force of circumstances made reason (3) by far the most important.

By the time of the Shoup Reports, the deduction had risen to 25 percent of remuneration income (although a ceiling was imposed).[144] A compromise device of this sort was not acceptable to Shoup. He rigorously rejected the thinking underlying (3) and warned that recognition of such an institution would promote evasion by taxpayers not able to claim the deduction and would lead to the complete undermining of the tax structure. Moreover, he believed that the reasoning behind (2) required the application of the same deduction to not only remuneration income but farm and business income as well, and therefore he concluded that in the final analysis only (1) furnished any justification for its preservation. Shoup personally felt that full abrogation of this discriminatory deduction was desirable, but in practice he found it difficult to recommend total repeal, for it was not possible to uncover another source of income which would permit a decrease in the general rate schedule to the extent necessary in order to balance the increased tax burden that abolition of the deduction would have induced. Be that as it may, he was of the opinion that if (1) was to be the sole grounds for recognition, the amount granted should be severely restricted; accordingly he proposed a reduction to 10 percent.[145]

Without pressure from the occupation forces, it is doubtful that so sweeping a change, cutting at a single stroke a special deduction available

[142] Income Tax Law of 1920, art. 15. For certain forms of remuneration income, though, two similar deductions were made available as early as 1913. Income Tax Law of 1899, arts. 4-4–4-5, as amended by Law No. 13 of 1913.

[143] FIRST REPORT OF THE TAX SYSTEM INVESTIGATION COMMISSION, SEPARATE VOLUME 73–74 (1960).

[144] Income Tax Law, art. 9(iv), as amended by Law No. 142 of 1947, but prior to amendment by Law No. 71 of 1950.

[145] 1 FIRST SHOUP REPORT 68–73.

to the overwhelming majority of individuals required to pay income tax, could have ever taken place. The Shoup recommendations shocked the Japanese government. For some time afterwards government officials held daily conferences with General Headquarters, SCAP to discuss the issue, and eventually they were able to negotiate the latter's consent to hold the reduction to 15 percent.[146] The following year, upon the Shoup Mission's return, it suggested in a very strong tone in its Second Report that farmers, fishermen, and — financial conditions permitting — other individual proprietors should also be given an "earned income credit" of 10 percent.[147] Presumably this statement was stimulated by a general belief among the mission's members that the lowering of the remuneration income deduction to only 15 percent meant that their proposals of the year before had been disregarded. This portion of the Second Report was never enforced.

Here was an event clearly recording the differences in outlook between the mission and the Japanese government. Among the many controversies concerning the taxation of income since the end of the war, one constantly recurrent theme, not only in the field of tax policy but in that of administration too, has been whether in fact the income tax burden is equitably imposed on all categories of income recipients.[148] In other words, is it not true that the tax on persons receiving remuneration income, where withholding blocks all chance of evasion, is in practice heavier than that borne by farmers and businessmen? The preponderant portion of today's income tax revenue is collected at source. Expressed in numerical terms, according to 1960 tax statistics, remuneration income recipients constitute 85 percent of the total taxpayers of the income tax, business income recipients including members of the free professions about 8 percent, and agricultural income recipients no more than 3 percent.[149] Over the past decade there has been a gradual expansion in the percentage occupied by recipients of remuneration income among all taxpayers, a trend intensified by the steady rise in national income and repeated reductions in the income tax.[150] Any number of reasons may be cited why the income of those receiving remuneration income has increased more rapidly than that of others; two are that the remunerative form of income has grown quicker within national income in recent years than other forms and that it has become a common practice for high-income recipients to incorporate and turn themselves into employees on a salary.[151]

[146] Income Tax Law, art. 9(v), as amended by Law No. 71 of 1950, but prior to amendment by Law No. 56 of 1956.

[147] Second Shoup Report 1.

[148] First Report of the Tax System Investigation Commission, Separate Volume 74–75.

[149] These percentages were computed by the author based on the absolute amounts of revenue given in Shuzei Kyoku, note 37, at 48–49, 51–53.

[150] See *ibid.*, at 48–49.

[151] Upon the basis of this trend, Bronfenbrenner and Kogiku sharply criticize the Japanese income tax as degenerating into "little more than a disguised payroll tax." Bronfenbrenner and Kogiku, note 38, at 243.

In terms of the nature of the peculiar factors involved, it is difficult to delineate objectively and numerically the extent that these reasons rather than defective tax enforcement operate and the degree to which the reputed faulty balance in tax burdens is actually present among different types of taxpayers. Nevertheless, the public at large intuitively feels that wage earners are taxed far heavier than other taxpayers.[152] In these circumstances, the remuneration income deduction has persistently expanded since it was sliced by Shoup, with the ceiling limitation and the percentage of the deduction both increasing gradually.

It is self-evident that any tax system which treats the remuneration income deduction as an allowance to compensate for the squeeze of more efficient tax collection is somewhat tainted. Doubtless, where the burdens of different taxpayers appear out of balance, the correct course is to seek the remedy in better administration. This, in fact, has been the very line of approach pursued as far as possible by the Japanese government in its attempt to bring about improvement, but in every tax system some realistic adjustments are necessary. Within the government, the common feeling is that, despite a general awareness that it is undesirable to eliminate inequality by means of such a deduction, its employment for this purpose must be tolerated to a certain extent as a necessary evil.[153]

Another subject of special treatment is severance income. Its taxable income consists of one half the amount remaining after deducting from the amount of receipts the portion applicable to one year's employment, of a certain prescribed sum determined according to the ages at which the recipient began and ceased employment, multiplied by the number of years of employment.[154] The years-of-employment factor is a special one in keeping with the particular character of severance income, while the purpose of the reduction by one half is to soften the effect of progressive rates on income arising irregularly and only once.[155]

In the case of two other forms of extraordinary income, assignment and occasional income, first 150,000 yen (417 dollars) is deducted and then only half the remainder taxed.[156] With forestry income, the same 150,000 is de-

[152] FIRST REPORT OF THE TAX SYSTEM INVESTIGATION COMMISSION, SEPARATE VOLUME 35–38.

[153] See, for example, *ibid.*, at 75.

[154] Income Tax Law, art. 9(1)(vi); Income Tax Law Enforcement Regulations, arts. 7-4, 7-6–7-7.

[155] Even assuming that expenses have been incurred in producing the severance income, they are considered covered by this special deduction. The problem of deducting contributions into a severance-pay fund by a wage earner does not arise since in the computation of taxable income the majority can be subtracted under the deduction for social-insurance fees. However, if, as an exception, a lump sum instead of an annuity is paid out of a qualified retirement annuity fund (see note 137 above), while this constitutes severance income, the special deduction applies only to the amount remaining after subtracting the quantity contributed to the fund during his term of employment by the person receiving this payment. Income Tax Law, art. 9(2); Income Tax Law Enforcement Regulations, art. 7-18.

[156] Income Tax Law, art. 9(1)(viii)–(ix).

ducted initially, but in place of the one-half reduction the application of progressive rates is mollified by computing the amount of tax by the so-called "divide by five, multiply by five" formula which will be described later.[157] The 150,000 yen deduction is not a blanket figure in lieu of expenses, but rather places minor amounts of extraordinary income outside the area subject to taxation for reasons of administrative convenience. Consequently, the general principle applies and expenses may be subtracted separately.[158]

The next step is to bring together all the income calculated separately under each category. However, the consolidation resulting, called the "amount of total income," [159] does not cover all income, despite its title, for here too there are some exceptions. Thus, severance and forestry income, instead of being added to the other amounts, are taxed separately as two distinct classes of income.[160] The exclusion of severance income from unitary taxation is understandable in light of its peculiar quality as a single lump-sum payment received on leaving work by a wage earner employed many years; but for forestry income, taking into account the facts that other types of extraordinary income (assignment and occasional income) are subject to the unitary tax and that forestry income includes amounts acquired regularly year after year through periodic logging by those controlling large tracts of forest, it is most difficult to find a rational basis for its segregation, the only conclusion possible being that it is purely a product of political considerations.[161] Interest income too, if receivable in payment prior to March 31, 1963, has been placed outside the unitary tax as a temporary special measure with only 10 percent withholding imposed at source.[162]

In consolidating the different categories of income, a loss produced under one category is joined with the income of the other categories in a prescribed order.[163] Capital losses (assignment losses) are fully deductible without limitation, there being no restriction such as exists in the United States.[164]

[157] *Ibid.*, art. 9(1)(viii).
[158] *Ibid.*, art. 9(1)(vii)–(ix).
[159] *Ibid.*, art. 9(1).
[160] *Ibid.*, art. 9(1)(vi)–(vii).
[161] The manner in which forestry income is taxed produces strange results. On the one hand, the burden on owners of large stands of timber, whose income arises regularly just as business income does, is unduly light, while, on the other side, the burden on irregular forestry income from a casual cutting made once in a lifetime is heavier than that on assignment and occasional income. The irrational character of this treatment has been pointed out by the Tax System Investigation Commission, but its modification still remains an unfinished task for the future. First Report of the Tax System Investigation Commission, Separate Volume 361–64.
[162] Tax Special Measures Law, art. 3.
[163] Income Tax Law, art. 9-3. On March 31, 1963, this date was extended to March 31, 1965, by Law No. 65 of 1963.
[164] Concerning the Manner of Treating the Income Tax Law as Amended August, 1953, National Tax Agency Circular, *Chokusho* (Direct Tax Division — Income Tax Section) 1-1, Jan. 5, 1954, 25.

But deduction of losses produced as a result of the transfer of certain assets not ordinarily necessary to the living of the individual, such as precious metals, works of art, and country villas, is confined to assignment income, while, to the same effect, losses relating to occasional income or derived from activities recognizable as chiefly hobbies or recreation — for example, those of a horse owner — may not be carried over into income categories different from the one in which they arose.[165] The general consolidation of losses also applies to severance income and forestry income, despite their separate taxation.

Needless to say, this consolidation does not include income prescribed as nontaxable by law. Besides such items as pensions for the sick and injured,[166] specified prizes honoring a conspicuous contribution to learning,[167] and assignment income (capital gain) from assets ordinarily necessary for living,[168] nontaxable income involves several important concessions made for economic policy reasons. Consequently, interest on postal savings,[169] interest on either deposits of 500,000 yen (1,389 dollars) or less or national, local, and company bonds or other specified valuable securities up to an equivalent face value obtained through a National Saving Society,[170] and assignment income from valuable securities, other than that resulting from continually recurrent transactions, the acquisition or disposal of the stock of the controlling shareholders in a family company, or market cornering operations,[171] are not taxed.

Persons filing a Blue Return (that is, taxpayers approved by the tax authorities who keep accounting records meeting certain fixed standards)[172] may carry over three years and back one year net losses arising in the

[165] Income Tax Law, art. 9-3(1); Income Tax Law Enforcement Regulations, art. 7-19; Income Tax Law Basic Circular, 185.

[166] Income Tax Law, art. 6(ii).

[167] *Ibid.*, art. 6(xii).

[168] *Ibid.*, art. 6(v); Income Tax Law Enforcement Regulations, art. 4.

[169] Income Tax Law, art. 6(iv).

[170] National Saving Societies Law, Law No. 64 of 1941, art. 4. National Saving Societies were originally created during the war in order to increase saving as special organizations extending facilities to their members. All interest paid in consideration was made nontaxable as an incentive. A bit later even banks were authorized to form these societies. Today, alongside the nontaxation of interest from postal savings, the societies continue to function as institutions excluding interest on small deposits or investments from taxation. The maximum deposit or investment not taxable, though, has gradually increased until in the 1962 tax revision it became 500,000 yen. A person may participate in only one National Saving Society at a time.

[171] Income Tax Law, art. 6(vi); Income Tax Law Enforcement Regulations, art. 4-3–4-5. Concerning the meaning of "valuable securities," see the essay by Shinichiro Michida, "The Legal Structure for Economic Enterprise: Some Aspects of Japanese Commercial Law," in this volume.

[172] Income Tax Law, art. 26-3; Income Tax Law Enforcement Regulations, arts. 26-3–26-6; Income Tax Law Enforcement Rules, arts. 9–19-3. For further information on the Blue Return system, see 4 FIRST SHOUP REPORT D56–59, SECOND SHOUP REPORT 53–55, and TAX BUREAU, note 36, at 123–25.

computation of any single year's income.[173] With the carry-over the loss is deductible from income; in the case of the carry-back, tax is re-computed and a refund claimed for the difference between this figure and the amount previously paid.[174] Furthermore, even without a Blue Return, a three-year carry-over is recognized for losses arising in the computation of fluctuating income, losses produced regarding business assets damaged in a disaster, or losses resulting from a disaster or theft for which the deduction for miscellaneous losses is available.[175]

Computation of Income for the Juridical Persons' Tax

Since the juridical persons' tax lacks deductions corresponding to the personal deductions of the income tax, the two concepts of "computation of income" and "computation of taxable income" contained therein are in fact one and the same. The required computation is made once in each "business year."[176] The business year need not be twelve months in length but of any duration which the juridical person chooses to select.[177] In almost all respects it is synonymous with the notion of the accounting period employed by accountants. However, for tax purposes, if a business year in excess of twelve months is adopted, each twelve-month period is deemed one business year.[178]

In the computation process there is no special classification of income such as is present in the income tax; instead, the income of a business year is broadly defined as the amount remaining after deducting the period's "total outlays" from its "total proceeds."[179] The Juridical Persons' Tax Law does, though, resemble its sister statute in that it fails to provide a basic definition of income. Despite the establishment of many rules relating to the specific computation of taxable income, such as whether certain operative facts give rise to proceeds or items not to be included in outlays, no uniform definition of what generally constitutes a "proceed" or an "outlay" has been enacted. Be that as it may, the concept of a juridical person's income is essentially the same as that of "profit" in business accounting, while proceeds and outlays are equivalent to the accounting terms "revenues" and "expenses." Generally speaking, then, proceeds are all facts other than capital transac-

[173] Income Tax Law, art. 9-4(1)–(2), (5); Income Tax Law Enforcement Regulations, art. 8-2.

[174] Income Tax Law, art. 36; Income Tax Law Enforcement Regulations, arts. 39–39-3.

[175] Income Tax Law, art. 9-4(3)–(4), (6); Income Tax Law Enforcement Regulations, arts. 8-2–8-3.

[176] *Geschäftsjahr* in German. See Juridical Persons' Tax Law, art. 9(1).

[177] *Ibid.*, art. 7. Most large Japanese companies whose stock is listed on the stock exchange select a business year of six months. However, other medium- and small-sized concerns generally fix their business year at twelve months.

[178] *Ibid.*, art. 7(4).

[179] *Ibid.*, art. 9(1).

tions which increase net worth;[180] outlays are all facts other than capital transactions which reduce net worth.[181]

Although at present, as has already been noted, "income" under the income tax embraces receipts from all possible sources, this characteristic is for the most part a postwar phenomenon. Formerly, as in Great Britain, taxable individual income covered only that arising from specified ordinarily recurrent sources, not capital gains and occasional income. On the other hand, the story of the tax on juridical persons has been quite different. Juridical persons being by nature profit-seeking entities, all their income irrespective of source has been fully taxable from the very outset.[182] Today, the personal and corporate concepts of income have grown together, but in certain details a few variations yet remain. To indicate one such instance, juridical persons are permitted to write up or down, within the limits prescribed by tax law, the book value of assets held by them and thereby produce proceeds or outlays for tax purposes because inherently they are assumed to base their calculations upon the keeping of proper accounting records, while a comparable privilege is not extended to individuals.[183] Again, since the juridical persons' tax rate is not progressive, unlike the income tax, no special treatment is conferred on extraordinary or occasional income; nor does any rule exist similar to the American provisions granting preferential treatment to capital gains.

Income for purposes of the juridical persons' tax is computed in accordance with the general maxims of business accounting used to determine profit and loss. The broad statutory provision that a juridical person's income is total proceeds minus total outlays has remained unchanged since the commencement of corporate taxation in 1899, but over the years the concrete content of this rule has steadily undergone change commensurate with the development in the principles of accounting. Numerous special stipulations have been enacted into law in order to unify and adjust taxable income computation with proper accounting doctrine. Thus, the Meiji era's treatment of asset depreciation as a problem of revaluation loss rather than a deductible expense would be out of the question today. A similar case is the manner in which the tax authorities once dealt with a capital transaction involving neither a revenue nor an expense. They interpreted "capital" to mean solely stated capital and consequently adhered to the viewpoint that a premium[184] paid in excess of par on purchasing stock constituted in-

[180] Juridical Persons' Tax Law Basic Circular, National Tax Agency Circular, *Chokuhō* (Direct Tax Division—Juridical Persons' Tax Section) 1–100, Sept. 25, 1950, 51.

[181] *Ibid.*, 52.

[182] Income Tax Law of 1899, art. 4(1)(i).

[183] Juridical Persons' Tax Law Enforcement Regulations, arts. 17–17-2; Income Tax Law Basic Circular, 216.

[184] The no-par share system was introduced into Japan by revision of the Commercial Code in 1950 (COMMERCIAL CODE art. 199, as amended by Law No. 167 of 1950), but in actual practice, even today, par shares far exceed the no-par variety. Moreover, on increasing capital,

come, an interpretation upheld by the former Administrative Court.[185] When the juridical persons' tax system was completely revised pursuant to the recommendations of the Shoup Mission, this traditional construction was abandoned, and now capital for tax purposes includes not only stated capital but capital surplus ("appropriated funds from capital" in the Juridical Persons' Tax Law) as well.[186] Therefore, today both premiums of this sort[187] and surplus from a reduction in capital are excluded from taxable income.[188]

The postwar advances made in business accounting have been striking. The systematic movement to rationalize accounting methods and bring uniformity, as far as possible, to the techniques of business administration cannot escape the attention of even the casual observer. Typical examples are the publication in 1949 of draft "Principles of Business Accounting,"[189] prepared by a government inquiry commission established to investigate the business accounting system, and the creation in 1950 of regulations to unify the formal appearance of company financial statements required to be submitted to the Ministry of Finance under the Securities Exchange Law upon the occasion of a stock offering.[190]

This progress in accounting has had a great impact on the computation of income for the juridical persons' tax. Its fruits have been incorporated into the Juridical Persons' Tax Law where the rules of computation have been systematically filled in and organized point by point. Nor can we ignore the significant role the Shoup Reports played in implementing this development, for it was the 1950 changes which took the first major legislative step forward along this road.

In order to satisfy the demands of tax equity by standardizing the procedures for determining taxable income, innumerable technical rules dealing with the computation process have been adopted. For example, depreciation

---

a company normally allots the new shares resulting from the increase to its shareholders at par value, collection of a premium being exceptional. Recently, though, it has become common to offer a portion of these new shares to the general public at market value.

[185] Takaoka Uchiwata Kabushiki Kaisha (Takaoka Whipped Cotton Company) v. Ōsaka Zeimu Kantoku Kyoku-chō (Director, Osaka Tax Supervision Bureau), Administrative Court, Dec. 20, 1920, 31 GYŌSEI SAIBANSHO HANKETSU ROKU (Record of Administrative Court Judgments) [hereafter cited GYŌ-HAN] 1027; Runapāku Kabushiki Kaisha v. Tōkyō Zeimu Kantoku Kyoku-chō (Director, Tokyo Tax Supervision Bureau), Administrative Court, May 6, 1913, 24 GYŌ-HAN 424.

[186] Juridical Persons' Tax Law, art. 13(1). The statutory terminology is "capital, etc.," "capital" referring to the Commercial Code definition limiting the term to the par value of par shares (COMMERCIAL CODE art. 284-2(1)) and the "etc." pulling in capital surplus.

[187] *Ibid.*, art. 9-2.

[188] *Ibid.*, arts. 9-4–9-5.

[189] Kigyō Kaikei Seido Chōsa Kai (Business Accounting System Investigation Commission), Keizai Antei Hombu (Economic Stabilization Board), *Kigyō Kaikei Gensoku* (Principles of Business Accounting), in KAIKEI ZENSHO (Complete Accounting Materials) 14–23 (Watanabe ed. 1962).

[190] Regulations Concerning the Terms, Form, and Method of Preparing Financial Statements, Etc., Securities Exchange Commission Regulation No. 18 of 1950.

expenses enterable in outlays are limited to an amount computed according to the useful life legally prescribed for the fixed asset concerned;[191] detailed provisions specify the methods of depreciation[192] and inventory valuation[193] which may be utilized; and the setting up of a reserve for bad debts[194] or other reserves or allowances chargeable to outlays[195] must conform with standards prescribed by law.

It should be remembered, though, that tax law imposes some adjustments on what is profit from the standpoint of proper business accounting, and therefore taxable income is an original concept which may differ somewhat in amount from the figure arrived at in accordance with standard accounting practice. Besides sundry exemptions, diverse forms of accelerated depreciation, and allowance and reserve systems permitting the deduction of expenses in excess of that recognized by good accounting practice, authorized pursuant to various economic policies, in some cases the whole amount of dividends received by a juridical person need not be entered in proceeds.[196] Moreover, as in the income tax, the juridical persons' tax and the juridical persons' inhabitants' tax are not deductible outlays.[197]

Compared with the orthodox approach of the income tax, several interesting and unusual phases of the computation of income for the juridical persons' tax deserve particular comment. Gratuitous contributions made by an individual, whether charitable or otherwise, may be deducted as a necessary expense only if they clearly relate to a business activity.[198] In

[191] See pp. 601–04 below.

[192] Juridical Persons' Tax Law, art. 9-8; Juridical Persons' Tax Law Enforcement Regulations, arts. 21-3–21-4, 21-6.

[193] Juridical Persons' Tax Law, art. 9-7; Juridical Persons' Tax Law Enforcement Regulations, art. 20.

[194] Juridical Persons' Tax Law Enforcement Regulations, arts. 14–14-5.

[195] See *ibid.*, arts. 14-6–15-15.

[196] Prior to and throughout 1961, all dividends received by one juridical person from another domestic juridical person were not taxed. A legislative change enacted in that year provided that from 1962 on where dividends received by a juridical person exceed those it pays out in the same business year, 25 percent of the excess must be entered in proceeds and taxed. Juridical Persons' Tax Law, art. 9-6(1) (see note 76 above); Juridical Persons' Tax Law Enforcement Regulations, art. 18-4; Tax Special Measures Law, art. 42-2; Tax Special Measures Law Enforcement Order, art. 27-3.

[197] Juridical Persons' Tax Law, art. 9(2).

[198] Income Tax Law Basic Circular, 266. The individual, however, is not left entirely out of the picture. In order to encourage socially desirable donations, the Income Tax Law was amended in the spring of 1962 to institute a new "deduction for contributions." The tax credit technique was adopted instead of a special deduction from income because the progressive rates of the income tax produce considerable disparity in the degree which an income deduction favors individual taxpayers subject to taxation at different brackets. Because of almost a complete lack of any tradition of personal giving for public purposes in Japanese society, the tax system for a long while diverged greatly in the way it dealt with corporate and individual contributions. The creation of this new deduction, despite a large variation in the specific rules applicable, has finally brought about a rough balance in the tax system between these two forms of contribution. Income Tax Law, art. 15-6, added by Law No. 44 of 1962. Also see ZEISEI CHŌSA KAI (Tax System Investigation Commission), TŌSHIN OYOBI SONO

the case of a juridical person, formerly the deduction of any contribution having even the slightest tinge of a business expense was permitted, for the basic composition of the income computation process called for deducting as outlays all disbursements diminishing net worth. Today, however, to be entered in outlays, a contribution must either come within a specific framework formulated pursuant to the amount of the juridical person's capital and taxable income[199] or be of a type or to an organization designated by the Minister of Finance as being strongly in the public interest.[200] In other words, the present rule sanctions a set sum as a business expense in accordance with a formal uniform standard and then, over and above this, recognizes the exemption of separate amounts for the reason that they are in the public interest.[201] Another area in which it has become necessary to impose some controls is that of entertainment expenses. Extravagant expenditure of company entertainment allowances, items of personal consumption often being thrown in, is an evil born out of the heavy taxation which followed the war. How to handle this perplexing issue developed into a painful ordeal for the Japanese tax administration. In search of a remedy, the law since 1954 has limited the extent to which a juridical person may include its expenditures for entertainment in outlays, and at present, after having undergone several changes, the rule states flatly that 20 percent of such disbursements may not be deducted if they exceed a specified maximum.[202]

Juridical persons filing a Blue Return may also carry net losses over and back. Such losses, known in the juridical persons' tax as "deficits," are deductible in business years beginning within five normal years after the commencement of the business year immediately following the one in which

---

SHINGI NO NAIYŌ TO KEIKA NO SETSUMEI (Report and an Explanation of the Content and Progress of Deliberations) [hereafter cited FINAL REPORT OF THE TAX SYSTEM INVESTIGATION COMMISSION], TŌSHIN BESSATSU (Separate Volume of the Report) [hereafter cited SEPARATE VOLUME] 566–72 (1961), and 2 ZEISEI CHŌSA KAI (Tax System Investigation Commission), TŌSHIN KANKEI SHIRYŌ SHŪ (Collection of Materials Relating to the Report) [hereafter cited FINAL REPORT OF THE TAX SYSTEM INVESTIGATION COMMISSION MATERIALS] 1014–24 (1962).

199 Juridical Persons' Tax Law, art. 9(3) (main sentence); Juridical Persons' Tax Law Enforcement Regulations, arts. 7–7-2.

200 Juridical Persons' Tax Law, art. 9(3) (proviso); Juridical Persons' Tax Law Enforcement Regulations, art. 8.

201 Strictly speaking, the framework for including contributions within outlays based on the amount of capital and taxable income, brought about by the 1961 amendments, is also really made up of two elements. Thus, in order to encourage science and technology as well as educational pursuits generally, it involves, in addition to the former generally recognized inclusion of contributions in outlays aspect, the approval of contributions up to a prescribed amount to certain agencies for experimentation and research, specified schools, organizations granting scholarships, etc., without the need of formal designation by the Minister of Finance. In this sense, the rules permitting contributions to be deducted up to the limit set by the capital and taxable income standard also include a tax exemption for policy reasons.

202 Tax Special Measures Law, art. 62; Tax Special Measures Law Enforcement Order, arts. 38–39. Also see FIRST REPORT OF THE TAX SYSTEM INVESTIGATION COMMISSION, SEPARATE VOLUME 345–50.

the deficit arose[203] or within one normal year prior to the business year of the deficit.[204] Furthermore, as in the income tax, even without a Blue Return the carry-over of losses to assets resulting from a disaster is recognized.[205] The variation between natural and juridical persons in the length of time allowed for the carry-over is primarily a product of the differing historical backgrounds of the two statutes.

The Juridical Persons' Tax Law possesses a concept peculiar to Japanese corporate income taxation—that of "liquidation income." Besides the regular income of each business, the juridical persons' tax also imposes separate rates on the liquidation income created by a dissolution or merger. "Liquidation income" is a special form of income, meaning, in the case of dissolution, the amount that the residual assets of a juridical person exceed its capital at the time of dissolution[206] and, in the case of merger, the amount that the total value of the shares of stock and money given by the juridical person produced by the merger to the shareholders of the juridical person being merged exceeds the capital of the latter at the time of merger.[207] Described in somewhat different terms, "liquidation income" involves a portion composed of retained earnings accumulated prior to the dissolution or merger and a portion formed from income realized due to the dissolution or merger itself. Although it may be possible to understand the taxation of the latter, why the former, consisting of undistributed profit upon which the regular juridical persons' tax has already been imposed, should be taxed once more, must assuredly bewilder the reader. Actually, though, despite its formal designation as "juridical persons' tax," the tax on liquidation income is really composite in nature—one part being equivalent to the juridical persons' tax levied on the income of each business year and the other to the personal income tax on the profits of a juridical person after they have been distributed into the hands of its shareholders. Consequently, liquidation income is subject to more than one rate. A burden equivalent to that of the income tax is imposed on the portion made up of accumulated reserves already taxed by the regular juridical persons' tax (computed in accordance with the average income tax burden borne by dividend income today) and one combining both the corporate and personal taxes on the remainder.[208] In order to complete the scheme, the income tax complements the special juridical persons' tax levy by providing that funds received by

[203] Juridical Persons' Tax Law, art. 9(5); Juridical Persons' Tax Law Enforcement Regulations, arts. 6(2), 9-2.

[204] Juridical Persons' Tax Law, art. 26-4; Juridical Persons' Tax Law Enforcement Regulations, art. 30.

[205] Juridical Persons' Tax Law, art. 9(6); Juridical Persons' Tax Law Enforcement Regulations, art. 10.

[206] Juridical Persons' Tax Law, art. 13(1)(i).

[207] *Ibid.*, art. 13(1)(ii).

[208] *Ibid.*, art. 17(1)(iii).

shareholders from a subsequent distribution of the liquidation income are tax free.[209]

Taxation of liquidation income has been a feature of the Japanese tax system since its first major reform in 1920.[210] This notion of imposing a special levy under the juridical persons' tax in accordance with a general estimate of the average income tax rate on profits attributable to shareholders was, of course, a convenient expedient to ease the administration of tax collection in this area. It is by no means difficult to imagine how this method of rough approximation must have struck Shoup, in his zealous quest for a perfectly pure global income tax. It must have seemed to him a weird and strangely grotesque institution. The system recommended by his mission[211] did away with this device and replaced it with the more conventional technique of taxing the shareholders directly on funds distributed during liquidation, the distribution being treated either as a constructive dividend[212] or a constructive capital gain.[213] However, Japanese officials charged with tax administration felt that in actual application it would be too much to expect individual taxpayers to comprehend the theoretical computations required for a correct declaration of income under the new system, and they concluded that the traditional practice of placing a general estimate of the burden on the source at the entity level was far more practical and secure. Consequently, when on economic grounds the income taxation of capital gains from an assignment of valuable securities was abolished in 1953, this aspect of the Shoup plan gave way to a revival of the old liquidation income formula.[214]

Depreciation, Economic Incentive Measures, and the Income Tax Family Employee Deduction

The Japanese income tax system contains a number of fairly specialized institutions relating to the computation of income, peculiarly characteristic of the system, which could not be accorded their just due in a general discussion of the sort given above. One of these is the depreciation system.

We have already noted that the development of business accounting has led to the gradual filling in of the details of income computation. Provisions

[209] Income Tax Law, art. 6(vii)–(viii).

[210] Income Tax Law of 1920, arts. 3 (Class I) D, 11.

[211] 1 First Shoup Report 112–13.

[212] Income Tax Law, art. 5, as amended by Law No. 71 of 1950, but prior to amendment by Law No. 173 of 1953.

[213] *Ibid.*, art. 10-2, as added by Law No. 71 of 1950, but prior to amendment by Law No. 173 of 1953.

[214] *Ibid.*, art. 6(vii)–(viii), as amended by Laws No. 173 of 1953 and No. 35 of 1961; Juridical Persons' Tax Law, art. 13, as added by Law No. 174 of 1953 and amended by Law No. 45 of 1962.

similar to the rules of the Juridical Persons' Tax Law have also been introduced into the Income Tax Law for the computation of individual business income, as far as the nature of this category of income permits. Consequently, present-day tax law incorporates almost all the methods utilized by standard accounting practice to value inventories and depreciate assets, classifies and prescribes regulations governing them by type, and, under certain fixed rules, broadly recognizes a free choice among the methods which one may apply provided that a method once selected will continue to be employed.[215] These provisions were not an aspect of tax law before the war and can be pointed to as a good example of the contribution made by the Shoup recommendations to the modernization of tax legislation. For instance, the Japanese depreciation system is now equipped with many features not appearing in the tax law of other nations. An examination of some of these peculiarities is instructive in showing the emphasis which Japanese income tax law places on accounting doctrine.

The first unique distinction of the depreciation system is its use of legally prescribed useful lives. That is to say, unlike the new guideline lives or Bulletin "F" in the United States and the useful life tables determined for internal use within the government by West Germany's tax administration,[216] the law has set out the useful life of every possible form of fixed asset in the minutest detail, and a business enterprise may deduct depreciation as an expense only where it calculates this amount in accordance with these tables.[217] Negotiation between business and government to determine the acceptable length of useful lives does not fit traditional Japanese methods of operation, and, in fact, the lives set by tax law decisively control those actually employed by business. Of course, if a legal useful life patently fails to meet a particular concern's needs, it may be reduced with the consent of the tax authorities.[218] The useful life tables are regularly expanded and amended as a matter of course to keep them up to date, and in 1961 they

[215] Income Tax Law, art. 10-3; Income Tax Law Enforcement Regulations, arts. 10, 10-3, 12-13–12-17; Income Tax Law Enforcement Rules, arts. 1-3–5-3; Juridical Persons' Tax Law, art. 9-8; Juridical Persons' Tax Law Enforcement Regulations, arts. 21–21-7; Juridical Persons' Tax Law Enforcement Rules, arts. 3–8.

[216] WORLD TAX SERIES, TAXATION IN THE FEDERAL REPUBLIC OF GERMANY 7/3.3 (1963).

[217] Income Tax Law Enforcement Regulations, arts. 10(3), 10-3(2); Income Tax Law Enforcement Rules, arts. 1-3, 5-2(1); Juridical Persons' Tax Law Enforcement Regulations, arts. 21-2(1), 21-6(2); Juridical Persons' Tax Law Enforcement Rules, arts. 3-2, 7-8(1); Ministerial Order Concerning the Useful Lives, Etc., of Fixed Assets, Ministry of Finance Order No. 50 of 1951; Concerning the Treatment of the Separate Tables of the Ministerial Order Concerning the Useful Lives, Etc., of Fixed Assets, National Tax Agency Circular, *Chokusho* (Direct Tax Division — Income Tax Section) 1–111, Sept. 25, 1951; Details for Machinery and Apparatus and Individual Lives, National Tax Agency, October 1961; Normal Period of Use of Machinery and Apparatus, National Tax Agency, October, 1961.

[218] Income Tax Law Enforcement Regulations, art. 10(4)–(5); Income Tax Law Enforcement Rules, arts. 4-2–4-4; Juridical Persons' Tax Law Enforcement Regulations, art. 21-2(2)–(3); Juridical Persons' Tax Law Enforcement Rules, arts. 7-2–7-4.

underwent a complete revision meant to take into account the present-day rapidity of technological innovation which went far beyond even these normal periodic changes.[219] Consequently, in that year the length of all useful lives was reduced notably.[220]

Second, while an individual proprietor must include in necessary expenses the amount of depreciation computed under tax law pursuant to the above useful lives regardless of the amount of depreciation really deducted internally within the business,[221] juridical persons need enter in outlays only the quantity computed in fact for accounting purposes provided that it is within the scope allowed by tax law,[222] and those filing a Blue Return may carry over for five years the amount within these bounds not actually deducted in the past.[223] Therefore, despite the standardization and control which results from the legal determination of useful lives, within the pattern set the depreciation permitted is extremely liberal.

Third, among the various methods of depreciation, free use of the declining-balance method is recognized for all tangible fixed assets, including buildings.[224] There is no condition, such as exists in the United States and West Germany, that the amount of depreciation taken in accordance therewith must remain within a fixed framework based on the straight-line method.

Fourth, nearly ten special accelerated depreciation plans have been established on the grounds of various industrial policies, such as, promoting business rationalization and modernizing small- and medium-sized enter-

[219] See FIRST REPORT OF THE TAX SYSTEM INVESTIGATION COMMISSION, SEPARATE VOLUME 169–90; FINAL REPORT OF THE TAX SYSTEM INVESTIGATION COMMISSION, SEPARATE VOLUME 62–65.

[220] Representative of the length of useful lives applied are the following general figures based on the legal useful life tables: wooden factory buildings 8–20 years, nonwooden factory buildings 15–55 years, wooden office buildings 27–30 years, nonwooden office buildings 25–75 years, wooden hotel buildings 25–27 years, nonwooden hotel buildings 22–65 years, dams used to generate hydroelectric power 80 years, steel electric transmission towers 50 years, large steel fishing vessels 14 years, large oil tankers 16 years, other steel vessels 16–18 years, trucks 4–5 years, buses 5 years, taxis 3–4 years, milling machinery 14–16 years, baking machinery 14 years, cold-storage machinery 17 years, spinning machinery 12–17 years, textile machinery 13–19 years, dye-control machinery 7–10 years, plywood-manufacturing machinery 13 years, paper-manufacturing machinery 15–18 years, sulfuric-acid-manufacturing machinery 8–10 years, rayon-manufacturing machinery 9–11 years, cement-manufacturing machinery 8–19 years, iron-and-steel-manufacturing machinery 15–18 years, automobile-manufacturing machinery 13–16 years, railroad-rolling-stock-manufacturing machinery 14 years, and machinery for lumbering 15 years. Ministerial Order Concerning the Useful Lives, Etc., of Fixed Assets, Separate Tables I–II.

[221] Concerning the Manner of Treating the Amended Income Tax Law, *Chokusho* (Direct Tax Division — Income Tax Section) 1–12, Jan. 26, 1952, 23.

[222] Juridical Persons' Tax Law Enforcement Rules, arts. 3–3-2.

[223] Juridical Persons' Tax Law Enforcement Rules, art. 3-6.

[224] Income Tax Law Enforcement Regulations, art. 12-13(1); Juridical Persons' Tax Law Enforcement Regulations, art. 21-3(1).

prise.[225] A typical pattern calls for adding to normal depreciation in the first year a one-third write-off of the acquisition value of the fixed asset and then prorating the depreciation yet remaining over the rest of the asset's useful life. There is, though, nothing comparable to the British "investment allowance" wherein the book value of the asset is not reduced and which, therefore, actually operates as a subsidy.

Another singular characteristic of Japanese income taxation, which has lent color to the tax changes enacted throughout the period of industrial reconstruction that set in soon after the Shoup reforms, has been the trial of numerous special measures formulated to accomplish certain economic objectives. Change after change, piled one on top of the other, has been enacted into legislation of limited and normally short duration. The forms of incentive involved can be classified into many types. The special depreciation systems were but one example. Others are various reserves and allowances, chargeable to business expense in order to encourage the accumulation of working capital, and the even more direct device of a straight tax exemption. Let us glance quickly at a few of these items not touched on elsewhere.

Reserves and allowances which may be charged off as a business expense involve not only those of a sort common to all enterprise, such as a reserve for bad debts, a reserve for price fluctuations, and an allowance for severance pay, but also those applicable to more specialized operations like an allowance for special repairs,[226] a reserve for extraordinary casualties (for casualty-insurance companies),[227] and a reserve for drought (for electric-power companies).[228] Some of these reserves and allowances conform to their original accounting function and amounts entered therein qualify as proper expenses in terms of sound accounting practice, but in many instances tax law, emphasizing the need for uniformity, has established a fixed standard to which private enterprise normally responds by seeking to retain its earnings through making deductions up to the allowable maximum. For example, the reserve for bad debts is not thought of as an allowance calculated separately by each individual concern according to its past experience in the rate of defaulted debts, as is the case in America and Germany; instead, a standard across-the-board limitation based on multiplying the debts at the end of a business year by a prescribed percentage for the particular

[225] Tax Special Measures Law, arts. 11–18, 43–52; Tax Special Measures Law Enforcement Order, arts. 6–10, 27-4–30; Designation of Machinery and Other Equipment and Periods Subject to the Application of the Provisions of Article 11, Paragraph (1), Item (i), and Article 43, Paragraph (1), Item (i), of the Tax Special Measures Law, Ministry of Finance Notification No. 186 of 1961.

[226] Income Tax Law Enforcement Regulations, arts. 10-10–10-15; Juridical Persons' Tax Law Enforcement Regulations, arts. 15–15-6.

[227] Juridical Persons' Tax Law Enforcement Regulations, arts. 14-14–14-21.

[228] Juridical Persons' Tax Law Enforcement Regulations, arts. 14-6–14-8.

kind of business activity being carried on is imposed for all.[229] This reserve's roots may be traced back to the First Shoup Report,[230] but despite many subsequent restrictions placed on the extent to which funds may be transferred to it, its use as a means to retain income far exceeds anything anticipated by Shoup.

Similar traits are equally visible in the allowance for severance pay and the reserve for price fluctuations. Employment of the former is quite common, for Japanese tax law has only recently recognized special treatment for pension funds comparable to the American "employees' trust," the usual course being to retain within the business in the form of a reserve those funds which will eventually be paid out to employees on leaving work.[231] The allowance resembles the German reserve for future pension payments to employees[232] in that it involves an appropriation of funds within the business; but, unlike the German system — which with the American and British plans assumes that contributions will be set aside in accordance with actuarial principles applicable to life insurance — it possesses its own peculiar structure taking as its base the amount of severance pay that would be necessary if at the end of each business year all the employees should decide to leave work en bloc.[233] The latter reserve for price fluctuations consists of

[229] Income Tax Law Enforcement Regulations, arts. 10-5–10-9; Juridical Persons' Tax Law Enforcement Regulations, arts. 14–14-5.

[230] 2 First Shoup Report 141–42.

[231] The single lump-sum payment to the employee on leaving work is traditional in Japan, but formerly its actual employment was limited to government officials and at most a portion of the large companies. Recently, though, consciousness concerning the retirement annuity system has intensified within the business world and gradually the cases where a concern establishes its own annuity plan have increased. Reflecting these conditions, private enterprise strongly urged that, besides the internal allowance for severance pay, Japan should also adopt the American and British qualified pension-plan system where a fund is set up outside the business for the purpose of paying retirement annuities. This desire was finally realized in the 1962 amendments (Juridical Persons' Tax Law, arts. 2(2), 12-2; Juridical Persons' Tax Law Enforcement Regulations, arts. 1-5–1-7, 10-7; Juridical Persons' Tax Law Enforcement Rules, art. 1-2). The system enacted is essentially the same as that found in the United States and Great Britain, but it involves one feature peculiar to it alone. Since it presupposes the setting aside of a large amount of money for a lengthy period as a retirement annuity fund free from the income and juridical persons' taxes, a light tax (in form a special juridical persons' tax) of 1.2 percent of the amount of the fund is imposed on the fund itself (that is, the portion accumulated from contributions borne by the employer and the profit from the fund's operations) as a kind of interest surcharge for the deferral of income taxation from the time the concern makes its contribution until the employee actually receives his annuity (Juridical Persons' Tax Law, arts. 2(2), 17(1)(ii)).

An enterprise may elect to use either the allowance for severance pay or the qualified retirement annuity system, or both together, provided that they do not overlap, but in view of the tendency of private enterprise to place considerable importance on the internal retention of capital within the business, it seems likely that the allowance for severance pay system will continue widely utilized in the future.

[232] World Tax Series, Taxation in the Federal Republic of Germany 7/2.4d. (1963).

[233] Income Tax Law Enforcement Regulations, arts. 10-16–10-24; Juridical Persons' Tax Law Enforcement Regulations, arts. 15-7–15-15. In Japan the amount of severance pay due normally differs depending upon whether the employee leaves work at his own rather than his employer's convenience. For the computation involved here, the former is assumed to be the case.

a specific amount, established anew at the end of each business year and based on the amount of inventories at that time, which is charged back into proceeds and then re-established ("scrubbed out and replaced")[234] at the end of the succeeding business year by first a reversing entry and then a new entry calculated in exactly the same manner.[235] Although an attempt has been made to rationalize it in conformity with its initial aim by cutting the rate at which it may be accumulated, depending upon whether the commodity concerned is one subject to extreme price variation (for example, international merchandise), it remains the one among all the legally recognized reserves and allowances most deeply tainted with income retention qualities. West Germany possesses a somewhat similar system,[236] but Japan's is considerably broader in application. Properly speaking, its function has become such that it might better be called a "special reserve to give management a freer hand in financing business operations."

The important special measures exempting interest on certain deposits and capital gain from the assignment of valuable securities have already been mentioned. The special export income deduction to stimulate foreign trade[237] and the exemption of manufacturing profit from new important industries[238] are two other significant measures deserving citation. The latter dates back to 1913, when Japanese capitalism was in its adolescence.[239] In spite of the recent imposition of strong restrictions on both its scope and the items covered, this outright immunity from taxation remains with us as a crude relic of a bygone day. It is of a sort typical to underdeveloped countries but has no place in an advanced industrial nation and ought to be repealed. The Shoup Reports failed to touch upon it, possibly because they overlooked its existence.

A new and extremely interesting institution, representative of fundamental changes taking place within Japanese society, is the deduction for family employees in the income tax, usually referred to as the "exclusive employee deduction."[240] Formerly, the Income Tax Law reflected the traditional family organization known as the "House." From the law's very beginning,

[234] *Araigae.*

[235] Tax Special Measures Law, arts. 19, 53; Tax Special Measures Law Enforcement Order, arts. 10-2–11, 30-2–31.

[236] WORLD TAX SERIES, TAXATION IN THE FEDERAL REPUBLIC OF GERMANY 6/6.6 (1963).

[237] Tax Special Measures Law, arts. 21–23, 55–57-2; Tax Special Measures Law Enforcement Order, arts. 13–15-2, 33–34-2; Tax Special Measures Law Enforcement Regulations, arts. 7-3–9, 21.

[238] Income Tax Law, art. 20; Income Tax Law Enforcement Regulations, arts. 15–18; Income Tax Law Enforcement Rules, arts. 8-2–8-5; Juridical Persons' Tax Law, art. 6; Juridical Persons' Tax Law Enforcement Regulations, arts. 2–5; Juridical Persons' Tax Law Enforcement Rules, arts. 1-4–1-8.

[239] Income Tax Law of 1899, art. 5-2, as added by law No. 13 of 1913; Cabinet Order No. 69 of 1913.

[240] See Income Tax Law, art. 11-2.

all income of the "members of a House"[241] living together was combined with that of the "head of the House" and taxed to him.[242] When after the war a revision of the Civil Code brought about the demise of this body as a legally recognized group, the tax law concept of "members of a House living together"[243] was merely repainted to read "relatives living together";[244] yet taxation of the household unit as a whole through consolidation of all the income of the extended family over several generations was maintained. It was the Shoup Reports which finally destroyed this scheme.[245] Pursuant to their recommendations, Japan's income tax took a sharp turn in a direction away from the family and toward the individual as the basic taxable unit. Consequently, today, featuring such aspects as the completely separate taxation of the income of husband and wife, the tax system has become the most thoroughly individualistic found anywhere in the world.

However, despite this legal transformation in the manner of taxing income, the realities of family living did not alter anywhere near so abruptly. One perplexing problem was how to treat the compensation paid family members employed in the business activities of an individual proprietorship. It is indeed quite correct that originally the practice of an owner of a business paying wages for family labor had been almost nonexistent. The business belonged to the family and both its finances and those of the household were normally controlled by one and the same person: their common head. While the penetration of individualistic thought, which reached its pinnacle in the new postwar Constitution, has been, to say the least, remarkable, it has not reached the point where family labor is considered the same as a general contract of employment; great differences between town and country in the manner in which such labor is regarded are still present.

Accordingly, if compensation paid by an individual proprietor to the members of his family is to be regarded as a freely deductible expense in the computation of his business income, it is clear that the lack of objective standards of control will leave the way open for the inevitable manipulation of the tax burden through the device of apparent wages. Under the pre-

[241] The Japanese term used here is *kazoku*, a word normally translated as "family." However, etymologically the Chinese characters making it up literally mean "members of a House" and in prewar legal language it was used to represent the oriental extended family. Today, both legally and in common usage, it has come to mean a much more limited body centering around parents and children in the English sense of the word "family." To convey both meanings, in this essay the prewar employment of the term is translated as "members of a House" and the postwar concept as "family."

[242] See Income Tax Law of 1887, art. 1(1).

[243] *Dōkyo kazoku*. See Income Tax Law of 1940, arts. 14(2), 15(2), 19, 20(2), 21(4), 25(4), 31(2).

[244] *Dōkyo shinzoku*. Income Tax Law, arts. 8(1)–(2), 14(2), prior to amendment by Law No. 71 of 1950.

[245] 1 First Shoup Report 73–76.

existing system, the lumping of family income meant that, no matter how the income was allocated among its respective components, the burden on the family as a whole remained unchanged, but today, when the individual is the unit, how this allocation is made strongly affects the various burdens. Shoup also foresaw the possibility of abuse here and recommended that the loophole be closed by combining compensation paid family members by an individual proprietor with his own income.[246] Provisions adopting this suggestion were in fact enacted into the Income Tax Law at the same time that consolidated taxation of the household was repealed.[247]

However, it was absolutely impossible to stabilize the tax structure pursuant to this pattern. The major source of disruption was the widespread transformation of individual proprietorships into organized juridical persons. This "incorporation" process developed into one of the most significant factors which the postwar tax system has had to face, and it is not going too far to state that the fundamental cause of this phenomenon was a reaction to the fact that the individual entrepreneur was not permitted to deduct compensation for family labor. When a business becomes a separate entity, family members employed in it become its officers and employees, and suitable compensation for their services becomes a deductible outlay of the business and wages to the members; thus, unlike the case of the sole proprietorship, the entity works a transmutation of business income into remuneration income with all the attendant advantages. Not only do the members of the family lighten their income tax through dividing up their income among themselves, but the tax base for the local business activity tax levied on the net profit of the enterprise is reduced and, consequently, there is a drop in the amount of this tax payable.

Although the establishment of new juridical persons has progressed at breakneck speed, naturally not all individual entrepreneurs have been able to become entities. Once the nature of the phenomenon became generally understood, a fierce debate arose as to whether or not rules ought to be introduced into the income tax to permit the controlled deduction of compensation for family labor. Even the possibility of placing restrictions directly on the wages paid by these jerry-built companies was considered.[248] Among many of these entities there are some whose actual structure, despite the formal payment of wages, differs not in the least from the sole proprietor who fails to separate his business accounts from his family finances. Of

[246] *Ibid.*, at 74.

[247] Income Tax Law, art. 11-2, as added by Law No. 71 of 1950, but prior to amendment by Law No. 53 of 1952.

[248] See Shiozaki, *Kokuzei ni Kan-suru Tōmen no Sho-Mondai* (Current Problems Concerning National Taxation), in NIHON SOZEI KENKYŪ KYŌKAI (Japan Tax Research Association), KŌWA JŌYAKU-GO NO NIHON ZEISEI (The Japanese Tax System After the Peace Treaty) 511, 518 (Nihon Sozei Kenkyū Kyōkai Dai San Kai Kenkyū Taikai Kiroku (Record of the Third Study Convention of the Japan Tax Research Association) ed. 1951); FIRST REPORT OF THE TAX SYSTEM INVESTIGATION COMMISSION, SEPARATE VOLUME 60.

course, if a payment of wages is clearly fictitious or the amount paid is inordinately high, it is possible to undertake administrative measures which will recognize deduction of the sum only within reasonable bounds. For the great majority of juridical persons, however, one could not even begin to point out those which merely serve as a sham and, even though a family company is concerned, in principle, there is no rationale running through the tax system which would permit disallowing the deduction of compensation paid family executives. On the other hand, while the actual circumstances involved are quite similar, the time is still not ripe to line up individual entrepreneurs beside juridical persons and recognize the free deduction of compensation for family labor based upon decisions made within the family. Doubtless, the most desirable course would be to regard the matter as a problem of administration and place it in the hands of the tax authorities to be dealt with case by case in accordance with the peculiar circumstances involved, but, in view of the present state of family labor in Japan, this would be in terms of realistic tax administration an enormously difficult task to accomplish. Here, then, was a major dilemma facing the authorities.

The solution ultimately adopted was somewhat generalized, serving as a compromise between several conflicting elements. One result, devised as a link in the chain of steps taken, was the exclusive employee deduction now under discussion. When first incorporated into the Income Tax Law in 1952, it was restricted to persons filing a Blue Return and recognized the deduction by individual proprietors as a necessary expense of compensation paid for family labor, provided that the amount actually paid each family employee did not exceed 50,000 yen (about 139 dollars) per calendar year.[249] The limitation to taxpayers filing a Blue Return was part of an intentional policy to encourage the widespread use of Blue Returns among single entrepreneurs and rested upon the common knowledge that those authorized to file a Blue Return must clearly distinguish their business accounts from family finances.

Structurally, although a maximum restriction is placed on the amount deductible, the system plainly presupposes that the entrepreneur actually pays wages and deducts them as an operating expense.[250] Nevertheless, the popular denomination of this system as a separate special "deduction" hints at what may in fact be its true nature. After 1952, subsequent amendments expanded its application to cover spouses and increased the maximum amount deductible concomitant with the gradual rise in the basic deduction.[251] The most far-reaching change occurred in the 1961 revision, which

[249] Income Tax Law, art. 11-2(2), as added by Law No. 53 of 1952, but prior to amendment by Law No. 173 of 1953.

[250] Income Tax Law, art. 11-2; Concerning the Treatment of the Income Tax Law (Excluding Income Tax at Source Relationships) as Amended in March, 1961, National Tax Agency Circular, *Chokusho* (Direct Tax Division — Income Tax Section) 1–85, Dec. 12, 1961, 32.

[251] The "basic deduction" is a concept equivalent to the taxpayer's own "personal exemption" in the United States.

made the system available even to individuals filing a White Return (general taxpayers not authorized to file a Blue Return).[252] In this instance, since it would be extremely difficult to determine whether the average White Return taxpayer, who normally possesses scanty accounting records, had actually paid the wages deducted and preservation of the old requirement could easily have become a farce, the new rules literally granted an "exclusive employee deduction"; no inquiry is conducted into the fact of payment and the mere stroke of a pen claiming the deduction of a specified amount paid to family employees meeting certain conditions is recognized without question. The composition of this new deduction for White Return taxpayers, as a necessary expense subtractable from business income and as "constructive" remuneration income of the family member rendering services, makes it quite apparent that it functions both as a special device to adjust the differences between natural and juridical persons in the treatment of consideration for family labor and as a means to strike a balance between individual Blue and White Return taxpayers. Today the maximum deduction allowed persons filing a Blue Return is 120,000 yen (about 333 dollars),[253] and the flat deduction for others 70,000 yen (about 194 dollars).[254] From a theoretical standpoint, this disparity may seem strange, but it is aimed at preservation of the policy seeking to expand the use of Blue Returns. Moreover, even for Japan, with its relatively low income level, the amounts deductible have been kept extremely small.[255]

A tax system which recognizes the payment of wages between husband and wife through the device of an exclusive employee deduction may well give rise to the impression that postwar Japanese society is even more individualistic than that of the West. Again, it is possible that granting a deduction to White Return entrepreneurs without requiring proof of an actual expenditure will result in wage earners objecting that they are being discriminated against and businessmen favored. The elements involved, such as the state of family labor in Japan, the influence on the tax burden under various conditions of the various taxes on individuals and juridical persons, the lack of a balance between natural and juridical persons and White and Blue Return taxpayers, the demand for equity of burdens, and the desire not to isolate the tax system from the demands of reality, and so on ad infinitum, are not only numerous but extremely complex. Sufficient space is lacking to do them all justice, but the seeming discrepancies in the deduction for

[252] Income Tax Law, art. 11-2(3).
[253] *Ibid.*, art. 11-2(2).
[254] *Ibid.*, art. 11-2(3).
[255] Japanese per-capita national income for fiscal year 1961 (April 1961 to March 1962) was 149,806 yen (about 416 dollars). Japan Times, Dec. 12, 1962, p. 2, col. 5–6. Also see SHŌWA 37 NENDO ZUSETSU NIHON NO ZAISEI (1962 Graphic Japanese Public Finance) 41 (Aoshika ed. 1962) and SHŌWA 37 NENDO KEIZAI HAKUSHO (1962 Economic White Paper) 326–27, 391 (Keizai Kikaku-chō (Economic Planning Agency) ed. 1962).

family employees can be understood only when we perceive that this system is a realistic and practicable one precariously balanced astride a score of highly intricate factors.

Some Comments on the Concept of Income

The usual course in any discussion of income and its computation is to begin by considering just what is "income." Feeling, though, that the reader would prefer first to get acquainted with what is most likely an unfamiliar system, up to now I have only described the particulars and have had little to say about the general concept. We have, however, reached the point where it seems proper to include a few comments on the latter topic.

The British, American, and West German systems are representative of different approaches toward taxable income; the British and American positions present two extremes and Germany stands somewhere in between. Thus, in Great Britain taxable income consists only of that prescribed in specific schedules, regarded as derived from ordinarily recurrent sources, while capital gains and casual receipts are excluded.[256] On the other hand, the American income tax is typical of those systems which treat income from every source, including capital gains, as taxable.[257] Germany employs a concept which, although it is based on that of Britain, is broader in scope, for it includes income derived from various speculative transactions and the assignment of either a business or shares of stock in a company that amount to a "substantial interest."[258]

Where does Japan place on a scale running from the British to the American position? As has been noted already, the Japanese personal and corporate income taxes began their development from two quite divergent starting points. The taxation of juridical persons has always been permeated with the idea that any increase in net worth produces income and that every form of income received after the entity's establishment, irrespective of source, is subject to tax. The personal income tax, quite the contrary, was initially founded upon a proposition quite similar to the British one, casual receipts not derived from a profit-making business activity being nontaxable. Although undoubtedly this approach was adopted under the influence of the British system, various realistic considerations of tax enforcement were also at work. Be that as it may, conceptually it governed the Japanese personal income tax for a great many years, and it was only an increase in the general tax burden produced by a growth in the demands of public finance which, through a gradual expansion of the subject matter taxed, finally led to its demise. The revolt against this tradition began in 1938 when severance

[256] World Tax Series, Taxation in the United Kingdom 6/1.1 (1957).

[257] World Tax Series, Taxation in the United States 6/1.2a. (1963).

[258] World Tax Series, Taxation in the Federal Republic of Germany 6/1.2, 6/1.6c., 6/1.8, 9/7.3 (1963).

income was taxed for the first time[259] and gained momentum during the war in the amendment of an "extraordinary profits tax," enacted a few years earlier separate from the formal income tax, so that it imposed a fairly heavy burden on capital gains from the assignment of such property as immovables, ships, and mining industrial rights.[260] The end of the war saw another step forward with the abolition of the extraordinary profits tax in 1946 [261] and the incorporation of its taxable subject matter into the income tax without change under the name of "assignment income." [262] Finally, in the next year, personal income as an all-inclusive conception was rounded out by expanding capital gains to cover assignments of valuable securities and inaugurating the taxation of occasional or casual income, such as prizes.

Today the inclusion of capital gains in taxable income is balanced by the full deduction of capital losses from other income. Moreover, although before the Shoup Reports, aside from the basic and dependency deductions, only those items deductible in the "computation of income" stage — such as business and capital losses (assignment losses) — were permitted to be subtracted in the even more inclusive "computation of taxable income" process (all personal and family expenditures being strictly disregarded), since then the personal income tax has allowed within certain limits the deduction of extraordinary losses — namely, casualty losses and medical expenses. These, while personal in nature, bring about a reduction in the individual taxpayer's ability to pay tax.[263] Accordingly, when we take these factors into account, it becomes quite apparent that taxable income in the income tax has grown very close to the net worth accretion theory of income found in the juridical persons' tax.[264]

However, in spite of the fact that the basic pattern of the income tax has been thus set for a good many years, it has failed to attain anywhere near a semblance of adequate stability. The problem lies with capital gains, which have constituted an incessant source of disturbance, amendment after amendment regularly being brought up for discussion. Undeniably every national income tax system worthy of the name must tax capital gains, but how this is to be accomplished presents a wide variety of issues requiring solution.

[259] Income Tax Law of 1920, arts. 2(iv), 3(Class II) C, as amended by Law No. 43 of 1938.

[260] Extraordinary Profits Tax Law, Law No. 20 of 1935, arts. 3(1)(iii), 11-2, as amended by Laws No. 49 of 1939 and No. 49 of 1942.

[261] By Law No. 14 of 1946.

[262] Income Tax Law of 1940, arts. 12(1)(xi), as amended by Law No. 14 of 1946.

[263] That is, by means of the "deduction for medical expenses" (Income Tax Law, art. 11-5) and the "deduction for miscellaneous losses" (*ibid.*, art. 11-4).

[264] However, neither the National Tax Agency nor the courts has seen fit to go so far in their official pronouncements. They have rather chosen to build up gradually the doubtful areas under the heading of "miscellaneous income" case by case. See, for example, Income Tax Law Basic Circular, 151; Yoshimura v. Japan, Tokyo High Court, May 10, 1950, 3 KŌTŌ SAIBANSHO KEIJI HANREI SHŪ (A Collection of Criminal High Court Cases) 185. Also see CHU, ZEIHŌ TO KAIKEI GENSOKU (Tax Law and the Principles of Accounting) 473–77, 559–69 (1953).

An extended general discussion of the nature of income as a concept is given in *ibid.*, at 287–399.

Shoup, in his fastidious pursuit of a complete taxation of every type of capital gain and other casual income, sought to meet one of the major objections to this form of taxation by proposing the introduction of a complicated formula to average tax over several years; this was intended to soften the effect of progressive rates on income of a kind arising all at once in a single calendar year.[265] In the beginning, his plan was adopted in its entirety, but soon after it underwent a number of unavoidable changes, about which I shall have more to say later. Here, though, the mere necessity of change should be mentioned with some emphasis, for it explains why the present tax system fails to apply a single clear-cut theory. In comparison with other categories of income, capital gains incorporate heterogeneous elements, a fact clearly reflected by the various sorts of resistance which arise whenever any attempt is made to include capital gains and losses within taxable income. Shoup emphasized that there is no substantial economic difference between capital gains and other income and that the utmost effort should be exerted to abolish its privileged treatment.[266] However, the problem which seemed to concern him most was gain from transactions in shares of stock; among all the different forms which capital gains may take, it is difficult to understand why his reports in their discussion of the general topic placed so much emphasis upon this particularly specialized one. It is indeed true that gain from stock transactions possesses the fewest special elements and is by nature suitable for taxation in the same way as ordinary income, but, where capital gains in general concern us, I cannot in all honesty pronounce peremptory judgment that they are in no way different from other classes of income.

Viewed either in terms of the national economy or from the individual taxpayer's standpoint, taxing capital gains in exactly the same manner as other income involves a taxation of capital element which creates widespread hostility. The average person does not normally regard an increase in the value of his property as giving rise in and of itself to income. Even when the property is sold and the gain from the price increase realized, the public tends to feel that a tax on this amount is a capital levy, since it is no longer possible to replace the asset with another of equivalent economic value by means of the proceeds remaining from the sale. This attitude becomes apparent when the property has been used for a fixed purpose within either the home or a business and is particularly pronounced when it has been held over a long period of time. There cannot be the slightest doubt that taxation of capital gains strongly interferes with property transactions.[267]

[265] 1 FIRST SHOUP REPORT 89–93; 3 *ibid.*, at B1–5.

[266] 3 *ibid.*, at B10–12.

[267] This is not my view alone. See, for example, Smith, *Tax Treatment of Capital Gains*, in 2 STAFF OF HOUSE COMM. ON WAYS AND MEANS, 86TH CONG., 1ST SESS., TAX REVISION COMPENDIUM 1233 (Comm. Print 1959), which explains clearly and lucidly the essential nature of capital gains taxation and proposes specific methods for carrying it out. Similar views in greater detail are also expressed in SMITH, FEDERAL TAX REFORM 119–55 (1961). Cf. SELTZER, THE NATURE AND TAX TREATMENT OF CAPITAL GAINS (1951).

Resistance of this sort has resulted in the building up of a variety of exceptions to capital gains taxation in Japanese income tax law. One extreme case of special treatment is the deferred taxation of gain due to compulsory expropriation by the state provided the item is replaced.[268] Again, rules, comparable to those in American tax law, have been established which do not recognize the realization of income from the sale and replacement or exchange of certain assets, such as household property, because it is not desirable in terms of policy.[269] The Shoup Reports went so far as to recommend that not only gain actually realized through a sale or exchange for consideration, but also the imputed benefit produced where the transfer is by gift, bequest, or inheritance be liquidated and taxed to the decedent or donor.[270] Initially this suggestion was faithfully enacted into the Income Tax Law.[271] In 1952, though, the portion dealing with inheritance was replaced by a provision that the heir should succeed to the acquisition value of the property in the hands of the decedent.[272] However, the balance of the rule, which related to gifts and bequests, remained a factor in Japanese income taxation for a number of years. Finally, in the 1962 amendments, owing to the ill repute with which it was held by both front-line tax officials and taxpayers, this provision was modified and now, in this case too, the donor or his heir may elect that the donee or legatee shall succeed to his predecessor's acquisition value.[273] It is difficult to convince a taxpayer that a mere rise in the price of an asset amounts to income, and the tax officials were constantly perplexed over how best to explain to the taxpayer why he must pay income tax on a gift to another when he himself realized no benefit whatsoever from the transfer.

Capital losses, although somewhat easier to deal with, have not been free from their own peculiar problems. In 1961, the Tax System Investigation Commission examined this matter thoroughly and in the spring of 1962 its recommendations became law. Basically two problems were considered. First, where should the line be drawn between a capital loss and a loss of assets considered a nondeductible disposal of income or property? The term "capital loss" is not a technical term employed by Japanese statutory law and has been used in this essay, in the case of the Income Tax Law, as the equivalent of "assignment losses" (the counterpart of assignment income).[274]

[268] Tax Special Measures Law, arts. 31–34, 64–65-2.

[269] For example, Tax Special Measures Law, arts. 35–38-2; Tax Special Measures Law Enforcement Order, arts. 24–25-2; Tax Special Measures Law Enforcement Regulations, arts. 17–18.

[270] 1 FIRST SHOUP REPORT 91–92; 3 *ibid.*, at B12–13.

[271] Income Tax Law, arts. 5-2, 10(4), as amended by Law No. 71 of 1950, but prior to amendment by Law No. 53 of 1952.

[272] Income Tax Law, arts. 5-2, 10(4), as amended by Law No. 53 of 1952, but prior to amendment by Law No. 44 of 1962.

[273] Income Tax Law, arts. 5-2(3), 10(5). Of course, if the election is not made, the old rule remains in effect.

[274] Strictly speaking, the words "assignment losses" (*jōto sonshitsu*) do not appear in the Income Tax Law either, but they constitute the term normally employed in commentaries on

In addition to this concept, which encompasses losses derived from assignment income transactions producing a loss rather than a gain,[275] Japan also possesses a special "deduction for miscellaneous losses," to be taken in the computation of taxable income, permitting the deduction of those extraordinary losses which, in spite of their personal nature, result solely from disaster or theft.[276] The relationship between this deduction and capital losses inevitably became part of the general issue. For example, if an individual tears down an old house in order to construct a new one, the result is a voluntary disposal of property and not a capital loss;[277] nor is the scope of the deduction for miscellaneous losses broad enough to cover the matter.[278] Formerly, the same thinking applied to an individual's destruction of a store used by him in his business,[279] but this rule was inconsistent with the conception of income in the juridical persons' tax which views such action as an outlay per se[280] and led to a breakdown in the aspect of equality of treatment between natural and juridical persons under the personal and corporate income taxes. Again, losses due to the performance of a nonbusiness-connected surety obligation or the inability of a bankrupt bank to repay a deposit are neither an assignment loss nor covered by the deduction for miscellaneous losses. But it is overly harsh to look upon them as a voluntary disposal of income, and there are those who hold the opinion that such losses should be deductible as a capital loss, as in the United States.

The second problem considered by the commission was the reasonableness of allowing the general unconditional deduction from all income of assignment losses and those subject to the deduction for miscellaneous losses. Is it rational to permit a millionaire to subtract from his extremely large annual income the loss of a palatial villa destroyed by fire? Each year's income is a yardstick by which we measure the taxpayer's ability to pay, but, if we accept the unconditional setoff against it of the loss of property that is the product of many years of accumulation, it is tantamount to granting a property owner insurance on his asset equal to the effective rate of his income tax burden. Undeniably this course of action is a bit too magnanimous for the tax system of a poor state. Great Britain matches its nontaxation of capital gains by completely refusing to consider these capital losses. Despite its simplicity, the British practice has much to say for it.[281]

---

it. The various references to "capital losses" in the Shoup Reports were regularly translated into Japanese as "assignment losses." See, for example, 1 FIRST SHOUP REPORT 90.

[275] Income Tax Law, art. 9-3(1).

[276] Income Tax Law, art. 11-4; Income Tax Law Enforcement Regulations, art. 12-25.

[277] See FINAL REPORT OF THE TAX SYSTEM INVESTIGATION COMMISSION, SEPARATE VOLUME 549; 2 FINAL REPORT OF THE TAX SYSTEM INVESTIGATION COMMISSION MATERIALS 955.

[278] See Income Tax Law Basic Circular, 327(1).

[279] See FINAL REPORT OF THE TAX SYSTEM INVESTIGATION COMMISSION, SEPARATE VOLUME 551.

[280] Concerning the Treatment of the Acquisition Value, Etc., of Fixed Assets, National Tax Agency Circular, *Chokuhō* (Direct Tax Division — Juridical Persons' Tax Section) 1–28, March 1, 1960, 11.

[281] On this second problem see also FIRST REPORT OF THE TAX SYSTEM INVESTIGATION COMMISSION, SEPARATE VOLUME 371–72.

The answers provided by the 1962 changes are disarmingly uncomplicated. Concerning the idea that the deduction for miscellaneous losses should be expanded and losses to assets, other than those considered a free disposal of income or property by the income recipient, should be deducted, it was decided that the pre-existing structure of the deduction for miscellaneous losses should be preserved essentially intact. Assorted reasons were given for arriving at this conclusion, such as the difficulty of delineating the scope of losses to be recognized as deductible, the dubious propriety of granting the broad deduction of property losses which, in terms of the concept of taxable income as it is adapted to the taxpayer's ability to pay, are not related to activities giving rise to the generation of income, and the need, if the deduction is to be permitted over a wide area from all types of income, to establish as far as possible a precise maximum restriction on the amount that might be subtracted.[282] However, the composition of necessary expenses was expanded in regard to the loss of an individual entrepreneur's business-connected fixed assets, which prior to the changes had been accorded a somewhat narrower scope as necessary expenses than was available for the outlays of a juridical person, to include even intentional losses of the sort wherein a shopowner destroys his own shop.[283]

Regarding the second problem, there was general agreement that the unrestricted deduction of asset losses from all income under the deduction for miscellaneous losses had indeed gone too far and that some restraints were necessary. The possibility of establishing a fixed amount as a maximum limitation was examined, but it was decided that any attempt to impose a uniform deductible limit would be in the final analysis a strictly arbitrary one. Accordingly, the 1962 amendments took the path of least resistance and excluded losses relating to those assets not ordinarily required in the daily life of the individual, such as precious stones, works of artistic value, villas, and so on, from the subject matter of the deduction for miscellaneous losses.[284] These losses were not entirely left out in the cold, though, for it was provided that they would be deemed an assignment loss and that they might be deducted solely from assignment income of the year in which they arose or in the following year.[285]

THE QUESTION OF A RETREAT FROM THE PRINCIPLE OF GLOBAL TAXATION IN REGARD TO PERSONAL INCOME

It has been asserted by some scholars that developments in the Japanese personal income tax system since the Shoup Reports have taken a course,

[282] See FINAL REPORT OF THE TAX SYSTEM INVESTIGATION COMMISSION, SEPARATE VOLUME 553–54. The commission rejected the suggestion that the deduction for miscellaneous losses should be expanded to cover losses due to the performance of a non-business-connected surety obligation or a defaulted bank deposit. Cf. Income Tax Law, art. 10-6(2).

[283] Income Tax Law, art. 10(2); Income Tax Law Enforcement Regulations, art. 9-10(2).

[284] Income Tax Law, arts. 9-3(1), 11-4; Income Tax Law Enforcement Regulations, art. 7-19.

[285] Income Tax Law, arts. 9-3(1), 10(3); Income Tax Law Enforcement Regulations, art. 9-11.

completely unacceptable to the mission, which leads back toward a "*schedular or classified*" income tax and a "return to pre-war Japanese traditions and practices."[286] The Shoup system's relentless pursuit of an ideal global personal income tax and the subsequent gradual relaxation of the unitary composition of that tax, which at one point was completely rewritten in accordance with the Shoup pattern, are irrefutable facts that may not be ignored in any honest account of the road followed by Japanese income taxation since the end of the occupation. Therefore, consideration of the validity of the scholars' assertion seems an apt topic to conclude our discussion of the computation of income in Japan.

Different deductions and tax rates for separate categories of income, the practice under the prewar schedular income tax, tend to become quite arbitrary and certainly ought to be avoided. On the other hand, it is no easy task to pour all sorts of income into a single mold. No matter what method one may choose to follow, it is impossible in actual practice to avoid some imperfections. The various factors underlying the breakdown in the Shoup plan are extremely complex and cannot be dismissed with the simple generalization that they amount to a return to former Japanese traditions and practices.

Shoup attempted to create a modern and effective progressive income tax by attacking the rather rough technique formerly employed — which sought to mollify the effect of progressive tax rates on capital gains through incorporating only one half into taxable income — and made the complete taxation of such gains, as well as that of other forms of extraordinary and occasional income, and the full deduction of capital losses the cornerstone of his proposals. He also, though, took the graduated rates of the tax into account by recommending the introduction of a form of tax averaging for not only extraordinary income but also other irregular or fluctuating normal income, such as manuscript fees and proceeds from fishing.[287]

Shoup's involved proposal called for the spreading of tax over anywhere from five to twenty years in accordance with the particular character of the income. To give a concrete example, suppose the spreading was to take ten years. Here one tenth of the "fluctuating income" would be added to other income and the effective rate for the sum determined. Then, the remaining nine tenths of the fluctuating income would be multiplied by this rate and the amount of tax so computed provisionally collected in the first year. Subsequently, the taxpayer could gradually liquidate his burden by claiming an annual credit for one ninth of the amount of tax collected in the beginning, provided that each year for the next nine years he added one ninth of the remaining fluctuating income to his other income. The result was that year by year, as new fluctuating income arose, the adjusting calculation became more and more complicated. I do not know whether so intricate

[286] Bronfenbrenner and Kogiku, note 37 above, at 241, 242–43.

[287] 1 First Shoup Report 89–90; 3 *ibid.*, at B1–5.

a system has been put into operation anywhere else in the world, but in any event Japan, with one exception, wrote it into law.[288] The sole exception related to the maximum length of the period. An adjustment covering a span from five to twenty years was just too complicated for the authorities to handle, and in order to ease tax administration a flat five-year term was enacted for all spreading. Shoup expressed the opinion that the procedure concerned would not prove intolerable, despite its complexity, because the actual number of taxpayers with income of this sort was limited,[289] but once in operation taxpayers and tax officers alike found themselves incessantly stung by the tortuous computations required. Again, while the longer period might have been better, the five-year term dictated by the needs of practical administration was too short to have any appreciable effect on the tax burden, a point regarding which those receiving severance income, among the various types of income recipients covered, were particularly vociferous in their dissatisfaction.[290]

Although in the past the overwhelming majority of severance-pay payments made in Japan have been in the form of a lump-sum disbursement and not a continuing annuity, they are by nature a deferred payment of wages earned during prior service which will form the employee's principal means of support after discharge. For many salaried men with low earnings, this sum is the largest single payment of money received during an entire lifetime. To such persons taxation of severance income is an issue charged with deep emotion, for these funds represent long years of hard labor and constitute the mainstay of a worker's livelihood in his declining years. In regard to income of this sort, the Shoup method of tax averaging was far too harsh, and as early as 1952 it became apparent that revision was essential. It was replaced by a technique whereby the receipts of severance income would be segregated from other income and then, after deducting 150,000 yen (417 dollars), half the remainder taxed entirely separately at the regular rates.[291] Later changes raised the amount of the deduction over and over again until today it is calculated through multiplying the number of years one has worked by certain fixed amounts for each year of work based upon one's age at the commencement and termination of employment. Taxation of only one half the remainder following the deduction, though, remains unchanged.[292] As with an arbitrary schedular income tax, probably no one

[288] Income Tax Law, arts. 14–14-2, as amended by Law No. 71 of 1950, but prior to amendment by Law No. 53 of 1952.

[289] 3 FIRST SHOUP REPORT B3–4.

[290] The Shoup Reports did not actually touch on the taxation of severance income, but it was included within the purview of the tax-averaging formula for fluctuating income as being the only satisfactory course following per se from Shoup's analysis.

[291] Income Tax Law, art. 9(1) (vi), as amended by Law No. 53 of 1952, but prior to amendment by Law No. 52 of 1954.

[292] Income Tax Law, art. 9(1)(vi).

can answer "yes" with assurance to the question, "Does taxing severance income in this way strike a fair balance between it and the taxation of other income?" But preservation of the Shoup formula would most certainly have had even more undesirable results and in all likelihood would have caused the public to feel that it was being made the butt of some cruel and capricious trick. Placement of severance income outside the framework of global taxation cannot be pigeonholed simply as a step back into the past.[293]

It is indeed true, however, that the forestry income "divide by five multiply by five" [294] tax formula harks back to a prewar precedent. "Divide by five multiply by five" is a method whereby the amount of tax that would apply to only one fifth of the forestry income is determined and then multiplied by five to arrive at the total tax due;[295] in a sense, it amounts to an expedient to write off and be done with tax averaging in a single year. Although, in comparison with the more normal technique of spreading tax over several years, it fails to avoid some theoretical flaws, it is an unavoidable fact of life that the hard realities of practical tax administration decree to a certain extent the employment of simplified devices. When we consider the case of a person engaged in selective logging as a business to whom forestry income accrues annually, it is easy to visualize how the computation of tax spreading over a stretch of five years will increase in complexity year by year until in the end it ceases to be practicable. As already noted, the major disputes concerning forestry income relate to whether it ought to be taxed apart from other income and all its various forms lumped together and subjected to a single method of taxation — not whether the "divide by five multiply by five" device itself is rational. Of course, it is somewhat muddle-headed thinking to justify the restoration of the prewar formula merely on the grounds of the importance of forest resources, but future revision, when and if it occurs, will pursue a course which, while taking into account convenient and practical operation, elaborates measures more finely shaped to accomplish equitable taxation than the broad black strokes painted in the Shoup scheme.

Assignment income (capital gains) and occasional income also returned to the pre-Shoup pattern of deducting 150,000 yen (417 dollars) followed by the global taxation of only one half of the remainder.[296] Naturally this "half-taxing" is but a convenient means to soften the effect of the progressive rates and has no other theoretical rationale; it is somewhat more favorable to the

[293] Bronfenbrenner and Kogiku refer somewhat incorrectly, but with considerable precedent, to "severance income" as "retirement income." Severance income is paid not only on retirement but at any time an employee satisfying certain conditions terminates the ties with his employer. See, for example, Bronfenbrenner and Kogiku, note 37 above, at 243.

[294] *Go-bun go-jō*.

[295] Income Tax Law, art. 13(1).

[296] Income Tax Law, art. 9(1) (viii)–(ix).

taxpayer than "divide by five multiply by five," being roughly equivalent to a "divide by twenty multiply by twenty" formula.[297] As a generalization, "half-taxing" was restored because spreading over only five years employs too short a period, while further lengthening and classifying the term in accordance with various forms of income would unnecessarily complicate the tax structure and its administration. It would be possible to go on for pages with this topic, but space limitations require that I bring it to an end with the remark that capital gains taxation has produced countless problems. The Japanese experience raises considerable doubt about whether the idea of fully taxing capital gains, so strongly asserted with conviction by Shoup, is in fact axiomatic for a fair and equitable tax system.

In addition, the manner of taxing fluctuating income, such as manuscript fees and income from fishing, was simplified. Here, too, the five-year spreading provision was abandoned. In its place, the amount of this income in the current year which exceeds the average of income of this type for the past two years is subjected to a tax adjustment employing the "divide by five multiply by five" formula.[298] Moreover, recently a new category of "extraordinary income" was established for that income for which there is some hesitancy to use the rough "half-taxing" technique applied to capital gains. It consists of such items as a baseball player's bonus, the down payment for the use of a patent, and furlough pay (pay given to an employee during a period of temporary work stoppage for which the employee is not responsible), and is also granted the benefits of "divide by five multiply by five."[299]

The techniques set forth above to tax different forms of unusual income may well merit criticism as being far too compartmentalized and failing to clarify the structural interrelationship among the forms. Undoubtedly, systematic organization remains a problem for the future, but tax spreading, as proposed by Shoup, was an overly simple device to deal with complex phenomena, and this very fact made its actual application within the tax system extremely complicated. Thus, it is quite easy to understand how this compartmentalization came about through a search for various subtle refinements in both the character of the device and the nature of the phenomena — two sides of what was essentially a single weakness in the Shoup plan.

In this connection, the remarks of the present Prime Minister of Japan, Hayato Ikeda, strike a fitting note upon which to bring our long discussion to an end. The better portion of his professional life as a civil servant was devoted to the administration of taxation. As Minister of Finance he carried on the negotiations with the Shoup Mission, and later he occupied a supervisory position in regard to the subsequent revision of the Shoup system.

[297] Of course, in the effect on specific brackets there is at times a considerable difference between "half-taxing" and "divide by twenty multiply by twenty."

[298] Income Tax Law, art. 14; Income Tax Law Enforcement Regulations, art. 13.

[299] Income Tax Law, art. 14; Income Tax Law Enforcement Regulations, arts. 12-29–13.

His long experience with tax matters lends particular significance to his words.[300]

Dr. Shoup's party was composed solely of scholars who made academically logical recommendations, but, if I may say so frankly, I believe that there are some points which are overly theoretical and conceptual. One such manifestation is the assumption that the final issue is always whether or not an item is income, and that, provided it is income, any and everything without discrimination should be taxed at the same rate; such an approach fails to treat tax law as an active and living thing. To present a short example, in the building of a hydroelectric dam there are farming families who must be pushed off farm land which has been handed down from their ancestors for generations. While they receive a good price for the purchase, they have to immediately bear a sizable tax simply because it is a capital gain. Rational or not, it is absolutely impossible to tax income produced under such circumstances at exactly the same rate applicable to ordinary income. A "tax law which ignores human sentiment" [301] will not succeed. Here, in order to do away with a mere tax in name only, the law was subsequently amended, but there are still many other similar instances. Although all called "income," such items as severance income, assignment income, and forestry income differ from that income which arises from trade, and it is improper to tax them fully at the normal tax rate. It is my feeling that it is desirable to digest thoroughly the peculiar circumstances and conditions under which various sorts of income have been obtained and then impose taxation fitted to the actual situation. Revision in this sense was partially enacted in a recent session of the National Diet, but many matters requiring change yet remain.

[300] Ikeda, Kinkō Zaisei (Balanced Public Finance) 122–23 (1952).
[301] *Ninjō.*

COMMENTARY: PART III

Arthur Taylor von Mehren

THE employer-employee relationship in Japan had traditionally been considered an extension of the family relationship. Although the patriarchal basis of the relationship is gradually disappearing, the status of labor in Japan is very different from that known in the West since the Industrial Revolution. The lingering force of family and community ties affects the attitudes toward the employment relation of both employer and employee and adds to the normal deterrents to the mobility of labor — the difficulties and expenses of moving to a new location or learning a new trade. Consequently, many Japanese employees and employers view employment as a lifetime relationship,[1] indeed, as heritable within the family.[2] Moreover, a substantial portion of the employee's compensation is often in various fringe benefits — housing, company vacation plans, benefits for children — of a kind that ties the individual closely to the establishment.[3]

Some aspects of Japanese employment relationships fit within a rather traditional framework; but, in other respects, the realities of labor relations lie very far from the close-knit, stable, and homogenous group-life characteristic of the older Japan.[4] Marxist assumptions about labor relations as an expression of the class struggle are very important, even among men who are non-Communist in orientation. Open struggle is thus, for many Japanese, the norm to which industrial cooperation and peace is the exception. Consequently, the field contains divergent political and social ideals antithetical both to the ideals of the traditional society and to those underlying the dominant democratic institutions of government; these ideals are capable

Note. At various places, the conference participant who suggested or particularly emphasized a point is named.

[1] Judge Tanabe.

[2] These same traits seem to be emerging at various points in Western employment relations. For example, severe union restrictions on entry into certain highly skilled trades are not infrequently associated with preferential entry treatment for children of union members.

[3] The rise in fringe benefits in the United States has also tended to tie an employee to his job.

[4] Professor Beardsley. Mr. Oppler pointed out that on the national political scene, the leading political parties are in violent disagreement on ultimate ends and appropriate procedures.

not only of disrupting the harmony of an individual establishment but also of dividing the entire society.[5]

In the light of these two characteristics, several aspects of Japanese labor relations were discussed, especially the reliance on power rather than persuasion.[6] In the United States, both sides basically accept the structure and values of the society, and labor relations is largely a struggle for economic advantage. In Japan, when labor difficulties arise, the struggle tends to proceed with violence and seeks goals more ideological than economic. In part, this violence reflects the difficulty, discussed in Part One, encountered in resolving disputes once a group's informal methods of dispute resolution have broken down and its harmony is shattered.[7] Moreover, as Kohji Tanabe remarked, because labor mobility is low in Japan and employees are often very firmly attached to a single employer, conditions in the establishment frequently have to be rather bad before a strike will be called; thus pressures tend to build up to explosive force before they are released. The overwhelmingly superior strength of employers in some industries reinforces this tendency by engendering a feeling of desperation on the part of the workers.

In this connection, the emergence of a considerable reliance on formal arbitration may be of great significance. Arbitration represents a form of dispute resolution potentially capable of handling those employment problems for which traditional forms no longer yield socially acceptable results.[8] At the same time, the availability of effective forms of dispute resolution should operate to reduce somewhat the political focus and the violence currently characteristic of Japanese labor relations. Without arbitration, labor has had a choice only of the polar opposites of submission and violence. Should arbitration prove able to adjust the competing demands of labor for an increased share of the national product and of management for the right to control its operations, the Japanese labor movement will become increasingly similar to that in the United States, primarily seeking specific economic concessions. It should be recognized, however, that labor arbitration developed in the United States primarily as a basis for the settlement of disputes arising under a contract and that it does not, in itself, provide a basis for deciding how the basic claims of the parties should be adjusted.

The violence of Japanese labor relations finds its scholarly counterpart in a certain academic "ruthlessness," described by Ishikawa in his essay.

[5] Professor Beardsley remarked that cultural anthropologists usually try to interpret a society as a harmonious whole. But this assumption, however appropriate for relatively simple societies, clearly does not fit complex societies. Thus, the realities and values of Japanese village life and of Japanese labor relations may be very different.

[6] Professor Gellhorn particularly emphasized this point.

[7] Professor Kawashima.

[8] Professors Kawashima and Gellhorn.

Scholarly discussions of labor law tend to become an aspect of sociopolitical or socioeconomic crusades. There was a considerable measure of agreement at the conference that Japanese labor-law scholars are not sufficiently objective. The ordinary premise of legal scholarship is that the scholar, in commenting on legal matters, is committed to accept the premises and values underlying the legal system. Of course, he is perfectly free to hold and argue other values as well. But these assertions and arguments should not take on the guise of an objective exposition of the existing system. Japanese scholars too frequently confuse their own value commitments with purportedly objective commentaries.[9] For example, Ishikawa told how one Japanese professor, after elaborating his theory on a certain point, was asked to explain a Supreme Court case reaching the opposite conclusion. His disdainful reply was that case study was unrewarding and that the particular decision, regardless of reasoning, was just plain wrong. Robert Bellah suggested that this lack of objectivity represents in part a reaction to the suppression of divergent viewpoints during the 1930s, Japanese scholars of today feeling, as it were, a need to stand up and be counted.

The discussion of Japanese labor-relations law closed with some remarks on the role of lawyers in labor relations. Ishikawa stated that lawyers play a large role in labor negotiations. However, in his judgment, there are still today very few good labor lawyers. Yasuharu Nagashima noted that Sōhyō attracts most of the good labor attorneys.[10] Neither Zenrō[11] nor the employers have had much luck in attracting labor lawyers.

The discussion of Yoshio Kanazawa's paper, "The Regulation of Corporate Enterprise: The Law of Unfair Competition and the Control of Monopoly Power," began with the statement that, while various European countries are today strengthening their antimonopoly laws, Japan is weakening hers.[12] In effect, Japan is returning to a position closer to the one she had before the American occupation, strong pressure for cartelization coming from export industries; the strict trade laws of other nations, particularly those of the United States, with quota limitations on imports, encourage compulsory cartelization. It is also to be remembered that exporting industries are far more significant to the Japanese than to the American economy.

In evaluating the impact of cartels on the Japanese economy, it is significant that restraints, just as in prewar Japan, are more often achieved by informal controls than by formal cartels.[13] Even government pressure is typically exerted informally, through purchasing contracts, import quotas

[9] Mr. Rabinowitz and Professor Kawashima.
[10] Sōhyō is a militant, socialist, labor organization. It is not, however, Communist-dominated.
[11] Zenrō is a smaller, more moderate labor group.
[12] Professor Yazawa.
[13] Professor Lockwood.

and controls, government investment, and direct suggestion.[14] Of course, as various governmental controls such as exchange restrictions are removed, the effectiveness of informal governmental regulation will diminish.

William Lockwood observed that the Japanese economy must be competitive to a significant degree in order to explain the recent very high rate of growth. The Japanese economy appears as a blend of extreme competition — especially in the domestic area — mixed with collusion. Kanazawa noted that today a significant trend toward merger exists in Japan, with the number of both cartels and oligopolies increasing.

In spite of its history of failure, the Japanese antimonopoly law enlists considerable political support. Bills to exempt a large part of domestic industry from the coverage of the law have failed to pass on three separate occasions. The law's support comes principally from the socialists, consumers, small farmers, and small-enterprise groups.[15] Such support may not represent a belief that competition is valuable because of the increased efficiency and lower prices which it thus fosters, but an attempt to restrain the power of capital within the society. Moreover, to the extent that the government faces the prospect of losing some of its informal bases for controlling private enterprise, it may find a useful weapon in the antimonopoly law.[16] The annual reports of the Fair Trade Commission noting the degree of monopolization in various industries have the valuable effect of informing public opinion and preparing it for possible future changes in governmental policy toward cartels.[17]

The conference discussion of the final three essays, by Michida, Yazawa, and Uematsu, owing to considerations of time and the rather more detailed and technical nature of their subject matter, could only touch upon a few points that seemed of particular interest.

Discussion of Shinichiro Michida's essay on commercial law began with a proposal that the specific problems of product-liability insurance, the filing of security interests, and the use of checks be considered. Robert Braucher remarked that claims for monetary damage for breach of warranty are still very infrequent in Japan. To the extent that breach-of-warranty actions serve the function of controlling product quality, other techniques are available and applied. The Fair Trade Commission has been taking steps against misleading advertising,[18] violation of food-control laws are punished by fines,[19] and the sale of drugs is licensed and strictly controlled.[20] In June

[14] Professor Lockwood and Mr. Calhoun.

[15] Professor Yazawa.

[16] Mr. Coleman and Professor Yazawa.

[17] Professor Yazawa.

[18] Professor Yazawa.

[19] Procurator A. Nagashima.

[20] Mr. Rabinowitz.

1959, more than two hundred thousand items of hair dye and wave lotion were seized and destroyed by the Ministry of Welfare as adulterated cosmetics under the Drug Law.[21] In many situations, the police exercise an informal control, even though no legal basis exists for their activity.[22] The recent appearance of a consumer's research magazine provides a further quality check by offering the consumer some information about inferior goods.[23] However, to the extent that an action for breach of warranty serves to compensate the injured for losses, no real surrogate exists in contemporary Japanese practice. In line with traditional concepts, the manufacturer apologizes and pays a small indemnity. Social security, in particular medical insurance, serves in some measure to remove the pressure for adequate compensation. Nonetheless, the absence of litigation respecting breach of warranty suggests that the traditional Japanese attitudes toward dispute resolution, noted earlier in other contexts, still persist. Despite the absence of litigation for consumer claims, however, and despite the fact that the codes do not provide for warranty and disclaimer clauses, manufacturers have used clauses similar to those used in America. Though product-liability insurance does not now exist, the introduction of this institution, through borrowing from other systems, may be possible without changing the law.

Attention next turned to an institution of Japanese commercial law, the *jōto tampo* (security by assignment), developed by the courts without any clear statutory basis. The jōto-tampo transaction permits a debtor to take possession of goods while vesting the title in the creditor, and it is the Japanese equivalent of the American chattel mortgage, conditional sale, and similar security devices. It takes many forms. There is no general provision for public registration, although registration is separately provided for many particular types of security transactions. In the past there has been reluctance to disclose to the public details of business operations, but this reluctance is losing ground as the Securities Exchange Law and the Commercial Code now provide access to corporate financial information. Moreover, the type of notice filing embodied in the American Uniform Commercial Code could be adopted and would preserve secrecy respecting the details of security transactions, merely giving public notice that a security transaction may exist.

The problems of place of registration and convenience in checking public records and obtaining credit information were discussed, and it was agreed that difficult legislative questions are posed. Robert Braucher outlined the analogous problems arising in the United States in the drafting and enactment of the Uniform Commercial Code, and Makoto Yazawa reported on unofficial legislative research on the registration of jōto tampo now under

[21] Professor Michida. The present Drug Law is Law No. 145 of 1960. The statute in effect in 1959 was the Drug Law of 1948, Law No. 197 of 1948.

[22] Mr. Blakemore.

[23] Mr. Coleman.

way in Tokyo under the auspices of the Matsumoto Foundation. Takaaki Hattori and Kohji Tanabe remarked that, judging from the litigated cases, a jōto tampo was frequently placed on chattels of such small value that recording them would be impractical. They doubted that the creation of an integrated recording system would solve the problems arising from the use of jōto tampo in such cases. Michida stated that jōto-tampo transactions are often substantial, providing the basis for credit on shipments of ore or of large quantities of cotton moving from importer to distributor or manufacturer and then to their subsidiaries. In many cases banks become the jōto-tampo creditor. One company has estimated that a simplified notice-filing registration system for security interests in general might save it some billion yen over a ten-year period. Hattori suggested that jōto tampo is subject to many abuses. Michida urged that protection against frauds depends more on extreme care in granting credit than on legal safeguards. If personal-property security could be effectively registered and expeditiously checked, many of the problems inherent in jōto tampo could be avoided. Until solutions are developed, the law's choice is between rules like those found in the written law that favor a more static economy and institutions like jōto tampo that encourage economic growth and risk taking.

Consideration of Makoto Yazawa's essay concentrated on a discussion of "corporate democracy." The term is not particularly felicitous but was taken to mean principally that shareholders should be provided with rather full information respecting corporate activities and given an opportunity to make recommendations respecting policy and some kinds of corporate decisions.[24] Traditionally, and still to a large extent today, Japanese corporations are reluctant to make public disclosure. Moreover, the general Japanese reluctance to litigate carries over into the area of corporate management so that stockholders' suits and related phenomena are most exceptional.

Discussion of the problem area dealt with by Morio Uematsu in his essay was limited to consideration of a recent proposal of the Tax System Investigation Commission to disregard any transaction designed to avoid taxes, a topic not actually touched on in the essay.[25] The proposal is obviously attractive from the point of view of the tax administrator. However, whatever the desirability of closing loopholes in the interest of equal taxation to parties equally situated, this proposal carries the dangers that a taxpayer will be unable to predict his tax incidence in advance and

[24] As explained by Professors Jennings and Loss.

[25] ZEISEI CHŌSA KAI (Tax System Investigation Commission), KOKUZEI TSŪSOKU HŌ NO SEITEI NI KAN-SURU TŌSHIN — ZEISEI CHŌSA KAI DAI NI TŌSHIN (Report Concerning Establishment of the National Tax Common Provisions Law — Second Report of the Tax System Investigation Commission) 4 (July 5, 1961); ZEISEI CHŌSA KAI (Tax System Investigation Commission), KOKUZEI TSŪSOKU HŌ NO SEITEI NI KAN-SURU TŌSHIN NO SETSUMEI — TŌSHIN BESSATSU (Explanation of the Report Concerning Establishment of the National Tax Common Provisions Law — Separate Volume of the Report) 11–14 (July 5, 1961).

that the rule will be administered in an arbitrary or discriminatory fashion.[26] Tax law is only beginning to receive recognition as a legal discipline in the departments of law, and there are few competent tax lawyers and even fewer legal scholars in the field. Consequently, proposals for changes in the Japanese law do not have the benefit of informed and rigorous criticism by scholars and professionals outside the government.[27] It is to be hoped that there will be serious consideration of the disadvantages of such a general provision as that discussed here before deciding that it warrants adoption.

It should be remarked that the taxpayer today enjoys substantially greater protection through administrative and judicial review than was the case before World War II.[28] However, many taxpayers still seem reluctant to litigate tax problems, perhaps fearing that if they cause present difficulties they will inevitably be disadvantaged in the long run.[29]

[26] It is interesting to note that, because of political opposition to this proposal in the autumn of 1961, the Ministry of Finance decided to put it aside for "further . . . careful study" and thereby indefinitely postponed its enactment into law. See Kokuzei Tsūsoku Hō no Seitei ni Tsuite (Concerning the Establishment of the National Tax Common Provisions Law), Tax Bureau, Ministry of Finance Release No. 26–1, c. Dec. 1961.

[27] Mr. Coleman.

[28] Professor Kaneko.

[29] Mr. Y. Nagashima.

LAWS, ORDERS, AND RELATED MATERIALS CITED

TABLE OF CASES

INDEX

LAWS, ORDERS, AND RELATED MATERIALS CITED

Prepared by Rex Coleman

The following sections provide lists of the types of legal and administrative materials employed in Japan in modern times and titles of such materials cited in this volume. Wherever an English translation of the item is available, except for the major codes which have been translated many times and for which numerous versions are available, it is given in each essay at the point in the text where the particular item is first cited. However, the reader should be forewarned that few of these translations are entirely accurate, being in most cases a mere approximation of the original language, and that they should be used with considerable caution. All translations printed in the text were especially prepared for this volume and are not taken from the sources noted.

Legal and Administrative Materials Issued by the Japanese Government Since 1868

Chokugo — Imperial Speech[1]
A speech made by the Emperor.

Chokurei — Imperial Order
An Order under the Meiji Constitution issued in the Emperor's name in regard to matters under his direct authority. Those which did not become the subject of Laws under the new Constitution retained the same effect as Cabinet Orders (by Law No. 72 of 1947, art. 2).

Chokusho — Imperial Writ[2]
A writing issued by the Emperor under the Meiji Constitution indicating imperial intent which was not generally published.

Fukenrei — Prefectural Order[3]
An Order issued by a prefectural governor under the Meiji Constitution in execution of his official powers or pursuant to a special delegation of authority (mandate). Those which did not become the subject of Laws under the new Constitution retained the same effect as local governmental Regulations (Local Autonomy Law Enforcement Rules, art. 3).

Fukoku — Decree
A type of law issued by the Dajōkan (Great Council of State) from 1868 (1st year of Meiji) until 1886 (19th year of Meiji). They were generally effective throughout the entire country and not just within governmental agencies.

[1] See note 10 below.
[2] See note 10 below.
[3] See note 6 below.

FUTATSU — Pronouncement

A type of order issued to the general public by the Dajōkan (Great Council of State), a Minister or the director of an administrative agency from 1873 (6th year of Meiji) until 1886 (19th year of Meiji).

HŌRITSU — Law

A statute enacted by the Diet.

HŌREI — Laws and Orders

A general term encompassing Laws and Orders.

JŌREI — Ordinance[4]

An enactment by the legislative branch of a local government. It must not conflict with a valid Law or Order. These are, in effect, local statutes (Local Autonomy Law, art. 14).

KAKUREI — Cabinet Order (Prewar)[5]

An Order of the Cabinet under the Meiji Constitution issued by the Prime Minister. These are now treated as Orders of the Prime Minister's Office (Cabinet Order No. 14 of 1947, para. (2)).

KITEI — Rule

A lesser form of regulation issued by the courts to deal with administrative matters.

KISOKU — Regulation

(1) An Order-like measure issued by the executive branch of a local government (Local Autonomy Law, art. 15).

(2) Orders prescribed by law to be issued by certain agencies and commissions, and Orders issued by various independent agencies.

(3) Procedural rules issued by the courts (CONST. art. 77).

(4) Rules of meetings, proceedings, and internal discipline within the Diet (CONST. art. 58 (2)).

KOKUJI — Notification

A form used to give public notice of specific administrative action. It deals with the general disposition of certain matters and, unlike Orders, does not supplement the content of Laws. However, this principle is not always followed scrupulously (National Administrative Organization Law, art. 14 (1)).

KUNREI — Instruction

Directions from a higher to a lower level within one governmental agency (National Administrative Organization Law, art. 14 (2)). Normally the same agency does not employ both Instructions and Circulars, but exceptionally some (e.g., the National Tax Agency) issue both with Instructions covering matters of more general application.

MEIREI — Order[6]

[4] See note 6 below.

[5] See note 6 below.

[6] Prior to the Constitution of 1946, English translations of Japanese legal terms seem almost uniformly to have translated *Meirei* in the sense given in (1) and its various forms, such as *Chokurei, Kakurei,* and *Shōrei,* as "Ordinance," apparently in the belief that this word most closely approximated the German *Verordnung* and the French *Ordonnance*. The official English version of the new Constitution introduced the term "Cabinet Order" for *Seirei* and since its enforcement the custom seems to have grown up of continuing the word "Ordinance" only

(1) A general term for all types of Orders. Under the Meiji Constitution they covered Imperial Orders, Cabinet Orders, and Ministerial Orders, while under the new Constitution they include Cabinet Orders, Prime Minister's Office Orders, Ministerial Orders, and certain Regulations (National Administrative Organization Law, art. 12).

(2) A specific directive issued by an administrative agency to a certain person or organization calling for the performance or nonperformance of a prescribed action.

(3) Directions from a higher to a lower government officer concerning the performance of official duties.

(4) A determination by a court other than a ruling or judgment.

OBOEGAKI — Memorandum

An Order from the Supreme Commander for the Allied Powers to the Japanese government during the Occupation. Usually it required certain action of a legal nature to be taken.

SAISOKU — Detailed Rule

Specialized provisions issued by the National Personnel Authority.

SEIREI — Cabinet Order (Postwar)[7]

Orders issued by the Cabinet in order to execute provisions of the Constitution and Laws (CONST. art. 73 (vi)).

SHIREI — Directive

(1) Orders issued by the Supreme Commander for the Allied Powers during the Occupation. Only three were issued, the last on September 22, 1945. In legal effect they were superior to the Constitution.

(2) Directives now issued by the National Personnel Authority. They are not Orders, but deal with general action taken in carrying out the Authority's Regulations and other matters.

SHŌCHOKU — Imperial Edict[8]

General term for Imperial Writs, Imperial Rescripts, and other acts by the Emperor.

SHŌREI — Ministerial Order[9]

An Order issued by a Minister within his sphere of competence to enforce a Law or Cabinet Order, or under his general duty to administer.

SHŌSHO — Imperial Rescript[10]

---

for *Sōrifurei* and *Shōrei,* though considerable confusion can be found in various texts. For example, SHOUP MISSION TO THE SUPREME COMMANDER FOR THE ALLIED POWERS, REPORT ON JAPANESE TAXATION (1949) often refers to *Tsūtatsu* (Circulars) as "Ordinances." Because Japanese administrative law specialists deal with only one concept — *Meirei* — here, we feel it unwise to use two different terms and therefore have settled on "Order," the English word closest to the actual meaning of the Japanese term. "Ordinance" has been restricted solely to the translation of the statute-like enactments of local governments, such as prefectures and cities, called *Jōrei* in Japanese.

[7] See note 6 above.

[8] See note 10 below.

[9] See note 6 above.

[10] Traditionally scholars writing in English have exercised little care in distinguishing between *Chokusho, Shōchoku, Shōsho,* and *Chokugo,* calling all, at one time or another, by the title "Imperial Rescript." See, for example, the English version of CONST. art. 98(1) where *Shōchoku* is translated "Imperial Rescript" and SANSOM, THE WESTERN WORLD AND JAPAN 464 (1951)

A writing issued by the Emperor to publish some action taken by him within his peculiar competence.

SŌRIFUREI — Prime Minister's Office Order[11]

An Order from the Prime Minister's Office equivalent to a Ministerial Order.

TATSU — Notice

Directions from the Dajōkan (Great Council of State) or one of the ministries to a government office in accord with a Decree. Used prior to 1886 (19th year of Meiji).

TSŪCHŌ — Circular

Old title for *Tsūtatsu*. The term was changed since the character for *chō* did not appear among standard *kanji* on their adoption.

TSŪTATSU — Circular

Internal directions sent from a higher to lower level within one governmental agency (National Administrative Organization Law, art. 14 (2)). They are issued under the authority of the head of the agency and may not conflict with a Law or Order.

LEGAL AND ADMINISTRATIVE MATERIALS CITED IN THIS VOLUME

* Measures repealed or abrogated prior to or no longer effective on October 1, 1962.

† Measures suspended but not repealed prior to October 1, 1962.

A. Imperial Speeches

* Imperial Speech on Education (*Kyōiku Chokugo*) October 30, 1890.

B. Laws, Great Council of State Decrees and Tokugawa Legislation

Administrative Case Litigation Law (*Gyōsei Jiken Soshō Hō*) Law No. 139 of 1962.

Administrative Exceptions Review Law (*Gyōsei Fufuku Shinsa Hō*) Law No. 160 of 1962.

* Administrative Execution Law (*Gyōsei Shikkō Hō*) Law No. 84 of 1900.

Administrative Scrivener Law (*Gyōsei Soshi Hō*) Law No. 4 of 1951.

* Administrative Trial Law (*Gyōsei Saiban Hō*) Law No. 48 of 1890.

Admission Tax Law (*Nyūjōzei Hō*) Law No. 96 of 1954.

Agricultural Movables Credit Law (*Nōgyō Dōsan Shinyō Hō*) Law No. 30 of 1933.

Aircraft Hypothec Law (*Kōkūki Teitō Hō*) Law No. 66 of 1953.

* Aircraft Manufacturing Business Law (*Kōkūki Seizō Jigyō Hō*) Law No. 41 of 1938.

* Amended Criminal Regulations (*Kaitei Ritsurei*) Great Council of State Decree No. 206 of 1873.

Ammonium Sulphate Industry Rationalization and Ammonium Sulphate Export

---

where even a *Chokugo* is designated a "Rescript." "Rescript" in its basic English meaning would seem to involve a writing, which is certainly not the case with *Chokugo* and need not be the case with *Shōchoku*. Accordingly, we have restricted the word to *Shōsho* and have assigned new terms for the other concepts.

[11] See note 6 above.

Adjustment Extraordinary Measures Law (*Ryūan Kōgyō Gōrika oyobi Ryūan Yushutsu Chōsei Rinji Sochi Hō*) Law No. 173 of 1954.

* Appeal and Revision Procedure (*Kōso Jōkoku Tetsuzuki*) Great Council of State Decree No. 93 of 1875.

Attorneys Law (*Bengoshi Hō*) Law No. 205 of 1949.

* Attorneys Law of 1933 (*Bengoshi Hō*) Law No. 53 of 1933.

* Attorneys Law of 1893 (*Bengoshi Hō*) Law No. 7 of 1893.

Automobile Damage Compensation Security Law (*Jidōsha Songai Baishō Hoshō Hō*) Law No. 97 of 1955.

Automobile Hypothec Law (*Jidōsha Teitō Hō*) Law No. 187 of 1951.

* Automotive Traffic Business Activities Law (*Jidōsha Kōtsū Jigyō Hō*) Law No. 52 of 1931.

Aviation Law (*Kōkū Hō*) Law No. 231 of 1952.

* Bail Ordinance (*Hoshaku Jōrei*) Great Council of State Decree No. 17 of 1877.

Bankruptcy Law (*Hasan Hō*) Law No. 71 of 1922.

Bills Law (*Tegata Hō*) Law No. 20 of 1932.

* Bills of Exchange and Promissory Notes Ordinance (*Kawase Tegata Yakusoku Tegata Jōrei*) Great Council of State Decree No. 17 of 1882.

Board of Audit Law (*Kaikei Kensa In Hō*) Law No. 73 of 1947.

* Businessmen Organization Law (*Jigyōsha Dantai Hō*) Law No. 191 of 1948.

Canal Law (*Unga Hō*) Law No. 16 of 1913.

Central Wholesale Market Law (*Chūō Oroshiuri Ichiba Hō*) Law No. 32 of 1923.

Checks Law (*Kogitte Hō*) Law No. 57 of 1933.

Child Welfare Law (*Jidō Fukushi Hō*) Law No. 164 of 1947.

Civil Code (*Mimpō*) Laws No. 89 of 1896 and No. 9 of 1898.

* Civil Code of 1890 (*Mimpō*) Laws No. 28 and No. 98 of 1890.

Civil Procedure Costs Law (*Minji Soshō Hiyō Hō*) Law No. 64 of 1890.

Coal Mining Industry Rationalization Extraordinary Measures Law (*Sekitan Kōgyō Gōrika Rinji Sochi Hō*) Law No. 156 of 1955.

* Code of a Hundred Articles (*O-Sadamegaki Hyakkajō*) Tokugawa legislation issued in 1742.

Code of Civil Procedure (*Minji Soshō Hō*) Law No. 29 of 1890.

* Code of Criminal Instruction (*Chizai Hō*) Great Council of State Decree No. 37 of 1880.

Code of Criminal Procedure (*Keiji Soshō Hō*) Law No. 131 of 1948.

* Code of Criminal Procedure of 1922 (*Keiji Soshō Hō*) Law No. 75 of 1922.

* Code of Criminal Procedure of 1890 (*Keiji Soshō Hō*) Law No. 96 of 1890.

Commerce and Industry Societies Central Depository Law (*Shōkō Kumiai Chūō Kinko Hō*) Law No. 14 of 1936.

* Commerce and Industry Society Law (*Shōkō Kumiai Hō*) Law No. 53 of 1943.

Commercial Code (*Shōhō*) Law No. 48 of 1899.

* Commercial Code of 1890 (*Shōhō*) Law No. 32 of 1890.

Commercial Code Enforcement Law (*Shōhō Shikō Hō*) Law No. 49 of 1899.

Construction Industry Law (*Kensetsu-gyō Hō*) Law No. 100 of 1949.

Construction Machinery Hypothec Law (*Kensetsu Kikai Teitō Hō*) Law No. 97 of 1954.

Court Law (*Saibansho Hō*) Law No. 59 of 1947.
* Court Organization Law (*Saibansho Kōsei Hō*) Law No. 6 of 1890.
Credit Depository Law (*Shinyō Kinko Hō*) Law No. 238 of 1951.
Customs Tariff Law (*Kanzei Teiritsu Hō*) Law No. 54 of 1910.
Day Laborer's Health Insurance Law (*Hiyatoi Rōdōsha Kenkō Hoken Hō*) Law No. 207 of 1953.
Drug Law (*Yakuji Hō*) Law No. 145 of 1960.
* Drug Law of 1948 (*Yakuji Hō*) Law No. 197 of 1948.
Electric Resource Development Promotion Law (*Dengen Kaihatsu Sokushin Hō*) Law No. 283 of 1952.
Electronic Industry Promotion Extraordinary Measures Law (*Denshi Kōgyō Shinkō Rinji Sochi Hō*) Law No. 171 of 1957.
* Elimination of Excessive Concentration of Economic Power Law (*Kado Keizai-ryoku Shūchū Haijo Hō*) Law No. 207 of 1947.
Emergency Unemployment Countermeasures Law (*Kinkyū Shitsugyō Taisaku Hō*) Law No. 89 of 1949.
* Enterprise Profits Tax Law (*Eigyō Shūeki Zei Hō*) Law No. 11 of 1926.
Enterprise Security Law (*Kigyō Tampo Hō*) Law No. 106 of 1958.
* Enterprise Tax Law (*Eigyō Zei Hō*) Law No. 33 of 1940.
* Enterprise Tax Law of 1896 (*Eigyō Zei Hō*) Law No. 33 of 1896.
Eugenic Protection Law (*Yūsei Hogo Hō*) Law No. 156 of 1948.
Explosives Control Penal Rules (*Bakuhatsu-butsu Torishimari Bassoku*) Great Council of State Decree No. 23 of 1884.
Export-Import Transactions Law (*Yushutsunyū Torihiki Hō*) Law No. 299 of 1952 (former title "Export Transactions Law").
* Export Society Law (*Yushutsu Kumiai Hō*) Law No. 27 of 1925.
Export Transactions Law (*Yushutsu Torihiki Hō*) Former title of the Export-Import Transactions Law; title changed by Law No. 188 of 1953.
Extraordinary Interest Adjustment Law (*Rinji Kinri Chōsei Hō*) Law No. 181 of 1947.
* Extraordinary Profits Tax Law (*Rinji Ritoku Zei Hō*) Law No. 20 of 1935.
Factory Hypothec Law (*Kōba Teitō Hō*) Law No. 54 of 1905.
* Factory Law (*Kōba Hō*) Law No. 46 of 1911.
Family Affairs Determination Law (*Kaji Shimpan Hō*) Law No. 152 of 1947.
Family Registration Law (*Kōseki Hō*) Law No. 224 of 1947.
Fiber Industry Equipment Extraordinary Measures Law (*Seni Kōgyō Setsubi Rinji Sochi Hō*) Law No. 130 of 1956.
Fishing Industry Foundation Hypothec Law (*Gyogyō Zaidan Teitō Hō*) Law No. 9 of 1925.
Food Control Law (*Shokuryō Kanri Hō*) Law No. 40 of 1942.
Food Sanitation Law (*Shokuhin Eisei Hō*) Law No. 233 of 1947.
Foreign Exchange and Foreign Trade Control Law (*Gaikoku Kawase oyobi Gaikoku Bōeki Kanri Hō*) Law No. 228 of 1949.
* Forms for Pleadings (*Sotō Bunrei*) Great Council of State Decree No. 247 of 1873.
* Formulary for the Shogun's Decision of Suits (*Go Seibai Shikimoku*) A law issued by Yasutoki Hojo in 1232.

Harbor Transport Business Activities Law (*Kōwan Unsō Jigyō Hō*) Law No. 161 of 1951.
Health Insurance Law (*Kenkō Hoken Hō*) Law No. 70 of 1922.
Hypothecation Securities Law (*Teitō Shōken Hō*) Law No. 15 of 1931.
Immovable Property Recording Law (*Fudōsan Tōki Hō*) Law No. 24 of 1899.
* Important Export Commodities Industrial Society Law (*Jūyō Yushutsu-hin Kōgyō Kumiai Hō*) Law No. 28 of 1925.
Income Tax Law (*Shotoku Zei Hō*) Law No. 27 of 1947.
* Income Tax Law of 1940 (*Shotoku Zei Hō*) Law No. 26 of 1940.
* Income Tax Law of 1920 (*Shotoku Zei Hō*) Law No. 11 of 1920.
* Income Tax Law of 1899 (*Shotoku Zei Hō*) Law No. 17 of 1899.
* Industrial Society Law (*Kōgyō Kumiai Hō*) Law No. 62 of 1931.
* Industry Society Law (*Sangyō Kumiai Hō*) Law No. 34 of 1900.
Inheritance Tax Law (*Sōzoku Zei Hō*) Law No. 73 of 1950.
Inquest of Prosecution Law (*Kensatsu Shinsakai Hō*) Law No. 147 of 1948.
International Telegraph and Telephone Stock Company Law (*Kokusai Denshin Denwa Kabushiki Kaisha Hō*) Law No. 301 of 1952.
Japan Air Lines Stock Company Law (*Nihon Kōkū Kabushiki Kaisha Hō*) Law No. 154 of 1953.
* Japan Steel Stock Company Law (*Nippon Seitetsu Kabushiki Kaisha Hō*) Law No. 47 of 1933.
* Judge Disciplinary Law (*Hanji Chōkai Hō*) Law No. 68 of 1890.
Judge Impeachment Law (*Saibankan Dangai Hō*) Law No. 137 of 1947.
Judicial Affairs Directions (*Saiban Jimu Kokoroe*) Great Council of State Decree No. 103 of 1875.
Juridical Persons' Tax Law (*Hōjin Zei Hō*) Law No. 28 of 1947.
* Juridical Persons' Tax Law of 1940 (*Hōjin Zei Hō*) Law No. 24 of 1940.
† Jury Law (*Baishin Hō*) Law No. 50 of 1923.
Juvenile Law (*Shōnen Hō*) Law No. 168 of 1948.
* Juvenile Law of 1922 (*Shōnen Hō*) Law No. 42 of 1922.
* Labor Disputes Mediation Law (*Rōdō Sōgi Chōtei Hō*) Law No. 57 of 1926.
Labor Relations Adjustment Law (*Rōdō Kankei Chōsei Hō*) Law No. 25 of 1946.
Labor Standards Law (*Rōdō Kijun Hō*) Law No. 49 of 1947.
Labor Union Law (*Rōdō Kumiai Hō*) Law No. 174 of 1949.
* Law Concerning Adjustment, Etc., of the Disposition of Valuable Securities (*Yūka Shōken no Shobun no Chōsei Tō ni Kan-suru Hōritsu*) Law No. 8 of 1947.
Law Concerning Atomic Energy Damage Compensation Indemnification Contracts (*Genshiryoku Songai Baishō Hoshō Keiyaku ni Kan-suru Hōritsu*) Law No. 148 of 1961.
Law Concerning Compensation of Atomic Energy Damage (*Genshiryoku Songai no Baishō ni Kan-suru Hōritsu*) Law No. 147 of 1961.
Law Concerning Exclusion from Application, Etc., of the Law Concerning the Prohibition of Private Monopoly and the Maintenance of Fair Trade (*Shiteki Dokusen no Kinshi oyobi Kōsei Torihiki no Kakuho ni Kan-suru Hōritsu no Tekiyō Jogai Tō ni Kan-suru Hōritsu*) Law No. 138 of 1947.

Law Concerning Financial Business Activities by Cooperative Societies (*Kyōdō Kumiai ni yoru Kinyū Jigyō ni Kan-suru Hōritsu*) Law. No. 183 of 1949.

Law Concerning Foreign Investment (*Gaishi ni Kan-suru Hōritsu*) Law No. 163 of 1950.

* Law Concerning Limitation of Local Taxes (*Chihō Zei Seigen ni Kan-suru Hōritsu*) Law No. 37 of 1908.

* Law Concerning Local Taxes (*Chihō Zei ni Kan-suru Hōritsu*) Law No. 24 of 1926.

Law Concerning Normalization of the Operation of Enterprises Related to Environment Sanitation (*Kankyō Eisei Kankei Eigyō no Unei no Tekisei-ka ni Kan-suru Hōritsu*) Law No. 164 of 1957.

Law Concerning Pension Security Financing Carried on by the People's Finance Public Depository (*Kokumin Kinyū Kōko ga Okonau Onkyū Tampo Kinyū ni Kan-suru Hōritsu*) Law No. 91 of 1954.

Law Concerning Restrictions, Etc., on the Assignment of Shares of Stock and Interests in Stock Companies and Limited Liability Companies Whose Purpose Is to Issue Daily Newspapers (*Nikkan Shimbunshi no Hakkō o Mokuteki to Suru Kabushiki Kaisha oyobi Yūgen Kaisha no Kabushiki oyobi Mochibun no Jōto no Seigen Tō ni Kan-suru Hōritsu*) Law No. 212 of 1951.

* Law Concerning Temporary Measures for the Compensation, Etc., of Judges (*Saibankan no Hōshū Tō no Ōkyūteki Sochi ni Kan-suru Hōritsu*) Law No. 65 of 1947.

* Law Concerning the Control of Important Industries (*Jūyō Sangyō no Tōsei ni Kan-suru Hōritsu*) Law No. 40 of 1931.

Law Concerning the Control of Insurance Solicitation (*Hoken Boshū no Torishimari ni Kan-suru Hōritsu*) Law No. 171 of 1948.

Law Concerning the Maintenance of Order in Court, Etc. (*Hōtei Tō no Chitsujo Iji ni Kan-suru Hōritsu*) Law No. 286 of 1952.

Law Concerning the Organization for Computation of Casualty Insurance Premium Rates (*Songai Hoken Ryōritsu Sanshutsu Dantai ni Kan-suru Hōritsu*) Law No. 193 of 1948.

Law Concerning the Organization of Medium and Small Enterprise Organizations (*Chūshō Kigyō Dantai no Soshiki ni Kan-suru Hōritsu*) Law No. 185 of 1957.

Law Concerning the Preservation of Liquor Tax and Liquor Industry Societies, Etc. (*Shuzei no Hozen oyobi Shurui-gyō Kumiai Tō ni Kan-suru Hōritsu*) Law No. 7 of 1953.

Law Concerning the Prohibition of Private Monopoly and the Maintenance of Fair Trade (*Shiteki Dokusen no Kinshi oyobi Kōsei Torihiki no Kakuho ni Kan-suru Hōritsu*) Law No. 54 of 1947.

Law Concerning the Promotion of the Export Marine Products Industry (*Yushutsu Suisan-gyō no Shinkō ni Kan-suru Hōritsu*) Law No. 154 of 1954.

Law Concerning the Punishment of Acts of Violence, Etc. (*Bōryoku Kōi Tō Shobatsu ni Kan-suru Hōritsu*) Law No. 60 of 1926.

Law Concerning the Regulation of the Method of Acts of Dispute in the Electricity Business and the Coal Mining Industry (*Denki Jigyō oyobi Sekitan*

Kōgyō ni okeru Sōgi Kōi no Hōhō no Kisei ni Kan-suru Hōritsu) Law No. 171 of 1953.
Law Concerning the Special Case of the Official Authority of Assistant Judges (*Hanji-ho no Shokken no Tokurei ni Kan-suru Hō*) Law No. 146 of 1948.
Law Concerning the Suspension of the Jury Law (*Baishin Hō no Teishi ni Kan-suru Hōritsu*) Law No. 88 of 1943.
Law Enforcing the Commercial Code Amendment Law (*Shōhō-chū Kaisei Hōritsu Skikō Hō*) Law No. 73 of 1938.
* Law for the Elimination of Zaibatsu Family Control (*Zaibatsu Dōzoku Shihai-ryoku Haijo Hō*) Law No. 2 of 1948.
Law for the Application of Laws (*Hōrei*) Law No. 10 of 1898.
* Law for the Special Situation of Litigation in Administrative Cases (*Gyōsei Jiken Soshō Tokurei Hō*) Law No. 81 of 1948.
Law to Establish the Land Adjustment Commission (*Tochi Chōsei Iinkai Setchi Hō*) Law No. 292 of 1950.
Law Repealing the Japan Steel Stock Company Law (*Nippon Seitetsu Kabushiki Kaisha Hō Haishi Hō*) Law No. 240 of 1950.
Leased House Law (*Shakuya Hō*) Law No. 50 of 1921.
Leased Land Law (*Shakuchi Hō*) Law No. 49 of 1921.
* Leased Land and Leased House Mediation Law (*Shakuchi Shakuya Chōtei Hō*) Law No. 41 of 1922.
Legal Examination Law (*Shihō Shiken Hō*) Law No. 140 of 1949.
Legal Scrivener Law (*Shihō Shoshi Hō*) Law No. 197 of 1950.
Limited Liability Company Law (*Yūgen Kaisha Hō*) Law No. 74 of 1938.
Livelihood Protection Law (*Seikatsu Hogo Hō*) Law No. 144 of 1950.
Local Autonomy Law (*Chihō Jichi Hō*) Law No. 67 of 1947.
Local Public Enterprise Labor Relations Law (*Chihō Kōei Kigyō Rōdō Kankei Hō*) Law No. 289 of 1952.
Local Public Servants Law (*Chihō Kōmuin Hō*) Law No. 261 of 1950.
Local Tax Law (*Chihō Zei Hō*) Law No. 226 of 1950.
* Local Tax Law of 1948 (*Chihō Zei Hō*) Law No. 110 of 1948.
* Local Tax Law of 1940 (*Chihō Zei Hō*) Law No. 60 of 1940.
* Local Tax Regulations (*Chihō Zei Kisoku*) Great Council of State Decree No. 16 of 1880.
* Local Tax Regulations of 1878 (*Chihō Zei Kisoku*) Great Council of State Decree No. 19 of 1878.
Machinery Industry Promotion Extraordinary Measures Law (*Kikai Kōgyō Shinkō Rinji Sochi Hō*) Law No. 154 of 1956.
* Machine Tool Manufacturing Business Law (*Kosaku Kikai Seizō Jigyō Hō*) Law No. 40 of 1938.
Marine Disaster Determination Law (*Kainan Shimpan Hō*) Law No. 135 of 1947.
Marine Transportation Law (*Kaijō Unsō Hō*) Law No. 187 of 1949.
Medium and Small Enterprise and Others' Cooperative Societies Law (*Chūshō Kigyō Tō Kyōdō Kumiai Hō*) Law No. 181 of 1949.
Medium and Small Enterprise Severance Pay Mutual Aid Law (*Chūshō Kigyō Taishokkin Kyōsai Hō*) Law No. 160 of 1959.

* Medium and Small Enterprise Stabilization Law (*Chūshō Kigyō Antei Hō*) Law No. 294 of 1952.
* Mercantile Society Law (*Shōgyō Kumiai Hō*) Law No. 25 of 1932.
Minimum Wage Law (*Saitei Chingin Hō*) Law No. 137 of 1959.
Mining Hypothec Law (*Kōgyō Teitō Hō*) Law No. 55 of 1905.
Mining Industry Law (*Kōgyō Hō*) Law No. 289 of 1950.
Minor Offenses Law (*Kei Hanzai Hō*) Law No. 39 of 1948.
* Monetary Obligation Temporary Mediation Law (*Kinsen Saimu Rinji Chōtei Hō*) Law No. 26 of 1905.
Mortgage Debenture Trust Law (*Tampo-zuki Shasai Shintaku Hō*) Law No. 52 of 1905.
Mujin Business Law (*Mujin-gyō Hō*) Law No. 42 of 1931.
Mutual Bank Law (*Sōgo Ginkō Hō*) Law No. 199 of 1951.
National Annuity Law (*Kokumin Nenkin Hō*) Law No. 141 of 1959.
National Administrative Organization Law (*Kokka Gyōsei Soshiki Hō*) Law No. 120 of 1948.
* National Bank Ordinance (*Kokuritsu Ginkō Jōrei*) Great Council of State Decree No. 349 of 1872.
* National General Mobilization Law (*Kokka Sōdōin Hō*) Law No. 55 of 1938.
National Public Servants, Etc., Severance Allowance Law (*Kokka Kōmuin Tō Taishoku Teate Hō*) Law No. 182 of 1953.
National Public Servants Law (*Kokka Kōmuin Hō*) Law No. 120 of 1947.
National Public Servants Mutual Aid Societies Law (*Kokka Kōmuin Kyōsai Kumiai Hō*) Law No. 128 of 1958.
National Saving Societies Law (*Kokumin Chochiku Kumiai Hō*) Law No. 64 of 1941.
National Tax Collection Law (*Kokuzei Chōshū Hō*) Law No. 147 of 1959.
National Tax Common Provisions Law (*Kokuzei Tsūsoku Hō*) Law No. 66 of 1962.
National Tax Violations Control Law (*Kokuzei Hansoku Torishimari Hō*) Law No. 67 of 1900.
* Newspaper Law (*Shimbunshi Hō*) Law No. 41 of 1909.
Non-Litigious Cases Procedure Law (*Hishō Jiken Tetsuzuki Hō*) Law No. 14 of 1898.
Occupation Stabilization Law (*Shokugyō Antei Hō*) Law No. 141 of 1947.
* Organization of Cities (*Shisei*) Law No. 1 of 1888.
* Organization of Towns and Villages (*Chōsonsei*) Law No. 1 of 1888.
* Outline of the New Criminal Law (*Shinritsu Kōryō*) Enforced in 1870 but never promulgated. Reprinted in [MEIJI 3 NEN] HŌREI ZENSHO ([1870] Complete Laws and Orders) 572.
Passport Law (*Ryoken Hō*) Law No. 267 of 1951.
Patent Law (*Tokkyo Hō*) Law No. 121 of 1959.
* Patent Law of 1921 (*Tokkyo Hō*) Law No. 96 of 1921.
Patent Specialist Law (*Benrishi Hō*) Law No. 100 of 1921.
* Peace Police Law (*Chian Keisatsu Hō*) Law No. 36 of 1900.
* Peace Preservation Law (*Chian Iji Hō*) Law No. 54 of 1941.
* Peace Preservation Law of 1925 (*Chian Iji Hō*) Law No. 46 of 1925.

Penal Code (*Keihō*) Law No. 45 of 1907.
* Penal Code of 1880 (*Keihō*) Great Council of State Decree No. 36 of 1880.
Pension Law (*Onkyū Hō*) Law No. 48 of 1923.
People's Finance Public Depository Law (*Kokumin Kinyū Kōko Hō*) Law No. 49 of 1949.
* Personal Affairs Mediation Law (*Jinji Chōtei Hō*) Law No. 11 of 1939.
Personal Surety Law (*Mimoto Hoshō Hō*) Law No. 42 of 1933.
* Petroleum Industry Law (*Sekiyu-gyō Hō*) Law No. 26 of 1934.
Postal Law (*Yūbin Hō*) Law No. 165 of 1947.
Prostitution Prevention Law (*Baishun Bōshi Hō*) Law No. 118 of 1956.
Public Corporation, Etc., Labor Relations Law (*Kōkyō Kigyō-tai Tō Rōdō Kankei Hō*) Law No. 257 of 1948.
Public Medium and Small Enterprise Finance Depository Law (*Chūshō Kigyō Kinyū Kōko Hō*) Law No. 138 of 1953.
Public Notary Law (*Kōshōnin Hō*) Law No. 53 of 1908.
Public Procurators' Office Law (*Kensatsuchō Hō*) Law No. 61 of 1947.
* Publication Law (*Shuppan Hō*) Law No. 15 of 1893.
Radio Law (*Dempa Hō*) Law No. 131 of 1950.
Railroad Hypothec Law (*Tetsudō Teitō Hō*) Law No. 53 of 1905.
* Recording Law (*Tōki Hō*) Law No. 1 of 1886.
* Recourse Law (*Sogan Hō*) Law No. 105 of 1890.
Road Traffic Business Activities Hypothec Law (*Dōro Kōtsū Jigyō Teitō Hō*) Law No. 204 of 1952.
* Road Traffic Control Law (*Dōro Kōtsū Torishimari Hō*) Law No. 130 of 1947.
Road Traffic Law (*Dōro Kōtsū Hō*) Law No. 105 of 1960.
Road Transport Vehicle Law (*Dōro Unsō Sharyō Hō*) Law No. 185 of 1951.
* Rules for the Organization of the Great Court of Judicature and Various Other Courts (*Dai Shin In Sho-Saibansho Shokusei Shōtei*) Great Council of State Decree No. 91 of 1875.
School Education Law (*Gakkō Kyōiku Hō*) Law No. 26 of 1947.
Securities Exchange Law (*Shōken Torihiki Hō*) Law No. 25 of 1948.
Ship's Crew Insurance Law (*Senin Hoken Hō*) Law No. 73 of 1939.
* Sorts of and Restrictions on the Enterprise Tax and Miscellaneous Taxes Among Local Taxes (*Chihō Zei-chū Eigyō Zei Zasshu Zei no Shurui oyobi Seigen*) Great Council of State Decree No. 39 of 1878.
State Compensation Law (*Kokka Baishō Hō*) Law No. 125 of 1947.
* Statement of the Form of Government (*Seitaisho*) June 11, 1868.
* Stock Exchange Ordinance (*Kabushiki Torihiki Jōrei*) Great Council of State Decree No. 107 of 1874.
Subversive Activities Prevention Law (*Hakai Katsudō Bōshi Hō*) Law No. 240 of 1952.
Supreme Court Justice Popular Review Law (*Saikō Saibansho Saibankan Kokumin Shinsa Hō*) Law No. 136 of 1947.
* Synthetic Petroleum Manufacturing Business Law (*Jinzō Sekiyu Seizō Jigyō Hō*) Law No. 52 of 1937.
Tax Special Measures Law (*Sozei Tokubetsu Sochi Hō*) Law No. 26 of 1957.
Tax Specialist Law (*Zeirishi Hō*) Law No. 237 of 1951.

* Tenant Farming Mediation Law (*Kosaku Chōtei Hō*) Law No. 18 of 1924.
* Trade Society Law (*Bōeki Kumiai Hō*) Law No. 74 of 1937.
Trust Business Law (*Shintaku-gyō Hō*) Law No. 65 of 1922.
Trust Law (*Shintaku Hō*) Law No. 62 of 1922.
Unemployment Insurance Law (*Shitsugyō Hoken Hō*) Law No. 146 of 1947.
Vocational Training Law (*Shokugyō Kunren Hō*) Law No. 133 of 1958.
Welfare Annuity Insurance Law (*Kōsei Nenkin Hoken Hō*) Law No. 115 of 1954.
Women's Guidance Home Law (*Fujin Hodō In Hō*) Law No. 17 of 1958.
Workmen's Accident Compensation Insurance Law (*Rōdōsha Saigai Hoshō Hoken Hō*) Law No. 50 of 1947.

C. Cabinet Orders (Postwar), Imperial Orders, and Great Council of State Notices

* Alien Registration Order (*Gaikokujin Tōroku Rei*) Imperial Order No. 207 of 1947.
Automobile Damage Compensation Security Law Enforcement Order (*Jidōsha Songai Baishō Hoshō Hō Shikō Rei*) Cabinet Order No. 286 of 1955.
Cabinet Order Concerning the Designation of the Designated Cities of Article 252-19, Paragraph (1) of the Local Autonomy Law (*Chihō Jichi Hō Dai 252 Jō no 19, Dai 1 Kō no Shitei Toshi no Shitei ni Kan-suru Seirei*) Cabinet Order No. 254 of 1956.
Cabinet Order Fixing the Amount of Automobile Damage Compensation Security Business Assessment, Etc. (*Jidōsha Songai Baishō Hoshō Jigyō Fukakin Tō no Kingaku o Sadameru Seirei*) Cabinet Order No. 316 of 1955.
Closed Institutions Order (*Heisa Kikan Rei*) Imperial Order No. 74 of 1947.
* Court Organization Regulations (*Saibansho Kansei*) Imperial Order No. 40 of 1886.
Emigration and Immigration Control Order (*Shutsunyūkoku Kanri Rei*) Cabinet Order No. 319 of 1951.
Food Emergency Measures Order (*Shokuryō Kinkyū Sochi Rei*) Emergency Imperial Order No. 86 of 1946.
* Holding Company Liquidation Commission Order (*Mochikabu Kaisha Seiri Iinkai Rei*) Imperial Order No. 233 of 1946.
* Imperial Order Concerning the Restriction, Etc., of Securities Holdings by Companies (*Kaisha no Shōken Hoyū Seigen Tō ni Kan-suru Chokurei*) Imperial Order No. 567 of 1946.
Important Industry Organizations Order (*Jūyō Sangyō Dantai Rei*) Imperial Order No. 831 of 1941.
* Income Tax Law of 1887 (*Shotoku Zei Hō*) Imperial Order No. 5 of 1887.
Income Tax Law Enforcement Regulations (*Shotoku Zei Hō Shikō Kisoku*) Imperial Order No. 110 of 1947.
Juridical Persons' Tax Law Enforcement Regulations (*Hōjin Zei Hō Shikō Kisoku*) Imperial Order No. 111 of 1947.
Justice Staff Regulations and Operating Rules (*Shihō Shokumu Teisei*) Great Council of State Notice of August 3, 1872.

Local Autonomy Law Enforcement Rules (*Chihō Jichi Hō Shikō Kitei*) Cabinet Order No. 19 of 1947.

Local Tax Law Enforcement Order (*Chihō Zei Hō Shikō Rei*) Cabinet Order No. 245 of 1950.

* Matter Concerning Enforcement of the Law Concerning Local Taxes (*Chihō Zei ni Kan-suru Hōritsu Shikō ni Kan-suru Ken*) Imperial Order No. 339 of 1926.

Ministry of Justice Organization Order (*Hōmu-shō Soshiki Rei*) Cabinet Order No. 384 of 1952.

National Tax Common Provisions Law Enforcement Order (*Kokuzei Tsūsoku Hō Shikō Rei*) Cabinet Order No. 135 of 1962.

* Poisonous Foods and Beverages Control Order (*Yūdoku Inshoku-butsu Torishimari Rei*) Imperial Order No. 52 of 1946.

* Public Utilities Order (*Kōeki Jigyō Rei*) Cabinet Order No. 343 of 1950.

* Regulations for the Appointment of Judges (*Hanji Tōyō Kisoku*) Great Council of State Notice No. 101 of 1884.

Tax Special Measures Law Enforcement Order (*Sozei Tokubetsu Sochi Hō Shikō Rei*) Cabinet Order No. 43 of 1957.

D. Cabinet Orders (Prewar), Ministerial Orders, Regulations, Rules, Ministerial Notices, and Ministerial Pronouncements

* Advocate Regulations (*Daigennin Kisoku*) Ministry of Justice Pronouncement A (*Kō*) No. 1 of 1876.

* Attorneys Examination Regulations (*Bengoshi Shiken Kisoku*) Ministry of Justice Order No. 9 of 1893.

Automobile Damage Compensation Security Law Enforcement Regulations (*Jidōsha Songai Baishō Hoshō Hō Shikō Kisoku*) Ministry of Transportation Order No. 66 of 1955.

Central Labor Relations Commission Regulations (*Chūō Rōdō Iinkai Kisoku*) Central Labor Relations Commission Regulation No. 1 of 1949.

Civil Procedure Regulations (*Minji Soshō Kisoku*) Supreme Court Regulation No. 2 of 1956.

Criminal Procedure Regulations (*Keiji Soshō Kisoku*) Supreme Court Regulation No. 32 of 1948.

* Enforcement Regulations of the Law Concerning Local Taxes (*Chihō Zei ni Kan-suru Hōritsu Shikō Kisoku*) Ministry of Finance and Ministry of Home Affairs Order of Nov. 27, 1926.

Family Registration Law Enforcement Regulations (*Kōseki Hō Shikō Kisoku*) Ministry of Justice Order No. 94 of 1947.

* Holding Company Liquidation Commission Order Enforcement Regulations (*Mochikabu Kaisha Seiri Iinkai Rei Shikō Kisoku*) Cabinet, Ministry of Finance and Ministry of Justice Order No. 1 of 1946.

Income Tax Law Enforcement Rules (*Shotoku Zei Hō Shikō Saisoku*) Ministry of Finance Order No. 29 of 1947.

Juridical Persons' Tax Law Enforcement Rules (*Hōjin Zei Hō Shikō Saisoku*) Ministry of Finance Order No. 30 of 1947.

Labor Standards Law Enforcement Regulations (*Rōdō Kijun Hō Shikō Kisoku*) Ministry of Welfare Order No. 23 of 1947.

Legal Training and Research Institute Rules (*Shihō Kenshūjo Kitei*) Supreme Court Rule No. 6 of 1947.

Local Tax Law Enforcement Regulations (*Chihō Zei Hō Shikō Kisoku*) Prime Minister's Office Order No. 23 of 1954.

Ministerial Order Concerning the Certified Audit of Financial Statements *Zaimu Shohyō no Kansa Shōmei ni Kan-suru Shōrei*) Securities Exchange Commission Regulation No. 4 of 1951.

Ministerial Order Concerning the Useful Lives, Etc., of Fixed Assets (*Kotei Shisan no Taiyō Nensū Tō ni Kan-suru Shōrei*) Ministry of Finance Order No. 50 of 1951.

Ministry of Justice Integrated Research Institute Rules of Organization (*Hōmu Sōgō Kenkyūjo Soshiki Kitei*) Ministry of Justice Order No. 2 of 1952.

* National Public Park Control Regulations (*Kokumin Kōen Kanri Kisoku*) Ministry of Welfare Order No. 19 of 1949.

National Tax Common Provisions Law Enforcement Regulations (*Kokuzei Tsūsoku Hō Shikō Kisoku*) Ministry of Finance Order No. 28 of 1962.

* Provisional Regulations for the Official Duties of Judges of Instruction (*Kyūmon Hanji Shokumu Kari-Kisoku*) Ministry of Justice Notice No. 47 of 1876.

Regulation Concerning Inquiry and Hearing by the Fair Trade Commission (*Kōsei Torihiki Iinkai no Shinsa oyobi Shimpan ni Kan-suru Kisoku*) Fair Trade Commission Regulation No. 5 of 1953.

Regulation Concerning Notification Pursuant to the Provisions of Article 8 of the Law Concerning the Prohibition of Private Monopoly and the Maintenance of Fair Trade (*Shiteki Dokusen no Kinshi oyobi Kōsei Torihiki no Kakuho ni Kan-suru Hōritsu Dai 8 Jō no Kitei ni yoru Todokeide ni Kan-suru Kisoku*) Fair Trade Commission Regulation No. 2 of 1953.

* Regulations Concerning Continuous Trial in Civil Procedure (*Minji Soshō no Keizoku Shinri ni Kan-suru Kisoku*) Supreme Court Regulation No. 27 of 1954.

Regulations Concerning Legal Apprentices (*Shihō Shūshūsei ni Kan-suru Kisoku*) Supreme Court Regulation No. 15 of 1948.

Regulations Concerning the Solicitation of Proxy Voting Rights of Listed Shares (*Jōjō Kabushiki no Giketsuken no Dairi Kōshi no Kanyū ni Kan-suru Kisoku*) Securities Exchange Commission Regulation No. 13 of 1948.

Regulations Concerning the Terms, Form and Method of Preparing Financial Statements, Etc. (*Zaimu Shohyō Tō no Yōgo, Yōshiki oyobi Sakusei Hōhō ni Kan-suru Kisoku*) Securities Exchange Commission Regulation No. 18 of 1950.

School Education Law Enforcement Regulations (*Gakkō Kyōiku Hō Shikō Kisoku*) Ministry of Education Order No. 11 of 1947.

Tax Special Measures Law Enforcement Regulations (*Sozei Tokubetsu Sōchi Hō Shikō Kisoku*) Ministry of Finance Order No. 15 of 1957.

Workmen's Accident Compensation Insurance Law Enforcement Regulations (*Rōdōsha Saigai Hoshō Hoken Hō Shikō Kisoku*) Ministry of Labor Order No. 22 of 1955.

E. Notifications, Circulars, and Other National Government Materials

Automobile Damage Compensation Liability Insurance Rate Validation (*Jidōsha Songai Baishō Sekinin Hoken Ryōritsu Ninka*) Ministry of Finance Notification No. 466 of 1955.

Concerning the Establishment of the National Tax Collection Law Basic Circular (*Kokuzei Chōshū Hō Kihon Tsūtatsu no Seitei ni Tsuite*) National Tax Agency Circular, *Chōchō* (Collection Division — Collection Section) 4–5, Jan. 27, 1960.

Concerning the Evaluation of an Amount Equivalent to the Rent of Company Houses, Dormitories, Etc. (*Shataku, Ryō Tō no Chintairyō Sōtō Gaku no Hyōka ni Tsuite*) National Tax Agency Circular, *Chokusho* (Direct Tax Division — Income Tax Section) 2–94, Nov. 4, 1952.

Concerning the Manner of Treating the Amended Income Tax Law (*Kaisei-go no Shotoku Zei no Toriatsukai-kata ni Tsuite*) National Tax Agency Circular, *Chokusho* (Direct Tax Division — Income Tax Section) 1–12, Jan. 26, 1952.

Concerning the Manner of Treating the Income Tax Law as Amended August, 1953 (*Shōwa 28 Nen 8 Gatsu Kaisei Shotoku Zei Hō no Toriatsukai-kata ni Tsuite*) National Tax Agency Circular, *Chokusho* (Direct Tax Division — Income Tax Section) 1–1, Jan. 5, 1954.

Concerning the Operation of the Basic Circular Relating to the Income Tax Law (Collection at Source Portion) (*Shotoku Zei Hō ni Kan-suru Kihon Tsūtatsu (Gensen Chōshū Bun) no Unyō ni Tsuite*) National Tax Agency Circular, *Chokusho* (Direct Tax Division — Income Tax Section) 2–62, July 5, 1951.

Concerning the Revision of the Treatment of Payment in Kind, Etc., of Commutation Passes (*Tsūkin-yō Teiki Jōshaken no Genbutsu Kyūyo Tō ni Tai-suru Toriatsukai no Kaisei ni Tsuite*) National Tax Agency Circular, *Chokusho* (Direct Tax Division — Income Tax Section) 2–109, Nov. 2, 1961.

Concerning the Treatment of Remuneration Income for an Amount Equivalent to the Rent of Company Houses, Dormitories, Etc. (*Shataku, Ryō Tō no Chintairyō Sōtō Gaku ni Tai-suru Kyūyo Shotoku no Toriatsukai ni Tsuite*) National Tax Agency Circular, *Chokusho* (Direct Tax Division — Income Tax Section) 2–61, Aug. 11, 1952.

Concerning the Treatment of Remuneration Income for an Amount Equivalent to the Rent of Company Houses, Dormitories, Etc. (*Shataku, Ryō Tō no Chintairyō Sōtō Gaku ni Tai-suru Kyūyo Shotoku no Toriatsukai ni Tsuite*) National Tax Agency Circular, *Chokusho* (Direct Tax Division — Income Tax Section) 2–109, Oct. 24, 1951.

Concerning the Treatment of Remuneration Income for an Amount Equivalent to the Rent of Company Houses, Dormitories, Etc. (*Shataku, Ryō Tō no Chintairyō Sōtō Gaku ni Tai-suru Kyūyo Shotoku no Toriatsukai ni Tsuite*) National Tax Agency Circular, *Chokusho* (Direct Tax Division — Income Tax Section) 2–78, Aug. 13, 1951.

Concerning the Treatment of the Acquisition Value, Etc., of Fixed Assets (*Kotei Shisan no Shutoku Kagaku Tō no Toriatsukai ni Tsuite*) National Tax

Agency Circular, *Chokuhō* (Direct Tax Division — Juridical Persons' Tax Section) 1–28, March 1, 1960.

Concerning the Treatment of the Income Tax Law (Excluding Income Tax at Source Relationships) as Amended in March, 1961 (*Shōwa 36 Nen 3 Gatsu Kaisei Shotoku Zei Hō (Gensen Shotoku Zei Kankei o Nozoku) no Toriatsukai ni Tsuite*) National Tax Agency Circular, *Chokusho* (Direct Tax Division — Income Tax Section) 1–85, Dec. 12, 1961.

Concerning the Treatment of the Income Tax on Day and Night Watchmen Fees (*Nitchokuryō Mata wa Shukuchokuryō ni Tai-suru Shotoku Zei no Toriatsukai ni Tsuite*) National Tax Agency Circular, *Chokusho* (Direct Tax Division — Income Tax Section) 2–28, March 12, 1955.

Concerning the Treatment of the Income Tax on Day and Night Watchmen Fees (*Nitchokuryō Mata wa Shukuchokuryō ni Tai-suru Shotoku Zei no Toriatsukai ni Tsuite*) National Tax Agency Circular, *Chokusho* (Direct Tax Division — Income Tax Section) 2–12, Feb. 15, 1954.

Concerning the Treatment of the Separate Tables of the Ministerial Order Concerning the Useful Lives, Etc., of Fixed Assets (*Kotei Shisan no Taiyō Nensū Tō ni Kan-suru Shōrei Beppyō no Toriatsukai ni Tsuite*) National Tax Agency Circular, *Chokusho* (Direct Tax Division — Income Tax Section) 1–111, Sept. 25, 1951.

Designation of Machinery and Other Equipment and Periods Subject to the Application of the Provisions of Article 21, Paragraph (1), Item (i), and Article 43, Paragraph (1), Item (i), of the Tax Special Measures Law (*Sozei Tokubetsu Sochi Hō Dai 21 Jō, Dai 1 Kō, Dai 1 Gō oyobi Dai 43 Jō, Dai 1 Kō, Dai 1 Gō no Kitei no Tekiyō o Ukeru Kikai Sono Ta no Setsubi oyobi Kikan o Shitei*) Ministry of Finance Notification No. 186 of 1961.

Designation of Merchandise Provided for in Article 24-2, Paragraph (1), of the Law Concerning the Prohibition of Private Monopoly and the Maintenance of Fair Trade (*Shiteki Dokusen no Kinshi oyobi Kōsei Torihiki no Kakuho ni Kan-suru Hōritsu Dai 24 Jō no 2, Dai 1 Kō ni Kitei-suru Shōhin Shitei*) Fair Trade Commission Notification No. 18 of 1953.

Details for Machinery and Apparatus and Individual Lives (*Kikai oyobi Sōchi no Saimoku to Kobetsu Nensū*) National Tax Agency, Oct., 1961.

General Plan for the Guidance of Legal Apprentices (*Shihō Shūshūsei Shidō Yōkō*) *Nikki-hatsu* (Legal Training and Research Institute Daybook Entry) No. 320 of 1954.

Income Tax Law Basic Circular (*Shotoku Zei Hō Kihon Tsūtatsu*) National Tax Agency Circular, *Chokusho* (Direct Tax Division — Income Tax Section) 1–1, Jan. 1, 1951.

Inheritance Tax Law Basic Circular (*Sōzoku Zei Hō Kihon Tsūtatsu*) National Tax Agency Circular, *Chokushi* (Direct Tax Division — Assets Tax Section) 10, Jan. 28, 1959.

Juridical Persons' Tax Law Basic Circular (*Hōjin Zei Hō Kihon Tsūtatsu*) National Tax Agency Circular, *Chokuhō* (Direct Tax Division — Juridical Persons' Tax Section) 1–100, Sept. 25, 1950.

Municipal Tax Ordinance (Model Provisions) (*Shi-chō-son Zei Jōrei* (*Junsoku*))

Autonomy Agency Circular, *Ji-otsu Shi-hatsu* (Tax Affairs Bureau — Municipal Tax Section) No. 20, May 14, 1954.

Normal Period of Use of Machinery and Apparatus (*Kikai oyobi Sōchi no Tsūjō no Shiyō Jikan*) National Tax Agency, Oct., 1961.

* Notes on the Local Tax Regulations (*Chihō Zei Kisoku Bikō*) Ministry of Home Affairs Communication of May 27, 1880.

Prefectural Tax Ordinance (Model Provisions) (*Fu-ken Zei Jōrei* (*Junsoku*)) Autonomy Agency Circular, *Ji-hei Fu-hatsu* No. 30, Aug. 1, 1955.

Specific Unfair Trade Practices in the Animal and Whale Meat, Etc., Canning Industry (*Chikuniku, Kujiraniku Tō no Kanzume-gyō ni okeru Tokutei no Fukōsei na Torihiki Hōhō*) Fair Trade Commission Notification No. 1 of 1961.

Specific Unfair Trade Practices in the Marine Transport Industry (*Kaiun-gyō ni okeru Tokutei no Fukōsei na Torihiki Hōhō*) Fair Trade Commission Notification No. 17 of 1959.

Specific Unfair Trade Practices in the Miso Industry (*Miso-gyō ni okeru Tokutei no Fukōsei na Torihiki Hōhō*) Fair Trade Commission Notification No. 13 of 1953.

Specific Unfair Trade Practices in the Newspaper Industry (*Shimbun-gyō ni okeru Tokutei no Fukōsei na Torihiki Hōhō*) Fair Trade Commission Notification No. 3 of 1955.

Specific Unfair Trade Practices in the Soy Sauce Industry (*Shōyu-gyō ni okeru Tokutei no Fukōsei na Torihiki Hōhō*) Fair Trade Commission Notification No. 12 of 1953.

Specific Unfair Trade Practices in the Textbook Business (*Kyōkasho-gyō ni okeru Tokutei no Fukōsei na Torihiki Hōhō*) Fair Trade Commission Notification No. 5 of 1956.

F. Local Government Ordinances

Ordinance Concerning Assembly, Parade en Masse, and Mass Demonstrations (*Shūkai, Shudan Kōshin oyobi Shūdan Jii-undō ni Kan-suru Jōrei*) Tokyo Metropolitan Ordinance No. 44 of 1950.

Ordinance Concerning Parades and Mass Demonstrations (*Gyōretsu Kōshin Shūdan Jii-undō ni Kan-suru Jōrei*) Niigata Prefectural Ordinance No. 4 of 1949.

TABLE OF CASES

Japanese Reporters Cited and Their Standard Abbreviations

Dai Shin In Keiji Hanketsu Roku (Record of Great Court of Judicature Criminal Judgments)
Abbreviation: Dai-han Keiroku

Dai Shin In Keiji Hanrei Shū (A Collection of Criminal Great Court of Judicature Cases)
Abbreviation: Dai-han Keishū

Dai Shin In Minji Hanketsu Roku (Record of Great Court of Judicature Civil Judgments)
Abbreviation: Dai-han Minroku

Dai Shin In Minji Hanrei Shū (A Collection of Civil Great Court of Judicature Cases)
Abbreviation: Dai-han Minshū

Fuhō Kōi ni Kan-suru Kakyū Saibansho Minji Saiban Reishū (A Collection of Civil Cases in the Inferior Courts Concerning Torts)

Gyōsei Jiken Saiban Reishū (A Collection of Judicial Precedents Concerning Administrative Cases)
Abbreviation: Gyōsai Reishū

Gyōsei Saibansho Hanketsu Roku (Record of Administrative Court Judgments)
Abbreviation: Gyō-han

Hanrei Jihō (The Case Journal)

Hanrei Times (The Law Times Report)

Hōgaku (Jurisprudence)

Hōritsu Hyōron Zenshū (A Complete Critique of the Law)
Abbreviation: Hyōron

Hōritsu Shimbun (The Law News)
Abbreviation: Shimbun

Hōritsu Shimpō (The New Law Report)

Kakyū Saibansho Keiji Saiban Reishū (A Collection of Criminal Cases in the Inferior Courts)
Abbreviation: Kakyū Keishū

Kakyū Saibansho Minji Saiban Reishū (A Collection of Civil Cases in the Inferior Courts)
Abbreviation: Kakyū Minshū

Katei Saiban Geppō (The Family Trial Monthly Reporter)
Abbreviation: Kasai Geppō

Kōsei Torihiki Iinkai Shinketsu Shū (A Collection of Fair Trade Commission Decrees)
Abbreviation: Shinketsu Shū

Kōtō Saibansho Keiji Hanketsu Tokuhō (High Court Criminal Decisions Special Reporter)

Kōtō Saibansho Keiji Hanrei Shū (A Collection of Criminal High Court Cases)
Abbreviation: Kō-han Keishū

Kōtō Saibansho Keiji Saiban Tokuhō (High Court Criminal Trials Special Reporter)
Abbreviation: Tokuhō

KŌTŌ SAIBANSHO MINJI HANREI SHŪ (A Collection of Civil High Court Cases)
Abbreviation: KŌ-HAN MINSHŪ
RŌDŌ HŌREI TSŪSHIN (Labor Legislation News)
RŌDŌ IINKAI SOKUHŌ (Labor Relations Commissions' Rapid Reporter)
RŌDŌ KANKEI MINJI SAIBAN REISHŪ (A Collection of Civil Cases Concerning Labor)
Abbreviation: RŌ-MINSHŪ
SAIBAN SUISHI (Essential Trial Reports)
SAIBANSHO JIHŌ (The Court Journal)
SAIKŌ SAIBANSHO KEIJI HANREI SHŪ (A Collection of Criminal Supreme Court Cases)
Abbreviation: SAI-HAN KEISHŪ
SAIKŌ SAIBANSHO MINJI HANREI SHŪ (A Collection of Civil Supreme Court Cases)
Abbreviation: SAI-HAN MINSHŪ

CASES BY COUNTRY

Austria

England (Listed by Case Name and Court)

Queen's Bench Division

Court of Common Pleas

France (Listed by Case Name)

France (Listed Chronologically)

Germany (Listed Chronologically)

Japan (Listed by Case Name)

Japan (Listed Chronologically)

May 28, 1958: Yajima v. Japan, Supreme Court, Grand Bench, 12 SAI-HAN KEISHŪ 1718 290
Aug. 29, 1958: Judgment, Tokyo District Court, HANREI JIHŌ no. 168, at 28 459
Sept. 10, 1958: Hoashi v. Japan, Supreme Court, Grand Bench, 12 SAI-HAN MINSHŪ 1969 252
Sept. 19, 1958: Japan v. Kamada, Supreme Court, II Petty Bench, 12 SAI-HAN KEISHŪ 3047 452
Sept. 19, 1958: Yamamoto v. Japan, Supreme Court, II Petty Bench, 12 SAI-HAN KEISHŪ 3127 451
Oct. 9, 1958: Honda Giken Saitama Rōdō Kumiai (Honda Giken Saitama Labor Union) v. Honda Giken Kōgyō Kabushiki Kaisha (Honda Giken Industrial Co.), Saitama Local Labor Relations Commission, RŌDŌ IINKAI SOKUHŌ no. 438, at 6 465
Nov. 5, 1958: Uematsu v. Kusui, Takamatsu District Court, 9 KAKYŪ MINSHŪ 2182 409
Nov. 24, 1958: Chijiiwa v. Honda Giken Kōgyō Kabushiki Kaisha (Honda Giken Industrial Co.), Tokyo District Court, 9 RŌ-MINSHŪ 1013 465
Dec. 24, 1958: Fujita v. Yamae Mokuzai Kabushiki Kaisha (Yamae Lumber Co.), Tokyo District Court, 9 RŌ-MINSHŪ 984 469
Dec. 25, 1958: Japan v. Ando, Tokyo District Court, HANREI JIHŌ no. 177, at 5 290
Jan. 27, 1959: Japan v. Kim, Gifu District Court, HANREI JIHŌ no. 183, at 5 293
March 24, 1959: Yamaki v. Yūgen Kaisha Kubota Shōji (Kubota Commercial Limited Liability Co.), Tokyo District Court, 10 KAKYŪ MINSHŪ 545 48
March 30, 1959: Japan v. Sakata (Sunakawa Case), Tokyo District Court, 10 KAKYŪ KEISHŪ 776, translated into English in 4 JAPANESE ANN. INTL. L. 97 (1960) 422
April 18, 1959: Arai v. Kyōei Kasai Hoken Sōgo Kaisha (Kyoei Mutual Fire Insurance Co.), Kobe District Court, 10 KAKYŪ MINSHŪ 781 407
April 24, 1959: Nakayama v. Yamaichi Suisan Kabushiki Kaisha (Yamaichi Marine Products Co.), Kofu District Court, 10 KAKYŪ MINSHŪ 820 404, 409
June 16, 1959: Japan v. Hagiwara, Tokyo High Court, 12 KŌ-HAN KEISHŪ 635 283
June 25, 1959: Judgment, Supreme Court, I Petty Bench (unreported case) 93
July 18, 1959: Nihon Kayaku Kabushiki Kaisha (Japan Chemical Co.) v. Nihon Kayaku Rōdō Kumiai (Japan Chemical Labor Union), Central Labor Relations Commission, RŌDŌ IINKAI SOKUHŌ no. 467, at 236 451
Aug. 8, 1959: Japan v. Ito, Tokyo District Court, 14 SAI-HAN KEISHŪ 1282 235
Aug. 10, 1959: Japan v. Suzuki (Matsukawa Case), Supreme Court, Grand Bench, 13 SAI-HAN KEISHŪ 1419 179, 290
Oct. 3, 1959: Japan v. Doishita, Osaka District Court, HANREI JIHŌ no. 202, at 22 309
Sept. 23, 1959: Japan v. Ato (Yakai Case), Hiroshima High Court, HANREI JIHŌ no. 201, at 11 179
Dec. 16, 1959: Japan v. Sakata, Supreme Court, Grand Bench, 13 SAI-HAN KEISHŪ 3225, translated into English in 4 JAPANESE ANN. INTL. L. 103 (1960), and JUDGMENT UPON THE CASE OF THE SO-CALLED "SUNAKAWA CASE" (General Secretariat of the Supreme Court trans., 1960) 238, 422
Dec. 26, 1959: Takehara v. Doishita, Supreme Court, III Petty Bench, 13 SAI-HAN KEISHŪ 1427 315
Jan. 20, 1960: Okutani v. Nomura, Osaka High Court, 13 KŌ-HAN MINSHŪ 10 404
April 28, 1960: Japan v. Oka, Tokyo District Court (unreported case) 331
April 28, 1960: Miyamoto v. Gaimu Daijin (Minister of Foreign Affairs), Tokyo District Court, 11 GYŌSAI REISHŪ 1217 253, 254

Switzerland

United States (Listed by Case and Court)

United States Supreme Court

United States Court of Appeals

United States District Court

New Jersey Supreme Court

National Labor Relations Board

INDEX

Bei Fragen zur Produktsicherheit wenden Sie sich bitte an:
If you have any questions regarding product safety,
please contact:

Walter de Gruyter GmbH
Genthiner Straße 13
10785 Berlin
productsafety@degruyterbrill.com